Commentary
on
Mark

Commentary
on
Mark

by

Henry Barclay Swete

THE GREEK TEXT

with

INTRODUCTION, NOTES and INDEXES

KREGEL PUBLICATIONS
Grand Rapids, Michigan 49501

COMMENTARY ON MARK
Published in 1977, by Kregel Publications, a
division of Kregel, Inc. All rights reserved.

Printed in the United States of America

Library of Congress Cataloging in Publication Data

Bible. N.T. Mark. Greek. 1977.
    Commentary on Mark.
    (Kregel Reprint Library series)
    Reprint of the ed. originally published in 1913 by
Macmillan, London, under title: The Gospel according
to Mark.
    Includes bibliographical references and indexes.
    1. Bible. N. T. Mark — Commentaries. I. Swete,
Henry Barclay, 1835-1917. II. Title.
BS2581.1977   226'.3'077   77-79193
ISBN 0-8254-3715-6

CONTENTS

PREFACE
to the Third Edition

THE present edition is little more than a reprint of the second. A few corrections and additions have been made, chiefly in the footnotes; the most important of these being the insertion at p. 404 of the Greek fragment which follows 'Mark' xvi. 14 in the Freer MS. of the Four Gospels.

Of one important source of new knowledge I have been unable to make as much use as I could have wished. Professor Deissmann and Dr A. Thumb in Germany, and Professor J. H. Moulton and Dr G. Milligan in Great Britain, have taught us how much the papyri and the inscriptions have to contribute to the study of New Testament Lexicography. Most of their researches have appeared since the publication of the first edition of this book, and it would be impossible to avail myself of them without a serious interference with the plates. I can only refer the reader to the published papers and books of the above-mentioned scholars, and in particular to the Lexical Notes contributed by Dr Moulton and Dr Milligan to the *Expositor,* and to the work which, it is understood, will be based upon them.

The conclusions with regard to New Testament Grammar which have been drawn from the non-literary papyri are not as yet, in my opinion, established beyond doubt, and I am therefore content still to rely upon the authority of Winer-Moulton, Winer-Schmiedel, and Blass. But the subject is one upon which I desire to keep an open mind, and the time may come when this commentary will call for a more extensive revision in this respect than I am at present prepared to undertake.

H. B. S.

PREFACE
to the Second Edition

THE years which have gone by since the first issue of this Commentary have been singularly fruitful in publications bearing upon the study of the Gospels. In the work of preparing a second edition for the press these new helps have not been left out of sight; and from several of them—more particularly from Dr Chase's and Dr Salmond's articles in the third volume of Dr Hastings' *Dictionary of the Bible*, the second volume of Professor Theodore Zahn's *Einleitung in das Neue Testament*, Sir J. C. Hawkins' *Horae Synopticae*, and Mr P. M. Barnard's *Biblical Text of Clement of Alexandria*—much assistance has been derived. If my conclusions have not often been modified, it is not because I have failed to reconsider them in the light of these and other recent contributions to Biblical knowledge.

I am glad also to acknowledge my debts to the kindness of reviewers, and of not a few private friends and some unknown correspondents, who have pointed out errors or deficiencies in the first edition of my book. These corrections have all, as I trust, received respectful attention, although in some cases the plan of the work has refused to lend itself to the proposed changes, or after full consideration I have found myself unable to accept them.

In the preface to the first edition I expressed a desire to discuss more fully at a future time some of the larger questions raised by the Gospel of St Mark. This purpose has not been fulfilled. The book has been revised throughout; the critical apparatus has been enlarged by the use of the fresh evidence printed in Mr Lake's *Texts from Mount Athos*, of which advanced sheets were sent to me through the kindness of the author; the foot-notes have been here and there expanded or re-written. But the pressure of other work and the call of fresh studies have precluded me from attempting the dissertations which I had intended to write. My book therefore goes forth under its original limitations. But I am confident that younger students will be found to fulfil the task which I am constrained to leave. The growing interest manifested in all problems connected with the Gospels, and more especially the earliest of the Gospels, justifies the expectation that the next generation of New Testament scholars will carry our knowledge more than one step nearer to the fulness and certainty which all must desire to attain.

H. B. S.

PREFACE
to the First Edition

THE earliest of extant commentators on St Mark urges as his apology for undertaking so serious a task the neglect which that Evangelist appeared to have suffered at the hands of the great teachers of the Church. While each of the other Gospels had received separate treatment, the Gospel according to St Mark, so far as he could discover, had been passed by, as if it needed no elucidation or none which could not be gathered from expositions of St Matthew and St Luke.

If this plea can no longer be used, it is still true that St Mark has gained far less attention than he deserves. The importance of his work as an independent history, and the beauty of its bright and unartificial picture of our Lord's life in Galilee, are at length generally recognised; but no monograph has yet appeared which makes full use of the materials at the disposal of the expositor.

I cannot claim to have supplied this deficiency in the present volume, nor has it been my aim to do so. I am content to offer help to those who desire to enter upon the serious study of the Gospels. Such study should begin, as it appears to me, with the Gospel which I believe to be the earliest of the four and, throughout a large part of the narrative, the nearest to the common source.

My chief aids have been the concordances of Bruder and Moulton-Geden, the grammatical works of Winer-Moulton, Winer-Schmiedel, Burton, and Blass, and the Greek text, introduction, and notes of Westcott and Hort. Next to these, I have learnt most from the concordance to the LXX. compiled by Hatch and Redpath, the text and indices of Niese's Josephus, and the illustrations from the later Greek literature which are to be found in the pages of Field, Grinfield, Grotius, Kuinoel, Kypke, and Wetstein, together with those which Deissmann has collected from the papyri. For Aramaic forms I have consulted Kautzsch and Dalman, and for Jewish thought and customs the well-known works of the elder Lightfoot, Schöttgen, Schürer, Streane, Taylor, Weber, and Wünsche. Of ancient expositors Origen, Jerome, Victor of Antioch, Bede, and Theophylact have supplied valuable help; among those of recent times I have consulted with advantage Schanz and Knabenbauer, Meyer-Weiss and Holtzmann. But no effort has been made to collect and tabulate the views of the commentators upon disputed points; it has been thought that a mere list of authorities, apart from a detailed statement of the grounds on which their opinions are based, could render little assistance to the student and might discourage individual effort. Nor have I appealed to any expositor, ancient or modern, until an effort had been made to gain light from a careful study of the Gospel itself. A prolonged examination of the text, and a diligent use of the lexical and grammatical helps to which reference has already been made, will almost invariably guide the student to a true interpretation of St Mark's rugged yet simple sentences. It is chiefly in the attempt to penetrate the profound sayings of our Lord, which this Evangelist reports in their most compact form, that valuable assistance may be gained from the suggestiveness of Origen and the devout insight of Bede and Bengel.

The text of Westcott and Hort has been generally followed; the few changes which I have permitted myself to make consist chiefly of the introduction within square brackets of words which the *New Testament in Greek* either omits or relegates to the margin. Even if we regard as proved the contention of Dr Salmon that " what Westcott and Hort have restored is the text which had the highest authority at Alexandria in the third century "—i.e. that it is " early Alexandrian," rather than strictly " neutral "—we may still reasonably prefer this text on the whole to any other as a basis for the interpretation of the Gospels. At the same time it is desirable that the student should have before him materials for forming a judgement upon all important variants, or at least discriminating between the principal types of text, and explaining to himself the grounds upon which any particular reading is to be preferred. With the view of enabling him to do this, I have printed above the commentary an apparatus of various readings, largely derived from the apparatus of Tischendorf's eighth critical edition, which has been simplified and to some extent revised and enriched.

It had been part of my original plan to discuss in additional notes and dissertations some of the points raised by this Gospel which seemed to require fuller investigation. But as the work grew under my hands, it became apparent that this purpose could not be carried into effect without unduly increasing the size of the volume and at the same time delaying, perhaps for some years, the publication of the text and notes. If strength is given to me, I hope to return to my task at a future time; meanwhile I have thrown into the form of an Introduction a portion of the materials which had been collected, and I trust that the present work may be regarded as complete in itself within the narrower limits which circumstances have prescribed.

It would be difficult to overestimate what I owe to the kindness of friends. While in each case I am responsible for the final form assumed by the text, apparatus, and notes, I desire to acknowledge with sincere gratitude the generous assistance which has enabled me to make them what they are. To the Bishop of Durham I am indebted for permission to use the WH. text of St Mark as far as I might find it convenient to do so. My colleague, Professor J. Armitage Robinson, has supplied me with copious notes upon the readings of the Armenian version, and has also frequently verified and corrected my references to the Sinaitic Syriac and the other Syriac versions. Mr F. C. Conybeare has contributed a photograph of the page of an Armenian MS. in which the last twelve verses of the Gospel are ascribed to the "presbyter Ariston." From Mr F. C. Burkitt I have received much valuable help, especially in the earlier chapters of St Mark, in reference to the readings of the Old Latin and the treatment of various points connected with Syriac and Aramaic words. Mr H. S. Cronin has given me access to his yet unpublished collation of the new fragments of cod. N, and to the results of a fresh examination of cod. 2^{pe}; and through the kindness of Mr A. M. Knight I have been permitted to use the proof-sheets of a new edition of Field's *Otium Norvicense* (pt. iii.). Not less important service of another kind has been rendered by Mr J. H. Srawley, who has revised the proofs and supplied materials for the index of subject-matter, and by Dr W. E. Barnes, to whom I owe many corrections which have been embodied in the sheets or appear in the list of *corrigenda*. Lastly, it is due to the workmen and readers of the University Press to acknowledge their unvarying attention to a work which has necessarily made large demands upon their patience and skill.

Few readers of this book will be more conscious of its shortcomings than the writer is. The briefest of the Gospels is in some respects the fullest and the most exacting; the simplest of the books of the New Testament brings us nearest to the feet of the Master. The interpreter of St Mark fulfils his office so far as he assists the student to understand, and in turn to interpret to others, this primitive picture of the Incarnate Life. To do this in any high degree demands such a preparation of mind and spirit as can rarely be attained; to do it in some measure has been my hope and aim.

Domine Deus...quaecumque dixi in hoc libro de tuo, agnoscant et tui; si qua de meo, et Tu ignosce et tui.

H. B. S.

INTRODUCTION

1

Personal History of Mark[1]

1. The Roman praenomen *Marcus* was in common use among Greek-speaking peoples from the Augustan age onwards. The inscriptions offer abundant examples from every part of the Empire, and from every rank in society.

The following are examples of the widespread use of the Greek name. Attica: *CIG* 191 γραμματεὺς βουλῆς καὶ δήμου Μ. Εὐκαρπίδου Ἀζηνιεύς. 192 Σφήττιοι...Ἐπίγονος Μάρκου, Ἱπποκράτης Μάρκου. 254 Μ. Ἀναφλύστιος. Lydia: 3162 Μ. ταμίας. 3440 Μηίονες Μ. καὶ Νεῖκος. Mysia: 3664 Μ. Ῥούφου μύστης. Nubia: 5109 Μ. στρατιώτης. Cyrene: 5218 Μ. Μάρκου. Sicily: 5644 Μαάρκου υἱὸς Μαάρκελλος. Italy: 6155 Μάαρκος Κοσσούτιος Μαάρκου ἀπελεύθερος. The last two inscriptions justify the accentuation Μᾶρκος, which has been adopted in this edition after Blass: see his comm. on Acts xii. 25, and his *Gramm. d. NTlichen Griechisch*, § 4. 2.

In all these instances the name stands by itself in accordance with Greek practice. The same is true of its later Christian use; thus we have a Marcus who was the first Gentile Bishop of Jerusalem (Aelia), a Marcus who was a Valentinian leader contemporary with Irenaeus, and another who was eighth Bishop of Alexandria; even at Rome the *praenomen* occurs as a single name in the case of Pope Marcus († 336). Christian inscriptions of the fourth century collected by Prof. Ramsay in the neighbourhood of Laodiceia combusta supply several examples of the same kind.

[1] The first two sections of this Introduction have been reproduced in part from articles published in the *Expositor* (v. vi. pp. 80 ff., 268 ff.).

Mitth. d. k. d. arch. Instituts (Athen. Abth.) 1888, p. 233 ff.:
55 τῷ ποθεινοτάτῳ μου υἱῷ Μάρκῳ πρεσβυτέρῳ. 56 Μάρκῳ καὶ
Παύλῳ. 61 Μάρκῳ διακόνῳ.

In the N.T. the name occurs eight times (Acts xii. 12, 25, xv.
37, 39, Col. iv. 10, Philem. 24, 2 Tim. iv. 11, 1 Pet. v. 13). In the
Acts it is the surname of a Jew of Jerusalem whose name was
John (xii. 12 Ἰωάνου τοῦ ἐπικαλουμένου Μάρκου, 25 Ἰωάνην τὸν
ἐπικληθέντα Μᾶρκον, xv. 37 Ἰωάνην τὸν καλούμενον [ἐπικ. אᶜCD
min^nonn] Μᾶρκον, 39 τὸν Μᾶρκον): the Epistles use Μάρκος by
itself and without the article, as if it were the only or at least
the familiar name by which the person to whom they refer was
known[1].

The N. T. bears witness to the readiness of the Palestinian Jew
to adopt or accept a secondary name, whether of Aramaic or
foreign origin[2]. Latin names were frequently used in this way,
whether epithets such as Justus (Acts i. 23), Niger (*ib.* xiii. 1),
Secundus, xx. 4, *cognomina* like Paulus, Lucanus, Silvanus, or
praenomina, of which Caius (Γάιος Acts xix. 29, Rom. xvi. 23,
1 Cor. i. 14, 3 Jo. 1) and Lucius (Acts xiii. 1) are examples.
Marcus is an exact parallel to Caius and Lucius, except that in
the Acts, where St Mark appears in Jewish surroundings, his
Jewish name precedes, and the Roman *praenomen* which he had
assumed occupies the place of the *cognomen*.

For other examples of the use of Marcus as a secondary name see
Dittenberger *inscr. Att. aet. Rom.* 1137 Λεύκιος ὁ καὶ Μ., Μαρα-
θώνιος παρατρίβης, 1142 Ἅλιος ὁ καὶ Μ. Χολλείδης ἔφηβος (time of
L. Verus and Commodus); Ramsay *ap. op. cit.* 92 Αὔρ. Μάρκῳ.

2. The mother of John Mark was a Mary who was a member of
the Church at Jerusalem (Acts xii. 12). She was clearly a woman
of some means and a conspicuous person in the Christian community. Her house (τὴν οἰκίαν Μαρίας)[3] is approached by a porch
(πυλών): a slave girl (παιδίσκη), probably the portress (ἡ θυρωρός, Jo. xviii. 16, 17), opens the door; there is an upper room or

---

[1] It seems to have been rarely borne
by Jews; cf. Chase, in Hastings *D. B.*
iii., p. 245.
[2] On the witness of Josephus to the

same fact see Deissmann, *Bibl. Studia*
(E. T.), p. 314.
[3] See foot-notes to Mc. xiv. 14, 52.

guestchamber large enough to receive a concourse of the brethren (ἦσαν ἱκανοὶ συνηθροισμένοι). It is to Mary's house that Peter naturally turns his steps, when released from prison; he is content to leave in the hands of the party who are assembled there the duty of communicating the tidings of his escape to the rest of the Church ('Ιακώβῳ καὶ τοῖς ἀδελφοῖς)[1]. John is not mentioned in this narrative, except for the purpose of distinguishing his mother Mary from others of the same name; but it is reasonable to suppose that he was present, and that he was already a believer, and intimate with St Peter and the heads of the Church at Jerusalem.

Conjecture has connected the name of John Mark with certain incidents in the Gospel history. In the Dialogue of Adamantius *de recta fide* (Lommatzsch, xvi. 259) we read: Μᾶρκος οὖν καὶ Λουκᾶς ἐκ τῶν ἑβδομήκοντα καὶ δυοῖν ὄντες Παύλῳ τῷ ἀποστόλῳ εὐηγγελίσαντο. Epiphanius (*haer.* 21. 6) adds: εἷς ἐτύγχανεν ἐκ τῶν ἑβδομήκοντα δύο τῶν διασκορπισθέντων ἐπὶ τῷ ῥήματι ᾧ εἶπεν ὁ κύριος Ἐὰν μή τις μου φάγῃ τὴν σάρκα κτλ. The statement is probably as baseless as many others which are due to that writer; it may be that the reference to Jo. vi. 66 has arisen from what is said of John Mark in Acts xiii. 13, xv. 38. That he was the νεανίσκος of Mc. xiv. 51 f. is not unlikely: see note *ad loc.* Bede's supposition that he was a Priest or Levite, which is probably borrowed from the comm. of Ps.-Jerome, or from the preface to Mark in mss. of the Vulgate (cf. Wordsworth-White, p. 171 "Marcus evangelista...sacerdotium in Israhel agens, secundum carnem levita"), rests ultimately upon Mark's connexion with the Levite Barnabas.

John was at Jerusalem during the famine of 45–6, when Barnabas and Saul visited the city for the purpose of conveying to the Church the alms of the brethren at Antioch; and on their return they took him back with them to Syria (Acts xii. 25). He may have attracted them as the son of a leading member of the Church at Jerusalem, and possibly also by services rendered during the distribution of the relief fund which revealed in him a capacity for systematic work. If we assume his identity with the Mark of St Paul's Epistles, there was doubtless another reason. Barnabas was still leader of the Christian body at Antioch; he

[1] On the interesting traditions connected with the house of John Mark see Zahn, *Einleitung* ii. 212 f., and the note in this commentary on Mc. xiv. 13 ff., 51 f.

had been sent there by the mother Church (Acts xi. 22), and
Saul's position in the Antiochian brotherhood was as yet
evidently subordinate (*ib.* 25, 30, xii. 25, xiii. 1 f.). It was for
Barnabas to seek fresh associates in the work, and John was a
near relative of Barnabas (Col. iv. 10 ὁ ἀνεψιὸς Βαρνάβα¹).
Whether the father of John had been uncle to Joseph of Cyprus
(Acts iv. 36), or the mother his aunt, is unknown; but the relationship accounts for the persistent favour which Barnabas
extended to Mark.

Mark's association with the Antiochian leaders was doubtless for
the purpose of rendering assistance to them in their growing work.
As Saul had been brought from Tarsus (Acts xi. 25 f.), so Mark
was now taken from Jerusalem; the same verb συνπαραλαβεῖν is
used again in xv. 37, 38, and seems distinctly to indicate the
position which Mark was called to fill—that of a coopted colleague
of inferior rank (cf. Gal. ii. 1 ἀνέβην...μετὰ Βαρνάβα συνπαραλα-
βὼν καὶ Τίτον)². It was natural that when the Holy Spirit
designated Barnabas and Saul for a new field of work, Mark
should accompany them. The general character of his duties is
now expressly stated; it was personal service, not evangelistic, to
which he was called (εἶχον δὲ καὶ Ἰωάνην ὑπηρέτην)³. Blass defines this service too strictly when he comments " velut ad bap-
tizandum⁴"; Mark may have been required to baptize converts
(cf. Acts x. 48, 1 Cor. i. 14), but his work would include all those
minor details which could safely be delegated to a younger man,
such as arrangements for travel, the provision of food and lodging,
conveying messages, negotiating interviews, and the like.

An examination of the passages where ὑπηρέτης is used in Biblical Greek will shew that the word covers a wide range of offices:
cf. e.g. Prov. xiv. 35 δεκτὸς βασιλεῖ ὑ. νοήμων (a courtier; similarly
Sap. vi. 4, Dan. iii. 46); Mt. v. 25 μήποτέ σε παραδῷ ὁ κριτὴς τῷ
ὑπηρέτῃ (the officer of a court); Mc. xiv. 54 συνκαθήμενος μετὰ τῶν
ὑπηρετῶν (temple police); Lc. i. 2 ὑπηρέται γενόμενοι τοῦ λόγου, Acts

---

¹ On ἀνεψιός see Bp Lightfoot *ad loc.*
² Cf. Ramsay, *St Paul the Traveller*,
p. 71: "he was not essential to the
expedition; he had not been selected by
the Spirit; he had not been formally
delegated by the Church of Antioch; he

was an extra hand, taken by Barnabas
and Saul on their own responsibility."
³ Acts xiii. 5. For ὑπηρέτην D reads
ὑπηρετοῦντι αὐτοῖς: E substitutes ἔχοντες
μεθ᾽ ἑαυτῶν καὶ Ἰ. εἰς διακονίαν.
⁴ *Acta App.*, p. 146.

xxvi. 16 ὑπηρέτην καὶ μάρτυρα (a person employed in the service of the Gospel); Lc. iv. 20 ἀποδοὺς τῷ ὑπηρέτῃ (the synagogue minister or ןֵזַּח)[1]. Official service, not of a menial kind, is the prevalent idea of the word which distinguishes it from δοῦλος on the one hand, and to some extent from διάκονος on the other: see Trench, *syn.* 9. Θεράπων is similarly used in reference to Joshua (Exod. xxxiii. 11, LXX.).

For such forms of ministry John possessed perhaps a natural aptitude (2 Tim. iv. 11 εὔχρηστος εἰς διακονίαν), and his assistance would be invaluable to the two Apostles, whose time was fully occupied with the spiritual work of their mission. But it was rendered only for a short time. At Perga in Pamphylia he left his colleagues, and returned to Jerusalem (Acts xiii. 13 ἀποχω-ρήσας ἀπ' αὐτῶν ὑπέστρεψεν εἰς Ἱεροσόλυμα). If St Luke records the fact in words which are nearly colourless, the censure which he represents St Paul as having subsequently passed upon Mark's conduct at this juncture is severe and almost passionate (xv. 38 ἠξίου τὸν ἀποστάντα ἀπ' αὐτῶν ἀπὸ Παμφυλίας καὶ μὴ συνελθόντα αὐτοῖς εἰς τὸ ἔργον, μὴ συνπαραλαμβάνειν τοῦτον). Nevertheless, as Professor Ramsay has pointed out[2], there is something to be said on Mark's behalf. He was not sent to the work by the Spirit or by the Church, as Barnabas and Saul had been. The sphere of the mission, moreover, had not been revealed at the first; and when the Apostles determined to leave the seacoast and strike across the Taurus into the interior, he may have considered himself free to abandon the undertaking. He had left Jerusalem for work at Antioch, and had not engaged himself to face the dangers of a campaign in central Asia Minor (2 Cor. xi. 26); and he may have felt that duty to his mother and his home required him to break off at this point from so perilous a development of the mission.

To Barnabas, at any rate, Mark's withdrawal did not appear in the light of a desertion, nor was St Paul unwilling to be associated with him again in the work at Antioch; for from Acts xv. 37 it

---

[1] Dr Chase (in Hastings, *D. B.* iii. p. 245 f.) suggests that the word may be used in this sense of John Mark, translating, "and they had with them also John, the synagogue minister."

[2] *The Church in the Roman Empire*, p. 61; *St Paul the Traveller*, p. 90.

would seem that he was with the Apostles there till the eve of the second missionary journey. St Paul, however, declined to accept the cousin of Barnabas as a companion in another voyage to Asia Minor, and Mark consequently set out with Barnabas alone. Whilst Paul went by land through the Cilician Gates, Barnabas sailed with Mark to Cyprus. In the first soreness of the separation each turned to the home of his family. Barnabas was Κύπριος τῷ γένει, for Levite though he was, he belonged to a Hellenistic family which had settled in the island (Acts iv. 36), and Mark was also probably a Cypriot Jew on one side[1]. Unfortunately the author of the Acts leaves the two men at this point, and there is no early or even moderately trustworthy tradition to carry on the thread of Mark's story. The Acts of Barnabas (περίοδοι Βαρνάβα), a work ascribed to St Mark, but of the fourth, or, in its present form, the fifth century, represents the Apostle as suffering martyrdom in Cyprus, and adds that after his death Mark set sail for Egypt, and evangelised Alexandria. The book as a whole is quite unworthy of credit, but it is not improbable that Mark proceeded from Cyprus to Egypt, whether in company with Barnabas or after his death.

Barnabas was still alive and at work when St Paul wrote 1 Cor. ix. 5 (ἢ μόνος ἐγὼ καὶ Βαρνάβας οὐκ ἔχομεν ἐξουσίαν μὴ ἐργάζεσθαι;), i.e. in A.D. 57, or according to Harnack 52–3. In the Clementine Homilies Barnabas is represented as doing evangelistic work in Egypt (i. 9 &c.). McGiffert conjectures, but without probability, that B. was the author of 1 Peter, which with Ramsay he places in the reign of Domitian (*Hist. of Christianity in the Apostolic age*, p. 597 ff.).

A widespread series of traditions connects St Mark with the foundation of the Alexandrian Church[2]. According to Eusebius, whose statement is possibly based on Julius Africanus or an older authority[3], his first successor in the care of that Church was appointed in Nero's eighth year, i.e. A.D. 61–2. If the date

---

[1] On Jewish settlements in Cyprus see Schürer II. ii. pp. 222, 232 (E. T.), or ed. 3 (1898) iii. p. 27 n. ; and cf. Acts xi. 19, 20, xxi. 16.

[2] Against this must be placed the fact to which Chase (Hastings, *D. B.* ii. 248) calls attention, that "the great Alex-andrian Fathers, Clement and Origen, make no reference to any sojourn or work of Mark in that city."

[3] Cf. Lipsius, *Die Apocryphen Apostelgeschichten*, ii. 2, p. 323; Harnack, *Chronologie*, p. 123 f.

is approximately correct, it may be that of the departure of Mark from Alexandria after the completion of his mission there. Such a hypothesis helps to account for part at least of the long interval between Mark's separation from St Paul and his reappearance in St Paul's company at Rome.

The following are the chief early authorities: Eus. *H.E.* ii. 16 φασὶν ἐπὶ τῆς Αἰγύπτου στειλάμενον τὸ εὐαγγέλιον ὃ δὴ καὶ συνεγράψατο κηρύξαι, ἐκκλησίας τε πρῶτον ἐπ᾽ αὐτῆς Ἀλεξανδρείας συστήσασθαι. *Ib.* 24 Νέρωνος δὲ ὄγδοον ἄγοντος τῆς βασιλείας ἔτος πρῶτος μετὰ Μάρκον τὸν εὐαγγελιστὴν τῆς ἐν Ἀλεξανδρείᾳ παροικίας Ἀννιανὸς τὴν λειτουργίαν διαδέχεται. Cf. Hieron. *de virr. ill.* 8 "adsumpto itaque evangelio quod ipse confecerat[1] perrexit Aegyptum...mortuus est autem octavo Neronis anno et sepultus Alexandriae succedente sibi Anniano." *Const. Ap.* vii. 46 τῆς δὲ Ἀλεξανδρέων Ἀννιανὸς πρῶτος ὑπὸ Μάρκου τοῦ εὐαγγελιστοῦ κεχειροτόνηται. Epiph. *haer.* li. 6 ὁ Μᾶρκος...γράψας τὸ εὐαγγέλιον ἀποστέλλεται ὑπὸ τοῦ ἁγίου Πέτρου εἰς τὴν τῶν Αἰγυπτίων χώραν. Cf. *Mart. Rom.* (Apr. 25) "Alexandriae natalis b. Marci evangelistae...Alexandriae S. Aniani episcopi qui b. Marci discipulus eiusque in episcopatu successor... quievit in Domino."

We have assumed the identity of John Mark of the Acts with Mark of the Pauline Epistles. It is placed beyond reasonable doubt by Col. iv. 10, where St Paul refers in one sentence to the relationship which existed between Mark and Barnabas, and the hesitation which the Colossians would naturally feel as to receiving the man who had forsaken the Apostles on occasion of their first visit to Asia Minor (Μᾶρκος ὁ ἀνεψιὸς Βαρνάβα, περὶ οὗ ἐλάβετε ἐντολάς Ἐὰν ἔλθῃ πρὸς ὑμᾶς, δέξασθε αὐτόν[2]). Mark, it appears, had thought of visiting the Churches of the Lycus valley some time before the writing of the Colossian letter, perhaps when he was on the point of leaving Cyprus; and St Paul had on that occasion sent orders to Colossae that he was to be received. There is nothing to shew that the visit took place; if our hypothesis is correct, it was abandoned for the mission to Egypt. The latter was now at an end, and Mark had proceeded to Rome.

---

[1] An inference from the ambiguous phrase of Eusebius. Bishop J. Wordsworth (*Ministry of Grace*, p. 603 f.) suggests that "the close connection of Alexandria with Rome" was "due probably at first to the mission of St Mark from the imperial city." But it is explained as easily by the constant communication between the two cities.

[2] See Lightfoot *ad loc.*; for δέξασθε comp. Mc. vi. 10, ix. 37, and *Didache* c. 11.

There, perhaps to his surprise, he found St Paul a prisoner. A complete reconciliation took place, and the ὑπηρέτης of the first missionary journey became the συνεργός of the Roman imprisonment (Col. iv. 11, Philem. 24). The fact is the more remarkable, because of all the Jewish Christians in Rome at this time only three were loyal to St Paul, Aristarchus, Jesus Justus, and Mark; his other colleagues, Epaphras, Demas, Luke, were Gentiles. The Apostle's grief was alleviated by the ministry of his Jewish friends (ἐγενήθησάν μοι παρηγορία), and especially no doubt by the revival of his old association with Mark. After this Mark seems to have returned to the East, for in 2 Tim. iv. 11, Timothy, who is apparently at Ephesus (cf. *v.* 19), is directed to "pick up Mark" on his way to Rome (Μᾶρκον ἀναλαβὼν ἄγε μετὰ σεαυτοῦ[1]). The reason which is given assigns to Mark his precise place in the history of the Apostolic age; he was εὔχρηστος εἰς διακονίαν. Not endowed with gifts of leadership, neither prophet nor teacher, he knew how to be invaluable to those who filled the first rank in the service of the Church, and proved himself a true *servus servorum Dei.*

Mark's early history had connected him with St Peter, and it is therefore no surprise to find him described by St Peter (1 Pet. v. 13) as his 'son[2].' The Apostle who had been most prominent in the beginnings of the Church of Jerusalem must have known Mary and her son John from the time of their baptism, and may have been the instrument of their conversion. Yet ὁ υἱός μου does not involve spiritual relationship of this kind, which is more naturally expressed, as in the Pauline Epistles, by τέκνον (cf. 1 Cor. iv. 17, Phil. ii. 22, Philem. 10, 1 Tim. i. 2, 18, 2 Tim. i. 2, ii. 1, Tit. i. 4). Rather it is the affectionate designation

---

[1] Lightfoot, *Biblical Essays*, p. 407.

[2] The Petrine authorship of 1 Peter may be assumed, notwithstanding the recent attempt of Professor McGiffert to assign that epistle to Barnabas (*History of Christianity in the Apostolic Age*, p. 598 ff.). It is difficult to follow him when he writes (p. 599 f.): "that Barnabas should speak of him (Mark) as his son was very natural, but it is not likely that any one else would do it save Paul himself"; the epithet is surely at least as appropriate on the lips of St Peter. As to the 'Paulinism' of 1 Peter see Hort, *Romans and Ephesians*, p. 169: "St Peter makes them [the thoughts derived from St Paul] fully his own by the form into which he casts them, a form for the most part unlike what we find in any epistle of St Paul."

of a former pupil, who as a young disciple must often have sat at his feet to be catechised and taught the way of the Lord, and who had come to look upon his mother's old friend and teacher as a second father, and to render to him the offices of filial piety.

But the Mark of 1 Peter is not merely described as St Peter's son; he is represented as being with that Apostle at Rome[1].

The words are: ἀσπάζεται ὑμᾶς ἡ ἐν Βαβυλῶνι συνεκλεκτὴ καὶ Μᾶρκος ὁ υἱός μου. 'Babylon' has been identified with (1) the city on the Euphrates, (2) a fortress in Egypt now Old Cairo[2], (3) Rome. The evidence in favour of the last is summarised by Lightfoot, *Clement*, ii. p. 492, Salmon, *Introduction to the N.T.*[7], p. 439 ff., and Hort, *First Epistle of St Peter*, p. 5 f.; the first and second identifications are without ancient authority, and beset with difficulties. Blass (*Philology of the Gospels*, p. 27 ff.) regards St Peter as having proceeded to Babylon from Antioch (Gal. ii. 11) shortly after A.D. 46. But apart from Strabo's statement that Babylon was at this time a desert, which Blass seeks to minimise, the facts which Josephus (*ant.* xviii. 9 sqq.) relates as to the condition of the Jews in Babylonia render this hypothesis highly improbable.

According to the constant and probably true tradition which brings St Peter to Rome, that Apostle suffered martyrdom there in the time of Nero and at the same time as St Paul (Dionysius of Corinth ap. Eus. ii. 25 ἐμαρτύρησαν κατὰ τὸν αὐτὸν χρόνον). "The expression (as Lightfoot urges, *Clement*, ii. p. 499) must not be too rigorously pressed, even if the testimony of a Corinthian could be accepted as regards the belief in Rome," or, we may add, the testimony of a bishop who lived in the latter half of the second century as regards matters of fact which belong to the history of the first. Lightfoot himself placed the martyrdom of St Peter in A.D. 64, and that of St Paul in A.D. 67; but if the two martyrdoms may be dissociated, it is open to consideration whether St Paul's was not the earlier.

Harnack[3], who holds that the two Apostles suffered together in A.D. 64, refers to Clem. 1 Cor. 6 τούτοις τοῖς ἀνδράσιν (sc. Πέτρῳ καὶ

---

[1] Cf. Jerome *de virr. ill.* 8 "meminit huius Marci et Petrus in prima epistula, sub nomine Babylonis figuraliter Romam significans."

[2] See Pearson's *Minor Th. Works* (ed.

Churton), ii. p. 353 ff.; and cf. A. J. Butler, *Ancient Coptic Churches*, i. p. 155 ff.

[3] *Chronologie*, p. 708 ff.; cf. C. H. Turner, *Chronology of the N. T.* (in Hastings, *Dictionary of the Bible*). That the

Παύλῳ)...συνηθροίσθη πολὺ πλῆθος ἐκλεκτῶν οἵτινες πολλαῖς αἰκίαις καὶ βασάνοις...ὑπόδειγμα κάλλιστον ἐγένοντο. But the words of Clement do not necessarily imply that the Apostles and the πολὺ πλῆθος suffered at the same time, or that the martyrdom of the Apostles took place at the first outbreak of the persecution. Nor does the fact that St Peter was believed to have been buried in the Vatican amount to a proof that he was among the first sufferers. Early as the tradition is (cf. Eus. *H.E.* ii. 25), it may rest upon inference only.

An examination of 1 Peter supplies more than one reason for believing the Epistle to have been written subsequently to St Paul's death. (1) It is addressed to the Christian communities of Pontus, Galatia, Cappadocia, Asia, and Bithynia, some of which were distinctly Pauline Churches and had received letters from St Paul during his imprisonment. It was transmitted to them by the hands of Silvanus, a well-known colleague of St Paul. It contains reminiscences of two of St Paul's writings, the Epistle to the Romans and the Epistle to the Ephesians[1]. The conclusion can scarcely be avoided that at the time when it was written St Paul had finished his course. The care of the Churches had fallen on St Peter; the two oldest associates of St Paul had transferred their services to the surviving Apostle; both had originally been members of the Church of Jerusalem, and, when the attraction of the stronger personality had been withdrawn, both had returned to their early leader. St Peter on his part is careful to shew by the character of his letter and by his selection of colleagues that he has no other end than to take up and carry on the work of St Paul. (2) Further, it has been pointed out by Professor Ramsay that 1 Peter contemplates a state of things in Asia Minor which did not exist before A.D. 64, and was hardly realised before the middle of the eighth decade of the century[2]. Reasons have been advanced for hesitating to push the year of St Peter's death so far forwards as 75, or beyond 70[3]; but even 68, the last year

---

martyrdom of St Peter took place in A.D. 64 is also maintained by Chase (Hastings, *D. B.* iii. 777 f.); cf. Zahn, *Einleitung*, ii. p. 19.

[1] Sanday and Headlam, *Romans*, p. lxxiv. ff.; Hort, *Romans and Ephesians*, p. 168; Salmon, *Intr. to the N. T.*[7], p. 442 ff.

[2] *The Church and the Empire*, p. 279 ff. Cf. *Exp.* iv. viii. 285 ff.

[3] Dr Sanday in the *Expositor*, iv. vii. p. 411 f.

of Nero's reign, will leave time for a considerable interval during which Mark may have ministered to St Peter at Rome.

Of the services rendered by Mark to Barnabas or to St Paul the tradition of the Church preserves but the faintest traces; in post-canonical Christian writings his name is persistently associated with St Peter.

An exception occurs in *Const. Ap.* ii. 57 τὰ εὐαγγέλια ἅ...οἱ συνεργοὶ Παύλου παρειληφότες κατέλειψαν ὑμῖν Λουκᾶς καὶ Μᾶρκος, and another in Hipp. *haer.* vii. 30 τούτους [sc. τοὺς λόγους] οὔτε Παῦλος ὁ ἀπόστολος οὔτε Μᾶρκος...ἀνήγγειλαν. But the former writer has perhaps been influenced by the order of the Gospels with which he was familiar; and the latter seems in this passage to have strangely confused St Mark with St Luke (see Duncker's note *ad loc.*).

3. One of the oldest and most trustworthy of Christian traditions represents Mark as St Peter's interpreter, and as the author of a collection of memoirs which gave the substance of St Peter's teaching.

The chief authorities are as follows: (1) *Asiatic and Western.* Papias ap. Eus. *H.E.* iii. 39 καὶ τοῦθ᾽ ὁ πρεσβύτερος ἔλεγε· Μᾶρκος μέν, ἑρμηνευτὴς Πέτρου γενόμενος, ὅσα ἐμνημόνευσεν ἀκριβῶς ἔγραψεν, οὐ μέντοι τάξει, τὰ ὑπὸ τοῦ χριστοῦ ἢ λεχθέντα ἢ πραχθέντα. οὔτε γὰρ ἤκουσε τοῦ κυρίου οὔτε παρηκολούθησεν αὐτῷ· ὕστερον δέ, ὡς ἔφην, Πέτρῳ, ὃς πρὸς τὰς χρείας ἐποιεῖτο τὰς διδασκαλίας, ἀλλ᾽ οὐχ ὥσπερ σύνταξιν τῶν κυριακῶν ποιούμενος λόγων. ὥστε οὐδὲν ἥμαρτε Μᾶρκος, οὕτως ἔνια γράψας ὡς ἀπεμνημόνευσεν· ἑνὸς γὰρ ἐποιήσατο πρόνοιαν, τοῦ μηδὲν ὧν ἤκουσε παραλιπεῖν ἢ ψεύσασθαί τι ἐν αὐτοῖς¹. Iren. iii. 1. 1 μετὰ δὲ τὴν τούτων [sc. τοῦ Πέτρου καὶ τοῦ Παύλου] ἔξοδον Μᾶρκος, ὁ μαθητὴς καὶ ἑρμηνευτὴς Πέτρου, καὶ αὐτὸς τὰ ὑπὸ Πέτρου κηρυσσόμενα ἐγγράφως ἡμῖν παραδέδωκε. *Ib.* 10. 6 "Marcus interpres et sectator Petri initium evangelicae conscriptionis fecit sic." Fragm. Murat. *ad init.* "[Marcus...(?) ali]quibus tamen interfuit et ita posuit²." Tertullian *adv. Marc.* iv. 5 "licet et Marcus quod edidit Petri affirmetur, cuius interpres Marcus." (2) *Alexandrian.* Clement, *hypotyp.* ap. Eus. *H.E.* vi. 14 τὸ δὲ κατὰ Μᾶρκον ταύτην ἐσχηκέναι τὴν οἰκονομίαν· τοῦ Πέτρου δημοσίᾳ ἐν Ῥώμῃ κηρύξαντος τὸν λόγον καὶ πνεύματι τὸ εὐαγγέλιον ἐξειπόντος τοὺς παρόντας πολλοὺς ὄντας παρακαλέσαι τὸν Μᾶρκον ὡς ἂν ἀκολουθήσαντα αὐτῷ πόρρωθεν καὶ μεμνημένον τῶν λεχθέντων ἀναγράψαι τὰ εἰρημένα, ποιήσαντα δὲ τὸ εὐαγγέλιον μεταδοῦναι τοῖς δεομένοις αὐτοῦ. ὅπερ ἐπιγνόντα τὸν Πέτρον προτρεπτικῶς μήτε κωλῦσαι μήτε προτρέψασθαι. (Cf. Eus. ii. 15 γνόντα

---

¹ For the interpretation of this passage see Westcott, *Canon of the N. T.*⁶, p. 74 f.; Lightfoot, *Supernatural Religion*, p. 163 ff.; Zahn, *Gesch. d. NTli-*

chen Kanons, i. p. 871 ff.; Link, in *Studien u. Kritiken*, 1896, 3.

² Comp. Lightfoot, *S. R.*, p. 205 ff.; Zahn, *op. cit.*, ii. p. 14 ff.

δὲ τὸ πραχθέν φασι τὸν ἀπόστολον, ἀποκαλύψαντος αὐτῷ τοῦ πνεύματος, ἡσθῆναι τῇ τῶν ἀνδρῶν προθυμίᾳ, κυρῶσαί τε τὴν γραφὴν εἰς ἔντευξιν ταῖς ἐκκλησίαις· Κλήμης ἐν ἕκτῳ τῶν ὑποτυπώσεων παρατέθειται τὴν ἱστορίαν.) *Adumbr. in* 1 *Petr.* v. 13 : "Marcus Petri sectator palam praedicante Petro evangelium Romae coram quibusdam Caesareanis equitibus et multa Christi testimonia proferente, petitus ab eis ut possent quae dicebantur memoriae commendare, scripsit ex his quae Petro dicta sunt evangelium quod secundum Marcum vocitatur." Origen ap. Eus. vi. 25 δεύτερον δὲ [τῶν τεσσάρων εὐαγγελίων] τὸ κατὰ Μᾶρκον ὡς Πέτρος ὑφηγήσατο αὐτῷ ποιήσαντα. Jerome gathers up the substance of the traditions recorded by Papias and Clement (*de virr. ill.* 8); but elsewhere he follows Origen (see p. xxi).

It will be observed that while the two lines of tradition have much in common, they are by no means identical, and probably depend on sources partly or wholly distinct. The Asiatic tradition goes behind St Mark's work as an Evangelist, and describes the nature of his services to St Peter. He had been the Apostle's interpreter. According to its usual meaning in later Greek, the ἑρμηνευτής is the secretary or dragoman who translates his master's words into a foreign tongue[1].

Thus when Joseph as an Egyptian prince communicates with his brethren from Palestine he uses the services of an interpreter (Gen. xlii. 23 ὁ γὰρ ἑρμηνευτὴς ἀνὰ μέσον αὐτῶν ἦν). St Paul directs that the gift of tongues shall not be exercised in Christian assemblies unless there be an interpreter at hand (1 Cor. xiv. 28 ἐὰν δὲ μὴ ᾖ διερμηνευτής (v.l. ἑρμηνευτής), σιγάτω ἐν τῇ ἐκκλησίᾳ).

Now John Mark had enjoyed opportunities of becoming a serviceable interpreter to an Aramaic-speaking Jew. As a resident in Jerusalem he was familiar with Aramaic; as a Jew who on one side at least was of Hellenistic descent, he could doubtless make himself understood in Greek. His Graeco-Latin surname implies something more than this; he had probably acquired in Jerusalem the power of reading and writing the Greek which passed current in Judæa and among Hellenistic Jews. Simon Peter on the other hand, if he could express himself in Greek at all, could scarcely have possessed sufficient knowledge of the language to address a Roman congregation with success. In the phrase ἑρμηνευτὴς

---

[1] For a different view see Zahn, *Einleitung*, ii. pp. 209, 218 ff.

Πέτρου γενόμενος we catch a glimpse of St Mark's work at Rome during St Peter's residence in the city[1].

The traditions differ also as to some important points connected with the origin of the Gospel. Papias suggests and Irenaeus expressly says that it was written after St Peter's death; Clement of Alexandria on the other hand states that the Apostle knew and permitted or even approved the enterprise. He adds that Mark wrote at the request of the Roman hearers of St Peter; but this feature in the story bears a suspicious resemblance to the account which the Muratorian fragment gives and Clement repeats in reference to the Gospel of St John. On the whole, notwithstanding St Mark's Alexandrian connexion, the Alexandrian tradition appears to be less worthy of credit than the Asiatic. Clement indeed attributes it to "the elders of olden time" (παράδοσιν τῶν ἀνέκαθεν πρεσβυτέρων τέθειται), meaning probably Pantaenus and others before him. But it must have passed through several hands before it reached Clement, whereas the statement of Papias came from a contemporary of St Mark[2].

John the presbyter, on whose witness Papias relies, describes the character of St Mark's work with much precision. It was not an orderly or a complete account of the Lord's words or works. Mark had no opportunity of collecting materials for such a history, for he had not been a personal follower of Christ, and depended upon his recollections of St Peter's teaching; and that teaching was not systematic, but intended to meet the practical requirements of the Church. On the other hand there was no lack of industry or of accuracy on the part of the Evangelist; he was careful to omit nothing that he had heard and could recall, and in what he recorded he kept strictly to the facts. It will be observed that John does not describe St Mark's work as a 'Gospel.'

---

[1] Jerome ad Hedib. 11 suggests that St Peter may have employed more than one interpreter, basing his belief on the differences of style which distinguish 1 and 2 Peter ("ex quo intellegimus pro necessitate rerum diversis eum usum interpretibus"). The argument applies with greater force to 1 Peter as compared with St Mark; the evangelist was assuredly not the interpreter who supplied the Epistle with its Greek dress.

[2] The Alexandrian elders were so imperfectly informed as to the relative age of the Gospels that according to Eusebius (H. E. vi. 14) they held προγεγράφθαι τῶν εὐαγγελίων τὰ περιέχοντα τὰς γενεαλογίας.

It was a record of St Peter's teaching or preaching (τῆς διδασκαλίας, cf. Iren. l.c. τὰ ὑπὸ Πέτρου κηρυσσόμενα). Yet it was certainly limited to the Apostle's reminiscences of the ministry of Christ (τὰ ὑπὸ τοῦ χριστοῦ ἢ λεχθέντα ἢ πραχθέντα), and thus in its general scope answered precisely to the book which was afterwards known as εὐαγγέλιον κατὰ Μᾶρκον. Later forms of the story exaggerate St Peter's part in the production. Even Origen seems to represent the Apostle as having personally controlled the work (ὡς Πέτρος ὑφηγήσατο αὐτῷ), whilst Jerome (*ad Hedib.*) says that the Gospel of St Mark was written "Petro narrante et illo scribente."

> The subscriptions which are appended to St Mark's Gospel in certain cursive MSS. enter into further details, e.g. 293 subscr. ἐγράφη ἰδιοχείρως αὐτοῦ τοῦ ἁγίου Μάρκου...καὶ ἐξεδόθη παρὰ Πέτρου...τοῖς ἐν Ῥώμῃ οὖσι πιστοῖς ἀδελφοῖς. Others add ὑπηγορεύθη (or διηγορεύθη) ὑπὸ Πέτρου, or ἐπεδόθη Μάρκῳ τῷ εὐαγγελιστῃ. On the other hand the subscriptions to the versions recognise Mark's authorship without mention of St Peter: e.g. "explicit evangelium secundum Marcum" (Latin Vulgate); ⲉⲩⲁⲅⲅⲉⲗⲓⲟⲛ ⲍⲱⲏⲥ ⲕⲁⲧⲁ ⲙⲁⲣⲕⲟⲛ (Memph.); ܐܘܢܓܠܝܘܢ (Sin. and Cur. Syriac); ܐܘܢܓܠܝܘܢ ܩܕܝܫܐ ܕܡܪܩܘܣ ܕܐܟܪܙ ܘܣܒܪ ܒܪܘܡܝ (Peshitta; similarly Harclean). The last of these seems to be an attempt to combine the Papias tradition with the ordinary attribution to Mark; the Gospel is a record of preaching at Rome, but the preaching is Mark's and not St Peter's.

4. One personal reminiscence of St Mark survives in a few authorities of Western origin. According to Hippolytus (*Philos.* vii. 30) he was known as ὁ κολοβοδάκτυλος, and the epithet is repeated and explained in the Latin prefaces to the Gospel. A Spanish MS. of the Vulgate, *cod. Toletanus* (saec. VIII), says: "*colobodactilus* est nominatus ideo quod a cetera corporis proceritatem (*sic*) digitos minores habuisset[1]"; whilst the ordinary Vulgate preface states that the Evangelist after his conversion amputated one of his fingers in order to disqualify himself for the duties of the Jewish priesthood ("amputasse sibi post fidem pollicem dicitur ut sacerdotio reprobus haberetur"). The explanation is ingenious,

---

[1] Wordsworth and White, p. 171.

but it is evidently based upon the conjecture that Mark, like Barnabas, belonged to the tribe of Levi. An attempt was made by Dr Tregelles[1] to shew that the word is used by Hippolytus as an equivalent for 'deserter,' in reference to Mark's departure from Perga. But this account of the matter can hardly be regarded as satisfactory; it is far-fetched at the best; and so offensive a nickname is not likely to have attached itself to the Evangelist in Roman circles, where he was known as St Paul's faithful colleague. The word itself determines nothing as to the cause of the defect, or its extent; it may have been congenital, or due to accident; it may have affected both hands or all the fingers of one hand or one finger only[2]. The preface in *cod. Toletanus* seems to ascribe it to a natural cause. No authority can be allowed to a document of this kind, but the statement is not in itself improbable; at all events there seems to be no reason for setting aside the literal meaning of the word, or for doubting that it describes a personal peculiarity which had impressed itself on the memory of the Roman Church. Such a defect, to whatever cause it was due, may have helped to mould the course of John Mark's life; by closing against him a more ambitious career, it may have turned his thoughts to those secondary ministries by which he has rendered enduring service to the Church.

Κολοβός is either (1) of stunted growth, or (2) mutilated. Both senses occur when the word is used as part of a compound; the former appears in κολοβανθής, κολοβοκέρατος, κολοβοτράχηλος, the latter in κολοβόκερκος (Lev. xxii. 23 LXX., where it is coupled with ὠτότμητος), κολοβόριν (Lev. xxi. 18); cf. 2 Regn. iv. 12 κολοβοῦσιν τὰς χεῖρας αὐτῶν καὶ τοὺς πόδας αὐτῶν.

As to the time and manner of St Mark's death we have no trustworthy information. Jerome, as we have seen, fixes his death in the eighth year of Nero, at Alexandria; but the statement seems to be merely an unsound inference from the Eusebian date for the succession of Annianus. The Paschal Chronicle assigns to Mark the crown of martyrdom[3], but the story cannot be

---

[1] *Journal of Classical and Sacred Philology*, 1855, p. 224 f.
[2] Dr Chase (in Hastings, *D. B.* iii. p. 247) suggests that " the word may refer to some mutilation or malformation of the *toes*, resulting in lameness."
[3] *Chron. Pasch.*: ἐπὶ τούτου τοῦ Τραιανοῦ καὶ Μᾶρκος ὁ εὐαγγελιστὴς καὶ ἐπί-

traced back further than the fourth or fifth century, when it is found in the *Acts of Mark*, an *apocryphon* of Alexandrian origin[1]; the particulars as they were elaborated at a later time may be seen in Nicephorus, or in the Sarum lections for his festival[2]. No reference is made to the fact in the prefaces to the Vulgate, or by Jerome, though he relates that Mark was buried at Alexandria[3].

σκοπος 'Αλεξανδρείας γενόμενος...ἐμαρτύρησεν.

[1] See Lipsius, *Apostelgesch.* ii. 2, p. 321 ff.

[2] Niceph. Call. *H. E.* ii. 43 εἰς τὴν 'Αλεξάνδρειαν πάλιν ἐπάνεισιν, ὅπου δὴ τὰς διατριβὰς ποιούμενος ἦν ἐν τοῖς Βουκέλου ὀνομαζομένοις μετά τινων ἀδελφῶν παρρησίᾳ τὸν χριστὸν κηρύσσων. οἱ τοίνυν τῶν εἰδώλων θεραπευταὶ αἴφνης αὐτῷ ἐπιθέμενοι σχοινίοις τοὺς πόδας διαλαβόντες ἀπηνέστερον εἶλον...οὕτω δὴ συρόμενος τὸ πνεῦμα παρατίθησι τῷ θεῷ. Procter and Wordsworth, *Sanctorale*, col. 262 f. The day of his martyrdom was Pharmouthi 30 in the Egyptian Kalendar, and VIII Kal. Mai=Apr. 28 in the Roman (Lipsius, *op. cit.*, p. 335).

[3] For the traditional connexion of St Mark with the Church of Aquileia and the translation of his body to Venice see the *Acta Sanctorum* (Apr. 25), and as to the latter point cf. Tillemont, *Mémoires*, ii. pp. 98 f., 513; Lipsius, *op. cit.*, p. 346 ff. On the mission to Aquileia Ado of Vienne († 874) writes (*Chron.* vi., Migne *P. L.* cxxiii. col. 78): "Marcus evangelista evangelium quod Romae scripserat Petro mittente primum Aquileiae praedicavit, itaque...ad Aegyptum pervenit." The extension of the older story (Eus. *H. E.* ii. 16) in this passage is instructive. The mosaic at St Mark's, Venice, which represents the removal of the Evangelist's body is described by Ruskin, *St Mark's Rest*, p. 109 ff.; for his account of St Mark's see *Stones of Venice*, ii. p. 56 ff.

History of the Gospel in the Early Church

1. A work which was ascribed by contemporaries to a disciple and interpreter of St Peter, and believed to consist of carefully registered reminiscences of the Apostle's teaching, might have been expected to find a prompt and wide circulation in Christian communities, especially at Rome and in the West, where it is said to have been written. Yet the letter addressed to the Corinthian Church by Clement of Rome, c. A.D. 95, contains no certain reference to the Gospel according to St Mark, although it quotes sayings which bear a close affinity to the Synoptic record.

Clem. R. 1 *Cor.* 23, πρῶτον μὲν φυλλορροεῖ, εἶτα βλαστὸς γίνεται, εἶτα φύλλον...εἶτα σταφυλὴ παρεστηκυῖα, reminds the reader of Mc. iv. 28, 29; but the passage in Clement is part of a quotation (cf. γραφή...ὅπου λέγει) which occurs again in Ps.-Clem. 2 *Cor.* 11 and appears to be derived from some Christian apocryphon (cf. Lightfoot *ad loc.*), so that the reference, if there be any, is indirect. In Clem. 1 *Cor.* 15, οὗτος ὁ λαὸς τοῖς χείλεσιν με τιμᾷ, ἡ δὲ καρδία αὐτῶν πόρρω ἄπεστιν ἀπ' ἐμοῦ, Isa. xxix. 13 is cited in words which are nearer to Mc. vii. 6 than to the LXX., but the quotation is given by Mt. in an almost identical form, and Clement (cod. A) differs from both Evangelists and from the LXX., writing ἄπεστιν for ἀπέχει. The passage had probably (Hatch, *Essays*, p. 177 f.) been detached from its context and abbreviated by some compiler of *testimonia* before the middle of the first century, and, if so, no argument can be built upon the general coincidence of the form used by Clem. with that which appears in Mc. *Ib.* 1 *Cor.* 46, οὐαὶ τῷ ἀνθρώπῳ ἐκείνῳ· καλὸν ἦν αὐτῷ εἰ οὐκ ἐγεννήθη, agrees fairly well with Mc. xiv. 21, but still more exactly with Mt. xxvi. 24, and may have been cited from a pre-evangelical tradition.

The same may be said of the writings of Ignatius, Polycarp, and Barnabas. Bishop Westcott, after a careful examination, arrives at the conclusion that "no Evangelic reference in the

Apostolic Fathers can be referred certainly to a written record[1]."
Yet these writers with Clement represent the chief centres of
both East and West—Rome, Antioch, Smyrna, and perhaps
Alexandria. If we add other documents of the same period—
the *Didache*, the so-called second Epistle of Clement, the Epistle
to Diognetus, the martyrdom of Polycarp, the fragments of Papias
and the Elders—the general result will not be different[2]. On the
other hand the *Shepherd*, which is the next document emanating
from the Roman Church, and cannot be placed later than A.D. 156,
while it may possibly belong to the first years of the second
century, seems clearly to shew the influence of the second Gospel.

Herm. *sim.* ix. 20 οἱ τοιοῦτοι οὖν δυσκόλως εἰσελεύσονται εἰς
τὴν βασιλείαν τοῦ θεοῦ...τοῖς τοιούτοις δύσκολόν ἐστιν εἰς τ. β.
τ. θ. εἰσελθεῖν (cf. Mc. x. 23, 24; Mt. has merely πλούσιος εἰσελεύ-
σεται εἰς τ. β. τῶν οὐρανῶν, and Lc. drifts further away from the
Marcan form of the saying). Ib. *mand.* ii. 2 ἔνοχος ἔσῃ τῆς ἁμαρτίας
(cf. Mc. iii. 29). On the general question as to the use of our four
Gospels by Hermas see Dr C. Taylor, *Witness of Hermas*, p. 5 ff.

In Justin, again, we have an echo of Christian opinion at
Rome, and though the point is open to dispute, there is ground
for believing that he not only refers to the second Gospel, but
identifies it with the "memoirs of Peter."

Dial. 106 τὸ εἰπεῖν μετωνομακέναι αὐτὸν Πέτρον ἕνα τῶν ἀποστόλων
καὶ γεγράφθαι ἐν τοῖς ἀπομνημονεύμασιν αὐτοῦ γεγενημένον καὶ τοῦτο
μετὰ τοῦ καὶ ἄλλους δύο ἀδελφοὺς υἱοὺς Ζεβεδαίου ὄντας μετωνομακέναι
ὀνόματι τοῦ Βοανεργές, ὅ ἐστιν υἱοὶ βροντῆς, σημαντικὸν ἦν τὸν
αὐτὸν ἐκεῖνον δι' οὗ καὶ τὸ ἐπώνυμον Ἰακὼβ τῷ Ἰσραὴλ ἐπικληθέντι
ἐδόθη. It is clear from this that Justin knew certain Ἀπομνημονεύματα Πέτρου which contained the words ὄνομα Βοανεργές, ὅ
ἐστιν υἱοὶ βροντῆς, or their substance. But the actual words occur
in Mc. iii. 17, and in no other evangelical record[3]. The assumption that they were borrowed not from our second Gospel but
from Pseudo-Peter appears to be arbitrary, notwithstanding the
support of some great names (Harnack, *Bruckstücke d. Ev. d.
Petrus*, p. 37 ff., and Sanday, *Inspiration*, p. 310). A second
reference to Mc. has been found in *Dial.* 88 τέκτονος νομιζομένου

---

[1] *Canon of the N. T.*[6], p. 63.
[2] Ignatius has (*Eph.* 16) the Marcan
phrase τὸ πῦρ τὸ ἄσβεστον, but cf. Mt. iii.
12 = Lc. iii. 17; all the passages rest on
Isa. lxvi. 24. In Polyc. *Philipp.* 5 (τοῦ
κυρίου ὃς ἐγένετο διάκονος πάντων) there is

possibly a reminiscence of the saying in
Mc. ix. 35, ἔσται...πάντων διάκονος, but it
is too uncertain to establish direct indebtedness.
[3] See the writer's *Akhmîm Fragment*,
p. xxxiii. ff.; *J. Th. St.* ii. p. 6 ff.

(Mc. vi. 3); other passages might be quoted, but they relate to contexts which are common to Mc. and Mt. or Lc., or to the non-Marcan verses xvi. 9—20 (see Intr. § xi.).

Meanwhile the Gospel was known and used by more than one of the earlier Gnostic sects, and in other heretical circles both in East and West.

Thus Heracleon (ap. Clem. Al. *strom.* iv. 72) in a catena of extracts from the Synoptic Gospels cites Mc. viii. 38; cf. Zahn, *Gesch. d. NTlichen Kanons*, i. p. 741 f. Irenaeus (i. 3. 3) refers to the use of Mc. v. 31 by a Valentinian school, and Mc. i. 13 is distinctly quoted by the Eastern Valentinians, Clem. *exc.* 85 (αὐτίκα ὁ κύριος μετὰ τὸ βάπτισμα γίνεται πρῶτον μετὰ θηρίων ἐν τῇ ἐρήμῳ). A Docetic sect mentioned by Irenaeus manifested a preference for the Second Gospel (iii. 11. 7 "qui autem Iesum separant a Christo et impassibilem perseverasse Christum passum autem Iesum dicunt, id quod secundum Marcum est praeferentes evangelium"). But a mistake may perhaps lurk in this statement. Basilides, we know (Clem. *strom.* vii. 17), professed to have received instruction from one Glaucias, who is styled an interpreter of Peter. If this Gnostic rival of St Mark wrote a Gospel, it is possible that the words of Irenaeus refer to the Gnostic Gospel, and not to the true St Mark. In Pseudo-Peter there are distinct indications of the use of St Mark (*Akhmîm Fragment*, p. xl.). The Ebionite Clementine Homilies also shew an acquaintance with it, e.g. xix. 20 τοῖς αὐτοῦ μαθηταῖς κατ᾽ ἰδίαν ἐπέλυε τῆς τῶν οὐρανῶν βασιλείας μυστήρια (Mc. iv. 34); a reference to Mc. xii. 29 in *hom.* iii. 51 is less certain, but probable (cf. Sanday, *Gospels in the second century*, p. 177 f.). Hippolytus (*phil.* vii. 30) strangely represents St Mark's Gospel as forming part of the canon of Marcion[1]. But apart from Marcion the Second Gospel seems to have found no opponents in early Christian communities, heretical or catholic.

The early circulation of St Mark's Gospel is further attested by its place among the primary Gospels, which were regarded, perhaps before the middle of the second century, as a sacred quaternion.

This idea is first expounded by Irenaeus iii. 11. 8 ἐπειδὴ τέσσαρα κλίματα τοῦ κόσμου ἐν ᾧ ἐσμεν εἰσὶ καὶ τέσσαρα καθολικὰ πνεύματα, κατέσπαρται δὲ ἡ ἐκκλησία ἐπὶ πάσης τῆς γῆς...εἰκότως (*consequens est*) τέσσαρας ἔχειν αὐτὴν στύλους...ἐξ ὧν φανερὸν ὅτι ὁ τῶν ἁπάντων τεχνίτης Λόγος, ὁ καθήμενος ἐπὶ τῶν χερουβὶμ καὶ συνέχων τὰ πάντα, φανερωθεὶς τοῖς ἀνθρώποις ἔδωκεν ἡμῖν τετράμορφον τὸ εὐαγγέλιον (*quadriforme evangelium*), ἑνὶ δὲ πνεύματι συνεχόμενον. But the conception of a τετράμορφον εὐαγγέλιον does not seem to have

---

[1] Marcion was probably acquainted with St Mark (cf. Westcott, *Canon*[6], p. 316 n.; Zahn, *Geschichte*, p. 675).

originated with the Bp of Lyons. Dr C. Taylor (*Witness of Hermas,* i. *passim*) with much probability traces it to Hermas, i.e. to the generation before Irenaeus. Between Hermas and Irenaeus we have the witness of Tatian, whose *Diatessaron* reveals the fact that the four Gospels which had received general recognition were none other than those of the present canon. Moreover there is reason to believe (J. R. Harris, *Diatessaron,* p. 56) that Tatian's Harmony was not the first attempt of its kind; certainly the harmonising of portions of the Synoptic narrative appears to have begun before his time.

If it be asked why St Mark's Gospel took its place among the four, the answer must be that in the belief of the post-Apostolic Church it was identified with the teaching of St Peter. It did not appeal in any special manner to the interests of the Ancient Church, or, like the first and fourth of our Gospels, bear an Apostolic name. It was saved from exclusion, and perhaps from oblivion, by the connexion of its writer with St Peter. Thus its position in the primitive canon bears witness to a general and early conviction that it was the genuine work of the *interpres Petri.*

In Irenaeus the identification of the work of St Mark with the Second Gospel is formal and complete. The great Bishop of Lyons is "the first extant writer in whom, from the nature of his work, we have a right to expect explicit information on the subject of the Canon[1]," and he does not disappoint our expectations here. He quotes our Gospel repeatedly, he quotes it as St Mark's, and he declares the author to have been St Peter's disciple and interpreter.

Iren. iii. 10. 6 "Marcus interpres et sectator Petri initium evan-gelicae conscriptionis fecit sic : *initium evangelii Iesu Christi filii Dei,*" etc. (Mc. i. 1—3). Elsewhere Irenaeus quotes *verbatim* Mc. i. 24 (iv. 6. 6), v. 31 (i. 3. 3), 41, 43 (v. 13. 1), viii. 31 (iii. 16. 5), 38 (iii. 18. 6), ix. 23 (iv. 37. 5), 44 (ii. 32. 1), x. 38 (i. 21. 3), xiii. 32 (ii. 28. 6), xvi. 19 (iii. 10. 6). The last of these passages shews that the Gospel as he possessed it included the supplementary verses, and that he attributed the whole to Mark : "in fine autem evangelii ait Marcus *Et quidem Dominus Iesus, postquam locutus est eis, receptus est in caelum, et sedet ad dexteram Dei.*"

[1] Lightfoot, *Supernatural Religion,* p. 271.

The century ends with the witness of an anonymous Roman writer, the author of the so-called Muratorian fragment, and that of Tertullian, who represents the belief of the daughter Church of Carthage.

The Muratorian writer recognised four Gospels ("tertio secundum Lucam...quarti evangeliorum Iohannis"), and the single line which is all that remains of his account of St Matthew and St Mark doubtless refers to St Mark. The words are *quibus tamen interfuit et ita posuit*. *Quibus* may be regarded as the second half of *aliquibus*, the first two syllables having perished with the preceding leaf of the MS., or *quibus tamen* may represent οἷς δὲ in the Greek original[1]. The sentence cannot mean that St Mark was on certain occasions a personal attendant on our Lord, as the next sentence ("Lucas...Dominum...nec ipse vidit in carne")[2] clearly shews, and must therefore refer to St Peter's teaching[3], which Mark reported carefully so far as he had opportunity. This may be either a reminiscence of the words of Papias (οὐδὲν ἥμαρτε Μᾶρκος, οὕτως ἔνια γράψας ὡς ἀπεμνημόνευσεν), or part of an independent Roman tradition. In either case it is important as evidence of Roman opinion at the end of the second century.

Tertullian's belief is clearly shewn in *adv. Marc.* iv. 2, 5 "nobis fidem ex apostolis Ioannes et Matthaeus insinuant, ex apostolicis Lucas et Marcus instaurant...licet et Marcus quod edidit Petri affirmetur, cuius interpres Marcus." His references to Mark are few, but some of them at least admit of no doubt; they will be found in Rönsch, *d. N. T. Tertullians*, p. 148 ff.

From the end of the second century the literary history of St Mark is merged in that of the canon of the Four Gospels. The Gospel according to Mark holds its place in all ancient versions of the New Testament and in all early lists of the canon. No voice was raised against its acceptance; East and West, Catholics and heretics, tacitly recognised its authority. The evidence comes from all the great centres of Christian life; from Edessa and Antioch, from Jerusalem and Asia Minor, from Alexandria and the banks of the Nile, as well as from Rome, Carthage, and Gaul.

The Gospel according to St Mark was contained in the Old Syriac version (it appears in both the Curetonian and Sinaitic

---

[1] So Chase in Hastings, *D. B.* iii. p. 247.
[2] Lightfoot, *S. R.* p. 271.
[3] See on the other hand Zahn, *Einlei-*

tung, ii. pp. 200, 201. A later tradition represented St Mark as one of the Seventy (Adamant. *Dial.* p. 10 (ed. Bakhuyzen), Epiph. *haer.* 51 § 6).

texts), in the Egyptian versions, both Bohairic and Sahidic, and in the oldest forms of the Old Latin. It finds a place in all the catalogues which enumerate the Gospels, both Eastern and Western (see Westcott, *Canon*, app. D; Preuschen, *Analecta*, p. 138 ff.).

2. But while no doubts are expressed by any early writer as to the genuineness of St Mark, it cannot be denied that the Gospel received comparatively little attention from the theologians of the ancient Church. This relative neglect is noticeable from the very first. It has been pointed out that with the exception of Hermas the Apostolic fathers contain no clear reference to St Mark, and that their quotations as a whole are in closer agreement with the first Gospel than with the second[1]. But it is doubtful whether the earliest post-apostolic writers of the Church made use of written Gospels at all. Papias expresses the general feeling of the age which succeeded the Apostles when he records his preference for "the living voice," i.e. the oral testimony of the elders who yet survived from the first generation; even the Memoirs of St Peter would not be widely used so long as the stream of oral tradition continued to flow. This consideration may serve to account for the absence of quotations from St Mark in such writers as Clement of Rome and Ignatius of Antioch. It is less easy to explain the apparent neglect of this Gospel long after it had taken its place in every Greek codex of the Gospels and in every version of the New Testament. The commentator known as Victor of Antioch, a compiler whose date is certainly not earlier than the fifth century, complains that, while St Matthew and St John had received the attention of a number of expositors, and St Luke also had attracted a few, his utmost efforts had failed to detect a single commentary upon St Mark.

Victor, *hypoth.*: πολλῶν εἰς τὸ κατὰ Ματθαῖον καὶ εἰς τὸ κατὰ Ἰωάννην...συνταξάντων ὑπομνήματα, ὀλίγων δὲ εἰς τὸ κατὰ Λουκᾶν, οὐδενὸς δὲ ὅλως, ὡς οἶμαι, εἰς τὸ κατὰ Μᾶρκον ἐξηγησαμένου, ἐπεὶ μηδὲ μέχρι τήμερον ἀκήκοα καὶ τοῦτο πολυπραγμονήσας παρὰ τῶν σπουδὴν ποιουμένων τὰ τῶν ἀρχαιοτέρων συνάγειν πονήματα κτλ.

---

[1] Sir J. C. Hawkins (*Hor. Syn.* p. 179) finds a correspondence between "the degree of familiarity with the language of the three Gospels which appears to have existed among Christians" and the relative adaptation of the Gospels "for the purposes of catechetical or other teaching." Traces of such adaptation are fewest in St Mark, and this fact suggests a reason for the comparative neglect of St Mark in the sub-apostolic age.

The cause is doubtless partly to be sought in the *prestige* attaching to the first Gospel, which was regarded as the immediate work of an Apostle, and the greater fulness of both St Matthew and St Luke. St Mark offered, after all, merely a disciple's recollections of his master's teaching. There was little in St Mark which was not to be found in St Matthew or St Luke, or in both. Moreover, St Mark was believed even by Irenaeus to have been written after St Matthew; and from this view men passed by easy steps to the conclusion that the second Gospel was a mere abridgement of the first.

Iren. iii. 1. 1 ὁ μὲν δὴ Ματθαῖος...γραφὴν ἐξήνεγκεν εὐαγγελίου τοῦ Πέτρου καὶ τοῦ Παύλου ἐν Ῥώμῃ εὐαγγελιζομένων...μετὰ δὲ τὴν τούτων ἔξοδον Μᾶρκος κτλ. Victor, *hypoth.* ἰστέον ὅτι μετὰ Ματθαῖον Μᾶρκος ὁ εὐαγγελιστὴς συγγραφὴν ποιεῖται. Aug. *de cons. evv.* i. 3, 4 " isti quatuor evangelistae...hoc ordine scripsisse perhibentur : primum Matthaeus, deinde Marcus...Marcus eum subsecutus tanquam pedissequus et breviator eius videtur. cum solo quippe Ioanne nihil dixit, solus ipse perpauca, cum solo Luca pauciora, cum Matthaeo vero plurima et multa paene totidem atque ipsis verbis sive cum solo sive cum ceteris consonante."

Such an estimate of St Mark was sufficient to counterbalance the weight which was attached to this Gospel as the work of St Peter's interpreter.

Something may be learnt as to the relative importance of the Gospels in the judgement of the Ancient Church from the order in which they are placed in catalogues and MSS. The two principal groupings are as follows:

(1) Mt. Mc. Lc. Jo. (or Mt. Mc. Jo. Lc.);

(2) Mt. Jo. Lc. Mc. (or Jo. Mt. Lc. Mc., or Jo. Mt. Mc. Lc., or Mt. Jo. Mc. Lc.[1]).

The first is that of nearly all the Greek MSS. and of the great majority of the catalogues and ecclesiastical writers, and in its secondary form it appears in the Curetonian MS. of the Old Syriac, and in the Cheltenham list. The second is the order of

---

[1] Gregory, *Prolegomena*, p. 137 f.; Sanday, *Studia Biblica*, iii. p. 259 f.; Nestle, *Textual Criticism of the N.T.* (E. T.), p. 161 f. The O. L. MS. *k* has the order Jo. Lc. Mc. Mt., whilst Ambrosiaster and the list of ' the Sixty Books' have Mt. Lc. Mc. Jo., where the Apostolic Gospels are placed first and last, but Mc. retains its usual Western position.

the Gospels in Codex Bezae and one Greek cursive, in certain Old Latin MSS. (a b e f ff q r), the Gothic version and the Apostolical Constitutions, in the Latin stichometry of Codex Claromontanus, in Tertullian, and in the vocabularies of the Egyptian versions. Each of these groupings rests upon an intelligible principle. The second, which embodies the original order of the West (cf. Tert. *adv. Marc. l.c.*), places in the first pair the Gospels which were ascribed to Apostles, and after them those which were the work of followers of the Apostles. The first, which ultimately prevailed in the West as well as in the East, arranges the four according to the supposed *ordo scribendi*[1]. In both the relative inferiority of St Mark is apparent; in (1) he follows Mt. as his *pedissequus*; in (2) he is preceded not only by the two Apostles, but usually also by St Luke. The two exceptions are probably due to a mixture of (2) with (1); the scribe began with the Western order, but when he reached the *apostolici*, he reverted to the customary arrangement, in which Mark precedes Luke according to the order of time[2].

Another indication of the attitude of the ancient Church towards the Gospel of St Mark is to be found in the distribution of the evangelical symbols among the Four Evangelists. From the time of Irenaeus the four Gospels were associated in Christian thought with the four Cherubim of Ezekiel, and the corresponding ζῷα of the Apocalypse. Irenaeus (iii. 11. 8) quotes the Apocalypse only, but he calls the living creatures Cherubim, and refers to Ps. lxxix. (lxxx.) 2 LXX. (ὁ καθήμενος ἐπὶ τῶν χερουβείμ, ἐμφάνηθι). It is the Eternal Word, he says, Who sits upon the Cherubim, and their four aspects represent His fourfold manner of operation (πραγματεία, *dispositio*); the lion answers to His royal office and sovereign authority and executive power (τὸ ἔμπρακτον αὐτοῦ καὶ ἡγεμονικὸν καὶ βασιλικόν); the

---

[1] Cf. Clem. Al. in Eus. *H. E.* vi. 14.

[2] The Rev. H. T. Tilley informs me that in the tower of Wolston Church near Rugby there is a fifteenth century bell which bears the inscription + MARCVS · MATHEVS · LVCAS · IOHES, and that some tiles at Malvern Priory Church, dated 1456, give the same order. It may have come from the Commentary on the Apocalypse which is printed under the name of Victorinus of Pettau, where the Evangelists are mentioned in this order (Migne, *P. L.* v., col. 324).

calf symbolises His sacrificial and priestly character; the human face, His coming in human nature; the flying eagle, the gift of the Spirit descending on His Church. The Gospels accordingly, which reflect the likeness of Christ, possess the same characteristics; St John sets forth the Lord's princely and glorious generation from the Father, St Luke emphasises His priestly work, St Matthew His human descent, St Mark His prophetic office:

Iren. *l.c.* Μᾶρκος δὲ ἀπὸ τοῦ προφητικοῦ πνεύματος τοῦ ἐξ ὕψους ἐπιόντος τοῖς ἀνθρώποις τὴν ἀρχὴν ἐποιήσατο λέγων Ἀρχὴ τοῦ εὐαγγελίου Ἰησοῦ Χριστοῦ, ὡς γέγραπται ἐν Ἠσαΐᾳ τῷ προφήτῃ, τὴν πτερωτικὴν εἰκόνα τοῦ εὐαγγελίου δεικνύων· διὰ τοῦτο δὲ καὶ σύντομον καὶ παρατρέχουσαν τὴν καταγγελίαν πεποίηται· προφητικὸς γὰρ ὁ χαρακτὴρ οὗτος.

Thus Irenaeus, it is clear, regards the Eagle as the symbol of St Mark, whilst St Matthew, St Luke and St John are represented by the Man, the Calf, and the Lion respectively. This interpretation of the symbols is followed in the lines prefixed to the Gospel-paraphrase of Juvencus, according to which

"Marcus amat terras inter caelumque volare,
    Et vehemens aquila stricto secat omnia lapsu."

But the method by which it was reached is so arbitrary that later writers did not hesitate to rearrange them at discretion. Thus in the notes on the Apocalypse attributed to Victorinus of Pettau the Eagle is assigned to St John and the Lion to St Mark. Through the influence of Jerome this became the popular view, and impressed itself on mediaeval art, although it was based on grounds not more reasonable than those which led Irenaeus to the opposite conclusion.

Hieron. *in Marcum tract.* ad init. "in Marco leonem in heremo personat...qui in heremo personat utique leo est." Cf. Victorin. *in Apoc.* c. iv. (Migne, *P.L.* v. *l.c.*) "simile leoni animal Marcum designat in quo vox leonis in heremo rugientis auditur...Marcus itaque Evangelista sic incipiens...leonis habet effigiem."

Other arrangements were freely proposed. Thus in the Pseudo-Athanasian *Synopsis*[1] Matthew is the man, Mark the calf, Luke

[1] Migne, *P. G.* xxviii., col. 431 : τέσσαρα γὰρ εἶδε χερουβεὶμ οὗτος ὁ προφήτης...τὸ δεύτερον ὅμοιον μόσχῳ, τουτέστι τὸ κατὰ Μᾶρκον εὐαγγέλιον. The second symbol is attributed to the second Evangelist.

the lion, John the eagle. Augustine finds the lion in Matthew,
the man in Mark, the calf in Luke, the eagle in John. He
complains with justice of the puerility of deciding the character
of a book from the opening sentences, and not from the general
purpose and aim of the writer; and he justifies his assignment of
the man to St Mark on the ground that the second Gospel sets
forth the human life of Christ rather than His royal descent, or
His priestly office.

> *De cons. evv.* i. 9 "de principiis enim librorum quandam coniec-
> turam capere voluerunt, non de tota intentione Evangelistarum...
> Marcus ergo, qui neque stirpem regiam neque sacerdotalem vel cog-
> nationem vel consecrationem narrare voluit et tamen in eis versatus
> ostenditur quae homo Christus operatus est, tantum hominis figura
> in illis quatuor animalibus significatus videtur."

A table will shew the extent of these variations[1].

	Irenaeus.	*Victorinus.*	*Augustine.*	*Ps.-Athanasius.*
MT.	Man	Man	Lion	Man
Mc.	Eagle	Lion	Man	Calf
Lc.	Calf	Calf	Calf	Lion
Jo.	Lion	Eagle	Eagle	Eagle.

It will be seen at a glance that while in three out of the four
distributions St Matthew is the Man, St Luke the Calf, and
St John the Eagle, to St Mark each of the symbols is assigned in
turn. This fact illustrates with curious precision the difficulty
which the ancient Church experienced in forming a definite
judgement as to the place and office of his Gospel[2]. Irenaeus
indeed has rightly seized upon the rapid movement of the narrative as one of its features, and Augustine calls attention to
another and deeper characteristic, the interest which the writer
shews in the humanity of the Lord. But it remained for a later
age to realise and appreciate to the full the freshness and exactness of the first-hand report which has descended to us from the
senior Apostle through the ministry of John Mark.

[1] A fuller treatment will be found in Zahn, *Forschungen*, ii. p. 257 ff.

[2] See Professor Lawlor's *Chapters on the Book of Mulling* (p. 17 ff.) for an interesting discussion of the evangelical symbols in connexion with certain Irish MSS. "in which, while the text followed the Vulgate order, the symbols adhered to that of the older versions."

3

Place and Time of Writing, and Original Language

1. According to the prevalent belief of the ancient Church St Mark wrote his Gospel in Rome and for the Roman Church. Chrysostom transfers the place of composition to Egypt, but he is sufficiently refuted by the testimony of Clement of Alexandria and Origen.

For the Alexandrian evidence see p. xxii f. Chrysostom's words (*prooem. in Mt.*) are as follows: καὶ Μᾶρκος δὲ ἐν Αἰγύπτῳ τῶν μαθητῶν παρακαλεσάντων αὐτὸν αὐτὸ τοῦτο ποιῆσαι (sc. συνθεῖναι τὸ εὐαγγέλιον, as the context shews). The error has possibly arisen from the statement of Eusebius (*H. E.* ii. 16), Μᾶρκον πρῶτόν φασιν ἐπὶ τῆς Αἰγύπτου στειλάμενον τὸ εὐαγγέλιον ὃ δὴ συνεγράψατο κηρύξαι: cf. Jerome, *de virr. ill.* 8 "adsumpto itaque evangelio quod ipse confecerat perrexit Aegyptum." Epiphanius for once expresses himself with greater care (*haer.* li. 6 ἐν Ῥώμῃ ἐπιτρέπεται τὸ εὐαγγέλιον ἐκθέσθαι, καὶ γράψας ἀποστέλλεται ὑπὸ τοῦ ἁγίου Πέτρου εἰς τὴν τῶν Αἰγυπτίων χώραν). The subscriptions to the Gospels vary; while the majority of those which fix upon a locality are in favour of Rome, others refer only to the preaching of the Gospel at Alexandria, e.g. a codex quoted by Mill has ἐπεδόθη Μάρκῳ τῷ εὐαγγελίστῃ καὶ ἐκηρύχθη ἐν Ἀλεξανδρείᾳ καὶ πάσῃ τῇ περιχώρῳ αὐτῆς (cf. Ps. Ath. *synops.* 76). Tischendorf mentions the subscription ἐγράφη...ἐν Αἰγύπτῳ as found in certain MSS. which he does not specify.

2. But if the Gospel was written at Rome or for the Church of Rome, at what time was it written? 'After the departure (ἔξοδον[1])

---

[1] For ἔξοδος in this sense cf. Lc. ix. 31, 2 Pet. i. 15, Jos. *ant.* iv. 8. 2 (ἐπ' ἐξόδου τοῦ ζῆν). The citation from Irenaeus which follows Victor's argument (Possin. *cat.* p. 5, Cramer, p. 264) begins μετὰ τὴν τοῦ κατὰ Ματθαῖον εὐαγγελίου ἔκδοσιν, and Grotius (*Annot.* p. 523) quotes μετὰ τούτου ἔκδοσιν from "an old MS."; but the Latin of Irenaeus *post vero horum excessum* supports the printed Greek text.

xl / Commentary on Mark

of St Peter and St Paul,' says Irenaeus; 'while St Peter was yet
alive,' is the answer of the Alexandrians. The former is the more
credible witness, whether we consider his relative nearness to the
age of St Mark, or his opportunities of making himself acquainted
with the traditions of Rome and Asia Minor.

According to the subscriptions of many of the later uncials and
cursive MSS. of Mc., the Gospel was written in the tenth or twelfth
year after the Ascension[1]. This computation is doubtless based
on the tradition which represents Peter as taking up his abode in
Rome in the second year of Claudius (Eus. *H. E.* ii. 14, Hieron.
de virr. ill. 1). If we dismiss this story, we are left free to adopt
the *terminus a quo* fixed by Irenaeus and at least implied in the
statement of Papias. It is more difficult to settle the *terminus ad
quem*. As we have seen, Jerome's date for the death of St Mark
(the 8th year of Nero) rests upon a mistake[2]. The Paschal
Chronicle with greater probability places it in the reign of
Trajan; the young man who was the ὑπηρέτης of Saul and
Barnabas in A.D. 47–8 might have lived to see the last decade of
the first century[3]. On the other hand an earlier date is suggested
by the circumstances under which, if we accept the Alexandrian
tradition, the Gospel was composed. The request for a written
record of St Peter's teaching would naturally be made soon after
the Apostle's death, while the Church was still keenly conscious
of its loss. Thus we are led to think of A.D. 70[4] as a probable
limit of time, and this conclusion is to some extent confirmed
by the internal evidence of the Gospel. The freshness of its
colouring, the simplicity of its teaching, the absence of any indication that Jerusalem had already fallen when it was written,
seem to point to a date earlier than the summer of A.D. 70.

3. It may be assumed that a Gospel written for Roman believers in the first century was composed in Greek. Even if Greek
was not the predominant language of the capital, it certainly pre-

---

[1] The form is usually ἐξεδόθη μετὰ
χρόνους ι΄ (or ιβ΄) τῆς τοῦ χριστοῦ ἀναλήψεως (so codd. G²KS and many cursives); cf. Thpht. *prooem. in Mc.* τὸ κατὰ
Μᾶρκον εὐαγγέλιον μετὰ δέκα ἔτη τῆς τοῦ

χριστοῦ ἀναλήψεως συνεγράφη ἐν Ῥώμῃ.
Cf. Harnack, *Chronologie*, pp. 70, 124.
[2] See pp. xviii. f., xxvii.
[3] Comp. Harnack, *op. cit.*, p. 652.
[4] See p. xxii. f.

vailed among the Roman Jews and the servile class from which the early Roman Church was largely recruited[1]. The Gospel of St Peter's interpreter, if of Roman origin, was doubtless written in the language which was employed by St Paul when he addressed the Christians of Rome, and by Clement when he wrote in the name of the Christians of Rome to the Church at Corinth. A Latin Gospel would have appealed to comparatively few of St Peter's Roman friends. Moreover it can scarcely be doubted that Greek and not Latin was the tongue into which St Mark had been accustomed to render St Peter's Aramaic discourses, whether at Jerusalem or at Rome. Bishop Lightfoot indeed maintains the opposite[2], on the ground that the Apostle knew Greek enough to address a Greek-speaking people without the aid of an interpreter. But the scanty knowledge of colloquial Greek which sufficed the fisherman of Bethsaida Julias in his intercourse with Galileans, may well have proved inadequate for sustained discourses delivered at Rome. The occasions would have been few when the Apostle would have needed to use the Latin tongue, and it is at least uncertain whether Mark, a Jew probably born and brought up in Jerusalem, could have rendered him assistance here.

A few MSS. (e.g. codd. 160, 161) in their subscriptions to St Mark support the view that the Gospel was originally composed in Latin, and the form of words which they adopt (ἐγράφη Ῥωμαιστὶ ἐν Ῥώμῃ) suggests the origin of the mistake. The same error appears in the subscriptions to the Peshitta and Harclean Syriac (see p. xxvi.); on the other hand the preface to the Latin Vulgate is content to say, "evangelium in Italia (or "in Italiae partibus") scripsit." Yet it was once believed that the autograph of St Mark existed in a MS. of the Latin Vulgate at Venice (Simon, *hist. critique* ii. p. 114, and Dobrowsky, *Fragm. Pragense Ev. S. Marci vulgo autographi* (Prague, 1778); cf. Gregory, *prolegg.* p. 185, Scrivener-Miller, ii. pp. 84, 259).

Professor Blass[3] maintains that St Mark's Gospel was originally written in Aramaic, and that Papias, who knew the Gospel only in

---

[1] The evidence is stated most fully by Caspari, *Quellen zur Geschichte des Taufsymbols*, iii. p. 267 ff.; a useful summary may be seen in Sanday and Headlam's

Commentary on Romans, p. lii. ff.
[2] *Clement*, ii. p. 494.
[3] *Philology of the Gospels* (1898), p. 196 ff.

a Greek form, mistook a translation for the original. Blass supports his theory by two arguments: (1) "Luke in the first part
of his Acts followed an author who had written in Aramaic.
Mark is very likely to be the author who first published these
stories; he seems therefore to be Luke's Aramaic authority. If
Mark's Acts were written in Aramaic, his Gospel originally was
written in Aramaic also." (2) "Secondly, the textual condition of
St Mark's Gospel suggests the idea that there existed a plurality
of versions of a common Aramaic original." It is difficult to
take the first of these arguments very seriously. Granting that
St Mark wrote a book of Acts in Aramaic, it is manifestly unsafe
to infer that Aramaic was also the original language of his
Gospel; for Mark was *ex hypothesi* bilingual, and he would use
either Aramaic or Greek according to circumstances. The second
argument is supported by examples which open an interesting
field of enquiry, but cannot be regarded as supplying a secure
basis for so large an inference. When he adds that the Aramaic
words in St Mark are "relics of the original, preserved by the
translation," Blass seems to overlook the fact that they are followed
in almost every case by a rendering into Greek. A translator
might have either translated the Aramaic or transliterated it; but
transliteration followed by interpretation savours of an original
writer.

But the theory of an Aramaic original has to meet a stronger
objection. A translator may shew a partiality for certain words
and constructions by employing them as often as the author
gives him the opportunity. But an examination of St Mark's
vocabulary and style reveals peculiarities of diction and colouring
which cannot reasonably be explained in this way. Doubtless
there is a sense in which the book is based upon Aramaic
originals; it is in the main a reproduction of Aramaic teaching,
behind which there probably lay oral or written sources, also
Aramaic. But the Greek Gospel is manifestly not a mere translation of an Aramaic work. It bears on every page marks of the
individuality of the author. If he wrote in Aramaic, he translated
his book into Greek, and the translation which we possess is his

own. But such a conjecture is unnecessary, as well as at variance
with the witness of Papias.

Blass's supposition that "Papias's presbyter knew of different
Greek forms of Matthew besides the Hebrew (or Aramaic) original,
but in the case of Mark, the interpreter of Peter, he knew only
one Greek form of that Gospel, and nothing at all of an Aramaic
original," imputes to this contemporary witness something worse
than ignorance. It is evident that 'the presbyter' means to contrast the original work of St Mark with the many attempts which
had been made to translate the λόγια of St Matthew.

4

Vocabulary, Grammar, and Style

1. A complete vocabulary of St Mark[1] will be found at the end of this volume. It contains some 1330 distinct words, of which 60 are proper names. This is not the place to attempt a full analysis of the Greek of St Mark, but it may be useful to the student to have access to a few tables which will enable him to form some estimate of the relation in which St Mark's vocabulary stands to that of other writers in the New Testament.

i. Words in St Mark (excepting proper names) which occur in no other N.T. writing :

* ἀγρεύειν, * ἄλαλος, ἀλεκτοροφωνία, ἀλλαχοῦ, * ἀμφιβάλλειν, * ἄμφ-οδον, ἀνακυλίειν, ἄναλος, * ἀναπηδᾶν, * ἀναστενάζειν, ἀπόδημος, ἀποστε-γάζειν, ἀφρίζειν, † βοανηργές, * γναφεύς, * δισχίλιοι, * δύσκολος, εἶτεν, * ἐκθαμβεῖσθαι, * ἐκθαυμάζειν, ‡ ἐκπερισσῶς, * ἐναγκαλίζεσθαι, * ἐνειλεῖν, ‡ ἔννυχα, * ἐξάπινα, * ἐξουδενεῖν, ‡ ἐπιράπτειν, ‡ ἐπισυντρέχειν, ἐσχάτως, † ἐφφαθά, * θαμβεῖσθαι, * θυγάτριον, * καταβαρύνειν, * καταδιώκειν, * κατα-κόπτειν, * κατευλογεῖν, * κατοίκησις, κεντυρίων, ‡ κεφαλιοῦν, † κορβάν, † κούμ, * κυλίειν, κωμόπολις, * μηκύνειν, * μογιλάλος, μυρίζειν, νουνεχῶς, ξέστης, οὐά, * παιδιόθεν, παρόμοιος, * περιτρέχειν, * πρασιά, προσαύλιον, ‡ προμεριμνᾶν, * προσάββατον, * προσκεφάλαιον, προσορμίζεσθαι, * προσ-πορεύεσθαι, ‡ πυγμῇ, * σκώληξ, σμυρνίζειν, ‡ σπεκουλάτωρ, στασιαστής, στιβάς, * στίλβειν, * συμπόσιον, * συνθλίβειν, * συνλυπεῖσθαι, * σύσσημον, † ταλειθά, ‡ τηλαυγῶς, τρίζειν, * τρυμαλιά, * ὑπερηφανία, ‡ ὑπερπερισσῶς, * ὑπολήνιον, Φοινίκισσα, * χαλκίον.

(Words in this list marked by an asterisk occur in the LXX. Thick type denotes that Mt. or Lc. uses another word in the same place. Transliterations peculiar to Mc. are distinguished by †, and other words which appear to be ἅπαξ λεγόμενα, by ‡.)

[1] 'Mc.' xvi. 9 ff. is not included in this examination of the Marcan vocabu-lary. Its words will be found, however, in the Index of Greek Words at the end of the volume.

ii. Words peculiar to St Mark and one or both of the other Synoptists:

ἀγανακτεῖν, ἀγγαρεύειν (Mt.), ἀγέλη, ἄγναφος (Mt.), ἀγορά, ἀγρός, ἀλάβαστρος, ἁλεεύς, ἁλίζειν (Mt.), ἀνάγαιον (Lc.), ἀναθεματίζειν (Lc.), ἀνακράζειν (Lc.), ἀνασείειν (Lc.), ἄνιπτος (Mt.), ἀντάλλαγμα (Mt.), ἀπαίρειν, ἁπαλός (Mt.), ἀπαρνεῖσθαι, ἀποδημεῖν, ἀποκεφαλίζειν, ἀποκυλίειν, ἀποστάσιον (Mt.), ἀρχισυνάγωγος (Lc.), ἄσβεστος, ἀσκός, ἀσφαλῶς (Lc.), αὐτόματος (Lc.), ἀφεδρών (Mt.), βαπτιστής, βάτος (Lc.), βλάπτειν (Lc.), βουλευτής (Lc.), γαλήνη, γενέσια (Mt.), γονυπετεῖν (Mt.), δερμάτινος (Mt.), διαβλέπειν, διαγίνεσθαι (Lc.), διαλογίζεσθαι, διανοίγειν (Lc.), διαπερᾶν, διαρήσσειν, διαρπάζειν (Mt.), διασπᾶν, διαφημίζειν (Mt.), δύνειν (Lc.), δυσκόλως, εἰσπορεύεσθαι, ἑκατονταπλασίων, ἐκδίδοσθαι, ἐκπλήσσεσθαι, ἐκπνεῖν (Lc.), ἔκστασις (Lc.), ἐκτινάσσειν, ἐκφύειν (Mt.), Ἑλληνίς (Lc.), ἐλωΐ (Mt.), ἐμπαίζειν, ἐμπτύειν, ἐνδιδύσκειν (Lc.), ἐξαίφνης (Lc.), ἐξανατέλλειν (Mt.), ἐξανιστάναι (Lc.), ἐπανιστάναι (Mt.), ἐπίβλημα, ἐπιγραφή, ἐπιλύειν (Lc.), ἐπισκιάζειν, ἐπισυνάγειν, ἐρήμωσις (LXX.), εὔκοπος, Ἡρωδιανός, θέρος, θηλάζειν, θορυβεῖσθαι (Lc.), θόρυβος, ἱματίζειν (Lc.), ἰχθύδιον (Mt.), καθέδρα (Mt.), κακολογεῖν, κάμηλος, Καναναῖος (Mt.), καταγελᾶν, κατακλᾶν (Lc.), κατάλυμα (Lc.), καταμαρτυρεῖν (Mt.), κατασκηνοῖν, καταστρέφειν, καταφιλεῖν, καταχεῖν (Mt.), κατεξουσιάζειν (Mt.), κεράμιον (Lc.), κῆνσος (Mt.), κλοπή (Mt.), κοδράντης (Mt.), κολοβοῦν (Mt.), κοπάζειν (Mt.), κοράσιον (Mt.), κράσπεδον, κρημνός, κτῆμα, κυλλός (Mt.), κυνάριον (Mt.), κωφός, λαμά (Mt.), λατομεῖν (Mt.), λεγιών, λέπρα, λεπρός, λεπτόν (Lc.), λύτρον (Mt.), μακρός (Lc.), μάτην (LXX., Mt.), μεσονύκτιον (Lc.), μνημόσυνον, μόδιος, μοιχᾶσθαι (Mt.), μονόφθαλμος, Ναζαρηνός (Lc.), νῆστις (Mt.), νόσος, νυμφών, οἰκοδεσπότης, ὄμμα, ὀνικός (Mt.), ὀρθῶς (Lc.), ὅριον, ὁρκίζειν, ὁρμᾶν, ὀρύσσειν, ὀρχεῖσθαι, ὀψέ (Mt.), παρακούειν (Mt.), παραλυτικός, παραπορεύεσθαι (Mt.), παραφέρειν (Lc.), πέδη (Lc.), πεζῇ (Mt.), πενθερά, περιβλέπεσθαι (Lc.), περίλυπος, περισσῶς, περίχωρος, πετρώδης (Mt.), πήρα, πίναξ, πνίγειν (Mt.), πόρρω (LXX.), προβαίνειν, προσκυλίειν (Mt.), προσπίπτειν, προστάσσειν, προστρέχειν (Lc.), πρύμνα (Lc.), πρωτοκαθεδρία, πρωτοκλισία, πύργος, πυρέσσειν (Mt.), ῥάκος (Mt.), ῥαφίς (Mt.), ῥύσις (Lc.), σαβαχθανεί (Mt.), Σαδδουκαῖος, σανδάλιον (Lc.), σέβεσθαι (LXX.), σίναπι, σινδών, σιωπᾶν, σκληροκαρδία (Mt.), σκύλλειν, σπᾶν (Lc.), σπαράσσειν (Lc.), σπλαγχνίζεσθαι, σπόριμον, στάχυς, στέγη, στρωννύναι, στυγνάζειν (Mt.), συμβούλιον, συνακολουθεῖν (Lc.), συνανακεῖσθαι, συνζευγνύειν (Mt.), συνζητεῖν (Lc.), συνκαθῆσθαι (Lc.), συνκαλεῖν (Lc.), συνλαλεῖν, συνπνίγειν, συνπορεύεσθαι (Lc.), συνσπαράσσειν (Lc.), συντηρεῖν, Σύρος, σφυρίς, τέκτων (Mt.), τελώνης, τελώνιον, τίλλειν, τετρακισχίλιοι, τρίβος (LXX.), τρύβλιον (Mt.), ὑποκριτής, φάντασμα (Mt.), φέγγος, φραγελλοῦν (Mt.), χοῖρος, χρῆμα (Lc.), ψευδομαρτυρεῖν, ψευδόχριστος (Mt.), ψιχίον (Mt.).

iii. Words peculiar to St Mark and St John's Gospel:

ἀκάνθινος, ἐνταφιασμός, θυρωρός, Ἱεροσολυμείτης, κύπτειν, μισθωτός, νάρδος πιστικός, πλοιάριον, προσαίτης, πτύειν, ῥαββουνεί, ῥάπισμα, τριακόσιοι, ὠτάριον.

iv. Words peculiar to St Mark, one of the other Synoptists, and St John :

ἄρωμα (Lc.), γαζοφυλάκιον (Lc.), ἐμβριμᾶσθαι (Mt.), ἱμάς (Lc.), κράβαττος (Lc.), μοιχεία (Mt.), ὄψιος (Mt.), πλέκειν (Mt.), ῥαββεί (Mt.), σπόγγος (Mt.), φανερῶς (Lc.), ὡσαννά (Mt.).

v. Words peculiar to St Mark and the Pauline Epistles (including Hebrews):

ἀββά, ἀλαλάζειν, ἁμάρτημα, ἀναμιμνήσκειν, ἀποβάλλειν, ἀποπλανᾶν, ἀποστερεῖν (LXX.), ἀφροσύνη, ἀχειροποίητος, βαπτισμός, εἰρηνεύειν, ἔκφοβος, ἐξορύσσειν, εὔκαιρος, εὐκαίρως, ἡδέως, ὁλοκαύτωμα, περιφέρειν, πορνεύειν, προλαμβάνειν, συναποθνήσκειν, τρόμος, ὑστέρησις.

vi. Words peculiar to St Mark, one of the other Synoptists, and the Pauline writings :

ἀγρυπνεῖν (Lc.), ἀδημονεῖν (Mt.), ἀκυροῦν (Mt.), ἀπιστία (Mt.), ἀπόκρυφος (Lc.), ἀποτάσσεσθαι (Lc.), ἄρρωστος (Mt.), ἀρτύειν (Lc.), ἀσύνετος (Mt.), ἄτιμος (Mt.), γόνυ (Lc.), διαπορεύεσθαι (Lc.), διδασκαλία (Mt.), διηγεῖσθαι (Lc.), ἐκλύεσθαι (Mt.), ἐκφέρειν (Lc.), ἐνέχειν (Lc.), ἔνταλμα (Mt.), ἐξαυτῆς (Lc.), ἐπαισχύνεσθαι (Lc.), ἐπιτάσσειν (Lc.), ἐρημία (Mt.), εὐκαιρεῖν (Lc.), θῆλυς (Mt.), θλίβειν (Mt.), θροεῖσθαι (Mt.), καθαιρεῖν (Lc.), μάστιξ (Lc.), μεταμορφοῦσθαι (Mt.), μωρός (Mt.), νεότης (Lc.), οἰκοδομή (Mt.), πανταχοῦ (Lc.), πάντοθεν (Lc.), παράδοσις (Mt.), παραιτεῖσθαι (Lc.), παράπτωμα (Mt.), παρατηρεῖν (Lc.), περικαλύπτειν (Lc.), περικεῖσθαι (Lc.), πλεῖστος (Mt.), πρόσκαιρος (Mt.), προσκαρτερεῖν (Lc.), σβεννύναι (Mt.), σπόρος (Lc.), σύνεσις (Lc.), σχολάζειν (Lc.), ὑποδεῖσθαι (Lc.), χαλᾶν (Lc.), χειροποίητος (Lc.).

vii. Words peculiar to St Mark and the Catholic Epistles :

δαμάζειν (Jas.), δωρεῖσθαι (2 Pet.).

viii. Words peculiar to St Mark, one other N.T. writer, and the Catholic Epistles :

ἀγαθοποιεῖν (Lc., 1 Pet., 3 Jo.), ἀγνοεῖν (Paul, 2 Pet.), ἄγριος (Mt., Jude), ἀσέλγεια (Paul, 1 Pet., 3 Jo.), θερμαίνεσθαι (Jo., Jas.), λαῖλαψ (Lc., 2 Pet.), πολυτελής (Paul, 1 Pet.), στενάζειν (Paul, Jas.), συντρέχειν (Lc., 1 Pet.), τρέμειν (Lc., 2 Pet.).

ix. Words peculiar to St Mark and the Apocalypse, or to St Mark, the Apocalypse, and one other N.T. writer :

δρέπανον, καυματίζειν (Mt.), λευκαίνειν, μεγιστάν, μέλι (Mt.), μύλος (Mt.), πορνεύειν (Paul), πορφύρα (Lc.), πτῶμα (Mt.), στολή (Lc.), φύλλον (Mt.), χλωρός, χοῦς.

Such tables may easily be multiplied[1] with the help of the index at the end of this volume and a good concordance. But

---

[1] For a good comparative table of the 'characteristic' words in Mc., see Hawkins, *Hor. Syn.*, p. 10 f.

those which are given above suffice to bring out certain features
in St Mark's vocabulary. Of the 1270 distinct words (excluding
proper names) which it contains, 80 are peculiar to St Mark,
about 150 are shared only by St Matthew and St Luke, and 100
more are among the less widely distributed words of the New
Testament. This is not a large proportion of peculiar or unusual
words. St Luke's Gospel has more than 250 ἅπαξ λεγόμενα,
besides a large number of words common only to itself and the
Pauline writings[1]. On the other hand the ἅπαξ λεγόμενα of
St Mark, if not relatively numerous, are often striking; while he
has comparatively few of the compounds in which the later Greek
delighted, we meet in his pages with such survivals as εἶτεν,
παιδιόθεν, such colloquialisms as κεντυρίων, ξέστης, πιστικός,
σπεκουλάτωρ, and such transliterations as κορβάν, ταλειθὰ κούμ,
ἐφφαθά, ῥαββουνεί. If we might generalise from these features
of St Mark's Greek as compared with the Greek of St Luke, we
should be led to conclude that the writer was a foreigner who spoke
Greek with some freedom, but had not been accustomed to employ
it for literary purposes[2]. He is not at a loss for an unusual word
when it is wanted to convey his meaning or give point to his
narrative, but under ordinary circumstances he is comparatively
limited in his choice, and he displays no familiarity with the
habits of the Hellenistic writers of his age.

2. The Greek of St Mark's Gospel is characterised by peculiarities of construction and style which force themselves upon
the attention of every student. A few of these may be particularly mentioned.

(a) Frequent use of εἶναι and ἐλθεῖν with a participle : i. 6 ἦν...
ἐνδεδυμένος...καὶ ἔσθων, 33 ἦν...ἐπισυνηγμένη, 39 ἦλθεν κηρύσσων,
40 ἔρχεται...προσκαλῶν, ii. 3 ἔρχονται φέροντες, 5 ἦσαν καθήμενοι καὶ
διαλογιζόμενοι, v. 5 ἦν κράζων καὶ κατακόπτων ἑαυτόν, ix. 4 ἦσαν
συνλαλοῦντες, x. 32 ἦσαν...ἀναβαίνοντες...καὶ ἦν προάγων, xiii. 13
ἔσεσθε μισούμενοι, 23 ἔσονται πίπτοντες, xv. 43 ἦν προσδεχόμενος.

---

[1] See Plummer, *St Luke*, p. lii. ff.

[2] Sir J. C. Hawkins (*Hor. Syn.*, p. 106)
has collected a list of 26 "rude, harsh,
obscure or unusual words or expressions
in St Mark," and points out (p. 171) that

"the non-classical words...occur with
considerably more frequency in the
special vocabulary of St Mark than in
those of the other Synoptists." Comp.
Encycl. Bibl. ii. 1767 f.

(*b*) Multiplication of participles: i. 21 προσελθὼν ἤγειρεν...
κρατήσας, 41 σπλαγχνισθεὶς ἐκτείνας...ἤψατο, v. 25 ff. οὖσα...καὶ
παθοῦσα...καὶ δαπανήσασα...καὶ μηδὲν ὠφεληθεῖσα ἀλλὰ...ἐλθοῦσα,
ἀκούσασα...ἐλθοῦσα ἥψατο, xiv. 67 ἰδοῦσα...ἐμβλέψασα λέγει, xv. 43
ἐλθὼν...τολμήσας εἰσῆλθεν.

(*c*) Use of article with infinitives and sentences: i. 14 μετὰ τὸ
παραδοθῆναι τὸν Ἰωάνην, iv. 6 διὰ τὸ μὴ ἔχειν ῥίζαν, v. 4 διὰ τὸ αὐτὸν...
δεδέσθαι καὶ διεσπάσθαι ὑπ᾽ αὐτοῦ κτλ., ix. 23 τὸ εἰ δύνῃ, xiv. 28 μετὰ
τὸ ἐγερθῆναί με.

(*d*) Frequent use of εὐθύς, which occurs 34 times in Mc. i.—ix.
and 7 times in x.—xvi.

(*e*) Use of ἄν in such sentences as iii. 11 ὅταν αὐτὸν ἐθεώρουν,
vi. 56 ὅπου ἂν εἰσεπορεύετο...ὅσοι ἂν ἥψαντο, xi. 19 ὅταν ἐγένοντο.

(*f*) Use of broken or imperfect constructions, in cases of parenthesis (ii. 22, iii. 16—18, vii. 19), or mixture (ii. 1, iv. 15, 26,
30—31, vi. 8, 11, viii. 2, xiii. 34), or extreme compression (v. 30,
vi. 43, viii. 8), or ellipse (x. 40).

(*g*) *Constructio ad sensum:* ix. 20 ἰδὼν αὐτὸν τὸ πνεῦμα, xiii. 14
τὸ βδέλυγμα...ἑστηκότα.

(*h*) Repetition of negative: i. 44 μηδενὶ μηδὲν εἴπῃς, v. 3 οὐδὲ...
οὐκέτι οὐδεὶς ἐδύνατο, xvi. 8 οὐδενὶ οὐδὲν εἶπαν.

(*i*) Frequent use and careful discrimination of prepositions:
e.g. i. 39, ii. 1, 2, 10, 13, iii. 8, iv. 7, 19, 21, vi. 5, 6, vii. 3, 31, ix.
42, x. 11, 22, 24, xi. 4, xii. 1, 17, xiii. 51; cf. ἀποκυλίειν, ἀνακυλίειν,
xvi. 3 f.[1]

3. Such examples, however, give no just conception of St
Mark's general style. The body of the work consists of a series
of sentences connected by the simplest of Greek copulas, each
contributing a fresh fact to the reader's knowledge, and each
by its vivid and distinct presentation of the fact claiming his
close attention. St Mark knows how to compress his matter,
where a multitude of words would only weaken the effect, or
where the scheme of his work forbids greater fulness; on the
other hand, when words can heighten the colouring or give life
to the picture, they are used without regard to brevity and with
little attention to elegance.

---

[1] To these stylistic peculiarities may
be added (*j*) a frequent use of the ' historic present '—151 instances are quoted
as against 78 in Mt. and 4 or 6 in Lc.;
(*k*) preference of καὶ to δέ; (*l*) use of
asyndeton (Hawkins, *Hor. Syn.*, pp. 108 ff.,
113 ff., 120 ff.); and (*m*) disposition to
employ pleonastic forms (Salmond, in
Hastings, *D.B.* iii. p. 251).

For instances of compression see especially Mark's summaries of our Lord's teaching or of the comments of the hearers, e.g. i. 27, ii. 7, viii. 29, xii. 38—40 (comp. Mt.). For his habit of adding word to word where one might have sufficed see i. 32 ὀψίας...ὅτε ἔδυσεν ὁ ἥλιος, 35 πρωὶ ἔννυχα λίαν, v. 26 (see above 2 § b), vi. 25 εὐθὺς μετὰ σπουδῆς, vii. 13 τῇ παραδόσει ᾗ παρεδώκατε, viii. 25 διέβλεψεν καὶ ἀπεκατέστη καὶ ἐνέβλεπεν, 37 ὑπερπερισσῶς ἐξεπλήσσοντο, xii. 14 ἔξεστιν δοῦναι...δῶμεν ἢ μὴ δῶμεν;, 44 πάντα ὅσα εἶχεν ἔβαλεν, ὅλον τὸν βίον αὐτῆς, xiv. 3 ἀλάβαστρον νάρδου πιστικῆς πολυτελοῦς, 68 οὔτε οἶδα οὔτε ἐπίσταμαι, xv. 1 εὐθὺς πρωί, xvi. 8 τρόμος καὶ ἔκστασις. Under the same head may be placed the frequent instances in which a statement is made first in a positive and then in a negative form or the reverse (e.g. i. 22, ii. 27, iii. 29, v. 19, x. 45).

Two other points, which the tables do not shew, deserve to be emphasised here : (1) the relatively frequent use of certain characteristic words ; (2) the use of certain ordinary words in an uncommon and sometimes enigmatic sense.

Examples of (1) are : ἀκάθαρτος[11] (in the term πνεῦμα ἀκάθαρτον), ἀναβλέπειν[6], διαλογίζεσθαι[7], ἐκθαμβεῖσθαι[4], εἰσπορεύεσθαι[8], ἐκπορεύεσθαι[10], ἐμβλέπειν[4], ἐμβριμᾶσθαι[3], ἐναγκαλίζεσθαι[2], ἐξουσία[10], ἐπερωτᾶν[25], ἐπιτάσσειν[5], ἐπιτιμᾶν[9], εὐαγγέλιον[7], θαμβεῖσθαι[3], μεθερμηνεύεσθαι[3], παραλαμβάνειν[4], παραπορεύεσθαι[4], περιβλέπεσθαι[6], πλήρωμα[3], προάγειν[6], προσκαλεῖσθαι[9], πωροῦσθαι (πώρωσις)[2], συνζητεῖν[6], ὑπάγειν[15], φιμοῦσθαι[2]. Under the second head we may place ἐνεῖχεν (vi. 19), πυγμῇ (vii. 3), ἀπέχει (xiv. 41), ἐπιβαλών (xiv. 72).

Further, St Mark gives movement to his history by the remarkable freedom with which he handles his tenses.

Changes of tense occur (1) with a corresponding difference of meaning : v. 15 ff. τὸν δαιμονιζόμενον...ὁ δαιμονισθείς, vi. 14 ff. ἐγήγερται...ἠγέρθη, vii. 35 ἐλύθη...ἐλάλει...διεστείλατο...διεστέλλετο, ix. 15 ἐξεθαμβήθησαν......ἠσπάζοντο, xv. 44 τέθνηκεν......ἀπέθανεν : (2) apparently for the purpose of giving life to a dialogue : ix. 34 ff. ἐπηρώτα...λέγει...εἶπεν, xi. 27 ἔρχονται...καὶ ἔλεγον...εἶπεν... λέγουσιν...λέγει.

Thus present, perfect, imperfect, aorist, are interchanged, not through ignorance of the laws of the Greek language, or with conscious artificiality, but from a keen sense of the reality and living interest of the facts. Sometimes the historical tenses are used almost exclusively throughout a paragraph (e.g. ii. 3— 10, xv. 20—24) ; more frequently they alternate with the imperfect and aorist (e.g. iv. 35—41, vi. 30—51). Even in indirect narration the present and perfect are freely used (ii. 1, xv. 44, 47, xvi. 4), when the writer desires to place the reader for the moment in the speaker's point of view. On the other hand St Mark frequently uses the imperfect in a sense which is scarcely distinguishable from the aorist, except that it conveys the impression of an eye-witness describing events which passed under his own eye (cf. e.g. v. 18, vii. 17, x. 17, xii. 41, xiv. 55).

Much has been written as to a supposed tendency on the part of this writer to adopt Latin words and forms of speech. The occurrence of such words as δηνάριον, κεντυρίων, κοδράντης, κράβαττος, λεγιών, ξέστης, σπεκουλάτωρ, and such a phrase as ἱκανὸν ποιεῖν, lends a *prima facie* support to this view. But some of these Latinisms occur in other Gospels as well as in St Mark, and it may be doubted whether they prove more than a familiarity with the vulgar Greek of the Empire, which freely adopted Latin words and some Latin phraseology[1]. Nevertheless their relatively frequent occurrence in St Mark is one indication amongst others of his larger acquaintance with the Greek which was spoken in the Roman world, and it accords well with the tradition which represents the writer of this Gospel as a professional 'interpreter,' and as having resided for some years in Rome.

[1] Blass, *Philology of the Gospels*, p. 211 f.

5

Contents, Plan, and Sources

1. Attempts were made at an early time to break up the Gospels into sections corresponding more or less nearly to the nature of the contents. Besides the stichometry which measured the text by lines[1], and the 'Ammonian' sections which divided it in such a manner as to shew its relation to that of the other Gospels, there were systems of capitulation under which it was arranged in paragraphs for reading. Two such systems survive in cod. B and cod. A respectively. In the former, which is the more ancient[2], St Mark is broken up into 62 sections as against 170 in St Matthew and 152 in St Luke; in the system represented by cod. A[3] (the so-called κεφάλαια maiora or τίτλοι) St Mark has 48 sections, St Matthew 68, and St Luke 83[4].

> The following table will enable the student to compare the capitulation of codd. BA with the paragraphing adopted in the text of Westcott and Hort. Italics are used where two of the three systems coincide; where the three agree the verse-numbers are printed in thick type.

Cod. B	Cod. A	WH.
I. *1*		I. *1*
		2
9		*9*
12		*12*

---

[1] For the variations of the stichometry in St Mark see *Studia Biblica*, p. 268 f.; J. R. Harris, *Stichometry*, p. 49; *J. Th. St.* i. p. 444 f., ii. p. 250; the majority of the subscriptions in mss. give 1600. The Ammonian sections fluctuate between 232 and 242 (Gregory, *Prolegg.*, i. p. 152 f.; cf. Burgon, *Last twelve verses*, p. 310 f.). On the Church lessons in St Mark see Gregory, p. 162, Scrivener-Miller, p. 80 ff.

[2] Found also in cod. Ξ.

[3] Found also in codd. CNRZ$_1$ and possibly of Alexandrian origin; cf. *J. Th. St.*, i. p. 419.

[4] Cod. D has a system peculiar to itself, in which Mc. is divided into 148 sections (Scrivener, *Codex Bezae*, p. xx.).

Cod. B	Cod. A	WH.
14		*14*
		16
21		*21*
	I. 23	
29	**29**	**29**
	32	*32*
35		*35*
38		
	40	*40*
II. *1*		II. *1*
	II. 3	
13	**13**	•**13**
15		*15*
18		*18*
23		*23*
III. **1**	III. **1**	III. **1**
7		**7**
	13	*13*
14		
		20
		31
IV. *1*		IV. *1*
	IV. **2**	
10		*10*
		21
		24
		26
		30
		33
35	**35**	**35**
V. **1**	V. **1**	V. **1**
21		*21*
	22	
	25	
VI. **1** *b*		
		VI. **1**
6 *b*		**6** *b*
	VI. **7**	
14	**14**	**14**
30		*30*
	34	
45		*45*
	47	
53		*53*
VII. **1**	VII. **1**	VII. **1**
17		
24		*24*
	25	

Cod. B	Cod. A	WH.
		26
27		27
		32
43		43
53		53
	66	66
XV. *1*		XV. *1*
16		*16*
		20 *b*
24		
		33
38		
42	XV. 42	42
XVI. *1*		XVI. *1*
		[9]

The τίτλοι which precede the Gospel in cod. A give the contents of the successive chapters as follows[1]:

Τοῦ κατὰ Μᾶρκον εὐαγγελίου αἱ περιοχαί.

α΄. περὶ τοῦ δαιμονιζομένου. β΄. περὶ τῆς πενθερᾶς Πέτρου. γ΄. περὶ τῶν ἰαθέντων ἀπὸ ποικίλων νόσων. δ΄. περὶ τοῦ λεπροῦ. ε΄. περὶ τοῦ παραλυτικοῦ. ϛ΄. περὶ Λευὶ τοῦ τελώνου. ζ΄. περὶ τοῦ ξηρὰν ἔχοντος χεῖρα. η΄. περὶ τῆς τῶν ἀποστόλων ἐκλογῆς. θ΄. περὶ τῆς παραβολῆς τοῦ σπόρου. ι΄. περὶ τῆς ἐπιτιμήσεως τοῦ ἀνέμου καὶ τῆς θαλάσσης. ια΄. περὶ τοῦ λεγεῶνος. ιβ΄. περὶ τῆς θυγατρὸς τοῦ ἀρχισυναγώγου. ιγ΄. περὶ τῆς αἱμορροούσης. ιδ΄. περὶ τῆς διαταγῆς τῶν ἀποστόλων. ιε΄. περὶ Ἰωάννου καὶ Ἡρώδου. ιϛ΄. περὶ τῶν πέντε ἄρτων. ιζ΄. περὶ τοῦ ἐν θαλάσσῃ περιπάτου. ιη΄. περὶ τῆς παραβάσεως τῆς ἐντολῆς τοῦ θεοῦ. ιθ΄. περὶ τῆς Φοινικίσσης. κ΄. περὶ τοῦ μογιλάλου. κα΄. περὶ τῶν ἑπτὰ ἄρτων. κβ΄. περὶ τῆς ζύμης τῶν Φαρισαίων. κγ΄. περὶ τοῦ τυφλοῦ. κδ΄. περὶ τῆς ἐν Καισαρίᾳ ἐπερωτήσεως. κε΄. περὶ τῆς μεταμορφώσεως τοῦ Ἰησοῦ. κϛ΄. περὶ τοῦ σεληνιαζομένου. κζ΄. περὶ τῶν διαλογιζομένων τίς μείζων. κη΄. περὶ τῶν ἐπερωτησάντων Φαρισαίων. κθ΄. περὶ τοῦ ἐπερωτήσαντος αὐτὸν πλουσίου. λ΄. περὶ τῶν υἱῶν Ζεβεδαίου. λα΄. περὶ Βαρτιμαίου. λβ΄. περὶ τοῦ πώλου. λγ΄. περὶ τῆς ξηρανθείσης συκῆς. λδ΄. περὶ ἀμνησικακίας. λε΄. περὶ τῶν ἐπερωτησάντων τὸν κύριον ἀρχιερέων καὶ γραμματέων Ἐν ποίᾳ ἐξουσίᾳ ταῦτα ποιεῖς; λϛ΄. περὶ τοῦ ἀμπελῶνος. λζ΄. περὶ τῶν ἐγκαθέτων διὰ τὸν κῆνσον. λη΄. περὶ τῶν Σαδδουκαίων. λθ΄. περὶ τῶν γραμματέων. μ΄. περὶ τῆς τοῦ κυρίου ἐπερωτήσεως. μα΄. περὶ τῆς τὰ δύο λεπτά. μβ΄. περὶ τῆς συντελείας. . μγ΄. περὶ τῆς ἡμέρας καὶ ὥρας. μδ΄. περὶ τῆς ἀλειψάσης τὸν κύριον μύρῳ. με΄. περὶ τοῦ πάσχα. μϛ΄. περὶ

---

[1] For the variants of codd. LΔ see Tregelles, p. 486 f. ; for the capitulation of cod. Amiatinus and other MSS. of the Latin Vulgate, cf. Wordsworth and White, p. 174; and for tables of Latin *tituli*, Thomasius, *opera*, i. p. 303 sqq.

παραδόσεως προφητεία.   μζ΄. ἄρνησις Πέτρου.   μή΄. περὶ τῆς αἰτή-
σεως τοῦ κυριακοῦ σώματος.

The following conspectus shews the contents as they are
arranged in the present edition.

2. We are now in a position to consider how far the contents group themselves into larger sections[1], revealing the existence of a

---

[1] Zahn (*Einleitung*, ii. p. 224 ff.) divides the Gospel, apart from the introduction and appendix, into five very unequal parts (i. 16—45, ii. 1—iii. 6, iii. 7—vi. 13, vi. 14—x. 52, xi. 1—xvi. 8).

Dr Salmond (in Hastings, *D. B.*, iii. 249) suggests a division in accordance with the geographical data (i. 14—vii. 23, vii. 24—ix. 50, x. 1—31, x. 32—xv. 47).

purpose or plan in the mind of the writer. Even a hasty examination will shew that the book deals with two great themes,
the Ministry in Galilee (i. 14—ix. 50), and the Last Week at
Jerusalem (xi. 1—xvi. 8), and that these sections are connected
by a comparatively brief survey of the period which intervened
(x. 1—52). The first fourteen verses of the Gospel are evidently
introductory; the last twelve have the character of an appendix,
which links the Gospel history with the fortunes of the Church
in the Apostolic age.

The first of the two great sections of St Mark bears manifest
signs of brevity and compression, especially in certain parts of the
narrative. On the other hand there are indications of the writer's
desire to follow the order of events, as far as his information
permitted him to do so. It is shewn by the notes of time and
place which· continually occur.

The following are examples: παράγων παρὰ τὴν θάλασσαν (i. 16)...
καὶ προβὰς ὀλίγον (19)...καὶ εἰσπορεύονται εἰς Καφαρναούμ, καὶ εὐθὺς
τοῖς σάββασιν εἰσελθὼν εἰς τὴν συναγωγήν (21)...καὶ εὐθὺς ἐκ τῆς
συναγωγῆς ἐξελθόντες (29)...ὀψίας δὲ γενομένης (32)...καὶ πρωὶ ἔννυχα
λίαν ἀναστὰς ἐξῆλθεν (35)...καὶ εἰσελθὼν πάλιν εἰς Καφ. δι᾽ ἡμερῶν (ii. 1)
...καὶ ἐξῆλθεν πάλιν παρὰ τὴν θάλασσαν (13)...καὶ παράγων (14)...καὶ
εἰσῆλθεν πάλιν εἰς συναγωγήν (iii. 1)...καὶ...ἀνεχώρησεν πρὸς τὴν θάλασσαν (7)...καὶ ἀναβαίνει εἰς τὸ ὄρος (13)...καὶ ἔρχεται εἰς οἶκον (20)...
καὶ πάλιν ἤρξατο διδάσκειν παρὰ τὴν θάλασσαν (iv. 1)...καὶ ὅτε ἐγένετο
κατὰ μόνας (10)...καὶ λέγει αὐτοῖς ἐν ἐκείνῃ τῇ ἡμέρᾳ ὀψίας γενομένης
Διέλθωμεν εἰς τὸ πέρας (35)...καὶ ἦλθον εἰς τὸ πέραν (v. 1)...καὶ
διαπεράσαντος τοῦ Ἰησοῦ ἐν τῷ πλοίῳ πάλιν (21)...καὶ ἐξῆλθεν ἐκεῖθεν
(vi. 1)...καὶ περιῆγεν τὰς κώμας (7)...καὶ ἀπῆλθον ἐν τῷ πλοίῳ εἰς
ἔρημον τόπον (32)...καὶ διαπεράσαντες ἐπὶ τὴν γῆν ἦλθον εἰς Γεννησαρέτ
(53)...ἐκεῖθεν δὲ ἀναστὰς ἀπῆλθεν εἰς τὰ ὅρια Τύρου (vii. 24)...καὶ
πάλιν ἐξελθὼν ἐκ τῶν ὁρίων Τύρου ἦλθεν διὰ Σιδῶνος εἰς τὴν θάλασσαν
(31)...καὶ εὐθὺς ἐμβὰς εἰς τὸ πλοῖον...ἦλθεν εἰς τὰ μέρη Δαλμανουθά
(viii. 10)...καὶ...πάλιν ἐμβὰς ἀπῆλθεν εἰς τὸ πέραν (13)...καὶ ἔρχονται
εἰς Βηθσαιδάν (22)...καὶ ἐξῆλθεν...εἰς τὰς κώμας Καισαρίας (27)...καὶ
μετὰ ἡμέρας ἓξ...ἀναφέρει αὐτοὺς εἰς ὄρος ὑψηλόν (ix. 2)...καὶ καταβαινόντων αὐτῶν ἐκ τοῦ ὄρους (9)...καὶ εἰσελθόντος αὐτοῦ εἰς οἶκον (28)...
κἀκεῖθεν ἐξελθόντες ἐπορεύοντο διὰ τῆς Γαλειλαίας (30)...καὶ ἦλθον εἰς
Καφαρναούμ (33).

It is impossible to resist the impression that the writer
who constructed this chain of sequence believed himself to be
presenting his facts upon the whole in the order of their actual

occurrence; and this impression is not weakened by the occasional dropping of a link (as e.g. at i. 40, ii. 23, vii. 1), for such exceptions suggest that he was unwilling to go beyond his information, and that the indications of order which he gives are sound so far as they go. This view is supported by the absence of his favourite εὐθύς at the points of transition; at such times the writer vouches for the relative order only, and not for the immediate succession of the events. The kind of sequence which he aims to establish is consistent with the omission of many incidents or discourses, and with the bringing into close proximity of others which were separated by considerable intervals, but not with a disregard of chronological order; nor is it his habit to group together materials of similar character, or which appeared to illustrate the same principle[1].

But granting that the writer intended to follow the relative order of time, is there reason to suppose that he has succeeded? Can we recognise in this part of his work the steady and natural development of events which possesses historical verisimilitude?

The answer makes itself distinctly heard by the careful student. He observes a progress in the history of the Galilean Ministry, as it is depicted by St Mark, which bears the stamp of truth. The teaching of Christ is seen to pass through a succession of stages in an order which corresponds to His method of dealing with men: first there is the synagogue homily, then the popular instruction delivered in the larger auditorium supplied by the sea-shore or the neighbouring hills, then the teaching by parables of the multitudes who had proved themselves incapable of receiving spiritual truth, and lastly the initiation of a select few into the mysteries of the Kingdom, which they were afterwards to proclaim to the world. And

---

[1] Dr Sanday, however, (Smith, *D.B.*[2], i. p. 1224, cf. Hastings, *D.B.*, ii. p. 613) finds some instances of this: "Some sections (according to Holtzmann, ii. 23—iii. 6, iv. 21—25, ix. 33—50, x. 2—31, xi. 23—26) shew marks of artificial composition." Mr C. H. Turner (Hastings, *D.B.*, i. pp. 406, 410) expresses himself with less reserve: "even if the sections as wholes are in chronological order, the events within each section are obviously massed in groups"; "within his first section St Mark certainly groups events by subject-matter rather than by time." The general attitude of St Mark towards chronological order is stated in a few careful sentences by Dr Salmond, in Hastings, *D. B.*, iii. p. 255.

the course of events as sketched by St Mark answers to this progress in the teaching and partly explains it. We see the crowd growing daily in numbers and enthusiasm, the opportunities of teaching increased, the necessity arising for a division of labour, the consequent selection and training of the Twelve; and on the other hand, the growing hostility of the Scribes, their reinforcement from Jerusalem, their alliance with the party of Herod, the unintelligent and dangerous excitement of the common people, the awakened curiosity of Antipas. As we look more closely into St Mark's picture, the plan of the Ministry begins to shape itself. We see that it includes (1) the evangelisation of the lake-side towns and country, both in the tetrarchy of Antipas and in that of Philip; (2) the extension of this work to the rest of Galilee during intervals of enforced withdrawal from the lake-district; and (3) the instruction and disciplining of the men who were ultimately to carry the preaching of the Divine Kingdom to the ends of the earth. The whole of this complicated process moves onwards in St Mark's history in so easy and natural a manner that we are scarcely conscious of the movement until we come to analyse the contents of the Gospel. But in fact the scheme is developed step by step, each incident forming a distinct link in the sequence[1].

According to Papias St Mark wrote ἀκριβῶς, οὐ μέντοι τάξει, and this has been taken to mean that, while his recollections were faithfully reproduced, he made no attempt to arrange them chronologically[2]. But τάξις is order of any kind, and its precise meaning must be interpreted by the context in which it occurs. In this case the context supplies a clue, for Papias goes on to say that St Peter taught οὐχ ὥσπερ σύνταξιν τῶν κυριακῶν ποιούμενος λόγων, i.e. not with the view of producing a literary work. A σύνταξις is a set treatise which follows the rules of orderly composition; thus the writer of 2 Maccabees at the end of his task (xv. 39) finds comfort in the reflexion τὸ τῆς κατασκευῆς τοῦ λόγου τέρπει τὰς ἀκοὰς τῶν ἐντυγχανόντων τῇ συντάξει. Papias himself claims that his *logia* were compiled συντακτικῶς: οὐκ ὀκνήσω δέ σοι καὶ ὅσα ποτὲ παρὰ τῶν πρεσβυτέρων καλῶς ἔμαθον καὶ καλῶς ἐμνημόνευσα συνκατατάξαι (*al.*

---

[1] The solitary exception is the explanatory episode of the Baptist's death (vi. 17—29).

[2] For various explanations of this omission see Salmon, *Intr.*[7] p. 91.

συντάξαι) ταῖς ἑρμηνείαις. St Mark's work, being a mere echo of St Peter's ἀπομνημονεύματα, was not in this sense orderly; it belonged to a different category from the artificial treatises which were in fashion, and for the most part was a mere string of notes connected in the simplest way. The structure of the Second Gospel is wholly in harmony with this view. The paragraphs, often extremely brief, are connected by the simplest of Greek copulas. Τότε, which abounds in St Matthew, is not once used by St Mark as a note of transition; οὖν, St John's favourite copula, is employed in narration only by the writer of the supplementary verses; δέ occurs in this connexion but four times in the first nine chapters. Yet in the longer subsections the writer of this Gospel shews himself willing to vary the monotony of the repeated καί by the use of ἀλλά, γάρ, ἰδού, or by dispensing with copulas of any kind. His invariable use of καί at the commencement of a paragraph[1] may therefore be attributed to the deliberate purpose of connecting his notes together in the least artificial manner; and this feature of his work sufficiently explains the words of Papias.

When we pass from the narrative of the Galilean Ministry (i. 14—ix. 50) to the brief summary of the Judaean and Peraean journeys which followed it, St Mark's manner changes perceptibly. He is still, at least in c. x., a compiler of ὑπομνηματισμοί, but his memoranda are no longer accompanied by notes of time, and the notes of place are few (x. 1, 17, 32, 46). When Jerusalem is reached such indications of fuller knowledge appear again; the succession of the events is carefully noted, and the places where they occurred are specified (e.g. xi. 1, 11, 12, 15, 19, 20, 27; xii. 41; xiii. 1, &c.). The hand of the writer to whom we owe the first great section of the book is clearly to be seen in the last. Yet there is a change of manner which is perhaps not wholly due to the difference of theme. The narrative of the Passion is on a scale which is out of all proportion to that on which the Ministry is drawn. The subsections become noticeably longer; instruction holds a more prominent position; the terseness of the earlier sayings is exchanged for specimens of more prolonged teaching (e.g. xi. 23—25, xii. 24—27, 29—31, 38—40); a whole chapter (xiii.) is occupied by a single discourse; the style is more varied, and the monotonous καί gives place more frequently to δέ or some other equivalent. These are among the signs which point to a

[1] See above, p. xlviii. n.

partial use in these chapters of a source distinct in character from that which supplied the materials of the first nine or ten chapters.

3. The tradition which from the days of Irenaeus has identified the Second Gospel with the teaching of St Peter is too early and too consistent to be wholly set aside, unless the internal evidence of the book requires us to abandon it. There is certainly but little in this Gospel which did not fall within the limits of St Peter's personal knowledge. He may have been present on all the occasions in our Lord's life to which St Mark refers except the Baptism, the Temptation, and the Crucifixion and the scenes which followed it. On certain occasions he was one of three selected witnesses. It is true that the figure of Simon Peter does not loom large in the Second Gospel, and some pages in the history where he fills a prominent place are wanting in St Mark; it is St Matthew who relates the high commendation passed upon Peter's confession of faith, while St Mark gives only the story of his subsequent miscarriage; the story of Peter's walking on the sea, and of the stater in the fish's mouth, are also in Matthew only; indeed the only long paragraph in Mark which concerns St Peter is the account of his three-fold denial of the Master.

This difficulty presented itself to the acute mind of Eusebius of Caesarea, and he met it by what is probably on the whole the true explanation of the facts—the Apostle's reluctance to call attention to himself in a record of the words and works of Christ; *dem. ev.* iii. 3 ταῦτα μὲν οὖν ὁ Πέτρος εἰκότως παρασιωπᾶσθαι ἠξίου· διὸ καὶ Μᾶρκος αὐτὰ παρέλιπεν, τὰ δὲ κατὰ τὴν ἄρνησιν αὐτοῦ εἰς πάντας ἐκήρυξεν ἀνθρώπους...Μᾶρκος μὲν ταῦτα γράφει, Πέτρος δὲ ταῦτα περὶ ἑαυτοῦ μαρτυρεῖ. Such reticence may indeed serve to disarm suspicion when we remember that the Pseudo-Peter writes in the first person (*Ev. Petr. ad fin.* ἐγὼ δὲ Σίμων Πέτρος καὶ Ἀνδρέας ὁ ἀδελφός μου), and that the same feature appears in other Christian pseudonymous literature.

But if tokens of Petrine origination are not prominent in St Mark's Gospel, they are not wanting altogether, and the unobtrusiveness of those which meet the eye of the careful student increases his sense of their importance. Thus, while the Second Gospel omits a series of incidents relating to St Peter which find a place in the first and third (e.g. Mt. xiv. 28 f., xv. 15,

xvi. 18, xvii. 24 ff., xviii. 21, Lc. v. 3 ff., xii. 41, xxii. 31), and contains no such incident which the other Synoptists omit, it occasionally identifies St Peter where St Matthew and St Luke are indefinite.

Simon, Peter, or Simon Peter is mentioned 28 times by Mt., 25 by Mc., 27 by Lc. Of Mc.'s references to the name in separate contexts four are peculiar to him (Mc. i. 36, xi. 21, xiii. 3, xvi. 7), whilst, except in the passages cited above, Mt. has no reference which is not shared by one or both of the other Synoptists. Lc. has four (viii. 45, xxii. 8, xxiv. 12, 34), but the last two are found elsewhere (Jo. xx. 3 ff., 1 Cor. xv. 5).

There are other facts which point to the same conclusion. The reader of the Synoptist Gospels is frequently struck by the appearance in St Mark of minute details or touches which suggest first-hand knowledge. This impression may be partly due to St Mark's characteristic style, though on the other hand it is possible that the style itself may have been moulded by intercourse with an eye-witness. Such striking phrases as ἐμβριμησάμενος αὐτῷ εὐθὺς ἐξέβαλεν αὐτόν (i. 43), περιβλεψάμενος αὐτοὺς μετ᾽ ὀργῆς συνλυπούμενος ἐπὶ τῇ πωρώσει τῆς καρδίας αὐτῶν (iii. 5), περιεβλέπετο ἰδεῖν τὴν τοῦτο ποιήσασαν (v. 32), ἀνέπεσαν πρασιαὶ πρασιαί (vi. 40), can hardly be attributed to the fancy of a compiler. Certainly no amount of realism will account for the scores of unexpected and independent details with which St Mark enriches the common narrative ; as Bishop Westcott observes, "there is perhaps not one narrative which he gives in common with St Matthew and St Luke to which he does not contribute some special feature[1]."

Examples may be found in Mc. i. 14 f., 20, 27, 29, 33, 35 ff., ii. 2, 3, 4, 13, 15, 23, iii. 4, 7, 9, 14 f., 17, 20 f., 31, 32, 34, iv. 33, 34, 35, 36, 38, v. 13, 20, 21, 26, vi. 1, 5, 30, 32, 37, 45, 48, 51, 53, 56, vii. 24, 26, 31, viii. 12, 22 ff., 34, ix. 13, 15 ff., 28, 33 ff., x. 16, 21 ff., 32, 46 ff., xi. 8, 11, 13, 16, 19, 20 f., 27, xii. 12, 35, 37, 41, 43, xiii. 3, xiv. 40, 58, 59, 65, 66, 67, 72, xv. 7, 8, 21, 23, 25, 41, 44, 45, 46, xvi. 1, 3, 4, 5, 8.

Was St Peter the eye-witness who supplied this mass of independent information ? There are three narratives in the Synoptic tradition which must have been derived originally from

---

[1] Westcott, *Introduction to the Study of the Gospels*, p. 562.

St Peter, St John, or St James; and there is one of which St Peter alone was competent to give a full account. A comparison of St Mark's account of these incidents ought to throw light upon the question.

(1) Mc. v. 37—43 (Mt. ix. 23—25, Lc. viii. 51—56). Mc. alone distinguishes the successive stages of the Lord's way to the dead child (οὐκ ἀφῆκεν οὐδένα μετ' αὐτοῦ συνακολουθῆσαι εἰ μή κτλ....καὶ ἔρχονται εἰς τὸν οἶκον...καὶ εἰσελθών...εἰσπορεύεται ὅπου ἦν τὸ παιδίον); in Mc. only the Lord's words are preserved in Aramaic, and the child's age is mentioned at this point to account for her rising and walking (περιεπάτει, ἦν γὰρ ἐτῶν δώδεκα); lastly, it is Mc. only who connects this miracle with the departure from Capernaum which followed (vi. 1). (2) Mc. ix. 2—13 (Mt. xvii. 1—13, Lc. ix. 28—36). Here Mt. is in some respects fuller than Mc., and seems to have had access to another tradition. But Mc. has several striking features, some of which point to Peter as their source. Such a phrase as στίλβοντα λευκὰ λίαν οἷα γναφεύς κτλ., the untranslated "Rabbi" of Peter's 'answer,' the explanatory clause οὐ γὰρ ᾔδει τί ἀποκριθῇ, the mention of the suddenness with which the vision vanished (ἐξάπινα περιβλεψάμενοι οὐκέτι οὐδένα εἶδον), the reference to the reticence which the three practised (τὸν λόγον ἐκράτησαν... συνζητοῦντες κτλ.)—are just such personal reminiscences as St Peter might have been expected to retain. (3) Mc. xiv. 33—42 (Mt. xxvi. 37—46, Lc. xxii. 40—46). Here Mt. agrees with Mc., yet a close examination reveals the greater originality of Mc., and some probable traces of a Petrine source; thus it is Mc. only who preserves the Aramaic ἀββά, and the Σίμων of the Lord's address to Peter; moreover the characteristic οὐκ ᾔδεισαν τί ἀποκριθῶσιν αὐτῷ clearly comes from the same mind which supplied the similar note in the Marcan account of the Transfiguration. (4) Mc. xiv. 54, 66—72 (Mt. xxvi. 58, 69—75, Lc. xxii. 54—62). All the Synoptic accounts here depend on St Peter, for St John's report (Jo. xviii. 17—18, 25—27) is quite distinct. But Mc.'s narrative manifests special knowledge of the lesser details (e.g. ἦν...θερμαινόμενος πρὸς τὸ φῶς, ἰδοῦσα τὸν Πέτρον θερμαινόμενον, εἰς τὸ προαύλιον, ἐκ δευτέρου, ἐπιβαλών). His dialogue also has greater freshness and verisimilitude; comp. καὶ σὺ μετὰ τοῦ Ναζαρηνοῦ ἦσθα τοῦ Ἰησοῦ with Mt.'s καὶ σὺ ἦσθα μετὰ Ἰησοῦ τοῦ Γαλειλαίου, and the answer οὔτε οἶδα οὔτε ἐπίσταμαι σὺ τί λέγεις (Mc.) with the tamer οὐκ οἶδα τί λέγεις (Mt.), οὐκ οἶδα αὐτόν, γύναι (Lc.).

The internal evidence does not amount to a proof of Petrine origination. But it is entirely consistent with the tradition which represents St Mark as specially indebted to St Peter; and the tradition is at once too early and too wide-spread to be abandoned unless the evidence of the Gospel itself renders its acceptance impossible.

It is another question whether the present book can be assigned as a whole to St Peter or even to St Mark[1]. The last twelve verses, as we shall see, almost certainly belong to another hand; the first verse is possibly no part of the original work. To St Mark and not to St Peter must probably be ascribed the episode of the Baptist's martyrdom, the story of the νεανίσκος in Gethsemane, such explanatory notes as vii. 3—4, 19 b, and the interpretations of Aramaic words and names. It may be doubted whether the long discourse of c. xiii. was derived from St Peter's teaching; indeed the note in v. 14 (ὁ ἀναγινώσκων νοείτω) seems to point distinctly to a written source which St Mark has incorporated. At xiv. 1 we come upon the traces of another source; the words ἦν δὲ τὸ πάσχα καὶ τὰ ἄζυμα μετὰ δύο ἡμέρας have the air of a new beginning and are not in St Mark's style, and the incident which follows, although it might have formed a suitable introduction to a detached narrative of the Passion, breaks St Mark's order of time, carrying us back, as St John shews, to the day before the Lord's entry into Jerusalem. Thus it is probable that at this point St Mark has availed himself of an earlier document, into which he has worked his recollections of St Peter's teaching and such other materials as his own residence at Jerusalem had placed within his reach[2].

On the whole it seems safe to assume as a working theory of the origination of the Gospel that its main source is the teaching of St Peter, which has supplied nearly the entire series of notes descriptive of the Galilean Ministry, and has largely influenced the remainder of the book. But allowance must probably be made, especially in the last six chapters, for the use of other authorities, some perhaps documentary, which had been familiar to the Evangelist before he left the Holy City.

[1] The present writer has risen from his study of the Gospel with a strong sense of the unity of the work, and can echo the *requiescat Urmarkus* which ends a recent discussion. But he is not prepared to express an opinion as to the nature and extent of the editorial revision which St Mark's original has undergone.

[2] For an account of the attempts made by critics since the time of Baur to discover a 'tendency' or a dogmatic purpose in the Second Gospel, see Salmond in Hastings, *D.B.* iii. p. 260; and on the supposed Paulinisms of St Mark cf. *Encycl. Bibl.* ii. p. 1844.

6

Comparison of Mark With the Other Synoptists

If we accept the traditional account of the origin of St Mark's work, the writer was far from regarding it in the light of a 'Gospel,' i.e. as one of a series of attempts to produce a record of the life of Christ. It is not impossible that the present headline Ἀρχὴ τοῦ εὐαγγελίου Ἰησοῦ Χριστοῦ may be due to a later hand; the superscription Κατὰ Μᾶρκον was certainly added by a generation which had conceived the idea of a tetrad of Gospels. The interpreter of Peter, if he gave a title to his book, was doubtless content to call it by such a name as we find in Justin— Ἀπομνημονεύματα Πέτρου.

But though originally an independent work, St Mark stands to the first and third of our present Gospels in a relation which is not accidental or artificial, but vital. When the three writings are compared together, they are found to deal with the same great cycles of events, and to describe them in words which are often nearly identical. The literary problem which arises from this remarkable fact belongs to the general Introduction of the Gospels, and cannot be usefully discussed here[1]; nor, indeed, is it one which directly concerns the student of St Mark. But he will do well to take note of the distinctive features of the second Gospel as compared with the first and the third, and to examine

[1] For a comprehensive treatment of the subject the reader may be referred to Professor Stanton's article *Gospels* in the second volume of Dr Hastings' *Dictionary of the Bible*. An elaborate and able article on the same subject in *Encyclopaedia Biblica* is unhappily disfigured, more especially in the section on the 'Credibility of the Synoptics,' by the dogmatic statement of conclusions which are quite insufficiently supported.

their bearing upon the origin and character of the book upon which he is engaged.

The following table will shew how far the First and Third Gospels cover the ground which is covered by St Mark, and the relative order which they follow. For the contents of the sections see § v. p. li ff.

Mc.	Mt.	Lc.
I. 1		
2—8	III. 1—12	III. 1—6, 15—17
9—11	13—17	21—22
12—13	IV. 1—11	IV. 1—13
14—15	12—17	14—15
16—20	18—22	[V. 1 ff.]
21—28		IV. 31—37
29—31	VIII. 14—15	38—39
32—34	16	40—41
35—39		42—44
40—45	2—4	V. 12—16
II. 1—12	IX. 1—8	17—26
13—14	9	27—28
15—17	10—13	29—32
18—22	14—17	33—39
23—28	XII. 1—8	VI. 1—5
III. 1—6	9—14	6—11
7—12	15—21	17—19
13—19^a	X. 1—4	12—16
19^b—30	XII. 22—32	XI. 14—26
31—35	46—50	VIII. 19—21
IV. 1—9	XIII. 1—9	4—8
10—12	10—15	9—10
13—20	18—23	11—15
21—25		16—18
26—29		
30—32	31—32	XIII. 18—19
33—34	34	
35—41	VIII. 23—27	VIII. 22—25
V. 1—13	28—32	26—33
14—17	33—34	34—37
18—20		38—39
21—34	IX. 18—22	40—48
35—43	23—26	49—56
VI. 1—6	XIII. 53—58	IV. 16—30
7—13	IX. 35—X. 1, X. 5—XI. 1	IX. 1—6
14—16	XIV. 1—2	7—9
17—29	3—12	III. 19—20

Mc.	Mt.	Lc.
30—44	13—21	IX. 10—17
45—52	22—33	
VII. 1—13	XV. 1—9	
14—23	10—19	
24—30	21—28	
31—37	29 ff.—31	
VIII. 1—10	32—39a	
11—13	39b—XVI. 4	
14—21	XVI. 5—12	
22—26		
27—30	13—20	18—21
31—33	21—23	22
34—IX. 1	24—28	23—27
IX. 2—8	XVII. 1—8	28—36
9—13	9—13	
14—29	14—20	37—43a
30—32	22—23	43b—45
33—37	XVIII. 1—5	46—48
38—40		49—50
41—50	6—9	
X. 1	XIX. 1—2	
2—12	3—9	
13—16	13—15	XVIII. 15—17
17—22	16—22	18—23
23—27	23—26	24—27
28—31	27—30	28—30
32—34	XX. 17—19	31—34
35—45	20—28	
46—52	29—34	35—43
XI. 1—11	XXI. 1—11	XIX. 29—45a
12—14	18—19	
15—19	12—17	45b—48
20—25	19b—22	
27—33	23—27	XX. 1—8
XII. 1—12	33—46	9—19
13—17	XXII. 15—22	20—26
18—27	23—33	27—38
28—34	34—40	
35—37a	41—45	41—44
37b—40	XXIII. 1—38	45—47
41—44		XXI. 1—4
XIII. 1—2	XXIV. 1—2	5—6
3—13	3—14	8—19
14—23	15—25	20—24
24—27	29—31	25—28
28—29	32—33	29—31
30—32	34—35	32—33
33—37	42—44	36

Mc.		Mt.		Lc.	
XIV.	1—2	XXVI.	1—5	XXII.	1—2
	3—9		6—13		
	10—11		14—16		3—6
	12—16		17—19		7—13
	17—21		20—25		14, 21—23
	22—25		26—29		17—20
	26—31		30—35		31—39
	32—42		36—46		40—46
	43—50		47—56		47—53
	51—52				
	53—65		57—68		54^{a}, 63—71
	66—72		69—75		56—62
XV.	1—15	XXVII.	1—26	XXIII.	1—25
	$16—20^{a}$		$27—31^{a}$		
	$20^{b}—22$		$31^{b}—33$		$26—33^{a}$
	23—32		34—44		$33^{b}—43$
	33—37		45—50		$44—45^{a}$
	38—41		51—56		$45^{b}—55$
	42—47		57—61		50—55
XVI.	1—8	XXVIII.	1—20		56—XXIV.

1. It appears from this table that out of the 106 sections of the genuine St Mark there are but three (excluding the head-line) which are wholly absent from both St Matthew and St Luke; and of the remaining 102, 96 are to be found in St Matthew, and 82 in St Luke. On the other hand, as the table shews with equal distinctness, there are large portions of St Matthew and St Luke (e.g. Mt. i.—ii., v.—vii., Lc. i.—ii., ix. 51—xviii. 14) which are either entirely wanting in St Mark, or represented there only by an occasional fragment. This is but a rough statement of the case, but it suffices to indicate the relation of St Mark to the other Synoptists[1] in regard to the extent of the fields which they respectively occupy.

2. Further, the table reveals a marked difference of order in that part of the common narrative which belongs to the Galilean Ministry. From the beginning of the journeyings to Jerusalem to the Resurrection the order of the sections differs but slightly. St Matthew (xxi. 19 f.) brings the withering of the fig-tree into immediate connexion with the sentence pronounced upon it, and

[1] Compare Mr W. C. Allen's paper in *Exp. T.* xii., p. 279 ff. (*The dependence of St Matt. i—xiii upon St Mark*).

St Luke (xxii. 21 f.) places the detection of Judas after the distribution of the Eucharist. With these exceptions the order of Mc.
x. 1—xvi. 8 is generally followed by St Matthew and St Luke.
But in the sequence of the events narrated in Mc. i. 14—ix. 50
there is no such consensus. St Luke, indeed, is generally in fair
agreement with St Mark, where the two are dealing with the same
events; but St Matthew's displacements of the Marcan order are
numerous and serious in the earlier chapters.

> The chief differences of order in St Luke are as follows : (1) the
> charge of collusion with Beelzebul follows the arrival of the
> mother and brethren; (2) the parable of the mustard seed is
> detached from that of the sower and stands in a later context;
> (3) the preaching at Nazareth is placed at the outset of the
> Ministry. St Matthew's order is essentially different from
> St Mark's as far as Mc. vi. 13, although from that point the
> two are in almost complete agreement.

It may be taken as a *prima facie* argument in favour of St
Mark's order that it is "confirmed either by St Matthew or St
Luke, and the greater part of it by both[1]." Moreover, when one
of the other Synoptists strikes out a path peculiar to himself,
his order usually has less verisimilitude, and is open on internal
grounds to suspicion.

> Thus (1) when Mt. places the gathering of crowds from Decapolis
> and Judaea at the very outset of the Ministry (Mt. iv. 25), there
> can be little doubt that he antedates a state of things which Mc.
> rightly places at a later stage (Mc. iii. 7 ff.). (2) The crossing to
> the Gadarene (Gerasene) country, if preparatory to an evangelistic
> tour in the Decapolis, seems to come too early in Mt.'s order,
> and on the other hand he places the calling of the Apostles too
> late; in Mc. both incidents occupy places which accord with what
> appears to be the natural course of events. (3) The synagogue
> scene at Nazareth, which Lc. fixes before the commencement of the
> Lord's residence at Capernaum, bears upon its surface the evidence
> of a later date (cf. Lc. iv. 23 ὅσα ἠκούσαμεν γενόμενα εἰς τὴν Καφαρ-
> ναούμ κτλ.). (4) Again the notes of time and place in Mc. are
> frequently precise where in Lc. they disappear, or exist only in a
> weakened form—e.g. Mc. i. 22 εὐθὺς τοῖς σάββασιν (Lc. ἐν τοῖς σ.),
> ii. 1 εἰσελθὼν πάλιν εἰς Καφαρναούμ δι' ἡμερῶν (Lc. ἐγένετο ἐν μιᾷ τῶν
> ἡμερῶν), iv. 35 ἐν ἐκείνῃ τῇ ἡμέρᾳ (Lc. ἐν μιᾷ τῶν ἡμερῶν)—whilst in

---

[1] Mr F. H. Woods in *Studia Biblica*, ii. p. 62; cf. Dr Sanday's remarks in
Smith's *D.B.*[2] (p. 1224).

Mt. the incidents have sometimes fallen into new surroundings which are inconsistent with those assigned to them in Mc. or Lc. or in both; comp. e.g. Mt. viii. 1 καταβάντος δὲ αὐτοῦ ἀπὸ τοῦ ὄρους (Lc. ἐν τῷ εἶναι αὐτὸν ἐν μιᾷ τῶν πόλεων), ix. 18 ταῦτα αὐτοῦ λαλοῦντος (Mc. and Lc. place the preceding parables in other contexts).

3. The comparison of St Mark's matter with that of the corresponding narratives in St Matthew and St Luke has been to some extent anticipated in the preceding section (p. lxiii ff.). But it may be useful to illustrate a little more fully the relative fulness of St Mark's knowledge in matters of detail[1]. The following examples are taken from the first four chapters of the Gospel.

Mc.	Mt.	Lc.
i. 20 ἀφέντες τὸν πατέρα αὐτῶν Ζεβεδαῖον ἐν τῷ πλοίῳ μετὰ τῶν μισθωτῶν ἀπῆλθον ὀπίσω αὐτοῦ.	iv. 22 ἀφέντες τὸ πλοῖον καὶ τὸν πατέρα αὐτῶν ἠκολούθησαν αὐτῷ.	v. 11 καταγαγόντες τὰ πλοῖα ἐπὶ τὴν γῆν ἀφέντες πάντα ἠκολούθησαν αὐτῷ.
i. 35 πρωὶ ἔννυχα λίαν ἀναστὰς ἐξῆλθεν καὶ ἀπῆλθεν εἰς ἔρημον τόπον κἀκεῖ προσηύχετο.		iv. 42 γενομένης δὲ ἡμέρας ἐξελθὼν ἐπορεύθη εἰς ἔρημον τόπον.
i. 43 καὶ ἐμβριμησάμενος αὐτῷ εὐθὺς ἐξέβαλεν αὐτόν, καὶ λέγει αὐτῷ κτλ.	viii. 4 καὶ λέγει αὐτῷ κτλ.	v. 14 καὶ αὐτὸς παρήγγειλεν αὐτῷ κτλ.
ii. 2 καὶ συνήχθησαν πολλοὶ ὥστε μηκέτι χωρεῖν μηδὲ τὰ πρὸς θύραν.		
ii. 23 ἤρξαντο ὁδὸν ποιεῖν τίλλοντες τοὺς στάχυας.	xii. 1 ἤρξαντο τίλλειν στάχυας καὶ ἐσθίειν.	vi. 1 ἔτιλλον οἱ μαθηταὶ αὐτοῦ καὶ ἤσθιον τοὺς στάχυας.
iii. 6 ἐξελθόντες οἱ Φαρισαῖοι εὐθὺς μετὰ τῶν Ἡρῳδιανῶν κτλ.	xiii. 14 ἐξελθόντες δὲ οἱ Φαρισαῖοι κτλ.	vi. 11 αὐτοὶ δέ κτλ.
iii. 14 προσκαλεῖται οὓς ἤθελεν αὐτός... καὶ ἐποίησεν δώδεκα...ἵνα ὦσιν μετ' αὐτοῦ καὶ ἵνα ἀποστέλλῃ αὐτοὺς κη-	x. 1 προσκαλεσάμενος τοὺς δώδεκα μαθητὰς αὐτοῦ ἔδωκεν αὐτοῖς ἐξουσίαν κτλ.	vi. 13 προσεφώνησεν τοὺς μαθητὰς αὐτοῦ, καὶ ἐκλεξάμενος ἀπ' αὐτῶν δώδεκα....

---

[1] Cf. Papias ap. Eus.: ἑνὸς...ἐποιήσατο πρόνοιαν, τοῦ μηδὲν ὧν ἤκουσε παραλιπεῖν.

Mc.	Mt.	Lc.
ρύσσειν καὶ ἔχειν ἐξουσίαν κτλ.		
iii. 19—21 ἔρχεται εἰς οἶκον· καὶ συνέρχεται πάλιν ὁ ὄχλος, ὥστε μὴ δύνασθαι αὐτοὺς μηδὲ ἄρτον φαγεῖν. καὶ ἀκούσαντες οἱ παρ᾽ αὐτοῦ ἐξῆλθον κρατῆσαι αὐτόν, ἔλεγον γὰρ ὅτι ἐξέστη.		
iv. 10 ὅτε ἐγένετο κατὰ μόνας, ἠρώτων αὐτὸν οἱ περὶ αὐτὸν σὺν τοῖς δώδεκα κτλ.	xiii. 10 προσελθόντες οἱ μαθηταὶ εἶπαν αὐτῷ κτλ.	viii. 9 ἐπηρώτων δὲ αὐτὸν οἱ μαθηταὶ αὐτοῦ κτλ.
iv. 34 κατ᾽ ἰδίαν δὲ τοῖς ἰδίοις μαθηταῖς ἐπέλυεν πάντα.		
iv. 36 παραλαμβάνουσιν αὐτὸν ὡς ἦν ἐν τῷ πλοίῳ, καὶ ἄλλα πλοῖα ἦν μετ᾽ αὐτοῦ.	viii. 23 ἐμβάντι αὐτῷ εἰς πλοῖον ἠκολούθησαν αὐτῷ οἱ μαθηταὶ αὐτοῦ.	viii. 22 αὐτὸς ἐνέβη εἰς πλοῖον καὶ οἱ μαθηταὶ αὐτοῦ.
iv. 38 καὶ αὐτὸς ἦν ἐν τῇ πρύμνῃ ἐπὶ τὸ προσκεφάλαιον καθεύδων.	viii. 24 αὐτὸς δὲ ἐκάθευδεν.	viii. 23 πλεόντων δὲ αὐτῶν ἀφύπνωσεν.
iv. 39 ἐπετίμησεν τῷ ἀνέμῳ καὶ εἶπεν τῇ θαλάσσῃ Σιώπα, πεφίμωσο.	viii. 26 ἐπετίμησεν τοῖς ἀνέμοις καὶ τῇ θαλάσσῃ.	viii. 24 ἐπετίμησεν τῷ ἀνέμῳ καὶ τῷ κλύδωνι τοῦ ὕδατος, καὶ ἐπαύσαντο.

When St Mark does not add to our knowledge, his presentation of a fact or saying is often distinct from that which it assumes in St Matthew and St Luke, and has the appearance of being the original from which one or both of the other accounts have been derived.

The following examples from the same chapters may suffice:

Mc.	Mt.	Lc.
i. 16 Σίμωνα καὶ Ἀνδρέαν τὸν ἀδελφὸν Σίμωνος.	iv. 18 δύο ἀδελφούς, Σίμωνα τὸν λεγόμενον Πέτρον	

Mc.	Mt.	Lc.
	καὶ Ἀνδρέαν τὸν ἀ-δελφὸν Σίμωνος.	
i. 26 σπαράξαν αὐ-τόν.		iv. 35 ῥίψαν αὐτὸν εἰς τὸ μέσον...μηδὲν βλάψαν αὐτόν.
ii. 12 τὸν κράβατ-τον.	ix. 6 τὴν κλίνην.	v. 24 τὸ κλινίδιον.
ii. 17 καλέσαι... ἁμαρτωλούς.	ix. 13 καλέσαι... ἁμαρτωλούς.	v. 32 καλέσαι ἁ-μαρτωλοὺς εἰς μετά-νοιαν.
ii. 21 εἰ δὲ μή, αἴρει τὸ πλήρωμα ἀπ᾽ αὐτοῦ τὸ καινὸν τοῦ παλαιοῦ.	iv. 16 αἴρει γὰρ τὸ πλήρωμα αὐτοῦ ἀπὸ τοῦ ἱματίου.	v. 36 εἰ δὲ μήγε, καὶ τὸ καινὸν σχίσει καὶ τῷ παλαιῷ οὐ συμφωνήσει τὸ ἐπί-βλημα τὸ ἀπὸ τοῦ καινοῦ.
iii. 16 καὶ ἐπέθηκεν ὄνομα τῷ Σίμωνι Πέ-τρον, καὶ Ἰάκωβον.	x. 2 Σίμων ὁ κα-λούμενος Πέτρος... καὶ Ἰάκωβος.	vi. 14 Σίμωνα ὃν καὶ ὠνόμασεν Πέ-τρον...καὶ Ἰάκωβον.
iv. 11 ὑμῖν τὸ μυ-στήριον δέδοται.	xiii. 11 ὑμῖν δέ-δοται γνῶναι τὰ μυ-στήρια.	viii. 9 ὑμῖν δέδο-ται γνῶναι τὰ μυστή-ρια.
iv. 21 ἔρχεται ὁ λύχνος.	v. 15 καίουσιν λύχνον.	viii. 16 λύχνον ἅψας.
iv. 22 οὐ γάρ ἐσ-τιν κρυπτὸν ἐὰν μὴ ἵνα κτλ.	x. 26 οὐδὲν γάρ ἐστιν κεκαλυμμένον ὃ οὐκ κτλ.	viii. 17 οὐ γάρ ἐστιν κρυπτὸν ὃ οὐ κτλ.
iv. 31 ὡς κόκκῳ.	xiii. 31 ὁμοία ἐσ-τὶν...κόκκῳ.	xiii. 19 ὁμοία ἐσ-τὶν κόκκῳ.

Although in several of these instances St Mark's mode of expressing himself is briefer than that which is preferred by the other Synoptists, his style is not on the whole distinguished by brevity. On the contrary his treatment of incident is constantly fuller than theirs, partly through the habit, already illustrated, of filling up his picture with an abundance of minute details, partly from his way of (1) presenting facts in a vivid and pictorial form, and (2) interpreting character and conduct.

Examples of (1) may be found in the story of the Gerasene demoniac, the narrative of the cleansing of the αἱμορροοῦσα and the raising of the child of Jairus, the Baptist's martyrdom, the discussion arising out of the question about κοιναὶ χεῖρες, the healing of the Syrophoenician girl, the epileptic boy, and the son of Timaeus, the scribe's question, the anointing at Bethany. This feature in Mc. is most apparent when he is compared with Mt.

Lc. has a fulness of his own, but it is of another character, and largely due to a literary style; cf. Mc. ii. 22 with Lc. v. 37 f., v. 1 with Lc. viii. 26, v. 17 with Lc. viii. 37, viii. 30 with Lc. ix. 21, viii. 34 with Lc. ix. 23, ix. 32 with Lc. ix. 45, xi. 8 with Lc. xix. 37, xiii. 7 f. with Lc. xxi. 9 ff.

The following may serve as illustrations of (2): Mc. i. 41 σπλαγχνισθείς, i. 43 ἐμβριμησάμενος, iii. 5 μετ᾽ ὀργῆς συνλυπούμενος, v. 30 ἐπιγνοὺς ἐν ἑαυτῷ τὴν ἐξ αὐτοῦ δύναμιν, v. 36 παρακούσας τὸν λόγον λαλούμενον, vi. 19 ἐνεῖχεν αὐτῷ κτλ., vi. 20 ἐφοβεῖτο...πολλὰ ἠπόρει καὶ ἡδέως αὐτοῦ ἤκουεν, vi. 52 ἦν αὐτῶν ἡ καρδία πεπωρωμένη, vii. 19 καθαρίζων πάντα τὰ βρώματα, x. 21 ἐμβλέψας αὐτῷ ἠγάπησεν αὐτόν, x. 22 στυγνάσας ἐπὶ τῷ λόγῳ, xv. 15 βουλόμενος τῷ ὄχλῳ τὸ ἱκανὸν ποιῆσαι, xvi. 8 οὐδενὶ οὐδὲν εἶπον, ἐφοβοῦντο γάρ.

As a result of this characteristic fulness of St Mark, some eighty verses in his Gospel find no direct parallel in the other Synoptists. Although he seldom introduces a narrative or a parable which is not also found in St Matthew or St Luke, the aggregate of matter peculiar to the Second Gospel cannot fall much below one-sixth of the whole book.

In one respect, indeed, St Mark is concise where the other Evangelists are full. With a single exception (c. xiii.) he represents the longer discourses of St Matthew and St Luke by a few compact sentences. Thus, the Sermon on the Mount finds only an occasional echo in the Second Gospel (e.g. iv. 21, ix. 50, x. 11); the long charge to the Twelve (Mt. x.) is reduced by St Mark to a few verses (vi. 8—11); of the final denunciation of the Pharisees, which occupies a whole chapter in St Matthew (xxiii.), St Mark gives merely a specimen (xii. 38—40). Such public teaching as St Mark reports is chiefly parabolic (ii. 19—22, iii. 23—27, iv. 3—32, vii. 15, xii. 1—9); yet his parables are few in comparison with those of either Matthew or Luke. On the other hand instructions delivered privately to the Twelve are sometimes given more at length by St Mark than by the other two Synoptists (cf. e.g. vii. 18—23, viii. 17—21, ix. 33—50, xiii. 34—37). And such sayings as St Mark records are often, like his narrative, characterised by touches which possess a singular freshness and originality.

The following are examples: i. 14 πεπλήρωται ὁ καιρός, ii. 27 τὸ σάββατον διὰ τὸν ἄνθρωπον ἐγένετο καὶ οὐχ ὁ ἄνθρωπος διὰ τὸ σάββατον,

iii. 23 πῶς δύναται Σατανᾶς Σατανᾶν ἐκβάλλειν; 26 ἀλλὰ τέλος ἔχει, 29 ἔνοχος ἔσται αἰωνίου ἁμαρτήματος, iv. 8 ἀναβαίνοντα καὶ αὐξανόμενα, 13 οὐκ οἴδατε τὴν παραβολὴν ταύτην κτλ., vii. 13 παρόμοια τοιαῦτα πολλὰ ποιεῖτε, vii. 27 ἄφες πρῶτον χορτασθῆναι τὰ τέκνα, viii. 21 οὔπω συνίετε; ix. 23 τὸ Εἰ δύνῃ, πάντα δυνατὰ τῷ πιστεύοντι, ix. 29 τοῦτο τὸ γένος ἐν οὐδενὶ δύναται ἐξελθεῖν εἰ μὴ ἐν προσευχῇ, x. 30 μετὰ διωγμῶν, xi. 22 ἔχετε πίστιν θεοῦ, xii. 27 πολὺ πλανᾶσθε, xii. 34 οὐ μακρὰν εἶ ἀπὸ τῆς βασιλείας τοῦ θεοῦ, xiv. 36 πάντα δυνατά σοι.

To sum up these remarks. It would appear that the relation of St Mark to the other Synoptists is that of an early but fragmentary record towards records of a somewhat later origin[1] and more complex character. In compass St Mark falls far short of the other two[2], but he excels them in approximation to chronological order and in life-like representation of the facts[3]. His narrative moves in a more contracted field; he reports but one of our Lord's longer discourses in full, and comparatively few of His sayings and parables. But where the three Synoptists are on common ground, St Mark is usually distinguished by signs of the minuter knowledge which comes from personal observation or from personal contact with an eye-witness[4].

[1] For a discussion of this point see Hastings, *D. B.* iii. 259 f., *Enc. Bibl.* ii. 1847 f.; the literature upon it will be found in Moffatt, *Historical N. T.*, p. 262 f.

[2] Jerome, *de virr. ill.* 8, "Marcus... breve scripsit evangelium."

[3] On the 'genius' of St Mark's Gospel see Salmond in Hastings, *D.B.*, p. 253 ff.

[4] Mr F. P. Badham in *St Mark's Indebtedness to St Matthew* uses the picturesqueness of St Mark's narrative as an argument against his priority; see e.g. p. 44: "consider the frequently trivial character of these details...consider, too, the tendency to emphasise the marvellous. With the phenomena of the Apocryphal Gospels before our eyes it will surely be reckoned a sign of decadence that our Second Evangelist dilates so exuberantly on the Gadarene's ferocity and the epileptic's paroxysm." The comparison of St Mark with the Apocryphal Gospels is unfortunate. It calls attention to the essential difference between the real and the realistic, a report based upon a first-hand authority and an historical romance. For a criticism of Mr Badham's method the student may be referred to Mr A. Wright's *Some N. T. problems*, p. 256 ff.

7

Use of the Old Testament by Mark

This Gospel contains 68 distinct references to the Old Testament, of which 25 are either formal[1] or nearly verbal quotations. Only seven of the references are peculiar to St Mark.

In the following table quotations are distinguished by an asterisk; (Mt.), (Lc.), indicate that the passage is used by St Matthew or St Luke in a corresponding context; a dagger before a Marcan reference shews that it contains a quotation peculiar to St Mark.

*Gen.	i. 27	Mc. x. 6 (Mt.)
*	ii. 24	x. 7 f. (Mt.)
	xviii. 14	x. 27 (Mt., Lc.)
	xxxvii. 20	xii. 7 (Mt., Lc.)
	xxxviii. 8	xii. 19 (Mt., Lc.)
*Exod.	iii. 6	xii. 26 (Mt., Lc.)
*	xx. 12	vii. 10^a, x. 19 (Mt.)
*	xx. 12—17	x. 19 (Mt., Lc.)
*	xxi. 17	vii. 10^b (Mt.)
*	xxiv. 8	xiv. 24 (Mt.)
Lev.	xiii. 49	i. 44 (Mt., Lc.)
*	xix. 18	xii. 31, 33 (Mt., Lc.)
Num.	xxvii. 17	vi. 34 (Mt.)
*Deut.	iv. 35	† xii. 32
	v. 16	vii. 10 (Mt.)
	v. 17—20	x. 19 (Mt., Lc.)
*	vi. 4	xii. 29, 32
	vi. 5	xii. 33 (Mt., Lc.)
	xiii. 1	xiii. 22 (Mt.)
	xxiv. 1	x. 4 (Mt.)
*	xxiv. 14	† x. 19
	xxv. 5	xii. 19 (Mt., Lc.)
	xxx. 4	xiii. 27 (Mt.)
1 Sam. xv. 22		† xii. 33

[1] The formal quotations in Mc. are 19; see *Introduction to the O. T. in Greek*, pp. 382, 391.

1 Sam.	xxi. 6	Mc. ii. 26 (Mt., Lc.)
1 Kings	xxii. 17	vi. 34 (Mt.)
2 Kings	i. 8	i. 10 (Mt.)
Esther	v. 3, vii. 2	vi. 23
Job	xlii. 2	x. 29 (Mt.)
*Ps.	xxii. 1	xv. 34 (Mt.)
	xxii. 7	xv. 29 (Mt.)
	xxii. 19	xv. 24 (Mt., Lc.)
	xli. 9	† xiv. 18
*	xlii. 6	xiv. 34 (Mt.)
	lxix. 22	xv. 36 (Mt.)
*	cx. 1	xii. 36, xiv. 62 (Mt., Lc.)
*	cxviii. 22 f.	xii. 10 (Mt., Lc.)
*	cxviii. 25 f.	xi. 9 (Mt.)
Isa.	v. 1—2	xii. 1 (Mt., Lc.)
	vi. 9 f.	iv. 12 (Mt., Lc.)
	xiii. 10	xiii. 24 (Mt.)
	xix. 2	xiii. 8 (Mt., Lc.)
*	xxix. 13	vii. 6 (Mt.)
	xxxiv. 4	xiii. 25 (Mt.)
*	xl. 3	i. 3 (Mt., Lc.)
*	lvi. 7	xi. 17ª (Mt., Lc.)
	lxii. 2	vi. 11 (Mt.)
*	lxvi. 24	† ix. 48
Jer.	v. 21	† viii. 18
*	vii. 11	xi. 17ᵇ (Mt., Lc.)
Ezek.	xii. 2	† viii. 18
	xvii. 23	iv. 32 (Mt., Lc.)
	xxxiv. 5	vi. 34 (Mt.)
Dan.	ii. 28, 29, 45	xiii. 7 (Mt., Lc.)
	iv. 12, 21	iv. 32 (Mt.)
	vii. 13	xiii. 26, xiv. 62 (Mt., Lc.)
	ix. 27	xiii. 14 (Mt.)
	xi. 31	xiii. 14 (Mt.)
*	xii. 1	xiii. 19 (Mt.)
*	xii. 11	xiii. 14 (Mt.)
Joel	iii. 13	† iv. 29
Mic.	vii. 6	xiii. 12 (cf. Mt., Lc.)
Zech.	ii. 10	xiii. 27 (Mt.)
	viii. 6	x. 27 (Mt.)
	ix. 11	xiv. 24 (Mt.)
*	xiii. 7	xiv. 27 (Mt.)
*Mal.	iii. 1	i. 2 (Mt., Lc.)
	iv. 5	ix. 12 (Mt.)

A comparison of the formal and direct quotations with the Cambridge manual edition of the LXX.[1] will shew that while St

---

[1] A more detailed comparison is given by Mr W. C. Allen in *Exp. Times*, xii. (1900–1) pp. 187 ff., 281 ff.

Mark is generally in fair agreement with the MS. which on the whole presents the LXX. in its relatively oldest form, there are some remarkable variations.

In the following list thick type is used where the text of the Cambridge LXX. diverges from the text of St Mark as edited in this volume.

Mc. i. 2 ἰδοὺ ἀποστέλλω τὸν ἄγγελόν μου πρὸ προσώπου σου, ὃς κατασκευάσει τὴν ὁδόν σου.

Mc. i. 3 φωνὴ βοῶντος ἐν τῇ ἐρήμῳ Ἑτοιμάσατε τὴν ὁδὸν Κυρίου, εὐθείας ποιεῖτε τὰς τρίβους αὐτοῦ.

Mc. vii. 6 ὁ λαὸς οὗτος τοῖς χείλεσίν με τιμᾷ, ἡ δὲ καρδία αὐτῶν πόρρω ἀπέχει ἀπ᾽ ἐμοῦ· μάτην δὲ σέβονταί με, διδάσκοντες διδασκαλίας ἐντάλματα ἀνθρώπων.

Mc. vii. 10ᵃ τίμα τὸν πατέρα σου καὶ τὴν μητέρα σου.

Mc. vii. 10ᵇ ὁ κακολογῶν πατέρα ἢ μητέρα θανάτῳ τελευτάτω.

Mc. ix. 48 ὁ σκώληξ αὐτῶν οὐ τελευτᾷ καὶ τὸ πῦρ οὐ σβέννυται.

Mc. x. 6 ἄρσεν καὶ θῆλυ ἐποίησεν αὐτούς.

Mc. x. 7 f. ἕνεκεν τούτου καταλείψει ἄνθρωπος τὸν πατέρα αὐτοῦ καὶ τὴν μητέρα, καὶ ἔσονται οἱ δύο εἰς σάρκα μίαν.

Mc. x. 19 μὴ φονεύσῃς, μὴ μοιχεύσῃς, μὴ κλέψῃς, μὴ ψευδομαρτυρήσῃς, μὴ ἀποστερήσῃς, τίμα τὸν πατέρα σου καὶ τὴν μητέρα.

Mc. xi. 9 ὡσαννά· εὐλογημένος ὁ ἐρχόμενος ἐν ὀνόματι Κυρίου.

Mc. xi. 17ᵃ ὁ οἶκός μου οἶκος προσευχῆς κληθήσεται πᾶσιν τοῖς ἔθνεσιν.

Mc. xi. 17ᵇ σπήλαιον λῃστῶν.

Mal. iii. 1 ἰδοὺ ἐξαποστέλλω τὸν ἄγγελόν μου, καὶ ἐπιβλέψεται ὁδὸν πρὸ προσώπου μου.

Isa. xl. 3 φωνὴ βοῶντος ἐν τῇ ἐρήμῳ Ἑτοιμάσατε τὴν ὁδὸν Κυρίου, εὐθείας ποιεῖτε τὰς τρίβους τοῦ θεοῦ ἡμῶν.

Isa. xxix. 13 ἐγγίζει μοι ὁ λαὸς οὗτος ἐν τῷ στόματι αὐτοῦ, καὶ ἐν τοῖς χείλεσιν αὐτῶν τιμῶσίν με, ἡ δὲ καρδία αὐτῶν πόρρω ἀπέχει ἀπ᾽ ἐμοῦ· μάτην δὲ σέβονταί με, διδάσκοντες ἐντάλματα ἀνθρώπων καὶ διδασκαλίας.

Exod. xx. 12 (Deut. v. 16) τίμα τὸν πατέρα σου καὶ τὴν μητέρα.

Exod. xxi. 16 (17) ὁ κακολογῶν πατέρα αὐτοῦ ἢ μητέρα αὐτοῦ τελευτήσει θανάτῳ.

Isa. lxvi. 24 ὁ...σκώληξ αὐτῶν οὐ τελευτήσει (τελευτᾷ Α), καὶ τὸ πῦρ αὐτῶν οὐ σβεσθήσεται.

Gen. i. 27 ἄρσεν καὶ θῆλυ ἐποίησεν αὐτούς.

Gen. ii. 24 ἕνεκεν τούτου καταλείψει ἄνθρωπος τὸν πατέρα αὐτοῦ καὶ τὴν μητέρα αὐτοῦ,...καὶ ἔσονται οἱ δύο εἰς σάρκα μίαν.

Exod. xx. 12—17 τίμα τὸν πατέρα σου καὶ τὴν μητέρα...οὐ μοιχεύσεις, οὐ κλέψεις, οὐ φονεύσεις, οὐ ψευδομαρτυρήσεις.

Deut. xxiv. 14, Α οὐκ ἀποστερήσεις.

Ps. cxvii. (cxviii.) 25, 26 σῶσον δή...εὐλογημένος ὁ ἐρχόμενος ἐν ὀνόματι Κυρίου.

Isa. lvi. 7 ὁ...οἶκός μου οἶκος προσευχῆς κληθήσεται πᾶσιν τοῖς ἔθνεσιν.

Jer. vii. 11 σπήλαιον λῃστῶν.

Mc. xii. 10 λίθον ὃν ἀπεδοκίμασαν οἱ οἰκοδομοῦντες, οὗτος
ἐγενήθη εἰς κεφαλὴν γωνίας· παρὰ
Κυρίου ἐγένετο αὕτη, καὶ ἔστιν
θαυμαστὴ ἐν ὀφθαλμοῖς ἡμῶν.

Ps. cxvii. (cxviii.) 22 f. τὸν
λίθον ὃν ἀπεδοκίμασαν οἱ οἰκοδομοῦντες, οὗτος ἐγενήθη εἰς κεφαλὴν
γωνίας· παρὰ Κυρίου ἐγένετο αὕτη,
καὶ ἔστιν θαυμαστὴ ἐν ὀφθαλμοῖς
ἡμῶν.

Mc. xii. 26 εἶπεν...Ἐγὼ ὁ θεὸς
Ἀβραὰμ καὶ θεὸς Ἰσαὰκ καὶ θεὸς
Ἰακώβ.

Exod. iii. 6 εἶπεν Ἐγώ εἰμι ὁ
θεὸς...Ἀβραὰμ καὶ θεὸς Ἰσαὰκ
καὶ θεὸς Ἰακώβ.

Mc. xii. 29 f. ἄκουε, Ἰσραήλ·
Κύριος ὁ θεὸς ἡμῶν Κύριος εἷς
ἐστιν· καὶ ἀγαπήσεις Κύριον τὸν
θεόν σου ἐξ ὅλης [τῆς] καρδίας
σου καὶ ἐξ ὅλης τῆς ψυχῆς σου
καὶ ἐξ ὅλης τῆς διανοίας σου καὶ ἐξ
ὅλης τῆς ἰσχύος σου.

Deut. vi. 4 f. ἄκουε, Ἰσραήλ·
Κύριος ὁ θεὸς ἡμῶν Κύριος εἷς
ἐστιν· καὶ ἀγαπήσεις Κύριον τὸν
θεόν σου ἐξ ὅλης τῆς διανοίας σου
καὶ ἐξ ὅλης τῆς ψυχῆς σου καὶ ἐξ
ὅλης τῆς δυνάμεώς σου.

Mc. xii. 31 ἀγαπήσεις τὸν
πλησίον σου ὡς σεαυτόν.

Lev. xix. 18 ἀγαπήσεις τὸν
πλησίον σου ὡς σεαυτόν.

Mc. xii. 32 οὐκ ἔστιν ἄλλος
πλὴν αὐτοῦ.

Deut. iv. 35 οὐκ ἔστιν ἔτι
(ἄλλος Α) πλὴν αὐτοῦ.

Mc. xii. 36 εἶπεν Κύριος τῷ
κυρίῳ μου Κάθου ἐκ δεξιῶν μου
ἕως ἂν θῶ τοὺς ἐχθρούς σου ὑποκάτω τῶν ποδῶν σου.

Ps. cix. (cx.) 1 εἶπεν ὁ κύριος τῷ
κυρίῳ μου Κάθου ἐκ δεξιῶν μου
ἕως ἂν θῶ τοὺς ἐχθρούς σου ὑποπόδιον τῶν ποδῶν σου.

Mc. xiii. 14 τὸ βδέλυγμα τῆς
ἐρημώσεως.

Dan. xii. 11 (LXX.) τὸ βδέλυγμα τῆς ἐρημώσεως.

Mc. xiii. 19 θλίψις οἷα οὐ
γέγονεν...

Dan. xii. 1 (Th.) θλίψις οἷα
οὐ γέγονεν...

Mc. xiv. 24 τὸ αἷμα...τῆς διαθήκης.

Exod. xxiv. 8 τὸ αἷμα τῆς διαθήκης.

Mc. xiv. 27 πατάξω τὸν ποιμένα, καὶ τὰ πρόβατα διασκορπισθήσονται.

Zach. xiii. 7 πατάξατε τοὺς ποιμένας καὶ ἐκσπάσατε τὰ πρόβατα.

Mc. xiv. 34 περίλυπος...ἡ
ψυχή.

Ps. xli. (xlii.) 6 περίλυπος...ἡ
ψυχή.

Mc. xv. 34 ὁ θεός μου ὁ θεός
μου, εἰς τί ἐγκατέλιπές με;

Ps. xxi. (xxii.) 1 ὁ θεὸς ὁ θεός
μου...ἵνα τί ἐγκατέλιπές με;

The variations, it will be seen, are not numerous or extensive,
but they are sometimes well marked and of considerable interest.
Details have been discussed, as far as space permitted, in the
footnotes; but attention may be called here to a few points.
(1) St Mark manifests an occasional leaning towards the text of
cod. A (Gen. ii. 24 [?], Exod. xx. 13 ff. (order), xxi. 16, Deut. vi. 4,
Zach. xiii. 7). (2) In a few remarkable instances he agrees with
the other Synoptists against the LXX. (Isa. xxix. 13, xl. 3,

Zach. xiii. 7, Mal. iii. 1). (3) While his LXX. quotations usually exhibit the same text as St Matthew's and St Luke's, he is here and there independent of one or both (Exod. xx. 13 ff., Deut. vi. 4, Ps. xxi. (xxii.) 1, cix. (cx.) 1).

With few exceptions (e.g. i. 2, 3) St Mark's references to the Old Testament occur in his report of the words of our Lord or of those who conversed with Him. But the commentary will make it probable that our Evangelist was intimately acquainted with the language of the Greek Bible[1]. To the LXX. he was probably indebted for nearly all that he knew of Greek as a written language[2], as well as for the form in which his conceptions of the Messiah and the Kingdom of GOD were generally cast.

[1] See also § IV. of this Introduction.

[2] Sir J. C. Hawkins (*Hor. Syn.* pp. 108, 162 ff.) points out that, to judge by the list of words peculiar to St Mark, his acquaintance with the LXX. was less intimate than either St Matthew's or St Luke's. The test, however, is not conclusive, merely establishing a probability that Mc. had other resources, such as those which a ἑρμηνευτής might not unnaturally possess, which rendered him more independent of the LXX. vocabulary than the other Synoptists.

8

External Conditions of the Life of Christ as Depicted by Mark

1. Two sections of Palestine make up the field of St Mark's history, Galilee (ἡ Γαλειλαία[1]), and Judaea (ἡ 'Ιουδαία χώρα or simply ἡ 'Ιουδαία); and two cities stand prominently forward as the centres of the movement, Capernaum (Καφαρναούμ), and Jerusalem (in Mc. always 'Ιεροσόλυμα). Adjacent regions are also mentioned, into some of which the scene occasionally passes— Idumaea, Peraea (πέραν 'Ιορδάνου), Phoenicia (περὶ Τύρον καὶ Σιδῶνα, τὰ ὅρια Τύρου καὶ Σιδῶνος), Decapolis (ἡ δεκάπολις, Δεκάπολις), Gennesaret, 'the land of the Gerasenes' (ἡ χώρα τῶν Γερασηνῶν); and other towns and villages—Nazareth (Ναζαρέτ), Bethsaida, Dalmanutha (? Magdala or Mageda), Caesarea (Καισαρία ἡ Φιλίππου), Tyre, Sidon, Jericho, Bethphage, Bethany. The river Jordan, the 'wilderness' of Judaea (ἡ ἔρημος), the waste or common ground in the neighbourhood of the towns of Galilee and Gaulonitis (ἔρημοι τόποι, ἐρημία), the lake (ἡ θάλασσα τῆς Γαλειλαίας, or ἡ θάλασσα), the Galilean and Peraean hills (τὸ ὄρος, τὰ ὄρη), a 'high mountain' in the North which is probably Hermon, and the Mount of Olives (τὸ ὄρος τῶν ἐλαιῶν), complete the geographical surroundings of the narrative.

[1] The name is spelt thus in cod. B throughout St Mark except i. 9 and xvi. 7, and uniformly in the O.T. (Jos. xx. 7, xxi. 32, 3 Regn. ix. 11, 4 Regn. xv. 29, 1 Chron. vi. 76, Isa. ix. 1). Winer-Schmiedel, § 5, 13 a, classes Γαλειλαία with κρείνειν, μεισεῖν, πολεῖται. But though analogy may have had weight, it is probable that Γαλειλαία is a genuine attempt to reproduce the sound of the Hebrew word, and that the diphthong answers to the long vowel in גְּלִילָה. Cf. WH. *Notes*, p. 155.

If we consider the extent of our Lord's itinerations, this list will appear singularly meagre. During the period covered by Mc. i. 14—ix. 50 He seems to have evangelised in person or through the Twelve every part of Galilee, and a portion at least of the vaguely defined region east of the Jordan which was known as the Decapolis, besides undertaking a journey through Phoenicia and across the Lebanon. These missionary journeys led Him through all the towns and larger villages (κωμοπόλεις) of the most densely populated part of Palestine; but though St Mark relates the fact (i. 38 ff., vi. 6 ff.), he is silent as to the names of the places visited. Nor again, graphic as he is, does he stop to describe the effect produced upon fishermen of the little inclosed freshwater lake by their first sight of the Mediterranean and of the glories of Lebanon and Hermon. The Evangelist keeps strictly to his purpose, and allows himself to enter into details only when they illustrate the matter which is in hand. He is more concerned to set forth the character and method of the Ministry than the names of its localities. Nevertheless the indications of place are distinct enough to fix the geographical surroundings of almost every important incident, if we may assume that St Mark's order is roughly chronological. Of the events reported in c. x. 1—31 no more can be said than that they took place in Judaea or in Peraea (x. 1). But in both the greater sections of the history (i. 14—ix. 50, x. 32—xvi. 8) localisation can be carried into details.

This is obvious in x. 32—xvi. 8; but a little examination will shew that it is true also of the earlier section. Capernaum or its neighbourhood on the west side of the Lake is the scene of i. 16—38, ii. 1—iii. 12, iii. 20—iv. 36, v. 21—43, vi. 53—vii. 23, ix. 33—50, whilst v. 1—20, vi. 32—47, vii. 32—viii. 9, 22—26 belong to the eastern shore, and iv. 37—41, vi. 48—52, viii. 14—21, to the Lake itself; journeyings through Galilee, Phoenicia, Abilene and Ituraea occupy i. 39—45, iii. 13—19, vi. 1—13, 30—31, vii. 24—31, viii. 27—ix. 32. This accounts for the whole section i. 14—ix. 50 with the exception of vi. 14—29, which consists of an explanatory episode and belongs, as we learn from an independent source, to Machaerus on the east of the Dead Sea. In many cases we can locate separate incidents yet more precisely. Thus the events of i. 21—34, ii. 1—12, ix. 33—50, are expressly connected with Capernaum; others belong to Gerasa, Gennesaret, Bethsaida, Nazareth, the neighbourhoods of Tyre and Caesarea Philippi. The exact locality however is more frequently described than named; the writer is usually content to place the event in its physical surroundings—in a house, on the road, by the side of the lake, among the hills, or wherever it may have occurred—but information of this kind is rarely withheld.

This method of localising the incidents imparts distinctness and movement to the history, while it does not burden the reader's memory with mere lists of names. At the same time it offers guidance in the construction of an intelligible plan of the Ministry. We can see quite clearly that the Ministry in Galilee found its centre in Capernaum; there it begins and ends (i. 21, ix. 33). Other Gospels couple Chorazin with Capernaum (Mt. xi. 21 ff., Lc. x. 13 ff.); St Mark mentions no other town on the west shore of the lake, and thus fixes attention on the head-quarters of the movement. Capernaum was the home of Simon and Andrew (i. 29) and Levi (ii. 15); from Capernaum easy access could be had, not only to every part of the lake-district, but, by means of the great roads which were within reach, to every part of Palestine. The roads brought people together from east and west, north and south (iii. 8), and at other times carried the Lord and the Twelve upon their errand of preaching the Gospel to the rest of Galilee. So far as we can judge, it belonged to our Lord's design to evangelise the Tetrarchy thoroughly, while He made the lake-side the centre of His work. In St Mark we can see how the wider purpose was worked into the narrower. The itinerations occur at intervals determined by circumstances; whenever the enthusiasm of the crowd rose to a dangerous height, or the hostility of the Scribes at Capernaum or of the court-party at Tiberias rendered a temporary withdrawal expedient, the Lord used the interval either in evangelistic work (i. 35 ff., vi. 1 ff.), or in intercourse with the Twelve, for which leisure and privacy were gained by travel (vii. 24 ff., viii. 27 ff.). Towards the end of the Ministry in Galilee the latter employment predominated, and in this fact it is impossible not to see the working out of a Divine plan. The solitudes of Lebanon and Hermon afforded an unrivalled scene for the teaching

of the laws of the Kingdom to the future Apostles and their
initiation into the mystery of the Passion.

Besides the journey from Judaea to Galilee (i. 14), the Gospel
describes (i.) three voyages on the lake, with visits to places in the
neighbourhood, (ii.) three inland journeys in Galilee, (iii.) three
longer journeys. The particulars are as follows: i. 1. From
Capernaum to the land of the Gerasenes and back (iv. 35, v. 1,
21). 2. From some point on the west shore, probably north
of Capernaum, to the neighbourhood of Bethsaida, and back to
Gennesaret (vi. 32, 53). 3. From some point on the east shore to
the neighbourhood of Dalmanutha, and from thence to Bethsaida
(viii. 10, 22). ii. 1. Circuit of Galilee; return to Capernaum
(i. 39, ii. 1). 2. Visit to the hill-country; return to Capernaum
(iii. 13). 3. Circuit of the villages beginning with Nazareth;
return to the lake (vi. 1, 6, 32). iii. 1. From Capernaum to
Phoenicia, through Sidon, and round to Decapolis and the lake
(vii. 24, 31). 2. From Bethsaida to the neighbourhood of Caesarea
Philippi, thence northwards to Hermon; return through Galilee to
Capernaum (viii. 27—ix. 33). 3. From Capernaum to Judaea and
Peraea (x. 1).

For the identification of the various sites see the commentary
upon the text, and the maps. It is to be understood that the dotted
lines in the latter give merely the probable direction of the routes.

2. Into the political conditions of the countries where our
Lord worked or travelled, St Mark allows his readers only a passing
glimpse. He is almost obviously indifferent as to precise details of
this kind. Herod Antipas is introduced as 'the king' (vi. 14, in a
context where both Mt. and Lc. are careful to write ὁ τετραάρχης).
There is nothing to shew that when Christ crossed the lake to
Bethsaida or Gerasa He entered another tetrarchy, or that He
came under the authority of the *legatus Syriae* when He visited
Phoenicia, and under that of the Procurator of Judaea when He
reached Jericho. Yet if St Mark's history is placed in the light
of these facts, it is seen to be in full accord with them. Tyre
and Sidon, Caesarea Philippi, and even Bethsaida Julias are
recognised as places of relative safety, where the Lord can shelter
for a time from the intrigues of Herod. On the other hand, He is
represented as being aware that in going up to Jerusalem He is
encountering greater peril than in Galilee; there He will be
delivered to Gentile officials (τοῖς ἔθνεσιν), and die by a Roman
punishment. If the writer of this Gospel does not display a

knowledge of the complex political life which prevailed in Palestine at the time, his reticence is not due to ignorance.

3. On the state of religion in Galilee and Judaea St Mark is less reserved. The synagogues in Galilee, the Temple and Precinct at Jerusalem, control the ecclesiastical life of the two provinces; in the North the ἀρχισυνάγωγοι, in the South the ἀρχιερεῖς, are the ecclesiastical authorities. But in both the religious teachers of the people are the Scribes—οἱ γραμματεῖς, as St Mark uniformly calls them—and we meet them everywhere, at Capernaum (ii. 6), among the villages under Hermon (ix. 14), and at Jerusalem. Of the two great religious sects which divide religious opinion, the Pharisees are found both in Galilee and Judaea; of the Sadducees St Mark makes no mention till he reaches the last scenes at Jerusalem. In these the Pharisaic Scribes fall into the background, and their place is taken by the Sadducean priesthood which dominates the capital. There is a delicate mark of truth in this sudden but unannounced change, of which indications may be found everywhere in the last five chapters of the Gospel. On the first morning after His entrance into the Precinct the Lord comes into collision with the hierarchy through His action in the matter of the temple-market. From that moment they take the lead in seeking His death: they head the deputation from the Sanhedrin which demands to know His authority; they negotiate with Judas for the betrayal; a servant of the High Priest seems to have been foremost in the arrest; the Lord is taken from Gethsemane to the High Priest's Palace, and, though other members of the Sanhedrin are present, the condemnation is evidently the act of the priesthood, and it is from them that the Procurator learns the nature of the charge. Even Pilate could detect the motive which inspired them. For traditionalism, which concerned the Scribes so deeply, they cared little; but they could not suffer a superior, and if Jesus were the Christ, or were generally regarded in that light, their supremacy was at an end. Thus Jesus was condemned in the end not for His supposed contempt of the Law, written or oral, but for His acceptance of the Messianic character. The result is widely different from what the

experience of Galilee would have led the reader to expect; but it is fully explained by the change of circumstances which St Mark assumes but does not stop to relate.

Not less interesting is the light which the Evangelist throws upon the religious and social condition of the mass of the Jewish people. There is here again a marked distinction between the North and the South, though our attention is hardly called to it. In Galilee we find ourselves in the midst of a population which on the whole is rural; the towns are for the most part κωμοπόλεις, and round them are uninhabited spaces, high ground, cornfields (τὰ σπόριμα), open country dotted with villages and farms (ἀγροί). The history moves among the working classes, the fishermen and husbandmen who were the backbone of the lake-side people. At Tiberias and Machaerus the court of Antipas attracted men of another stamp, and on the occasion of the Tetrarch's birthday we see the "heads of Galilee" (οἱ πρῶτοι τῆς Γαλειλαίας) mingling with high officials and military tribunes (οἱ μεγιστᾶνες, οἱ χιλί-αρχοι). But at Capernaum the only indications of proximity to a seat of government are the τελώνιον which faces the shore, and the "Herodians" with whom the local Pharisees take counsel. The most striking feature here is the vast throng (ὁ ὄχλος, οἱ ὄχλοι) which surrounds the Prophet of Nazareth all day long and day after day. It is replenished from all parts of Syria, but the bulk of the crowd must always have come from the lake-side towns and villages (cf. vi. 55). This crowd is uniformly friendly and indeed enthusiastic, intent in the first instance upon getting its sick healed or watching and admiring the miracles, but also attracted by a teaching which was strangely unlike that of other Rabbis (i. 21, 27). Many elements were mingled in this Galilean audience; a few were themselves Rabbis, and these were at least secretly hostile; the majority were doubtless members of synagogues and men of unblemished orthodoxy (cf. Acts x. 14), but there was also a large following of persons who had no place in the religious life of Judaism (τελῶναι καὶ ἁμαρτωλοί, ii. 15), but were not averse to religious instruction such as Jesus offered. Our Lord was touched by their enthusiasm; it revealed a yearning for guidance which deserved better shepherding than it received at the hands of their official guides (vi. 34). But He was at the same time grieved by the immaturity and obtuseness which rendered the masses impervious to directly spiritual teaching, and indeed unworthy of it (iv. 11 ff.). Even the picked companions of His journeys in Galilee retained much of the callousness and blindness which belonged to their environment (viii. 17, 21). Hence the Galilean teaching of Christ was limited to elementary lessons of truth, or, if it went further, was clothed in parables (iv. 11 f.).

Of the Jerusalemites this Gospel tells us little, but there are indications that the influences at work among them were widely different. The Lord had friends and disciples in Jerusalem and the neighbourhood—the household of Simon at Bethany (xiv. 3), Joseph of Arimathaea, the owner of Gethsemane, and the master of the house in the city where the last supper was eaten. But it may be doubted whether the Galilean Prophet was popular in the city. The crowds who escorted Him to Jerusalem, and who hung on His words in the Court of the Gentiles, were largely made up of Galileans and visitors; the crowd of citizens which thronged up to the Praetorium when the news of His arrest spread through the city, was chiefly interested in the opportunity of pressing its claims upon Pilate (xv. 8), and yielded to the importunity of the ἀρχιερεῖς (xv. 11). The report that Jesus had threatened to destroy the Temple easily turned the scale of feeling against Him; no release was attempted, no hands were laid on the party who had brought about His crucifixion, no sympathy was extended to Him on the cross by the passers-by, who mocked His sufferings (xv. 29). On the other hand our Lord's attitude at Jerusalem shews that He was brought face to face there with questions quite distinct from those which met Him in Galilee. He was no longer under a government which, though pagan in spirit, preserved the forms of Judaism; the shadow of the Roman *imperium* lay upon Jerusalem, and He was called there to vindicate His Messiahship, and to settle the apparently conflicting claims of Caesar and GOD.

4. The Gospel abounds with minute references to the external features of life.

Its vocabulary is rich in words which describe clothing (ἱμάτιον, χιτών, στολή, κράσπεδον, πορφύρα, σινδών, ζώνη, σανδάλιον, ὑπόδημα, ἱμάς), food (ἄρτος, οἶνος, ὄξος, λάχανον, ἰχθύδιον, ζύμη, μέλι, βρῶμα, κλάσμα), the house and its parts (οἶκος, οἰκία, αὐλή, προαύλιον, πυλών, θύρα, ἀνάγαιον, κατάλυμα, στέγη, δῶμα, ἀφεδρών), utensils and tools (μόδιος, λύχνος, λυχνία, πίναξ, τρύβλιον, ποτήριον, ἀσκός, ἀλάβαστρος, ξέστης, κράβαττος, κλίνη, πήρα, κόφινος, σφυρίς, μάχαιρα, κεράμιον, μύλος), coins (ἀργύριον, χαλκός, δηνάριον, κοδράντης, λεπτόν, κόλλυβος), divisions of time (ὥρα (τρίτη, ἕκτη), πρωί, πρωία, ὀψέ, ὀψία, μεσονύκτιον, ἀλεκτοροφωνία), religious practices (βαπτισμός, καθαρισμός, κορβάν, σάββατον, προσάββατον, παρασκευή, παράδοσις, συναγωγή, συνέδριον, ἱερόν, γαζοφυλάκιον, ἑορτή, θυσία, ὁλοκαύτωμα, νηστεία, εὐλογεῖν, εὐχαριστεῖν, ὑμνεῖν), marriage (γαμίζειν, γαμεῖν, γαμεῖσθαι, νυμφίος, νυμφών, γυνή, πενθερά, βίβλος ἀποστασίου), service (διάκονος, ὑπηρέτης, δοῦλος, μισθωτός, θυρωρός, παιδίσκη), punishment (δέρειν, βασανίζειν, ἀποκεφαλίζειν, φυλακή, δέσμιος, σταυρός), agriculture and other rural pursuits (σπόριμα, πρασιά, ἀμπελών, ὑπολήνιον, φραγμός, πύργος, δρέπανον, θερισμός, γεωργός), trade (ἐκδιδόναι, ἀντάλλαγμα, λύτρον), military matters (κεντυρίων, χιλίαρχος, σπεκουλάτωρ, σπεῖρα, λεγιών), boating and fishing (ἁλεεῖς, ἀμφιβάλλειν, δίκτυον, πλοῖον, πλοιάριον, πρύμνα, προσκεφάλαιον, προσορμίζεσθαι), animals (θηρία, κάμηλος, χοῖρος, κυνάριον, πῶλος, πετεινά, περιστερά), disease (πυρετός, λέπρα, κωφός, μογιλάλος, σπαράσσεσθαι, δαιμονίζεσθαι, μονόφθαλμος), treatment of the dead (ἐνειλεῖν, ἐνταφιασμός, μύρον, ἀρώματα). A considerable number of these words are used by no other N.T. writer.

Besides this free use of words which describe the visible surroundings of life, there are many less manifest but not less instructive traces of local knowledge; such as the references to pauperism which appear only in connexion with Judaea and Jerusalem (πτωχός, x. 21, xii. 42 f., xiv. 5, 7; προσαίτης, x. 46), and a similarly restricted use of λῃστής (xi. 17, xiv. 48) and στασιαστής (xiv. 7); the tacit assumption of the general employment of Aramaic, at least in Galilee, which underlies such Aramaisms as βοανηργές and ταλειθὰ κούμ; the careful choice of words which seem to imply that in Hellenised places, such as the Decapolis and the neighbourhood of Caesarea Philippi, the Lord's ministry was limited to the villages and open country, and that He did not enter the practically pagan towns.

St Mark's interests do not lie in the field of contemporary

history or political geography or in the social condition of Palestine. Every detail of this kind in his Gospel is merely incidental. But his passion for exact description, so far as it can be brought within the compass of his work, leads him unconsciously to supply a variety of information on these subjects, whilst his residence in Jerusalem and his personal relation to St Peter assure us that the information which he gives is first-hand and accurate.

9

Mark's Conception of the Person and Office of Our Lord

Whether the present headline of the Gospel in its fuller form is due to St Mark or not, it admirably expresses the idea of the book. It is *the Gospel of Jesus Christ, the Son of God*. St Mark begins (i. 2) by quoting two well-known Messianic passages (Mal. iii. 1, Isa. xl. 3), and tracing their accomplishment in the mission of the Baptist; and his next step is to shew that at His Baptism Jesus was declared to be the Beloved Son (i. 11). Thus he places in the forefront of the work the presupposition of our Lord's Messianic office and Divine Sonship, and all that follows is a record of the historical manifestation of the Christ.

According to St Mark the Lord began His Galilean Ministry in the character of the Baptist's successor, repeating St John's message, and carrying it a stage further (i. 15). His method, however, was new. John had appeared in the wilderness, Jesus shewed Himself in the heart of Galilee; John waited till men came to him, Jesus sought them out, and called them to follow Him (i. 17 ff.); John was a preacher only, Jesus on His first sabbath in Capernaum revealed His power over unclean spirits (i. 27), who at once recognised Him as the Holy One of God (i. 24), the Messiah (i. 34), and the Son of God (iii. 11, v. 7). But their premature and hostile testimony was refused and silenced, and the Lord proceeded to reveal Himself by other means. He began by applying to Himself the title *Son of man* (ii. 10), which, while it implied a relation to human weakness and mortality (viii. 31, ix. 9, 31, x. 33, 45, xiv. 21, 41), at the same time asserted His authority over all matters connected with the spiritual well-being of the human race; and in this capacity he claimed the right to forgive sins upon earth (ii. 10), to regulate the observance of the Sabbath (iii. 28), and to adjudge future rewards and punishments (viii. 38 f.).

But neither friends nor enemies could find an explanation of His extraordinary powers in a name which seemed to carry no assertion of a superhuman origin. At Nazareth the wisdom and the miracles of the Son of Mary excited both surprise and resentment (vi. 2, 3). His own family and friends saw in them indications of madness which called for interference and restraint (iii. 21). Learned scribes, who had come down from Jerusalem to enquire and report, hazarded the conjecture that He was possessed by the chief of the unclean spirits (iii. 22). Among the crowd, on the other hand, whispers were heard that Jesus was a prophet, and one of the same rank as the Prophets of the canon; possibly Elijah himself, the expected forerunner of the Messiah (vi. 15, ix. 11), or the Baptist restored to life (vi. 14, 16, viii. 28). The Twelve shared the general perplexity (iv. 41). There is no indication that any one in Galilee, while the Ministry was in progress, stumbled upon the truth, or that Jesus during this period either publicly or privately declared Himself to be the Christ.

The Twelve were the first to make the discovery, but they did not make it till our Lord's work in Galilee was practically at an end. He was on His way to Caesarea Philippi, with his back turned upon Capernaum and the Lake, when He raised the question of His own personality, and received from St Peter the immediate answer "Thou art the Christ" (viii. 29). For the Apostles the moment was decisive. Henceforth the Messiahship of Jesus was a part of their faith, and the ruling idea of their lives; they knew themselves to be Christ's (ix. 41). The Lord now began to speak to them freely of His future glory (viii. 38); to Peter and the two sons of Zebedee, whom he seems to have constituted His three witnesses (v. 37, ix. 2, xiv. 33), He granted a remarkable anticipation of it, which at once confirmed and interpreted St Peter's confession. The Transfiguration proved that Jesus was not a mere Prophet, not even Elijah, but greater than Elijah and Moses himself; it repeated the Divine assurance vouchsafed to the Baptist, that the Son of Mary was also the beloved or unique Son of GOD (ix. 7); it revealed Him for a moment clad in the glory of the Father, and thus rebuked the expectations which had begun to rise in minds that *savoured not the things of GOD*, while it encouraged hopes of a more than earthly magnificence. Raiment such as the Messiah wore at His Transfiguration *no fuller on earth could whiten* (ix. 3); all was celestial and superhuman in this vision of the glorified Christ.

Another revelation began simultaneously with that of the Lord's Messianic dignity. From the moment that St Peter confessed Him to be the Christ, Jesus set Himself to foretell His coming Passion (viii. 34); and the prediction was repeated more than once with growing clearness during the months which followed the Transfiguration (ix. 31, x. 33). But the doctrine of the Cross, while it perplexed and disquieted the Twelve, awoke no response in their hearts, and did not even penetrate their understandings (ix. 32, x. 32, 35 ff.). False ambitions were at work in them, shutting out the true conception of the Kingdom of GOD; and the Lord was occupied at this period in dispelling these errors, and teaching the primary laws of self-sacrifice and service (ix. 33 ff., x. 21—31, 35—45).

When at last the Lord approached Jerusalem to offer His own Sacrifice, the occasion for the reserve which He had practised in Galilee had passed away. His Messiahship was no longer a secret to be kept by the Twelve; it was openly recognised and acknowledged. At Jericho for the first time in this Gospel we hear the cry *Son of David* (x. 47). On the Mount of Olives the crowd acclaimed *the coming Kingdom of our father David* (xi. 10). In the parable of the vineyard the Lord openly represented Himself as *the Beloved Son* and *the Heir* (xii. 6, 7). His question on Ps. cx. 1, though it dealt only with the general subject of the Messianic dignity, was doubtless understood to refer to Himself. When Caiaphas asked *Art Thou the Christ?* the Lord, according to St Mark, replied without hesitation *I am*, adding words from the Book of Daniel which placed His early claim to be the Son of Man in connexion with the vision of a Messianic Kingdom (xiv. 62). It was as Messiah that He was condemned to the Cross, for *the King of the Jews* is but 'the Christ,' expressed in terms intelligible to a Roman judge. The banter with which He was assailed on the Cross proves that His claim to be Messiah was uppermost in the thoughts of the people of Jerusalem, from the hierarchy downwards: *let the Christ, the King of Israel, come down now from the cross; He calleth Elijah...let us see whether Elijah cometh to take Him down* (xv. 32—36).

The abrupt end of St Mark's work prevents us from ascertaining his conception of the Risen Christ. We do not know whether the original work was ever brought to a completion. But if it was, a comparison of Mc. xvi. 7 with Mt. xxviii. 7 suggests that St Mark, like St Matthew, proceeded to give an account of the meeting in Galilee[1]. In such a narrative, if it followed the general lines of Mt. xxviii. 16—20, our Evangelist's view of the Person and work of *Jesus Christ the Son of* GOD would have found its natural issue. The Lord had begun His ministry in Galilee by claiming authority over the spiritual forces which are at work in man's world (Mc. ii. 10, 27); this claim was renewed in His last utterances, and extended to things in heaven (Mt. xxviii. 18). He had foretold the catholic mission of His Gospel (Mc. xiii. 10, xiv. 9); before He left the world He provided for its worldwide propagation (Mt. xxviii. 19). He had been revealed as the Beloved Son (Mc. i. 11, ix. 7, xii. 6), and had identified His work with the operation of the Divine Spirit (Mc. iii. 29, 30); He now completed the revelation of His oneness with the Father and the Spirit by the command that all His disciples should be baptized *into the Name of the Father and of the Son and of the Holy Ghost.* He had taken the Twelve to be with Him in the association of a common life (Mc. iii. 14), and now He pledged Himself to be

---

[1] Cf. Pseudo-Peter, *ev.* 12, and see Mr F. C. Burkitt's *Two Lectures on the Gospels,* p. 28 ff. See also Mc. xiv. 28.

with them and with His whole Church *until the consummation of the age*.

St Mark does not write with a dogmatic purpose. But the Person whose movements are depicted in his vivid narrative is seen to be at once man and more than man. In every act and word the Christ of the second Gospel is revealed as the supreme Son of man and the only Son of GOD. No Gospel brings into clearer light the perfect humanity of the Lord. He can be touched (i. 41) and grieved and angered (iii. 5); He makes as though He does not hear (v. 36) or does not see (vi. 48), He is moved with indignation (x. 14), He permits Himself to use irony (xiv. 41); He sleeps from fatigue (iv. 38); He possesses a human spirit (ii. 8), soul (xiv. 34), and body (xv. 43), with all their capacities and their sinless limitations. He turns to see who has touched Him (v. 30); He asks questions, apparently for the purpose of gaining information (viii. 5). He submits Himself absolutely to the Father's will (xiv. 36); He disclaims the right to make the final award apart from the Father's predestination (x. 40); He professes Himself ignorant, as the Son, of the Father's appointed time (xiii. 32). On the other hand He claims an authority in the sphere of man's relations to GOD which is coextensive with the present order (ii. 10, 28); He knows precisely what is passing in men's minds and hearts, and the circumstances of their lives (ii. 5, 8, viii. 17, ix. 3 f., xii. 15, 44); He foresees and foretells the future, whether His own (viii. 31, 38) or that of individual men (x. 39, xiv. 27) and communities (xiii. 1 ff.); in the most trying situations He manifests absolute wisdom and self-adaptation; even in His death He extorts from a Roman centurion the acknowledgement that He was a supernatural person (xv. 39). The centurion's words express the conviction with which the student of St Mark rises from his examination of the Gospel; *truly this man was Son of GOD*. But for those who have before them the whole record of that supreme human life they bear a meaning of which the Roman could not have dreamt; we realise that the Sonship of Jesus was unique and essential. It was not a servant who was sent in the last resort to receive the fruits of the Divine Vineyard, but the only Son, Who is the Heir of GOD (xii. 2—7).

Limited as St Mark's work is to recollections of the Lord's Ministry and Passion, it is full of glimpses into His future relations to the world. *I came not to call the righteous but sinners* (ii. 17); *the Son of man...came...to give His life a ransom for many* (x. 45); *My blood of the covenant...is shed for many* (xiv. 24); *every one shall be salted with fire* (ix. 49); *the Bridegroom shall be taken away* (ii. 20); *the Son of man...shall come in the glory of His Father* (viii. 38); *the Gospel must first be preached to all the nations* (xiii. 10); *if any man willeth to come after me let him deny himself* (viii. 34); *have salt in yourselves, and be at peace one with another* (ix. 50); *have faith in GOD...pray...believe... forgive* (xi. 23 ff.); *what I say unto you I say unto all, Watch* (xiii. 37). These and similar sayings contain an almost complete outline of Christian soteriology and eschatology, and assert the principles of the new life which the Lord taught and exemplified and which His Spirit was to produce in the life of the future Church.

10

Authorities for the Text

1. The following Uncial MSS. contain the Greek text of St Mark in part or in whole.

ℵ.   Cod. Sinaiticus (IV.). Ed. Tischendorf, 1862. Ends at xvi. 8 (see § xi.).

A.   Cod. Alexandrinus (V.). Ed. E. M. Thompson, 1879.

B.   Cod. Vaticanus, 1209 (IV.). Ed. Cozza-Luzi, 1889. Ends at xvi. 8 (see § xi.).

C.   Cod. Ephraemi (V.). Ed. Tischendorf, 1843. Contains Mc. i. 17—vi. 31, viii. 5—xii. 29, xiii. 19—xvi. 20.

D.   Cod. Bezae (VI.). Ed. F. H. A. Scrivener, 1864; reproduced in heliogravure by the Camb. Univ. Press[1], 1899. Contains Mc., except xvi. 15—20, which is in a later hand.

E.   Cod. Basiliensis (VIII.).

F.   Cod. Boreelianus (IX.). Contains Mc. i. 1—41, ii. 8—23, iii. 5—xi. 6, xi. 27—xiv. 54, xv. 6—39, xvi. 19—20.

G.   Cod. Seidelianus I. (IX. or X.). Contains Mc. i. 13—xiv. 18, xiv. 25—xvi. 20.

H.   Cod. Seidelianus II. (IX. or X.). Contains Mc. i. 1—31, ii. 4—xv. 43, xvi. 14—20.

I.   Fragm. Petropolitanum (V.). Ed. Tischendorf, *mon. sacr. ined., nov. coll.* i., 1855. Contains Mc. ix. 14—22, xiv. 58—70.

K.   Cod. Cyprius (IX.).

L.   Cod. Regius (VIII.). Ed. Tischendorf, *mon. sacr. ined.,* 1846. Contains Mc. i. 1—x. 15, x. 30—xv. 1, xv. 20—xvi. 20; the shorter ending precedes xvi. 9 (see § xi.).

M.   Cod. Campianus (IX.).

---

[1] A useful collation of D with Gebhardt's text is printed in Nestle's *N.T. Gr. supplementum* (Lips., 1896).

N. Cod. Purpureus (VI.). Ed. Tischendorf, *mon. sacr. ined.*, 1846 ; an edition including the new St Petersburg fragments has been published by the Rev. H. S. Cronin in *Texts and Studies*, v. 4 (Cambridge, 1899). Contains v. 20—vii. 4, vii. 20—viii. 32, ix. 1—x. 43, xi. 7—xii. 19, xiv. 25—xv. 23, xv. 33—42.

P. Cod. Guelpherbytanus (VI.). Ed. Tischendorf, *mon. sacr. ined., nov. coll.* vi., 1869. Contains i. 2—11, iii. 5—17, xiv. 13—24, 48—61, xv. 12—37.

S. Cod. Vaticanus 354 (x.).

Tᵈ. Cod. Borgianus (VII.). Contains Mc. i. 3—8, xii. 35—37.

U. Cod. Nanianus (IX. or X.).

V. Cod. Moscuensis (IX.).

Wᵇ. Fragm. Neapolitanum (VIII. or IX.). Contains Mc. xiii. 21—xiv. 67.

Wᶜ. Fragm. Sangallense (IX.). Contains Mc. ii. 8—16.

Wᵈ. Fragm. Cantabrigiense (IX.). Contains Mc. vii. 3—4, 6—8, 30—viii. 16, ix. 2, 7—9. Ed. J. R. Harris (in an Appendix to his *Diatessaron of Tatian*, 1890).

Wᶠ. Fragm. Oxoniense aed. Chr. (IX.). Contains Mc. v. 16—21, 22—28, 29—35, 35—40.

Wᵍ. Fragm. Londiniense (IX.). Contains Mc. i. 1—42, ii. 21— v. 1, v. 29—vi. 22, x. 50—xi. 13.

Wʰ. Fragm. Oxoniense Bodl. (IX.). Contains Mc. iii. 15—32, v. 16—31.

Wˡ. Fragm. Parisiense I. (VII.). Contains Mc. xiii. 34—xiv. 29.

Wᵐ. Fragm. Parisiense II. (VII. or VIII.). Contains Mc. i. 27—41.

Wᵒ. Fragm. Mediolanense (IX.). Contains Mc. i. 12—24, ii. 26—iii. 10.

X. Cod. Monacensis (X.). Contains Mc. vi. 47—xvi. 20 ; many verses in xiv.—xvi. are defective.

Γ. Cod. Oxoniensis (IX. or X.). Contains Mc. i. 1—iii. 34, vi. 21—xvi. 20.

Δ. Cod. Sangallensis (IX. or X.). Ed. Rettig, 1836. On the text of this MS. in Mc. see WH., *Intr.* §§ 209, 225, 229, 307, 352 ; Nestle, *Textual Criticism of the N.T.*, p. 72.

Θᵇ. Fragm. Petropolitanum I. (VII.). Contains Mc. iv. 24—35, v. 14—23.

Θᶠ. Fragm. Porfirianum (VI.). Contains Mc. i. 34—ii. 12, with some *lacunae*.

Π. Cod. Petropolitanus (IX.). Contains Mc., except xvi. 18— 20, which is in a later hand.

Σ.   Cod. Rossanensis (VI.).   Ed. Gebhardt and Harnack, 1883. Contains Mc., except xvi. 14—20.

Φ.   Cod. Beratinus (VI.).   Ed. Batiffol, 1886.   Contains Mc. i. 1—xiv. 62.

Ψ.   Cod. Athous Laurae (VIII. or IX.).   Contains Mc. ix. 5—xvi. 20; the shorter ending precedes xvi. 9[1].

Ω.   Cod. Athous Dionysii (VIII. or IX.).

ב.   Cod. Athous Andreae (IX. or X.).   Contains Mc. i. 1—v. 40, vi. 18—viii. 35, ix. 19—xvi. 20.

ד[10].   Fragm. Sinaiticum (V.).   Ed. J. R. Harris, *Biblical Fragments*, 1890.   Contains Mc. i. 11—22, ii. 21—iii. 3, iii. 27—iv. 4, v. 9—20.

ד[11].   Fragm. Sinaiticum (VI.).   Ed. J. R. Harris, *op. cit.*   Contains Mc. xii. 32—37.

ד[12].   Fragm. Sinaiticum (VII.).   Ed. J. R. Harris, *op. cit.*, and in Mrs Lewis's *Syriac MSS.*, p. 103.   Contains Mc. xiv. 29—45, xv. 27—xvi. 10; the shorter ending precedes xvi. 9.

פ.   Fragm. Parisiense (VIII.).   Ed. Amélineau, ap. *Notices et Extraits*, xxxiv. ii. pp. 370, 402 ff.   Contains Mc. xvi. 6—18; the shorter ending precedes xvi. 9[2].

ז.   Fragm. Oxyrhynchitanum (V. or VI.).   Ed. Grenfell and Hunt, *Oxyrhynchus papyri*, i., 1898.   Contains Mc. x. 50 f., xi. 11 f.

For the Freer MS. of the Four Gospels see p. 404.

2.   The cursive Greek MSS. which contain this Gospel are far too numerous to be recited here.   According to Gregory (*Prolegomena* (1884—94), pp. 616, 717, 1310, the known cursive MSS. of the Gospels are 1287, besides 953 lectionaries; Mr Miller (Scrivener's *Introduction* (1894), i. p. 283, 396* f.) enumerates 1326 Gospels and 980 lectionaries.   The following list is limited to those which are frequently cited in the *apparatus*.

1.   Basle, Univ. Libr. (X.).   Ed. K. Lake in *Texts and Studies*, VII. 3, 1902.

[3]13.   Paris, Nat. Libr. (XIII.); wants Mc. i. 20—45.

28.   Paris, Nat. Libr. (XI.).

33.   Paris, Nat. Libr. (IX. or X.); wants Mc. ix. 31—xi. 11, xiii. 11—xiv. 59.

59.   Cambridge, Gonville and Caius Coll. (XII.); cf. J. R. Harris, *Origin of the Leicester Codex.*

---

[1] On the text of this Codex in Mc. see *J. Th. St.*, i. p. 290 ff., and *Studia Biblica*, v. 2, pp. 97—104; the latter gives also a complete transcript of the Marcan fragment (pp. 105—122).

[2] For this MS. Nestle proposes the symbol T[1] (*Textual Criticism of the N. T.*, pp. 70, 74).

[3] For these MSS. see Dr T. K. Abbott, *Collation of four important MSS.*, 1877; cf. J. R. Harris, *On the origin of the Ferrar Group*, 1893.

66. Cambridge, Trin. Coll. (x. or xiii.).

³69. Leicester, Libr. of Town Council (xv.); cf. J. R. Harris, *op. cit.*

109. London, Brit. Mus. (xiv.).

118. Oxford, Bodl. Libr. (xiii.).

³124. Vienna, Imp. Libr. (xii.).

131. Rome, Vat. Libr. (xiv. or xv.).

157. Rome, Vat. Libr. (xii.).

209. Venice, S. Mark's Libr. (xiv. and xv.).

238. Moscow, Libr. of the Holy Synod (xi.).

242. Moscow, Libr. of the Holy Synod (xii.).

282. Paris, Nat. Libr. (xii.).

299. Paris, Nat. Libr. (x. or xi.).

³346. Milan, Ambr. Libr. (x. or xi.).

435. Leyden, Univ. Libr. (x.).

482 (= p^{scr}, 570 Miller). London, Brit. Mus. (xiii.).

556 (= 543 Greg.). Burdett-Coutts collection (xii.). See Scrivener, *Adversaria crit. sacr.*, p. 1 ff.

565 (= 2^{pe} Tisch., = 81 WH., = 473 Miller). St Petersburg, Imp. Libr. (ix. or x.). Edited by Belsheim, 1885; corrections of his text are supplied in an appendix to Mr Cronin's edition of cod. N (*Texts and Studies*, v. 4, p. 106 ff.).

569 (7^{pe} Tisch., = 475 Scriv.), St Petersburg, Imp. Libr. (xi.).

604 (= 700 Greg.), London, Brit. Mus. (xi.). Collation published by H. C. Hoskier, 1890.

736 (= 718 Greg.), Cambridge, in the possession of the editor.

1071. Athos, Laur. 104 A (xii.). See the Rev. K. Lake's description and collation in *Studia Biblica*, v. 2, p. 132 ff.

3. The ancient versions of St Mark used in this edition are the Latin, Syriac, Armenian, Egyptian, Gothic, and Ethiopic.

I. *Latin* (latt).

(a) Old Latin (lat^{vt}).

The following MSS. are cited as offering a more or less purely pre-Hieronymian text.

a. Cod. Vercellensis (iv.). Ed. Bianchini, *evang. quadr.*, 1749; Belsheim, 1894. Wants Mc. i. 22—34, iv. 17—25, xv. 15—xvi. 20; xvi. 7—20 is supplied by a later hand.

b. Cod. Veronensis (v.). Ed. Bianchini, *op. cit.* Wants Mc. xiii. 9—19, xiii. 24—xvi. 20.

c.   Cod. Colbertinus (XII.).   Ed. Sabatier, 1751; Belsheim, 1888.

d.   Cod. Bezae (VI.).   The Latin version of Cod. D (*q. v.*).

e.   Cod. Palatinus (V.).   Ed. Tischendorf, 1847.   Contains Mc. i. 20—iv. 8, iv. 19—vi. 9, xii. 37—40, xiii. 2—3, 24—27, 33—36.

f.   Cod. Brixianus (VI.).   Ed. Bianchini, *op. cit.*; Wordsworth and White in the Oxford Vulgate, 1891.   Wants Mc. xii. 5—xiii. 32, xiv. 53—62, xiv. 70—xvi. 20.

ff. (= ff², Tisch. Greg. Scriv.).   Cod. Corbeiensis II. (VI.).   Ed. Belsheim, 1887.   Wants a few verses in Mc. vi., xvi.

g. (= g¹, Tisch. Greg. Scriv.).   Cod. Sangermanensis I. (VIII.).   Collated by Wordsworth and White, who cite it in Mc. as G.

i.   Cod. Vindobonensis (VI. or VII.).   Ed. Belsheim, 1885.   Wants i. 1—ii. 16, iii. 29—iv. 3, x. 2—32, xiv. 37—xv. 32, xv. 40—xvi. 20.

k.   Cod. Bobiensis (IV. or V.).   Ed. Wordsworth Sanday and White, *O. L. Bibl. texts* ii., 1886.   Contains viii. 8—11, 14—16, 19—xvi. 8, and the shorter ending (see § xi.).

l.   Cod. Vratislaviensis (VII.).   Ed. H. F. Haase, 1865—6.

n.   Cod. Sangallensis I. (V.).   Ed. Wordsworth Sanday and White, *op. cit.*   Contains vii. 13—31, viii. 32—ix. 10, xiii. 2—20, xv. 22—xvi. 13.

o.   Cod. Sangallensis II. (VII.).   Ed. Wordsworth Sanday and White, *op. cit.*   Contains xvi. 14—20.

q.   Cod. Monacensis (VII.).   Ed. White, *O. L. Bibl. texts* iii., 1888.   Wants i. 7—22, xv. 5—36.

r.   Cod. Dublinensis (VI. or VII.).   Ed. T. K. Abbott, *ev. versio antehier.*, 1884.   Wants xiv. 58—xv. 8, xv. 32—xvi. 20 ; many *lacunae*.

t.   Cod. Bernensis (V. or VI.).   Ed. Wordsworth, *O. L. Bibl. texts* ii., 1886.   Contains i. 2—23, ii. 22—27, iii. 11—18.

(β)   Vulgate (lat^vg).   Ed. Wordsworth and White.

II. *Syriac* (syrr).

(a)   Old Syriac (syrr^sin cu).

This version exists in two MSS., which appear to represent different recensions.

Cod. Sinaiticus (IV. or V.).   Ed. Bensly Harris and Burkitt, 1894.   Wants Mc. i. 1—11, i. 44—ii. 20, iv. 19—40, v. 27—vi. 4; ends at xvi. 8.

Cod. Curetonianus (V.).   Ed. Cureton, 1858; a fresh edition is in progress under the care of F. C. Burkitt (*Texts and Studies*).   Contains only xvi. 17—20.

(β)   Vulgate Syriac or Peshitta (syr^pesh). Ed. Leusden and Schaaf, 1717; P. E. Pusey and G. H. Gwilliam, 1901.

(γ)   Harclean (syr^hcl). Ed. White, 1778.

(δ)   Palestinian (syr^hier). Ed. Lagarde, 1892; Mrs Lewis and Mrs Gibson, 1899. Contains Mc. i. 1—11, 35—44, ii. 1—12, 14—17, 23—iii. 5, v. 24—34, vi. 1—5, 14—30, vii. 24—37, viii. 27—31, 34—39, ix. 16—30, 32—40, x. 32—45, xi. 22—25, xii. 28—44, xv. 16—32, 43—xvi. 20.

III.   *Armenian* (arm).

The only critical edition of the Armenian text is that of Zohrab (Venice, 1805), whose margin gives variants, without however naming the codices from which they are taken. Uscan's edition (Amsterdam, 1666) is valueless to the critic, as having been freely corrected by the Latin Vulgate. The most recent study of the Armenian version is the article by Mr F. C. Conybeare in Hastings' *Dict. of the Bible* (1898). Some interesting facts about Uscan's edition are given by Simon (*Hist. Crit. des Versions*, 1690, pp. 196 ff.)[1].

IV.   *Egyptian* (aegg).

(a)   Memphitic or Bohairic (me). Ed. D. Wilkins, 1717. A new edition by Mr G. Horner with a translation and copious *apparatus criticus* has been issued by the Clarendon Press (1898).

(β)   Thebaic or Sahidic (the). A list of the MSS. is printed in G. Zoega's *Catalogus codd. Copticorum* (Romae, 1810). The known fragments of St Mark (Gregory, iii. p. 864) are i. 36—38, i. 41—44, ii. 2—4, ii. 7—9, ii. 12—ix. 16,

---

[1] This account of the Armenian version has been supplied by Dr J. Armitage Robinson. He adds: "According to the Armenian historians this version was translated from Syriac and afterwards subjected to a careful revision by the aid of Greek MSS. Internal evidence affords striking confirmation of this view (see *Euthaliana*, Texts and Studies III. ii. pp. 72 ff.). Two conspicuous elements of the version are (1) the Old Syriac, as now represented for us in St Mark by the Sinai palimpsest, and (2) the text represented by the Greek

cursives known as the Ferrar group; see e.g. (1) viii. 4; (2) iii. 18, iv. 24, viii. 14, xi. 9. The relation of the Ferrar group itself to the Syriac is a vexed question. Striking correspondences are also to be noted with 1–28–209, with 2^pe, and with 604; many too with D and with k; some, both in this Gospel and in the others, with the first hand of ℵ. Noteworthy is xiv. 25 οὐ μὴ προσθῶ πεῖν D (2^pe) a f arm: it is curious that for a Semitic idiom like this no Syriac attestation is forthcoming."

ix. 19—xiv. 26, xiv. 34—xv. 41, xvi. 20—"about three quarters of [the] Gospel" (Scrivener-Miller, ii. p. 131).

A full account of these versions is given by Mr Forbes Robinson in Hastings' *Dictionary* (i. 668 ff.).

V. *Gothic* (go).

Ed. Gabelentz and Löbe, 1836 ; Massmann, *Ulfilas*, 1857 ; Stamm-Heyne, *Ulfilas*, 1878 ; Skeat, *Gospel of St Mark in Gothic*, 1882. The extant fragments of Mark contain i. 1—vi. 30, vi. 53—xii. 38, xiii. 16—29, xiv. 4—16, xiv. 41—xvi. 12.

VI. *Ethiopic* (aeth).

Ed. T. P. Platt, 1830 (but cf. Gregory, *prolegg.*, p. 899 f.). See *Ethiopic Version*, in Hastings, i. 791 f.

11
Alternative Endings of the Gospel

In some of our authorities the Gospel according to St Mark ends with the words καὶ οὐδενὶ οὐδὲν εἶπαν, ἐφοβοῦντο γάρ (xvi. 8). Other MSS. and Versions add the twelve verses which follow in the Received Text, whilst others again, usually as an alternative, present a short ending which consists of only two sentences, and is wholly independent of the printed supplement.

1. Eusebius of Caesarea in his book of *Questions and Solutions concerning the Passion and Resurrection of the Saviour*[2] represents an apologist[3] as seeking to remove a supposed inconsistency in the Gospels by throwing doubt upon the genuineness of Mc. xvi. 9 ff.

Quaest. ad Marin. ap. Mai *nov. patr. bibl.* iv. p. 255 f. ὁ μὲν γὰρ τὴν τοῦτο φάσκουσαν περικοπὴν ἀθετῶν εἴποι ἂν μὴ ἐν ἅπασιν αὐτὴν φέρεσθαι τοῖς ἀντιγράφοις τοῦ κατὰ Μᾶρκον εὐαγγελίου· τὰ γοῦν ἀκριβῆ τῶν ἀντιγράφων τὸ τέλος περιγράφει...ἐν τοῖς λόγοις...'ἐφοβοῦντο γάρ.' ἐν τούτῳ γὰρ σχεδὸν ἐν ἅπασι τοῖς ἀντιγράφοις τοῦ κατὰ Μᾶρκον εὐαγγελίου περιγέγραπται τὸ τέλος, τὰ δὲ ἐξῆς σπανίως ἔν τισιν ἀλλ' οὐκ ἐν πᾶσι φερόμενα περιττὰ ἂν εἴη. For a full discussion of this passage see WH., *Notes*, p. 30 f. The textual statement for which Eusebius appears to make himself responsible is reproduced by Jerome (*ad Hedib.* 3 "Marci testimonium...in raris fertur evangeliis, omnibus Graeciae libris paene hoc capitulum non habentibus"), and by Victor of Antioch (in Mc. xvi. 1 ἐπειδὴ δὲ ἔν τισι τῶν ἀντιγράφων πρόσκειται...'ἀναστὰς δέ κτλ.'...ἐροῦμεν ὡς δυνατὸν ἦν εἰπεῖν ὅτι νενόθευται τὸ παρὰ Μάρκῳ τελευταῖον ἔν τισι φερόμενον. Victor's commentary ends accordingly with xvi. 8, for the note on xvi. 9 and the attempt to reestablish the authority of *vv.* 9—20 which follow in Cramer are clearly due to other sources (WH., *Notes*, p. 35).

---

[1] On the subject of this chapter see now Zahn, *Einleitung*, ii. p. 227 ff. (Leipzig, 1899); a useful summary of the literature is given by Salmond in Hastings, *D. B.* iii. p. 253.

[2] On this work see Bp Lightfoot's art. *Eusebius* in *D. C. B.* (ii. p. 338 f.).

[3] Dean Burgon (*Last twelve verses*, p. 47) suspected that Eusebius met "with the suggestion in some older writer (in Origen probably)." Dr Hort (*Notes*, p. 32) agrees with him, and points out that in this case "the testimony as to MSS. gains in importance by being carried back to a much earlier date and a much higher authority."

The two great codices which have come down to us from the fourth century corroborate this evidence. Both B and ℵ bring the Gospel to an end at ἐφοβοῦντο γάρ, as "the accurate copies" cited by the apologist in Eusebius were wont to do. In both the words are followed by the subscription; but in B the scribe has left a column blank after ΚΑΤΑ ΜΑΡΚΟΝ, which has been taken to mean that he was acquainted with a text of St Mark which did not end at *v.* 8, although his own copy failed him at that point.

The Gospel ends thus in the two MSS.:

<table>
<tr><td align="center">Cod. B.</td><td align="center">Cod. ℵ.</td></tr>
<tr><td>ϹΤΑϹΙϹ ΚΑΙ ΟΥΔΕΝΙ ΟΥ</td><td>ϹΤΑϹΙϹ ΚΑΙ ΟΥ ></td></tr>
<tr><td>ΔΕΝ ΕΙΠΟΝ ΕΦΟΒΟΥΝ</td><td>ΔΕΝΙ ΟΥΔΕΝ ΕΙ ></td></tr>
<tr><td>ΤΟ ΓΑΡ :</td><td>ΠΟΝ ΕΦΟΒΟΥΝ</td></tr>
<tr><td></td><td>ΤΟ ΓΑΡ' : :</td></tr>
<tr><td>> Κ̄ΑΤᾹ ></td><td></td></tr>
<tr><td>> Μ̱ΑΡΚΟΝ̱̄ ></td><td>≥Ε̄ΥΑΓΓΕ̄̄ ></td></tr>
<tr><td></td><td>> ΛΙΟΝ ></td></tr>
<tr><td></td><td>≥Κ̄ΑΤᾹ ΜᾹΡΚΟΝ̱ ></td></tr>
</table>

Witness of a similar kind is borne by the cursive MS. 22, which places τέλος after both *v.* 8 and *v.* 20, and after the first τέλος has the note ἔν τισι τῶν ἀντιγράφων ἕως ὧδε πληροῦται ὁ εὐαγγελιστής, ἐν πολλοῖς δὲ καὶ ταῦτα φέρεται. In like manner "some of the more ancient Armenian MSS. have εὐαγγέλιον κατὰ Μάρκου after both *v.* 8 and *v.* 20" (WH., *Notes, l.c.*); a few Ethiopic MSS. appear to omit everything after *v.* 8 (Sanday, *Appendices ad N. T.*, p. 195). To this must now be added the testimony of the Sinaitic Syriac, which ends the Gospel at ἐφοβοῦντο γάρ, followed immediately by the subscription and the opening of St Luke. Other documentary evidence of a less direct character will come into view as we proceed.

2. Of the two endings found in MSS. and versions which do not stop short at *v.* 8, it will be convenient to discuss the shorter first. It occurs in four uncial MSS. whose testimony must be given in full.

Cod. L.	Cod. 7¹².
εΦοΒογΝ	. . . . . εΦο
το γαρ'·	[Βογντο Γ]αρ > > > >
∧ ∧ ∧ ∧ ∧ ∧ ∧	> > > >
Φερετε πογ	> > > >
και ταγτα	[εγαγγελ]ιοΝ̄
Παντα Δε τα παρη	[κατα μα]ρκοΝ
γγελμεΝα τοιC	[παΝτα Δε τα πα
περι τοΝ πετροΝ	ρηγγελμεΝα τοιC
Cγντομωc εΞη	περι τοΝ πετροΝ
γγιλαΝ· μετα	Cγντομωc εΞηΓ
Δε ταγτα και αγτοc	γειλαΝ μετα Δε]¹
ο ι͞c, απο αΝατοληc	ταγτα και αγτοc
και αχρι Δγcεωc	ι͞c απο αΝατοληc
εΞαπεcτιλεΝ Δι	αχρι Δγcεωc εΞα
αγτωΝ το ιεροΝ	πεcτειλεΝ Δι αγ
και αΦθαρτοΝ κη	τωΝ το ιεροΝ και
ργγμα· τηc αιω	αΦθαρτοΝ κηργ
Νιογ cωτηριαc·	γμα τηc αιωΝιογ
εcτηΝ Δε και	cωτηριαc αμηΝ
ταγτα Φερο	εcτιΝ Δε και ταγτα
μεΝα μετα το	Φερομενα μετα
εΦοΒογΝτο	το εΦοΒογΝτο Γαρ
Γαρ·	αΝαcταc Δε πρωϊ
ΑΝαcταc Δε πρωϊ	πρωτη cαΒΒατογ
πρωτη cαΒΒατογ	εΦαΝη πρωτοΝ
κτλ. ... cημειωΝ.	μαρια τη μαγΔα
αμηΝ.	ληΝη παρ ηc
κ͟τ͟α μαρκοΝ	εκΒεΒληκει επτα
	Δαιμονια εκειΝη
	πορεγθ[ειcα] απηΓ
	γειλεΝ [τοιc] με
	(cetera desiderantur)

---

¹ I owe this restoration (πάντα δὲ... μετὰ δὲ) to Mr Burkitt, who points out that, since 7¹² has 25 lines to the column, 5 lines are lost before ταῦτα καὶ αὐτός. He adds, however, that as the note ἔστιν κτλ. is "in a smaller character" (*Syriac MSS.*, p. 104), φέρεταί που καὶ ταῦτα may have stood before πάντα.

<table>
<tr><td align="center">Cod. ק.</td><td align="center">Cod. Ψ.</td></tr>
</table>

Cod. ק.	Cod. Ψ.

εφοΒογΝΤο
ΓΑΡ·

^ ^ ^ ^ ^

[ΠΑΝΤΑ] Δε ΤΑ
[ΠΑΡΗ]ΓΓεΛΜεΝΑ
ΤοΙC Περι ΤοΝ
[ΠεΤΡοΝ] CγΝ
ΤοΜωC εξΗΓ
ΓεΙΛΑΝ·
ΜεΤΑ Δε ΤΑγΤΑ
ΚΑΙ ΑγΤοC ο ΙC
εφΑΝΗ ΑγΤοΙC
ΑΠ ΑΝΑΤοΛΗC
Τογ ΗΛΙογ ΚΑΙ ΑΧΡΙ
ΔγCεωC εξεΠε
CΤεΙΛεΝ ΔΙ Αγ
ΤωΝ Το ΙεΡοΝ
ΚΑΙ ΑφθΑΡΤοΝ
ΚΗΡγΓΜΑ ΤΗC
ΔΙωΝΙογ CωΤΗ
ΡΙΑC ΑΜΗΝ·

^ ^ ^ ^ ^

εΙΧεΝ ΓΑΡ ΑγΤΑC
ΤΡοΜοC ΚΑΙ εΚ
CΤΑCΙC ΚΑΙ ογ
ΔεΝΙ ογΔεΝ εΙ
ΠοΝ εφοΒογ
Το ΓΑΡ·
ΑΝΑCΤΑC Δε...ΠΙω[CΙΝ]

(*cetera desiderantur*)

εφοΒογΝΤο ΓΑΡ : f̂

ΠΑΝΤΑ Δε ΤΑ ΠΑΡΗΓΓεΛΜεΝΑ ΤοΙC Περι ΤοΝ
ΠεΤΡοΝ CγΝΤοΜωC. εξΗΓΓεΙΛΑΝ : ΜεΤΑ
Δε ΤΑγΤΑ. ΚΑΙ ΑγΤοC ΙC εφΑΝΗ ΑΠο ΑΝΑΤοΛΗC
ΚΑΙ ΜεΧΡΙ ΔγCεωC εξΑΠεCΤεΙΛεΝ ΔΙ ΑγΤωΝ
Το ΪεΡοΝ ΚΑΙ ΑφθΑΡΤοΝ ΚΗΡγΓΜΑ ΤΗC ΔΙω
ΝΙογ CωΤΗΡΙΑC ΑΜΗΝ :

ΕCΤΙΝ ΚΑΙ ΤΑγΤΑ φεΡοΜεΝΑ
ΜεΤΑ Το εφοΒογΝΤο ΓΑΡ.

ΑΝΑCΤΑC Δε ΚΤΛ. .. CΗΜεΙωΝ. ΑΜΗΝ.
εγΑΓΓεΛΙοΝ ΚΑΤΑ ΜΑΡΚοΝ

It is obvious that the archetype of L ק¹² ends at ἐφοβοῦντο γάρ, and that the scribes on their own responsibility have added two endings with which they had met in other MSS., preferring apparently the shorter one, since it is in each case placed first. But each codex has its own way of dealing with the supplementary matter. In ק¹² the subscription εὐαγγέλιον κατὰ Μᾶρκον has been retained after *v.* 8, where it stood in the archetype; in L,

and possibly also in ב[12], each ending is preceded by a brief note
of origin; in ק there are no such notes, but the scribe, after
writing the shorter ending, returns to *v.* 8 and annexes the
longer ending to it. Cod. Ψ, which stands alone in placing
the shorter ending immediately after ἐφοβοῦντο γάρ, without
either break or note[1], seems to have descended from an archetype
which had the shorter ending only, though the scribe of Ψ
proceeds to give the longer with the usual prefatory note. Since
the formula ἔστιν δὲ καὶ ταῦτα φερόμενα μετὰ τὸ ' ἐφ. γάρ ' is
common to L Ψ ב[12], we must suppose that these MSS., notwithstanding other features which attest independence, drew at this
point from the same relatively early archetype.

Besides these uncial authorities the shorter ending finds a place
in the margin of the cursive MS. 274 and of the Harclean Syriac,
in the margin of two important MSS. of the Bohairic or Memphitic
version[2], and in several MSS. of the Ethiopic, where it stands in the
text between *v.* 8 and *v.* 9 without note or break[3]. One authority
which is still extant gives the shorter ending only—the O.L. MS.
k, in which Mc. ends: "omnia autem quaecumque prae|cepta erant
et qui cum puero (*sic*) erant | breviter exposuerunt posthaec | et
ipse hī⁸ adparuit · et ab orientē· | usque · usque in orientem ·
misit | per illos · sanctam · et incorruptam · [praedicationem⁴] |
salutis aeternae · amen."

As the shorter ending has not been printed with the text, it may
be convenient to give it here with an *apparatus.*

πάντα δὲ τὰ παρηγγελμένα τοῖς περὶ τὸν Πέτρον συντόμως ἐξήγγειλαν.
μετὰ δὲ ταῦτα καὶ αὐτὸς ὁ Ἰησοῦς ἐφάνη αὐτοῖς, καὶ ἀπὸ ἀνατολῆς καὶ
ἄχρι δύσεως ἐξαπέστειλεν δι᾽ αὐτῶν τὸ ἱερὸν καὶ ἄφθαρτον κήρυγμα τῆς
αἰωνίου σωτηρίας.

παντα...μετα δε] hiat ב | om και αυτος me^{codd (mg)} aeth^{codd} | ο Ιησους
LP] om ο Ψ ב ο κυριος I. aeth^{codd} | εφανη αυτοις (ק) me^{codd (mg)} aeth^{codd}]

[1] Gregory, *prolegg.,* p. 445 : "nihil
adnotationis ante πάντα δέ noster inter-
ponit, quod antiquiorem sibi vindicare
fontem videretur, nisi fortasse vocabula
ἐφάνη, μέχρι, ἀμήν seriorem textus con-
formationem testarentur."

[2] "In A, at the end of *v.* 8, in the
break, as if referring to the last twelve
verses, is a gloss [in Arabic] 'this is the

chapter expelled in the Greek'" (Oxford
edition, p. 480).

[3] So WH.², *Notes,* pp. 38, 44 ; see
however Sanday, *App.,* p. 195.

[4] "Ha" which stands here in the
margin refers, as Dr Sanday points out,
to *praedicationis* (i.e. praedicationem)
which the corrector has written at the
foot of the page.

om L⊓ 274^{mg} syr$^{hcl (mg)}$ om αυτοις Ψ k | και 2° k (me$^{codd (mg)}$) aeth^{codd}]
om rell | απο] απ ፆ | απο ανατολης (ανατολων 274^{mg} cf. me$^{codd (mg)}$)]
+ του ηλιου ፆ me$^{codd (mg)}$ aeth^{codd} | om και 3° ⊓ k | αχρι] μεχρι Ψ | δυ-
σεως] orientem k | εξεπεστ. ፆ | σωτηριας] + αμην Ψ ⊓ ፆ 274^{mg} k syr$^{hcl (mg)}$
me$^{cod A (mg)}$ aeth^{codd}.

For cod. L see the facsimile in Burgon, *Last twelve verses*, p. 112,
and Tischendorf, *mon. sacr. ined.*, 1846; for cod. Ψ, Gregory, *Prolegg.*
ii. p. 445, Lake, *Texts from Mt Athos*, p. 122; for cod. ⊓^{12}, Mrs
Lewis, *Catal. of Syriac MSS. on Mt Sinai*, p. 103 f.; for cod. ፆ,
Amélineau, *Notices et extraits* xxxiv. ·ii. p. 402 ff.; for cod. 274,
Tischendorf, *N. T. Gr.*⁸ i. p. 404; for *syr*^{hcl}, White's edition, i.
p. 258; for *me*, Sanday, *Appendices ad N. T.*, p. 187, and *Coptic
Version of the N. T.*, Oxf., 1898, i: p. 480 ff.; for *aeth*, Sanday, *op.
cit.*, p. 195; *k* is printed in full in *O. L. Bibl. Texts*, ii. p. 23.

As to the origin of this ending there can be little doubt. It
has been written by some one whose copy of the Gospel ended at
ἐφοβοῦντο γάρ, and who desired to soften the harshness of so
abrupt a conclusion, and at the same time to remove the impression which it leaves of a failure on the part of Mary of Magdala
and her friends to deliver the message with which they had been
charged. Terrified as they were, he adds, they recovered themselves sufficiently to report to Peter the substance of the Angel's
words. After this the Lord Himself appeared to the Apostles
and gave them their orders to carry the Gospel from East to
West; and these orders, with His assistance, were loyally fulfilled.

The style of this little paragraph, as Dr Hort[1] observes, bears
some resemblance to that of St Luke's prologue, but it is certainly
as little as possible in harmony with the manner of St Mark.
Perhaps it may without rashness be attributed to a Roman hand[2];
a Western origin is suggested by the pointed references to the
westward course of the Apostolic preaching.

One or two verbal similarities may suggest Clement, cf. 1 Cor.
6 κῆρυξ γενόμενος ἔν τε τῇ ἀνατολῇ καὶ ἐν τῇ δύσει, and with ἱερὸν καὶ
ἄφθαρτον cf. *ib.* 33 ἱεραῖς καὶ ἀμώμοις. On the other hand some of
the more striking words are characteristic of Ps.-Clement 2 Cor.
(e.g. συντόμως, ἐξαποστέλλειν, ἄφθαρτος).

---

[1] WH., *Intr.*, p. 298 f.
[2] Nestle (in Hastings, *D. B.*, iii. p. 13)
suggests Egypt as its birth-place, and
Dobschütz (*Texte u. Unters.* xi. 1. p. 73 f.)

conjectures that it is taken from the
Κήρυγμα Πέτρου, which, as he contends,
was written as an appendix to Mc.

The place it occupies in *k* and its occurrence in other versions, and in the four uncials where it is given with considerable variations of text and setting, point to an early date, and there is nothing either in the vocabulary or the manner to forbid this view. On the other hand it must always have had a very limited acceptance, for no trace of it has been found in any Greek or Latin Christian writing. It was overshadowed almost from the first by the superior merits of the longer ending.

3. The longer ending follows *v.* 8 without break in every known Greek MS. except the two which end at ἐφοβοῦντο γάρ (א B) and the four which append both endings as partially attested alternatives (L Ψ ר¹² ק). It is found or at one time occupied a place without alternative in the uncial MSS. AC(D)EFGHKM(N¹) SUVXΓΔ(ΠΣ)Ωב, in all cursive MSS., in the Old Latin MSS. c ff g l n o q, in the Curetonian form of the Old Syriac, in the Memphitic and Gothic. Moreover, it appears as the recognised ending of St Mark in the earliest Christian writings which bear definite traces of the influence of the second Gospel. There are indications of its use in Hermas, and Justin appears to refer to *v.* 20, whilst *v.* 19 is expressly quoted by Irenaeus as the work of St Mark.

For Hermas see Dr C. Taylor's *Hermas and the Four Gospels*, p. 57 ff. Justin either has our fragment in view or stumbles unaccountably upon its phraseology when he writes (*ap.* i. 45): οἱ ἀπόστολοι αὐτοῦ ἐξελθόντες πανταχοῦ ἐκήρυξαν. Other "early evidence for the twelve verses" may be seen in a paper contributed by Dr Taylor to the *Expositor* for 1893 (IV. viii., p. 71 ff.). These writers, however, may have known the fragment in another connexion; in Irenaeus it is quoted as a true part of this Gospel: iii. 10. 6 "in fine autem evangelii ait Marcus *Et quidem dominus Iesus*," &c.

Thus on the whole it seems safe to conclude that at Rome and at Lyons in the second half of the second century the Gospel ended as it does now. If the last twelve verses did not form part of the autograph, there is nothing to shew when they were attached to the Gospel. But they must have been very generally accepted as the work of St Mark soon after the middle of the second century, if not indeed at an earlier time. It is significant

---

[1] See Cronin, *Codex purpureus Petropolitanus*, p. xxviii.

that a writer of such wide knowledge as Irenaeus entertained no doubt as to their genuineness.

4. The present ending of the Gospel stands in evident contrast with the formal and somewhat turgid manner of the shorter ending. Although it contains an abundance of words and phrases which differentiate it from the rest of the book, yet like St Mark's genuine work, it might have been written by a bilingual Jew of the first generation who had been nourished upon the vocabulary of the LXX., and accustomed to translate Aramaic into Greek. But the two fragments are distinguished by a more serious and indeed fundamental difference. While the shorter ending was evidently composed with the view of completing St Mark's work, the last twelve verses of the common text are as clearly part of an independent composition. They form an epitome of the appearances of the Risen Christ from the moment of the Resurrection to the Ascension, followed by a brief summary of the subsequent work of the Apostles. Instead of taking up the thread dropt at the end of xvi. 8, the longer ending begins with a statement which, if not inconsistent with xvi. 1—8, presupposes a situation to which the earlier verses of the chapter offer no clue. It is clear that the subject of ἀναστάς...ἐφάνη has been indicated in the sentence which immediately preceded; but v. 8 is occupied with another subject. The writer of v. 9 introduces Mary of Magdala as if she were a person who had not been named before, or not referred to recently; but St Mark has already mentioned her thrice in the previous sixteen verses. Moreover, both the structure and the general purpose of this ending are remarkably distinct from those which distinguish the genuine work of Mark. Instead of a succession of short paragraphs linked by καί and an occasional δέ, we have before us in xvi. 9—20 a carefully constructed passage, in which μετὰ δὲ ταῦτα, ὕστερον δέ, ὁ μὲν οὖν, ἐκεῖνος δέ, mark the successive points of juncture. The purpose is didactic and not simply or in the first instance historical; the tone is Johannine rather than Marcan. The author wishes to exhibit the slow recovery of the Apostles from their unbelief, and the triumphant power of faith (ἠπίστησαν...οὐδὲ ἐπίστευσαν...

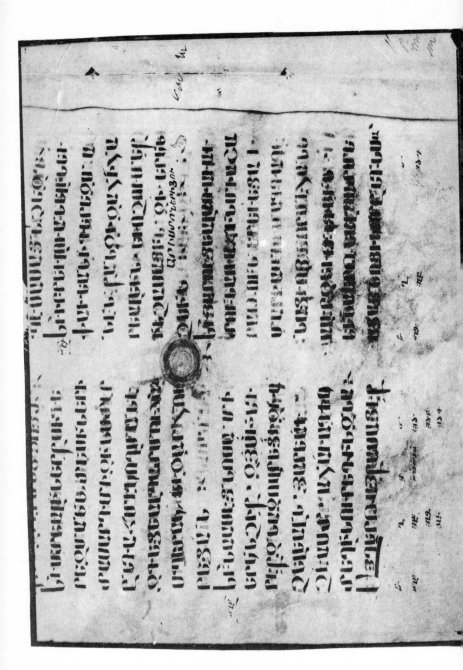

FACSIMILE OF EDSCHMIATZIN MS.

ὠνείδισεν τὴν ἀπιστίαν αὐτῶν...ὁ πιστεύσας σωθήσεται...ἐκεῖνοι δὲ ἐξελθόντες ἐκήρυξαν πανταχοῦ). He carries the Risen Lord beyond the sphere of history to His place at the Right Hand of GOD, and recognises His cooperation in the work of the Church during the age which followed the Ascension. The historian has given place to the theologian, the interpreter of St Peter to the scholar of St John.

5. A recent discovery assigns a name to the author of this fragment. In November 1891 Mr F. C. Conybeare found in the Patriarchal Library of Edschmiatzin an Armenian MS. of the Gospels written A.D. 989, in which the last twelve verses of St Mark are introduced by a rubric written in the first hand, *Of the presbyter Ariston*[1]. Mr Conybeare with much probability suggests that the person intended is the Aristion who is mentioned by Papias as one of the disciples of the Lord.

Papias (Eus. *H. E.* iii. 39) is quoted as saying : εἰ δέ που καὶ παρηκολουθηκώς τις τοῖς πρεσβυτέροις ἔλθοι, τοὺς τῶν πρεσβυτέρων ἀνέκρινον λόγους...ἅ τε Ἀριστίων καὶ ὁ πρεσβύτερος Ἰωάννης οἱ τοῦ κυρίου μαθηταὶ λέγουσιν. Eusebius adds : καὶ ἄλλας δὲ τῇ ἰδίᾳ γραφῇ παραδίδωσιν Ἀριστίωνος τοῦ πρόσθεν δεδηλωμένου τῶν τοῦ κυρίου λόγων διηγήσεις. Papias frequently cited him by name in his Λογίων κυριακῶν ἐξηγήσεις (Eus. *l.c.*: Ἀριστίωνος δὲ καὶ τοῦ πρεσβυτέρου Ἰωάννου αὐτήκοον ἑαυτόν φησι γενέσθαι· ὀνομαστὶ γοῦν πολλάκις αὐτῶν μνημονεύσας ἐν τοῖς αὐτοῦ συγγράμμασι τίθησιν αὐτῶν παραδόσεις).

Through Mr Conybeare's kindness a photograph is given of the leaf which bears the name of Ariston. He has sent me the following note in explanation of the facsimile.

" In this codex verse 8 of ch. xvi. ends at the beginning of a line, in the second column of a page. The line is partly filled up with the vermilioned flourishes which indicate that the Gospel proper of Mark is ended. Verse 9 however is begun on the next line, and the whole 12 verses are completed in the same large uncials as the rest of the Gospels. As it were by an afterthought the scribe adds the title *Ariston Eritzou* just above the flourishes mentioned, and within the columnar space. It is written in vermilioned smaller uncials identical in character with those which at the foot of each column denote the Ammonian canons, and also with those which the scribe uses to complete a word at the end of a line, thereby preserving the symmetry of the lines and avoiding the necessity of placing the last one or two letters of a word by themselves at the

[1] *Expositor*, IV. viii. p. 241 ff.

beginning of a fresh line. The title therefore was added by the first hand ; or, if not by him, at least by the διορθωτής. In any case it is contemporary and must have stood in the older copy transcribed, from which also were perhaps transferred the fifth century full-page illuminations included in the existing codex. At first it was intended to omit the title, but on second thoughts it was added. If the scribe had from the first meant to keep it, he would have left room for it, instead of cramping it in above the terminal flourishes. That he regarded Mark proper as ending with verse 8, is further shewn by the large circular boss consisting of concentric circles of colour added against the end of verse 8 between the columns. The paler tints in the photograph correspond to vermilion in the codex ; and the vermilioned lettering of the title was so faint in the positive sent to Mr Conybeare from Edschmiatzin in 1895, that he has strengthened it with ink for the preparation of the present facsimile. The parchment of the codex is so thin and fine that the writing on the back of the page here and there shews through in the photograph."

Though neither Eusebius nor Papias as quoted by Eusebius says that Aristion committed his διηγήσεις to writing, nothing is more likely than that they were collected and published by those who heard them. To such a collection, made under the influence of the school of St John, this summary of post-Resurrection history may well have belonged, and in the exemplar which was the archetype of the codices known to Irenaeus it had been judged worthy to complete the unfinished work of the Evangelist. While the shorter ending passed over to Carthage and established itself in some circles at Alexandria, Rome and Gaul were quick to perceive the higher claims of this genuine relic of the first generation, and it took its place unchallenged in the fourfold Gospel of the West.

6. The documentary testimony for the longer ending is, as we have seen, overwhelming. Nevertheless, there are points at which the chain of evidence is not merely weak but broken. Besides the fact that in the fourth century, if not in the third, the 'accurate copies' of the Gospel were known to end with xvi. 8, and that in the two great fourth century Bibles which have come down to us the Gospel actually ends at this point, those who maintain the genuineness of the last twelve verses have to account for the early circulation of an alternative ending, and for the ominous silence of the Ante-Nicene fathers between

Irenaeus and Eusebius[1] in reference to a passage which was of so much importance both on historical and theological grounds. When we add to these defects in the external evidence the internal characteristics which distinguish these verses from the rest of the Gospel, it is impossible to resist the conclusion that they belong to another work, whether that of Aristion or of some unknown writer of the first century[2].

[1] See Zahn, *Einleitung*, ii. p. 227.

[2] Dr Salmon (*Introduction to the N.T.*, p. 151) writes in reference to the last twelve verses of this Gospel, "We must ascribe their authorship to one who lived in the very first age of the Church. And why not to St Mark?" St Mark, undoubtedly, has more than one manner; he writes with greater freedom when he is stating facts on his own knowledge than when he is compiling his recollections of St Peter's teaching. But is there anything in the Gospel, whether in its opening verses or elsewhere, which resembles the rhythmical structure and didactic tone of the present ending? Unless we entirely misjudge the writer of the second Gospel, the last twelve verses are the work of another mind, trained in another school.

12

Commentaries

We have already seen that this Gospel received little or no attention from the great commentators of the first five centuries. The commentary ascribed to Origen in a Paris MS. (Omont, *Manuscrits grecs de la bibl. nat.*, p. 180) is identical with the work of Victor (Harnack, *Gesch. d. altchr. Lit.*, p. 389; cf. Huet, *Origeniana*, iii., app. § iv.; see also Westcott, 'Origen,' in *D. C. B.* iv., p. 112). In *Anecdota Maredsolana* (III. ii. p. 319 sqq., 1897), Dom Morin has printed some interesting homilies on St Mark which he attributes to Jerome[1], but the treatment is allegorical and practical rather than exegetical in the strict sense. A few fragments which are found among the exegetical works of Theodore of Mopsuestia are probably taken from his other writings (Fritzsche, *fragm. Th. Mops.*, p. 84). Chrysostom is said by Suidas to have written on St Mark, but the statement needs confirmation[2].

The earliest extant commentary on the second Gospel is that which bears the name of " Victor, presbyter of Antioch."

In the Oxford MS. used by J. Cramer (*Catenae in Evangelia*, 1840) the argument is said to be ἐκ τῆς εἰς αὐτὸν (τὸν Μᾶρκον) ἑρμηνείας τοῦ ἐν ἁγίοις Κυρίλλου Ἀλεξανδρείας. Other MSS. have the same attribution, but the majority ascribe the work to Victor (Simon, *hist. crit. du N. T.*, p. 427). For an account of the MSS. and editions of this commentary see Burgon, *Twelve last verses of St Mark*, p. 272 ff. It was first published by Possinus in the *Catena Graecorum Patrum in ev. sec. Marcum* (Rome, 1673); see Burgon, p. 270.

---

[1] Two commentaries upon St Mark are printed in the appendix to Jerome (Migne, *P.L.* xxx. coll. 560 sqq., 590 sqq.). Collections on St Mark from the works of Gregory the Great will be found in *P.L.* lxxix. coll. 1052, 1178.

[2] See Bardenhewer, *Patrologie*, p. 313.

VICTOR OF ANTIOCH is otherwise unknown, but his personality is of little importance, since he professes to limit himself to the task of a compiler (συνεῖδον τὰ κατὰ μέρος καὶ σποράδην εἰς αὐτὸ εἰρημένα παρὰ τῶν διδασκάλων τῆς ἐκκλησίας συναγαγεῖν, καὶ σύντομον ἑρμηνείαν συντάξαι). Burgon (*op. cit.*, p. 275 f.) has shewn that while Chrysostom's homilies on St Matthew supply the backbone of the work, Origen is freely used, and there are at least occasional references to St Basil, Apollinaris, Theodore of Mopsuestia, Titus of Bostra, and Cyril of Alexandria. A suggestion of Schanz[1] that the bulk of the commentary belongs to the school of Antioch is not supported by a solitary reference to Nestorius, which points the other way. Rather it seems to be the work of an industrious compiler who is willing to use all the materials at his disposal. Yet as Burgon points out[2], Victor is not a catenist in the ordinary sense, for he speaks occasionally in his own person, and rarely quotes his authorities by name. The popularity of his work in the Eastern Church is shewn by the multiplication of copies; it survives in more than fifty codices of the Gospels[3]. As to the time of its composition Dr Hort writes[4]: "it probably belongs to Cent. V. or VI., but there is no clear evidence to fix the date"; Dean Burgon, less cautiously: "[the] date...may be assigned to the first half of the fifth century —suppose A.D. 425—450." A conjecture which placed it a century later would perhaps be nearer to the truth.

Next in point of age to Victor of Antioch comes our country-man BAEDA [† 735]. Bede's commentaries on St Mark and St Luke were written at the desire of Acca, Bishop of Hexham. A passage from a letter to Acca prefixed to the commentary on St Mark describes Bede's method: "quae in patrum venerabilium exemplis invenimus hinc inde collecta ponere curabimus, sed et nonnulla propria ad imitationem sensus eorum ubi oportunum videbitur interponemus." He complains in the preface to Luke of the difficulties which in a monastic cell beset such

---

[1] *Commentar*, p. 53. The passage quoted runs: εἰ ἄλλος ἐν ἄλλῳ ἐστὶ κατὰ τοὺς λόγους τοῦ Νεστορίου ἔδει εἰπεῖν Ἐν σοί ἐστιν ὁ υἱός μου ὁ ἀγαπητὸς ἐν ᾧ εὐδό-

κησα (Cramer, p. 272).
[2] *Op. cit.*, p. 277.
[3] *Ib.* pp. 60, 278 ff.
[4] *Notes*, p. 34.

work—"ipse mihi dictator simul notarius et librarius"—but tells us that he has nevertheless contrived to collect materials from all the great Latin fathers, Ambrose, Augustine, Gregory and Jerome. To the commentary of Jerome on St Matthew most of his exposition of Mark appears to be due; but the work is by no means devoid of independent merit, and perhaps its best features are those which it owes to the insight and devotion of Bede himself. Printed in Migne, *P. L.* xcii.

Under the name of WALAFRID STRABO († 750) we have (1) the *Glossa ordinaria*, and (2) a few notes on St Mark (Migne, *P. L.* cxiii., cxiv.).

THEOPHYLACT, Archbishop of Achridia (*Ochrida*) in Bulgaria (fl. c. A.D. 1077), has expounded St Mark with considerable fulness in his Ἑρμηνεία εἰς τὰ τέσσαρα εὐαγγέλια (Simon, iv., p. 390 ff.). Simon's judgement ("les commentaires de Théophylacte...sont plutôt des abrégés de S. Chrysostome que de véritables commentaires") is manifestly less applicable to this Gospel than to the others, if Chrysostom left no genuine work on St Mark; certainly Theophylact's commentary on St Mark is of considerable importance for the exposition of the Gospel, and in the dearth of older expositions invaluable. Printed in Migne, *P. G.* cxxiii.

EUTHYMIUS ZIGABENUS, a monk of Constantinople (fl. c. A.D. 1115), is also a follower of Chrysostom (*prooem. in Mt.*: μάλιστα μὲν ἀπὸ τῆς ἐξηγήσεως τοῦ ἐν ἁγίοις πατρὸς ἡμῶν Ἰωάννου τοῦ χρυσοστόμου, ἔτι δὲ καὶ ἀπὸ διαφόρων ἄλλων πατέρων συνεισενεγκόντος τινά). But unlike Theophylact he regards St Mark as scarcely deserving of a separate commentary, since 'the second Gospel is in close agreement with the first, excepting where the first is fuller' (συμφωνεῖ λίαν τῷ Ματθαίῳ πλὴν ὅταν ἐκεῖνός ἐστι πλατύτερος). His notes on Mark are therefore generally mere cross-references to those on Matthew; here and there, however, where Mark differs from Matthew or relates something which is peculiar to himself, useful comments will be found. Printed in Migne, *P. G.* cxxix.

BRUNO ASTENSIS († 1125) contributes a brief exposition, of which the author writes: "non multum quidem nos laborare necesse erit quoniam valde pauca ibi dicuntur quae in Matthaeo exposita non sint." Printed in Migne, *P. L.* clxv.

Rupertus Tuitiensis (Rupert of Deutz, † 1135): *in vol. iv. Evangelistarum commentariorum liber unus* (Migne, *P. L.* clxvii.).

(?) Thomas Aquinas († 1274): *catena aurea in iv. Evangelistas.*

Albertus Magnus († 1289) : *commentarius in Marcum.*

Dionysius Carthusianus († 1417): *in iv. Evangelia.*

Faber Stapulensis († 1527): *commentarii initiatorii in iv. Evangelia.*

Desiderius Erasmus († 1536): *paraphrasis in N.T.*

Jo. Maldonatus († 1583): *commentarii in iv. Evangelistas.*

Cornelius a Lapide († 1637): *commentaria in iv. Evangelia.*

Among later writers on the four Gospels good work of varying merit and usefulness may be found in the commentaries of Bengel, Elsner, Grotius, Kuinoel, Kypke, and Wetstein. The last century produced many expositions of St Mark, and others have appeared since 1900. It must suffice to specify the following:

Fritzsche, K. F. A.: *Evangelium Marci*, Lips., 1830.

Meyer, H. A. W.: in the *Krit.-exegetischer Kommentar*, first ed., 1832; ninth ed. (Meyer-Weiss), 1901.

Alford, H.: in *the Four Gospels*, London, 1849.

Alexander, J. A.: *Gospel acc. to St Mark*, Princeton, 1858.

Lange, J. P.: in the *Theol.-homiletisches Bibelwerk*, first ed., 1858; fourth ed., 1884.

Klostermann, A.: *das Markusevangelium*, Göttingen, 1867.

Weiss, B.: *das Markusevangelium*, Berlin, 1872; *die vier Evangelien*, Leipzig, 1900.

Morison, Jas.: *Commentary on the Gospel acc. to St Mark*, London, 1873.

Cook, F. G.: in the *Speaker's Commentary on the N.T.*, vol. I., London, 1878.

Riddle, M. R.: in Schaff's *Popular Commentary on the N.T.*, Edinburgh, 1878–82.

Plumptre, E. H. (in the *N.T. Commentary for English readers*), London, 1879.

SCHANZ, P.: *Commentar über das Evangelium d. h. Marcus*, Freiburg-im-Breisgau, 1881.

MACLEAR, G. F. (in the *Cambridge Greek Testament*), Cambridge, first ed., 1883; last reprint, 1899.

CHADWICK, G. A.: *the Gospel acc. to St Mark* (in the Expositor's Bible), London, 1887.

LUCKOCK, H. M.: *Footprints of the Son of Man as traced by St Mark*, London, 1889.

HOLTZMANN, H. J.: in the *Hand-commentar*, Freiburg-im-Breisgau, 1892; third edition, 1901.

KNABENBAUER, J.: *Commentarius in Evangelium sec. Marcum* (in the *Cursus scripturae sacrae*), Paris, 1894.

GOULD, E. P.: *a critical and exegetical commentary on the Gospel acc. to St Mark* (in the International Critical Commentary), Edinburgh, 1896.

BRUCE, A. B.: *St Mark* (in the *Expositor's Greek Testament*), London, 1897.

MENZIES, A.: *the Earliest Gospel: a historical study of the Gospel acc. to Mark*, London, 1901.

WELLHAUSEN, J.: *Das Evangelium Marci.* Berlin, 1903.

GRESSMANN, H., and KLOSTERMANN, E.: *Die Evangelien.* I. *Markus.* Tübingen, 1907.

WOHLENBERG, G.: *Das Evangelium des Markus* (in Th. Zahn's *Kommentar zum N.T.*). Leipzig, 1910.

The following are a few of the least obvious abbreviations employed in the footnotes:

BDB. Brown Driver and Briggs, *Hebrew and English Lexicon of the O.T.* (Oxford, 1892—).

Blass, *Gr.* F. Blass, *Grammar of N.T. Greek.* Translated by H. St J. Thackeray (London, 1898).

Burton. E. de W. Burton, *Syntax of the Moods and Tenses in N.T. Greek* (Edinburgh, 1894).

Dalman, *Gr.* G. Dalman, *Grammatik d. Jüdisch-Palästinischen Aramäisch* (Leipzig, 1894).

Dalman, *Worte.* G. Dalman, *Die Worte Jesu* bd. 1 (Leipzig, 1898): the English translation (*The Words of Jesus*, 1, Edinburgh, 1902) appeared too late to be quoted in this edition.

D.C.A. Smith and Cheetham, *Dictionary of Christian Antiquities.*

D.C.B. Smith and Wace, *Dictionary of Christian Biography and Doctrines.*

Deissmann. G. A. Deissmann, *Bible Studies.* Translated by A. Grieve (Edinburgh, 1901).

Delitzsch. N.T. in Hebrew (Leipzig, 1892).

Euth. Euthymius Zigabenus.

Exp. The *Expositor.*

Exp. T. The *Expository Times.*

Field, *Notes.* F. Field, *Notes on the translation of the N.T. = Otium Norvicense* iii., edited by A. M. Knight (Cambridge, 1899).

Hastings, *D. B.* J. Hastings, *Dictionary of the Bible* (Edinburgh, 1898—1902).

J. B. L. The *Journal of Biblical Literature.*

J. Th. St. The *Journal of Theological Studies.*

Nestle, *T.C.* E. Nestle, *Textual Criticism of the N.T.* Translated by W. Edie and A. Menzies (London, 1901).

SH. Sanday and Headlam, *Commentary on the Epistle to the Romans* (Edinburgh, 1895).

Thpht. Theophylact.

Vg. The Latin Vulgate.

Victor. 'Victor of Antioch' (in Cramer's *Catena*).

WH. Westcott and Hort, *N.T. in Greek* (Cambridge, 1881); WH.[2], second edition (1896).

WM. Winer-Moulton, *Grammar of N.T. Greek*, 8th Engl. ed. (Edinburgh, 1877).

WSchm. Winer-Schmiedel, *Grammatik d. NTlichen Sprachidioms* (Göttingen, 1894—).

Zahn, *Einl.* Th. Zahn, *Einleitung in das N.T.* (Leipzig, 1897—9).

In substance and style and treatment the Gospel of St Mark is essentially a transcript from life. The course and issue of facts are imaged in it with the clearest outline. If all other arguments against the mythic origin of the Evangelic narratives were wanting, this vivid and simple record, stamped with the most distinct impress of independence and originality, totally unconnected with the symbolism of the Old Dispensation, totally independent of the deeper reasonings of the New, would be sufficient to refute a theory subversive of all faith in history. The details which were originally addressed to the vigorous intelligence of Roman hearers are still pregnant with instruction for us. The teaching which 'met their wants' in the first age finds a corresponding field for its action now....The picture of the sovereign power of Christ battling with evil among men swayed to and fro by tumultuous passions is still needful, though we may turn to St Matthew and St John for the ancient types or deeper mysteries of Christianity or find in St Luke its inmost connexion with the unchanging heart of man.— Bishop Westcott.

ΑΡΧΗ τοῦ εὐαγγελίου Ἰησοῦ Χριστοῦ §[υἱοῦ θεοῦ]. I **1.**
§ r

κατα Μαρκον 𝔎BF] pr ευαγγελιον ADEHKLMUΓΔΠΣΦ min^pl το κ. Μ. (αγιον)
ευαγγελιον min^sat mu

I. 1 αρχη του ευ.] ευαγγελιον syr^hier | υιου θεου 𝔎^aBDL] υιου του θεου AEFHKMSU
VΓΔΠΣΦ min^pl latt syrr^pesh hcl (mg) arm me go aeth Ir^2 Or^pl Amb Hier^1 Aug (om 𝔎* 28
[Ιησ. tantum 28*] 255 syr^hier Ir^1 Or^4 Bas Hier^2)

I. 1. SUPERSCRIPTION.

1. ἀρχὴ τοῦ εὐαγγελίου 'I. X.] Possibly an early heading which arose from the fusion of an original title ΕΥΑΓΓΕΛΙΟΝ Ι͞Υ Χ͞Υ with the note ἀρχή that marked the beginning of a new book (Nestle, *Exp.*, Dec. 1894; *Intr.* pp. 163, 261; see on the other hand Zahn, *Einl.* ii. p. 220 ff., 235). Yet the sentence is intelligible if regarded as a title prefixed to the book by the writer or editor; for a similar opening comp. Hosea i. 1 (LXX.), ἀρχὴ λόγου Κυρίου ἐν Ὡσῆε; see also Prov. i. 1, Eccl. i. 1, Cant. i. 1, &c. Or it may have been intended to refer to the immediate sequel. Irenaeus connects it with *v.* 2: ἀπὸ τοῦ προφητικοῦ πνεύματος...τὴν ἀρχὴν ἐποιήσατο λέγων Ἀρχή...ὡς γέγραπται, κτλ.; and so Origen (*in Jo.* t. vi. 24). Others with more probability find the ἀρχή in the events described in *v.* 4 ff., e.g. Basil *c. Eun.* ii. 15, ὁ δὲ Μᾶρκος ἀρχὴν τοῦ εὐαγγελίου τὸ Ἰωάννου πεποίηκε κήρυγμα: Victor, Ἰωάννην οὖν τελευταῖον τῶν προφητῶν ἀρχὴν εἶναι τοῦ εὐαγγελίου φησίν. The starting-point varies with the position of the writer; Mt. sees it in the ancestry and birth of the Messiah,

Lc., in the birth of the Baptist; Jo. (but see Jo. xv. 26) looks back to the ἀρχή in which the Word was with GOD; St Paul, using the word 'Gospel' in a wider sense, sees a fresh beginning in the foundation of each of the churches (Phil. iv. 15). That Mc. begins his Gospel with the ministration of the Baptist is one indication amongst many that he preserves the earliest form of the evangelical tradition, in which the record of the Birth and Childhood did not find a place.

Εὐαγγέλιον (in class. Greek usually pl., εὐαγγέλια) from Homer downwards is the reward accorded to a bearer of good tidings, but in later writers (e.g. Lucian, Plutarch) the good news itself. The LXX. use it only in 2 Regn. iv. 10, and in the class. sense, for in 2 Regn. xviii. 22, 25 we should probably read εὐαγγελία (cf. *v.* 20). In the N.T. the later sense alone occurs, but with some latitude of application; see *v.* 15 n. Εὐ. 'I. X. is 'the good tidings concerning J. C.' (gen. of the obj.), as revealed in His life, death, and resurrection. The phrase is unique in the Gospels, which elsewhere have τὸ εὐ. τοῦ θεοῦ (i. 14), τὸ εὐ. τῆς βασιλείας,

1

§ P   2   §² *Καθὼς γέγραπται ἐν τῷ Ἠσαΐᾳ τῷ προφήτῃ*
§ t   *Ἰδοὺ ἀποστέλλω τὸν ἄγγελόν μου* §*πρὸ προσώπου*

2 καθως אBKLΔΠ* 1 33 209 604 2ᵖᵉ alᵖᵃᵘᶜ Or al] ως ADEFHMPSUVΓΠ²ΣΤ
Ir Or¹ al | εν τω Ησαια τω προφητη אB(D)LΔ (1 22 al) 33 604 1071 alⁿᵒⁿⁿ latt
syrrᵖᵉᵉʰ ʰᶜˡ(ᵐᵍ) ʰⁱᵉʳ armᶜᵒᵈᵈ me Ir¹ Or⁴ al] εν τοις προφηταις AEFHKMPSUVΓΠΣΦ
syrʰᶜˡ(ᵗˣᵗ) armᶻᵒʰ aeth Ir²ˡᵃᵗ | om ιδου...την οδ. σου Bas Epiph Victorin | ιδου]+εγω
אALPΓΔΠΣΦ minᶠᵉʳᵉᵒᵐⁿ vgᵉᵈ syrʰᶜˡ arm go aeth Or⁴ (om BD 28 latt Irⁱⁿᵗ) | αποστελω
א alᵖᵃᵘᶜ me

or simply τὸ εὐ. (i. 15). If the heading
was added early in the second century
we might understand by εὐ. here a
record of the Lord's life and words:
for the earliest exx. of this use of
the word see Ign. *Philad.* 5, 8, *Did.
App.* 8, 11, 15, Justin *ap.* i. 66; and
cf. Zahn, *Gesch. des N. T. Kanons*, i.
p. 162.

υἱοῦ θεοῦ] The evidence for the
omission of these words is weighty, but
meagre. WH. (*Notes*, p. 23) relegate
them to the margin as a secondary
reading, but hold that " neither reading can be safely rejected." Possibly
the heading existed almost from the
first in two forms, with and without
υἱ. θ. The phrase υἱὸς θεοῦ or ὁ υἱ. τ.
θ. occurs in Mc. iii. 11, v. 7, xv. 39;
cf. i. 11, ix. 7, xii. 6, xiii. 32, xiv. 61.

2—8. THE PREPARATORY MINISTRY
OF JOHN THE BAPTIST (Mt. iii. 1—12,
Lc. iii. 1—6, 15—17; cf. Jo. i. 6—31).

2. *καθὼς γέγραπται*] A LXX. formula = כַּכָּתוּב (4 Regn. xiv. 6, xxiii. 14,
2 Paral. xxiii. 18, xxv. 4, xxxiii. 32,
xxxv. 12, Tob. i. 6). Mc. employs it
again in ix. 13, xiv. 21, and it occurs
in Lc.ᵉᵛ·, ᵃᶜᵗ·, and frequently in St
Paul; Jo. (vi. 31, xii. 14) seems to
prefer καθώς ἐστιν γεγραμμένον. The
perf. gives the sense of perpetuity;
the 'litera scripta' abides. See WM.,
p. 339.

The apodosis to καθώς κτλ. is wanting, unless we find it in *v.* 4. For a
similar omission see the opening clause
of 1 Tim. (i. 3, 4). For other possible
constructions cf. Nestle, *Intr.* p. 261.

ἐν τῷ Ἠσαΐᾳ τῷ προφήτῃ] The quotations are from Mal. iii. 1, Is. xl. 3.

In the parallels Mt. iii. 3, Lc. iii. 1—6
(cf. Jo. i. 23) Malachi is not quoted, but
his words are used by the two Synoptists
in another connexion (Mt. xi. 10, Lc.
vii. 27). Origen (*in Jo.* t. vi. 24)
remarks that Mc. is here δύο προφητείας ἐν διαφόροις εἰρημένας τόποις
ὑπὸ δύο προφητῶν εἰς ἐν συνάγων. That
he quotes the two under one name
did not escape the notice of Porphyry
(Hier. *tr. in Mc.*); Jerome (on Mt.)
answers: " nomen Isaiae putamus ad-
ditum scriptorum vitio...aut certe
de diversis testimoniis scripturarum
unum corpus effectum." The latter
solution is not improbable. Mc. (or
his source) may have depended upon
a collection of excerpts in which Mal.
iii. 1 stood immediately before Is. xl.
3, possibly on a leaf headed ΗϹΑΙΑϹ.
A similar confusion occurs in Iren.
iii. 20. 4, where quotations from Micah
(vii. 19) and Amos i. 2 are preceded
by the formula *Amos propheta* ait.
On the use of such collections see
Hatch, *Essays*, p. 203 ff.; SH., *Romans*,
pp. 264, 282. The reading is hotly
contested in Burgon-Miller, *Causes
of Corruption*, p. 111 f.

ἰδοὺ...τὴν ὁδόν σου] LXX. ἰδοὺ ἐξαποστέλλω τὸν ἄγγελόν μου, καὶ ἐπιβλέψεται ὁδὸν πρὸ προσώπου μου. Both
Mt. (xi. 10) and Lc. (vii. 27) read with
Mc. κατασκευάσει and σου, and trans-
pose πρὸ προσώπου σου, but both
add ἔμπροσθέν σου after ὁδόν σου.
The LXX. ἐπιβλέψεται presupposes the
vocalisation פִּנָּה, whereas κατασκευάσει
represents פִּנָּה (Resch, *Paralleltexte
zu Lucas*, p. 114); Symm. (ἀποσκευάσει)
and Theod. (ἐτοιμάσει) agree with the

σου, ὃς κατασκευάσει τὴν ὁδόν σου. ³φωνὴ βοῶντος 3
ἐν τῇ ἐρήμῳ Ἑτοιμάσατε τὴν ὁδὸν⁋ Κυρίου, εὐθείας   ⁋ G
ποιεῖτε τὰς τρίβους αὐτοῦ. ⁴ἐγένετο Ἰωάνης ὁ βαπ- 4
τίζων ἐν τῇ ἐρήμῳ κηρύσσων βάπτισμα μετανοίας

2 την οδον σου]+εμπροσθεν σου ΑΓΔΠ²Σ al min^pl f ff g vg^ed syr^hcl arm go me Or
3 αυτου] του θεου υμων D 34^mg a b c f ff t (dei nostri) syr^hcl (mg) go Ir^int vid bis (ante deum
nostrum)   4 εγενετο] pr και ℵ* | Ιωανης B] Ιωαννης codd^fere omn | ο βαπτ. ℵBLT^dΔ
33 me] om ο A(D)ΡΓΠΣΦ al syr^pesh arm | εν τη ερ. βαπτ. D 28 604 latt (exc f)
syr^pesh | κηρυσσων] pr και ℵADLΔΣΦ al latt syrr arm me (om και B 33 73 102)

Gospels. For σου the Heb. supplies
no justification : it is perhaps due to
the compiler of the excerpts (see last
note), who has blended Mal. *l.c.* with
Exod. xxiii. 20.

πρὸ προσώπου σου] Victor : καθάπερ
...ἐπὶ τῶν βασιλέων οἱ ἐγγὺς τοῦ ὀχή-
ματος ἐλαύνοντες οὗτοι τῶν ἄλλων εἰσὶ
λαμπρότεροι.

3. φωνὴ...τρίβους αὐτοῦ] So the
LXX. exactly, except that for the last
word, following the Heb., they give
τοῦ θεοῦ ἡμῶν—a reading which has
found its way into some Western texts
of Mc. (see vv. ll.). Origen (*in Jo. l.c.*),
Jerome (*in Mal.* iii.), and Victor notice
this remarkable divergence of the
Synoptists from the LXX. The passage
is quoted also by Jo. (i. 23), but he
stops at Κυρίου.

Tregelles connects ἐν τῇ ἐρήμῳ with
ἑτοιμάσατε, following the M. T.; but
the absence in the Greek of any
parallelism corresponding to בָּעֲרָבָה
justifies the ordinary punctuation
which is common to the Gospels and
the LXX., and it is supported by Jewish
interpretation (Delitzsch *ad l.*).

4. ἐγένετο Ἰωάνης κτλ.] 'There
arose John the Baptizer in the wilderness, preaching' &c. For this use of
ἐγένετο cf. 2 Pet. ii. 1, 1 Jo. ii. 18; and
especially Jo. i. 6, where it begins a
sentence with equal abruptness. On
the forms Ἰωάνης, Ἰωάννης see WH.,
Notes, p. 166; Winer-Schmiedel, p. 57 ;
Blass, p. 11. Mt. (iii. 1) has παραγίνεται,
Lc. (iii. 3) ἦλθεν. Ὁ βαπτίζων is nearly

= ὁ βαπτιστής, as in vi. 14, 24 (cf. 25);
on this use of the participle see Lightfoot on Gal. i. 23. If with all the
uncials except B and with the versions
we read καὶ κηρύσσων, the descriptive
clause will run on to the end of the
verse ('John the Baptizer... and
preacher,' &c.).

ἐν τῇ ἐρήμῳ] Mt. connects this
with κηρύσσων and adds τῆς Ἰουδαίας.
According to Lc. (i. 80, iii. 3) the
Baptist was ἐν ταῖς ἐρήμοις till his call
came, and then went to the Jordan ;
Mt. and Mc., writing in view of Isa. xl.
3, draw no distinction between the
ἔρημος and the Jordan valley. The
wilderness of Judah or Judaea (מִדְבַּר
יְהוּדָה, LXX. (A), τὴν ἔρημον Ἰούδα,
Jud. i. 16) has been described as
a region "piled up from the beach of
the Dead Sea to the very edge of the
central plateau" (G. A. Smith, *Hist.
Geogr.* p. 263), and, from an opposite
point of view, as "the barren steeps in
which the mountains break down to
the Dead Sea" (Moore, *Judges*, p. 32);
Engedi seems to have been the most
southerly town of this district (Moore,
l.c., referring to Josh. xv. 61 f.). It
was in the wilderness of Engedi that
David had sought a retreat (1 Sam.
xxiv. 1), and the same neighbourhood
would naturally have offered itself to
John, whose childhood had been spent
in the hill country of Judaea (Lc. i.
39).

κηρύσσων βάπτισμα...ἁμαρτιῶν] The
vox clamantis (Isa. *l.c.*, cf. Jo. i. 23)

5 εἰς ἄφεσιν ἁμαρτιῶν. ⁵καὶ ἐξεπορεύετο πρὸς αὐτὸν
πᾶσα ἡ Ἰουδαία χώρα καὶ οἱ Ἱεροσολυμεῖται πάντες,
καὶ ἐβαπτίζοντο ὑπ' αὐτοῦ ἐν τῷ Ἰορδάνῃ ποταμῷ,

5 ἐξεπορευοντο EFHLSVΓ latᵛᵗⁿᵒⁿⁿ go | παντες και εβ. ℵᶜ·ᵃBDLTᵈΔΣ 28 33
1071 a b q t vg syrᵖᵉˢʰ arm me] και εβ. π. ΑΡΓΠ al syrʰᶜˡ go 13 al om παντες Φ minᵖᵃᵘᶜ
f om και ℵ* 69 a | om ποταμω D 604 a b c

was the cry of a herald (קְרָא is rendered indifferently by βοᾶν and κηρύσσειν, cf. Dan. iii. 4, LXX. and Theo-
dotion), proclaiming a religious rite
which was to be at once the expression
and the pledge of repentance (μετανοίας, gen. of inner reference. WM., p.
235), and had remission of sins for its
purpose and end (εἰς ἄφ., WM., p. 495).
The baptism of John was strictly
speaking εἰς μετάνοιαν (Mt. iii. 11, Acts
xix. 3; cf. Wünsche, neue Beiträge,
p. 385); it was εἰς ἄφεσιν only inasmuch as it prepared for the ἐν β. εἰς
ἄφεσιν ἁμαρτιῶν of the Christian
Creed. Ambr. in Lc. ii.: "aliud fuit
baptisma paenitentiae, aliud gratiae
est"; Victor: προοδοποιῶν παραγέγονε
καὶ προετοιμάζων, οὐ τὴν δωρεὰν χαρι-
ζόμενος ... ἀλλὰ προπαρασκευάζων τὰς
ψυχάς. Ἄφεσις belongs properly to
the Messianic Kingdom (Mc. ii. 5 ff.),
in which it is associated with the
Baptism of the Spirit (Acts ii. 38).
The Law itself offered forgiveness of
external offences through external
rites; the new order, anticipated in the
Psalms and Prophets and beginning
with John, proclaimed a full forgiveness citra sacrificia levitica (Bengel).
On the form βάπτισμα see Mc. vii.
4, note, and Lightfoot on Col. ii. 12:
neither βάπτισμα nor βαπτισμός is
known to the LXX., and the verb is
used of a religious purification only
in Sir. xxxi. (xxxiv.) 30. Μετάνοια is
nearly restricted to the non-canonical
books (Prov.¹ Sap.³ Sir.³); ἄφεσις,
though frequent, occurs nowhere in
the Greek O.T. in the sense of forgiveness, although the ἐνιαυτὸς ἀφέσεως
(Lev. xxv. 10) is the archetype of an

era of spiritual remission (Lc. iv. 21).
In the N.T. both words are used with
some reserve (ἄφεσις¹⁸, μετάνοια²²) except perhaps by Lc. (ἄφ.¹⁰, μετ.¹¹).
   5. ἐξεπορεύετο...πάντες] Judaea is
personified, as in Gen. xli. 57 πᾶσαι αἱ
χῶραι ἦλθον. So Mt.; Lc. (iii. 7) prefers to speak of ἐκπορευόμενοι ὄχλοι.
With ἡ Ἰ. χώρα (Vg. Iudaeae regio)
cf. the similar phrases in Lc. iii. 1,
Acts xvi. 6, xviii. 23; ἡ Ἰουδαία γῆ
occurs in Jo. iii. 22, ἡ χῶρα τῶν Ἰουδαίων
in Acts x. 39, ἡ χ. τῆς Ἰουδαίας in Acts
xxvi. 20. More usually we have simply
ἡ Ἰουδαία (e.g. Mc. iii. 7, x. 1, xiii. 14).
For the limits of Judaea see Joseph.
B. J. iii. 3. 5, and comp. Neubauer,
géogr. du Talmud, p. 59 ff., G. A.
Smith, Hist. Geogr., c. xiii. Mt. adds
καὶ πᾶσα ἡ περίχωρος τοῦ Ἰορδάνου, i.e.
the Jordan valley (כָּל־כִּכַּר הַיַּרְדֵּן, Gen.
xiii. 10); some came from Galilee, as
Simon, Andrew, and John (Jo. i. 35 ff.),
and Jesus Himself. Οἱ Ἱεροσολυμεῖται
(on the breathing see WH., p. 313, and
on the termination in -είτης, WH.,
Notes, p. 154: for the form comp. 4
Macc. xviii. 5, Jo. vii. 25, Joseph. ant.
xii. 5. 3); distinguished from ἡ Ἰ. χῶρα
as a conspicuous portion of the whole,
cf. Isa. i. 1, ii. 1, iii. 1—not only the district in general, but the capital itself,
poured out its contribution of visitors.
   Πᾶσα, πάντες, like the Heb. כֹּל, are used
with some looseness: cf. Mt. ii. 3 πᾶσα
Ἱεροσόλυμα. The movement was practically universal. The long-cherished
desire for a revival of prophecy
(1 Macc. iv. 46, xiv. 41, cf. Mt. xi.
9, 32) seemed to have been realised;
hence this exodus to the Jordan.
   ἐβαπτίζοντο] Both the exodus and

ἐξομολογούμενοι τὰς ἁμαρτίας αὐτῶν. ⁶καὶ ἦν ὁ 6
Ἰωάνης ἐνδεδυμένος τρίχας καμήλου καὶ ζώνην δερματίνην περὶ τὴν ὀσφὺν αὐτοῦ, καὶ ἔσθων ἀκρίδας καὶ

6 και ην אBLTᵈ 33 2ᵖᵉᵐᵍ b d al vg] ην δε ΑΔΡΓΔΠΣΦ al | τριχας] δερρην D a
(pellem) | om και ζωνην...αυτου D a b d ff t | εσθιων ADLᶜᵒʳʳΡΓΠ alᵖˡ

the baptisms were continuous ; comp.
Jo. iii. 23, and contrast the aorists in
Acts ii. 41, 1 Cor. i. 13f., x. 2, xii. 13.
Ὑπ' αὐτοῦ determines the voice of
ἐβαπτ., 'they received baptism at the
hands of John' (cf. v. 9) ; the middle
is also used, as in 4 Regn. v. 14,
Judith xii. 7, Acts xxii. 16, 1 Cor. x. 2.
For Josephus's account of the baptism
of John see ant. xviii. 5. 2, and on the
question of its relation to proselyte-
baptism, cf. Schürer II. ii. 319 ff. Ἐν
τῷ Ἰορδ. ποταμῷ (cf. εἰς τὸν Ἰορδ., v. 9,
note): so Mt.; "im Jordanstrome"
(Schanz). Ἰ. ποταμός is regarded as a
single term, needing but one article
(synthetical apposition, cf. WM., p.
72 f.).

ἐξομολ. τὰς ἁμ. αὐτῶν] Evidence of
μετάνοια. Ἐξομολογεῖσθαι in Biblical
Greek is usually to give glory to GOD
(=הוֹדָה לְ), a phrase especially common
in the Psalms ; see also Mt. xi. 25,
Rom. xiv. 11. The rarer ἐξομολ. ἁμαρτίας occurs in Dan. ix. 20 (LXX.), where
Th. has ἐξαγορεύειν, the usual equivalent in the LXX. of the Hithp. of יָדָה.
Ἐξαγορεύειν does not occur in the
N. T., but ἐξομολ. τὰς ἁμαρτίας is used
in James v. 16 as well as by Mt., Mc.
in this place ; see also Barnabas (19),
Clement of Rome (1 Cor. 51), Ps.
Clement (2 Cor. 8), Tert. pat. 15,
paen. 10, 12.

6. ἦν...ἐνδεδυμένος κτλ.] Elijah had
worn a sheepskin mantle (μηλωτή,
3 Regn. xix. 19; cf. Heb. xi. 37, Clem.
R. 1 Cor. 17) and a leathern girdle
(4 Regn. i. 8 ζώνην δερματίνην περιεζω-
σμένος τὴν ὀσφὺν αὐτοῦ); and a similar
costume had become the traditional
dress of the prophet (Zech. xiii. 4

ἐνδύσονται δέρριν τριχίνην; cf. Mt. vii.
15). Δέρριν has been transferred from
Zech. l.c. into some representatives of
the 'Western' text of Mc.; see vv. ll.
But John's ἔνδυμα ἀπὸ τριχῶν καμήλου
(Just. dial. 88) was probably not a
camel's skin, but an ordinary garment
of sackcloth (σάκκος τρίχινος, Apoc. vi.
12) woven from the rough hair of the
animal ; J. Lightfoot ad loc. points
out that the Talmud speaks of such
a garment (בגד מצמר גמלים). Cf.
Victor : σαφέστερον ὁ Ματθαῖός φησιν
ὡς τὸ ἔνδυμα αὐτοῦ ἦν ἀπὸ τριχῶν
καμήλου· Euth. : τρίχας οὐχὶ ἀκατερ-
γάστους ἀλλ' ὑφηφασμένας, and see
Joseph. ant. xvi. 4, B. J. i. 17. Hieron.
op. imp.: "non de lana cameli habuit
vestimentum...sed de asperioribus
setis." The crowd did not go out to
see ἄνθρωπον ἐν μαλακοῖς ἠμφιεσμένον
(Mt. xi. 8), but one who inherited the
poverty as well as the power of Elijah.
Jerome claims the Baptist as the
head of the monastic order: "mona-
chorum princeps Johannes Baptista
est." With the constr. ἐνδεδ. τρίχας
cf. Apoc. i. 13, xix. 14.

καὶ ἔσθων] Mt. ἡ δὲ τροφὴ ἦν αὐτοῦ.
It was "wilderness food" (Gould). Certain locusts were accounted 'clean':
Lev. xi. 22, 23, ταῦτα φάγεσθε ἀπὸ
τῶν ἑρπετῶν...τὴν ἀκρίδα (חָגָב) καὶ τὰ
ὅμοια αὐτῇ. "The Gemarists feign
that there are 800 kinds...of such
as are clean" (J. Lightfoot ad loc.):
Hieron. adv. Jovin. ii. 6, "apud orien-
tales...locustis vesci moris est." It
was perhaps in ignorance of this fact,
perhaps from encratite tendencies,
that some ancient commentators
understood by ἀκρίς in this place a

7 μέλι ἄγριον. ⁷καὶ ἐκήρυσσεν λέγων Ἔρχεται ὁ
¶ q ἰσχυρότερός μου ὀπίσω μου, οὗ οὐκ εἰμὶ ἱκανὸς¶
κύψας λῦσαι τὸν ἱμάντα τῶν ὑποδημάτων αὐτοῦ.

7—8 και ελεγεν αυτοις εγω μεν υμ. βαπτ. εν υδ. ερχ. δε οπ. μου ο ισχυροτ. μου ου
ουκ ειμι ικ. λυσαι τ. ιμ. των υποδ. αυτου και αυτος υμ. βαπτιζει εν πν. αγ. D (a) (ff).

7 εκηρυσσεν] εκεκραγεν Γ | ισχυρος A min¹ | om μου 2° B Or¹ | om οπισω μου Δ
min¹ ff t | om κυψας D 28 256 1071 2ᵖᵉ a b c f g Amb

kind of vegetable food (cf. Euth.); see
J. R. Harris, *Fragments of Ephrem*,
p. 17 f. As to the wild honey of
Palestine (ἄγριον, Vg. *silvestre*, Wycliffe, "hony of the wode"), cf. 4 Regn.
iv. 39, Ps. lxxix. (lxxx.) 14, and see
Exod. iii. 8, Deut. xxxii. 13, Judg.
xiv. 8, 1 Sam. xiv. 25; also Joseph.
B. J. iv. 8. 3, where it is named among
the products of the plain of Jericho.
The Sinaitic (Mt.) and Jerusalem
Syriac versions render μέλι ἄγριον
'mountain honey' (cf. Lc. xii. 28 in
Syrr.ˢⁱⁿ·ᶜᵘ·); the Ebionite Gospel had
the curious gloss (from Exod. xvi. 31,
Num. xi. 8) οὗ ἡ γεῦσις ἦν τοῦ μάννα
ὡς ἐγκρὶς ἐν ἐλαίῳ: cf. Resch, *Paralleltexte zu Mt. u. Mc.*, p. 56. The
name μέλι ἄγριον (*mel silvestre*) was
also given by the ancients to a
vegetable product: Diod. Sic. xix. 94,
φύεται...ἀπὸ τῶν δένδρων καὶ μέλι πολὺ
τὸ καλούμενον ἄγριον: Plin. *H. N.* xix.
8, "est autem mel in arundinibus col-
lectum." But it is unnecessary in the
present case to go beyond the natural
meaning.
Ἔσθειν = ἐσθίειν, a Homeric form
which "occurs Mc.¹ and probably Mc.¹,
Lc.⁴, mostly in the participle"(WH.²,
Notes, p. 152 f., cf. WSchm., p. 127,
Blass, p. 54). In the LXX. the shorter
form of the participle is frequent in
cod. B.

7. καὶ ἐκήρυσσεν λέγων Ἔρχεται κτλ.]
A second stage in the Baptist's preaching—the heralding of the Christ. Lc.
(iii. 15) mentions that he was led to
it by the growing belief in his own
Messiahship. Ὁ ἰσχυρότερός μου: cf.

Lc. xi. 22. Mt. inverts the sentence (ὁ
δὲ ὀπ. μου ἐρχ. ἰσχυρότερος...); comp.
Jo. i. 15, where the ground of the
superiority is found in the preexistence
of Messiah (ὅτι πρῶτός μου ἦν). Οὗ...
αὐτοῦ : see WM., p. 184 f.
οὐκ εἰμὶ ἱκανός] Cf. Exod. iv. 10
(LXX.). Ἱκανός εἰμι in the N. T. is followed by an inf., as here (Burton,
§ 376), by ἵνα (Mt. viii. 8), or by πρός
τι (2 Cor. ii. 16). Jo. (i. 27) substitutes
ἄξιος for ἱκανός; see Origen *in Jo.*
t. vi. 36 (20).
κύψας λῦσαι τὸν ἱμάντα κτλ.] Κύψας
is a touch peculiar to Mc. and ex-
punged by D and some other Western
authorities. For λῦσαι...ὑπόδ. αὐτοῦ
(Mc. Lc.) Mt. substitutes τὰ ὑποδήματα
βαστάσαι, cf. Victor, and Origen (*in Jo.*
t. vi. 34), who suggests, ἀκόλουθόν γε
μηδενὸς σφαλλομένου τῶν εὐαγγελιστῶν
...ἀμφότερα κατὰ διαφόρους καιροὺς
εἰρηκέναι τὸν βαπτιστήν: similarly
Aug. *de cons.* ii. 30. Both were
servile acts connected with the use of
the bath, and possibly suggested by
the baptismal rite (Bengel : "ad bap-
tismum...calcei exuebantur"): see Ps.
lx. 10, and Lc. xv. 22, where the
slaves offer ὑποδήματα. Plautus *trin.*
ii. 1 speaks of slaves known as *sandali-
ferae*: and cf. Lucian *Herod.* 5, ὁ δέ
τις μάλα δουλικῶς ἀφαιρεῖ τὸ σανδάλιον.
For ἱμάς (*corrigia*) see Isa. v. 27 (LXX.)
οὐδὲ μὴ ῥαγῶσιν οἱ ἱμάντες τῶν ὑποδημάτων αὐτῶν. Victor : ἱμ. φησὶ τὸν
σφαιρωτῆρα (Gen. xiv. 23) τοῦ ὑπο-
δήματος. Euth. : τὸν ἐκ λώρου δεσμόν.
For λῦσαι in this connexion see Exod.
iii. 5 (LXX.) and Polyc. Mart. ἐπειρᾶτο

⁸ἐγὼ ἐβάπτισα ὑμᾶς ὕδατι, αὐτὸς δὲ βαπτίσει ὑμᾶς 8
πνεύματι ἁγίῳ.

⁹ Καὶ ἐγένετο ἐν ἐκείναις ταῖς ἡμέραις ἦλθεν 9
Ἰησοῦς ἀπὸ Ναζαρὲτ τῆς Γαλειλαίας καὶ ἐβαπτίσθη

8 εγω]+μεν ΑΔΡΓΔΠΣΦ al (om μεν אBLTᵈ 33 69 al² b c ff t vg Or¹) | υδατι] pr
εν ΑΔLPTᵈΓΠΣΦ (om εν אBHΔ 16 33 al pauc Or¹) | om υμας 2° א* (hab אᶜ·ᵃ) b |
τνευματι] pr εν אΑDHPTᵈΓΔΠΣΦ al a c f ff r me Or¹ (om εν BL b t vg) | αγιω]+και πυρι
PΦ al syrʰᶜˡ*   9 om και 1° B | om και εγενετο a | Ιησους] pr o DMΓΔΠΣΦ al | Ναζαρετ
אBLΓΔ 33 69ᶜᵒʳʳ a b d f Or] Ναζαρατ ΑΡΣ Ναζαρεθ DEFHKMUVΠΦ minᵐᵘ vg me go

καὶ ὑπολύειν ἑαυτόν, μὴ πρότερον τοῦτο
ποιῶν. Οὗ..αὐτοῦ, cf. vii. 25, and see
WM., p. 184 f.

8. ἐβάπτισα] Mt., Lc., βαπτίζω.
The aor. represents John's course as
already fulfilled in view of the coming
of Messiah : cf. the epistolary ἔγραψα
scripsi, and ἔπεμψα misi (WM., p.
347). Ὕδατι...πνεύματι 'with water,'
'with the Spirit,' dat. of manner or
instrument (WM., p. 271) : ἐν ὕδατι,
ἐν πν. are used (Mt. Lc. Jo. i. 33, 34,
Acts i. 5) in reference to the spheres,
material and spiritual, in which the
action is performed (WM., p. 483 ff.).
For the correlation of ὕδωρ and
πνεῦμα see also Jo. iii. 5, iv. 14, vii.
38, 39, Acts i. 5, Tit. iii. 5. Mt.,
Lc. add καὶ πυρί. The effusion of
the Spirit was a well-known characteristic of the Messianic age (see Isa. xliv.
3, Ezek. xxxvi. 25—27, Joel ii. 28), but
the phrase βαπτίζειν πνεύματι is new,
though Joel (LXX.) has ἐκχεῶ and Ezek.
ῥανῶ. Πν. ἅγιον is the Holy Spirit in
operation ; contrast τὸ πν. (i. 10, 12),
τὸ πν. τὸ ἅγ. (iii. 29), the Holy Spirit
regarded as a Divine Power.

9—11. The Baptism (Mt. iii. 13—
17, Lc. iii. 21—22 ; cf. Jo. i. 32—34).

9. καὶ ἐγένετο...ἦλθεν] A Hebra-
ism, וַיְהִי...; also καὶ ἐγ. (or ἐγ. δέ)...
καί : both constructions occur in the
LXX., e.g. Gen. iv. 3, 8, and the N. T.,
but Mc. has only the first. For καὶ
ἐγένετο followed by the inf. see Mc. ii.
23, and on the whole subject consult
WM., p. 760 n., Burton, § 357 f. Ἐν

ἐκείναις ταῖς ἡμέραις, another Hebraism = בַּיָּמִים הָהֵם. Cf. Exod. ii. 11,
Jud. xviii. 1, &c., and in the N. T. Mt.
iii. 1, Mc. viii. 1, xiii. 17, 24, Lc. ii. 1,
iv. 2, Acts ii. 18, vii. 41, &c. ; ἐν ἐκείνῃ
τῇ ἡμέρᾳ occurs in nearly the same sense
Lc. xvii. 31, Jo. xvi. 23, 26. As a
note of time the phrase is somewhat
indefinite, but like τότε (Mt. iii. 13) it
brings the narrative which follows into
general connexion with the preceding
context. Here e.g. it connects the
arrival of Jesus at the Jordan with
the stage in the Baptist's ministry described in. 7, 8. Euth.: ἡμέρας δὲ νῦν
φησιν ἐν αἷς ἐκήρυσσε...ὁ Ἰωάννης.

ἀπὸ Ναζαρὲτ τῆς Γαλειλαίας] Mt.,
ἀπὸ τῆς Γ. ; the exact locality had
been mentioned by him in ii. 23.
Mc.'s ἀρχή does not carry him behind
the Lord's residence at Nazareth ; to
the first generation Jesus was ὁ ἀπὸ N.
(Jo. i. 46, Acts x. 37), or ὁ Ναζαρηνός
(Mc. i. 24, xiv. 67, xvi. 6) or Ναζωραῖος
(Lc.¹ Jo.³ Acts³)—on the two forms
see Dalman Gr. d. Aram. p. 141 n.
Ναζαρέτ (-ρέθ, -ράθ, -ρά are also found,
but not in Mc., see WH., Notes, p. 160)
is unknown to the O. T. and to Josephus ; and its insignificance seems to
be implied by the explanatory notes
which accompany the first mention of
the place in Mt. ii. 23, Lc. ii. 39, and
here : perhaps also by the question of
Jo. i. 46. The onomastica revel in
etymologies, e.g. "N. flos aut virgultum
eius vel munditiae aut separata vel
custodita" ; the first was based on a

10 εἰς τὸν Ἰορδάνην ὑπὸ Ἰωάνου. ¹⁰καὶ εὐθὺς ἀναβαίνων ἐκ τοῦ ὕδατος εἶδεν σχιζομένους τοὺς οὐρανοὺς καὶ τὸ

9 εις τ. Ιορδ. υπο Ιωαν. ℵBDL 33 al] υπο Ιωαν. εις τ. Ιορδ. ΑΡΓΔΠΣΦ al^{pler} f syr^{hcl} arm go aeth | Ιορδ.]+ποταμον syr^{hier}   10 ευθεως ΑΡΓΠ om D a b t | εκ ℵBDLΔ 33 al go] απο ΑΡΓΔΠΣΦ al^{pler} | σχιζομενους] ηνυγμενους D latt (apertos, aperiri) syr^{hier} | το πνευμα]+του θεου arm

supposed reference to the נֵצֶר in Isa. xi. 1. Delitzsch (*Z. f. d. l. Th.*, 1876) proposed to connect the name with נָצְרַת, Aram. נַצְרַת (Dalman, p. 119, prefers נָצְרַת, Aram. נֵצְרָה, נָצְרַת), a watch-tower, in reference to its position on the flank of a hill commanding a wide prospect. On the situation see G. A. Smith's *H. G.*, p. 432 f. and Merrill, *Galilee*, p. 122. Τῆς Γαλειλαίας (Mt. xxi. 11, Lc. i. 26) is the topographical gen., cf. WM., p. 234. Ἡ γῆ ἡ Γαλειλαία, or simply ἡ Γ., occurs in the LXX. as far back as Jos. xx. 7, xxi. 32; cf. 3 Regn. ix. 11, 4 Regn. xv. 29, 1 Par. vi. 76 (61), Isa. ix. 1 (viii. 23), and answers to גְּלִילָה, גָּלִיל, a roll, or ring, hence a circuit of country: see G. A. Smith, *H. G.*, p. 413 ff., cf. Joseph. *B. J.* iii. 3. 1. From Nazareth the journey to the place of the Baptism would lie along the Esdraelon as far as Bethshan, and then down the valley of the Jordan. On the locality of the Baptism see G. A. Smith, *H. G.*, p. 496.

καὶ ἐβαπτίσθη...ὑπὸ Ἰ.] Mt. adds that the journey was taken for this purpose (τοῦ βαπτισθῆναι). Εἰς τὸν Ἰορδάνην (WM., p. 517 f.)=ἐν τῷ Ἰορδάνῃ (i. 5), but with the added thought of the immersion, which gives vividness to the scene. In every other instance βαπτίζειν εἰς is followed by the acc. of the purpose (εἰς μετάνοιαν, εἰς ἄφεσιν) or of the object to which the baptized are united (εἰς Χριστὸν Ἰησοῦν, εἰς τὸν Μωυσῆ, εἰς τὸν θάνατον). Ὑπὸ Ἰωάνου (cf. i. 5, note), as the rest—μετὰ τῶν δούλων ὁ δεσπότης (Euth. Zig.).

10. καὶ εὐθύς κτλ.] Εὐθύς (Wy-

cliffe, *anoon*) is characteristic of Mc. —"ein Lieblingswort des Marcus,' Schanz—occurring Mc.⁴¹ Mt.¹⁹ Lc.⁷; Mt. shews a similar partiality for τότε. In the LXX. (Gen. xv. 4, xxxviii. 29) καὶ εὐθύς=וְהִנֵּה=καὶ ἰδού, a phrase which, though common in the other Gospels, is not used by Mc. Of the forms εὐθύς, εὐθέως the first only occurs in Mc.; the second predominates in the rest of the N. T. (³²⁄₁₂).

ἀναβαίνων ἐκ τοῦ ὕδατος] Out of the river into which He had descended: cf. Jos. iv. 18, ἐξέβησαν οἱ ἱερεῖς...ἐκ τοῦ Ἰορδάνου, Jer. xxix. 20 (xlix. 19), ὥσπερ λέων ἀναβήσεται ἐκ μέσου τοῦ Ἰορδάνου. Mt.'s ἀπὸ τοῦ ὕδατος is less graphic, giving merely the point of departure: cf. Acts xxv. 1, Apoc. vii. 2. Lc. adds προσευχόμενος, cf. Mc. i. 25, vi. 46, Lc. ix. 28.

εἶδεν σχιζομένους τοὺς οὐρανούς] The subject is Ἰησοῦς (v. 9). Some interpreters, influenced by Jo. i. 32 ff., have regarded ἀναβαίνων as a *nom. pendens*, and understood ὁ Ἰωάνης after εἶδεν: cf. Tindale, "John saw heavens open" (so even in Mt.). It was permitted to the Baptist to share the vision as a witness (Jo. *l.c.* ἑώρακα καὶ μεμαρτύρηκα), but the vision was primarily for the Christ.

σχιζομένους] Vg. *apertos*, with the 'Western' text, from Mt. (ἠνεώχθησαν οἱ οὐρανοί, cf. Lc.); in the true text of Mc. both the word and the tense are more graphic—'He saw the heaven in the act of being riven asunder.' Bengel: "dicitur de eo quod antea non fuerat apertum." Σχίζειν is used of a garment (Isa. xxxvi. 22, Jo. xix. 24), a veil (Lc. xxiii. 45), a net (Jo. xxi. 11), rocks (Zech. xiv. 4, Isa.

πνεῦμα ὡς περιστερὰν καταβαῖνον εἰς αὐτόν.   ¹¹καὶ 11

10 ως] ωσει ΜΡΣΦ al | καταβαινον]+και μενον ℵΔ^(forte spat vac) 33 262 al b ff t vg me aeth | εις BD 13 69 al^pauc a g] επ ℵALΡΓΔΠΣΦ al^pler

xlviii. 21, Mt. xxvii. 51), and wood (Gen. xxii. 3): *scindere caelum* occurs in Silius Italicus i. 535 f. Ἀνοίγειν is the usual word in this connexion (Gen. vii. 11, Ps. lxxvii. (lxxviii.) 23, Isa. xxiv. 18, lxiv. 1, Acts vii. 56, Apoc. iv. 1, xix. 11): cf. esp. Ezek. i. 1, ἠνοίχθησαν οἱ οὐρανοὶ καὶ εἶδον ὁράσεις θεοῦ. Orig. *in Jo. fragm.* (Brooke, ii. 238), ἄνοιξιν δὲ ἢ σχίσιν οὐρανῶν αἰσθητικῶς οὐκ ἔστιν ἰδεῖν, ὁπότε οὐδὲ τῶν παχυτέρων σωμάτων. Jerome in Matt. *l.c.* "aperiuntur autem caeli non reseratione elementorum, sed spiritualibus oculis." This vision of the rending heavens seems to have symbolised the outcome of Christ's mission: cf. Jo. i. 51.

καὶ τὸ πνεῦμα] Mt. πνεῦμα θεοῦ (cf. Gen. i. 2), Lc. τὸ πν. τὸ ἅγιον. The art. either looks back to i. 8, 'the (Holy) Spirit already mentioned,' or more probably indicates the Person of the Spirit, as in Jo. i. 32, 33, Acts x. 19, xi. 12, &c.

ὡς περιστεράν] Mt. ὡσεὶ π., Lc. σωματικῷ εἴδει ὡς π. Jerome: "non veritas sed similitudo monstratur." The Ebionite Gospel paraphrased: ἐν εἴδει περιστερᾶς κατελθούσης καὶ εἰσελθούσης εἰς αὐτόν. Cf. Justin *dial.* 88, ὡς περιστερὰν τὸ ἅγιον πνεῦμα ἐπιπτῆναι ἐπ᾽ αὐτὸν ἔγραψαν οἱ ἀπόστολοι, and see other references in Resch, *Parallceltexte zu Luc.*, p. 15 f. The vision corresponds to that of Gen. i. 2, where מְרַחֶפֶת suggests the motion of a bird; cf. *Chagigah* (ed. Streane) 15 A. The dove is a familiar image in Hebr. poetry; see esp. Ps. lxviii. 13 (Cheyne), Cant. ii. 12 ; F. C. Conybeare (*Exp.* IV. ix. 436) produces illustrations from Philo, e.g. *quis rer.*

div. her. 25, ἡ θεία σοφία...συμβολικῶς ...τρυγὼν καλεῖται: ib. 48, περιστερᾷ μὲν ὁ ἡμέτερος νοῦς...εἰκάζεται, τῷ δὲ τούτου παραδείγματι (i.e. the Divine λόγος) ἡ τρυγών. In the *Protev.*, c. 9, Joseph is said to have been marked by a like phenomenon : ἰδοὺ περιστερὰ...ἐξῆλθεν ἐπὶ τὴν κεφαλὴν Ἰωσήφ. On the significance of the symbol, cf. Mt. x. 16, Tert. *bapt.* 8, and the Greek commentators *ad l.*, e.g. Victor: ἐν εἴδει περιστερᾶς...τὸ πνεῦμα ἔρχεται τὸν ἔλεον τοῦ θεοῦ καταγγέλλον τῇ οἰκουμένῃ, ἅμα καὶ δηλοῦν ὅτι τὸν πνευματικὸν ἀπόνηρον εἶναι χρὴ καὶ πρᾷον, ἁπλοῦν τε καὶ ἄδολον.

καταβαῖνον εἰς αὐτόν] The κατάβασις answers to the ἀνάβασις of i. 10; cf. the play upon these compounds in Jo. iii. 13, Eph. iv. 9, 10. For εἰς αὐτόν, Mt., Lc. prefer ἐπ᾽ αὐτόν : only Jo. (i. 33) has καὶ ἔμενεν ἐπ᾽ αὐτόν (cf. Isa. xi. 2; see vv. ll. here). The immanence of the Spirit in Jesus was at once the purpose of the Descent and the evidence of His being the Christ; see note on next verse.

11. καὶ φωνή κτλ.] Victor: ἡ ἀγγελική τις ἦν ἢ καὶ ἑτέρα ἐκ προσώπου τοῦ πατρός. For exx. of such voices in the O. T. see Gen. xxi. 17, xxii. 11, 15, Exod. xix. 19, xx. 22, 1 Kings xix. 12, 13. In the Gospels the Father's Voice is heard thrice, at the Baptism and Transfiguration (cf. 2 Pet. i. 17) and before the Passion (Jo. xii. 28). The Voice was audible or articulate only to those who had 'ears to hear' (Jo. v. 37, xii. 29): comp. the scoff of the Jew in Orig. *c. Cels.* i. 41, τίς ἤκουσεν ἐξ οὐρανοῦ φωνῆς ; On its relation to the בַּת קוֹל see Edersheim, *Life and Times*, i. p. 285.

§ ז
¶ P
¶ syr[hier]
§ W°
§ syr[sin]

φωνὴ ἐγένετο ἐκ τῶν οὐρανῶν Cὺ εἶ ὁ υἱός μου, ὁ ἀγαπητός· §ἐν σοὶ¶ εὐδόκησα.¶

12 §12 Καὶ εὐθὺς § τὸ πνεῦμα αὐτὸν ἐκβάλλει εἰς τὴν

11 εγενετο ℵ[c.a]ABLP al[pler] lat[vet pler vg] syrr arm me] om ℵ*D ff g t ηκουσθη 28 2[pe] | ουρανων]+λεγων syr[hier]+και λεγει arm | σοι ℵBDLPΔΣז 1 13 22 33 69 604 2[pe] al a t vg me al] ω ΑΓΠΦ al b d g | ηυδοκησα D[corr] EFHVΓΔ al 12 το πνευμα]+το αγιον D

σὺ εἶ ὁ υἱός μου, ὁ ἀγαπητός] So Lc., after Ps. ii. 7; Mt., οὗτός ἐστιν κτλ. The words point to Gen. xxii. 2 and perhaps also to Isa. xlii. 1 (cf. Mt. xii. 18). Ἀγαπητός in the LXX. answers to יָחִיד (μονογενής, *unicus*, cf. Hort, *Two Diss.* p. 49 f.) in seven instances out of fifteen; in the N. T., where the word is much more frequent, it is exclusively a title of Christ, or applied to Christians as such. As a Messianic title (cf. Mc. ix. 7, xii. 6, 2 Pet. i. 17, Eph. i. 6 (ὁ ἠγαπημένος), Col. i. 13 (ὁ υἱὸς τῆς ἀγάπης αὐτοῦ), where however see Lightfoot), it indicates a unique relation to God; thus in Rom. viii. 31 τοῦ ἰδίου υἱοῦ is substituted for τοῦ ἀγαπητοῦ υἱ. of Gen. xxii. 16. The title is frequent as a name of Messiah in the *Ascension of Isaiah* (ed. Charles, p. 3 &c.; see also Hastings, *D. B.* ii. 501; cf. *Test. XII. patr.* Benj. 11, ἀναστήσεται... ἀγαπητὸς Κυρίου) and is used in the Targum of Jonathan on Isa. xlii. 1.

ἐν σοὶ εὐδόκησα] Latt., *in te complacui.* Mt., ἐν ᾧ εὐδ. Εὐδοκεῖν ἐν= חָפֵץ בְּ 2 Regn. xxii. 20, Mal. ii. 17, or רָצָה בְּ Ps. xliii. (xliv.) 4, cxlvi. (cxlvii.) 11. The reference is probably to Isa. xlii. 1 רָצְתָה נַפְשִׁי (LXX. προσεδέξατο, Th. ηὐδόκησεν); the exact phrase occurs in Isa. lxii. 4. In Lc. an early Western reading substitutes ἐγὼ σήμερον γεγέννηκά σε (from Ps. ii. 7), cf. Just. *dial.* 103; in the *G. acc. to the Hebrews* the two sayings seem to have been combined (Epiph. *haer.* xxx. 13). Acc. to Jerome (on Isa. xi. 2) the Nazarene Gospel had the interesting gloss, "Fili mi, in omnibus prophetis expectabam te ut venires et requiescerem in te; tu es enim requies mea."

The aor. εὐδόκησα does not denote merely "the historical process by which God came to take pleasure in Jesus during his earthly life" (Gould), but rather the satisfaction of the Father in the Son during the preexistent life; cf. Jo. i. 2, xvii. 24. Thus it corresponds to the perf. רָצְתָה of Isa. xlii. 1; cf. Driver, *Tenses in Hebr.* § 9, Burton, § 55.

Theodore of Mopsuestia, in the interests of his Christology, held that the εὐδοκία arose from the foreseen perfection of the Man with whom the Word united Himself (*Minor Epp.* ii. p. 294 ff.). According to his view the Son in whom God took pleasure was not the Word, but the ἀναληφθεὶς ἄνθρωπος (ib. i. 63, 260; Migne, *P. G.* lxvi. 705—6).

12—13. The Temptation (Mt. iv. 1—11, Lc. iv. 1—13).

12. *καὶ εὐθὺς τὸ πνεῦμα κτλ.*] For καὶ εὐθύς see i. 10 n. Ἐκβάλλει, Vg. *expellit*; other Latin texts (a, f) have *duxit*, *eduxit*: Wycliffe, "puttide hym (forth)." Mt. has simply ἀνήχθη... ὑπὸ τοῦ πνεύματος, Lc. ἤγετο ἐν τῷ πνεύματι. Ἐκβάλλειν is used for the power exercised by Christ over the δαιμόνια (e.g. i. 34). But *expellit* and "driveth" (A.V.) or "driveth forth" (R.V.) are perhaps too strong in this context, cf. Mt. ix. 38, Mc. i. 43, Jo. x. 4; ἐκβάλλειν=הוֹצִיא in 2 Chron. xxiii. 14, xxix. 5 (see Guillemard, *G. T., Hebraistic ed.* p. 20). At the most the word denotes here only a pressure upon the spirit (Victor: ἕλκει), not an irresistible

ἔρημον. ¹³ καὶ ἦν ἐν τῇ ἐρήμῳ τεσσεράκοντα ἡμέρας 13
πειραζόμενος ὑπὸ τοῦ σατανᾶ, καὶ ἦν μετὰ τῶν
θηρίων· §καὶ οἱ ἄγγελοι διηκόνουν αὐτῷ. §G

13 εν τη ερ.] pr εκει ΕΓΗΜΓΔΠ^corr ΦΣΤ al^pl syrr arm go aeth εκει sine εν τ. ε. ΚΠ*
1 28* 69 124 131 209 604 2^pe al syr^sin arm | ημερας]+και τεσσαρακοντα νυκτας (vel
κ. ν. τ.) LM 13 33 al vg syr^helmg me aeth | πειραξομενος] pr και D | οι αγγελοι] om
οι ΑΜ⁷ 33 al

power. Mt. adds the purpose (πει-
ρασθῆναι ὑπὸ τοῦ διαβόλου). Cf. Hilary
in Matt., "significatur libertas Spiritus
sancti, hominem suum iam diabolo
offerentis"; Jerome *in Matt. l.c.*, "du-
citur autem non invitus aut captus,
sed voluntate pugnandi."
εἰς τὴν ἔρημον] To be distinguished
apparently from the ἔρημος of i. 4.
Christian tradition from the time of
the Crusades points to the Quaran-
tania *(Jebel Kuruntul)*, a rugged limestone height which rises 1000 feet a-
bove the plain of Jericho (cf. Josh.
xvi. 1); the Arabs on the other hand
select the conical hill '*Osh el Ghu-
râb.* The Gospels give no indication
beyond the fact that the Lord went
to the place from the Jordan.
13. τεσσεράκοντα ἡμέρας...σατανᾶ]
The same limit of time occurs in the
lives of Moses and Elijah (Exod. xxxiv.
28, 1 Kings xix. 8), and again in the
life of Christ (Acts i. 3); for other
exx. of the number in Scripture see
Trench, *Studies in the Gospels*, p. 13 ff.
Mc., Lc. make the Temptation coextensive with the 40 days; Mt. seems
to connect the limit of time with the
fasting, and to place the Temptation
at the end of the days. Comp. in
support of the Marcan tradition Clem.
hom. xi. 35, xix. 2; Orig. *hom. in
Luc.* 29. Πειράζειν in the LXX. is used
of man tempting GOD, and of GOD
tempting man, but not of Satanic
suggestions: in 1 Chron. xxi. 1 we
have ἐπέσεισεν in this connexion: in
1 Macc. i. 15 ἐπειράθησαν (א^c.a?) approaches to the latter sense, but the

reading is more than doubtful. In
the N. T. this meaning is common
(cf., besides the present context and
its parallels, 1 Cor. vii. 5, Gal. vi. 1,
Heb. ii. 18, Apoc. ii. 10, iii. 10); in
Mt. iv. 3, perhaps also in 1 Thess. iii.
5, ὁ πειράζων=ὁ σατανᾶς. See Mayor
on James i. 13.
ὑπὸ τοῦ σατανᾶ] Mt., Lc., ὑπὸ τοῦ
διαβόλου. The LXX. translate הַשָּׂטָן by
ὁ διάβολος in Job i., ii., and Zech. iii.;
σατάν is used in the sense of an adversary in 3 Regn. xi. 14, 23, ὁ σατανᾶς
appears first in Sir. xxi. 27 (30). In
the N. T. ὁ σατανᾶς or Σατανᾶς (Mc. iii.
23, Lc. xxii. 3) is invariably the Adversary κατ᾽ ἐξοχήν, and the name
is freely used by the Synoptists and
St Paul, and in the Apocalypse. On
the history of the Jewish belief in
Satan see Cheyne, *Origin of the Psalter*, p. 282 f., Schultz, *O. T. Theology*,
ii. p. 274 ff., Edersheim, *Life &c.* ii.
p. 755 ff., Charles, *Enoch*, pp. 52 ff.,
119, Weber, *Jüd. Theologie*, ed. 2,
p. 251 f.
ἦν μετὰ τῶν θηρίων] Comp. 2 Macc.
v. 27, Ἰούδας...ἀναχωρήσας ἐν τοῖς ὄρεσιν (i.e. probably the wilderness of
Judaea), θηρίων τρόπον διέζη. In Ps.
xc. (xci.) 13 the promise of victory over
the θηρία follows immediately after
that of angelic guardianship, cited by
the Tempter in Mt. iv. 6. But this
peculiarly Marcan touch may be simply
meant to accentuate the loneliness of
the place; cf. Victor: οὕτως ἄβατος ἦν
ἡ ἔρημος ὡς καὶ θηρίων πλήρης ὑπάρχειν:
it was not such an ἔρημος as John
tenanted, but a haunt of the hyaena,

14   ¹⁴Καὶ μετὰ τὸ παραδοθῆναι τὸν Ἰωάνην ἦλθεν ὁ
Ἰησοῦς εἰς τὴν Γαλειλαίαν κηρύσσων τὸ εὐαγγέλιον

14 και μετα BD a (c) syr^sin] μετα δε ℵALΓΔΠΣΦ⁷ al latt^vt mu vg syrr^pesh hel go
aeth | τον Ιωαν.] om τον AEFG*H al | ο Ιησους] om ο AV^corrΓΠ⁷ al | κηρυσσων] pr
διδασκων και L

jackal, and leopard (cf. Tristram,
Land of Israel, p. 240; G. A. Smith,
H. G., p. 316 f.). The mystical refer-
ence to the Second Adam (Gen. ii. 19),
which some have imagined, seems, as
Meyer has well said, out of place in
this narrative; see, however, Trench,
Studies, p. 9 f.

καὶ οἱ ἄγγελοι διηκόνουν αὐτῷ] Apparently during the forty days, the
imperf. corresponding with ἦν...πειρα-
ζόμενος...ἦν. Mt. seems to limit this
ministry to the end (τότε προσῆλθον).
Comp. Gen. xxviii. 12, Jo. i. 51, Heb.
i. 14; esp. the hymn in 1 Tim. iii. 16,
ἐδικαιώθη ἐν πνεύματι, ὤφθη ἀγγέλοις.
The διακονία may refer to the supply
of physical (1 Kings xix. 5 ff.) or
spiritual (Dan. x. 19 ff.) needs. Such
a ministration, while it attests the
human weakness of the Lord, bears
witness also to His Sonship; cf. Clem.
Al. *exc. Theod.* § 85 ὡς ἂν ἤδη βασιλεὺς
ἀληθὴς ὑπ' ἀγγέλων ἤδη διακονεῖται.

14—15.   FIRST PREACHING IN
GALILEE (Mt. iv. 12—17, Lc. iv.
14—15).

14.   μετὰ τὸ παραδοθῆναι τὸν Ἰωά-
νην] A definite *terminus a quo* for
all that follows: cf. Mt., ἀκούσας δὲ ὅτι
Ἰωάνης παρεδόθη. Παραδίδωμι (in the
LXX. generally the equivalent of נתן)
acquires its special meaning from the
context; the most usual complement is
εἰς (τὰς) χεῖρας (τῶν) ἐχθρῶν or the like,
but we find also π. εἰς θάνατον 2 Chr.
xxxii. 11, εἰς προνομήν (Isa. xxxiii. 23),
εἰς σφαγήν (xxxiv. 2). Here we may
supply εἰς φυλακήν, as in Acts viii. 3,
xxii. 4; cf. Lc. iii. 20, Jo. iii. 24. The
events of Jo. ii. iii. must be placed
before the commencement of the Synoptic Ministry. If Mark is silent as
to the previous work in Galilee and

Judaea, he does not "exclude it"
(Gould); it lies outside his subject
—perhaps outside his information.
From Mc.'s point of view the Lord's
Ministry begins where the Baptist's
ends : "Ioanne tradito, recte ipse
incipit praedicare; desinente lege,
consequenter oritur evangelium" (Jerome).

ἦλθεν] Mt., ἀνεχώρησεν. This journey to Galilee was in fact a withdrawal
from Judaea, where the tidings of
John's imprisonment (Mt.), and still
more the growing jealousy of the
Pharisees towards the new Teacher
(Jo. iv. 1), rendered a longer stay
dangerous or unprofitable. Though
Galilee was under the jurisdiction of
Antipas, His mission there would not
expose Him at first to the tetrarch's
interference (cf. Mc. vi. 14, Lc. xiii.
31 f., xxiii. 8). It was Jerusalem, not
Galilee, that shed the blood of the
prophets; in any case it was clear that
Jerusalem would not tolerate His
teaching; Galilee offered a better
field (cf. Jo. iv. 45). The Greek commentators think of the move only as
an escape from peril (Theod. Heracl.,
ἵνα ἡμᾶς διδάξῃ μὴ ἀποπηδᾶν τοῖς κινδύνοις : Victor, διετήρει ἑαυτόν); but the
other motive should be kept in view.

εἰς τὴν Γαλειλαίαν] Jo. adds πάλιν,
and states the route (iv. 4 διὰ τῆς
Σαμαρίας). Cana was visited on the
way to Capernaum (Jo. iv. 46).

κηρύσσων τὸ εὐαγγέλιον τοῦ θεοῦ]
Contrast i. 4 κηρύσσων βάπτισμα
μετανοίας. Both proclamations urged
repentance, and both told of good
tidings; but μετάνοια predominated in
the one, εὐαγγέλιον in the other. The
preaching of Jesus began, as a regular
mission, with the silencing of John:

τοῦ θεοῦ ¹⁵καὶ λέγων ὅτι Πεπλήρωται ὁ καιρός, 15
καὶ ἤγγικεν ἡ βασιλεία τοῦ θεοῦ· μετανοεῖτε, καὶ
πιστεύετε ἐν τῷ εὐαγγελίῳ.

14 του θεου] pr της βασιλειας ΑΔΓΔΠΣΦ⸆ al a f g vg syrᵖᵉˢʰ go aeth 15 και
λεγων ΒΚΛΜΔΠΦ alᵖˡᵉʳ a b vg syrrᵖᵉˢʰ ʰᵉˡ me] om και ℵᵃΑDEFGHSUΣ⸆ 1071 al
f ff g t go om και λεγ. ℵ* c syrˢⁱⁿ Or | πεπληρωνται οι καιροι D a b c ff g r t | om εν
36ᵉᵛ 481 b f vg Or

cf. Mt. iv. 17, ἀπὸ τότε ἤρξατο. He
took up the Baptist's note, but added
another. Τὸ εὐαγγέλιον τοῦ θεοῦ (εὐ.
θεοῦ) is a Pauline phrase (Rom. i. 1,
xv. 16, 2 Cor. xi. 7, 1 Thess. ii. 8, 9),
used however also by St Peter (1 Pet.
iv. 17). The gen. probably denotes
the source : the Gospel which comes
from GOD, of which GOD (the Father)
is the Author and Sender ; cf. v. 1 ;
see, however, the more inclusive view
advocated by SH. (on Rom. i. 1). The
insertion of τῆς βασιλείας (vv. ll.) is
due to a desire to explain an unusual
phrase : see next verse.

15. ὅτι Πεπλήρωται ὁ καιρός κτλ.]
The substance of the new proclamation. "Οτι is here 'recitative' (WM.,
p. 683 n.), as in i. 37, 40, ii. 12, and
frequently in Mc. For πληροῦσθαι
used of time, cf. Gen. xxix. 21, πεπλή-
ρωνται (מָלְאוּ?) αἱ ἡμέραι—a phrase frequently occurring in the LXX.; and
for its connexion with καιρός see Tob.
xiv. 5 (B), Esth. ii. 12 (A). Καιρός
(usually = עֵת or מוֹעֵד) is the 'season,'
the 'opportune moment' (see esp. Eccl.
iii. 1—8), with an ethical outlook,
χρόνος being merely the time, considered as a date : see Trench, syn.
§ vii. and cf. Lightfoot on 1 Thess. v. 1.
Thus St Paul speaks of the πλήρωμα
τοῦ χρόνου (Gal. iv. 4), when he has in
view the place of the Incarnation in
the order of events, but of the πλήρ.
τῶν καιρῶν (Eph. i. 10), when he thinks
of the Divine οἰκονομία. Here the
thought is that of the opportuneness
of the moment. The season fixed in
the foreknowledge of GOD (Acts i. 7),

and for which the whole moral guidance of the world had prepared, was
fully come. It is not so much in
regard to Galilee that the words are
spoken as in reference to the world
and humanity considered as a whole.
See Lux Mundi, Essay iv.

καὶ ἤγγικεν ἡ βασιλεία τοῦ θεοῦ]
Acc. to Mt. (iii. 2) this announcement
had been anticipated by John. Mt.
has usually ἡ βασ. τῶν οὐρανῶν (τοῦ θ.
only in vi. 33, xii. 28, xix. 24, xxi. 31,
43), but the two expressions are nearly
equivalent (see Schürer II. ii. 171,
Bevan on Dan. iv. 26, Stanton, J. and
Chr. Messiah, p. 208 f.). The term
possibly originated in the language of
Daniel—see esp. ii. 24, vii. 22 (Nestle,
Marginal., p. 41), and cf. Stanton, p.
211—and there are parallels in pre-
Christian literature, e.g. Ps. Solom.
xvii. 23, ἀναστήσει αὐτοῖς τὸν βασιλέα
αὐτῶν...εἰς τὸν καιρὸν ὃν ἴδες. On the
Rabbinical use of the term see Stanton, p. 214 f. A yearning for a Divine Kingdom pervades the history
of Israel, and the new preaching in
announcing its realisation probably
found the phrase ready. For a fresh
and invigorating if incomplete view of
the subject see Ecce Homo cc. iii., iv.
Ἤγγικεν, appropinquavit, 'hath drawn
near,' is nigh; cf. Isa. lvi. 1, Thren. iv.
19, Ezek. vii. 7, &c. (קָרַב or קָרוֹב);
Mc. xiv. 42, Lc. x. 9, 11, 1 Pet. iv. 7.

μετανοεῖτε, καὶ πιστεύετε κτλ.] See
on v. 14. For the connexion of
μετάνοια and πίστις cf. Acts xx. 21,
Heb. vi. 1. Πιστεύειν ἐν (בְּ הֶאֱמִין)
occurs in Ps. lxxvii. (lxxviii.) 22, cv.

16   ¹⁶Καὶ παράγων παρὰ τὴν θάλασσαν τῆς Γαλειλαίας εἶδεν Σίμωνα καὶ Ἀνδρέαν τὸν ἀδελφὸν Σίμωνος
ἀμφιβάλλοντας ἐν τῇ θαλάσσῃ, ἦσαν γὰρ ἁλεεῖς.

16 και παραγων אBDL 13 33 69 604 al latt syr^{sin pesh} arm me] περιπατων δε
ΑΓΔΠΣΦ al^{pl} syr^{hcl (txt)} | Σιμωνος אBLMΦ min^{pauc} a arm me] του Σ. AE^{corr}Δ 1 69 al^{nonn}
αυτου του Σ. E*FHKSUVΠΣΦ⁷ al^{mu} syr^{hcl} go αυτου DGΓ 33 al latt^{vt pl vg} syrr aeth |
αμφιβαλλοντας אABDE* al] βαλλοντας E^{corr}MΓΠ^{corr} al+αμφιβλησTρον ΑΓΔΠΣΦ⁷
2^{pe mg} al b ff+αμφιβλησTρα 1 al+Tα δικτυα D 13 28 69 134 346 2^{pe txt} a c f g
vg | αλιεις אB^{corr}(D)ΓΠ al

(cvi.) 12 (cf. 24), Jer. xii. 6, and elsewhere, frequently however with a v. l.
which omits ἐν. In the N. T. the
construction is perhaps unique (see
Westcott on Jo. iii. 15, and Ellicott
on Eph. i. 13—on its occurrence in
Ign. *Philad.* 8, cf. Lightfoot *ad l.*); nor
do we elsewhere hear of believing the
Gospel (see however 'Mc.' xvi. 15,
16); faith is regarded as primarily
due to the Person of whom the Gospel
speaks (cf. e.g. Jo. xiv. 1). Yet faith
in the message was the first step; a
creed of some kind lies at the basis
of confidence in the Person of Christ,
and the occurrence of the phrase π.
ἐν τῷ εὐαγγελίῳ in the oldest record of
the teaching of our Lord is a valuable
witness to this fact. Τὸ εὐαγγέλιον is
the nucleus of Christian teaching
already imparted in the announcement ἤγγικεν, κτλ. For other meanings see note on i. 1.

16—20. CALL OF THE FIRST FOUR
DISCIPLES (Mt. iv. 18—22; cf. Lc. v.
1 ff.).

16. καὶ παράγων παρὰ τὴν θάλασσαν
κτλ.] Mt. περιπατῶν δέ; see vv. ll.
here. Παράγων intrans. (=עָבַר) occurs in the LXX. (Ps. cxxviii. (cxxix.)
8, cxliii. (cxliv.) 4) and N. T. (Mt.
Mc. Jo. Paul), but the construction
with παρά seems to stand alone; see
however 3 Macc. vi. 16, κατὰ τὸν ἱππό-
δρομον παρῆγεν. Mt. and Mc. carry
the reader at once to the lake-side;
Lc. prefaces the preaching at Caper-

naum with the synagogue-scene at
Nazareth: see Mc. vi. 1, note.

τὴν θάλασσαν τῆς Γ.] So Mt., Mc., or
more usually 'the Sea.' Jo. adds (vi. 1)
or substitutes (xxi. 1) τῆς Τιβεριάδος.
Lc. prefers λίμνη to θάλασσα, and in
v. 1 calls it ἡ λ. Γεννησαρέτ, apparently
from the district known as Γεννησαρέτ
on its western shore (Mc. vi. 53): cf.
Joseph. *B.J.* iii. 10. 7, ἡ λ. Γεννησάρ, 1
Macc. xi. 67, τὸ ὕδωρ τοῦ Γ. The O. T.
name is יָם כִּנֶּרֶת, θάλασσα Χενάρα
(Χενέρεθ, Χενερώθ), Num. xxxiv. 11,
Jos. xiii. 27. On the topography of
the Lake see G. A. Smith, *H. G.*
c. xxi.

εἶδεν Σίμωνα καὶ Ἀνδρέαν] Σίμων is
a Hellenized form of Συμεών (=שִׁמְעוֹן,
Gen. xxix. 33, cf. Apoc. vii. 7); both
forms are used in reference to Simon
Maccabaeus, 1 Macc. ii. 3, 66, to whose
reputation the popularity of this name
is probably due (Lightfoot, *Gal.*, p.
268). The Apostle is called Συμεών
in Acts xv. 14, 2 Pet. i. 1 (אA); the
Synoptists call him Σίμων up to the
choosing of the Apostles, after which
he is Πέτρος (but see Mt. xvi. 16, 17,
xvii. 25, Mc. xiv. 37, Lc. xxii. 31, xxiv.
34), a name which Mt. anticipates here
(iv. 18, Σ. τὸν λεγόμενον Π.). For a fuller
discussion see Hort, *St Peter*, p. 151 ff.,
or Chase, in Hastings' *D. B.* iii. p. 756.
Ἀνδρέας is a true Greek name (Herodotus vi. 126), but instances occur of
its use by Jews (Smith's *D. B.*, ed. 2,
i. 128); and Andrew appears in com-

¹⁷καὶ εἶπεν αὐτοῖς ὁ Ἰησοῦς Δεῦτε ὀπίσω μου, καὶ 17
ποιήσω §ὑμᾶς γενέσθαι ἁλεεῖς ἀνθρώπων. ¹⁸καὶ εὐθὺς 18 § C
ἀφέντες τὰ δίκτυα ἠκολούθησαν αὐτῷ. ¹⁹καὶ προβὰς 19

17 om o Ιησους Φ | om γενεσθαι 1 13 28 69 118 209 604 1071 al b syrʳᵉⁱⁿᵖᵉˢʰ
aeth | αλιεις BᶜᵒʳʳDΓΠ   18 ευθυς אL 33] ευθεως ABCD al pl | τα δικτυα אBCL al
vg arm me]+αυτων ΑΓΔΠΣΦ٦ alᵖˡᵉʳ f g syrr go aeth παντα D a b c ff τα λινα
604 | ηκολουθουν B   19 προβας]+εκειθεν א*ΑΓΔΠΣΦ٦ alᵖˡᵉʳ (אᶜ·ᵃ 33 post ολιγ.)
c f vg syrʰᶜˡ arm go aeth

pany with Greeks in Jo. xii. 20 f. The
brothers came from Bethsaida (Jo. *l.c.*,
i. 44, cf. Mc. vi. 45 n.), but at this time
resided in Capernaum (Mc. i. 29); the
father's name was Jonas (Mt. xvi.
17), or John (Jo. i. 42, xxi. 15—17).
Andrew had been a disciple of the
Baptist (Jo. i. 35, 40), but apparently
both A. and S. had for some time followed Jesus, witnessing His miracles
in Galilee (Jo. ii. 2, 7) and Jerusalem
(ib. 13, 23), and baptizing in His
Name (Jo. iii. 22, iv. 2); after His
return to Galilee they had gone back
to Capernaum and resumed their fishing.

ἀμφιβάλλοντας ἐν τῇ θαλάσσῃ] Mt.
βάλλοντας ἀμφίβληστρον εἰς τὴν θάλασσαν: cf. Hab. i. 17, ἀμφιβαλεῖ τὸ ἀμφίβληστρον αὐτοῦ, and see vv. ll. here.
Mc. alone uses ἀμφιβάλλειν absolutely;
cf. however οἱ ἀμφιβολεῖς, Isa. xix. 8.
On the synonyms ἀμφίβληστρον, δίκτυον (Mc. i. 18, 19), σαγήνη (Mt. xiii.
47), see Trench *syn.*, § lxiv.: ἀμφ.
and σαγήνη occur together in Hab. i.
16, cf. Isa. xix. 8. On ἀμφιβ. εἰς, ἐν,
see WM., p. 520.

ἦσαν γὰρ ἁλεεῖς] The form ἁλεεῖς
predominates in the best MSS. of the
LXX. (Isa. xix. 8 א*B*, Jer. xvi. 16
א*B*, Ezek. xlvii. 10 B*A (but Job
xl. 26 ἁλιέων); cf. WH., *Notes*, 151. On
the fish of the Lake of G. see Sir
C. W. Wilson in Smith's *D. B.*, ed. 2,
ii. p. 1074; Merrill, *Galilee*, p. 43 f.

17. καὶ εἶπεν αὐτοῖς κτλ.] The
brothers are in their boat, Jesus
speaks from the shore; cf. Jo. xxi.
4, 5. Δεῦτε ὀπίσω μου = לְכוּ אַחֲרַי, 4

Regn. vi. 19; other forms are ἔρχεσθαι
(Mc. viii. 34), ἀπέρχεσθαι (Mc. i. 20),
ἀκολουθεῖν ὀπίσω (Mt. x. 38), or
simply ἀκολουθεῖν w. dat. (Mc. ii. 14,
viii. 34 b, Jo. i. 43, &c.); for ὑπάγειν
ὀπίσω with a very different sense, see
Mc. viii. 33. On the form of the
sentence see Burton § 269 c.

καὶ ποιήσω...ἀνθρώπων] Mt. omits
γενέσθαι (לִהְיוֹת); see WM., p. 757,
and C. W. Votaw, *Use of the Infinitive*,
p. 7. Ἁλεεῖς ἀνθρώπων: so Mt.; Lc.
ἀπὸ τοῦ νῦν ἀνθρώπους ἔσῃ ζωγρῶν. For
the metaphor, cf. Prov. vi. 26, Jer.
xvi. 16, 2 Tim. ii. 26, and cf. Pitra,
Spic. Solesm. iii. 419 ff.; as to its influence on early Christian thought
and art see the articles 'fish,' 'fisherman' in *D. C. A.* In Clem. Alex.
hymn. in Chr. the Lord Himself is
the ἁλιεὺ[ς] μερόπων | τῶν σωζομένων |
πελάγους κακίας | ἰχθῦς ἁγνοὺς | κύματος
ἐχθροῦ | γλυκερᾷ ζωῇ δελεάζων. The
anulus piscatoris worn by the Pope
is of mediaeval origin (*D. C. A.* ii. p.
1807). Erasmus appositely remarks,
"piscantes primum piscatus est
Jesus."

18. καὶ εὐθὺς ἀφέντες τὰ δίκτυα]
So Mt.; Lc., who appears to follow
another tradition (cf. Latham, *Pastor
pastorum*, p. 197 f.), and connects the
call with a miraculous draught of
fishes, concludes (v. 11): καταγαγόντες
τὰ πλοῖα ἐπὶ τὴν γῆν ἀφέντες πάντα ἠκ.
αὐτῷ.

19. καὶ προβὰς κτλ.] Another pair
of brothers (Mt. ἄλλους δύο ἀδελφούς),
called shortly after the first pair
(ὀλίγον, Mc. only). Ἰάκωβος, *Iacobus*

ὀλίγον εἶδεν Ἰάκωβον τὸν τοῦ Ζεβεδαίου καὶ Ἰωάνην
τὸν ἀδελφὸν αὐτοῦ, καὶ αὐτοὺς ἐν τῷ πλοίῳ καταρ-
20 τίζοντας τὰ δίκτυα, ²⁰ καὶ εὐθὺς ἐκάλεσεν αὐτούς. καὶ
ἀφέντες τὸν πατέρα αὐτῶν Ζεβεδαῖον ἐν τῷ πλοίῳ
¶ 13
§ e   μετὰ τῶν μισθωτῶν ἀπῆλθον ¶ ὀπίσω §αὐτοῦ.

---

19 om ολιγον ℵ*ΣΦ (προβ. ολιγον sine εκ. BDL min^nonn a b ff g syrr^sin pesh me)
20 ευθυς (ευθεως ACDΓΔII al min^pl) ante αφ. transpon Δ 124 al c ff syr^pesh arm |
απηλθον οπισω αυτου] ηκολουθησαν αυτω D latt

= יַעֲקֹב LXX. Ἰακώβ (Gen. xxv. 26 and
throughout O. T.), English 'James'
(through *Ital.* Giacomo, Mayor) from
Wycliffe onwards. Ἰωάνης (for the
orthography, see on i. 4)=יְהוֹחָנָן, יוֹחָנָן,
(LXX., Ἰωανάς, Ἰωανάν, Ἰωνά, but in
2 Paral. xxviii. 12, 1 Esdr. viii. 38,
cod. B uses Ἰωάνης, and Ἰωάννης
occurs in cod. A, 1 Esdr. *l. c.*, 1
Macc. ii. 1 sq.). The father, who
is mentioned as present (*infra*), was
one Ζεβεδαῖος = זַבְדִּי or rather זְבַדְיָה,
for which the LXX. have Ζαβδειά in
2 Esdr. viii. 8, x. 20, and Ζαβαδαίας
in 1 Esdr. ix. 35, or Ζαβδαῖος, ib. 21;
the mother was Salome, see Mc. xv.
40—on the form of the name cf. Dalman, p. 122. Τὸν ἀδελφὸν αὐτοῦ implies
that John was the younger or the
less important at the time; cf. τὸν
ἀδελφὸν Σίμωνος (*v.* 16). Προβὰς
ὀλίγον, i.e. along the shore (i. 16)
towards Capernaum (ii. 1).
καὶ αὐτούς] Mc. only. Vg. *et ipsos*,
'they too': cf. Lc. i. 36, Acts xv. 27, 32
(Blass); the exx. of καὶ αὐτός with
a finite verb, adduced by Knabenbauer, are inapposite. James and
John, like Simon and Andrew, were
in their boat (ἐν τῷ πλ.), though not
similarly occupied. Καταρτίζοντας τὰ
δίκτυα, Vg. *componentes retia*: Wycliffe, "makynge nettis," Tindale, A.V.,
R.V., "mending their nets," cf. Jerome:
"ubi dicitur *componentes* ostenditur
quod scissa fuerant." Καταρτίζειν is
used of rebuilding a ruin (2 Esdr. iv.

12, 13), and in surgery, of setting a
bone, or bringing the broken parts
together (Galen). In a metaphorical
sense the word is a favourite with
St Paul (see Lightfoot on Gal. vi. 1,
1 Thess. iii. 10), but it is also used in
1 Pet. v. 10. Here it may include the
whole preparation (see Heb. x. 5, xi.
3) of the nets for another night's
fishing. Comp. the different account
in Lc. v. 2.
20. καὶ εὐθὺς ἐκάλεσεν αὐτούς] On
εὐθύς see *v.* 10, note. Mt. omits it
here, but places εὐθέως before ἀφέντες,
as in *v.* 18. The call was doubtless
as before, *v.* 17; and the voice was as
familiar and as authoritative in the
second case as in the first.
ἀφέντες τὸν πατέρα] See the archetype of this parting in 1 Kings xix.
20 f., and cf. Mc. x. 28, 29. Mt. brings
out more fully the relative greatness
of the sacrifice in this case: ἀφέντες
τὸ πλοῖον καὶ τὸν πατέρα αὐτῶν. In
both cases the abandonment was
complete (Lc. ἀφέντες πάντα); all left
what they had to leave. Mc.'s μετὰ
τῶν μισθωτῶν has been thought to
imply comparative prosperity, but the
two pairs of brothers were partners
in the fishing industry (Lc. v. 7, 10),
so that there was at least no social
difference. Of μισθωτοί we hear again
in connexion with other businesses
(Jo. x. 12, 13, cf. Mt. xx. 1).
ἀπῆλθον ὀπίσω αὐτοῦ. Mt. ἠκολούθησαν αὐτῷ. See note on i. 17.

²¹ Καὶ εἰσπορεύονται εἰς Καφαρναούμ· καὶ εὐθὺς 21
τοῖς σάββασιν [εἰσελθὼν] εἰς τὴν συναγωγὴν ἐδίδασκεν.

21 om εισπ. εις Κ. και ευθ. syrˢⁱⁿ | εισεπορευοντο D 33 61 a b f go | Καπερναουμ
ACLΓΠ alᵖˡ | ευθυς ℵL 1 28 33 131 1071] ευθεως ABCD rell minᵖˡ | om εισελθων
ℵCLΔ 28 69 346 2ᵖᵉ al pauc me syrrˢⁱⁿ ᵖᵉˢʰ Orᵇⁱˢ (hab ABDΓΠΣΦ al latt syrʰᶜˡ arm
go aeth) | την συν.] +αυτων Δ syrᵖᵉˢʰ

21—28. CASTING OUT AN UNCLEAN
SPIRIT IN THE SYNAGOGUE AT CAPER-
NAUM (Lc. iv. 31—37).
21. καὶ εἰσπ. εἰς Καφαρναούμ] Cf.
Mt. iv. 13 καταλιπὼν τὴν Ναζαρὰ ἐλθὼν
κατῴκησεν εἰς Κ.; Lc. iv. 31 (after the
Sabbath at Nazareth) κατῆλθεν εἰς Κ.
In Mc. the entrance into Capernaum
follows the walk by the Sea, but εἰσπ.
does not of course exclude a previous
arrival from Nazareth. Καφαρναούμ
(Καπερν. is a 'Syrian' corruption,
WH., Notes, p. 160): Mt. adds τὴν
παραθαλασσίαν ἐν ὁρίοις Ζαβουλὼν καὶ
Νεφθαλείμ, in ref. to Isa. viii. 23 (ix.
1). The name כְּפַר נָחוּם, 'Nahum's
village,' is unknown to the O. T., but
Josephus mentions a κώμην Κεφαρνω-
κὸν λεγομένην (vit. 72) and a fountain
called Capharnaum in Gennesar (πηγῇ
...Καφαρναοὺμ αὐτὴν οἱ ἐπιχώριοι λέγουσιν, B. J. iii. 10. 8), identified by some
with 'Ain-et-Tin close to Khan Minyeh,
by others with 'Ain-et-Tabigah. The
site has been sought either at Khan
Minyeh, at the N. end of the plain
(so G. A. Smith, H.G. p. 456; Enc.
Bibl. i. p. 696 ff.), or at Tell Hum 2½
miles N.E. of Khan M. (see Wilson,
Recovery of Jerusalem, p. 342 ff., and
the other authorities quoted in Names
and Places, s.v.). Jerome onomast.
says, "usque hodie oppidum in Gal-
ilaea." On the Talmudic references
see Neubauer, géogr. du Talmud, p.
221. Tell Hum is now a wilderness
of ruins, half buried in brambles and
nettles; among them are conspicuous
the remains of a large synagogue
built of white limestone (Wilson, l.c.).
On the strange statement of Hera-

cleon, οὐδὲ πεποιηκώς τι λέγεται ἐν αὐτῇ
ἢ λελαληκώς see Origen in Joann.
t. x. 11.

καὶ εὐθὺς τοῖς σάββασιν] On the first
sabbath after the call of the Four. Σάββατα (so Joseph. ant. iii. 6. 6, and even
Horace, sat. i. 9. 69) is perhaps pl.
only in form = Aram. שַׁבְּתָא; cf. however τὰ ἄζυμα, τὰ γενέσια, and the like.
The LXX. use both σάββατον and σάββατα for 'a sabbath,' cf. Exod. xvi. 23,
xx. 8 f., xxxi. 15; but σάββατον does
not appear in cod. B before 4 Regn. iv.
23. Mc. uses the sing. in ii. 27, 28, vi.
2, xvi. 1, and it is the prevalent form
in the N. T.; σάββατα occurs as a
true plural in Acts xvii. 2. The meta-
plastic dat. σάββασιν is normal in the
N.T.; "B twice has σαββάτοις," WH.,
Notes, p. 157 (in Mt. xii. 1, 12). On
τοῖς σ. with or without ἐν see WM.,
p. 274.

εἰσελθὼν εἰς τὴν συναγωγὴν ἐδίδασκεν]
He was engaged in teaching in the
synagogue, when the event about to
be recorded took place. The rejection of εἰσελθών by some good authorities (?'Alexandrian') may be justified
by such passages as i. 39, x. 10, xiii. 9.
The 'pregnant' use of εἰς is not to be
attributed to confusion of εἰς with ἐν;
see WM., p. 516 ff. Τὴν συν.; there was
probably but one (see Lc. vii. 5). The
synagogue teaching of Christ seems to
have been characteristic of the earlier
part of His ministry: we hear no more
of it after Mc. vi. 2. On the Synagogue
as an institution see Schürer II. ii. 52 ff.
The word occurs abundantly in the
Pentateuch (LXX.) for עֵדָה or קָהָל, the
congregation of Israel (see Hort, Chr.

§ q ¶ a   §²²καὶ ἐξεπλήσσοντο ἐπὶ¶ τῇ διδαχῇ αὐτοῦ, ἦν γὰρ 22
¶ ד   διδάσκων αὐτοὺς ὡς ἐξουσίαν ἔχων καὶ οὐχ ὡς¶ οἱ

22 οι γραμματεις]+αυτων CMΔΣ 33 al c f syrr aeth+et farisaei e

Ecclesia, p. 4 ff.) : later on it is used
for any assembly (Prov. v. 14 ἐν μέσῳ
συναγωγῆς καὶ ἐκκλησίας, 1 Macc. xiv.
28 ἐπὶ συναγωγῆς μεγάλης ἱερέων), esp.
a religious assembly, Ps. Sol. xvii. 8 ;
but as denoting a place of assembly it
is almost peculiar to the N. T., and
occurs chiefly in the Synoptists and
Acts (Jo. vi. 59, xviii. 20, James ii.
2 are not real exceptions). Teaching was a chief purpose of the synagogues ; Phil. *de Sept.* 2 calls them
διδασκαλεῖα φρονήσεως. It arose out
of the Scripture lections (Lc. iv. 16,
Acts xiii. 15), which were followed by
a דְּרָשָׁה or exposition. The expositor
(דַּרְשָׁן) was not an officer of the synagogue, but any competent Israelite
who was invited by the officers. Hence
the synagogue supplied invaluable
opportunities to the first preachers of
the Gospel.

22. καὶ ἐξεπλήσσοντο κτλ.] So Mt.
vii. 28 f., Lc. iv. 32. Ἐκπλ., though
used from Homer downwards, is rare
in the LXX. (Eccl.¹ Sap.¹ Macc.³) and
in the N. T. is limited to Mt., Mc.,
Lc.ᵉᵛ·, ᵃᶜᵗ. For ἐπὶ τῇ δ. see WM⁴., p. 491
('over'=at). The amazement was due
to the manner of the teaching. It was
authoritative, and that not on certain
occasions only, but in general (ἦν διδάσκων, periphrastic imperf., cf. Blass,
Gr. p. 203 f.). Its note was ἐξουσία,
Justin, *apol.* i. 14, contrasting our
Lord with the Greek σοφισταί says :
βραχεῖς δὲ καὶ σύντομοι παρ᾽ αὐτοῦ λόγοι γεγόνασιν· οὐ γὰρ σοφιστὴς ὑπῆρχεν
ἀλλὰ δύναμις θεοῦ ὁ λόγος αὐτοῦ ἦν.
The frequenters of the synagogue were
chiefly struck by the Lord's tone of
authority ; there was no appeal to
Rabbis greater or older than Himself,
His message came direct from GOD.
The same character pervades all our

Lord's conduct : cf. i. 27, ii. 10, xi. 28 ff.
The source of this ἐξουσία is the Father
(Mt. xxviii. 18, Jo. v. 27, x. 18, xvii.
2) ; the Son delegates His authority
to His servants (Mc. vi. 7, xiii. 34, Jo.
i. 12). On the distinction between δύναμις and ἐξουσία see Mason, *Conditions of O. L.'s Life*, p. 98 : " authority
is not always power delegated, [nor is
it always] a rightful power...the distinction is rather between the inward
force or faculty...and the external
relationship." For the use of ὡς with
the part. to denote the manner of an
action cf. Burton, § 445.

καὶ οὐχ ὡς οἱ γρ.] Οἱ γρ., generic
art., ' the Scribes as a class.' On the
functions of this class see Schürer II.
i. 306 ff. ; Robertson Smith, *O.T.J.C.*
42 ff. The classical γραμματεύς is the
secretary or clerk of a public body;
γραμματεῖς τῆς βουλῆς, τῆς γερουσίας,
τοῦ δήμου are mentioned in the inscriptions, cf. Hicks, *Inscr. of Ephesos*,
p. 8, and Blass on Acts xix. 35. In
the LXX. γραμματεῖς first appear in
connexion with the Egyptian ἐργοδιῶ-
κται, and Deissmann has shewn (*Bibelst.*
p. 106 f.) that the papyri employ the
word for a class of military officers,
presumably those who kept the regis-
ter of the army (cf. Driver on Deut.
xx. 5, Moore on Jud. v. 14). In the
later sense of a Biblical scholar the
word first occurs in 1 Esdr. viii. 3,
2 Esdr. vii. 6 : cf. 1 Macc. vii. 12,
2 Macc. vi. 18 ; the Gospels know no
other. But the γραμματεῖς had before
this time become a dominant factor in
Jewish life, the recognised teachers of
Israel, taking their place in the Sanhedrin with the representatives of priesthood and people (Mc. xv. 1). 'Scribe'
(Latt. *scriba*) unfortunately lays stress
on the etymological sense of the word

γραμματεῖς. ²³καὶ εὐθὺς ἦν ἐν τῇ συναγωγῇ αὐτῶν 23
ἄνθρωπος ¶ ἐν πνεύματι ἀκαθάρτῳ, καὶ ἀνέκραξεν   ¶ t
²⁴λέγων Τί ἡμῖν καὶ σοί, Ἰησοῦ Ναζαρηνέ; ἦλθες 24
ἀπολέσαι ἡμᾶς; οἶδά σε τίς εἶ, ὁ ἅγιος τοῦ θεοῦ. ¶   ¶ Wᵒ

23 om ευθυς ACDΓΔΠΣΦ al latt syrr arm go aeth (hab ℵBL 1 33 131 209 me Or) |
om αυτων DL 72 b c e ff g | ανεκραξεν] + φωνη μεγαλη 1071   24 τι] pr εα
ℵᶜˑᵃACLΓΔΠΣΦ al syrʰᵉˡ arm go Orˡ Eus³ (om εα ℵ*BD 102 157 2ᵖᵉ latt syrʳᵃⁱⁿ ᵖᵉˢʰ
me aeth) | οιδαμεν ℵLΔ arm me aeth Or² Eus⁴

⟨γραμματεῖς = ‎סֹפְרִים‎); 'lawyer' (νομικός
Mt.¹ Lc.⁶) is scarcely better: Lc.'s
νομοδιδάσκαλος (v. 17, cf. Acts v. 34)
is perhaps the most exact title. On
the relation of our Lord's teaching to
the Law and its authorised expounders
see Hort, *Jud. Chr.* p. 14 ff. Ἦν γὰρ
διδάσκων is a little wider than ἐδίδασκεν above; as He proceeded, the
note of authority rang out more and
more clearly.

23. καὶ εὐθὺς ἦν κτλ.] Mc. and Lc.
only. Lc. omits εὐθύς and αὐτῶν; both
words as they stand in Mc.belong to the
completeness of the picture; the events
occurred at a definite time and place,
on that Sabbath during the sermon in
the synagogue of the Capharnaites.

ἄνθρωπος ἐν πνεύματι ἀκαθ.] Lc.
ἄνθρ. ἔχων πνεῦμα διαμονίου ἀκαθάρτου
—an easier phrase. For [εἶναι] ἐν
πνεύματι cf. Mt. xxii. 43, Mc. v. 2,
xii. 36, Lc. ii. 27, Rom. viii. 9, I Cor.
xii. 3, Apoc. i. 10. Ἐν is not here instrumental or indicative of manner
(Blass, *Gr.* p. 131): rather it represents
the person who is under spiritual influence as moving in the sphere of
the spirit. Most of the exx. refer
to the Holy Spirit, but there is nothing in the formula to forbid its
application to evil spirits in their
relation to men under their control.
Πνεῦμα ἀκάθαρτον appears already in
Zech. xiii. 2 (= ‎רוּחַ הַטֻּמְאָה‎); ἀκάθαρτος and ἀκαθαρσία are ordinarily used
in Leviticus for the ceremonial pollution which banishes from the Divine

presence. This idea of estrangement
from GOD probably predominates in
the present phrase: cf. Victor: διὰ τὴν
ἀσέβειαν καὶ τὴν ἀπὸ θεοῦ ἀναχώρησιν,
adding however—what should not
perhaps be excluded—διὰ τὸ πάσαις
ταῖς αἰσχραῖς καὶ πονηραῖς ἐφήδεσθαι
πράξεσιν.

καὶ ἀνέκραξεν κτλ.] Ἀνακράζειν (LXX.;
late Gk.) is used again of the cry of a
demoniac in Lc. viii. 28; and of the
cry of human terror (Mc. vi. 49) or
excitement (Lc. xxiii. 18). Lc. adds
here φωνῇ μεγάλῃ (cf. I Regn. iv. 5
and Mc. *infra*, v. 26).

24. τί ἡμῖν καὶ σοί κτλ.] = ‎מַה־לָּנוּ‎
‎וָלָךְ‎: cf. Jos. xxii. 24, Jud. xi. 12,
2 Regn. xvi. 10, 3 Regn. xvii. 18; the
phrase was used also in class. Gk., see
Wetstein on Mt. viii. 29 and WM., p.
731. 'What have we in common with
Thee?' Cf. Mc. v. 7, and esp. 2 Cor.
vi. 14, τίς γὰρ μετοχὴ δικαιοσύνῃ καὶ
ἀνομίᾳ κτλ. Ἡμῖν = τοῖς δαιμονίοις,
'us, as a class'; only one seems to
have been in possession in this case,
but he speaks for all. Ναζαρηνός is
the Marcan form (cf. xiv. 67, xvi. 6);
Mt., Lc. (xviii. 37), Jo., Acts, give
Ναζωραῖος. On the origin of the two
forms see Dalman, p. 141 n.

ἦλθες ἀπολέσαι ἡμᾶς;] Probably a
second question, parallel to τί ἡμῖν
κ. σ.: 'didst Thou come (hither from
Nazareth, or perhaps, since ἡμᾶς is
generic, into the world) to work our
ruin, to destroy and not to save, in
our case?' Contrast Lc. xix. 10. The

25 ²⁵καὶ ἐπετίμησεν αὐτῷ ὁ Ἰησοῦς λέγων Φιμώθητι καὶ

25 om λεγων ℵ*A*ᵛⁱᵈ | εξ αυτου] εκ του ανθρωπου D (8ᵖᵉ) latt (exc f) απ αυτου ΗLΣ
33 alᵖˡ+πνευμα ακαθαρτον D (8ᵖᵉ) b c e ff g q go aeth | αυτου] αυτων 1071

Saviour of men must needs be the Destroyer of unclean spirits. See the use made of this context against Marcionism by Tertullian, *adv. Marc.* iv. 7.

οἶδά σε τίς εἶ κτλ.] See James ii. 19 τὰ δαιμόνια πιστεύουσιν καὶ φρίσσουσιν, and cf. also Lc. iv. 41, Mc. v. 7, Acts xix. 15. Orig. *in Jo.* t. xxviii. 15, δύναται καὶ πονηρὰ πνεύματα μαρτυρεῖν τῷ Ἰησοῦ καὶ προφητεύειν περὶ αὐτοῦ. For the special meaning of οἶδα as opposed to γινώσκω (Acts *l.c.*) see Lightfoot on Gal. iv. 9, Rom. vii. 7, 1 Cor. ii. 11 : οἶδα is absolute, γινώσκω relative. At this stage the evil spirits merely knew as a matter of fact that Jesus was the Messiah : experience of His power came later on. The slightly pleonastic σέ is common to Mc. and Lc. here, and perhaps is due to an Aramaic original (Delitzsch, יְדַעְתִּיךָ מִי אַתָּה); for the attraction cf. Mt. xxv. 24. Ὁ ἅγιος τοῦ θεοῦ : cf. Ps. cv. (cvi.) 16, Ἀαρὼν τὸν ἅγιον Κυρίου : 4 Regn. iv. 9, ἄνθρωπος τοῦ θεοῦ ἅγιος. The Apostles learnt afterwards to adopt the title (John vi. 69, cf. 1 Jo. ii. 20, Apoc. iii. 7). Employed in this way it distinguished the Christ from all other consecrated persons. Victor : ἅγιος ἦν καὶ ἕκαστος τῶν προφητῶν.. διὰ τοῦ ἄρθρου τὸν ἕνα σημαίνει τῶν ἄλλων ἐξαίρετον. Ὁ δίκαιος is also used (Acts xxii. 14, James v. 6 : the two stand together in Acts iii. 14). But it was the ἁγιότης of Jesus—His absolute consecration to God (Jo. x. 36, xvii. 19)—which struck terror into the δαιμόνια. Bede : "praesentia Salvatoris tormenta sunt daemonum."

25. ἐπετίμησεν αὐτῷ] Sc. τῷ ἀνθρώπῳ, but in effect the spirit, as the words that follow shew; cf. v. 8.

Ἐπιτιμᾶν, Vg. *comminari*, Wycliffe and Rheims "threaten," other Engl. vv., "rebuke" ; the strict meaning of the word is 'to mete out due measure,' but in the N. T. it is used only of censure ; cf. 2 Tim. iv. 2, where it stands between ἐλέγχειν and παρακαλεῖν : Jude 9 (Zach. iii. 2), ἐπιτιμήσαι σοι Κύριος. With these two exceptions it is limited to the Synoptists.

φιμώθητι καὶ ἔξελθε] The rebuke takes the form of a double command : Euth., ἐξουσιαστικὸν τὸ φιμ. καὶ τὸ ἔξελθε. The offence was two-fold: (1) The confession οἶδά σε κτλ., coming inopportunely and from unholy lips ; cf. i. 34, Acts xvi. 18, and see Tert. *Marc.* iv. 7, "increpuit illum...ut invidiosum et in ipsa confessione petulantem et male adulantem, quasi haec esset summa gloria Christi si ad perditionem daemonum venisset": (2) the invasion of the man's spirit by an alien power. Φιμοῦν occurs in its literal sense in Deut. xxv. 4, cited in 1 Cor ix. 9, 1 Tim. v. 18; φιμοῦσθαι is in the LXX. (4 Macc. i. 35, ℵV) and N.T. uniformly metaphorical, Vg. *obmutescere*. The word is not a vulgar colloquialism, as Gould's rendering suggests ; it occurs in this sense in good late writers (Josephus, Lucian, &c.) ; see, however, Kennedy, *Sources*, p. 41. In Mt. xxii. 34, 1 Pet. ii. 15 we find the active similarly used, cf. Prov. xxvi. 10 Th. φιμῶν ἄφρονα φιμοῖ χόλους. For ἔξελθε see v. 8, ix. 25. The summons to depart was in this case the penalty for unprovoked interruption ; the δαιμόνιον was the aggressor. An exodus was possible, since the human personality, although overpowered, remained intact, awaiting the Deliverer : cf. iii. 27, Lc. xi. 21 ff.

ἔξελθε ἐξ αὐτοῦ. ²⁶καὶ σπαράξαν αὐτὸν τὸ πνεῦμα 26
τὸ ἀκάθαρτον καὶ φωνῆσαν φωνῇ μεγάλῃ ἐξῆλθεν
ἐξ αὐτοῦ. §²⁷καὶ ἐθαμβήθησαν ἄπαντες, ὥστε 27 § Wᵐ
συνζητεῖν αὐτοὺς λέγοντας Τί ἐστιν τοῦτο; δι-

26 και εξηλθεν το πν. το ακ. και σπαραξας αυτον και κραξας φωνη μεγ. εξηλθεν απ
αυτου D (e) (ff) | om το πν. B 102 | φωνησαν ℵBL 33 (1071) Or] κραξαν AC(D)ΓΔΠΣΦ
alᵖˡᵉʳ | εξ] απ C(D)ΜΔΣ 33 alᵐᵘ   27 εθαμβησαν D Or | παντες ACDΓΔΠ al | αυτους
ℵB b e ff q] προς αυτους GLSΦ minᵐᵘ προς εαυτ. ACDΓΔΠΣ al minᵖˡ προς αυτον
2ᵖᵉᵐᵍ | λεγοντες ACE*ΜΔᶜᵒʳʳ 13 33 238 346 736 | om τι εστιν τουτο D evᵖᵃᵘᶜ b c e ff q
arm

26. καὶ σπαράξαν...ἐξῆλθεν] The
spirit obeyed, but displayed his
malice (Apoc. xii. 12); cf. Lc. ῥίψαν
αὐτὸν εἰς τὸ μέσον ἐξῆλθεν.. μηδὲν
βλάψαν αὐτόν. Σπαράξαν, Vg. 'dis-
cerpens; the verb is used in reference
to a spirit again in Mc. ix. 20 (συνεσπ.)
26, Lc. ix. 39, 42 (συνσπ.). The later
usage of the word inclines towards
the meaning 'convulse'; see 2 Regn.
xxii. 8, but esp. Dan. viii. 7, where
וַיְשַׁלִּיכֵהוּ אַרְצָה is translated by Th.
ἔριψεν αὐτὸν ἐπὶ τὴν γῆν, but by LXX.
ἐσπάραξεν αὐτὸν ἐπὶ τὴν γῆν. From
the second instance it is clear that, on
the hypothesis of a Hebrew or Aramaic
original, Lc.'s ῥίψαν may represent
the same word as Mc.'s σπαράξαν, and
that the latter implies no laceration,
so that Lc.'s (perhaps editorial) note
μηδὲν βλ. αὐτόν is justifiable. The
reading of D in ix. 20 (ἐτάραξεν) and
in Lc. ix. 42 (συνετ.) is a serviceable
gloss. For the mystical interpretation see Greg. M. hom. in Ezek. i.
12. 24, "quid est quod obsessum
hominem antiquus hostis quem pos-
sessum non discerpserat deserens
discerpsit, nisi quod plerumque dum
de corde expellitur acriores in eo
tentationes generat?" Φωνῆσαν φωνῇ
μεγάλῃ, using for the last time the
human voice through which he had
so long spoken. Lc. has connected
φωνῇ μεγάλῃ with the cry τί ἐμοὶ κ. σ.,
and omits it here.

27. καὶ ἐθαμβήθησαν ἄπαντες]

Amazement (v. 22) deepened into
awe. Lc. ἐγένετο θάμβος ἐπὶ πάντας.
Θαμβεῖσθαι, ἐκθαμβεῖσθαι are used in
the N. T. only by Mc., but occur
occasionally in the Lxx.; in class.
Gk. the words are found chiefly in
poetry, and θαμβεῖν is intrans.; cf.
1 Regn. xiv. 15, and the reading of
D here. Θάμβος is connected with
ἔκστασις in Acts iii. 10, and the verb
with φοβεῖσθαι in Mc. x. 32.

ὥστε συνζητεῖν αὐτούς]=Lc. συνε-
λάλουν πρὸς ἀλλήλους. Συνζητεῖν is
usually followed by πρός (ix. 14,
Acts ix. 29), or the dative (viii. 11,
Acts v. 9), or a dependent clause
giving the subject of debate (ix. 10);
see vv. ll. here. Here, as again in
xii. 28, it is used absolutely: 'they
discussed.' The word is predominantly Marcan; see Hawkins, Hor.
Syn. p. 10.

τί ἐστιν τοῦτο; διδαχὴ καινή] Lc.
τίς ὁ λόγος οὗτος; ὅτι κτλ. Mc.
gives the incoherent and excited
remarks of the crowd in their natural
roughness: the Western and traditional texts attempt to reduce them
to literary form. For διδαχὴ καινή see
v. 22. There was now another element which was new: the ἐξουσία
was manifested in accompanying acts
—κατ' ἐξουσίαν καί κτλ. Exorcism
was not unknown among the Jews
of this period, cf. Mt. xii. 27, Acts
xix. 13 (on the latter reference see
Blass, and cf. Edersheim i. 482); but

δαχὴ καινή· κατ᾽ ἐξουσίαν καὶ τοῖς πνεύμασιν τοῖς
28 ἀκαθάρτοις ἐπιτάσσει καὶ ὑπακούουσιν αὐτῷ. ²⁸καὶ
ἐξῆλθεν ἡ ἀκοὴ αὐτοῦ εὐθὺς πανταχοῦ εἰς ὅλην
τὴν περίχωρον τῆς Γαλειλαίας.
29   ²⁹Καὶ εὐθὺς ἐκ τῆς συναγωγῆς ἐξελθὼν ἦλθεν εἰς

27 διδαχη καινη κατ εξ. אBL 33 102 (1 28* 2ᵖᵉ*) (604)] τις η διδ. η καινη αυτη οτι
κατ εξ. (A)ΓΔΠΣΦ al minᵖˡ f vg syrrᵖᵉˢʰ ʰᶜˡ arm go τις η διδ. εκεινη η καιν. αυτ. η
εξουσια οτι D τις η διδ. (η καιν.) αυτ. κατ εξ. b c e ff (q) r (syrˢⁱⁿ)   28 εξηλθεν δε
ΑΓΠ al | om ευθυς א* 1 28 33 al b c e ff q syrˢⁱⁿ arm | om πανταχου א*ΑΔΓΔΠΣΦ
minᵖˡ c f ff vg syrr arm go (hab (אᶜ·ᵃ) BC(L) 69 124 b e q me) | της Γαλ.] της Ιουδαιας
א* του Ιορδανου 28+και πολλοι ηκολουθησαν αυτω syrˢⁱⁿ   29 om ευθυς D c e ff g
syrrˢⁱⁿᵖᵉˢʰ aeth | εξελθων ηλθεν B(D)(Σ) 1 22 69 124 604 al f g syrʰᶜˡ⁽ᵐᵍ⁾ arm aeth]
εξελθοντες ηλθον אAC(F)(L)Γ(Δ)ΠΦ minᵖˡ syrᵖᵉˢʰ ʰᶜˡ ᵗˣᵗ εξελθων ηλθον ff syrˢⁱⁿ ᵛⁱᵈ

it consisted in the use of magical
formulae, not in the power of a direct
command. The tone of authority
adopted by Jesus was extended even
(καί) to the uncontrollable wills of
spirits who defied all moral obligations (τοῖς πν. τοῖς ἀκαθ., an order
which emphasises the adj., cf. Eph.
iv. 30, 1 Thess. iv. 8), and even in that
sphere it received attention (καὶ ὑπ.
αὐτῷ, cf. iv. 41). For διδαχὴ καινή cf.
Acts xvii. 19, and for the sense of
καινός as compared with νέος see Mc.
ii. 21, 22. The freshness and vigour
of the teaching, and not merely its
novelty, attracted attention.

κατ᾽ ἐξουσίαν] Lc. ἐν ἐξουσίᾳ καὶ
δυνάμει. With κατ᾽ ἐξ. 'in the way of
authority' cf. Rom. iv. 16, ἵνα κατὰ
χάριν, Phil. ii. 3, μηδὲν κατ᾽ ἐριθίαν
μηδὲ κατὰ κενοδοξίαν. Lc.'s καὶ δυνάμει
brings into sight another factor (see
i. 22, note), in the act, which however
was not in the forefront of men's
thoughts at the time. Καὶ τοῖς πνεύμασιν...'even the demons obey His
word,' cf. iv. 41 καὶ ὁ ἄνεμος καὶ ἡ
θάλασσα. See Lc. x. 17, 20. Ὑπακούουσιν αὐτῷ: Lc. ἐξέρχονται.

28. καὶ ἐξῆλθεν...πανταχοῦ] From
that hour (εὐθύς) the new Teacher's
fame (ἀκοή, Vg. rumor) spread in all
directions. Ἀκοή is (1) 'hearing' (e.g.
in the common LXX. phrase ἀκοῇ

ἀκούειν); (2) in pl., 'the organs of hearing' (Mc. vii. 35, Acts xvii. 20); (3) the
thing heard, 'hearsay,' 1 Regn. ii. 24
(שְׁמֻעָה), Isa. liii. 1, cf. Rom. x. 16, 17,
where (3) passes back into (1).

εἰς ὅλην τὴν π. τῆς Γ.] Either=εἰς
ὅλην τὴν Γαλειλαίαν (τῆς Γ. being epexe-
getical of τ. π.), or 'into all the district
round G.'; Wycliffe, "the cuntree of
G."; Tindale, Cranmer, &c., "the
region bordering on G." The latter
accords with Mt.'s summary (iv. 24,
ἀπῆλθεν ἡ ἀκοὴ αὐτοῦ εἰς ὅλην τὴν
Συρίαν) and with usage: cf. ἡ π. τοῦ
Ἰορδάνου (Gen. xiii. 10, 11, Mt. iii. 5),
τῶν Γερασηνῶν (Lc. viii. 37), Ἱερουσαλήμ (2 Esdr. xiii. 9); and on the other
hand see Deut. iii. 13 πᾶσαν περίχωρον
Ἀργόβ. A third interpretation is 'the
whole of that part of Galilee which lay
round Capernaum.' But for this εἰς
ὅλην τὴν π. Καφαρναούμ would have
sufficed, for there was no need at present to contrast the Galilean περίχωρος
with the tetrarchy of Philip which had
not yet been mentioned; moreover the
report could not have been limited to
the W. of the Jordan. Lc., however,
seems to incline to the narrowest
sense (εἰς πάντα τόπον τῆς περιχώρου).

29–31. HEALING OF SIMON'S
WIFE'S MOTHER (Mt. viii. 14–15,
Lc. iv. 38–39).

29. καὶ εὐθὺς ἐκ τῆς συν. ἐξελθὼν

τὴν οἰκίαν Σίμωνος καὶ Ἀνδρέου μετὰ Ἰακώβου καὶ
Ἰωάνου. ³⁰ἡ δὲ πενθερὰ Σίμωνος κατέκειτο πυρέσ- 30
σουσα, καὶ εὐθὺς λέγουσιν αὐτῷ περὶ αὐτῆς· ³¹καὶ 31
προσελθὼν ἤγειρεν αὐτὴν κρατήσας τῆς χειρός, καὶ
ἀφῆκεν αὐτὴν ὁ πυρετός, καὶ διηκόνει αὐτοῖς.¶   ¶ H

30 κατεκειτο δε η π. Σ. D latt (exc f) | om ευθυς b c ff g q syrr^{sin pesh} aeth
31 ηγειρεν αυτην κρατ. της χειρος] εκτεινας την χειρα κρατ. ηγ. αυτην D (b f q) |
χειρος]+αυτης ΑΓΔΠΣΦ al vg syrr arm me (om αυτ. אBL (D b q)) | πυρετος]+
ευθεως Α(D)ΓΔΠΣΦ al (b c e f ff q vg) syrr^{(sin) (pesh) hcl} go aeth (om ευθ. אBCL 1 28
33 al^{pauc} e arm me) | και διηκονει] pr και ηγερθη 16 syrr^{sin hcl} aeth

ἦλθεν] The narrative is still unbroken,
as κ. εὐθύς suggests, and ἐκ τῆς σ.
shews. We are carried back to the
end of v. 26, vv. 27, 28 being paren-
thetical. As soon as the congregation had broken up (Acts xiii. 43),
Jesus went to the house of Simon.
Ἐξελθὼν ἦλθεν, as it stands, is a 'sub-
singular' reading of B (see WH., Intr.
§ 308 ff.), but D gives ἐξελθ. δὲ ἐκ τῆς
συν. ἦλθεν, and Σ, καὶ ἐξελθ. εὐθὺς ἐκ
τῆς συν. ἦλθεν : with B are also a fair
number of important cursives (see vv.
ll.), and the sing. part. is supported
by Syr.^{sin.} and the O. L. ms. ff; besides, the roughness of B's text is in
its favour, and ἐξελθόντες ἦλθαν followed by μετὰ Ἰακώβου καὶ Ἰωάνου is
hardly tolerable; see however Zahn,
Einleitung ii. pp. 246, 252, where an
ingenious explanation is given of the
reading of א A. Τὴν οἰκίαν Σίμωνος
καὶ Ἀνδρέου. Mt., Lc. mention only
Simon (Mt., Πέτρου); the home was
probably his, since he was a married man, but shared by his brother.
Syr.^{sin.} has : "Andrew and James and
John were with Him" (? μετὰ Ἀνδρ.
κ. Ἰακ. καὶ Ἰω.). A house in Capernaum is frequently mentioned as the
rendez-vous of Jesus and the disciples
(Mc. ii. 1, iii. 27, vii. 24, ix. 33, x. 10).
Jerome : "utinam ad nostram domum
veniat...unusquisque nostrum febri-
citat."
30. ἡ δὲ πενθερὰ Σίμωνος] Simon
was therefore "himself also a married

man" before his call, and his wife
accompanied him afterwards in his
Apostolic journeys (1 Cor. ix. 5, cf.
Suicer s. v. γυνή); see the story told
of her by Clem. Alex. strom. vii. 11.
62 (Eus. H. E. iii. 30), and Clement's
statement, strom. iii. 6. 52 (cf. Hieron.
adv. Jovin. i. 26): ἡ καὶ ἀποστόλους
ἀποδοκιμάζουσι; Πέτρος μὲν γὰρ καὶ
Φίλιππος ἐπαιδοποιήσαντο. Her mother
(for πενθερά and the correlative νύμφη
see Mt. x. 35) 'kept her bed of a
fever,' decumbebat febricitans : κατακεῖσθαι is used of the sick by Galen,
and occurs again in this sense Mc. ii. 4,
Lc. v. 25, Jo. v. 3, 6, Acts ix. 33, xxviii.
8; cf. Mt. βεβλημένην καὶ πυρ. See
Field, Notes, p. 25. For πυρέσσουσα
Lc. has the professionally precise συν-
εχομένη πυρετῷ μεγάλῳ, 'in a high
fever,' and similarly ἠρώτησαν for the
simple λέγουσιν. The pl. is best explained as referring to οἱ περὶ τὸν
Σίμωνα. The Lord is told as soon
as He enters the house (εὐθύς); they
have waited till He returned from the
synagogue.
31. καὶ προσελθών κτλ.] He approached the sufferer, took her by the
hand, and raised her up. Lc. substitutes ἐπιστὰς ἐπάνω αὐτῆς ἐπετίμησεν
τῷ πυρετῷ (cf. Mc. i. 25, iv. 39). For
κρατήσας τ. χ. compare Mc. v. 41, ix. 27.
The aor. part. is one of 'antecedent
action,' see Burton § 134—rather
perhaps of concurrent action, the
grasp scarcely preceding and certainly

32   ³²'Οψίας δὲ γενομένης, ὅτε ἔδυσεν ὁ ἥλιος, ἔφερον
πρὸς αὐτὸν πάντας τοὺς κακῶς ἔχοντας καὶ τοὺς
33 δαιμονιζομένους· ³³καὶ ἦν ὅλη ἡ πόλις ἐπισυνηγμένη

32 εδυσεν BD 28] εδυ ℵACLΓΔΠΣΦ alᵖˡ | εφεροσαν D | om προς αυτον syrˢⁱⁿ |
κακως εχ.] transil ℵ* ad κακ. εχ. (v. 34)+νοσοις ποικιλαις D b c e ff g q syrˢⁱⁿ ᵛⁱᵈ | om
και τους δαιμ. syrˢⁱⁿ

coinciding with the lifting of the
prostrate form ; cf. Blass, *Gr.*, p. 197.
The genitive is partitive (WM., p. 252);
for an ex. from the LXX. see Gen.
xix. 16. With the whole narrative
compare Acts xxviii. 8—another case
of miraculous recovery from fever.

καὶ διηκόνει αὐτοῖς] The prostration
which attends early convalescence
found no place ; she at once assumed
her usual function in the household (cf.
Lc. x. 40, Jo. xii. 2). Jerome: "natura
hominum istiusmodi est ut post febrim
magis lassescant corpora, et incipi-
ente sanitate aegrotationis mala sen-
tiant; verum sanitas quae confertur a
Domino totum simul reddit." The
service was probably rendered at the
Sabbath meal; cf. Joseph. *vit.* 54 ἕκτῃ
ὥρα καθ' ἣν τοῖς σάββασιν ἀριστοποι-
εῖσθαι νόμιμόν ἐστιν ἡμῖν. For διακονεῖν
'to wait at table' cf. Lc. *l.c.*, xvii. 8, xxii.
26, 27, Acts vi. 2. Victor: ἀνεχώρουν
ὡς ἐν σαββάτῳ ἐπὶ ἐστίασιν εἰς τὸν οἶκον
τοῦ μαθητοῦ. Αὐτοῖς Mc., Lc.: Mt.,
αὐτῷ. The Lord, Who had restored
her, was doubtless the chief object
of her care. Jerome: "et nos mini-
stremus Iesu."

32—34. MIRACLES AFTER SUNSET
(Mt. viii. 16, Lc. iv. 40—41).

32. οψίας δὲ γενομένης, ὅτε ἔδυσεν
ὁ ἥλιος] For the phrase ὀψία ἐγένετο
cf. Judith xiii. 1. Mt. omits ὅτε
ἔδυσεν ὁ ἥ., Lc. changes it into δύνοντος
τοῦ ἡλίου: comp. the similar discrepancy in the readings of Mc. xvi. 2
(ἀνατείλαντος s. ἀνατέλλοντος τοῦ ἡλίου).
Lc.'s recension is probably intended
to leave time before dark for the
miracles that follow. On the Sabbath the crowds would not bring

their sick before sunset, cf. Victor:
οὐχ ἁπλῶς πρόσκειται τὸ ' δύνοντος τοῦ
ἡλίου,' ἀλλ' ἐπειδὴ ἐνόμιζον μὴ ἐξεῖναί
τινι θεραπεύειν σαββάτῳ, τούτου χάριν
τοῦ σαββάτου τὸ πέρας ἀνέμενον. For
ἔδυσα = ἔδυν see WSchm., p. 109, and
cf. vv. ll.

ἔφερον κτλ.] Case after case arrived (imperf.); Mt. προσήνεγκαν, Lc.
ἤγαγον, with less realisation of the
scene. In using the Marcan tradition
Lc. has changed the position of
ποικίλαις νόσοις : cf. what is said of
φωνῇ μεγάλῃ *supra*, v. 26. Κακῶς
ἔχειν (Ezech. xxxiv. 4) is not uncommon
in the Gospels (Mt.⁷ Mc.⁴ Lc.²). Καὶ
τοὺς δαιμονιζομένους: Mt. δ. πολλούς (cf.
Mc. *infra*, v. 34). Δαιμόνια have not
yet been mentioned by that name, yet
the verb is used as if familiar to the
reader. The corresponding classical
form is δαιμονᾶν, and δαιμονίζεσθαι is
rare before the N. T.; there is no
trace of it in the Gk. O. T., but it
occurs in the later literary Greek in
reference to the insane. In the N. T.
its use is nearly limited to the participles δαιμονιζόμενος, δαιμονισθείς, in
the sense of a person possessed by a
δαιμόνιον: cf. Acts x. 38, τοὺς κατα-
δυναστευομένους ὑπὸ τοῦ διαβόλου.

33. καὶ ἦν ὅλη ἡ πόλις κτλ.] See
note on i. 5. Ἐπισυνάγειν is a strengthened form of συνάγειν found in late
Greek and frequent in the LXX., normally implying a large or complete
gathering, cf. 1 Macc. v. 10, 16, Mt.
xxiii. 37, Mc. xiii. 27, Lc. xii. 1 ; cf.
ἐπισυντρέχειν, Mc. ix. 25. Πρὸς τὴν
θύραν : the acc. dwells on the thought
of the flocking up to the door which
preceded, and the surging, moving,

πρὸς τὴν θύραν. ³⁴καὶ ἐθεράπευσεν πολλοὺς κακῶς 34
ἔχοντας ποικίλαις νόσοις, §καὶ δαιμόνια πολλὰ ἐξέ-   § a
βαλεν· καὶ οὐκ ἤφιεν λαλεῖν τὰ δαιμόνια, §ὅτι   § θ͘
ἤδεισαν αὐτὸν [Χριστὸν εἶναι].

33 προς την θυραν (πρ. τη θυρα U πρ. τας θυρας 28 124 2ᵖᶜ)]+αυτου D c ff g q
syrˢⁱⁿ   34 και εθερ. αυτους και τους δαιμονια εχ. εξεβαλεν αυτα απ αυτων και ουκ
ηφ. αυτα λαλειν οτι ηιδισαν αυτον και εθερ. π. κ. εχοντας ποικ. ν. και δαιμ. π.
εξεβαλεν D | om κακως..νοσοις syrˢⁱⁿ | om ποικ. νοσ. Lℵ* (hab ℵᶜ·ᵃ) | τα δαιμ. λαλ.
B αυτα λαλειν D | χριστον ειναι BLΣ 1 28 33 69 alˢᵃᵗᵐᵘ g syrʰᵉˡ arm me aethᴛ] τον
χⁿ ειναι ℵᶜ·ᵃCGM al om ℵ*ADEFKSUVΓΔΘᶠΦ al a b c e f ff q vg syrrˢⁱⁿᵖᵉˢʰ go

mass before it: cf. ii. 2, xi. 4, and
contrast Jo. xviii. 16, ἱστήκει πρὸς τῇ
θύρᾳ.

34 καὶ ἐθεράπευσεν κτλ.] For θεραπεύειν to attend on a patient, to treat
medically, see Tobit ii. 10 (ℵ), ἐπορευό-
μην πρὸς τοὺς ἰατροὺς θεραπευθῆναι.
It is in Mt. and Mc. the nearly constant
word for Christ's treatment of disease;
ἰᾶσθαι occurs only in Mt. viii. 8, 13,
xiii. 15 (LXX.), xv. 28, Mc. v. 29. The
treatment was not tentative; πολλούς
is either coextensive with πάντας (v.
32, cf. Mt.), or it implies that if
all could not approach the Lord that
night, there were many that did and
were healed (on Mt. see Hawkins, Hor.
Syn., p. 96). Lc. adds the method of
individual treatment: ἑνὶ ἑκάστῳ αὐτῶν τὰς χεῖρας ἐπιτιθείς. The diseases
were various—ποικίλαις: cf. π. ἐπιθυμίαι (2 Tim. iii. 6), ἡδοναί (Tit. iii. 3),
δυνάμεις (Heb. ii. 4), διδαχαί (Heb.
xiii. 9).

καὶ δαιμόνια πολλὰ ἐξέβαλεν] The
class. δαίμων (Mt. viii. 31) or δαιμόνιον
is simply a power belonging to the
unseen world but operating upon men
here (θεὸς ἢ θεοῦ ἔργον Arist.; μεταξύ
ἐστι θεοῦ καὶ θνητοῦ Plat.). In Biblical Greek the word took a bad sense
through its appropriation to heathen
deities (Deut. xxxii. 17, Ps. xcv. (xcvi.)
5, Bar. iv. 7, cf. 1 Cor. x. 20, 21), regarded either as שֵׁדִים genii (?) (see
Driver on Deut. l. c., Cheyne, Origin
of the Psalter, p. 334f.) or אֱלִילִים. In

Tobit, under Persian influence, the
conception of evil δαιμόνια is developed (Tob. iii. 8, Ἀσμόδαυς (-δαῖος ℵ) τὸ
πονηρὸν δαιμόνιον); a further progress
is made in Enoch (c. xvi.), where however the Greek has πνεύματα. Joseph.
B. J. vii. 6. 3 identifies them with the
spirits of the wicked dead (τὰ καλούμενα
δαιμόνια, ταῦτα δὲ πονηρῶν ἐστιν ἀνθρώπων πνεύματα τοῖς ζῶσιν εἰσδυόμενα).
On the later Jewish demonology see
Edersheim, Life and Times, ii., app.
viii., or the subject may be studied in
J. M. Fuller's intr. to Tobit (Speaker's
Comm.) or in Weber Jüd. Theologie
pp. 251—9; cf. F. C. Conybeare in
J.Q.R. 1896, and the arts. Demon,
Demons in Hastings, D.B., and Enc.
Bibl. The N.T. uses δαιμόνια as = πνεύ-
ματα ἀκάθαρτα, adopting the accepted
belief and the word supplied by the
LXX. Ἐξέβαλεν: see note on i. 12.
Mt. adds λόγῳ—a command sufficed.

καὶ οὐκ ἤφιεν λαλεῖν] Cf. i. 25. Lc.
fills in this brief statement, representing the spirits as κράζοντα καὶ λέγοντα
ὅτι Σὺ εἶ ὁ υἱὸς τοῦ θεοῦ. Ἤφιεν, so
Mc. xi. 16; cf. ἀφίομεν Lc. xi. 4. Ἀφίω,
ἀφιέω, ἀφίημι seem to have been all
in use (WH., Notes, p. 167, Blass, Gr.,
p. 51): ἀφίω occurs in the best MSS. of
the LXX., 1 Esdr. iv. 50, Eccl. v. 11, and
ἀφιέω in Sus. (LXX.) 53 τοὺς δὲ ἐνό-
χους ἠφίεις, cf. Phil. leg. ad Cai. 1021.
Ἤδεισαν αὐτόν: see on οἶδά σε i. 24;
and contrast Jo. x. 14 γινώσκουσί με
τὰ ἐμά. Χριστὸν (or τὸν χριστόν) εἶναι

§ syr^hier 35 [35]§ Καὶ πρωὶ ἔννυχα λίαν ἀναστὰς ἐξῆλθεν [καὶ
36 ἀπῆλθεν] εἰς ἔρημον τόπον κἀκεῖ προσηύχετο. [36] καὶ
37 κατεδίωξεν αὐτὸν Cίμων καὶ οἱ μετʼ αὐτοῦ, [37] καὶ

35 εννυχα ℵBCDLΘ^f 28 33 al] εννυχον ΑΓΔΠΣΦ al^pler | om αναστας D 226 a c | om εξηλθεν και 1071 b d e q | om και απηλθεν B 28 56 102 235 2^pe ff g | ερημ. τοπ.] pr τον D | και εκει AD | προσηυξετο D   36 κατεδιωξεν ℵBMSU 28 40 604 vg al] κατεδιωξαν ACDLΓΔΘ^fΠΣΦ a b c e f ff g q syrr | ο Σιμων ΑCΓΔΘ^f ο τε Σ. ΚΠ 1071 οι μετ αυτ.] om οι B + ησαν Δ

is strongly supported, yet may have been an early gloss from Lc.; cf. Victor: τὸ δὲ τελευταῖον Μᾶρκος οὐκ ἔχει. But in any case it probably strikes a true note. It does not seem as though the knowledge of the δαιμόνια went beyond the fact of our Lord's Messiahship; both ὁ ἅγιος τοῦ θεοῦ and ὁ υἱὸς τ. θ. are Messianic titles.

35—39. Withdrawal from Capernaum, and First Circuit of Galilee (Lc. iv. 42—44).

35. καὶ πρωὶ ἔννυχα λίαν κτλ.] Πρωὶ may be the morning watch—the φυλακὴ πρωία (Ps. cxxix. = cxxx. 6), as in Mc. xiii. 35; but in the present context the simpler meaning seems preferable —'early,' so early that it was still quite dark: cf. λίαν πρωί (xvi. 2) = ὄρθρου βαθέως (Lc. xxiv. 1) = πρωὶ σκοτίας ἔτι οὔσης (Jo. xx. 1). Ἔννυχος is used by the poets from Homer downwards, and in the prose of the later Gk., cf. 3 Macc. v. 5. With the adv. ἔννυχα (ἅπ. λεγ.) compare πάννυχα (poet. and late Gk.);. Hesych. quotes νύχα = νύκτωρ. The Vg. *diluculo valde* fails to give the force of ἔννυχα (Euth. ἀντὶ τοῦ νυκτὸς ἔτι οὔσης). In Lc. this touch of intimate acquaintance with the circumstances is lost (γενομένης δὲ ἡμέρας ἐξελθών). Ἐξῆλθεν: i.e. out of the house and town. It is difficult to believe that the reading ἐξ. καὶ ἀπῆλθεν is not a conflation which happens to have secured a consensus of the great majority of the authorities (see vv. ll.), although under the circumstances it must retain its place in the text: ἀπῆλθεν is probably from vi. 32, 46. The ἔρημος τόπος (Mc. Lc.) was doubtless in the neighbourhood of Capernaum: cf. vi. 31 ff., Lc. ix. 10.

κἀκεῖ προσηύχετο] Cf. Ps. v. 4, lxxxvii. (lxxxviii.) 14. These words reveal the purpose of the sudden withdrawal. Sunrise would bring fresh crowds, new wonders, increasing popularity. Was all this consistent with His mission? Guidance must be sought in prayer. Comp. vi. 46, xiv. 32, Lc. vi. 12, ix. 18, 28, xi. 1. Victor: οὐκ αὐτὸς ταύτης δεόμενος...ἀλλʼ οἰκονομικῶς τοῦτο ποιῶν. Ambros. *in Lc.* v.: "quid enim te pro salute tua facere oportet quando pro te Christus in oratione pernoctat?" There is truth in both remarks, but they overlook the εὐλάβεια of the Incarnate Son which made prayer a necessity for Himself (Heb. v. 7, 8).

36. καὶ κατεδίωξεν αὐτὸν Σίμων κτλ.] Vg. *Et persecutus est eum S.* Simon (whose personal narrative we clearly have here) started in pursuit of Him with Andrew and James and John (οἱ μετʼ αὐτοῦ, cf. *v.* 29; Bengel: "iam Simon est eximius"), and tracked Him to His retreat. Καταδιώκω (an ἅπ. λεγ. in the N.T. but freq. in LXX., where it usually = רָדַף) has an air of hostility: Gen. xxxi. 36, τί τὸ ἀδίκημά μου...ὅτι κατεδίωξας ὀπίσω μου; yet cf. Ps. xxii. (xxiii.) 6, τὸ ἔλεός σου καταδιώξεταί με. Simon's intention at least was good; the Master seemed to be losing precious opportunities and must be brought back. Yet see note on *v.* 31.

εὗρον αὐτὸν καὶ λέγουσιν αὐτῷ ὅτι Πάντες ζητοῦσίν
σε. ³⁸ καὶ λέγει αὐτοῖς Ἄγωμεν ἀλλαχοῦ εἰς τὰς 38
ἐχομένας κωμοπόλεις ἵνα καὶ ἐκεῖ κηρύξω, εἰς τοῦτο

37 κ. ευρον αυτον και λεγ. אBL θ meᶜᵒᵈ aeth] κ. ευροντες αυτ. λεγ. ΑCΓΔΘᶠΠΦ
al κ. ευροντες αυτον ειπον Σ κ. οτε ευρον αυτον λεγ. D | dicentes b c | σε ζητουσιν
ΑFΘᶠΠ 1071   38 om αλλαχου ACᶜᵒʳʳDΓΔΘᶠΠΣΦ latt syrr go (hab אBC*L 33
arm me aeth) | εχομενας (εχομενα B)] ενγυς D | κωμοπολεις] κωμας και εις τας πολεις
D latt syrrˢⁱⁿ ᵖᵉˢʰ

37. καὶ εὗρον αὐτόν κτλ.] Lc.'s account apparently is not based on the
Marcan tradition, and in form at least
conflicts with it: in Lc. the ὄχλοι pur-
sue Jesus and stay Him; from Mc. we
learn that in fact the attempt was
made by the disciples. Tatian endeavours to harmonise the two traditions, in the order Mc. i. 35—38, Lc.
iv. 42, 43. Πάντες ζητοῦσίν σε, i.e. all
the Capharnaites and others on the
spot. Cf. Jo. vi. 24, 26, xiii. 33. The
quest was prompted by very mixed
motives.

38. καὶ λέγει αὐτοῖς Ἄγωμεν ἀλλαχοῦ κτλ.] In Lc. similar words are
addressed to the crowd, but the occasion is clearly the same. Ἄγωμεν,
intrans., as in Mc. xiv. 42; Jo. xi. 7,
15, 16, xiv. 31, and as ἄγε in Homer
and the poets: 'let us go elsewhere';
ἀλλαχοῦ = ἄλλοσε or ἀλλαχόσε, as
πανταχοῦ, i. 28, = πάντοσε or παντα-
χόσε: the latter forms are not used in
N. T. Gk. Ἀλλαχοῦ occurs here only
in N. T.; cf. ἀλλαχόθεν, Jo. x. 1.

εἰς τὰς ἐχομένας κωμοπόλεις] Into the
neighbouring country towns (Wycliffe,
"the nexte townes and citees," after
Vg., in proximos vicos et civitates:
comp. the reading of D). Ὁ ἐχόμενος =
ὁ πλησίον is freq. in the LXX., but uncommon in the N. T., cf. Lc. xiii. 33;
Acts xiii. 44, xx. 15, xxi. 26; Heb. vi.
9: the phrase "is used of local con-
tiguity and also of temporal connexion" (Westcott on Heb. l.c.). Κωμόπολις—an ἅπ. λεγ. in the N. T. and not

found in the LXX., though Aq. and
Theod. seem to have used it in Josh.
xviii. 28 (Field)—occurs in Strabo
(pp. 537, 557), and in Joseph. (ant.
xi. 86). According to J. Lightfoot
it is the כָּפָר as distinguished from
the עִיר (cf. Schürer II. i. 155)—the
small country town, whether walled
or not, or partly fortified (cf. Euth. ἡ
ἐν μέρει μὲν ἀτείχιστος ἐν μέρει δὲ τε-
τειχισμένη). There were many such
in Galilee: Joseph. B. J. iii. 3. 2, πόλεις πυκναὶ καὶ τὸ τῶν κωμῶν πλῆθος
πανταχοῦ πολυάνθρωπον διὰ τὴν εὐ-
θηνίαν. Lc. has merely πόλις in this
context. Such small towns are called
indifferently κῶμαι or πόλεις; cf. Lc.
ii. 4, Jo. vii. 42.

ἵνα καὶ ἐκεῖ κτλ.] The Lord's primary
mission was to proclaim the Kingdom
(i. 14); dispossessing demoniacs and
healing the sick were secondary and
in a manner accidental features of His
work. Εἰς τοῦτο γὰρ ἐξῆλθον (Mc.) is
interpreted for us by Lc. ὅτι ἐπὶ τοῦτο
ἀπεστάλην. Ἐξῆλθον does not refer to
His departure from Capernaum (v. 35),
but to His mission from the Father
(Jo. viii. 42, xiii. 3); whether it was so
understood at the time by the disciples is of course another question.
The thought, though perhaps unintelligible to those about Him, was
present to His own mind from the
first, as even the Synoptists shew (Lc.
ii. 49). Bengel: "primi sermones Iesu
habent aenigmatis aliquid, sed paullatim apertius de se loquitur."

39 γὰρ ἐξῆλθον. ³⁹καὶ ἦλθεν κηρύσσων εἰς τὰς συνα-
γωγὰς αὐτῶν εἰς ὅλην τὴν Γαλειλαίαν καὶ τὰ δαιμόνια
ἐκβάλλων.

40   ⁴⁰ Καὶ ἔρχεται πρὸς αὐτὸν λεπρὸς παρακαλῶν
αὐτὸν [καὶ γονυπετῶν], λέγων αὐτῷ ὅτι Ἐὰν θέλῃς,

38 εξηλθον אBCL 33] εξεληλυθα ADΓΠΣΦ al εληλυθα Δ (Θʳ) 2ᵖᵉ minˢᵃᵗ ᵐᵘ
39 ηλθεν אBL syrʰⁱᵉʳ me aeth] ην ACDΓΔΘʳΠΣΦ latt syrʳˢⁱⁿ ᵖᵉˢʰ ʰᶜˡ arm go | εις τας
συναγωγας אABCDKLΔΘʳΠ 1 69 al] εν ταις συναγωγαις EFGMSUVΓΣΦ (εν τας
συναγωγας) alᵖˡ   40 παρακαλων] ερωτων D | και γονυπετων אL 1 209 300 736* 2ᵖᵉ
alᵖᵃᵘᶜ e f q vg arm] κ. γ. αυτον ACΔΘʳΠΣΦ al syrr me aeth om BDGΓ minᵖᵃᵘᶜ
a b c ff g | λεγων] pr και א°·ᵃACDLΓΔΘʳΠΣΦ al | οτι εαν θελης אAΓΔΠ al minᵖˡ
syrˢⁱⁿ] κυριε ο. ε. θ. B κυριε ε. θ. CLΣ c e ff g arm go aeth ο. ε. θ. κυριε ΘʳΦ 28 εαν
θελης (D) 69 71 238 b f q vg syrᵖᵉˢʰ | δυνη B

39. καὶ ἦλθεν κηρύσσων κτλ.] A
tour of synagogue preaching follows,
extending through the whole of Galilee
(Mc., cf. Mt. iv. 23), and if we accept
the reading Ἰουδαίας (see WH., Notes,
p. 57) in Lc. iv. 44, through Judaea
also ; Judaea is occasionally used by
Lc. inclusively (i. 5, perhaps also vii.
17, Acts ii. 9, x. 37), but not as = Galilee. See the references to this synagogue preaching in Lc. xxiii. 5, Jo.
xviii. 20. Such a cycle may have
lasted many weeks or even months
(see Lewin, fast. sacr., § 1245, Edersheim, Life and Times, i. p. 501, and
on the other hand Ellicott, Lectures,
p. 168), although only one incident has
survived. Εἰς τὰς συναγωγάς : where-
ever He went, He entered the synagogue and proclaimed His message
there ; εἰς ὅ. τ. Γαλειλαίαν adds the
locality, = ἐν ὅλῃ τῇ Γαλειλαίᾳ (cf. Mt.
iv. 23), but with the added thought of
the movement which accompanied the
preaching. Mc. has fused into one the
two clauses ἦλθεν εἰς ὅ. τ. Γ. (cf. i. 14),
and ἐκήρυσσεν εἰς τὰς συν. αὐτῶν (cf. i.
21).

40—45. CLEANSING OF A LEPER
(Mt. viii. 2—4, Lc. v. 12—16).

40. ἔρχεται πρὸς αὐτὸν λεπρός]
Though the purpose of this circuit was
preaching, miracles were incidentally
performed. One is selected, possibly

as the first of its class, or as having
made the deepest impression. All
the Synoptists relate it, but in different contexts. Λεπρός (מְצֹרָע, צָרוּעַ),
' suffering from leprosy,' is in the
Gospels used as a noun. Lepers were
evidently a numerous class of sufferers
in Palestine in our Lord's time, cf. Mt.
x. 8, xi. 5 ; Lc. xvii. 12, perhaps at all
times (Lc. iv. 27), as indeed the elaborate provisions of Lev. xiii., xiv. seem
to shew. The approach of this leper
(προσελθών, Mt.) to Jesus is remarkable ; cf. Lev. xiii. 45, 46, Lc. xvii. 12
(πόρρωθεν). He came near enough to
be touched (v. 41). The event took
place ἐν μιᾷ τῶν πόλεων, i.e. in one of
the κωμοπόλεις of Galilee where the
Lord was preaching, but doubtless
outside the gate (Lev. l.c.).

παρακαλῶν αὐτὸν κ. γονυπετῶν] The
entreaty begins at the first sight of the
Lord ; when the leper has come up
with Him, the prostration follows.
Γονυπετεῖν (Polyb., but not LXX.) occurs
also in Mt. xvii. 14, xxvii. 29, and Mc.
x. 17 ; in this place the words καὶ γον.
are open to doubt (see vv. ll.), yet as
they are not from Mt. (προσεκύνει) or
Lc. (πεσὼν ἐπὶ πρόσωπον) it is difficult
to regard them as an interpolation.
For λέγων ὅτι see i. 15 note.

ἐὰν θέλῃς, δύνασαί με καθαρίσαι] So
Mt., Lc., but with a prefixed Κύριε.

δύνασαί με καθαρίσαι. ⁴¹καὶ σπλαγχνισθεὶς ἐκτείνας 41
τὴν χεῖρα αὐτοῦ ἥψατο καὶ λέγει αὐτῷ Θέλω, καθαρίσθητι. ¶ ⁴²καὶ εὐθὺς ἀπῆλθεν ἀπ᾽ αὐτοῦ ἡ λέπρα, 42 ¶ F, Wᵐ

41 και 1° אBD a b e] ο δε ις ΑΓΔ al | σπλαγχνισθεις] οργισθεις D a ff r* Eph om
b g | αυτου ηψατο]+αυτου D 7ᵖᵉ lattᵖˡ ηψ. αυτου ΑΓΔΘᶠΠ alᵖˡ | om αυτω א 1 209 c ff
42 και 1°]+ειποντος αυτου ΑΓΔΘᶠΠΣΦ minᵖˡ f q vg syrʰᵉˡ arm go aeth | om
απηλθεν απ αυτου η λ. και syrˢⁱⁿ | εκαθαρισθη אBᶜᵒʳʳDEKMSUΓΠ alᵖˡ

Contrast the petition in Mc. ix. 22,
and the Lord's method of dealing with
the two cases. On the force of the
apodosis see Burton § 263. For δύνα-
σαι=δύνῃ (Mc. l.c.) see WH., Notes,
p. 168. Καθαρίζειν=καθαίρειν (טִהַר),
the term used for the ceremonial
cleansing of a leper in Lev. xiii., xiv.,
is transferred in the Gospels to the
actual purging of the disease.

41. καὶ σπλαγχνισθείς κτλ.] On the
'Western' reading ὀργισθείς see WH.,
Notes, p. 23: "a singular reading, perhaps suggested by v. 43 (ἐμβριμησάμενος), perhaps derived from an extraneous source." Nestle thinks that
it may be "an instance of a difference in translation"; see his Intr.,
p. 262. Ὀργή is attributed to our Lord
in Mc. iii. 5, but under wholly different
circumstances; nor is Ephraem's explanation satisfactory: "quia dixit
Si vis, iratus est" (Moesinger, p. 144);
for at this stage in the story there is
nothing to suggest anger, and σπλ.
is obviously in keeping with ἐκτ. τ. χ.
α. ἥψατο. In the N. T. σπλαγχνίζεσθαι
is limited to the Synoptists: in the
LXX., Prov. xvii. 5 ὁ δὲ ἐπισπλαγχνι-
ζόμενος (A, σπλ.) ἐλεηθήσεται (where
the Gk. is the converse of the Heb.)
seems to be the only instance of its
use in a metaphorical sense; for the
literal sense of the verb and its
derivatives, see 2 Macc. vi. 7, 8, 21,
vii. 42, ix. 5, 6. It is remarkable that,
while σπλάγχνα was used in classical
Gk. for the seat of the affections, the
verb appears first in Biblical Greek:
see Lightfoot on Phil. i. 8, "perhaps
a coinage of the Jewish dispersion."

Delitzsch renders here, וַיְּרַחֶם עָלָיו
but רַחֵם is represented in the LXX. by
ἐλεῶ or οἰκτείρω. The σπλάγχνα Ἰησοῦ
Χριστοῦ (Phil. l.c.) are a favourite
topic with the author of the Ep. to
the Hebrews (see ii. 17, iv. 15, v. 2).

ἐκτείνας τὴν χεῖρα αὐτοῦ ἥψατο]
Contrast i. 31, κρατήσας τῆς χειρός;
the action is adapted to the circumstances. Even after the Ascension
the Apostles remembered the out-
stretched Hand (Acts iv. 30). As
specimens of patristic exegesis see
Origen c. Cels. i. 48: νοητῶς μᾶλλον ἢ
αἰσθητῶς Ἰησοῦς ἥψατο τοῦ λεπροῦ,
ἵνα αὐτὸν καθαρίσῃ, ὡς οἶμαι, διχῶς.
Victor: διὰ τί δὲ ἅπτεται τοῦ λεπροῦ
καὶ μὴ λόγῳ ἐπάγει τὴν ἴασιν;...ὅτι ἀκαθαρσία κατὰ φύσιν οὐχ ἅπτεται Σωτῆρος
...καὶ ὅτι κύριός ἐστι τοῦ ἰδίου νόμου.

θέλω, καθαρίσθητι] So Mt., Lc. The
Lord's human will is exercised here in
harmony with the Divine: contrast
Mc. xiv. 36, where it remains in harmony by submission. The subject
may be studied further by comparing
Mt. xv. 32, xxiii. 37; Mc. iii. 13, vi.
48, vii. 24; Lc. xii. 49; Jo. vii. 1, xvii.
24, xxi. 22. For a singular misunder-
standing created by an ambiguity in the
Latin version see Jerome in Matt.:
"non ergo ut plerique Latinorum
putant...legendum volo mundare, sed
separatim [volo, mundare]."

42. καὶ εὐθὺς...ἐκαθερίσθη] Mc.'s
text seems here to be a conflation of
Mt. (καὶ εὐθέως ἐκ. αὐτοῦ ἡ λέπρα) and
Lc. (καὶ εὐθέως ἡ λ. ἀπῆλθεν ἀπ᾽ αὐτοῦ).
But it is possible that Mt. and Lc.
have each preserved a portion of the
original tradition, and the general

¶ W⁵ 43 καὶ ἐκαθερίσθη.¶ ⁴³καὶ ἐμβριμησάμενος αὐτῷ εὐθὺς
¶ syrˢⁱⁿ 44 ἐξέβαλεν αὐτόν, ⁴⁴καὶ λέγει αὐτῷ ῞Ορα μηδενὶ¶ μηδὲν
εἴπῃς, ἀλλὰ ὕπαγε σεαυτὸν δεῖξον τῷ ἱερεῖ, καὶ
προσένεγκε περὶ τοῦ καθαρισμοῦ σου ἃ προσέταξεν

43 om ευθυς εξεβαλεν αυτον και syrˢⁱⁿ   44 om μηδεν ℵADLΔ 33 69 124 604
al latt syrᵖᵉˢʰ me aeth | ιερει] αρχιερει 33 69 vg

phenomena agree with this hypothesis. For the form ἐκαθερίσθη (Mt.
Mc.) see WH.,*Notes*, p. 150,and Winer-
Schm., p. 50. With the whole narrative it is instructive to compare
4 Regn. v. 6—14. Of Naaman too
ἐκαθαρίσθη is used.

43. καὶ ἐμβριμησάμενος αὐτῷ κτλ.]
᾿Εμβριμᾶσθαι (Aesch. *Sept. c. Theb.* 46,
of the snorting of the horse) is to speak
or act sternly: cf. Dan. xi. 30 (LXX.)
῾Ρωμαῖοι...ἐμβριμήσονται αὐτῷ, in reference to the attitude of C. Popilius
Laenas towards Antiochus (Bevan on
Daniel *l.c.*); in Lam. ii. 6, ἐμβριμήματι
ὀργῆς αὐτοῦ=בְּזַעַם־אַפּוֹ. But the idea
of anger is not inherent in the word;
see Jo. xi. 33, 38, where it is used of
our Lord's attitude towards Himself;
rather it indicates depth and strength
of feeling expressed in tone and manner. A close parallel to the present
passage is to be found in Mt. ix. 30.
In neither case can we discover any
occasion for displeasure with the
subject of the verb: the Vg. *comminatus est* (Wycliffe, "thretenyde hym")
is too harsh, nor is there any apparent
room for ἐπιτίμησις, unless by anticipation. We may paraphrase, ' He
gave him a stern injunction': cf.
Hesych. ἐμβριμῆσαι· κελεῦσαι. A summary dismissal followed—εὐθὺς ἐξέβαλεν αὐτόν: on ἐκβάλλω cf. *v.* 12. Vg.
eiecit illum; Wycliffe, "putte hym
out"; Tindale, "sent him away," and
so A.V.; R.V. "sent him out." If the
first rendering is too strong, the last
seems to fall short of the original,
which involves at least some pressure
and urgency.

44. καὶ λέγει αὐτῷ κτλ.] The words
reveal in part the need for this stern
and curt manner. If the man remained even a few minutes, a crowd
would collect; if he went away to
spread the news, the danger of interruption to the Lord's work of preaching would be yet greater. He must
go at once, keep his secret, and fulfil
the immediate duty which the Law
imposed. ῞Ορα μηδενὶ μηδὲν εἴπῃς (Mt.
omits μηδέν): for the double negative
cf. Rom. xiii. 8. How grave the
danger which Jesus sought to avert
ultimately became is apparent from
Jo. vi. 15.

ἀλλὰ ὕπαγε κτλ.] So Mt.; Lc. ἀπελθὼν δεῖξον σ. τ. ἱ.; cf. Lc. xvii. 14, in
a narrative peculiar to the third
Gospel, πορευθέντες ἐπιδείξατε ἑαυτοὺς
τοῖς ἱερεῦσιν. All depend on Lev. xiii.
49 δείξει τῷ ἱερεῖ [τὴν ἀφήν], xiv. 2
ᾗ ἂν ἡμέρᾳ καθαρισθῇ καὶ προσαχ-
θήσεται τῷ ἱερεῖ. ῞Υπαγε=לֵךְ, as in
ii. 11, v. 19, and frequently: a use of
ὑπάγειν which, though classical, is unknown to the LXX.

καὶ προσένεγκε κτλ.] Mt. προσένεγ-
κον: on the two forms see WSchm.,
p. 111 f. Περὶ τοῦ καθαρισμοῦ σου,
in the matter of, in reference to
the ceremonial purification required
by the Law; cf. Lev. xiv. 32 εἰς
τὸν καθαρισμὸν αὐτοῦ. So καθ. is
always used in the Gospels (cf. Lc. ii.
22, Jo. ii. 6, iii. 25); in the Epistles
(2 Pet. i. 9, Heb. i. 3) the deeper
sense comes into sight. ῾Α (ὅ, Mt.;
καθώς, Lc.) προσέταξεν Μωυσῆς, see
Lev. xiv. 4 ff. The Mosaic origin of
the Levitical and Deuteronomic legis-

Μωυσῆς εἰς μαρτύριον αὐτοῖς.¶ ⁴⁵ὁ δὲ ἐξελθὼν ἤρξατο 45 ¶ syr^hier
κηρυσσειν πολλὰ καὶ διαφημίζειν τὸν λόγον, ὥστε
μηκέτι αὐτὸν δύνασθαι φανερῶς εἰς πόλιν εἰσελθεῖν,

44 Μωσης ACEGLMSUΓ al^pl   45 om πολλα D latt

lation is accepted as belonging to the recognised belief (cf. vii. 10, x. 3, 4, Jo. vi. 32, vii. 19), and not set forth by our Lord as part of His own teaching; see Sanday, *Inspiration*, p. 413 ff. There was no revolt on His part against 'Moses,' still less any disposition to detach the Jew from the obedience he still owed to the Law: cf. Hort, *Jud. Chr.*, p. 30.

εἰς μαρτύριον αὐτοῖς] The phrase occurs again in vi. 11 and xiii. 9, cf. Lc. ix. 5, εἰς μ. ἐπ' αὐτούς. For εἰς μαρτύριον in the LXX. see Prov. xxix. 14 (לְעֵד), Hos. ii. 12 (14), Mic. i. 2, vii. 18 (לְעֵד). The cure of the leper would witness to the priests (αὐτοῖς=τοῖς ἱερεῦσιν suggested by τῷ ἱερεῖ above) that there was a Prophet amongst them (2 Kings v. 8); the knowledge that λεπροὶ καθαρίζονται (Mt. xi. 5) might lead them to suspect that the Messiah had come. WM., p. 183, interprets αὐτοῖς of the Jews, but they are not in question: indeed it was not the Lord's purpose that the miracle should be generally known—it was enough to leave the guides of the nation without excuse, if they rejected Him (Jo. v. 36, xv. 24). Αὐτοῖς however is not like ἐπ' αὐτούς necessarily hostile; whether the witness saved or condemned them would depend on their own action with regard to it. Victor's exposition is too harsh: τουτέστιν, εἰς κατηγορίαν τῆς αὐτῶν ἀγνωμοσύνης. Comp. Jerome: "si crederent, salvarentur; si non crederent, inexcusabiles forent." Οὕτως (writes Origen *in Jo.* t. ii. 34) εἰς μαρτύριον τοῖς ἀπίστοις οἱ μάρτυρες μαρτυροῦσι καὶ πάντες οἱ ἅγιοι.

45. ὁ δὲ ἐξελθὼν κτλ.] He left the presence of Christ (ἐξελθών corresponds

to ἐξέβαλεν), only to tell his tale to every one he met. For this use of κηρύσσειν cf. v. 20, vii. 36; the adverbial πολλά occurs again in iii. 12, v. 10, 23, 38, 43, ix. 26, with the meaning 'much' or 'often.' Both senses are almost equally in place here. An oriental with a tale not only tells it at great length, but repeats it with unwearied energy. Ἤρξατο κηρύσσειν: cf. ii. 23, iv. 1, v. 17, etc., and see Blass, *Gr.*, p. 227.

καὶ διαφημίζειν τὸν λόγον] Διαφημίζειν (Vg. *diffamare*), a word of the later Greek, not in LXX.; cf. Mt. ix. 31, xxviii. 15. Τὸν λόγον=הַדָּבָר, the tale; Tindale, "the dede," A.V., "the matter"; cf. 1 Macc. viii. 10 ἐγνώσθη ὁ λόγος, Acts xi. 22 ἠκούσθη δὲ ὁ λόγος: Lc. here, διήρχετο ὁ λόγος. Euth. understands by τὸν λόγον the words of Jesus (θέλω, καθαρίσθητι). But Victor is doubtless right: τουτέστι, τὴν παράδοξον θεραπείαν.

ὥστε μηκέτι αὐτὸν δύνασθαι κτλ.] The result was, as Jesus had foreseen, another enforced retreat, and the abandonment of His synagogue preaching; if He entered a town, it could only be at night or in such a manner as not to attract attention (cf. Jo. vii. 10, οὐ φανερῶς ἀλλ' ὡς ἐν κρυπτῷ). But in general He lodged henceforth outside the walls (ἔξω, cf. xi. 19) in the neighbouring open country (ἐπί with dat. of place = on, i.e. remaining in, the locality, WM., 489: for ἔρημοι τόποι cf. i. 35). The interval was spent in prayer: Lc. ἦν ὑποχωρῶν ἐν ταῖς ἐρήμοις καὶ προσευχόμενος. On ὥστε μηκέτι see WM., p. 602. The inability was of course relative only: He could not enter the towns to any good purpose, or indeed without endangering the success of His

ἀλλὰ ἔξω ἐπ᾽ ἐρήμοις τόποις ἦν· καὶ ἤρχοντο πρὸς
αὐτὸν πάντοθεν.

2
§ syrʰⁱᵉʳ

1   ¹ § Καὶ εἰσελθὼν πάλιν εἰς Καφαρναούμ δι᾽ ἡμερῶν,
2 ἠκούσθη ὅτι ἐν οἴκῳ ἐστίν· ²καὶ συνήχθησαν πολλοὶ

45 επ ℵBLΔ minᵖᵃᵘᶜ] εν ACDΓΘ'ΠΣΦ al | om ην B 102 om ην και b e | παντοθεν
ℵABCDKLMSΔΘ'ΠΣΦ 1 33 1071 alⁿᵒⁿⁿ] πανταχοθεν EGUVΓ al

II 1 εισελθων ℵBDL 28 33 604 alᵖᵃᵘᶜ a c arm me aeth] εισηλθεν ACEFGKMΣΦ al
b d e f ff q vg syrrᵖᵉˢʰʰᶜˡ go | om παλιν S e | Καπερναουμ ACLΓΘ'Π alᵖˡ | ηκουσθη]
pr και ACDΓΔΘ'ΠΣΦ al lattᵛᵗ ᵖˡ ᵛᵍ syrrᵖᵉˢʰʰᶜˡ go | εν οικω] εις οικον ACΓΔΘ'ΠΦ al gᵛⁱᵈ
2 και 1°]+ευθεως ACDΓΔΘ'ΠΣΦ al pler a c e f ff g q syrʰᶜˡ go

mission; of physical danger as yet
there was none.

καὶ ἤρχοντο πρὸς αὐτὸν πάντοθεν]
Lc. συνήρχοντο ὄχλοι πολλοὶ ἀκούειν
καὶ θεραπεύεσθαι. He could still deliver His message, but not in the
synagogues, where He willed to
preach at this stage in His ministry.
Πάντοθεν, cf. Lc. xix. 43, Heb. ix. 4;
so the LXX. (Jer. xx. 9, Sus. 22 Th.,
Sir. li. 7 (10)); the prevalent form
in Attic prose is πανταχόθεν (vv. ll.).

II. 1—12. HEALING OF A PARA-
LYTIC IN A HOUSE AT CAPERNAUM.
THE FORGIVENESS OF SINS. (Mt. ix.
1—8, Lc. v. 17—26.)

1. καὶ εἰσελθὼν πάλιν κτλ.] The
circuit (i. 39) is now over, ended
perhaps prematurely by the indiscre-
tion of the leper (i. 45); and the Lord
returns to Capernaum. Εἰσελθών,
an anacoluthon, cf. WM., p. 709 ff.
and vv. ll.; πάλιν looks back to the
visit before the circuit (i. 21 ff.).
According to Mt. the Lord appears
to have arrived by boat from the
other side of the lake, but the impression is perhaps due simply to
Mt.'s method of grouping events; in
Lc. as in Mc. the healing of the paralytic follows the healing of the leper.
Mt. in this context calls Capernaum
τὴν ἰδίαν πόλιν, probably, as Victor
suggests, διὰ τὸ πολλάκις ἐκεῖσε ἐπιδημεῖν: Lc. ἐν μιᾷ τῶν πόλεων. Δι᾽ ἡμερῶν
(Lc. ἐν μιᾷ τῶν ἡμερῶν), Vg. post dies,
Euth., ἀντὶ τοῦ 'διελθουσῶν ἡμερῶν
τινῶν': for this use of διά see WM.,

p. 476 f. and Lightfoot on Gal. ii. 1,
and cf. Dion. Hal. ant. x. διὰ πολλῶν
ἡμερῶν, and the class. διὰ χρόνου. The
note of time is to be attached to εἰσελθών, not to ἠκούσθη, and covers the
interval between the first visit to
Capernaum and the second; as to the
length of the interval it suggests
nothing. See note on i. 39.

ἠκούσθη ὅτι ἐν οἴκῳ ἐστίν] Men
were heard to say 'He is indoors.'
'Ηκούσθη impers., Vg. auditum est:
cf. 2 Esdr. xvi. 1, 6, Jo. ix. 32; in Acts
xi. 22 we have ἠκούσθη ὁ λόγος: cf.
Blass, Gr., p. 239, who suggests a
personal construction here. The reading εἰς οἶκον (WM., 516, 518) is attractive, but the balance of authority
is distinctly against it in this place.
The house was probably Simon's (i. 29),
but ἐν οἴκῳ is not=ἐν τῷ οἴκῳ: the
sense is 'at home,' 'indoors,' cf. 1 Cor.
xi. 34, xiv. 35.

2. καὶ συνήχθησαν πολλοί κτλ.] Cf.
i. 33. The concourse was so great
as to choke the approaches to the
house, 'so that even the doorway
could hold no more,' Vg. ita ut non
caperet neque ad ianuam. The θύρα
or house-door seems to have opened
on to the street in the smaller Jewish
houses (cf. xi. 4, πρὸς θύραν ἔξω ἐπὶ τοῦ
ἀμφόδου); no προαύλιον or πρόθυρον
(xiv. 68) would intervene between the
door and the street, nor would there
be a θυρωρός (Jo. xviii. 16) to exclude
unwelcome visitors. Τὰ πρὸς τὴν
θύραν is simply the neighbourhood of

ὥστε μηκέτι χωρεῖν μηδὲ τὰ πρὸς τὴν θύραν, καὶ
ἐλάλει αὐτοῖς τὸν λόγον. ³καὶ ἔρχονται φέροντες 3
πρὸς αὐτὸν παραλυτικὸν αἰρόμενον ὑπὸ τεσσάρων.
⁴καὶ μὴ δυνάμενοι προσενέγκαι αὐτῷ διὰ τὸν ὄχλον 4
ἀπεστέγασαν τὴν στέγην ὅπου ἦν, ⁸καὶ ἐξορύξαντες   § H

2 αυτοις] προς αυτους D b c ff q | τον λογον] om τον D   3 ερχ. προς αυτον τινες
παραλ. φερ. Φ | υπο] απο L επι Δ παρα yˢᶜʳ   4 προσενεγκαι אBL 33 al f vg
syrʰᶜˡ me aethʰ] προσεγγισαι ACDΓΔΘᶠΠΣΦ al minᵖˡᵉʳ a b c e ff g syrᵖᵉˢʰ arm go | δια
τον οχλον] απο του οχλου D armᵛⁱᵈ | om εξορυξαντες D latᵛᵗ ᵖˡᵉʳ syrᵖᵉˢʰ aeth

the door on the side of the street : cf.
πρὸς τὴν θάλασσαν, iv. 1 : on the acc.
cf. i. 33. For χωρεῖν *capere* see Gen.
xiii. 6, 3 Regn. vii. 24 (38), Jo. ii. 6,
xxi. 25 ; and on ὥστε μηκέτι…μηδὲ see
notes on i. 44, 45.

καὶ ἐλάλει αὐτοῖς τὸν λόγον] The
preaching meanwhile proceeded within (imperf.). Ὁ λόγος=τὸ εὐαγγέλιον
occurs with various explanatory genitives, e.g. τοῦ θεοῦ, τοῦ κυρίου (Acts viii.
14, 25), τῆς σωτηρίας, τῆς χάριτος, τοῦ
εὐαγγελίου (Acts xiii. 26, xiv. 3, xv. 7),
τοῦ σταυροῦ (1 Cor. i. 18), τῆς καταλλαγῆς
(2 Cor. v. 19), τῆς ἀληθείας (Col. i. 5) ;
but the term (like ἡ ὁδός, τὸ θέλημα,
&c.) was also used by itself in the first
generation ; cf. Mc. iv. 14 ff., 33, Acts
viii. 4, x. 44, xiv. 26, xviii. 5. To
αὐτὸς ἦν διδάσκων Lc. adds καὶ
δύναμις Κυρίου ἦν εἰς τὸ ἰᾶσθαι αὐτόν :
on which see Mason, *Conditions*, &c.,
p. 97.

3. καὶ ἔρχονται φέροντες κτλ.] Mt.
καὶ ἰδοὺ προσέφερον αὐτῷ, Lc. κ. ἰδοὺ
ἄνδρες φέροντες. Mc. alone mentions
that the bearers were four. They
reach the outskirts of the crowd, but
are stopped before they can approach
the door. For αἰρόμενον cf. Ps. xc.
(xci.) 12, cited in Mt. iv. 6. Παραλυτικός (not class. or in LXX.) is used
by Mt., Mc. in this context, and by Mt.
also in cc. iv. 24, viii. 6 ; Lc. seems to
avoid it (v. 18, ἄνθρωπον ὃς ἦν παρα-
λελυμένος, 24 τῷ παραλελυμένῳ).

4. καὶ μὴ δυν. προσενέγκαι] Vg.,
cum non possent offerre eum illi ;

for προσενέγκαι the 'Western' and
traditional texts read προσεγγίσαι,
possibly a correction due to the
absence of αὐτόν. Cf. Lc. μὴ εὑρόντες ποίας εἰσενέγκωσιν αὐτόν. Nothing
daunted, they mounted on the roof (so
Lc. alone expressly, ἀναβάντες ἐπὶ τὸ
δῶμα, cf. Acts x. 9), by an external
staircase, the existence of which in
Palestinian houses of the period is
implied in Mc. xiii. 15.

ἀπεστέγασαν τὴν στέγην κτλ.]
Ἀποστεγάζω (ἅπ. λεγ. in the N. T.)
is used by Strabo (iv. 4), and by
Symmachus in Jer. xxix. 11 (xlix. 10)
for יְתִּ֑יב, LXX. ἀπεκάλυψα. The un-
roofing was, according to Lc., limited
to the removal of the tiles (διὰ κεράμων :
see however W. M. Ramsay, *Was Christ
born*, &c., p. 63 f.) just over the spot
where the Lord sat. It was done by
'digging up' the place (ἐξορύξαντες).
Ἐξορύσσειν is chiefly used of putting
out the eyes (Jud. xvi. 21, 1 Regn. xi.
2, Gal. iv. 15) ; the housebreaker is
said διορύσσειν (Mt. vi. 19) ; Joseph.
ant. xiv. 15. 12 uses ἀνασκάπτειν similarly. It is difficult to realise the
circumstances. The Lord was clearly
in a room immediately under the roof.
The ὑπερῷον would answer to the
conditions, and it appears to have
been a favourite resort of Rabbis when
they were engaged in teaching ; cf.
Lightfoot *ad l.*, Vitringa *de Syn.* 145,
Edersheim, *Life and Times*, i. 503 ;
the last-named writer suggests a roofed
gallery round the αὐλή. But it may

χαλῶσι τὸν κράβαττον ὅπου ὁ παραλυτικὸς κατέ-
5 κειτο. ⁵καὶ ἰδὼν ὁ Ἰησοῦς τὴν πίστιν αὐτῶν λέγει
τῷ παραλυτικῷ Τέκνον, ἀφίενταί σου αἱ ἁμαρτίαι.

4 κραβακτον ℵ item 9, 11, 12 κραββατον B^corrV grabattum a e grabatum c d f g ff |
οπου 2° ℵBDL a g] εφ ω ACEGΘ^fΦ al latt^vt pl er vg syrr arm me go aeth εφ ο Γ | ην ο
παραλ. κατακειμενος D   5 τεκνον] pr θαρσει C+μου ℵ* syr^hier me | αφιενται
B 28 33 a c e ff vg syrr go] αφιονται Δ αφεωνται ℵACDLΓΘ^fΠΣ(Φ) al | σου αι αμ.
ℵBDGLΔ 1 33 69 al^nonn] σοι αι αμ. σου AC³EHKM²SUVΓΠΣΦ al a c d f q

be doubted whether a fisherman's
house in Capernaum would have been
provided with such conveniences.
The next step was to lower (χαλῶσι
= Lc. καθῆκαν) the pallet on which the
man lay (Lc. the man, bed and all).
For χαλᾶν cf. Jer. xlv. (xxxviii.) 6,
ἐχάλασαν αὐτὸν εἰς τὸν λάκκον, Acts
ix. 25, 2 Cor. xi. 33. Κράβαττος, said
to be a Macedonian word (Sturz, dial.
Mac., p. 175 f.), does not occur in the
LXX., but is used by Aq. in Amos iii. 12
for עֶרֶשׂ (see Jerome's remarks ad l.),
and in the N. T. by Mc. (in this context and vi. 55), Jo. (v. 8 ff.), and Lc.
(Acts v. 15, where it is distinguished
from κλίνη—see Blass, ad l., ix. 33);
from the N. T., perhaps, it has passed
into Ev. Nicod. 6, Act. Thom. 50, 51.
It was used by certain writers of the
New Comedy. For the forms of the
word (κράβατος, κράβακτος—so ℵ¹⁰₁₁, cf.
κραβάκτιον, Grenfell, Gk. papyri ii. p.
161—κράββατος, κράββατος) see Winer-
Schm., p. 56, and n. ; in Latin it became grabātus (Catullus and Martial);
modern Greek retains it in the form
κρεββάτι (Kennedy, Sources of N. T.
Gk., p. 154). The classical equivalents
are ἀσκάντης, σκίμπους(Phryn. σκίμπους
λέγε ἀλλὰ μὴ κράββατος), σκιμπόδιον.
Clem. Al. paed. i. 6 substitutes σκίμ-
ποδα here; see also the story related
by Sozom. H. E. i. 11. The κράβαττος
or σκίμπους was the poor man's bed
(Seneca, ep. mor. ii. 6, where gra-
batus goes with sagum and panis
durus et sordidus), small and flexible,
and therefore better adapted for the
purpose of the bearers than the κλίνη

which Mt. and Lc. substitute. Lc.,
who seems to feel the difficulty as to
κλίνη, uses κλινίδιον as the story ad-
vances (v. 19).

5. καὶ ἰδὼν ὁ Ἰ. τὴν πίστιν αὐτῶν]
So Mt., Lc.; Victor: οὐ τὴν πίστιν
τοῦ παραλελυμένου ἀλλὰ τῶν κομισάν-
των. Ephrem: "See what the faith
of others may do for one." Ambros.
in Lc. v. 20, "Magnus Dominus
qui aliorum merito ignoscit aliis...si
gravium peccatorum diffidis veniam,
adhibe precatores, adhibe ecclesiam"
—an application of the words which,
as the history of Christian doctrine
shews, needs to be used with caution.
For ἰδεῖν πίστιν (Bengel: "opero-
sam") cf. 1 Macc. xiv. 35, James ii.
18. Λέγει τῷ παραλυτικῷ: Mt. εἶπεν
τ. π., Lc. εἶπεν.

τέκνον, ἀφίενταί σου αἱ ἁμαρτίαι]
'Child, thy sins are receiving forgiveness.' Τέκνον is used of disciples and
spiritual children (Mc. x. 24, 1 Cor. iv.
14, 17, &c.; see Intr., p. xx f.); for the
contrast between τέκνον and παιδίον
see Westcott on Jo. xxi. 5. Victor:
τὸ δὲ 'τέκνον' ἢ καὶ αὐτῷ πιστεύσαντι
ἢ κατὰ τῆς δημιουργίας λέγει. In either
case it is intended to cheer and win
confidence (Schanz: "Jesus den
Kranken mit dem gewinnenden τέκνον
anredet"), a point of which Lc.'s
ἄνθρωπε loses sight. Ἀφίενται, di-
mittuntur, see vv. ll. here and in v. 9,
and cf. Mt. ix. 2, 5.—The forgiveness
is regarded as continuous, beginning
from that hour (see however Burton,
§ 13, who calls ἀφ. an "aoristic present"). Lc. has ἀφέωνται (a Doric

⁶ἦσαν δέ τινες τῶν γραμματέων ἐκεῖ καθήμενοι καὶ 6
διαλογιζόμενοι ἐν ταῖς καρδίαις αὐτῶν ⁷Τί οὗτος 7
οὕτως λαλεῖ; βλασφημεῖ· τίς δύναται ἀφιέναι ἁμαρ-

6 αυτων]+λεγοντες D lat^vt^exc fq   7 τι] οτι B 482 om b c | om ουτως min²⁰ c
syr^pesh arm | om ουτως λαλει b q | λαλει βλασφημει אBDL a f ff vg me] λ. βλασφημιας
ΑΓΓ(Δ)ΠΣΦ al c syrr^(pesh) hcl arm go aeth

perfect, Winer-Schm., p. 119, cf. Blass,
Gr., p. 51), regarding the ἄφεσις,
from another point of view, as complete, although enduring in its effects.
Jewish thought connected forgiveness
with recovery: "there is no sick man
healed of his sickness until all his sins
have been forgiven him" (Schöttgen
ad l.).

6. ἦσαν δέ τινες τῶν γραμματέων
κτλ.] The first appearance of the
Scribes in the Synoptic narrative; cf.
supra i. 22. Lc. Φαρισαῖοι καὶ νομοδι-
δάσκαλοι (cf. Mc. ii. 16), adding οἱ
ἦσαν ἐληλυθότες ἐκ πάσης κώμης τῆς
Γαλειλαίας καὶ Ἰουδαίας καὶ Ἰερουσαλήμ:
i.e., the local Galilean Rabbis had now
been reinforced by others from the
capital, some of them possibly members of the Sanhedrin (see Mc. iii. 22).
The suspicions of the Pharisees of
Jerusalem had been roused before
Jesus left Judaea (Jo. iv. 1, 2), and
they had decided to watch His movements in Galilee (cf. Jo. i. 19, 24).
The Scribes were seated (καθήμενοι
Mc., Lc.), probably in the place of
honour near the Teacher (cf. xii. 38,
39).

διαλογιζόμενοι ἐν ταῖς καρδίαις
αὐτῶν] Mt. εἶπαν ἐν ἑαυτοῖς (cf. Mc.,
v. 8); in the immediate presence of
Jesus communication was impossible.
Like many of the finer points this
passes out of sight in Lc. (ἤρξαντο
διαλογίζεσθαι). For the two senses of
διαλογισμός see Lightfoot on Phil. ii.
14. The καρδία is the source and
seat of deliberative thought, cf. Mc.
vii. 21, Lc. ii. 35, ix. 47. As the
centre of the personal life, it is the

sphere not only of the passions and
emotions, but of the thoughts and
intellectual processes, at least so far
as they go to make up the moral
character. Thus διάνοια may be distinguished from καρδία (Mc. xii. 30,
Lc. i. 51), as one of the contents from
the seat and source; see Lightfoot on
Phil. iv. 7, and Westcott on Hebrews
viii. 10 (cf. p. 115 f.). Yet in the LXX.
διάνοια is for the most part used as a
rendering of לֵב or לֵבָב, with καρδία
as an occasional variant; see e.g. Exod.
xxxv. 9, Deut. vi. 5, Job i. 5.

7. τί οὗτος οὕτως λαλεῖ; βλασφη-
μεῖ] Comp. Mt. οὗτος βλασφημεῖ, Lc.
τίς ἐστιν οὗτος ὃς λαλεῖ βλασφημίας;
For βλασφημεῖν = λαλεῖν βλασφημίας
cf. 2 Macc. x. 34, xii. 14, Mt. xxvi.
65, Jo. x. 36, Acts xiii. 45, &c.: the
more usual constructions are βλ. τινα
(τι), εἴς τινα, ἔν τινι, and in class. Gk.,
περί, κατά τινος (WM., p. 278). Used
absolutely the word is understood
of the sin of blasphemy (sc. εἰς τὸν
θεόν, cf. Dan. iii. 96 (29), LXX., Apoc.
xvi. 11). The offence was a capital
one (Mt. xxvi. 65 f.), and the normal
punishment stoning (Lev. xxiv. 15,
16, 1 Kings xxi. 13, Jo. x. 33,
Acts vii. 58). The blasphemy in the
present instance was supposed to
lie in the words ἀφίενταί σου αἱ ἁμ.
(οὕτως λαλεῖ), by which the Lord
seemed to claim a Divine prerogative: cf. Jo. x. 36, Mt. xxvi. 65.

τίς δύναται...εἰ μὴ εἷς ὁ θεός;] See
Exod. xxxiv. 6, 7, Isa. xliii. 25, xliv.
22. On the O. T. doctrine of Forgiveness see Schultz, ii. 96: on the
Rabbinic doctrine, Edersheim, i. p.

§ F 8 τίας εἰ μὴ εἷς ὁ θεός ; ⁸⁸καὶ εὐθὺς ἐπιγνοὺς ὁ Ἰησοῦς

τῷ πνεύματι αὐτοῦ ὅτι οὕτως διαλογίζονται ἐν

§ Wᶜ ἑαυτοῖς ⁸λέγει αὐτοῖς Τί ταῦτα διαλογίζεσθε ἐν ταῖς

9 καρδίαις ὑμῶν ; ⁹τί ἐστιν εὐκοπώτερον, εἰπεῖν τῷ

8 om ευθυς D 28 64 565 a b c ff g q syrᵖᵉˢʰ arm aeth | om αυτου D 258 a b c e ff q |
όm ουτως B 102 a g r | διαλογιζονται] pr αυτοι ACΓΔΘ'ΠΣ 13 22 33 69 1071 minᵐᵘ
syrʰᵉˡ go | εαυτοις] αυτοις L min² | λεγει אBL 33 e f vg] ειπεν ACDΓΔΘ'Π alᵖˡ
a b c ff g q | om αυτοις B 102 ff arm | om ταυτα L

508 ff. For εἷς solus (Lc. μόνος) cf.
Mc. x. 18. Mt. omits this clause.

8. καὶ εὐθὺς ἐπιγνοὺς ὁ Ἰ. τῷ πνεύματι αὐτοῦ] The Lord at once became
conscious of the thoughts which occupied those about Him. Ἐπιγνούς (so
Lc.; Mt. ἰδών): cf. Mc. v. 30, ἐπιγνοὺς
ἐν ἑαυτῷ: the verb describes the fuller
knowledge gained by observation or
experience (cf. Lightfoot on Col. i. 6,
9)—the locus classicus is 1 Cor. xiii.
12, ἄρτι γινώσκω ἐκ μέρους τότε δὲ
ἐπιγνώσομαι. The recognition was in
the sphere of his human spirit, and
was not attained through the senses;
there was not even the guidance of
external circumstances, such as may
have enabled Him to 'see the faith'
of the friends of the paralytic. He
read their thoughts by His own consciousness, without visible or audible
indications to suggest them to Him.
For τὸ πνεῦμα, used in reference to
our Lord's human spirit, see Mt.
xxvii. 50, Mc. viii. 12. His spirit,
while it belonged to the human nature of Christ, was that part of
His human nature which was the immediate sphere of the Holy Spirit's
operations, and through which, as we
may reverently believe, the Sacred
Humanity was united to the Divine
Word. Wycliffe glosses "by the holy
goost"; Tindale rightly, "in his
spreete." On our Lord's power of
reading the thoughts of men see Jo.
ii. 24, 25, xxi. 17. In the O. T. this
power is represented as Divine, e.g.
Ps. cxxxviii. (cxxxix.) 2 σὺ συνῆκας
τοὺς διαλογισμούς μου, cf. Acts i. 24,

xv. 8 ὁ καρδιογνώστης θεός. Its presence
in Jesus clearly made a deep impression on His immediate followers.
See Mason, Conditions, &c., p. 164 ff.

ὅτι οὕτως διαλ. ἐν ἑαυτοῖς]=Mt. τὰς
ἐνθυμήσεις αὐτῶν, Lc. τοὺς διαλογισμοὺς
αὐτῶν. For τί ταῦτα διαλογίζεσθε Mt.
has ἵνα τί ἐνθυμεῖσθε πονηρά, whilst Lc.
simply omits ταῦτα.

9. τί ἐστιν εὐκοπώτερον κτλ.] Mt.
τί γάρ... The second question justifies
the first : 'why think evil...for which
is easier...?' Τί...ἤ=πότερον...ἤ (W-
M., p. 211). To the scribes the answer would seem self-evident; surely
it was easier to say the word of absolution than the word of healing (εἰπεῖν...ἤ εἰπεῖν), since the latter involved an appeal to sensible results.
Jerome: "inter dicere et facere multa
distantia est; utrum sint paralytico
peccata dimissa, solus noverat qui
dimittebat." Anticipating this reply
the Lord utters the word which they
deemed the harder, with results
which proved His power. But His
question, sinking into minds prepared
to receive it, suggests an opposite
conclusion; the word of absolution
is indeed the harder, since it deals
with the invisible and eternal order.
In speaking with authority the word
of absolution Christ had done the
greater thing; the healing of the
physical disorder was secondary and
made less demand on His power.
But this answer does not lie upon
the surface; the question presented
no enigma at the time; and Christ
does not stop to interpret His words,

παραλυτικῷ Ἀφίενταί σου αἱ ἁμαρτίαι, ἢ εἰπεῖν
Ἔγειρε καὶ ἆρον τὸν κράβαττόν σου καὶ περιπάτει;
¹⁰ἵνα δὲ εἰδῆτε ὅτι ἐξουσίαν ἔχει ὁ υἱὸς τοῦ ἀνθρώπου 10
ἐπὶ τῆς γῆς ἀφιέναι ἁμαρτίας—λέγει τῷ παραλυτικῷ

9 ἀφιενται...περιπατει] εγειρε αρον τον κραβ. σου και υπ. εις τ. οικον σου η ειπειν
αφαιωνται σοι αι αμ. D | αφιενται (ℵB 28 565)] αφεωνται AC(D)ΛΓΔΘ˙ΠΣ(Φ) al | σου
αι αμ. ℵBEFGHKLMUVΠΣ minˢᵃᵗ ᵐᵘ] σοι αι αμ. ACDSWᶜΓΔΘᶠΦ σοι αι αμ. σου a c f q
syrrᵖᵉˢʰ ʰᶜˡ arm me go aeth | εγειρε ℵACDEFGHKMSVΓΘˢΠΣΦ 1 33 alᵐᵘ] εγειρου
BL 28 εγειραι UWᶜΔΘᶠ minᵖˡ | om και 1° CDL 1 syrᵖᵉˢʰ arm | περιπατει ΑΒΓΠ
al minᶠᵉʳᵉ ᵒᵐⁿ b c e f q vg syrrᵖᵉˢʰ ʰᶜˡ me aeth] υπαγε ℵLWᶜΔ υπ. εις τον οικον σου D
33 a ff vg arm   10 επι τ. γ. αφ. αμ. ℵCDHLMWᶜΔΘᶠΣ alᵐᵘ latt syrᵖᵉˢʰ me arm
go] αφ. επι τ. γ. αμ. AEFGKSUVΓΠ 1 69 al syrʰᶜˡ αφ. αμ. επι τ. γ. ΒΦ 142 157

but leaves them to germinate where they found soil. Εὐκοπώτερόν ἐστιν occurs here in the three Synoptists, and again in Mc. x. 25 (Mt. Lc.) and Lc. xvi. 17; for εὔκοπος see Sir. xxii. 15, 1 Macc. iii. 18, and εὐκοπία occurs in 2 Macc. ii. 25; the words belong to the later Greek from Aristophanes onwards. Ἔγειρε: WH. prefer ἐγείρου, the reading of BL 28; see note on v. 11.

10. ἵνα δὲ εἰδῆτε ὅτι κτλ.] ‘But—be the answer what it may—to convince you that the word of absolution was not uttered without authority, I will confirm it by the word of healing of which you may see the effects.’ On the construction see Blass, Gr., p. 286 f. Ἐξουσίαν ἔχει, Mt., Mc., Lc., not = potest, potestatem habet, as the Latin versions render, followed by the English versions from Wycliffe onwards, but "hath authority": cf. i. 22, 27. This ἐξουσία is not in conflict with the δύναμις of GOD (ii. 7), but dependent on it. It is claimed by the Lord as the Son of Man, i.e. as belonging to Him in His Incarnate Life as the ideal Man Who has received the fulness of the Spirit (cf. i. 10, Jo. xx. 23), and as Head of the race: cf. Jo. v. 26.

ὁ υἱὸς τοῦ ἀνθρώπου] Used here for the first time in the Synoptic narrative: cf. ii. 28, viii. 31, 38, ix.

9, 12, 31, x. 33, 45, xiii. 26, xiv. 21, 41, 62. The LXX. has (οἱ) υἱοὶ τοῦ ἀνθρώπου (בְּנֵי־הָאָדָם), Eccl. iii. 18, 19, 21, and υἱὸς ἀνθρώπου (בַּר־אֱנָשׁ), Dan. vii. 13 (LXX. and Th.) and (בֶּן־אָדָם), Ezek. ii. 1, &c., Dan. viii. 17. The term is usually thought to be based on Dan. vii. 13, but see Westcott, add. note on Jo. i. 51, and on the interpretation of Dan. l.c. cf. Stanton, J. and C. Messiah, p. 109, and Bevan, Daniel, p. 118 f. Comp. also Charles, B. of Enoch, p. 312 ff., and on the use of υἱὸς τοῦ ἀνθρ. by our Lord and in the early Church, see Stanton, p. 239 ff.; G. Dalman, Die Worte Jesu i., p. 191 ff.; the careful investigations by Dr Jas. Drummond in J. Th. St. ii. pp. 350 ff., 539; and the art. Son of Man in Hastings, D.B. iv.

ἐπὶ τῆς γῆς ἀφιέναι ἁμαρτίας] In contrast to an implied 'in Heaven,' cf. Lc. ii. 14, ἐν ὑψίστοις...ἐπὶ γῆς: Mt. xvi. 19, Col. i. 20, ἐπὶ τῆς γῆς...ἐν τοῖς οὐρανοῖς. The ratification of the absolving words belongs to another order (Mt. l.c.): the act of absolution, which is committed to the Son of Man as such, takes place in man's world, and is pronounced by human lips, either those of the Son of Man Himself or of men who receive His Spirit and are sent by Him for that end (Jo. xx. 23). Such absolutions do not invade

11 ¹¹*Coὶ λέγω, ἔγειρε, ἆρον τὸν κράβαττόν σου καὶ*
12 *ὕπαγε εἰς τὸν οἶκόν σου. ¹²καὶ ἠγέρθη, καὶ εὐθὺς*
ἄρας τὸν κράβαττον ἐξῆλθεν ἔμπροσθεν πάντων·
ὥστε ἐξίστασθαι πάντας καὶ δοξάζειν τὸν θεὸν
¶ Θʳ   *[λέγοντας] ὅτι Οὕτως¶ οὐδέποτε εἴδαμεν.¶*
¶ syrʰⁱᵉʳ

11 εγειραι LUWᶜΔ alˢᵃᵗᵐᵘ εγειρον K+και AWᶜΔΘʳΙΙ al   12 ηγ. και ευθυς
ℵB(C*) L 33 meᶜᵒᵈ] ηγ. ευθεως και AC³WᶜΓΔΘʳΠΣΦ al syrr go aeth ευθεως ηγ. και
D om ευθ. b c e ff q | εμπροσθεν ℵBL 604] εναντιον ACDWᶜΓΔΠΣ al ενωπιον WᵉΘʳΦ
33 1071 alᵖᵃᵘᶜ | λεγοντας ℵACLWᶜΓΔΘʳΠΣΦ] om B b και λεγειν D arm | ειδαμεν
CD (ειδομεν ℵᶜ·ᵃBLWᶜΓ al ιδομεν AKMVII al)] εφανη εν τω Ισραηλ ℵ*

the prerogative of GOD, since they ultimately proceed from Him, and become effective only on conditions which He prescribes.

λέγει τῷ παραλυτικῷ] Mt. τότε κτλ.: Lc. εἶπεν τῷ παραλελυμένῳ. It is instructive to observe how a note which clearly belongs to the common tradition receives a slightly different form from each of the Synoptists.

11. σοὶ λέγω, ἔγειρε] The absolution was declaratory (ἀφίενται), the healing is given in the form of a command, for the recipient must co-operate. Ἔγειρε, like ἄγε, is used intransitively; see Winer-Schm., p. 126; ἐγείρου (vv. ll. *v.* 9) seems to be a grammatical correction; ἐγείραι (Mt. ix. 5, 6, Mc. *ad l.*, Lc. v. 24, vi. 8, viii. 54, Jo. v. 8) is possibly an itacism, yet see WSchm. p. 126.

ἆρον τὸν κράβ. σου] Cf. Jo. v. 8. The κράβαττος without its burden could easily be carried by one man if in good health. That the paralytic could do this was proof of his complete recovery. Taken with ὕπαγε εἰς τὸν οἶκόν σου (Mt. Mc.), the command points to his being an inhabitant of Capernaum, and not one of the crowd from outside. He would therefore remain as a standing witness to Jesus.

12. καὶ ἠγέρθη, καὶ εὐθύς κτλ.] The command received prompt (εὐθύς, Mc.

only) obedience: the paralytic rose (ἠγέρθη, raised himself), took the pallet on his back or under his arm and, the crowd giving way, passed out into the street (ἐξῆλθεν, Mc.; Mt. Lc. ἀπῆλθεν), in the sight of (ἔμπροσθεν = ἐνώπιον = לִפְנֵי, cf. Guillemard on Mt. v. 16) the whole company.

ὥστε ἐξίστασθαι πάντας κτλ.] Mt. ἰδόντες δὲ ἐφοβήθησαν: Lc. ἔκστασις ἔλαβεν ἅπαντας. For the moment the general amazement was too great for words (cf. v. 42, vi. 51): when they spoke, it was to glorify GOD for the authority committed to humanity in the person of Jesus (Mt. τὸν δόντα ἐξουσίαν τοιαύτην τοῖς ἀνθρώποις). According to Lc. the restored paralytic had set the example (ἀπῆλθεν...δοξάζων τὸν θεόν).

λέγοντας ὅτι Οὕτως οὐδέποτε εἴδαμεν] Lc. εἴδαμεν παράδοξα σήμερον. The contrast between this astonishment at the physical cure, and the silence with which the absolution had been received, did not escape the ancient expositors: cf. Victor: τὸ μεῖζον ἐάσαντες τὴν τῶν ἁμαρτιῶν ἄφεσιν τὸ φαινόμενον θαυμάζουσιν. Ἰδεῖν οὕτως is an unusual construction for ἰδ. τοιαῦτα, but see Mt. ix. 33, οὐδέποτε ἐφάνη οὕτως; for εἴδαμεν cf. WH., *Notes*, p. 164: Blass, *Gr.*, p. 45. Lc. has given the sense in other words; both accounts convey the same impression of unbounded surprise.

¹³ Καὶ ἐξῆλθεν πάλιν παρὰ τὴν θάλασσαν· καὶ 13
πᾶς ὁ ὄχλος ἤρχετο πρὸς αὐτόν, καὶ ἐδίδασκεν αὐτούς. ¹⁴§καὶ παράγων εἶδεν Λευεὶν τὸν τοῦ Ἀλφαίου 14 § syr^hior
καθήμενον ἐπὶ τὸ τελώνιον, καὶ λέγει αὐτῷ Ἀκολούθει
μοι· καὶ ἀναστὰς ἠκολούθησεν αὐτῷ.

13 om παλιν D 13 | παρα] εις ℵ* (π. ℵ^c.ᵃ) | om ο D* | ηρχοντο 1071   14 παρα-
γων]+ῑς FGHΓ min^nonn | Λευειν ℵ^c.ᵃBE*LMΣΦ (Λευιν CE²FGHSUV Λευει ℵ* Λευι
AKSΓΔΠ 33 al^mu)] Ιακωβον D 13 69 124^txt a b c d e ff g r

13—14. CALL OF LEVI (Mt. ix. 9,
Lc. v. 27—28).

13. καὶ ἐξῆλθεν πάλιν κτλ.] Probably as soon as the crowd was dispersed and the excitement had subsided. Ἐξῆλθεν, i.e. from the house
and the town, cf. i. 35: with ἐξ. παρά
comp. Acts xvi. 13, ἐξήλθομεν ἔξω τῆς
πύλης παρὰ ποταμόν: the way out led
Him to the seaside, Vg. ad mare, i.e.
ad oram maris. Πάλιν—a note frequently struck by Mc., cf. ii. 1, iii.
1, 20, iv. 1, &c.—refers not to ἐξ.,
but to παρὰ τ. θάλασσαν, cf. i. 16;
once again He found Himself, as at
the beginning of His Ministry, by
the side of the lake.

καὶ πᾶς ὁ ὄχλος ἤρχετο κτλ.] As
soon as He is seen there, the crowd
reassembles as thick as ever (πᾶς),
and the teaching, interrupted in the
house, begins afresh by the lake. The
imperfects ἤρχετο...ἐδίδασκεν, as contrasted with ἐξῆλθεν, point to the
continuance of the process, perhaps
at intervals, through the day. Only
Mc. notes the teaching by the seaside
on this occasion.

14. καὶ παράγων κτλ.] As He
teaches, or at intervals between the
instructions, He passes on along the
shore. Παράγων εἶδεν: the same words
are used at the call of Simon and
Andrew (i. 16): cf. also Jo. ix. 1;
even in moving from place to place
the Lord was on the watch for opportunities. Λευεὶν τὸν τοῦ Ἀλφαίου
(so Mc. only: Lc. ὀνόματι Λευείν: Mt.
ἄνθρωπον...λεγόμενον Ματθαῖον). Λευείς

(Λευεί, וֵי.) occurs in 1 Esdr. ix. 14 as
the proper name of a Jew of the time
of the exile, and is used in Heb. vii. 9
for the patriarch; cf. Λευίς Joseph. ant.
i. 19. 7. In Origen c. Cels. i. 62 the
true reading is Λευής, and not, as was
formerly supposed, Λεβής: see WH.,
Intr., p. 144 (ed. 2, 1896). Ἀλφαῖος,
Vg. Alphaeus, was also the name of
the father of the second James (Mc. iii.
18): hence apparently the 'Western'
reading Ἰάκωβον in this context, see
vv. ll., and Ephrem's comment "He
chose James the publican," ev. con-
cord. exp. p. 58: cf. Photius in
Possin. caten. in Mc. p. 50: δύο ἦσαν
τελῶναι ἐκ τῶν δώδεκα, Ματθαῖος καὶ
Ἰάκωβος.

τοῦ Ἀλφαίου] Ἀλφαῖος = Aram.
חַלְפַי, cf. Syrr.^sin. (Lc.)pesh. ܚܠܦܝ. Whether
it is identical with Κλωπᾶς (Jo. xix.
25) is more than doubtful, see Lightfoot, Galatians, p. 267 n.; against
that view is the spelling of the latter
word in Syrr.^pesh. hier. with ܒ instead of
ܦ. On the identity of Λευείς with
Ματθαῖος see note on iii. 18.

καθήμενον ἐπὶ τὸ τελώνιον] Capernaum was on the Great West road
which led from Damascus to the
Mediterranean (G. A. Smith, Hist.
Geogr., p. 428), and like Jericho had
its establishment of τελῶναι and its
τελώνιον, but the tolls were here collected for the tetrarch and not for the
Emperor (Schürer I. ii. 68). Τελώνιον
(Vg. teloneum, cf. Tert. de bapt. 12;
used in modern Greek, Kennedy,

15   ¹⁵ Καὶ γίνεται κατακεῖσθαι αὐτὸν ἐν τῇ οἰκίᾳ
αὐτοῦ, καὶ πολλοὶ τελῶναι καὶ ἁμαρτωλοὶ συνανέ-

15 γίνεται אBL 33 565 604] εγενετο ACDΓΔΠΣΦ al latt | κατακεισθαι αυτ.] pr. εν
τω ACWᶜΓΠΣΦ alᵖˡᵉʳ f q vg syrrᵖᵉˢʰʰᶜˡ arm me εν τω κατακλιθηναι Δ κατακειμενων
αυτων D a b c e ff

p. 154) is, (1) the toll (Strabo, xvi.
1. 27, τελώνιον ἔχει καὶ τοῦτ᾽ οὐ μέτριον),
(2) the toll-house (Wycliffe, "tolbothe,"
Tindale, "receyte of custome"), as
in this context. Levi was seated,
doubtless amongst other τελῶναι (v.
15), 'at' (ad) the office. Ἐπί c.
acc. in the N. T. often answers the
question 'whither?' (Blass, Gr., p. 136),
cf. iv. 38, Lc. ii. 25, Acts i. 21 : the
phrase is here common to Mt., Mc.,
Lc.

καὶ λέγει αὐτῷ Ἀκολούθει μοι] See
note on i. 17. The command was
practically a call to discipleship, involving the complete abandonment of
his work. Disciples who were fishermen could return to their fishing at
pleasure (cf. Jo. xxi. 3); not so the
toll-collector who forsook his post.
Yet Levi did not hesitate: ἀναστὰς
ἠκολούθησεν αὐτῷ, Mt., Mc.; Lc.,
thinking of the life which was thus
begun, writes ἠκολούθει, and adds καταλιπὼν πάντα. The call was given
by One Who knew that the way
had been prepared for its acceptance. How the preparation had been
made can only be conjectured : possibly, as in the case of the first four,
through the Baptist, Lc. iii. 12. Cf.
Tert. l. c., "nescio quorum fide uno
verbo Domini suscitatus teloneum
dereliquit." To Porphyry, who saw in
Matthew's prompt obedience proof of
the mental weakness of Christ's disciples, Jerome replies that it rather
attests the magnetic power exerted
on men by His unique personality.
15—17. FEAST IN LEVI'S HOUSE
(Mt. ix. 10—13, Lc. v. 29—32).
15. καὶ γίνεται ... καὶ] Mt. καὶ
ἐγένετο...καὶ ἰδού: Lc. drops the
Hebraic turn of the sentence. Κατα-

κεῖσθαι, used of the sick in i. 30, ii. 4,
refers here and in xiv. 3 to persons
at table (see Amos vi. 4); cf. Judith
xiii. 15, Lc. v. 29, 1 Cor. viii. 10, and
in class. Greek, Plato, Symp. 185 D.
Mt. prefers ἀνακεῖσθαι, which is more
usual in this sense in Biblical Greek
(LXX., 1 Esdr. iv. 10, Tob. ix. 6 (א),
Mc. xiv. 18, &c.), so Mc. just below
(συνανέκειντο); the Vg. endeavours to
distinguish between the two (cum
accumberet...simul discumbebant). Ἐν
τῇ οἰκίᾳ αὐτοῦ : so Lc. ; Mt., speaking
of his own house, omits αὐτοῦ—a house
to its owner or tenant is simply ἡ οἰκία.
A second house in Capernaum is now
thrown open to Jesus and His disciples, cf. i. 29. On αὐτοῦ (nearly =
ἐκείνου) cf. WM., pp. 183, 788.

πολλοὶ τελῶναι κτλ.] So Mt. ; Lc.
ἦν ὄχλος πολὺς τελωνῶν καὶ ἄλλων. It
was, as Lc. says, a μεγάλη δοχή, a
'reception,' which, if intended in the
first instance to do honour to the
Master (αὐτῷ), included many of Levi's
friends and colleagues. Τελώνης occurs
in Mc. only in this context. Τελωνεῖν
'to impose taxes' is used in 1 Macc.
xiii. 39 (εἴ τι ἄλλο ἐτελωνεῖτο ἐν Ἱερουσαλήμ, μηκέτι τελωνείσθω, cf. x. 29, 30)
of dues exacted from the Jews under
the Syrian domination. The τελώνης
or tax-farmer was a well-known
personage at Athens in the time of
Aristophanes, and not popular; cf.
Ar. Eq. 247 f., παῖε παῖε τὸν πανοῦργον...
καὶ τελώνην καὶ φάραγγα καὶ Χάρυβδιν
ἁρπαγῆς. The Vg. renders the word
by the title of the corresponding
officer at Rome, publicanus; but the
τελῶναι of the Gospels corresponded
more nearly to the portitores. With
the τελῶναι were ἁμαρτωλοί : the two
classes are found together again in

κεͺντο τῷ ᾽Ιησοῦ καὶ τοῖς μαθηταῖς αὐτοῦ· ἦσαν γὰρ
πολλοί· καὶ ἠκολούθουν αὐτῷ ¹⁶καὶ [οἱ] γραμματεῖς 16

15 συνανεκειντο] pr ελθοντες AC* | και ηκολουθουν (-θησαν ACDΓΠΣΦ) αυτω] pr
οι D b f vg et omisso και a c e ff q arm   16 και (om και ΒΔ me) οι (om οι ℵWᶜᵛⁱᵈ)
γρ. των Φαρ. (ℵ)BL(Wᶜᵛⁱᵈ)Δ 33 b meᶜᵒᵈ] και οι γρ. και Φαρ. ACDΓΠΦ al οι δε γρ. και
οι Φαρ. Σ 604 armᵛⁱᵈ

Mt. ix. 19, Lc. xv. 1. Fritzsche cites
Lucian *Necyom.* 11, μοιχοὶ καὶ πορνο-
βοσκοὶ καὶ τελῶναι καὶ κόλακες καὶ
συκοφάνται καὶ τοιοῦτος ὅμιλος τῶν
πάντα κυκώντων ἐν τῷ βίῳ. But ἁμ. is
probably used in this connexion with
some latitude: sometimes it refers to
the outcasts of society (Lc. vii. 37),
but as used by the Scribes it would
include non-Pharisees e.g. Sadducees (so frequently in the Psalms
of Solomon, Ryle and James, pp.
xlvi, 3 f.), Gentiles (Galatians ii. 15,
Lightfoot's note), or even Hellenizing
Jews (1 Macc. ii. 44, 48). Many of
the men thus branded in Capernaum
were probably guilty of no worse
offence than abstaining from the
official piety of the Pharisees, or
following proscribed occupations (Lc.
xix. 7, 8), or were of Gentile extraction, or merely consorted with
Gentiles (Acts x. 28): cf. Mt. xviii. 17
ὁ ἐθνικὸς καὶ ὁ τ. The word ἁμαρτωλός belongs to the later Greek, but
was probably a colloquialism in
earlier times (cf. Ar. *Thesm.* 1111);
in the LXX. it is specially common
in Pss. (where it mostly = רָשָׁע) and
in Sirach.

συνανέκειντο τῷ ᾽Ιησοῦ κτλ.] So
Mt. Συνανακεῖσθαι (3 Macc. v. 39)
occurs again in vi. 22, and in Lc. vii.
49, xiv. 10, 15; Jo. appears to prefer
ἀνακεῖσθαι σύν (xii. 2). ᾽Ιησοῦ is the
N. T. form of the dat. (WM., p. 77);
in Deut. iii. 21, xxxi. 23, Jos. i. 1, &c.
᾽Ιησοῖ is the reading of Cod. B (in
Jos. iv. 15 of A also). Μαθητής is
here used by Mc. for the first time; it
occurs in Cod. A of Jer. xiii. 21, and
again in xx. 11, xxvi. (xlvi.) 9, and not

elsewhere in the LXX., but it is used
by Plato for the adult pupil of a
philosopher (*Prot.* 315 A). The Biblical μαθητής is the pupil (תַּלְמִיד) of
a religious teacher, such as a Rabbi,
or a Prophet who assumed the office
of διδάσκαλος. On the pupils of the
Scribes see Schürer II. i. p. 324; cf.
the reference to them in Aboth i. 1
(Taylor, *Sayings*, &c., p. 25). The
master followed by his pupils was
a familiar sight in Galilee; it was
the teaching which was new.

ἦσαν γὰρ πολλοί] These words appear to refer to τελ. κ. ἁμ., reasserting
the singular fact just mentioned—
an editorial note, or possibly one
belonging to the earliest form of
the tradition. If καὶ ἠκολούθουν
αὐτῷ is to be connected (WH.) with
the antecedent clause, it must be
taken to refer to the fact that a
number of this class had already
begun to follow Jesus, probably in
consequence of His words of forgiveness to the paralytic, as well as
through the example of Levi. But
see next note.

15—16. καὶ ἠκολούθουν αὐτῷ κτλ.]
So the words should probably be
connected and read. Jesus was followed to Levi's house by enemies
as well as (καί) disciples. ᾽Ακολουθεῖν
in the Gospels usually implies moral
attraction, and it may be to the
rarity of the ordinary meaning that
the disturbance of the text is due:
D (οἱ καὶ...καὶ...καὶ εἶδαν) mediates between the two texts. Οἱ γραμματεῖς
τῶν Φαρισαίων: those of the Scribes
who belonged to the Pharisees, cf.
Acts xxiii. 9, τινὲς τῶν γραμματέων

τῶν Φαρισαίων· καὶ ἰδόντες ὅτι ἐσθίει μετὰ τῶν
ἁμαρτωλῶν καὶ τελωνῶν ἔλεγον τοῖς μαθηταῖς αὐτοῦ
¶ Wᶜ Ὅτι μετὰ τῶν τελωνῶν¶ καὶ ἁμαρτωλῶν ἐσθίει;
§ i 17 §¹⁷καὶ ἀκούσας ὁ Ἰησοῦς λέγει αὐτοῖς ὅτι Οὐ χρείαν
ἔχουσιν οἱ ἰσχύοντες ἰατροῦ, ἀλλ᾿ οἱ κακῶς ἔχοντες·
¶ syrʰⁱᵉʳ οὐκ ἦλθον καλέσαι δικαίους ἀλλὰ ἁμαρτωλούς.¶

16 καὶ ἰδόντες ℵBLΔWᶜ] om καὶ ACΓΠΣΦ lattᵛᵗᵖˡᵛᵍ armᵛⁱᵈ καὶ ειδαν D | οτι εσθιει
B 33 565] οτι ησθιεν ℵDL c vg αυτον εσθιοντα ACWᶜΓΔΠΣΦ al a f q go | αμαρτ. κ.
τελ. BDL* 33 565 a b c g q vgᶜᵒᵈᵈ] τελ. κ. αμαρτ. ℵACLᶜᵒʳʳWᶜΓΔΠΣΦ al f ff syrrᵖᵉˢʰ ʰᶜˡ
arm go | οτι] pr τι ACΓΔΠΣΦ al διὰ τι ℵD | τελ. κ. αμ.] τελ. κ. των αμ. B αμ. κ. των
τελ. D a aeth | εσθιει 2° (ℵBD minᵖᵃᵘᶜ a b c ff εσθιετε GΣ 124 604 syrʰᶜˡ)]+και πινει
ACEFHKLΓΔΠΦ al c f vg syrrᵖᵉˢʰ ʰᶜˡ me go aeth+και πινετε GΣ 124 604 syrʰᶜˡ+ο
διδασκαλος υμων ℵC (ante εσθ.) LΔ 69 1071 al c f vg me aeth   17 om αυτοις D
1 209 a b c ff g q | οτι BD 1071] om cett | ου] ου γαρ CL 1071 c f ff vg | αλλα B |
αμαρτωλους]+εις μετανοιαν CΓ al a c f g syrʰⁱᵉʳ (om εις μ. ℵABDKLΔΠΣΦ al b f ff q vg
syrrᵖᵉˢʰ ʰᶜˡ arm me aeth)

τοῦ μέρους τῶν Φαρισαίων. Mt. has
οἱ Φαρισαῖοι, Lc., combining Mt. and
Mc., οἱ Φ. καὶ οἱ γρ. αὐτῶν.

καὶ ἰδόντες ὅτι κτλ.] The changes of
order (15, τελ. κ. ἁμ., 16, ἁμ. κ. τελ.
(1°), τελ. κ. ἁμ. (2°)) are singular and,
if original, can hardly be accidental.
Possibly Mc. means to shew that in
the thoughts of these Scribes, though
not in their words, the charge of
being in the company of sinners was
foremost. Here, at least, the Master
had, as they supposed, revealed His
departure from the standard of the
O. T. (Ps. i. 1). For ἰδεῖν ὅτι (see
vv. ll.) cf. ix. 25.

ἔλεγον τοῖς μαθηταῖς κτλ.] Not yet
daring to remonstrate with the Master; they have learnt caution from the
experience related in ii. 8. Ὅτι is
here = τί; (Mt., Lc., διὰ τί;): cf. ix. 11,
28, and for the LXX., 1 Chron. xvii. 6
(ὅτι = מָה;), Jer. ii. 36 (= מַה); see
WM., p. 208, n. 5, and Burton,
§ 349. To eat with Gentiles was an
offence recognised even by Pharisaic
Christians (Acts xi. 3, cf. Gal. ii. 11 f.),
and publicans and sinners were ranked
in the same category with Gentiles
(1 Cor. v. 11).

After ἐσθίει Mt. supplies ὁ διδάσκαλος ὑμῶν: Lc. includes the disciples
(ἐσθίετε καὶ πίνετε).

17. καὶ ἀκούσας ὁ Ἰησοῦς] The
remark does not escape Him: cf.
v. 36. Οὐ χρείαν ἔχουσιν οἱ ἰσχ.
κτλ.: so the three Synoptists (Lc.,
ὑγιαίνοντες = ἰσχύοντες). The proverb
in some form was not unknown to
pagan writers, e.g. Pausanias ap.
Plutarch. apophth. Lacon. 230 F, οὐδ᾿
οἱ ἰατροί, ἔφη, παρὰ τοῖς ὑγιαίνουσιν
ὅπου δὲ οἱ νοσοῦντες διατρίβειν εἰώθα-
σιν: Diog. Laert. Antisth. vi. 1. 6,
οἱ ἰατροί, φησί, μετὰ τῶν νοσούντων
εἰσὶν ἀλλ᾿ οὐ πυρέττουσιν: the last
words present an application to which
Jesus does not refer, but which is implied in the use of the saying.

οὐκ ἦλθον κτλ.] Lc. οὐκ ἐλήλυθα,
adding εἰς μετάνοιαν—a true gloss,
but perhaps not so well in keeping with the proverbial form of
the saying as the terser ending.
There is no need to say that the
physician's aim is the restoration of
the patient to health. For early
homiletic applications see Justin M.,
apol. i. 15, οὐ γὰρ τοὺς δικαίους οὐδὲ
τοὺς σώφρονας εἰς μετάνοιαν ἐκάλεσεν

¹⁸ Καὶ ἦσαν οἱ μαθηταὶ 'Ιωάνου καὶ οἱ Φαρισαῖοι 18
νηστεύοντες. καὶ ἔρχονται καὶ λέγουσιν αὐτῷ Διὰ

18 οἱ Φαρισαιοι ℵABCDKMΠ al b c e f ff q vg syrr^{gw hcl} arm me go] οι των Φαρισαιων
EFGHLSUVΓΔΠΣ 1 33 al a g l syr^{sch} οι Φαρισαιων Φ

ὁ Χριστός, ἀλλὰ τοὺς ἀσεβεῖς καὶ ἀκο-
λάστους καὶ ἀδίκους. Ps. Clem. 2 Cor.
2, τοῦτο λέγει ὅτι δεῖ τοὺς ἀπολλυμέ-
νους σῴζειν· ἐκεῖνο γάρ ἐστιν μέγα καὶ
θαυμαστόν, οὐ τὰ ἑστῶτα στηρίζειν ἀλλὰ τὰ πίπτοντα. The contrast of ἁμαρτωλός and δίκαιος appears first in Ps.
i. 5. The question who are the δίκαιοι whom Christ did not come to
call has exercised interpreters here
and in Lc. xv. 17. In such contexts
the relatively righteous can hardly
be in view, since all are ἁμαρτωλοί
in the sight of GOD and of Christ
(Rom. iii. 23, 1 John i. 8). Hence
Macarius Magnes, iv. 18, argues that
the δίκαιοι are the Angels. But since
our Lord speaks only of those within
the sphere of His mission, the explanation is inadmissible. Rather His
reference is to the Pharisees, on the
assumption that they were what they
professed to be, and the saying in
this respect should not be pressed
beyond its immediate application:
cf. Jerome: "sugillat scribas et Pharisaeos, qui iustos se aestimantes peccatorum et publicanorum consortia
declinabant"; we need not add with
Thpht.: κατ' εἰρωνείαν γὰρ τοῦτό φησιν.
The point of it is that if the guests
were ἁμαρτωλοί, it was in such company the physician of souls might be
sought, and not under opposite circumstances. For this view of sin as
a disease comp. Isa. i. 4 ff. and liii.
5, τῷ μώλωπι αὐτοῦ ἡμεῖς ἰάθημεν.
Mt. inserts between the proverb and
its application a reference to Hosea
vi. 6 q. v. With ἦλθον cf. ἐξῆλθον,
i. 38, and note there; x. 45, Jo. i. 11,
iii. 2, &c.

18—22. QUESTION OF FASTING :
THE OLD AND THE NEW (Mt. ix. 14
—17, Lc. v. 33—39).
18. καὶ ἦσαν οἱ μαθηταί κτλ.] Vg. et

erant...ieiunantes, 'were fasting' not
(as WM., p. 438) 'were used to fast' ;
cf. Lc. νηστεύουσιν πυκνά; on this imperf. see Blass, Gr., p. 198 f., Burton,
§ 34. If Levi's entertainment fell on
a Sunday or a Wednesday night, the
disciples of Jesus were feasting after
the disciples of stricter schools had
begun one of their weekly fasts. The
Law required abstinence only on the
Day of the Atonement (ἡ νηστεία,
Acts xxvii. 9), but the stricter Jews
practised it on the second and fifth
days of every week (Schürer II. ii.
119). For the practice of the disciples
of the Pharisees (i.e. the pupils of
Pharisaic Rabbis) see Lc. xviii. 12,
νηστεύω δὶς τοῦ σαββάτου, Didache
7 = Apost. Const. vii. 23, νηστεύουσι
γὰρ δευτέρᾳ σαββάτων καὶ πέμπτῃ, and
J. Lightfoot on Mt. ix. 14. The
disciples of John (mentioned again in
Jo. i. 35, iii. 25, cf. Acts xix. 2 ff.)
naturally inherited John's asceticism
(Mt. xi. 18). Tatian omits this explanatory note, which is peculiar to Mc.

καὶ ἔρχονται κτλ.] Not apparently
the disciples of John or of the Pharisees, but the Scribes, who have now
gathered courage from confidence in
the goodness of their cause: cf. Lc.
οἱ δὲ εἶπαν. Mt. gives another account: προσέρχονται αὐτῷ οἱ μαθηταὶ
'Ιωάνου, and alters the question accordingly (διὰ τί ἡμεῖς κτλ.). Tatian
ignores the difference, adopting Lc.'s
form. Later harmonists imagine the
same question to be put in varying
form by the disciples and the guests,
e.g. Aug. de cons. ii. 26. 62, who is
followed by Bede: "colligendum a
pluribus hanc Domino objectam esse
quaestionem et a Pharisaeis scilicet
et a discipulis Joannis et a convivis
vel aliis quibusdam." The uncertainty
thus imported into the history is

τί οἱ μαθηταὶ Ἰωάνου καὶ οἱ μαθηταὶ τῶν Φαρισαίωι·
νηστεύουσιν οἱ δὲ σοὶ μαθηταὶ οὐ νηστεύουσιν; καὶ
19 εἶπεν αὐτοῖς ὁ Ἰησοῦς ¹⁹Μὴ δύνανται οἱ υἱοὶ τοῦ
νυμφῶνος ἐν ᾧ ὁ νυμφίος μετ᾽ αὐτῶν ἐστιν νηστεύειν;
ὅσον χρόνον ἔχουσιν τὸν νυμφίον μετ᾽ αὐτῶν οἱ
20 δύνανται νηστεύειν· ²⁰ἐλεύσονται δὲ ἡμέραι ὅταν

18 οι μαθ. τ. Φαρ. ℵBC*L 33 565 e aeth] οι τ. Φ. C²DΓΔΠΣΦ al c vg syrr^pesh hcl οι
Φαρισαιοι min^pauc a f ff arm οι απο τ. Φ. οι μαθ. τ. Φ. 1071 om A | om μαθηται 4° B
127 2^pe   19 om ο Ιησ. D 28 b i q | του νυμφ.] nuptiarum b ff vg | om οσον
χρονον ... νηστευειν DU 1 33 604 al^pauc a b e ff g i syr^pesh aeth | μεθ εαυτων
ΑΓΛΓΔΠΣΦ al

surely a worse evil than any doubt that can arise as to the precise accuracy of one of the reports.

οἱ δὲ σοὶ μαθηταί κτλ.] They still stop short of a direct attack upon the Master; cf. v. 24.

19. μὴ δύνανται;] Vg. numquid possunt? Μή expects a negative answer (WM., p. 641, Blass, Gr., p. 254); cf. e.g. Mt. vii. 9, 10, Jo. iii. 4, James ii. 14. Lc., as often, turns the sentence into another form with a slightly different sense: μὴ δύνασθε...ποιεῖν νηστεῦσαι; in Mt. and Mc. δύνανται points to the moral impossibility; they might be made to fast, but it would not be a fast worthy of the name.

οἱ υἱοὶ τοῦ νυμφῶνος] = בְּנֵי הַחֻפָּה, known in class. Greek as νυμφευταί, and in the later literary style as παράνυμφοι or παρανύμφιοι. For νυμφών (= παστός, Joel ii. 16) cf. Tobit vi. 14, 17, and for the idiom 'sons of,' &c., 1 Macc. iv. 2 οἱ υἱοὶ τῆς ἄκρας = 'the men of the citadel'; see Trench, Studies, p. 170 n. The Lord perhaps designedly adopts the Baptist's own metaphor (Jo. iii. 29), substituting however οἱ υἱοὶ τοῦ νυμφῶνος for ὁ φίλος τοῦ νυμφίου: on the distinction between the two see Edersheim i. 355, and Moore on Judges xiv. 11, 20. The rôle of the 'best man' was over; twelve disciples had taken the place of the one fore-runner. In the present connexion the title 'sons of the bride-chamber' had perhaps a further appropriateness; it was in fact an answer to the cavil of v. 18, for "apparently by Rabbinic custom all in attendance on the bridegroom were dispensed from certain religious observances in consideration of their duty to increase his joy" (Hort, Judaistic Christianity, p. 23).

ἐν ᾧ ὁ νυμφίος κτλ.] So the Lord identifies Himself with the Bridegroom of O.T. prophecy (Hos. ii. 20, &c.), i.e. God in His covenant relation to Israel, a metaphor in the N.T. applied to the Christ (Mt. xxv. 1, Jo. iii. 28, 29, Eph. v. 28 ff., Apoc. xix. 7, &c.). Victor: ποῖος νυμφίος; ὁ μέλλων νυμφεύεσθαι τὴν ἐκκλησίαν...τί ἐστιν ἡ νύμφευσις; ἀρραβῶνος δόσις, τουτέστι πνεύματος ἁγίου χάρις. Ἐν ᾧ Mc., Lc. = ἐφ᾽ ὅσον Mt., cf. Mc., infra, ὅσον χρόνον. For νηστεύειν Mt. substitutes πενθεῖν. Fasting was fitting for the house of mourning, not for a time of rejoicing: cf. Judith viii. 6, ἐνήστευε πάσας τὰς ἡμέρας τῆς χηρεύσεως αὐτῆς. With ὅσον χρόνον ἔχουσιν cf. xiv. 7, ἐμὲ δὲ οὐ πάντοτε ἔχετε [μεθ᾽ ἑαυτῶν]: Jo. xiii. 33, ἔτι μικρὸν μεθ᾽ ὑμῶν εἰμι. Ὅσον χρόνον is the acc. of duration, WM., p. 288. Tatian again (cf. v. 18) omits the words which Mc. adds.

20. ἐλεύσονται δὲ ἡμέραι κτλ.]

ἀπαρθῇ ἀπ᾽ αὐτῶν ὁ νυμφίος, καὶ τότε νηστεύσουσιν
ἐν ἐκείνῃ τῇ ἡμέρᾳ. §²¹οὐδεὶς §ἐπίβλημα ῥάκους 21 § Wᵍ
§ syrˢⁱⁿ
§ἀγνάφου ἐπιράπτει ἐπὶ ἱμάτιον παλαιόν· εἰ δὲ μή,   §᷄

20 απαρθη] αρθη C 13 28 64 69 124 346 | εν εκειναις ταις ημεραις ΓΠ² al minᵖˡᵉʳ
a b c e f vg me   21 ουδεις] pr και EFHUVΓΠ al+δε DGM | επισυνραπτει D |
ιματιω παλαιω ΑΓΔΠΣΦ᷄ al | μη] μηγε ΚΔΠ*Σ minⁿᵒⁿⁿ

There must be a limit to the joyous
life of personal intercourse. The saying as far as νηστεύσουσιν is reported
in identical words in Mt., Mc., Lc.
For the phrase ἐλεύσονται ἡμ. see
Lc. xxi. 6, and with the whole verse
compare Jo. xvi. 20. Ὅταν ἀπαρθῇ,
Vg. *cum auferetur*—rather perhaps,
cum ablatus fuerit; ὅταν leaves the
moment uncertain, while of the certainty of the future occurrence there
is no question : cf. Burton, § 316.
Ἀπαίρεσθαι, here only used of Christ's
departure; but cf. Isa. liii. 8, αἴρεται
ἀπὸ τῆς γῆς ἡ ζωὴ αὐτοῦ. Καὶ τότε
νηστεύσουσιν : a prophecy, not a command ; the Lord anticipates that
fasting will remain as an institution
of the Church after the Passion, and
regulates its use (Mt. vi. 16). Comp.
Acts xiii. 2, 3, xiv. 23, *Didache* 7, 8,
ὑμεῖς δὲ νηστεύσατε τετράδα καὶ παρασκευήν. The fast before Easter was
from the end of the second century
specially connected with this saying
of Christ: Tert. *ieiun.* 2, "certe in
evangelio illos dies ieiunii deter-
minatos putant in quibus ablatus est
Sponsus, et hos esse iam solos legitimos
ieiuniorum Christianorum...de cetero
indifferenter ieiunandum ex arbitrio,
non ex imperio." Cf. *Const. Ap.* v. 18
ἐν ταῖς ἡμέραις οὖν τοῦ πάσχα νηστεύετε
...ἐν ταύταις οὖν ἤρθη ἀφ᾽ ἡμῶν. Even
in regard to the Paschal fast there
was at first no rigid uniformity; cf.
Iren. (*ap.* Eus. v. 24) who remarks :
ἡ διαφωνία τῆς νηστείας τὴν ὁμόνοιαν
τῆς πίστεως συνίστησι. Ἐν ἐκείνῃ τῇ
ἡμέρᾳ=(Lc.) ἐν ἐκείναις ταῖς ἡμέραις,
for which see Mc. i. 9 note. On the
change introduced by the Gospel into

the ordinance of fasting, see Victor :
οὐκ ἀνάγκη...ἀλλὰ γνώμη, δι᾽ ἀρετήν.
Bede aptly compares Acts ii. 13. Cf.
the *logion* : ἐὰν μὴ νηστεύσητε τὸν
κόσμον οὐ μὴ εὕρητε τὴν βασιλείαν τοῦ
θεοῦ (*Oxyrhynchus Papyri*, i. p. 3).

21. οὐδεὶς ἐπίβλημα κτλ.] The two
parables that follow occupy the same
position in the three Synoptists, and
doubtless are meant to illustrate the
answer to the question of v. 18. Ἐπίβλημα ῥάκους ἀγνάφου, Vg. *adsumen-
tum panni rudis*, is explained by
Lc. as ἐπίβλημα ἀπὸ ἱματίου καινοῦ.
Ῥάκος is a rag, whether of old stuff
(Jer. xlv. (xxxviii.) 11, παλαιὰ ῥάκη), or,
as here, newly torn from the piece : e.g.
Artemidorus (27) uses it of the strips
of cloth wound round a mummy. In
the present case the ῥάκος is ἄγναφον
(=ἄγναπτον, ἄκναπτον)—torn off from
a piece which had not gone through
the hands of the γναφεύς. Γναφεύς
(Mc. ix. 3)=בֹּצֵעַ, Aram. קַצְרָא, occurs
thrice in the LXX. (4 Regn. xviii. 17,
Isa. vii. 3, xxxvi. 2) in connexion
with "the fuller's field"—possibly a
bleaching ground at Jerusalem ; cf.
Joseph. *B. J.* v. 4. 2, τὸ τοῦ γναφέως
προσαγορευόμενον μνῆμα. Comp. the
account of the martyrdom of James
'the Just,' Euseb. *H. E.* ii. 23 : λαβὼν...εἷς τῶν κναφέων τὸ ξύλον ἐν ᾧ
ἀπεπίεζε τὰ ἱμάτια κτλ. Ἐπίβλημα,
'a patch,' cf. Jos. ix. 11 (5), Symm.,τὰ
σανδάλια ἐπιβλήματα ἔχοντα : for ἐπιράπτει (WH., *Notes*, p. 163, Blass,
Gr., p. 10) Mt., Lc. have ἐπιβάλλει.
εἰ δὲ μή κτλ.] Εἰ δὲ μή (Lc. εἰ δὲ
μήγε), Vg. *alioquin*, 'if otherwise' :
see Blass, *Gr.*, p. 260, and cf. Mt. vi.
1, Jo. xiv. 2, Apoc. ii. 5.

αἴρει τὸ πλήρωμα ἀπ᾽ αὐτοῦ τὸ καινὸν τοῦ παλαιοῦ,
§ t 22 καὶ χεῖρον σχίσμα γίνεται. ²²καὶ οὐδεὶς §βάλλει
οἶνον νέον εἰς ἀσκοὺς παλαιούς—εἰ δὲ μή, ῥήξει ὁ
οἶνος τοὺς ἀσκούς, καὶ ὁ οἶνος ἀπόλλυται καὶ οἱ
ἀσκοί [—ἀλλὰ οἶνον νέον εἰς ἀσκοὺς καινούς].

21 αρει H | το πλ. απ αυτου ℵ (om το) AB (αφ εαυτ.) ΚΔΠ*Σ 33 al^mu] om απ
CLΠ²Φ min^pl aeth om απ αυτου D 13 28 69 124 a b f ff i q vg | του παλαιου] pr απο
D 13 etc | om και...γινεται L   22 μη] μηγε CLM²Σ al^pauc | ρησσει ΑΓΔΠΣΦ℩ al c e ff
q syrr^sin pesh hcl arm me aeth | ο οινος 1°]+ο νεος AC²ΓΔΠΣΦ℩ e f syr^hcl go aeth | ο
οινος απολλυται και οι ασκοι BL me] ο οινος και οι ασκοι απολουνται D a b e ff οι ασκ.
απολλυται και οι οινος εκχειται 124 syrr arm ο οιν. εκχειται και οι ασκ. απολουνται
ℵ*ΑΓΔΠΣΦ℩ al c f q vg me go aeth | om αλλα...καινους D a b ff i | καινους]+
βλητεον ℵ^c.a ACΛΓΔΠΣΦ℩ al c e f q vg (syrr) me go arm aeth+βαλλουσιν syrr^sin pesh
(om ℵ*B) | ad fin vers add και αμφοτεροι συντηρουνται min^pauc e f g aeth

αἴρει τὸ πλήρωμα ἀπ᾽ αὐτοῦ] Mt.
αἴρει...τὸ πλ. αὐτοῦ ἀπὸ τοῦ ἱματίου.
In each case it seems best to identify
τὸ πλήρωμα with τὸ ἐπίβλημα, and to
take αὐτοῦ as =τοῦ ἱματίου. In adopting this view it is not necessary to
give up the passive sense of πλήρωμα for which Lightfoot contends
(*Colossians*, p. 323 ff.); for as he
points out, the patch may be so
called "not because it fills the hole,
but because it is itself fulness or
full measure as regards the defect."
As ἐπίβλημα is the piece laid on or
applied to the rent, so πλήρωμα is
the same piece as filled in and become the complement (Vg. *supplementum*). Τὸ καινὸν τοῦ παλαιοῦ, the
new complement of the old garment;
the contrast of καινός (νέος), παλαιός, is
frequent in the N.T., perhaps through
the influence of this saying, and the
examples are interesting: Rom. vii. 6,
Eph. iv. 22 ff., Col. iii. 9 f., Heb. viii. 13.
For παλαιός as applied to a garment
cf. Deut. viii. 4, Isa. l. 9, li. 6.
καὶ χεῖρον σχίσμα γίνεται] 'And a
worse rent is the result' (Wycliffe,
"more brekynge is maad"). Cf. Lc.'s
paraphrase, and Philo, *de creat. princ.*
11, οὐ μόνον ἡ διαφορότης ἀκοινώνητον,
ἀλλὰ καὶ ἡ ἐπικράτεια θατέρου ῥῆξιν
ἀπεργασομένη μᾶλλον ἢ ἕνωσιν. For

σχίσμα cf. i. 10: elsewhere in the N.T.
the word is used in an ethical sense
(Jo. vii. 43, 1 Cor. i. 10, &c.).
22. καὶ οὐδεὶς βάλλει κτλ.] So Lc.;
Mt. οὐδὲ βάλλουσιν. The worn-out
ἀσκός passed into a proverb, see Job
xiii. 28, Ps. cxviii. (cxix.) 83: comp.
especially Jos. ix. 10 (4), ἀσκοὺς οἴνου
παλαιοὺς καὶ κατερρωγότας: ib. 19 (13),
οὗτοι οἱ ἀσκοὶ τοῦ οἴνου οὓς ἐπλήσαμεν
καινούς, καὶ οὗτοι ἐρρώγασιν. The
wine-skins in the parable are as yet
whole, but thin and strained by use,
and unable to resist the strength of
the newly fermented wine. The contrast is here between νέος and παλαιός:
νέος is *recens* (Vg. *novellus*), freshly
made, in reference to time: for οἶνος
νέος cf. Isa. xlix. 26, Sir. ix. 10. A
full treatment of the synonyms καινός,
νέος may be found in Trench, *syn.* 10,
or in Westcott on Heb. viii. 8, xii. 24.
εἰ δὲ μή κτλ.] Mt., Lc. εἰ δὲ μήγε:
see on *v.* 21. If any one is so unwise
as to become an exception to the
rule, he will lose both wine and skins.
Mc.'s brevity is noticeable; both Mt.
and Lc. distinguish the manner of the
loss in the two cases—ὁ οἶνος ἐκχεῖται
(ἐκχυθήσεται) καὶ οἱ ἀσκοὶ ἀπόλλυνται
(ἀπολοῦνται). Similarly in the next
clause Mt. supplies βάλλουσιν, Lc.
βλητέον. Attempts have been made

²³§ *Καὶ ἐγένετο*¶ *αὐτὸν ἐν τοῖς σάββασιν διαπορεύ-* 23 § syrʰⁱᵉʳ
εσθαι διὰ τῶν σπορίμων, καὶ οἱ μαθηταὶ αὐτοῦ ἤρξαντο ¶ F
ὁδὸν ποιεῖν τίλλοντες τοὺς στάχυας. ²⁴*καὶ οἱ Φαρι-* 24

23 εγενετο]+παλιν D 13 69 124 346 a ff q vg pr παλιν Φ | om εν Φ 1071 | δια-
πορευεσθαι BCD] παραπορ. אALΓΔΠΣΦⁿ al lattᵛᵗ ᵖˡᵉʳ ᵛᵍ πορ. 13 69 124 | om αυτου
D 435 ff | οδον ποιειν τιλλοντες אACLΓΔΠΦⁿ] οδοποιειν τιλλοντ. BGH 13 69 124 346
τιλλειν D 26ᵉᵛ b c e ff g t+εσθιειν c e ff

in the MSS. to assimilate Mc.; see
vv. ll. The contrast between *νέος,*
καινός is preserved by the three Synoptists, but it has been missed in
the Vg., *vinum novum in utres no-*
vos. On the connexion of these parables with the context see Hort, *Jud.*
Chr., p. 24. The general teaching
is that men "nova non accepturos
esse nisi novi fierent" (Hilary). The
old system was not capable of being
patched with mere fragments of the
new, and still less could the old man
receive the new spirit and life. For
some special applications of the principle cf. Trench, *Studies*, p. 180 ff.

23—28. CORN-FIELD INCIDENT.
QUESTION OF THE SABBATH. (Mt. xii.
1—8, Lc. vi. 1—5.)

23. *καὶ ἐγένετο...διαπορεύεσθαι*] *Et*
factum est ut...ambularet (f); cf.
ii. 15, and see Burton, § 360. Lc.
has the same construction, and agrees
with Mc. also in the order of events:
Mt., who begins *ἐν ἐκείνῳ τῷ καιρῷ*
ἐπορεύθη, places this incident much
later. *Ἐν τοῖς σάββασιν* (*τοῖς σ.* Mt.,
ἐν σαββάτῳ Lc.: see note on i. 21),
'on the sabbath'; in Lc. 'Western'
and 'Syrian' authorities add *δευτερο-*
πρώτῳ, cf. WH., *Notes*, p. 58. *Δια-*
πορεύεσθαι, a common LXX. word
(usually = הָלַךְ or עָבַר), is rare in the
N. T., occurring, besides this context,
Lc.ᵉᵛ·², ᵃᶜᵗ·¹, Paul¹; the construction
varies, the verb being used absolutely,
or followed by acc. with or without
prep.; for *διαπ. διά* cf. Prov. ix. 12 c,
Soph. iii. 1. The fields were probably
in the neighbourhood of Capernaum;
there is no charge of having exceeded

the Sabbath day's journey (Acts i. 12,
cf. Joseph. *ant.* xiii. 8. 4, *οὐκ ἔξεστιν*
δ' ἡμῖν οὔτε ἐν τοῖς σάββασιν οὔτ' ἐν
τῇ ἑορτῇ [*τῇ πεντηκοστῇ*] *ὁδεύειν*). *Τὰ*
σπόριμα: in the LXX., *σπόριμος*=זָרֻעַ
(Gen. i. 29) or זֵרוּעַ (Lev. xi. 37); *σπό-*
ριμα="sown land," "corn-fields" (V.
sata), is found in a papyrus of c. A.D.
346, and seems to have been familiar
in colloquial Greek of cent. i, for it
belongs to the common tradition of
the Synoptic Gospels.

ἤρξαντο ὁδὸν ποιεῖν τίλλοντες] Mt.
ἤρξαντο τίλλειν, Lc. *ἔτιλλον.* Ὁδὸν
ποιεῖν is properly, like *ὁδοποιεῖν*, to
make a road, or make one's way, and
suggests that the party was pushing
its way through the corn where there
was no path; Euth.: *ἵνα προβαίνειν*
ἔχοιεν. But *ὁδὸν ποιεῖσθαι* is used
(Herod., Xen., Dion. Hal., Joseph.,
&c.) of simple advance (Vg. *coeperunt*
praegredi, v. l. *progredi*), and *ὁδ.*
ποιεῖν probably bears that meaning
here; cf. Jud. xvii. 8 *τοῦ ποιῆσαι ὁδὸν*
αὐτοῦ (לַעֲשׂוֹת דַּרְכּוֹ, but see Moore,
Judges, p. 385 f.). As they went
they plucked the ears and ate (*καὶ*
ἐσθίειν Mt.; *καὶ ἤσθιον* Lc., who adds
ψώχοντες ταῖς χερσίν). Permission to
pluck and eat ears of standing corn
was given by the Law, provided that
no instrument was used, Deut. xxiii.
24 (26): *συλλέξεις ἐν ταῖς χερσίν σου*
στάχυς καὶ δρέπανον οὐ μὴ ἐπιβάλῃς.

24. *καὶ οἱ Φαρισαῖοι κτλ.*] See
notes on ii. 16, 18. The Master is
again attacked through the disciples.
Mt. supplies *οἱ μαθηταί σου* before
ποιοῦσιν, Lc. represents the question
as addressed to the disciples (*τί*

σαῖοι ἔλεγον αὐτῷ Ἴδε τί ποιοῦσιν τοῖς σάββασιν ὃ
25 οὐκ ἔξεστιν; ²⁵καὶ ἔλεγεν αὐτοῖς Οὐδέποτε ἀνέγνωτε
τί ἐποίησεν Δαυεὶδ ὅτε χρείαν ἔσχεν καὶ ἐπείνασεν
§ W° 26 αὐτὸς καὶ οἱ μετ' αὐτοῦ; §²⁶ εἰσῆλθεν εἰς τὸν οἶκον
τοῦ θεοῦ ἐπὶ 'Αβιαθὰρ ἀρχιερέως, καὶ τοὺς ἄρτους τῆς

---

24 ποιουσιν]+οι μαθηται σου DMΣ 1 13 28 69 124 346 al lat^{vt(exce)} syrr^{sin hcl} arm
go aeth+οι μαθ. 1071 | τοις σαββασιν] pr εν EGHLSUVΓΣ   25 ελεγεν ΑΒΓΔΠ]
λεγει ℵCL 33 604 1071 al αποκριθεις ειπεν D a pr αυτος ΑΓΔΠ al   26 εισηλθεν] pr
πως ℵACLΓΔΠΣΦ⁷ latt syrr arm al (om π. BD t) | om επι Αβ. αρχ. D 271 a b e f f i t
syr^{sin} | αρχ.] pr του ΑCΔ (τ. ιερ.) ΠΣΦ⁷ 1 33 69 al

ποιεῖτε). Ἴδε (= רְאֵה), not ἰδού (=
הִגֵּה); cf. iii. 34, xi. 21, xiii. 1, 21, xv.
4, 35, xvi. 6. The offence was being
openly committed under the very eyes
of the Master. Plucking corn was
considered as equivalent to reaping,
the hand taking the place of the
sickle, and reaping on the Sabbath
was forbidden (Exod. xxxiv. 21, τῷ
ἀμήτῳ κατάπαυσις; cf. J. Lightfoot on
Mt. xii. 2). Τί ποιοῦσιν τοῖς σαββ. ὃ
οὐκ ἔξεστιν; sc. ποιεῖν τοῖς σάββασιν.
Mt. simplifies the construction by
writing ποιοῦσιν ὃ οὐκ ἔξεστιν ποιεῖν ἐν
σαββάτῳ, and similarly Lc. The act
was not unlawful in itself, but only in
regard to the occasion.

25. καὶ ἔλεγεν αὐτοῖς Οὐδέποτε
ἀνέγνωτε κτλ.] The Lord concedes
the principle for the moment, content
with pointing out that rules of this
kind admit of exceptions. Οὐδ. ἀνέγν.,
an appeal to an authority which they
recognised and of which they were professed students. The formula is frequently used by our Lord, cf. xii. 10,
26, Mt. xii. 5, xix. 4, xxi. 16 (οὐδέποτε,
οὐδέ, or οὐκ ἀνέγν.;).

τί ἐποίησεν Δαυείδ κτλ.] The
reference is to 1 Sam. xxi. 1—6, but
the words χρείαν ἔσχεν καὶ ἐπείνασεν
are an inference from the facts, added
to bring out the parallel. David and
his men find their counterpart in the
Son of David and His disciples.

26. εἰσῆλθεν εἰς τὸν οἶκον τοῦ θεοῦ]
I.e., the Tabernacle: cf. Jud. xviii.

31, 1 Regn. i. 7, 24. It was at this
time in Nob (Νομβά, Νομμά (B), Νοβά
(A), Νόβ (ℵ)), a town of Benjamin (Neh.
xi. 32) near Jerusalem (Isa. x. 32
Heb.). Mt. πῶς εἰσῆλθεν (cf. vv. ll.
here), Lc. ὡς εἰσ.

ἐπὶ 'Αβιαθὰρ ἀρχιερέως] Vg. sub A.
principe sacerdotum: cf. 1 Macc. xiii.
42, ἔτους πρώτου ἐπὶ Σίμωνος ἀρχιερέως.
Lc. iii. 2, ἐπὶ ἀρχιερέως Ἄννα καὶ
Καιάφα. Polyc. mart. 21, ἐπὶ ἀρχιερέως
Φιλίππου Τραλλιανοῦ. 'Επί='in the
time of,' as in Acts xi. 28 ἐγένετο ἐπὶ
Κλαυδίου: when an anarthrous title
is added to the personal name, the
period is limited to the term of
office: 'in the days when A. was
highpriest.' Τοῦ ἀρχ. (AC) is perhaps
a correction. The clause is peculiar
to Mc., and may be an editorial
note. It is in conflict with the account in 1 Sam. l.c. where the high-
priest at the time of David's visit
to Nob is Ahimelech (אֲחִימֶלֶךְ, lxx.,
codd. BA, 'Αβ(ε)ιμέλεχ, but in 1 Regn.
xxx. 7, 2 Regn. viii. 17, 'Αχειμέλεχ),
not Abiathar, Ahimelech's son and
successor (1 Sam. xxii. 20). The confusion between Ahimelech and Abiathar seems to have begun in the text
of the O. T., where (both in M.T. and
lxx.) we read of Ahimelech the son
of Abiathar as high-priest in the time
of David (2 Sam. viii. 17, cf. Driver,
ad l., 1 Chron. xviii. 16, xxiv. 6). The
clause is omitted by Mt., Lc., see
Hawkins, H. S., p. 99.

προθέσεως ἔφαγεν οὓς οὐκ ἔξεστιν φαγεῖν εἰ μὴ τοὺς
ἱερεῖς, καὶ ἔδωκεν καὶ τοῖς σὺν αὐτῷ οὖσιν. ²⁷καὶ 27
ἔλεγεν αὐτοῖς Τὸ σάββατον διὰ τὸν ἄνθρωπον ἐγένετο

26 προσθεσεως D (cf. Nestle *Intr.* p. 237) | ους...ουσιν] και εδωκεν τοις μετ αυτου
ουσιν ους ουκ εξεστιν φαγειν ει μη τοις ιερευσιν D | τους ιερεις אBL] τοις ιερευσιν
ACDΓΔΠ al τοις αρχιερευσι Φ+μονοις ΔΦ 13 33 69 al^pauc lat^{vtmu}+μονον 1071
27—28 και ελεγεν...ωστε] λεγω δε υμιν Daceffit   27 εγενετο] εκτισθη 1 131
209 604 syrr^{sin pesh}

τοὺς ἄρτους τῆς προθέσεως] Vg. *panes
propositionis* (Wycliffe, "loues of pro-
posicioun"); cf. Heb. ix. 2, ἡ πρόθεσις
τῶν ἄρτων, *propositio panum*. The
'shewbread' as set before GOD is
called לֶחֶם הַפָּנִים, ἄρτοι ἐνώπιοι (Exod.
xxv. 29), προκείμενοι (Exod. xxxix. 18
(36)), τοῦ προσώπου (1 Regn. xxi. 6),
τῆς προσφορᾶς (3 Regn. vii. 34=48).
(Οἱ) ἄρτοι (τῆς) προθέσεως occurs also in
1 Regn. *l.c.*, but as a paraphrase for
קֹדֶשׁ, and in 2 Chron. iv. 19 it stands
for לֶחֶם הַפָּנִים; but elsewhere it =
עֶרֶד־לָחֶם (Exod. xl. 21 (23), &c.) or in
Chron., לֶחֶם־הַמַּעֲרָכֶת (1 Chr. ix. 32); i.e.,
it points to the ordered rows upon the
table rather than to their ceremonial
import. See however Deissmann,
Bibelstudien, p. 155 f. (E. Tr., p. 157).
It was one of the glories of Judas
Maccabaeus that he restored the use
of the shewbread (2 Macc. x. 3, τῶν
ἄρτων τὴν πρόθεσιν ἐποιήσαντο).

οὓς οὐκ ἔξ. φαγεῖν εἰ μὴ τοὺς ἱερεῖς]
'Which it was not lawful that any
should eat except the priests': so Lc.;
Mt. has the more usual construction
ἔξεστιν...τοῖς ἱερεῦσιν. On the law of
the shewbread see Lev. xxiv. 5,
Joseph. *ant.* iii. 10. 7, οἱ δὲ τοῖς ἱερεῦσιν
πρὸς τροφὴν δίδονται. But the prohibition does not seem to have been
absolute; cf. 1 Sam. xxi. 4. Οὐκ ἔξεστιν
is taken out of the mouth of the
Scribes, and used in their sense (*v.* 24):
it was at least as unlawful to eat
the shewbread as to pluck and eat
corn on the Sabbath.

καὶ ἔδωκεν καὶ τοῖς σὺν αὐτῷ οὖσιν]
Cf. *v.* 25, οἱ μετ' αὐτοῦ. An O. T. phrase

(see Gen. iii. 6). Delitzsch renders:
וַיִּתֶּן־גַּם לַאֲנָשִׁים אֲשֶׁר אִתּוֹ. The companions were in David's case παιδάρια,
נְעָרִים, i.e. personal followers, the
nucleus of the crowd who gathered
round him in the cave of Adullam
(1 Sam. xxii. 2). The contrast between these men and the peaceful
disciples of Jesus is great, but it only
serves to add force to the argument.

27. Mt. gives another argument:
the priests in the temple were compelled to violate the strict law of the
Sabbath, their duties being in fact
doubled on that day (Numb. xxviii. 9);
if the exigencies of the temple justified their conduct, a greater than
the temple was here to justify the
disciples. He adds a quotation from
Hos vi. 6, which he had previously
cited in connexion with the saying of
v. 17 (Mt. ix. 13).

τὸ σάββατον...διὰ τὸ σάββατον] Mc.
only; cf. Hawkins, *H.S.* p. 99. Comp.
2 Macc. v. 19, οὐ διὰ τὸν τόπον τὸ
ἔθνος, ἀλλὰ διὰ τὸ ἔθνος τὸν τόπον ὁ
κύριος ἐξελέξατο. The Rabbis themselves occasionally admitted the principle; see Schöttgen *ad l.* and the
passage cited by Meyer from *Mechilta*
in Exod. xxxi. 13: "the Sabbath is
delivered unto you, and ye are not
delivered to the Sabbath." Our Lord's
words rise higher, and reach further:
at the root of the Sabbath-law was
the love of God for mankind, and not
for Israel only. Cf. Ephrem: "the
Sabbath was appointed not for God's
sake, but for the sake of man." Bengel: "origo et finis rerum spectanda;
benedictio sabbati (Gen. ii. 3) hominem

¶ † 28 καὶ οὐχ ὁ ἄνθρωπος διὰ τὸ σάββατον. ²⁸ὥστε¶
κύριός ἐστιν ὁ υἱὸς τοῦ ἀνθρώπου καὶ τοῦ σαββάτου.
3 1 ¹Καὶ εἰσῆλθεν πάλιν εἰς συναγωγήν, καὶ ἦν ἐκεῖ
2 ἄνθρωπος ἐξηραμμένην ἔχων τὴν χεῖρα· ²καὶ παρετή-

27 om και ουχ ο ανθρ. δ. το σ. syrsin | om και 2° AC³ΓΠ alpl   III 1 συνα-
γωγην] pr την ACDLΣΦ٦ al (om אB) | εξηραμμενην] ξηραν D   2 παρετηρουντο
AC*DΔΣT minpauc

spectat." For a similar antithesis cf.
1 Cor. xi. 9. Ὁ ἄνθρωπος, man, i.e.
humanity ; cf. Eccl. i. 3, iii. 19.
28. ὥστε κύριός ἐστιν κτλ.] Wycliffe,
"and so mannes sone is also lord of the
sabath." Κύριος γάρ ἐστιν, Mt. ; Κ. ἐστιν,
Lc. In Mc. the sequence of the thought
is clear. The Sabbath, being made for
man's benefit, is subject to the control of the ideal and representative
Man, to whom it belongs. On ὥστε
with the indic. mood see WM., p. 377,
Burton § 237, and cf. Mc. x. 8. Κύριος
is here perhaps rather 'owner' than
'master'—בַּעַל הַשַּׁבָּת, cf. Gen. xlix.
23, Jud. xix. 22. On ὁ υἱ. τ. ἀνθρ. see
v. 10 n. Tatian, followed by the O. L.
cod. a, places after this verse c. iii. 21
(q.v.), as if it was His doctrine of the
Sabbath which led our Lord's relatives
to suspect insanity.

III. 1—6. Healing of a Withered
Hand on the Sabbath (Mt. xii. 9—
14, Lc. vi. 6—11).

1. καὶ εἰσῆλθεν πάλιν εἰς συναγω-
γήν] Another scene in a synagogue.
Πάλιν points back to i. 21 (cf. ii. 1,
13 ; iii. 20, iv. 1) unless, with Bengel,
we interpret "alio sabbato." Εἰς
συναγωγήν, not εἰς τὴν σ., as in i.
21, (vi. 2), where the synagogue is
localised ; here the reader's thought
is limited to the fact that the event
took place in a synagogue. Cf. Jo.
vi. 59, xviii. 20, James ii. 2 ; similarly we speak of going 'to church'
or being 'in church' when no particular building is in view. Mc.
suggests, and Mt. seems distinctly
to state (μεταβὰς ἐκεῖθεν ἦλθεν), that
this visit to the synagogue followed

immediately after the cornfield incident ; Lc. places it on another Sabbath (ἐν ἑτέρῳ σαββάτῳ). St Augustine's reply (de cons. ev. 81, "post
quot dies in synagogam eorum venerit...non expressum est") is not
wholly satisfactory ; the two traditions if not absolutely inconsistent
are clearly distinct, Lc. perhaps possessing information unknown to Mc.
and Mt. Cod. D meets the difficulty
by omitting ἑτέρῳ in Lc.

καὶ ἦν ἐκεῖ ἄνθρωπος κτλ.] For ξη-
ραίνομαι (=יָבֵשׁ) see 3 Regn. xiii. 4,
Zach. xi. 17. Jo. (v. 3) mentions ξη-
ροί as a class of chronic invalids ; in
the present instance the paralysis of
the hand was not congenital, but as
Bengel says "morbo aut verbere," as
the past participle implies—a point
which Mt.'s ξηράν overlooks. Τὴν
χεῖρα, 'his hand,' cf. v. 3, vv. ll. ;
for exx. of the predicative use of the
art. see Blass, Gr. p. 158. Lc. adds
that the hand was ἡ δεξιά. Jerome
says that the Gospel according to
the Hebrews represented the man
as pleading his case with the Lord :
"caementarius eram, manibus victum
quaeritans ; precor te, Iesu, ut mihi
restituas sanitatem ne turpiter mendi-
cam cibos."

2. καὶ παρετήρουν αὐτόν] Cf. Ps.
xxxvi. (xxxvii.) 12, παρατηρήσεται
(זֹמֵם) ὁ ἁμαρτωλὸς τὸν δίκαιον: Dan.
vi. 11, Sus. 12, 16 (Th.). The middle
is more frequent, but παρατηρεῖν occurs
in Susanna and in Lc. xx. 20. Polybius
(xvii. 3. 2) couples παρατηρεῖν with
ἐνεδρεύειν. This hostile sense is not
however inherent in the word, which

ρουν αὐτὸν εἰ τοῖς σάββασιν θεραπεύσει αὐτόν, ἵνα
κατηγορήσωσιν αὐτοῦ. ³καὶ λέγει τῷ ἀνθρώπῳ τῷ 3
τὴν χεῖρα ἔχοντι ξηράν¶ "Εγειρε εἰς τὸ μέσον. ⁴καὶ 4 ¶ ㄱ¹⁰
λέγει αὐτοῖς "Εξεστιν τοῖς σάββασιν ἀγαθοποιῆσαι

2 τοις σ.] pr εν ℵCDHM min¹ me | θεραπευει ℵΔΣ | κατηγορησουσιν DΣ   3 τω
την χ. εχ. ξηραν BL 565 a me aeth] τω την ξ. χ. εχ. ℵC*Δ 33 τω εξηραμμενην εχ.
τ. χ. Aᶜᵒʳʳ(D)ΓΠΣΦㄱ al go | εγειραι UΓΦ | εις το μεσον (εν μεσω D c)] pr και στηθι
D c aeth   4 εξεστιν] pr τι E* 1 118 131 arm | τοις σαββ.] pr εν ADE al 2ᵖᵒ me
go | αγαθοποιησαι] αγαθον ποιησαι ℵ τι αγ. π. D e arm

merely means (Lightfoot on Gal. iv.
10) to observe minutely, going along
as it were with the object for the
purpose of watching its movements.
Lc. uses the middle here and in xiv.
1. Παρατηρεῖν εἰ, to watch whether;
cf. Blass, *Gr.* p. 211.

εἰ τοῖς σάββασιν θεραπεύσει] According to the Rabbinical rule relief
might be given to a sufferer on the
Sabbath only when life was in danger (Schürer II. ii. 104). Since in
the present case postponement was
clearly possible, a charge might lie
against Jesus before the Sanhedrin
if He restored the hand; and they
watched Him closely in the hope that
this opportunity might be given (ἵνα
κατηγορήσωσιν αὐτόν). According to
Mt. they even challenged Him by
asking Εἰ ἔξεστι τοῖς σάββασιν θεραπεύειν; The question afterwards put
to them by Jesus (Mc.) does not
exclude this account of the matter
(Victor, εἰκὸς δὲ ἀμφότερα γεγενῆ-
σθαι); but Lc.'s comment (ᾔδει τοὺς
διαλογισμοὺς αὐτῶν) seems to be inconsistent with it, and the additional
matter in Mt. clearly belongs to another occasion (Mt. xii. 11, 12=Lc.
xiii. 15, xiv. 5).

3. καὶ λέγει τῷ ἀνθρώπῳ κτλ.] His
knowledge of their purpose (Lc.) did
not deter Him: comp. Dan. vi. 10.
His first step was to bring the man
out into the body of the synagogue
where he could be seen by all (Mc.,
Lc.); there should be no secrecy and

no need for παρατήρησις in the matter, since a principle was involved:
comp. Jo. xviii. 20. "Εγειρε εἰς τὸ μέσον, a pregnant construction: 'arise
[and come] into the midst'; cf. examples in Blass, *Gr.* p. 122. Lc. in-
terpolates καὶ στῆθι, and adds καὶ ἀναστὰς ἔστη—details which Mc. leaves
to be imagined. The purpose of the
command is clear. The miracle was
intended to be a public and decisive
answer to the question 'Will He work
His cures on the Sabbath?'

4. καὶ λέγει αὐτοῖς κτλ.] The Lord
anticipates their question (cf. ii. 8).
Lc. prefixes ἐπερωτῶ ὑμᾶς. His questioning of the Rabbis began in childhood (Lc. ii. 46): in the method there
was nothing unusual, still less disre-
spectful; see J. Lightfoot on Lc. *l. c.*
The present question puts a new
colour on that which was in their
minds; for θεραπεύειν He substitutes ἀγαθοποιῆσαι, which raises the
principle. Ἀγαθοποιεῖν (formed on
the analogy of the class. κακοποιεῖν)
is a word of the LXX. (=הֵיטִיב), for
which class. Gk. used εὖ ποιεῖν or
εὐεργετεῖν. In Tob. xii. 13, 1 Macc.
xi. 33 ἀγαθὸν ποιεῖν has been substituted by some of the scribes, and the
same tendency appears here; but the
compound is well supported in the
N.T., especially in 1 Peter, where,
besides ἀγαθοποιεῖν (*quater*), we find
ἀγαθοποιΐα and ἀγαθοποιός. *Η κακοποιῆσαι raises the startling alternative: 'if good may not be done on

ἢ κακοποιῆσαι, ψυχὴν σῶσαι ἢ ἀποκτεῖναι; οἱ δὲ
5 ἐσιώπων. ⁵καὶ περιβλεψάμενος αὐτοὺς μετ᾽ ὀργῆς,
§ P   συνλυπούμενος §ἐπὶ τῇ πωρώσει τῆς καρδίας αὐτῶν,

4 η] pr μαλλον 28 124 | αποκτειναι] απολεσαι LΔ 1 124 209 2ᵖᵉ latt syrᵖᵉˢʰ arm |
εσιωπησαν (L)ΣΦ a g q   5 επι τ. πωρωσει] επι τ. πηρωσει 17 20 arm super caeci-
tate(m) cordis a b e f q vg επι τ. νεκρωσει D syrˢⁱⁿ super emortua corda c ff i r

the Sabbath, are you prepared to
justify evildoing on that day?' I.e.,
Was it unlawful on the Sabbath to
rescue a life from incipient death
(ψυχὴν σῶσαι), and yet lawful to
watch for the life of another, as
they were doing at the moment?
Was the Sabbath a day for malefi-
cent and not for beneficent action?
Ἀποκτεῖναι is used of a judicial sentence, Jo. xviii. 31; Lc. substitutes
here the more usual ἀπολέσαι.

οἱ δὲ ἐσιώπων: whether from policy,
or shame (ix. 34), or simply because
they had no answer ready (Lc. xx.
26).

5. καὶ περιβλεψάμενος αὐτούς]
Except in Lc. vi. 10 (the parallel to
this context) περιβλέπεσθαι is used by
Mc. only (iii. 5, 34, v. 32, ix. 8, x. 23,
xi. 11), and five times out of six in
reference to the quick searching
glance round the circle of His friends
or enemies, which St Peter remembered as characteristic of the Lord:
see Ellicott, Lectures, pp. 25, 176.
Bengel: "vultus Christi multa nos
docuit." For the use of περιβλ. in
the LXX. cf. Exod. ii. 12, 3 Regn. xxi.
(xx.) 40, Tob. xi. 5. Μετ᾽ ὀργῆς: there
was anger in the look or attending it
(cf. μετὰ δακρύων Acts xx. 31, Heb.
xii. 17). Anger is attributed to the
Lamb, Apoc. vi. 16, 17: it is "legiti-
mate in the absence of the personal
element" (Gould), i.e. if not vindictive,
and not inconsistent with a gentle
character (Mt. xi. 29).

συνλυπούμενος ἐπί κτλ.] Mc. only.
The anger was tempered by grief:
comp. 1 Esdr. ix. 2, πενθῶν ὑπὲρ τῶν
ἀνομιῶν τῶν μεγάλων τοῦ πλήθους.

Συνλυπεῖσθαι, Vg. contristari, implies
sorrow arising from sympathy, either
with the sorrow of another (cf. Ps.
lxviii. (lxix.) 21, where the ὁ συνλυπούμενος answers to ὁ παρακαλῶν),
or, as here, with his unconscious
misery. With this sorrow of Christ
for sinners comp. Eph. iv. 30. Sorrow
is predicated of Jesus again in Mt.
xxvi. 37. Συνλυπούμενος pres., in contrast with περιβλεψάμενος aor., points
to the abiding nature of this grief:
the look was momentary, the sorrow
habitual. Cf. Oxyrhynch. log. 3 πονεῖ
ἡ ψυχή μου ἐπὶ τοῖς υἱοῖς τῶν ἀνθρώπων. Πώρωσις τῆς καρδίας occurs again
in Eph. iv. 18, where it is a characteristic of pagan life: in this respect
unbelieving Israel was on a level with
untaught heathendom (Rom. xi. 25);
even the Apostles suffered at times
from this same malady (Mc. viii. 17).
Πωροῦσθαι is 'to grow callous,' and
πώρωσις in medical language is the
formation of the hard substance
(πῶρος, callus) which unites the frac-
tured ends of a broken bone; transferred to things spiritual, it is the
process of moral ossification, which
renders men insensible to spiritual
truth. Cod. D and the Sin. Syriac
express the result by substituting
νέκρωσις: so some O.L. texts, super
emortua illorum corda. The idea
seems to be derived from Isa. vi. 10,
where the LXX. has ἐπαχύνθη...ἡ καρδία
τοῦ λαοῦ τούτου, but Jo. (xii. 40) paraphrases ἐπώρωσεν αὐτῶν τὴν καρδίαν.
The Vg. renders super caecitate(m)
cordis eorum (Wycliffe, "on the blynd-
nesse of her harte," followed by
Tindale and Cranmer), reading appa-

λέγει τῷ ἀνθρώπῳ Ἔκτεινον τὴν χεῖρά σου· §καὶ   § F.
ἐξέτεινεν, καὶ ἀπεκατεστάθη ἡ χεὶρ αὐτοῦ.¶ ⁶καὶ 6 ¶ syrʰⁱᵉʳ
ἐξελθόντες οἱ Φαρισαῖοι εὐθὺς μετὰ τῶν Ἡρῳδιανῶν
συμβούλιον ἐδίδουν κατ᾽ αὐτοῦ ὅπως αὐτὸν ἀπολέσωσιν.

5 om σου BEMSUVΓΦ꜔ minⁿᵒⁿⁿ | εξετεινεν]+την χειρα αυτου syrʰⁱᵉʳ | απεκατεσταθη
(ℵABLPΓΔΠ² al) αποκ. (DΠ*Φ minˢᵃᵗ ᵐᵘ)] απεκατεστη C 565 | η χειρ αυτ. (om
syrʰⁱᵉʳ)]+ευθεως D ff i+υγιης ως η αλλη C³LΓ al+ως η α. syrˢⁱⁿ ʰⁱᵉʳ   6 om ευθυς
DL al b c ff g i q aeth | εδιδουν BL 13 28 69 124 346 604] εποιησαν ℵCΔ 238 736
1071 2ᵖᵉ alᵖᵃᵘᶜ εποιουν ΑΡΓΠΣΦ al lattᵛᵗ ᵖˡ ᵛᵍ arm go ποιουντες D | om κατ αυτου syrˢⁱⁿ |
απολεσουσιν Σ

rently πηρώσει: cf. Job xvii. 7, B, πεπώρωνται...οἱ ὀφθαλμοί μου, where ℵᶜ·ᵃA have the variant πεπήρωνται. See however *J. Th. St.* iii. 1, p. 81 ff., where Dr J. Armitage Robinson maintains that πώρωσις acquired by use the sense of πήρωσις.

λέγει τῷ ἀνθρώπῳ] As He had turned to the paralytic, ii. 10, 11. A command in each case precedes the healing; recovery comes through faith and obedience. With the whole scene comp. 3 Regn. xiii. 6.

ἀπεκατεστάθη ἡ χείρ] Mt. adds ὑγιὴς ὡς ἡ ἄλλη. For this use of ἀπεκ. cf. Mc. viii. 25. The verb is frequent in the later Gk. and in the LXX.; in the N.T. (exc. Heb. xiii. 19) its use is always more or less distinctly Messianic, and based perhaps on Mal. iv. 5 (see on Mc. ix. 12). Each miracle of healing was an earnest in an individual case of the ἀποκατάστασις πάντων (Acts iii. 21). For the double augment see WH., *Notes*, p. 162, and Blass, *Gr.*, p. 39.

6. καὶ ἐξελθόντες οἱ Φ. εὐθύς] The Pharisees left the synagogue mad with rage (ἐπλήσθησαν ἀνοίας, Lc.) and lost no time (εὐθύς, Mc. only) in plotting revenge. Lc. speaks only of an informal discussion (διελάλουν πρὸς ἀλλήλους), Mc., Mt. of a council or consultation (συμβούλιον—in Prov. xv. 22 it is Th.'s word for סוד, LXX. συνέδρια). Συμβ. διδόναι occurs here only in the N.T.; the usual phrases

are σ. λαμβάνειν (Mt.⁵) or ποιεῖν (Mc. xv. 1, with a variant ἑτοιμάζειν). Ἐδίδουν (ἐποίουν) perhaps implies that the consultation held that day was but one of many; the last is described in xv. 1. Ὅπως αὐτὸν ἀπολέσωσιν represents the purpose and ultimate issue of their counsels (cf. Burton, § 207)—not however without reference to the means to be employed. Lc. gives the immediate subject of debate—τί ἂν ποιήσαιεν τῷ Ἰησοῦ, and Mc.'s form implies the question Πῶς αὐτὸν ἀπολέσωμεν; (WM., p. 374).

μετὰ τῶν Ἡρῳδιανῶν] Mc. only. Tindale, "with them that belonged to Herode." The Ἡρῳδιανοί appear again in the same company c. xii. 13=Mt. xxii. 16, and some understanding between the two parties is implied also in Mc. viii. 15. Josephus (*ant.* xiv. 15. 10) speaks of τοὺς τὰ Ἡρῴδου φρονοῦντας, but the term Ἡρῳδιανός occurs only in Mt., Mc. Adjectives in -ανός denote partisanship (Blass on Acts xi. 26). An Herodian party, so far as it found a place in Jewish life, would be actuated by mixed motives; some would join it from sympathy with the Hellenising policy of the Herod family, others because they "saw in the power" of that family "the pledge of the preservation of their national existence" (Westcott in Smith's *B.D.*², s.v.). The latter would have certain interests in common with the Pharisees, and

7   ⁷Καὶ ὁ Ἰησοῦς μετὰ τῶν μαθητῶν αὐτοῦ ἀνεχώρησεν πρὸς τὴν θάλασσαν· καὶ πολὺ πλῆθος ἀπὸ τῆς
8 Γαλειλαίας ἠκολούθησεν καὶ ἀπὸ τῆς Ἰουδαίας ⁸καὶ

7 Ιησους]+γνους 1071 | προς] εις DHP min^nonn παρα 13 28 69 124 1071 | πολυ
πληθος] πολυς οχλος D latt | ηκολουθησεν] om D 28 124 a (b c) e ff i q syr^sin post Ιουδ.
transp אBΔ 238 1071 f vg+αυτω Φ

might have readily joined them in
an effort to suppress a teacher who
threatened the *status quo*; although,
as Bengel quaintly suggests, "fortasse non magnopere curabant Sabbatum." The Pharisees on their
part, without any great affection for
the Herods, could acquiesce in their
rule as the less of two evils. H.
the Great had made bids for their
support (Schürer I. i. pp. 419, 444 f.),
and Lc. shews (xiii. 31 f., xxiii. 10)
that they were not unwilling to use
Antipas as an ally against Jesus, or
even to act as emissaries of the
Tetrarch.

7—12. SECOND GREAT CONCOURSE
BY THE SEA (Mt. xii. 15—21, Lc. vi.
17—19).

7. καὶ ὁ Ἰησοῦς...ἀνεχώρησεν] Ἀναχωρεῖν is used, esp. by Mt., of withdrawal from danger, Mt. ii. 12 ff., iv. 12,
xiv. 13; in the present context Mt.
makes this meaning clear by adding
γνούς. Jesus withdrew from the town
to the seaside because He was aware of
the plot. He and His would be safer
on the open beach, surrounded by
crowds of followers, than in the narrow
streets of Capernaum. His friends
would prevent an arrest; in case of
danger, a boat was at hand. Εἰς is
the usual preposition after ἀναχωρεῖν
(Mt. ii. 14, &c.): πρός gives the direction or locality of the retreat (cf. ii. 2).
On the policy of this retreat see Bede:
"neque adhuc venerat hora passionis
eius, neque extra Ierusalem fuit locus
passionis."

καὶ πολὺ πλῆθος κτλ.] Cf. i. 28, 37,
45; ii. 13. Πλῆθος is frequent in Lc.;

for πολὺ πλ. cf. Lc. xxiii. 27, Acts xiv.
1, xvii. 4. On the prominence given to
the adj. see WM., p. 657; the normal
order occurs when the words are repeated in v. 8. The punctuation of
this paragraph is open to some doubt;
we may either keep ἠκολούθησεν for
the Galileans, assigning the other factors in the crowd to ἦλθον (v. 8), or we
may begin a new sentence at πλῆθος
πολύ, or at ἀκούοντες. WH. and R.V.
adopt the former view, but the repeated ἀπό seems to point to the con-
tinuity of the words from καὶ πολύ to
Ἰδουμαίας, and probably to Σιδῶνα:
comp. Lc. πλῆθος πολύ...οἳ ἦλθαν.

7—8. καὶ ἀπὸ τ. Ἰουδαίας κτλ.] The
Galilean following is now supple-
mented by others from south, east,
and north. Judaea had already sent
Pharisees and Scribes (Lc. v. 17), and
now, perhaps as a result of the synagogue preaching mentioned in Lc. iv.
45, adds its contribution to the Lord's
willing hearers. Jerusalem is named
separately, as in Isa. i. 1, Jer. iv. 3,
Joel iii. 20; cf. i. 5. Ἡ Ἰδουμαία,
named here only in the N.T.=אֱדוֹם
in the LXX. (Isa. xxxiv. 5, 6, &c.).
The victories of Judas Maccabaeus
(1 Macc. v. 3) and John Hyrcanus
(Joseph. *ant.* xiii. 9. 1) had gone
far to remove the barrier between
Edom and Israel, and the Edomite
extraction of the Herods brought the
two peoples nearer: "in our Lord's
time Idumaea was practically a part
of Judaea with a Jewish [circumcised]
population" (G. A. Smith, *Hist. Geogr.*
p. 240; cf. Joseph. *ant.* xiii. 9. 1). Moreover in Roman times Idumaea was

ἀπὸ Ἱεροσολύμων καὶ ἀπὸ τῆς Ἰδουμαίας καὶ πέραν
τοῦ Ἰορδάνου καὶ περὶ Τύρον καὶ Σιδῶνα, πλῆθος
πολύ, ἀκούοντες ὅσα ποιεῖ, ἦλθον πρὸς αὐτόν. ⁹καὶ 9
εἶπεν τοῖς μαθηταῖς αὐτοῦ ἵνα πλοιάριον προσκαρτερῇ

8 om και απο της Ιδουμ. ℵ* 1 118 131 209 258 c ff syrˢⁱⁿ arm | περαν] pr οι
D f | περι] pr οι ΑΔΡΓΠΣΦ rell a vg syrʰᵉˡ go arm | Σιδωνα] pr οι περι D | om
πληθ. πολυ a b c syrˢⁱⁿ | ακουοντες ℵΒΔ 1 13 69 al latt (exc a) me go aeth] ακουσαντες
ΑΣDLΡΓΠΣΦal | οσα] a CD min² a i r vg me | ποιει ΒL syrᵛⁱᵈ] εποιει ℵΑΣDΡΓΔΠΣΦ
al latt me | ηλθαν D ηλθεν U   9 πλοιαρια Β

used loosely for the south border-
land of Judaea; cf. Joseph. *c. Ap.*
ii. 9 ἡ μὲν Ἰδουμαία τῆς ἡμετέρας χώρας
ἐστὶν ὅμορος κατὰ Γάζαν κειμένη : *ant.*
v. 1. 22 ἡ μὲν Ἰούδα λαχοῦσα πᾶσαν
αἱρεῖται τὴν καθύπερθεν Ἰδουμαίαν παρα-
τείνουσαν μὲν ἄχρι τῶν Ἱεροσολύμων,
τὸ δ᾽ εὖρος ἕως τῆς Σοδομίτιδος λίμνης
καθήκουσαν. Thus Judaea and Idumaea together represent the South.
The East too sent its contribution
from Peraea (πέραν τοῦ Ἰορδάνου, i.e.
ἀπὸ τοῦ πέραν τ. Ἰ.). Ἡ Περαία
(Joseph. *B. J.* iii. 3. 3) is both in
LXX. and N.T. simply πέραν τοῦ
Ἰορδάνου = יַרְדֵּן־הַיַּרְדֵּן, cf. Isa. ix. 1
(viii. 23), Mt. iv. 25, Mc. x. 1. According to Josephus *l.c.* Peraea extended
on the East of Jordan from Machaerus
to Pella, i.e. it lay chiefly between the
Jabbok and the Arnon ; but, like
Idumaea, the name seems to have
been somewhat loosely applied (G. A.
Smith, p. 539); Mt. in a similar list
(iv. 25) substitutes Decapolis for
Peraea : see note on Mc. v. 20. From
the North-West came inhabitants of
the Phoenician sea-coast (περὶ Τύρον
καὶ Σιδῶνα = τῆς παραλίου Τύρου καὶ
Σιδῶνος, Lc.); the district is called
Φοινίκη in Acts xi. 19, xv. 3, xxi. 2,
and in the LXX. (1 Esdr. ii. 16 ff.,
2 Macc. iii. 5, &c.), but not in the
Gospels, where it is simply τὰ μέρη
or τὰ ὅρια Τύρου κ. Σιδῶνος (Mt. xv.
21, Mc. vii. 24). The network of
roads which covered Galilee facilitated

such gatherings ; see G. A. Smith,
p. 425 ff.

πλῆθος πολύ κτλ.] Cf. πολὺ πλῆθος
v. 7, note; the emphasis is no longer
on the magnitude of the concourse,
but on its cause. The fame of the
miracles (cf. i. 28, 45) had brought
them together, and also, as Lc. adds,
the fame of the teaching (ἦλθαν ἀκοῦσαι
αὐτοῦ καὶ ἰαθῆναι). Ἀκούοντες ὅσα
ποιεῖ, ἦλθον: for ἀκούοντες we expect
ἀκούσαντες (see vv. ll.), but the pres.
part. may denote that the rumour on
the strength of which they started
continued and increased in strength
(WM., p. 429; Burton § 59, who calls
it " the present of past action still in
progress "); in ποιεῖ we hear the report as it is passed from one to another
in the crowd. Ὅσα, 'how many things'
rather than ' how great,' = ' all that' ;
cf. Mc. iii. 28, v. 19, vi. 30, x. 21 ;
Lc. viii. 39; Acts xiv. 27, xv. 4, 12.

9. καὶ εἶπεν...ἵνα κτλ.] On εἰπεῖν
ἵνα see WM., p. 422. Πλοιάριον, Vg.
navicula, probably here a light boat
in contrast with a fishing smack
(πλοῖον), as in Jo. vi. 22, 24, xxi. 8
(cf. Westcott). Προσκαρτερεῖν (Acts⁶,
Paul³, here only in the Gospels) is
rendered in the Vg. by *perseverare*,
perdurare, *instare*, *adhaerere*, *pa-
rere*, *servire*, and here by *deservire*:
in Mc. the English versions from
Tindale have had the happy rendering
'wait on.' The boat was to keep
close to the shore, moving when He

10 αὐτῷ διὰ τὸν ὄχλον, ἵνα μὴ θλίβωσιν αὐτόν· ¹⁰πολ-
λοὺς γὰρ ἐθεράπευσεν, ὥστε ἐπιπίπτειν αὐτῷ ἵνα
¶ W° 11 αὐτοῦ ἅψωνται ὅσοι εἶχον μάστιγας.¶ ¹¹καὶ τὰ
πνεύματα τὰ ἀκάθαρτα, ὅταν αὐτὸν ἐθεώρουν, προσέ-
§ t πιπτον αὐτῷ καὶ §ἔκραζον λέγοντα ὅτι Cὺ εἶ ὁ υἱὸς

9 αυτον]+πολλοι D a ff + οι οχλοι 13 28 69 124 346   10 εθεραπευεν ΚΙΙ min²
latᵛᵗ ᵖˡ vg me | αυτω] pr εν D latt   11 και πν. ακαθ. D | οταν]+ουν D | εθεωρουν
(ℵBCDGLΔΣ 13 33 69 1071 al)] εθεωρει ΑΡΓΠΦ | προσεπιπταν B προσεπιπτεν EHSUV
al | εκραζεν EHMSUV al | λεγοντες ℵDK minᵖᵃᵘᶜ | συ ει]+ο χριστος CMPΦ 16 121 syrʰᶜˡ*

moved, so as to be ready at any
moment to receive Him ; comp. Lc.
v. 3. On the present occasion He
does not seem to have used it; the
work of healing kept Him on the
land as long as it was possible to
remain there. There was no shrinking
from contact with the crowd, but only
a provision against a real danger—ἵνα
μὴ θλίβωσιν αὐτόν. For the literal
sense of θλίβω cf. Mt. vii. 14 τεθλιμμένη
ἡ ὁδός: both in LXX. and N.T. it is used
with few exceptions metaphorically.

10. πολλοὺς γὰρ ἐθεράπευσεν κτλ.]
On θεραπεύειν see note on i. 34. For
πολλούς, Mt. has πάντας : see note on
i. 34: all were healed who touched
Him or on whom He laid hands.

ὥστε ἐπιπίπτειν αὐτῷ] The enthusiasm grew till it became dangerous :
the sufferers threw themselves on
Him in their eagerness, or impelled
by the crowd. For ἐπιπίπτειν τινί
(more usually ἐπί τινα or τινι) see
2 Regn. xvii. 9, Job vi. 16, Judith xv. 6.
The action is not always hostile (cf.
Acts xx. 10), but it implies suddenness,
and usually some degree of passion ;
Field (Notes, p. 25) adduces Thuc. vii.
84, ἐπέπιπτόν τε ἀλλήλοις καὶ κατεπά-
τουν. In the present case it was
natural enough, yet perilous. Ἵνα
αὐτοῦ ἅψωνται: contact was thought
to be a condition, since it was often
the concomitant, of healing (Mc. i. 41,
v. 27 ff., vi. 56, viii. 22 ; cf. Lc. ἐζήτουν
ἅπτεσθαι αὐτοῦ, ὅτι δύναμις παρ' αὐτοῦ
ἐξήρχετο καὶ ἰᾶτο πάντας).

ὅσοι εἶχον μάστιγας] For this use
of μάστιγες see Mc. v. 29, 34, Lc.
vii. 21 νόσων καὶ μαστίγων. Μάστιξ
represents disease or suffering as a
Divine scourge used for chastisement ;
comp. Prov. iii. 12, cited in Heb. xii. 6 ;
the idea is frequent in the O.T. and
' Apocrypha,' cf. e.g. Ps. lxxiii. 4, 5,
Jer. v. 3, Tob. xiii. 14 (18), 2 Macc.
iii. 34, ix. 11, Ps. Sol. x. 1, but the
noun does not appear in the LXX. as
interchangeable with νόσος: possibly
even in the N.T. it carries with it the
thought of greater suffering, as well
as of a more direct visitation of
God.

11. καὶ τὰ πνεύματα τὰ ἀκάθ. κτλ.]
For πνεῦμα ἀκάθαρτον = δαιμόνιον see
i. 23 note. Ὅταν αὐτὸν ἐθεώρουν =
the class. ὅτε or ὁπότε θεωροῖεν (Madv.
§ 134 b); see Burton, §§ 290, 315, and
cf. WM., p. 388, Blass, Gr. p. 207 :
' whenever, as often as, they caught
sight of Him.' Προσέπιπτον—an act
of homage (Acts xvi. 29) akin to
adoration (cf. Ps. xciv. (xcv.) 6,
προσκυνήσωμεν καὶ προσπέσωμεν αὐτῷ),
now, as it seems, for the first time
offered to Jesus since the commencement of His ministry ; subsequently
such prostrations were frequent (Mc.
v. 6, 33, vii. 25). The contrast between
ἐπιπίπτειν (v. 10) and προσπίπτειν is
striking and perhaps not accidental.

καὶ ἔκραζον κτλ.] Κράζω is used of
the wild cry of the demoniacs also in
i. 23, v. 5, 7, ix. 26. The words of
the cry go beyond the confession of

τοῦ θεοῦ. ¹²καὶ πολλὰ ἐπετίμα αὐτοῖς ἵνα μὴ αὐτὸν 12
φανερὸν ποιήσωσιν.

¹³Καὶ ἀναβαίνει εἰς τὸ ὄρος καὶ προσκαλεῖται οὓς 13

12 ποιησωσιν] ποιωσιν B²DKLΠ* 13 69 al^pauc+οτι ηδεισαν τον χριστον αυτον ειναι
CΦ 2 pe^corr w^scr corr a+οτι ηδ. αυτον b ff g q t

i. 24, for ὁ υἱὸς τοῦ θεοῦ, however interpreted, is more definite than ὁ ἅγιος.
Comp. Mt. iv. 6, ὁ διάβολος λέγει αὐτῷ
Εἰ υἱὸς εἶ τοῦ θεοῦ κτλ. The earliest
confession of the Sonship seems to
have come from evil spirits, who knew
Jesus better than he was known by
His own disciples—τὰ δαιμόνια πιστεύουσιν (James ii. 19).

12. καὶ πολλὰ ἐπετίμα αὐτοῖς κτλ.]
Cf. i. 25, 43. The purpose of the
censure was to prevent a premature
divulgence of His true character: cf.
Phil. ii. 6, οὐχ ἁρπαγμὸν ἡγήσατο τὸ
εἶναι ἴσα τῷ θεῷ. Mt. reminds his
readers of Isa. xlii. 1—4, which he
sees fulfilled in our Lord's freedom
from personal ambition. Πολλὰ
ἐπετίμα, Vg. vehementer commina-
batur: πολλά as an adverb is characteristic of Mc., cf. v. 10, 23, 43, ix. 26.
Mt. has the less vivid ἐπετίμησεν
αὐτοῖς: Lc. omits the circumstance.
Φανερὸν ποιεῖν = φανεροῦν occurs only
here and in Mt.'s parallel. The φανέ-
ρωσις was postponed only; cf. iv. 22,
Rom. xvi. 26; it was not yet the
time for a general manifestation (Jo.
vii. 6 f., xvii. 6), and the δαιμόνια were
possibly aware that their revelations
could only work mischief at this
stage. "Nec tempus erat, neque hi
praecones" (Bengel). Bede compares
Ps. xlix. (l.) 16.

13—19 a. SECOND WITHDRAWAL
FROM CAPERNAUM, AND CHOICE OF
THE TWELVE (Mt. x. 1—4, Lc. vi.
12—16).

13. καὶ ἀναβαίνει κτλ.] Lc. ἐγένετο δὲ
ἐν ταῖς ἡμέραις ταύταις ἐξελθεῖν, again
implying an interval where Mc.'s
narrative seems to be continuous
(comp. Mc. iii. 1); in Mt. the order

is entirely different. Ἀναβαίνει, the
historical present, frequent in Mc.
(e.g. i. 21, 40, ii. 15, 18, iii. 4, 8; cf.
Hawkins, p. 113 ff.); τὸ ὄρος as in vi.
46—the hills above the Lake (τὰ ὄρη,
v. 5), cf. ἡ θάλασσα (ii. 13, iii. 7):
any other mountain is specified, e.g.
ix. 2, xi. 1. Similarly in Gen. xix. 17
τὸ ὄρος (הָהָר) is the heights above the
Jordan valley, and in Jud. i. 19, the
hill country of Judah (ἡ ὀρινή, Lc. i. 39,
65). With the phrase ἀναβαίνειν εἰς
τὸ ὄ. compare Mt. v. 1, xiv. 23, xv. 29.

The purpose of this retreat to the
hills is stated by Lc.: ἐγένετο...ἐξελ-
θεῖν αὐτὸν...προσεύξασθαι, καὶ ἦν δια-
νυκτερεύων ἐν τῇ προσευχῇ τοῦ θεοῦ.
A crisis had been reached, for which
special preparation must be made.
"A way was prepared in that night of
prayer upon the hills whereby an
organic life was imparted to the little
community...Our Lord takes counsel
of the Father alone,...when the morning comes [Lc. ὅτε ἐγένετο ἡμέρα] His
resolve is distinct, and it is forth-
with carried out" (Latham, Pastor
pastorum, p. 238). It was the first
Ember night; Victor: τοὺς ἡγουμένους
διδάσκων τῆς ἐκκλησίας πρὸ τῶν γινο-
μένων ὑπ' αὐτῶν χειροτονιῶν διανυκτε-
ρεύειν ἐν προσευχῇ.

καὶ προσκαλεῖται οὓς ἤθελεν αὐτός
κτλ.] The King chooses His ministers:
the selection is His act and not
theirs: Jo. vi. 70, xv. 16, Acts i. 2.
For other instances of the exercise of our Lord's human will, see
i. 41, vii. 24, ix. 30, Jo. xvii. 24,
xxi. 22; and for its renunciation,
xiv. 36, Jo. v. 30. Bengel: "volebat, ex voluntate Patris." Two steps
(Mc., Lc.; the point is not noticed by

14 ἤθελεν αὐτός, καὶ ἀπῆλθον πρὸς αὐτόν. ¹⁴καὶ ἐποίησεν δώδεκα, [οὓς καὶ ἀποστόλους ὠνόμασεν,] ἵνα
ὦσιν μετ᾽ αὐτοῦ, καὶ ἵνα ἀποστέλλῃ αὐτοὺς κηρύσσειν

14 δώδεκα post ινα ωσιν D a c i vg | ους και απ. ωνομασεν אBC* vid Δ 13 28 69 124
238 346 syrhcl(mg) me (aeth)] om AC²DLPΣ(Φ) minpl latt syrreinposhhcl(txt) go arm |
om ινα 2° B | αποστελει Φ | κηρυσσειν] pr και αποστολους ωνομασεν του Φ+το ευαγγε-
λιον D b e f ff g i q

Mt.) appear in this ἐκλογή: (1) the
summoning of an inner circle of
disciples; (2) the appointment of
twelve of their number to a special
office. Προσκαλεῖσθαι (vocare ad se,
Vg.), first in Gen. xxviii. 1, is from
this time forth frequently used of
the summons of Christ whether to
the μαθηταί or the ὄχλος (Mc.⁸).
Those who were summoned in this
instance ἀπῆλθον πρὸς αὐτόν—more
perhaps than venerunt (Vg.): in
coming they finally parted with the
surroundings of their previous life.

14. καὶ ἐποίησεν δώδεκα] Out of
those who answered His summons
He again selected twelve : Lc. ἐκλεξά-
μενος ἀπ᾽ αὐτῶν δώδεκα; Victor: ἦσαν
γὰρ πλείους οἱ παρόντες. These He appointed (ἐποίησεν, Mc.). For ποιεῖν in
this sense see 1 Regn. xii. 6 (ὁ ποιήσας
τὸν Μωυσῆν καὶ τ. Ἀαρών), Acts ii. 36,
Heb. iii. 2 (Westcott), Apoc. v. 10;
the Vg. fecit ut essent, &c. presupposes
the Western reading ἐποίησεν ἵνα ὦσιν
ιβ´ μετ᾽ αὐτοῦ. The number (1) seems
to have reference to the tribes of Israel,
to whom the Twelve were originally
sent (Mt. x. 6, 23); (2) it suggests their
relation to the larger Israel as patriarchs and princes of the new Kingdom
(Mt. xix. 28, Lc. xxii. 30, Apoc. xxi.
12, 14). Cf. Barn. 8. 3, οἷς ἔδωκεν τοῦ
εὐαγγελίου τὴν ἐξουσίαν, οὖσιν δεκαδύο
εἰς μαρτύριον τῶν φυλῶν.

οὓς καὶ ἀποστόλους ὠνόμασεν] See
vv. ll.: the words look like an interpolation from Lc., and it has been
suggested that their omission by D
and other 'Western' authorities is an

instance of 'Western non-interpola-
tion'; but the external evidence is
too strong in their favour to permit
their ejection from the text of Mc.,
even if Mc. vi. 30 does not presuppose
their presence here. The name was
not perhaps given at the time, but it
was given by the Lord; He not only
created the office but also (καὶ) imposed the title. Ἀπόστολος is used
by the LXX. only in 3 Regn. xiv. 6 (A),
where it = שָׁלוּחַ, cf. Isa. xviii. 2 Symm.
ἀποστέλλων ἀποστόλους (= צִירִים, Aq.
πρεσβευτάς). For the history and
N.T. use of the word see Lightfoot,
Galatians, p. 92 ff.; Hort, Ecclesia,
p. 22 ff.

ἵνα ὦσιν μετ᾽ αὐτοῦ κτλ.] Two immediate purposes of the creation of
an Apostolate : (1) such closer association with the Master as was impossible for the general body of μαθηταί,
(2) a mission based on the special
training thus imparted. Association
with Christ was at once the training
of the Twelve, and if they were faithful, their reward (Jo. xvii. 24). For
its effects see Acts iv. 13. On ποιεῖν
ἵνα cf. Blass, Gr. p. 226.

14—15. ἵνα ἀποστέλλῃ κτλ.] Hence
the name of their office. On ἀποστέλλω as distinguished from πέμπω see
Westcott on Jo. xx. 21 (add. note); for
κηρύσσω cf. i. 4, 14, and vv. ll. here;
the substance of the original Apostolic κήρυγμα was (Mt. x. 7), Ἤγγικεν ἡ
βασιλεία τῶν οὐρανῶν. A second part
of their commission was to exorcise and
to heal; Mc. mentions only exorcism,
but cf. Mt. (x. 1). For this work au-

¹⁵καὶ ἔχειν ἐξουσίαν §ἐκβάλλειν τὰ δαιμόνια. ¹⁶καὶ ¹⁵₁₆ § Wʰ
ἐποίησεν τοὺς δώδεκα· καὶ ἐπέθηκεν ὄνομα τῷ Σίμωνι
Πέτρον, ¹⁷καὶ Ἰάκωβον τὸν τοῦ Ζεβεδαίου καὶ Ἰω- 17

15 εχειν] εδωκεν αυτοις D b c fff i t vg aeth | εξουσιαν]+θεραπευειν τας νοσους και
AC²DΡΓΠΣΦ minᶠᵉʳᵉᵒᵐⁿ latt syrr arm go   16 και εποιησεν τ. δωδ. אBC*ΔΦ
aethᶜᵈ] om AC²DLΡΓΠΣ minᵖˡ latt syrr arm me go aethᵉᵈᵈ πρωτον Σιμωνα 13 69
124 346 | επεθηκεν αυτοις ονοματα 1071 | τω Σ. ονομα ΑΡΓΠΣΦ al minᵖˡᵉʳ Σ. ονομα D

thority was necessary (ἔχειν ἐξουσίαν
ἐκβάλλειν, cf. Mt. ἔδωκεν αὐτοῖς ἐξουσίαν κτλ.); authority delegated from
Christ was to be the note of their
ministry, as authority delegated from
the Father had been the note of the
Master's (see i. 22, ii. 10). Their
mission was identical in its purposes
with His, but secondary, and dependent on His gifts.

16. καὶ ἐποίησεν τοὺς δώδεκα] The
thread of v. 14 is picked up after the
parenthesis ἵνα ὦσιν...τὰ δαιμόνια—'and
so He created the Twelve.' Δώδεκα
now has the article, cf. iv. 10, vi. 7, &c.:
so Lc. x. 1 ἀνέδειξεν...ἑβδομήκοντα δύο,
ib. 17 οἱ ἑβδομήκοντα δύο, Acts vi. 3
ἄνδρας...ἑπτά, xxi. 8 ὄντος ἐκ τῶν ἑπτά.
For ποιεῖν cf. v. 14, note.

καὶ ἐπέθηκεν ὄνομα τῷ Σίμωνι Πέτρον]
For ἐπιθεῖναι ὄνομα cf. 4 Regn. xxiv.
17, and on the practice of imposing
characteristic names on scholars, see
Schöttgen, ad l.; Bengel: "domini
nota est dare cognomen." The construction thus begun is broken off by
the intervention of another train of
thought. Mc. is (as it seems) about to
continue καὶ τῷ Ἰακώβῳ...καὶ Ἰωάνῃ ἐπέθηκεν ὄνομα Βοανηργές, when it occurs
to him that a list of the twelve will
naturally follow ἐποίησεν τοὺς δώδεκα.
Hence he proceeds as if he had written
Σίμωνα ᾧ ἐπέθηκεν ὄνομα Πέτρον. WH.
regard καὶ...Σίμωνι as a parenthesis,
but a parenthesis in such a context is
almost intolerable. Such added names
are common in the N.T., cf. Acts i.
23 Βαρσαββᾶν ὃς ἐπεκλήθη Ἰοῦστος,
iv. 36 Ἰωσὴφ ὁ ἐπικληθεὶς Βαρνάβας,

xii. 12 Ἰωάνου τοῦ ἐπικαλουμένου Μάρκου: in Acts a similar formula is used
in Simon's case (x. 5, 18, 32, xi.
13), but only when that Apostle is
mentioned by or to persons outside
the Church; elsewhere in the Acts
and in the Gospels he is henceforth Πέτρος or Σίμων Πέτρος, the
latter especially in St John. Πέτρος
= Κηφᾶς (Jo. i. 42), i.e. אָפֵּכְ (cf.
פֵּבְּים, Job xxx. 6, Jer. iv. 29), Syr.
ܟܐܦܐ, a rock, or usually a detached piece of rock, a stone (cf.
Hort, First Epistle of St Peter, p. 152).
"The title appears to mark not so
much the natural character of the
Apostle as the spiritual office to which
he was called" (Westcott): cf. Victor,
ἵνα προλάβῃ τὸ ἔργον ἡ κλῆσις προφη-
τικῶς. The name was actually given
at the first call of Simon (Jo. l.c.), but
apparently not appropriated till he
became an Apostle. Mc.'s ἐπέθηκεν
leaves the time undetermined, so that
Augustine (de cons. 109) may be right:
"hoc recolendo dixit, non quod tum
factum sit." Justin appears to refer
to this verse, dial. 106: μετωνομακέναι
αὐτὸν Πέτρον ἕνα τῶν ἀποστόλων, καὶ γεγράφθαι ἐν τοῖς ἀπομνημονεύμασιν αὐτοῦ
γεγενημένον καὶ τοῦτο (cf. Intr. p. xxx).

17. καὶ Ἰάκωβον...καὶ Ἰωάνην] Sc.
ἐποίησεν. For these Apostles see
note on i. 19. They follow next after
Peter (πρῶτος Σίμων, Mt.), either because they shared with him the
prerogative of a title imposed by the
Lord, or because with him they were
afterwards singled out for special

¶ P ἄνην τὸν ἀδελφὸν τοῦ Ἰακώβου ¶—καὶ ἐπέθηκεν
αὐτοῖς ὄνομα *Βοανηργές*, ὅ ἐστιν Υἱοὶ βροντῆς—
18 ¹⁸καὶ Ἀνδρέαν καὶ Φίλιππον καὶ Βαρθολομαῖον καὶ

17 του Ιακωβου] αυτου Ιακ. ΑΓΣ al αυτου G min^pauc syr^sin om του CKSΔ | ονομα
BD min³ syr^pesh] ονοματα ℵACLΓΔΠΣΦ al min^pl latt syr^hel arm me go aeth | βοανηρ-
γες ℵABCKLMΔ²Π* 1 33 69 al^pauc] βοανεργης D βοανεργες EFGHUVΓΠ²Φ min^pl
βοαναργες Δ* βανηρεγεζ 604 βανηρεγες 2^pe | om ο εστιν υιοι βρ. syr^sin

privileges (Mc. v. 37, ix. 2, xiv. 32;
Acts i. 13, where the titles are not
mentioned, has the same order).

καὶ ἐπέθηκεν αὐτοῖς ὄνομα Βοανηργές
κτλ.] Dalman, *Gr.* pp. 112 n., 158 n.,
suggested that Βοανηργές is a corruption of Βανηρογές (בְּנֵי־רֹגֶז), and similar
forms occur in two important cursives
(see vv. ll.), and in the Syriac versions,
which have the meaningless ܒܢܝ
ܪܓܫܝ, and the Armenian (*Bane-
reges*). More recently (*Worte Jesu*,
p. 39, n. 4) he has proposed to regard
either o or a as an intrusion into
the text. Others have justified the
prevalent form by such partial analogies as Σόδομα = סְדֹם, Ῥοωβώθ =
רְחֹבוֹת. The second factor in Βοανηργές is hardly less perplexing. The
Syriac root ܪܓܫ is never used of
thunder, and the ordinary Heb. for
thunder is רַעַם (Syr. ܪܥܡܐ).
Jerome (on Dan. i. 7) proposed *Bene-
reem* or *Baneraem* (בְּנֵי־רַעַם), but without Greek authority. In Job xxxvii. 2
רֹגֶז appears to be used for the rumbling
of the storm, and this seems to point
to the quarter where a solution may
be found. The υἱοὶ βροντῆς (=οἱ
βροντῶντες, Euth.) were probably so
called not merely from the impetuo-
sity of their natural character (cf. e.g.
Mc. ix. 38, Lc. ix. 54), but, as Simon
was called Peter, from their place in
the new order. In the case of James
nothing remains to justify the title
beyond the fact of his early martyrdom, probably due to the force of his

denunciations (Acts xii. 2): John's
νοητὴ βροντή (Orig. *Philoc.* xv. 18) is
heard in Gospel, Epistles, and Apocalypse; see esp. Trench, *Studies*, p.
144 f., Westcott, *St John*, p. xxxiii;
and for the patristic explanations cf.
Suicer s. v. Βροντή. Victor: διὰ τὸ
μέγα καὶ διαπρύσιον ἠχῆσαι τῇ οἰκουμένῃ τῆς θεολογίας τὰ δόγματα.

18. καὶ Ἀνδρέαν καὶ Φίλιππον] As
Simon Peter's brother, Andrew follows
the first three, although πρὸς τοὺς τρεῖς
οὐκ ἦλθεν (2 Regn. xxiii. 23); cf. Mc.
xiii. 3, Acts i. 13; Mt. and Lc. place
him second. He appears again in
connexion with Philip in Jo. xii. 22.
Both Ἀνδρέας and Φίλιππος are purely
Greek names, whilst Σίμων is Συμεών
Hellenised (note on i. 16): the three
men came from the same town, Bethsaida (Jo. i. 44), where Hellenising influences were at work; see note on
viii. 22.

καὶ Βαρθολομαῖον] Βαρθολομαῖος
(only in the Apostolic lists)=בַּר־תַּלְמַי,
Syr.^sin.pesh. ܒܪ ܬܘܠܡܝ, the son of
Talmai or Tolomai: cf. Βαριωνᾶ Mt.
xvi. 17=[υἱὸς] Ἰωάνου Jo. xxi. 15, Βαρ-
τιμαῖος=ὁ υἱὸς Τιμαίου (Mc. x. 46). The
name תַּלְמַי (M.T. תַּלְמָי) occurs in Num.
xiii. 22, Josh. xv. 14, Judg. i. 10,
2 Sam. iii. 3, xiii. 37, 1 Chron. iii. 2,
and among its Greek equivalents in
codd. BA are Θαλμεί, Θαλμαί, Θολμεί,
Θολαμαί; Josephus has Θολομαῖος (*ant.*
xx. 1. 1). Only the patronymic of
this Apostle appears in the lists, but
he is probably identical with the
Ναθαναήλ of Jo. i. 46 ff., xxi. 2 (see

Ματθαῖον¶ *καὶ Θωμᾶν καὶ Ἰάκωβον τὸν τοῦ Ἀλφαίου*   ¶ t

18 Ματθαιον B*D] Ματθαιον ℵ (sed alibi plerumque Μαθθ.) AB²CLΓΔΠΣΦ al min^{omn vid} + τον τελωνην 13 69 124 209 604 1071 syr^{hel(mg)} arm

Westcott *ad ll.*). If so, he was from Cana, and his introduction to the Lord was due to Philip, whom he follows in the lists of Mt. Mc. Lc. Tradition (Eus. *H. E.* v. 10) gave him India as his field of Apostolic work.

καὶ Ματθαῖον καὶ Θωμᾶν] The two names are associated, in varying order (Μ. κ. Θ., Mc. Lc.; Θ. κ. Μ., Mt.), by the three Synoptists; in Acts they are separated by Bartholomew. Mt. adds ὁ τελώνης to his own name. Ματθαῖος, Syrr.^{sin. cu. pesh.} ܡܬܝ, is either like Ματθίας an abbreviated form of מַתִּתְיָהוּ (1 Chron. xxv. 21 Ματθίας, A)—so Dalman, *Gr.* p. 142, *Worte J.*, p. 40 f.—or connected with מַתַּי, *vir*. That Matthew is identical with Levi seems to follow from Mt. ix. 9 ff. compared with the parallels in Mc., Lc. But some expositors ancient as well as modern have distinguished the two, e.g. Heracleon (ap. Clem. Al. *strom.* iv. 9, ἐξ ὧν Ματθαῖος, Φίλιππος, Θωμᾶς, Λευίς, καὶ ἄλλοι), and perhaps Origen (*Cels.* i. 62). No difficulty need be felt as to the double name, of which the Apostolic list has already yielded examples. Θωμᾶς = תָּאוֹמָא (= תָּאוֹם Gen. xxxviii. 27), cf. Dalman, p. 112, is interpreted by Jo. xi. 16, xx. 24, xxi. 2 (ὁ λεγόμενος Δίδυμος, the twin). According to the *Acta Thomae* (cf. Eus. *H.E.* i. 13) his personal name was Judas (ἔλαχεν ἡ Ἰνδία Ἰούδᾳ Θωμᾷ τῷ καὶ Διδύμῳ). In Jo. xiv. 22 Syr.^{cu.} has 'Judas Thomas' and Syr.^{sin.} 'Thomas' for Ἰούδας οὐχ ὁ Ἰσκαριώτης: see Lightfoot, *Galatians*, p. 263 n. If there were three Apostles of the name of Judas, the substitution of a secondary name in the case of one of them was natural enough.

καὶ Ἰάκωβον τὸν τοῦ Ἀλφαίου] So Mt. : Lc.^{ev. act.} Ἰάκωβος Ἀλφαίου : so called no doubt to distinguish him from Ἰάκωβος ὁ τοῦ Ζεβεδαίου. Ἀλφαῖος (= חַלְפַי, cf. Χαλφεί, 1 Macc. xi. 70) is perhaps identical with Κλωπᾶς, Jo. xix. 25 : if he is the Κλεόπας = Κλεόπατρος of Lc. xxiv. 18, the latter name must be simply a Greek substitute for the Aramaic name (cf. Lightfoot, *Galatians*, p. 267 n., Dalman, p. 142 n.). If the identification of Ἀλφαῖος with Κλωπᾶς is correct, this James was also known in the Apostolic Church as ὁ μικρός : his mother was a Mary, and he had a brother Joses (= Joseph); cf. Mc. xv. 40. There is no reason for regarding him as a brother of Levi, or as one of the 'brothers' of the Lord (see notes on ii. 14, vi. 3).

Θαδδαῖον] Aram. תַּדַּי, תַּדְרַי (Dalman, *Gr.*, p. 143 ; *Worte J.*, p. 41). Both in Mt. and Mc. the Western text gives Λεββαῖος (WH., *Notes*, pp. 11, 24), either an attempt to identify this Apostle with Levi (H.), or another rendering of his name (from לֵב, *cor*, as Θαδδαῖος is from שַׁד, Syr. ܐܕܬܐ *mamma*). In Lc.^{ev. act.} his name is given as Ἰούδας Ἰακώβου : cf. Orig. *praef. ad Rom.* : "eundem quem... Marcus Thaddaeum dixit, Lucas Iudam Iacobi scripsit...quia moris erat binis vel ternis nominibus uti Hebraeos." This Judas is apparently referred to in Jo. xiv. 22 as οὐχ ὁ Ἰσκαριώτης. For fuller particulars see Nestle, in Hastings, *D. B.* iv. p. 741 f.

Σίμωνα τὸν Καναναῖον] So Mt. ; Lc.^{ev.} Σίμωνα τὸν καλούμενον ζηλωτήν, Lc.^{act.} Σίμων ὁ ζηλωτής. Καναναῖος like Θαδδαῖος is a descriptive name, not a native of

καὶ Θαδδαῖον καὶ Cίμωνα τὸν Καναναῖον ¹⁹καὶ Ἰούδαν 19
Ἰσκαριώθ, ὃς καὶ παρέδωκεν αὐτόν.

18 Θαδδαιον] Λεββαιον D a b ff i q | Καναναιον אBCDLΔ 33 565 latt syrʳˢⁱⁿ ᵖᵉˢʰ ᵛⁱᵈ
arm me aeth] Κανανιτην ΑΓΠΣΦ al min ᶠᵉʳᵉ ᵒᵐⁿ syrʰᶜˡ go   19 Ισκαριωθ אBCLΔ
33 2ᵖᵉ al²] Σκαριωθ D aᵛⁱᵈ b ff i q vg Ισκαριωτην ΑΓΠΣΦ al minᵖˡᵉʳ (syrˢⁱⁿ ᵖᵉˢʰ arm)
syrʰᶜˡ me go

Cana (Καναῖος), nor a Canaanite (Χανα-
ναῖος, כְּנַעֲנִי), but, as Lc. interprets it, a
zealot (קַנְאָנָא, Syr.ˢⁱⁿ·ᵖᵉˢʰ· ܩܢܢܐ),
cf. Exod. xx. 5, Deut. iv. 24 אֵל קַנָּא,
LXX. θεὸς ζηλωτής, and in reference to
devout Israelites 1 Esdr. viii. 69, A,
2 Macc. iv. 2 ; the model of a true
ζηλωτής was Phinehas, 4 Macc. xviii.
12. The later Zealots were a fanatical
party originating among the Pharisees
(Schürer I. ii. 80 n., 229 f.). This
Simon cannot have belonged to the
more advanced Zealots who were
associated with sedition and outrage
(cf. Joseph. ant. xviii. 1, B. J. iv.
3. 9, &c.), but he may have been
before (Gal. i. 14) and even after
(Acts xxi. 20) his call a scrupulous
adherent to the forms of the Law.
Yet it is difficult to suppose this of
one who belonged to the inner circle
of our Lord's disciples, and the analogy
of other secondary names in the list
leads us to regard the name as descriptive of personal character only. As
the first Simon was 'rocklike,' so the
second was characterized by jealousy
for what he conceived to be right or
true. Possibly he was a man who
under other teaching might have developed into the fanatic or bigot, but
who learnt from the Master to cherish
only the ' fire of love.'

19. Ἰούδαν Ἰσκαριώθ] So xiv. 10,
Lc. vi. 16; elsewhere ὁ Ἰσκαριώτης
(Mt. x. 4, xxvi. 14, Lc. xxii. 3 (ὁ
καλούμενος), Jo. xii. 4, xiii. 2, 26, xiv.
22). Ἰσκαριώθ appears to = אִישׁ קְרִיּוֹת:
for the form Ἰσκαριώτης comp. Joseph.
ant. vii. 6. 1, Ἵστοβος = אִישׁ טוֹב.
There is some difficulty in identifying

Kerioth ; in Josh. xv. 25, to which
reference is usually made, the word is
but part of the name Kerioth-Hezron ;
in Jer. xlviii. 24, 41 Kerioth (LXX.,
Καριώθ) is a town of Moab distinct
apparently from Kiriathaim, one or
the other of which Tristram (Land of
Moab, p. 275) is disposed to identify
with Kureiyat, S.E. of Ataroth on the
east side of the Dead Sea. In Jo. vi.
71 the name of the town is given as
Καρυώτος by א* and some good cursives (ἀπὸ Καρυώτου), and the same
reading appears in D at Jo. xii. 4,
xiv. 22 ; cf. Lightfoot, Bibl. Essays,
p. 143 f. If this Judas came from a
town east of the Dead Sea, he was
possibly one of the newly arrived disciples (Mc. iii. 8)—a circumstance
which would perhaps account for his
position at the end of the list. His
father Simon (Ἰούδας Σίμωνος Jo.⁴) was
also of the same town (Jo. vi. 71, Ἰούδαν Σίμωνος Ἰσκαριώτου, א*BCGL).
See Zahn, Einl. ii. p. 561, and the artt.
in Hastings and Encycl. Bibl.

ὃς καὶ παρέδωκεν αὐτόν] Mt. ὁ καὶ
παραδοὺς αὐτόν, Lc. ὃς ἐγίνετο προδότης
(cf. Acts i. 16, τοῦ γενομένου ὁδηγοῦ
τοῖς συλλαβοῦσιν Ἰησοῦν), Jo. xii. 4 ὁ
μέλλων αὐτὸν παραδιδόναι, xviii. 2, 5 ὁ
παραδιδοὺς αὐτόν. In one form or another the terrible indictment is rarely
absent where the name of this Apostle
is mentioned. For παραδιδόναι comp.
note on i. 14, and on the use of the
aor., Blass, Gr. p. 198. Καί calls
attention to the identity of the
traitor with the Apostle, and contrasts the treachery of Judas with the
choice of Christ.

20 Καὶ ἔρχεται εἰς οἶκον· ²⁰καὶ συνέρχεται πάλιν
ὁ ὄχλος ὥστε μὴ δύνασθαι αὐτοὺς μηδὲ ἄρτον φαγεῖν.
21 ²¹καὶ ἀκούσαντες οἱ παρ' αὐτοῦ ἐξῆλθον κρατῆσαι

19 ερχεται ℵ*ΒΓ alᵖᵃᵘᶜ b e i ff syrˢⁱⁿ] ερχονται ℵᶜ·ᵃCLΔΠΣΦ al minᵖˡᵉʳ e q vg syrrᵖᵉˢʰ ʰᶜˡ arm go : εισερχονται D | οικον] pr τον 2ᵖᵉ   20 συνερχεται] ερχεται M c syrˢⁱⁿ arm συνερχονται Π* minᵖᵃᵘᶜ syrᵖᵉˢʰ | ο οχλος (ℵᶜ·ᵃABDLᶜᵒʳʳ minⁿᵒⁿⁿ)] om o ℵ*CEFGKL*ΤΠΣΦ alᵖˡᵉʳ | om αυτους D go | μηδε ABKLUΔΠ* minⁿᵒⁿⁿ] μητε ℵCDEFGΣΦ alᵖˡᵉʳ | αρτους D   21 ακουσαντες οι παρ αυτου (ακ. οι αδελφοι αυτου syrrᵛⁱᵈ)] οτε ηκουσαν περι αυτου οι γραμματεις και οι λοιποι D latᵛᵗᵖˡᵉʳ go

19 b—30. QUESTION OF THE SOURCE OF THE LORD'S POWER TO EXPEL δαιμόνια (Mt. xii. 22—32, Lc. xi. 14 —26; cf. Mt. ix. 32—34, Lc. xii. 10).

19. καὶ ἔρχεται εἰς οἶκον] Compared with v. 13 the words imply an interval during which the Lord descends from the mountain and returns to Capernaum (Lc. vii. 1). Lc. introduces here the discourse ἐπὶ τόπου πεδινοῦ which corresponds on the whole to Mt.'s 'Sermon on the Mount,' and the harmonists from Tatian onwards place it—rightly as it seems—in this position. Mc., to whom the Sermon is unknown, passes without notice to his next fact, and the English reader's sense of the relation of the sequel to what has gone before is further confused by the verse division. The house entered is probably Simon's (i. 29); for the omission of the article cf. ii. 1.

20. καὶ συνέρχεται πάλιν κτλ.] Apparently in the house and at the house-door; cf. i. 32, ii. 2. For πάλιν see note on ii. 1. Ὥστε μὴ...μηδέ, Vg. ita ut non possent neque panem manducare, 'so that they could not even,' &c.; the reading ὥστε μὴ... μήτε could only="ita ut n. p. neque panem manducarent" (WM., p. 614, Blass, Gr. p. 265). Ἄρτον φαγεῖν, to take food (of any kind) = אָכַל לֶחֶם, as in Gen. iii. 19, xliii. 16, Exod. ii. 20, &c. The difficulty must often have arisen during the height of the Lord's popularity; for another in-

stance see Mc. vi. 31. Bede exclaims, "Quam beata frequentia turbae confluentis, cui tantum studii ad audiendum verbum Dei."

21. καὶ ἀκούσαντες οἱ παρ' αὐτοῦ κτλ.] Cf. Prov. xxix. 39 (xxxi. 21) οἱ παρ' αὐτῆς=תֵיתָהּ. In Sus. 33 (cf. 30) οἱ παρ' αὐτῆς are Susanna's parents, children, and other relatives (Th.), or her parents and dependents (Lxx.); in 1 Macc. ix. 44 (ℵV, but τοῖς ἀδελφοῖς, A), xi. 73, xii. 27, xiii. 52, xv. 15, xvi. 16, 2 Macc. xi. 20, the phrase is used in a wider sense of adherents, followers, &c., cf. Joseph. ant. i. 11, περιτέμνεται καὶ πάντες οἱ παρ' αὐτοῦ. Thus the Syr.ˢⁱⁿ 'His brethren' or the Vg. sui fairly represents its general sense; "his kynnesmen" (Wycliffe), or "kynesfolkes" (Geneva) is too definite; the context, however, shews that this is practically what is meant. Clearly οἱ παρ' αὐτοῦ cannot be the Scribes and Pharisees, as Ð, which substitutes οἱ γραμματεῖς καὶ οἱ λοιποί, and Victor: νομίζω...περὶ τῶν Φαρισαίων καὶ γραμματέων λέγειν τὸν εὐαγγελιστήν. Either disciples or relatives are intended, and as the former were on the spot, ἀκούσαντες ἐξῆλθον could hardly apply to them. We are thus led to think of His family at Nazareth, whose coming is announced in v. 31. The incident of vv. 22—30 fills the interval between their departure and arrival. For κρατεῖν in this sense, cf. xii. 12, xiv. 1, 46.

22 αὐτόν, ἔλεγον γὰρ ὅτι Ἐξέστη. ²²καὶ οἱ γραμματεῖς
οἱ ἀπὸ Ἱεροσολύμων καταβάντες ἔλεγον ὅτι Βεελζεβοὺλ ἔχει, καὶ ὅτι Ἐν τῷ ἄρχοντι τῶν δαιμονίων

21 εξεσταται αυτους D* (εξεσται D²) *exentiat eos* a b d ff i q εξεσταται 13 69
εξισταται 346 εξεστι min^pauc   22 οι απο I.] pr και H al^pauc a | Βεεζεβουλ B

ἔλεγον γὰρ ὅτι Ἐξέστη] On the aor.
see Burton, § 47; as to the meaning
cf. Euth., παρεφρόνησε, and the Vg.
here, "in furorem versus est." The
same charge was brought against St
Paul, Acts xxvi. 24, cf. 2 Cor. v. 13,
εἴτε γὰρ ἐξέστημεν, θεῷ. For ἐξέστην
in this sense see Isa. xxviii. 7, Hos.
ix. 7. The family of Jesus were
doubtless inspired by a desire for His
safety, but their interpretation of
His enthusiasm implied want of
faith in Him, cf. Jo. vii. 5; the
Mother perhaps was overpersuaded
by the brethren. Tatian strangely
places this verse in connexion with the
narrative of Mc. ii. 23—28 (Hill,
Diatess., p. 71; see above, p. 50).

22. καὶ οἱ γραμματεῖς κτλ.] Mt. οἱ
Φαρισαῖοι, Lc. τινὲς ἐξ αὐτῶν. The
Pharisaic Scribes from Jerusalem
had been from the first the insti-
gators of the opposition (Lc. v. 17; cf.
Mc. ii. 6, vii. 1). The present attack
arose out of the healing of a possessed man who recovered sight and
speech (Mt. Lc.); voices were heard
in the crowd asking Μήτι οὗτός ἐστιν ὁ
υἱὸς Δαυείδ; (Mt. xii. 23), and the
Jerusalem Scribes were thus tempted
to suggest another explanation. For
καταβῆναι ἀπὸ Ἱερ. cf. Lc. ii. 51, x.
30 f., Acts viii. 26.

Βεελζεβοὺλ ἔχει] The form *Beelze-
bub*, which occurs in Syrr.^sin. cu. pesh. and
in most mss. of the Vulg., but in no
Greek ms., comes from 2 Kings i. 2, 6
בְּבַעַל זְבוּב אֱלֹהֵי עֶקְרוֹן, where the LXX.
render ἐν τῷ (τῇ) Βάαλ μυῖαν θεὸν Ἀκκα-
ρών, but Symm. had παρὰ τοῦ Βεελζεβοὺβ
θεοῦ Ἐκρών. The derivation of Βεελζεβοὺλ is obscure: some connect
the second factor of the name with

זְבֶל, whence זְבוּל, a Talmudic word
for dung (so Dalman, p. 105 n.),
others with זְבָל, habitation: cf.
Kautzsch, p. 9, Dalman, *l.c.* Neubauer (*Stud. Bibl.* i. p. 55) suggests
that זְבוּל is a dialectal form of זְבוּר,
a bee, so that Βεελζεβοὺλ = Βεελζε-
βούρ: but the conjecture has not
much to recommend it. We have then
to choose between 'Lord of dung'
and 'Lord of the habitation'; to the
latter the apparent play upon זְבוּל
in Mt. x. 25 (τὸν οἰκοδεσπότην Β.
ἐπεκάλεσαν) lends some support; if
the former is adopted, 'dung' is
used as an opprobrious name for
idols (J. Lightfoot on Mt. xii. 24),
and the application of the word to
the prince of the unclean spirits
points to the old belief in the connexion of idols with δαιμόνια: see
note on Mc. i. 34. The form Βεεζε-
βούλ, given by B here and by ℵB in
Mt. x. 25, xii. 24, Lc. xi. 15, 18, 19,
is admitted by WH. into the text
(*Notes*, p. 166); but it is difficult to
regard it as anything but a phonetic
corruption, perhaps a softening of the
original word. With Βεελζ. ἔχει cf.
Jo. vii. 20, where a similar charge
comes from the ὄχλος at Jerusalem.
Even of the Baptist some had said
Δαιμόνιον ἔχει (Mt. xi. 18). The charge
brought against our Lord was perhaps equivalent to that of using
magic: see Hastings, iii. p. 211 a.

ἐν τῷ ἄρχοντι κτλ.] In the power
and name of the chief of the unclean spirits: cf. Mt. xii. 28 ἐν πνεύματι θεοῦ, Lc. xi. 20 ἐν δακτύλῳ θεοῦ.
With ὁ ἄρχων τῶν δ. cf. ὁ τοῦ κόσμου
ἄρχων (Jo. xiv. 30), ὁ ἄρχων τοῦ κόσμου

ἐκβάλλει τὰ δαιμόνια. ²³καὶ προσκαλεσάμενος αὐτοὺς 23
ἐν παραβολαῖς ἔλεγεν αὐτοῖς Πῶς δύναται Σατανᾶς
Σατανᾶν ἐκβάλλειν; ²⁴καὶ ἐὰν βασιλεία ἐφ᾽ ἑαυτὴν 24

23 αυτοις]+ο κυριος Ιησους D a ff g r+o Ιησους U 1071 b c (al)

τούτου (Jo. xvi. 11), ὁ ἄρχων τῆς
ἐξουσίας τοῦ ἀέρος (Eph. ii. 2). The
authority is not denied, but limited
to its proper sphere : ἐν ἐμοὶ οὐκ ἔχει
οὐδέν (Jo. xiv. 30).

23. καὶ προσκαλεσάμενος αὐτούς]
See on iii. 13. The remark of the
Scribes, if made openly, was not
audible to Jesus, but He knew their
thoughts (Mt. Lc.): cf. ii. 8. He
beckoned them to Him, and they
came, little suspecting His purpose.

ἐν παραβολαῖς ἔλεγεν : in half-veiled,
proverb - like teaching. Παραβολή,
which occurs here for the first time,
is the usual LXX. rendering of מָשָׁל,
cf. Num. xxiii. 7 ff. (ἀναλαβεῖν παραβολήν), 3 Regn. iv. 28=v. 12 (ἐλάλησεν
Σαλωμὼν τρισχιλίας παραβολάς), Ps.
lxxvii. (lxxviii.) 2 (ἀνοίξω ἐν παραβολαῖς τὸ στόμα μου, cited in Mt. xiii.
35); the other rendering being παροι-
μία, which gives its Greek title to
the Book מִשְׁלֵי. The Synoptists use
the former in reference to the teaching of Jesus, St John (x. 6, xvi. 25,
29) the latter. A παραβολή is properly a comparison (Mc. iv. 30), and
a kind of παράδειγμα (Arist. Rhet. ii.
20), an illustration drawn from life
or nature. This meaning prevails in
the Gospels, but the sense suggested
by the Hebrew equivalent, a gnomic
saying (cf. Prov. i. 6), shews itself occasionally, e.g. Lc. iv. 23 ; the present
instance may be regarded as intermediate. A distinction between παρ-
οιμία and παραβολή appears perhaps
first in Sir. xlvii. 17, ἐν ᾠδαῖς καὶ παροιμίαις καὶ παραβολαῖς (Heb. בְּשִׁיר מָשָׁל
חִידָה וּמְלִיצָה, cf. Prov. i. 6). 'Parable'
comes to us through the 'European'

O.L. and Vg., and appears in Wycliffe :
Tindale substituted 'similitude' (cf.
similitudo of the 'African' O.L.), but
the familiar word re-appears in Cranmer and A.V.

πῶς δύναται Σατανᾶς κτλ.] The Lord
does not use Βεελζεβούλ, but the ordinary name for the Chief of the evil
spirits ; the occasion was too grave
for banter. Only Mc. reports this
saying, which goes to the heart of
the matter. The Scribes' explanation was morally impossible : the δαιμόνια could not be expelled through
collusion with their Chief. For Σατανᾶς cf. note on i. 13. Σατανᾶν, i.e.
τὰ δαιμόνια regarded as Satan's representatives and instruments. The
identification is instructive as throwing light on the manifoldness of Satanic agency. For the form of the
question cf. Mt. xii. 29, 34, Lc. vi. 42,
Jo. vi. 52.

24—25. καὶ ἐὰν βασιλεία κτλ.] The
first καί seems to be merely a connecting link with v. 23 : the two
that follow (vv. 25, 26) coordinate
the three cases of the divided kingdom, the divided house, and the divided Satan (WM., pp. 543, 547). For
ἐφ᾽ ἑαυτήν, 'in relation to itself,' Mt.
substitutes the explanatory καθ᾽ ἑαυτῆς, returning however to ἐπί just
afterwards (ἐφ᾽ ἑαυτόν). Οὐ δύναται
σταθῆναι=ἐρημοῦται, Mt., Lc.; similarly for οὐ δυνήσεται στῆναι Lc. has
πίπτει—both probably interpretations : cf. Burton, §§ 260, 262. For
the phrase which Mc. uses cf. Ps.
xvii. (xviii.) 39, xxxv. (xxxvi.) 13 :
the corresponding Heb. is לֹא יְכֹל קוּם.
If the difference between σταθῆναι
and στῆναι is to be pressed in this

25 μερισθῇ, οὐ δύναται σταθῆναι ἡ βασιλεία ἐκείνη· ²⁵καὶ
ἐὰν οἰκία ἐφ᾽ ἑαυτὴν μερισθῇ, οὐ δυνήσεται ἡ οἰκία
26 ἐκείνη στῆναι. ²⁶καὶ εἰ ὁ σατανᾶς ἀνέστη ἐφ᾽ ἑαυτὸν
καὶ ἐμερίσθη, οὐ δύναται στῆναι ἀλλὰ τέλος ἔχει.
§ ۱¹⁰ 27 ²⁷ἀλλ᾽ οὐ δύναται οὐδεὶς εἰς τὴν οἰκίαν τοῦ §ἰσχυροῦ
εἰσελθὼν τὰ σκεύη αὐτοῦ διαρπάσαι ἐὰν μὴ πρῶτον

25 δυνησεται אBCLΔ 1071 a i vg] δυναται ADΓΠΣΦ al b c e f ff q syrr | στηναι
BKLΠ] εστaναι D σταθηναι אAEFGHMSUVΓΔΣΦ al   26 ει] εαν D | ανεστη εφ
εαυτον] σαταναν εκβαλλει D a b c e ff g i q r | και εμερισθη ου א°·ᵃBL] και μεμερισται
ου AC²ΓΠΣΦ al syrrᵛⁱᵈ arm me go al εμερισθη και ου א*C*ᵛⁱᵈΔ f vg μεμερισται (-θαι D*)
εφ εαυτον ου D | στηναι אBCL] σταθηναι ADΓΔΠΦ al minᵒᵐⁿ ᵛⁱᵈ+η βασιλεια αυτου
D a b g i q r | τελος] pr το D   27 αλλ]και C²ᵛⁱᵈG om ADΓΠΣΦ al lattᵛᵗ ᵖˡ ᵛᵍ syrr
go | ου δυν. ουδεις אBC*Δ] ουδεις δυναται ADLΓΠΣΦ al latt syrr arm go | εις την οικ.
του ισχ. εισελθ. τα σκ. (א)BCLΔ 33 1071 syrrˢⁱⁿ ᵖᵉˢʰ me aeth] τα σκ. του ισχ. εισελθ.
εις τ. οικ. ADΓΠΣΦ۱ al latt syrʰᶜˡ arm go τα σκ. του ισχ. G

place, it must lie in the fact that
the body politic takes up and keeps
a position (cf. Lc. xviii. 11, 40, xix.
8) whilst the building stands as an
inert mass ; but the use of στῆναι
in the third clause is against this
distinction. Jerome : " quomodo concordia parvae res crescunt, ita dis-
cordia maximae dilabuntur."

26. καὶ εἰ ὁ σατανᾶς ἀνέστη...ἐμέ-
ρίσθη] This clause might have run
on the same lines as the other two
(καὶ ἐὰν ὁ Σ. ἀναστῇ...καὶ μερισθῇ κτλ.),
i.e., as involving a supposition which
will probably be fulfilled (Burton,
p. 250, cf. Blass, Gr. p. 214); but
the three Synoptists agree in representing the action of Satan as a matter
of fact: 'suppose Satan to have actually risen against himself...then he is
at this moment in an unstable condition, his end has come.' Ἐμερίσθη,
i.e. Satan in his corporate capacity, as
representing the Kingdom of evil; cf.
1 Cor. i. 12, μεμέρισται ὁ χριστός.

ἀλλὰ τέλος ἔχει] Cf. Lc. xxii. 37.
A phrase frequent in class. Gk. (cf.
e.g. Plat. Legg. 717 E, τῶν ἤδη τέλος
ἐχόντων=τῶν νεκρῶν). Mt., Lc. add
here in almost identical words εἰ [δὲ]

ἐγὼ ἐν Βεελζεβούλ...ἄρα ἔφθασεν ἐφ᾽
ὑμᾶς ἡ βασιλεία τοῦ θεοῦ.

27. ἀλλ᾽ οὐ δύναται οὐδείς κτλ.]
Another παραβολή. Mt. gives it in
a form almost exactly the same as
this ; Lc. resets the picture. The
connexion of thought is : 'so far from
being in league with Satan, I am
his conqueror, for he is too strong
an οἰκοδεσπότης to witness with equa-
nimity the spoiling of his goods.' Ὁ
ἰσχυρός possibly hints at the claims
of Satan as a usurper of Divine authority (cf. e.g. Mt. iv. 9, 2 Cor. iv.
4), since ἰσχυρός or ὁ ἰσχ. in the
LXX. frequently represents אֵל or
הַגִּבּוֹר. The parable itself is based
on Isa. xlix. 24, 25.

τὰ σκεύη αὐτοῦ] Lc. τὰ ὑπάρχοντα
αὐτοῦ. Cf. Gen. xxxi. 37 (πάντα τὰ
σκεύη τοῦ οἴκου μου), Lc. xvii. 31 (τὰ
σκ. αὐτοῦ ἐν τῇ οἰκίᾳ), 2 Tim. ii. 20f.;
how inclusive the word can be is seen
from Acts x. 11, σκεύός τι ὡς ὀθόνην.
For διαρπάσαι... διαρπάσει Mt. has
ἁρπάσαι...διαρπάσει, as if the result
were to be even more thorough than
could have been anticipated ; for διαρπάζειν cf. Gen. xxxiv. 27. Lc., who
describes the Strong One as armed to

τὸν ἰσχυρὸν δήσῃ, καὶ τότε τὴν οἰκίαν αὐτοῦ διαρπάσει. ²⁸ἀμὴν λέγω ὑμῖν ὅτι πάντα ἀφεθήσεται 28
τοῖς υἱοῖς τῶν ἀνθρώπων, τὰ ἁμαρτήματα καὶ αἱ
βλασφημίαι ὅσα ἐὰν βλασφημήσωσιν· ¶ ²⁹ὃς δ' ἂν 29 ¶ i

27 την οικ. 2°] τα σκευη syrˢⁱⁿ ᵛⁱᵈ | διαρπασει] διαρπαξει D διαρπαση AEFGKUV
ΓΠ²Σ۹   28 αι βλασφ.] om αι DKMSUVΓΠ al | οσα ℵBDE*GHΔΠ* al] οσας
ACE¹FKLMSUVΓΠ²ΣΦ 2ᵖᵉ | om οσ. αν βλασφ. a b c e ff g i q r Cypr² Ambrtr

the teeth (καθωπλισμένος), and keeping guard, mentions his πανοπλία and
σκῦλα among his goods (τὰ ὑπάρχοντα
αὐτοῦ): the picture seems to be ampli-
fied from Isa. l.c. (LXX.). In this
fuller form of the parable three stages
can be distinguished in the vanquish-
ing of Satan: (1) a personal victory
(δήσῃ Mc., νικήσῃ Lc., cf. Jo. xvi. 33,
Apoc. iii. 21), (2) the disarming of the
defeated οἰκοδεσπότης, (3) the spoiling
(διαρπάσει) and distribution (διαδίδω-
σιν) of his ill-gotten gains (σκῦλα).
Cf. Victor: ἐπειδὴ σκεύη τῶν δαιμόνων
γεγόνασιν οἱ ἄνθρωποι...ἀδύνατον ἦν
ἀφαιρεθῆναι τοὺς δαίμονας τὴν οἰκείαν
κτίσιν ἀλλ' ἢ πρότερον αὐτῶν ἡττη-
θέντων. The initial victory was won
at the Temptation.

Both Mt. and Lc. add here ὁ μὴ
μετ' ἐμοῦ, κτλ.; see the complementary
canon in Mc. ix. 40.

28. ἀμὴν λέγω ὑμῖν occurs here for
the first time in Mc. (Mt.³⁰ Mc.¹³
Lc.⁶ Jo.²⁵); in Jo. ἀμήν is constantly
doubled, cf. Num. v. 22 (Heb.), 1
Esdr. ix. 47 (B), 2 Esdr. xviii. 6 (Heb.).
The adv. אָמֵן is rendered by γένοιτο
in Deut. xxvii. 15 ff.: the transliteration ἀμήν appears first in 1 Chron.
xvi. 36. On the different uses of
Amen in the O. and N. T., see an
article in J. Q. R., Oct. 1896. The
Amen of the Gospels is what the
writer in J. Q. R. calls "introductory," i.e. it opens a sentence, as in
1 Kings i. 36, Jer. xi. 5, xxviii. 6
(Heb.); but it is sharply distinguished
from the O. T. exx. inasmuch as it
affirms what is to follow, not what

has just been said. The form ἀμὴν
λέγω ὑμῖν is characteristic of Him
who is ὁ Ἀμήν (Apoc. iii. 14). Here
Mt. has merely λέγω ὑμῖν, but the
occasion suits the graver style. The
logical victory is followed by the most
solemn of His warnings.

πάντα ἀφεθήσεται κτλ.] See ii. 5 ff.
There is one exception to the ἐξουσία
of the Son of Man in the forgiveness
of sins, which He proceeds to state.
Τοῖς υἱοῖς τῶν ἀνθρώπων=Mt. τοῖς
ἀνθρώποις: for the phrase (=בְּנֵי־אָדָם)
see Dan. ii. 38 Th. (cf. LXX.), Eph. iii.
5; Log. 3; cf. Hawkins, Hor. Syn.
p. 56. Τὰ ἁμαρτήματα, Mt. πᾶσα
ἁμαρτία: ἁμάρτημα, which is fairly
common in the LXX., is limited in the
N. T. to this context and Paul² (Rom.
iii. 25, 1 Cor. vi. 18); as distinguished
from ἁμαρτία it is 'an act of sin,'
whilst ἁμαρτία is strictly the principle
(SH., Romans, p. 90); but the distinction is in the case of ἁμαρτία
repeatedly overlooked. See note on
next verse.

καὶ αἱ βλασφημίαι] They had charged Him with blasphemy (ii. 7), and
were therefore themselves grievous offenders
in this way. But blasphemies against
the Son of Man (Mt., Lc. xii. 10)
formed no exception to His mission
of forgiveness. Ὅσα ἐὰν βλασφημή-
σωσιν—a constructio ad sensum
(=ὅσας κτλ.); cf. Deut. iv. 2, v. 28
(WM., p. 176 n.); on ἐάν=ἄν see
Burton, § 304.

29. ὃς δ' ἂν βλασφημήσῃ κτλ.]
Mt. ἡ δὲ τοῦ πνεύματος βλασφημία,
Lc. τῷ δὲ εἰς τὸ ἅγιον πνεῦμα βλασ-

¶ c βλασφημήσῃ εἰς τὸ πνεῦμα τὸ ἅγιον¶, οὐκ ἔχει ἄφεσιν
εἰς τὸν αἰῶνα, ἀλλὰ ἔνοχός ἐστιν αἰωνίου ἁμαρτή-
30 ματος. ³⁰ὅτι ἔλεγον Πνεῦμα ἀκάθαρτον ἔχει.

29 om εις τον αιωνα D min^pauc a b e f ff q vg Cypr² | εστιν ABCΓΠΦ⁊ al 1 69 al^mu b
syrr me go Ath Cypr¹] εσται אDLΔΣ 33 al^pauc a e f ff q vg arm Cypr^test | αμαρτηματος
אBLΔ 28 33 565 (αμαρτιας C*^vidD 13 69 346 Ath) latt^pler syr^sin me go Cypr⅔] κρισεως
AC²ΓΠΣΦ⁊ al f tol syr^pesh hcl aeth   30 εχει] pr αυτον C εχειν D a b c e f ff g q

φημήσαντι. For πνεῦμα ἅγιον see
Mc. i. 8, and for τὸ πνεῦμα, i. 10, 12 ;
τὸ πν. τὸ ἅγιον occurs again in Mc.
xiii. 11, Lc. ii. 26, iii. 22, Jo. xiv. 26,
Acts i. 16, v. 32, &c., and in the LXX.
Ps. l. (li.) 13, Isa. lxiii. 11 (רוּחַ קָדְשׁוֹ,
קָדְשִׁי). The repeated article brings
the holiness of the Spirit into prominence (cf. Eph. iv. 30, 1 Thess. iv. 8,
where see Lightfoot), contrasting it
with the ἀκαθαρσία of the evil spirits.
The charge Βεελζεβοὺλ ἔχει was
directed in fact against the πνεῦμα
Ἰησοῦ (Acts xvi. 7)—not the human
spirit of the Son of Man, but the
πνεῦμα θεοῦ (Mt. iii. 16) which per-
vaded and controlled it. For an
early extension of this saying cf.
Didache 11.

οὐκ ἔχει ἄφεσιν κτλ.] To identify
the Source of good with the im-
personation of evil implies a moral
disease for which the Incarnation
itself provides no remedy ; ἄφεσις
avails only where the possibility of
life remains. Εἰς τὸν αἰῶνα in the
LXX.=לְעֹלָם, 'in perpetuity' (Exod.
xxi. 6, xl. 13), or with a negative,
'never more' (2 Regn. xii. 10, Prov.
vi. 33); in the N. T. it gains a wider
meaning in view of the eternal relations
which the Gospel reveals. Ὁ αἰών is
indeed the present world (=ὁ αἰὼν
οὗτος, ὁ ἐνεστώς) in Mc. iv. 19, the
future life being distinguished from
it as αἰὼν ὁ ἐρχόμενος (Mc. x. 30); and
εἰς τὸν αἰῶνα in Mc. xi. 14 is used in
the narrower sense. In this place
however it is interpreted by Mt. as
inclusive of both αἰῶνες (οὔτε ἐν

τούτῳ τῷ αἰῶνι οὔτε ἐν τῷ μέλλοντι),
and this interpretation is supported
by the context in Mc.

ἀλλὰ ἔνοχός ἐστιν αἰωνίου ἁμαρτή-
ματος] 'But lies under the consequences of an act of sin which belongs
to the sphere of the world to come':
Vg. *reus erit aeterni delicti* (Wycliffe,
"gilti of euerlastynge trespas"). Ἔνοχος is used in the N. T. with a dative
of the person or body to whom one is
responsible (τῇ κρίσει, τῷ συνεδρίῳ,
Mt. v. 22), and a genitive of the
penalty (e.g. θανάτου Mc. xiv. 64, δου-
λείας Heb. ii. 15), or of the offence
(cf. 2 Macc. xiii. 6, τὸν ἱεροσυλίας ἔνοχον), or of that against which the
offence is committed (τοῦ σώματος κ.
τοῦ αἵματος τοῦ κυρίου, 1 Cor. xi. 27).
The man is in the grasp of his sin,
which will not let him go without a
Divine ἄφεσις, and to this sin, since it
belongs to the eternal order, the power
exercised by the Son of Man on earth
does not apply. Αἰώνιος in the N. T.
seems never to be limited to the
present order, as it often is in the LXX.
(cf. e.g. Gen. ix. 12, Lev. vi. 18 (11)),
always reaching forward into the life
beyond (as in the frequent phrase
ζωὴ αἰώνιος) or running back into a
measureless past (Rom. xvi. 25, 2 Tim.
i. 9). On the αἰώνιον ἁμάρτημα see the
interesting remarks of Origen, *de orat.*
27, *in Jo.* t. xix. 14, and comp. Heb.
vi. 4 ff., 1 Jo. v. 16, with Bp Westcott's
notes. Bengel: "peccata humana sunt,
sed blasphemia in Spiritum sanctum
est peccatum satanicum."

30. ὅτι ἔλεγον κτλ.] I.e., it was
this suggestion which called forth the

³¹ Καὶ ἔρχονται ἡ μήτηρ αὐτοῦ καὶ οἱ ἀδελφοὶ 31
αὐτοῦ, καὶ ἔξω στήκοντες ἀπέστειλαν πρὸς αὐτὸν
καλοῦντες αὐτόν. ³²καὶ ἐκάθητο περὶ αὐτὸν¶ ὄχλος, 32 ¶ Wʰ
καὶ λέγουσιν αὐτῷ Ἰδοὺ ἡ μήτηρ σου καὶ οἱ ἀδελφοί
σου ἔξω ζητοῦσίν σε. ³³καὶ ἀποκριθεὶς αὐτοῖς λέγει 33
Τίς ἐστιν ἡ μήτηρ μου καὶ οἱ ἀδελφοί; ³⁴καὶ περι- 34

31 και ερχ. ℵBCDGLΔ 1 13 69 1071 alᵖᵃᵘᶜ latt syrᵖᵉˢʰ me go aeth] ερχ. ουν
ΑΓΠΣΦ¶ al syrʰᶜˡ (ερχεται ℵDG latᵛᵗ⁶) | οι αδ. (αυτ.) και η μητηρ αυτου ΑΓΠ al minᵖˡᵉʳ
syrʰᶜˡ arm | στηκοντες BC*Δ 28] σταντες ℵ εστηκοτες CᶜᵒʳʳGL minᵖᵃᵘᶜ εστωτες ΑΔΓΠΣΦ¶
al | καλουντες ℵBCL 1 13 28 69 al] φωνουντες DΓΠΣΦ¶ al ζητουντες Α   32 περι
αυτ. οχλος] προς αυτ. ο. ℵ* προς τον οχλον D | οχλος]+πολυς 1071 και λεγουσιν] ειπον
δε ΑΓΠΣΦ¶ al syrʰᶜˡ go | σου 2°]+και αι αδελφαι σου ΑDEFHMSUVΓ minᵐᵘ
a b c f ff q syrʰᶜˡ⁽ᵐᵍ⁾ go (om ℵBCGKLΔΠ 1 13 33 69 alⁿᵒⁿⁿ e vg syrᵖᵉˢʰ arm me aeth)
33 απεκριθη...λεγων ΑDΓΠΣΦ al | και 2°] η Α(D)EFHKMSΓΠΣΦ¶ c e f q r syrˢⁱⁿ arm
34 om και 1° B

Lord's utterance on the Eternal Sin.
Mc. only; perhaps an editorial note.
Jerome: "[Marcus] caussas tantae
irae manifestius expressit."

31—35. THE ERRAND OF THE
BROTHERS AND THE MOTHER OF
JESUS, AND THE TEACHING BASED
UPON IT (Mt. xii. 46—50, Lc. viii.
19—21).

31. καὶ ἔρχονται ἡ μήτηρ κτλ.] See
note on v. 21. Mt. explicitly connects this incident with the foregoing (ἔτι αὐτοῦ λαλοῦντος). The
mother of Jesus does not appear
again in Mc., but is mentioned in vi. 3
(ὁ υἱὸς τῆς Μαρίας) in company with
the brothers; see notes on vi. 3 and
comp. Acts i. 14.

ἔξω στήκοντες] On στήκω see WH.,
Notes, p. 169. Mt. ἱστήκεισαν ἔξω.
They were crowded out, as in the
case of the paralytic, ii. 4; cf. Lc.
οὐκ ἠδύναντο συντυχεῖν αὐτῷ διὰ τὸν
ὄχλον. Naturally they were unwilling
to disclose their errand (iii. 21), and
therefore contented themselves with
asking for an interview. Καλοῦντες:
on the reading see Nestle, T. C., p. 263.

32. καὶ ἐκάθητο περὶ αὐτὸν ὄχλος]
The scene is similar to that in c. ii.
1 ff., but the Scribes seem to have
left, and the Lord is surrounded by a

crowd of friends (not ὁ ὄχλος), amongst
whom the Apostles and other μαθηταί
form an inner circle (v. 34). The
message is passed from one to
another till it reaches Jesus.

ἰδοὺ ἡ μήτηρ κτλ.] The addition
καὶ αἱ ἀδελφαί σου is "Western and
probably Syrian" (WH., Notes, p. 24).
The sisters of Jesus are mentioned
in vi. 3 as living at Nazareth (ὧδε
πρὸς ἡμᾶς). But they would scarcely
have taken part in a mission of this
nature, and the addition was probably
suggested by vi. 3 or by ἀδελφή in
v. 35.

33. καὶ ἀποκριθεὶς αὐτοῖς λέγει]
Not to His relatives who are still
without, but τῷ λέγοντι αὐτῷ (Mt.),
and through His informant to the
audience. The interruption affords,
as so often, an opportunity for fresh
teaching; it is instruction and not
censure which is the purpose of the
Lord's answer. Ἀποκριθείς is the
later Gk. for ἀποκρινάμενος (Blass,
Gr., pp. 44, 177); so LXX. and N. T.;
ἀπεκρίνατο appears however in Mc.
xiv. 61, and a few other passages.
The phrase ἀποκριθεὶς λέγει or εἶπεν
is a LXX. equivalent for וַיַּעַן וַיֹּאמֶר
(Gen. xviii. 27, &c.).

τίς ἐστιν ἡ μήτηρ μου κτλ.] This

¶ Γ βλεψάμενος τοὺς περὶ αὐτὸν κύκλῳ¶ καθημένους λέγει
35 Ἴδε ἡ μήτηρ μου καὶ οἱ ἀδελφοί μου. ³⁵ ὃς ἂν ποιήσῃ
τὸ θέλημα τοῦ θεοῦ, οὗτος ἀδελφός μου καὶ ἀδελφὴ
καὶ μήτηρ ἐστίν.

34 περιβλ. κυκλω τ. π. αυτον ΑΓΠΣΦ⁷ alᵖˡᵉʳ syrʰᵉˡ (arm) go περιβλ. τους κυκλω D |
om κυκλω 16 61 syrrˢⁱⁿ ᵖᵉˢʰ⁽ᵛⁱᵈ⁾ | ιδου ADGKMΔΠΣ 1 13 al | μου 2°]+ουτοι εισιν 1071
35 os αν B b c me] os γαρ αν ΝACDLΔΠΣΦ⁷ al minᵒᵐⁿᵛⁱᵈ f ff q vg syrr arm go | τα
θεληματα B | αδελφη]+μου CΠΦ⁷ minᵖᵃᵘᶜ a vg syrr me aeth | μητηρ]+μου H* alᵐᵘ
a (1) syrrˢⁱⁿ ᵖᵉˢʰ me al

relative renunciation of kinship appears at the outset of the Ministry
(Jo. ii. 4) and continues to the end
(Jo. xix. 26), and a similar attitude is
urged upon the disciples (Mc. x. 29).
But it is a relative attitude only (Mt.
x. 37), and is perfectly consistent
with tender care for kinsmen, as the
saying on the Cross shews : cf. 1 Tim.
v. 4, 8. Victor : δείκνυσιν ὅτι πάσης
προτιμᾷ συγγενείας τοὺς κατὰ τὴν πίστιν
οἰκείους· ταῦτα δὲ ἔφη οὐκ ἀποδοκιμάζων
πάντως τὴν μητέρα καὶ τοὺς ἀδελφούς.
Ambrose : " neque tamen iniuriose
refutantur parentes, sed religiosiores
copulae mentium docentur esse quam
corporum." At the present moment
the relatives of Jesus were forfeiting
their claim to consideration by op-
posing His work (Mt. x. 35). Here
again His knowledge of the unspoken
purposes of men appears ; for He
could hardly have been informed of
the nature of their errand.

34. περιβλεψάμενος τοὺς περὶ αὐτόν]
For περιβλ. cf. note on iii. 5. Who
those round Him were appears from
Mt., ἐκτείνας τὴν χεῖρα αὐτοῦ ἐπὶ
τοὺς μαθητὰς αὐτοῦ. Stretching forth
the hand was another characteristic
movement (Mc. i. 41), which may well
have accompanied the searching and
inclusive glance. Οἱ μαθηταί need
not be limited to the Apostles : cf.
Lc. vi. 17.

Ἴδε ἡ μήτηρ] Cf. v. 32, ἰδοὺ ἡ μ.
On the difference between ἰδού and
ἴδε see WM., p. 319. Both are re-

garded as interjections (en, ecce), and
not as verbs.

35. ὃς ἂν ποιήσῃ τὸ θέλημα τοῦ
θεοῦ] Mt. τοῦ πατρός μου τοῦ ἐν
οὐρανοῖς (perhaps a reminiscence of
the Lord's Prayer) ; Lc. interprets
the phrase οἱ τὸν λόγον τοῦ θεοῦ
ἀκούοντες καὶ ποιοῦντες—the particular fulfilment of the Father's Will in
which those who were present were
then engaged. The bond which
unites the family of GOD is obedience
to the Divine Will. This was the end
of the life of the Incarnate Son (Jo.
v. 30, &c., Mt. xxvi. 42), and is the
aim of the adopted children (Mt. vi.
10, vii. 21). Τὸ θέλημα became a
recognised term (SH. on Rom. ii. 18);
τὰ θελήματα (B) is an O. T. equivalent
(Chase, Lord's Prayer, p. 39 f.).

καὶ ἀδελφή] So Mt. also. See v. 31.
The word would have its fitness in
the teaching even if the sisters were
not among the relatives without ;
doubtless the ὄχλος contained women
as well as men who were attached
followers: cf. Lc. viii. 2, 3, Mc. xv. 40.
Our Lord, however, characteristically
lays stress on the works which reveal
faith and are the truest note of His
next of kin.

καὶ μήτηρ] Jerome : "isti sunt mater
mea qui me quotidie in credentium
animis generant." But the form of
the sentence (ὃς ἂν ποιήσῃ...οὗτος
ἀδελφὸς...καὶ μήτηρ) seems to forbid
this mysticism in details. Hilary's
interpretation is truer to the text:

¹Καὶ πάλιν ἤρξατο διδάσκειν παρὰ τὴν θάλασσαν. ι **4**
καὶ συνάγεται πρὸς αὐτὸν ὄχλος πλεῖστος, ὥστε
αὐτὸν εἰς πλοῖον ἐμβάντα καθῆσθαι ἐν τῇ θαλάσσῃ,
καὶ πᾶς ὁ ὄχλος πρὸς τὴν θάλασσαν ἐπὶ τῆς γῆς
ἦσαν. ²καὶ ἐδίδασκεν αὐτοὺς ἐν παραβολαῖς πολλά, 2
καὶ ἔλεγεν αὐτοῖς ἐν τῇ διδαχῇ αὐτοῦ ³Ἀκούετε. 3

IV 1 παρα] προς D | συναγεται ℵBCLΔ 13 28 69 124 604] συνηχθη DΠΣΦ⅂ al
minᵖˡᵉʳ latt syrrˢⁱⁿʰᵉˡ συνηχθησαν A 2ᵖᵉ alˢᵃᵗ ᵐᵘ syrᵖᵉˢʰ go arm aeth | οχλος] ο λαος D |
πλειστος ℵBCLΔ] πολυς ADΠΣΦ⅂ minᶠᵒʳᵗᵉᵒᵐⁿ | πλοιον ℵB*CKLMΠΣΦ⅂ 1 33 al go]
pr το AB²DΔ al minᵖˡᵉʳ me | εν τη θαλ.] περαν της θαλασσης D παρα την θαλ. 131
circa mare d circa litus (maris), ad l., a b c proxime l. c ff | προς την θαλασσαν] περαν
της θαλασσης D | om επι της γης D latᵛᵗ syrˢⁱⁿ | ην επι της γης 1071   2 πολλαις D
3 ακουσατε C 2ᵖᵉ alᵖᵃᵘᶜ

"respondit…quicunque voluntati paternae obsecutus est, eum esse et
patrem et sororem et matrem…propinquitatum omnium ius atque nomen
iam non de conditione nascendi sed de
ecclesiae communione retinendum."
He justly adds: "ceterum non fastidiose de matre sua sensisse existimandus est, cui in passione positus
maximae sollicitudinis tribuerit affectum."

IV. 1—9. TEACHING BY PARABLES.
THE PARABLE OF THE SOWER. (Mt.
xiii. 1—9, Lc. viii. 4—8.)

1. καὶ πάλιν κτλ.] Πάλιν (see on
ii. 1) looks back to ii. 13, iii. 7. Mt.
places this new teaching by the sea
immediately after the indoor scene of
iii. 31—35 (xiii. 1, ἐν τῇ ἡμέρα ἐκείνῃ
ἐξελθὼν ὁ Ἰ. τῆς οἰκίας); in Lc. this
order is inverted. For παρὰ τὴν θάλ.
see ii. 13.

καὶ συνάγεται] The pres. (Burton,
§ 14) places the scene before us, the
crowds flocking together as the Lord
begins to speak. The gathering was
even greater than on former occasions—ὄχλος πλεῖστος: cf. πολὺ πλῆθος
iii. 7, 8. Mt. and Lc. are less precise
(ὄχλοι πολλοί, ὄχλου πολλοῦ), but Lc.
adds καὶ τῶν κατὰ πόλιν ἐπιπορευομέ
νων, i.e. the audience came from the
other towns as well as from Capernaum.

ὥστε αὐτόν κτλ.] He was seated at
first on the beach (Mt. xiii. 1), but
when He saw the crowd hurrying
down, He took refuge in a boat (cf.
iii. 9)—possibly Simon's (Lc. v. 3), but
if so, no stress is laid upon the fact,
for πλοῖον is anarthrous in the best
text of Mc. and Mt. "The whole
multitude" (all were by this time
assembled) stood (ἦσαν = ἱστήκει, Mt.)
on the land facing (πρός, WM., p. 504)
the sea, the sloping beach (Mc.) forming a theatre from which He could
be seen and heard by all. Thpht.
ἵνα κατὰ πρόσωπον ἔχων πάντας ἐν
ἐπηκόῳ πάντων λέγοι. Cf. Victor:
κάθηται ἐν τῷ πλοίῳ ἁλιεύων καὶ σαγη
νεύων τοὺς ἐν τῇ γῇ.

2. καὶ ἐδίδασκεν κτλ.] He began
a series of parables ; ἐν παραβολαῖς
πολλά, i.e. as D rightly interprets, παρα
βολαῖς πολλαῖς. Mt.'s aor. (ἐλάλησεν)
is less exact, while Lc., who limits
himself here to the Parable of the
Sower, has nothing to mark the commencement of a new course of teaching
(εἶπεν διὰ παραβολῆς). On παραβολή
see iii. 23 note. Ἐν τῇ διδ. αὐτοῦ, in
the course of His teaching, = ἐν τῷ
διδάσκειν αὐτόν (cf. xii. 38).

3. ἀκούετε] A characteristic summons to attend—"ad sedandum populi
strepitum" (Bengel); cf. Mt. xv. 10,
xxi. 33, Mc. vii. 14.   It finds its

§ i   4 ἰδοὺ ἐξῆλθεν ὁ σπείρων σπεῖραι· §4καὶ ἐγένετο ἐν τῷ
¶ ᛣ10 σπείρειν¶ ὃ μὲν ἔπεσεν παρὰ τὴν ὁδόν, καὶ ἦλθεν τὰ
§ c   5 πετεινὰ καὶ κατέφαγεν αὐτό. §5καὶ ἄλλο ἔπεσεν ἐπὶ
      τὸ πετρῶδες [καὶ] ὅπου οὐκ εἶχεν γῆν πολλήν, καὶ

3 σπειραι ℵ*Bᛣ seminare a b c d e ff g] pr του ℵc.aACLΔΠΣΦ ad seminandum f vg
+τον σπορον αυτου F minnonn go om σπειραι D   4 om εγενετο DF minpauc latt
(exc a) syrrsin pesh | σπειραι D | τα πετεινα]+του ουρανου DGM minnonn a i q   5 αλλα
D 33 2pe alpauc | τα πετρωδη ℵ* (το πετρωδες ℵc.a) D 1 33 2pe alpauc lattpler | και οπου
B avid]και οτι D b c ff οπου rell

prototype in the famous זרע of Deut.
vi. 4 (Mc. xii. 29): but see also Gen.
xxiii. 5, 13, Jud. v. 3, 1 Regn. xxii. 7,
12, &c. Mt., Lc., omit it here; Lc.
omits also the ἰδού which follows and
strengthens the call (cf. iii. 32).

ἐξῆλθεν ὁ σπείρων σπεῖραι] Ὁ σπ.
(so also Mt., Lc.), the sower (see on
i. 4), i.e. the particular sower contemplated in the parable, the representative of his class (WM., p. 132). Σπεῖραι
=τοῦ σπείρειν (Mt.), τοῦ σπεῖραι (Lc.),
the inf. of purpose which may be used
with or without the article (Burton,
§§ 366, 397): both uses occur together
in Lc. ii. 23, 24: παραστῆσαι...καὶ τοῦ
δοῦναι.

4. καὶ ἐγένετο κτλ.] The pleonastic
καὶ ἐγέν. (cf. i. 9) is abandoned by Mt.,
Lc. Ἐν τῷ σπείρειν, in the process of
sowing: the article points back to
σπεῖραι, whilst the change of tense
brings into view the succession of
acts which constitutes the sowing.
In σπεῖραι the whole is gathered up
in a single purpose; it is ἐν τῷ
σπείρειν, as the sower carries out his
purpose, that the things happen
which are about to be related. This
delicate train of thought is lost
in Mt.

4 ff. ὃ μέν...καὶ ἄλλο...καὶ ἄλλο...
καὶ ἄλλα] Mt. ἃ μέν...ἄλλα δέ...ἄλλα
δέ...ἄλλα δέ: Lc. ὃ μέν...καὶ ἕτερον...
καὶ ἕτερον...καὶ ἕτερον. Cf. WM., p.
130. Some part of the seed (ὃ μέν),
i.e. some seeds (ἃ μέν), fell by the side
of the road (παρά, Mt. Mc. Lc.; WM.,

p. 502); not of course that the sower
deliberately sowed the pathway, but
that he partly missed his aim, as in
such rapid work must needs happen;
or he had not time to distinguish
nicely between the pathway and the
rest of the field. Cf. Victor: οὐκ
εἶπεν ὅτι αὐτὸς ἔρριψεν, ἀλλ' ὅτι ἔπεσεν.

καὶ ἦλθεν κτλ.] Lc. καὶ κατεπατήθη
καὶ...κατέφαγον αὐτό. But in the interpretation he adds nothing to correspond to this new feature, which
has possibly been suggested by the
mention of ὁδός. The birds would
be on the spot immediately and leave
little for the passers by to spoil;
moreover the point of the illustration
is that the seed, if unable to penetrate
the soil, will presently be stolen away.
For καταφαγεῖν, comedere, used in
reference to the clean sweep which
birds make of food, see Gen. xl. 17,
3 Regn. xii. 24, xiv. 11 (cod. A), xvi. 4,
xx. 24 (cod. A).

5. 'And another (portion) fell upon
the rocky (part of the field)': τὸ
πετρῶδες = Mt. τὰ πετρώδη, Lc. (less
precisely) τὴν πέτραν. Πετρώδης does
not occur in the LXX., or in the N.T.
except in this context (Mt., Mc.), but
it is used in good Greek (Soph., Plat.,
Arist.); the word implies not a stone-
strewn surface, as the English versions
except R.V. suggest, but rock thinly
coated with soil and here and there
cropping up through the earth—a
characteristic feature in the cornlands

εὐθὺς ἐξανέτειλεν διὰ τὸ μὴ ἔχειν βάθος γῆς· ⁶καὶ 6
ὅτε ἀνέτειλεν ὁ ἥλιος ἐκαυματίσθη, καὶ διὰ τὸ μὴ
ἔχειν ρίζαν ἐξηράνθη. ⁷καὶ ἄλλο ἔπεσεν εἰς τὰς 7
ἀκάνθας, καὶ ἀνέβησαν αἱ ἄκανθαι καὶ συνέπνιξαν

5 εξανετειλεν] εξεβλαστησεν 1 13 28 118 124 346 604 | γης] της γης B την γην D
6 και οτε ανετ. ο ηλιος ℵBCDLΔ 1071 ff i q vg me] ηλιου δε ανατειλαντος ΑΠΣΦ al
minᶠᵒʳᵗᵉᵒᵐⁿ a c f | εκαυματισθη ℵACLΔΠΣΦ] εκαυματισθησαν BD a e | εξηρανθησαν
D (604) e   7 αλλος ℵ* αλλα ℵᶜ·ᵃ 28 33 alᵖᵃᵘᶜ e | εις ℵABLΔΠΣΦ al minᵖˡ lattᵖˡ]
επι CDM² 33 604 2ᵖᵉ alⁿᵒⁿⁿ b me | απεπνιξαν 33 604 alⁿᵒⁿⁿ

of Galilee, still to be noted by the
traveller among the hills which slope
down to the Lake. Καὶ ὅπου κτλ. Καὶ
if genuine is probably epexegetic
(WM., p. 545 f.); Mt. omits it without
detriment to the sense. The πετρώ-
δες was that part of the ground where
the earth was shallow.

καὶ εὐθὺς ἐξανέτειλεν κτλ.] Mt. here
agrees with Mc. almost *verbatim*; Lc.
compresses greatly (καὶ φυέν). Ἐξα-
νατέλλω in the LXX. is trans., see Gen.
ii. 9, Ps. cxlvi. (cxlvii.) 8, but ἀνατέλλω
is used transitively of vegetable
growth (Gen. iii. 18, cf. Is. lxi. 11).
Nearness to the warm surface induced rapid growth, but it also led to
the shortening of the young plant's
life. Βάθος γῆς: Syr.ˢⁱⁿ· adds 'below
its root.' The reading of D, 'because
the earth had no depth,' does not suit
the context so well; both in οὐκ εἶχεν
(*v.* 5) and διὰ τὸ μὴ ἔχειν (2°, *v.* 6) it is
the seed which is the subject of the
verb.

6. καὶ ὅτε ἀνέτειλεν κτλ.] In Mc.'s
simpler style καί merely adds a fresh
particular, without regard to the
logical connexion. Here there is in
fact a contrast (cf. Mt. ἡλίου δὲ ἀνατείλαντος). The plant grew rapidly
in the warm Eastern night (comp.
Jon. iv. 10, ἐγενήθη ὑπὸ νύκτα), but
as soon as the sun grew hot it lan-
guished and withered. Ἐκαυματίσθη
is a word of the later Greek (Plutarch, &c.), not used in the LXX., but
occurring again in Apoc. xvi. 8, 9:

'it felt the burning heat' (καῦμα),
was scorched; Latt., *aestuavit*, *ex-
aestuavit*. The same illustration
occurs in James i. 11, ἀνέτειλεν γὰρ
ὁ ἥλιος σὺν τῷ καύσωνι καὶ ἐξήρανεν
τὸν χόρτον. See also Mc. xi. 20, 21,
Jo. xv. 6, 1 Pet. i. 24 (Isa. xl. 7). In
this case the withering is due to the
very cause which led to rapid growth
—the shallowness of the soil which
did not permit the plant to develop
its roots. For διὰ τὸ μὴ ἔχειν ρίζαν
Lc. has the remarkable variant διὰ τὸ
μὴ ἔ. ἰκμάδα. Cf. Jer. xvii. 8, ἐπὶ
ἰκμάδα βαλεῖ ρίζαν αὐτοῦ· οὐ φοβηθή-
σεται ὅταν ἔλθῃ καῦμα—a passage
which may have suggested the Lucan
gloss, if it be such.

7. καὶ ἄλλο ἔπεσεν εἰς τὰς ἀκάνθας]
'And another (portion) fell into the
thorns.' Mt. ἐπὶ τὰς ἀκ., Lc. ἐν μέσῳ
τῶν ἀκανθῶν: when the clause is repeated in the interpretation (Mt. xiii.
22, Lc. viii. 14), both agree with Mc.
Cf. Lc. x. 36, τοῦ ἐμπεσόντος εἰς τοὺς
λῃστάς (30, λῃσταῖς περιέπεσεν).

ἀνέβησαν αἱ ἄκανθαι] Lc. συνφυεῖσαι.
Mc.'s word, retained by Mt., is more
fully descriptive of the process: the
thorns not only grew with the wheat,
but grew faster and higher. For
ἀναβαίνειν (= עָלָה) 'to mount up,' used
of vegetation, see Gen. xli. 5, Deut.
xxix. 23 (22), especially Isa. v. 6,
xxxii. 13.

συνέπνιξαν] Mt., Lc. ἀπέπνιξαν: in
the interpretation all have συνπνίγειν;
the Latin versions use *suffocare* with-

¶ e 8 αὐτό, καὶ καρπὸν οὐκ ἔδωκεν. ⁸καὶ ἄλλα ἔπεσεν ¶ εἰς
τὴν γῆν τὴν καλήν, καὶ ἐδίδου καρπόν, ἀναβαίνοντα·
καὶ αὐξανόμενα· καὶ ἔφερεν εἰς τριάκοντα καὶ εἰς

8 αλλα ℵ*ᶜ·ᵇBCL 28 33 124 e] αλλο ℵᶜ·ᵃADΔΠΣΦ al minᵖˡ lattᵖˡ | εις 1°] επι
CΣ 1 28 118 124 a b | αυξανομενα ℵB 1071] αυξανομενον ACDLΔ 238 αυξανοντα ΠΣΦ
al minᶠᵉʳᵉᵒᵐⁿ | φερει D 124 604 2ᵖᵉ | εις 2°, 3°, 4° ℵC*Δ 28 604 2ᵖᵉ alᵖᵃᵘᶜ] εις...εν...εν
BL (εις, εν bis L) εις...και...και εν 1071 εν ter AC²DEFGHKMUVΠΣΦ minᵖᵉʳᵐᵘ ἔν
ter lattᵖˡᵉʳ syrᵖᵉˢʰ ᵛⁱᵈ

out distinction. Συνπν. suits Mc.'s context best, for he adds καὶ καρπὸν οὐκ ἔδωκεν, which Mt., Lc. omit. The thorns, crowding round the wheat and keeping off light and air, effectively prevented the yielding of fruit, and ultimately (but this is not the point on which Mc. dwells) killed it off. For the distinction between ἀποπν., συνπν., comp. Lc. viii. 33, 42 ; and for the use of συνπν. in reference to plants, Theophrast. *plant.* vi. 11. 6, δένδρα συμπνιγόμενα. Καρπὸν οὐκ ἔδωκεν : καρπὸν φέρειν, ποιεῖν are more usual phrases ; but cf. Mt. xiii. 8, and see next note.

8. καὶ ἄλλα ἔπεσεν εἰς τὴν γῆν τὴν καλήν] 'And other (seeds) fell into the good soil.' Wycliffe, "in to good lond." Mt. ἐπὶ τ. γ. τ. καλήν, Lc. εἰς τ. γ. τ. ἀγαθήν. Καλήν calls attention to that which met the eye ; ἀγαθήν to the nature and condition of the soil. The repetition of the article (τὴν γ. τὴν κ., not τὴν κ. γ.) gives prominence to the adjective : the seeds now in view not merely fell into the ground (in contrast with those which fell εἰς ἀκάνθας or ἐπὶ τὸ πετρῶδες), but into ground specifically good : cf. Jo. x. 11, 14, ὁ ποιμὴν ὁ καλός. Blass, *Gr.* p. 158. Ἐδίδου... ἔφερεν, a continuous process, contrasted with ἔπεσεν. Διδόναι καρπόν (נָתַן פְּרִי, Ps. i. 3) includes the formation of the wheat ear, which under the circumstances would be concurrent with the growth of the young wheat (ἀναβαίνοντα καὶ αὐξανόμενα). For ἀνα-

βαίνειν, now applied to the wheat, see on v. 7 and reff. there ; the Vg., following the reading αὐξανόμενον, wrongly interprets it of the ear (*fructum ascendentem et crescentem*) and so the English versions except R.V. With αὐξανόμενα compare Col. i. 6, 10, and for φέρειν (καρπόν) see Jo. xii. 24, xv. 2 ff.

εἰς τριάκοντα κτλ.] The text here is embarrassing. Of the possible readings (εἰς...εἰς...εἰς : ἐν...ἐν...ἐν : ἔν...ἔν...ἔν : εἰς...ἐν...ἐν) the last is perhaps the best supported, and has been adopted by W H.; but the change of preposition is meaningless and intolerably harsh, and it has the appearance of being due to a partial assimilation of v. 8 to v. 20. Εἰς (ἐν) answers to בְ 'at the rate of,' cf. BDB., p. 90; Harcl. represents it by ܒ. If we read ⲈⲚ *ter*, there is something to be said for printing it ἔν : the triple εἰς occurs in 1 Regn. x. 3, and elsewhere, and ἔν will accord here with Mt.'s ὁ μέν, ὁ δέ...ὁ δέ. The Vg. has *unum* both here and in v. 20; hence Wycliffe, "oon thritty fold," &c.

τριάκοντα...ἑξήκοντα...ἑκατόν] Even the highest rate of increase named here is not extravagant : cf. Gen. xxvi. 12, εὗρεν...ἑκατοστεύουσαν κριθήν, and see Wetstein and J. Lightfoot *ad l.* The fertility of Esdraelon and of the volcanic soil of the Hauran was prodigious, and there were rich cornfields about the Lake which may have justified these figures : cf. G. A. Smith, *H. G.* pp. 83, 439 ff., 612; Merrill, *Galilee*, p. 20 ff.

ἐξήκοντα καὶ εἰς ἑκατόν. ⁹καὶ ἔλεγεν Ὃς ἔχει ὦτα 9
ἀκούειν ἀκουέτω.

¹⁰Καὶ ὅτε ἐγένετο κατὰ μόνας, ἠρώτων αὐτὸν οἱ 10
περὶ αὐτὸν σὺν τοῖς δώδεκα τὰς παραβολάς. ¹¹καὶ 11
ἔλεγεν αὐτοῖς Ὑμῖν τὸ μυστήριον δέδοται τῆς βασι-

9 ος εχει ℵBC*DΔ] ο εχων ℵc.aAC²LΠΣΦ al minforte omn | ακουετω]+και ο συνιων
συνιετω D a b ff i syrhcl(mg)   10 ηρωτων (vel -τουν) ℵABCLΔΦ 33] ηρωτησαν ΠΣ
al minpl c f ff vg επηρωτων D επηρωτησαν 604 | οι π. α. σ. τ. δωδεκα] οι μαθηται
αυτου D 13 28 69 124 346 2pe a b c ff g i q syrsin Orint | τας παραβολας] την παρα-
βολην ΑΠΣ al minpl syrpesh go aeth τις η παραβολη αυτη D 13 28 69 124 346 2pe
a b c f ff g i l q Orint φρασον ημιν την παραβολην Φ   11 το μυστηριον δεδοται
ℵBC* vidL] δεδ. το μ. ΑΚΠ al minpauc (syrsin) δ. γνωναι το μ. C²DΔ al minpl lattvt pl vg
syrrpesh hier aeth δ. γν. τα μυστηρια GΣΦ minnonn syrhcl arm

9. ὃς ἔχει ὦτα κτλ.] The parable
ends as it began with a solemn call to
attention; the picture might easily
be regarded as a pleasant picture and
no more. With one exception (Apoc.
xiii. 9) the present formula is found
only in contexts ascribed to our
Lord (Mt. xi. 15, xiii. 9 [=Mc. iv. 9],
43, Mc. iv. 23, Lc. xiv. 35, Apoc. ii.
7, 11, 17, 29, iii. 6, 13, 22). The
forms vary slightly; besides that
which is given in the text we have
εἴ τις ἔχει ὦτα ἀκούειν ἀκουέτω (Mc.
iv. 23), ὁ ἔχων ὦτα ἀκουέτω (Mt.), ὁ
ἔχων ὦτα ἀκούειν ἀκουέτω (Lc.), ὁ ἔχων
οὖς ἀκουσάτω (Apoc. ii., iii.) and εἴ τις
ἔχει οὖς ἀκουσάτω (Apoc. xiii. 9). For
the inf. after ἔχει see Blass, Gr., p.
226. For the idea cf. Deut. xxix.
3 (lxx., 4), Isa. vi. 10, Ezek. iii. 27.
Wetstein (on Mt. xi. 15) quotes from
Philo the phrase ἀκοὰς (or ὦτα) ἔχειν
ἐν τῇ ψυχῇ. Cf. Euth., ὦτα νοητά.
Some Gnostic sects saw in these
words an encouragement to find in
the Parable of the Sower mysteries
which the Church did not recognise;
cf. Hippol. haer. v. 8, τουτέστι, φησίν,
οὐδεὶς τούτων τῶν μυστηρίων ἀκροατὴς
γέγονεν εἰ μὴ μόνοι οἱ γνωστικοὶ τέλειοι.
Cf. viii. 9, διὰ τοῦτο εἴρηκε...Ὁ ἔχων
κτλ., ὅτι ταῦτα οὐκ ἔστι πάντων ἀκούσ-
ματα.

10—12. REASONS FOR THE USE OF
PARABLES (Mt. xiii. 10—15, Lc. viii.
9—10).

10. ὅτε ἐγένετο κατὰ μόνας] Probably when the public teaching of the
day was over. Κατὰ μόνας (frequently
used in lxx. for לְבַד), Vg. singularis,
is relative only: He was apart from
the multitude, but the Twelve and
other disciples (οἱ περὶ αὐτὸν σὺν τοῖς
δ.) shared His solitude; cf. Lc. ix.
18, ἐν τῷ εἶναι αὐτὸν προσευχόμενον
κατὰ μόνας συνῆσαν αὐτῷ οἱ μαθηταί.
The succinct ἠρώτων αὐτόν...τὰς παραβολάς (WM., p. 284) is expanded by
Mt. (διὰ τί ἐν παραβολαῖς λαλεῖς αὐτοῖς;) and Lc. (τίς αὕτη εἴη ἡ παραβολή;): the latter narrows the enquiry to the particular parable, but,
as the answer shews, it raised the
whole question of parabolic teaching.

11. ὑμῖν τὸ μυστήριον δέδοται] The
variations in the other Synoptists are
instructive (ὑμῖν δ. γνῶναι τὰ μυστήρια Mt. Lc.). Γνῶναι interprets
δέδοται, but like other interpretations
of Christ's words, does not exhaust its
sense. The mystery was given to the
disciples, and the knowledge of it
followed in due time; but the gift was
more than knowledge, and even independent of it. Μυστήριον occurs here
only in the Gospels; its later use in

λείας τοῦ θεοῦ, ἐκείνοις δὲ τοῖς ἔξω ἐν παραβολαῖς
12 τὰ πάντα γίνεται· ¹²ἵνα βλέποντες βλέπωσι καὶ μὴ
ἴδωσιν, καὶ ἀκούοντες ἀκούωσι καὶ μὴ συνίωσιν, μή
ποτε ἐπιστρέψωσιν καὶ ἀφεθῇ αὐτοῖς.

11 τ. εξωθεν B | τα παντα] om τα אDKΠ 28 124 2ᵖᵉ alᵖᵃᵘᶜ | γινεται] λεγεται DΣ
28 64 124 2ᵖᵉ a b c ff g i q   12 βλεπωσιν (βλεψ. 1071)] pr μη E*FGHΔ minᵖᵃᵘᶜ
syrˢⁱⁿ Or | om μη ιδωσιν Δ syrˢⁱⁿ Orᵇⁱˢ | ακουωσιν (-σωσιν CM 33 69 124 alᵖᵃᵘᶜ)] pr
μη Δ | συνωσιν D*L al minᵖᵃᵘᶜ Orᶜᵒᵈᵇⁱˢ | επιστραφωσι 604 | αφεθη אBCDLΔΣΦ al
minᵖˡ Or⅟₄] αφεθησεται ΑΚΠ minᵖᵃᵘᶜ αφεθησομαι D* αφησω Dᵇ (dimittam d (ff) g i q r) |
αυτοις]+τα αμαρτηματα (αυτων) AD(Δ)ΠΦ (604) lattᵛᵗ ᵖˡ ᵛᵍ me (syrrˢⁱⁿ ᵖᵉˢʰ)+τα παραπτωματα Σ minᵖᵃᵘᶜ

the N.T. is limited to Paul[21] and Apoc.[4]. The lxx. employ it in Daniel[6] (for רָז, a secret of state), Tob.[1], Judith[1], Sap.[4], Sir.[4], 2 Macc.[1]; in Daniel ii. 28 ff., 47, Sap. ii. 22 the word passes into the theological sense which it exclusively has in the N.T.; see Hatch, *Essays*, p. 58. 'The mystery of the Kingdom of God' is the content of the Gospel (τὸ μ. τοῦ χριστοῦ, Eph. iii. 4, Col. iv. 3, τοῦ θεοῦ, Col. ii. 2, τοῦ εὐαγγελίου, Eph. vi. 19, τῆς πίστεως, 1 Tim. iii. 9, τῆς εὐσεβείας, 1 Tim. iii. 16), i.e. Christ Himself as revealing the Father, and fulfilling His counsels. As given to the Apostles it was still a secret, not yet to be divulged, nor even except in a small degree intelligible to themselves. On the Pauline sense of μυστήριον see Lightfoot on Col. i. 26. Τὰ μυστήρια (Mt. Lc.) loses sight of the unity of the gift, and belongs to a somewhat later form of the common tradition.

ἐκείνοις δὲ τοῖς ἔξω] Vg. "illis autem qui foris sunt"; 'but to those, the men who are outside,' i.e. the ὄχλος as contrasted with the μαθηταί, cf. xii. 7, Lc. xii. 38. Lc. τοῖς δὲ λοιποῖς, Mt. simply ἐκείνοις δέ. The words must not be understood as a reproach; they merely state the fact. Οἱ ἔξω are 'non-disciples,' who are as yet outside the pale—a Rabbinical phrase (הַחִיצוֹנִים) for Gentiles or unorthodox

Jews (see J. Lightfoot *ad h. l.*, Bp Lightfoot on Col. iv. 5); οἱ ἐκτός is similarly used in Sir. *prol.* l. 4: οἱ ἔξωθεν, which has some support here, is used by St Paul (1 Tim. iii. 7). To such, while they remained outside, the mystery was not committed in our Lord's lifetime; nevertheless, they received what they could. On exoteric teaching among Greek philosophers cf. A. Gellius *N. A.* xx. 4, and for the practical application of the principle by the later Church see Cyril. Hier. *catech.* vi. 29.

ἐν παραβολαῖς τὰ πάντα γίνεται] Vg. *in parabolis omnia fiunt*: 'the whole is transacted in parables,' i.e. the mystery takes the form of a series of illustrative similitudes. Euth.: τὰ π. γ., τὰ τῆς διδασκαλίας δηλονότι.

12. ἵνα βλέποντες κτλ.] An adaptation of Isa. vi. 9, 10, lxx., ἀκοῇ ἀκούσετε καὶ οὐ μὴ συνῆτε καὶ βλέποντες βλέψετε καὶ οὐ μὴ ἴδητε...μή ποτε...ἐπιστρέψωσιν καὶ ἰάσομαι αὐτούς: the whole passage is quoted by Mt. with the preface ἀναπληροῦται αὐτοῖς ἡ προφητεία Ἡσαίου ἡ λέγουσα: cf. John xii. 39 f., Acts xxviii. 25 ff. Ἵνα, which is not part of the quotation, explains the purpose of the parabolic teaching in regard to those who, after long attendance on Christ's Ministry, were still 'without'; it was intended to fulfil the sentence of judicial blindness pronounced on those who will not see.

¹³Καὶ λέγει αὐτοῖς Οὐκ οἴδατε τὴν παραβολὴν 13
ταύτην, καὶ πῶς πάσας τὰς παραβολὰς γνώσεσθε;
¹⁴ὁ σπείρων τὸν λόγον σπείρει. ¹⁵οὗτοι δέ εἰσιν οἱ ¹⁴₁₅

14 σπερει ℵ

Bengel: "iam ante non videbant; nunc accedit iudicium divinum." Mt. substitutes ὅτι for ἵνα, 'I speak in parables, because they cannot see—the sentence is already working itself out in their incapacity to understand.' The result, however, is due to themselves: cf. Thpht. βλέποντες· τοῦτο τοῦ θεοῦ· μὴ βλέπωσι· τοῦτο τῆς κακίας αὐτῶν. Cf. Iren. iv. 29. 1: "unus et idem Deus his quidem qui non credunt...infert caecitatem, quemadmodum sol in his qui propter aliquam infirmitatem oculorum non possunt contemplari lumen eius."

The distinction between βλέπειν and ἰδεῖν corresponds here to that between ἀκούειν and συνίειν. The Syriac versions and the Vg. (ut videntes videant et non videant) fail to notice this. Καὶ ἀφεθῇ αὐτοῖς (impers.) is preferred by Mc. to καὶ ἰάσομαι αὐτοὺς which Mt., Jo. and Acts borrow from the LXX.; in form at least it is nearer to the original (וְרָפָא לֹו: see Delitzsch ad l.); for ἀφ. impers. cf. Mt. xii. 31, 32, Lc. xii. 10, James v. 15. On the reading ἀφεθήσομαι see WM., p. 630 f.

13—20. INTERPRETATION OF THE PARABLE OF THE SOWER (Mt. xiii. 18—23, Lc. viii. 11—15).

13 ff. The disciples' question had implied that they needed to have the parable of the Sower explained to them. To this point the Lord now addresses Himself. Mc. alone prefaces the interpretation with a rebuke—οὐκ οἴδατε κτλ. 'Ye know not (or, "Know ye not?"—so all the English versions) what this first parable means: how then will you come to understand the parables which are to follow?' Οἶδα is used in reference to a knowledge which comes from intuition or insight, γινώσκω of that which is gained by experience or acquaintance (see Lightfoot on 1 Cor. ii. 11). An initial want of spiritual insight boded ill for their prospect of becoming apt interpreters of parabolic teaching. Cf. Sir. iii. 29, καρδία συνετοῦ διανοηθήσεται παραβολήν. Καὶ πῶς; 'how then?' cf. Lc. xx. 44, Jo. xii. 34. Πάσας τὰς παραβολάς, not 'parables in general' (πάσας παραβολάς), but 'all the parables which you are to hear from Me.'

14. ὁ σπείρων τὸν λόγον σπείρει] That which the sower sows is the word. Lc. more explicitly, ὁ σπόρος ἐστὶν ὁ λόγος. 'The sower' is not interpreted. Theophylact's view (τίς οὖν ἐστιν ὁ σπείρων; αὐτὸς ὁ χριστός) is correct (cf. Mt. xiii. 37), if it be borne in mind that Christ acts through His Spirit in the Church. For the sense of ὁ λόγος see note on ii. 2. Mt. adds τῆς βασιλείας, Lc. τοῦ θεοῦ; in the phraseology of Mc. it is usually unqualified (ii. 2, iv. 14—20, 33, viii. 32 [xvi. 20]). For the comparison of teaching to sowing see Philo, de agr. 2, ὁ νοῦς...τὰς ἀπὸ τῶν σπαρέντων καὶ φυτευθέντων ὠφελείας εἴωθε καρποῦσθαι...ἐν διανοίᾳ καρποὺς ὠφελιμωτάτους οἴσει [sc. τὰ σπαρέντα] καλὰς καὶ ἐπαινετὰς πράξεις. Ὁ σπείρων here is not simply, as in v. 2, the sower, whoever he may be, but the sower to whom the parable refers; the same remark applies to τὴν ὁδόν (v. 15), τὰ πετρώδη (v. 16), τὰς ἀκάνθας (v. 18), τὴν γῆν (v. 20).

15. οὗτοι δέ κτλ.] A compressed note which it is difficult to disentangle. Lc. gives the general sense, οἱ δὲ παρὰ τὴν ὁδόν εἰσιν οἱ ἀκούσαντες. As the words stand in Mc. we must either

παρὰ τὴν ὁδὸν ὅπου σπείρεται ὁ λόγος, καὶ ὅταν
ἀκούσωσιν εὐθὺς ἔρχεται ὁ σατανᾶς καὶ αἴρει τὸν
16 λόγον τὸν ἐσπαρμένον εἰς αὐτούς. ¹⁶καὶ οὗτοί εἰσιν
ὁμοίως οἱ ἐπὶ τὰ πετρώδη σπειρόμενοι, οἳ ὅταν ἀκούσωσιν τὸν λόγον εὐθὺς μετὰ χαρᾶς λαμβάνουσιν

15 οπου] οις D 69² ff g syrᵖᵉˢʰ | οπ. σπειρ. ο λογος] qui neglegenter verbum suscipiunt
a b (c) p q r οι ακουοντες τον λογον syrˢⁱⁿ ᵛⁱᵈ | και οταν] οι οτ. B | om ευθυς 1 118 syrˢⁱⁿ
arm | αιρει] αφερει D αρπαζει אCΔ | εις αυτους B 1 13 28 69 alᵖᵃᵘᶜ] εν αυτοις אCLΔ
c meᵉᵈᵈ syrʰᶜˡ⁽ᵐᵍ⁾ εν ταις καρδιαις αυτων DΠΣΦ al minᵖˡ lattᵛᵗ ᵖˡ ᵛᵍ syrrˢⁱⁿ ᵖᵉˢʰ ʰᶜˡ⁽ᵗˣᵗ⁾
go arm απο της καρδιας αυτων A l aeth   16 om ομοιως D 1 13 28 69 alᵖᵃᵘᶜ
a b c ff g i q | σπειρομενοι]+λογοι M | οι οταν] om οι B* (hab B³?) | om ευθυς D 1 28
alᵖᵃᵘᶜ c ff i q syrˢⁱⁿ | λαμβανουσιν] δεχονται 1 131 209 alᵖᵃᵘᶜ

translate "these are they by the
wayside where," &c., leaving the construction incomplete, or "these are
they by the wayside, (namely those who
are) where," &c. The analogy of *v.* 16
points rather to the former rendering;
the Evangelist has written καὶ ὅταν for
οἳ ὅταν, forgetting that a relative clause
ought to follow οὗτοι. Οἱ παρὰ τὴν
ὁδόν, sc. πεσόντες or (as in Mt.) σπαρέντες: the hearers are identified with
the seed, and not, as we might expect, with the soil. Since this identification is common to Mt., Mc., Lc.,
it probably belongs to the essence of
Christ's teaching, and represents a
"truth both of nature and of grace;
the seed sown...becomes the plant
and bears the fruit, or fails of bearing
it; it is therefore the representative,
when sown, of the individuals of
whom the discourse is" (Alford, on
Mt. xiii. 19).

ὅταν ἀκούσωσιν] On each occasion,
as soon as their hearing of the
message, or of any part of it, is
complete.

εὐθὺς ἔρχεται ὁ σατανᾶς κτλ.] Mt.
ἔρχεται ὁ πονηρός (cf. Mt. v. 37, vi. 13,
xiii. 38, 1 Jo. ii. 13, &c.). Lc. εἶτα
ἔρχεται ὁ διάβολος. For ὁ σ. see note
on Mc. i. 13. Εὐθύς retains its proper
sense; the birds lose no time, nor
does Satan. With this interpretation

of τὰ πετεινά comp. Eph. ii. 2, vi. 12.
Τὸν ἐσπαρμένον εἰς αὐτούς leaves the
region to which the word had pene-
trated undetermined; Mt.'s ἐν τῇ
καρδίᾳ (cf. Lc.) represents it as having
entered the intellectual life, which
is less in accord with this part of the
parable. Lc. adds Satan's purpose,
ἵνα μὴ πιστεύσαντες σωθῶσιν: cf. 'Mc.'
xvi. 16. The perf. part. ἐσπαρμένον
(Mt. Mc.) indicates that the sowing
was completed, and the seed not yet
disturbed when Satan arrived (Burton,
§ 154).

16. καὶ οὗτοί εἰσιν κτλ.] 'On the
same principle of interpretation (ὁ-
μοίως) those who are sown on the rocky
places are,' &c. Οἱ σπειρόμενοι, qui
seminantur, the class of persons to
whom belongs τὸ σπείρεσθαι ἐπὶ τὰ π.
Cf. Burton, § 123, and contrast οἱ
σπαρέντες in *v.* 20, where the notion
of time comes in. In one sense 'the
word is sown,' in another the hearers
are the seed; see above on *v.* 15.

εὐθὺς μετὰ χαρᾶς λαμβάνουσιν αὐτόν]
Cf. *v.* 5, εὐθὺς ἐξανέτειλεν. The joy
of the enthusiastic hearer corresponds
to the bursting through the soil of the
fresh green blade—a visible response
to the sower's work. Lc. substitutes
for λαμβ. the warmer δέχονται (cf. Acts
xi. 1, xvii. 11, 1 Thess. i. 6, ii. 13,
James i. 21).

αὐτόν, ¹⁷καὶ οὐκ ἔχουσιν ῥίζαν ἐν ἑαυτοῖς ἀλλὰ πρόσ- 17
καιροί εἰσιν· εἶτα γενομένης θλίψεως ἢ διωγμοῦ ¶ διὰ   ¶ a
τὸν λόγον ¶ εὐθὺς σκανδαλίζονται.   ¹⁸καὶ ἄλλοι εἰσὶν 18 ¶ syrsin

---

17 ῥιζαν] υδωρ V | προκαιροι F | η] και D c f ff i q vg | σκανδαλισθησονται D
18 αλλοι] ουτοι AC²ΠΣΦ al 33 minᵖˡ f q go aeth om αλλ. εισιν 1 13 28 124 604 alᵐᵘ
syrᵖᵉˢʰ arm

---

17. οὐκ ἔχουσιν ῥίζαν] The seed
of the word has not driven its way
into the soil. With this use of ῥίζα
cf. 4 Regn. xix. 30, Job xix. 28, Sap.
iii. 15, iv. 3, Sir. i. 6, 20, Isa. xl. 24;
and contrast Deut. xxix. 18 (Heb.
xii. 15), 1 Macc. i. 10.

ἐν ἑαυτοῖς] So Mt.; Lc. omits the
words. The hearer of the Gospel is
at once plant (ὁ σπειρόμενος or σπαρείς)
and soil; the roots which the seed
under normal conditions throws out
are within, in his heart, the seat of
the personal life. In the case now
contemplated the heart is πετρώδης;
there has been a πώρωσις within (iii. 5)
which stops the development of the
roots.

ἀλλὰ πρόσκαιροί εἰσιν] Vg. sed tem-
porales sunt : 'but (so far from being
well rooted) they are short-lived';
Lc. πρὸς καιρὸν πιστεύουσιν. Nearly
all the English versions paraphrase
πρόσκ. εἰσιν, e.g. Wycliffe, "thei ben
temporal, that is lasten a lytil tyme";
Tindale, Cranmer, Geneva, A. V.
"endure but a time" or "for a time":
"for a season" (Heb. xi. 25) has perhaps been avoided as ambiguous in
this connexion. Πρόσκαιρος, though
common in the later Gk., is rare in
the Greek of the Bible, occurring
only in 4 Macc. xv. 2, 2 Cor. iv.
18, Heb. l. c., besides the present
context.

εἶτα γενομένης κτλ.] Εἶτα, 'then,'
as the next step consequent upon the
non-development of the roots; cf.
εἶτεν (v. 28). Θλίψεως ἢ διωγμοῦ (Lc.
πειρασμοῦ, crushing sorrow of any
kind, or in the particular form of

persecution. Θλίψις (on the accentuation see WM., p. 56 n.), though rarely
used in non-Biblical Greek and only
in its literal sense, is common both in
LXX. and N.T.; in the former it is
usually an equivalent of צר or one of
its cognates. It is coupled with ἐλεγ-
μός (4 Regn. xix. 3), στενοχωρία (Esth.
A 7 (xi. 8), Is. viii. 22, Rom. ii. 9, viii.
35), ὀδύνη (Ps. cxiv. (cxvi.) 3), ἀνάγκη
(Ps. cxviii. (cxix.) 143, Zeph. i. 15,
2 Cor. vi. 4, 1 Th. iii. 7), ὀνειδισμός (Is.
xxxvii. 3), διωγμός (2 Thess. i. 4); its
opposites are πλατυσμός (cf. Ps. iv. 1),
ἀνάπαυσις (cf. Hab. iii. 16), εἰρήνη (Zach.
viii. 10), ἄνεσις (2 Th. i. 7). See Lightfoot on 1 Th. iii. 7, 2 Th. i. 7. For
διωγμός, another too familiar word in
Apostolic times, see x. 30, 2 Macc.
xii. 23, Acts viii. 1, xiii. 50. The two
words correspond here to the fierce
heat which withers the rootless plant
(v. 6): cf. Ps. cxx. (cxxi.) 6, Is. xxv. 4,
xlix. 10, Jer. xvii. 8. Διὰ τὸν λόγον is
a new point, which is not represented
in the parable: cf. xiii. 13, διὰ τὸ
ὄνομά μου.

σκανδαλίζονται] Σκανδαλίζειν occurs
in Dan. xi. 41, LXX. (= נִכְשַׁל), Sir. ix. 5,
xxiii. 8, xxxv. 15, Pss. Sol. xvi. 7, and
in Aq., Symm., but perhaps not elsewhere except in the N.T. and Church
writers; and whereas σκάνδαλον is
used occasionally in its literal sense
(Judith v. 1, Isa. viii. 14, Aq., 1 Pet.
ii. 8), the verb seems to be limited to
the sphere of ethics. Lc. interprets
it here of apostasy (ἀφίστανται), but
there may be moral stumbling which
falls short of that : see Mc. xiv. 27.

18. καὶ ἄλλοι εἰσὶν κτλ.] Another

οἱ εἰς τὰς ἀκάνθας σπειρόμενοι· οὗτοί εἰσιν οἱ τὸν
§ e 19 λόγον ἀκούσαντες, ¹⁹καὶ αἱ §μέριμναι τοῦ αἰῶνος καὶ ἡ
ἀπάτη τοῦ πλούτου καὶ αἱ περὶ τὰ λοιπὰ ἐπιθυμίαι
εἰσπορευόμεναι συνπνίγουσιν τὸν λόγον, καὶ ἄκαρπος
20 γίνεται. ²⁰καὶ ἐκεῖνοί εἰσιν οἱ ἐπὶ τὴν γῆν τὴν καλὴν
σπαρέντες, οἵτινες ἀκούουσιν τὸν λόγον καὶ παρα-

---

18 εις ABDLΠΣΦ al min^forte omn] επι אCΔ me | om ουτοι εισιν AC²ΠΣ (non Φ)
al 33 al^pl f q go aeth ακουσαντες (א)BCDLΔ 13 69 124 346 1071 al^pauc me] ακουοντες
ΑΠΣΦ al min^pl latt syr^hcl go aeth   19 αιωνος] βιου D 604 latt^vt+τουτου ΑΠΣΦ al
min^pl f syr^pesh arm me go aeth | η απατη (αγαπη Δ) του πλουτου] απαται του κοσμου
D(b) g i q ηδοναι του κοσμου c eff | om και αι π. τ. λ. επιθυμιαι D 1 28 604 a b c e ff i q
arm | ακαρποι γινονται D 124 b c e ff g i q   20 εκεινοι אBCLΔ] ουτοι ADΠΣΦ al
min^forte omn latt syr^hcl go aeth Or

---

class consists of those who are sown
upon the thorns : cf. *v.* 16, οὗτοι δέ
εἰσιν οἱ κτλ. The construction is
broken after ἀκούσαντες (Mt. Mc.);
we expect, what Lc. gives, καὶ...συν-
πνίγονται.

19. αἱ μέριμναι κτλ.] The thorns
of the spiritual soil. Αἱ μ. τοῦ αἰῶνος:
the cares of the age (usually ὁ αἰὼν
οὗτος), the present course of events—
wider than Lc.'s μέριμναι τοῦ βίου (or
βιωτικαί Lc. xxi. 34). For other N.T.
warnings against worldly care see Mt.
vi. 25 ff. (= Lc. xii. 22 ff.), Lc. x. 41,
xxi. 34; Phil. iv. 6, 1 Pet. v. 7. With
ἀπάτη τοῦ πλούτου comp. ἀπάτη ἀδικίας
(2 Th. ii. 10), τῆς ἁμαρτίας (Heb. iii. 13);
the confusion of ἀπάτη with ἀγάπη
in some MSS. finds an interesting parallel in 2 Pet. ii. 13. Αἱ περὶ τὰ λοιπὰ
ἐπιθυμίαι is peculiar to Mc.; Lc.'s
equivalent is ἡδοναὶ τοῦ βίου, but Mc.
is again more comprehensive; cf.
Euth.: συμπεριλαβὼν πᾶσαν βλαβε-
ρὰν ἐπιθυμίαν, where however βλαβ.
narrows the reference unduly if it
suggests only such desires as are
vicious in themselves (see 1 Jo. ii.
15 ff. with Westcott's notes). On this
interpretation of the ἄκανθαι see Herm.
sim. ix. 20; for the phrase αἱ περί
κτλ., see WM., p. 240.

εἰσπορευόμεναι συνπ. τ. λόγον] The
ἐπιθυμίαι enter the heart together
with the λόγος and in greater strength,
gathering round it (for συνπν. see
v. 7) and excluding from it the action
of the understanding and the affections which are as light and warmth
to the spiritual plant.

ἄκαρπος γίνεται]=καρπὸν οὐκ ἔδωκεν
(*v.* 7): Lc. οὐ τελεσφοροῦσιν. The
fruit does not mature itself, and so
the word proves in their case fruitless.
For the metaphorical use of ἄκαρπος
see Sap. xv. 4, σκιαγράφων πόνος ἄκαρπος: Eph. v. 11, Tit. iii. 14, 2 Pet.
i. 8.

20. ἐκεῖνοι...οἵτινες] 'Those who
are such as,' &c. Ἐκεῖνοι contrasts this
last class with οὗτοι (*vv.* 15, 16) and
ἄλλοι (*v.* 18): cf. Jo. ix. 9, ἄλλοι...ἄλλοι
...ἐκεῖνος. For ὅστις as distinguished
from ὅς see Lightfoot on Gal. iv. 24
and 2 Th. i. 9. The timeless σπειρόμενοι (*vv.* 16, 18) is now exchanged
for σπαρέντες—'those who· in the
parable were represented as sown,'
&c.: those of this type (1) hear the
word (Lc. adds ἐν καρδίᾳ καλῇ καὶ
ἀγαθῇ), (2) accept it, (3) yield fruit.
Παραδέχονται (Exod. xxiii. 1, 3 Macc.
vii. 12, Acts xvi. 21, xxii. 18, Heb.
xii. 6) goes beyond λαμβάνουσιν (*v.* 16),

δέχονται καὶ καρποφοροῦσιν ἐν τριάκοντα καὶ ἐν
ἑξήκοντα καὶ ἐν ἑκατόν.
²¹ Καὶ ἔλεγεν αὐτοῖς ὅτι Μήτι ἔρχεται ὁ λύχνος 21

20 εν...εν...εν ℵDEFGHKMUVII (ἕν latt me go arm)] om εν 2° BC* vid et 3° B
min^perpauc   21 οτι BL] om ℵACDΔΠΣΦ al min^pl | ερχεται] απτεται D 13 69 124
al c e ff g i r *adfertur* b (aeth)

cf. Mt. συνιείς (probably in contrast
to the ἀσύνετοι of Isa. vi. 10), Lc. κατέ-
χουσιν.

    καὶ καρποφοροῦσιν κτλ.] For καρπο-
φορεῖν (Xen., Theophr. &c.) see Hab.
iii. 17 (=פָּרַה), Sap. x. 7, Mc. iv. 28 ;
and in the metaphorical sense Rom.
vii. 4, 5, Col. i. 6 (middle, see Lightfoot), 10. Lc. adds ἐν ὑπομονῇ, "the
opposite of ἀφίστανται, v. 13" (Plummer). For ἐν...ἐν...ἐν Blass (*Gr.* p. 146)
would write ἐν...ἐν...ἕν, cf. Mt. ὁ μὲν...
ὁ δέ...ὁ δέ : but εν is probably the
equivalent of בְּ, 'at the rate of'; see
note on *v.* 8. The employment of this
detail in the interpretation by Mt.,
Mc. is remarkable. Lc. omits it, but
it clearly asserts a principle which
is as true in the kingdom of GOD as
in nature. Cf. Victor: τέταρτον οὖν
μέρος ἐσώθη καὶ οὐδὲ τοῦτο ἐπ' ἴσης
καρποφορεῖ. The comment of Theophylact serves to throw light upon
the estimate of Christian perfection
formed by a later age : οἱ μέν εἰσι
παρθένοι καὶ ἐρημικοί, ἄλλοι μιγάδες
καὶ ἐν κοινοβίῳ, ἕτεροι λαϊκοὶ καὶ ἐν
γάμῳ. (Cf. Jerome on Mt. xiii.)

21—25. PARABOLIC WARNINGS AS
TO THE RESPONSIBILITY OF HEARING
THE WORD (Lc. viii. 16—18; cf. Mt. v.
15, x. 26, vii. 2, xiii. 12, xxv. 29; Lc.
xi. 33, xii. 2, vi. 38, xix. 26).

21. καὶ ἔλεγεν occurs with remarkable frequency in this chapter (*vv.* 9,
11, 13 (λέγει), 21, 24, 26, 30, 35 (λέγει)).
Possibly its repetition indicates that
the editor had before him here a
number of detached sayings of uncertain order, which he has thus
strung together without note of time.
Several of these sayings are given by
Mt. in other contexts (see last note),

or occur in a slightly different form
which suggests a double rendering of
the same Aramaic words : cf. Lc. viii.
16 with xi. 33, viii. 17 with xii. 2, viii.
18 with xix. 26 (A. Wright *ad l.*). These
phenomena at first sight throw doubt
upon the Marcan sequence in this
place, and it is worthy of notice that
Tatian passes from *v.* 20 to *v.* 29 ; but
the inner coherence of the sayings
with the preceding context supports
Mc., and, unless they were repeated
on other occasions, it is probably Mt.'s
order which is at fault.

    μήτι ἔρχεται ὁ λύχνος] Vg. *num-
quid venit lucerna?* Μήτι expects a
negative answer, cf. e.g. Pilate's question (Jo. xviii. 35) μήτι ἐγὼ Ἰουδαῖός
εἰμι ; and see on Mc. xiv. 19. With
ἔρχεται the commentators compare
Liban. *ep.* 358 ἡ δὲ (ἐπιστολὴ) ἔρχεται.
The reading of D (ἅπτεται for ἔρχεται :
cf. Lc. ἅψας) is a harmonising gloss,
unless, as has been ingeniously suggested, we may see in it a retransla-
tion of *accēditur* (*accenditur*), Harris,
Cod. Bez., p. 89. Ὁ λύχνος "a lanterne"
(Wycliffe); rather, the lamp (on the
article see *v.* 3), as contrasted with
the λαμπάς or torch: see exx. in
Trench, *syn.* § xlvi, and cf. *Lamp,
Lantern*, in Hastings, *D.B.* iii. The
λύχνος when at rest is placed on
a stand—λυχνία—a later form of λυχ-
νίον or λυχνεῖον = λυχνοῦχος—used in
the LXX. for the מְנוֹרָה of the Tabernacle (Exod. xxv. 31, &c., esp. xl. 4,
εἰσοίσεις τὴν λυχνίαν καὶ ἐπιθήσεις τοὺς
λύχνους). In the present context the
λύχνος is the word, the λυχνία the
hearer or body of hearers (cf. Apoc.
i. 20) ; in Lc. xi. 34, Apoc. xxi. 23
the metaphor is applied somewhat

ἵνα ὑπὸ τὸν μόδιον τεθῇ ἢ ὑπὸ τὴν κλίνην, οὐχ ἵνα
22 ἐπὶ τὴν λυχνίαν τεθῇ ; ²²οὐ γὰρ ἔστιν κρυπτὸν ἐὰν
μὴ ἵνα φανερωθῇ, οὐδὲ ἐγένετο ἀπόκρυφον ἀλλ' ἵνα
23 ἔλθῃ εἰς φανερόν. ²³εἴ τις ἔχει ὦτα ἀκούειν ἀκουέτω.

21 ινα v. τ. μ. τεθη] v. τ. μ. τεθηναι ℵ* | επι] υπο ℵB*Σ 13 33 69 1071 | τεθη 2°]
επιτεθη ΑΠ al^pl   22 εστιν]+τι ℵACEFGLSVΔΠ²ΣΦ min^permu c f vg syr^pesh arm
go (om τι BDHKMUΠ* min^sat mu b e ff i q aeth) | εαν μη ινα ℵBΔ (1 13 28 69 604
al^perpauc)] εαν μη ΑCΚΛΠΣ 33 209 al^pauc αλλ ινα D 49 b ff i q o εαν μη
EFGHMSUVΦ | ελθη εις φανερον] φανερωθη B (syr^pesh) aeth

differently. When the word has been
proclaimed, its purpose is defeated if
it be concealed by the hearers ; when
the lamp comes in, who would put
it under the *modius* or the couch
of the *triclinium*? Μόδιος (Mt. v.
15, Lc. xi. 33,—in viii. 16 Lc. has
σκεῦος) = 16 sextarii, a sixth of a
μέδιμνος (?=סְאָה), a peck rather than
a bushel (so all the English versions),
is a Latinism common, as the reff.
shew, to the three Synoptists ; the
word had doubtless been adopted
into colloquial Greek. The reading
ὑπὸ τὴν λυχνίαν is rightly called by
Holtzmann "ein Beispiel ältesten
Textverderbs"; cf. WH., *Notes*, p. 24.
This saying brings before us the
commonest furniture of a Galilean
home, and the details add to its
picturesqueness—ὁ λύχνος, ἡ λυχνία,
ὁ μόδιος, ἡ κλίνη.

22. οὐ γὰρ ἔστιν κρυπτόν κτλ.] Vg.
non enim est aliquid, &c., cf. Mt.
οὐδὲν γάρ κτλ. and vv. ll. here ; 'for
there is not [anything] hidden (Mt.
κεκαλυμμένον, Lc. xii. 2 συγκεκαλυμ-
μένον) except with a view to its
future manifestation, neither did it
become a secret [to remain a secret],
but on the contrary (ἀλλά) that it
might pass into the light of day.'
The interpretation of the parable
takes the form of a parallelism after
the manner of Proverbs and Sirach.
While asserting a great principle of
the Divine government, our Lord
corrects a false impression which
might have arisen from the mention

of a μυστήριον (v. 11). If the Gospel
was for the moment treated as a
secret, this was so only because
temporary secrecy was essential to
its successful proclamation after the
Ascension. Those to whom the secret
was now confided were charged with
the responsibility of publishing it
then. The λυχνία must be ready to
receive and exhibit the λύχνος as
soon as the appropriate time had
come.

Κρυπτός and ἀπόκρυφος are both
O. T. words : cf. esp. Dan. ii. 22, Th.
αὐτὸς ἀποκαλύπτει βαθέα καὶ ἀπόκρυφα
(מְסַתְּרָתָא) ; ib. 47, lxx., ὁ ἐκφαίνων
μυστήρια κρυπτά. On ἀπόκρυφος cf.
Lightfoot on Col. ii. 3. Ἐὰν μὴ ἵνα φ.,
'except for the purpose of being revealed'; for ἐὰν μή without a verb see
Blass, *Gr.* p. 216. Ἀλλ' ἵνα answers
to ἐὰν μὴ ἵνα (Blass, *Gr.* p. 269), but
(ag. Blass) there is a perceptible difference of meaning : see the paraphrase
attempted above. Similarly ἔστιν and
ἐγένετο, though relating to the same
set of facts, present them in different
lights ; what 'is' now hidden from
us 'became' so through the will of
GOD working its way through darkness to the perfect light. Thpht.
τί γὰρ ἦν κρυφιώτερον θεοῦ ; ἀλλ'
ὅμως καὶ οὗτος ἐφανερώθη ἐν σαρκί.
Bengel : "id axioma valet de rebus
naturae, de sensibus et actionibus
hominum malis et bonis in statu
naturali et spirituali, de mysteriis
divinis."

23. εἴ τις ἔχει ὦτα κτλ.] See on

²⁴ Καὶ ἔλεγεν αὐτοῖς Βλέπετε τί ἀκούετε· ἐν ᾧ 24
μέτρῳ μετρεῖτε μετρηθήσεται ὑμῖν καὶ §προστεθή-　　§Θᵇ
σεται ὑμῖν. ²⁵§ὃς γὰρ ἔχει, δοθήσεται αὐτῷ· καὶ ὃς 25 §ᵃ
οὐκ ἔχει, καὶ ὃ ἔχει ἀρθήσεται ἀπ᾽ αὐτοῦ.
²⁶ Καὶ ἔλεγεν Οὕτως ἐστὶν ἡ βασιλεία τοῦ θεοῦ, 26

24 ακουετε]+και προστεθησεται υμιν τοις ακουουσιν 13 69 346 556 arm | αντιμετρη-
θησεται 1071 | και προστεθ. υμιν] om DG 114 2ᵖᵉ b e g+τοις ακουουσιν ΑΘᵇΠΣΦ al
1 33 69 alᵖˡ q syrr arm　　25 εχει] pr αν DE*FHKΘᵇ αν εχη ΑΕ²G(M)SUVΠ |
δοθησεται] προστεθησεται D 271

v. 9. The warning is needed for the
Apostles as for the rest.

24. βλέπετε τί ἀκούετε] Lc. βλ. οὖν
πῶς ἀκούετε. In Mc.'s form of the
saying βλέπειν is to consider : 'look
well what it is that ye hear,' i.e. weigh
its meaning ; be not as those who
βλέποντες οὐ βλέπουσιν (Mt. xiii. 13).
Thpht. πρὸς νηφαλιότητα διεγείρει τοὺς
μαθητάς...μηδὲν ὑμᾶς τῶν λεγομένων
παρ᾽ ἐμοῦ διαφευγέτω. Cf. Heb. ii.
1 f.

ἐν ᾧ μέτρῳ κτλ.] 'You shall be paid
back (Lc. ἀντιμετρηθήσεται) in your
own measure.' The proverb occurs in
several contexts (Mt. vii. 2, Lc. vi.
38) with different applications : here
the sense is : 'your attention to the
teaching will be the measure of the
profit you will receive from it.' Euth.
ἐν ᾧ μέτρῳ μετρεῖτε τὴν προσοχήν, ἐν
τῷ αὐτῷ μετρηθήσεται ὑμῖν ἡ γνῶσις.
The μέτρον however is not intellectual
merely, but spiritual ; its capacity
depends on the moral condition of
the hearer. Bengel : "est cor cum
sua capacitate, cupiditate, studio im-
pertiendi aliis, obsequio." Nor is the
return limited by it : καὶ προστεθήσεται
ὑμῖν (Mt. περισσευθήσεται), i.e. the
λόγος when received by one who is
not an ἀκροατὴς ἐπιλησμονῆς exceeds
his immediate power of assimilation ;
he is rich beyond his measure, richer
than he knows.

25. ὃς γὰρ ἔχει κτλ.] Another proverbial saying, found also in other
connexions (Mt. xiii. 12, xxv. 29, Lc.

xix. 26). Here the sense is : 'for the
appropriation of any measure of Divine truth implies a capacity for
receiving more ; and each gift, if as-
similated, is the forerunner of another';
Bede : "qui amorem habet verbi
dabitur illi etiam sensus intellegendi
quod amat." But the converse is
also true : 'incapacity for receiving
truth leads to a loss of truth already
in some sense possessed.' The para-
doxical form of the original tradition
is removed by Lc. who writes ὃ δοκεῖ
ἔχειν ἀρθήσεται. But the paradox is
characteristic of Christ's sayings (cf.
e.g. viii. 35, x. 31), and it is true : the
man both 'has' and 'has not': cf.
Rom. ii. 20, 2 Tim. iii. 5. With ἀρθήσεται ἀπ᾽ αὐτοῦ cf. Mt. xxi. 43, xxv.
28, 29. On the readings ὃς ἔχει, ὃς ἂν
ἔχει (ἔχῃ) see Blass, *Gr.*, p. 217.

26—29. PARABLE OF THE AUTO-
MATIC ACTION OF THE SOIL (Mc. only).

26. καὶ ἔλεγεν κτλ.] The record of
the public teaching seems to begin
again here ; the unexplained parable
belongs to the ὄχλος, not to the μαθηταί (see below *v.* 33 f.). The parable
which follows is peculiar to Mc., unless we accept the improbable theory
of Weiss and Holtzmann that it forms
one side of the picture of which the
other is preserved in the Parable of
the Tares (Mt. xiii. 24 ff.). There are
verbal coincidences, e.g. καθεύδη (cf.
Mt., *v.* 25), χόρτον...σῖτον (cf. Mt., *vv.*
26, 30), θερισμός (cf. Mt., *v.* 30) ; but
both the purpose and the story differ

¶ a 27 ὡς ἄνθρωπος βάλῃ¶ τὸν σπόρον ἐπὶ τῆς γῆς ²⁷καὶ
καθεύδῃ καὶ ἐγείρηται νύκτα καὶ ἡμέραν, καὶ ὁ
σπόρος βλαστᾷ καὶ μηκύνεται, ὡς οὐκ οἶδεν αὐτός.
28 ²⁸αὐτομάτη ἡ γῆ καρποφορεῖ, πρῶτον χόρτον, εἶτεν

26 ως ℵBDLΔ 13 28 33 69 alᵖᵃᵘᶜ me] ως εαν (αν, οταν) ACΘᵇΠΣΦ al minᵖˡ lattᵛᵗᵖˡᵛᵍ
go al | βαλλη F βαλλει minᵖᵃᵘᶜ | om τον D 2ᵖᵉ   27 καθευδει EFHU 33 69
alᵐᵘ | εγειρεται ℵEFGHLM 69 alᵖᵃᵘᶜ εγερθη D | βλαστα BC*DLΔ 2ᵖᵉ alᵖᵃᵘᶜ] βλαστανη
ℵAC²GKMSUVΘᵇΠΣΦ minᵖˡ βλαστανει EFH 33 alᵐᵘ | μηκυνεται BDHΣ minⁿᵒⁿⁿ]
μηκυνηται ℵACLΔII alᵖˡ   28 αυτοματη]+γαρ ΔΠΣΦ al lattᵛᵗᵖˡᵛᵍ go pr οτι D
2ᵖᵉ arm | ειτεν bis B*(L)Δ (cf. ℵ)] ειτα bis AB²CDII al minᶠᵒʳᵗᵉ ᵒᵐⁿ

widely. Tatian places Mc.'s parable
immediately before the Tares, an
order which has much to recommend
it.

οὕτως...ὡς ἄνθρωπος βάλῃ] The regular construction would have been ὡς
ἐὰν ἄνθρ. βάλῃ (cf. 1 Th. ii. 7), or ὡς
ἄνθρ. βαλών (cf. 1 Cor. ix. 26, Jas. ii.
12) or ὃς ἂν βάλῃ. There is a partial
parallel to the anomalous ὡς...βάλῃ in
xiii. 34, ὡς ἄνθρωπος...ἐνετείλατο. Τὸν
σπόρον: as in Lc. viii. 5, τὸν σπ. αὐτοῦ,
or perhaps generic, seed of any kind.
In the series βάλῃ...καθεύδῃ...ἐγείρ-
ηται, &c., the first verb alone stands
in the aor., the act of sowing being
"single and transient" (Madvig, § 128);
for the conjunction of aor. and pres.
cf. Jo. iii. 16, 1 Pet. iv. 6. Σπόρος,
sowing or seed time, is used in the
later Biblical Gk. as nearly = σπέρμα,
where the reference is to the seed as
used by the sower, not to the particular grain ; cf. Deut. xi. 10, Lc.
viii. 5, 11, 2 Cor. ix. 10 (contrast
σπέρμα in Mc. iv. 31, 1 Cor. xv. 38).

27. καὶ καθεύδῃ καὶ ἐγείρηται] Cf.
Ps. iii. 6, ἐγὼ ἐκοιμήθην καὶ ὕπνωσα·
ἐξηγέρθην. The process goes on νύκτα
καὶ ἡμέραν, not merely νυκτὸς καὶ
ἡμέρας (v. 5), but occupying the νυχθή-
μερον: cf. Lc. ii. 37, where the point
is that Anna's whole life was given to
devotion; Jo. iv. 52 (Westcott's note).
The order ν. καὶ ἡ. is usual (cf. Gen.
i. 5, &c.), and appropriate in this
context where καθεύδῃ precedes.

Βλαστᾷ = βλαστάνει. Βλαστάω occurs
also in Eccl. ii. 6, Hermas Sim. iv. 1,
δένδρα τὰ μὲν βλαστῶντα τὰ δὲ ξηρά:
cf. WSchm. p. 125. Μηκύνεσθαι is
an ἅπ. λεγ. in the N. T., but cf.
Isa. xliv. 14, ξύλον...ὑετὸς ἐμήκυνεν
(יְגַדֵּל). The middle emphasises the
activity of growth internal to the plant.
Into this mystery of growth however
the sower cannot penetrate : it takes
place ὡς οὐκ οἶδεν αὐτός, after a manner
which baffles his understanding. Vg.
"dum nescit ille," Wycliffe, "while he
wote not," and similarly the other
English versions before 1611, regarding ὡς as an adverb of time ; A.V.,
R.V. "he knoweth not how."

28. αὐτομάτη ἡ γῆ καρποφορεῖ] Vg.
ultro enim terra fructificat. Αὐτόματος is used of the spontaneous produce of uncultivated land (Lev. xxv.
5, 11, 4 Regn. xix. 29, = סָפִיחַ) : cf.
Plat. polit. 272 A, καρποὺς οὐχ ὑπὸ
γεωργίας φυομένους ἀλλ' αὐτομάτης
ἀναδιδούσης τῆς γῆς. Bengel's remark
is true and weighty : "non excludi-
tur agricultura et caelestis pluvia
solesque." Here however the thought
is that when man has done his
part, the actual process of growth
is beyond his reach or comprehen-
sion ; he must leave it to the apparently spontaneous action of the
soil. In the N. T. the word occurs
again but once (Acts xii. 10). Cf.
Philo, de incorr. mund. 944, ἀπαυ-

§στάχυν, εἶτεν πλήρη σῖτον ἐν τῷ στάχυι. 29 ὅταν 29 § a
δὲ παραδοῖ ὁ καρπός, εὐθὺς ἀποστέλλει τὸ δρέπανον,
ὅτι παρέστηκεν ὁ θερισμός.
30 Καὶ ἔλεγεν Πῶς ὁμοιώσωμεν¶ τὴν βασιλείαν τοῦ 30 ¶ a

28 σταχυν] σταχυας D | πληρη σιτον ℵAC^{2}LΔΠΦ al min^{pl}] πληρες σιτος B πληρης ο σιτος D πληρης σιτον C^{*vid}Σ πληρες σιτον min^{2} πληροι σιτον min^{pauc} me^{codd}
29 παραδοι ℵ*BDΔ 2^{pe}] παραδω ℵ$^{c.a}$ABLΘ^{b}ΠΣΦ al min$^{fere\ omn}$ | εξαποστελλει 13 69 346
30 πως ℵBCLΔ min^{pauc} b e syr$^{hcl\ mg}$] τινι ADΠΣΦ al min^{pl} c f ff i q vg syrr$^{pesh\ hcl\ (txt)}$ arm me go aeth Or | ομοιωσομεν C 1 604 al^{pauc} latt ομοιωσω K 28 69 al^{pauc} arm^{cod}

τοματίζουσα ἡ τοῦ ἔτους ὥρα παρέχεται. On καρποφορεῖν see *v.* 20: here it is loosely used in reference to the incipient stages of the fruitbearing plant.

πρῶτον χόρτον κτλ.] Vg. *primum herbam, deinde spicam, deinde plenum frumentum.* With πρῶτον...εἶτεν ...εἶτεν cf. πρῶτον...ἔπειτα (1 Cor. xv. 46, 1 Th. iv. 16), πρῶτον...εἶτα (1 Tim. iii. 10): εἶτεν (Blass, *Gr.* p. 20) is a very rare, originally Ionic, form of εἶτα, for which see note on *v.* 17. Χόρτος is properly herbage suitable for pasture (see e.g. vi. 39, Jo. vi. 10); here it is the green blade of corn, as in Mt. xiii. 26. The next stage is that of the στάχυς (ii. 23, cf. Gen. xli. 6 ff. = שִׁבֹּלֶת), to which succeeds the πλήρης σῖτος (Job v. 26, σῖτος ὥριμος κατὰ καιρὸν θεριζόμενος). Not improbably Mc. or his early copyists wrote πλήρης σῖτον: see WH., *Notes*, p. 24, and *J. Th. St.* i., p. 121.

29. ὅταν δὲ παραδοῖ ὁ καρπός] Vg. *cum se produxerit fructus.* Cf. Mt. xiii. 26, ὅτε δὲ ἐβλάστησεν ὁ χόρτος καὶ καρπὸν ἐποίησεν. Παραδοῖ (conj. aor. = παραδῷ, see WH., *Notes*, p. 175, WSchm., p. 121, Blass, *Gr.* p. 49) is either 'permits,' 'allows,' a sense supported by such writers as Herod., Xen., Polyb. (e.g. Polyb. xxii. 24. 9, τῆς ὥρας παραδιδούσης), or rather perhaps, 'yields [itself]' for which Jos. xi. 19 (AF) is quoted (οὐκ ἦν πόλις ἥτις οὐ παρέδωκεν τοῖς υἱοῖς Ἰσραήλ = (B) ἣν οὐκ ἔλαβεν Ἰ.); cf. 1 Pet. ii. 23 ὃς...παρεδίδου 'gave Himself up,' 'yielded,' 'surrendered.' Compare the Complutensian text of Hab. iii. 17 (LXX.), which for συκῆ οὐ καρποφορήσει reads ἡ σ. οὐ μὴ παραδῷ τὸν καρπὸν αὐτῆς.

ἀποστέλλει τὸ δρέπανον] Sc. ὁ ἄνθρωπος (*v.* 26); the time has again come for the intervention of the agriculturist. The phrase is borrowed from Joel iii. (iv.) 13: ἐξαποστείλατε (שִׁלְחוּ, cf. Field, *Notes*, p. 26) δρέπανα ὅτι παρέστηκεν τρυγητός: cf. Apoc. xiv. 15, πέμψον τὸ δρέπανόν σου...ὅτι ἐξηράνθη ὁ θερισμὸς τῆς γῆς. Δρέπανον is the later form of the Attic δρεπάνη (cf. δρεπανηφόρος in 2 Macc. xiii. 2), used in LXX.(12) and N.T.(2). Παρέστηκεν, not 'is at hand,' Vg. *adest*, or 'stands by,' as in the phrase οἱ παρεστηκότες (xiv. 47, &c.), but 'is ready' for the reaper, as the O.T. shews: cf. Joel *l.c.* where it = בָּשַׁל and Exod. ix. 32, ἡ γὰρ κριθὴ παρεστηκυῖα (= אָבִיב).

Of the interpretation of this interesting parable only a few leading points can be stated here. The functions of the sower end with the sowing, those of the reaper begin with the harvest; all that lies between is left to the mysterious laws of growth cooperating with the soil, the sunshine, and the rain. Christ came to sow, and will come to reap: the rest belongs to the invisible working of His Spirit in the Church and in the soul.

30—32. Parable of the Mustard Seed (Mt. xiii. 31–32, Lc. xiii. 18–19).

30. πῶς ὁμοιώσωμεν...θῶμεν; (delib.

31 θεοῦ, ἢ ἐν τίνι αὐτὴν παραβολῇ θῶμεν ; ³¹ ὡς κόκκῳ
σινάπεως, ὃς ὅταν σπαρῇ ἐπὶ τῆς γῆς, μικρότερον ὂν
32 πάντων τῶν σπερμάτων τῶν ἐπὶ τῆς γῆς—³²καὶ ὅταν

30 τινι ℵBC*LΔ minⁿᵒⁿⁿ Or] ποια AC²DΘᵇΠΣΦ minᵖˡ | θωμεν ℵBC*LΔ 28 63 alᵖᵃᵘᶜ
b (e) syrʰᵉˡ me Or] παραβαλωμεν AC²DΘᵇΠΣΦ al minᵖˡ lattᵛᵗᵖˡᵛᵍ syrrᵖᵉˢʰʰᶜˡ⁽ᵗˣᵗ⁾ arm
31 ως] ομοια εστιν D cᵛⁱᵈ meᵛⁱᵈ | κοκκω ℵBDΔΠ*ΣΦ minⁿᵒⁿⁿ] κοκκον ACLΘᵇΠ² al
minᵐᵘ lattᵛⁱᵈ | om os ℵ* (hab ℵᶜ·ᵃ) | μικροτερον ℵBD*LMΔ 13* 28 33 131 179 235
258 1071 alᵖᵃᵘᶜ] μικροτερος ACD²ΘᵇΠΣΦ al minᵖˡ go | ον] εστιν (Δ)C(D)MΘᵇΠΣΦ al
minᵖˡ lattᵛᵗᵖˡᵛᵍ arm go | των επι της γης] om C 271 b e a εισιν ε. τ. γ. D

conj., WM., p. 356, Blass, *Gr.*, p. 210).
Lc. (who has placed this parable and
the parable which follows it in Mt.
in quite another context) retains the
double question which Mt. has lost;
for the form cf. Isa. xl. 18. 'How
are we to depict the kingdom of God?
in what new light can we place it?'
The Lord, as a wise teacher, seems to
take His audience into His counsels,
and to seek their help (cf. Blass, *Gr.*,
p. 166). But the parable is ready,
and follows without a break.

31. ὡς κόκκῳ σινάπεως] Wycliffe,
"as a corn of seneueye." Answer to
πῶς ὁμοιώσωμεν κτλ.; two constructions seem to be combined—ὡς κόκκον
[θήσομεν] and κόκκῳ [ὁμοιώσομεν].
Κόκκος is here a grain or seed, as in
κ. σίτου Jo. xii. 24, 1 Cor. xv. 37; in
the LXX. κόκκος is the scarlet dye
(Lam. iv. 5, Heb. עָזוֹת, Sir. xlv. 11,
Heb. שָׁנִי), more usually τὸ κόκκινον
(cf. Mt. xxvii. 28, &c.), produced from
the berry-like grub which feeds on
the *ilex coccifera*. The σίναπι is probably *sinapis nigra*, which, though
but a herb (λάχανον Mt. xiii. 32),
grows to a great height in the warm
valley of the Jordan, forming branches
and assuming the appearance of a
small tree (Lc. xiii. 19, ἐγένετο εἰς
δένδρον). The point of the parable
lies in the contrast between the relatively small seed and the size to
which the plant attains; cf. Mt. xvii.
20 = Lc. xvii. 6. The disproportion
seems to have been proverbial. Pa-

tristic writers refer also to the pro-
perties of the mustard seed e.g.
Hilary (*in Mt.*): " grano sinapis seip-
sum Dominus comparavit acri maxime
...acrius virtus et potestas tribula-
tionibus et pressuris accenditur." But
this, if designed, is quite in the background of the thought.

ὅταν σπαρῇ ἐπὶ τῆς γῆς] Mt. and Lc.
particularise : the mustard is sown
not in the open plain like the wheat,
but ἐν τῷ ἀγρῷ, εἰς κῆπον (3 Regn. xx.
[xxi.] 2); it is a garden herb. Μικρότερον ὂν πάντων τῶν σπερμάτων] : the
construction is again involved : we
expect ὁ (sc. σπέρμα) μικρ. ὄν...γῆς,
ὅταν σπαρῇ κτλ., or as in Mt. ὁ μικρ.
μέν ἐστιν...ὅταν δέ κτλ. The verse
reads like a rough note translated
without any attempt to remove grammatical difficulties. On the use of
the comp. when the superlative seems
to be required see WM., p. 303. The
seed is relatively the least of seeds,
i.e. in proportion to the plant. For
one of several possible applications
cf. Jerome *in Mt.* xiii. : " praedicatio
evangelii minima est omnibus dis-
ciplinis...hominem Deum, Deum mor-
tuum, scandalum crucis praedicans.
Confer huiuscemodi doctrinam dog-
matibus philosophorum...sed illa cum
creverit, nihil mordax, nihil vividum,
nihil vitale demonstrat."

32. καὶ ὅταν σπαρῇ takes up the
thread of ὃς ὅταν σπ., broken by the
intruded participial clause. For ἀναβαίνει, *ascendit*, see above, v. 7. Mt.
and Lc. exaggerate the growth (γίνεται

σπαρῇ, ἀναβαίνει καὶ γίνεται μεῖζον πάντων τῶν
λαχάνων καὶ ποιεῖ κλάδους μεγάλους, ὥστε δύνασθαι ὑπὸ τὴν σκιὰν αὐτοῦ τὰ πετεινὰ τοῦ οὐρανοῦ
κατασκηνοῖν.

³³ Καὶ τοιαύταις παραβολαῖς πολλαῖς ἐλάλει 33
αὐτοῖς τὸν λόγον, καθὼς ἠδύναντο ἀκούειν· ³⁴ χωρὶς 34
δὲ παραβολῆς οὐκ ἐλάλει αὐτοῖς, κατ' ἰδίαν δὲ τοῖς
ἰδίοις μαθηταῖς ἐπέλυεν πάντα.

32 μειζων DFGHKMSUΔΠΣΦ min^pl | κατασκηνοιν B* (-νουν ℵAB²CDL al)] κατα-
σκηνωσ[αι] Δ^vid   33 om πολλαις C*^vidLΔ 1 28 33 131 604 al^nonn b c e syr^pesh arm
me^codd aeth | om καθως ηδυν. ακουειν Φ   34 χωρις δε] και χωρις BΦ 604 me syr^pesh |
καθ ιδιαν B*DΔ | τοις ιδιοις μαθ. ℵBCLΔ 1071 Or] τ. μαθ. αυτου ADΘ^bΠΣΦ al
min^fere omn | απελυεν Θ^b

δένδρον, ἐγένετο εἰς δ.), whilst Mc.
adheres to the fact: it becomes the
tallest of garden herbs—a δενδρολά-
χανον, as Theophrastus calls such
towering succulent plants (hist. plant.
i. 3, 4). For λάχανον see Gen. ix. 3,
Prov. xv. 17, Lc. xi. 42, Rom. xiv. 2;
for ποιεῖν κλάδους cf. Ezech. xvii. 8 τοῦ
ποιεῖν βλαστούς.

καὶ ποιεῖ κτλ. refers to Dan. iv. 9
(12), Th., ἐν τοῖς κλάδοις αὐτοῦ κατῴ-
κουν (v. 18 κατεσκήνουν) τὰ ὄρνεα (LXX.
τὰ πετεινὰ) τοῦ οὐρανοῦ κτλ.: cf. Ps.
ciii. (civ.) 12, Ezech. xvii. 23. Κατασκηνοῖν: see WH., Notes, p. 173;
WSchm., p. 116 n., Blass, Gr. p. 48.

The parable supplied the followers
of the Gnostic Marcus with materials
for one of their mystic formulas:
Iren. i. 13. 2, ἡ ἀνεννόητος καὶ ἄρρητος
χάρις...πληθύναι ἔν σοι τὴν γνῶσιν αὐτῆς, ἐγκατασπείρουσα τὸν κόκκον τοῦ
σινάπεως εἰς τὴν ἀγαθὴν γῆν.

The three parables of the Sower,
the Growth, and the Seed, direct
attention successively to the soil, the
hidden life working in the seed, and
the seed itself in its relation to the
final results of the sowing. Any impression of failure derived from the
first parable is corrected by the
second and the third. While the
first two regard the Kingdom of

Heaven in its operations upon the
individual, the third represents it as
an imperial power, destined to over-
shadow the world.

33—34. GENERAL LAW OF PARA-
BOLIC TEACHING (Mt. xiii. 34).

33 f. τοιαύταις παραβολαῖς πολλαῖς]
The parables just given are to be
regarded as specimens, a few out of
many. Even Mt.'s ταῦτα πάντα ἐλάλησεν
...ἐν παραβολαῖς must not be taken
as limiting the parables to the seven
which he relates. Ἐλάλει αὐτοῖς τὸν
λόγον: the subject of the teaching
was the same as at the outset (ii. 2)—
the word of the Kingdom—though
the method was new. Καθὼς ἠδύναντο
ἀκούειν: comp. Jo. xvi. 12, 1 Cor. iii. 2,
Heb. v. 12 f., xii. 20. Χωρὶς δὲ παραβολῆς κτλ., 'but apart from a parable,'
except in a parabolic form, He did
not speak to them (sc. τοῖς ὄχλοις,
Mt.), i.e. at this stage of His ministry;
with the form of the sentence comp.
Jo. i. 3, Philem. 14, Heb. ix. 18.
Mt. finds in this a fulfilment of Ps.
lxxviii. 2 f.

κατ' ἰδίαν δέ κτλ.] Wycliffe, "bi hem-
silf," by themselves. Κατ' ἰδίαν (for
the form καθ' ἰδίαν see WH., Notes,
p. 145) = κατὰ μόνας, v. 10—when the
crowd had dispersed and He was left
with His immediate followers. Τοῖς

¶ Θᵇ 35   ³⁵Καὶ λέγει¶ αὐτοῖς ἐν ἐκείνῃ τῇ ἡμέρᾳ ὀψίας
36 γενομένης Διέλθωμεν εἰς τὸ πέραν. ³⁶καὶ ἀφέντες
τὸν ὄχλον παραλαμβάνουσιν αὐτὸν ὡς ἦν ἐν τῷ
37 πλοίῳ, καὶ ἄλλα πλοῖα ἦν μετ' αὐτοῦ. ³⁷καὶ γίνεται

35 om το 1071   36 και αλλα]+δε AC²DEFGHKMSUVΠΣΦ (om δε אBC*LΔ
minᵖᵃᵘᵉ) | πλοια אABCDKMΔΠΣ 1 13 33 69 1071 alⁿᵒⁿⁿ] πλοιαρια EFGHLSUVΦ
alᵖˡ | πλ. ην (ησαν אDΔ) μετ αυτ.] τα οντα μετ αυτ. πλ. 1 28 604 2ᵖᵉ alᵖᵃᵘᶜ armᵛⁱᵈ

ἰδίοις μαθ., possibly suggested by κατ'
ἰδ., =τοῖς μαθηταῖς αὐτοῦ (Jo. xiii. 1),
but emphasising the relation. Ἐπιλύειν is used of interpreting dreams
(Gen. xl. 8, xli. 8, 12, Aq.=συγκρίνειν,
ἀπαγγέλλειν, LXX.), and of deciding a
question (Acts xix. 39); ἐπίλυσις in
2 Pet. i. 20 = the exposition of Scripture. Mc. has given us our Lord's
ἐπίλυσις of one of the parables (v.
14 ff.): exposition now regularly followed (ἐπέλυεν πάντα) the public teaching. Cf. Orig. c. Cels. iii. 46, ἐπέλυεν
…προτιμῶν παρὰ τοὺς ὄχλους τοὺς τῆς
σοφίας αὐτοῦ ἐπιθυμοῦντας.

35—41. STILLING OF THE WIND
AND SEA (Mt. viii. 23—27, Lc. viii.
22—25).

35. ἐν ἐκείνῃ τῇ ἡμέρᾳ links on the
sequel with iv. 1 ff., and therefore with
iii. 20 ff. Lc. seems to have lost this
note of time, but preserves the general
order (ἐγένετο δὲ ἐν μιᾷ τῶν ἡμερῶν);
Mt. transfers this miracle and the
next into another context.

ὀψίας γενομένης] Late in the afternoon, but probably before sunset; for
the crowd had not yet left the shore;
see however i. 32, Jo. vi. 16, 17.
The immediate purpose of the crossing was perhaps to disperse the
crowd before nightfall. Διέλθωμεν,
'let us go through'; so Lc., Mt.
uses ἀπελθεῖν. Διαπερᾶν is the usual
word (v. 21, vi. 53), διέρχεσθαι being
more appropriate to travelling by
land (Lc. ii. 15, xvii. 21, Jo. iv. 4,
Acts viii. 4, &c.), or, if used of the
water, meaning to wade (Ps. lxv.

(lxvi.) 12) rather than to cross.
Τὸ πέραν: sc. τῆς θαλάσσης, cf. v. 1.

36. καὶ ἀφέντες τὸν ὄχλον κτλ.] See
the two striking incidents which Mt.
connects with this departure (viii.
18—22). The Lord was already on
board (Mc. iv. 1)—a point which Mt.
(ἐμβάντι αὐτῷ) and Lc. (αὐτὸς ἐνέβη)
overlook,—and He now put to sea
(Lc. ἀνήχθησαν) without going ashore
to make preparations (ὡς ἦν, Vg. ita
ut erat). Euth.: ὡς ἦν, ἀντὶ τοῦ ὡς
ἐκάθητο ἐν τῷ πλοίῳ. For the phrase
cf. 4 Regn. vii. 7 (ὡς ἔστιν=כַּאֲשֶׁר הִיא);
Fritzsche cites Lucian, As. 24, ἀφῆκαν
ὡς ἦν ἐν τῷ δεσμῷ. For παραλ. see
Acts xv. 39: in the Gospels the word
is commonly used of the Lord 'taking'
the Twelve, e.g. ix. 2, x. 32, xiv. 33,
cf. Jo. xiv. 3; but here the disciples,
as owners and navigators of the boat,
'take' Him with them. Mc. alone
adds that other boats started with
them, either as an escort, or through
eagerness to follow the Rabbi; these
were probably scattered by the storm,
or soon turned back again. One boat
seems to have sufficed for the Twelve
and the Lord, see vi. 32, 45; otherwise
we might suppose the ἄλλα πλοῖα to
be those of other disciples.

37. γίνεται λαῖλαψ μεγάλη κτλ.]
Mt. speaks only of the σεισμὸς μέγας
on the water which resulted. Lc. on
the other hand adds to the picture,
possibly from his knowledge of the
locality, κατέβη λ. ἀνέμου εἰς τὴν λίμνην.
The cyclonic wind which arose swept
down upon the lake from the hills
through the ravines on the W. shore:

λαῖλαψ μεγάλη ἀνέμου, καὶ τὰ κύματα §ἐπέβαλλεν §ᵃ
εἰς τὸ πλοῖον, ὥστε ἤδη γεμίζεσθαι τὸ πλοῖον.
³⁸καὶ αὐτὸς ἦν ἐν τῇ πρύμνῃ ἐπὶ τὸ προσκεφάλαιον 38
καθεύδων· καὶ ἐγείρουσιν αὐτὸν καὶ λέγουσιν αὐτῷ
Διδάσκαλε, οὐ μέλει σοι ὅτι¶ ἀπολλύμεθα; ³⁹καὶ 39 ¶ ᵃ

37 μεγαλου C e | επεβαλλεν ABCGHKSVΔΠ²ΣΦ minᵖˡ lattᵛᵗᵖˡᵛᵍ] επεβαλεν אEFL
MΠ* minˢᵃᵗᵐᵘ εβαλεν D ενεβαλεν (U) minᵖᵃᵘᶜ | om ωστε...το πλ. א* (hab אᵃ) | ηδη
γεμ. το πλ.] αυτο ηδη γεμ. AEFHKMSUVΠ(Σ)Φ 13 69 124 346 syrrᵖᵉˢʰ ʰᶜˡ ⁽ᵗˣᵗ⁾ arm
go | γεμιζεσθαι] βυθιζεσθαι G 1 33 alⁿᵒⁿⁿ καταποντιζεσθαι minᵖᵃᵘᶜ 38 εν
אABCDLΔ minⁿᵒⁿⁿ] επι ΠΣΦ al minᵖˡ | επι προσκεφαλαιου D 131 | εγειρουσιν אB*
C*ΔΠ minᵖᵃᵘᶜ] διεγειρουσιν AB²C²LΠ²ΣΦ al minᵖˡ διεγειραντες (om και sq) D 28 69
604 2ᵖᵉ εγειραντες 13 69 alᵖᵃᵘᶜ

cf. G. A. Smith, *H. G.* p. 441 f. For
λαῖλαψ see Ps. liv. (lv.) 9, Aq. (=LXX.,
καταιγίς), Job xxi. 18, Sir. xlviii. 9
(סְעָרָה), Jer. xxxii. 18 = xxv. 32
(סַעַר), 2 Pet. ii. 17.

καὶ τὰ κύματα ἐπέβαλλεν κτλ.] 'The
waves came crowding up into the
boat.' For various uses of ἐπιβάλλειν
intrans. cf. Tob. vi. 11, Judith xi. 12,
1 Macc. iv. 2, 2 Macc. iii. 3, Mc. xiv.
72, Lc. xv. 12 : of classical exx.
Plat. *Phaedr.* 248 A comes fairly
near to the sense of the present context : ξυμπεριφέρονται πατοῦσαι ἀλλήλας καὶ ἐπιβάλλουσαι. If we follow
these analogies εἰς is not 'against,'
but 'so as to enter'; the point is not
the violence of the waves, but the
filling of the boat.

ὥστε ἤδη γεμίζεσθαι] Mt. ὥστε...
καλύπτεσθαι, Lc. συνεπληροῦντο, adding καὶ ἐκινδύνευον (Jon. i. 4). For
γεμίζεσθαι cf. Lc. xiv. 23, Apoc. xv. 8.

38. *καὶ αὐτὸς...προσκεφάλαιον*] Peculiar to Mark ; the other Synoptists
notice only that He slept (Mt. ἐκάθευδεν,
Lc. ἀφύπνωσεν). Comp. Jon. i. 5, 'Ιωνᾶς
δὲ κατέβη εἰς τὴν κοίλην τοῦ πλοίου καὶ
ἐκάθευδεν. Our Lord's work for the
day was done; the navigation belonged
to others, and He took the opportunity of repose. He was in the stern
(Acts xxvii. 29, 41), where He would
not interfere with the working of the
ship, on the head-rest—προσκεφάλαιον,

properly a pillow (πρὸς κεφαλῆς, Gen.
xxviii. 11, 1 Regn. xxvi. 11 ff., 1 Esdr.
iii. 8, Ezech. xiii. 18, 20), here possibly
a rower's cushion (see Smith, *Ship-
wreck*, p. 126 ff.) ; the art. indicates
that there was but one on board, or
in that part of the boat. According
to the later Greek interpreters, it was
merely a wooden head-rest (Thpht.
ξύλινον δὲ πάντως ἦν τοῦτο), possibly
a stage or platform ; cf. Macgregor,
*Rob Roy on the Jordan*⁴, p. 321.
See however Hesychius *ad v.*: τὸ
δερμάτινον ὑπηρέσιον ἐφ᾽ ᾧ καθέζονται
οἱ ἐρέσσοντες. Sleep is attributed to
our Lord in this context only ; but it
is probably implied in i. 35, and in
passages which describe His vigils as
if they were exceptional. The fact
that He slept is rightly regarded by
Leo M. (*ad Flav.*) as fatal to a
Eutychian view of His Person : "dor-
mire evidenter humanum est." Yet,
as Ambrose says (*in Lc.*), "exprimitur
securitas potestatis quod...solus in-
trepidus quiescebat." On αὐτός see
WM., p. 187.

διδάσκαλε] Mt. κύριε, Lc. ἐπιστάτα
—all probably = Rabbi, cf. Mt. xvii. 4
with Mc. ix. 5, Lc. ix. 33, and Jo. i.
39. The touch of natural resentment
at His seeming neglect which is seen
in Mc.'s οὐ μέλει σοι, disappears in Mt.
and Lc. For the phrase see Tob. x.
5, Lc. x. 40.

διεγερθεὶς ἐπετίμησεν τῷ ἀνέμῳ καὶ εἶπεν τῇ θαλάσσῃ Cιώπα, πεφίμωσο. καὶ ἐκόπασεν ὁ ἄνεμος,
§ a 40 καὶ ἐγένετο γαλήνη μεγάλη. ⁴⁰§καὶ εἶπεν αὐτοῖς Τί
41 δειλοί ἐστε; οὔπω ἔχετε πίστιν; ⁴¹καὶ ἐφοβήθησαν

39 εγερθεις D 28 69 604 2ᵖᵉ alᵖᵃᵘᶜ | και ειπεν τη θαλ.] και τη θαλ. και ειπεν D 1 118
131 209 604 b c e ff i q arm | πεφιμωσο] και φιμωθητι D   40 εστε]+ουτως ΑΣΠΣΦ
al minᶠᵉʳᵉᵒᵐⁿ syrr arm go (om אBDLΔ 2ᵖᵉ latt me aeth) | ουπω אBDLΔ minᵖᵃᵘᶜ
lattᵛᵗᵖˡᵛᵍ arm me aeth] πως ουκ ΑΣΠΣΦ al 33 alᵖˡ f syrr go

39. διεγερθεὶς κτλ.] They had no
need to repeat their cry; it had the
effect of fully arousing Him. From
Wycliffe onwards the English versions
follow the Vg. exsurgens, "He rose
up," or "He arose"; R.V. rightly, "He
awoke." The rebuking of the wind
and sea presents a striking analogy to
that of the unclean spirit in i. 25.
The Sea is personified (cf. Ps. cv.
(cvi.) 9), or perhaps regarded as the
instrument of adverse powers ; but
comp. xi. 14, 23, for exx. of dramatic
commands to inanimate objects. Mc.
alone gives the words of the rebuke :
πεφίμωσο (Wycliffe, "wexe doumb"),
be still and continue so (WM., p.
395 f.), stronger than φιμώθητι (i. 25).

καὶ ἐκόπασεν κτλ.] Κοπάζειν is used
of water in repose after a storm or a
flood, Gen. viii. 1 ff., Jon. i. 11, 12 ; of
fire, Num. xi. 2 ; of wind again in Mc.
vi. 51. The wind, as if weary of a
fruitless struggle, "sank to rest," and
the result was (ἐγένετο) a "great
calm" : the little lake rapidly settled
down again into its normal state of
repose. Γαλήνη in Biblical Greek occurs only in this context and in Ps.
cvi. (cvii.) 29, Symm.

40. τί δειλοί ἐστε ;] Mt. with less
probability makes the rebuke precede
the stilling of the storm. In classical
Greek δειλία is the extreme opposite
of θρασύτης, the mean being ἀνδρεία
(see Trench, syn. § x.). The δειλός is
the man who lacks physical or moral
courage and therefore fails to do his
duty in danger : Arist. rhet. i. 9, ἀν-

δρεία δέ, δι᾽ ἣν πρακτικοί εἰσι τῶν καλῶν
ἔργων ἐν τοῖς κινδύνοις—δειλία δὲ τοὐναν-
τίον. Jewish ethical writers connect
δειλία with an evil conscience (Sap.
iv. 20, xvii. 11). In the N. T. a new
element enters into the conception ;
δειλία is connected with ὀλιγοπιστία
(Mt. here) and ἀπιστία (Apoc. xxi. 8) ;
it is excluded by πίστις. Thus it
becomes a sin of the first rank, for
which the δεύτερος θάνατος is reserved.
Hence the warning now, and again
before the end (Jo. xiv. 27). The
πνεῦμα δειλίας is not of God (2 Tim.
i. 7) ; it is the opposite of the πνεῦμα
δυνάμεως which was in Christ, and
comes of faith.

οὔπω ἔχετε πίστιν ;] Not yet, after
months of discipleship. Comp. viii.
17, Jo. xiv. 9, Heb. vi. 12. Faith in
its fulness (Mt. viii. 26) was still
wanting to them ; or as Lc. puts the
matter, if they had faith, it was not
ready at hand for use in time of need
(ποῦ ἡ πίστις ὑμῶν ;). This is the first
of a series of censures on the Apostles
for their lack of faith or understanding ; see vii. 18, viii. 17, 21, 33, ix. 19,
[xvi. 14], Mt. xiv. 31, xvi. 8, xvii. 20.

41. ἐφοβήθησαν φόβον μέγαν] An
awe of the Presence of Christ generi-
cally different from the fear which
sprang from want of faith in Him
—indeed its direct opposite. This
miracle came home to the Apostles
above any that they had witnessed.
It touched them personally : they had
been delivered by it from imminent
peril. It appealed to them as men

φόβον μέγαν, καὶ ἔλεγον πρὸς ἀλλήλους⁋ Τίς ἄρα   ⁋ a
οὗτός ἐστιν, ὅτι καὶ ὁ ἄνεμος καὶ ἡ θάλασσα §ὑπα-   § syrˢⁱⁿ
κούει αὐτῷ;

¹Καὶ ἦλθον εἰς τὸ πέραν τῆς θαλάσσης εἰς τὴν ι **5**.
χώραν τῶν Γερασηνῶν.⁋ ²καὶ ἐξελθόντος αὐτοῦ ἐκ 2 ⁋ Wˢ

41 ο ανεμος] οι ανεμοι אᶜ·ᵃDE 1 33 131 1071 alⁿᵒⁿⁿ b c f i q me aeth | υπακουει
αυτω אᶜBL] αυτω υπακουει א*CΔ 1 13 28 69 alᵖᵃᵘᶜ υπακουουσιν αυτω ΑΠΣΦ al minᵖˡ
b c d e f vg arm me go υπακουουσιν D   V ι ηλθεν CGLMΔ | θαλασσης] λιμνης
604 | Γερασηνων א*BD latt] Γαδαρηνων ΑCΠΣΦ al minᵖˡ syrrᵖᵉˢʰ ʰᶜˡ (txt) go Γεργεσηνων
אᶜ·ᵃLUΔ 1 28 33 604 107·1 alⁿᵒⁿⁿ syrrˢⁱⁿ ʰᶜˡ (mg) arm aeth Or   2 εξελθοντος αυτου
אBCLΔ 1 13 69 604 alᵖᵃᵘᶜ b f syrr arm me aeth] εξελθοντι αυτω ΑΠΣΦ al minᵖˡ
g i q vg go εξελθοντων αυτων D c e ff

used to the navigation of the Lake. Thus it threw a new and aweful light on the Person with Whom they daily associated. For φοβεῖσθαι φόβον μέγαν (cogn. acc., WM., p. 281) comp. Jon. i. 10, 1 Pet. iii. 6, 14 (Isa. viii. 12).
ἔλεγον πρὸς ἀλλήλους κτλ.] To Him they said nothing, their awe kept them silent (cf. Jo. xxi. 12). But as they worked the ship while He perhaps was resting again, the question went round τίς ἄρα οὗτός ἐστιν (Mc. Lc.)= ποταπός ἐστιν Mt. Ἄρα is illative; 'in view of what we have just witnessed, what can we say of Him?' Cf. Mt. xviii. 1, xix. 25 ; Lc. i. 66, and see WM., p. 556. Wycliffe, "who, gessist thou, is this?" Τίς...ὅτι, cf. Blass, *Gr.* p. 293 n.
καὶ ὁ ἄνεμος καὶ ἡ θάλασσα] Not only the demons (i. 27), but, what to these sea-going men was a greater marvel, the wind and the sea. For a promise of the further extension of this power of Christ over the creation see 1 Cor. xv. 25 ff., Heb. ii. 5 ff.
An exquisite homiletical treatment of the story may be found in Aug. *serm.* 63 : "audisti convicium, ventus est; iratus es, fluctus est...periclitatur navis, periclitatur cor tuum...oblitus es Christum ; excita ergo Christum, recordare Christum, evigilet in te Christus, considera illum...imperavit Christus mari, facta est tranquillitas.

quod autem dixi ad iracundiam, hoc tenete regulariter in omnibus tentationibus vestris."
V. 1—13. CASTING OUT OF THE LEGION (Mt. viii. 28—32, Lc. viii. 26—33).
1. ἦλθον εἰς κτλ.] Lc. recasts the whole sentence : κατέπλευσαν εἰς τὴν χ. τῶν Γερ., ἥτις ἐστὶν ἀντίπερα τῆς Γαλειλαίας. They reached the land of the Gerasenes right over against the Galilean shore. For τὸ πέραν see iv. 35.
τῶν Γερασηνῶν] So Lc. In Mt. Γαδαρηνῶν is the best attested reading. The 'Western' text substitutes Γερασηνῶν for Γαδ. in Mt., the 'Syrian' on the other hand changes Γερασηνῶν into Γαδ. in Mc. and Lc. ; whilst the 'Alexandrian' text reads Γεργεσηνῶν in all three : see WH., *Notes*, p. 11. Origen (*in Ioann.*, t. vi. 41) supports Γεργ. on purely internal grounds : Γέρασα δὲ τῆς Ἀραβίας ἐστὶ πόλις οὔτε θάλασσαν οὔτε λίμνην πλησίον ἔχουσα... Γάδαρα γὰρ πόλις μέν ἐστι τῆς Ἰουδαίας ...ἀλλὰ Γέργεσα ἀφ' ἧς οἱ Γεργεσαῖοι πόλις ἀρχαία περὶ τὴν νῦν καλουμένην Τιβεριάδα λίμνην περὶ ἣν κρημνὸς προσκείμενος τῇ λίμνῃ (cf. t. x. 12 (10)). Jerome, who like Origen knew Palestine, bears witness to the existence of a Gergesa on the E. shore of the lake (*de situ*, p. 130: "et hodieque super montem viculus demonstratur iuxta

τοῦ πλοίου [εὐθὺς] ὑπήντησεν αὐτῷ ἐκ τῶν μνημείων
3 ἄνθρωπος ἐν πνεύματι ἀκαθάρτῳ, ³ὃς τὴν κατοίκησιν εἶχεν ἐν τοῖς μνήμασιν, καὶ οὐδὲ ἁλύσει οὐκέτι

2 om ευθυς B b c e ff i syrr^sin pesh hcl arm | απηντησεν ΑΠΣΦ al min^pl   3 μνημειοις
DH min^mu | ουδε אBCDLΔ 33 2^pe] ουτε ΑΠΣΦ al min^pl | αλυσει BC*L 33 2^pe c e]
αλυσεσιν אAC²DΔΠΦ al min^pl b f ff i l q vg syrr arm me go aeth ουτε αλυσεσιν ουτε
πεδες 1071 | om ουκετι AC²ΠΣΦ al min^pl i q syrr me go aeth

stagnum Tiberiadis"). Almost directly
opposite to Mejdel on the Ghuweir are
the ruins now known as *Kersa* (Wilson,
Recovery of Jerusalem, p. 369) or
Kursi: the nature of the place answers
fairly well to the description in *vv.* 11 ff.
where see note; comp. Thomson, *Land
and the Book*, pp. 374 f. But the Arabic
name, which means a 'stool,' may be
merely descriptive (Schumacher, *Jaulân*, p. 179); and there seem to be philo-
logical difficulties in the way of an identification of *Kursi* with either Gerasa or
Gergesa. The Decapolitan city Gerasa,
Jerash (Joseph. *B.J.* i. 4. 8, iii. 3), was
thirty miles to the S.E., and, as Origen
saw, impossible (see however Burkitt in
J.B.L. xxvii. ii. (1908)). On the other
hand the neighbourhood of the lake-
side Gerasa might perhaps be loosely
described as Gadarene territory; Gadara, *Um Keis* (Joseph. *B.J.* iv. 7),
was but 6 miles S.E. of the southern
extremity of the Lake, and Josephus
(*vit.* 9, 10) mentions Γαδαρηνῶν καὶ
Ἱππηνῶν κώμας αἳ δὴ μεθόριοι τῆς Τιβεριάδος...ἐτύγχανον κείμεναι.

2. ἐξελθόντος...εὐθύς κτλ.] The
Lord had but just landed (Lc. ἐπὶ τὴν
γῆν) when the incident occurred. Ὑπαν-
τᾶν is common to Mt., Mc., Lc.; for ἐκ
τῶν μνημείων Lc. has ἐκ τῆς πόλεως,
but apparently in the sense of 'belonging to the town,' for he agrees
with Mt. that the man had his residence in the tombs. "There do not
appear to be any rock-hewn tombs
near Kersa; but the demoniac may
possibly have lived in one of those
tombs built above ground" which
were "much more common in Galilee

than has been supposed" (Wilson,
l.c.). Μνημεῖον is used of both, see
Mt. xxvii. 60, Lc. xi. 47.

ἄνθρωπος ἐν πνεύματι ἀκαθάρτῳ] Ἐν =
in the sphere of, under the influence
of: see note on i. 23. Mt. δύο δαιμονιζόμενοι, cf. δύο τυφλοί, Mt. xx. 30,
where Mc. and Lc. mention one only.
As Victor remarks, τοῦτο οὐ διαφωνίαν
ἐμφαίνει, since the mention of one demoniac does not exclude the presence
of a second, unless it is expressly stated
that he was alone: still it indicates
either a distinct or a blurred tradition. Mc.'s description is too minute
in other respects to permit us to
suppose that it is defective here.

3. τὴν κατοίκησιν εἶχεν ἐν τοῖς μν.]
Vg. *domicilium habebat in monu-
mentis.* On the practice of haunting
sepulchral chambers see Ps. lxvii.
(lxviii.) 7, LXX. τοὺς κατοικοῦντας ἐν
τάφοις, Isa. lxv. 4 ἐν τοῖς μνήμασιν...
κοιμῶνται. Κατοίκησις is an ἅπ. λεγ.
in the N.T.; in the LXX. it is fairly
distributed (=מוֹשָׁב), together with
the non-classical κατοικεσία. Μνῆμα
and μνημεῖον are used with nearly
equal frequency in the LXX.; in the N.T.
μνῆμα is relatively rare (Mc.¹ Lc.^ev. 3, act. 2,
Apoc.¹, against about 40 exx. of μνημεῖον).

3—4. καὶ οὐδὲ ἁλύσει κτλ.] Not
even (οὐδέ) fetters availed any longer
(οὐκέτι); the malady had grown upon
him to such an extent that coercive
measures were now fruitless. Διὰ τὸ
αὐτὸν...συντετρίφθαι: reason for the
statement just made: 'since the ex-
periment had often been made and
proved futile.' Διὰ with the inf. here

οὐδεὶς ἐδύνατο αὐτὸν δῆσαι, ⁴διὰ τὸ αὐτὸν πολλάκις 4
πέδαις καὶ ἁλύσεσι δεδέσθαι, καὶ διεσπάσθαι ὑπ᾽
αὐτοῦ τὰς ἁλύσεις καὶ τὰς πέδας συντετρίφθαι, καὶ
οὐδεὶς ἴσχυεν αὐτὸν δαμάσαι. ⁵καὶ διὰ παντὸς 5
νυκτὸς καὶ ἡμέρας ἐν τοῖς μνήμασιν καὶ ἐν τοῖς ὄρεσιν
ἦν κράζων καὶ κατακόπτων ἑαυτὸν λίθοις. ⁶καὶ 6

3 εδυνατο] ετολμα M   4 δια το...συντετριφθαι] οτι πολλακις αυτον δεδεμενον
πεδες και αλυσεσιν εν αις εδησαν διεσπακεναι και τας πεδας συντετριφεναι D (sim ff i q
vg) δια το αυτον πολλας πεδας και αλυσεις (hucusque syrˢⁱⁿ) αις εδησαν αυτον διεσπακεναι
και συντετριφεναι 1 28 131 209 (604) alˢⁿᵗᵐᵘ δια το πολλ. αυτ. πεδαις και αλυσεσιν αις
εδησαν διεσπακεναι και τας πεδας σιντετριφθεναι 2ᵖᵉ | και μηδενα αυτον ισχυιν δαμασαι
D 604 | δαμασαι] δησαι A om ℵ* (hab ℵᶜ·ᵃ)   5 και δια παντος νυκτος] νυκτος δε
D b c e ff i q κ. δια πασης ν. 604 | εν τοις ορεσιν και εν τοις μνημειοις D (b e i q) | κραζων]
κραζον D κραυγαζων 69 124 225 346 | εαυτον] αυτον D

"expresses the evidence rather than the cause" (Burton, § 408). Πέδαις καὶ ἁλύσεσι, Vg. compedibus et catenis, with fetters and manacles; Wycliffe, "in stockis and cheynes"; cf. Ps. civ. (cv.) 18, 3 Macc. iv. 9, Acts xii. 7, and Lightfoot, Philippians, p. 8: Horace, ep. i. 16, 76 "in manicis et | compedibus saevo te sub custode tenebo." The perfects δεδέσθαι, διεσπάσθαι, συντετρίφθαι refer to actions "whose result was existing not at the time of speaking, but at an earlier time" (Burton, § 108). It is as if the writer's imagination had caught the words of the neighbours as they told the tale of their repeated failures (οὐ δυνάμεθα αὐτὸν δῆσαι, πολλάκις γὰρ δέδεται κτλ.), and he had embodied them without a change of tense. The scene reminds the reader of Samson, Jud. xvi. 8, 9, ἔδησεν αὐτὸν...καὶ διέσπασεν τὰς νευρέας (διέρρηξεν, A; cf. Lc., v. 29, διαρήσσων τὰ δεσμά). Διασπᾶσθαι is more than 'to be torn apart,' rather 'torn to shreds': cf. Jud. xvi. 9, Jer. x. 20, Acts xxiii. 10; συντρίβεσθαι is 'to be crushed' or 'broken into pieces,' like glass or pottery or a bone; cf. Mc. xiv. 3, Jo. xix. 36, Apoc. ii. 27.

4. καὶ οὐδεὶς ἴσχυεν αὐτὸν δαμάσαι] In its logical connexion the clause

belongs to the evidence introduced by διά, so that we should expect καὶ μηδένα ἰσχύειν. Mc. however reverts to the ind. imperf. of v. 3. On ἰσχύειν=δύνασθαι see Field, Notes, p. 26 f. Δαμάζειν is used properly of wild animals: see however James iii. 7, 8, with Mayor's note. Even iron ὁ δαμάζων πάντα (Dan. ii. 40, LXX.) failed in the present case.

5. νυκτὸς καὶ ἡμέρας] I.e. at intervals during the night and the day (see note on iv. 27); yet without any long intermission—practically διὰ παντός, cf. Deut. xxxiii. 10, Lc. xxiv. 53, Heb. ix. 6.

ἐν τοῖς ὄρεσιν] At times he left the shelter of the tombs for the open downs, and his cry was heard among the hills.

κράζων καὶ κατακόπτων ἑαυτόν] For κράζειν used of demoniacs or the possessing spirits see i. 26, iii. 11, ix. 26. St Paul transfers it to the domain of the Spirit of God, Rom. viii. 15, Gal. iv. 6. The word suggests strong emotion, which may be either good or evil. For κατακόπτειν, Vg. concidere, to cut to pieces (here only in N.T.) cf. 2 Chron. xxxiv. 7 (κ. λεπτά), Jer. xxi. 7 (κ. ἐν στόματι μαχαίρας); his body may in this way have been gashed and scarred all over, for (Lc.) χρόνῳ

ἰδὼν τὸν Ἰησοῦν ἀπὸ μακρόθεν ἔδραμεν καὶ προσε-
7 κύνησεν αὐτόν, ⁷καὶ κράξας φωνῇ μεγάλῃ λέγει Τί
ἐμοὶ καὶ σοί, Ἰησοῦ, υἱὲ τοῦ θεοῦ τοῦ ὑψίστου;
§ a 8 ὁρκίζω σε τὸν θεόν, μή με §βασανίσῃς. ⁸ἔλεγεν γὰρ

6 om απο AKLMΠΣΦ min^nonn | προσεκυνησεν] προσεπεσεν F | αυτων ABCLΔ
min^pauc] αυτω NDΠΣΦ min^nonn   7 λεγει] ειπεν D al min^pl | υψιστου] ζωντος A
syr^hcl(mg)   8 ελεγεν γαρ] και ελεγεν N

ἱκανῷ οὐκ ἐνεδύσατο ἱμάτιον. Field
(*Notes*, p. 27) defends the Wycliffite
rendering "betynge hymsilf," quoting
Chrysostom for this use of κατακόπτειν; but λίθοις seems to determine
its meaning in this context; cf.
Syrr.^sin. pesh. Mt. adds that the man
was a source of danger to passers by,
so that people avoided that way (i.e.
apparently the way from the shore
over the hills). At times a paroxysm
seized him (Lc. συνηρπάκει αὐτόν,
ἠλαύνετο ἀπὸ τοῦ δαιμονίου), and then
he was at his worst. Nevertheless
the man did not attempt suicide;
"servatus est homo ne, ut porci, in
mare se praecipitaret" (Bengel).

6. καὶ ἰδών κτλ.] Ἀπὸ μακρόθεν
(WM., p. 753 f.) occurs again viii. 3,
xi. 13, xiv. 54, xv. 40, "ein dem Mark.
besonders beliebter Pleonasmus"
(Meyer-Weiss); it occurs also Mt.²,
Lc.², Apoc.³, and is fairly common in
the LXX.; cf. 4 Regn. xix. 25, A; 2 Esdr.
iii. 13, xxii. 43, Ps. xxxvii. (xxxviii.)
12 (N^c.a.ART), cxxxvii. (cxxxviii.) 6,
cxxxviii. (cxxxix.) 2 : Aq. has εἰς ἀπὸ
μ., 4 Regn. xix. 25. Μακρόθεν itself
is a late Greek equivalent for πόρρωθεν (Blass, *Gr*. p. 59). Ἔδραμεν—at
first perhaps with hostile intentions.
The onrush of the naked yelling
maniac must have tried the newly
recovered confidence of the Twelve.
We can imagine their surprise when,
on approaching, he threw himself on
his knees; comp. iii. 11, τὰ πνεύματα...
προσέπιπτον. Προσκυνεῖν is rarely
used in the Gospels in reference to
these acts of prostration exc. in Mt.

(only here and Mc. xv. 19, Lc. xxiv.
52, Jo. ix. 38).

7. καὶ κράξας] Lc. ἀνακράξας (cf.
Mc. i. 23). The words of the cry
begin as in Mc. *l.c.* (where see note)
by repudiating fellowship and intercourse (τί ἐμοὶ καὶ σοί;). With υἱὲ
τοῦ θεοῦ cf. ὁ ἅγιος τοῦ θεοῦ in the
earlier incident. Τοῦ ὑψίστου, not in
Mt., but probably original; ὁ ὕψιστος or (as a proper name) Ὕψιστος
=עֶלְיוֹן אֵל or עֶלְיוֹן, in LXX. frequently
from Gen. xiv. 18, 19 onwards: in
the N.T. it occurs only in passages
with an O.T. ring, Lc. i. 32, 35, 76;
vi. 35, viii. 28, Heb. vii. 1 (where see
Westcott's note), or in sayings attributed to the possessed (here, and
in Acts xvi. 17). This name, which
Israel used in common with other
monotheists and even pagans, seems
to have been displaced in Christian
Gentile circles by words which gave a
fuller view of GOD as revealed in
Christ—Κύριος, θεός, ὁ πατήρ.

μή με βασανίσῃς] Mt. ἦλθες ὧδε
πρὸ καιροῦ βασανίσαι ἡμᾶς; a remarkable variation which has the air
of originality. The unclean spirits recognise that βασανισμός awaits them;
it is only a question of time; cf. *Act.
Thom.* § 42, τοῦ καιροῦ ἡμῶν μηδέπω
ἐνεστῶτος... and on καιρός see Mc. i.
15 note. The ill-sounding words βά-
σανος βασανίζω βασανισμός meet the
reader constantly in the Books of the
Maccabees in descriptions of physical
torture; in Wisdom they are used in
reference to the plagues of Egypt
(Sap. xi. 9, xii. 23, &c.). The N.T.

αὐτῷ Ἔξελθε, τὸ πνεῦμα τὸ ἀκάθαρτον, ἐκ τοῦ
ἀνθρώπου. ⁹καὶ ἐπηρώτα αὐτόν Τί ὄνομά σοι ; καὶ 9
λέγει αὐτῷ Λεγιὼν ὄνομά μοι [ἐστίν],¶ §ὅτι πολλοί   ¶ a
ἐσμεν. ¹⁰καὶ παρεκάλει αὐτὸν πολλὰ ἵνα μὴ αὐτὰ 10   § ¶¹⁰
ἀποστείλῃ ἔξω τῆς χώρας. ¹¹ἦν δὲ ἐκεῖ πρὸς τῷ 11

8 εκ] απο A 33 alᵖᵃᵘᶜ f i q vg   9 τι σοι ον. εστιν D latt Orⁱⁿᵗ | λεγει αυτω]
απεκριθη λεγων EFGHSUVIIᵐᵍ minᵖˡ | λεγιων ℵ*B*CDLΔ latt syrr me] λεγεων
(ℵᶜ)AB²ΠΣΦ al minᶠᵒʳᵗᵉ ᵒᵐⁿ | μοι]+εστιν B(D) 69 124 238 346 latᵛᵗ ᵖˡ ᵛᵍ arm
10 παρεκαλει ℵBCDLΠΣΦ minᵖˡ b e f i q vg go] παρεκαλουν AΔ⅂ 1 28 2ᵖᵉ alᵖᵃᵘᶜ
c ff syrˢⁱⁿ arm go+οι δαιμονες syrˢⁱⁿ | αυτα BCΔ] αυτους DEFGHSUVΣΦ⅂ αυτον ℵ
KLII minᵖᵃᵘᶜ b e syrᵖᵉˢʰ aeth   11 προς τα ορη (ⴔ) minᵖᵃᵘᶜ ᵛⁱᵈ

tranfers them to the spiritual consequences of sin : cf. Mt. xviii. 34, Lc.
xvi. 23, Apoc. xx. 10. Mc. alone retains the form of adjuration which
accompanied this despairing appeal.
Ὁρκίζειν τινὰ κατὰ Κυρίου (τοῦ θεοῦ) is
the lxx. form (3 Regn. ii. 43, cf. Mt.
xxvi. 63), but the present construction
occurs again in Acts xix. 13, 1 Thess.
v. 27 ; cf. ὁρκίζω σε…τὸν θεὸν τοῦ
Ἀβραάν κτλ. in the long Jewish in-
cantation printed by Deissmann, Bibelstudien, p. 28 ff. (= E. Tr. p. 274 ff.).

8. ἔλεγεν γάρ κτλ.] 'He had been
saying'; cf. Burton, § 29. The command probably followed the words τί
ἐμοὶ…ὑψίστου; With ἔξελθε cf. i. 25,
ix. 25. Τὸ πν. τὸ ἀκάθ., nom. for vocative ; see WM., p. 227 f. and Blass,
Gr. p. 86 f.

9. καὶ ἐπηρώτα] Lc. ἐπηρώτησεν.
The imperfect carries on the narrative of the conversation. The question is probably a reply to the appeal
μή με βασανίσῃς. Who was the suppliant ? was it the man or his op-
pressor ? This was the first point to
be determined. Αὐτόν, cf. Euth. : τὸν
ἄνθρωπον μὲν ἐπηρώτα· πρὸς τὸ πλῆθος
δὲ τῶν ἐν αὐτῷ δαιμόνων διέβαινεν ἡ
ἐρώτησις.

Λεγιὼν ὄνομά μοι κτλ.] Legio made
its way not only into the later Greek,
both Hellenistic and literary (Plutarch, i. 1072, Mt. xxvi. 53), but probably into the Aramaic of Palestine ;

it is found in Rabbinical writings
(לגיון, pl. לגיונין, Dalman, Gr., p. 149)
and in early Aramaic inscriptions
(S. A. Cook, Glossary, p. 67 s.v. לגיונא),
and it survives in Lejjun, the modern
name of a site usually identified with
Megiddo (G. A. Smith, H.G. pp. 386,
407). To a Palestinian of our Lord's
time the name would connote not only
vast numbers—the strength of the
legion often reached 5000 to 6000
men (Marquardt, ii. 389, 441)—and
submission to a superior will (Bengel :
"uni parebant ut legio imperatori");
but the miseries of a military occupation by a foreign power (on the
history of the Roman legion in Syria
see Schürer II. i. p. 50 ff.); even such
small bodies of irregular troops as
served under Herod Antipas and
Philip knew how to harass and plun-
der (Lc. iii. 14). For other exx. of
possession by more than one unclean
spirit cf. 'Mc.' xvi. 9, Lc. xi. 26 ; cf.
Tertull. anim. 25, "septenarii spiritus,
ut in Magdalena, et legionarii numeri,
ut in Geraseno."

10. παρεκάλει αὐτὸν πολλά] The
sing. is used because the spirits,
speaking by the voice of the man, are
still regarded as a single ego; the imperfect implies repetition. Πολλά, Vg.
multum, cf. i. 45, vi. 20; 80 μακρά
Mc. xii. 40, πυκνά Lc. v. 33.

ἔξω τῆς χώρας] Vg. extra regionem,

12 ὄρει ἀγέλη χοίρων μεγάλη βοσκομένη· ¹²καὶ παρε-
§ a κάλεσαν §αὐτὸν λέγοντες Πέμψον ἡμᾶς εἰς τοὺς
13 χοίρους, ἵνα εἰς αὐτοὺς εἰσέλθωμεν. ¹³καὶ ἐπέτρεψεν
αὐτοῖς. καὶ ἐξελθόντα τὰ πνεύματα τὰ ἀκάθαρτα

11 om μεγαλη DLU˥ minᵖᵃᵘᶜ b e ff i go | βοσκομενων אᶜ·ᵃALΔ minᵖᵃᵘᶜ b d q
12 παρεκαλεσαν אBCLΔΠᵐᵍΣΦ˥ 1 28 alᵖˡ c go syrʰᶜˡ] παρεκαλουν ADKMΠᵗˣᵗ minⁿᵒⁿⁿ
b f ff i q vg | αυτον]+παντες οι δαιμονες AEFGHSUVIIᵐᵍΣΦ˥ a syrʰᶜˡ arm+οι δαιμονες
KMΠᵗˣᵗ minⁿᵒⁿⁿ b c ff i q vg syrˢⁱⁿ ᵖᵉˢʰ+παντα τα δαιμονια 604 2ᵖᵉ+τα δαιμονια D e f |
λεγοντα D | απελθωμεν D   13 και επετρ. αυτοις]+ευθεως ΑΠΣ (Φ˥ ευθ. ο ι̅σ̅) al
minᵖˡ f vg και ευθεως κ̅σ̅ ι̅η̅σ̅ επεμψεν αυτους εις τους χοιρους D και ο Ι. επεμψεν
αυτους 604 2ᵖᶜ

sc. τῶν Γερασηνῶν. Lc. has the remarkable variation εἰς τὴν ἄβυσσον, which may have the double meaning, (1) "into the depths of the sea" (so ἄβυσσος is frequently used in the LXX., cf. e.g. Isa. lxiii. 13); (2) into the place of punishment (Apoc. ix. 1, &c.). An attempt has been made (*Exp.* IV. iv. p. 377) to treat these two versions of the demoniac's words as renderings of nearly identical Aramaic; but it is probably safer to regard Lc.'s phrase as interpretative. The man feared nothing worse than expulsion from his native hills; the spirits dreaded a graver punishment. Bede: "hostis humanae salutis non exiguum sibi ducit esse tormentum ab hominis laesione cessare."

11. ἦν δὲ ἐκεῖ κτλ.] Within sight, but (Mt.) at some distance. The herd was a large one (μεγάλη Mc., cf. πολλῶν Mt., ἱκανῶν Lc.), numbering ὡς δισχίλιοι (Mc. only). Πρὸς τῷ ὄρει: 'at,' on the side of the mountain, cf. Lc. xix. 37 πρὸς τῇ καταβάσει τοῦ ὄρους—a construction more frequent in the LXX. than in the N.T. (WM., p. 493).

ἀγέλη χοίρων μεγάλη] For the number see *v.* 13. The O.T. mentions ἀγέλαι προβάτων (1 Regn. xvii. 34), αἰγῶν (Cant. iv. 1, vi. 4), καμήλων (Isa. lx. 6); an ἀγ. χοίρων was perhaps hardly to be found W. of the Jordan and its lakes: even the word χοῖρος is unknown to the LXX. who use ὗς in the few passages where they have oc-

casion to mention the unclean animal. On the moral difficulty which the destruction of the swine has been felt to present see Plummer, *St Luke*, p. 228 f.

βοσκομένη] For the middle voice of this verb cf. Gen. xli. 2, Job i. 14, Isa. xi. 6, etc. The swine were under the control of swineherds (οἱ βόσκοντες *v.* 14): for this class see Lc. xv. 15.

12. παρεκάλεσαν] Contrast ἐσσε παρεκάλει (*v.* 10), κράξας...λέγει (*v.* 7). The Spirits at length dissociate themselves from the man, for they know that their hold over him is at an end, and the plural is consequently used; cf. *v.* 13.

πέμψον] Mt. ἀπόστειλον: for the difference of meaning see on iii. 14. Lc. avoids both verbs (ἵνα ἐπιτρέψῃ αὐτοὺς εἰς ἐκείνους εἰσελθεῖν). The Lord's ὑπάγετε (Mt.) was permissive only: they were left free to go if they would.

13. καὶ ἐπέτρεψεν αὐτοῖς] See last note. The reading of D (εὐθέως κύριος Ἰησοῦς ἔπεμψεν αὐτοὺς εἰς τοὺς χοίρους) loses sight of an important distinction. The permission shewed how completely the spirits were subject to His will: Clem. *Hom.* xix. 14, ὡς μηδὲ τοῦ εἰς χοίρους εἰσελθεῖν ἄνευ τῆς αὐτοῦ συγχωρήσεως ἐξουσίαν ἔχοντες. Cf. Tertull. *fug.* 2: "nec in porcorum gregem diaboli legio habuit potestatem nisi eam de Deo impetrasset," and Thpht. *ad loc.*

καὶ ἐξελθόντα κτλ.] Ἐξελθεῖν and εἰσελθεῖν are regularly used in refer-

εἰσῆλθον εἰς τοὺς χοίρους, καὶ ὥρμησεν ἡ ἀγέλη κατὰ
τοῦ κρημνοῦ εἰς τὴν θάλασσαν, ὡς δισχίλιοι, καὶ
ἐπνίγοντο ἐν τῇ θαλάσσῃ.

¹⁴Καὶ οἱ βόσκοντες αὐτοὺς ἔφυγον¶ §καὶ ἀπήγ- 14 ¶ a
γειλαν εἰς τὴν πόλιν καὶ εἰς τοὺς ἀγρούς· καὶ ἦλθον   §Θᵇ

---

13 αγελη]+πασα 1071 | ως δισχιλιοι] ως ͵β (ras 1 lit ante ͵β Bʔ) B ως χιλιοι H pr
ησαν δε AC²ΠΡΦ⅂ al minᵖˡ a f i l (arm) go pr ησαν γαρ minᵖᵃᵘᶜ syrʰᶜˡ   14 αυτους]
τους χοιρους ΑΠ alᵖˡ syrʰᶜˡ arm go | ανηγγειλαν EFGHSUVΔ alᵖˡ | ηλθον ℵᶜ·ᵃ
ABKLMUΠ*ΣΦ⅂ 33 alⁿᵒⁿⁿ syrʰᶜˡ me go] εξηλθον ℵ*CDEFGHSVΔΠ² minᵖˡ
b c e f f f i vg syrˢⁱⁿ ᵖᵉˢʰ arm aeth om H alᵖᵃᵘᶜ

---

ence to possession: cf. Mc. i. 25, 26,
vii. 29, 30, Mt. xii. 43, Lc. viii. 30,
xi. 26, Jo. xiii. 27. Τὰ πνεύματα τὰ
ἀκάθαρτα, cf. τὸ πνεῦμα τὸ ἀκάθαρτον
(v. 7). The corporate unity which
resulted from their identification with
the man's personality is now lost : see
on v. 11. Εἰς τοὺς χοίρους. Patristic
writers point out the fitness of the
coincidence which brought unclean
spirits into fellowship with the most
unclean of beasts: e.g. Macarius Magnes iii. 11, οὐ προβάτων ἀγέλας οὐδ'
ἵππων οὐδὲ βοῶν λαβεῖν σπουδάζομεν,
ταῦτα γὰρ τὰ ζῷα καθαρὰ καὶ ἀμύσακτα,
ἀλλὰ χοίρων ὑπόσμων καὶ ἀτάκτων
ἄθροισμα. The moral was readily
drawn: Clem. Hom. x. 6, ἐπεὶ οὖν
ἀλόγοις ζῴοις ἐοικότα πράξαντες ἐκ τῆς
ψυχῆς ὑμῶν τὴν ἀνθρώπου ψυχὴν ἀπω-
λέσατε, ὥσπερ χοῖροι γενόμενοι δαιμόνων αἰτήματα ἐγένεσθε.

ὥρμησεν ἡ ἀγέλη κτλ.] Vg. magno
impetu grex praecipitatus est; Wycliffe, "with a great birre the flok
was cast doun." Driven to madness
by a new and sudden impulse the herd
rushed to its destruction. Ὁρμᾶν is
used of the unreasoning onrush of a
crowd, 2 Macc. ix. 2, x. 16, xii. 22,
Acts vii. 57, xix. 29. Κατὰ τοῦ κρημνοῦ, "down from the steep," WM.,
p. 477. Κρημνός = יוֹבַּ, 2 Chron.
xxv. 12. Of Kersa Schumacher (p.
180) reports : "steep precipices at a

slight distance from the Lake…are
numerous." Ὡς δισχίλιοι: the number
is given by Mc. alone. Dr Plummer
(St Luke, p. 231) remarks that it "may
be an exaggeration of the swineherds
or owners," adding, "Had the number
been an invention of the narrator,
we should have had 4000 or 5000 to
correspond with the legion."

ἐπνίγοντο] suffocati sunt, Lc. ἀπε-
πνίγη ; Mt. more vaguely, ἀπέθανον ἐν
τοῖς ὕδασιν. The word is used in 1 Regn.
xvi. 14 f. of the effect of possession
by an evil spirit.

14—17. THE GERASENES ALARMED
AND HOSTILE (Mt. viii. 33—34, Lc. viii.
34—37).

14. καὶ οἱ βόσκοντες κτλ.] The
χοιροβόσκοι fled, narrowly escaping
the fate of the herd, and reported the
matter in Gerasa and the country
places round the town (καὶ εἰς τοὺς
ἀγρούς, Mc. Lc., cf. Mc. vi. 36, 56,
xv. 21). Καὶ ἦλθον ἰδεῖν, i.e. the townsfolk and the countryside poured down
to the place where Jesus was apparently still halting by the Lake; cf. Mt.
πᾶσα ἡ πόλις ἐξῆλθεν εἰς ὑπάντησιν τῷ
Ἰησοῦ. Their immediate object was
to see what had happened (τὸ γεγονός);
but finding all quiet again, they went
down to the shore (ἔρχονται πρὸς τὸν Ἰ.
Mc., cf. Lc.) and there witnessed a
scene more remarkable than that
which the swineherds had described.

15 ἰδεῖν τί ἐστιν τὸ γεγονός. ¹⁵καὶ ἔρχονται πρὸς τὸν
Ἰησοῦν, καὶ θεωροῦσιν τὸν δαιμονιζόμενον καθήμενον
ἱματισμένον καὶ σωφρονοῦντα, τὸν ἐσχηκότα τὸν
§ Wʳ 16 λεγιῶνα· καὶ ἐφοβήθησαν. ¹⁶καὶ §διηγήσαντο αὐτοῖς
§ Wʰ οἱ ἰδόντες πῶς §ἐγένετο τῷ δαιμονιζομένῳ, καὶ περὶ

15 τον δαιμ.] pr αυτον D | om καθημενον Δ minᴾᵉʳᵖᵃᵘᶜ e | ιματισμενον] pr και
ACΠΦ⁷ al minᵖˡ q syrˢⁱⁿ ʰᶜˡ arm go (om και אBDLΔΣ) | om τον εσχηκοτα τον λεγιωνα
D minᵖᵉʳᵖᵃᵘᶜ lattᵛᵗ ᵛᵍ (ᶜᵒᵈᵈ ᵖˡᵉʳ)   16 και διηγησαντο] διηγ. δε DEFHUV alᵐᵘ
e f i q και διηγ. δε 1071 | ιδοντες] ειδοτες Δ | εγενετο τω δαιμ.] εσωθη ο δαιμονισθεις
1 209

15. θεωροῦσιν τὸν δαιμονιζόμενον
κτλ.] For θεωρεῖν cf. iii. 11, xii. 41,
xv. 40. Ὁ δαιμονιζόμενος is timeless
(see note on i. 4), the man who, as
they knew him, belonged to the class
of demoniacs: see WM., p. 444, Burton
§ 123. Contrast ὁ δαιμονισθείς (v. 18),
where the fact of the possession being
now at an end is emphasised. Καθ.,
ἱμ., σωφρ., "cum antea fuisset sine
quiete, vestibus, rationis usu" (Bengel). Καθήμενον, as a disciple (Lc. ii.
46, x. 39). Lc. adds here παρὰ τοὺς
πόδας τοῦ Ἰησοῦ, the technical phrase
for the position of the scholar (Acts
xxii. 2, cf. Schürer II. i. 326).

ἱματισμένον] Before he took his seat
among the disciples he had been
clothed (cf. Lc. viii. 27), perhaps
with a spare χιτών belonging to one
of the Twelve. Though ἱματισμός is
fairly common, the verb has not been
detected elsewhere in Greek literature, yet here it is used both by Mc.
and Lc., who also share καθήμ. and
σωφρονοῦντα—a coincidence difficult
to explain except on the hypothesis
of a common Greek tradition or document, or on that of one of the two
Evangelists having borrowed from the
other. Σωφρονεῖν is opposed to ὑπερ-
φρονεῖν (Rom. xii. 3), and ἐκστῆναι (2
Cor. v. 13); the σώφρων goes with the
νηφάλιος, the κόσμιος, the σεμνός (1
Tim. iii. 2, Tit. ii. 2), σωφροσύνη with
αἰδώς (1 Tim. ii. 9). These conceptions
however belong to a developed Chris

tian ethic; in the present passage
the word scarcely rises above its
ordinary Greek sense. Cf. Arist.
rhet. i. 9. 9 σωφροσύνη δὲ ἀρετὴ δι' ἣν
τὰς ἡδονὰς τοῦ σώματος οὕτως ἔχουσιν
ὡς ὁ νόμος κελεύει· ἀκολασία δὲ τού-
ναντίον. 4 Macc. i. 31 σωφρ. δὴ τοίνυν
ἐστὶν ἐπικράτεια τῶν ἐπιθυμιῶν. The
man was not simply sanae mentis
(Vg.), but free from the slavery of
headstrong passions, master of himself
again. Τὸν ἐσχηκότα τὸν λεγιῶνα emphasises the contrast between his present
state and that from which he had
been just set free; the words are not
in Lc. and may be an editorial note
due to Mc. For the perf. part. see
Burton, § 156; while ἱματισμένον describes a condition which belongs to
the time indicated by θεωροῦσιν, ἐσχηκότα goes back behind it, to a state
which had ceased to exist, 'who had
had the Legion'; so the MSS. of the
Vg. which retain the clause (qui
habuerat legionem). Καὶ ἐφοβήθησαν,
cf. iv. 41; both events excited the awe
which attends the supernatural.

16. καὶ διηγήσαντο κτλ.] The townsfolk turned to those who had witnessed
everything—the Twelve, and perhaps
a few bystanders—and learnt from
them the whole story. Διηγεῖσθαι (a
common equivalent of ספר in the LXX.
but relatively rare in the N.T., Mt.²
Lc.ᵉᵛ·², ᵃᶜᵗ·³ Heb.¹) well expresses the
voluminousness of the Eastern story-
teller; cf. ix. 9.

τῶν χοίρων. ¹⁷ καὶ ἤρξαντο παρακαλεῖν αὐτὸν ἀπελ- 17
θεῖν ἀπὸ τῶν ὁρίων αὐτῶν.

¹⁸ Καὶ ἐμβαίνοντος αὐτοῦ εἰς τὸ πλοῖον παρεκάλει 18
αὐτὸν ὁ δαιμονισθεὶς ἵνα μετ᾽ αὐτοῦ ᾖ. ¹⁹ καὶ οὐκ 19
ἀφῆκεν αὐτόν, ἀλλὰ λέγει αὐτῷ ῞Υπαγε εἰς τὸν οἶκόν
σου πρὸς τοὺς σούς, καὶ ἀπάγγειλον αὐτοῖς ὅσα §ὁ   § a
κύριός σοι πεποίηκεν καὶ ἠλέησέν σε.   ²⁰ καὶ ἀπῆλθεν 20

17 ηρξ. παρακαλειν] παρεκαλουν D 225 604 2ᵖᵉ a | απελθειν] ινα απελθη D | απο]
εκ Δ   18 εμβαινοντος אABCDKLMΔΠΣ⸆ 1 33 124 alⁿᵒⁿⁿ] εμβαντος EFGHSUVΦ
minᵖˡ | παρεκαλει] ηρξατο παρακαλειν D lattᵛᵗᵖˡ ᵛᵍ   19 και 1° אABCKLMΔΠ 1 33
f l vg syrᵖᵉˢʰ ʰᶜˡ me go] και ο Ιησους 69 arm o δε I. D rell b c e ff g i aeth | απαγ-
γειλον] διαγγειλον D 1 13 28 69 131 209 346 604 αναγγειλον ΑΛΠΣΦ⸆ al | ο κυριος] ο
θεος D 238 | πεποιηκεν אABCLΠΣ⸆ minᵖᵉʳᵐᵘ me] εποιησεν DKΦ minⁿᵒⁿⁿ | και ηλ.] κ.
οτι ηλ. D b c ff i syrᵖᵉˢʰ (ⁿᵒⁿ ˢⁱⁿ)

17. καὶ ἤρξαντο κτλ.] Ephrem
(conc. exp. ev. p. 75) represents the
Gerasenes as hostile from the first.
It is difficult to say how far this little
town within Gadarene territory may
have fallen under pagan influences—
the owners and keepers of the swine
were surely indifferent Jews—but
their unwillingness to receive Christ
was probably due to the fear that His
miraculous powers might bring upon
them further losses. The demand
for His departure was unanimous acc.
to Lc.: ἠρώτησεν αὐτὸν ἅπαν τὸ πλῆθος
τῆς περιχώρου. The only parallel in
the Galilean Ministry is the expulsion from Nazareth (Lc. iv. 29). The
ὅρια would be the bounds of the district attached to Gerasa, cf. Mt. ii. 16,
xv. 39, Mc. vii. 24, 31.

18—20. THE RESTORED DEMONIAC
SENT TO EVANGELISE (Lc. viii. 38—39).
18. ἐμβαίνοντος αὐτοῦ κτλ.] As He
was going on board, the released demoniac begged to be taken with Him
as a disciple: cf. Mc. iii. 14, Lc. xxii.
59. Thpht.'s explanation is quite unnecessary (ἐφοβεῖτο γὰρ μήποτε μόνον
εὑρόντες αὐτὸν οἱ δαίμονες πάλιν ἐπέλ-
θωσιν αὐτῷ). For ὁ δαιμονισθείς see
note on ὁ δαιμονιζόμενος, v. 15; atten-

tion is now called to his deliverance;
the possession was a thing of the
past. On the constr. παρεκάλει...ἵνα
see Burton, § 200, and cf. v. 10
supra.

19. καὶ οὐκ ἀφῆκεν αὐτόν] Lc. ἀπέ-
λυσέν δὲ αὐτόν. The request is refused, because the man is wanted for
immediate service. The eastern shore
of the Lake was for the present closed
against Jesus and the Twelve. A preparatory publication of the demoniac's
story was necessary in anticipation of
a later visit (vii. 31 ff.). What had
been prohibited in Galilee (i. 43 f.) is
under other circumstances not only
permitted but commanded in Decapolis: cf. Eccl. iii. 7, καιρὸς τοῦ σιγᾶν
καὶ καιρὸς τοῦ λαλεῖν.

εἰς τὸν οἶκόν σου πρὸς τοὺς σούς] Cf.
ii. 11. The man's first duty was to
his own house (where he had long
been a stranger, Lc. viii. 27), and his
relatives and acquaintances. Comp.
1 Tim. v. 4, 8. His tale was to be
told in his own circle first. Οἱ σοί:
cf. τὸ σόν, Mt. xx. 14; τὰ σά, Lc. vi. 30.
For ἀπάγγειλον Lc. has διηγοῦ (see on
v. 16).

ὅσα ὁ κύριός σοι κτλ.] On ὅσα see
iii. 8 note, and infra, v. 20. Lc. ὁ θεός:

§ N καὶ ἤρξατο κηρύσσειν ἐν τῇ Δεκαπόλει §ὅσα ἐποίησεν
¶ ¹⁰ αὐτῷ ὁ Ἰησοῦς, καὶ πάντες ἐθαύμαζον.¶

21   ²¹Καὶ διαπεράσαντος τοῦ Ἰησοῦ ἐν τῷ πλοίῳ
πάλιν εἰς τὸ πέραν, συνήχθη ὄχλος πολὺς ἐπ᾽ αὐτόν·

21 om εν τω πλοιω D 1 28 2ᵖᵉ a b c e syrˢⁱⁿ arm | εις το περαν παλιν אD 2ᵖᵉ a b c ff g
i q syrᵘᵗʳ | επ] προς DN 13 28 69 346 2ᵖᵉ

ὁ κύριος is here = Κύριος as in Lc. i. 6,
&c., either יְהֹוָה or אֲדֹנָי, as repeatedly
in the LXX.; ὁ κ. is used of Jesus by
Mc. only in xi. 3 where it possibly
= ὁ διδάσκαλος (Jo. xiii. 13). Euth.:
οὐκ εἶπεν Ὅσα ἐγὼ πεποίηκα· τῷ πατρὶ
τὸ θαῦμα ἐπιγραφόμενος. Πεποίηκεν
καὶ ἠλέησεν: the combination of tenses
expresses two sides of the transaction,
its historical completeness and its
permanent results. The act of mercy
was momentary, the consequences
would be before the eyes of those
who listened to his tale. On such
combinations see WM., p. 339. In some
cases the perfect appears to bear a
sense almost undistinguishable from
that of the aorist, ib., p. 340, Burton,
§§ 80, 88; but here the change of tense
can be conveyed in a translation: cf.
R.V. 'hath done,' 'had mercy.' In
the next verse where an ordinary
narrative is in view Mc. writes ἐποίησεν. For ποιεῖν τί τινι cf. Mt.
xxvii. 22. Ὅσα, which belongs properly to πεποίηκεν, is loosely carried
on to ἠλέησεν, before which we should
expect ὡς.

20. ἤρξατο κηρύσσειν ἐν τῇ Δεκα-
πόλει] Lc. καθ᾽ ὅλην τὴν πόλιν i.e.
Gerasa. The Decapolis (G. A. Smith,
H. G. p. 595 ff., Schürer II. ii. 94 ff.)
was strictly a confederation of Greek
cities, perhaps originally ten in number. Pliny H. N. v. 18. 74 mentions
Damascus, Philadelphia, Raphana,
Scythopolis (the O.T. Bethshan), Gadara, Hippos, Dios, Pella, Gerasa
(now Jerash), Kanatha: but he
warns his readers that the names
varied in different lists. As a geographical name the word was prob-

ably used with a corresponding laxity,
and the territory of each city in the
league was regarded as the local
'Decapolis.' If so, the Decapolis of
the Gospels (Mt. iv. 25, Mc. v. 20,
vii. 31) may be sought for in the
neighbourhood of Gadara and Hippos,
which bordered on the Lake (Joseph.
B.J. iii. 3. 1, πρὸς ἔω δὲ Ἱππηνῇ τε καὶ
Γαδάροις ἀποτέμνεται [ἡ Γαλιλαία] καὶ
τῇ Γαυλωνίτιδι). See note on vii. 31
infra. Κηρύσσειν: the man became
a κῆρυξ, sharing in his measure the
ministry of Christ and the Apostles
(i. 14, iii. 14). For the moment the
result was merely to excite astonishment (ἐθαύμαζον).

21—34. ON HIS RETURN TO THE
WESTERN SHORE THE LORD IS CALLED
TO HEAL THE CHILD OF JAIRUS, AND
ON HIS WAY THITHER IS TOUCHED BY
A WOMAN IN THE CROWD (Mt. ix. 18—
22, Lc. viii. 40—48).

21. διαπεράσαντος…εἰς τὸ πέραν]
Τὸ πέραν is here the Western shore;
the place of landing is apparently
Capernaum. See below, v. 22. For
διαπερᾶν ('cross the water') cf. vi. 53,
Acts xxi. 2.

συνήχθη κτλ.] The contrast is remarkable; on the E. side He had
been desired to depart; on the W.,
ἀπεδέξατο αὐτὸν ὁ ὄχλος (Lc.). The
reading of אD looks back to iv.
1: 'again a great multitude assembled.' Ἐπί with acc. of a person is
not common (WM., p. 508), and when
preceded as here by a verb which implies rest it is a little difficult; the
multitude had come together at the
first sight of the boat putting out
from Gerasa, and as soon as He had

καὶ ἦν παρὰ τὴν θάλασσαν.¶ ²²καὶ ἔρχεται εἰς τῶν 22 ¶ Wᶠ
ἀρχισυναγώγων, §ὀνόματι 'Ιάειρος, καὶ ἰδὼν αὐτὸν   § Wᶠ
πίπτει πρὸς τοὺς πόδας αὐτοῦ· ²³καὶ παρεκάλει 23
αὐτὸν πολλὰ λέγων ὅτι Τὸ θυγάτριόν μου ἐσχάτως
ἔχει· ἵνα ἐλθὼν¶ ἐπιθῇς τὰς χεῖρας αὐτῇ, ἵνα σωθῇ   ¶ Θᵇ
καὶ ζήσῃ. ²⁴§καὶ ἀπῆλθεν μετ' αὐτοῦ.   24 § syrʰⁱᵉʳ

21 om και ην Dbcefffiq syrˢⁱⁿ aeth   22 και 1°]+ιδου ACP alᵖˡc f l syrʰᶜˡ
arm go | εις] τις D | om ονοματι Ιαειρος Daeffi | om ιδων αυτον D e ιδ. τον Ιησουν
N | προς] παρα N   23 παρεκαλει ΒΔΔΙΣΦ] παρακαλει אACLN 33 1071 2ᵖᵉ
alⁿᵒⁿⁿ παρακαλων Dabeffiq | om πολλα D albcfffiq | ινα ελθων...αυτη] ελθε αψαι
αυτης εκ των χειρων σου Dbiq syrˢⁱⁿ | om αυτη N | ινα σωθη και ζηση אBCDLΔ 13 69
346 604 2ᵖᵉ] οπως σ. κ. ζησεται ΑΝΠΣΦ   24 απηλθεν] υπηγεν D 124 επορευετο 604

landed, it swarmed down upon Him
—a *constr. praegnans.* Ἦν παρὰ τὴν
θάλασσαν may merely mean, ' He was
by the Sea'; cf. WM., p. 503, Blass,
Gr. p. 138.

22. ἔρχεται εἰς τῶν ἀρχισυναγώγων]
The teaching is interrupted by an
arrival. Mt. (ix. 18) places this incident in an entirely different context;
Lc. agrees with Mc. For εἰς τῶν
ἀρχισ. Mt. has ἄρχων εἷς, Lc. ἄρχων
τῆς συναγωγῆς here, but ἀρχισυνάγωγος further on (viii. 49). In a small
synagogue there might be but one
such officer (Lc. xiii. 14); in larger
synagogues there were sometimes
several (Acts xiii. 15, xiv. 2, D). The
ἀρχισυνάγωγος (רֹאשׁ הַכְּנֶסֶת) was the
supervisor of the worship of the
synagogue (Schürer II. ii. p. 63 ff.),
but not (as Irenaeus v. 13. 1 calls him)
an ἀρχιερεύς: his functions were not
priestly but administrative only. For
a later distinction between ἄρχοντες
τ. συναγωγῆς and ἀρχισυνάγωγοι see
W. M. Ramsay, *Exp.* v. i. p. 272 ff.

'Ιάειρος] = יָאִיר, LXX. 'Ιαείρ, Num.
xxxii. 41, Jud. x. 3 f.; in Esth. ii. 5,
1 Esdr. v. 31 'Ιάειρος; Syrr. ˢⁱⁿ·ᵖᵉˢʰ· have
Joarash. For the Jair of Judges Josephus (*ant.* v. 7) gives 'Ιάρης (Niese),
but with the variants 'Ιαείρης, 'Ιάειρος.
In view of these facts it is arbitrary
to derive 'Ιάειρος from יָעִיר, as if

it arose out of the story itself
(Cheyne, in *Encycl. Bibl.* s. v.). Both
the earlier Jairs were Gileadites.
Victor remarks: τὸ ὄνομα κεῖται διὰ
τοὺς 'Ιουδαίους τοὺς εἰδότας τὸ γεγονός.
More probably, because it was familiar
to the first generation of believers;
cf. xv. 21. Bengel: " quo tempore
Marcus hoc scripsit [? Petrus hoc
dixit] Jairus eiusve filia adhuc repe-
riri in Palestina potuit." The name
occurs also in Lc., but not in Mt.

πίπτει πρὸς τ. πόδας αὐτοῦ] Mt. προσεκύνει αὐτόν: see on *v.* 6. The prostration is the more remarkable as that
of a dignitary in the presence of a
crowd. His dignity was forgotten in
the presence of a great sorrow; he
recognised his inferiority to the Prophet who had the power to heal.

παρεκάλει κτλ.] On πολλά see *v.* 10,
note. Θυγάτριον, cf. vii. 25 : a diminutive of affection used in later Greek
(Plutarch, Athenaeus); in the N. T.
peculiar to Mc. Lc. adds that she was
μονογενής (cf. vii. 12, ix. 38). 'Εσχάτως
ἔχει, also peculiar to Mc., a phrase
condemned by the Atticists, see Lob.
Phryn. p. 389; Josephus has (*ant.* ix.
8. 6) ἐν ἐσχάτοις εἶναι, cf. Vg. here,
in extremis est. Wycliffe², "is nyʒ
deed." Mt. substitutes ἄρτι ἐτελεύ-
τησεν, Lc. ἀπέθνησκεν.

ἵνα ἐλθὼν ἐπιθῇς κτλ.] For the
ellipsis see WM., p. 396. Either παρα-

Καὶ ἠκολούθει αὐτῷ ὄχλος πολύς, καὶ συνέθλιβον
25 αὐτόν. ²⁵καὶ γυνὴ οὖσα ἐν ῥύσει αἵματος δώδεκα
26 ἔτη, ²⁶καὶ πολλὰ παθοῦσα ὑπὸ πολλῶν ἰατρῶν καὶ
¶ syrˢⁱⁿ   δαπανήσασα τὰ παρ' αὐτῆς πάντα καὶ μηδὲν¶ ὠφελη-
27 θεῖσα ἀλλὰ μᾶλλον εἰς τὸ χεῖρον ἐλθοῦσα, ²⁷ἀκού-

25 γυνη]+τις DNII al minᵖˡ   26 τα παρ αυτης ABLNΣ al minᶠᵉʳᵉ¹⁰⁰] τα παρ
εαυτης ℵCKΔII minᵐᵘ τα εαυτης D τα υπαρχοντα αυτης Φ τα παρ αυτη 736

καλῶ or θέλω may be mentally supplied: cf. vv. 10, 18, and see Burton,
§§ 202, 203. Mt. gives a simple imperative (ἀλλὰ ἐλθὼν ἐπιθές), and so
the Western text in Mc.; cf. Vg.
veni impone manus; Mc.'s broken
construction reflects the anxiety of
the speaker. The Greek expositors
contrast the superior faith of the
centurion (Mt. viii. 8). For the use
of imposition of hands in healing see
vi. 5, vii. 32, viii. 23, 25, [xvi. 18];
Acts ix. 17, xxviii. 8; as a primitive
form of benediction (Gen. xlviii. 14ff.)
in common use among the Jews
(Mason, Baptism and Conf. p. 10,
cf. Hastings, D. B. iii. p. 84 f.), it was
adopted by our Lord, and employed
in the Church in various rites to
symbolise and convey gifts whether
of healing or of grace. Ἵνα σωθῇ καὶ
ζήσῃ is not a hendiadys: 'that she
may be healed (of her disorder) and
her life may be spared.' For σῴζειν
'to restore to health,' in cases where
the disease is not fatal, see vv. 28, 34,
vi. 56, x. 52.

24. ἀπῆλθεν μετ' αὐτοῦ] The Lord
rose and followed the synagogue-
ruler, and after him went the Twelve
(Mt.), and a vast crowd (Lc.), eager
to see another wonder. The crowd
pressed round Him, leaving Him
scarce space to move (συνέθλιβον
αὐτόν, Mc.) or even to breathe
(συνέπνιγον αὐτόν, Lc.). Συνθλίβω
(Sir. xxxiv. 14=xxxi. 17), Mc. only;
cf. θλίβειν, Mc. iii. 9, ἀποθλίβειν,
Lc. viii. 45.

25. γυνὴ οὖσα ἐν ῥύσει] So Lc.;
Mt. γ. αἱμορροοῦσα. For εἶναι ἐν ῥ.
see WM., p. 230: ἐν ῥ. in a condition
of, i.e. suffering from, hemorrhage.
Fritzsche compares ἦν ἐν τῇ νόσῳ
Soph. Aj. 271. Ῥύσις is used in Lev.
xv. 2 ff. for זוֹב; αἱμορροεῖν occurs in
the same context (v. 33). The trouble
had lasted as many years (12) as Jair's
child had lived, cf. infra, v. 42; Bengel: "uno tempore initium miseriae
et vitae habuerant." For a curious
use made of this number by the
Valentinian Gnostics see Iren. i. 3.
3.

26. πολλὰ παθοῦσα ὑπὸ πολλῶν
ἰατρῶν] She had suffered much at
the hands of many physicians: cf.
Mt. xvi. 21, πολλὰ παθεῖν ἀπὸ τῶν
πρεσβυτέρων. Both ὑπό and ἀπό are
used with verbs of passive signification to denote the agent: Blass, Gr.
pp. 125 f., 135. For some of the pre-
scriptions ordered by the Rabbinical
experts see J. Lightfoot on this verse.
Δαπανήσασα τὰ παρ' αὐτῆς πάντα, Vg.
et erogaverat omnia sua; cf. iii. 21 οἱ
παρ' αὐτοῦ, Lc. x. 7 τὰ παρ' αὐτῶν,
Phil. iv. 18 τὰ παρ' ὑμῶν, and see
Field, Notes, p. 27; the phrase is
equivalent to ὅσα εἶχεν, ὅλον τὸν βίον
αὐτῆς (xii. 44), which might indeed be
little enough, as the last reference
shews. In Lc. BD Syr.ˢⁱⁿ· omit the
corresponding words ἰατροῖς προσανα-
λώσασα ὅλον τὸν βίον αὐτῆς, and WH.
exclude them from margin as well as
text. For varying estimates of the
physician in later Jewish writings see

σασα τὰ περὶ τοῦ Ἰησοῦ, ἐλθοῦσα ἐν τῷ ὄχλῳ
ὄπισθεν ἥψατο τοῦ ἱματίου αὐτοῦ· ²⁸ἔλεγεν γὰρ ὅτι 28
Ἐὰν ἅψωμαι κἂν τῶν ἱματίων αὐτοῦ, σωθήσομαι.¶ ¶ Wᵗ
²⁹§καὶ εὐθὺς ἐξηράνθη ἡ πηγὴ τοῦ αἵματος αὐτῆς, 29 § Wᵍ
§καὶ ἔγνω τῷ σώματι ὅτι ἴαται ἀπὸ τῆς μάστιγος.   § Wᶠ

27 τα περι ℵ*BC*Δ] om τα ℵᶜAC²DLNΠΣΦ minᶠᵉʳᵉᵒᵐⁿ | εν τω οχλω] εις τον
οχλον N 13 28 69 124 346 | του ιματιου] pr του κρασπεδου M 1 33 1071 alᵖᵃᵘᶜ
28 ελεγεν γαρ (λεγουσα D 604 2ᵖᵉ b c ff i q aeth)]+εν εαυτη DKNΠΣ 1 33 209 604 2ᵖᵉ
alⁿᵒⁿⁿ a c ff i q arm | εαν (+μονον 33 arm) αψ. καν των ιματιων (του ιματιου ℵ 33) αυτ.
ℵBCLΔ 49ᵉᵛ] καν των ιματιων αυτ. (του ιματιου εαυτου D) αψ. ADΠ al minᶠᵉʳᵉᵒᵐⁿ

Tobit ii. 10 (B and ℵ texts)—an
interesting parallel—and on the other
hand Sir. xxxviii. 1 ff. Holtzmann
quotes from the Mishna a sentence
which seems to shew that they were
in ill odour with the Rabbis (Kid-
dushim, iv. 14, "medicorum optimus
dignus est gehenna"). Μηδὲν ὠφεληθεῖσα, as her experience told her;
οὐδὲν ὠφ. would have merely stated the
fact; see, however, Blass, Gr. p. 255.
Εἰς τὸ χεῖρον ἐλθοῦσα : cf. ἐπὶ τὸ χεῖρον
προκόπτειν (2 Tim. iii. 13).

27. τὰ περὶ τοῦ Ἰησοῦ] I.e. the
report of His powers of healing; cf.
Lc. xxiv. 14, Acts xxiv. 10, Phil.
ii. 23.

ἐλθοῦσα ἐν τῷ ὄχλῳ ὄπισθεν] She
mixed with the crowd which followed
the Lord and contrived to make her
way to the front, immediately behind
Him. For a similar touch of delicate
feeling cf. Gen. xviii. 10.

ἥψατο τοῦ ἱματίου αὐτοῦ] The part
touched was the κράσπεδον (Mt. Lc.),
i.e. the edge of the outer garment.
The Law required every Jew to attach
to the corners of his quadrangular
covering tassels, which according to
later usage consisted of three threads
of white wool twisted together with a
cord of blue; see Num. xv. 38 f. :
ποιησάτωσαν ἑαυτοῖς κράσπεδα (צִיצִת)
ἐπὶ τὰ πτερύγια τῶν ἱματίων αὐτῶν...
καὶ ἐπιθήσετε ἐπὶ τὰ κράσπεδα τῶν
πτερυγίων κλῶσμα ὑακίνθινον; Deut.

xxii. 12: στρεπτὰ ('twists') ποιήσεις
σεαυτῷ ἐπὶ τῶν τεσσάρων κρασπέδων
(גְּדִלִים) τῶν περιβολαίων σου (see
Driver, ad l.). Interesting details will
be found in Hastings, D. B. i. p. 627, ii.
p. 68 ff., and Encycl. Bibl. ii. p. 1565.
The Lord doubtless conformed to the
precept of the Law, though he afterwards censured the Scribes for their
ostentatious obedience (Mt. xxiii. 5).
The κράσπεδον may have been either
one of the tassels, or the corner from
which it hung (so the LXX. in Deut.
l.c., Zach. viii. 23). One corner with
its tassel was behind Him, and on
this the woman laid her hand (ἐλθοῦσα
...ὄπισθεν).

28. ἔλεγεν] Mt. adds ἐν ἑαυτῇ :
the words were unspoken. Ἐὰν...
κἂν has caused trouble to the copyists, but κἂν qualifies τῶν ἱματίων
(WM., p. 730), cf. Vg. si vel resti-
mentum eius tetigero; similarly we
find ἵνα...κἂν in vi. 56, and Acts
v. 15 (where see Blass, and cf. his
Gr. pp. 19, 275). Mt. substitutes
μόνον for κἂν without materially
modifying the sense. Τῶν ἱματίων,
'the clothes,' general and inclusive,
as in v. 30 infra. On the expectation of a cure by contact comp. iii.
10, and on σωθήσομαι see v. 23
supra.

29. εὐθὺς ἐξηράνθη κτλ.] The
hemorrhage ceased: Lc., using perhaps a medical term (cf. Plummer,

30 ³⁰καὶ εὐθὺς ὁ Ἰησοῦς ἐπιγνοὺς ἐν ἑαυτῷ τὴν ἐξ αὐτοῦ
δύναμιν ἐξελθοῦσαν, ἐπιστραφεὶς ἐν τῷ ὄχλῳ ἔλεγεν
31 Τίς μου ἥψατο τῶν ἱματίων; ³¹καὶ ἔλεγον αὐτῷ οἱ
¶ Wʰ   μαθηταὶ αὐτοῦ Βλέπεις τὸν ὄχλον συνθλίβοντά σε,¶

30 την εξ αυτου δυναμιν εξελθ.] την δ. (+την Dᵃ armᵛⁱᵈ) εξελθ. απ. αυτου D
31 λεγουσιν DN 2ᵖᵒ (a) e i q

Luke, pp. lxv, 235), ἔστη ἡ ῥύσις. For
ξηραίνω in the sense of drying up a
spring cf. 3 Regn. xvii. 7, Jer. xxviii.
(li.) 36, ξηρανῶ τὴν πηγὴν αὐτῆς: ἡ
πηγὴ τοῦ αἵματος is from Lev. xii. 7.
Ἔγνω τῷ σώματι ὅτι ἴαται: she knew
from her bodily sensations, cf. ii. 5,
ἐπιγνοὺς...τῷ πνεύματι, dat. of sphere
(WM., p. 270). Ἴαται transfers the
reader into the region of the woman's thoughts : the conviction flashed
through her mind, Ἴαμαι: 'I have received a permanent cure.' The perf.
pass. of ἰάομαι occurs here only in
Biblical Greek, for ἴαμαι in 4 Regn.
ii. 21, Hos. xi. 3 is middle; but ἰάθην,
ἰαθήσομαι are repeatedly used in
a passive sense both in LXX. and
N.T. For μάστιξ *plaga* see iii. 10,
note.

30. εὐθὺς ὁ Ἰησοῦς κτλ.] The Lord
also experienced an instantaneous
sensation in the sphere of His consciousness (ἐν ἑαυτῷ), amounting to
a definite knowledge of the fact;
for ἐπιγνοὺς as contrasted with ἔγνω
(*v.* 29) see note on ii. 8. He was
fully aware that this power had gone
forth from Him—τὴν ἐξ αὐτοῦ δύναμιν
ἐξελθοῦσαν—not as Vg., *virtutem
quae exierat de eo*, but "virtutem
quae de eo [erat] exisse": cf. Lc.
ἔγνων δύναμιν ἐξελθοῦσαν ἀπ' ἐμοῦ, Vg. *novi
virtutem de me exisse*. Τὴν ἐξ
αὐτοῦ, that which belonged to Him
and from time to time proceeded
from Him; ἐξελθοῦσαν, "the substantive part. as object," Burton, § 458;
cf. Acts xxiv. 10, Heb. xiii. 23. That
miraculous energy went forth from
Jesus was notorious, cf. vi. 14; con-

trast the disavowal of personal power
on the part of the Apostles, Acts iii.
12. The Gk. commentators are careful to point out that the Lord's power
did not leave Him when it went forth
to heal; the movement is not to be
understood τοπικῶς ἢ σωματικῶς (Victor, Thpht.).

ἐπιστραφεὶς ἐν τῷ ὄχλῳ] Ἐπεστρά-
φην in a middle sense : cf. Sap. xvi. 7,
Mt. x. 13, Mc. viii. 33, Jo. xxi. 20.
The Lord turned and questioned the
crowd which pressed upon Him from
behind (*vv.* 24, 27). The act of turning was characteristic; see viii. 33,
Lc. vii. 9, 44, ix. 55 &c. The question
seems to imply that He needed information; see Mason, *Conditions*,
&c. p. 149 f.; on the other hand cf.
Jerome, *tract. in Mc.*: "nesciebat
Dominus quis tetigisset? quomodo
ergo quaerebat eam? quasi sciens, ut
indicaret...ut mulier illa confiteatur
et Deus glorificetur."

The order τίς μου...τῶν ἱμ. may
perhaps be intended to bring together
the two persons of the toucher and
the Touched, cf. *v.* 31, τίς μου ἥψατο;
see however WM., p. 193.

31. ἔλεγον αὐτῷ οἱ μαθηταί] Lc.
εἶπεν ὁ Πέτρος. That the remark was
Peter's might have been inferred from
its hasty criticism, and a certain tone
of assumed superiority, which at a
later time called for a severe rebuke;
cf. viii. 32 ff.

On the spiritual significance of
συνθλίβειν and ἅπτεσθαι see Victor :
ὁ πιστεύων εἰς τὸν σωτῆρα ἅπτεται
αὐτοῦ · ὁ δὲ ἀπιστῶν θλίβει αὐτὸν καὶ
λυπεῖ. Compare especially Aug. *serm.*

καὶ λέγεις Τίς μου ἥψατο; ³²καὶ περιεβλέπετο ἰδεῖν 32
τὴν τοῦτο ποιήσασαν. ³³ἡ δὲ γυνὴ φοβηθεῖσα καὶ 33
τρέμουσα, εἰδυῖα ὃ γέγονεν αὐτῇ, ἦλθεν καὶ προσέπεσεν αὐτῷ καὶ εἶπεν αὐτῷ πᾶσαν τὴν ἀλήθειαν.
³⁴ὁ δὲ εἶπεν αὐτῇ Θυγάτηρ, ἡ πίστις σου σέσωκέν 34
σε· ὕπαγε εἰς εἰρήνην,¶ καὶ ἴσθι ὑγιὴς ἀπὸ τῆς   ¶ syrʰⁱᵉʳ
μάστιγός σου.

---

31 ηψατο]+των ιματιων arm   33 τρεμουσα]+δι ο πεποιηκει λαθρα D 50 124
604 736 (1071) 2ᵖᵒ (6ᵖᵉ) a ff i arm | ο γεγονεν] το γεγονος N | αυτη] pr επ ΑΝΠΣ al
minᵖˡ c f vg επ αυτην Φ 13 66 alᵖᵃᵘᵉ | προσεπεσεν αυτω] προσεκυνησεν αυτον C προσεκ.
αυτω 6ᵖᵉ | αληθειαν] αιτιαν 1 13 28 69 346 (arm)   34 θυγατηρ BD] θυγατερ
ℵACᶜLΝΔΠΣΦ al minᶠᵒʳᵗᵉ ᵒᵐⁿ | υπαγε] πορευου N 604

62; Bede *ad l.*: "quem turba passim comitans comprimit, una credula mulier Dominum tangit."

32. περιεβλέπετο ἰδεῖν κτλ.] The Lord's only reply was to look round with a prolonged (imperf.) and scrutinising gaze (iii. 5, 34) which revealed to Him the individual who had stolen a cure. Ἰδεῖν is the inf. of purpose, Burton, § 366; on the distinction between ἰδεῖν and βλέπειν see note on iv. 12. The use of the fem. (τὴν ποιήσασαν) is anticipatory: 'the person who had done this and who proved to be a woman.' Or it may refer to Christ's knowledge of the fact —'whom He knew to be a woman.' Her 'woman's touch' (Bruce) had revealed her sex.

33. ἡ δὲ γυνή κτλ.] Lc. adds ἰδοῦσα ...ὅτι οὐκ ἔλαθεν. She was detected partly by her nearness to Christ,—a position from which she could not withdraw, on account of the crowd— partly by her own consciousness (εἰδυῖα ὃ γέγονεν αὐτῇ). She felt the Lord's eye resting on her, and knew herself discovered. The fear and trembling with which she came forward are not fully explained by the Western gloss δι' ὃ πεποιήκει λάθρα (WH., *Notes*, p. 24); a deeper psychology would take into account the excitement of the moment and the spiritual effort. For the combination φοβ. καὶ τρέμ. cf. Jud. ii. 28 (B), Dan. v. 19 (Th.), 4 Macc. iv. 10, 1 Cor. ii. 3, 2 Cor. vii. 15, Eph. vi. 5, Phil. ii. 12. The inward movement expressed itself in visible signs of excitement.

πᾶσαν τὴν ἀλήθειαν] 'The whole truth.' Cf. Jo. xvi. 13 (τὴν ἀλ. π.) and Westcott's note. Lc. gives the details. The confession revealed both the purpose (δι' ἣν αἰτίαν) and effect (ὡς ἰάθη παραχρῆμα). Moreover it was made publicly (ἐνώπιον παντὸς τοῦ λαοῦ). Bede: "ecce quo interrogatio Domini tendebat."

34. θυγάτηρ = θύγατερ: so the LXX. (codd. BA) in Ruth ii. 2, 22; iii. 1; cf. WH., *Notes*, p. 158. With this use of θυγάτηρ cf. τέκνον (ii. 5), παιδία (Jo. xxi. 5). Ἡ πίστις σου σέσωκέν σε: 'thy restoration is due to thy faith,' cf. x. 52, Lc. xvii. 19—a statement which does not of course exclude the complementary truth that she was healed by power proceeding from the person of Christ (*v.* 30). Christ's purpose in detecting her was to perfect her faith by confession (Rom. x. 10); this end being now gained, she is free to reap the fruits of her venture. Jerome: "nec dixit 'Fides tua te salvam factura est,' sed 'salvam fecit.'"

ὕπαγε εἰς εἰρήνην] Lc. πορεύου εἰς

¶ Wᶜ 35   ³⁵῍Ετι αὐτοῦ λαλοῦντος¶ ἔρχονται ἀπὸ τοῦ ἀρχι-
§ Wᶜ   συναγώγου λέγοντες ὅτι Ἡ θυγάτηρ §σου ἀπέθανεν·
36 τί ἔτι σκύλλεις τὸν διδάσκαλον ;   ³⁶ὁ δὲ Ἰησοῦς
παρακούσας τὸν λόγον λαλούμενον λέγει τῷ ἀρχι-

35 om ετι N   36 ο δε I.]+ευθεως AC(N)ΠΦ al minᵖˡ a syrʰᶜˡ go | παρακουσας
ℵ*ᶜ·ᵇBLΔ e] ακουσας ℵᶜ·ᵃACDNΠΣΦ al minᶠᵒʳᵗᵉᵒᵐⁿ latt (exc e) al | τον λογον λαλ.]
τον λογ. τον λαλ. B τουτον τον λογ. D τον λογ. ευθεως λαλ. Σ

εἰρ.,' go and enjoy peace'; an O. T.
phrase = לְכִי לְשָׁלוֹם 1 Regn. i. 17 :
cf. 1 Regn. xxix. 7, 2 Regn. xv. 9.
The Vg. *vade in pace* answers better
to the tamer πορ. ἐν εἰρήνῃ (Acts xvi.
36, James ii. 16, where see Mayor's
note). Ἴσθι ὑγιὴς ἀπὸ τῆς μ. σου, 'be
sound (and therefore free) from thy
scourge': i.e. continue so from this
time forth; cf. Mt. ἐσώθη ἡ γυνὴ ἀπὸ
τῆς ὥρας ἐκείνης. With ὑγ. ἀπό cf.
Rom. ix. 3 ἀνάθεμα εἶναι ἀπό. For
μάστιξ see note on iii. 10.
   Acc. to *Ev. Nicod.* i. 7 (B) the
woman's name was Veronica. Eusebius (*H.E.* vii. 18) relates a tradition
that she was a native of Caesarea
Philippi or Paneas, where a brazen
statue of her in the act of kneeling
before the Saviour had been seen by
himself. Macarius Magnes (i. 6) represents her as a princess of Edessa,
and as μέχρι τοῦ νῦν ἀοίδιμον ἐν τῇ
μέσῃ τῶν ποταμῶν. For the mass of
legend which has gathered round
the story see Thilo, *Cod. apocr.* i.
560 n.
   35—43. RAISING OF THE DEAD
CHILD (Mt. ix. 23—26, Lc. viii. 49—
56).
   35. ἔτι αὐτοῦ λαλοῦντος] So Lc.:
the exact phrase occurs in Gen. xxix.
9, LXX. The coincidence was a happy
one for the αἱμορροοῦσα, for the new
arrival at once diverted the attention
of the crowd. Ἀπὸ τοῦ ἀρχισυναγώγου:
he was present (*v.* 36), so that the
words = ἀπὸ τῆς οἰκίας τοῦ ἀρχ. (Euth.);
cf. Lc. παρὰ τοῦ ἀρχ. Ἔρχονται,
"man kommt" (Lc. ἔρχεταί τις); cf.

λέγουσιν, i. 30 (Meyer). Ἀπέθανεν =
τέθνηκεν (Lc.); see Burton, § 47.
   τί ἔτι σκύλλεις κτλ.] Tindale: "why
diseasest thou the master any further?" Lc. μηκέτι σκύλλε. Σκύλλειν is
properly to flay or to mangle (Aesch.
Pers. 577), but in later Greek 'to
harass, annoy' (Euth. ἀντὶ τοῦ περι-
σπᾷς, ἐνοχλεῖς); cf. 3 Macc. iii. 25 μεθ'
ὕβρεως καὶ σκυλμῶν, ib. vii. 5 μετὰ
σκυλμῶν ὡς ἀνδράποδα, Mt. ix. 36.
Here and in Lc. vii. 6 the verb means
scarcely more than 'to trouble,' 'put
to inconvenience' (Vg. *vexare*). Τὸν
διδάσκαλον = רַבָּנָא (רַבָּן), Dalman,
Worte Jesu, p. 278; cf. Mc. xiv. 14.
The remark shews that the power of
raising the dead was not yet generally
attributed to Jesus; only one instance,
so far as we know, had occurred, and
that not in the Lake district (Lc. vii.
11 ff.). Victor : ἐνόμισαν μηκέτι αὐτοῦ
χρείαν εἶναι διὰ τὸ τεθνηκέναι αὐτήν,
οὐκ εἰδότες ὅτι δυνατὸς ἦν καὶ ἀποθαν-
οῦσαν ἀναστῆσαι.
   36. παρακούσας τὸν λόγον λαλού-
μενον] On the construction see WM.,
p. 436. In the LXX. παρακούειν is uniformly to hear without heeding, to
neglect or refuse to hear, or to act
as if one did not hear; cf. Ps. xxxix.
13 Symm., 1 Esdr. iv. 11, Esther
iii. 3, 8, vii. 4 (παρήκουσα = הֶחֱרִישְׁתִּי),
Tob. iii. 4, Isa. lxv. 12 (παρηκούσατε =
לֹא שְׁמַעְתֶּם): and so the word is used
in Mt. xviii. 17 bis; whilst παρακοή
is the reverse of ὑπακοή (Rom. v. 19,
2 Cor. x. 6, Heb. ii. 2). The Lord
heard the words said (for λαλ. see
WM., p. 436, Burton, § 458, and note

συναγώγῳ Μὴ φοβοῦ· μόνον πίστευε. ³⁷καὶ οὐκ 37
ἀφῆκεν οὐδένα μετ᾽ αὐτοῦ συνακολουθῆσαι, εἰ μὴ
τὸν Πέτρον καὶ Ἰάκωβον καὶ Ἰωάνην τὸν ἀδελφὸν
Ἰακώβου. ³⁸καὶ ἔρχονται εἰς τὸν οἶκον τοῦ ἀρχι- 38
συναγώγου, καὶ θεωρεῖ θόρυβον καὶ κλαίοντας καὶ

37 ουδε ενα D | μετ αυτου συνακ. ℵBCLΔ] αυτω συνακολουθησαι EFGHMSUV
Π²(Σ)Φ αυτω ακολουθησαι ΑΚΠ* minᵖᵃᵘᶜ παρακολουθησαι αυτω D 1 28 124 209 604
2ᵖᵉ | τον Πετρον] om τον ADLΠ al minᵒᵐⁿ ᵛⁱᵈ   38 ερχονται ℵABCDFΔ 1 33
alᵖᵃᵘᶜ b e i q syrᵖᵉˢʰ me] ερχεται LNΠΣΦ al minᵖˡ a c f ff go syrʰᵉˡ arm aeth | τον
οικον]την οικιαν Δ 604 2ᵖᵉ | εθεωρει D | om και 3° DΦ al minᵖˡ lattᵛᵗ ᵖˡ me | κλαιοντων
και αλαλαζοντων D 2ᵖᵉ

on v. 30 supra), but spoke as if He
had not heard, passed them by in
silence and followed His own course.
Contrast Act. Ioann. 17 (ed. James,
p. 22 f.), ὑφ᾽ ἑκάστου ἡμῶν καλούμενος
οὐχ ὑπομένει παρακοῦσαι ἡμῶν, and cf.
Field's note ad l.

μόνον πίστευε] Lc. μ. πίστευσον,
faith being viewed as an act rather
than as a state. With μόνον tantummodo cf. Mt. viii. 8.   There was no
cause for fear, unless the man's faith
broke down.

37. The crowd is not suffered to
approach the house. Lc., perhaps
with less exactness, represents the
Lord as dismissing them on reaching
the house (ἐλθών...οὐκ ἀφῆκεν εἰσελθεῖν : cf. Mc.'s οὐκ ἀφῆκεν...καὶ ἔρχονται). Συνακολουθεῖν is a rare compound
in Biblical Greek (2 Macc. ii. 4, 6 ; in
N. T. only here and in xiv. 51, Lc.
xxiii. 49); comp. ἠκολούθει in v. 24—
the crowd followed, but there was no
bond of fellowship to keep them with
Him to the end.

εἰ μὴ τὸν Πέτρον κτλ.] Even of the
Apostles only three are permitted to
enter ; so careful is the Lord not to
invade at such a time the seclusion
of the home life. Three were sufficient as witnesses (Mt. xviii. 16) ;
and the same triad were chosen on
other occasions when privacy was
desired (ix. 2, xiv. 33).

The order of the names is the same

as in Mc.'s list of the Apostles (iii.
16), and it is maintained in ix. 2, xiii.
3, xiv. 33 ; Mt. on the whole agrees
(x. 2, xvii. 1) :. Lc. on the other hand
usually writes Π. καὶ Ἰωάνης καὶ Ἰάκωβος (viii. 51, ix. 28, Acts i. 13), though
his Gospel preserves the older order
in the Apostolic list (Lc. vi. 14). See
note on Mc. iii. 16. The single article
in Mc. before the three names seems
to represent the three as a body. But
the practice of the Evangelist varies ;
thus in ix. 2 we have τὸν Π. καὶ τὸν
Ἰάκ. καὶ Ἰω., while in xiv. 33 an article
stands in WH.'s text (though the
margin agrees with v. 37) before each
name. For τὸν ἀδελφὸν Ἰακ. see i.
16, 19 notes.

38. θεωρεῖ...ἀλαλάζοντας πολλά]
The Lord has dismissed one crowd
only to find the house occupied by
another (θόρυβον=ὄχλον θορυβούμενον,
Mt.). For the moment He stands
gazing at the strange spectacle (θεωρεῖ, cf. xii. 41). Θόρυβος is the uproar
of an excited mob (xiv. 2, Acts xx. 1,
xxi. 34).   The καί which follows is
epexegetic (WM., p. 345); the up-
roarious crowd within consisted of
mourners. Ἀλαλάζειν is 'to shout,'
whether for joy (so often in the
Psalms, e.g. Ps. xlvi. (xlvii.) 1, ἀλαλάξατε τῷ θεῷ), or in lamentation, cf.
Jer. iv. 8, κόπτεσθε καὶ ἀλαλάξατε.
The correction ὀλολύζοντας proposed
by Naber is unnecessary ; even if

39 ἀλαλάζοντας πολλά· ³⁹καὶ εἰσελθὼν λέγει αὐτοῖς Τί
θορυβεῖσθε καὶ κλαίετε; τὸ παιδίον οὐκ ἀπέθανεν
40 ἀλλὰ καθεύδει. ⁴⁰καὶ κατεγέλων αὐτοῦ. αὐτὸς δὲ
ἐκβαλὼν πάντας παραλαμβάνει τὸν πατέρα τοῦ

39 κλαιετε] pr τι D 28 b f ff i q   40 αυτος δε ℵBCDLΔ 33 latt (exc e) me]
ο δε ΑΝΙΙΣ al minᵖˡ syrʰᶜˡ⁽ᵗˣᵗ⁾ arm ο δε ῑ Μ𝚽 minᵖᵃᵘᶜ syrᵖᵉˢʰ | παντας] τους οχλους εξω
D latᵛᵗᵖˡ

ἀλαλάζειν is to be taken in its ordinary
sense, the heartless uproar was an
ἀλαλαγμός rather than an ὀλολυγμός.
The mourners were probably professional; among them were musicians
(αὐληταί, Mt.), and wailing women
(αἱ θρηνοῦσαι, Jer. ix. 17); "even the
poorest of Israel will afford his dead
wife not less than two minstrels and
one woman to make lamentations"
(J. Lightfoot), and this was the house
of an ἀρχισυνάγωγος. On the shallowness of the feeling which prompted
these demonstrations see Sir. xxxviii.
16 ff.

39. εἰσελθών κτλ.] The Lord entered the court, and expostulated.
For Mc.'s τί θορυβεῖσθε and Lc.'s
milder μὴ κλαίετε, Mt. has the sterner
ἀναχωρεῖτε, which may have followed
when the call to silence had proved
in vain. Οὐκ ἀπέθανεν ἀλλὰ καθεύδει
is enigmatical; καθεύδειν may = τεθνηκέναι, as in Dan. xii. 2 (LXX. and
Th.), 1 Th. v. 10; cf. κοιμᾶσθαι in Jo.
xi. 11 ff., but this sense seems to be
excluded when the verb is placed in
contrast with ἀποθανεῖν. Hence some
have declined to regard this miracle
as a raising of the dead (see Trench,
Miracles, p. 182 f.). But the fact of
the child's death was obvious to the
bystanders, and is apparently assumed
by the Evangelists, at least by Lc.
(εἰδότες ὅτι ἀπέθανεν). The Lord's
meaning seems to be: 'a death from
which there is to be so speedy an
awakening can only be regarded as a
sleep.' Cf. Bede: "hominibus mor-
tua, qui suscitare nequiverant, Deo
dormiebat." Ambrose: "fleant ergo

mortuos suos qui putant mortuos; ubi
resurrectionis fides est, non mortis
est species, sed quietis."

40. κατεγέλων αὐτοῦ] So Mt., Mc.,
Lc. The compound is used in the
N. T. only in this context, but it is
common in classical Gk. and in the
LXX, e.g. Ps. xxiv. (xxv.) 2, Prov. xvii.
5, 4 Macc. vi. 20. The Engl. versions
rightly lay stress on the scornfulness
of the laughter expressed by κατά
(e.g. Wycliffe, "thei scorneden hym";
Tindale, "they lawght him to scorne").
On the gen. see WM., p. 537 n. According to the Gk. expositors the
Lord suffered these hirelings to de-
ride Him in order to prevent them
from saying afterwards that the child
was not really dead (Thpht. ὡς ἂν μὴ
ἔχωσιν ὕστερον λέγειν ὅτι κάτοχος (cata-
leptic) ἐγένετο). But it is unnecessary
to seek for any such explanation; ἡ
ἀγάπη πάντα ὑπομένει.

αὐτὸς δὲ ἐκβαλὼν πάντας κτλ.] On
ἐκβάλλω see i. 12. In this case some
pressure was needed, for it was the
interest of these paid mourners to
remain. There is a sternness manifested in their ejection which finds a
counterpart on other occasions when
our Lord is confronted with levity or
greed; cf. xi. 15, Jo. ii. 15. Jerome:
"non enim erant digni ut viderent
mysterium resurgentis, qui resusci-
tantem indignis contumeliis deride-
bant." Αὐτὸς δέ, 'He on His part,'
Vg. *ipse vero*. Παραλαμβάνει, cf. iv.
36. Five persons enter the chamber
of death by His invitation. In the
O. T. instances of the raising of the
dead the prophet is alone (1 K. xvii.

παιδίου καὶ τὴν μητέρα καὶ τοὺς μετ᾽ αὐτοῦ, καὶ
εἰσπορεύεται ὅπου ἦν τὸ παιδίον·⁋ ⁴¹καὶ κρατήσας 41 ⁋ Wᶜ, ⊃
τῆς χειρὸς τοῦ παιδίου λέγει αὐτῇ Ταλειθά, κούμ·
ὅ ἐστιν μεθερμηνευόμενον Τὸ κοράσιον, σοὶ λέγω,
ἔγειρε. ⁴²καὶ εὐθὺς ἀνέστη τὸ κοράσιον καὶ περιεπάτει, 42

40 μετ αυτου]+οντας D | το παιδιον]+ανακειμενον ACNΠΦ al minᵖˡ+κατακειμενον
Σ 604 arm   41 της χειρος] την χειρα D | ταλειθα (ταλιθα אACLNII al arm)]
ραββι· θαβιτα D thabitha (tabitha etc.) a b c ff i r vgᶜᵒᵈᵈ tabea acultha e | κουμ
אBCLMNΣ 1 33 1071 alⁿᵒⁿⁿ ff] κουμι (A)DΔΠΦ al minᵖˡ lattᵛᵗ ᵖˡ (ᵛᵍ) syrrᵖᵉˢʰ ᵇᶜˡ arm
me aeth | εγειραι UΦ minˢᵃᵗ ᵐᵘ εγειρον minᵖᵃᵘᶜ

19 ff., 2 K. iv. 33), and this seems to
have been the case also at the raising
of Tabitha (Acts ix. 40). Our Lord,
knowing the issue (Jo. xi. 41, 42),
chooses to work in the presence of
witnesses, not excepting the mother,
though He ejects the jeering hirelings who were not in sympathy
with His purpose. Euth.: τὸν μὲν οὖν
πατέρα καὶ τὴν μητέρα...παρέλαβε θεατὰς
τοῦ θαύματος ὡς οἰκείους ἐκείνῃ, τοὺς δὲ
μαθητὰς ὡς οἰκείους ἑαυτῷ. Εἰσπορεύεται ὅπου=εἰσπ. εἰς τὸ ὑπερῷον (Acts
ix. 39) ὅπου.

41. κρατήσας τῆς χειρὸς τοῦ παιδίου]
Wycliffe, "he heeld the hond of the
damysel"; Tindale rightly, "toke
the mayden by the honde." See WM.,
p. 252; Blass, Gr. p. 101; and cf. i.
31, ix. 27. He addresses Himself to
the personality, not to the body only
(λέγει αὐτῇ: cf. Lc. vii. 14, Jo. xi. 43);
comp. Jo. v. 28, οἱ ἐν τοῖς μνημείοις
ἀκούσουσιν. Αὐτῇ i.e. τῷ παιδίῳ, a
constructio ad sensum: cf. Blass, Gr.
p. 166.

ταλειθά, κούμ] (קוּמִי) טְלִיתָא קוּם (Dalman, p. 118 n., 266 n.; with ταλειθά
cf. the use of טָלֶה, טְלָאִים in 1 Sam.
vii. 9, Isa. xl. 11, lxv. 25). On the
strange corruptions of these Aramaic
words in some Western texts see
Chase, Syro-Latin Text, p. 109 f.;
tabita for talitha found its way into
our earlier English versions, Tindale,
as well as Wycliffe. For other Ara-

maic words preserved by Mc., see
vii. 34, xiv. 36; and on the general
subject of Aramaisms in the Gospels,
Schürer II. i. 9. Ὅ ἐστιν μεθερμηνευόμενον, a phrase common to Mt.,
Mc., Jo., and Acts; other forms are
ὃ λέγεται μεθερμ., ὃ ἑρμηνεύεται, οὕτως
γὰρ μεθερμηνεύεται. Μεθερμηνεύειν (a
late compound for the class. ἑρμη-
νεύειν) is already used in reference
to the translation of Hebrew into
Greek in the prologue to Sirach (l. 19).
Τὸ κοράσιον: the word is late and
colloquial (Lob. Phryn. p. 74), and
survives in modern Gk. (Kennedy,
Sources, p. 154); in the LXX. where
it usually represents נַעֲרָה, it is fairly
common from Ruth onwards; in the
N. T. it is used only of the girl in
this narrative and of the daughter of
Herodias. On the nom. (τὸ κοράσιον)
see v. 8 note, and cf. Lc. ἡ παῖς,
ἐγείρου.

42. εὐθὺς ἀνέστη...καὶ περιεπάτει]
The effect was instantaneous (παραχρῆμα, Lc.), the child rose and walked
(imperf., since the act was continuous,
and not, like the rising, momentary;
cf. Jo. v. 9, Acts iii. 8). Strength returned as well as life: cf. Lc. vii. 15
(ἤρξατο λαλεῖν), Jo. xi. 44 (ἐξῆλθεν...
ἄφετε αὐτὸν ὑπάγειν). Ἦν γὰρ ἐτῶν
δώδεκα justifies περιεπάτει—the child
was of an age to walk; the correction
in D has arisen from a failure to
understand γάρ. For the gen. of

ἦν γὰρ ἐτῶν δώδεκα· καὶ ἐξέστησαν εὐθὺς ἐκστάσει
43 μεγάλη. ⁴³καὶ διεστείλατο αὐτοῖς πολλὰ ἵνα μηδεὶς
γνοῖ τοῦτο· καὶ εἶπεν δοθῆναι αὐτῇ φαγεῖν.

6. I ¹§Καὶ ἐξῆλθεν ἐκεῖθεν, καὶ ἔρχεται εἰς τὴν πατρίδα
§ syrʰⁱᵉʳ

42 ην γαρ] ην δε D 2ᵖᵉ 7ᵖᵉ latt | δωδεκα (δεκα δυο Φ 1)] pr ωσει ℵCΔ pr ως 1 33 604
alᵖᵃᵘᶜ arm | εξεστησαν+παντες D c f ff i q+οι γονεις αυτης 736 8ᵖᵉ alᵖᵃᵘᶜ | om ευθυς 2°
ADNΠΣΦ al minᵖˡ latt syrr arm go al (hab ℵBCLΔ 33 me aeth)   43 om πολλα
D latᵛᵗᵖˡ | γνοι ABDL] γνω ℵCNΔΠΣΦ al | δοθηναι] δουναι D   VI 1 και ερχεται
ℵBCLΔ] κ. ηλθεν ANΠΣΦ al minᵖˡ Or καπηλθεν D (sic)

time cf. Lc. ii. 37, 42, iii. 23, Acts
iv. 22. For a patristic homily on the
three miracles of raising the dead
recorded in the Gospels see Aug.
serm. 98 (Migne).

ἐξέστησαν κτλ.] On ἐξίστασθαι see
note on ii. 12, and for ἔκστασις in this
sense xvi. 8, Lc. v. 26, Acts iii. 10.
The nearly equivalent phrase ἐκστῆναι
ἔκστασιν μεγάλην occurs in Gen. xxvii.
33. Εὐθύς is not necessarily otiose:
the astonishment was instantaneous
and complete.

43. διεστείλατο κτλ.] Two directions follow the miracle: (1) the facts
are not to be made public, (2) the
restored child is to receive nourish-
ment. The purpose of (1) was partly
to prevent idle curiosity, and the excitement which would check spiritual
work (cf. i. 44 note, vii. 36), partly
to gain time for His departure (vi. 1
note). In (2) we have fresh evidence
of the sympathetic tenderness of the
Lord, and His attention to small
details in which the safety or comfort
of others was involved. In the excitement of the moment the necessity
of maintaining the life which had
been restored might have been overlooked. But life restored by miracle
must be supported by ordinary means;
the miracle has no place where human
care or labour will suffice. Chrys.:
οὐκ αὐτὸς δίδωσιν, ἀλλ' ἐκείνοις κελεύει·
ὥσπερ καὶ ἐπὶ τοῦ Λαζάρου εἶπε Λύσατε
αὐτόν. Victor sees in this command
evidence of the reality of the miracle:
εἰς ἀπόδειξιν τοῦ ἀληθῶς αὐτὴν ἐγεγέρθαι

καὶ οὐ δοκήσει τινὶ καὶ φαντασία, referring to Lc. xxiv. 41 f.; cf. Iren. v.
13. 1, Jerome, *tract. in Mc.* ad l.

Διαστέλλειν is properly to divide or
distinguish: cf. e.g. Gen. xxx. 35, 40,
Deut. x. 8. In the mid. the word in
later Gk. has acquired the meaning
'to give an explicit order,' 'to enjoin': Jud. i. 19, Judith xi. 12, Ezech.
iii. 18 ff., and this sense it uniformly
bears in the N. T. (Mc.⁵, Acts¹; cf.
the pres. part. pass. in Heb. xii. 20).
With the conj. γνοῖ cf. παραδοῖ, iv. 29
note, and WM., p. 360. For the inf.
δοθῆναι see Burton, §§ 337, 391; for
φαγεῖν, almost=βρῶμα, cf. vi. 37, Jo.
iv. 33.

VI. 1—6 a. Departure from Capernaum: Preaching at Nazareth
(Mt. xiii. 53—58; cf. Lc. iv. 16—30).

1. ἐξῆλθεν ἐκεῖθεν] From the house
of Jairus (cf. v. 39, εἰσελθών), but also
from Capernaum; cf. Mt. xiii. 53,
μετῆρεν ἐκεῖθεν, where there is no
mention of Jairus in the context.
The purpose was probably to escape
from the enthusiasm of the crowd,
who, notwithstanding the charge to
conceal what had occurred (v. 43),
must soon hear of the miracle.

εἰς τὴν πατρίδα αὐτοῦ] I.e. to Nazareth, cf. Lc. iv. 23, 24; the word can
be used of a town, cf. Phil. *leg. ad
Cai.* 36, ἔστι δέ μοι Ἱεροσόλυμα πατρίς.
Neither Mt. nor Mc. mentions Nazareth here, but Mc. i. 9, 24, Jo. i. 46
imply that the Lord was regarded
by the Galileans as a Nazarene;
His birth at Bethlehem was forgotten

αὐτοῦ καὶ ἀκολουθοῦσιν αὐτῷ οἱ μαθηταὶ αὐτοῦ.
²καὶ γενομένου σαββάτου ἤρξατο διδάσκειν ἐν τῇ 2
συναγωγῇ· καὶ οἱ πολλοὶ ἀκούοντες ἐξεπλήσσοντο
λέγοντες Πόθεν τούτῳ ταῦτα, καὶ τίς ἡ σοφία ἡ
δοθεῖσα τούτῳ, καὶ αἱ δυνάμεις τοιαῦται διὰ τῶν

2 γενομενου σαββατου] ημερα σαββατων D (ff) i (q) r | οι πολλοι BL 13 28 69 346]
om οι ℵACDΔΠΣΦ al minᵖˡ | ακουσαντες DFHLNΔΙΙ al om b c e | εξεπλησσοντο]+επι
τη διδαχη αυτου D minᵖᵃᵘᶜ latt (exc e) syrᵖᵉˢʰ arm | ταυτα]+παντα ℵC² (απαντα C*)
(Δ) τουτο παντα 1071 | τουτο 2° ℵBCLΔ me] αυτω ΑDΠΣΦ al minᶠᵒʳᵗᵉᵒᵐⁿ | αι
δυναμεις τοιαυται δ. τ. χ. α. γινομεναι ℵ*⁽ᶜ⁾B(LΔ) 33 (vg) me] δυν. τοιαυται δ. τ. χ. α.
γινονται AC²EFGHM(N)SUVΣ (αι δυν.) Φ 1 13 28 69 alᵐᵘ a e ινα και δυν. τοι. δ. τ. χ.
α. γεινωνται D (sim C* b f i q ff r arm) | δια των χειρων] δ. τ. χειλεων cᵛⁱᵈ (per labia)

(cf. Jo. vii. 41, 42), and even if it had
been notorious, the village where His
family lived (v. 3), and where He had
passed His youth (Lc. iv. 16), might
well be called His πατρίς. Lc. places
this visit, of which he has preserved a
much fuller account, at the outset of
the Ministry, but without note of
time.

ἀκολουθοῦσιν αὐτῷ οἱ μαθ. αὐτοῦ] It
was not a private visit to His family;
He came as a Rabbi, surrounded by
His scholars.

2. γενομένου σαββάτου] Vg. facto
sabbato, 'when Sabbath had come.'
Lc. ἐν τῇ ἡμέρᾳ τῶν σαββάτων. He
took His place in the synagogue as
the reader (Ambr. "ille ita ad omnia
se curvavit obsequia ut ne lectoris
quidem adspernaretur officium"). Lc.
describes the whole scene from the
recollections of some eyewitness, perhaps the Mother of the Lord. The
Scripture expounded was Isa. lxi. 1, 2.
Ἤρξατο διδάσκειν = ἐδίδασκεν, Mt., cf.
Lc. ἤρξατο λέγειν. A similar phrase is
used in i. 45, iv. 1, v. 20, vi. 34, viii.
31, always apparently with reference
to a new departure. It was perhaps
the first time He had taught officially
in His own town, and but for the
hostility of the Nazarenes it might
have been the beginning of a course
of teaching there. On this use of
ἄρχεσθαι cf. WM., p. 767.

οἱ πολλοί...ἐξεπλήσσοντο] Mt. ὥστε
ἐκπλήσσεσθαι αὐτούς, Lc. πάντες ἐμαρ-
τύρουν αὐτῷ. Mc. is more exact: the
majority were impressed, but there
was an undercurrent of dissatisfaction
which in the end prevailed. For
ἐξεπλ. cf. i. 22.

πόθεν τούτῳ ταῦτα κτλ.] A change
had come over Him for which they
could not account; the workman had
become the Rabbi and the worker of
miracles. Of His wisdom they had
evidence in His discourse; it was a
gift (ἡ δοθεῖσα) and not the result of
study (Jo. vii. 15); it had shewn itself
in childhood (Lc. ii. 40, 47), and now
was revealed again in the man. But
whence and what was it (πόθεν; τίς;)?
And the miracles—such miracles as
report said were being wrought from
time to time (γινόμεναι) by His instru-
mentality (διὰ τῶν χειρῶν αὐτοῦ, cf.
Acts v. 12, xix. 11), whence were
these? No similar powers distinguished any other member of the
family, mother or brothers or sisters;
why should they distinguish Him?
(Mt. πόθεν οὖν τούτῳ ταῦτα πάντα;).
Jerome: "mira stultitia Nazaren-
orum; mirantur unde habeat sapien-
tiam Sapientia, et virtutes Virtus."
On τίς ἡ σ. see Blass, Gr. p. 176. Αἱ
δυνάμεις...γινόμεναι, sc. τί: 'what mean
such miracles wrought,' &c. For δύναμις, a miracle, see vi. 5, 14.

3 χειρῶν αὐτοῦ γινόμεναι; ³ οὐχ οὗτός ἐστιν ὁ τέκτων,
ὁ υἱὸς τῆς Μαρίας καὶ ἀδελφὸς Ἰακώβου καὶ Ἰωσῆτος

3 ο τεκτων ο υιος] ο του τεκτονος υιος και 13 33 69 604 2ᵖᵒ alᵖᵃᵘᶜ a b c e i (arm)
aeth om ο τεκτων syrʰᵉˡʰⁱᵉʳ (cf. Or infr) | της Μαριας] om της ΑΔΠ alᵖˡ | Ιωσητος]
Ιωσηφ ℵ 121 b e f q vg aeth Ιωση ΑΟΝΠΣΦ al minᵖˡ syrr go arm

3. ὁ τέκτων] Mt. ὁ τοῦ τέκτονος
υἱός. To the sneer of Celsus τέκτων
ἦν τὴν τέχνην Origen (Cels. vi. 36)
replies οὐδαμοῦ τῶν ἐν ταῖς ἐκκλησίαις
φερομένων εὐαγγελίων τέκτων αὐτὸς ὁ
Ἰησοῦς ἀναγέγραπται. "He either for-
got this passage or, perhaps more
probably, did not hold Mc. responsible
for the words of the Galileans" (W H.,
Notes, p. 24: see however the app.
crit. above). As the son of a τέκτων
Jesus would naturally have learnt τὴν
τεκτονικήν (see Lightfoot and Schöttgen ad loc.). This inference, if it was
no more, was early drawn: cf. Justin,
dial. 88, τὰ τεκτονικὰ ἔργα ἠργάζετο ἐν
ἀνθρώποις ὤν, ἄροτρα καὶ ζυγά, and the
answer to the scoffing question of
Libanius (Thdt. H. E. iii. 18). Τέκτων
is properly an artificer in wood, but
it is occasionally used of a worker in
metals (1 Regn. xiii. 19 τέκτων σιδήρου),
and several of the Fathers held Joseph
to have been a smith (see Thilo, Cod.
apocr. N. T. i. p. 368 f. n.). Mystical
reasons were found for the Lord's
connexion with one or other of these
trades; thus Hilary (on Mt. xiv.)
writes : "Fabri erat filius ferrum igne
vincentis, omnem saeculi virtutem
iudicio decoquentis," and Ambrose
(on Lc. iii. 25): "hoc typo patrem
sibi esse demonstrat qui Fabricator
omnium condidit mundum." The
family continued to be engaged in
manual labour to the third generation;
see the story of the grandsons of Jude
in Eus. H. E. iii. 20, τὰς χεῖρας τὰς
ἑαυτῶν ἐπιδεικνύναι, μαρτύριον τῆς αὐ-
τουργίας τὴν τοῦ σώματος σκληρίαν
καὶ τοὺς ἀπὸ τῆς συνεχοῦς ἐργασίας
ἐναποτυπωθέντας ἐπὶ τῶν ἰδίων χειρῶν
τύλους παριστάντας. Of the particulars of Joseph's work, and of the
interest manifested in it by the Child
Jesus, the apocryphal Gospels have
much to tell: see Thilo l.c.

ὁ υἱὸς τῆς Μαρίας] The absence of
any reference to Joseph in Mc. is
noteworthy; contrast Lc. iii. 23, iv.
22, Jo. i. 45, vi. 42. He was still
alive in our Lord's thirteenth year
(Lc. ii. 41 ff.), but there is no evidence
of his life having been prolonged
further; according to Protev. 9 Joseph
was already an old man before the
Birth of Jesus, and all the later
notices of the Lord's Mother (e.g.
Jo. ii. 1 ff.; Mc. iii. 31 ff.; Jo. xix.
25 ff.) confirm the supposition that
he died before the Ministry began.
The Arabic Historia Josephi (cc. 14,
15) places his death in our Lord's
eighteenth year, when Joseph had
reached the age of 111.

ἀδελφός] On this relationship see
Lightfoot (Galatians, "The Brethren
of the Lord") and J. B. Mayor (St
James, Introd.). Lightfoot disposes
of Jerome's view (cf. de vir. ill. 2)
that the 'brothers' were cousins, sons
of "Mary the sister of the Lord's
Mother," and on the whole supports
the alternative, which was widely held
by Catholics of the fourth century,
that they were sons of Joseph by a
former marriage. This belief is traced
by Origen (in Matt. x. 17) to the
apocryphal Gospel of Peter, and it
finds some support in the Protevan-
gelium (c. 9). On the other hand the
more obvious interpretation, which
makes the brothers sons of Joseph
and Mary, born after the Birth of
Jesus, was apparently accepted by
Tertullian (cf. adv. Marc. iv. 29, de

καὶ ᾽Ιούδα καὶ Σίμωνος ; καὶ οὐκ εἰσὶν αἱ ἀδελφαὶ
αὐτοῦ ὧδε πρὸς ἡμᾶς ; καὶ ἐσκανδαλίζοντο ἐν αὐτῷ.

3 om οὐκ syr^hier

carn. Chr. 7), who does not shew any
consciousness of departing in this
matter from the Catholic tradition of
his time.

The names of the four brothers are
given only here and in Mt. xiii. 55 ;
Mt.'s order is ᾽Ιάκωβος, ᾽Ιωσήφ, Σίμων,
᾽Ιούδας. The loyalty of the family
to the traditions of the O.T. appears
in the selection : Joseph named his
firstborn after Jacob, and his other
sons after the greater patriarchs.

᾽Ιακώβου] This James is mentioned
as ὁ ἀδελφὸς τοῦ κυρίου in Gal. i. 19 ;
see also Joseph. *ant.* xx. 9. 1, τὸν
ἀδελφὸν ᾽Ιησοῦ τοῦ λεγομένου Χριστοῦ,
᾽Ιάκωβος ὄνομα αὐτῷ, and Hegesippus
ap. Euseb. *H. E.* ii. 23. His eminence
in the Church at Jerusalem, to which
Heg. refers, is implied in Acts xii. 17,
xv. 13, xxi. 18, and in Gal. ii. 9, 12,
where he is classed with Peter and
John (οἱ δοκοῦντες στῦλοι εἶναι) ; by a
somewhat later age he was regarded
as an ἐπίσκοπος, and even (in Ebionite
circles) as ἐπισκόπων ἐπίσκοπος (*Clem.
Hom. ad init.*), or *archiepiscopus*
(*Recogn.* i. 73, cf. Hort, *Clem. Recogn.*
p. 116 f.). In the heading of his
own letter he describes himself simply
as θεοῦ καὶ κυρίου ᾽Ιησοῦ Χριστοῦ
δοῦλος. For further particulars see
Mayor, p. xxxvi ff., and Hort, *Ecclesia,*
p. 76 ff., who suggests that " he was
at some early time after the persecution of Herod taken up into the
place among the Twelve vacated by
his namesake."

᾽Ιωσῆτος] The name is another
form of ᾽Ιωσήφ ; see Mt. xiii. 55 and
cf. Mc. xv. 40, 47 with Mt. xxvii. 56 ;
also Acts iv. 36, where for ᾽Ιωσὴφ ὁ
ἐπικληθεὶς Βαρνάβας the R.T. reads
᾽Ιωσῆς. Lightfoot's difficulty (*Galatians,* p. 268, n. 1) seems to be met
by Dalman's view (p. 75) that יוסי
was a Galilean abbreviation of יוֹסֵף ;

cf. the Rabbinic forms which he quotes,
pp. 139, 143. For the Hellenised
termination -ῆς, gen. -ῆτος, see Blass,
Gr. p. 30 f. This brother is mentioned
only here and in the parallel passage
of Mt. ; the Joses of Mc. xv. 40 f. is
another person (see note there).

᾽Ιούδα] The Judas who styles himself (Jude 1) ᾽Ιούδας ᾽Ιησοῦ Χριστοῦ
δοῦλος ἀδελφὸς δὲ ᾽Ιακώβου. If he
was the third brother (or fourth,
according to Mt.'s order) born after
B.C. 4, his age at this time could
not have been thirty, and his
grandsons might well have been men
in middle life during the reign of
Domitian (Euseb. *H. E.* iii. 20). St
Paul speaks of the Lord's brothers as
married men (1 Cor. ix. 5).

Σίμωνος] Mentioned only here and
in Mt. xiii. 55 : for the form of the
name see note on i. 16. The Symeon
who succeeded James as Bishop of
Jerusalem was, according to Hegesippus, a son of Clopas, Joseph's
brother (Euseb. *H. E.* iii. 11).

αἱ ἀδελφαί] Mt. adds πᾶσαι. Epiphanius *haer.* lxxviii. 9 gives the
names of two—Salome and Mary,
but his statement possibly rests upon
a confused recollection of Mc. xv.
40 ; for other accounts see Thilo,
Cod. apocr. p. 363 n. The sisters
of Jesus are not mentioned elsewhere (cf. however Mc. iii. 32 v.l.),
even in Acts i. 14 where the mother
and brothers appear among the disciples at Jerusalem. They were settled
at Nazareth (ὧδε πρὸς ἡμᾶς), and possibly were already married women
whose duties tied them to their
homes ; while the brothers passed
from unbelief (Jo. vii. 5) to faith, the
sisters were perhaps scarcely touched
by the course of events.

ἐσκανδαλίζοντο ἐν αὐτῷ] So Mt. Lc.
passes over this intermediate stage of

+ ⁴καὶ ἔλεγεν αὐτοῖς ὁ Ἰησοῦς ὅτι Οὐκ ἔστιν προφήτης
ἄτιμος εἰ μὴ ἐν τῇ πατρίδι αὐτοῦ καὶ ἐν τοῖς συγγε-
5 νεῦσιν αὐτοῦ καὶ ἐν τῇ οἰκίᾳ αὐτοῦ. ⁵καὶ οὐκ ἐδύνατο
§ syrˢⁱⁿ §ἐκεῖ ποιῆσαι οὐδεμίαν δύναμιν, εἰ μὴ ὀλίγοις ἀρρώ-

+ πατρ. αυτου אᶜABCDΠΣΦ] πατρ. εαυτου א*L 13 69 346 pr ιδια אᶜAL | τοις συγγε-
νευσιν B*D²EFGHLNUVΔΣ 1 33 69 1071 alˢᵃᵗ ᵐᵘ] τ. συγγενεσιν אᵃAB²CD*K²MSΠΦ
minᵖˡ τη συγγενεια K* minᵖᵉʳᵖᵃᵘᶜ cognatione lattᵛᵗ ᵖˡ ᵛᵍ (arm) | om αυτου אᵃAC²DEF
GHMSUVII alᵖˡ a f go arm   5 ουκ εδυνατο...ποι.] non faciebat b c e (ff) noluit
facere a f i q r

feeling, but adds afterwards ἐπλήσθησαν πάντες θυμοῦ. Amazement rapidly
gave place to jealous suspicion, and
jealousy to anger. The σκάνδαλον
was the fact that the Lord till lately
had been one of themselves. For
σκανδαλίζεσθαι see note on iv. 17,
and for σκ. ἔν τινι cf. Mt. xi. 6, xxvi.
31 f.; the construction occurs also
in Sir. ix. 5, xxiii. 8, xxxv. 15 (xxxii.
19). The Nazarenes found their
stumblingblock in the person or circumstances of Jesus; He became a
πέτρα σκανδάλου (1 Pet. ii. 7, 8, Rom.
ix. 33) to those who disbelieved. The
Cross enormously increased the difficulties of belief for those who expected external display; see 1 Cor.
i. 23, Gal. v. 11. But for such there
were difficulties from the first.

4. καὶ ἔλεγεν αὐτοῖς κτλ.] An answer to the objection which He anticipates (Lc.), that the Capharnaites
had been more favoured than His
own fellow-townsmen. In His own
city He would have been received
with less alacrity; people are slow to
credit with extraordinary powers one
who has lived from childhood under
their observation. For οὐκ ἔστιν προφ.
ἄτιμος εἰ μή κτλ. (Mt. Mc.) Lc. substitutes οὐδεὶς προφήτης δεκτός ἐστιν
ἐν τῇ πατρίδι αὐτοῦ: Jo., who seems
to regard Judaea as the πατρίς (cf.
Westcott ad l. and Origen in Cor-
derius, p. 138), has a reminiscence
of the saying in its earlier form (iv.
44, αὐτὸς γὰρ Ἰησοῦς ἐμαρτύρησεν ὅτι
προφ. ἐν τῇ ἰδίᾳ πατρίδι τιμὴν οὐκ ἔχει).

Comp. Oxyrhynch. log. 6. The Lord
here assumes the rôle of the Prophet
which was generally conceded to Him
(vi. 15, viii. 28, Mt. xxi. 11, 46, Lc.
xxiv. 19, Jo. iv. 19, vi. 14, vii. 40,
ix. 17, Acts iii. 22, vii. 37). Συγγενεῦ-
σιν = συγγενέσιν: for the form cf.
1 Macc. x. 89 (אᶜ·ᵃA), Lc. ii. 44 (LXΔΛ
1, 13, 33, 69, al.); see WH., Notes,
p. 158, WSchm., p. 89, Blass, Gr.,
p. 27. Of the ἀτιμία cast upon the
Lord by His kindred and family (ἡ
οἰκία αὐτοῦ) see exx. in iii. 21, Jo.
vii. 3 f.

5. οὐκ ἐδύνατο...ποιῆσαι] Mt. οὐκ
ἐποίησεν. Origen (on Mt. x. 19) has
an interesting comment on Mc.'s
phrase: οὐ γὰρ εἶπεν Οὐκ ἤθελεν· ἀλλ'
Οὐκ ἠδύνατο, ὡς ἐρχομένης μὲν ἐπὶ τὴν
ἐνεργοῦσαν δύναμιν συμπράξεως ὑπὸ
πίστεως ἐκείνου εἰς ὃν ἐνήργει ἡ δύναμις
κωλυομένης δὲ ἐνεργεῖν ὑπὸ τῆς ἀπιστίας.
To work a miracle upon a responsible
human being it was necessary that
faith on the part of the recipient
should concur with Divine power;
neither was effectual without the
other : οὔτε τὰ ἐνεργήματα τῶν δυνάμεων
χωρὶς πίστεως τῆς τῶν θεραπευομένων
...οὔτε ἡ πίστις, ὁποία ποτ' ἂν ᾖ, χωρὶς
τῆς θείας δυνάμεως. Faith was necessary also on the part of the worker of
the miracle (see Mt. xvii. 19, 20), but
in our Lord's case this condition was
always satisfied (Mc. xi. 21 f., Jo. xi.
41).

εἰ μὴ ὀλίγοις ἀρρώστοις κτλ.] Cf.
'Mc.' xvi. 18, ἐπὶ ἀρρώστους χεῖρας
ἐπιθήσουσιν, and for other instances

στοις ἐπιθεὶς τὰς χεῖρας ἐθεράπευσεν· ¶ ⁶καὶ ἐθαύμασεν ὁ   ¶ syrʰⁱᵉʳ
διὰ τὴν ἀπιστίαν αὐτῶν.

Καὶ περιῆγεν τὰς κώμας κύκλῳ διδάσκων. ⁷καὶ 7
προσκαλεῖται τοὺς δώδεκα καὶ ἤρξατο αὐτοὺς ἀπο-
στέλλειν δύο δύο, καὶ ἐδίδου αὐτοῖς ἐξουσίαν τῶν

6 εθαυμασεν ℵBE*ᵛⁱᵈ 2ᵖᵉ alᵖᵃᵘᶜ] εθαυμαζεν ACDLΠΣΦ al minᵖˡ | απιστιαν] πιστιν D
(sed incredulitatem d)   7 προσκαλειται…δυο δυο] προσκαλεσαμενος τους ιβ μαθητας
απεστειλεν αυτους ανα β̄ D latᵛᵗ syrˢⁱⁿ | των πν. των ακαθ.] pr κατα Δ 238 al aeth
om των bis CΔ

of the imposition of hands in such cases, Mc. v. 23, vii. 32, viii. 23, 25. These works of healing at Nazareth must, it would appear, have preceded the scene in the synagogue, which was immediately followed by the Lord's expulsion from the town (Lc. iv. 28 ff.).

6. ἐθαύμασεν] His wonder, as well as the limitation of His power, was real and not apparent only. Cf. Mt. viii. 10, where the Lord expresses wonder at a high degree of faith under conditions where faith was not to be expected. The surprises of life, especially those which belong to its ethical and spiritual side, created genuine astonishment in the human mind of Christ. Θαυμάζειν is usually followed in the N.T. by ἐπί with dat. (Lc. iv. 22, xx. 26, Acts iii. 12), περὶ with gen. (Lc. ii. 18) or an acc. of the object (Lc. vii. 9, xxiv. 12, Acts vii. 31). Διά with acc. points to the cause of the sensation which the Lord experienced. Cf. WM., p. 497.

6b—13. ANOTHER CIRCUIT OF GALILEE; MISSION OF THE TWELVE (Mt. ix. 35—x. 1, x. 5—xi. 1, Lc. ix. 1—6).

6b. περιῆγεν τὰς κώμας] Another circuit of the villages and towns (Mt. τὰς πόλεις πάσας) of Galilee (cf. Mc. i. 38 f.). Κύκλῳ does not limit the tour to the neighbourhood of Nazareth, but implies that, after passing from town to town, He came back to a point near that from which He started, i.e. the neighbourhood of the Lake; see vi. 32. Διδάσκων: Mt.

adds ἐν ταῖς συναγωγαῖς αὐτῶν, καὶ κηρύσσων…καὶ θεραπεύων. His work, as usual, included (1) Synagogue-teaching, (2) proclamation of the Kingdom in houses or by the roadside, (3) incidental miracles of healing. Unbelief no longer prevented the manifestation of His power. For περιάγειν intr. with acc. loci cf. Mt. ix. 35, xxiii. 15.

7. προσκαλεῖται τοὺς δώδεκα] The Twelve are now a recognised body, who can be summoned as such at the pleasure of the Head. Προσκ. implies authority, cf. Mc. xv. 44, Lc. xv. 26. It is, however, characteristic of our Lord that His summons is by no means limited to disciples: cf. iii. 23, προσκ. αὐτούς, sc. τοὺς γραμματεῖς: vii. 14, viii. 34, προσκαλ. τὸν ὄχλον. With τοὺς δώδεκα cf. οἱ ἔνδεκα 'Mc.' xvi. 14, οἱ ἑβδομήκοντα δύο (Lc. x. 17), οἱ ἑπτά (Acts xxi. 8).

ἤρξατο αὐτ. ἀποστέλλειν] This was the ultimate purpose of their selection (iii. 15, where see note). The time had now come for testing the results of their preparatory training.

δύο δύο] As in LXX., Gen. vi. 19 f., vii. 2 f., 9, 15. Vg. binos, in pairs = ἀνὰ δύο (cf. D here), a Hebraism which Delitzsch renders שְׁנַיִם שְׁנַיִם; cf. WM., p. 312, Blass, Gr., p. 145. On the purpose of this arrangement see Latham, Pastor p., p. 297 f. Thpht. cites Eccl. iv. 9, ἀγαθοὶ δύο ὑπὲρ τὸν ἕνα. Galilee was now evangelised in six different directions. The pairs

8 πνευμάτων τῶν ἀκαθάρτων. ⁸καὶ παρήγγειλεν αὐτοῖς
ἵνα μηδὲν αἴρωσιν εἰς ὁδὸν εἰ μὴ ῥάβδον μόνον, μὴ
9 ἄρτον, μὴ πήραν, μὴ εἰς τὴν ζώνην χαλκόν, ⁹ἀλλὰ

8 αρωσιν אCLΔΦ 13 69 2ᵖᵉ alᵖᵃᵘᶜ | μη αρτον μη πηραν אBCLΔ 33 me aeth] μη π.
μη α. ΑΠΣΦ al minᵖˡ latt syrr arm μητε π. μητε α. D 2ᵖᵉ a go   9 αλλ EFGH
KMΔΠ alᵖˡ

were probably arranged as in the
Apostolic lists, as Victor suggests.
ἐδίδου αὐτοῖς ἐξουσίαν κτλ.] Cf. iii.
14. ἔχειν ἐξ. ἐκβάλλειν τὰ δαιμόνια.
Ἐδίδου: He was occupied in giving
them their authority (imperf.), and
while doing so, He charged them
(aor.) etc. Ἐξουσία is the note of the
authorised servants, as it was that of
the Master Himself, cf. i. 27, xiii. 34.
Τῶν πνευμάτων: gen. of the object, cf.
Jo. xvii. 2, Rom. ix. 21, 1 Cor. ix. 12 ;
other constructions are in use, as ἐπί
with acc. (Lc. ix. 1) or gen. (Apoc. ii.
26, xiv. 18, xx. 6), ἐπάνω τινός (Lc. xix.
17) or κατά τινος (Jo. xix. 11). On πν.
ἀκάθαρτα see i. 23 note.
Mt., Lc. extend the commission to
the healing of diseases and the preaching of the Kingdom. Both preaching
and healing were in fact included, cf.
Mc. v. 12.
8. παρήγγειλεν αὐτοῖς ἵνα κτλ.] Ἵνα
is used after παραγγέλλω again in
2 Thess. iii. 12 ; after παρακαλῶ it
is frequent (1 Cor. i. 10, xvi. 12, 15,
2 Cor. vii. 6, xii. 8). In all these
cases the telic use of ἵνα is in the
background of the thought, but the
sense is hardly distinguishable from
that of the ordinary construction with
the inf., or from a direct imperative ;
cf. Lc. here (εἶπεν...μηδὲν αἴρετε). Εἰς
ὁδόν, as a travelling outfit: Lc. more
explicitly, εἰς τὴν ὁδόν, for this particular journey. For the anarthrous
phrase cf. Mc. x. 17, Lc. xi. 6.
εἰ μὴ ῥάβδον μόνον κτλ.] Mt. (μηδὲ
ῥάβδον) and Lc. (μήτε ῥ.) exclude
even this—an early exaggeration of
the sternness of the command, for it
is impossible to assent here to Augustine's ruling (de cons. ev. ii. 75)

"utrumque accipiendum est a Domino
Apostolis dictum." The staff was the
universal companion of the traveller,
whatever else he might lack ; see
Gen. xxxii. 10 (11), ἐν γὰρ τῇ ῥάβδῳ
μου διέβην τὸν Ἰορδάνην, and with
the whole passage comp. Exod. xii.
11. Much forethought was ordinarily
expended on a journey, cf. Tob. v. 17,
and the delightful picture in Jos. ix.
10 (4) ff. Μή...μή...μή carry on the
construction ἵνα μηδὲν αἴρωσιν (cf. Mt.
Lc.). The order is ascensive : 'no
bread, no bag to carry what they
could buy, no money to buy with.'
This point is missed in Lc., and in
the later text of Mc. (cf. Vg. non
peram non panem). Πήρα is a leathern
bag to carry provisions, cf. 4 Regn. iv.
42 (cod. א, Compl.), Judith x. 5, xiii.
10, 15 ; Suidas: πήρα ἡ θήκη τῶν
ἄρτων. The word is found from Homer
downwards. On the significance of
this direction cf. Victor : ὥστε καὶ
ἀπὸ τοῦ σχήματος δεικνύναι πᾶσιν ὑμᾶς
ὅσον ἀφεστήκατε χρημάτων ἐπιθυμίας.
Μὴ εἰς τὴν ζώνην χαλκόν—'not a copper
for your girdle,' Lc. μήτε ἀργύριον 'nor
a silver piece' (shekel or drachma);
Mt. μὴ κτήσησθε χρυσὸν μηδὲ ἄργυρον
μηδὲ χαλκόν. The girdle served as a
purse for small change (cf. the classical
phrase εἰς ζώνην δίδοσθαι), or, when
secrecy was necessary, for considerable sums of money (Suet. Vitell.
16, "zona se aureorum plena circum-
dedit"), but on this occasion it was
to be empty; much less was the
missioner to carry a βαλλάντιον (Lc.
x. 4).
9. ἀλλὰ ὑποδεδεμένους κτλ.] A sudden break in the construction, suggestive of the disjointed notes on

ὑποδεδεμένους σανδάλια· καὶ μὴ ἐνδύσασθε δύο χι
τῶνας.¶ ¹⁰καὶ ἔλεγεν αὐτοῖς ʽΟπου ἐὰν εἰσέλθητε εἰς 10 ¶ ᵉ

9 ενδυσασθε B* 33 alᵖᵃᵘᵉ] ενδυσασθαι B²SII* al ενδυσησθε אACDΔII²Φ al minᵖˡ a
me go arm ενδεδυσθαι LNΣ minᵐᵘ

which the Evangelist depended. The
writer, forgetting that he has used
ἵνα, falls back upon the ordinary construction of παραγγέλλω with the inf.
(oratio variata, WM., p. 724, Buttmann, p. 330, Blass, Gr. p. 286;
Bengel compares xii. 38, θελόντων
περιπατεῖν...καὶ ἀσπασμούς); others
with less probability regard ὑποδε
δεμ. [εἶναι]...ἐνδύσασθαι (vv. ll.) as
'infinitive imperatives,' cf. Burton,
§ 365. If we read ἐνδύσασθε, another change follows, from the oratio
obliqua to the o. recta; see other
N. T. exx. in WM., p. 725. For ὑποδ.
σανδάλια Mt. has μηδὲ ὑποδήματα (cf.
Lc. x. 4). Σανδάλιον and ὑπόδημα are
both used in the LXX. as equivalents
of נַעַל (for σανδ. see Jos. ix. 11 (5), Isa.
xx. 2, Judith x. 4, xvi. 9); in the
N. T., σανδ. occurs again only in Acts
xii. 8; the form סנדל is found in Rabbinical writings (Schürer II. i. p.
44 n.). The σανδάλιον was in Greece
part of the woman's attire (Becker,
Charicles, p. 447), but in the East it
appears to have been used by men
also, esp. perhaps in travelling. There
seems to be no warrant for distinguishing σανδ. and ὑπόδημα: σανδ.
may have been used here and in Acts
l. c. (see Blass) in order to avoid
writing ὑποδεδέσθαι ὑποδήματα. If so,
Mc. is here again at issue with Mt.;
see note on v. 8 (εἰ μὴ ῥ. μόνον).

δύο χιτῶνας] One χιτών (בְּתֹנֶת)
sufficed, cf. Jo. xix. 23, τὰ ἱμάτια...ὁ
χιτών: to possess two was a sign of
comparative wealth, cf. Lc. iii. 11.
Two were however sometimes worn
at the same time, esp. perhaps in
travelling; see Joseph. ant. xvii. 5.
7, τὸν ἐντὸς χιτῶνα, ἐνεδεδύκει γὰρ δύο:
cf. Mc. xiv. 63. It is the wearing of

two on this journey which is prohibited (μὴ ἐνδ.); Mt. and Lc. extend
the prohibition to the possession of
two (Mt. μηδὲ δύο χιτῶνας, sc. κτή
σησθε: Lc. μήτε δ. χ. ἔχειν).
On the general purpose of these
directions see Latham, p. 290 ff. No
hardship was suffered by the Apostles in consequence (Lc. xxii. 35), while
an important lesson was taught to
the future Church: comp. Mt. x. 10
with 1 Tim. v. 18. For the mystical
interpretation see Origen in Jo. t. i.
27 (25): αὐτός ἐστιν ἡ ὁδός, ἐφ᾿ ἣν
ὁδὸν οὐδὲν αἴρειν δεῖ...αὐτάρκης γάρ ἐστι
παντὸς ἐφοδίου αὕτη ἡ ὁδός: ib. t. vi.
19; de princ. iv. 18; and cf. Bigg,
Christian Platonists, p. 137 f.

10. καὶ ἔλεγεν αὐτοῖς κτλ.] The
directions given above imply that
the missionaries were to look for free
entertainment. The Lord adds two
general rules for their guidance in
this matter: (1) 'during your visit to
any town remain in the same house,'
(2) 'do not force yourselves on an unwilling people or quit them without
solemn warning.'

ὅπου ἐὰν εἰσέλθητε κτλ.] The house
was not to be chosen at haphazard,
but by a careful selection of the fittest (Mt.); Jerome in Mt. ix., "apostoli
novam introeuntes urbem scire non
poterunt quis qualis esset. ergo
hospes fama eligendus est populi et
indicio vicinorum." Having made their
choice, they were to be content with
the fare it offered, and not to change
their lodging unnecessarily (cf. Lc. x.
7). St Paul seems to have followed
this rule in his mission to the Gentiles; see Acts xvi. 15, xvii. 5—7,
xviii. 7; only during his captivity at
Rome do we find him dwelling ἐν ἰδίῳ
μισθώματι. Contrast the care with

11 οἰκίαν, ἐκεῖ μένετε ἕως ἂν ἐξέλθητε ἐκεῖθεν. ¹¹καὶ ὃς
ἂν τόπος μὴ δέξηται ὑμᾶς μηδὲ ἀκούσωσιν ὑμῶν,
ἐκπορευόμενοι ἐκεῖθεν ἐκτινάξατε τὸν χοῦν τὸν ὑπο-
12 κάτω τῶν ποδῶν ὑμῶν εἰς μαρτύριον αὐτοῖς. ¹²καὶ
13 ἐξελθόντες ἐκήρυξαν ἵνα μετανοῶσιν, ¹³καὶ δαιμόνια

11 ος αν τοπος μη δεξηται אBLΔ 13 28 69 124 346 syrʰᶜˡ⁽ᵐᵍ⁾ me aeth] ος αν μη
δεξ. C*ᵛⁱᵈ 1 209 syrˢⁱⁿ οσοι εαν μη δεξωνται AC²DNΠΣΦ al minᵖˡ latt syrrᵖᵉˢʰ ʰᶜˡ⁽ᵗˣᵗ⁾
arm οσοι ου μη δεξωνται 1071 | om τον υποκατω D 33 604 2ᵖᵉ latt (exc c) syrˢⁱⁿ arm
aeth | αυτοις]+αμην λεγω υμιν ανεκτοτερον εσται Σοδομοις η Γομορροις εν ημερα κρισεως
η τη πολει εκεινη ANΠΣΦ al minᵖˡ a f q syrr go aeth   12 εκηρυξαν אBCDLΔ
syrrᵖᵉˢʰ ʰᶜˡ⁽ᵐᵍ⁾ go] εκηρυσσον ANΠΣΦ al minᶠᵒʳᵗᵉ ᵒᵐⁿ latt | μετανοωσιν BDL me]
μετανοησωσιν אACΔΠΦ al minᶠᵒʳᵗᵉ ᵒᵐⁿ μετανοησουσιν NΣ

which the next age found it necessary to guard itself against an abuse of this privilege of the itinerant preacher; *Didache* 11: πᾶς δὲ ἀπόστολος ἐρχόμενος πρὸς ὑμᾶς δεχθήτω ὡς Κύριος· μενεῖ δὲ ἡμέραν μίαν, ἐὰν δὲ ᾖ χρεία, καὶ τὴν ἄλλην· τρεῖς δε ἐὰν μείνῃ, ψευδοπροφήτης ἐστίν κτλ.

11. ὃς ἂν τόπος μὴ δέξηται κτλ.] The giving or withholding hospitality in this case was not a personal matter; it was a visible sign of acceptance or rejection of the Master and the Father Who sent Him (Mt. x. 40, Lc. x. 16), and therefore an index of the relation in which the inhabitants as a whole stood to the eternal order. Mt. extends the principle to the case of the individual householder who refuses hospitality. For δέχεσθαι in the sense of hospitable or courteous reception comp. Acts xxi. 17, 2 Cor. vii. 15, Gal. iv. 14, Col. iv. 10, Heb. xi. 31. Μηδὲ ἀκ. ὑμῶν: 'nor will they even give you a hearing.'

ἐκπορευόμενοι ἐκεῖθεν] I.e. ἐκ τοῦ τόπου ἐκείνου. Mt. ἔξω τῆς οἰκίας ἢ τῆς πόλεως ἐκείνης: see last note. Ἐκτινάξατε τὸν χοῦν. Cf. Lc. x. 11, εἴπατε Καὶ τὸν κονιορτὸν (Mt. x. 14) τὸν κολληθέντα ἡμῖν ἐκ τῆς πόλεως ὑμῶν εἰς τοὺς πόδας ἀπομασσόμεθα, and Acts xiii. 51, where Paul and Barnabas are said to have acted upon this

precept at Pisidian Antioch. The act was understood to be a formal disavowal of fellowship, and probably also an intimation that the offender had placed himself on the level of the Gentiles, for it is a Rabbinical doctrine that the dust of a Gentile land defiles. The Israelite who rejected the Messiah became as an ἐθνικός, cf. Mt. xviii. 17. The garments were sometimes shaken with the same purpose (Acts xviii. 6).

εἰς μαρτύριον αὐτοῖς] Cf. i. 44, xiii. 9. The action just prescribed was not to be performed in a contemptuous or vindictive spirit, but with a view to its moral effect: either it would lead to reflexion and possibly repentance, or at least it would justify God's future judgment (cf. Mt. x. 15, Lc. x. 12). The reference to Sodom and Gomorrah inserted by A and a few of the later uncials is from Mt.

12. ἐκήρυξαν ἵνα μετανοῶσιν] On this use of ἵνα see note on παρήγγειλεν ...ἵνα (v. 8). Μετάνοια was the theme of their preaching, μετανοεῖτε its chief summons; cf. i. 15, Lc. xxiv. 47, Acts xx. 21. Further, its aim and purpose were to produce repentance, and from this point of view ἵνα retains its telic force: cf. Vg. *praedicabant ut paenitentiam agerent*. The pres. μετανοῶσιν represents the repentance as a

πολλὰ ἐξέβαλλον, καὶ ἤλειφον ἐλαίῳ πολλοὺς ἀρρώστους καὶ ἐθεράπευον.
¹⁴§Καὶ ἤκουσεν ὁ βασιλεὺς Ἡρῴδης, φανερὸν γὰρ 14 § syrʰⁱᵉʳ

13 ἐξέβαλλον אABLΣΦ al minᵖˡ latt] ἐξέβαλον CM 33 alᵖᵃᵘᶜ | ηλ. ελ. π. αρρ. κ. εθερ.]
ἀλείψαντες ελ. π. αρρ. εθερ. D b c(g)i q r | αρρ. post εθ. transp syrˢⁱⁿ | εθεραπευοντο
ΝΠΣ minᵖᵃᵘᶜ f   14 Ηρωδης]+την ακοην ιυ M 13 69 736 1071 alᵖᵃᵘᶜ

state and not merely an act following
upon the preaching.

13. δαιμόνια πολλὰ ἐξέβαλλον] They
found themselves invested with the
same authority over unclean spirits
which had been the earliest note of
the Master's mission (i. 23), and from
time to time they exercised it (imperf.). But they were not invariably
successful (ix. 18); and when they
succeeded, it was through a believing
use of the Master's Name ('Mc.' xvi.
17, Lc. ix. 49).

ἤλειφον ἐλαίῳ π. ἀρρώστους] Euth.:
εἰκὸς δὲ καὶ τοῦτο παρὰ τοῦ κυρίου
διδαχθῆναι τοὺς ἀποστόλους. Oil was
much used in medical treatment: cf.
Lc. x. 34, Joseph. B. J. i. 33. 5.
Galen (cited by J. B. Mayor) calls it
ἄριστον ἰαμάτων πάντων τοῖς ἐξηραμ-
μένοις καὶ αὐχμώδεσι σώμασιν: Isaiah
(i. 6) complains, οὐκ ἔστιν μάλαγμα
ἐπιθεῖναι οὔτε ἔλαιον οὔτε καταδέσμους.
See also J. Lightfoot ad loc. and
Schöttgen on James v. 14. As used
by the Apostles and followed by immediate results, it was no more than
a sign of healing power, but it served
perhaps to differentiate their miracles
from those performed by the Master,
Who does not appear to have employed any symbol but His own hands
or saliva. After His departure the
Apostles and other disciples laid
their hands upon the sick ('Mc.' xvi.
18, Acts xxviii. 8, Iren. ii. 32. 4), but
the use of oil held its place at least
among Jewish Christians (James, l.c.).
Traces of a ritual use of the unction of
the sick appear first among Gnostic
practices of the second century (Iren.
i. 21. 5); on the later ecclesiastical

rite see the authorities cited in D.C.A.
ii. p. 2004 f. Victor remarks: σημαίνει
οὖν τὸ ἀλειφόμενον ἔλαιον καὶ τὸ παρὰ
τοῦ θεοῦ ἔλεον καὶ τὴν ἴασιν τοῦ νοσή-
ματος καὶ τῆς καρδίας τὸν φωτισμόν·
ὅτι γὰρ ἡ εὐχὴ τὸ πᾶν ἐνήργει παντί
που δῆλον· τὸ δὲ ἔλαιον ὧς γε οἶμαι
σύμβολον τούτων ὑπῆρχε. Bede finds
in this Apostolic practice a precedent for the Western use of unction
with which he was familiar: "unde
patet ab ipsis apostolis hunc sanctae
ecclesiae morem esse traditum ut
energumeni vel alii quilibet aegroti
ungantur oleo pontificali benedictione
consecrato."

ἐκήρυξαν...ἐξέβαλλον...ἤλειφον] The
change of tense is perhaps intended
to mark the incidental character of
the miracles. The preaching is regarded as a whole, the miracles are
mentioned as occurring from time to
time during the course of the preaching. The traditional text misses this
point; cf. Vg. praedicabant...eicie-
bant...unguebant.

14—16. THE FAME OF JESUS
REACHES THE TETRARCH (Mt. xiv. 1—
2, Lc. ix. 7—9).

14. καὶ ἤκουσεν ὁ βασιλεὺς Ἡρ.]
Mt. adds τὴν ἀκοὴν Ἰησοῦ, Lc., τὰ γινόμενα πάντα. Mt. distinctly connects
this with the circuit of Galilee which
began at Nazareth (xiv. 1, ἐν ἐκείνῳ
τῷ καιρῷ). It was not so much the
miracles at Capernaum, as the stir
throughout the entire tetrarchy (Lc. τὰ
γινόμενα πάντα) and the great diffusion
of the movement caused by the mission
of the Twelve, which attracted the attention of Antipas. The court, even
if located at Tiberias, could regard

ἐγένετο τὸ ὄνομα αὐτοῦ, καὶ ἔλεγον ὅτι Ἰωάνης ὁ
βαπτίζων ἐγήγερται ἐκ νεκρῶν, καὶ διὰ τοῦτο ἐνερ-

14 ελεγον B (D -γοσαν) min^perpauc a b ff Aug^cons] ελεγεν אACLNΔΠΣ al min^pl
c f i q vg syrr me arm go ειπεν τοις πασιν αυτου Φ | ο βαπτιζων] ο βαπτιστης DS 13 28
33 69 124 346 604 (baptista a b c f i q vg) | εγηγερται אBDLΔ 33 604] ηγερθη CNΠ^mg
ΣΦ al ανεστη AKΠ^txt

with indifference the preaching of a
local prophet, so long as it was limited
to the Jewish lake-side towns; but
when it was systematically carried into
every part of the country, suspicion was
aroused. Ὁ βασιλεύς = ὁ τετραάρχης
(Mt. Lc.). Mc. does not use the latter
word, and Mt. falls back on βασιλεύς
in the course of his narrative (xiv. 9);
cf. Acts iv. 26, 27, Justin, dial. 49 (ὁ
βασιλεὺς ὑμῶν Ἡρῴδης), Ev. Petr. 1
(Ἡρ. ὁ βασιλεύς), Ev. Nic. prol.
(Ἡρῴδου βασιλέως τῆς Γαλιλαίας).
Victor: ὁ δὲ Μᾶρκος καὶ ἕτεροι δέ τινες
ἀδιαφόρως καὶ βασιλέα καλοῦσιν εἴτε
ἀπὸ τῆς τοῦ πατρὸς συνηθείας εἴτε καὶ
ἀδεέστερον ἔτι τῇ φωνῇ κεχρημένοι. A
tetrarch was in fact a petty king, and
may have been called βασιλεύς as an act
of courtesy: he possessed a jurisdiction
with which the Imperial authorities
were ordinarily reluctant to interfere
(Lc. xxiii. 7). Yet an attempt to
claim the title from Caligula led to
the downfall of Antipas: Joseph. ant.
xviii. 7. 2. On the life and character
of Antipas see Schürer I. ii. 17 ff.
φανερὸν γάρ κτλ.] Notoriety was
inevitable, although it was not desired;
cf. iii. 12, vii. 24. Bengel: "Iesus
prius non innotuit...sero aula accipit
novellas spirituales." What especially
arrested Herod's attention was the
common report (ἔλεγον: see vv. ll.
and cf. Field, Notes, p. 28) that the
new prophet was a resuscitated John.
As Elijah was thought to have re-
appeared in John, so John had returned to life in his successor.
Origen (in Jo. t. vi. 30) suggests that
the Baptist and our Lord were so like
in personal appearance ὥστε διὰ τὸ
κοινὸν τῆς μορφῆς Ἰωάννην τε Χριστὸν

ὑπονοεῖσθαι τυγχάνειν καὶ Ἰησοῦν Ἰωάννην: cf. however his remarks in Mt.
t. x. 20. For ὁ βαπτίζων see i. 4.
Ἐγήγερται, 'has risen' and is therefore alive and amongst us again: cf.
1 Cor. xv. 20. Ἠγέρθη (Mt. Lc., and
below, v. 16) is scarcely distinguishable in a translation (cf. xvi. 6, and see
Burton, 52 f.), but the perf. concerns
itself less with the historical fact and
more with the result.
διὰ τοῦτο ἐνεργοῦσιν αἱ δυν. ἐν αὐτῷ]
In life John did no miracle (Jo. x. 41),
but John risen from the dead might
well be supposed to have brought with
him new and supernatural powers (ἐκ
τῆς ἀναστάσεως προσέλαβε τὸ θαυματουργεῖν, Thpht.), or, as Origen (in Mt. t.
x. 20) suggests, the same powers turned
into a new channel: ᾤετο ὁ Ἡρῴδης
τὰς ἐν Ἰωάννῃ δυνάμεις ἐν μὲν τῷ Ἰωάννῃ
ἐνηργηκέναι τὰ τοῦ βαπτίσματος καὶ τῆς
διδασκαλίας...ἐν δὲ τῷ Ἰησοῦ τὰς τερα-
στίους δυνάμεις. Ἐνεργοῦσιν, Vg. in-
operantur, 'are operative,' intrans.,
as in Gal. ii. 8, Eph. ii. 2, Phil. ii. 13
(τὸ ἐνεργεῖν): cf. Sap. xv. 11, ψυχὴν
ἐνεργοῦσαν. More usually ἐνεργεῖν is
followed by an acc. of the thing
effected, cf. 1 Cor. xii. 6, 11, Gal. iii. 5,
Eph. i. 11, 20, while ἐνεργεῖσθαι is
used intransitively, e.g. Rom. vii. 5,
2 Cor. i. 6, Eph. iii. 20, Col. i. 29; for
a further distinction noticed in St
Paul see Lightfoot on Gal. v. 6. On
the construction ἐνεργ. ἔν τινι see
Lightfoot on Gal. ii. 8, and for other
instances cf. Eph. i. 20, ii. 2, 1 Thess.
ii. 13. Αἱ δυνάμεις, the miraculous
powers of which report spoke; for
δύναμις in this sense see 1 Cor. xii. 10,
28, Gal. iii. 5 (Lightfoot)—more usually,
the miraculous acts which the powers

γοῦσιν αἱ δυνάμεις ἐν αὐτῷ· ¹⁵ἄλλοι δὲ ἔλεγον ὅτι 15
Ἡλείας ἐστίν· ἄλλοι δὲ ἔλεγον ὅτι Προφήτης, ὡς εἷς
τῶν προφητῶν. ¹⁶ἀκούσας δὲ ὁ Ἡρῴδης ἔλεγεν ῝Ον 16
ἐγὼ ἀπεκεφάλισα Ἰωάνην, οὗτος ἠγέρθη.
¹⁷Αὐτὸς γὰρ ὁ Ἡρῴδης ἀποστείλας ἐκράτησεν 17

15 om δε 1° FMUV syrʰᵉˡ arm | om προφ. ως D b c ff i πρ. η ως ΔΦ 1 alᵖᵃᵘᶜ syrʰᵉˡ
arm πρ. εστιν ως AC²Π al minᵖˡ a f q vg go | ως εις των προφ.] om a τις των αρχαιων
ανεστη 33   16 ελεγεν] ειπεν ADΠ | ουτος Ιωαννης ηγερθη ℵ* ουτος I. αυτος ηγερθη ℵᵃ
ουτος εκ νεκρων ηγερθη D ουτος εστιν αυτος ηγ. εκ νεκρων ΑΠ(Σ)Φ al minᵖˡ b q go
syrʰᵉˡ arm o. ε. α. ηγ. απο των ν. CN alᵖᵃᵘᶜ Orˡ + οτι ACΔΠ me go   17 αυτος γαρ ο]
ο γαρ ℵᶜ·ᵃ L me go

effect (vi. 2, Acts xix. 11, 2 Cor.
xii. 12).

15. ἄλλοι δὲ ἔλεγον κτλ.] While all
were agreed as to the wonder-working
power of Jesus, opinions differed as to
His personality. Those who saw the ab-
surdity of identifying Him with John,
took Him for Elijah, with whom John
had refused to be identified (Jo. i.
21). This opinion was perhaps widely
spread in Galilee, where no suspicion
seems to have been as yet entertained
of His Messiahship. If Elijah must
come before Messiah (ix. 11), why
should not this be Elijah? Cf. viii.
28, and note on ix. 11. Others again
were content to say that Jesus was a
prophet of the highest order, the equal
of the Prophets of the O. T. canon (οἱ
προφῆται, Tob. xiv. 4 (ℵ), 5, Acts iii.
21, 24 f.). Ὡς εἷς τῶν προφητῶν : cf.
Jud. xvi. 7, 11 (codd. BA), ἔσομαι ὡς
εἷς τῶν ἀνθρώπων, on a par with other
men (כְּאַחַד הָאָדָם). In Lc. this belief
takes another form : προφήτης τις τῶν
ἀρχαίων ἀνέστη (cf. Sir. xlix. 10 (12))
—the name of Jeremiah was especially connected in the popular expectation (Mt. xvi. 14) with the hope of
a revival of the prophetic order. This
hope, which seems to have been based
on Deut. xviii. 15, appears in the
Maccabean age (1 Macc. iv. 46, xiv.
41), and was revived by the appearance of the Baptist (Jo. i. 21). Jesus
Himself claimed to be a Prophet (see
note on v. 4).

16. ἀκούσας δὲ ὁ Ἡρῴδης κτλ.]
Ἀκούσας takes up the thread which
had been dropped in v. 14, where
instead of continuing καὶ ἔλεγεν ῝Ον
κτλ., the Evangelist goes off into
the parenthesis φανερὸν γάρ...προφη-
τῶν. Herod was at first in doubt
which of these conjectures to accept
(Lc., διηπόρει), but finally decided in
favour of the first. His conscience
turned the scale in its favour. Lc. represents him as still sceptical (Ἰωάνην
ἐγὼ ἀπεκεφάλισα· τίς δέ ἐστιν οὗτος ;) ;
in Mc. fear has changed a reasonable
doubt into credulity : ‘I put John to
death, and now he has risen to condemn me.’ This conviction is the
more significant since Herod's frank
worldliness probably predisposed him
to Sadducean views (comp. Mt. xvi.
11 with Mc. viii. 15). Euth.: ὁ φονεύσας
φοβεῖται τὸν πεφονευμένον· τοιοῦτος
γὰρ ὁ κακός. For the construction
ὃν...Ἰωάνην οὗτος see WM., p. 205 :
for the late verb ἀποκεφαλίζω cf. Ps.
cli. 7 : Kennedy, Sources, p. 130.
Ἠγέρθη : has risen (as a fact): see
note on v. 14.

On the treatment of this verse in
the Eusebian canons see Nestle, Text.
Crit. p. 263 f.

17—29. EPISODE OF JOHN'S IM-
PRISONMENT AND DEATH (Mt. xiv.
3—12; cf. Lc. iii. 19—20).

17. αὐτὸς γάρ κτλ.] Mc. is here
much fuller than Mt., while Lc. gives
but a bare summary of the causes of

τὸν Ἰωάνην καὶ ἔδησεν αὐτὸν ἐν φυλακῇ διὰ Ἡρῳδιάδα τὴν γυναῖκα Φιλίππου τοῦ ἀδελφοῦ αὐτοῦ, ὅτι

17 και εδ. αυτον εν φυλακη] εν φυλ. και εδ. αυτον A | εν φυλακη (εν τη φ. ς
min^(pauc vid))] και εβαλεν εις φυλακην D 13 28 69 124 346 604 a b f ff i syr^(hier ed) arm | om
την γυναικα B* (hab B^(mg))

the imprisonment. Certain coincidences (comp. *vv.* 17, 22, 23, 26, 28,
29 with Mt. xiv. 3, 6, 8, 9, 21, 22)
point to the dependence of Mt. and
Mc. on a common source which Mt.'s
sense of the secondary importance of
the narrative has perhaps led him to
abbreviate. Αὐτός answers to the
emphatic ἐγώ of *v.* 16: the first step
at least had been taken by Herod
himself, who had sent (to Aenon? cf.
Jo. iii. 23; on the position see Tristram, *Bible Places*, p. 234) to have
John arrested. For this sense of
κρατεῖν see xii. 12, xiv. 1 ff. The
events can be placed with some precision. John was still baptizing
during the Lord's early ministry in
Judaea, after the first Passover (Jo.
iii. 23 f.). But before Jesus left
Judaea (Mt. iv. 12), certainly before
He began His ministry in Galilee
(Mc. i. 14), the Baptist was already
a prisoner. On the other hand his
death had not long preceded the
report of the new Prophet's successes.
He was alive for some time after the
beginning of the Galilean ministry
(Mt. xi. 2 ff., Lc. vii. 18), and the tidings
of the murder of the Baptist seem to
have brought the recent circuit to an
end (Mt. xiv. 12, 13). Hence, while the
narrative of Mc. vi. 17, 18 carries us
back to the interval which follows
i. 13, Mc. vi. 21—29 is but slightly
out of its chronological order. Ἐν
φυλακῇ: cf. ἐν τῇ φυλακῇ (*v.* 28) and
ἐν τῷ δεσμωτηρίῳ (Mt. xi. 2). Josephus
ant. xviii. 5. 2 gives the locality of
the imprisonment : ὁ μὲν ὑποψίᾳ τῇ
Ἡρῴδου δέσμιος εἰς τὸν Μαχαιροῦντα
πεμφθεὶς τὸ προειρημένον φρούριον
ταύτῃ κτίννυται. For a description of
this formidable fortress see *B. J.* vii.
6. 1, and for the local history and

topography see G. A. Smith, *H. G.*
p. 569 f., Schürer I. ii. p. 250 f. n.,
Neubauer, *G. du T.* p. 40, Tristram,
Land of Moab, p. 253 ff. Machaerus
(מכור, *M'khawr*) overlooked the
Dead Sea, perched on the wild heights
opposite to the wilderness of Judaea
(i. 4); the tragedy of the Baptist's
death was enacted within view of the
scene of his early work. The citadel
stood on the summit of a cone, a
small but almost impregnable circular
keep, within which Tristram noticed
two dungeons with "small holes still
visible in the masonry where staples
of wood and iron had once been
fixed."

διὰ Ἡρῳδιάδα τὴν γυναῖκα Φιλίππου]
Her first husband was not Philip the
tetrarch (Lc. iii. 1, cf. Mc. viii. 27),
but another half-brother of Antipas,
son of Herod the Great by Mariamne
daughter of Simon. Joseph. *ant.*
xviii. 5. 4, Ἡρῳδιὰς δὲ αὐτῶν ἡ ἀδελφὴ
γίνεται Ἡρῴδῃ Ἡρῴδου τοῦ μεγάλου
παιδὶ γεγονότι ἐκ Μαριάμμης τῆς τοῦ
Σίμωνος τοῦ ἀρχιερέως...καὶ αὐτοῖς Σαλώμη γίνεται μεθ᾽ ἧς τὰς γονὰς Ἡρῳδιὰς
...Ἡρῴδῃ (sc. τῷ Ἀντίπᾳ) γαμεῖται, τοῦ
ἀνδρὸς τῷ ὁμοπατρίῳ ἀδελφῷ διαστᾶσα
ζῶντος. From the Gospels it appears
that this Herod also bore the name
of Philip, and it is arbitrary to assume
with Holtzmann that this is an error.
Herodias herself was a granddaughter
of Herod the Great (child of Aristo-
bulus, Herod's son by the other
Mariamne), and therefore niece to
both Philip her first husband and
Antipas.

ὅτι αὐτὴν ἐγάμησεν] Γαμεῖν is used
here in its proper sense = *uxorem
ducere* : for γαμεῖν = *nubere* see x. 12,
1 Cor. vii. 28, 34. Antipas so far
yielded to public opinion as to divorce

αὐτὴν ἐγάμησεν· ¹⁸ἔλεγεν γὰρ ὁ ᾿Ιωάνης τῷ ῾Ηρῴδη 18
ὅτι Οὐκ ἔξεστίν σοι ἔχειν τὴν γυναῖκα τοῦ ἀδελφοῦ
σου. ¹⁹ἡ δὲ ῾Ηρῳδιὰς ἐνεῖχεν αὐτῷ καὶ ἤθελεν αὐτὸν 19
ἀποκτεῖναι, καὶ οὐκ ἠδύνατο· ²⁰ὁ γὰρ ῾Ηρῴδης ἐφο- 20
βεῖτο τὸν ᾿Ιωάνην, εἰδὼς αὐτὸν ἄνδρα δίκαιον καὶ

19 ηθελεν] εζητει C* a b c d i q | αποκτειναι] απολεσαι C*

his first wife before he married Herodias. She was a daughter of Aretas
the Nabathaean king of Petra, and
her father subsequently severely chastised Antipas for his faithlessness
(Joseph. *ant.* xviii. 5. 1).

18. ἔλεγεν γὰρ ὁ ᾿Ιωάνης] John
was, like Elijah, no frequenter of courts
(Mt. xi. 8), and the message was perhaps sent by his disciples (cf. Mt. xi. 2);
see on the other hand *v.* 20, which
implies some personal intercourse between Antipas and John. That the
Baptist should have visited the court
at Tiberias is inconceivable, but he
might have shewn himself more
than once at times when Herod was
at Machaerus (cf. 1 Kings xvii. 1,
xviii. 1 ff., xxi. 17 ff., 2 Kings i. 15).

οὐκ ἔξεστιν κτλ.] In Mt. the denunciation is general (οὐκ ἔξ. σοι ἔχειν
αὐτήν); Mc. adds the principal ground
on which the union is attacked. Antipas as a Jew was under the law of
Lev. xviii. 16. John's conduct is a
notable instance of "boldness in rebuking vice" (1549 Collect for St J.
Baptist's day).

19. ἡ δὲ ῾Ηρῳδιὰς ἐνεῖχεν αὐτῷ]
Herod silenced the Baptist by sending him down to the dungeons, and
dismissed the matter from his mind.
Not so Herodias; her resentment
could be satisfied only by the Baptist's death. Ἐνεῖχεν, Vg. *insidiabatur.* Wycliffe, "leide aspies to him";
Tindale, "layd wayte for him"; R.V.,
"set herself against him." For this
intrans. use of ἐνέχειν cf. Gen. xlix.
23, ἐνεῖχον αὐτῷ (וַיִּשְׂטְמֻהוּ), Ambr. *intendebant in eum,* Lyons Pent. *insidiati sunt ei*) κύριοι τοξευμάτων (see

Field, *Notes,* p. 28 f.): Lc. xi. 53,
δεινῶς ἐνέχειν, Vg. *graviter insistere.*
The grammarians suggest an ellipsis
of χόλον (Blass, *Gr.* p. 182, cf. WM.,
p. 742; cf. Herod. i. 118, vi. 119,
viii. 27). Hesychius gives the general
sense: ἐνέχει· μηνσικακεῖ. Dr Plummer (*J. Th. St.,* i., p. 619) compares
the English provincialism 'to have
it in with' (or 'for') 'a man,' i.e. 'to
be on bad terms or have a quarrel
with him.' Αὐτῷ may be regarded
as the *dat. incommodi* (WM., p. 265).
Ἤθελεν...καὶ οὐκ ἠδύνατο—the power
was wanting, not the will. The imperfects indicate the normal attitude
of Herodias toward the Baptist.

20. ὁ γὰρ ῾Ηρῴδης ἐφοβεῖτο τὸν ᾿Ιωά
νην] The tradition in Mt. is strangely
different: θέλων αὐτὸν ἀποκτεῖναι ἐφο
βήθη τὸν ὄχλον ὅτι ὡς προφήτην αὐτὸν
εἶχεν. The end of this sentence occurs again with unimportant variations in Mt. xxi. 26, and is perhaps a
reminiscence of that context. Mc.'s
account has the ring of real life:
Herod was awed by the purity of
John's character, feared him as the
bad fear the good (Bengel: "venerabilem facit sanctitas...argumentum
verae religionis timor malorum"). The
attitude of Ahab towards Elijah is
remarkably similar; it is Jezebel, not
Ahab, who plots Elijah's death (1
Kings xix. 2). Ἄνδρα δίκαιον καὶ ἅγιον,
blameless in his relations to his fellowmen and to GOD. The order is ascensive, as in Apoc. xxii. 11; for ἅγιος κ.
δίκαιος see Acts iii. 14, Rom. vii. 12.
Δικαιοσύνη is also coupled with ὁσιό
της (Sap. ix. 3, Lc. i. 75, Eph. iv. 24)
and εὐσέβεια (1 Tim vi. 11, Tit. ii. 12).

ἅγιον, καὶ συνετήρει αὐτόν, καὶ ἀκούσας αὐτοῦ πολλὰ
21 ἠπόρει, καὶ ἡδέως αὐτοῦ ἤκουεν. ²¹καὶ γενομένης
§ Γ ἡμέρας εὐκαίρου, §ὅτε Ἡρῴδης τοῖς γενεσίοις αὐτοῦ
δεῖπνον ἐποίησεν τοῖς μεγιστᾶσιν αὐτοῦ καὶ τοῖς

20 ηποροι ℵBL me] εποιει ACDNΔΠΣΦ al min^forte omn latt syrr arm go al (a εποιει
13 28 69 346 556 (b) (c) (vg^codd))   21 γενεσιοις] γενεθλιοις Dᵃ (-χλιοις D*) | εποιησεν
ℵBCDLΔ 13 28 69 124] εποιει ΑΠΣΦ al min^pl

On εἰδώς see i. 24 note. Εἰδὼς αὐτὸν
δίκαιον καὶ ἅγιον = εἰδ. ὅτι δίκαιος ἦν καὶ
ἅγιος.

καὶ συνετήρει αὐτόν] protected him,
Vg. custodiebat eum, Wycliffe, "kepte
him," Tindale, Cranmer, Geneva, "gave
him reverence," A.V. "observed him":
R.V. "kept him safely" (" contra
Herodiadem," Bengel). Συντηρεῖν,
which belongs to the later Greek, is
common in the Apocr. (Tob.² Sir.¹⁴ 1,
2 Macc.¹¹.), and occurs also in Prov.⁽¹⁾,
Ezek.⁽¹⁾, and Dan. (LXX.⁴ Th.²), meaning
'to keep' (e.g. τὸν νόμον, τὰς ἐντολάς),
or 'preserve' (e.g. Sir. xvii. 22, χάριν
...ὡς κόρην συντηρήσει). Of the former
meaning there is an example in
Lc. ii. 19; the latter is illustrated
by Mt. ix. 17, and is clearly required
here.   Possibly under the circumstances Antipas regarded imprisonment as the best safeguard. From
time to time during his visits to Machaerus he had the Baptist brought
up from the dungeon, and gave him
audience.   These repeated interviews (imperf.) pleased Antipas (ἡδέως
ἤκουεν, cf. Lc. xxiii. 8) at the time,
bracing his jaded mind as with a
whiff of desert air.   At the same
time they perplexed him (ἠπόρει),
leaving behind a tangle of confused
thoughts and purposes which led to
no definite course of action. This
psychological picture—the portrait of
a δίψυχος ἀνήρ (Bruce)—is one of great
interest for the Christian teacher and
the student of human nature. For
πολλά used adverbially see i. 45, iii. 12,
v. 10, 43; and for the reading πολλὰ
ἐποίει (Vg. multa faciebat) see WH.,
Notes, p. 25; Field, Notes, p. 29 f.;

Nestle, Text. Crit., p. 264. Ἀπορεῖν
is less usual than ἀπορεῖσθαι, but see
Sap. xi. 5, 17, and Lc. ix. 7 (διηπόρει).

21. γενομένης ἡμέρας εὐκαίρου] Vg.
cum dies oportunus accidisset. Herodias found her opportunity (cf.
2 Macc. xiv. 29, εὔκαιρον ἐτήρει, Mt.
xxvi. 16, ἐζήτει εὐκαιρίαν: the adjective
occurs again in Heb. iv. 16, εἰς εὔκαιρον
βοήθειαν). It was supplied by the
birthday of Antipas: cf. Gen. xl. 20ff.
In Attic Gk. τὰ γενέσια is used of
commemorations of the dead, the
birthday feast of a living man being
τὰ γενέθλια or ἡ γενέθλιος ἡμέρα
(2 Macc. vi. 7); see Lob. Phryn.
p. 103, Rutherford, N. Phr., p. 184.
But the later Gk. neglects or even
reverses this distinction; cf. Polyc.
mart. 18, ἐπιτελεῖν τὴν τοῦ μαρτυρίου
αὐτοῦ ἡμέραν γενέθλιον (see Suicer s.v.
γενέθλιος); Joseph. ant. xii. 4. 7, ἑορ-
τάζοντες τὴν γενέσιον ἡμέραν. An effort
has been made in the interests of a
particular scheme of chronology to
interpret τὰ γενέσια as the day of
Herod's accession (Wieseler, syn. p.
266 ff.); on this see Schürer I. ii.
p. 26 n.

τοῖς μεγιστᾶσιν κτλ.] Vg. principibus et tribunis et primis Galilaeae.
Μεγιστᾶνες (μεγιστάν), freq. in the
later books of the LXX., esp. 1 Esdr.
Sir., Jer., Dan., in the N. T. used
again Apoc. vi. 15, xviii. 23; cf.
Joseph. ant. xi. 3. 2, vit. 23, 31; a
word of the later Gk. (Lob. Phryn.
p. 147, Sturz, de dial. Mac., p. 182):
the Vg. equivalent is usually magnates, but the Gk. word was taken
over by later writers under the Empire (Tac., Suet.). Cf. Dan. v. 1 (Th.),

χιλιάρχοις καὶ τοῖς πρώτοις τῆς Γαλειλαίας, ²²καὶ 22
εἰσελθούσης τῆς θυγατρὸς αὐτῆς τῆς Ἡρωδιάδος καὶ
ὀρχησαμένης, ἤρεσεν τῷ Ἡρῴδη καὶ τοῖς συνανα-
κειμένοις. ὁ δὲ βασιλεὺς εἶπεν τῷ κορασίῳ Αἴτησόν
με ὃ ἐὰν θέλῃς, καὶ δώσω σοι· ¶ ²³καὶ ὤμοσεν αὐτῇ 23 ¶ Wᵍ
Ὅτι ἐάν με αἰτήσῃς δώσω σοι ἕως ἡμίσους τῆς

22 αυτης της Ηρ. ΑϹΝΓΠΣΦ al minᶠᵉʳᵉᵒᵐⁿ latᵛᵗᵖˡ vg syrʰᶜˡ (της Ηρ. 1 118 209 b c f
syrʳˢⁱⁿᵖᵉˢʰ arm me go aeth)] αυτου Ηρ. אBDLΔ 2ᵖᵉ 238 | ηρεσεν אBC*L 33 c ff me
arm] και αρεσασης ΑϹ³DΝΓΠΣΦ al minᵖˡ a b f i q vg go | αιτησαι א (N) | ο θελεις D
minᵖᵃᵘᶜ (latt) ο εαν θελεις N om syrˢⁱⁿ | και δωσω σοι ο εαν θ. ΚΠ* κ. δ. σ. εως ημ. της
βασ. μου syrˢⁱⁿ   23 ωμοσεν] ωμολογησεν F | αυτη]+πολλα D 2ᵖᵉ 604 latᵛᵗ arm+μετα
ορκου (om οτι...της βασ. μου) syrˢⁱⁿ | οτι εαν BΔ 124 alᵖᵃᵘᶜ] οτι ο εαν אΑϹLΠΣΦ al
minᵖˡ latt ει τι αν D | om με HL 13 69 alᵖᵃᵘᶜ b c q vg me | αιτηση N | εως ημισεως S
ε. ημισεος Π² ε. ημισου Κ ε. ημισυ LNΔΣ και το ημισυ D καν το ημ. 2ᵖᵉ

ὁ βασιλεὺς ἐποίησεν δεῖπνον μέγα τοῖς
μεγιστᾶσιν αὐτοῦ (LXX. τοῖς ἑταίροις
αὐτοῦ) = לְרַבְרְבָנוֹהִי. The χιλίαρχος
(Jo. xviii. 12, Acts xxi.—xxv. passim; see Blass on Acts xxi. 31) was
properly the tribunus militum, who
commanded a Roman cohort; here
he is doubtless the corresponding
officer in the army of the tetrarch.
As the μεγιστᾶνες were the highest
civil dignitaries, so the χιλίαρχοι were
the chief military officers of Galilee
and Peraea (cf. Apoc. vi. 15, οἱ βασιλεῖς τῆς γῆς καὶ οἱ μεγιστᾶνες καὶ οἱ
χιλίαρχοι). With these were invited
the leading provincials, οἱ πρῶτοι τῆς
Γαλ., cf. οἱ πρῶτοι τοῦ λαοῦ, τῆς πόλεως, τῆς νήσου, τῶν Ἰουδαίων (Lc.
xix. 47, Acts xiii. 50, xxv. 2, xxviii. 7,
17), τῶν Φαρισαίων, τῶν Ἱεροσολυμιτῶν
(Joseph. vit. 5, 7). The three classes
are distinguished by the repetition of
the article: cf. WM., p. 160.
    22. εἰσελθούσης...καὶ ὀρχησαμένης]
Antipas, true to the Greek tastes of
his family, permits licentious dancing
after the δεῖπνον (see reff. in Wetstein
on Mt. xiv. 6), and the principal ὀρ-
χηστρίς is the daughter of Herodias.
Notwithstanding the weighty documentary evidence by which it is supported, the reading τῆς θυγ. αὐτοῦ

Ἡρωδιάδος (WH.), which represents
the girl as bearing her mother's name
and as the daughter of Antipas, can
scarcely be anything but an error,
even if a primitive one; her name
was Salome and she was the grand-
niece, not the daughter of Antipas
(see note to v. 17, and cf. Justin, dial.
49, τῆς ἐξαδέλφης αὐτοῦ τοῦ Ἡρῴδου).
Αὐτῆς τῆς Ἡρ. yields an excellent
sense, emphasising the fact that for
the sake of gratifying her resentment
this haughty woman, the daughter of
a king and wife of a tetrarch, submitted her child to a degradation
usually limited to ἑταῖραι.
    ἤρεσεν τῷ Ἡρῴδη: the man who, in
another mood, had found pleasure in
the preaching of John (v. 20). Οἱ συν-
ανακείμενοι, his guests: cf. 3 Macc. v.
39, Lc. vii. 49, xiv. 10, 15.
    ὁ δὲ βασιλεύς] see note on v. 14.
Τῷ κορασίῳ: cf. v. 41, 42. For κοράσιον used of a girl of marriageable
age cf. Esth. ii. 9, ἤρεσεν αὐτῷ τὸ κοράσιον; and see Kennedy, Sources, p.
154. Salome was afterwards married
to Philip the tetrarch, and after his
death to another member of the
Herod family (Joseph. ant. xviii. 5. 4).
    22, 23. αἴτησόν με ὃ ἐὰν θέλῃς κτλ.]
Esther is still in the writer's mind;

24 βασιλείας μου. ²⁴καὶ ἐξελθοῦσα εἶπεν τῇ μητρὶ
αὐτῆς Τί αἰτήσωμαι; ἡ δὲ εἶπεν Τὴν κεφαλὴν Ἰωάνου
25 τοῦ βαπτίζοντος. ²⁵καὶ εἰσελθοῦσα εὐθὺς μετὰ
σπουδῆς πρὸς τὸν βασιλέα ᾐτήσατο λέγουσα Θέλω
ἵνα ἐξαυτῆς δῷς μοι ἐπὶ πίνακι τὴν κεφαλὴν Ἰωάνου

24 η δε εξελθ. ACDΓΠ a b f syrr go | αιτησωμαι אABCDGLNΔΣ 28 33 124 346
al[pauc]] αιτησομαι EFHKMSUVΓΠΦ min[pl] | του βαπτιζοντος אBLΔ 28 syr[hcl] go] του
βαπτιστου ACDNΓΠΣΦ al min[fereomn] latt al   25 om ευθυς DL min[pauc] a b c i l q
me | om μετα σπουδης D a b c i q syr[sin] | ητησατο λεγουσα] ειπεν DΔ 1 28 al[pauc] a b ff
vg syr[sin pesh] arm | om θελω ινα D 2[pe] a b ff i q | θελω ινα...δως] δος D | om εξαυτης
D min[pauc] c f go

cf. Esth. v. 3 f., καὶ εἶπεν ὁ βασιλεύς Τί
θέλεις, Ἐσθήρ ;...ἕως τοῦ ἡμίσους τῆς
βασιλείας μου, καὶ ἔσται σοι (A adds,
v. 6, τί τὸ αἴτημά σου καὶ δοθήσεταί σοι).
For αἰτεῖν τινά τι see WM., p. 284,
and for ἡμίσους=ἡμίσεος, Lob. *Phryn.*
p. 347 ; cf. Blass, *Gr.*, p. 27. Ὤμοσεν αὐτῇ : Mt. μετὰ ὅρκου ὡμολόγησεν
αὐτῇ, cf. Heb. vi. 16.
24. ἐξελθοῦσα εἶπεν...Τί αἰτήσωμαι;]
Leaving the banqueting room when
her part was finished, Salome joins
her mother in the women's apart-
ments and enquires eagerly ' What am
I to ask for myself?' With αἰτήσωμαι
(delib. conj., WM., p. 356, Burton,
§ 168 f.) comp. Herod's αἴτησον, αἰτήσῃς : in the girl's mind the uppermost
thought is her own advantage. See
James iv. 2, 1 Jo. v. 14, 15, with
Mayor's and Westcott's notes ; and
cf. Blass, *Gr.*, p. 186. The answer
of Herodias is ready : ' the head of
John.' Thus, as Mt. says, in the outrage that followed the daughter was
προβιβασθεῖσα ὑπὸ τῆς μητρὸς αὐτῆς
—not an uncommon feature in the
history of crime. The unfortunate use
of this incident by Chrysostom in his
quarrel with the Empress Eudoxia is
familiar to students of Church History
(Socr. *H. E.* vi. 18). Τοῦ βαπτίζοντος,
Vg. *baptistae;* see on *v.* 14, and cf.
τοῦ βαπτιστοῦ, *v.* 25.
25. εἰσελθοῦσα εὐθὺς μετὰ σπουδῆς]
The girl seems to have entered at

once into the spirit of her mother's
thirst for revenge, whether because
she shared Herodias's aversion to
the stern preacher, or rejoiced in the
opportunity of shewing the power she
had gained over her stepfather. Μετὰ
σπουδῆς, Exod. xii. 11, Ps. lxxvii.
(lxxviii.) 33, Sap. xix. 2, Ezech. vii. 11,
Sus. 50 (74), 3 Macc. v. 24, Lc. i. 39 ;
other phrases in LXX. and N. T. are
ἐν σπουδῇ, κατὰ σπουδήν, ἐπὶ σπουδῆς.
Θέλω ἵνα (WM., p. 422 f.) occurs again
in x. 35, Jo. xvii. 24 ; the conjunction
is often dropped (x. 36, 51, xiv. 12,
xv. 9, al.), the subjunctive being in
such cases perhaps simply ' deliberative '; see Burton, § 171. Ἐξαυτῆς,
i.e. ἐξ αὐτῆς τῆς ὥρας, ' at once, here
and now '; elsewhere limited within
the N.T. to Acts[4] Paul[1], a word of
the later Gk., see Lob. *Phryn.* 47 ;
Wetstein *ad loc.* cites exx. of its use
in Philo, Josephus and Polybius. This
demand for the immediate delivery of
the head seems to locate the banquet
at Machaerus ; cf. Mt. ὧδε—a supposition surely not excluded by the presence of the πρῶτοι τῆς Γαλειλαίας.
Herod the Great had built a large
and splendid palace at Machaerus
(Joseph. *B. J.* vii. 6. 2, cf. Schürer
I. ii. 27 n., Hastings, *D. B.* iii. p. 196 f.).
Ἐπὶ πίνακι, Vg. *disco* : the word is
used in the same sense in Lc. xi. 39,
τὸ ἔξωθεν τοῦ ποτηρίου καὶ τοῦ πίνακος :
for other meanings cf. 4 Macc. xvii. 7,

τοῦ βαπτιστοῦ. ²⁶καὶ περίλυπος γενόμενος ὁ βασι- 26
λεὺς διὰ τοὺς ὅρκους καὶ τοὺς ἀνακειμένους οὐκ ἠθέλησεν ἀθετῆσαι αὐτήν· ²⁷καὶ εὐθὺς ἀποστείλας ὁ 27
βασιλεὺς σπεκουλάτορα ἐπέταξεν ἐνέγκαι τὴν κεφαλὴν αὐτοῦ· ²⁸καὶ ἀπελθὼν ἀπεκεφάλισεν αὐτὸν 28
ἐν τῇ φυλακῇ καὶ ἤνεγκεν τὴν κεφαλὴν αὐτοῦ ἐπὶ
πίνακι καὶ ἔδωκεν αὐτὴν τῷ κορασίῳ, καὶ τὸ κοράσιον

25 βαπτιστου] βαπτιζοντος L   26 ο βασιλευς]+ως ηκουσεν D c ff i | ανακειμενους
BC*LΔ 42] συνανακ. אAC²DNΓΠΣΦ al min^fere omn | ηθελεν Π* 1 209 1071   27 om
ευθυς c ff i vg syr^sin | om ο βασιλευς D 1 28 604 al^paue latt syr^sin hier | σπεκουλατωρα Γ
min^sat mu | ενεγκαι אBCΔ] ενεχθηναι ADLNΓΠΣΦ | αυτου]+επι πινακι CΔ min^paue c g vg
28 και 1°] ο δε ADΓΠ al | om αυτην 1° LΔ 1 b c q syr^pesh arm

Lc. i. 63 (πινακίδιον). The banquet
suggested the use of a plate, but this
piece of grim irony was due, it may
be hoped, to the older woman (cf. Mt.
xiv. 8; Justin, dial. l.c.).

26. περίλυπος γενόμενος ὁ β.] The
sense of περίλυπος is well illustrated
by the following passages where it
occurs: Gen. iv. 6, 1 Esdr. viii. 71
(σύννους καὶ π.), 72, Dan. ii. 12 (στυγνὸς
καὶ π., LXX.), Lc. xviii. 23. Mt. has
merely λυπηθείς. Herod's grief was
genuine, if shallow : it is unnecessary
to suppose that he was dissembling
(Jerome, "iustitiam praeferebat in facie, quum laetitiam haberet in mente").
Διὰ τοὺς ὅρκους: for the pl. see 2 Macc.
iv. 34, vii. 24. Thpht., ἔδει δὲ ἐπιορ-
κῆσαι...οὐ πανταχοῦ γὰρ τὸ εὐορκεῖν
καλόν. Jerome asks, "Si patris, si
matris postulasset interitum, facturus
fuerat an non?" Οὐκ ἠθέλησεν ἀθετῆσαι αὐτήν, 'would not break faith
with her, set aside her claims,' "disappoint her" (Field): cf. Lc. x. 16,
1 Th. iv. 8; the word is more commonly used of things than of persons,
e.g. ἀθετεῖν τὴν ἐντολήν (Mc. vii. 9),
τὴν χάριν (Gal. ii. 21), διαθήκην (Gal.
iii. 15), πίστιν (1 Tim. v. 12), ὁρκισμόν
(1 Macc. vi. 62). For the sense 'to
break faith' cf. Ps. xiv. (xv.) 4, ὁ
ὀμνύων τῷ πλησίον καὶ οὐκ ἀθετῶν

(וְלֹא יָמֵר), where the P.B. version
renders "disappointeth him not."

27. ἀποστείλας...σπεκουλάτορα] Mt.
πέμψας (omitting σπ.). Σπεκουλάτωρ,
speculator or less accurately spicu-
lator, in the later Heb. ספקלטור
(J. Lightfoot and Schöttgen ad loc.),
is (1) a spy or scout, (2) an officer
attached to a legion for the purpose
of keeping the look-out and of carrying dispatches; (3) since such military
officers were frequently employed to
carry out a sentence, an executioner
(σπ. ὁ δήμιος λέγεται στρατιώτης,
Thpht.). The word occurs in the N.T.
here only, but is of fairly frequent
use in pagan and Rabbinic literature,
and in the Acta Martyrum; see the
reff. in Wetstein ad loc. or in Schürer
I. ii. 62 f. n. As illustrations of the
meaning which the word bears in
Mc., it may be sufficient to quote
Seneca de ira i. 16, "centurio supplicio
praepositus condere gladium specu-
latorem iubet": de benef. iii. 25,
"speculatoribus occurrit ... cervicem
porrexit." See the full discussion in
Archbp Benson's Cyprian, p. 505 n., f.
Ἐπέταξεν ἐνέγκαι. On the v. l.
ἐνεχθῆναι cf. Blass, Gr., p. 230.

28. ἀπελθών...τῇ μητρὶ αὐτῆς] For
ἀποκεφαλίζω see v. 16: for πίναξ, v.

29 ἔδωκεν αὐτὴν τῇ μητρὶ αὐτῆς. ²⁹καὶ ἀκούσαντες οἱ
μαθηταὶ αὐτοῦ ἦλθαν καὶ ἦραν τὸ πτῶμα αὐτοῦ καὶ
ἔθηκαν αὐτὸ ἐν μνημείῳ.

30　　³⁰Καὶ συνάγονται οἱ ἀπόστολοι πρὸς τὸν Ἰησοῦν,

¶ go　καὶ ἀπήγγειλαν αὐτῷ πάντα ὅσα ἐποίησαν¶ καὶ ὅσα

28 εδωκεν 2°] ηνεγκεν C 33 53ᵉᵛ meᶜᵒᵈ syrˢⁱⁿ (arm) | om αυτην 2° D 33 256 a c f i
vg syrᵖᵉˢʰ arm aeth　　29 αυτο ABCLΓΔΠΣΦ al] αυτον ℵ 346 om 556 | μνημειω]
pr τω DΦ minᵐᵘ　　30 οσα 1°] pr και ΑΓΠΦ al minᵖˡ go syrʰᵉˡ | εδιδ. και εποιησαν
ΚΠ* εποιησεν και εδιδαξεν syrˢⁱⁿ ᵛⁱᵈ | om οσα 2° ℵ*C* 1 alᵖᵃᵘᶜ latt(exc e) syrˢⁱⁿ

25: for κοράσιον, v. 22. The Evangelists draw a veil over the treatment which the head received from
Herodias and Salome. For the legends
connected with its subsequent fate
see Sozom. H. E. vii. 21, Papebroch,
Acta Sanctorum. The 'Decree of
Gelasius' mentions an anonymous
writing "de inventione capitis beati
Johannis baptistae," adding "non-
nulli eas catholicorum legunt." The
Cathedral Church of Amiens claims
to be in present possession of the
head. In the Sarum Calendar Aug.
29 is marked *Decollatio Jo. Bapt.*;
the *Inventio capitis* was sometimes
identified with the *Decollatio* (see
Bede *ad loc.*), but more commonly
observed on Feb. 24. On the cause
of John's martyrdom Victor quaintly
remarks: μοιχεία καὶ ὄρχησις καὶ ὅρκος
τοῦ βαπτιστοῦ ἀφεῖλεν τὴν κεφαλήν,
καὶ παραιτητέα γε ταῦτα τοῖς εὖ φρο-
νοῦσιν.

29. καὶ ἀκούσαντες...ἐν μνημείῳ] For
other notices of the disciples of John
see ii. 18, Jo. i. 35, iii. 25, iv. 1, Acts
xix. 1 f. Τὸ πτῶμα (Mt. Mc.), the
headless body, the corpse, cf. Mt.
xxiv. 28, and Apoc. xii. 8, 9; πτ. is
also used in this sense by the LXX.,
see Ps. cix. (cx.) 6 (=יְוֵה), Ezech.
vi 5 (AQΓ,=פֶּגֶר). It was probably
buried in one of the rock tombs
round Machaerus (Mc. ἐν μνημείῳ);
but it was believed to have been
found at Sebaste (Samaria) in the
time of Julian, when the bones were

burnt and the dust was scattered by
the pagan party (Thdt. H. E. iii. 3);
some portion of the remains, however,
were secured by Christians, and preserved as relics (H. R. xxi.). Both
the Baptist and our Lord received
honourable burial; contrast the fate
of the two Apocalyptic witnesses
(Apoc. xi. 9).

Mt. (xiv. 12, 13) adds that after the
burial the disciples of John made
their way to Jesus with the tidings,
and that the Lord's movements were
affected by what He heard from them:
see note on the next verse.

30—44. RETURN TO THE SEA.
FEEDING OF THE FIVE THOUSAND
(Mt. xiv. 13—21; Lc. ix. 10—17; Jo.
vi. 1—13).

30. καὶ συνάγονται οἱ ἀπόστολοι]
The Twelve have now earned the title
ἀπόστολοι which had been given to
them apparently at the time of their
selection (iii. 14); "apta huic loco
appellatio" (Bengel). Mc. does not
use it again; in the later narrative
of Lc. it becomes an official name
(Lc. xvii. 5, xxii. 14, xxiv. 10, Acts
passim). See Hort, *Ecclesia*, p. 22 f.
Their present mission fulfilled, they
return from various parts of Galilee
to headquarters, i.e. the place where
the Master had probably arranged to
be, and reported (Mc. ἀπήγγειλαν,
Lc. διηγήσαντο) particulars (ὅσα...ὅσα)
of their work and teaching. For the
combination ποιεῖν (τε) καὶ διδάσκειν
cf. Acts i. 1; Lc. omits ἐδίδαξαν here.

ἐδίδαξαν.¶ ³¹καὶ λέγει αὐτοῖς Δεῦτε ὑμεῖς αὐτοὶ κατ᾽ 31 ¶ ꜱʏʀʰⁱᵉʳ
ἰδίαν εἰς ἔρημον τόπον, καὶ ἀναπαύσασθε ὀλίγον.
ἦσαν γὰρ οἱ ἐρχόμενοι καὶ οἱ ὑπάγοντες πολλοί, καὶ
οὐδὲ φαγεῖν εὐκαίρουν.¶ ³²καὶ ἀπῆλθον ἐν τῷ πλοίῳ 32 ¶ ᴄ
εἰς ἔρημον τόπον κατ᾽ ἰδίαν. ³³καὶ εἶδαν αὐτοὺς 33

31 λεγει] ειπεν ADNΓΠ al | δευτε υ. α. κατ ιδιαν] υπαγωμεν D c ff i | εις] επ
ℵ*LΔ | αναπαυσασθε ABCMΔ min^nonn] αναπαυεσθε ℵDLNΓΠΣΦ al min^pl | ευκαιρουν
(ηυκ. CKMUΠΦ al)] ευκαιρως (-ρος D*) ειχον D   32 και απηλθον...πλοιω] και
αναβαντες εις το πλοιον απ. εις ερημον τοπον D latt (exc b)

Their return seems to have synchronised with the arrival of John's disciples (Mt.), and to have helped to determine the Lord's course.

31. καὶ λέγει αὐτοῖς Δεῦτε κτλ.] 'Come apart by yourselves—away from the crowd—and rest for a while.' Two things pointed to a temporary withdrawal from public work, (1) the danger of arrest by order of Antipas, who might think it desirable to follow up his murder of John by silencing John's successor ; (2) the Apostles' need of rest. Mc. recognises only the latter. On δεῦτε see i. 17, and on κατ᾽ ἰδίαν, iv. 34. Ὑμεῖς αὐτοί, 'ye by yourselves' (cf. Jo. vi. 15); or perhaps, 'ye yourselves'—even workers must now and again halt to take breath. Ἀναπαύσασθε gives the idea of the momentary rest better than the present (see vv. ll.); the verb is well illustrated by Exod. xxiii. 12, Dan x. 20 (LXX.). Ὀλίγον, of time here, as of space in c. i. 19. For εἰς ἔρημον τόπον (Mt. Mc.), Lc. has εἰς πόλιν καλουμένην Βηθσαιδά, and Jo. πέραν τῆς θαλάσσης τῆς Γαλειλαίας τῆς Τιβεριάδος. The ἔρημος τόπος may well have been in the neighbourhood of a town (see i. 35, 45); the conflate reading in Lc., εἰς τ. ἐρ. πόλεως καλουμένης Βηθσ., is probably right as an interpretation. Jo.'s recollection that the spot lay across the Lake shews that Bethsaida Julias is intended ; see note on v. 45.

οἱ ἐρχόμενοι καὶ οἱ ὑπ.] The articles distinguish two distinct streams of people : cf. xi. 9. The departures and the new arrivals left no intervals for refreshment, and not even leisure for a meal ; cf. iii. 20. Εὐκαιρεῖν was condemned by the purists (Lob. Phryn., p. 125, εὐκ. οὐ λεκτέον ἀλλ᾽ εὐ σχολῆς ἔχειν; cf. Sturz, dial. Alex. p. 168 f.); it occurs again in Acts xvii. 21, 1 Cor. xvi. 12 ; cod. D substitutes εὐκαίρως ἔχειν here. The word seems to be found first in Polybius (Blass on Acts l.c.) and is common in Philo, but has no place in the LXX. Comp. the interesting practical reflexion in Bede : "magna temporis illius felicitas de labore docentium simul et discentium studio demonstratur : qui utinam nostro in aevo rediret ! "

32. ἀπῆλθον ἐν τῷ πλοίῳ] The rendez-vous was therefore close to the Lake, probably near Capernaum, as τῷ πλ. suggests. The boat took an easterly course and they landed perhaps a little south of Bethsaida, on the edge of the plain now known as el-Batîhah (Schumacher, Jaulân, p. 106, Butaiha, Smith, H. G. p. 457)— "a part of the old lake basin...sown two or three times during the year... and grazed by the buffalo herds...in its north western part...covered with ruins." For ἔρημος τόπος see i. 35, 45.

33. καὶ εἶδαν...καὶ ἔγνωσαν πολλοί] Many witnessed the departure ; the course of the boat could be seen by all, even perhaps the landing of the party on the opposite shore. The

ὑπάγοντας καὶ ἔγνωσαν πολλοί, καὶ πεζῇ ἀπὸ
πασῶν τῶν πόλεων συνέδραμον ἐκεῖ καὶ προῆλθον
αὐτούς. ³⁴καὶ ἐξελθὼν εἶδεν πολὺν ὄχλον, καὶ 34
ἐσπλαγχνίσθη ἐπ᾽ αὐτούς, ὅτι ἦσαν ὡς πρόβατα

33 υπαγοντας]+οι οχλοι (ϛ) 13 69 124 al^nonn | εγνωσαν B*D 1 118 209] επεγνωσαν ℵAB²ΛΓΔΠΣΦ al min^pl+αυτους ℵAKLMNUΔΠΣ min^mu f q syrr me aeth+αυτον EFGHSVΓΦ min^sat mu (om αυτ. BD 1 13 28 118 131 209 al^pauc a ff vg) | εκει και προηλθον αυτους ℵB (προσ. ΛΔ) al^perpauc vg (arm) me] και προηλθον αυτον εκει syr^pesh εκει και συνηλθον αυτου D (28 604) b εκει κ. ηλθον αυτου 2^pe (a) (d ff i r) και ηλθον εκει 1 om 209 al^perpauc προς αυτους και συνηλθον προς αυτον 33 εκει και προηλθον αυτους και συνηλθον (συνεδραμον A) προς αυτον (A)EFGHKM(N)UV(Γ)Π(Σ)Φ min^fere omn f q syr^hcl aeth   34 ειδεν]+ο Iησους (A)(D)EFGHKMNS(U)VΔ(Π) al | επ αυτους ℵBDΓ min^perpauc] επ αυτοις ΑΛΓΔΠΣΦ al min^pl | om ως προβατα ℵ* (hab ℵ^c)

Lord was recognised, and the report of His return spread rapidly (Mt. ἀκούσαντες).

πεζῇ ... συνέδραμον ... καὶ προῆλθον] The crowd went round by land—πεζῇ as contrasted with ἐν τῷ πλοίῳ—cf. Acts xx. 13, μέλλων αὐτὸς πεζεύειν, where Blass remarks, "πεζεύειν de terrestri (non necessario pedestri) itinere." Across the Lake from *Tell Hum* or *Khan Minyeh* is scarcely more than four miles; by land the distance to the upper part of Batîhah could hardly be above ten (Sanday, *Fourth Gospel*, p. 120), unless they went by road and crossed the Jordan by the bridge. If there was little wind, it would be easy to get to the place before a sailing boat. On the reading καὶ προῆλθον αὐτούς see the important discussion in WH., *Intr.*², pp. 95 f., 327; for the construction προελθεῖν τινα cf. Lc. xxii. 47 : Vg. *praevenerunt eos.* Mc. alone has preserved this interesting detail.

34. ἐξελθὼν εἶδεν πολὺν ὄχλον] It was not till He had landed (cf. v. 2; Dr Hort (*l.c.*) prefers "came out of His retirement in some sequestered nook") that the crowd came into sight. He knew then that His effort to find a retreat had failed, yet no impatience revealed itself in His manner. On the contrary, He was

touched (ἐσπλαγχνίσθη, cf. i. 41) by their earnestness of purpose, and bade them welcome (Lc. ἀποδεξάμενος αὐτούς), as if their presence had been desired. Σπλαγχνίζεσθαι ἐπί τινα occurs also in Mt. xv. 32, Mc. viii. 2, ix. 22; other constructions are σπλ. ἐπί τινι Mt. xiv. 14, Lc. vii. 13, περί τινος Mt. ix. 36. 'Επ᾽ αὐτούς = 'towards them,' as those to whom His compassion went forth ; ἐπ᾽ αὐτοῖς would represent the multitude as the object on which it rested.

ὅτι ἦσαν ὡς πρόβατα κτλ.] The ground of His compassion. The blind zeal of the common people shewed both their need of a leader and their readiness to follow one who offered them what their official teachers failed to supply. The phrase ὡς πρ. μὴ ἔχοντα ποιμένα occurs also in another context (Mt. ix. 36). It is based on the O.T. (Num. xxvii. 17, 3 Regn. xxii. 17, 2 Chron. xviii. 16, Judith xi. 19) where however בַּאׁן אֲשֶׁר אֵין לָהֶם רֹעֶה is uniformly rendered πρ. οἷς (ποίμνιον ᾧ) οὐκ ἔστιν ποιμήν. The implied contrast between the false pastors and the True is worked out in Jo. x. 11—16; for other references to the pastoral character of our Lord cf. Mc. xiv. 27, Heb. xiii. 20, 1 Pet. ii. 25. Ἤρξατο διδάσκειν αὐτοὺς πολλά: Lc. ἐλάλει αὐτοῖς περὶ τῆς βασιλείας τοῦ θεοῦ,

μὴ ἔχοντα ποιμένα· καὶ ἤρξατο διδάσκειν αὐτοὺς
πολλά. ³⁵καὶ ἤδη ὥρας πολλῆς γενομένης προσ- 35
ελθόντες αὐτῷ οἱ μαθηταὶ αὐτοῦ ἔλεγον ὅτι Ἔρημός
ἐστιν ὁ τόπος, καὶ ἤδη ὥρα πολλή· ³⁶ἀπόλυσον 36
αὐτούς, ἵνα ἀπελθόντες εἰς τοὺς κύκλῳ ἀγροὺς καὶ
κώμας ἀγοράσωσιν ἑαυτοῖς τί φάγωσιν. ³⁷ὁ δὲ 37
ἀποκριθεὶς εἶπεν αὐτοῖς Δότε αὐτοῖς ὑμεῖς φαγεῖν.

34 om πολλα syrˢⁱⁿ   35 γενομενης ΑΒΛΓΔΠΣΦ al minᶠᵒʳᵗᵉᵒᵐⁿ] γινομενης אD
latt | προσηλθον...λεγοντες Ν om αυτω א*ADKL minᵖᵃᵘᶜ a b i ffᵛⁱᵈ vg syrˢⁱⁿ arm aeth
(hab אᶜΒΓΔΣΦ al minᵖˡ syrr me al) | ελεγον] λεγουσιν αυτω 1071   36 αυτους] τους
οχλους arm | κυκλω] εγγιστα D 604 latt | και κωμας] om Δ syrˢⁱⁿ και εις τας κ. D |
αγορασωσιν pr ινα D | τι φαγωσιν Β(D)LΔ 28 a ff i syrˢⁱⁿ me] pr βρωματα א αρτους τι
γαρ φαγωσιν ουκ εχουσιν ΑΝ (א φαγουσιν) ΓΠΣΦ al minᵖˡ (b) f syrrᴾᵉˢʰʰᶜˡ (arm) aeth

adding καὶ τοὺς χρείαν ἔχοντας θερα-
πείας ἰᾶτο (cf. Mt.). Ἤρξατο : " denuo,
ut si antea non docuisset " (Bengel).
Their first need was teaching—first at
least in His sight; but teaching, as
at other times, brought opportunities
of healing disease. The Lord, as He
taught, sat on the rising ground above
the plain (Jo. ἀνῆλθεν εἰς τὸ ὄρος καὶ
ἐκεῖ ἐκάθητο μετὰ τῶν μαθητῶν αὐτοῦ,
cf. Mt. v. 1).

35. ἤδη ὥρας πολλῆς γενομένης] Vg.
cum iam hora multa fieret; Mt.,
ὀψίας δὲ γενομένης, Lc., ἡ δὲ ἡμέρα
ἤρξατο κλίνειν; cf. Bede, "horam mul-
tam vespertinum tempus dicit." Mc.'s
phrase ὥρα πολλή, which is repeated
at the end of the verse, occurs also
in Dion. Hal. ii. 54, ἐμάχοντο ἄχρι
πολλῆς ὥρας, "to a late hour." That
Lc.'s interpretation is right appears
from v. 47. Since the passover was
at hand (Jo.), it was near the time
of the spring equinox, and the sun
set about 6 p.m.; the miracle was
probably wrought an hour or so before sunset. Προσελθόντες ἔλεγον κτλ.
According to Jo. the thought of providing for the multitude had presented
itself to our Lord some hours before,
when He first saw them coming to
Him (vi. 5, θεασάμενος ὅτι πολὺς ὄχλος
ἔρχεται).

36. ἀπόλυσον αὐτούς] For ἀπόλύω
='dismiss,' see Tob. x. 12 (א), Mc.
vi. 45, viii. 3, 9, Acts xiii. 3, xv. 30,
33, xix. 41. Εἰς τοὺς κύκλῳ ἀγροὺς καὶ
κώμας does not exclude the supposition that Bethsaida was near, cf.
Jos. xxi. 12, τοὺς ἀγρ. τῆς πόλεως καὶ
τὰς κώμας αὐτῆς. The 'Western' text
(WH., Notes, p. 25) substitutes ἔγ-
γιστα for κύκλῳ; cf. Vg. in proximas
villas et vicos. Ἀγροί, villae, are the
scattered farms, cf. v. 14; for the
single article in the gender of the
first noun, see WM., p. 158. Τί φάγωσιν (WM., p. 210), Mt. βρώματα, Lc.
ἐπισιτισμόν. Lc. adds (ἵνα) καταλύσω-
σιν, a necessity scarcely less pressing,
considering the time of year, and
that the crowd contained women and
children. For this our Lord provided
shortly afterwards in the way proposed by the disciples (vv. 45, 46).
Food was a more immediate want,
and more difficult to supply.

37. δότε αὐτοῖς ὑμεῖς φαγεῖν] Mt.
prefixes οὐ χρείαν ἔχουσιν ἀπελθεῖν—
an answer to ἀπελθόντες of v. 36, as
the emphatic ὑμεῖς (WM., p. 190)
replies to ἵνα...ἀγοράσωσιν ἑαυτοῖς. Of
this conversation between our Lord
and the Twelve we have two independent accounts, St Peter's (Mc.,
abbreviated in Mt., Lc.) and St John's.

καὶ λέγουσιν αὐτῷ Ἀπελθόντες ἀγοράσωμεν δηναρίων
38 διακοσίων ἄρτους καὶ δώσωμεν αὐτοῖς φαγεῖν; ³⁸ ὁ
δὲ λέγει αὐτοῖς Πόσους ἔχετε ἄρτους; ὑπάγετε,
ἴδετε. καὶ γνόντες λέγουσιν Πέντε, καὶ δύο ἰχθύας.

37 δωσωμεν ℵBD 13 33 69 124 346 2ᵖᵉ] δωσομεν ALΔ alᵖᵃᵘᶜ lattᵛⁱᵈ δωμεν ΓΠΣ al
minᵖˡ | φαγειν 2°] + ινα εκαστος βραχυ λαβη 13 69 124 346 ινα φαγωσιν 2ᵖᵉ
38 ιδετε] pr και ΑΓΔΠ al | γνοντες] ελθοντες ℵ* (γν. ℵᶜ·ᵃ) επιγνοντες 1071 | λεγου-
σιν] + αυτω ADMᵐᵍ 13 69 al | πεντε] + αρτους D 2ᵖᵉ a c ff syrr

A comparison shews that the words ἀπελθόντες ἀγοράσωμεν κτλ. belong in part to Philip, and πέντε καὶ δύο ἰχθύας to Andrew. On the whole "the superiority in distinctness and precision is all on the side of St John" (Sanday, *l.c.* p. 121; cf. Lightfoot, *Bibl. Essays*, p. 182). For an attempt to bring the two accounts into precise agreement see Aug. *de cons. ev.* ii. 96. With his conclusion we may heartily concur: "ex qua universa varietate verborum, rerum autem sententiarumque concordia, satis apparet salubriter nos doceri nihil quaerendum in verbis nisi loquentium voluntatem."

ἀπελθόντες ἀγοράσωμεν κτλ.] A conflation, as appears from Jo. vi. 5—7, of the Lord's question πόθεν ἀγοράσωμεν ἄρτους ἵνα φάγωσιν οὗτοι; and Philip's answer διακοσίων δηναρίων ἄρτοι κτλ. Δηναρίων διακοσίων, at the cost of 200 denarii, the gen. of price, WM., p. 258. On the *denarius* see Madden's *Jewish Coinage*, p. 245 ff., Hastings, *D. B.* iii. p. 427 f.; the mean value at this time is stated to have been 9½*d*. It was the labourer's daily wage (Mt. xx. 2 ff.): two *denarii* were sufficient to pay the expenses of a πανδοχεῖον for at least a day or two (Lc. x. 35); the costly oil of spikenard poured on the Lord by Mary of Bethany was worth three hundred or more (Mc. xiv. 5, note); five hundred was a typically large debt (Lc. vii. 41). Two hundred of these silver pieces may well have been more than the Twelve had in their γλωσσό-

κομον (Jo. xii. 6). Yet even this outlay would have been inadequate: Jo. οὐκ ἀρκοῦσιν αὐτοῖς ἵνα ἕκαστος βραχύ λάβῃ. Δώσωμεν is possibly an aor. conj., cf. WSchm., pp. 107, 120. WH. prefer δώσομεν, on which see Blass, *Gr.*, p. 212.

38. πόσους ἔχετε ἄρτους;] This question interprets the previous one. They were not called to imagine impracticable schemes of charitable action, but to give what they had (cf. 2 Cor. viii. 12). Bede: "non nova creat cibaria, sed acceptis eis quae habuerant discipuli."

γνόντες λέγουσιν] The discovery was made (Jo.) by Andrew, and the supply belonged, it appears, not to the Twelve, but to a lad in the crowd (ἔστιν παιδάριον ὧδε ὃς ἔχει...). Jo. alone (Orig. *in Mt.* xi. 2) mentions that the cakes were made of barley-flour (ἄρτοι κρίθινοι), i.e. of the coarsest and cheapest kind, the food of the working man: cf. Jud. v. 8 (A), vii. 13, 4 Regn. iv. 42: for the relative cost of wheat and barley see 4 Regn. vii. 18 and Apoc. vi. 6 (χοῖνιξ σίτου δηναρίου καὶ τρεῖς χοίνικες κριθῶν δηναρίου). For ἰχθύας, Jo. has ὀψάρια (cf. Num. xi. 22, πᾶν τὸ ὄψον τῆς θαλάσσης). The fish—two to five loaves—were a mere relish, and probably pickled or cooked: for the use of cooked fish with bread see Jo. xxi. 9, 13. Taricheae at the S.W. corner of the Lake derived its name from the curing of fish. Some of the older commentators find mysteries in the numbers: e.g. Thpht. πέντε ἄρτοι οἱ Μωσαικοὶ λόγοι, ἰχθύες

³⁹καὶ ἐπέταξεν αὐτοῖς ἀνακλιθῆναι πάντας συμπόσια 39
συμπόσια ἐπὶ τῷ χλωρῷ χόρτῳ.   ⁴⁰καὶ ἀνέπεσαν 40
πρασιαὶ πρασιαὶ κατὰ ἑκατὸν καὶ κατὰ πεντήκοντα.

39 ανακλιθῆναι אB*GΦ 1 13 28 64 604 1071 2ᵖᵉ alⁿᵒⁿⁿ Or] ανακλιναι AB²DLNΓΔΠΣ
al minᵖˡ Or | συμπ. συμπ.] κατα την συνποσιαν D om a syrˢⁱⁿ ᵛⁱᵈ | επι] εν B*
40 om πρασιαι 2° אLΔ minᵖᵃᵘᶜ | κατα bis אBD 2ᵖᵉ me] ανα bis ALNΓΔΠΣΦ al
minᶠᵉʳᵉᵒᵐⁿ (om ανα 2° 33 alᵖᵃᵘᶜ Or)

δὲ δύο, οἱ τῶν ἁλιέων λόγοι, ὁ Ἀπόστολος καὶ τὸ Εὐαγγέλιον. Similarly
Aug. in Jo. tract. xxiv.

39. ἐπέταξεν αὐτοῖς ἀνακλιθῆναι] The
command was given through the
Twelve (Lc. κατακλίνατε αὐτούς, Jo.
ποιήσατε τοὺς ἀνθρώπους ἀναπεσεῖν).
For ἀνακλίνεσθαι and ἀναπίπτειν used
of taking places on a couch before a
meal see Mt. viii. 11, Lc. xiii. 29; Lc.
xi. 37, Jo. xiii. 12. Order was secured
by breaking up the crowd into companies (συμπόσια, Mc., κλισίας, Lc.).
In the LXX. συμπόσιον οἴνου = מִשְׁתֵּה
הַיַּיִן (Esther, Sirach), but συμπόσιον
occurs without οἴνου in the first three
books of Maccabees, and apparently
in the wider sense. The form preferred by D (συμποσία) is also to be
found in Sirach and 3 Macc.; Lc.'s
more precise term occurs in 3 Macc.
vi. 31. The construction συμπόσια
συμπόσια = ἀνὰ or κατὰ συμπόσια is
Hebraistic: cf. Exod. viii. 14 (10), συνή-
γαγον αὐτοὺς θιμωνιὰς θιμωνιάς חֳמָרִם
חֳמָרִם), and πρασιαὶ πρασιαί in the
next verse: see also Mc. vi. 7 (WM.,
pp. 312, 581, Blass, Gr. p. 145). On
the construction ἀνακλ. πάντας συμπόσια
see WM., pp. 282, 663 ff.

ἐπὶ τῷ χλωρῷ χόρτῳ] See note on
v. 32. The place supplied in the
early spring a natural carpet on which
thousands could recline in comfort;
cf. Jo. ἦν δὲ χόρτος πολὺς ἐν τῷ τόπῳ.
Χλωρὸς χόρτος, faenum viride, is
'green food,' i.e. growing grass or
crops, as contrasted with dry fodder:
cf. Gen. i. 30, Isa. xv. 6, xxxvii. 27,
Apoc. viii. 7. The epithet is not
otiose or merely picturesque; it indi-

cates the season of the year, and thus,
so far as it goes, supports the existing
text of Jo. vi. 4 (cf. WH., Notes, p.
77 ff.).

40. ἀνέπεσαν πρασιαὶ πρασιαί] The
act implies trust on the part of the
crowd (Bengel: "fides populi"). The
συμπόσια took the form of rectangular
garden beds. Πρασιαί occurs in Homer, Od. viii. 127, where the Sch.
interprets αἱ τῶν φυτειῶν τετράγωνοι
σχέσεις, and reappears in Theophrastus and in the LXX. (Sir. xxiv. 31
μεθύσω μου τὴν πρασιάν): cf. Euth.:
πρασιαὶ αἱ τετραγωνοειδεῖς [συναγωγαί]·
τοιαῦται γὰρ αἱ τῶν κήπων πρασιαί.
Mc. probably uses the word to convey
the notion of regularity of form, not
of variety of colouring (Farrar, Life,
i. p. 402); the πρασιά, unless otherwise
defined (πρ. ἀνθῶν) is the bed of
garden herbs (λαχανιά, Hesych.), as its
probable etymology shews. See the
somewhat similar comparison, quoted
from the Talmud by J. Lightfoot ad
loc., of Jewish scholars to the rows
of vines in a vineyard, planted שׁוּרוֹת
שׁוּרוֹת.

κατὰ ἑκατὸν καὶ κατὰ πεντήκοντα]
The groups consisted roughly of fifty,
in other cases of a hundred each;
cf. Lc. ὡσεὶ ἀνὰ πεντήκοντα. Mt. omits
all these details—the greenness of the
grass, the orderly distribution of the
crowd, the size of the groups; nor do
they find a place in the recollections
of St John, though he remembers the
number of the party as a whole (ἀνέπεσαν...ὡς πεντακισχίλιοι). The purpose of the arrangement was probably
to prevent a dangerous scramble for
the food, or at any rate, confusion and

41 ⁴¹καὶ λαβὼν τοὺς πέντε ἄρτους καὶ τοὺς δύο ἰχθύας,
ἀναβλέψας εἰς τὸν οὐρανόν, εὐλόγησεν καὶ κατέκλασεν
τοὺς ἄρτους καὶ ἐδίδου τοῖς μαθηταῖς ἵνα παρατιθῶσιν
42 αὐτοῖς, καὶ τοὺς δύο ἰχθύας ἐμέρισεν πᾶσιν. ⁴²καὶ
43 ἔφαγον πάντες καὶ ἐχορτάσθησαν· ⁴³καὶ ἦραν

41 κατεκλασεν τ. α. και] κλασας τ. α. ℵ* 33 | τοις μαθ.]+αυτου ΑΔΓΠ al | παρατι-
θωσιν ℵ*BLM*ΔΠ* minᵖᵃᵘᶜ] παραθωσιν ℵᶜΑDM²ΝΓΠ²ΣΦ al minᵖˡ | αυτοις] κατεναντι
αυτων D latt τω οχλω M*   42 om παντες 1* 33 (209*) arm

disorder (cf. 1 Cor. xiv. 33, 40), and
to secure an easy and rapid distribution : twelve men could serve fifty
to one hundred companies in a comparatively short time. Incidentally
the division into companies made
the counting of the multitude a
simple matter, and accounts for the
same number being given by the
four evangelists.

41. καὶ λαβὼν τοὺς πέντε ἄρτους
κτλ.] The cakes and fish were
brought to Him (Mt. xiv. 18), probably in a κόφινος (cf. v. 43), and the
Lord took the basket, or one of the
cakes, into His hands. The action
marked Him as the Master and
Host; cf. xiv. 22, Lc. xxiv. 30, Acts
xxvii. 35. Ἀναβλέψας εἰς τὸν οὐρανόν (Mc. Mt. Lc.) : the attitude of
prayer (vii. 34, Jo. xi. 41 ; for the
O.T. see Job xxii. 26, and cf. 1 K. viii.
22, Ps. xxviii. 2, lxxiii. 4, cxxxiv. 2),
specially characteristic of Him Who
knew no sin (contrast Lc. xviii. 13).
The ancient Liturgies have transferred this feature to the institution of the Eucharist (Brightman,
Liturgies, pp. 20, 51, 133, &c.; cf.
the words of the Roman canon, "ele-
vatis oculis ad te," &c.). Εὐλόγησεν
(Mt. Mc. Lc.)=εὐχαριστήσας (Jo.); a
similar variation occurs in the account of the first Eucharist, where
εὐχαριστεῖν is used of the blessing of
the Bread by Lc., Paul (1 Cor. xi.),
and of the blessing of the Cup by
Mt., Mc., Lc.; the two verbs are
practically synonymous, the blessing

being in fact in the form of a thanks-
giving (cf. 1 Tim. iv. 3, 4); the Cup,
in reference to which the three Synoptists use εὐχαριστεῖν, is called by
St Paul τὸ ποτήριον τῆς εὐλογίας ὃ
εὐλογοῦμεν. The recognised form of
blessing was (Edersheim, i. p. 684):
"Blessed art Thou, O Lord our God,
King of the world, Who bringest
forth bread from the earth." Κατέκλασεν : so Lc.; Mt. κλάσας. The
simple verb is used in all our accounts of the Eucharistic fraction (cf.
ἡ κλάσις τοῦ ἄρτου, Acts ii. 42); perhaps the compound points here to
the breaking of each cake into several pieces (cf. κατακόπτω, v. 5). The
distribution was entrusted to the
Twelve : ἐδίδου (Mc. Lc.) may imply
that they came to Him at intervals to
be replenished, but is perhaps more
naturally understood of the repeated
action involved in the gift to each
of them severally (cf. Jo. διέδωκεν).
The fish was no doubt distributed
in the same way, though Mc. for the
sake of brevity writes ἐμέρισεν πᾶσιν :
cf. Jo. ὁμοίως καὶ ἐκ τῶν ὀψαρίων.
Ἵνα παρατιθῶσιν=Lc. παραθεῖναι : for
this sense of the verb cf. Lc. x. 8
ἐσθίετε τὰ παρατιθέμενα ὑμῖν. Cf. Origen *in Jo*. t. xiii. 34, λαμβάνει δὲ τὰ
βρώματα ὁ μὲν πολὺς τῶν μαθητευομένων
ἀπὸ τῶν μαθητῶν Ἰησοῦ...οἱ δὲ τοῦ
Ἰησοῦ μαθηταὶ ἀπ᾽ αὐτοῦ τοῦ Ἰησοῦ.

42. ἐχορτάσθησαν] Vg. *saturati
sunt*. The food more than sufficed
(contrast Jo. vi. 7). All had as much
as they would, even of the fish (Jo.

κλάσματα δώδεκα κοφίνων πληρώματα καὶ ἀπὸ τῶν
ἰχθύων. ⁴⁴καὶ ἦσαν οἱ φαγόντες τοὺς ἄρτους πεντα- 44
κισχίλιοι ἄνδρες.
⁴⁵Καὶ εὐθὺς ἠνάγκασεν τοὺς μαθητὰς αὐτοῦ ἐμ- 45

43 κλασματα BLΔ] κλασματων ℵ 13 69 124 209 346 το περισσευσαν των κλασματων
604 | κοφινων πληρωματα ℵB 1 13 69 124 209 346] κοφινους πληρωματα LΔ κοφινους
πληρεις ΑΔΓΠΣΦ rell min^pl   44 om τους αρτους ℵD 1 28 604 2^pe vg (syr^sin) arm |
πεντακισχιλιοι] pr ως (vel ωσει vel ωσπερ) ℵ (ως) 2^pe (ωσπερ) al^nonn arm   45 ευθυς]
+εξεγερθεις D a b c ff i q

ὅσον ἤθελον). Ἔχορτ. is common to
the Synoptists; Jo. uses ἐνεπλήσθη-
σαν. For the former word cf. Lightfoot on Phil. iv. 12, Kennedy, *Sources*,
p. 82; it is fairly distributed in the
N. T. (Mt.⁴ Mc.⁴ Lc.⁴ Jo.¹ Cath.¹ Paul¹,
Apoc.¹), but in the LXX. limited to
Pss.⁹, Job¹, Jer.¹, Lam.¹ (=יְשַׂבַּע), Tob.¹.
43.   ἦραν κλάσματα] Mt. τὸ περισσεῦον τῶν κλ., Lc. τὸ περισσεῦσαν
αὐτοῖς (sc. τῷ ὄχλῳ) κλ. So the Master directed: Jo. συναγάγετε τὰ πε-
ρισσεύσαντα κλάσματα ἵνα μή τι ἀπό-
ληται. For κλάσμα (ἄρτου) cf. Jud.
xix. 5 (A, =ψωμὸς ἄρτου B), Ezech.
xiii. 19. Δώδεκα κοφίνων πληρώματα,
in apposition to κλ., ' wherewith was
filled twelve hampers': cf. Mt. δ.
κοφίνους πλήρεις, Jo. ἐγέμισαν δ. κοφίνους κλασμάτων. Mc. uses πλ. κοφ.
again in viii. 20: for a discussion of
πλήρωμα see note on ii. 21. Κόφινος
is common to the four accounts. The
word is used by Aq. in Gen. xl. 16 for
a bread-basket (סַל), and by the LXX.
in Jud. vi. 19 (B, =κανοῦν A) for the
basket (also סַל) in which Gideon places
cooked meat; in Ps. lxxx. (lxxxi.) 6
it is the pot-shaped basket (דּוּד) in
which the Israelite during the Egyptian oppression carried his clay or
bricks. A "stout wicker basket"
appears to be intended, "as distinguished from the soft flexible
'frails'" (Westcott, on St John). The
κόφινος is contrasted in the Gospels
with· the σφυρίς (viii. 19, 20), for
which see note on viii. 8. In Rome

it was the characteristic appendage of
the poorer class of Jews (Juv. iii. 14,
vi. 542, "quorum cophinus faenum-
que supellex"; see J. E. B. Mayor's
note). The twelve κόφινοι were possibly those in which the Apostles
had carried what they needed for
their recent circuit of Galilee; cf.
Euth., δώδεκα κόφινοι...ἵνα καὶ οἱ δώδεκα ἀπόστολοι διαβαστάσωσιν τοὺς
κοφίνους. With the excess of the
miraculous supply above the requirements of the people comp. 4 Regn.
iv. 44, ἔφαγον καὶ κατέλιπον κατὰ τὸ
ῥῆμα Κυρίου.
44.   ἦσαν ... πεντακισχίλιοι ἄνδρες]
The number was doubtless roughly
calculated by counting the συμπόσια
(note on *v.* 39); cf. Mt. Lc. ὡσεί,
Jo. ὡς, πεντ. The men perhaps alone
composed the groups, but the women and children were not neglected
(Mt.).
On the miracle as a whole Victor
well remarks: θαυμάσιον μὲν οὖν τὸ
πραχθέν...θαυμάσιον δὲ οὐκ ἔλαττον τὸ
μὴ ἀεὶ τῇ ἐξουσίᾳ χρῆσθαι πρὸς τὴν
τῶν τροφῶν εὐπορίαν.

45—52. WALKING ON THE SEA
(Mt. xiv. 22—33, Jo. vi. 16—21).
45.   εὐθὺς ἠνάγκασεν...εἰς τὸ πέραν]
For once the Lord put a severe strain
upon the loyalty of the Twelve. His
command was in direct conflict with
all that seemed to be reasonable and
right. He had led them to the place
that very day, and now required them
at once to leave it. On other occasions He led the way (see x. 32,

βῆναι εἰς τὸ πλοῖον καὶ προάγειν εἰς τὸ πέραν πρὸς
46 Βηθσαιδάν, ἕως αὐτὸς ἀπολύει τὸν ὄχλον. ⁴⁶καὶ

45 om εις το περαν 1 118 209 syrˢⁱⁿ | προς] εις 1 28 209 2ᵖᵉ Or a b i q in contra a |
Βηθσαιδαν אBLΠΦ al minᵖˡ c f ff q vg arm] Βηθσαιδα Δ (Βησ.) Σ minⁿᵒⁿⁿ | απολυει
אBDL 1] απολυσει E*ΚΓ 28 69 604 minⁿᵒⁿⁿ απολυση AE²FGHMNSUVΠΣΦ minᵖˡ | τους
οχλους 1071

xiv. 28, Jo. x. 4); now He would
only undertake to follow them. The
Synoptists throw no light on the
situation, but it is explained by St
John (vi. 14, 15). The enthusiasm of
the multitude was not limited to a
recognition of the Lord's prophetic
office: they were on the point of
seizing His person and proclaiming
Him King. "No malice on the part
of the Scribes could have been so
fatal...as their giving of a political
turn to the movement...He hurried
the disciples on board that they might
not catch the contagion of the idea"
(Latham, Pastor p., p. 307). Origen
in Jo. t. xxviii. 23 : μὴ παρέχων μηδὲ
τούτοις ἀφορμήν, φιλοῦσιν αὐτὸν καὶ
βουληθεῖσιν ἂν μετὰ τῶν θελόντων
ποιῆσαι αὐτὸν βασιλέα.

πρὸς Βηθσαιδάν] Mt. stops short at
πέραν ; Jo. says, ἤρχοντο πέραν τῆς
θαλάσσης εἰς Καφαρναούμ. Both Mc.
and Mt. represent the Twelve as
landing eventually εἰς Γεννησαρέτ (vi.
53, Mt. xiv. 34). The direction of the
boat was therefore ultimately west-
wards, and this fact has led to a
conjecture that there was a Western
Bethsaida (Reland, Stanley, Tristram),
which has been identified with 'Ain et-
Tabigha (Tristram, Bible Places, p.
315); in support of this theory it has
been urged that Jo. (xii. 21) mentions
a Βηθσ. τῆς Γαλειλαίας (see, however,
Merrill, Galilee, p. 27). But there is
no direct evidence for the existence
of two Bethsaidas on the Lake, and
the Bethsaida of which Josephus
speaks (ant. xviii. 2. 1, B.J. ii. 9. 1,
iii. 10. 7) was in Philip's tetrarchy
and therefore on the East bank of the
Jordan. Unless Lc. has misunder-

stood his source, the starting-point
of the boat was near this town (Lc.
ix. 10, see note on v. 32), and the
Lord directed the Twelve to cross to
the town in the first instance (Bengel : "terminus navigationis non to-
tius sed ex parte "). In this case τὸ
πέραν is here not the Western shore,
but the opposite side of the little bay
which lay between the sloping ground
where the miracle was wrought and
Philip's new city—an alternative which
presented itself to Bede (ad l.). Τὸ
πέραν is interpreted by πρὸς Βηθσαιδάν. Why they did not reach
Bethsaida, but landed on the Western
shore, appears as we proceed. On the
form Βηθσαιδάν see WH., Notes, p.
160, WSchm., pp. 62 f., 91 ; and for
the question of locality, the articles in
Hastings, D.B., and Encycl. Bibl.

ἕως αὐτὸς ἀπολύει τὸν ὄχλον] ' While
He for His part dismisses the multitude.' Mt. ἕως οὖ ἀπολύσῃ : see Burton,
§ 321 ff., esp. §§ 326, 330; Blass, Gr.
p. 219. The shortness of the interval
suggested agrees with the view that
the original destination of the boat
was Bethsaida Julias.

46. καὶ ἀποταξάμενος] Mt. has
ἀπολύσας. Mc. changes the word.
The dismissal (v. 36) was friendly
and courteous, if peremptory ; nothing in His manner betrayed anxiety or consciousness of their intentions. Ἀποτάσσεσθαι is (in late Gk.,
see Lob. Phryn. p. 24) to bid farewell to friends ; cf. Lc. ix. 61, Acts
xviii. 18, 21, 2 Cor. ii. 13. It is
possible that αὐτοῖς may = τοῖς μαθηταῖς αὐτοῦ, and that Mt. has mis-
interpreted the pronoun ; but if so,
Mc. omits altogether the dismissal of

ἀποταξάμενος αὐτοῖς ἀπῆλθεν εἰς τὸ ὄρος προσεύξασθαι. ⁴⁷καὶ §ὀψίας γενομένης ἦν τὸ πλοῖον ἐν μέσῳ 47 §X
τῆς θαλάσσης, καὶ αὐτὸς μόνος ἐπὶ τῆς γῆς. ⁴⁸καὶ 48
ἰδὼν αὐτοὺς βασανιζομένους ἐν τῷ ἐλαύνειν, ἦν γὰρ
ὁ ἄνεμος ἐναντίος αὐτοῖς, περὶ τετάρτην φυλακὴν

46 ανηλθεν 1 209   47 και οψ.] οψ. δε N | ην]+παλαι D 1 28 209 251 iam
a b i | εν μεση τη θαλασση D 2ᵖᵉ | om μονος arm   48 ιδων] ιδεν AKMVXII* ειδεν
EFGHSˢⁱˡUΓΠ² alᵖˡ | βασ. εν τω ελαυνειν] βασ. και ελαυνοντας D 2ᵖᵉ a b ff i q ελαυνοντας
κ. βασ. 604 | περι τετ. φυλ. τ. νυκτος] om syrˢⁱⁿ pr και ADXΓΠ alᵖˡ

the people, which was the next step
and an important one. On the whole
the Vg. is probably right in referring
both ἀπολύει and ἀποταξάμενος to the
crowd (dum dimitteret populum...
cum dimisisset eos), though it misses
the significant change of verb. Προσεύξασθαι, inf. of aim or object; cf.
Blass, Gr. p. 223.

ἀπῆλθεν εἰς τὸ ὄρος] When all were
gone He returned to the higher
ground (cf. Jo. vi. 3, 15), partly to
escape the crowd (ἀνεχώρησεν, Jo.),
but chiefly to pray (οἷα ἄνθρωπος, Victor; χρήσιμον γὰρ ταῖς προσευχαῖς καὶ
τὸ ὄρος καὶ ἡ νὺξ καὶ ἡ μόνωσις, Euth.);
cf. i. 35. Another crisis had come;
the way to further usefulness in Galilee seemed to be blocked, partly by
the attitude of Antipas, partly by the
unreasoning enthusiasm of the people;
He needed counsel and strength for
the immediate future.

47—48. ὀψίας γενομένης κτλ.] More
than an hour must have passed since
the conversation before the miracle
(see note on v. 35), and the sun had
now probably set: cf. Jo. vi. 17,
σκοτία ἤδη ἐγεγόνει. Meanwhile a stiff
breeze had sprung up, and it was
against the rowers (Mc. Mt.), blowing
probably from the N. or N.W. and
raising so much sea (Jo.) as to distress
them (βασανιζομένους) as well as to
alter their course. The Paschal moon
gave light enough to reveal the boat
struggling with the waves (βασανιζό-
μενον Mt.), and well out to sea (Mc.

ἐν μέσῳ τῆς θαλάσσης, Mt. σταδίους
πολλοὺς ἀπὸ τῆς γῆς: for the reading of D in Mc. (ἦν πάλαι) see
WH., Notes, p. 25). The Lord, who
was now alone on the land, realised
their position and, breaking off His
vigil, went down to the sea and took
the direction of the boat.

For ὀψία = the early hours of the
night see Judith xiii. 1, Mc. xiv. 17,
Jo. xx. 19. Βασανίζω has already
occurred in v. 7 (q.v.); the different
applications of the word in this context by Mt. and Mc. are instructive
as shewing the degree of latitude
which the Synoptists allowed themselves in dealing with the common
tradition, even when they retained its
actual terms. For a metaphorical
use of the verb cf. Sir. iv. 17, 2 Pet.
ii. 8. On βασ. ἐν τῷ ἐλ. see Blass,
Gr. p. 237. Ἄνεμος ἐναντίος, cf. Acts
xxvii. 4.

48. περὶ τετάρτην φυλακήν κτλ.] The
Lord reached the boat about 3 a.m.
(cf. WM., p. 506); Mt., more precisely,
τετάρτη φυλακῇ. Cf. Macar. Magn.
iii. 6, τετάρτη τῆς νυκτὸς φυλακή ἐστιν
ἡ δεκάτη τῆς νυκτὸς ὥρα, μεθ' ἣν ὑπο-
λείπονται τρεῖς ὑστεραῖαι ὥραι. Mc.
and Mt. count four watches in the
night after the Roman system; see
Mc. xiii. 35, and cf. Acts xii. 4 (Blass).
Lc. on the other hand (xii. 38) seems
to follow the Jewish division into
three. Φυλακή occurs in this sense in
the LXX. (Jud. vii. 19, 1 Regn. xi. 11,
Ps. lxxxix. (xc.) 4, cxxix. (cxxx.) 6, cf.

τῆς νυκτὸς ἔρχεται πρὸς αὐτοὺς περιπατῶν ἐπὶ τῆς
49 θαλάσσης· καὶ ἤθελεν παρελθεῖν αὐτούς. ⁴⁹οἱ δὲ
ἰδόντες αὐτὸν ἐπὶ τῆς θαλάσσης περιπατοῦντα ἔδοξαν
50 ὅτι φάντασμά ἐστιν, καὶ ἀνέκραξαν· ⁵⁰πάντες γὰρ
αὐτὸν εἶδαν καὶ ἐταράχθησαν. ὁ δὲ εὐθὺς ἐλάλησεν

48 ηθελεν] ηθελησεν D | om και ηθ. παρ. αυτους G   49 οτι φαντασμα εστιν
אBLΔ 33] φαντ. ειναι ADNXΓΠΣΦ al minᵖˡ latt me   50 ειδον AΓΔΠ² ιδον
KLMXVII* | om και εταραχθ. syrˢⁱⁿ | και ευθεως ελαλ. μ. α. ο Ιησους N

Thren. ii. 19). Ἔρχεται πρὸς αὐτούς.
Jo. says that when they caught sight
of the Lord they had rowed ὡς σταδίους
εἴκοσι πέντε ἢ τριάκοντα. Since the
lake was forty stades broad (Joseph.
B. J. iii. 10. 7), this agrees fairly well
with Mc.'s ἐν μέσῳ τῆς θαλάσσης, if
we allow for the tortuous course of
the boat, her general direction (N.E.
to S.W. by W.), and the interval between the Lord's departure from the
hill and arrival at the spot where
they saw Him. Περιπατῶν ἐπὶ τῆς
θαλάσσης, Mc. and Jo.; Mt. π. ἐπὶ
τὴν θάλασσαν. The gen. points to
the apparent solidity of the water
under His feet (cf. ἐπὶ τῆς γῆς, v. 47),
the acc. to His progress implied in
περιπατῶν; in v. 26 where the order
is different Mt. also prefers the gen.
The reader is left to complete the
picture; the Lord must be imagined
as walking on a seething sea, not
upon a smooth surface (Jo. ἡ θάλασσα
...διεγείρετο: cf. Victor, τῶν ἀνέμων
ἐναντία πνεόντων καὶ τῶν κυμάτων κατὰ
τοῦ ἀνέμου ἐγειρομένων, ἔμενεν ἐπὶ τῶν
ὑδάτων βαδίζων); now on the crest of
a wave, now hidden out of sight. It
was the darkest hour of the night,
and the moon had probably set; only
the outline of a human form could
be seen appearing from time to time,
and approaching the boat. The conception is found in Hebrew poetry,
but only in connexion with Divine
prerogatives, e.g. Job xxxviii. 16,
ἦλθες δὲ ἐπὶ πηγὴν θαλάσσης ἐν δὲ
ἴχνεσιν ἀβύσσου περιεπάτησας; in Sir.

xxiv. 5 Wisdom says ἐν βάθει ἀβύσσων
περιεπάτησα. For a mystical application see Aug. in Jo. tract. xxv.:
"venit...calcans fluctus, omnes tumo-
res mundi sub pedibus habens...quid
ergo timetis, Christiani? Christus loquitur Ego sum, nolite timere." Cf.
serm. 75.

ἤθελεν παρελθεῖν αὐτούς] Vg. volebat praeterire eos; the imperfect is
conative (Burton, p. 12); for the acc.
cf. Lc. xi. 42, xv. 29, Acts xvi. 8.
With the feigned purpose comp. Lc.
xxiv. 28, and see Mc. v. 36, vii. 27.
The purpose in each case was to try,
and by trial to strengthen faith (cf.
Jo. vi. 6).

49. ἔδοξαν ὅτι φάντασμά ἐστιν]
Wycliffe, "thei gessiden that it were
a fantum"; Tindale, "they supposed
it had been a sprete." Cf. Lc. xxiv.
37, ἐδόκουν πνεῦμα θεωρεῖν. Δοκεῖν in
this sense is followed almost indifferently by ὅτι or by acc. and inf.; for
δ. ὅτι see Mt. vi. 7, xxvi. 53, Lc. xii. 51,
xix. 11, Jo. v. 45, &c. Φάντασμα, an
apparition: here only and in Mt.;
cf. Job xx. 8 (A) ὥσπερ φάντασμα
νυκτερινόν. Φ. ἐστιν: the present represents the thought as it took shape
on their tongues: 'it is a phantom'
(cf. Mt.). For earlier evidence of a
popular belief in apparitions among
the Hebrew people see Job iv. 15 ff.,
xx. 8, and esp. Sap. xvii. 4, 15. Ἀνέ-
κραξαν: the appearance drew forth
a shriek of terror: cf. i. 23.

50. πάντες γὰρ αὐτὸν εἶδαν] It was
not the fancy of an individual; all

μετ' αὐτῶν, καὶ λέγει αὐτοῖς Θαρσεῖτε, ἐγώ εἰμι, μὴ
φοβεῖσθε. ⁵¹καὶ ἀνέβη πρὸς αὐτοὺς εἰς τὸ πλοῖον, 51
καὶ ἐκόπασεν ὁ ἄνεμος. καὶ λίαν ἐν ἑαυτοῖς ἐξ-
ίσταντο, ⁵²οὐ γὰρ συνῆκαν ἐπὶ τοῖς ἄρτοις, ἀλλ' ἦν 52
αὐτῶν ἡ καρδία πεπωρωμένη.

51 λιαν] om D 1 28 2ᵖᵉ b syrˢⁱⁿ arm + εκ περισσου (vel εκπερισσως vel περισσως)
ΑΔΝΧΓΠΣΦ al minᵖˡ syrʰᶜˡ arm (om ℵBLΔ syrᵖᵉˢʰ aeth) | εξισταντο] εξεπλησσοντο
1 118 209 + και εθαυμαζον ΑΔΝΧΓΠΣΦ al minᵖˡ a b f q syrrᵖᵉˢʰ ʰᶜˡ arm aeth (om ℵBLΔ
1 28 118 209 ᴏ i vg syrˢⁱⁿ me)   52 τοις αρτοις] τοις αυτοις Δ | αλλ ην ℵBLM²SΔ
33 alᵖᵃᵘᶜ syrʰᶜˡ⁽ᵐᵍ⁾ me] ην γαρ ΑΔΜ*ΝΧΓΠΣΦ minᵖˡ lattᵛᵗ ᵖˡ ᵛᵍ syrʰᶜˡ⁽ᵗˣᵗ⁾ arm aeth

the Twelve saw the Form on the
water, as all the Eleven afterwards
saw the Risen Christ. The fear was
momentary : it was relieved at once
by the well-known voice; cf. the similar circumstances in Lc. xxiv 37 ff.,
Apoc. i. 17 ff. For λαλεῖν μετά τινος
cf. Jo. iv. 27, ix. 37, xiv. 30 : the
phrase is probably preferred here to
the more usual λ. τινι or πρός τινα, as
implying familiar intercourse. Μετά
implies "mutual action" (WM., p. 471),
and with λαλεῖν, the exchange of conversation.

Θαρσεῖτε, ἐγώ εἰμι] For this use of
the imper. of θαρσεῖν (so always in the
Gospels and Acts, θαρρεῖν in Epp. ;
WH., Notes, p. 149) cf. x. 49, Mt. ix.
2, 22, Jo. xvi. 33, Acts xxiii. 11.
Ἐγώ εἰμι = 'It is I,' cf. Lc. xxiv. 39,
ἐγώ εἰμι αὐτός, and the use of אֲנִי,
LXX. ἐγώ, in the O.T. (BDB., p. 59).
In the Fourth Gospel the phrase
sometimes (viii. 24, 28, 58, xiii. 19)
rises to the level of its use in Deut.
xxxii. 39, Isa. xliii. 10; see Westcott
on Jo. viii. 24. Μὴ φοβεῖσθε : see
Burton, § 165. Augustine points the
moral of this little episode: "quomodo
eos volebat praeterire quos paventes
ita confirmat, nisi quia illa voluntas
praetereundi ad eliciendum illum cla-
morem valebat cui subveniri oportebat ?"

51. ἀνέβη πρὸς αὐτοὺς εἰς τὸ πλοῖον]
Cf. Jo. vi. 21, ἤθελον οὖν λαβεῖν αὐτὸν
εἰς τὸ πλοῖον (Westcott). Ἀνέβη, in-

stead of the usual ἐνέβη, perhaps to
depict the climb from the hollow of
the wave over the side of the boat.
Mt. ἀναβάντων αὐτῶν, i.e. the Lord
and Simon Peter. The latter had
gone down (καταβάς) into the water
and attempted to walk on it to the
Lord: Mt. (xiv. 28—31) alone relates
the incident. Upon the return of
Peter to the boat accompanied by the
Lord the wind at once fell : cf. iv. 39
(where see note on κοπάζειν).

ἐν ἑαυτοῖς ἐξίσταντο] The astonishment did not express itself in words;
for ἐν ἑαυτοῖς see ii. 8, v. 30. Mt.,
however, represents them as falling
at His feet with the exclamation
Ἀληθῶς θεοῦ υἱὸς εἶ. If this confession is in its right place, it anticipates St Peter's (Mt. xvi. 16, Mc. viii.
29). The excitement of the moment
may have given voice to a growing
impression which had not yet reached
the maturity of a definite judgment.
Victor points out that on the previous
occasion when a storm was stilled
they had been content to exclaim Τίς
ἄρα οὗτός ἐστιν; (iv. 41).

52. οὐ γὰρ συνῆκαν ἐπὶ τοῖς ἄρτοις]
Vg. non enim intellexerant de pani-
bus. Their amazement would have
been less had they realised the wonder of the preceding miracle ; "de-
buerant a pane ad mare concludere"
(Bengel). Somehow the miracles connected with the multiplication of food
failed to impress the Twelve (cf. viii.

53   ^{53} Καὶ διαπεράσαντες ἐπὶ τὴν γῆν ἦλθον εἰς Γεννη-

53 διαπερασαντες]+εκειθεν D 45 a b c ff i q | επι την γην ηλθον εις Γενν. אBLΔ 28 33 2^{pe}] ηλθ. επι την γην Γ. ΑΔΝΓΠΣ al min^{pl} latt syrr ηλθ. εις την γην Γενν. ΧΦ min^{pauc} arm^{zoh} om την γην me arm^{codd} om Γενν. i | Γεννησαρετ (Γεννσ. FHN 69 al^{nonn} ff q vg$^{codd\,aliq}$) אAB²LΜΓΔΣΦ 33 al a] Γεννησαρεθ B*(N)XII al min^{pl} f q vg me Γεννησαρ D b c (ff) syrr$^{sin\,pesh}$ pr εις 604

17 ff.); perhaps their administration of the food diverted their thoughts from the work wrought by the Lord. 'Επί 'in the matter of,' 'in reference to,' WM., p. 489, Blass, *Gr.* p. 137; συνιέναι ἐπί (but with gen. or acc.) occurs in Dan. xi. 37 (Th.); cf. σ. εἰς, Ps. xxvii. (xxviii.) 5; ἐν, 2 Esdr. xviii. (Neh. viii.) 12.

ἀλλ' ἦν αὐτῶν ἡ καρδία πεπωρωμένη] Vg. *erat enim* (see vv. ll.) *cor illorum obcaecatum*; Wycliffe, " her herte was blyndid." For πωροῦσθαι see note on iii. 5. The καρδία (ii. 6) includes the intelligence considered in its relation to the moral and spiritual life of men; cf. 2 Cor. iii. 14, ἐπωρώθη τὰ νοήματα αὐτῶν: Rom. i. 21, ἐσκοτίσθη ἡ ἀσύνετος αὐτῶν καρδία. Both σύνεσις and φρόνησις (for the distinction of these synonyms see Lightfoot on Col. i. 9) depend for their right exercise upon moral conditions.

53—56. MINISTRY IN THE PLAIN OF GENNESARET (Mt. xiv. 34—36).

53. διαπεράσαντες ἐπὶ τὴν γῆν ἦλθον] Jo. remembers another incident of this voyage which appears to be miraculous. When Jesus and Peter entered the boat and the wind ceased, they found themselves at once close to shore, εὐθέως ἐγένετο τὸ πλοῖον ἐπὶ τῆς γῆς εἰς ἣν ὑπῆγον: see Westcott's note; Euth. explains: πλησίον τῆς γῆς γενομένου τοῦ πλοίου. The phrase used by Mt., Mc. (διαπ. ἦλθον) merely sets forth the welcome ending of a laborious and hazardous crossing. Cf. Ps. cvi. (cvii.) 24 ff. 'Επὶ τὴν γῆν: cf. Acts xxvii. 44.

εἰς Γεννησαρέτ] In the end they landed neither at Bethsaida (v. 45) nor at Capernaum (Jo. vi. 17), but

a few miles to the south of the latter town, on the edge of the plain from which the lake took its usual name (Lc. v. 1, τὴν λίμνην Γεννησαρέτ, 1 Macc. xi. 67, τὸ ὕδωρ τοῦ Γεννησάρ, Joseph. *ant.* xviii. 2. 1, λίμνη Γεννησαρῖτις). On the form Γεννησάρ which occurs in D (Mt. Mc.), in many MSS. of the Old Latin and Vg., and in the Syriac versions, see Chase, *Syro-Latin·Text of the Gospels*, p. 105. Gennesaret is usually identified with the present *el-Ghuweir*, a semi-elliptical plain on the West shore between '*Ain-et-Tin* and *Mejdel*, three miles long and rather more than one mile in breadth. Josephus, who is enthusiastic in praise of the fertility of this district, writes (*B. J.* iii. 10. 8) παρατείνει δὲ τὴν Γεννησὰρ ὁμώνυμος χώρα θαυμαστὴ φύσιν τε καὶ κάλλος...μῆκος δὲ τοῦ χωρίου παρατείνει κατὰ τὸν αἰγιαλὸν τῆς ὁμωνύμου λίμνης ἐπὶ σταδίους τριάκοντα καὶ εὖρος εἴκοσι. For the descriptions of recent travellers see Stanley, *S. and P.*, pp. 374, 382; Wilson, *Recovery*, p. 338; Tristram, *B. P.*, p. 313; G. A. Smith, *H. G.*, p. 443 n.; Merrill, *Galilee*, p. 32 f. The place has lost the glories which Josephus praises; towns and villages, cultivated lands and vineyards are gone. But the visitor still finds much to admire—the pearly whiteness of the shell-strewn beach, the thickets of oleander blossoming along the watercourses, the profusion of wild flowers, the fine cliffs which guard the two extremities of the plain, and then recede to join the Galilean hills. In extent el-Ghuweir corresponds very nearly to the Batîhah which the Lord had just left; but

σαρέτ, §καὶ προσωρμίσθησαν. ⁵⁴καὶ ἐξελθόντων αὐτῶν 54 § go
ἐκ τοῦ πλοίου εὐθὺς ἐπιγνόντες αὐτὸν ⁵⁵περιέδραμον 55
ὅλην τὴν χώραν ἐκείνην, καὶ ἤρξαντο ἐπὶ τοῖς κραβάττοις τοὺς κακῶς ἔχοντας περιφέρειν ὅπου ἤκουον
ὅτι ἔστιν. ⁵⁶καὶ ὅπου ἂν εἰσεπορεύετο εἰς κώμας ἢ 56

53 om καὶ προσωρμισθησαν D 1 28 209 604 a b c ff i q r syrʳˢⁱⁿ ᵖᵉˢʰ arm   54 αυτον]
+οι ανδρες του τοπου εκεινου (και) AGΔ(Φ) 1 13 28 33 (69) (604) 1071 (2ᵖᵉ) alⁿᵒⁿⁿ c
arm (syrᵖᵉˢʰ)   55 περιδραμοντες (om και seq) ANXΓΠ alᵖˡ | χωραν אBLΔ 33
me] περιχωρον ADNXΓΠΣΦ minᵖˡ vg syrʰᶜˡ arm | κραβακτοις א κραβατοις F*XΔ
κραββατοις B²EH | οπου ηκουον] ηκουσθη א περιεφερον γαρ αυτους ο. αν ηκουσαν
D a (b ff i q) aeth | οτι εστιν] τον ιυ ειναι D a ff o. εκει εστιν ANXΓΠΣΦ al minᵖˡ
syrʰᶜˡ me arm   56 αν ABDLNII] εαν אXΓΔ

while the scene of the miracle was little more than a waste of pasture dotted with an occasional village or homestead, the plain to which He had now come was densely populated. The retirement and rest He had sought were at an end, as soon as He was seen on the beach of Gennesaret.

προσωρμίσθησαν] Vg. *adplicuerunt*; they brought the boat to her moorings, casting anchor, or lashing her to a post on the shore. The word is ἅπ. λεγ. in Biblical Greek, but both act. and mid. are classical, and there are examples of the 1st aor. pass. in a middle sense in late writers, e.g. Aelian and Dio Cassius.

54. εὐθὺς ἐπιγνόντες αὐτόν] It must have been early and hardly daylight (comp. vi. 48 with Jo. vi. 21); yet, as on the previous day when He left the neighbourhood of Capernaum (*v.* 33), there were people about who recognised Him and spread the news. For ἐπιγινώσκειν in the sense of personal recognition cf. Mt. xvii. 12, Lc. xxiv. 16, 31, Acts iv. 13.

55. περιέδραμον ὅλην τὴν χώραν] Mt. τὴν περίχωρον: the news was hastily carried round to all parts of the plain. Περιτρέχειν is ἅπ. λεγ. in the N. T.; but occurs in the LXX. (Amos viii. 12, Jer. v. 1, = טוֹשֵׁט).

Here it vividly depicts the circulation of the tidings throughout the *Ghuweir*. As the result, there came from every quarter streams of people bringing their sick for healing. For περιφέρειν see 2 Cor. iv. 10. With περιέδραμον...ἤρξαντο περιφέρειν comp. Mt.'s tamer ἀπέστειλαν...προσήνεγκαν. The sick were carried on their pallets (ἐπὶ τοῖς κραβάττοις: Mc. only, see note on ii. 4); the course of the bearers was shaped by the reports that reached them from time to time as to the Lord's movements (ὅπου ἤκουον ὅτι ἔστιν). Ἔστιν, the present, as if one caught the reply of those of whom inquiry was made: 'he is here,' or 'there.'

56. ὅπου ἂν εἰσεπορεύετο κτλ.] Whenever in His progress He entered a village, He found the sick laid in the open spaces ready for His healing. In strictness ἀγοραί would exist only in the towns, at Magdala and Capernaum and Chorazin and Bethsaida; but the word is apparently used here loosely to include other open spaces. Ἐν ταῖς πλατείαις (D), Vg. *in plateis*, which is followed by all the English versions except R.V., is perhaps from Acts iv. 15. Πόλεις and κῶμαι are classed together in Mt. x. 11, Lc. viii. 1, xiii. 22, κῶμαι and ἀγροί in vi. 36, Lc. ix. 12: the combination of the three covers every collection of dwellings large and

εἰς πόλεις ἢ εἰς ἀγροὺς ἐν ταῖς ἀγοραῖς ἐτίθεσαν τοὺς
ἀσθενοῦντας, καὶ παρεκάλουν αὐτὸν ἵνα κἂν τοῦ κρα-
σπέδου τοῦ ἱματίου αὐτοῦ ἅψωνται· καὶ ὅσοι ἂν
ἥψαντο αὐτοῦ ἐσῴζοντο.

7 1   ¹Καὶ συνάγονται πρὸς αὐτὸν οἱ Φαρισαῖοι καί
τινες τῶν γραμματέων ἐλθόντες ἀπὸ Ἱεροσολύμων.
2 ²καὶ ἰδόντες τινὰς τῶν μαθητῶν αὐτοῦ ὅτι κοιναῖς

56 εν ταις αγοραις] pr η ℵ εν ταις πλατειαις D 604 2ᵖᵉ b c f ff i q vg go | ετιθεσαν
ℵBLΔ minᵖᵉʳᵖᵃᵘᶜ] ετιθουν A(D)NΧΓΠΣΦ minᵖˡ | ηψαντο ℵBDLΔ 1 13 28 33 69 124
346 2ᵖᵉ a] ηπτοντο ANΧΓΠΣΦ minᵖˡ tangebant lattᵛᵗ ᵖˡ ᵛᵍ syrr αψωνται 604 | εσωζοντο]
διεσωζοντο ΝΣ 1 69 604 alᵖᵃᵘᶜ διεσωθησαν Δ εσωθησαν 33 2ᵖᵉ   VII 1 ελθοντες] pr οι
ΝΣ qui venerant a b f (q)   2 ιδοντες] ειδοτες D | οτι...εσθιουσιν ℵBLΔ 33] εσθιοντας
ADNΧΓΠΣΦ al minᵖˡ a go | κοιν. χ. τ. ε. ανιπτ.] non lotis manibus b c (syrrˢⁱⁿ ᵖᵉˢʰ aeth)

small. On the construction see WM.,
p. 384, Burton, § 315 f., Blass, Gr.
p. 207.

καὶ παρεκάλουν αὐτόν κτλ.] Again
and again the entreaty was heard.
The fame of the healing of the αἱμορροοῦσα had spread (Victor : ἡ γὰρ
αἱμορροοῦσα πάντας ἐδίδαξε φιλοσο-
φεῖν); so simple a means of obtain-
ing a cure appealed to the popular
imagination, and under the circumstances the Lord permitted its use.
Cf. Acts iv. 15, xix. 11 f. On the
κράσπεδον, and on κἂν, see v. 27, 28
notes.

ὅσοι ἂν ἥψαντο αὐτοῦ ἐσῴζοντο]
For the construction see the references at the end of the last note.
The aor. (see vv. ll.) points to the
momentariness of the touch in each
case ; the imperfect which ˙follows,
to the rapid succession of the cases.
Mt. again is less picturesque (ὅσοι
ἥψαντο διεσώθησαν). For σῴζεσθαι in
reference to physical restoration
see v. 28 ; on the orthography cf.
WSchm., p. 41.

VII. 1—13. QUESTION OF CERE-
MONIAL WASHINGS (Mt. xv. 1—9).

1. συνάγονται] See iv. 1, v. 21,
vi. 30. The Lord's person is the
rallying-point for both friends and
enemies; cf. Mt. xxv. 31, 32. Of the

Pharisees there has been no mention
since iii. 6 ; during the interval they
may have been occupied by their
intrigue with the Herodians, of which
perhaps we see the fruit in vi. 14.
Now that Jesus has returned to the
W. shore, they fall back upon their
old policy of insidious questioning.
The Scribes from Jerusalem (iii. 22)
are still with them, unless, as τινες...
ἐλθόντες suggests, these are another
party, newly arrived. Mt. is less precise : προσέρχονται τῷ Ἰ. ἀπὸ Ἱεροσ.
Φαρισαῖοι καὶ γραμματεῖς. Cf. Bede :
"non ad verbum audiendum...sed ad
movendas solum quaestiones pugnae
ad Dominum concurrunt."

2. ἰδόντες τινὰς...ὅτι...ἐσθίουσιν] A
mixture of the two constructions ἰδόντες τινὰς...ἐσθίοντας (cf. i. 10, vi. 48,
49) and ἰδ. ὅτι ἐσθίουσίν τινες (ii. 16,
ix. 25). The opportunity probably
arose during the passage of the party
through the plain (vi. 56); the loaves
were very possibly some of the κλάσματα with which their baskets had
been filled the night before, and
which now served them as an ἐφόδιον.

κοιναῖς χερσίν, τοῦτ᾽ ἔστιν ἀνίπτοις]
Κοινός, 'polluted,' 'ceremonially unclean,' occurs in 1 Macc. i. 47 θύειν
ὕεια καὶ κτήνη κοινά (A, V : ℵ*, πολλά),
ib. 62 φαγεῖν κοινά (for אמט, see Guil-

χερσίν, τοῦτ' ἔστιν ἀνίπτοις, ἐσθίουσιν τοὺς ἄρτους
—³οἱ γὰρ Φαρισαῖοι §καὶ πάντες οἱ Ἰουδαῖοι ἐὰν μὴ 3 § W^d

2 τους (om τους ΑΧΓΠ al) αρτους]+εμεμψαντο ΚΜΝSUΠΣΦ al min^pl κατεγνωσαν
D *vituperaverunt* latt^vt pl vg (syrr^pesh hcl arm)

lemard on Mt. xv. 11), cf. 4 Macc. vii. 6
γαστέρα ἐκοίνωσας (אַ: Α, ἐκοινώνησας)
μιεροφαγίᾳ : in the N.T., outside this
context, κοινός is similarly used in
Acts x. 14, 28, xi. 8, Rom. xiv. 14,
Heb. x. 29, Apoc. xxi. 27, and κοινοῦν
or κοινοῦσθαι (mid. and pass.) in
Acts x. 15, xi. 9, xxi. 28, Heb. ix. 13.
This use of κοινός corresponds to the
Rabbinic חֹל, חֻלְּאָ (Edersheim, ii.
9 n.); the κοινόν is the opposite of the
ἅγιον or καθαρόν (Westcott on Heb.
x. 29). Hence Mc.'s explanation, τ. ἔ.
ἀνίπτοις, must be taken to interpret
the word only in reference to the
particular case ; unwashed hands
were, for the purpose of eating, κοιναί.
For τοῦτ' ἔστιν as a formula of interpretation cf. Mt. xxvii. 46, Acts
i. 19, Rom. vii. 18, Heb. ii. 14; on the
question whether it is to be written
as two words see WSchm., p. 37, Blass,
Gr., pp. 18, 77. On ἐσθίειν τοὺς ἄρτους (τὸν ἄρτον, *v.* 5) see Dalman,
Worte, p. 92.

3—4. Another apparently editorial
note. There is no trace of it in Mt.
Cf. Zahn, *Einleitung*, ii. p. 241.

3. οἱ γὰρ Φ. καὶ πάντες οἱ Ἰουδαῖοι]
Except in the phrase ὁ βασιλεὺς
τῶν Ἰουδαίων (xv. 2 ff.), οἱ Ἰουδαῖοι is
used by Mc. here only ; in Mt. with
the same exception it is limited to
xxviii. 15, and in Lc. to vii. 3, xxiii. 51.
On Jo.'s use of the term see Westcott's
St John, Intr. p. lx. ; οἱ Ἰουδαῖοι are
in the Fourth Gospel the opposite of
the ὄχλος : "as 'the multitude' reflect the spirit of Galilee, 'the Jews'
reflect the spirit of Jerusalem" ; they
are "the representatives of the narrow
finality of Judaism." In some such
limited sense the term is probably
used here by Mc. and Mt. ; "the Jews"

who "all" hold the tradition of the
Elders are not the masses, but the
strict and orthodox minority who
supported the Scribes. Yet ceremonial purification was usual in religious
households (cf. Westcott on Jo. ii. 6),
and the Lord had probably conformed
to it at Nazareth ; He resists merely
the attempt to enforce it as an essential (Hort, *Jud. Chr.*, p. 29 f.). On the
origin and extent of these practices
see Schürer II. ii. p. 106 ff.

ἐὰν μὴ πυγμῇ νίψωνται τὰς χ.] Πυγμή
(Exod. xxi. 18, Isa. lviii. 4, = אֶגְרֹף)
is the closed hand, the fist—σύγ-
κλεισις δακτύλων, Suid.; cf. Pind. *Ol.*
7. 30, πυγμῇ νικήσαντα. The word is
used in late Gk. for the length of the
arm between the fist and the elbow ;
hence Euth. and Thpht. interpret
here ἄχρι ἀγκῶνος, i.e. thrusting the
arm into the water up to the elbow.
Cf. J. Lightfoot *ad l.*, and Edersheim, who renders עַד הַפֶּרֶק, "to
the wrist"; but it is difficult to see
how πυγμῇ can be made to bear the
meaning of ἕως τῆς πυγμῆς. The
reading πυκνά (Vg. *crebro*, Wycliffe
and the other English versions exc.
R.V., "oft") may be a gloss borrowed perhaps from Lc. v. 33, if it
be not due to corruption (cf. πύκμη,
D) ; the rendering of the Pesh.
(ܚܦܝܛܐܝܬ, i.e. ἐπιμελῶς, see Lc.
xv. 8) is another gloss which we have no
means of verifying (see however Morison, *St Mark, ad l.*); for the marginal
gloss in Syr.^hcl. see Field (*Notes*, p.
30 f.), who renders it ἀποκλύζοντες τῷ
ὕδατι τοὺς δακτύλους αὐτῶν. On the
whole it is perhaps best to take πυγμῇ
literally, 'with the fist,' i.e. either
with the hand held out with clenched
fingers while the attendant pours

πυγμῇ νίψωνται τὰς χεῖρας οὐκ ἐσθίουσιν, κρατοῦντες
¶ Wᵈ 4 τὴν παράδοσιν τῶν πρεσβυτέρων· ⁴καὶ¶ ἀπ' ἀγορᾶς

3 πυγμη AB (D πυκμη) LNWᵈΧΓΠΣΦ al minᵒᵐⁿᵛⁱᵈ *pugillo* c ff i q r (*momento* a *subinde* b *primo* d) arm Or] πυκνα ℵ vg me go *diligenter* syrrᵖᵉˢʰ ʰᶜˡ ⁽ᵗˣᵗ⁾ om Δ syrˢⁱⁿ | ουκ εσθ.]+(τον) αρτον D(M²) al a b c ff i syrˢⁱⁿ arm   4 απ αγορας]+οταν ελθωσιν D a b c ff i l q r (arm)

water over it (2 Kings iii. 11); or as Meyer-Weiss explains, "so dass sie die geballte Faust in die hohle Hand stecken, erstere in der letzteren reiben und drehen." In the first case the dat. is modal, in the second instrumental. A possible alternative is to treat πυγμῇ as the dat. of measure—'by elbow-length' (see above). But it must be confessed that no explanation hitherto offered is wholly satisfactory.

Νίπτειν, νίπτεσθαι are used of the feet (Gen. xviii. 4, 2 Regn. xi. 8, Jo. xiii. 5 ff., 1 Tim. v. 10), the hands (Exod. xxx. 19 ff., Lev. xv. 11, Ps. xxv. (xxvi.) 6), the face (Mt. vi. 17, Jo. ix. 7 ff.), in contrast to λούεσθαι, to bathe the whole body: cf. Jo. xiii. 10, ὁ λελουμένος οὐκ ἔχει χρείαν εἰ μὴ τοὺς πόδας νίψασθαι.

κρατοῦντες τὴν παράδοσιν τῶν πρεσβυτέρων] Cf. Joseph. *ant.* xiii. 10. 6, νόμιμα πολλά τινα παρέδοσαν τῷ δήμῳ οἱ Φαρισαῖοι ἐκ πατέρων διαδοχῆς ἅπερ οὐκ ἀναγέγραπται ἐν τοῖς Μωυσέως νόμοις. The rule, at least in its details, belonged not to the Torah, but to the Qabbalah (Taylor, *Pirqe Aboth*, pp. 120, 128), and to its non-canonical part (Edersheim, ii. p. 9). The Elders (זְקֵנִים) are here of course not the officers of the synagogue or members of the Sanhedrin, but such great teachers as Hillel and Shammai, or the scribes of former generations (cf. Heb. xi. 2, where οἱ πρ.=οἱ πατέρες, i. 1), perhaps especially the members of the 'Great Synagogue,' see *Aboth*, i. 1 ff., and Dr Taylor's account, p. 124; the παράδοσις τ. πρ. is the sum of the παραδόσεις πατρικαί (Gal. i. 14) after-

wards embodied in the Mishnah, which every Pharisee and disciple of the Pharisees sought to keep inviolate. On St Paul's attitude with regard to tradition cf. Hort, *Jud. Chr.*, p. 118, and cf. Lightfoot on 2 Th. ii. 15. For κρατεῖν παράδοσιν see 2 Th. *l.c.*, and cf. κρατεῖν διδαχήν, Apoc. ii. 14, 15, or with the gen., κρ. ὁμολογίας, Heb. iv. 14, where see Westcott's note. The affection with which even the Egyptian Jews in the second century before Christ clung to a similar tradition is illustrated in the Sibyllines, iii. 591 sq., ἀλλὰ μὲν ἀείρουσι πρὸς οὐρανὸν ὠλένας ἁγνὰς | ὄρθιοι ἐξ εὐνῆς ἀεὶ χέρας ἁγνίζοντες | ὕδατι. See J. Lightfoot on Mt. xv. 2 ff., and especially Edersheim, *Life*, ii. p. 9 ff.

4. καὶ ἀπ' ἀγορᾶς κτλ.] After mingling with men of all sorts in the open market, they purified the whole person before taking food. The Apostles had been ἐν ταῖς ἀγοραῖς (vi. 56), jostled by a mixed crowd, yet they had not even washed their hands. Ἀπ' ἀγορᾶς, Vg. *a foro*, 'after market'; a pregnant construction, see WM., p. 776 n., and cf. Theophrast. *char.* 16, περιρρανάμενος ἀπὸ ἱεροῦ. The purification was effected by sprinkling (cf. the ὕδωρ ῥαντισμοῦ of Num. xix. 9 ff., and the metaphorical use of the verb and substantive in Ps. l. (li.) 7, Zach. xiii. 1, Heb. x. 22, Apoc. xix. 13), or, according to the alternative reading (see vv. ll.), by dipping (cf. 4 Regn. v. 14, Judith xii. 7). But βαπτίσωνται suggests a standard which is Essene rather than Pharisaic, unless, as J. Lightfoot suggests, an immersion of the hands only is intended. Cf. how-

ἐὰν μὴ ῥαντίσωνται οὐκ ἐσθίουσιν, καὶ ἄλλα πολλά
ἐστιν ἃ παρέλαβον κρατεῖν,¶ βαπτισμοὺς ποτηρίων ¶ N
καὶ ξεστῶν καὶ χαλκίων. ⁵καὶ ἐπερωτῶσιν αὐτὸν 5

---

4 ῥαντισωνται אB 40 53 71 86 237 240 244 259 Euth] βαπτισωνται (-σονται,
-ζωνται, -ζονται) ADEFGHKLMNSUVXΓΔΠΣΦ latt syrr arm Or | α παρελαβον] απερ
ελαβον B | κρατειν] τηρειν D *servare* latt^{vt pl vg} | και χαλκιων (-κειων AL min^{sat mu})] om
syr^{sin}+και κλινων ADXΓΠΣΦ al min^{pl} latt syrr^{pesh hcl} go arm Or (om אBLΔ min^{perpauc}
syr^{sin} me)   5 και 1°] επειτα A^{corr}XΓΠΣ(Φ) al min^{pl} syrr^{(sin) hcl} go arm επειτα και Δ

---

ever Justin, *dial.* 46, where Trypho
mentions among ordinary Jewish practices τὸ βαπτίζεσθαι ἁψάμενόν τινος ὧν
ἀπηγόρευται ὑπὸ Μωσέως.

ἄλλα πολλά] I.e. in the way of
lustration or ceremonial purification,
besides the purification of the person.
For παραλαβεῖν as the correlative of
παραδοῦναι see 1 Cor. xv. 1, 3, 2 Thess.
iii. 6: κρατεῖν is the inf. of purpose
(Burton, § 366), cf. WM., p. 401.

βαπτισμοὺς ποτηρίων κτλ.] Cf. Heb.
ix. 10, διαφόροις βαπτισμοῖς, on which
see Westcott's note; the word does
not occur in the O.T., but βαπτίζεσθαι
ἀπὸ νεκροῦ is used in Sir. xxxi. (xxxiv.)
30 in reference to the law of Num.
xix. For Talmudic directions as to
the dipping of vessels see *Chagigah*
(ed. Streane, p. 115 ff.). The vessels
specified are (1) ποτήρια, ordinary
drinking cups (cf. ix. 41, xiv. 23, Lc.
xi. 39), whether of earthenware or
metal (Esth. i. 7, Apoc. xvii. 4), (2)
ξέσται, Vg. *urcei*, pitchers or ewers,
possibly of wood (Lev. xv. 12) or of
stone (Jo. ii. 6, λίθιναι ὑδρίαι, (3) χαλ-
κία, vessels of brass or copper, as pots
used in cooking (1 Regn. ii. 14, 2 Chron.
xxxv. 13, 1 Esdr. i. 12). Ξέστης (*sex-
tarius*) occurs in two MSS. of Lev. xiv.
10 (see Hastings, *D. B.* iv., art.
Weights) and in Joseph. *ant.* viii. 2. 9
(ὁ δὲ βάτος δύναται ξέστας ἑβδομήκοντα
δύο) as a measure; the word passed
into Rabbinic (קְסְטָא). The Western
addition καὶ κλινῶν (vv. ll.) is interesting and possibly genuine, though βαπτισμοὺς...κλινῶν seems an incongruous

combination; the mention of κλῖναι
(whether 'beds' or *triclinia*) may have
been suggested by the legislation of
Lev. xv. See WH., *Notes*, p. 25.

5. καὶ ἐπερωτῶσιν αὐτόν] The sentence broken off at the end of *v.* 2 is
resumed, but καί is repeated in forgetfulness that καὶ ἰδόντες remains
without a finite verb. The R.T. gets
rid of the anacoluthon by adding
ἐμέμψαντο to *v.* 2 (Vg. *cum vidissent...
vituperaverunt*). Ἐπερωτᾶν, *supra*
v. 9; cf. vii. 17, viii. 23, &c. The
word does not imply hostility, but the
question itself leaves no doubt of the
attitude of those who put it; cf. ii.
18, 24. The Pharisees and the Scribes
(οἱ Φ. καὶ οἱ γρ.) are distinguished as in
v. 1 ; they formed on this occasion two
parties, distinct though allied. Περιπατεῖν, here only in the Synoptic Gospels
in the ethical sense, which is fairly
common in St John (viii. 12, xii. 35
bis, 1 Jo. i. 6, &c.), and frequent in
St Paul; the idea is found in the
O.T., see Gen. v. 22 (where for the
LXX. εὐηρέστησεν τῷ θεῷ, Aq. renders
literally περιεπάτει σὺν τῷ θ.), Prov.
viii. 20, Eccl. xi. 9. For περιπ. κατά
(הָלַךְ בְּ) see Rom. viii. 4, xiv. 15, 2 Cor.
x. 2, 3, Eph. ii. 2 ; κατά indicates conformity with a rule or standard, WM.,
p. 500. The standard maintained by
the Scribes was that of the Halachah
(הֲלָכָה, the rule by which men must
' walk'). Mt., less idiomatically, παρα-
βαίνουσιν τ. παράδοσιν. For τ. παράδοσιν τ. πρ. see note on *v.* 3.

οἱ Φαρισαῖοι καὶ οἱ γραμματεῖς Διὰ τί οὐ περιπατοῦσιν οἱ μαθηταί σου κατὰ τὴν παράδοσιν τῶν
πρεσβυτέρων, ἀλλὰ κοιναῖς χερσὶν ἐσθίουσιν τὸν
6 ἄρτον ; ⁶ ὁ δὲ εἶπεν αὐτοῖς Καλῶς ἐπροφήτευσεν
Ἡσαίας περὶ ὑμῶν τῶν ὑποκριτῶν ὡς γέγραπται ὅτι

5 om και οι γραμμ. Δ | κοιναις ℵ*BD 1 28 33 118 209 604 2ᵖᵉ a i q vg me arm]
ανιπτοις ℵᶜˑᵃALXΓΔΠΣΦ al minᵖˡ b c f ff syrr go | χερσιν] pr ταις D 28   6 ο δε]
+αποκριθεις ADXΓΠ al minᵖˡ latt syrʰᶜˡ arm go | καλως] pr οτι ADXΓΠ al minᵖˡ |
επροφητευσεν ℵB*DLΔ 1 13 33 124 346 1071] προεφ. AB²XΓΠΣΦ al minᵖˡ | om των
υποκρ. syrˢⁱⁿ | ως γεγραπται] και ειπεν D ως ειπεν 1 2ᵖᵉ arm λεγων 604 e ff i qui dixit
a b | om οτι ADXΓΔΠ al minᵒᵐⁿ ᵛⁱᵈ

ἀλλὰ κοιναῖς κτλ.] Mt. paraphrases,
οὐ γὰρ νίπτονται τὰς χεῖρας ὅταν ἄρτον
ἐσθίωσιν. Mc., after the explanation
of vv. 2, 3, is able to give the words
as they were uttered. Τὸν ἄρτον=τοὺς
ἄρτους, v. 2 ; for the sing. with art. cf.
Jo. vi. 23 ; φαγεῖν ἄρτον (אֱכָל־לֶחֶם)
is usual, but the article points to
what is passing before the eyes.

6. ὁ δὲ εἶπεν αὐτοῖς κτλ.] The
time had come for plain speaking, for
the Scribes had called attention to
the very heart of the controversy
between Jesus and themselves. The
answer consists of two parts, (a) vv.
6—8, (b) 9—13; Mt. has both, but
inverts the order—perhaps rightly,
for the sharp retort διὰ τί καὶ ὑμεῖς...
is lost in Mc., and the stern ὑποκριταί
seems to come better after the exposure of their inconsistency than at
the outset.

καλῶς ἐπροφήτ. Ἡσαίας περὶ ὑμῶν]
I.e. 'Isaiah's denunciation of Israel
in his own day is admirably adapted
to your case.' For this sense of καλῶς
cf. xii. 32 (where it is followed by ἐπ᾽
ἀληθείας), Jo. iv. 17, viii. 48, xiii. 13,
and see Schöttgen ad l. ; for προφητεύειν περί with gen., 1 Pet. i. 10, other
constructions are πρ. ἐπί with acc.
(Am. vii. 15, 16, Jer. xxxii. 16 (xxv.
30)), πρ. τινί (Jude 14); on the position
of the augment (ἐπροφ.) cf. WSchm.,
p. 102.

τῶν ὑποκριτῶν] The charge of 'hy-

pocrisy' is here for the first time
directly laid at the door of the
Scribes ; yet see Mt. vi. 2, 5, 15,
vii. 5. Ὑποκριτής=חָנֵף occurs in Job
xxxiv. 30, xxxvi. 13 (LXX.), and in Job
xx. 5 (Aq.). In the Pss. of Solomon
ὑπόκρισις is a charge constantly
brought against the Sadducees by
the Pharisaic author, e.g. iv. 7, ἐξ-
άραι ὁ θεὸς τοὺς ἐν ὑποκρίσει ζῶντας
μετὰ ὁσίων (see Ryle and James,
ad l.). The Scribes may well have
been startled to hear the reproach
cast back upon themselves.

ὡς γέγραπται ὅτι] Cf. καθὼς γέγρ.,
i. 2 (note), and for ὅτι as introducing
a citation see ii. 17. The passage
quoted is Isa. xxix. 13. In the quotation Mt. and Mc. agree, whilst both
differ from the LXX. in two points.
(1) The LXX. gives (with M.T.) : ἐγγίζει
μοι ὁ λαὸς οὗτος ἐν τῷ στόματι αὐτοῦ
καὶ ἐν τοῖς χείλεσιν αὐτῶν τιμῶσίν με
(B), or in the shorter text of אA, ἐγγ.
μοι ὁ λ. οὗτος, ἐν τοῖς χ. αὐτῶν τιμῶσίν
με : in Mt., Mc. the sentence is abbreviated still further.   (2) The LXX.
has : διδάσκοντες ἐντάλματα ἀνθρώπων
καὶ διδασκαλίας. Here there is no
important variant in the MSS., yet
Mt., Mc. omit καὶ and place διδασκαλίας before ἐντ., without approaching nearer to the M.T. which gives
(R.V.) "their fear of me is a commandment of men which hath been taught
them" (cf. Aq. Symm. Th., ἐγένετο τὸ

ʽΟ λαὸς οὗτος τοῖς χείλεσίν με τιμᾷ, ἡ δὲ καρδία
αὐτῶν §πόρρω ἀπέχει ἀπ᾽ ἐμοῦ· ⁷μάτην δὲ σέβονταί 7 §Wᵈ
με, διδάσκοντες διδασκαλίας ἐντάλματα ἀνθρώπων.
⁸ἀφέντες τὴν ἐντολὴν τοῦ θεοῦ κρατεῖτε τὴν παρά- 8
δοσιν τῶν ἀνθρώπων.¶ ⁹καὶ ἔλεγεν αὐτοῖς Καλῶς 9 ¶ Wᵈ

6 ο λαος ουτος BD b c f i q vg] ουτ. ο λ. ℵΑLΧΓΔΠ al | τιμα] αγαπα D a b c (cf.
Clem-Al) τιμα και αγαπα aeth | απεχει] αφεστηκεν D απεστιν L 2ᵖᵉ εστιν Clem-Al² est
lattᵖˡ Clem-R Clem-Al¹ απεστη Δ   7 ενταλματα] pr και a c f (vg) | ανθρωπων]
+βαπτισμους ξεστων και ποτηριων και αλλα παρομοια α ποιειται τοιαυτα πολλα D
8 totum versum om syrˢⁱⁿ | αφεντες]+γαρ ΑΧΓΠΣΦ al minᵖˡ f vg syrr go | αν-
θρωπων]+βαπτ. ξεστ. κ. ποτ. κ. αλλα (om αλλα A alᵖᵃᵘᶜ) παρ. τοιαυτα πολλα ποιειτε
(A)(F)(Wᵈ)ΧΓΠΣΦ al minᵖˡ f vg syrr go arm aeth   9 om και ελ. αυτ. 28 syrˢⁱⁿ

φοβεῖσθαι αὐτοὺς ἐμὲ ἐντολὴ ἀνθρώπων
διδακτή). St Paul (Col. ii. 22) seems
to follow the LXX.; Justin has both
forms (dial. 78, 140, see Resch, Paralleltexte, p. 170). The facts are perplexing, but a solution is perhaps to
be sought in the direction to which
reference has been made in the note
on i. 2; see Hatch, Essays, p. 117 f.
The readings of D and some of the
Old Latin texts are interesting: see
vv. ll.; with ἀγαπᾷ cf. Ps. lxxvii.
(lxxviii.) 36. On the readings of
Clement of Rome see Intr. to O.T.
in Greek, p. 408, and on those of
Clement of Alexandria, Barnard, Biblical Text of Clement, p. 30 f.

7. μάτην δὲ σέβονταί με κτλ.] Μάτην
δέ represents וַתְּהִי, which the LXX.
read in place of M.T. וַתְּהִי; see Nestle
in Exp. T. xi. p. 330 f. The fruitlessness of the Pharisaic religion was due
to its self-imposed and external character. Διδασκαλία, a rare word in
Biblical Gk. (Prov.¹ Sir.² Rom.² Eph.¹
Col.¹), except in the Pastoral Epp.
(1 Tim.⁸ 2 Tim.³ Tit.⁴), is a doctrine, a
definite piece or course of instruction,
as contrasted with διδαχή, which is
properly an act or line of teaching (i.
22, 27, iv. 2), though διδαχή sometimes
(Rom. vi. 17, xvi. 17) is used in a
sense scarcely distinguishable from
διδασκαλία. The two words may be

studied in juxtaposition in Tit. i. 9 (see
Hort, Ecclesia, p. 191). Ἐντάλματα
is in apposition to διδ., 'inasmuch
as they teach doctrines (which are)
commandments of men'; cf. vi. 43,
ἦραν κλάσματα...πληρώματα (WM., p.
664 f.). The pl. perhaps points to
the multiplicity of the details, and the
absence of an underlying principle:
contrast ἐντολή, v. 8 (note), and cf.
Tit. i. 14, ἐντολαὶ ἀνθρώπων.

8. ἀφέντες τὴν ἐντολήν κτλ.] Perhaps a doublet of v. 9; Mt. has another form of the saying, corresponding more nearly with the next verse.
The Law of GOD (ἡ ἐντολή, Ps. cxviii.
(cxix.) 96, cf. 1 Tim. vi. 14, 2 Pet. ii. 21,
iii. 2) is regarded as an unit; ἐντολή is
properly a single commandment, but
seems to be here used in opposition
to·ἐντάλματα (v. 7) for the Law as a
whole, the manifold expression of the
one principle of love (Rom. xiii. 8 ff.,
Gal. v. 14). The ἐντολή is here the
Torah as contrasted with the Halachah. Τοῦ θεοῦ...τῶν ἀνθρώπων: the
Elders were but אֲנָשִׁים (Isa. l.c.); the
Torah was, as the Scribes themselves
believed, of GOD. A like claim is
made in the Talmud for the oral
tradition (cf. Taylor, Aboth, p. 119 ff.,
Streane, Chagigah, p. vi.), but this
does not seem to have been openly
maintained in our Lord's time.

ἀθετεῖτε τὴν ἐντολὴν τοῦ θεοῦ, ἵνα τὴν παράδοσιν
10 ὑμῶν τηρήσητε. ¹⁰ Μωυσῆς γὰρ εἶπεν Τίμα τὸν
πατέρα σου καὶ τὴν μητέρα σου· καί Ὁ κακολογῶν
11 πατέρα ἢ μητέρα θανάτῳ τελευτάτω· ¹¹ὑμεῖς δὲ
λέγετε Ἐὰν εἴπη ἄνθρωπος τῷ πατρὶ ἢ τῇ μητρί
Κορβάν (ὅ ἐστιν Δῶρον), ὃ ἐὰν ἐξ ἐμοῦ ὠφεληθῇς,

9 εντολην] βουλην Δ | τηρησητε (τηρητε Β)] στησητε D 1 28 209 2ᵖᵉ *statuatis* latᵛᵗ
syrrˢⁱⁿ ᵖᵉˢʰ arm goᵛⁱᵈ Cypr   10 Μωσης ΑΛΓ al minᵖˡ   11 εαν] ος αν Α 33 |
om ανθρωπος 33 ο ανθρ. 1071

9. καλῶς ἀθετεῖτε κτλ.] Καλῶς is
in part ironical (cf. Jo. iv. 17), but see
v. 6. For ἀθετεῖν see vi. 26; and for
the sense it bears here (nullify, eva-
cuate, reduce to a dead letter) cf. Isa.
xxiv. 16 (οὐαὶ τοῖς ἀθετοῦσιν· οἱ ἀθε-
τοῦντες τὸν νόμον), Gal. iii. 15 (ἀθ. διαθήκην), Heb. x. 28 (ἀθ. νόμον Μωυσέως).
The oral law was professedly a 'fence'
to the written law; in practice it
took its place and even reversed its
decisions. When the two were in com-
petition, the tradition was preferred :
cf. the frank saying of R. Jochanan
quoted by Dr Taylor *l.c.*, "words of
Soferim...are more beloved than words
of Torah." With the 'Western' reading στήσητε cf. Exod. vi. 4, 2 Esdr.
xix. 8, Heb. x. 9.

10. Μωυσῆς γὰρ εἶπεν κτλ.] An
instance of the tendency censured
in v. 9. Mt. ὁ γὰρ θεὸς εἶπεν. The
first citation is from the Divine Ten
Words, incorporated in 'Moses,' i.e.
the Pentateuch; cf. 2 Cor. iii. 15,
ἡνίκα ἂν ἀναγινώσκηται Μωυσῆς. The
passages, which follow the LXX. with
some slight variations, are from Exod.
xx. 12 (Deut. v. 16), xxi. 16 (17); cf.
Victor : ἐκ δύο νομίμων ἀπαιτεῖ τὴν εἰς
γονέας τιμὴν κατὰ βούλησιν θεοῦ, ἑνὸς
μὲν τοῦ κελεύοντος οὕτω ποιεῖν, ἑτέρου
δὲ τοῦ τιμωρουμένου τὸν ἐναντίως ποι-
οῦντα. In the second passage ὁ κακολογῶν (מְקַלֵּל) is scarcely (as Vg.,
Wycliffe, and the other English versions, exc. R.V.) 'he that curseth';

though קָלַל has this meaning (e.g. in
1 Regn. xvii. 43 where the LXX. renders
κατηράσατο), yet in Deut. xxvii. 16,
which closely corresponds with Exod.
xxi. 16, מַקְלֶה is represented by ὁ
ἀτιμάζων (cf. Guillemard on Mt. xv. 4).
The correction is clearly important in
view of the Lord's argument. Θανάτῳ
τελευτάτω (Mc. Mt.)=מוֹת יוּמַת; so
codd. AF in Exod. xxi. 16 (17), where
cod. B has τελευτήσει θ.

11. ὑμεῖς δὲ λέγετε κτλ.] You
(emph.) set yourselves against Moses
(cf. Jo. v. 45 ff.), for your tradition
(v. 9) permits, and under certain circumstances requires, a son to dis-
honour his parents. Ἐὰν εἴπη ἄνθρ.,
'suppose a man shall say,' Mt. ὃς ἂν
εἴπη. The apodosis would naturally
be, as in Mt., οὐ μὴ τιμήσει (see
Burton, § 260), but Mc. cuts the
sentence short in order to proceed
with the Lord's comment on the rule
(οὐκέτι ἀφίετε κτλ., v. 12).

κορβάν (ὅ ἐστιν δῶρον)] Another
Marcan Aramaism (but see Dalman, *Gr.*
p. 139 n.), with its explanatory Greek ;
cf. v. 41. Δῶρον represents קָרְבָּן Lev.³⁵,
Num.³⁹, 2 Esdr.¹ (קָרְבָּן) ; the transliteration does not occur in the LXX.
or apparently in the later Gk. versions of the O.T., or again in the
N.T., but cf. Joseph. *ant.* iv. 4. 4,
κορβάν...δῶρον δὲ τοῦτο σημαίνει κατὰ
Ἑλλήνων γλῶσσαν : c. *Ap.* i. 167, τὸν
καλούμενον ὅρκον κορβάν (citing Theo-

¹²οὐκέτι ἀφίετε αὐτὸν οὐδὲν ποιῆσαι τῷ πατρὶ ἢ τῇ 12
μητρί, ¹³ἀκυροῦντες §τὸν λόγον τοῦ θεοῦ τῇ παρα- 13 §ⁿ

12 ουκετι] pr και ΑΧΓΠΣΦ al minᵖˡ f vg syrr arm go pr οτι L | om τω πατρι η
τη μητρι Δ | τω πατρι]+αυτου ΑΧΠ al minᵖˡ | τη μητρι]+αυτου ΑΧΓΠ al minᵖˡ
13 τον λογον] την εντολην 1 | τη παραδοσει υμων]+τη μωρα D a b c ff i n q syrʰᶜˡ⁽ᵐᵍ⁾ δια
την παραδοσιν υμ. 1071

phrastus). A *qorban* is a consecrated
gift; the Temple treasury is called
κορβανᾶς in Mt. xxvii. 6, Joseph. *B. J.*
ii. 9. 4: cf. Cyprian, *de op. et el.* 15,
"Dominicum celebrare te credis quae
corban omnino non respicis?" In
Syriac ⟨⟩ is the Eucharist
itself, as the Christian offering. The
Scribes held that the mere act of de-
claring any property to be *qorban* alienated it from the service of the person
addressed; cf. Edersheim, *Life*, ii. p.
19: "it must not be thought that the
pronunciation of the votive word *qorban*..necessarily dedicated a thing to
the Temple; the meaning might be that
in regard to the person or persons
named the thing [so] termed was to be
considered as if it were *qorban*, laid on
the altar and put entirely out of their
reach." A son who took this way of
relieving himself from the support of a
father or mother was not only justified
in his unfilial conduct, but actually
prohibited from returning to his duty.
Victor: εἴτις ἀτιμίᾳ γονέων θυσίαν
ὑπόσχοιτο, λέγων θεῷ ποιήσειν δῶρα
καὶ θυσίας ἃ πατρὶ παρέχειν ὀφείλει,
τοῦτο[ν] λέγετε μηδὲ ἐξεῖναι τιμῆσαι
τὸν πατέρα. Origen (*in Matt.* t. xi. 9)
mentions a somewhat similar case
which had been reported to him by
a Jew: ἔσθ᾽ ὅτε, φησίν, οἱ δανεισταὶ
δυστραπέλοις περιπίπτοντες χρεώσταις
καὶ δυναμένοις μὲν μὴ βουλομένοις δὲ
ἀποδιδόναι τὸ χρέος ἀνετίθεσαν τὸ ὀφει-
λόμενον εἰς τὸν τῶν πενήτων λόγον—a
proceeding which prevented the debt-
or's escape. For ὠφελεῖσθαι, pass.,
see v. 26, Heb. xiii. 9; ἐκ points to
the source of the expected profit, cf.
WM., p. 458. The Vg. gives the
general sense of ὃ ἐὰν ἐξ ἐμοῦ ὠφε-

ληθῇς—*quodcumque ex me tibi pro-
fuerit*; cf. Euth.: ἀφιέρωται τῷ θεῷ
ὃ ἂν ἐξ ἐμοῦ κερδανεῖς. The son speaks
from the parent's point of view, which
regards his support as practically
secure: 'the assistance which thou
lookest to receive from me is now
irrevocably alienated.' For the Rabbinical *formulae* see J. Lightfoot and
Schöttgen *ad l.*

12. οὐκέτι ἀφίετε κτλ.] Mt. οὐ μὴ
τιμήσει: see last note. Origen: τῆς
πρὸς τοὺς γονεῖς τιμῆς μέρος ἦν καὶ τὸ
κοινωνεῖν αὐτοῖς τῶν βιωτικῶν χρειῶν.
Comp. the English Ch. catechism:
"my duty is...to love, honour, and
succour my father and mother." In
illustration of this use of τιμᾶν Jerome
produces 1 Tim. v. 3, 17; cf. Theod.
Mops. *ad l.*: "*honora*, hoc est, dili-
gentiam illis adhibe." With οὐκέτι
οὐδέν cf. v. 3, ix. 8, xii. 34, xiv. 25, xv.
5. The ὃ ἐάν of *v.* 11 excludes in the
hypothetical case all hope of material
assistance from the moment the *qorban* is uttered. Ποιεῖν τί τινι, sc.
ἀγαθόν, cf. v. 19, 20; the phrase may
have, as in English, an opposite sense,
cf. ix. 13. Thpht. points out that the
Scribes may have often been not dis-
interested in their judgement: αὐτοὶ
δὲ τὰ ἀφιερωθέντα κατήσθιον (cf. xii.
40).

13. ἀκυροῦντες κτλ.] Ἀκυροῦν is
stronger than ἀθετεῖν v. 9; but he
who habitually ἀθετεῖ, practically ἀκυροῖ, invalidates and, so far as in him
lies, repeals a law. The distinction
is well seen in Gal. iii. 15, 17, κεκυ-
ρωμένην διαθήκην οὐδεὶς ἀθετεῖ...νόμος
οὐκ ἀκυροῖ. Cf. ἄκυρον ποιεῖν in Prov.
i. 25 (=פָּרַע), v. 7 (=סוּר): ἀκυροῦν
occurs in 1 Esdr., 1, 4 Macc., and is

δόσει ὑμῶν ἢ παρεδώκατε· καὶ παρόμοια τοιαῦτα πολλὰ ποιεῖτε.

14 ¹⁴Καὶ προσκαλεσάμενος πάλιν τὸν ὄχλον ἔλεγεν 15 αὐτοῖς Ἀκούσατέ μου πάντες καὶ σύνετε. ¹⁵οὐδὲν ἔστιν ἔξωθεν τοῦ ἀνθρώπου εἰσπορευόμενον εἰς αὐτὸν

13 om η παρεδωκατε syrˢⁱⁿ ην π. 1071   14 παλιν אBDLΔ b ff i n q vg syrʰᶜˡ⁽ᵐᵍ⁾ me aeth] παντα ΑΧΓΠΣΦ al minᵖˡ f syrˢⁱⁿ ᵖᵉˢʰ ʰᶜˡ⁽ᵗˣᵗ⁾ arm go | ακουσατε BDHL 2ᵖᵉ alᵖᵃᵘᶜ] ακουετε אΑΧΓΔΠΣΦ al minᵖˡ | om μου Δ | om παντες אLΔ al me | συνετε BHLΔ 238] συνιετε אΑΧΓΠΣΦ al minᶠᵉʳᵉ ᵒᵐⁿ

fairly common in Aq.; in the N.T. it is limited to the context (Mc. Mt.), and Gal. *l.c.*

τῇ παραδόσει ὑ. ᾗ παρεδώκατε] Apparently the dat. of instrument, but cf. Mt. διὰ τὴν παράδοσιν, 'for the sake of your tradition.' For παραδιδόναι παράδοσιν see WM., p. 282, and for ᾗ, WM., p. 202 f. The 'Western' text glosses again, adding τῇ μωρᾷ; see vv. ll. Παρόμοια τοιαῦτα, 'such like things'; the Vg. keeps the tautology, *similia huiusmodi*. Παρόμοιος is ἅπ. λεγ. in Biblical Gk., though frequent in class. and late writers; for its exact meaning cf. Pollux cited by Wetstein: ὁ γὰρ παρόμοιος παρ' ὀλίγον ὅμοιός ἐστιν. Euth. adds the wholesome reflexion: φοβηθῶμεν οὖν καὶ ἡμεῖς, ὁ τοῦ Χριστοῦ λαός, μὴ καὶ καθ' ἡμῶν ταῦτα ῥηθείη.

14—23. TEACHING BASED UPON THE QUESTION (Mt. xv. 10—20).

14. καὶ προσκαλεσάμενος πάλιν τὸν ὄχλον] The question of *v.* 5 had been put and answered at a time of comparative privacy, which the Twelve had used for snatching a hasty meal. But the principle which had been asserted was too important to be dropped. It touched the heart of things, and was necessary for all. For προσκαλεῖσθαι see note on iii. 13; πάλιν (omitted by Mt.) points to an unnoticed dispersion of the Gennesaret crowd (vi. 55 f.). For ἀκούσατέ μου π. καὶ σύνετε Mt. has less pre-

cisely ἀκούετε καὶ συνίετε: cf. WM., p. 393 f., and contrast Mc. iv. 23, ix. 7, Eph. v. 17.

15. οὐδὲν ἔστιν ἔξωθεν κτλ.] A fundamental canon, differentiating the Kingdom of GOD from Pharisaic Judaism. Victor: ἐντεῦθεν ὁ καινὸς ἄρχεται νόμος ὁ κατὰ τὸ πνεῦμα. The merely external cannot defile man's spiritual nature (Euth., οὐδὲ γὰρ ἅπτεται τῆς ψυχῆς)—the converse of the principle that the merely external cannot purify it (Mt. xxiii. 25, 26, Heb. ix. 9 ff.). For οὐδὲν ἔξωθεν Mt. substitutes the explanatory οὐ τὸ εἰσερχόμενον εἰς τὸ στόμα, 'nothing in the way of food'; and similarly to τὰ ἐκπορευόμενα he adds ἐκ τοῦ στόματος. Even when thus limited the canon goes much further than a protest against the unwritten law of Scribism; its logical effect was to abrogate the Levitical distinction of meats clean and unclean. In defence of this distinction the Maccabean heroes had given their lives (1 Macc. i. 62 f., 4 Macc. vii. 6), and a Jewish crowd, even in Galilee, would probably have resented the principle now asserted by the Lord, had they understood it. But it was not understood even by the Apostles until long afterwards, Acts x. 14 ff.; for the time the Lord was content to drop the seed and leave it to germinate. Κοινοῦν is used in the N.T. only in the technical sense (*v.* 2 note), though the Vg., which renders it *coin-*

ὃ δύναται κοινῶσαι αὐτόν· ἀλλὰ τὰ ἐκ τοῦ ἀνθρώπου
ἐκπορευόμενά ἐστιν τὰ κοινοῦντα τὸν ἄνθρωπον.
¹⁷καὶ ὅτε εἰσῆλθεν εἰς οἶκον ἀπὸ τοῦ ὄχλου, ἐπη- 17
ρώτων αὐτὸν οἱ μαθηταὶ αὐτοῦ τὴν παραβολήν.
¹⁸καὶ λέγει αὐτοῖς Οὕτως καὶ ὑμεῖς ἀσύνετοί ἐστε; 18
οὐ νοεῖτε ὅτι πᾶν τὸ ἔξωθεν εἰσπορευόμενον εἰς τὸν

15 ο δυναται κοινωσαι] το κοινουν B | τα εκ του ανθρ. εκπ. אBDLΔ 33 2ᵖᵉ latt me
go aeth] τα εκπ. απ αυτου ΑΧΓΠ al syrʳᵖᵉˢʰʰᵉˡ arm | εστιν 2°] pr εκεινα ΑΔΧΓΠΣΦ
al minᵖˡ latt | τον ανθρωπον]+(16) ει τις εχει (ο εχων 1071 g) ωτα ακουειν ακουετω
ΑΔΧΓΔᶜᵒʳʳΣΦ al minᵖˡ latt syrr arm go aeth (om אBLΔ* 28 me)   17 οικον] pr
τον אΔ minᵖᵃᵘᶜ την οικιαν D 2ᵖᵉ alᵖᵃᵘᶜ | την παραβολην] περι της παραβολης ΑΧΓΠΣΦ
minᵖˡ arm go   18 ου] ουπω אLUΔ 1 604 alⁿᵒⁿⁿ f syrʰᵉˡ⁽ᵐᵍ⁾ | om εξωθεν Δ syrˢⁱⁿ |
om εις τον ανθρ. א

quinare in Mt. xv. and on its first
occurrence in Mc., retains the O.L.
communicare (Rönsch, *Itala*, p. 354)
throughout the rest of this chapter;
cf. the confusion of ἐκοίνωσας, ἐκοινώνησας in the mss. of 4 Macc. *l.c.*

ἀλλὰ τὰ ἐκ τοῦ ἀνθρώπου κτλ.] The
positive side of the canon; the source
of human defilement is internal to the
nature of man. Ὁ ἄνθρωπος, as in ii.
27, Jo. ii. 25, 1 Cor. ii. 11, =man, i.e.
men regarded as a generic unity. Τὰ
κοινοῦντα: on the art. with the predi-
cate see WM., p. 141 f. For *v.* 16 of
the R.T. see vv. ll. It has been introduced as the proper sequel to *v.* 14;
cf. iv. 9.

17. καὶ ὅτε εἰσῆλθεν κτλ.] A third
stage in the incident. To the crowd
the new law was stated in a parabolic
form; to the disciples it is now interpreted (cf. iv. 10 ff., 33 f.). Εἰς οἶκον,
whether Simon's house at Capernaum
(i. 29, ii. 1, &c.), or the house of some
disciple in one of the Gennesaret
villages, does not appear; in either
case it supplied a temporary rest.
For ἀπό 'away from' see WM., p. 463.
This detail is wanting in Mt., who on
the other hand is alone in attributing
the question of the disciples to Peter.
Whether from his position (πρῶτος,

Mt. x. 2) or from natural readiness to
speak, St Peter seems to have been
the usual spokesman, cf. Mc. viii. 29 ff.,
ix. 5, x. 28, xi. 21, xiii. 3, Mt. xv. 15,
Lc. viii. 45, xxii. 8. With ἐπηρώτων
...τὴν παραβολήν cf. iv. 10; Mt. εἶπεν
Φράσον ἡμῖν τὴν π.: the 'parable is
here little more than a proverbial
saying, as in Lc. iv. 23. See the
conversation which precedes this request in Mt. (xv. 12—14).

18. οὕτως καὶ ὑμεῖς ἀσύνετοί ἐστε;]
For οὕτως Mt. has ἀκμήν=ἔτι: οὕτως
is *sic* (Vg.) or *siccine* (Field) rather
than *tam*; in Gal. iii. 3, Heb. xii. 21
the juxtaposition of the adv. with the
adj. decides for the latter meaning.
Καὶ ὑμεῖς, 'ye (emph.) also' (Jo. vi.
68) as well as the crowd (cf. iv. 11).
Ἀσύνετος looks back to μὴ συνίωσιν
(Isa. vi. 9, cited Mc. iv. 12): the word
occurs also in Rom. i. 21, 31, x. 19.
The ἀσύνετος is the man who lacks
the discernment (ἡ δὲ σύνεσις κριτική,
Arist. *Eth. Nic.* vi. 11, cited by
Lightfoot on Col. i. 9) which comes
from the due use of the illuminated
intelligence; hence he is near of kin
to the ἀνόητος (Lc. xxiv. 25, Gal. *l.c.*;
cf. Mc. viii. 17, 2 Tim. ii. 7). Thus
ἀσύνετοι prepares for οὐ νοεῖτε which
immediately follows (Mt. Mc.).

19 ἄνθρωπον οὐ δύναται αὐτὸν κοινῶσαι, ¹⁹ὅτι οὐκ εἰσπορεύεται αὐτοῦ εἰς τὴν καρδίαν ἀλλ᾽ εἰς τὴν κοιλίαν,
καὶ εἰς τὸν ἀφεδρῶνα ἐκπορεύεται;—καθαρίζων πάντα
20 τὰ βρώματα. ²⁰ἔλεγεν δὲ ὅτι Τὸ ἐκ τοῦ ἀνθρώπου

18 ου δυναται αυτον κοινωσαι] ου κοινοι τον ανθρωπον ℵ syrˢⁱⁿ   19 οτι ουκ] ου
γαρ D a b i n q | εισπορευεται] εισερχεται D | om εις τ. αφεδρωνα syrˢⁱⁿ arm | αφεδρωνα]
οχετον D | εκπορευεται] εκβαλλεται ℵΦ minᵖᵃᵘᶜ syrˢⁱⁿ εξερχεται D | καθαριζων ℵABE
FGHLSXΔ 1 13 28 69 124 1071 2ᵖᵉ al Or] καθαριζον KMUVΓΠΣΦ minᵖˡ καθαριζει D
go και καθαριζει zˢᶜʳ arm   20 το...εκπορευομενον] quae exeunt latt

18—19. οὐ δύναται...ἐκπορεύεται]
Mc. only. The words state explicitly the principle involved in v.
15. ' Pollution' (τὸ κοινοῦσθαι) in the
sense contemplated by the Scribes
can be predicated only of that which
affects man's moral nature. There
was no question between Christ and
the Scribes as to external cleanliness,
for their censure rested purely on
religious grounds. It is therefore of
spiritual pollution only that He speaks.
The two spheres of human life, the
physical and the spiritual, are here distinct ; to confuse them, as the Scribes
did, is to ignore the commonest
facts of daily experience. 'Αφεδρών
is the class. ἄφοδος or ἀπόπατος, Vg.
secessus ; the word occurs in Biblical
Gk. only in this context (Mt. Mc.);
the LXX. use ἡ ἄφεδρος in another
connexion (Lev. xii. 9), employing
λυτρών in this sense (4 Regn. x. 27).
Cod. D substitutes ὀχετός in Mc., retaining ἀφ. in Mt.
Origen in Mt. t. xi. 14 has an interesting reference to the Eucharist : καὶ τὸ ἁγιαζόμενον βρῶμα...κατ᾽
αὐτὸ μὲν τὸ ὑλικὸν εἰς τὴν κοιλίαν χωρεῖ,
κατὰ δὲ τὴν ἐπιγινομένην αὐτῷ εὐχὴν...
ὠφέλιμον γίνεται...οὐχ ἡ ὕλη τοῦ ἄρτου
ἀλλ᾽ ὁ ἐπ᾽ αὐτῷ εἰρημένος λόγος ἐστὶν
ὁ ὠφελῶν τὸν μὴ ἀναξίως τοῦ κυρίου
ἐσθίοντα αὐτόν.
19. καθαρίζων πάντα τὰ βρώματα]
A note added by a teacher or editor
who has realised that in the preceding
words the Lord had really abrogated

the distinction between clean and
unclean food. ᷍ The true reading and
interpretation were known to Origen
(in Mt. t. xi. 12, κατὰ τὸν Μᾶρκον ἔλεγε
ταῦτα ὁ σωτὴρ καθαρίζων πάντα τὰ
βρώματα, δηλῶν ὅτι οὐ κοινούμεθα μὲν
ἐσθίοντες ἃ 'Ιουδαῖοί φασι κτλ.), who is
followed by Gregory Thaum. and
Chrysostom : see Field, Notes, p. 32.
This interesting reference to the interpretation put upon the Lord's words
by the Apostolic age (cf. Acts x. 15 ἃ
ὁ θεὸς ἐκαθάρισεν) is lost in the R.T.
(see vv. ll.). In support of καθαρίζων
see Scrivener-Miller, ii. p. 336 f., and
for a defence of καθαρίζον Burgon-
Miller, Causes of Corruption, p. 61 f.;
but few students of St Mark will
follow Mr Miller in rejecting καθαρίζων
on the ground that its distance from
λέγει (v. 18) is inconsistent with the
style of this Gospel. Field ad loc.
rightly points to iii. 30 for another
instance of a brief explanation paren-
thetically added by Mc. For the
interpretation which the supporters
of the R.T. propose to give to καθαρίζον cf. WM., pp. 669, 778 ; the view
that καθαρίζων is a nom. pendens in
agreement with ὁ ἀφεδρών scarcely
calls for consideration.
20. τὸ ἐκ τοῦ ἀνθρώπου κτλ.] See
v. 15 b. Mt. narrows the statement
(ἐκ τοῦ στόματος for ἐκ τοῦ ἀνθρώπου),
and anticipates the explanation (ἐκ
τῆς καρδίας ἐξέρχεται). 'Εκεῖνο, 'that,'
in contrast with τὰ ἔξωθεν (v. 15) ; see
Blass, Gr. p. 172.

§ἐκπορευόμενον, ἐκεῖνο κοινοῖ τὸν ἄνθρωπον· ²¹ἔσωθεν 21 § N
γὰρ ἐκ τῆς καρδίας τῶν ἀνθρώπων οἱ διαλογισμοὶ
οἱ κακοὶ ἐκπορεύονται, πορνεῖαι, κλοπαί, φόνοι,

20 εκεινα D latt   21, 22 πορνειαι κλοπαι φονοι μοιχειαι אBLΔ 604 me aeth]
πορνεια κλεμματα μοιχειαι φονος D μοιχειαι πορνειαι φονοι κλοπαι ΑΝΧΓΠΣΦ d minᵖˡ
f vg syrrˢⁱⁿ ʰᶜˡ μοιχ. κλοπ. πορν. φον. a b c d ff i q μοιχ. πορν. κλοπ. φον. syrᵖᵉˢʰ arm

21—22. ἔσωθεν γὰρ ἐκ τῆς καρδίας
κτλ.] Ἔσωθεν answers to ἔξωθεν (vv.
15, 18); for the contrast in this
reference see Mt. xxiii. 25, 26 (τὸ
ἐντός, τὸ ἐκτός), Lc. xi. 39, 40, 2 Cor.
iv. 16 (ὁ ἔξω ἄνθρωπος, ὁ ἔσω). Bede's
remark needs modification, but is just
on the whole: "animae principale non
iuxta Platonem in cerebro, sed iuxta
Christum in corde est." For καρδία
see ii. 6, 8, iii. 5, vi. 52, vii. 6; the
seat of the moral nature is in man
the source of moral defilement. The
Lord states the fact without explaining it; into the question of the origin
of evil in man He does not enter.
His teaching stands midway between
the O.T. doctrine of sin (e.g. Ps. li. 5,
Isa. liii. 6, Jer. xvii. 9, cf. Schultz, ii.
p. 292 ff.), and the Pauline doctrine
(cf. SH., Romans, p. 143 ff.). Διαλογισμοί, thoughts, elsewhere chiefly in
Lc. and Paul.

The list of sins which follows is
twice as full as in Mt., who, while
adding ψευδομαρτυρίαι, omits πλεονεξίαι, πονηρίαι, δόλος, ἀσέλγεια,
ὀφθαλμὸς πονηρός, ὑπερηφανία, ἀφροσύνη (Euth.: ὁ δὲ Μᾶρκος ἀπαριθμεῖται
καὶ ἕτερα, πλεονεξίαν, πονηρίαν, δόλον,
ἀσέλγειαν κτλ.). Moreover, in those
which are common to both the order
differs: Mt. seems to follow that of
the Decalogue as arranged in the M.T.
and in cod. A of the LXX., whilst Mc.
is in partial accord with cod. B (οὐ
κλέψεις, οὐ φονεύσεις). While both
lists begin with the διαλογισμοί, in
the specification which follows Mt.
limits himself to external sins, whilst
Mc. passes from these to mental acts
or habits (πλεονεξίαι...ἀφροσύνη). It

is instructive to compare with both
the catalogues of sins in Sap. xiv. 25 f.,
Rom. i. 29 ff., Gal. v. 20 f., Eph. iv.
31, v. 3 ff., Col. iii. 5 ff., Didache 5,
Hermas mand. viii. 5; cf. Harnack,
T. u. U. v. 1. p. 86 f. The last two
shew the influence of the Gospel lists,
whilst Wisdom has possibly suggested
some of its details; but in the Pauline
passages we strike a new vein; such
Gentile sins as εἰδωλολατρεία, φαρμα-
κία, and such peculiarly Greek vices
as κῶμοι, εὐτραπελία, αἰσχρολογία, are
naturally not represented in our
Lord's enumeration.

21. οἱ διαλογισμοὶ οἱ κακοί] Mt.
διαλογισμοὶ πονηροί. The commission
of any sin is preceded by a delibera-
tion, however rapid, in the mind of
the sinner; cf. ii. 6 ff., Lc. v. 22, Rom.
i. 21, James ii. 4. On διαλ. see Hatch,
Essays, p. 8. Οἱ δ., such inward deliberations regarded as a class of
mental acts; the addition of οἱ κακοί
marks off a part of the class, such as
are evil in themselves (κακοί), or mis-
chievous in their effects (πονηροί)—see
Trench, syn. xi.

πορνεῖαι κτλ.] The plurals indicate
successive acts of sin, as they emerge
from the inner source of human corruption; the more subtle tendencies
to evil which follow are in the singular (v. 22). Cf. Gal. v. 20 ζῆλος,
θυμοί, the spirit of rivalry, 'outbursts
of wrath' (Lightfoot), and see WM.,
p. 220. Κλοπαί: cod. D, κλέμματα, cf.
Herm. l.c. For this combination of
sins cf. Hos. iv. 2 φόνος καὶ κλοπὴ καὶ
μοιχεία κέχυται ἐπὶ τῆς γῆς.

22 ²²μοιχεῖαι, πλεονεξίαι, πονηρίαι, δόλος, ἀσέλγεια, ὀφθαλμὸς πονηρός, βλασφημία, ὑπερηφανία, ἀφρο-

22 πλεονεξια δολος πονηρια D | δολοι πονηριαι ασελγειαι 2ᵖᵉ | δολοι ασελγειαι arm

22. πλεονεξίαι] Vg. avaritiae; rather, impulses or acts of self-seeking. Cf. Plat. resp. ii. 359 c τὴν πλεονεξίαν, ὃ πᾶσα φύσις διώκειν πέφυκεν ὡς ἀγαθόν. This commonest corruption of human nature is not spared by our Lord (Lc. xii. 15), or by St Paul (Col. iii. 5 τὴν πλ. ἥτις ἐστὶν εἰδωλολατρία): the πλεονέκτης is classed by the latter with the πόρνος (1 Cor. v. 10, 11, Eph. v. 5), the κλέπτης, the μέθυσος (1 Cor. vi. 10), as his vice is here mentioned in the same breath with φόνοι and μοιχεῖαι; see also 2 Pet. ii. 14.

πονηρίαι] Vg. nequitiae, purposes or acts of malicious wickedness, cf. Mt. xxii. 18, Lc. xi. 39; in Rom. i. 29 πονηρία is in the same company as here (πονηρίᾳ πλεονεξίᾳ κακίᾳ).

δόλος] A besetting sin of Orientals, repeatedly illustrated and condemned in the O.T. (e.g. Gen. xxvii. 35, Deut. xxvii. 24, Ps. ix. 28 (x. 7)), and characteristic of our Lord's opponents (Mc. xiv. 1); its absence was a note of the true Israelite and of Christ Himself (Ps. xxiii. (xxiv.) 4, xxxi. (xxxii.) 2, Jo. i. 48, 1 Pet. ii. 22). It appears in Rom. i. 29, but not in the lists of sins which occur in Epistles addressed to Churches in which Gentiles largely predominated (Gal. Eph. Col.).

ἀσέλγεια] Vg. impudicitia. Cf. Gal. v. 20 πορνεία ἀκαθαρσία ἀσέλγεια, on which Lightfoot remarks: "a man may be ἀκάθαρτος and hide his sin; he does not become ἀσελγής, until he shocks public decency." The word, which is class., finds no place in the LXX. exc. in Sap. xiv. 26, 3 Macc. ii. 26, where Gentile habits are in view; in the N.T. it is used in the same connexion (Eph. iv. 19, 1 Pet. iv. 3). Here the reference is probably to the dissolute life of the Herodian court, and of the Greek cities of Galilee and

the Decapolis; if δόλος characterised the Jew, his Greek neighbour was yet more terribly branded by ἀσέλγεια.

ὀφθαλμὸς πονηρός] On the Hebrew belief in the evil eye see Lightfoot on Gal. iii. 1. The ἀνὴρ βάσκανος (אִישׁ רַע עָיִן Prov. xxviii. 22) was a dreaded enemy (Sir. xiv. 10, xxxiv. 13 (xxxi. 14, 15) κακὸν ὀφθαλμὸς πονηρός· πονηρότερον ὀφθαλμοῦ τί ἔκτισται;). Hence ' the evil eye' became a synonym for jealousy, or a jealous grudge; cf. Deut. xv. 9 וְרָעָה עֵינְךָ בְּאָחִיךָ, LXX., μὴ ...πονηρεύσηται ὁ ὀφθαλμός σου τῷ ἀδελφῷ σου, i.e. 'lest thou grudge him his due'; Tob. iv. 7 (B), μὴ φθονεσάτω σου ὁ ὀφθαλμὸς ἐν τῷ ποιεῖν σε ἐλεημοσύνην: cf. Mt. vi. 23, xx. 15. 'Οφθ. πονηρός is thus akin to φθόνος, but wider in meaning; the self-seeking which, not satisfied with appropriating more than its share (πλεονεξία), grudges and, where it can, withholds, diverts, or spoils that which falls to another.

βλασφημία] Mt. βλασφημίαι. Slander, detraction; cf. Eph. iv. 31, Col. iii. 8, 1 Tim. vi. 4. The Lord may have had in view the slanders perpetrated against Himself (Mc. iii. 28, cf. Mt. xii. 32).

ὑπερηφανία] Theophr. char. 24 ἔστι δὲ ὑ. καταφρόνησίς τις πλὴν αὐτοῦ τῶν ἄλλων—a Pharisaic sin (Lc. xviii. 9). The noun, though common in the LXX., occurs here only in the N.T., but the ὑπερήφανος appears in company with the ὑβριστής and the ἀλαζών in Rom. i. 30, and with the ἀλαζών and the βλάσφημος in 2 Tim. iii. 2; see Trench, syn. xxxix., and cf. Theod. Mops. on 2 Tim. l.c. ἀλαζόνες, καυχώμενοι ἔχειν ἃ μὴ ἔχουσιν· ὑπερήφανοι, μεγάλα φρονοῦντες ἐπὶ τοῖς οὖσιν. The sin of the latter lies not so much in exaggerating their endowments, as in claiming for themselves the merit of them. In

σύνη· ²³πάντα ταῦτα τὰ πονηρὰ ἔσωθεν ἐκπορεύεται 23
καὶ κοινοῖ τὸν ἄνθρωπον.
²⁴§Ἐκεῖθεν δὲ ἀναστὰς ἀπῆλθεν εἰς τὰ ὅρια Τύρου 24 § syrʰⁱᵉʳ

23 om παντα L | om τα πονηρα 1 604 2ᵖᵉ alᵖᵃᵘᶜ | εκπορευονται GKNΔ 28 736 yˢᶜʳ
alᵖᵃᵘᶜ   24 και εκειθεν αναστας A(D)NXΓII al minᶠᵉʳᵉᵒᵐⁿ | απηλθεν] εξηλθεν LΔ
ηλθεν M 28 al syrᵖᵉˢʰ arm Or | ορια אBDLΔ 1 13 28 69 209 346 604 2ᵖᵉ Or] μεθορια
ΑΝΧΓΠΣΦ al minᵖˡ

Biblical Gk. the opposite of ὑπερήφανος
is ταπεινός (עָנָו), see Prov. iii. 34,
James iv. 6, 1 Pet. v. 5.

ἀφροσύνη] The list culminates in
a word which may seem to imply a
relatively low degree of moral culpa-
bility. But ἄφρων like ἀσύνετος is a
word of strong censure on the lips of
Christ; see Lc. xi. 40, xii. 20 (cf.
μωρός, Mt. v. 22, vii. 26, xxv. 2). His
ἄφρων is the נָבָל of Ps. xiii. (xiv.) 1,
and the אֱוִיל or כְּסִיל of Proverbs; cf.
Schultz, ii. p. 284. Ἀφροσύνη is in
its Biblical use moral and not intellectual only—the shortsightedness
and wrongheadedness of unbelief and
sin; "a rooted incapacity to discern
moral and religious relations, leading
to an intolerant repudiation in practice of the claims which they impose"
(Driver, on Deut. xxii. 21). Euth. is
substantially right: ἀφρ. δὲ κυρίως τὸ
μὴ εἰδέναι τὸν θεόν.

23. πάντα ταῦτα κτλ.] These vicious
acts and principles constitute a real
profanation of human nature, and
they come from man himself. Euth.:
ἀρχαὶ γὰρ τούτων αἱ ἐπιθυμήσεις ἃς ἡ
καρδία πηγάζειν εἴωθεν. Mt. adds τὸ
δὲ ἀνίπτοις χερσὶν φαγεῖν οὐ κοινοῖ τὸν
ἄνθρωπον, but it seems more after our
Lord's manner to stop abruptly when
He has affirmed a great principle,
than to revert to the circumstances
which led Him to enunciate it.

24—30. IN THE REGION OF TYRE
AND SIDON. THE DAUGHTER OF A
SYROPHOENICIAN WOMAN DELIVERED
FROM AN EVIL SPIRIT (Mt. xv. 21—28).
24. ἐκεῖθεν δὲ ἀναστὰς ἀπῆλθεν] Mt.
καὶ ἐξελθὼν ἐκεῖθεν ὁ Ἰ. ἀνεχώρησεν.

The departure was a retreat. Not
only were the Pharisees scandalised
(Mt. xv. 12) by His denunciation of
the unwritten Law, but the discourse
in the synagogue of Capernaum, which
immediately followed or preceded it
(Jo. vi. 59 ff.), had alienated friends,
and Capernaum was again hostile and
perhaps unsafe; cf. iii. 7, vi. 31. The
policy of withdrawal from danger was
criticised by Celsus (Orig. c. Cels. i.
65 = Philoc. p. 107); Origen replies:
διδάσκων τοὺς μαθητὰς (Mt. x. 23)
παράδειγμα αὐτοῖς ἐγένετο εὐσταθοῦς
βίου οἰκονομοῦντος μὴ εἰκῆ μηδὲ ἀκαίρως
καὶ ἀλόγως ὁμόσε χωρεῖν τοῖς κινδύνοις.
The earliest withdrawal, as Celsus
pointed out, was during the Infancy
(Mt. ii. 13 ff.); the Lord's life was
threatened from the first. If He
safeguarded it, the motive was that it
might be freely given in due time
(Jo. x. 11, 15, 18). It was saved for
the Cross.

εἰς τὰ ὅρια Τ. καὶ Σ.] On ὅρια see
v. 17. The word may mean either
the boundaries or borders of a district,
or the territory of a city; see for the
former sense Gen. x. 19, xlvii. 21, and
for the latter Num. xxxv. 26, Jos. xiii.
26, and cf. BDB., s. vv. גְּבוּל, גְּבוּלָה.
Here, if we accept the reading of
אAB, τὰ ὅρια Τ. κ. Σ. (cf. iii. 8) appear
to be equivalent to the entire district
(Mt. μέρη) dominated by the two cities,
i.e. the coast of Phoenicia. Poli-
tically Phoenicia had formed part of
Syria since the days of Pompey:
geographically and ecclesiastically it
remained distinct (Acts xi. 19, xii. 20f.,
xxi. 2, Blass). According to Josephus

[καὶ Cιδῶνος]. καὶ εἰσελθὼν εἰς οἰκίαν οὐδένα ἤθελεν
25 γνῶναι, καὶ οὐκ ἠδυνάσθη λαθεῖν· ²⁵ ἀλλ᾽ εὐθὺς ἀκούσασα γυνὴ περὶ αὐτοῦ ἧς εἶχεν τὸ θυγάτριον αὐτῆς
πνεῦμα ἀκάθαρτον, ἐλθοῦσα προσέπεσεν πρὸς τοὺς
26 πόδας αὐτοῦ· ²⁶ ἡ δὲ γυνὴ ἦν Ἑλληνίς, Cύρα Φοινίκισσα

24 om καὶ Cιδῶνος DLΔ 28 2ᵖᵉ a b ff i n r syrˢⁱⁿ ʰⁱᵉʳ Or (hab אABNXΓΠCΦ al
minᵖˡ f q vg syrrᵖᵉˢʰ ʰᶜˡ arm go) | οικιαν] pr την DΦ al Or | ηθελησεν אΔ 13 69 124
346 2ᵖᵉ Or | ηδυνασθη אB] ηδυνηθη ADLNXΓ al minᵖˡ εδυνηθη KΔΠCΦ minᵖᵃᵘᶜ
25 αλλ ευθυς ακουσ. γυνη (א)BLΔ 33 f syrʰᶜˡ⁽ᵐᵍ⁾ me] γ. δε ευθεως (+ ως D*) ακουσ.
D syrˢⁱⁿ arm ακουσ. γαρ γ. ΑΝΧΓΠ*CΦ al minᵖˡ a n syrrᵖᵉˢʰ ʰᶜˡ ⁽ᵗˣᵗ⁾ al | εν π̄ν̄ι ακαθαρτω
13 28 69 346 2ᵖᵉ (armᵛⁱᵈ) | ελθουσα] εισελθουσα אLΔ 604 lattᵛᵗ ᵖˡ ᵛᵍ me   26 Cυρα
Φοινικισσα BEFGHMSᵗˣᵗVᵗˣᵗΧΓC 604 1071 alᵐᵘ] Cυρα Φοινισσα U minᵖᵃᵘᶜ a q Cυροφοι-
νικισσα אAK(L)SᵐᵍVᵐᵍΔΠΦ 1 alᵐᵘ go Cυροφοινισσα minᵖᵃᵘᶜ ᵛⁱᵈ b d f ff vg Φοινισσα(D) i

(B. J. iii. 3. 1, cf. ant. xix. 5. 6) it
embraced the whole seacoast and
plain—at least from Carmel northwards. Phoenicia, like the Decapolis,
was frankly pagan, and the Tyrians
bore a special illwill towards the Jews
(Joseph. c. Ap. i. 13). In crossing the
border the Lord passed into a Gentile
land. Phoenicians had sought Him
in Galilee (iii. 8), but He had no
mission to their country; His purpose
in entering it was retirement and not
public work. Εἰσελθὼν εἰς οἰκίαν: cf.
v. 17; on οὐδ. ἤθελεν γν., see ix. 30,
and for ἤθελεν, cf. vi. 48.

καὶ οὐκ ἠδυνάσθη λαθεῖν] On the
quasi-adversative sense of καί see
WM., p. 545. Ἠδυνάσθην or ἐδυνάσθην
is frequent in the LXX., cf. Gen. xxx.
8, Exod. xii. 39 (A), Jos. xv. 63, xvii.
12, Jud. i. 19, 32 (A), 2 Regn. iii. 11 ;
in the N.T. ἠδυνάσθην occurs here
(אB), and Mt. xvii. 16 (B). See
WSchm., p. 208 n. Λανθάνειν is one
of the rarer words of N.T. Greek,
occurring elsewhere Lc.² Heb.¹ 2 Pet.
The aor. inf. is usual after δύνασθαι
(Blass, Gr. p. 197).

25. ἀλλ᾽ εὐθὺς ἀκούσασα κτλ.] Cf.
vi. 33, 54 f. Even in Phoenicia He
was recognised. Τὸ θυγάτριον, cf. v.
23, 42: another child-applicant for
healing. Children as well as adults
were liable to the inroads of unclean

spirits, cf. ix. 21. The phenomena
and the belief which assigned them to
the agency of evil spirits were, as
it appears, not limited to Jews or to
the land of Israel (Acts xvi. 16 f.).
On ἧς...αὐτῆς, cf. WM., p. 185; Blass,
Gr. p. 175. Προσέπεσεν, see iii. 11, v. 33.

26. Ἑλληνίς, Cύρα Φοινίκισσα τῷ
γένει] Mt. Χαναναία. The woman was
a Gentile (f, vg., gentilis), probably
Greek-speaking, but descended from
the old stock of the Phoenicians of
Syria, who belonged to the Canaan-
ites of the O.T. Ἕλλην in the Acts
and Epistles is contrasted sometimes
with Ἰουδαῖος (Acts xiv. 1, Rom. i. 16,
ii. 9 f. &c., 1 Cor. i. 24, Gal. iii. 28),
sometimes with βάρβαρος (Rom. i. 14),
i.e. it represents either the Gentile as
such, or the civilised and generally
Greek-speaking Gentile (see Lightfoot's note on βάρβαρος, Col. iii. 11).
In the Gospels Ἕλλην, Ἑλληνίς
occur only here and in Jo. vii. 35,
xii. 20, and the word must in each
case be interpreted by the context.
The Phoenician language may have
lingered in country places round Tyre
and Sidon, as the Punic tongue was
still spoken in Augustine's time by
descendants of the old Phoenician
colony in N. Africa (Aug. ep. 209).
But in Ἑλλ., Cύρα Φ. τῷ γένει there is
surely an implied contrast between

τῷ γένει· καὶ ἠρώτα αὐτὸν ἵνα τὸ δαιμόνιον ἐκβάλῃ
ἐκ τῆς θυγατρὸς αὐτῆς. ²⁷καὶ ἔλεγεν αὐτῇ ῎Αφες 27
πρῶτον χορτασθῆναι τὰ τέκνα· οὐ γάρ ἐστιν καλὸν
λαβεῖν τὸν ἄρτον τῶν τέκνων καὶ τοῖς κυναρίοις

26 εκ] απο D 115 c ff om L 9   27 και ελ.] ο δε I. ειπεν ΑΝΧΓΠΣΦ min^pl
syr^hcl (arm) go

Phoenician extraction and Greek speech; cf. Euth., who however partly misunderstands his text: Ἑλληνὶς μὲν τὴν θρησκείαν, Σύρα δὲ τῇ διαλέκτῳ, Φοινίκισσα δὲ τῷ γένει: correct, Ἑ. μ. τ. θ. καὶ τὴν διάλεκτον, Σύρα Φοιν. δὲ τ. γ. The fem. of Ἕλλην occurs again in Acts xvii. 12; cf. 2 Macc. vi. 8. Σύρα Φοινίκισσα (also Σ. Φοίνισσα, Συροφοινίκισσα, Συροφοίνισσα, see vv. ll.), an inhabitant (or as here, a descendant of the old inhabitants) of Syrian Phoenicia (ἡ Συροφοινίκη, Justin. dial. 78), so called in contrast to the Carthaginian seacoast (Strabo xvii. 19 ἡ τῶν Λιβυφοινίκων γῆ). Συροφοῖνιξ occurs in Lucian deor. eccl. 4, and Syrophoenix in Juv. sat. viii. 159; on the late and rare form of the fem. see WSchm., p. 135 n., Blass, Gr., p. 63. The Clementines (hom. ii. 19, iii. 73) name the mother Justa, and the daughter Bernice. With τῷ γένει cf. Acts xviii. 2, 24.

ἠρώτα...ἵνα] Cf. παρεκάλει...ἵνα, v. 10. Mt. gives the words: ἐλέησόν με, κύριε, υἱὸς Δαυείδ· ἡ θυγάτηρ μου κακῶς δαιμονίζεται: cf. Mt. ix. 27, xx. 30, 31 (Mc. x. 47, 48). Such a formula as υἱὸς Δ. once used in public would soon become customary, but its occurrence in this narrative is remarkable; as yet, so far as we know, the title had been applied to Christ only once even in Galilee. On the contrast between this mode of addressing Him and that adopted by the δαιμόνια and, with an added ἀληθῶς, by the disciples, see Origen in Mt. t. xi. 17: συνάγαγε δὲ ἀπὸ τῶν εὐαγγελίων τίνες μὲν αὐτὸν καλοῦσιν υἱὸν Δαβίδ...τίνες δὲ υἱὸν θεοῦ...τίνες δὲ μετὰ τῆς ἀληθῶς προσ-

θήκης. καὶ γὰρ χρήσιμος, οἶμαι, ἔσται σοι ἡ τούτων συναγωγὴ πρὸς τὸ ἰδεῖν τὴν διαφορὰν τῶν προσιόντων.

27. ἄφες πρῶτον χορτασθῆναι τὰ τέκνα] The τέκνα are of course the Jews; cf. Isa. i. 2, Lc. xv. 31. They had the first claim, and by this principle not only the Lord's ministry, but the subsequent mission of the Church was regulated; see Mt. x. 5, 23, Acts i. 8, iii. 26, Rom. i. 16, ii. 9, 10. To Marcion, in whose Gospel this incident had no place, Tertullian (adv. Marc. iv. 7) well replies: "detrahe voces Christi mei, res loquentur." The conversation with this Phoenician woman merely calls attention to a rule which is everywhere apparent. Yet if the Jew justly claimed precedence, he had no exclusive right to the Gospel; πρῶτον implies that the Gentile would find his opportunity; cf. Mt. viii. 11, Acts xiii. 46, xxviii. 28. For ἄφες with the inf. cf. Mt. viii. 22, Mc. x. 14; the subjunctive follows in Mt. vii. 4, Mc. xv. 36. For χορτάζεσθαι saturari, see note on vi. 42.

Mt., who in the early part of this incident is on the whole much fuller than Mc., relates the circumstances which led to this reply (xv. 23, 24), but omits the words ἄφες...τὰ τέκνα.

οὐ γάρ ἐστιν καλὸν κτλ.] So Mt., Mc. Τὰ κυνάρια are τὰ κυνίδια τῆς οἰκίας (Origen)—the housedogs (τραπεζῆες κύνες Hom. Il. xxii. 69), as the dim. possibly indicates; though not children of the house, they have a place within its walls, and are fed, if not with the children's bread. Thus the term, which on Jewish lips was

28 βαλεῖν. ²⁸ἡ δὲ ἀπεκρίθη καὶ λέγει αὐτῷ Ναί, κύριε,
καὶ τὰ κυνάρια ὑποκάτω τῆς τραπέζης ἐσθίουσιν ἀπὸ
29 τῶν ψιχίων τῶν παιδίων. ²⁹καὶ εἶπεν αὐτῇ Διὰ
τοῦτον τὸν λόγον ὕπαγε· ἐξελήλυθεν ἐκ τῆς θυγα-
30 τρός σου τὸ δαιμόνιον. ³⁰καὶ ἀπελθοῦσα εἰς τὸν

28 om ναι D 13 69 604 2ᵖᵉ b c ff i syrˢⁱⁿ arm | και] και γαρ ALNXΓΠΣΦ al minᵖˡ
a f n q vg syrʰᶜˡ go αλλα και D b c ff i r | εσθιει ANXΓΠ al | ψιχιων] ψιχων D pr πιπ-
τοντων 1071 | παιδιων] παιδων (D) minᵖᵃᵘᶜ om 1071 + και ζωσιν syrʰⁱᵉʳ Tatᵈⁱᵃᵗ ᵃʳᵃᵇ

usually a reproach, is used by the Lord to open a door of hope through which the suppliant is not slow to enter (v. 28). On τὰ κυνάρια=τὰ ἔθνη see J. Lightfoot and Schöttgen on Mt. xv., and Bp Lightfoot on Phil. iii. 1. Jerome, after observing that the relative positions of Jew and Gentile have been reversed, exclaims "O mira rerum conversio! Israel quondam filius, nos canes." Origen suggests that the saying may have its application still: τάχα δὲ καὶ τῶν λόγων Ἰησοῦ εἰσί τινες ἄρτοι οὓς τοῖς λογικωτέροις ὡς τέκνοις ἔξεστι διδόναι μόνοις καὶ ἄλλοι λόγοι οἱονεὶ ψιχία ἀπὸ τῆς μεγάλης ἑστίας...οἷς χρήσαιντ' ἄν τινες ψυχαὶ ὡς κύνες. Tertullian thinks (de orat. 6) of the Bread of life which only the faithful can receive: "cetera enim nationes requirunt...ostendit enim quid a patre filii expectent."

28. ἡ δὲ ἀπεκρίθη καὶ λέγει] Her saying was in the strictest sense an answer: she laid hold of Christ's word and based her plea upon it. The usual phrase in the Synoptists is ἀποκριθεὶς λέγει (εἶπεν), or ἀπεκρίθη λέγων, but ἀπεκρίθη καὶ εἶπεν is common in St John. Λέγει, the historic present (Hawkins, H. S. p. 113 ff.); on its combination with an aor. see WM., p. 350.

ναί, κύριε, καὶ τὰ κυνάρια κτλ.] 'True, Rabbi; even (Mt. καὶ γάρ, 'for even') the dogs (of the house) are fed with the crumbs which the children leave.' Mt.,τῶν πιπτόντων ἀπὸ τῆς τραπέζης τῶν κυρίων αὐτῶν, 'with the crumbs which their masters let fall' (cf. Lc. xvi. 21).

The woman accepts and affirms the Lord's saying about the dogs; it serves her purpose; there is that in it on which she can build an argument; Euth., ἐπεὶ τοίνυν κυνάριόν εἰμι, οὐκ εἰμὶ ἀλλοτρία. For ναί see 2 Cor. i. 20, Apoc. i. 7, xiv. 13, xxii. 20; καί is here simply 'even,' as in i. 27, not 'and yet,' 'yet even'; for καὶ γάρ (the reading followed by A. V.) see Bp Ellicott on 2 Th. iii. 10. Ἐσθίειν ἀπό =אָכַל מִן, a Hebraism common in Biblical Gk. from Gen. ii. 16 onwards; cf. WM., p. 248 f. Two early variants are of interest; the Western text begins Κύριε, ἀλλὰ καί, sed et; at the end of the verse 'Tatian' and the earlier Syriac versions in Mt. add "and live."

29. διὰ τοῦτον τὸν λόγον ὕπαγε κτλ.] Mt. ὦ γύναι, μεγάλη σου ἡ πίστις· γενηθήτω σοι ὡς θέλεις. Cf. Victor: ὁ μὲν οὖν Ματθαῖος τὸ τῆς πίστεως ἐσημήνατο...ὁ δὲ Μάρκος τοῦ λόγου τὴν ἀρετήν. Tatian gives both answers, placing Mt.'s first. Throughout the incident Mt. and Mc. seem to depend on different sources, the only strictly common matter being the saying οὐκ ἔστιν καλόν κτλ. On ἐξελήλυθεν τὸ δαιμόνιον Bede remarks (with a reference to the baptismal exorcism of the Latin rite): "per fidem et confessionem parentum in baptismo liberantur a diabolo parvuli."

30. καὶ ἀπελθοῦσα κτλ.] Mt. καὶ ἰάθη ἡ θυγάτηρ αὐτῆς ἀπὸ τῆς ὥρας ἐκείνης. The result finds a parallel in the miracle of Jo. iv. 46 ff. Βεβλη-

οἶκον αὐτῆς εὗρεν τὸ παιδίον βεβλημένον ἐπὶ τὴν
κλίνην καὶ τὸ ⁸δαιμόνιον ἐξεληλυθός.　　　　　§ Wᵈ

³¹Καὶ πάλιν ἐξελθὼν ἐκ τῶν ὁρίων Τύρου ἦλθεν 31
διὰ Σιδῶνος εἰς τὴν θάλασσαν τῆς Γαλειλαίας ἀνὰ

30 ευρεν την θυγατερα βεβλημενην επι κτλ. D ευρεν το δαιμ. εξελ. και την θυγ.
βεβλ. επι της κλινης ΑΝΧΓΠΣΦ al minᵖˡ a n syrʰᶜˡ arm go ευρεν την θυγ. και το δαιμ.
εξελ. και αυτη βεβλημενη επι τ. κλ. syrˢⁱⁿ⁽ᵛⁱᵈ⁾　　31 εκ] απο 1071 | ηλθεν δια
Σιδωνος אBDLΔ 33 604 2ᵖᵉ lattᵛᵗ⁽ᵉˣᶜ q⁾ᵛᵍ syrʰⁱᵉʳ me aeth] και Σιδ. ηλθεν ΑΝΧΓΠΣΦ al
minᵖˡ q syrrˢⁱⁿ ᵖᵉˢʰ ʰᶜˡ arm go | εις אBDLΔ 1 33 69 124 209 282 346 604 2ᵖᵉ] προς ΑΝΧ
ΓΠΣΦ al minᵖˡ

μένον ἐπὶ τὴν κλίνην: the exhaustion
had not yet spent itself, though the
foul spirit was gone; cf. ix. 26. On
the place of this incident in the
Ministry, see Hort, *Jud. Chr.* p. 34:
" when at length the boon is granted
her, nothing is said to take away
from its exceptional and as it were
extraneous character; it remains a
crumb from the children's table."
Euth. treats the incident as prefigur-
ing the call of the Gentiles: προ-
ετύπου δὲ κατὰ ἀλληγορίαν ἡ Χαναναία
αὕτη γυνὴ τὴν ἐξ ἐθνῶν ἐκκλησίαν κτλ.
On the participle after εὗρεν see Blass,
Gr. p. 246.

31—37. RETURN TO THE DECA-
POLIS. HEALING OF A DEAF MAN
WHO SPOKE WITH DIFFICULTY (Mt. xv.
29, cf. 30, 31).

31. καὶ πάλιν ἐξελθών κτλ.] With
πάλιν ἐξελθών cf. ii. 13, xiv. 39, 40.
The last incident took place in the
neighbourhood of Tyre. The Lord
now leaves the ὅρια Τύρου and following the coast-line northwards across
the Leontes and perhaps through or
within sight of Zarephath (Σάρεπτα
τῆς Σειδωνίας, 3 Regn. xvii. 8, Lc. iv.
26), passes through Sidon. Σιδών,
Σειδών=צִידוֹן, *Saida*, some 20 miles
N. of Tyre on the Phoenician coast,
first mentioned in Gen. x. 15: in N.T.
cf. Mt. xi. 21 f.=Lc. x. 13 f., xv. 21=
Mc. vii. 24, 31, Mc. iii. 8=Lc. vi. 17,
Acts xxvii. 3. The traditional text
avoids the reference to the Lord's
passage through a Gentile city (vv.

ll.). He went through merely as a
traveller *en route* (for this use of διά
see Mc. ix. 30, Jo. iv. 4, 2 Cor. i. 16),
and in so large and busy a place may
easily have escaped notice. From
Sidon and the Mediterranean coast
He returned to (εἰς, for ἐπί or πρός, cf.
Blass, *Gr.* p. 124) the Sea of Galilee,
but to its eastern shore (ἀνὰ μέσον
τῶν ὁρίων Δεκαπόλεως). A road led
from Sidon across the hills (Merrill,
p. 58, G. A. Smith, p. 426); it crossed
the Leontes near the modern Belfort,
and climbing the ranges of the Lebanon, passed through the tetrarchy
of Abilene, and eventually reached
Damascus. The Lord probably left it
where it skirted Hermon, and striking
south kept on the east bank of the
Jordan till He reached the Lake
(see map). The long *détour* may have
served the double purpose of defeating
the immediate designs of His enemies
and providing " for the Apostles the
rest which He had desired to give
them before" (Latham, p. 333; cf. vi.
31). Ἀνὰ μέσον=בֵּין (Gen. i. 4, &c.);
the ὅρια τῆς Δ. are the districts under
the influence of the cities of the
Decapolis, see note on v. 20. No
mention is made of a passage through,
still less of a ministry in any of them;
but in the country round these cities
(G. A. Smith, p. 601) preaching and
the working of miracles are resumed,
probably among the Jewish or mixed
population prepared by the work of
the released demoniac (v. 20). The

¶ n 32 μέσον τῶν ὁρίων¶ Δεκαπόλεως.   ³²καὶ φέρουσιν αὐτῷ
κωφὸν καὶ μογιλάλον, καὶ παρακαλοῦσιν αὐτὸν ἵνα
33 ἐπιθῇ αὐτῷ τὴν χεῖρα.   ³³καὶ ἀπολαβόμενος αὐτὸν
ἀπὸ τοῦ ὄχλου κατ᾽ ἰδίαν ἔβαλεν τοὺς δακτύλους

31 Δεκαπολεως] pr της DWᵈΦ   32 om και 2° ALNXΓΠΣΦ al minᶠᵉʳᵉᵒᵐⁿ syrr
armᶜᵒᵈᵈ me go | μογγιλαλον B³EFHLNWᵈXΓΔ 28 33 69 157 262 346 alˢᵃᵗᵐᵘ | παρεκα-
λουν 33 arm | τας χειρας ℵ*NWᵈΔΣ 33   33 απολαβομενος] επιλ. E*Γ 131 271
alⁿᵒⁿⁿ λαβ. Δ 63ᶜᵒʳʳ | εβαλεν…αυτου 2°] επτυσεν εις τους δακτυλους αυτου και εβαλεν εις
τα ωτα του κωφου (αυτου Tat) και ηψατο της γλωσσης του μογγιλαλου Wᵈ Tatᵈⁱᵃᵗ ᵃʳᵃᵇ εβ.
τ. δακτ. αυτ. κ. πτυσας εις τα ω. αυτ. ηψατο τ. γλ. αυτ. syrˢⁱⁿ

Lord is again in the land of Israel, for Gaulanitis, though the towns were Hellenised, had belonged to the tribe of Manasseh (Jos. xiii. 29 f.), and still had a predominantly Jewish population (Schürer, II. i. 3).

32. φέρουσιν αὐτῷ κωφόν κτλ.] Mt. again is, at least in part, independent of Mc.; he locates the scene of the Lord's work in the Decapolis among the hills (ἀναβὰς εἰς τὸ ὄρος ἐκάθητο ἐκεῖ: cf. Mt. v. 1), and he represents Him as surrounded by the usual crowd of applicants for relief from various disorders (ὄχλοι πολλοὶ ἔχοντες μεθ᾽ ἑαυτῶν χωλούς, κυλλούς, τυφλούς, κωφούς, καὶ ἑτέρους πολλούς: cf. iv. 24), but describes no case in detail. The recovery of hearing by the deaf was a note of the Messianic age (Isa. xxxv. 5, xlii. 18), and had accompanied the Ministry in Galilee (Mt. xi. 5). In this case deafness was attended by such an impediment in the speech that the man was practically dumb (v. 37 ἀλάλους: cf. ix. 25 τὸ ἄλαλον καὶ κωφὸν πνεῦμα). Μογιλάλος (here only in N.T.) is probably from Isa. xxxv. 6 τρανὴ δὲ ἔσται γλῶσσα μογιλάλων: the word occurs also in Exod. iv. 11 (Aq., Symm., Th.=LXX. δύσκωφος), Isa. lvi. 10 (Aq., = LXX. ἐνεοί, Symm., Th., ἄλαλοι), and in each case it = אִלֵּם. Here the Vg. has mutum; Wycliffe follows with "a man deef and doumbe"; Tindale prefers "one that was deffe and stambed in his speech"; "had an impediment in his speech" (A.V.,

R.V.) begins with Cranmer. The stricter meaning is supported by ἐλάλει ὀρθῶς (v. 35). The variant μογγιλάλος, found also in MSS. of the LXX. (Isa. xxxv. 6, cf. Ps. lv. (lvi.), tit., where the Quinta has τῆς περιστερᾶς τῆς μογγιλάλου), is said to be a distinct word, a compound of μόγγος, 'thick-voiced' (WSchm., p. 65, see Steph.-Hase, s.v.; Exp. VII. vii. p. 566).

παρακαλοῦσιν…ἵνα ἐπιθῇ κτλ.] The Lord's ordinary sign of healing, familiar to every Jew through long use in Israel; cf. v. 23, vi. 5. For some reason which does not appear other symbols are employed in this case, such as suggest the presence of unusual difficulties. Τὴν χεῖρα, usually τὰς χεῖρας: yet see Mt. ix. 18.

33. ἀπολαβόμενος αὐτὸν…κατ᾽ ἰδίαν] Cf. 2 Macc. vi. 21, ἀπολαμβάνοντες αὐτὸν κατ᾽ ἰδίαν. Προσλαβέσθαι is used in nearly the same sense in viii. 32, cf. Acts xviii. 26; in ἀπολ. the isolation of the person who is taken comes more strongly into view. The Lord takes the μογιλάλος away with Him, because a crowd was gathered round them (ἀπὸ τοῦ ὄχλου, cf. Mt.), and He wished to be alone with the man (κατ᾽ ἰδίαν, iv. 34, vi. 31, 32, ix. 2, 28, xiii. 3). The miracles were usually wrought under the eyes of the crowd, but in special cases relative (v. 37) or even absolute (cf. viii. 23) privacy seems to have been necessary.

ἔβαλεν τοὺς δακτύλους κτλ.] The organs affected receive the signs of

αὐτοῦ εἰς τὰ ὦτα αὐτοῦ, καὶ πτύσας ἥψατο τῆς
γλώσσης αὐτοῦ. ³⁴καὶ ἀναβλέψας εἰς τὸν οὐρανὸν 34
ἐστέναξεν, καὶ λέγει αὐτῷ Ἐφφαθά, ὅ ἐστιν Δια-
νοίχθητι. ³⁵καὶ ἠνοίγησαν αὐτοῦ αἱ ἀκοαί, καὶ ἐλύθη 35

33 om αυτου 1° אL c i   34 εστεναξεν] ανεστεναξεν DWᵈΣ 13 69 124 346 | εφφεθα
אᶜD latt   35 και 1°]+ευθεως AEFGHKMNSUVWᵈ⁽ᵐᵍ⁾ΧΓΠΣΦ minⁱᵉʳᵉᵒᵐⁿ f vg
syrrᵖᵉˢʰʰᶜˡ arm go aeth | ηνοιγησαν אBDΔ 1] ηνοιχθησαν L διηνοιγησαν 124 604 2ᵖᵉ
διηνοιχθησαν ANWᵈΧΓΠΣΦ al minᵖˡ | ελυθη]pr ευθυς אLΔ (aeth) pr του μογγιλαλου Wᵈ

healing power; the ears are bored
(ἔβαλεν εἰς), the tongue is touched.
Πτύσας, see viii. 23, Jo. ix. 6 (Westcott). Saliva was regarded as remedial, but the custom of applying it
with incantations seems to have led
the Rabbis to denounce its use; see
Wetstein and Schöttgen ad l. Possibly to this Decapolitan it appealed
more strongly than any other symbol
that could have been employed. The
faith of a deaf man needed all the
support that visible signs could afford.
The use of the Lord's fingers and
saliva emphasised the truth that the
healing power proceeded from His own
person (cf. v. 30). Victor: δεικνὺς ὡς
πλουτεῖ τὴν τῆς θείας δυνάμεως ἐνέργειαν
καὶ τὸ ἐνωθὲν αὐτῷ ἀπορρήτως σῶμα.
On the remarkable variants in Wᵈ,
Syr.ˢⁱⁿ· see Nestle, Introd. p. 264 f.

34. ἀναβλέψας...ἐστέναξεν] For ἀναβλ. εἰς τὸν οὐρανόν see vi. 41, Jo. xi.
41, xvii. 1; St John's phrase is αἴρειν
(ἐπαίρειν) τοὺς ὀφθαλμούς, cf. Lc. xviii.
13. Ἐστέναξεν: cf. viii. 12 ἀναστενάξας τῷ πνεύματι αὐτοῦ. In both
cases perhaps the vast difficulty and
long delays of His remedial work were
borne in upon the Lord's human
spirit in an especial manner. So His
Church, or His Spirit in her, inwardly groans while waiting for the
redemption of the body (Rom. viii. 23,
26). Such a στεναγμὸς ἀλάλητος here
proceeds from the Lord's humanity.

ἐφφαθά] הִתְפַּתַּח, by assimilation
for Aram. הִתְפְּתַח, the ethpeel of פְּתַח
(Dalman, p. 202, 222), Syr. ܐܬܦܬܚ.

The earlier Syriac versions naturally
omit Mc.'s explanatory ὅ ἐστιν Διαν.
(it is in Syr.ʰᶜˡ·, ʰⁱᵉʳ·): the Latin transliterations are ephphetha, ephetha,
effetha, effeta and the like (Wordsworth
and White, p. 225). For Mc.'s use of
Aramaic words in the sayings of Christ,
see note on v. 41. On the word as
addressed to a deaf man Origen has
some interesting remarks (in Jo. t. xx.
20 (18)).

Both the word and the use of saliva
passed at an early time into the Baptismal rite as practised at Milan and
Rome: cf. Ambr. de myst., "aperite
igitur aures...quod vobis significavi-
mus cum apertionis celebrantes mysterium diceremus 'Ephphatha quod
est adaperire.'" The ceremony, which
was known as aurium apertio, and
immediately preceded the renunciation, is thus described in the 'Gelasian' Sacramentary (ed. Wilson, pp.
79, 115): "inde tangis (saliva oris sui
cum digito tangit) et nares et aures
de sputo et dicis ei ad aurem 'Effeta,
quod est adaperire, in odorem suavi-
tatis'"; comp. the more elaborate
ritual in the Sarum ordo ad facien-
dum catechumenum (Maskell, rit. i.
11) and the similar form in the modern
Roman Rituale. Bede refers also to
the versicle Domine labia mea (Ps. l.
(li.) 17).

For διανοίγειν cf. Lc. xxiv. 31 f., 45,
Acts xvi. 14.

35. ἠνοίγησαν αὐτοῦ αἱ ἀκοαί] On the
late aor. ἠνοίγην cf. WH., Notes, p. 170,
Deissmann, B. St. p. 189. It occurs again
Mt. xx. 33, Acts xii. 10, Apoc. xi. 19,

ὁ δεσμὸς τῆς γλώσσης αὐτοῦ καὶ ἐλάλει ὀρθῶς·
36 ³⁶καὶ διεστείλατο αὐτοῖς ἵνα μηδενὶ λέγωσιν· ὅσον
δὲ αὐτοῖς διεστέλλετο, αὐτοὶ μᾶλλον περισσότερον
37 ἐκήρυσσον. ³⁷καὶ ὑπερπερισσῶς ἐξεπλήσσοντο λέγοντες Καλῶς πάντα πεποίηκεν· καὶ τοὺς κωφοὺς
¶ syrʰⁱᵉʳ ποιεῖ ἀκούειν καὶ ἀλάλους λαλεῖν.¶

35 om αυτου 2° Wᵈ   36 διεστειλατο] ενετειλατο Δ | μηδενι]+μηδεν D 28 604
2ᵖᵉ | λεγωσιν] ειπωσιν ADNXΓΠ al minᵖˡ | οσον δε…αυτοι] οι δε αυτοι D* (b c ff i) |
αυτοις] pr αυτος EFGKMNSUVΓΠ alᵖˡ syrr arm go aeth | διεστελλετο] ενετελετο
(sic) Δ | περισσοτερως DWᵈ 61 1071   37 υπερεκπερισσως DU 1 209 435 604 om
Wᵈ | εξεπλησσοντο] pr παντες Wᵈ | και 2°] pr ως B me | αλαλους] pr τους ADNWᵈX
ΓΠΣΦ al minᶠᵉʳᵉ ᵒᵐⁿ

xv. 5, but ἠνεῴχθην is more frequent.
Ἀκοαί=ὦτα, as in 2 Macc. xv. 39; cf.
Lc. vii. 1, Acts xvii. 20, Heb. v. 11.

ἐλύθη ὁ δεσμός κτλ.] Cf. Lc. xiii.
16 οὐκ ἔδει λυθῆναι ἀπὸ τοῦ δεσμοῦ
τούτου where the reference is to an
infirm woman ἣν ἔδησεν ὁ σατανᾶς. It
belonged to the office of the Messiah
to release the captives of Satan (Isa.
xlii. 7 ἐξαγαγεῖν ἐκ δεσμῶν δεδεμένους,
xlix. 9 λέγοντες τοῖς ἐν δεσμοῖς Ἐξέλ-
θατε). The phrase ἐλύθη κτλ. does not
perhaps necessarily imply that the man
was 'tongue-tied' (Vg. solutum est vin-
culum linguae); however caused, the
impediment was a bondage from which
he rejoiced to be set free. Ἐλύθη...
ἐλάλει: the momentary act of libera-
tion gave birth to a new faculty of
articulate speech.

36. καὶ διεστείλατο αὐτοῖς ἵνα κτλ.]
Cf. v. 43. For some reason, special
perhaps to the particular case, privacy
was expedient after the miracle as
well as during the act of release. But
the charge seemed to defeat its own
end; not only was it ineffectual, but
its very vehemence increased the zeal
of those who spread the story. Ὅσον
...μᾶλλον: fuller forms are καθ' ὅσον
...κατὰ τοσοῦτο (Heb. vii. 20 ff.); ὅσῳ
...τοσούτῳ (Heb. x. 25) followed by a
comparative; cf. Vg. here, quanto...
tanto magis. The imperf. (διεστέλλετο) is apparently that of repeated

action (Burton, § 24); the charge
(διεστείλατο) was reiterated with the
effect described. Μᾶλλον περισσότερον, cf. WM., p. 300; Vg. magis
plus. The repetition of commands
which experience shewed to be ineffectual (i. 43 f.) is analogous to much
in the ordinary dealings of GOD with
man. Bede has the practical remark:
"volebat ostendere quanto studiosius
quantoque ferventius eum praedicare
debeant quibus iubet ut praedicent."

37. ὑπερπερισσῶς] Another ἅπ.
λεγ.; ὑπερπερισσεύειν occurs in St
Paul twice (Rom. v. 20, 2 Cor. vii. 4),
but for the adv. he prefers the
strengthened compound ὑπερεκπερισ-
σοῦ (-σῶς). For ἐκπλήσσεσθαι see i.
22, vi. 2, xi. 18; it expresses the
normal impression produced on the
mass of the people by both the teaching and the miracles. Mt., describing
the general effect of the miracles in
Decapolis, uses the milder term θαυμάζειν.

καλῶς πάντα πεποίηκεν] Mt. (but
without special reference to this miracle), ἐδόξασαν τὸν θεὸν Ἰσραήλ. The
partly pagan crowd recognised in the
miracles of Jesus the glory of the
GOD of Israel, in Whose Name Jesus
came; cf. v. 19, 20. To some it recalled Gen. i. 31, ἴδεν ὁ θεὸς τὰ πάντα
ὅσα ἐποίησεν καὶ ἰδοὺ καλὰ λίαν: cf.
Sir. xxxix. 16. Πεποίηκεν...ποιεῖ: the

¹Ἐν ἐκείναις ταῖς ἡμέραις πάλιν πολλοῦ ὄχλου ι
ὄντος καὶ μὴ ἐχόντων τί φάγωσιν, προσκαλεσάμενος
τοὺς μαθητὰς λέγει αὐτοῖς ²Cπλαγχνίζομαι ἐπὶ τὸν 2
ὄχλον, ὅτι ἤδη ἡμέραι τρεῖς προσμένουσιν [μοὶ] καὶ
οὐκ ἔχουσιν τί φάγωσιν· ³καὶ ἐὰν ἀπολύσω αὐτοὺς 3

VIII ι παλιν πολλου ℵBDGLMNΔΣΦ ι 13 28 33 59 61 69 73 209 242 346 1071
2ᵖᵉ al lattᵛᵗ(ᵉˣᶜq)ᵛᵍ syrˢⁱⁿ arm me go aeth] παμπολλου AEFHKSUVWᵈΧΓΠ 604 minᵖˡ
q syrr(ᵉˣᶜ ˢⁱⁿ) | οντος] συναχθεντος Wᵈ | προσκαλ.]+ο Ιησους EFGHSUVXΓ alᵖˡ f |
τους μαθητας]+παλιν Δ   2 επι τον οχλον]+τουτον L 1071 alᵖᵃᵘᶜ ε. του οχλου
τουτου D lattᵛᵗᵖˡᵛⁱᵈ (cf. syrrˢⁱⁿᵖᵉˢʰ arm) | ημεραι τρεις ℵALNWᵈΧΓΠΣ(Φ) al minᵖˡ]
ημεραις τρισι B ημερας τρεις Δ ι 69 2ᵖᵉ alⁿᵒⁿⁿ | προσμενουσιν] εισιν απο ποτε ωδε εισιν D
a b (c) d (ff) i (arm) | om μοι BD   3 και εαν...εκλυθησονται] και απολυσαι αυτους
νηστεις εις οικον ου θελω μη εκλυθωσιν D 604 (2ᵖᵉ) a b ff i q

act continues in its abiding effects.
The plurals κωφούς, ἀλάλους may include the classes represented by the
case of the μογιλάλος, or they may
refer to other miracles of the same
kind on the same occasion (cf. Mt.,
κωφοὺς λαλοῦντας). Ἀλάλους λαλεῖν,
perhaps an intentional *paronomasia* ;
see WM., p. 793 f. ; for a similar
juxtaposition of κωφός and ἄλαλος cf.
Ps. xxxvii. (xxxviii.) 14. Καὶ...καί,
WM., p. 547 ; ἀλάλους, anarthr., the
ἄλαλοι being usually identical with
the κωφοί.

VIII. 1—9. FEEDING OF THE
FOUR THOUSAND (Mt. xv. 32—39).

1. ἐν ἐκείναις ταῖς ἡμέραις] During
the period to which the preceding
incident belonged (see note on i. 9),
i.e. in the course of the Lord's journey
through the Decapolis (vii. 31). Πάλιν
πολλοῦ κτλ. The crowd which followed Him was so great that it
reminded the disciples of the crowds
on the western shore (iii. 20, iv. 1, v.
21), especially perhaps of the five
thousand men who assembled near
Bethsaida (vi. 34). Παμπόλλου (cf.
vv. ll.) is probably due to a misreading
of παλινπολλογ ; for the opposite
view see Burgon-Miller, *Causes of
Corruption*, p. 34. The word, though
classical, is unknown to Biblical Gk.
Προσκαλεσάμενος τ. μ.: in vi. 35 the

disciples take the first step. For
προσκαλεῖσθαι see note on iii. 13.

2. σπλαγχνίζομαι ἐπὶ τὸν ὄχλον]
The Lord had known the pangs of
hunger (Mt. iv. 2). Even under ordinary circumstances there was something in the sight of an eager crowd
which moved Him; see Mt. xiv. 14,
Mc. vi. 34. For σπλαγχνίζεσθαι see
note on i. 41. This crowd was suffering through its attendance upon Him :
ὅτι ἤδη ἡμέραι τρεῖς προσμένουσίν μοι
(Mt. Mc.). Προσμένειν τινί, to wait
upon ; see Sap. iii. 9 οἱ πιστοὶ ἐν
ἀγάπῃ προσμενοῦσιν αὐτῷ (sc. τῷ κυρίῳ),
Acts xi. 23, xiii. 43, and cf. προσκαρτερεῖν τινι Mc. iii. 9 (note). The construction ἤδη ἡμέραι τρεῖς προσμ. is
explained by treating ἤδη ἡ. τρ. as
a parenthesis (WM., p. 704), but it is
simpler to supply εἰσίν, and treat προσμένουσιν and ἔχουσιν as datives of the
participle. The reading of D is an
interpretation of a difficult phrase ;
the Vg. *iam triduo sustinent me* (q,
adherent mihi) evades the difficulty ;
the singular reading of B appears to
be a grammatical correction (cf. WM.,
p. 273).

οὐκ ἔχουσιν τί φάγωσιν: cf. v. 1 μὴ
ἐχόντων τί φ. The supply of food
was spent, for the stay had been
longer than they anticipated. In the
case of the Five Thousand, only a

νήστεις εἰς οἶκον αὐτῶν, ἐκλυθήσονται ἐν τῇ ὁδῷ· καί
4 τινες αὐτῶν ἀπὸ μακρόθεν εἰσίν. ⁴καὶ ἀπεκρίθησαν
αὐτῷ οἱ μαθηταὶ αὐτοῦ ὅτι Πόθεν τούτους δυνήσεταί
5 τις ὧδε χορτάσαι ἄρτων ἐπ᾽ ἐρημίας; ⁵καὶ ἠρώτα
§ C αὐτούς Πόσους ἔχετε ἄρτους; οἱ δὲ §εἶπαν Ἑπτά.
6 ⁶καὶ παραγγέλλει τῷ ὄχλῳ ἀναπεσεῖν ἐπὶ τῆς γῆς,

3 νηστις ℵΔ 604 al^nonn | και τινες ℵBLΔ 1 13 28 33 209 q syr^sin me] οτι και τ.
D latt^vt pl τινες γαρ ANW^dΧΓΠΣ al min^pl f vg syrr^(pesh)hcl arm go aeth | om απο
ANW^dΧΓΠΣΦ al min^pl | εισιν BLΔ me] ηκασιν ℵADNΣΦ 1 28 33 69 124 al^nonn ηκουσιν
EFGHKMSUVW^dΧΓΠ min^pl venerunt latt similiter syrr arm go aeth   4 οτι] και
ειπαν ℵ λεγοντες 106 251 282 (c) syr^hcl | δυν. τις] δυνη ut vid syr^sin arm | om ωδε DH
69 1071 b c ff i q go | ερημιας ℵBDLNW^dΧΓΠ²ΣΦ al min^pl latt^vid] ερημιαις ΑΚΔΠ*
min^nonn   5 ηρωτα ℵBLΔ] επηρωτα ADNW^dΠΣΦ al min^pl επηρωτησεν M
6 παραγγελλει ℵBDLΔ] παρηγγειλεν ACNW^dΧΓΠΣΦ al min^omn vid(exc1) vg rell

day seems to have passed, but no
provision had been made for more
than a few hours' absence from home.
On τί φάγ. see vi. 36.

3. ἐὰν ἀπολύσω αὐτοὺς νήστεις κτλ.]
Mt. ἀπολῦσαι...οὐ θέλω μήποτε κτλ.
The Lord anticipates the proposal
with which the Twelve were doubtless again ready (vi. 36 ἀπόλυσον
αὐτούς). Νῆστις, a classical word,
occurs here only (Mt. Mc.) in Biblical
Gk. Εἰς οἶκον αὐτῶν "to their home";
for εἰς οἶκον (ἐν οἴκῳ) in this sense see
ii. 1. For ἐκλύεσθαι of the faintness
caused by want of food see Jud. viii.
15 A (where B has ἐκλείπειν), 1 Regn.
xiv. 28, Isa. xlvi. 1, Thren. ii. 19,
1 Macc. iii. 7.

καί τινες αὐτῶν ἀπὸ μακρόθεν εἰσίν]
Mc. only. Gamala, Hippos, Gadara were
perhaps the nearest centres of population. The towns and villages of the
Decapolis were fewer, and at longer
distances from each other than those
of the populous western shore. Nothing is said here of κύκλῳ ἀγροὶ καὶ
κῶμαι where bread could be bought.
The Decapolitans, unlike the Five
Thousand, were in their own country,
and if dismissed would make their
way home. For ἀπὸ μακρόθεν, Vg. de
longe, see v. 6, note: on the variant
ἥκασιν cf. WM., p. 106.

4. ἀπεκρίθησαν...ὅτι Πόθεν κτλ.]

For the 'recitative' ὅτι cf. i. 15, 37,
40, ii. 12, iii. 11, 21, iv. 21, v. 23, 28,
35, vi. 4, 14, 15 bis, 18, 35, vii. 6, 20.
The objection raised by the Twelve
corresponds to the circumstances: at
Bethsaida they had urged the want
of means (ἀγοράσωμεν δηναρίων διακοσίων ἄρτους;)—in this thinly popu-
ated region they plead the scarcity of
food : cf. Mt. πόθεν ἡμῖν ἐν ἐρημίᾳ ἄρτοι
τοσοῦτοι κτλ. Gould's remark, "the
stupid repetition of the question is
psychologically impossible," is doubly
at fault. The question is not repeated
exactly, and such stupidity as it shews
is in accordance with all that we know
of the condition of the Apostles at
this period (cf. viii. 17 ff.). For χορτά-
ζειν see vi. 42, note, and for the gen.
cf. Ps. cxxxi. (cxxxii.) 15, and Blass,
Gr. p. 101. Ἐπ᾽ ἐρημίας, on the surface
of a desert, cf. WM., p. 468. Ἐρημία
occurs in the Gospels only in this context, and not a dozen times in Biblical
Gk.; the usual phrase is ἡ ἔρημος, ἔρημος τόπος or γῆ, see i. 3, 4, 12 f., 35.

5. πόσους...ἑπτά] The question is
the same as in vi. 38. With the
loaves, as before, there were a few
small fishes, as a relish (Mt. καὶ ὀλίγα
ἰχθύδια, see below, v. 7). For the use
of fish with bread see note on vi. 38.

6. παραγγέλλει] Mt. παραγγείλας—
another trace of the dependence of

καὶ λαβὼν τοὺς ἑπτὰ ἄρτους εὐχαριστήσας ἔκλασεν
καὶ ἐδίδου τοῖς μαθηταῖς αὐτοῦ ἵνα παρατιθῶσιν· καὶ
παρέθηκαν τῷ ὄχλῳ. ⁷καὶ εἶχαν ἰχθύδια ὀλίγα· καὶ 7
εὐλογήσας αὐτὰ εἶπεν καὶ ταῦτα παρατιθέναι. ⁸καὶ 8
ἔφαγον καὶ §ἐχορτάσθησαν, καὶ ἦραν περισσεύματα   §k

6 παρατιθωσιν ℵBCLMΔΦ 13 33 69 346 al^pauc] παραθωσιν ADNW^dΧΓΠΣ al
min^pl | τω οχλω] αυτοις 1071   7 ευλογησας] ευχαριστησας D q | ειπεν και ταυτα
ℵ^aBCLΔ 115 q] ειπεν και αυτα AEFGHKM^txtSUXΓΠ al^pl ειπεν αυτα V (ειπεν παρα-
θειναι αυτα 1071) και αυτους εκελευσεν D latt^vid(exc d) (arm^vid) | παρατιθεναι ℵ^aB(D)LM^mg
Δ min^pauc παρατεθηναι Α(Φ) min^pauc παραθειναι GM^txtNUVXΠΣ min^pl   8 εχορτασ-
θησαν]+παντες KM(N) 1 33 1071 al^nonn | περισσευματα κλασματων ABLNW^dΧΓΠΣΦ
al min^fereomnes] τα π. κλ. ℵC το περισσευμα των κλ. D 2^pe το περισσευσαν των κλ. 604
περισσευσαντα κλασματα 33 om κλασματων Δ k

Mt. on Mc., or of their use of a common Greek source. In the Feeding of the Five Thousand the direction is given to the Twelve; here apparently the Lord Himself addresses the crowd. No mention is made here of χλωρὸς χόρτος; the spring was now past, and the hills were bare.

λαβὼν...εὐχαριστήσας ἔκλασεν καὶ ἐδίδου] See notes on vi. 41. The insertion of καὶ παρέθηκαν τῷ ὄχλῳ here in Mc. seems to imply that the bread was blessed and distributed first—another detail which has escaped Mt. On εὐχαριστεῖν see Lob. *Phryn.* p. 18, Rutherford, *N. Phr.* p. 69.

7. καὶ εἶχαν ἰχθύδια ὀλίγα] See on v. 5. The form εἶχαν occurs again Acts xxviii. 2 (παρεῖχαν), Apoc. ix. 8 f., cf. εἴχαμεν, 2 Jo. 5, and elsewhere as a variant, see WH., *Notes*, p. 165, WSchm., p. 112. Ἰχθύδιον (Mt. also) is here a true diminutive; cf. A.V., R.V.

εὐλογήσας αὐτὰ εἶπεν καὶ ταῦτα παρατιθ.] The blessing was probably distinct from that of the loaves (see note on v. 6), but similar; εὐλογεῖν and εὐχαριστεῖν are practically synonymous, see Mt. xv. 36 τοὺς ἑπτὰ ἄρτους καὶ τ. ἰχθύας εὐχαριστήσας, and cf. Mc. vi. 41 ; see *J. Th. St.* iii. p. 163. For εἶπεν 'bade,' cf. v. 43, Lc. xii. 13, xix. 15 ; and on παρατιθέναι and its variants see Blass, *Gr.* p. 230, who chooses the

less definite παρατεθῆναι. Καὶ ταῦτα, these, as well as the loaves.

8. καὶ ἔφαγον καὶ ἐχορτάσθησαν] Cf. vi. 42. Περισσεύματα κλασμάτων, Mt. τὸ περισσεῦον τῶν κλ., as in xiv. 20, where Mc. has simply κλάσματα. Περίσσευμα is the opposite of ὑστέρημα (2 Cor. viii. 13, 14), that which is left or remains over when all present needs are satisfied; an active form περισσεία also occurs (Eccl.[13] Paul[4] Jas.[1]). Σπυρίς (in the N.T. σφυρίς, see WH., *Notes*, p. 148, WSchm., p. 63, Deissmann, *B. St.*, pp. 158, 185, a late form rejected by the Atticists, cf. Lob. *Phryn.* 43) is used by Herodotus and re-appears in comedy (Ar. *Pax* 1005) and in the later writers (Theophrastus, Epictetus, &c.). It is said to be akin to σπεῖρα, and to denote a basket of coiled or plaited materials, cord or reeds ; in Ar. *l. c.* it is an eel-basket (Κωπάδων ἐλθεῖν σπυρίδας), in Athen. 365 A (δεῖπνον ἀπὸ σπυρίδος) a dinner-hamper. Sometimes baskets of this sort were of considerable size, cf. Acts ix. 25, where Saul makes his escape in a σπυρίς (= σαργάνη, 2 Cor. xi. 33). That the word is here not a mere synonym of κόφινος is clear from the distinction in v. 20, q. v. The Vg. renders σφ. by *sportas*: Wycliffe has "leepis," reserving "coffyns" for κοφ. ; 'frails'

9 κλασμάτων ἑπτὰ σφυρίδας. ⁹ἦσαν δὲ ὡς τετρακισχίλιοι. καὶ ἀπέλυσεν αὐτούς.

10   ¹⁰Καὶ εὐθὺς ἐμβὰς [αὐτὸς] εἰς τὸ πλοῖον μετὰ
τῶν μαθητῶν αὐτοῦ ἦλθεν εἰς τὰ μέρη Δαλμανουθά.

8 σφυριδας אA*D] σπυριδας A²BCLNWᵈΧΓΔΠΣΦ al minᵒᵐⁿ ᵛⁱᵈ+πληρεις 13 33 69
1071 alⁿᵒⁿⁿ i   9 ησαν δε]+οι φαγοντες ACNWᵈΧΓΠΣΦ al minᵖˡ latt syrr arm go al |
τετρακισχιλιοι]+ανδρες GΔ 1071 alᵖᵃᵘᶜ a b c ff i q   10 ευθυς] αυτος D b i k |
εμβας] ανεβη...και D a f g k ενεβη...και 604 2ᵖᵉ+αυτος B | το πλοιον] om το L 1 28 33
69 124 209 604 alⁿᵒⁿⁿ | τα μερη] τα ορια D το ορος 28 syrˢⁱⁿ τα ορη N | Δαλμανουθα
(-νουνθα B dalmanunea arm)] Μελεγαδα D* Μαγαιδα D¹ ᵛⁱᵈ Μαγεδα 28 2ᵖᵉ Μαγδαλα
1 13 69 209 271 347 Magidan d Magedan a ff Magedam b i r Mageda c k Μαγεδαν
syrˢⁱⁿ ᵛⁱᵈ Magdal syrᵖᵃˡ ᵉᵈ ⁽ᴸᵃⁿᵈ⁾ Μαγδαλαν go

is the equivalent of σφ. in modern colloquial English (cf. Westcott on Jo. vi. 13), but it has not been admitted by the Revisers of the English Bible. See art. *Basket* in Hastings, *D.B.* i. p. 256. Probably the correspondence of the number of the σφυρίδες with that of the loaves is accidental, like the relation between the number of the loaves in the earlier miracle and that of the multitude (πέντε, πεντακισχίλιοι; to assign a σφυρίς to each pair of Apostles and the seventh to the Lord is as puerile as to infer from such a coincidence the untrustworthiness of the whole story.—Ἑπτὰ σφ. is in apposition to περισσεύματα (WM., p. 664); σφυρίδας is written inexactly for σφ. πλήρεις (Mt.), or σφυρίδων πληρώματα (*infra v.* 20).

9. ἦσαν δὲ ὡς τετρακισχίλιοι] Mt. ἦσαν τέτρ. ἄνδρες χωρὶς γυναικῶν καὶ παιδίων (as in xiv. 21). The number was probably ascertained as before by an orderly division of the crowd into συμπόσια of a certain size.

For a comparison of the details of the two miracles (Mc. vi. 35 ff., viii. 1 ff.) see Origen, Hilary, and Jerome on Mt. xv.; Jerome's quaint and terse summary may be quoted: "ibi v panes erant et ii pisces, hic vii panes et pauci pisculi; ibi super faenum discumbunt, hic super terram; ibi qui comedunt v millia sunt, hic iv millia; ibi xii cophini replentur, hic vii spor-

tae." Each of these fathers adds a mystical interpretation of some interest.

10—13. FRESH ENCOUNTER WITH THE PHARISEES NEAR DALMANUTHA (Mt. xv. 39 *b*—xvi. 5).

10. εὐθὺς ἐμβάς κτλ.] After dismissing the crowd the Lord Himself at once left the neighbourhood by boat; cf. vi. 45 f. His destination was Dalmanutha or Magadan (Mc. ἦλθεν εἰς τὰ μέρη Δ.=Mt. ἦλθ. εἰς τ. ὅρια Μαγαδάν; cf. Mc. vii. 24 with Mt. xv. 21). Neither name has been definitely identified, and the geographical question is complicated by the uncertainty of the text in both Gospels: in Mt. besides Μαγαδάν (or Μαγεδάν) we have the readings Μαγδαλά, Μαγδαλάν; in Mc., for Δαλμανουθά (B, Δαλμανουνθά), cod. D has Μελεγαδά (D*), Μαγαιδά (D¹)— a form which appears substantially in all true O.L. texts and in the Sinaitic Syriac. Dr J. R. Harris (*Cod. Bez.* p. 178) suggests that Δαλμανουθά represents the Syriac ‏ܠܡܢܥܘܬܐ‏=εἰς τὰ μέρη, and Dr Nestle inclines to a similar view (*Philol. Sacr.*, p. 17); on the other hand see Chase, *Syriac element*, &c. p. 146 n. Dalman (*Gr.* p. 133), with perhaps slightly more probability, suggests that Δαλμανουθά is a corrupt form of Μαγδαλουθά: cf. *Worte Jesu*, p. 52 f. Assuming that both Magadan and Dalmanutha are genuine names, we may accept as a

¹¹καὶ ἐξῆλθον οἱ Φαρισαῖοι καὶ ἤρξαντο συνζητεῖν[¶] 11 ¶ k
αὐτῷ, ζητοῦντες παρ᾽ αὐτοῦ σημεῖον ἀπὸ τοῦ οὐρανοῦ,

11 και (1°)...ηρξ.] και ηρξ. οι Φ. 33 c k | εξηλθοσαν D | αυτω] pr συν D | om ζητ.
παρ αυτου Δ | σημειον] pr ιδειν א 68 c

working hypothesis a modification of
Augustine's opinion (*cons. ev.* ii. 51
"non dubitandum est eundem locum
esse sub utroque nomine."); both places
must at least be sought in the same
neighbourhood. Was it to another
part of the eastern coast that the
Lord sailed, or did He cross to the
west side of the lake? Eusebius
(*onomast.*), who read Μεγαιδάν in Mc.,
adds καί ἐστι νῦν ἡ Μαγαιδανὴ περὶ
τὴν Γεράσαν. On the other hand it is
usually assumed that Μαγαδάν is another form of Magdala, i.e. el Mejdel
at the southern end of the plain of
Gennesaret, and that εἰς τὸ πέραν
(*v.* 13) implies a return from the
western to the eastern shore; on the
latter point cf. vi. 45. Robinson (*B.R.*
iii., p. 264) and Thomson (*Land* &c.,
p. 393) mention a site known as ed-
Delhemîyah near the junction of the
Yarmûk with the Jordan, some five
miles S. of the Lake (see map); if its
territory ran down to the shore (cf. v.
1), the locality is consistent with Mc.'s
account. Of a Magadan however in
this neighbourhood there is as yet no
trace: but the form like Μαγδαλά may
represent מִגְדַּל, as in Jos. xv. 37 where
Μαγαδὰ Γάδ (B) = Μαγδὰλ Γάδ (A). On
the whole question see *Encycl. Bibl.,*
s.v., and Hastings, *D.B.* iii. art. *Magadan.*

11. καὶ ἐξῆλθον οἱ Φ.] Mt. adds
καὶ Σαδδουκαῖοι—the only mention of
the Sadducees as present at any interview with our Lord during the
Galilean ministry; as the aristocratic
and priestly party they resided prin-
cipally at Jerusalem and in its neighbourhood. Some were possibly connected with the court of Herod (see
on *v.* 15), residing at Tiberias. Their
association with the Pharisees on this

occasion indicates the extent to which
the hostility of the latter was now
carried. Ἐξῆλθον, i.e. from Dalmanutha (cf. Mt. xv. 22), or possibly from
the towns on the W. coast. Their
appearance is an argument against
locating Dalmanutha on the S. of the
lake, but not perhaps an insuperable
one; the journey from Capernaum to
the S. end was not a serious one for
men who had been watching their
opportunity to retaliate.

ἤρξαντο συνζητεῖν αὐτῷ κτλ.] Bengel:
"ἤρξαντο...post pausam." Their plan
was to tempt Him by a leading question to commit Himself to a damaging
statement of His claims. Συνζητεῖν is
a favourite word with Mc. (i. 27, ix.
10, 14, 16, xii. 28), found also in
Lc.^{ev.2, act.2}; see note on i. 27.

ζητοῦντες...σημεῖον ἀπὸ τοῦ οὐρανοῦ]
In Lc. xi. 16, 29 the incident occurs
in another context; in Mt. it appears
in both (xii. 38 f., xvi. 1 f.). The
request may naturally have been repeated, but the substantial identity of
the answer, especially the recurrence
of the σημεῖον Ἰωνᾶ, is suspicious; that
the conversation is here at least in its
right place is attested by the agreement of Mt. and Mc. The demand
was for σημεῖα of a higher order than
the miracles (Bede: "signa quaerunt
quasi quae viderant signa non fue-
rint")—a visible or audible interposi-
tion of God (Mt. σημεῖον ἐπιδεῖξαι).
The manna is cited in Jo. vi. 30 f. as
such a sign; the Bath Qol might have
been regarded as another. Such wonders had more than once signalised the
ministry of Elijah (1 K. xviii. 38, 2 K.
i. 10 ff.). The more fruitful but more
human and less startling miracles of
the Gospel appealed less forcibly to a
generation which was possessed by a

12 πειράζοντες αὐτόν. ¹²καὶ ἀναστενάξας τῷ πνεύματι αὐτοῦ λέγει Τί ἡ γενεὰ αὕτη ζητεῖ σημεῖον; ἀμὴν λέγω [ὑμῖν] Εἰ δοθήσεται τῇ γενεᾷ ταύτῃ σημεῖον. 13 ¹³καὶ ἀφεὶς αὐτοὺς πάλιν ἐμβὰς ἀπῆλθεν εἰς τὸ πέραν.

12 αναστεναξας] στεναξας M* min^paue | αυτου] εαυτου AL 1071 om DM*Γ 1 282 b i l | ζητει σημειον ℵBCDLΔ 1 28 33 118 209 604 2^pe] σημειον επιζητει ΑΝΧΓΠΣΦ al min^pl Or | om υμιν BL (hab ℵACDNΧΓΠΣ al) | ει] ου Δ 5 13 69 124 346 1071 syrr^sin pesh me al 13 αφεις] καταλιπων ΝΣ | εμβας]+εις (το) πλοιον (ΑΕFG)ΗΚ(Μ) N(S)U(VΧ)ΓΠ(ΣΦ) min^mu lat^vt(excff) vg^ed syrr^sin(vid) pesh hcl arm me go (om ℵBCLΔ ff vg^codd opt)

passion for display (1 Cor. i. 22, cf. Bp Lightfoot *ad l.*). As Thpht. suggests: ἐνόμιζον...ὅτι οὐ δυνήσεται ἐξ οὐρανοῦ ποιῆσαι σημεῖον οἷα δὴ ἐν τῷ Βεελζεβοὺλ δυνάμενος ποιεῖν τὰ ἐν τῇ γῇ μόνα σημεῖα. On the two participles without intervening copula see WM., p. 433.

πειράζοντες αὐτόν] The second part. qualifies the first; the request had a purpose which did not appear on the surface of the words—it was of the nature of a test. Such a test or question may be friendly (Jo. vi. 6), or hostile (Mc. x. 2, xii. 15); in the present case the intention could scarcely have been doubtful to any who knew the men.

12. ἀναστενάξας τῷ πνεύματι] Ἀναστενάζειν, used here only in the N.T., occurs in the LXX. (Sir. xxv. 18, Thren. i. 4, 2 Macc. vi. 29; cf. Sus. 22, Th.). Like ἀνακράζειν (Mc. i. 23, vi. 49) and ἀναφωνεῖν (Lc. i. 42), it is more intense in meaning than the simple verb: the sigh seemed to come, as we say, from the bottom of the heart; the Lord's human spirit was stirred to its depths. On τῷ πνεύματι see ii. 8, note. Bede: "veram hominis naturam, veros humanae naturae circumferens affectus, super eorum dolet et ingemiscit erroribus." Obstinate sin drew from Christ a deeper sigh than the sight of suffering (see vii. 34, and cf. Jo. xiii. 21), a sigh in which anger and sorrow both had a part (iii. 4, note).

τί ἡ γενεὰ αὕτη κτλ.] Mt. γ. πονηρὰ

καὶ μοιχαλὶς σ. ἐπιζητεῖ: on μοιχαλίς, which occurs *infra* v. 38, see Orig. *in Mt.* t. xii. 4. The phrase ἡ γενεὰ αὕτη is used again v. 38, (ix. 19), xiii. 30, and is frequent in Mt. and Lc.; it appears to look back to the age of the Exodus, and to point to such passages as Deut. xxxii. 5, Ps. xcv. (xciv.) 10; cf. Acts ii. 40, Phil. ii. 15. As the generation which came out of Egypt resisted Moses, so the generation to which Jesus belonged resisted its greater Deliverer; see the parallel worked out, with a slightly different reference, in Heb. iv. 7 ff. On the question whether γενεά bears in the Gospels the wider sense of γένος see xiii. 30, note. For ἀμὴν λέγω cf. iii. 28, note.

εἰ δοθήσεται κτλ.] Mt. σημεῖον οὐ δ. εἰ μὴ τὸ σημεῖον Ἰωνᾶ κτλ. Cf. Orig. *in Ezech.* xiv. 20: 'ἐὰν υἱοὶ καὶ θυγατέρες ὑπολειφθῶσιν·' ἀντὶ τοῦ 'οὐχ ὑπολειφθήσονται'...οὕτω καὶ ὁ κύριος ἐν τῷ κατὰ Μάρκον εὐαγγελίῳ 'εἰ δοθήσεται,' τουτέστιν 'οὐ δοθήσεται.' The idiom is based on the use of אִם to commence an imprecation which is in fact a solemn form of negation; for other exx. in the LXX., cf. Gen. xiv. 23, Deut. i. 35, 3 Regn. i. 51, Ps. lxxxviii. (lxxxix.) 36, xcv. (xciv.) 11, Isa. lxiii. 8. This is the only ex. of its employment in the N.T., except where Ps. xcv. is cited (Heb. iii. 11, iv. 3, 5). See WM., p. 627, Burton § 272. The exception in Mt., εἰ μὴ τὸ σημεῖον Ἰωνᾶ (cf. Mt. xii. 40, Lc. xi. 30), points to the

¹⁴§ Καὶ ἐπελάθοντο λαβεῖν ἄρτους, καὶ εἰ μὴ ἕνα 14 § k
ἄρτον οὐκ εἶχον μεθ᾽ ἑαυτῶν ἐν τῷ πλοίῳ. ¹⁵ καὶ διε- 15
στέλλετο αὐτοῖς λέγων ᾽Ορᾶτε, βλέπετε ἀπὸ τῆς

14 επελαθοντο (-θεντο B*)]+οι μαθηται (αυτου) DUΦ 13 28 69 1071 al^{sat mu} c q | και
ει μη ενα αρτον ουκ ειχον] ει μη ενα α. ειχ. D a (k) ενα μονον αρτον εχοντες 1 13 28 69
209 346 604 2^{pe} (arm) *nisi unum panem quem habebant* (b) (c) d ff i q r om ει μη syr^{sin}
15 διεστελλετο (διεστειλ. EF 13 28 69 131 346 al^{pauc})] ενετειλατο Δ | ορατε] om D 1
118 209 2^{pe} a b ff i k r syr^{sin} arm+και C 13 28 69 124 al^{pauc} c f | om βλεπετε Δ 604
arm^{vid}

Resurrection as the supreme proof of
the Divine mission of Jesus, and one
which that generation was to receive:
cf. Acts ii. 32 ff.

13. καὶ ἀφεὶς αὐτούς κτλ.] Mt. καὶ
καταλιπὼν αὐτούς... His departure was
significant, an anticipation of the end
(Lc. xiii. 35); since there was no scope
for His ministry among these men, He
entered the boat again and crossed the
Lake. Thpht.: ἀφίησι τοὺς Φαρισαίους
ὁ Κύριος ὡς ἀδιορθώτους. Whether τὸ
πέραν is here the western or the
eastern shore, or merely a point on
the same shore where He was, cannot
be determined from the word (cf. iv.
35, v. 1, 21, vi. 45). The destination
on this occasion was Bethsaida (*v.* 22);
if "the parts of Dalmanutha" were
near the exit of the Jordan, the boat
must have traversed nearly the whole
length of the lake, from S. to N.E.

14—21. The Leaven of the Pharisees and the Leaven of Herod
(Mt. xvi. 5—12; cf. Lc. xii. 1).

14. καὶ ἐπελάθοντο λαβεῖν ἄρτους]
Mt. alters the setting of this incident
by placing it on or after the arrival
(ἐλθόντες...εἰς τὸ πέραν); in Mc. the
omission is discovered, as it appears,
while they are crossing (cf. *vv.* 14, 22).
Ordinarily, at least when in thinly
peopled neighbourhoods, the Twelve
carried the thin flat loaves of the
country in their πῆραι or κόφινοι—the
direction given in vi. 8 is clearly
exceptional. It probably rested with
Judas of Kerioth to purchase food for
the party (Jo. xii. 6), but owing perhaps to the sudden departure (*v.* 13),

or under the impression that the
fragments of the seven loaves were
amply sufficient, the matter had been
overlooked. When they came to
search their bread baskets only one
cake could be found (Mt. omits this
detail). ᾽Επελάθοντο is rendered by
the English pluperfect in all the
English versions except Wycliffe,
Rheims, and R.V.; cf. Burton § 48,
and see Field, *Notes*, p. 11. The
form ἐπελάθεντο (B*) is not uncommon
in the best mss. of the lxx.; see Jud.
iii. 7 (A), Ps. lxxvii. (lxxviii.) 11
(B*), Hos. xiii. 6, Jer. xiii. 21 (B* ℵ).
Μεθ᾽ ἑαυτῶν: cf. ix. 8, xiv. 7.

15. διεστέλλετο] Either 'during the
crossing He charged them'; or, 'He
charged them more than once' (Burton
§§ 21, 24; cf. vii. 36). Βλέπετε ἀπό
κτλ., Mt. προσέχετε ἀπό...'keep your
eye (mind) upon it with the view of
avoiding it'; cf. xii. 38 (WM., p. 280),
and see Wilcken in *Archiv f. Papy-
rusforschung*, iv. p. 568; other constructions are βλέπειν τινά (xiii. 9,
Phil. iii. 2), βλ. μή (xiii. 5, Col. ii. 8).
Ζύμη is used with an ethical reference
in two other contexts of the N.T.,
(1) in the parable of the leaven
(Mt. xiii. 33, Lc. xiii. 21), (2) in the
Pauline proverb μικρὰ ζ. ὅλον τὸ
φύραμα ζυμοῖ (1 Cor. v. 6 ff., Gal.
v. 9); on both these uses see Bp
Lightfoot's notes). The word represents a tendency working invisibly,
and, except in the Parable of the
leaven, an evil tendency, partly because ἡ ζ. γέγονεν ἐκ φθορᾶς (Plutarch,
cited by Lightfoot), partly owing to

16 ζύμης τῶν Φαρισαίων καὶ τῆς ζύμης Ἡρῴδου. ¹⁶καὶ
¶ Wd διελογίζοντο πρὸς ἀλλήλους ὅτι ἄρτους ¶ οὐκ ἔχουσιν. ¶
¶ k
17 ¹⁷καὶ γνοὺς λέγει αὐτοῖς Τί διαλογίζεσθε ὅτι ἄρτους
οὐκ ἔχετε ; οὔπω νοεῖτε οὐδὲ συνίετε ; πεπωρωμένην

15 Ηρωδου] των Ηρωδιανων G 1 13 28 69 346 2ᵖᵉ alᵖᵃᵘᶜ i k arm   16 προς
αλληλους] εν εαυτοις 1071 | οτι] pr λεγοντες ACLNXΓΔΠΣΦ al minᵖˡ f vg syrr arm
me go aeth | εχουσιν B 1 28 209 604 2ᵖᵉ c k syrˢⁱⁿ⁽ᵛⁱᵈ⁾] ειχαν D (a b c ff q) εχομεν
ℵAC(K)LNXΓΔΠΣΦ minᵖˡ f vg syrr arm aeth   17 διαλογιζεσθε]+εν ταις καρδιαις
υμων DUΦ 28 604 2ᵖᵉ alᵖᵃᵘᶜ a b c ff i q syrʰᶜˡ arm aeth (post ὑμ. add ολιγοπιστοι Φ 604
alᵖᵃᵘᶜ arm)+εν αυτοις M 13 61 69 346 8ᵖᵉ | πεπωρωμενην (πεπηρ. D* caecatum f vg)
syrˢⁱⁿ ᵛⁱᵈ] pr ετι AXΓΠΦ minᵖˡ f q vg syrr

the rigid exclusion of leaven during
the Passover and in certain other
sacrificial rites (Lev. ii. 11 πᾶσαν
θυσίαν οὐ ποιήσετε ζυμωτόν). In the
present case the ζ. was (Mt. xv. 12)
the teaching of the Pharisees, or
(acc. to Lc. xii. 1) the spirit of hypocrisy which their teaching encouraged.
Once admitted into the heart or into
a society, this principle would spread
until it rendered the spiritual service
of God impossible.

καὶ τῆς ζύμης Ἡρῴδου] The repetition of the art. implies the distinctness of the two tendencies indicated ;
in Mt. this point is overlooked (τῆς
ζ. τῶν Φαρισαίων καὶ Σαδδουκαίων). Τῶν
Σαδδουκαίων (Mt.) appears to answer to
Ἡρῴδου (Mc.). Herod was not formally
a Sadducee, i.e., he did not reject the
Pharisaic doctrine of a resurrection
(cf. vi. 16). But the worldliness of
the Herod family and of Antipas's
court was not far removed from the
temper of the Sadducean aristocrats ;
and the supporters of the Herod
dynasty were probably disposed to
Sadducean rather than Pharisaic
views. Mt. seems to have used
Σαδδουκαῖοι in this passage as roughly
equivalent to Ἡρῳδιανοί (Mc. iii. 6,
Mt. xxii. 16). 'The leaven of Herod'
was doubtless the practical unbelief
which springs from love of the world
and the immoralities to which in a
coarser age it led. Bede : "fermen-

tum Herodis est adulterium, homi-
cidium, temeritas iurandi, simulatio
religionis." There are occasions when
this tendency can ally itself with
punctilious externalism in religious
practice ; the two are never perhaps
fundamentally at variance. Both were
to be carefully shunned by the Twelve
and the future Church.

16. διελογίζοντο πρὸς ἀλλήλους κτλ.]
The mention of leaven led to a discussion among the Twelve as to their
mistake—how it arose, who was to
blame, how it could be rectified. For
διελογ. cf. ii. 6, 8 ; with πρὸς ἀλλ.
(Mt., ἐν ἑαυτοῖς) cf. πρὸς ἑαυτούς, xi.
31. Ὅτι ἄρτους κτλ. : Mt., λέγοντες
ὅτι Ἄρτους οὐκ ἐλάβομεν. Ὅτι is 'recitative'; their conversation turned on
the omission to provide themselves
with loaves.

17. γνοὺς λέγει] When He became
aware what they were saying, and
what had led to it; see ii. 8, note ;
ix. 33. On γινώσκειν see iv. 13 ; γνούς
is the aor. part. of antecedent action
(Burton, § 134). Ὅτι may again be
recitative : 'why discuss such a subject?" Mt. adds ὀλιγόπιστοι, perhaps
as the equivalent of what he afterwards omits (see below).

οὔπω νοεῖτε οὐδὲ συνίετε ;] Have ye
not yet learnt the habit of attending
to and reflecting upon the facts that
pass under your observation from day
to day ? For similar questions imply-

ἔχετε τὴν καρδίαν ὑμῶν; ¹⁸ὀφθαλμοὺς ἔχοντες οὐ 18
βλέπετε καὶ ὦτα ἔχοντες οὐκ ἀκούετε ; καὶ οὐ μνημονεύετε ¹⁹ὅτε τοὺς §πέντε ἄρτους ἔκλασα εἰς τοὺς 19 § k
πεντακισχιλίους, πόσους κοφίνους κλασμάτων πλήρεις
ἤρατε; λέγουσιν αὐτῷ Δώδεκα. ²⁰ὅτε τοὺς ἑπτὰ εἰς 20

18 και ου μνημονευετε] ουδε μνημ. D ουπω νοειτε ΝΣ ουπω νοειτε ουδε μνημ. 2ᵖᵉ
arm   19 εκλασα] pr ους (D) 13 69 346 k om εκλ. syrˢⁱⁿ arm   20 οτε BL 2ᵖᵉ]
+και אΔ vg pr και c syrᵖᵉˢʰ arm+δε ADXΓΠ al minᶠᵉʳᵉᵒᵐⁿ a ff i q syrʰᵉˡ go aeth+δε
και CN f

ing censure comp. Mc. iv. 13, 40, vii.
18, Jo. xiv. 9; for νοεῖν see vii. 18,
xiii. 14, and for συνιέναι, iv. 12, vi. 52,
vii. 14. Οὐδὲ συνίετε has no place in
Mt. who passes on to καὶ οὐ (οὐδὲ)
μνημονεύετε (v. 18). For the sequence
οὐ...οὐδέ see WM., p. 613.
πεπωρωμένην ἔχετε κτλ.] Wanting
in Mt. On πεπωρ. (Wycliffe, Tindale,
Cranmer, "blinded") see iii. 5, vi. 52;
as to the reading of D here cf. Chase,
Syro-Latin text, p. 42. The train of
thought is well explained by Bengel:
"ex corde indurato manat in visum
auditum et memoriam." For the
predicative use of the participle see
Blass, *Gr.* p. 158.
18. ὀφθαλμοὺς ἔχοντες κτλ.] They
were as men who possessed organs of
sight and hearing which they could
not or would not use. The words are
adapted from Jer. v. 21 ὀφθαλμοὶ αὐτοῖς καὶ οὐ βλέπουσιν, ὦτα αὐτοῖς καὶ
οὐκ ἀκούουσιν, Ezech. xii. 2 ἔχουσιν
ὀφθαλμοὺς τοῦ βλέπειν καὶ οὐ βλέπουσιν καὶ ὦτα ἔχουσιν τοῦ ἀκούειν καὶ
οὐκ ἀκούουσιν. The condition of the
Twelve was perilously near to that
of the judicially blinded multitude
(iv. 12 note). Οὐ μνημονεύετε; the
Lord blames a lapse of memory
which was due to heedlessness and
lack of spiritual vision. Their forgetfulness needed and found a spiritual
remedy (Jo. xiv. 26 ὁ δὲ παράκλητος
...ὑπομνήσει ὑμᾶς πάντα ἃ εἶπον ὑμῖν
ἐγώ). With the whole saying compare
Oxyrh. Logia 3, 8, and see Salmon's

Cath. and Univ. Sermons, vii. (on
'Colour-blindness').

19, 20. ὅτε τοὺς πέντε ἄρτους κτλ.]
Cf. vi. 41 κατέκλασεν τοὺς ἄρτους...
αὐτοῖς, viii. 6 ἔκλασεν...τῷ ὄχλῳ. The
ministerial action of the Twelve passes
out of sight in this review of the two
miracles (ἔκλασα εἰς...); the Lord's
breaking of the loaves was symbolical
of the munificence which fed the
multitudes; cf. Isa. lviii. 7 διάθρυπτε
πεινῶντι τὸν ἄρτον σου. For εἰς in this
reference see WM., p. 267, and esp.
Deissmann, *B. St.*, p. 117 f.; κλᾶν τινι
is the more obvious construction, cf.
Thren. iv. 4 ὁ διακλῶν οὐκ ἔστιν αὐτοῖς
(לָהֶם). Κοφίνους κλ.πλήρεις=κλάσματα
...κοφίνων πληρώματα (vi. 42); σφυρίδων πληρώματα κλασμάτων=περισσεύ-
ματα κλασμάτων...σφυρίδας (viii. 8).
For exx. of the double gen. σφυρίδων
...κλασμάτων see WM., p. 239; in this
instance the construction may perhaps be more conveniently explained
by regarding σφυρίδος πλήρωμα in the
light of a single noun—'a basketful,'
on which κλασμάτων depends as the
gen. of content (WM., p. 235). Lightfoot (*Colossians*, p. 326) compares
Eccl. iv. 6 πλήρωμα δρακὸς ἀναπαύσεως
...μόχθου, 'a handful of rest...of toil';
Fritzsche points to Eur. *Ion* 1069
κρατήρων πληρώματα. Κοφίνους...σφυ-
ρίδων. Wycliffe, "coffyns...leepis";
cf. *v.* 8, note.
λέγουσιν αὐτῷ Δώδεκα...Ἑπτά] Their
memory does not fail them as regards

τοὺς τετρακισχιλίους, πόσων σφυρίδων πληρώματα
κλασμάτων ἤρατε ; καὶ λέγουσιν [αὐτῷ] Ἑπτά.
21 ²¹καὶ ἔλεγεν αὐτοῖς Οὔπω συνίετε;
22 ²²Καὶ ἔρχονται εἰς Βηθσαιδάν. καὶ φέρουσιν αὐτῷ

20 ποσων σφυριδων πληρωματα κλασματων] ποσας σφυριδας κλ. D ποσ. σπ. κλ. πληρεις 604 2ᵖᵒ και ποσους κοφινους κλ. πληρεις Δ | ηρατε πληρεις 1071 | om αυτω ℵADNXΓΠΣΦ minⁱᵉʳᵉᵒᵐⁿ (a) b c f ff i k q syrrᴾᵉˢʰ ʰᶜˡ arm (hab BCLΔ 115 vg me aeth) 21 ουπω ℵCKLΔΠ 1 118 209 1071 al k] πως ουπω ADMNUXΣΦ minˢᵃᵗ ᵐᵘ a c ff i r vg syrr go πως ουν ουπω 13 69 124 346 f arm πως ου BEFGHSVΓ minᵖˡ b d q me aeth | συνιετε] συννοειτε D* νοειτε BD² 22 ερχονται ℵᶜ·ᵃBCDLΔ 13 28 33 69 124 346 1071 alᵖᵃᵘᶜ latt me arm go aeth] ερχεται ℵ*ANXΓΠ alᵖˡ syrr | Βηθσαιδαν ℵABLNX ΓΠΦ al minᵖˡ b (-δα CNΔ (βησσ.) Σ 1 28 33 69 alⁿᵒⁿⁿ c k vg syrr arm aeth)] Βηθανιαν D 262* a f ff i l q r go

their own part in the transaction, so far at least as it had its immediate reward.

21. καὶ ἔλεγεν αὐτοῖς Οὔπω συνίετε ;] Even now their powers of reflexion were not in exercise. Mt. represents the Lord as anticipating their riper thoughts (πῶς οὐ νοεῖτε ὅτι οὐ περὶ ἄρτων εἶπον ὑμῖν; προσέχετε δὲ ἀπὸ τῆς ζύμης τῶν Φ. καὶ Σ.), and adds that upon this they understood that the teaching of the Pharisees and Sadducees was the leaven of which they must beware. But Mc.'s stimulating question, which leaves the Twelve to think out the matter for themselves, is certainly more characteristic of our Lord's method of dealing with souls. Nor does the equation ζύμη = διδαχή at all exhaust the purpose of His reference to the two miracles of the loaves. The inability to understand a metaphor was but a part of their offence ; their anxiety about the want of bread had shewn a distrust of His power to provide which the experience of baskets twice refilled ought to have made impossible. It is ὀλιγοπιστία and not mere want of intelligence which He censures (Mt. xvi. 8).

22—26. ARRIVAL AT BETHSAIDA. A BLIND MAN RECOVERS SIGHT. (Mc. only.)

22. ἔρχονται εἰς Βηθσαιδάν] From Dalmanutha (viii. 10 q.v.). Bethsaida, sc. Julias ; see note on vi. 45. The remarkable reading of D and some other O.L. authorities (Βηθανίαν) either refers to an unknown Bethany on the Lake, or has arisen from a confusion of Bethsaida with the Bethany beyond Jordan (Jo. i. 28) where John baptized; the latter locality is excluded by its inland position. Bethsaida Julias was at this time more than a κώμη (vv. 23, 26, cf. Jo. i. 45), but it may have kept its old style in the popular speech ; or one of the villages in its territory may be intended in the sequel (cf. vi. 36).

φέρουσιν αὐτῷ τυφλόν κτλ.] A second miracle recorded only by Mc. (cf. vii. 32 ff.). There are some remarkable coincidences between the two narratives, both of language and of detail. The words φέρουσιν αὐτῷ …καὶ παρακαλοῦσιν ἵνα…πτύσας…ἀναβλέψας are common to both ; cf. also ἐπιλαβόμενος (viii. 23) with ἀπολ. (vii. 33). Both again agree in many of the circumstances : the withdrawal from the crowd, the touching of the organs affected, the strict charge to keep the matter close. Yet there is no room for suspecting either of the two miracles. Similarity of surroundings may have led to partial similarity of circumstances ; but the

τυφλὸν καὶ παρακαλοῦσιν αὐτὸν ἵνα αὐτοῦ ἅψηται.
²³καὶ ἐπιλαβόμενος τῆς χειρὸς τοῦ τυφλοῦ ἐξήνεγκεν 23
αὐτὸν ἔξω τῆς κώμης, καὶ πτύσας εἰς τὰ ὄμματα
αὐτοῦ, ἐπιθεὶς τὰς χεῖρας αὐτῷ, ἐπηρώτα αὐτόν Εἰ

22 τυφλον] + δαιμονιζομενον Δ   23 επιλαβ. της χειρος] λαβομενος την χειρα D |
εξηνεγκεν ΝΒCL(Δ) 33] εξηγαγεν ADNXΓΠΣΦ al min^{fere omn} | αυτω] αυτου ΑΚΔ 28
2^{pe} 1701 al^{pauc} f l vg (αυτου et αυτω syr^{hcl} me)

narratives are at the heart of the facts distinct.

τυφλόν] The first mention in Mc. of blindness as an infirmity for which a cure was sought from Christ: a second case occurs in x. 46 ff.; for cases in the other Gospels see Mt. ix. 27, xi. 5, xii. 22, xv. 30, xxi. 14, Jo. ix. 1 ff. Παρακ. αὐτ. ἵνα αὐτοῦ ἅψηται : cf. i. 41, x. 13; and for the converse, iii. 10, v. 27 ff., vi. 56. Παρακαλεῖν ἵνα: cf. v. 10, 18 (note). Αὐτοῦ = τοῦ τυφλοῦ, cf. WM., p. 186. ῞Απτεσθαι = nearly ἐπιτιθέναι τὰς χεῖρας: in Job i. 12 it is the LXX. rendering of יָד נָטָה: cf. Mc. i. 41, x. 13.

23. ἐπιλαβόμενος τῆς χειρός κτλ.] Cf. κρατήσας τῆς χειρός, i. 31, v. 41, ix. 27: ἐπιλαβέσθαι (τινός, τινά) occurs in Lc.^{ev. 5, act. 7}, 1 Tim.², Heb.², but in the other Gospels only here and Mt. xiv. 31. Like the κωφὸς μογιλάλος the blind man is taken apart (ἀπολαβόμενος, vii. 33), but since he cannot follow, the Lord leads him by the hand (Bengel: "ipse ducebat: magna humilitas"). For the double gen. (τῆς χειρὸς τοῦ τυφλοῦ) see WM., p. 252, Blass, Gr. p. 101; as Blass observes, the reading of D is in the style neither of classical nor of N.T. Greek; R.V. rightly, "he took hold of the blind man by the hand."

ἐξήνεγκεν αὐτὸν ἔξω τῆς κώμης] 'He brought him outside the village' (Wycliffe: "out of the streete"); the appeal had evidently been made in one of the thoroughfares or open spaces where a concourse might be expected. For this use of ἔξω cf. i. 45, xi. 19. The isolation was probably for the

sake of the blind man himself. Euth. remarks: οὐ γὰρ ἦσαν οἱ τῆς κώμης ταύτης οἰκήτορες ἄξιοι θεάσασθαι γινόμενον τὸ τοιοῦτον θαῦμα. But there is no ground for this supposition. Cf. v. 26.

πτύσας εἰς τὰ ὄμματα αὐτοῦ] Cf. vii. 33, note. The Lord condescends to use a popular remedy as a symbol of the healing power which resided in His own humanity. Suetonius ascribes a similar miracle to Vespasian: Vesp. 7 "e plebe quidam luminibus orbatus, item alius debili crure sedentem pro tribunali pariter adierunt... 'restituturum oculos si inspuisset, confirmaturum crus si dignaretur calce contingere'...utrumque temptavit, nec eventus defuit." See also Tac. hist. iv. 81. The poetical word ὄμμα is rare in Biblical Gk. (Prov.^5 Sap.² 4 Macc.³ Mt.¹ Mc.¹). Ἐπιθεὶς τὰς χεῖρας αὐτῷ : the laying on of hands is vouchsafed as an additional help to the blind man's faith. In some cases it seems to have been the only sign of healing used (vi. 5, Lc. iv. 40, xiii. 13).

ἐπηρώτα αὐτόν Εἴ τι βλέπεις;] For the imperf. cf. v. 9, viii. 27, 29. The question is regarded as a factor in a process which is passing before the reader's mind. On εἰ as a direct interrogative see WM., p. 639; the traditional text softens but at the same time weakens the sentence (see vv. ll.). The Lord recognises that the recovery of sight in this case will be gradual; Victor: σημαίνων ὡς ἀτελὴς τῶν προσαγόντων ἡ πίστις καὶ αὐτοῦ τοῦ πεπηρωμένου τὰς ὄψεις.

24 τι βλέπεις; ²⁴καὶ ἀναβλέψας ἔλεγεν Βλέπω τοὺς
25 ἀνθρώπους, ὅτι ὡς δένδρα ὁρῶ περιπατοῦντας. ²⁵εἶτα
πάλιν ἔθηκεν τὰς χεῖρας ἐπὶ τοὺς ὀφθαλμοὺς αὐτοῦ,
καὶ διέβλεψεν καὶ ἀπεκατέστη, καὶ ἐνέβλεπεν

23 βλεπεις BCD*Δ 2ᵖᵉ me aeth] βλεπει ℵAD²LNΧΓΠΣΦ al min^(fere omn) latt syrr
go arm   24 ελεγεν] ειπεν ℵ*C 1071 al^(pauc) λεγει DN | οτι ως δενδρα ορω περιπ.
ℵABC*LM^(txt)NΧΓΔΠΣΦ min^(pl) go] ως δ. περιπ. C²DM^(mg) 1 604 1071 al^(nonn) latt syrr
arm me aeth | περιπατουντα F 225   25 om ειτα syr^(pesh) arm | και διεβλεψεν
(ℵBC*LΔ 1 28 209 346)] και ηρξατο αναβλεψαι D b ff i r vg και εποιησεν αυτον
αναβλεψαι ANΧΓΠ al^(fere omn) a f q et uidit k syr^(sin uid (sic)) om syr^(pesh) κ. επ. αυτ. αναβλ.
και διεβλεψεν 13 69 (arm) | απεκατεστη ℵBCLΔ min^(pauc)] απεκατεσταθη (αποκ.)
A(D)N(U)ΧΓ(Π)ΣΦ al min^(pl) | και ενεβλεπεν ℵ°BL(Δ) 13 28 69 346] κ. εβλεψεν ℵ*
κ. ενεβλεψεν ACEGΓΠΣΦ al min^(permu) κ. ανεβλεψεν FM* min^(sat mu) ωστε αναβλεψαι D
latt

24. ἀναβλέψας ἔλεγεν κτλ.] At
the question the man involuntarily
raised his eyes. 'Αναβλέπειν is either
(a) to look up (vi. 41, vii. 34, xvi. 4) or
(b) to recover sight (x. 51, 52); the context determines the meaning in each
case. The same ambiguity appears in
certain other verbs compounded with
ἀνά, e.g. ἀνάγειν, ἀναδιδόναι, ἀναδύεσθαι,
ἀνακαλεῖν. Βλέπω τοὺς ἀνθρώπους κτλ.,
" I see men, for I perceive objects like
trees walking." As yet he can dis-
criminate a man from a tree of the
same height only by his movements;
the image reflected on the retina is
still indistinct; "nec caecus est nec
oculos habet" (Jerome). Cf. Jud. ix.
36 τὴν σκιὰν τῶν ὀρέων σὺ βλέπεις ὡς
ἄνδρας : Field compares the proverb
οὐδὲ ἀνθρώπους ἑώρων τοὺς ἀνθρώπους.
The reading of the R.T. which omits
ὅτι and ὁρῶ—" I see men like trees,
walking"—is easier, but comparatively
pointless. On the distinction between
βλέπω and ὁρῶ see iv. 12, note.
25. εἶτα πάλιν ἔθηκεν κτλ.] A
second application of the Lord's hand
completes the cure. Διέβλεψεν, ἀπεκατέστη, ἐνέβλεπεν, represent the completeness of the recovery in three
aspects; the man saw perfectly, his
faculty of sight was from that hour
restored, he was able henceforth to

examine every object and interpret
the phenomena correctly. The reading
of D latt. (ἤρξατο ἀναβλέψαι), while it
aims at removing a tautology, misses
the point of Mc.'s description; the
second imposition of hands, unlike the
first, was followed by perfect restoration. Διαβλέπειν, to see clearly, does
not occur in the LXX., but Aq. substitutes διάβλεψις for ἀνάβλεψις in Isa.
lxi. 1; in the N. T. its meaning is well
illustrated by Mt. vii. 5 = Lc. vi. 42
ἔκβαλε...τὴν δοκὸν καὶ τότε διαβλέψεις
ἐκβαλεῖν τὸ κάρφος, 'thou shalt gain
clearness of vision.' 'Εμβλέπειν, to turn
and fix the eyes upon (cf. Jud. xvi. 27
(A), 1 Esdr. iv. 33 (A), Mt. xix. 26, Mc.
x. 21, 27, xiv. 67, Jo. i. 36, 43), implies
the power to concentrate the attention
on a particular object : the construction is usually ἐμβλ. τινί or εἰς, but
ἐμβλ. τινά occurs in Jud. l.c., Isa. v.
12. Τηλαυγῶς, 'clearly, though at a
distance'; his sight served for distant
objects as well as for those near at
hand, so completely was it restored;
cf. Strabo xvii. 30 ἀφορῶνται δ' ἐν-
θένδε τηλαυγῶς αἱ πυραμίδες. The
adv. is ἅπ. λεγ. in the N. T.; the LXX.
use τηλαυγής (Lev. xiii. 2, 4, 19, 24,
Job xxxvii. 21, Ps. xviii. (xix.) 8),
τηλαύγημα (Lev. xiii. 23), τηλαύγησις
(Ps. xvii. (xviii.) 12). Δηλαυγῶς (vv. ll.),

τηλαυγῶs ἅπαντα.   ²⁶καὶ ἀπέστειλεν αὐτὸν εἰς οἶκον 26
αὐτοῦ λέγων Μηδὲ εἰς τὴν κώμην εἰσέλθῃς.

²⁷§ Καὶ ἐξῆλθεν ὁ Ἰησοῦs καὶ οἱ μαθηταὶ αὐτοῦ εἰς 27 § syrʰˡᵉʳ

25 τηλαυγωs ℵᶜABDNXΓΠΣΦ minᶠᵉʳᵉᵒᵐⁿ] δηλαυγωs ℵ*CLΔ δηλωs 33 | απανταs
AC²NXΓΠΣΦ minᵖˡ go om c k παντα D 2ᵖᵉ   26 εις τον οικον ℵᶜ·ᵃGMUXΔ alᵐᵘ
me | μηδε εις την κωμην εισελθης ℵᶜ (μη ℵ*) BL 1* 209 syrˢⁱⁿ me] μηδενι ειπης εις την
κωμην (εν τη κωμη) (c) k υπαγε εις τον οικον σου και μηδενι ειπης εις την κωμην D (q)
υπαγε εις τ. ο. σ. και εαν εις την κ. εισελθης 13 (28) 69 (346) 2ᵖᵉ et cum μηδεν ειπης
τινι Φ item omisso μηδε i et omisso μηδε εν τη κωμη b f ff vg υπ. εις τ. ο. σ. και μη εις
την κ. εισελθης a μηδε εις τ. κ. εισελθης αλλα υπ. εις τ. ο. σ. και οταν εις τ. κ. εισελθης
μηδενι ειπης εν τη κωμη arm μηδε εις τ. κ. εισελθης μηδε ειπης τινι εν τη κωμη ACEFG
HKMNSUVXΓΔΠΣ minᶠᵉʳᵉᵒᵐⁿ syrrᵖᵉˢʰ ʰᶜˡ⁽ᵗˣᵗ⁾ go aeth   27 εις τας κωμας Καισαριας
(-ρειας BKMSUΓΠ) ℵACEFHLNXΔΣΦ] εις Καισαριαν D a b ff i q r

besides being a word of doubtful authority, misses an important point.

As Gould rightly remarks (in opposition to Weiss): "we have no right to argue from this single case that gradualness was the ordinary method" of the Lord's working. On the contrary, the abnormal character of this incident is probably the cause of its being selected by the Evangelist or St Peter. Euth. is probably not far from the truth in his explanation of the slowness of the recovery: ἀτελῶs δὲ τὸν τυφλὸν τοῦτον ἐθεράπευσεν ὡs ἀτελῶs πιστεύοντα. For homiletic treatment cf. Bede : "paullatim et non statim repente curat quem uno mox verbo si vellet poterat curare, ut magnitudinem humanae caecitatis ostenderet, quae quasi pedetentim et per quosdam profectuum gradus ad lucem divinae visionis solet pervenire."

26. εἰs οἶκον αὐτοῦ] Our Lord seems to have desired that those who had been recently healed should seek the retirement of their own homes, cf. ii. 11, v. 19. The house was apparently away from the town : see next note.

μηδὲ εἰs τὴν κώμην εἰσέλθῃς] 'So far from holding any conversation with the people of the village, do not even enter it for the present : go straight home.' The reading is discussed at some length in WH., *Intr.*, § 140; a defence of the traditional

text is attempted by Burgon-Miller, *Causes of Corruption*, p. 273 f. Dr Hort points out that "the peculiar initial μηδέ has the terse force of many 'sayings as given by St Mark." Μηδέ is used with the imperative in the same sense (= *ne quidem*) in Eph. v. 3, 2 Thess. iii. 10, and with the infinitive by Mc. (ii. 2, iii. 20); but there is no precise parallel in the N. T. Jerome's mystical interpretation is curious : "vade in domum tuam, h. e. in domum fidei, h. e. in ecclesiam; ne revertaris in viculum Iudaeorum."

27—30. JOURNEY TO NEIGHBOURHOOD OF CAESAREA PHILIPPI. QUESTION AS TO THE LORD'S PERSON (Mt. xvi. 13—20, Lc. ix. 18—21).

27. καὶ ἐξῆλθεν ὁ Ἰησοῦς κτλ.] From Bethsaida the Lord and the Twelve moved northwards, following the course of the Jordan till they reached the neighbourhood of its sources ; the road may have lain entirely on the E. bank, or the party may have crossed the river below the waters of Merom where the bridge known as *Jisr benât Yakûb* joins the Jaulân to Galilee. The Caesarea to whose 'villages' they came was distinguished from that upon the coast of the Mediterranean (the Caesarea of the Acts, K. ἡ παράλιοs, at an earlier time Στράτωνος πύργος) as Caesarea Philippi : it was in Philip's tetrarchy (Lc. iii..1), and

τὰς κώμας Καισαρίας τῆς Φιλίππου· καὶ ἐν τῇ ὁδῷ
ἐπηρώτα τοὺς μαθητὰς αὐτοῦ λέγων αὐτοῖς Τίνα με
28 λέγουσιν οἱ ἄνθρωποι εἶναι; ²⁸ οἱ δὲ εἶπαν αὐτῷ

27 εν τη οδω και k | τινα] τι K   28 ειπαν ℵBC*²LΔ k syrᵖᵉˢʰ me ˊaeth] απε-
κριθησαν ADNXΓΠΦ al minᵒᵐⁿ ᵛⁱᵈ lattᵛᵗ⁽ᵉˣᶜᵏ⁾ ᵛᵍ syrʰᶜˡ arm go | om αυτω λεγοντες
ANXΓΠ alᵖˡ syrr go om αυτω f q arm om λεγοντες C² 33 alᵖᵃᵘᶜ

had been recently rebuilt in part by
Philip's munificence, and named after
Augustus, as Bethsaida had been re-
named Julias after the daughter of
the Imperator; Joseph. *ant.* xviii. 2. 1
Φίλιππος δὲ Πανεάδα τὴν πρὸς ταῖς
πηγαῖς τοῦ Ἰορδάνου κατασκευάσας ὀνομάζει Καισάρειαν· κώμην δὲ Βηθσαιδὰ
πρὸς λίμνη τῇ Γεννησαρίτιδι πόλεως
παρασχὼν ἀξίωμα...Ἰουλίᾳ θυγατρὶ τῇ
Καίσαρος ὁμώνυμον ἐκάλεσεν. In passing from one of Philip's new cities
to the other the Lord found Himself
in a more distinctly and aggressively
Hellenised country. The old name
of the town—Paneas, now Bânias—
marked it as sacred to the worship of
Pan; its second name connected it
with the worship of the Emperor, in
whose honour a temple had been
erected close to the old shrine of Pan
(Joseph. *ant.* xv. 10. 3). The population was chiefly Gentile (cf. Schürer
II. i. 133 ff.), yet, as this context shews,
not exclusively so, especially in the
suburbs, to which the Lord seems to
have confined Himself. The physical
surroundings of Caesarea are graphi-
cally described by Stanley, *S. and P.*
p. 397: "over an unwonted carpet of
turf...through a park-like verdure...
the pathway winds, and the snowy
top of the mountain itself is gradually
shut out from view by its increasing
nearness, and again there is a rush
of waters through deep thickets, and
the ruins of an ancient town...rise on
the hill side: in its situation, in its
exuberance of water, its olive groves,
and its view over the distant plain,
almost a Syrian Tivoli"; cf. G. A.
Smith, *H. G.*, p. 473 f. For the Tal-

mudic name, קְסָרִין or קְסָרְיוֹן, see
Neubauer, *Geogr. du Talm.*, p. 237.
Αἱ κῶμαι Καισαρίας (Mt. τὰ μέρη: cf.
note on vii. 24) are the villages and
small towns that clustered round
Caesarea, and belonged to its territory
(WM., p. 234)—its 'daughter towns';
so the phrase is used repeatedly in the
LXX. of Joshua and 1, 2 Chronicles.

ἐν τῇ ὁδῷ ἐπηρώτα τοὺς μαθ.] Probably
one of the chief purposes of the long
journey over a relatively unfrequented
road was to afford opportunities for
the instruction of the Twelve. The
Lord begins by eliciting their views
with regard to Himself. The Galilean
ministry was now practically at an end;
the way to the Cross was opening
before Him. Thus the moment had
come for testing the result upon the
Twelve of what they had seen and
heard, and preparing them for the
future. It was felt by Jesus Himself
to be a crisis of great moment, and
He prepared for it by prayer (Lc. ix.
18), as He had prepared for the first
circuit of Galilee (Mc. i. 35), and for
the selection of the Twelve (Lc. vi. 12).
For another important conversation
ἐν τῇ ὁδῷ cf. x. 32.

τίνα με λέγουσιν οἱ ἄνθρωποι εἶναι;]
Mt. τ. λ. οἱ ἄνθρ. εἶναι τὸν υἱὸν τοῦ ἀνθρώπου; Lc. τ. με οἱ ὄχλοι λ. εἶναι;
He asks for information, perhaps in
order to lead them to the further
question which follows, or it may
have been from a desire to ascertain
by the ordinary methods of human
knowledge what they would have had
opportunities of knowing, which were
denied to Him by the circumstances
of His position (cf. v. 30 b, note). Not

λέγοντες ὅτι ᾿Ιωάνην τὸν βαπτιστήν, καὶ ἄλλοι
᾿Ηλείαν, ἄλλοι δὲ ὅτι εἷς τῶν προφητῶν. ²⁹καὶ 29
αὐτὸς ἐπηρώτα αὐτούς ῾Υμεῖς δὲ τίνα με λέγετε
εἶναι ; ἀποκριθεὶς ὁ Πέτρος λέγει αὐτῷ Cὺ εἶ ὁ

28 οτι εις ℵBC*L me] ενα AC³NXΓΔΠΣΦ al minᶠᵉʳᵉᵒᵐⁿ (k) arm ως ενα D lattᵛᵗ⁽ᵉˣᶜᵏ⁾ᵛᵍ
29 επηρωτα αυτους ℵBC*DLΔ] λεγει αυτοις AC²NXΓΠΣ al minᵖˡ b (f) i vg (syrr) go
arm aeth (και...αυτοις om k) | αποκριθεις]+ δε ℵCDXΓΔΠ al pr και AN 33 al | ο χριστος]
+ ο υιος του θεου ℵL 157 (b) r syrʰⁱᵉʳ+ ο υι. τ. θ. του ζωντος 13 69 124 346 syrᵖᵉˢʰ

even the Pharisees ventured to discuss the Master in His presence.
28. ᾿Ιωάνην τὸν βαπτιστήν κτλ.] Sc.
λέγουσιν οἱ ἄνθρωποί σε εἶναι. These
conjectures have already been mentioned (vi. 14, 15, where see notes).
Matthew adds that some had singled
out the prophet Jeremiah—possibly
(Edersheim, ii. 79) on account of the
denunciatory character of one side of
our Lord's teaching, possibly (J. Lightfoot on Mt. xxvii. 9) because Jeremiah
occupied the first place in the order
traditionally assigned to the 'Latter
Prophets' (cf. Ryle, O. T. Canon, p.
225 ff.). Cf. the references to Jeremiah in 2 Macc. ii. 5 ff., xv. 14 f.; in
4 Esdr. ii. 18 the return of both Isaiah
and Jeremiah is anticipated, "mittam
tibi adiutorium pueros meos Isaiam
et Hieremiam"; see Weber, Jüd.
Theologie², p. 354. Few in Galilee, it
seems, had spoken of Jesus as Messiah (see however Mt. ix. 27), though
in Judaea this possibility had been
freely discussed (Jo. vii. 28—31, 41,
ix. 22), and even in Samaria (Jo. iv.
29), and perhaps in Phoenicia (Mt.
xv. 22). Perhaps the advent of a
national deliverer was not so anxiously
awaited in a country where members
of the Herod family were in power as
in Judaea under Roman sway; yet
see Jo. vi. 15.
29. καὶ αὐτός] Αὐτός is not emphatic, but, like ὁ δέ, serves to shew
that the previous speaker takes up
the conversation again. ῾Υμεῖς δὲ τίνα
κτλ. 'but ye'—in contrast to men
in general—'those without' (cf. iv.

11). Λέγετε, in your ordinary conversation, among yourselves or with
others. ᾿Αποκριθεὶς...λέγει: an instance
of the aor. part. of identical action
coupled with a pres., cf. Burton, § 141;
Mt., ἀποκρ. εἶπεν. All the Synoptists
attribute the answer to Peter, but
they report it differently. Mc.'s brief
σὺ εἶ ὁ χριστός becomes in Lc. τὸν
χριστὸν τοῦ θεοῦ, and in Mt., σὺ εἶ
ὁ χριστός, ὁ υἱὸς τοῦ θεοῦ τοῦ ζῶντος.
But in each of the forms the essence
of the confession is the same. In
the O. T. the priest or king is GOD's
Anointed : 1 Regn. xxvi. 9, 11 χριστὸν
Κυρίου (מְשִׁיחַ יְהוָה), 2 Regn. xxiii. 1
χρ. θεοῦ ᾿Ιακώβ (מְ׳ אֱלֹהֵי יַעֲקֹב), and
the ideal King of the Psalms is also
son of God (Ps. ii. 7, lxxxix. 26, 27);
cf. Enoch cv. 2, and on the import of
the last ref. Stanton, J. and Chr. M.,
p. 288. For a discussion of the title
as applied to Christ in the Gospels
see Dalman, Worte, i. p. 219 ff.,
and art. Son of God in Hastings,
D. B. iv. The epithet ὁ ζῶν is possibly
suggested by the pagan surroundings
of Caesarea; for its use in the O. T.
cf. Esth. vi. 13, viii. 13, Sir. xviii. 1,
Dan. v. 23 (LXX.), vi. 20 (21) (Th.), and
the constant phrases ζῇ Κύριος, ζῶ
ἐγώ, λέγει Κύριος: in the N. T. it occurs
again in Mt. xxvi. 63, Jo. vi. 57 (ὁ ζῶν
πατήρ), Rom. ix. 26, 2 Cor. vi. 16, 1 Th.
i. 9, 1 Tim. iii. 15, iv. 10, Heb. iii. 12,
ix. 14, x. 31, xii. 22, 1 Pet. i. 23, Apoc.
vii. 2, x. 6, xv. 7 (ὁ ζῶν εἰς τοὺς αἰῶνας
τῶν αἰώνων).

According to Mt. xiv. 33 (ἀληθῶς

30 χριστός. ³⁰καὶ ἐπετίμησεν αὐτοῖς ἵνα μηδενὶ λέγωσιν
περὶ αὐτοῦ.

31 ³¹Καὶ ἤρξατο διδάσκειν αὐτοὺς ὅτι Δεῖ τὸν υἱὸν
τοῦ ἀνθρώπου πολλὰ παθεῖν καὶ ἀποδοκιμασθῆναι
ὑπὸ τῶν πρεσβυτέρων καὶ τῶν ἀρχιερέων καὶ τῶν

30 λεγωσιν] ειπωσιν CDG   31 υπο ℵBCDGKLΠΣΦ] απο ΑΧΓΔ al minᵖˡ |
των αρχ. κ. των γρ.] om των bis AGKNΔΠΣ om των 1° FLΓ om των 2° ΧΦ

θεοῦ υἱὸς εἶ), Jo. vi. 69 (σὺ εἶ ὁ ἅγιος
τοῦ θεοῦ), this was not the first occasion upon which the Messiahship of
the Lord had been confessed by the
Twelve. Peter in particular had
known who He was from the first
(Jo. i. 41). But his belief is now
solemnly and formally professed, and
the Lord rewards this act of recognition on the part of His Apostle
with a remarkable promise which Mt.
alone has preserved (Mt. xvi. 17 ff., cf.
Hort, *Ecclesia*, p. 10 f.). On Mc.'s
omission of the reward cf. Victor : τὴν
γὰρ ἀκριβεστέραν περὶ τούτου διήγησιν
παρεχώρησεν ὁ παρὼν εὐαγγελιστὴς τῷ
Ματθαίῳ...ἵνα μὴ δόξῃ Πέτρῳ τῷ ἑαυτοῦ
χαρίζεσθαι διδασκάλῳ. Eusebius (*D.E.*
iii. 3) is perhaps more accurate : ταῦτα
μὲν οὖν ὁ Πέτρος εἰκότως παρασιωπᾶσθαι ἠξίου· διὸ καὶ Μᾶρκος αὐτὸ
παρέλιπεν.

30. καὶ ἐπετίμησεν αὐτοῖς κτλ.] Lc.,
ἐπιτιμήσας αὐτοῖς παρήγγειλεν. On
this use of ἐπιτιμᾶν cf. i. 25. The
censure which the word implies belongs here only to the disobedience
which the Lord has reason to anticipate (cf. i. 45, vii. 36); Vg. *comminatus
est eis ne cui dicerent.* Περὶ αὐτοῦ,
i.e. as Mt. explains, ὅτι αὐτός ἐστιν
ὁ χριστός. The spread of such a
rumour would have either precipitated the Passion, or prevented it at
the cost of substituting a national
and political movement for one which
was spiritual and universal.

31—33. THE PASSION FORETOLD ;
PETER REPROVED (Mt. xvi. 21—23,
Lc. ix. 22).

31. ἤρξατο διδάσκειν] Mt. ἀπὸ τότε
ἤρξατο Ἰησοῦς Χριστὸς δεικνύειν. It
was a new departure, beginning with
the moment when by the confession
of the Twelve he was acknowledged
to be the Christ. The Christ must
suffer (Lc. xxiv. 26, Acts xxvi. 23
παθητὸς ὁ χρ.) ; so prophecy had
clearly foretold (Acts viii. 32—35).
But the idea was nevertheless strange
and repulsive to the Jewish mind ;
see Westcott, *Study of the Gospels*,
p. 141, Stanton, p. 125 ff., Schürer II.
ii. p. 184 ff. ; quite other thoughts
were associated with the name of
Messiah. The Lord therefore does
not say as yet δεῖ τὸν χριστὸν πολλὰ
παθεῖν, but calls Himself as heretofore
τὸν υἱὸν τοῦ ἀνθρώπου (Mc. Lc.). Irenaeus (iii. 16. 5) quotes this passage
against the Docetic notion of an im-
passible Christ. For δεῖ cf. ix. 11,
xiii. 7, Lc. xxiv. 26, Acts xxiii. 11,
xxvii. 24, 1 Cor. xv. 25, Apoc. i. 1.
Πολλὰ παθεῖν : a frequent phrase in
reference to the Passion, cf. Mt. xvi.
21, Mc. ix. 12, Lc. ix. 22, xvii. 25; the
Lord suffered πολλά but not πολλάκις,
Heb. ix. 26.

ἀποδοκιμασθῆναι...ἀποκτανθῆναι...ἀνα-
στῆναι] A remarkably complete outline
of the Passion in its three stages : (1)
the official rejection of the Messiah by
the Sanhedrin, (2) His violent death,
(3) His victory over death. Καὶ ἀποδοκιμασθῆναι (Mc., Lc., omitted by Mt.)
looks back to Ps. cxvii. (cxviii.) 22 ;
cf. xii. 10, 1 Pet. ii. 4 ff. ; ἀποδοκι-
μάζειν (= DℵΩ Ps. *l.c.*) is to reject after
scrutiny, and implies an official test-

γραμματέων καὶ ἀποκτανθῆναι, καὶ μετὰ τρεῖς ἡμέρας
ἀναστῆναι. ⁋ ³²καὶ παρρησίᾳ τὸν λόγον⁋ ἐλάλει. καὶ 32 ⁋ syrʰⁱᵉʳ ⁋ N

31 μετα τρεις ημερας] (εν) τη τριτη ημερα 1 (13 28) 33 69 124 2ᵖᵉ alᵖᵃᵘᶜ d g arm aeth

ing and rejection of His claims. This
was to be conducted by the three
factors in the national council acting
together (ὑπὸ τῶν πρ. καὶ ἀρχ. καὶ γρ.
Mt., so Lc.), but each severally responsible and consenting to the verdict (ὑπὸ
τῶν πρ. καὶ τῶν ἀρχ. καὶ τῶν γρ., Mc.).
The words distinctly contemplate Jerusalem as the scene of the rejection,
for there only could the ἀρχιερεῖς
be found, or the three classes take
common action. The three are mentioned together again xi. 27, xiv. 43,
53 (οἱ ἀρχ. κ. οἱ γρ. κ. οἱ πρ.), xv. 1 (οἱ
ἀρχ. μετὰ τῶν πρ. καὶ γρ.). For the
γρ. see note on i. 22; the ἀρχιερεῖς
(Vg. summi sacerdotes, A.V. and
R.V., "chief priests") are the heads
of the priestly class, High Priest and
ex-High Priests, and other leading
members of the sacerdotal aristocracy;
cf. Acts iv. 6 ὅσοι ἦσαν ἐκ γένους
ἀρχιερατικοῦ, and see Blass ad l. and
Schürer ii. i. p. 177 ff. The πρεσβύτεροι (to be distinguished of course
from the elders of vii. 3, 5) appear to
have been the non-professional or lay
element in the Council—a survival
apparently of the γερουσία of Maccabean times (1 Macc. xii. 6, 3 Macc.
i. 8) and of the primitive זִקְנֵי־יִשְׂרָאֵל
(Exod. xvii. 5).

καὶ ἀποκτανθῆναι] So also Mt., Lc.;
this late pass. aor. occurs in 1 Macc.
ii. 9, and again in Mc. ix. 31 (cf.
WSchm., p. 128). Καὶ μετὰ τρεῖς
ἡμέρας ἀναστῆναι : Mt., Lc., καὶ τῇ
τρίτῃ ἡμέρᾳ ἐγερθῆναι. Ἐγείρομαι is
used of the Resurrection in Mc. (WH.)
exclusively, in Mt. and Lc. the two
verbs appear to be employed indiscriminately ; in doctrinal passages
ἐγείρομαι as a pass. in form suggests
the thought of ὁ ἐγείρας (Rom. iv.
24 f., viii. 11, 34, 1 Cor. xv. 14, 15, cf.
Ign. Trall. 9), but this is hardly

present to the writers of the Gospel
narrative. Μετὰ τρ. ἡμ.; so Mc. always (ix. 31, x. 34), except when he
uses διὰ τριῶν ἡμερῶν (xiii. 2, v.l., xiv.
58) in reference to the saying of Jo. ii.
19. Mt. also has μετὰ τρ. ἡμ. in xxvii.
63, but elsewhere he writes τῇ τρίτῃ
ἡμέρᾳ (xvi. 21, xvii. 23, xx. 19), and so
Lc., ix. 22, xviii. 33 (τῇ ἡμ. τῇ τρ.),
xxiv. 7, 46, Acts x. 40, and Paul
(1 Cor. xv. 4, τῇ ἡμ. τῇ τρ.). Mc.'s
phrase occurs also, with another reference, in Acts xxv. 1; cf. μετὰ τρεῖς
μῆνας (Acts xxviii. 11); μετὰ τρία ἔτη
Gal. i. 18; τῇ τρίτῃ Acts xxvii. 19.
Both phrases were perhaps suggested
by Hos. vi. 2, ὑγιάσει ἡμᾶς μετὰ δύο
ἡμέρας· ἐν τῇ ἡμέρᾳ τῇ τρίτῃ καὶ ἀνα-
στησόμεθα. The earliest tradition
seems to have inclined to the former,
modifying it however so as to retain a
reference to the third day. That μετὰ
τρεῖς ἡμέρας in this connexion is equivalent to ἐν τῇ τρίτῃ ἡμέρᾳ is clear from
the explanatory ἕως τῆς τρίτης ἡμέρας
in Mt. xxvii. 64; cf. Mt. xii. 40 where
the stay of the Lord in the grave is
described as "three days and three
nights"; see also Field, Notes, p. 11.
The easier phrase however soon superseded the harder, and is almost universal in early citations from the
Gospels (Resch, aussercan. Par. zu
Lc. p. 147 ff.), and in Creeds it is varied
only by the equivalent διὰ τριῶν ἡμερῶν or τριήμερον (Caspari, Quellen, iii.
p. 70 f.). On the singular renderings
of some O. L. texts see J. R. Harris,
Codex Bezae, p. 91. The Sinaitic
Syriac substitutes 'on the third day'
in Mc., but in Mt. xxvii. 63 retains
'after three days.'

32. παρρησίᾳ τὸν λόγον ἐλάλει] He
spake the saying (so probably here,
but cf. i. 45) without reserve (Wycliffe,
"pleynli," "openli"), in the presence of

προσλαβόμενος ὁ Πέτρος αὐτὸν ἤρξατο ἐπιτιμᾶν
§ n 33 αὐτῷ. ³³§ὁ δὲ ἐπιστραφεὶς καὶ ἰδὼν τοὺς μαθητὰς
αὐτοῦ ἐπετίμησεν Πέτρῳ καὶ λέγει "Υπαγε ὀπίσω

32 προσλαβομενος] προσκαλεσαμενος Γ | αυτω]+ne cui illa diceret (c) k+Domine
propitius esto nam hoc non erit a b n (syrˢⁱⁿ)   33 και ιδ. τ. μαθ. αυτου] om k |
Πετρω] pr τω ΑΣΧΓΔΠ | και λεγει] λεγων ΑΔΧΓΠ al lattᵛᵗ ᵖˡ ᵛᵍ syrʰᵉˡ go arm

all the Twelve (Euth. φανερῶς καὶ ἀπα-
ρακαλύπτως), and in plain, direct words.
Παρρησίᾳ (here only in the Synoptists)
is contrasted with ἐν κρυπτῷ (Jo. vii.
4): ἐν παροιμίαις (Jo. xvi. 25, cf. 29).
The more usual forms are μετὰ παρ-
ρησίας (Prov. x. 10, Acts ii. 29), ἐν
παρρησίᾳ (Sap. v. 1, Jo. xvi. 29); παρρησίᾳ is specially frequent in Jo. (vii.
13, 26, x. 24, xi. 14, 54, xvi. 25, xviii.
20). For the general sense and use of
the word see Lightfoot on Col. ii. 15.

προσλαβόμενος ὁ Πέτρος αὐτόν κτλ.]
To Peter such frankness seemed to
be indiscreet; such premonitions of
failure were at variance with all his
conceptions of the Christ. The Master
had manifested a momentary weakness; it was his duty as senior of the
Twelve to remonstrate. He took the
Lord aside a little, as if to ask a
question or to give some information
privately, perhaps in order to spare
the Master the pain of a public remonstrance, 'as if sparing Him,'
Syr.ˢⁱⁿ.(Bede: "ne praesentibus ceteris
condiscipulis magistrum videatur ar-
guere"). Προσλαβέσθαι (Mt. Mc.) is
used of the stronger or wealthier
coming to the help of the weaker or
poorer (Ps. xvii. (xviii.) 17 (אA), xxvi.
(xxvii.) 10, Acts xviii. 26, Rom. xiv. 1,
3, xv. 7), and carries here an air of
conscious superiority (cf. Hastings, D.
B., iii. p. 760 a). Something of this
officiousness had shewn itself already
in Simon Peter's relations to his
Master (i. 36); the tension of his
recent act of faith and the exaltation
of feeling which followed it probably
exaggerated a fault of natural character, and led to the astounding conduct
described in the next words.

ἤρξατο ἐπιτιμᾶν αὐτῷ] Mt. gives
the words: ἵλεώς σοι (1 Macc. ii. 21),
Κύριε, οὐ μὴ ἔσται σοι τοῦτο.

33. ὁ δὲ ἐπιστραφείς κτλ.] The
Lord turned sharply round as if to
face the speaker—a characteristic act,
see v. 30, Mt. ix. 22, Lc. vii. 9, 44, ix.
55, x. 23, xiv. 25, xxii. 61, xxiii. 28,
Jo. i. 38; for ἐπιστρέφεσθαι (ἐπιστρέ-
φειν) in this sense cf. v. 30, Jo. xxi. 20,
Acts ix. 40, Apoc. i. 12. On this, as
on a later occasion (Lc. xxii. 61), a
mere look might have sufficed to bring
Peter to repentance; but Jesus as He
turned caught sight of the rest of the
Twelve (ἰδὼν τοὺς μαθητὰς αὐτοῦ), who
were probably watching the scene with
interest, and perhaps shared Peter's
views. A public reproof was therefore necessary, and the Lord did not
spare His first Apostle; ἐπετίμησεν
Πέτρῳ, so Mc. only, apparently in
reference to v. 32, ἤρξατο ἐπιτιμᾶν, cf.
Bengel: "dum increpat, increpati-
onem meretur," a point which the
Vg. misses—coepit increpare...com-
minatus est. Mc., who does not record the Lord's commendation of
Peter, accentuates the reproof.

ὕπαγε ὀπίσω μου, Σατανᾶ] Cf. Mt.
iv. 10 ὕπαγε, Σατανᾶ—the words in
which the Lord before the beginning
of His public work dismissed the
Tempter, when he offered the kingdoms of the world on condition of receiving homage for them. This temptation was now renewed by Satan in
the person of the Apostle who desired
his Master to put from Him the
prospect of the Cross. It is unnecessary to suppose either that Peter
is here called 'Satan' (cf. Jo. vi. 70),
or that the word is to be understood

μου, Cατανᾶ· ὅτι οὐ φρονεῖς τὰ τοῦ θεοῦ ἀλλὰ τὰ
τῶν ἀνθρώπων.

³⁴Καὶ προσκαλεσάμενος τὸν ὄχλον σὺν τοῖς μα- 34
θηταῖς αὐτοῦ εἶπεν αὐτοῖς §Εἴ τις θέλει ὀπίσω μου   § syrʰⁱᵉʳ

34 ει τις ℵBC*DLΔ 604 1071 alᵖᵃᵘᶜ latt syrʰᵉˡ⁽ᵐᵍ⁾ arm Or] οστις AC²ΧΓΠΣΦ al
minᵖˡ syrr me go aeth | οπισω μου] om k

simply in its etymological sense, 'adversary' (Victor, ὅ ἐστιν ἀντικείμενε: see
note on i. 13). The Lord recognises
His great adversary in Peter, who for
the moment acts Satan's part. Thpht.:
ὁ σατανᾶς μόνος οὐ θέλει αὐτὸν παθεῖν
...Σατανᾶν ὀνομάζει τὸν Πέτρον ὡς τὰ
Σατανᾶ φρονοῦντα, cf. Macar. Magn.
iii. 27 οὐ Πέτρου τὸ ῥῆμα ἀλλ᾽ ὑποβολὴ
τοῦ σατανᾶ τὸ λεχθέν. Ὑπάγειν ὀπίσω
τινός (Mt., Mc. here: not in the true
text of Mt. iv. 10) is interpreted by
Origen in a favourable sense as
= ἀκολουθεῖν ὁ. τ.: διὰ μὲν τὴν πρόθεσιν, οὖσαν δεξιάν, λέγει αὐτῷ ⁰Υ. ὁ. μ.,
οἱονεὶ καταλιπόντι τὰ δι᾽ ὧν ἠγνόει...
ἀκολουθεῖν τῷ Ἰησοῦ. But ὑπάγειν is
not = ἐλθεῖν (v. 34); it implies removal, not approach, and ὀπίσω μου
in this connexion represents defeat
and banishment from the sight of the
conqueror, not a closer attachment to
the company of the Master; cf. Ps.
vi. 11 (ℵA), ix. 4, xlix. (l.) 17, Isa.
xxxviii. 17. If Peter identified himself with Satan, he must share Satan's
repulse and exile.

ὅτι οὐ φρονεῖς κτλ.] It is not merely
the officiousness of Peter which is
rebuked, but the graver error which
led him to interfere. His resistance to the thought of the Passion
revealed a deep cleavage between his
mind and the mind of GOD. The
illumination which had enabled him
to apprehend the Messiahship of Jesus (Mt. xvi. 17) left him still unable
to assimilate the λόγος τοῦ σταυροῦ.
On this fundamental point he was
not in sympathy with the Divine
order of things. Φρονεῖν τὰ τοῦ θεοῦ
= φρ. τὰ τοῦ πνεύματος, the opposite
of φρ. τὰ τῆς σαρκός (Rom. viii. 5) or

τὰ ἐπίγεια, τὰ ἐπὶ τῆς γῆς (Phil. iii. 19,
Col. iii. 2); such conformity with the
Divine Mind distinguished the Master
and is the aim of the true disciple
(Phil. ii. 5). It is interesting to see
how this Gospel phrase reflects and
expands itself in the Pauline Epistles.
For earlier instances of φρονεῖν τά
τινος cf. Esth. viii. 13, 1 Macc. x. 20,
and in non-Biblical Gk., Dem. in Phil.
3 οἱ τὰ Φιλίππου φρονοῦντες, Dion. H.
ii. οἱ φρονοῦντες τὰ τῆς ὀλιγαρχίας:
and for a practical application of the
present passage see Orig. in Mt. t. xii.
23 μὴ νομίσωμεν τοίνυν τὸ τυχὸν εἶναι
ἁμάρτημα φρονεῖν τὰ τῶν ἀνθρώπων,
δέον ἐν πᾶσι φρονεῖν τὰ τοῦ θεοῦ. Cf.
Iren. iii. 18. 4. Mt. prefixes σκάνδαλον
εἶ μου—words that reveal the reality
of the temptation which such a suggestion as Peter's presented to our
Lord, and serve to explain the warmth
with which he repels it.

34—ix. 1. PUBLIC TEACHING ON
SELF-SACRIFICE (Mt. xvi. 24—28, Lc.
ix. 23—27).

34. προσκαλεσάμενος τὸν ὄχλον κτλ.]
Mt. εἶπεν τοῖς μαθηταῖς αὐτοῦ, Lc.
ἔλεγεν δὲ πρὸς πάντας. Only Mc. calls
attention to the unexpected presence
of a crowd. Even in the villages of
Caesarea the Lord was recognised
and was followed by the Jewish population. The prediction of the Passion
was for the Twelve alone; but the
crowd could share with them the
great practical lessons which it suggested, and it needed them at this
moment when it was pressing with too
light a heart into the Kingdom of
God. Bengel: "doctrina catholica."

εἴ τις θέλει ὀπίσω μου ἐλθεῖν κτλ.]
The words are identically the same in

ἐλθεῖν, ἀπαρνησάσθω ἑαυτὸν καὶ ἀράτω τὸν σταυρὸν
35 αὐτοῦ καὶ ἀκολουθείτω μοι. ³⁵ὃς γὰρ ἐὰν θέλη

34 ελθειν ℵABC²KLΠΣ min^mu c g k l arm me Or] ακολουθειν C*DXΦ al 1 28 604
al^matmu a b f ff n q vg ελθ. και ακολ. Δ | απαρνησασθω...αρατω] επαρατω Δ | αυτου]
εαυτου ℵ

Mt. down to ἕνεκεν ἐμοῦ, and with one
exception there is no important variation in Lc. Such a saying uttered on
such an occasion would naturally impress itself verbally on the Twelve,
and gain currency in an identical
form. The phrase ἐλθεῖν ὀπ. μου is
not suggested by the ὕπαγε κτλ. of
v. 33 but by the eagerness of the
crowd or the presence of the Twelve:
see note on i. 17. To constitute a loyal
disciple three things were necessary.
(1) Ἀπαρνήσασθαι ἑαυτόν, to deny, i.e.
to refuse to recognise, to ignore, oneself. The verb occurs in Isa. xxxi. 7
ἀπαρνήσονται (יִמְאָסוּ) οἱ ἄνθρωποι τὰ
χειροποίητα αὐτῶν; in the N. T., besides this context, it is used in reference to the disciple who denies all
knowledge of his master (Lc. xxii. 34),
or the master who refuses to recognise the unworthy disciple (Lc. xii. 9):
ἀρνεῖσθαι is similarly employed by Mt.,
Lc., Jo., Jude, Paul. The idea is
very inadequately represented by the
current notions of 'self-denial' which
regard it as the abnegation of a
man's property or rights rather than
of himself: the true interpretation is
given by St Paul, Gal. ii. 19 f. ἀπέθανον,
ἵνα θεῷ ζήσω· Χριστῷ συνεσταύρωμαι,
ζῶ δὲ οὐκέτι ἐγώ, ζῇ δὲ ἐν ἐμοὶ Χριστός.
Cf. Thpht.: τί δέ ἐστι τὸ ἀπαρν. ἑαυτὸν
οὕτως ἂν μάθοιμεν ἐὰν γνῶμεν τί ἐστὶ τὸ
ἀρνήσασθαι ἕτερον. ὁ ἀρνούμενος ἕτερον
...οὐκ ἐπιστρέφεται, οὐ συμπάσχει, ἅτε
ἅπαξ ἀλλοτριωθείς. οὕτως οὖν καὶ ἡμεῖς
βούλεται τοῦ ἡμετέρου σώματος ἀφει-
δεῖν. Bede: "pensemus quomodo se
Paulus abnegaverat qui dicebat, 'Vivo
autem iam non ego.'" (2) Ἆραι τὸν
σταυρὸν αὐτοῦ, to put oneself into the
position of a condemned man on his
way to execution, i.e. to be prepared

to face extreme forms of shame and
loss. This reference to crucifixion
was perhaps not new to the Twelve
(Mt. x. 38); to the crowd at least it
must have been deterrent in a high
degree, suggesting a procession of
furciferi headed by Jesus and consisting of His followers. Such wholesale crucifixions had occurred within
memory (Schürer, II. i. p. 5) and
might be expected in case of a revolt.
Lc. adds καθ' ἡμέραν in view of Christian experience, which had learnt to
see the Cross in ordinary trials, but
the Lord's words were doubtless intended also to prepare His followers
for the supreme trial of faith. (3) Ἀκολουθεῖν, to persevere in the exacting
course of a personal following (cf. i.
18). Without this martyrdom itself
would be insufficient; cf. Victor:
ἐπειδὴ γάρ ἐστι καὶ πάσχοντα μὴ ἀκολουθεῖν ὅταν μὴ δι' αὐτόν τι πάθῃ, ἵνα μὴ
νομίσῃς ὅτι ἀρκεῖ τῶν κινδύνων ἡ φύσις,
προστίθησι καὶ τὴν ὑπόθεσιν ἵνα ταῦτα
ποιῶν αὐτῷ ἀκολουθῇς. The following is
to be habitual and permanent (ἀκολουθείτω, pres., cf. ἀπαρνησάσθω, ἀράτω).
35. ὃς γὰρ ἐὰν θέλῃ κτλ.] A saying
attributed to our Lord on more than
one other occasion (Mt. x. 39, Lc. xvii.
33, Jo. xii. 25). The key to its interpretation lies in the Biblical use of
ψυχή. In the O. T. ψ. is the usual
equivalent of נֶפֶשׁ, the conscious life
of feeling and desire (Schulz, ii. p.
246). The N. T. distinguishes this
life from merely physical animation
on the one hand (Mt. x. 28, cf. 4 Macc.
xiii. 14), and from the higher life of
the πνεῦμα on the other (1 Cor. ii. 14,
xv. 45, 1 Thess. v. 23, Heb. iv. 12).
Thus the ψυχή holds a mediating position between σῶμα and πνεῦμα (see Elli-

τὴν ψυχὴν αὐτοῦ σῶσαι, ἀπολέσει αὐτήν· ὃς δ'
ἂν ἀπολέσει τὴν ψυχὴν αὐτοῦ ἕνεκεν ἐμοῦ καὶ τοῦ
εὐαγγελίου, σώσει αὐτήν. ³⁶τί γὰρ ὠφελεῖ ἄνθρωπον 36

35 την ψυχην αυτου (1°)] τ. εαυτου ψ. B Or τ. ψ. εαυτου D² | ος δ αν απ. τ. ψ. αυτου]
om k | απολεσει 2° אBCD²ΓΔ al^nonn] απολεση ALXII al^pl | την ψυχην αυτου (2°)] τ.
εαυτου ψ. C³XII al 604 al^satmu | εμου και του ευαγγελιου] om εμου και D a b i m r arm
aeth om και του ευαγγ. 33 ff om και k^vid syr^sinvid | σωσει] pr ουτος C²EFGM^mgSUVΓ
al^pl 36 ωφελει אB(L) a n q arm] ωφελησει ACDXΓΠΣΦ al min^fereomn latt syr^hcl
Or ωφεληθησεται 33 | (τον) ανθρωπον א^c(A)B(C*D)KSUVΠΦ min^pl go (Or)] ανθρωπος
א*C³EFGHLMXΓΔΣ 1 33 69 al^nonn

cott, *Destiny of the creature* v.; Lightfoot on 1 Thess. *l. c.*), and the word is
used with a lower or higher reference
in different contexts; for exx. of the
former see Mt. ii. 20, vi. 25, Jo. x. 15 ff.,
Rom. xi. 3, Phil. ii. 30, and for the
latter, Mt. xi. 29, Mc. xiv. 34, Jo. xii.
27, Heb. vi. 19, 1 Pet. i. 22; the English versions seek to distinguish the
two uses by the double rendering
'life' and 'soul.' In the present saying both meanings are in view, and an
adequate translation is perhaps impossible. We may paraphrase : 'the
man whose aim in life is to secure
personal safety and success, loses the
higher life of which he is capable, and
which is gained by those who sacrifice
themselves in the service of Christ.'
The immediate reference is doubtless
to the alternative of martyrdom or
apostasy, but the saying admits of
wider application; cf. the form which
it takes in Jo. xii. 25, and the variations here in Mt., Lc. All self-seeking
is condemned as self-destruction, all
true self-sacrifice is approved as self-
preservation. Victor: ὃ δὲ λέγει τοιοῦ-
τόν ἐστιν Οὐκ ἀφειδῶν ὑμῶν ἀλλὰ
καὶ σφόδρα φειδόμενος ταῦτα ἐπιτάττω.
Bede : " ac si agricolae dicatur, ' Frumentum si servas, perdis; si seminas,
renovas.'"

⁵Ος δ' ἂν ἀπολέσει (Mt., Lc., ἀπολέσῃ)
is a construction which appears occasionally in Biblical Gk., cf. Jud. xi. 24
ἃ ἐὰν κληρονομήσει σε (B), Jer. xlix.
(xlii.) 4 ὁ λόγος ὃν ἂν ἀποκριθήσεται;

for N. T. exx. see WH., *Notes*, p. 172,
WM., p. 385, Blass, *Gr.* p. 217. Ἔνεκεν
ἐμοῦ (omitted in 'Western' texts) is
one of those striking claims upon the
absolute devotion of His followers
which reveal our Lord's consciousness
of a Divine right. The addition καὶ
τοῦ εὐαγγελίου is characteristic of Mc.;
cf. i. 1, 15, x. 29. Mc. alone of the Evangelists uses τὸ εὐαγγέλιον absolutely;
cf. Salmon, *H. E.* p. 37. For the contrast of σῴζειν and ἀπολλύναι comp.
1 Cor. i. 18, 2 Cor. ii. 15, James iv. 12;
similarly σωτηρία is opposed to ἀπώλεια, Phil. i. 28. Salvation is predicated
of the soul in Jas. i. 20, v. 15, 1 Pet. i. 9.
36. τί γὰρ ὠφελεῖ ἄνθρωπον κτλ.]
Self-sacrifice is the truest self-inter-
est, for (γάρ) a man gains nothing by
the acquisition of the whole world if
the penalty is his own personal life.
"The question is...between that life
which consists mainly in having, and
that which consists in being" (Gould).
The Lord seems to have in view
the temptation described in Mt. iv. 8
(see note on *v.* 33). For τί ὠφελεῖ or
ὠφελήσει cf. Hab. ii. 18 (מַה־הוֹעִיל),
Sap. v. 8, 1 Cor. xiv. 6, Heb. iv. 2 ; Mt.,
Lc., τί γὰρ ὠφεληθήσεται (ὠφελεῖται);
Clem. Al. *strom.* vi. 13, Ps.-Clem. *hom.*
6 τί τὸ ὄφελος: see Resch, p. 150 ff.
Κερδῆσαι...ζημιωθῆναι: for the contrast
cf. Phil. iii. 8. The population of the
northern towns, esp. perhaps of such
a town as Caesarea, was deeply occupied in the pursuit of wealth (cf.
Merrill, cc. viii., xvi.), as the frequent

κερδῆσαι τὸν κόσμον ὅλον καὶ ζημιωθῆναι τὴν ψυχὴν
37 αὐτοῦ ; ³⁷τί γὰρ δοῖ ἄνθρωπος ἀντάλλαγμα τῆς
38 ψυχῆς αὐτοῦ ; ³⁸ὃς γὰρ ἐὰν ἐπαισχυνθῇ με καὶ τοὺς

36 κερδησαι...ζημιωθηναι ℵBL] εαν κερδηση...ζημιωθη ACDXΓΔΠΣΦ al min^omn vid
syrr Or 37 τι γαρ ℵBLΔ 28 2^pe q me arm Or] η τι γαρ D* η τι AB²XΓΠΦ al
min^pl latt^vt(excq)vg syrr go aeth | δοι ℵ*B] δω ℵ°L δωσει ACDXΓΠΣΦ al min^omn vid latt
Or | ανθρωπος] pr o B | om δοι ανθρωπος Δ | αυτου] εαυτου B αυτω C   38 ος γαρ
εαν] ος εαν A ος δ αν D | επαισχυνθη με] επαισχυνθησεται εμε D

references in the Gospels to wealth
and worldly care suggest. The Lord
saw that the penalty was too often
the loss of the higher personal life
(ἑαυτὸν ζημιωθείς, Lc.). Ζημιοῦν is properly to confiscate or fine (1 Esdr. i.
36, viii. 24), but also to inflict a penalty of any kind (e.g. death, 2 Macc. iv.
48; loss of one's handiwork, 1 Cor. iii.
15); for ζ. τὴν ψ. cf. Prov. xix. 16
κακόφρων ἄνθρωπος ζημιωθήσεται· ἐὰν
δὲ λοιμεύηται, καὶ τὴν ψυχὴν αὐτοῦ προσ-
θήσει: Philo, ebr. 3 ζημιουμένους δὲ
πάντα, χρήματα, σώματα, ψυχάς. Lightfoot on Phil. l.c. cites a line from
Menander which is a partial parallel
to this saying of Christ: κέρδος πονηρὸν ζημίαν ἀεὶ φέρει. Cf. Origen in
Mt. t. xii. 28 κερδαίνει τὸν κόσμον ᾧ ὁ
κόσμος οὐ σταυροῦται· ᾧ δὲ κόσμος οὐ
σταυροῦται ἐκείνῳ ἔσται ζημία τῆς ψυχῆς
αὐτοῦ. The κόσμος is the external considered as a counter attraction to the
spiritual and eternal: cf. 1 Jo. ii. 15 ff.,
with Westcott's notes. For an early
comment on this saying of Christ see
Ps.-Clem. hom. § 6.

37. τί γὰρ δοῖ κτλ.] Another link
in the chain of reasoning. The man
is not a gainer by his transaction, for
(γὰρ) the loss he has suffered is irre-
parable. Ἀντάλλαγμα, commutatio, is
the price received in exchange for an
article of commerce; cf. Ruth iv. 7,
3 Regn. xx. (xxi.) 2 δώσω σοι ἀργύριον
ἀντάλλαγμα (A; B, ἄλλαγμα) ἀμπελῶνος, Job xxviii. 15 οὐ σταθήσεται αὐτῇ
(sc. τῇ σοφίᾳ) ἀργύριον ἀντάλλαγμα
αὐτῆς (cf. v. 17), and esp. Sir. xxvi. 14
οὐκ ἔστιν ἀντάλλαγμα πεπαιδευμένης

ψυχῆς, "no money can purchase (i.e.
there is nothing so valuable as) an
instructed, disciplined soul." The
saying before us carries the thought
of Jesus ben Sira further: there is
nothing which can take the place of
the soul in any man: comp. the fine
lines in Eur. Or. 1155 οὐκ ἔστιν οὐδὲν
κρεῖσσον ἢ φίλος σαφής, | οὐ πλοῦτος,
οὐ τυραννίς· ἀλόγιστον δέ τι | τὸ πλῆθος
ἀντάλλαγμα γενναίου φίλου. The idea
of the irredeemableness of the lost
soul (Wycliffe, "what chaungyng schal
a man ʒyve for his soule?" Tindale,
"what shall a man geve to redeme his
soule agayne?"), to which expositors
usually refer, does not lie in the word,
even if it is in the background of the
thought; for a redemptive price Mc.
uses λύτρον, see x. 45, note. On the
form δοῖ = δῷ conj. cf. iv. 29, v.
43, notes.

38. ὃς γὰρ ἐὰν ἐπαισχυνθῇ κτλ.]
This final γάρ carries us on to the
issue of human life, and places the
whole struggle between self-seeking
and self-sacrifice in the light of the
eternal order. The words retain their
Marcan form in Lc.; in Mt. they are
more general and at the same time
more dogmatic (μέλλει ἔρχεσθαι...καὶ
τότε ἀποδώσει κτλ.). Ὃς γὰρ ἐὰν ἐπαισχυνθῇ corresponds to ὃς γὰρ ἐὰν θέλῃ...
σῶσαι οf v. 35; μὲ καὶ τοὺς ἐμοὺς λόγους
looks back to ἕνεκεν ἐμοῦ καὶ τοῦ εὐαγγελίου. If some would lack physical
courage to face death, more would
fail through want of moral courage,
as St Peter himself did more than
once (xiv. 66 ff., Gal. ii. 11 ff.; con-

ἐμοὺς λόγους ἐν τῇ γενεᾷ ταύτῃ τῇ μοιχαλίδι καὶ
ἁμαρτωλῷ, καὶ ὁ υἱὸς τοῦ ἀνθρώπου ἐπαισχυνθήσεται
αὐτὸν ὅταν ἔλθῃ ἐν τῇ δόξῃ τοῦ πατρὸς αὐτοῦ μετὰ
τῶν ἀγγέλων τῶν ἁγίων.¶ ¹καὶ ἔλεγεν §αὐτοῖς Ἀμὴν Ι
λέγω ὑμῖν ὅτι εἰσίν τινες ὧδε τῶν ἑστηκότων οἵτινες

¶ syrʰⁱᵉʳ
9
§ N

38 λογους] om k | των αγιων]+αυτου F minᵖᵃᵘᶜ om I 209   IX I τινες ωδε των
εστηκοτων BD* a ff n q] ωδε τινες των εστ. (c) k syrˢⁱⁿ τινες των ωδε εστ. ℵ (εστωτων)
ACD²LNXΓΔΠΣΦ al minᶠᵉʳᵉᵒᵐⁿ f vg syrʰᵉˡ go arm τινες των εστ. ωδε I syrᵖᵉˢʰ me Or
om ωδε b i r | εστ.] +μετ εμου D 2ᵖᵉ a b ff n q r

trast Rom. i. 16, Gal. vi. 14, 2 Tim. i.
12, 16, 1 Pet. iv. 16). On the σκάνδαλον
τοῦ σταυροῦ in the first age see 1 Cor.
i. 18 ff.; and for a magnificent instance
of the spirit in which it could be met
cf. Tert. *de carne Chr.* 5, "salvus sum
si non confundar de domino meo;
'qui mei (inquit) confusus fuerit, confundar et ego eius.' alias non invenio
materias quae me per contemptum
ruboris probent bene impudentem et
feliciter stultum." For the compound
ἐπαισχύνεσθαι cf. Job xxxiv. 19, Ps.
cxviii. (cxix.) 6 (ℵ*A), Isa. i. 29 (A);
it occurs also in the parallel passage
of Lc., and seven times in the Pauline
Epp. and Hebrews. The construction
ἐπαισχ. τινά (τί) is found in Job *l.c.*,
Rom. i. 16, 2 Tim. i. 8, 16, Heb. xi. 16.

ἐν τῇ γενεᾷ ταύτῃ τῇ κτλ.] On γενεά
see viii. 12, note; for μοιχαλίς, Mt.
xii. 39, xvi. 4. The comparison of
Israel to a μοιχαλίς is adopted from
the prophets, esp. Hosea (ii. 2 (4) ff.),
and Ezekiel (xvi. 32 ff.); for ἁμαρτωλός
cf. Isa. i. 4 οὐαὶ ἔθνος ἁμαρτωλόν, but
the word is perhaps used here as
equivalent to πόρνη (Isa. i. 21, Jer. iii.
3). In either case the sin laid to the
charge of the Lord's own generation
is spiritual: their attitude towards
the Christ was evidence of apostasy
from GOD.

καὶ ὁ υἱὸς τ. ἀ. ἐπαισχυνθήσεται]
i.e. 'shall disown him'; cf. Lc. xii. 9
ὁ δὲ ἀρνησάμενος...ἀπαρνηθήσεται, and
the λόγος of 2 Tim. ii. 12, 13 εἰ ἀρνη-
σόμεθα, κἀκεῖνος ἀρνήσεται ἡμᾶς. For
the converse see Lc. xii. 8, Apoc. iii. 8 ff.

ὅταν ἔλθῃ ἐν τῇ δόξῃ κτλ.] The
earliest announcement of a glorious
παρουσία (excepting perhaps Mt. x. 32,
33). The δόξα anticipated is clearly
that of the Divine Presence, not of a
temporal kingdom; there is perhaps
an implied contrast to the δόξα τῶν
βασιλειῶν τοῦ κόσμου (Mt. iv. 8). For
τοῦ πατρὸς αὐτοῦ μετὰ τῶν ἀγγέλων
τῶν ἁγίων (Mt. αὐτοῦ), Lc. substitutes
αὐτοῦ καὶ τοῦ πατρὸς καὶ τῶν ἁγ. ἀγγ.,
perhaps a later form of the tradition
(Dalman, *Worte*, i. p. 158): yet cf.
Mt. xix. 28, xxv. 31, Mc. x. 37,
and esp. Jo. xvii. 5, 22, 24; Bengel:
"gloria...ut unigeniti." For the angelic
manifestation at the παρουσία see Mt.
xiii. 41, xxiv. 31, xxv. 31, Mc. xiii. 27,
2 Thess. i. 7; and for the relation of
the angels of GOD to the Son of Man,
Jo. i. 51, Heb. i. 6, Apoc. i. 1, xxii. 16.

IX. 1. καὶ ἔλεγεν αὐτοῖς κτλ.] A
separate note in Mc. (cf. iv. 21 ff.),
which in Mt. and Lc. has been fused
with the preceding context. The
words were probably spoken to the
Twelve privately after the crowd (viii.
34) had dispersed.

ἀμὴν λέγω ὑμῖν: cf. iii. 28, note.
So Mt.; Lc., λέγω δὲ ὑ. ἀληθῶς.
Jerome: "iurat Christus: debemus
Christo iuranti credere. quod enim
in V.T. dicitur, 'Vivo ego, dicit Dominus,' in N.T. dicitur, 'Amen amen
dico vobis.'"

εἰσίν τινες ὧδε τῶν ἑστηκότων κτλ.]
The statement was very possibly an
answer to some such enquiry, expressed

οὐ μὴ γεύσωνται θανάτου ἕως ἂν ἴδωσιν τὴν βασιλείαν τοῦ θεοῦ ἐληλυθυῖαν ἐν δυνάμει.

§ W⁴ 2   ²§ Καὶ μετὰ ἡμέρας ἓξ παραλαμβάνει ὁ Ἰησοῦς τὸν

1 γευσονται Ε*ΗΚLΝΧΣΦ 69 al^{mu} Or

or anticipated, as we find in xiii. 4 (πότε
ἔσται ταῦτα;). The prospect of seeing
the Son of Man in His glory must
have excited the liveliest hopes; the
Lord at once encourages and guides
this new enthusiasm by a prophecy
which events alone could fully interpret. Τινὲς ὧδε τῶν ἑστ. "some here
of those that stand by"; for this use of
οἱ ἑστ. cf. Mt. xxvi. 73, Jo. iii. 29, Acts
xxii. 25. In Mt. the phrase has been
changed into τ. τῶν ὧδε ἑστ., whilst
for ὧδε Lc. writes αὐτοῦ. For the
phrase γενέσθαι θανάτου cf. Jo. viii. 52
(Westcott), Heb. ii. 9; the phrase is
not found in the O.T., but the Talmud
has the corresponding טַעַם מִיתָה
(Schöttgen, i. p. 148), and the metaphorical use of γενέσθαι occurs in Job
xx. 18, Ps. xxxiii. (xxxiv.) 9, Prov.
xxix. 36 (xxxi. 18). Origen seeks (on
Jo. l. c.) to distinguish between γ.
θανάτου and θεωρεῖν θάνατον (Jo. viii.
51): ἄλλη μέν τις ἂν εἴη ὁρατικὴ τῆς
ψυχῆς δύναμις καὶ θεωρητική, ἄλλη δὲ ἡ
γνωστικὴ καὶ ἀντιληπτικὴ τῆς ποιότητος
κτλ.; but the distinction can hardly
be pressed in a context where the
words are not contrasted. Ἕως ἂν
ἴδωσιν κτλ., Vg. donec videant (cf. vi.
10, xii. 36, and see Burton § 322)
regnum dei veniens in virtute; for
the participle see v. 30, 36, notes; the
perf. implies that the event described
is at once a (potentially) realised fact,
and one which, when realised, will
abide; in one at least of its aspects
the prayer ἐλθάτω ἡ βασιλεία σου will
have been fulfilled.
    The question remains in what sense
these words were accomplished in
the lifetime of any who heard them.
Mt.'s substitution of τὸν υἱὸν τοῦ ἀνθρ.
ἐρχόμενον ἐν τῇ βασιλείᾳ for τὴν
βασιλείαν...ἐν δυνάμει (cf. Lc.) perhaps

indicates that the first generation
looked for a fulfilment in the παρουσία
(cf. 1 Thess. iv. 15). When the event
rendered that view untenable, it was
natural to connect the promise with
the vision which three of the Twelve
were privileged to see a week after
(v. 2 ff.). This interpretation occurs
already in the excerpta Theodoti ap.
Clem. Al. § 4 εἶδον οὖν καὶ ἐκοιμήθησαν
ὅ τε Πέτρος καὶ Ἰάκωβος καὶ Ἰωάννης.
Origen (in Mt. t. xii. 31 ταῦτα ἀνα-
φέρουσί τινες ἐπὶ τὴν μεθ' ἡμέρας ἕξ...
ἀνάβασιν τῶν τριῶν ἀποστόλων κτλ.)
dismisses it in favour of a mystical
sense which is not wholly satisfactory;
but the old Gnostic explanation survives in most of the patristic interpreters (Chrys., Thpht., Euth., etc.).
Many post-Reformation expositors
have thought of the fall of Jerusalem
as the fulfilment of the Lord's words.
A more satisfactory solution is that
which finds it in the coming of the
Spirit and the power manifested in
that triumphant march of the Gospel
through the Empire which was
already assured before the death of
at least some of the original apostolate: cf. Jo. xiv. 18, 19, xvi. 16 ff.,
Acts i. 8, Rom. xv. 17 ff., Col. i. 6.
Yet this view need not exclude a
secondary reference to the anticipation of the Lord's glory which was to
be vouchsafed almost immediately to
some of the Twelve. Mc., by detach-
ing the saying from the previous conversation (καὶ ἔλεγεν), seems to suggest
that it forms a link between the conversation and the event which follows.

    2–8. THE TRANSFIGURATION (Mt.
xvii. 1–8, Lc. ix. 28–36; cf. 2 Pet.
i. 16 ff.).

    2. μετὰ ἡμέρας ἕξ] So Mt.; Lc., μετὰ
τοὺς λόγους τούτους ὡσεὶ ἡμέραι ὀκτώ.

Πέτρον καὶ τὸν Ἰάκωβον καὶ Ἰωάνην, καὶ ἀναφέρει
αὐτοὺς εἰς ὄρος ὑψηλὸν κατ᾽ ἰδίαν μόνους· καὶ μετε-

2 τον Ιακωβον] om τον ΧΓΔ al | Ιωανην ΑΒΝΓΔ al 1071 al^pl] pr τον ℵCDKLUXII
al | αναφερει] αναγει DW^d 2^pe latt | υψηλον]+λιαν ℵ 52 124 altissimum b c ff i r | om
κατ ιδιαν 52 255 the | om μονους min^perpauc syr^sin arm me aeth | μετεμορφωθη]
μεταμορφουνται W^d pr εν τω προσευχεσθαι αυτον (ṽel αυτους) (13 28 69 124) 346 826 828
2^pe Or

The discrepancy is usually explained
by assuming that Lc.'s formula means
'on the octave'—αὐτὴν τὴν ἡμέραν καθ'
ἣν ἐφθέγξατο κἀκείνην καθ' ἣν ἀνήγαγεν
εἶπεν (Victor). But according to the
analogy of viii. 31 Mark's μετὰ ἡμ. ἓξ
should mean 'on the sixth day,' not on
the eighth. Perhaps a truer explanation is to be found in Lc.'s ὡσεί : limits
of time were less distinctly marked in
his later form of the tradition : cf. Lc.
iii. 23, ix. 14, xxii. 59. The Transfiguration is usually commemorated in
both Eastern and Western Calendars
on Aug. 6; the Armenian Calendar
however places it on the 7th Sunday
after Pentecost. No inference as
to the exact day or month can be
drawn from the Gospels; but the
circumstances point to the summer.
On the relation of this event to the
revelations of the preceding chapter
cf. Victor : ἐπεὶ πολλὰ περὶ κινδύνων
διελέχθη καὶ θανάτου καὶ τοῦ πάθους τοῦ
ἑαυτοῦ...δείκνυσιν αὐτοῖς καὶ ἀποκαλύπτει ταύτην [τὴν δόξαν αὐτοῦ], ἵνα μήτε
ἐπὶ τῷ οἰκείῳ θανάτῳ μήτε ἐπὶ τῷ τοῦ
δεσπότου λοιπὸν ἀλγῶσιν.

παραλαμβάνει ὁ Ἰ. τὸν Πέτρον κτλ.]
For παραλαμβάνειν in this sense cf. iv.
36, v. 40, x. 32. The Lord takes with
Him three witnesses (Tert. adv. Marc.
iv. 22 "tres de discentibus arbitros
futurae visionis et vocis assumit...'in
tribus,' inquit, 'testibus stabit omne
verbum'"); for other instances of the
choice of these three see v. 37, xiv.
33. Τὸν Ἰάκ. καὶ Ἰωάν. : the single
article contrasts the two, as brothers,
with Peter; for other groupings see
note on v. 37. Lc.'s order Πέτρον καὶ
Ἰωάνην καὶ Ἰάκωβον is that which the

three held in the light of history :
comp. Acts xii. 2 with Mc. iii. 17, v. 37.

ἀναφέρει αὐτοὺς εἰς ὄρος ὑψηλόν]
For ἀναφέρειν in this sense see 1 Esdr.
ii. 15, Dan. vi. 23, Lc. xxiv. 51. Lc.
ἀνέβη εἰς τὸ ὄρος προσεύξασθαι. The
prevalent tradition, which identifies
the mountain of the Transfiguration
with Tabor, is perhaps based on the
singular saying in the Gospel according to the Hebrews cited by Orig. in
Jo. t. ii. 12, ἄρτι ἔλαβέ με ἡ μήτηρ μου
τὸ ἅγιον πνεῦμα ἐν μιᾷ τῶν τριχῶν μου
καὶ ἀπένεγκέ με εἰς τὸ ὄρος τὸ μέγα
Θαβώρ (cf. Resch, Agrapha, p. 383).
The truth of this tradition is assumed
by Cyril of Jerusalem cat. xii. 16,
and by Jerome epp. 46, 108; and the
festival of the Transfiguration is
known to Eastern Christians as τὸ
Θαβώριον. If the locality was suggested by Ps. lxxxviii. (lxxxix.) 13
(Θαβὼρ καὶ Ἑρμωνιεὶμ τῷ ὀνόματί σου
ἀγαλλιάσονται, cf. Euseb. ap. Corder.
caten. l.c. ἐν τούτοις γὰρ οἶμαι τὰς πα-
ραδόξας τοῦ σωτῆρος ἡμῶν γεγονέναι
μεταμορφώσεις) the choice of Tabor
was unfortunate; this relatively low
rounded knoll (not 1000 feet above the
plain) was crowned by a fortress
(Joseph. B. J. iv. 1, 8), and at the
southern end of Galilee (cf. Ps. l. c.);
whilst Hermon, which rises to the
height of 9200 feet, overlooked Caesarea and offered a perfect solitude
(κατ᾽ ἰδίαν μόνους, cf. iv. 34, vi. 31).
One of its southern spurs became the
ὄρος ἅγιον of the Gospel (2 Pet. i. 18).

μετεμορφώθη ἔμπροσθεν αὐτῶν] Mt.,
Mc.; Lc., ἐγένετο ἐν τῷ προσεύχεσθαι
αὐτὸν (cf. Lc. iii. 21) τὸ εἶδος τοῦ
προσώπου αὐτοῦ ἕτερον. Μεταμορφοῦν

¶ W^d 3 μορφώθη ἔμπροσθεν¶ αὐτῶν. ³καὶ τὰ ἱμάτια αὐτοῦ ἐγένετο στίλβοντα λευκὰ λίαν οἷα γναφεὺς ἐπὶ τῆς 4 γῆς οὐ δύναται οὕτως λευκᾶναι. ⁴καὶ ὤφθη αὐτοῖς

3 εγενοντο ADGKLNVXΓΠ 1 1071 al^nonn | λιαν] om Δ b l r go aeth Or+ως χιων AD(K)NXΓ(Π)ΣΦ min^pl latt^vtplvg syrr^sinpesh me^edd go+ως το φως min^pauc Or | οια γναφευς (κν. Π* min^nonn)...λευκαναι] ως ου δυναται τις λευκαναι επι της γης D b i syr^pesh om X a n syr^sin om ουτως ADXΓΠΦ al min^pl f q vg go

occurs in Ps. xxxiii. (xxxiv.) tit., Symm. (=ἀλλοιοῦν, LXX., cf. Dan. vii. 28 Th. ἡ μορφή μου ἠλλοιώθη), and is adopted by St Paul with an ethical reference (Rom. xii. 2, SH., 2 Cor. iii. 18) and in partial contrast to μετασχηματίζειν. The latter verb might perhaps have been expected here, but "μεταμ. alone is adequate to express the completeness and significance of the change" (Lightfoot, *Philippians*, p. 129). "Was transfigured" (Vg. *transfiguratus est*) has held its place in all the English versions of Mc. from Wycliffe onwards, though 'transformed' is the rendering in Rom., 2 Cor. (Vg. *reformamini, transformamur*). An O.T. archetype of the Transfiguration is to be found in Exod. xxxiv. 29 δεδόξασται ἡ ὄψις τοῦ χρώματος τοῦ προσώπου αὐτοῦ (sc. Μωυσέως) ἐν τῷ λαλεῖν αὐτὸν αὐτῷ (cf. 2 Cor. iii. 7 ff.). Ἔμπροσθεν αὐτῶν: cf. 2 Pet. l.c. ἐπόπται γενηθέντες τῆς ἐκείνου μεγαλειότητος. For a mystical yet practical application see Orig. *in Mt.* t. xii. 36 sq. διαφόρους ἔχει ὁ Λόγος μορφάς, φαινόμενος ἑκάστῳ ὡς συμφέρει τῷ βλέποντι... εἰ δὲ θέλεις τὴν μεταμόρφωσιν τοῦ Ἰησοῦ ἰδεῖν ἔμπροσθεν τῶν ἀναβάντων εἰς τὸ ὑψηλὸν ὄρος κατ᾿ ἰδίαν σὺν αὐτῷ, ἴδε μοι τὸν ἐν τοῖς εὐαγγελίοις Ἰησοῦν...θεολογούμενον...καὶ ἐν τῇ τοῦ θεοῦ μορφῇ κατὰ τὴν γνῶσιν αὐτῶν θεωρούμενον. τούτων γὰρ ἔμπροσθεν μεταμορφοῦται ὁ Ἰησοῦς καὶ οὐδενὶ τῶν κάτω. Cf. *Philoc.* xv. ed. Robinson, p. 83 f., and Jerome *tr. in Mc.*: "vere enim in monte consistimus quando spiritaliter intellegimus." On the Synoptic narrative of the Transfiguration and the signific-

ance of the event see *Biblical and Semitic Studies* (N. Y. 1901), pp. 159—210.

3. καὶ τὰ ἱμάτια αὐτοῦ ἐγένετο στίλβοντα] Cf. Dan. vii. 9 Th. τὸ ἔνδυμα αὐτοῦ ὡσεὶ χιὼν λευκόν, Mt. xxviii. 3, Apoc. i. 13 f., xii. 1. Στίλβειν is used in the LXX. of the flashing of burnished brass or gold (1 Esdr. viii. 56, 2 Esdr. viii. 27) or steel (Nah. iii. 3) or of sunlight (1 Macc. vi. 39): cf. Joseph. *ant.* xix. 8. 2 ὁ ἄργυρος καταυγασθεὶς θαυμασίως ἀπέστιλβε. In the N.T. it does not occur again; Mt.'s equivalent here is ὡς τὸ φῶς, Lc. substitutes ἐξαστράπτων. The reading ὡς χιών (vv. ll.) is attractive, especially in view of the perennial snows on the summit of Hermon; but it is probably borrowed from Dan. *l.c.*, or from Mt. xxviii.

λευκὰ λίαν οἷα γναφεὺς κτλ.] No earthly fuller could have produced such a dazzling whiteness. On γναφεύς see ii. 21, note, and for λευκαίνειν in reference to clothing, cf. Isa. i. 18, Apoc. vii. 14, whence *candidati martyres* in the 'Te Deum.' This is Mc.'s special contribution to the picture; he makes no direct reference to the glory of the Lord's Face (Mt. ἔλαμψεν τὸ πρόσωπον αὐτοῦ ὡς ὁ ἥλιος, cf. Lc.).

4. ὤφθη αὐτοῖς Ἠλείας σὺν Μωυσεῖ] The vision was for the benefit of the disciples (αὐτοῖς, cf. ἔμπρ. αὐτῶν, v. 2). Ὤφθη is used not only for angelic (Jud. vi. 12, Lc. i. 11, xxii. 43) and Divine (Gen. xii. 7, Acts vii. 2, 30) appearances, but in reference to the Lord's self-revelations after the Resurrection (Lc. xxiv. 34, Acts ix. 17). The word does not imply either an

Ἡλείας σὺν Μωυσεῖ, καὶ ἦσαν συνλαλοῦντες τῷ
Ἰησοῦ. ⁵καὶ ἀποκριθεὶς ὁ Πέτρος λέγει τῷ Ἰησοῦ 5
Ῥαββεί, καλόν ἐστιν ἡμᾶς ὧδε εἶναι· καὶ ποιήσωμεν

4 Ἡλίας ℵALNXΓΔΠ | Μωσ. ACEFGHLMUXΓ | ησαν συνλαλουντες] ησ. λαλουντες
cᵃᵉʳ συνελαλουν D 1 2ᴾᵉ a n q   5 ποιησωμεν] (ει) θελεις ποιησω (vel ποιησωμεν) D
(13 28 69) 604 (1071) 2ᴾᵉ alᵖᵉʳᵖᵃᵘᶜ b ff i + ωδε C 2ᴾᵉ c ff

illusion or a dream; the three, acc.
to Lc., had been disposed to slumber,
but were thoroughly roused by the
occurrence and saw everything (δια-
γρηγορήσαντες δὲ εἶδαν τὴν δόξαν αὐτοῦ
καὶ τοὺς δύο ἄνδρας). How the vision
was impressed upon the eyes it is
useless to enquire.

Ἡλείας σὺν Μωυσεῖ] The best supported form of the latter name is
Μωυσῆς (-σέως, -σεῖ, -σέα), but Μωσῆς
and the terminations -σῆ, -σῇ, -σῆν are
also found in good MSS. of the LXX. and
N.T.; see WSchm., pp. 51, 94, WH.,
Notes, p. 165. Mc.'s order seems to
be based upon Mal. iv. 4 (iii. 23) ff.
ἀποστέλλω ὑμῖν Ἡλίαν…μνήσθητε νόμου
Μωσῆ. Elijah was expected and had
been lately in their thoughts (viii.
28, ix. 11); to their surprise he was
accompanied by Moses, for whom
they had not looked (see however
J. Lightfoot on Lc. ix. 30, and
Wünsche, neue Beiträge, p. 394).
The re-arrangement in Mt., Lc. (Μωυσῆς καὶ Ἡλείας, so Syrr.ˢⁱⁿ·ᵖᵉˢʰ· here,
and cf. v. 5) has the appearance of
being an historical correction. The
two men represented the Law and
the Prophets (Tert. adv. Marc. iv.
22, Aug. serm. 232); both were seen
to be in perfect harmony with the
Gospel represented by the Christ;
cf. Victor: δηλοῖ δὲ καὶ συνάφειαν
παλαιᾶς διαθήκης καὶ νέας. Their appearance refuted the charge of law-
breaking brought by the Scribes
against the Master; Thpht.: ὁ μὲν
νομοθετὴς ἦν, ὁ δὲ ζηλωτής· οὐκ ἂν
ὡμίλουν οἱ τοιοῦτοι προφῆται τῷ τὸν
νόμον λύειν δοκοῦντι εἰ μὴ ἤρεσκεν
αὐτοῖς ἃ λέγει.

ἦσαν συνλαλοῦντες τῷ Ἰησοῦ] The

general drift of the conversation was
remembered by Lc.'s informant (? St
John); it was in keeping with Christ's
recent teaching about the Passion:
ἔλεγον τὴν ἔξοδον αὐτοῦ ἣν ἤμελλεν
πληροῦν ἐν Ἱερουσαλήμ. Cf. Jerome,
tr. in Mc. ad l.: "lex enim et prophetae Christi passionem adnuntiant."
Συνλαλεῖν is followed either by the
dat., as in Mc. and Lc. here (cf. Exod.
xxxiv. 35, Lc. xxii. 4), or by a prep.
(μετά τινος, Mt. here, Acts xxv. 12;
πρός τινα, 3 Regn. xii. 14 (A), Lc. iv. 36).

5. ἀποκριθεὶς ὁ Πέτρος κτλ.] Apparently no word had been addressed
to Peter or his companions by any of
the glorified Three; yet Peter felt
that some response was called for.
For a similar use of ἀποκρίνεσθαι cf.
x. 24, xi. 14, xii. 35, xv. 12; Syr.ᵖᵉˢʰ·
and various forms of the O.L. omit it
here. The Synoptists agree in attributing the remark which follows to
Peter; no Apostle found it so hard to
learn the lesson καιρὸς τοῦ σιγᾶν καὶ
καιρὸς τοῦ λαλεῖν. Acc. to Lc. the
occasion was specially inopportune:
ἐγένετο ἐν τῷ διαχωρίζεσθαι αὐτοὺς ἀπ᾽
αὐτοῦ.

Ῥαββεί, καλόν ἐστιν ἡμᾶς ὧδε εἶναι]
The title of Rabbi had been given
to Jesus from the first (Jo. i. 38, 49,
iii. 2), and was probably the usual
name by which both disciples and
others addressed Him (Mt. xxiii. 7, 8,
Jo. vi. 25, xi. 8, Mc. x. 51, xi. 21, xiv.
45). Mt. translates it by κύριε, Lc.
by ἐπιστάτα (cf. Lc. v. 5, viii. 24, 45,
ix. 49, xvii. 13); Mc., after his manner,
retains where he can the Aramaic
word (cf. Dalman, Worte, i. pp. 269,
276). It needed no interpretation for
Gentile readers; yet see the 'Western'

§ Ψ   τρεῖς σκηνάς, σοὶ μίαν §καὶ Μωυσεῖ μίαν καὶ Ἠλείᾳ
6 μίαν. ⁶οὐ γὰρ ᾔδει τί ἀποκριθῇ, ἔκφοβοι γὰρ ἐγέ-
7 νοντο. ⁷καὶ ἐγένετο νεφέλη ἐπισκιάζουσα αὐτοῖς, καὶ

6 αποκριθη] λαλησει (vel -ση) Α(C³)DMNUΓΔΠΣΦ al min^{sat mu} *loqueretur* vel
diceret latt^{exck} (syrr) arm me the aeth | εκφοβοι γαρ εγενοντο ℵBDLΔΨ 33 2^{pe} latt^{vt pl vg}]
ησαν γαρ εκφ. (vel εμφ.) Α(Κ)Ν(U)ΧΓΠΣΦ al min^{pl} f vg

text of x. 51. Καλόν ἐστιν κτλ. "it
is good that we—the Apostles—are
here," implying 'it were good for us to
stay where we are.' Origen : τὸ νομι-
ζόμενον τῷ Πέτρῳ καλὸν οὐ πεποίηκεν ὁ
Ἰησοῦς. Victor : τί οὖν ὁ Πέτρος ὁ
θερμός;...ἐπιθυμεῖ ὁ μέλλων ἀγωνίζεσθαι
ἀναπαύσεως πρὸ τῶν ἀγώνων. εἰ γὰρ
τοῦτο γένοιτο, φησίν, οὐκ ἀναβησόμεθα
εἰς τὰ Ἰεροσόλυμα καὶ οὐκ ἀποθανεῖται.
καὶ ποιήσωμεν τρεῖς σκηνάς] Mt. εἰ
θέλεις, ποιήσω τρ. σκ. Σκηνάς, tents
or booths : Wycliffe, "tabernaclis" =
חֻכֹּת, as in Gen. xxxiii. 17, Lev. xix.
21, 2 Esdr. xviii. 14 ff., Ps. xxx. (xxxi.)
20. The materials would be found in
the brushwood which clothes the spurs
of Hermon—Jerome's question "numquid arbores erant in monte illo ?" is
unnecessary—and the ideal in Peter's
mind seems to be that of the annual
σκηνοπηγία (Lev. xxiii. 40 ff., 2 Esdr.
xviii. 14 ff.) ; he would anticipate it
by a week spent on this leafy height
in the presence of the three greatest
masters of Israel. Σοὶ μίαν καὶ Μ.
μίαν καὶ Ἠλ. μίαν. Jerome : "erras,
Petre...noli tria tabernacula quaerere,
cum unum sit tabernaculum evangelii,
in quo lex et prophetae recapitulanda
sunt" ; "si quando inaequales aequaliter honorantur, maioris iniuria est...
non enim sciebat quid diceret cum
Dominum cum servis aequaliter hon-
oraret." For a practical reflexion on
καλόν ἐστιν κτλ. cf. Bede : "O quanta
felicitas visioni Deitatis inter angel-
orum choros adesse perpetuo, si
tantum transfigurata Christi humani-
tas duorumque societas sanctorum ad
punctum visa delectat."
6. οὐ γὰρ ᾔδει τί ἀποκριθῇ] Vg.

non enim sciebat quid diceret : the
same phrase occurs in connexion with
the Agony (xiv. 40). Lc. substitutes
here μὴ εἰδὼς ὃ λέγει. The speaker
was so dazed by the awfulness of the
vision that he neither knew what to
say (for the subjunctive see WM.,
p. 374), nor yet what he was saying
when he spoke. Ἔκφοβοι γὰρ ἐγένοντο, not Peter only, but the Three,
became panic-stricken, were seized
with extreme alarm ; cf. the abrupt
ending of the Gospel, xvi. 8 ἐφοβοῦντο
γάρ. For ἔκφοβος see Deut. ix. 19,
Heb. xii. 21. Lc. connects this fear
with the next occurrence : ἐφοβήθησαν δὲ ἐν τῷ εἰσελθεῖν αὐτοὺς εἰς τὴν
νεφέλην.

7. καὶ ἐγένετο νεφέλη ἐπισκιάζουσα]
For this use of ἐγένετο cf. i. 4, note.
Each Synoptist adopts a different
construction : Mt. ἰδοὺ ν. ἐπεσκίασεν,
Lc. ἐγένετο ν. καὶ ἐπεσκίαζεν. The
cloud occurs as the symbol of the
Divine Presence in the theophanies
of the Exodus (Exod. xvi. 10, xix. 9,
16, xxiv. 15 f., xxxiii. 9, Lev. xvi. 2,
Num. xi. 25) and at the dedication of
the first Temple (1 Kings viii. 10;
cf. Ps. civ. 3, Nah. i. 3). It was expected to reappear in Messianic times
(2 Macc. ii. 8 ὀφθήσεται ἡ δόξα τοῦ
κυρίου καὶ ἡ νεφέλη, ὡς ἐπὶ Μωσῇ
ἐδηλοῦτο, ὡς καὶ ὁ Σαλωμών κτλ.). In
the N. T. it is connected with the
Transfiguration, the Ascension (Acts
i. 9) and the παρουσία (Mc. xiii. 26
(cf. Dan. vii. 13), xiv. 62, Apoc. i. 7).
The cloud of the Transfiguration was
φωτινή (Mt., cf. Apoc. xiv. 14) : when
the Synoptists add that it "overshadowed" the Apostles, the refer-

ἐγένετο φωνὴ ἐκ τῆς νεφέλης Οὗτός ἐστιν ὁ υἱός §μου,　§ Wᵈ
ὁ ἀγαπητός· ἀκούετε αὐτοῦ. ⁸καὶ ἐξάπινα περιβλεψά- 8
μενοι οὐκέτι οὐδένα εἶδον εἰ μὴ τὸν Ἰησοῦν μόνον
μεθ' ἑαυτῶν.

7 εγενετο 2° אBCLΔΨ] ηλθεν ADNXΓΠΣΦ al minᶠᵉʳᵉᵒᵐⁿ a b f i n ꝗ vg syrˢⁱⁿ om ι
(c) k (syrᵍʷ) pr ιδου 300 1071 ff | νεφελης]+λεγουσα ADLWᵈ⁽ˢⁱᶜ⁾ Ψ ι 28 33 69 124 736
all latt⁽ᵉˣᶜᵏ⁾ syr⁽ᵉˣᶜˢⁱⁿ⁾ armᶻᵒʰ aeth | ακουετε αυτου (αυτου ακ. ΑΝΧΓΠ)] pr ον εξε-
λεξαμην Wᵈ pr εν ω ευδοκησα אª pr εν ω ηυδ. Δ 8 εξαπινα] ευθεως DWᵈ 28 66ᵐᵍ
69 2ᵖᵉ statim a i n r vg om b | ει μη אBDNΣΨ 33 61 3ᵖᵉ alᵖᵃᵘᶜ latt me go aeth] αλλα
ACLXΓΔΠΦ al minᵖᵃᵘᶜ the | om μονον F | μεθ εαυτων post ειδον B 33 c f om Wᵈ
61 a ff l k (post μονον pos אACDLΣΦΨ cet b n vg arm me go aeth)

ence is to Exod. xl. 29 (35) ἐπεσκίαζεν
ἐπ' αὐτὴν (sc. τὴν σκηνήν) ἡ νεφέλη,
where ἐπισκιάζειν=בַּ֫שְׁ, to rest; cf.
Lc. i. 35 δύναμις ὑψίστου ἐπισκιάσει
σοι. The appearance was that of the
Shechinah: οἶμαι δ' ὅτι τὸν Πέτρον
ὁ θεὸς ἀποτρέπων τοῦ ποιῆσαι τρεῖς
σκηνάς...δείκνυσι κρείττονα...καὶ πολλῷ
διαφέρουσαν σκηνήν, τὴν νεφέλην...φω-
τεινὴ γὰρ πατρός, υἱοῦ, καὶ τοῦ ἁγίου
πνεύματος νεφέλη ἐπισκιάζει τοὺς Ἰησοῦ
γνησίους μαθητάς. (Orig. in Mt. t. xii.
42.) Cf. Ephrem, hom. in transf.:
ἔδειξεν αὐτῷ ὅτι οὐ χρῄζει τῆς σκηνῆς
αὐτοῦ· αὐτὸς γὰρ ἦν ὁ ποιήσας τοῖς
πατράσιν αὐτοῦ σκηνὴν νεφέλης ἐν τῇ
ἐρήμῳ...βλέπεις, Σίμων, σκηνὴν ἄνευ
κόπου, σκηνὴν κωλύουσαν καῦμα καὶ μὴ
ἔχουσαν σκότος;

καὶ ἐγένετο φωνὴ ἐκ τ. ν.] See note
on i. 11, and cf. Dalman, Worte, i. pp.
167 f., 226 ff. It is instructive to compare the four reports of this Voice.
Taking Mc.'s as the standard, we
note that, besides variations of order,
Mt. and 2 Peter add ἐν ᾧ (εἰς ὃν ἐγὼ)
εὐδόκησα, 2 Peter omits ἀκούετε αὐτοῦ,
and Lc. substitutes ἐκλελεγμένος for
ἀγαπητός. Ἐν ᾧ εὐδόκησα is probably
from the Voice at the Baptism; Lc.'s
ἐκλελεγμένος (cf. Lc. xxiii. 35, Enoch
xl. 5) is based on Isa. xlii. 1 בְּחִירִי,
LXX. ὁ ἐκλεκτός μου (Mt. xii. 18 ὁ ἀγαπητός μου): on the interchange of these
two titles of the Messiah see Resch,
l.c., p. 164. The essential difference

between this Voice and that which
was heard at the Baptism is the
ἀκούετε αὐτοῦ or αὐτοῦ ἀκ. which the
three Synoptists add here. The words
are from Deut. xviii. 15, 19, and seem
to be suggested by the appearance
of Moses. The Prophet like unto
Moses is identified with the Christ,
the beloved or elect Son; the allegiance due to Moses is now with
Moses' concurrence transferred to
Jesus. Victor: κἂν σταυρωθῆναι βου-
ληθῇ μὴ ἀντιπέσῃς· οὗτος γάρ ἐστι
περὶ οὗ λέγουσιν οὗτοι...δεῖ παθεῖν
...δεῖ ἀναστῆναι. For this use of ἀκούειν (nearly = ὑπακούειν) cf. Mt. xviii.
15 f., Jo. x. 8, 16, xviii. 37. The fears
of the three Apostles, already excited
by the vision (Mc.) and the bright
cloud (Lc.), were intensified by the
Voice (Mt., ἀκούσαντες οἱ μαθηταὶ ἔπεσαν ἐπὶ τὸ πρόσωπον αὐτῶν; cf. Apoc.
i. 17). In 2 Peter it is the Voice of
the Father rather than the visible
splendour of the Transfiguration to
which attention is called (φωνῆς ἐνε-
χθείσης αὐτῷ τοιᾶσδε ὑπὸ τῆς μεγαλο-
πρεποῦς δόξης. It was the first Voice
from heaven which the Apostles had
heard.

8. ἐξάπινα περιβλεψάμενοι κτλ.] The
Lord meanwhile had raised them up
from the ground (Mt.). When they
ventured to lift their eyes again
(Mt. ἐπάραντες δὲ τοὺς ὀφθαλμοὺς αὐτῶν) and to look round them, the

¶ W 9   ⁹ Καὶ καταβαινόντων¶ αὐτῶν ἐκ τοῦ ὄρους διεστείλατο αὐτοῖς ἵνα μηδενὶ ἃ εἶδον διηγήσωνται, εἰ μὴ
10 ὅταν ὁ υἱὸς τοῦ ἀνθρώπου ἐκ νεκρῶν ἀναστῇ.   ¹⁰καὶ
τὸν λόγον ἐκράτησαν, πρὸς ἑαυτοὺς συνζητοῦντες τί

9 εκ BDΨ 33 fˢᶜʳ iˢᶜʳ] απο אACLNXΓΔΠ alᵖˡ | διεστειλατο (-στελλετο CΣΦ 1)]
παρηγγειλεν Δ | ειδοσαν D | διηγησονται ΗΚΝΧΣ minⁿᵒⁿⁿ εξηγησ. 13 28 69 346 604 |
ει μη] εως ου 604 om א* (hab אᵃ)   10 και] οι δε 13 49 (69) 124 346 736 2ᵖᵉ οι
δε και 262 300 | εκρατησαν] ετηρησαν 604 | συνζητουντες] om k | τι εστιν] pr το M

vision was gone; of the august Three
Jesus alone remained (Lc. εὑρέθη Ἰησοῦς μόνος) with them on the Mount.
The Transfiguration was at an end,
and they saw before them only the
familiar form of the Master. The
words of Mc. are perhaps suggested
by Exod. ii. 12 περιβλεψάμενος δὲ ὧδε
καὶ ὧδε οὐχ ὁρᾷ οὐδένα : in the N.T.
the word is elsewhere used only in
reference to Christ (cf. iii. 5, note).
Ἐξάπινα=ἐξαπίνης occurs in the LXX.
about a dozen times, but in the
N. T. only here, the prevalent N. T.
form being ἐξαίφνης, ἐξέφνης (xiii. 36,
Lc.ᵉᵛ·²,ᵃᶜᵗ·²). Jerome brings out the spiritual significance of the disappearance
of Moses and Elijah: "sic vidi Moysen,
sic vidi prophetas, ut de Christo
intelligerem loquentes…ut non perma-
neam in lege et prophetis, sed per legem
et prophetas ad Christum perveniam."

9—13. CONVERSATION ABOUT ELI-
JAH DURING THE DESCENT (Mt. xvii.
9—13, cf. Lc. ix. 36 b).

9. καταβαινόντων αὐτῶν κτλ.] As
they descended from (ἐκ, as if issuing
from) the mountain (probably on the
following morning, cf. Lc. ix. 37) the
Lord enjoined secrecy. For διεστείλατο (Mt. ἐνετείλατο), cf. v. 43, note,
and for διηγεῖσθαι, v. 16. ῍Α εἶδον, Mt.
τὸ ὅραμα (cf. Exod. iii. 3, Num. xii. 6).
The concealment is for a limited
period—εἰ μὴ ὅταν (Mt. ἕως οὗ) ὁ υἱ. τ.
ἀ. ἐκ νεκρῶν ἀναστῇ (Mt. ἐγερθῇ). On
the phrase ἀναστῆναι ἐκ νεκρῶν see WM.,
p. 153 : ἐκ τῶν νεκρῶν occurs only in
Eph. v. 14, Col. i. 18, 1 Thess. i. 10, ἀπὸ
τῶν νεκρῶν in Mt. xiv. 2, xxvii. 64,

xxviii. 7 ; ἐκ νεκρῶν predominates also
in early patristic and symbolic use
(Hahn, Symb., ed. 3, p. 380).

10. τὸν λόγον ἐκράτησαν κτλ.] Vg.
"verbum continuerunt apud se"; Wycliffe, "thei heelden the word at hem
silf." Lc. interprets: καὶ αὐτοὶ ἐσίγησαν
καὶ οὐδενὶ ἀπήγγειλαν ἐν ἐκείναις ταῖς
ἡμέραις οὐδὲν ὧν ἑώρακαν. For κρατεῖν
=σιγᾶν the commentators quote Dan.
v. 12 where Th. renders אֶחֳרִין by
κρατούμενα. But N.T. usage is in
favour of translating ἐκράτησαν 'they
held fast' ("kept" R.V.), retained in
their memory (cf. vii. 3, 4, 8, 2 Thess.
ii. 15, Apoc. ii. 14 ff.). The λόγος in
this case is not the fact of the
Transfiguration, but the Lord's saying, especially what He had said
about rising from the dead ; they discussed this among themselves, not
venturing to ask Him the meaning
(τὸ ἀναστῆναι; Blass, Gr. p. 233 f.).
So little had they realised His earlier
words (viii. 31) ; if their attention was
arrested now, it was because the
Resurrection was made the limit of
their silence. For πρὸς ἑαυτοὺς συνζητεῖν cf. Lc. xxii. 23. Some interpreters (cf. Lat.ᵛᵍ·, Syr.ᵖᵉˢʰ·) connect
πρ. ἑαυτ. with ἐκράτησαν, cf. Euth.:
ἐκράτησαν πρὸς ἑαυτούς, πρὸς μηδένα
ἕτερον τοῦτον [τὸν λόγον] ἐξειπόντες.
But the construction seems to be
without example. Victor is probably
right : τὸν μὲν λόγον ἐκράτησαν, πρὸς
ἑαυτοὺς δὲ συνεζήτουν: so Syr.ˢⁱⁿ·.
During the days that preceded the
Passion the matter was often discussed
among the Three, or perhaps (ix. 32,

ἐστιν᾽⁣ τὸ ἐκ νεκρῶν ἀναστῆναι. ¹¹καὶ ἐπηρώτων αὐτὸν 11 ⁋n
λέγοντες ῞Οτι λέγουσιν οἱ γραμματεῖς ὅτι Ἠλείαν
δεῖ ἐλθεῖν πρῶτον; ¹²ὁ δὲ ἔφη αὐτοῖς Ἠλείας μὲν 12
ἐλθὼν πρῶτον ἀποκαθιστάνει πάντα· καὶ πῶς γέ-

10 το εκ νεκρων αναστηναι אABCLNXΓ(Δ)ΠΣΨ al minᵖˡ (k) q (syrʰᶜˡ) arm me
go aeth] οταν εκ ν. αναστη D 1 13 69 118 124 209 346 a b c f n vg (syrr) tot vers om ff
11 οτι 1°] πως ουν 13 69 124 346 quid ergo a f vg quid utique c om 27 60 me aeth | οι
γραμμ.] pr οι Φαρισαιοι και אL vg (om ABCDNXΓΔΠΣΦΨ al minᵒᵐⁿ ᵛⁱᵈ lattᵛᵗ syrr arm
me go) | om οτι 2° D 1 108 alᵖᵃᵘᶜ b ff i k q   12 εφη] αποκριθεις ειπεν ADNXΓΠΣΦ
al minᵒᵐⁿ ᵛⁱᵈ latt syrrˢⁱⁿ ʰᵉˡ arm go aeth | om μεν DLΨ 128 2ᵖᵉ latt aeth | πρωτος
אᶜDNXΣΨ 1071 pˢᶜʳ om 604 | αποκαθιστανει אᶜ (αποκαταστ. א*) B² (αποκατιστ. B*Ψ)
D (ut א*) LΔ 1 33 118 2ᵖᵉ 8ᵖᵉ] αποκαθιστα א*ΧΓΠΣΦ minᵖˡ αποκαταστησει C latt
arm me aeth | και πως אBCDLNXΓΣΦΨ minᵖˡ latt syrr arm me go] καθως AKMΔΠ
1071 alⁿᵒⁿⁿ syrʰᵉˡ⁽ᵐᵍ⁾ quia k

x. 34) among the Twelve. Συνζητοῦντες
κτλ. is a detail peculiar to Mc.

11. καὶ ἐπηρώτων…῞Οτι λέγουσιν
κτλ.] The train of thought is perhaps
that suggested by Mt. (τί οὖν κτλ.).
The three have been reflecting upon
the vision, and it has revived and
given fresh point to an old perplexity.
How was Elijah's appearance at the
Transfiguration to be reconciled with
the official doctrine of his return? As
Origen observes (in Mt. t. xiii. 1): ἡ
δὲ ἐν τῷ ὄρει ὀπτασία, καθ᾽ ἣν ὁ Ἠλίας
ἐφάνη, ἐδόκει μὴ συνᾴδειν τοῖς εἰρη-
μένοις, ἐπεὶ οὐ πρὸ τοῦ Ἰησοῦ ἔδοξεν
αὐτοῖς ἐληλυθέναι ὁ Ἠλίας ἀλλὰ μετ᾽
αὐτόν. The first ὅτι is interrogative
as in 1 Chron. xvii. 6 (= לָמָּה) and in
Mc. ii. 16 (note), ix. 28, cf. WM., p.
208 n.; in Mc. ll. cc. the R.V. (text)
treats ὅτι as a formula of citation, but
the context and the corresponding
words in Mt. support the other view;
see Field, Notes, p. 33. For the
dictum of the Scribes to which the
question refers see J. Lightfoot on Mt.
xvii.; it was an inference from Mal.
iv. 4 (iii. 23) ἀποστέλλω ὑμῖν Ἠλίαν…
πρὶν ἐλθεῖν ἡμέραν Κυρίου κτλ. In
Justin dial. 49, Trypho urges: πάντες
ἡμεῖς τὸν χριστὸν ἄνθρωπον ἐξ ἀνθρώπων προσδοκῶμεν γενήσεσθαι, καὶ τὸν
Ἠλίαν χρίσαι αὐτὸν ἐλθόντα…ἐκ δὲ τοῦ

μηδὲ Ἠλίαν ἐληλυθέναι οὐδὲ τοῦτον
ἀποφαίνομαι εἶναι. The Rabbinic traditions are collected by Edersheim,
ii. p. 706 ff. Cf. Mc. xv. 35 f.

12. Ἠλείας μὲν ἐλθὼν πρῶτον κτλ.]
'Elijah, it is true, cometh first.' For
this use of μέν with no following δέ
see WM., p. 719 f.; the counterbalanc-
ing clause is left to be supplied from
the question which succeeds. Mc.
substitutes ἀποκαθιστάνει for ἀποκατα-
στήσει (Mt.), converting the prophecy
into a proposition which may or may
not have been realised; 'as a proposition it is correct to say that Elijah's
coming and work precede those of the
Messiah.' Πάντα (Mt., Mc.) extends the
scope of the prophecy (ἀποκ. καρδίαν
πατρὸς πρὸς υἱὸν καὶ καρδίαν ἀνθρώπου πρὸς τὸν πλησίον), including in it
the ultimate purpose of the Messianic
kingdom; the Forerunner restores all
things by initiating the new order out
of which will come in due course a
true ἀποκατάστασις πάντων (Acts iii.
21). WH. print, "but with hesitation," the form ἀποκατιστάνει, on
which see their Notes, p. 168. Ἀπο-
καθιστάνειν = ἀποκαθιστάναι (Job v. 18)
or ἀποκαθιστᾶν (Ps. xv. (xvi.) 5) occurs
again in Acts i. 6 (Blass).

καὶ πῶς γέγραπται κτλ.] Instead of
solving the difficulty the Lord pro-

γράπται ἐπὶ τὸν υἱὸν τοῦ ἀνθρώπου ἵνα πολλὰ πάθη
13 καὶ ἐξουδενηθῇ; ¹³ἀλλὰ λέγω ὑμῖν ὅτι καὶ Ἡλείας
ἐλήλυθεν, καὶ ἐποίησαν αὐτῷ ὅσα ἤθελον, καθὼς
γέγραπται ἐπ᾽ αὐτόν.

12 ινα] pr ουχ syr^sin | εξουδενηθη BDΨ 2^pe] εξουθενηθη Σ(Φ) εξουδενωθη אACXΓΔΠ
69 al^pl   13 εληλυθεν] εληλυθει Δ ηδη ηλθεν C 1 604 al^pauc f i go^vid | και 2°...ηθελον]
et fecit quanta oportebat illum facere k | αυτω] pr εν LΠΨ 28 al^pauc (syrr) | ηθελον
אBC*DLΨ] ηθελησαν AC²ΓΠΣΦ min^omn vid | επ αυτον] εν αυτω Γ επ αυτω 604 περι
αυτου 13 28 69 346 de eo latt^vt pl vg

poses another, in which however the
true solution lies. He anticipates an
objection which would be sure to rise
in the minds of the Three. What then
(καὶ πῶς;) do the Scriptures mean when
they foretell a suffering Messiah? how
can the Passion follow the Restoration? It is unnecessary to suppose
that the order of Mc. has here been
disturbed, the true sequence being 11,
12^b, 12^a, i.e., that καὶ πῶς γέγραπται...
ἐξουδενηθῇ forms part of the disciples'
question. The Apostles would scarcely
have recognised the Scriptural basis
of the Lord's prediction in viii. 31.
Γέγραπται...ἵνα: the telic sense need
not be excluded (WM., p. 577); the
Scripture foretells and by foretelling
determines the issue; γέγρ. ὅτι is the
normal formula when a passage is
merely cited, e.g. vii. 6, xi. 17. Γέγρ.
ἐπί, 'it is written with reference to'
Him (cf. σπλαγχνίζεσθαι ἐπί, vi. 34,
viii. 2); the ordinary construction is
γέγρ. περί with gen. (xiv. 21, Lc. vii.
27, &c.). Καὶ ἐξουδενηθῇ : cf. Ps. xxi.
(xxii.) 6 ἐγὼ δέ εἰμι...ἐξουδένημα λαοῦ.
Isa. liii. 3 Symm. ἐξουδενωμένος καὶ
ἐλάχιστος ἀνδρῶν, Aq. (?) ἐξουδενωμένος, διὸ οὐκ ἐλογισάμεθα αὐτόν. There
are four forms of this verb—ἐξουδε-
νοῦν, -νεῖν, ἐξουθενοῦν, -νεῖν; see W.
Schm. p. 61, and Lob. Phryn. p. 182.
    13. ἀλλὰ λέγω ὑμῖν κτλ.] ' How-
ever (taking up the thread broken by
the last question) I tell you that
Elijah not only must come first, but
has moreover (καὶ) actually come (ἤδη

ἦλθεν, Mt.); and men did not recognise him (Mt.), and did with him (Mt.
ἐν αὐτῷ = בוֹ) as they would.' The
phrase ποιεῖν ὅσα (ἃ) θέλω (τινί), frequently used in the O.T. to represent
irresponsible or arbitrary action (e.g.
3 Regn. ix. 1, x. 13, Ps. cxiii. 11 (cxv.
3), Dan. viii. 4 (Th.), 2 Macc. vii. 16),
points with sufficient distinctness to
the murder of John by Antipas.
    καθὼς γέγραπται ἐπ᾽ αὐτόν] So Mc.
only. In this case Scripture had foretold the future not by prophecy but
by a type. The fate intended for
Elijah (1 Kings xix. 2, 10) had over-
taken John: he had found his Jezebel
in Herodias. Orig. in Mt.: ἄλλος δ᾽
ἂν εἴποι ὅτι τὸ 'ἀλλ᾽ ἐποίησαν' κτλ. οὐκ
ἐπὶ τοὺς γραμματεῖς ἀλλ᾽ ἐπὶ τὴν Ἡρῳδιάδα καὶ τὴν θυγατέρα αὐτῆς καὶ τὸν
Ἡρώδην ἀναφέρεται.
    The identification of Elijah with
John was so evident that, as Mt. adds,
it was understood by the Three at the
time (Mt. τότε συνῆκαν οἱ μαθηταὶ ὅτι
περὶ Ἰωάνου τοῦ βαπτιστοῦ εἶπεν αὐτοῖς.
On another and earlier occasion, according to Mt., it had been made in
express terms (Mt. xi. 14 εἰ θέλετε
δέξασθαι, αὐτός ἐστιν Ἡλείας ὁ μέλλων
ἔρχεσθαι). The reference in Mal. l. c.
to "the great and terrible day of
the Lord" led the ancient Church to
expect an appearance of Elijah himself before the end; cf. Justin dial.
49, Chrys. ad loc., Aug. tract. in Jo.
iv. 5, 6.

14—29. A DEMONIAC BOY SET FREE,

¹⁴§ Καὶ ἐλθόντες πρὸς τοὺς μαθητὰς εἶδαν ὄχλον 14 §1
πολὺν περὶ αὐτοὺς καὶ γραμματεῖς συνζητοῦντας πρὸς
αὐτούς. ¹⁵καὶ εὐθὺς πᾶς ὁ ὄχλος ἰδόντες αὐτὸν ἐξε- 15
θαμβήθησαν, καὶ προστρέχοντες ἠσπάζοντο αὐτόν.

14 ελθοντες...ειδον ℵBᶜᵒʳʳ (ειδαν B*) LΔΨ (ιδον) k arm] ελθων...ειδεν ACDINXΓ
ΠΣΦ al minᵒᵐⁿ ᵛⁱᵈ lattᵛᵗ ᵖˡ ᵛᵍ syrr me go aeth | περι] προς D 28 lattᵛᵗ ᵖˡ | γραμματεις] pr
τους D 1 13 38 69 124 604 2ᵖᵉ arm | προς αυτους] πρ. εαυτους C αυτοις ADNXΓΠΣΦ
minᵖˡ προς αυτον Ψ   15 ιδων...εξεθαμβηθη ΑΝΧΓΠ alᵖˡ a syrr go | προστρεχοντες
(προτρ. AC)] προσχεροντες D gaudentes (b) c d ff i k (cf. Tatᵈⁱᵃᵗ ᵃʳᵃᵇ)

AND THE SEQUEL (Mt. xvii. 14—20, Lc.
ix. 37—43).

14. ἐλθόντες πρὸς τοὺς μαθητάς κτλ.]
Returning to the plain where they
had left the nine (Euth.: μαθητὰς νῦν
τοὺς ἐννέα λέγει), they saw that they
were surrounded by a crowd of people
who were listening to a discussion
which was passing between the disciples and certain scribes (γραμματεῖς,
anarthrous: contrast οἱ γρ. v. 11). Mt.,
who throughout this narrative is much
briefer than Mc., writes simply ἐλθόν-
των πρὸς τὸν ὄχλον and does not seem
to know the cause which had brought
it together. The scribes were probably Rabbis attached to the local
synagogues, but as ready as the rest
of their class to seize an opportunity
of discrediting the disciples of Jesus
before the people. The absence of the
Master and the incapacity of the nine
furnished what they sought. (Victor:
δραξάμενοι γὰρ οἱ γραμματεῖς τῆς τοῦ
σωτῆρος ἀπουσίας περιέλκειν τοὺς μαθητὰς ὑπελάμβανον.) On εἶδαν see WH.,
Notes, p. 164. Ἐλθόντες...εἶδαν points,
as Zahn remarks (Einl. ii. p. 245 f.), to
the narrative having originated with
one of the three, doubtless Peter, who
has told his story in the form Ἐλθόντες...εἴδαμεν.

15. καὶ εὐθὺς πᾶς ὁ ὄχλος κτλ.] As
soon as Jesus came into sight the
Scribes lost the attention of the
crowd. The first feeling was one of
amazement, almost amounting to awe
(cf. i. 27). Both θαμβεῖσθαι and ἐκθαμβεῖσθαι are in the N. T. peculiar to

Mc. (for the latter cf. xiv. 33, xvi. 5,
6); ἔκθαμβος occurs in Acts iii. 10
συνέδραμεν πᾶς ὁ λαὸς πρὸς αὐτούς...
ἔκθαμβοι, a near parallel to the present
passage. Interpreters have found it
difficult to assign a cause for the
θάμβος in this instance. Some (cf.
Thpht., Euth.) have thought of a
radiance from the transfiguration still
brightening the Lord's Face (Euth.
εἰκὸς ἐφέλκεσθαί τινα χάριν ἐκ τῆς μεταμορφώσεως), recalling the glory on the
face of Moses (Exod. xxxiv. 29 f. ὡς δὲ
κατέβαινεν Μωυσῆς ἐκ τοῦ ὄρους...καὶ
ἦν δεδοξασμένη ἡ ὄψις τοῦ χρώματος
τοῦ προσώπου αὐτοῦ). But (1) no hint
of such a phenomenon is dropped by
Mc. in the context, (2) it would have
betrayed what the Lord desired to
keep secret, (3) the result is just the
opposite of that which followed the
appearance of Moses; of Moses it is
said ἐφοβήθησαν ἐγγίσαι αὐτοῦ, of
Jesus, προστρέχοντες ἠσπάζοντο αὐτόν.
The alternative is to fall back upon
Victor's explanation: αἰφνίδιον αὐτὸν
θεασάμενοι...ὁ πᾶς ὄχλος ἐξεθαμβήθη.
The sudden appearance of the Lord
when they thought Him far away on
Hermon amazed and awed them for
the moment. But the next impulse
was to hasten towards Him, drawn
by the irresistible attraction of His
Presence. The remarkable reading
of D and some O.L. texts (προσχαί-
ροντες, gaudentes, cf. Prov. viii. 30, and
see Tatian (Ciasca) ad. loc., 'hastening
for joy') deserves attention, but is
probably an early corruption (χερ for

§ syr^{hier}
¶ the

16 ¹⁶§καὶ ἐπηρώτησεν αὐτοὺς Τί συνζητεῖτε πρὸς αὐτούς ; ¶
17 ¹⁷καὶ ἀπεκρίθη αὐτῷ εἷς ἐκ τοῦ ὄχλου Διδάσκαλε,
ἤνεγκα τὸν υἱόν μου πρός σε, ἔχοντα πνεῦμα ἄλαλον·

16 αυτους אBDLΔΨ 1 28 209 2ᵖᵉ b c ff i k q vg arm me aeth] τους γραμματεις
ΑCΝΧΓΠΣΦ minᵖˡ a syrʳᵖᵉˢʰ ʰᶜˡ go | προς εαυτους א*ᶜ·ᵃΑGΜΓ 33 1071 alⁿᵒⁿⁿ εν υμιν D
lattᵛᵗᵖˡᵛᵍ om k   17 απεκριθη αυτω אBDLΔΨ 28 33 a b (c) k q me] αποκριθεις ειπεν
ΑCΙΝΧΓΠ(ΣΦ) minᵖˡ f vg syrr arm go | αλαλον]+και κοφον (sic) 1071

ρεχ) : for another instance of προστρέχειν in Mc. see x. 17. Ἡσπάζοντο αὐτόν:
the ἀσπασμός of the crowd would be
such as they were accustomed to accord
to their own Rabbis (cf. xii. 38, Mt. xxvi.
49 χαῖρε, ῥαββεί = רַבִּי לְךָ שָׁלוֹם).
16. ἐπηρώτησεν αὐτοὺς κτλ.] The
question shews that the Lord had at
once grasped the situation, and was
prepared to meet it. He addresses
the people, not noticing the Scribes ;
for the moment the crowd had been
with the Scribes in their attack on
the disciples, but already perhaps a
reaction had begun. The Lord took
the matter into His own hands, at
once relieving the disciples and disappointing the Scribes. Τί συνζητεῖτε
is a bona fide request for information;
the human mind of Christ acquires
knowledge by ordinary means ; cf.
viii. 27ᵇ, note. Πρὸς αὐτούς i.e. πρ.
τοὺς μαθητάς (cf. v. 14).
17. καὶ ἀπεκρίθη αὐτῷ εἷς ἐκ τοῦ
ὄχλου] The crowd preserved a discreet silence (cf. v. 34); the answer
came from an individual (εἷς) whose
interest in the matter was deeper than
any συνζήτησις. Lc. like Mc. represents the man as telling his tale from
the heart of the crowd (ἀνὴρ ἀπὸ τοῦ
ὄχλου ἐβόησεν); in Mt. he comes forward
and prostrates himself before Christ
(προσῆλθεν αὐτῷ … γονυπετῶν αὐτόν,
cf. Mc. i. 40). Without undue harmonising we may perhaps accept both
statements ; the man began his tale
in the crowd, but was presently called
or pushed forward by the people to
the feet of Jesus. The words of the

father are reported with more than
usual independence by the three Synoptists. Mt. gives us details which
are not to be gathered from Mc. and
Lc., yet his account is clearly much
compressed; in v. 15 he has brought
together words spoken by the father
at different points in the conversation
(cf. Mc. vv. 17, 22). Lc. again has
some particulars which are not in
Mc., the prayer ἐπιβλέψαι ἐπὶ τὸν
υἱόν μου ὅτι μονογενής μοί ἐστιν, the
statement that the spirit κράζει…καὶ
μόγις ἀποχωρεῖ κτλ. (see however Mc.,
v. 26). But on the whole Mc.'s account
is not only the fullest but has the
most verisimilitude, and Mc. alone has
preserved the undoubtedly original
tradition in vv. 20—24. For details
see the following notes.

διδάσκαλε] So Lc.; Mt. κύριε; both
doubtless = רַבִּי; see note on v. 5, and
cf. iv. 38. The word is here simply
a name of office, for the relation of
teacher and taught did not yet exist
between our Lord and the speaker.
ἤνεγκα τὸν υἱόν μου πρός σε κτλ.]
Ἤνεγκα, the historical aorist, R.V. 'I
brought'; the English idiom prefers
the perfect. The man had brought
his boy that morning under the impression that Jesus was there, and on
discovering that the Lord was on the
mountain had applied to the disciples
(v. 18). This feature of the story disappears in Mt., Lc.: in Mt. the father
says προσήνεγκα αὐτὸν τοῖς μαθηταῖς,
as if the application had been made
to them in the first instance (cf. v. 18).
Ἔχοντα πνεῦμα ἄλαλον: cf. v. 25 τὸ ἄλ.

[18]καὶ ὅπου ἐὰν αὐτὸν καταλάβῃ, ῥήσσει αὐτόν, καὶ 18
ἀφρίζει καὶ τρίζει τοὺς ὀδόντας καὶ ξηραίνεται· καὶ
εἶπα τοῖς μαθηταῖς σου ἵνα αὐτὸ ἐκβάλωσιν, καὶ οὐκ
ἴσχυσαν. [19]§ὁ δὲ ἀποκριθεὶς αὐτοῖς λέγει ˀΩ γενεὰ 19 § ב, the

18 ρησσει] ρασσει D 2^{pe} *applontat* d *allidit* vel *elidit* latt[vt pl vg] *collidit* k | om αυτον 2° ℵD k | ισχυσαν] ηδυνηθησαν 604 + εκβαλειν αυτο D 2^{pe} a b arm 19 αυτοις ℵABDLΔΠ*Ψ min[pl] vg syrr[sin hcl (txt)] arm me go] αυτω C^3(N)ΧΓ$Π^2$ΣΦ min[pl] q syrr[pesh hcl (mg)] om C* 13 40 60 124 (1071) al[pauc] k

καὶ κωφὸν πν.; for the concurrence of the two infirmities see vii. 32 ff., notes. The participle suggests the reason for which the boy had been brought. The effect produced upon the demoniac is transferred in thought to the δαιμόνιον: cf. Lc. xi. 14 δαιμόνιον...κωφόν. Mt. σεληνιάζεται (cf. Mt. iv. 24), perhaps in reference to the periodical return of the attacks: see next verse. The father's trouble was the greater because the boy was μονογενής (Lc., cf. Lc. vii. 12, viii. 42).

18. ὅπου ἐὰν αὐτὸν καταλάβῃ] Lc. πνεῦμα λαμβάνει αὐτόν. The seizures might occur anywhere, and they occurred frequently (πολλάκις Mt., Mc. *v.* 22). Κατάληψις, καταληπτός are used by Galen and Hippocrates in reference to fits, and persons subject to them. The effects of the seizure in the present case are described in detail: first there came a sudden scream (Lc.), then the patient was thrown upon the ground in a strong convulsion. Ῥήσσει, Lc. σπαράσσει, cf. Lc. ix. 42 ἔρρηξεν...καὶ συνεσπάραξεν, where Mc. (*v.* 20) has only συνεσπάραξεν: σπαράσσειν and συνσπαράσσειν describe the actual convulsion (see note on i. 26), ῥήσσειν appears to be used of the preliminary heavy fall (Euth.: ἀντὶ τοῦ 'καταβάλλει εἰς γῆν'). For this sense of the latter word cf. Sap. iv. 19 ῥήξει αὐτοὺς ἀφώνους πρηνεῖς; Kuinoel cites also Artemidorus (i. 62) ῥῆξαι τὸν ἀντίπαλον 'to give one's adversary a throw.' In this use ῥήσσειν approaches to the meaning of ῥάσσειν, ἀράσσειν, and cod. D, with the apparent concurrence of the Latin versions (see vv. ll.), substitutes ῥάσσει for it in this place; cf. the Wycliffite "hurtlith hym doun." After being dashed to the ground the patient (1) foamed at the mouth (ἀφρίζειν, poet. and late Gk., here only in the N.T.), (2) ground his teeth (τρίζειν, another N. T. ἅπ. λεγ., used of any sharp or grating sound, is here interpreted by τοὺς ὀδ., cf. Vg. *stridet dentibus*: the usual phrase is βρύχειν τοὺς ὀδ., LXX., Acts vii. 54, cf. ὁ βρυγμὸς τῶν ὀδόντων, Mt. viii. 12); and (3) appeared to shrivel, or perhaps 'became rigid' (3 Regn. xiii. 4), Vg. *arescit* (for ξηραίν. cf. iii. 1, note). Celsus gives a similar account of the symptoms of catalepsy: "homo subito concidit; ex ore spumae moventur...interdum tamen, cum recens est [morbus], hominem consumit (*med.* iii. 23, *de morbo comitiali* 3).

καὶ εἶπα τοῖς μαθηταῖς σου] Lc. ἐδεήθην τῶν μαθ. σ. The father expected the disciples to possess the Master's authority; possibly he knew that they had formerly used it with success (vi. 13); even the disciples of the Rabbis claimed this power (Lc. xi. 19 οἱ υἱοὶ ὑμῶν...ἐκβάλλουσιν [τὰ δαιμόνια]). It was a genuine surprise to him as well as to them to find that they were powerless in this case (οὐκ ἴσχυσαν, Mt.; Lc. οὐκ ἠδυνήθησαν: cf. v. 3, 4).

19. ὁ δὲ ἀποκριθεὶς αὐτοῖς κτλ.] The Synoptists, in marked contrast to the freedom with which the father's words are treated by them, give the reply

ἄπιστος, ἕως πότε πρὸς ὑμᾶς ἔσομαι; ἕως πότε
20 ἀνέξομαι ὑμῶν; φέρετε αὐτὸν πρός με. ²⁰καὶ ἤνεγκαν
αὐτὸν πρὸς αὐτόν. καὶ ἰδὼν αὐτὸν τὸ πνεῦμα εὐθὺς
συνεσπάραξεν αὐτόν, καὶ πεσὼν ἐπὶ τῆς γῆς ἐκυλίετο
21 ἀφρίζων. ²¹καὶ ἐπηρώτησεν τὸν πατέρα αὐτοῦ Πόσος

19 απιστος (-στε D)]+και διεστραμμενη 13 69 124 al^pauc   20 και ιδων...ευθυς]
ευθυς ουν Ψ om ευθυς D a b ff i q | ιδων] ιδον C²?³? SV min^nonn | συνεσπαραξεν אBCLΔ
33 conturbavit latt)] εσπαραξεν ΑΙΝΧΓΠΣΦΨ min^pl εταραξεν D | αυτον 4°] το παιδιον
13 28 69 346 2^pe puerum a b c ff i k r fu   21 αυτου]+λεγων 13 28 69 124 346 2^pe
a f arm

of Christ in nearly identical terms.
To Mc.'s ὦ γενεά (viii. 12, 38) ἄπιστος
Mt. and Lc. add καὶ διεστραμμένη, a
reminiscence possibly of Deut. xxxii.
5 (cf. Phil. ii. 15). The repeated ἕως
πότε (Mt., Mc.)—the Lord's *quousque
tandem*, cf. Jo. x. 24, Apoc. vi. 10,
and see WM., p. 591—has the ring of
originality rather than Lc.'s ἕως π. καί,
and Mc.'s abrupt φέρετε αὐτὸν πρός με
is superior to Lc.'s softened προσάγαγε
ὧδε τὸν υἱόν σου. But the answer is
substantially the same in all, and it is
the only feature in which they clearly
follow the same tradition. The Lord
replies to all whose feeling the father
had voiced (αὐτοῖς); the reproof ὦ γ.
ἄπιστος is general, perhaps purposely
so, including the Scribes, the people,
and the father (vv. 22, 23) so far as
their faith had been at fault, and
the disciples not the least (v. 29).
Πρὸς ὑμᾶς = μεθ' ὑμῶν (Mt.), cf. vi. 3 :
for ἀνέχεσθαί τινος see WM., p. 253,
and cf. Isa. xlii. 14, xlvi. 4, lxiii. 15;
in the N. T., outside this context, it
appears only in the Pauline Epp. and
Hebrews.

20. ἤνεγκαν αὐτόν] Cf. Lc. προσ-
ερχομένου αὐτοῦ. It is implied (cf.
φέρετε αὐτὸν πρός με, v. 19) that the
boy was not with his father in the
crowd, but in safe keeping not far off.
Ἰδὼν αὐτὸν τὸ πνεῦμα—not, as Winer
(WM., p. 710) and Blass (*Gr.* p. 283),
an anacoluthon (ἰδὼν αὐτὸν [ὁ παῖς], τὸ
πν. κτλ., cf. Syr.^sin.), but a *constructio*

ad sensum—the gender of the noun is
overlooked in view of the personal
action of the spirit; cf. Jo. xvi. 13 f.
ἐκεῖνος, τὸ πνεῦμα...ἐκεῖνος, where if the
masc. pronoun is suggested by ὁ παράκλητος (v. 7), its repetition would be
impossible but for the personal life
implied in τὸ πνεῦμα. Συνεσπάραξεν,
Vg. *conturbavit*; see notes on i. 26, ix.
18 : Lc. ἔρρηξεν αὐτὸν καὶ συνεσπάραξεν.
With the strengthened συνσπαράσσειν,
cf. συνπνίγειν (iv. 7), συντηρεῖν vi. 20,
συνπληροῦν Lc. viii. 23, συναρπάζειν Lc.
viii. 29, συνκαλύπτειν Lc. xii. 2. Ἐκυλίετο is ἅπ. λεγ. in the N. T., but
κυλισμός occurs in 2 Pet. ii. 22; the
verb, which is a later form of κυλίνδειν, is used freely in the LXX. (e.g.
κυλίειν λίθον, Jos. x. 18, 1 Regn. xiv.
33, Prov. xxvi. 27, κ. ἄρτον, Jud. vii.
13 (A); cf. also 4 Regn. ix. 33 (of
Jezebel's fall), Amos ii. 13 (of the
wheels of a cart). For ἀφρίζειν see
ix. 18.

21. καὶ ἐπηρώτησεν τὸν πατέρα κτλ.]
Mc. only (to 25ᵃ). Πόσος χρόνος ἐστὶν
ὡς... 'how long is it that (since)...?' Cf.
Gal. iv. 1 ἐφ' ὅσον χρόνον, Soph. *O. T.*
558 ΟΙ. πόσον τιν' ἤδη δῆθ' ὁ Λάιος
χρόνον | ΚΡ. δέδρακε ποῖον ἔργον; Ὡς
is used elliptically for ἀφ' οὗ; cf. vv.ll.
Γέγονεν, not ἐγένετο—the disorder was
manifestly still upon him. Ἐκ παιδιόθεν : 'from a little boy,' 'from a
mere child'; i.e. he was a παιδίον
when it first took him : his age at
the time is not mentioned, but he was

χρόνος ἐστὶν ὡς τοῦτο γέγονεν αὐτῷ; ὁ δὲ εἶπεν Ἐκ
παιδιόθεν· ²²καὶ πολλάκις καὶ εἰς πῦρ αὐτὸν ἔβαλεν 22
καὶ εἰς ὕδατα, ἵνα ἀπολέσῃ αὐτόν. ἀλλ᾽ εἴ τι δύνῃ,
βοήθησον ἡμῖν, σπλαγχνισθεὶς ἐφ᾽ ἡμᾶς.¶ ²³ὁ δὲ 23 ¶ I
'Ιησοῦς εἶπεν αὐτῷ Τὸ Εἰ δύνῃ, πάντα δυνατὰ τῷ

21 ως ℵ*AC³DXΓΠΦ al minᵖˡ go] εως B εξ ου ℵᶜ·ᵃC*LΔΨ 33 2ᵖᵉ (ex quo latt
similiter syrr arm me al) αφ ου ΝΣ 13 40 124 346 armᵛⁱᵈ | εκ παιδιοθεν
ℵBCGILNΔΣΦΨ 1 33 118 209 alᵖᵃᵘᵉ] παιδιοθεν A(X)ΓΠ minᵖˡ εκ παιδος D 2ᵖᵉ
22 πυρ] pr το AEFGMVΓΠ²Φ minˢᵃᵗ ᵐᵘ | δυνη ℵBDILΔΨ 1 28 118 209] δυνασαι
ACNXΓΠΣΦ minᵖˡ | ημιν]+κυριε DG (1) (262) 2ᵖᵉ a b g i q arm (idem post δυνη add ι
post ημας vero 262 1071)   23 om το DKNUΠΦ 13 28 69 124 131 1071 2ᵖᵉ alⁿᵒⁿⁿ
hab ℵABCLXΓΔΣΨ minᵖˡ | δυνη ℵ*BDNΔΣ 1 28 118 209] δυνασαι ℵᶜ·ᵃACLXΓΠΦΨ
al minᵖˡ+πιστευσαι AC³D(EHM)NX(Γ)ΠΦΨ minᵖˡ lattᵉˣᶜ ᵏ* syrr go Chrys (om πιστ.
ℵBC*LΔ 1 118 209 244 k* arm me aeth)

still a παῖς (Lc. ix. 42). The Attic
phrase is ἐκ παιδίου (cf. D) but from
Xenophon downwards παιδιόθεν takes
its place : the pleonastic ἐκ παιδιόθεν
is a survival of Homeric usage (cf.
e.g. Il. viii. 34, ἐξ οὐρανόθεν) which is
censured by the Atticists (Lob. Phryn.
p. 93), but found a place in late Gk. :
cf. v. 6 (ἀπὸ μακρόθεν), and WM.,
p. 752 f., Blass, Gr. p. 59.

22. καὶ πολλάκις καὶ εἰς πῦρ κτλ.]
The seizures were often accompanied
by a tendency to suicidal mania. Mt.
has simply (xvii. 15) πίπτει, but Mc.'s
αὐτὸν ἔβαλεν...ἵνα ἀπολέσῃ αὐτόν shews
that in the view of the father these
frequent mishaps were not accidental.
Καί...καί : the spirit had tried both
means of destruction. Πῦρ, ὕδατα
(מַיִם) ; Mt., τὸ πῦρ, τὸ ὕδωρ. Thpht.
ῥίπτεται δέ τις ὑπὸ δαίμονος εἰς πῦρ,
τὸ τοῦ θυμοῦ καὶ τὸ τῆς ἐπιθυμίας·
καὶ εἰς ὕδωρ, τὸ τῶν βιωτικῶν πραγμάτων κλυδώνιον. Εἴ τι δύνῃ : δύνασθαι
is used absolutely as in Lc. xii. 26,
2 Cor. xiii. 8; cf. WM., p. 743. The
man's faith had been shaken by the
failure of the disciples; contrast the
leper's ἐὰν θέλῃς, δύνασαι (i. 40). Possibly no miracle had been wrought in
this neighbourhood as yet, so that in
the struggle to believe the father had
no experience to assist him. The form

δύνῃ is poetical and late (WM., p. 90);
on its occurrence in the N. T. side by
side with δύνασαι cf. WH., Notes, p.
168, WSchm., p. 123 n. For σπλαγχνισθείς see note on i. 41 : ἡμῖν, ἡμᾶς,
i.e. both father and son.

23. τὸ Εἰ δύνῃ, πάντα δυνατὰ τῷ
πιστεύοντι] The Lord repeats the
father's words and places them in
contrast with the spiritual facts which
he had yet to learn: 'if thou canst:
for one who believes all things are
possible': i.e. it is for thee rather
than for Me to decide whether this
thing can be done; it can be if thou
believest (cf. xi. 23 f.). Thpht.: οὐ τῇ
οἰκείᾳ δυνάμει ἀλλὰ τῇ ἐκείνου πίστει
ἀνατίθησι τὴν θεραπείαν. Cf. Iren. iv.
37. 5 "omnia talia suae potestatis
secundum fidem ostendunt hominem."
Τὸ 'εἰ δύνῃ' is a nominativus abso-
lutus (WM., p. 226, cf. 135); for the
clause preceded by an article and
treated as a noun, cf. Rom. viii. 26
with SH.'s note, and Blass, Gr. p. 158.

From its extreme compression the
sentence has given trouble to scribes
and commentators. The Western
text followed by a majority of the
MSS. reads ὁ δὲ Ἰησοῦς εἶπεν Εἰ δύνῃ
(δύνασαι) πιστεῦσαι, πάντα δυνατὰ τῷ
πιστεύοντι : si potes credere, omnia
possibilia credenti. Attempts have

24 πιστεύοντι. ²⁴εὐθὺς κράξας ὁ πατὴρ τοῦ παιδίου
25 ἔλεγεν Πιστεύω· βοήθει μου τῇ ἀπιστίᾳ. ²⁵ἰδὼν δὲ
ὁ Ἰησοῦς ὅτι ἐπισυντρέχει ὄχλος ἐπετίμησεν τῷ
πνεύματι τῷ ἀκαθάρτῳ λέγων αὐτῷ Τὸ ἄλαλον καὶ
κωφὸν πνεῦμα, ἐγὼ ἐπιτάσσω σοι, ἔξελθε ἐξ αὐτοῦ

24 ευθυς] και ℵ*C* και ευθυς Ψ | ελεγεν]+μετα δακρυων A²C³DNXΓΠΣΦ al minᵖˡ
a b c f i q vg syrrᵖᵉˢʰ ʰᶜˡ go (om ℵA*BC*LΔΨ 28 604 k syrˢⁱⁿ arm me aeth) | πιστευω]
+κυριε C²NXΓΔΠΣ al minᶠᵉʳᵉ ᵒᵐⁿ a b c f (q) vg syrrᵍʷ ˢⁱⁿ Chrys   25 ιδων δε] και
οτε ειδεν D latt⁽ᵛⁱᵈ⁾ | οχλος] pr ο ℵALMSXΔΠΦΨ 28 33 69 124 1071 2ᵖᵉ al arm (om
BCDNΓΣ minᵖˡ) | το αλ. και κωφ. πν.] το πν. το αλ. και κωφ. AC³NXΓΠΣΦ al minᵖˡ |
om εγω ℵ* 33 | εξ] απ C*Δ minᵖˡ lattᵛⁱᵈ

been made, but with poor success, to
extort a better sense from this reading (e.g. εἰ δύνασαι, πίστευσαι), or
to amend it (εἰ δ., πίστευε). Some
who accept the shorter text place a
mark of interrogation after δύνῃ—
"sayest thou 'If thou canst'?" But
there is nothing in the context to
suggest a question, and the English
Revisers of 1881 rightly render " If
thou canst! all things are possible to
him that believeth," without marginal
variant.

24. εὐθὺς κράξας κτλ.] The father
instantly responds to the demand for
fuller trust on his part; his strength
of feeling shews itself in a cry as
piercing as that of the demoniac
son (Lc. ix. 39). He recognises that
the help he needs is in the first
instance help for himself and not for
his boy (βοήθει μου τῇ ἀπ., cf. v. 22
βοήθησον ἡμῖν). He believes (πιστεύω), but his faith is defective, and
its defect needs the Master's succour
(for this use of βοηθεῖν cf. 2 Cor. vi. 2,
Heb. ii. 18, iv. 16). Wycliffe : "Lord,
I bileue ; help thou myn unbileueful-
nesse." Bede : "uno eodemque tempore is qui necdum perfecte crediderat
simul et credebat et incredulus erat."
Victor : ἀρξάμενος οὖν πιστεύειν ἐδέετο
τοῦ σωτῆρος διὰ τῆς αὐτοῦ δυνάμεως
προσθεῖναι τὸ λοιπόν. Ἀπιστία is perhaps suggested by γενεὰ ἄπιστος (v. 19):
β. μου τῇ ἀπ. 'help my faith where

it is ready to fail,' nearly = μοι τῷ
ἀπίστῳ. With μου τῇ ἀπ. cf. v. 30
μου τῶν ἱματίων, Rom. xi. 14 μου
τὴν σάρκα : the position is perhaps
slightly emphatic, though WM. (p. 193)
appears to doubt this. Ἀπιστία, cf.
note on vi. 6. The reading μετὰ
δακρύων (' Western' and Syrian, WH.,
Notes, p. 25) is at least an interesting
gloss; for the phrase cf. Acts xx. 19,
31, Heb. v. 7, xii. 17.

25. ἰδὼν δὲ ὁ Ἰησοῦς κτλ.] The conversation then was not in the presence
of the crowd, but was interrupted by
its arrival. The Lord had probably
retired with the father and the boy
to a distance from the ὄχλος, but the
cries of both brought them running
to the spot and privacy became impossible. This has been overlooked
in the text of ℵA, where ὁ ὄχλος refers
to vv. 15, 17. Ἐπισυντρέχειν is apparently ἄπ. λεγ.; cf. however ἐπισυνάγειν i. 33; the LXX. has also
ἐπισυνεῖναι, ἐπισυνέχειν, ἐπισυνιστάναι,
and ἐπισυστρέφειν. Συντρέχειν is used
by Mc. in vi. 33: the double compound
perhaps calls attention to the return
of the crowd (cf. προστρέχοντες, v. 15)
after it had been for the time dispersed. There is no indication in
Mc. of the habit of using otiose compounds (WM., p. 25 f.) which disfigures
much of the later Gk.

ἐπετίμησεν τῷ πνεύματι κτλ.] Here
Mt. and Lc. rejoin Mc. Mc. however

καὶ μηκέτι εἰσελθῆς εἰς αὐτόν. ²⁶καὶ κράξας καὶ 26
πολλὰ σπαράξας ἐξῆλθεν· καὶ ἐγένετο ὡσεὶ νεκρός,
ὥστε τοὺς πολλοὺς λέγειν ὅτι Ἀπέθανεν. ²⁷ὁ δὲ 27
Ἰησοῦς κρατήσας τῆς χειρὸς αὐτοῦ ἤγειρεν αὐτόν, καὶ
ἀνέστη. ²⁸καὶ εἰσελθόντος αὐτοῦ εἰς οἶκον, οἱ μα- 28

26 om πολλα k | κραξας, σπαραξας ℵBCDL(Δ)Ψ] κραξαν, σπαραξαν AC³NXΓΠΣΦ
minᵖˡ | σπαραξας]+αυτον ℵ*ᶜ·ᵃ? AC³NXΓΠ al | εξηλθεν]+απ αυτου D lattᵉˣᶜ𐞥 | τους
πολλους] om τους CDNXΓΠΣΦ minᵖˡ go   27 της χειρος αυτου ℵBDLΔΨ 1 13 28 69
2ᵖᵉ alᵖᵃᵘᶜ] αυτον της χ. (αυτου) A(C*)C³NXΓΠΣΦ minᵖˡ | om και ανεστη k   28 εισελ-
θοντος αυτου ℵBCDLΔ 1 13 28 69 118 209 604 1071 latt] εισελθοντα αυτον ANXΓΠΦ
al minᵖˡ ελθοντα αυτον Σ | οικον] pr τον AM minᵖᵃᵘᶜ

alone gives the words of the rebuke
(for ἐπιτιμᾶν see note on i. 25). Τὸ
ἄλαλον καὶ κωφὸν πνεῦμα, a nom. used
as a vocative : cf. τὸ κοράσιον, v. 41,
and v. 19 supra, and see WM., p. 327,
Blass, Gr. p. 86. Κωφόν is a new
feature in the case (πν. ἄλαλον, v. 17),
but see note on vii. 32, and cf. Ps.
xxxvii. (xxxviii.) 14 with Ps. xxxviii.
(xxxix.) 3. Ἐγὼ ἐπιτάσσω σοι, 'I
enjoin thee' (Euth. : ἐγὼ...ὃν οἶδας):
since this spirit had refused to acknowledge the authority of the disciples, the Master emphasises His
personal claim to obedience. For
ἐπιτάσσειν cf. i. 27 ; for the emphatic
ἐγώ see x. 38 f., xiv. 58, and the Fourth
Gospel passim. Ἔξελθε ἐξ αὐτοῦ
ordinarily sufficed (i. 25, v. 8) ; in this
desperate case of periodical seizures
it was necessary to add καὶ μηκέτι
εἰσελθῆς. For the spiritual analogy
see Lc. xi. 24 ff.

26. κράξας καὶ πολλὰ σπαράξας κτλ.]
For the moment the only result was
a fresh seizure (see on v. 20) ; the
spirit wreaked its revenge on its
victim even in the act of quitting
its hold upon him. For the masc.
participles cf. v. 20 ἰδὼν...τὸ πνεῦμα.
The convulsions were violent and prolonged (πολλά, cf. iii. 12, note), and when
they ceased, the sufferer's strength
was exhausted ; a collapse followed ;
he lay motionless and pallid as a
corpse. For ἐξῆλθεν see note on v. 29 ;

ἐγένετο ὡσεὶ νεκρός : contrast Apoc.
i. 17. There was a general cry among
the crowd (τοὺς πολλοὺς λέγειν), 'He
is dead.' Οἱ πολλοί, cf. vi. 2, xii. 37 ;
Gregory, prolegg. p. 128 : "Marcus
ponit ὁ πολύς et οἱ πολλοί ubi πολύς
et πολλοί satis videntur esse." For
the aor. ἀπέθανον see Burton, § 47,
and cf. v. 35, 39, Jo. viii. 52. This
incident again is peculiar to Mc.;
Mt. has merely ἐξῆλθεν ἀπ᾽ αὐτοῦ τὸ
δαιμόνιον, Lc. ἰάσατο τὸν παῖδα.

27. κρατήσας τῆς χειρὸς αὐτοῦ] Cf.
i. 31, v. 41. The Lord seems to have
offered this help only where great
exhaustion had preceded ; cf. Acts
ix. 41, and contrast ii. 11 f. Ἀνέστη :
he rose from the ground where he
had been rolling (v. 20), and afterwards
lay prostrate. Lc. helps us to complete the picture : ἀπέδωκεν αὐτὸν τῷ
πατρὶ αὐτοῦ (cf. Lc. vii. 15), ἐξεπλήσσοντο δὲ πάντες ἐπὶ τῇ μεγαλειότητι τοῦ
θεοῦ (cf. Mc. i. 27, ii. 12, vii. 37). Mt.
adds—probably in reference to the
Lord's μηκέτι εἰσελθῆς—καὶ ἐθεραπεύθη
ὁ παῖς ἀπὸ τῆς ὥρας ἐκείνης (cf. Mt. ix.
22, xv. 28). The epileptic fits did not
return.

28. εἰσελθόντος αὐτοῦ εἰς οἶκον]
On the vv. ll. and construction see
Blass, Gr. p. 251 f. The Lord went
indoors, into the lodging where the
party were housed (εἰς οἶκον, cf. iii.
20, vii. 17), to escape from the enthusiasm of the crowd, and because

θηταὶ αὐτοῦ κατ᾽ ἰδίαν ἐπηρώτων αὐτόν ῞Οτι ἡμεῖς
29 οὐκ ἠδυνήθημεν ἐκβαλεῖν αὐτό; ²⁹καὶ εἶπεν αὐτοῖς
Τοῦτο τὸ γένος ἐν οὐδενὶ δύναται ἐξελθεῖν εἰ μὴ ἐν
προσευχῇ.
30   ³⁰Κἀκεῖθεν ἐξελθόντες [παρ]επορεύοντο διὰ τῆς

28 κατ ιδιαν post ειϲελθ. αυτου Ψ | οτι ℵBCLNXΓΔΣΨ al minᵖˡ] δια τι ADKΠΦ
736 1071 alⁿᵒⁿⁿ οτι διατι U 131 238 alᵖᵃᵘᶜ τι οτι minᵖᵃᵘᶜ   29 εν προσευχη]+και (τη)
νηστεια ℵᶜ·ᵇADLNXΓ(Δ)ΠΣΦΨ minᵒᵐⁿ ᵛⁱᵈ lattᵉˣᶜ ᵏ syrr⁽ˢⁱⁿ ᵖᵉˢʰ⁾ ʰᵉˡ (arm) (aeth) (om κ.
νηστ. ℵ*ᶜ·ᵃB k)   30 και εκειθεν ACNXΓΠ alᵖˡ | παρεπορευοντο ℵAB³CLNXΓΔΣΦ
(παρευοντο) Ψ al minᵒᵐⁿ ᵛⁱᵈ b d (ff) i k vg syrr arm me] επορευοντο B*D a c f go aeth

on such occasions further teaching
was impossible. He and the disciples
were now in privacy (κατ᾽ ἰδίαν Mt.,
Mc.), and the nine took occasion
to seek an explanation of their
failure (ἐπηρώτων, Mt. προσελθόντες
...εἶπαν), approaching Him probably
(as was their wont on these occasions) by one of their number
(? Andrew). ῞Οτι=διὰ τί, Mt. (Euth. :
τὸ ὅτι ἀντὶ τοῦ διὰ τί· οὕτω γὰρ εἶπεν ὁ
Ματθαῖος : cf. Blass, Gr. p. 176); see
note on v. 11 supra, and for the
circumstances of the failure, v. 18.

29. τοῦτο τὸ γένος κτλ.] Either
'this class of δαιμόνια,' or 'this kind'
generally, i.e. the δαιμόνια; cf. Thpht.:
ἢ τὸ τῶν σεληνιαζομένων ἢ ἁπλῶς πᾶν
τὸ τῶν δαιμόνων γένος. Γένος is a
nationality (vii. 26, Acts iv. 36), a
family (Acts iv. 6, vii. 13, xiii. 26,
xviii. 2, 24), or a species (Mt. xiii. 47),
or class of things (1 Cor. xii. 10).
Hence it is used of the spiritual
affinity which associates moral beings
of the same order or type of character (1 Pet. ii. 9). Similarly St Paul
speaks of πατριαί in heaven as well as
on earth (Eph. iii. 15). Ἐν οὐδενὶ δύναται ἐξελθεῖν, 'can take its departure
(i.e. be cast out, ἐξελθεῖν being in
such contexts practically the pass. of
ἐκβαλεῖν) in the strength of no power
(not as Euth. = οὐδενὶ ἑτέρῳ τρόπῳ) but
one,' i.e. in the strength of (believing)
prayer (xi. 23, 24); cf. Clem. Al. ecl.
proph. 15. The Lord seizes on the

essential weakness of their case. They
had trusted to the quasi-magical power
with which they thought themselves
invested; there had been on their
part no preparation of heart and
spirit. Spirits of such malignity were
quick to discern the lack of moral
power and would yield to no other.
To ἐν προσευχῇ the 'Western' and
'Syrian' text adds καὶ (τῇ) νηστείᾳ, but
the time for fasting was not yet (ii. 19);
comp. the similar gloss 1 Cor. vii. 5.
Mt., who omits this answer, has the
more obvious Διὰ τὴν ὀλιγοπιστίαν
ὑμῶν, to which he adds the sayings
about the grain of mustard seed and
the removal of mountains which are
found in other contexts (Lc. xvii. 6,
Mt. xxi. 21). Tatian combines Mt.'s
answer with Mc.'s, placing Mt.'s first,
and connecting Mc.'s with it by a γάρ.

30—32. The Passion again foretold (Mt. xvii. 22, 23; Lc. ix. 43—45).
30. κἀκεῖθεν ἐξελθόντες κτλ.] The
Lord and the Twelve now leave their
retreat at the foot of Hermon and
travel southwards. Their way to the
North had perhaps led them through
Gaulanitis and Ituraea (cf. viii. 22, 27,
note), but they return διὰ τῆς Γαλειλαίας
i.e. probably along the West bank of
the Jordan. Mt.'s συστρεφομένων ἐν
τῇ Γαλειλαίᾳ suggests that they broke
up into small parties which mustered
at certain points in the route (for
συστρέφεσθαι cf. 2 Regn. xv. 31, 4 Regn.
ix. 14, x. 9 etc.), the purpose being

Γαλειλαίας, καὶ οὐκ ἤθελεν ἵνα τις γνοῖ. ³¹ἐδίδασκεν 31
γὰρ τοὺς μαθητὰς αὐτοῦ καὶ ἔλεγεν αὐτοῖς ὅτι Ὁ υἱὸς
τοῦ ἀνθρώπου παραδίδοται εἰς χεῖρας ἀνθρώπων, καὶ
ἀποκτενοῦσιν⁋ αὐτόν, καὶ ἀποκτανθεὶς μετὰ τρεῖς ⁋ 33

30 γνοι ℵBCDL] γνω ΑΝΧΓΔΣΦΨ al min^{omn vid}   31 om αυτοις B (26^{ev} k) |
παραδοθησεται 69 604 arm^{vid} | ανθρωπων] ανθρωπου D ανομων Ψ^{salt*} + αμαρτωλων 604 |
αποκτεινουσιν D | om αποκτανθεις D min^{perp} a c k me | μετα τρεις ημερας ℵBC*D
LΔΨ b c i _post tertium diem_ a k q _in tres dies_ d syr^{hcl (mg)} me] τη τριτη ημερα
ΑCSNΧΓΠΣΦ al min^{omn vid} f r vg syrr^{sin pesh hcl (txt)} arm go aeth

perhaps to avoid attracting notice
(Mc. οὐκ ἤθελεν ἵνα τις γνοῖ): cf. vii. 24
and on γνοῖ = γνῶ, v. 43, note. The
reading παρεπορεύοντο, which is well
supported and perhaps genuine, conveys the idea that the transit was
made without unnecessary breaks:
"_obiter profecti sunt_...intenti viae
conficiendae, non invisendis hospitibus
aut instituendae plebi" (Fritzsche).

31. ἐδίδασκεν γάρ κτλ.] Reasons
of the Lord's desire to escape recognition. He was now fully occupied
with the training of the Twelve
(Latham, _Pastor past._ p. 351). A
journey through Upper Galilee, in
which He could attach Himself now to
one party of two or four Apostles and
now to another, afforded an opportunity of quiet teaching which might
never return. The substance of this
reiterated teaching (ἐδίδασκεν...ἔλε-
γεν) is the same as that of the first
prediction of the Passion near Caesarea (viii. 31), with one new element
—a reference to the Betrayal. Lc.
points out the occasion of this fresh
prediction of the Passion: ἐξεπλήσσοντο δὲ πάντες ἐπὶ τῇ μεγαλειότητι τοῦ
θεοῦ· πάντων δὲ θαυμαζόντων ἐπὶ πᾶσιν
οἷς ἐποίει εἶπεν κτλ. There was reason
to fear that this new outburst of enthusiasm would lead them to forget
His warning, or even frustrate His
purpose.

ὁ υἱὸς τοῦ ἀνθρώπου] Notwithstanding Peter's confession and the
revelation of His glory on Mt. Hermon
the Lord retains the old title which

asserts the truth of His humanity and
His liability to suffering.

παραδίδοται εἰς χεῖρας ἀνθρώπων]
Mt., Lc., μέλλει...παραδίδοσθαι. The
event is regarded as imminent and
indeed in process of accomplishment;
cf. Mt. xxvi. 2 μετὰ δύο ἡμέρας...παρα-
δίδοται: Bengel: "iam id agitur ut
tradatur"; for this use of the present
see WM., p. 331 ff., Burton, § 15, who
calls it (but inexactly) "the present
for the future." The instrument of
the betrayal—ὁ παραδιδούς, xiv. 42—
was in the company, and the Lord
could see the purpose already lying
as an undeveloped thought in his
heart (Jo. vi. 70 f.). On παραδιδόναι
see i. 14, note. Προδιδόναι _tradere_
does not occur in the N. T., but its
meaning is more or less imported by
the circumstances into παραδιδόναι,
which even in class. Gk. is patient of
a bad sense. Yet, as Origen (_in Mt._)
reminds us, παραδιδόναι may be used
with quite another purpose; in the
eternal counsels of God, the Father
delivered up the Son (Rom. viii. 32),
and the Son delivered up Himself
(Gal. ii. 20). Εἰς χεῖρας ἀνθρ. is less
precise than the corresponding words
in viii. 31 (ὑπὸ τῶν πρεσβυτέρων καὶ
τῶν ἀρχιερέων καὶ τῶν γραμματέων).
But on the other hand it is wider, and
prepares the Twelve for the further
revelation of x. 34 (παραδώσουσιν αὐτὸν
τοῖς ἔθνεσιν: cf. xiv. 41, εἰς τ. χ. τ.
ἁμαρτωλῶν. On the form ἀποκτανθῆναι,
and on μετὰ τρεῖς ἡμέρας = τῇ τρίτῃ
ἡμέρᾳ see viii. 31, note.

32 ἡμέρας ἀναστήσεται. ³²οἱ δὲ ἠγνόουν τὸ ῥῆμα, καὶ
ἐφοβοῦντο αὐτὸν ἐπερωτῆσαι.

33 ³³Καὶ ἦλθον εἰς Καφαρναούμ. καὶ ἐν τῇ οἰκίᾳ
γενόμενος ἐπηρώτα αὐτούς Τί ἐν τῇ ὁδῷ διελο-
34 γίζεσθε ; ³⁴οἱ δὲ ἐσιώπων,· πρὸς ἀλλήλους γὰρ

31 αναστησεται] εγερθησεται 1 13 69 346 26ᵉᵛ alᵖᵃᵘᶜ   33 ηλθον ℵBD (-θοσαν)
1 118 209 2ᵖᵉ alᵖᵃᵘᶜ a b c k vg syrᵖᵉˢʰ] ηλθεν ACLXΓΠΣΦΨ al minᵖˡ f q syrʳˢⁱⁿ ʰᶜˡ arm
me go aeth εισηλθεν 604 + o ι̅ς̅ 1071 | διελογιζεσθε] pr (vel add) προς εαυτους ANXΓΔ
ΠΣΦ minᵒᵐⁿ ᵛⁱᵈ f syrr arm go aeth   34 εσιωπησαν Ψ

32. οἱ δὲ ἠγνόουν τὸ ῥῆμα] They
remained in ignorance of the import
of the Lord's words, especially of the
saying about the Resurrection (cf. ix.
10), for of the Passion they had some
dim and sorrowful conception (Mt., καὶ
ἐλυπήθησαν σφόδρα). Lc. explains that
there was a Divine purpose in their
temporary ignorance : ἦν παρακεκαλυμ-
μένον ἀπ᾽ αὐτῶν ἵνα μὴ αἴσθωνται αὐτό.
They shrank from seeking enlighten-
ment (ἐφοβοῦντο αὐτὸν ἐπερωτῆσαι,
Mc.; similarly Lc.), partly from a natural
reluctance to enter upon a painful
subject, partly perhaps from their
recollection of the censure incurred
by Peter (viii. 33). There is weight
also in Bengel's remark : " de quavis
re facilius interrogant Iesum quam
de ipso; sic fit inter familiares."
Ἀγνοεῖν in the N. T. is chiefly a
Pauline word (Mc.¹, Lc. ᵉᵛ.¹,ᵃᶜᵗ.², Paul.²⁵,
Heb.¹, 2 Pet.¹). Ῥῆμα, a common word
in the LXX. and fairly frequent in the
N.T., occurs in Mc. only here and
xiv. 72.

33—37. RETURN TO CAPERNAUM.
QUESTION OF PRECEDENCE (Mt. xviii.
1—5, Lc. ix. 46—48).

33. καὶ ἦλθον εἰς Καφαρναούμ] Capernaum (i. 21, ii. 1, Jo. vi. 59) had
ceased to be the centre of the Ministry; but it was a convenient terminus to the northern journey, and
starting point for a fresh field of
work in the south; and Simon's or
Levi's house (i. 29, ii. 15) afforded a
shelter there. The Galilean Ministry

ends as it began at Capernaum. No
subsequent visit to the town is mentioned in the Gospels, although after
the Resurrection the Lord was seen
by the shore of the lake (Jo. xxi. 1 ff.)
and among the hills (Mt. xxviii. 16).

καὶ ἐν τῇ οἰκίᾳ γενόμενος κτλ.] When
they had reached the privacy of the
house the Lord questioned the Twelve
on a discussion He had overheard
during the journey (ἐν τῇ ὁδῷ, Vg.
in via, cf. viii. 3, 27). Evidently they
had not thought Him to be within
earshot (cf. x. 32 ἦσαν δὲ ἐν τῇ ὁδῷ...
καὶ ἦν προάγων); but He had detected
angry voices and knew the cause (Lc.
εἰδὼς τὸν διαλογισμὸν τῆς καρδίας αὐτῶν).

34. οἱ δὲ ἐσιώπων] Cf. iii. 4, Lc.
xx. 26. Euth.: ἐσιώπων αἰσχυνθέντες,
ὡς ἤδη καταγνωσθέντες. Ἐσιώπων...
διελέχθησαν : the discussion was at an
end and the silence which followed
the Lord's question continued until it
was broken by His words in v. 35.
Διελέχθησαν...τίς μείζων, 'they had
discussed (Burton, § 48) the question
who is greater (than the rest)'; Lc.,
more fully, τὸ τίς ἂν εἴη μείζων αὐτῶν;
Mt., who represents the Twelve as
themselves propounding the question
to Jesus, writes Τίς ἄρα μείζων ἐστὶν
ἐν τῇ βασιλείᾳ τῶν οὐρανῶν; The comparative has practically the force of a
superlative, see Blass, Gr. pp. 33, 141 f.,
and on the other hand WM., p. 305;
cf. Mt. xi. 11, xxiii. 11, 1 Cor. xiii. 13.
The question τίς μείζων was probably
suggested by the selection of the

διελέχθησαν ἐν τῇ ὁδῷ τίς μείζων. ³⁵καὶ καθίσας 35
ἐφώνησεν τοὺς δώδεκα καὶ λέγει αὐτοῖς Εἴ τις θέλει
πρῶτος εἶναι, ἔσται πάντων ἔσχατος καὶ πάντων
διάκονος. ³⁶καὶ λαβὼν παιδίον ἔστησεν αὐτὸ ἐν 36
μέσῳ αὐτῶν καὶ ἐναγκαλισάμενος αὐτὸ εἶπεν αὐτοῖς

34 διελεχθησαν] διηνεχθησαν 1 604 2ᵖᵉ | om εν τη οδω ADΔ a b f i q go | τις μειζων]
+εστιν ℵ τις μ. γενηται αυτων D 2ᵖᵉ τις αυτ. μ. ειη 13 69 346 τις ειη μ. minᵖᵃᵘᶜ τις
η μ. 1071   35 om και λεγει αυτοις...διακονος D k | εστω Δ | διακονος] δουλος M*
36 παιδιον] pr το D | αναγκαλισαμενος C(DL)

Three for the mysterious ascent of Hermon, and the prominence of Peter among the three (cf. Bede). Origen: ὅτι μὲν γὰρ οὐκ ἔστιν ἰσότης τῶν ἀξιουμένων τῆς βασιλείας τῶν οὐρανῶν κατειλήφεισαν (comparing Mt. v. 29). See Dalman, *Worte*, i. p. 92 f.

35. καὶ καθίσας ἐφώνησεν κτλ.] The Lord assumes the attitude of the Teacher (Mt. v. 1, xiii. 1, Lc. v. 3, 'Jo.' viii. 2), and calls the disciples (ἐφώνησεν, cf. x. 49, Tob. v. 9, not προσεκαλέσατο, cf. iii. 13, 23, vi. 7, viii. 1, 34)—all the Twelve (τοὺς δώδεκα), for the lesson He is about to give is needed by them all and by the whole future Church. How important it is appears from its repetition towards the end of the Lord's life (Lc. xxii. 24 ff., Mt. xxiii. 8 ff.; for other parallels see x. 42 ff., and the saying in x. 31). The intention of the Master is not to enact "a penal provision against seeking the mastery," but (cf. Lc. ix. 48) to point out the way to true greatness (Latham, *Pastor past.* p. 355). The spirit of service is the passport to eminence in the Kingdom of God, for it is the spirit of the Master Who Himself became διάκονος πάντων. The διάκονος is properly the attendant at table (i. 31, Lc. xxii. 27, Jo. ii. 9, xii. 2); for the later Christian history of the word see Hort, *Ecclesia*, p. 202 ff. A lower depth is sounded and a higher dignity offered in the πάντων δοῦλος of x. 44, q. v. With πρῶτος...ἔσχατος cf. x. 31. In

quite another sense the Lord is at once ὁ πρῶτος and ὁ ἔσχατος (Apoc. i. 17, ii. 6, xxii. 13).

36. λαβὼν παιδίον ἔστησεν αὐτό κτλ. The new rule of life just enunciated is illustrated by a visible example. A child is playing near (? Peter's: see note on i. 30; on the late tradition that the child was Ignatius of Antioch—ὁ θεοφόρος read as ὁ θεόφορος—see Lightfoot, *Ignatius*, i. p. 27), and the Lord calls it to Him (προσκαλεσάμενος, Mt.), places it by His side in the middle of the group (λαβὼν...ἔστησεν αὐτὸ ἐν μέσῳ αὐτῶν, Lc. ἐπιλαβόμενος...ἔστ. αὐτ. παρ' ἑαυτῷ), and then takes it into His arms (ἐναγκαλισάμενος αὐτό, Mc. only), cf. x. 16; the verb, which belongs to the later Gk., occurs in Prov. vi. 10, xxiv. 48 (33) and the noun ἐναγκάλισμα in 4 Macc. xiii. 21 (ℵA, but the text is possibly corrupt); Lc. (ii. 28) prefers the paraphrase δέχεσθαι εἰς τὰς ἀγκάλας. The act was accompanied by words of which Mt. preserves the fullest account. According to Mt. the Lord began, Ἀμὴν λέγω ὑμῖν Ἐὰν μὴ στραφῆτε καὶ γένησθε ὡς τὰ παιδία κτλ. (xviii. 3, 4). The words carry with them the assurance of their genuineness, answering the question τίς μείζων ('the most childlike and trustful, the least self-conscious and self-sufficient') and preparing for the next sentence (ὃς ἂν ἐν τῶν τοιούτων παιδίων κτλ.), the substance of which is common to the three Synoptists.

37 37 ʻῸς ἂν ἓν τῶν τοιούτων παιδίων δέξηται ἐπὶ τῷ
ὀνόματί μου, ἐμὲ δέχεται· καὶ ὃς ἂν ἐμὲ δέχηται, οὐκ
ἐμὲ δέχεται ἀλλὰ τὸν ἀποστείλαντά με.

38 38 ʼῈφη αὐτῷ ὁ Ἰωάνης Διδάσκαλε, εἴδαμέν τινα ἐν

37 ἓν] om DXΓ 124 alᵖᵃᵘᶜ εκ 13 69 346 2ᵖᵉ ex b c ff i q *unum ex* a f vg similiter
syrʰᶜˡ me go | των τοιουτων παιδ. ABDLNXΓΠΣΦ minᵖˡ latt Or] των παιδιων τουτων
ℵCΔ minᵖᵃᵘᶜ *talem puerum* armᵛⁱᵈ (cf. k syrˢⁱⁿ) | om εμε 1° ...δεχηται k om και ος αν
εμε δεχ. syrˢⁱⁿ | δεχηται (ℵ)BLΨ minᵖᵃᵘᶜ] δεξηται ACDNXΓΔΠΣΦ al minᵖˡ   38 εφη
ℵBΔΨ 1071 syrᵖᵉˢʰ me] απεκριθη (δε) A(D)NXΓΠΣΦ αποκριθεις δε εφη C και αποκριθεις
...ειπεν (λεγει) 69 (604) (b i k r vg syrʳˢⁱⁿʰᶜˡʰⁱᵉʳ arm) | ο Ιωανης] om ο ADNΓΠ al
+λεγων ALNXΓΠ alᵖˡ | εν] επι U minᵖᵃᵘᶜ om AXΓΠΦ al minᵖˡ

37. ὃς ἂν ἓν τῶν τοιούτων παιδίων
κτλ.] Mt. ἓν παιδίον τοιοῦτο, Lc. τοῦτο
τὸ παιδίον, i.e. this child regarded as
the representative of its class, or
rather of the class of disciples whom
it symbolises (see WM., p. 138). Cf.
Orig. *in Mt.*: ἐὰν οὖν, ὅπερ παρὰ τὴν
ἡλικίαν πάσχει τὰ παιδία...ἀπὸ λόγου, ὁ
τοῦ Ἰησοῦ μαθητὴς ἐταπείνωσεν ἑαυτόν...
μάλιστα δὲ τοὺς ὡς ὁ Λόγος ἀπέδειξε
στραφέντας...ἀποδεκτέον καὶ μιμητέον
κτλ. Chrys. παιδίον γὰρ ἐνταῦθα τοὺς
οὕτως ἀφελεῖς φησὶ καὶ ταπεινοὺς καὶ
ἀπερριμμένους παρὰ τοῖς πολλοῖς. He
who recognises and welcomes such,
because he sees in them the type of
character which Christ Himself approved and exhibited (Mt. xi. 29, Phil.
ii. 5 ff.), recognises and welcomes Christ
Himself—is a true and loyal disciple.
On δέχεσθαι see vi. 11, note, and
Dalman, *Worte*, i. p. 101 f.; ἐπὶ τῷ
ὀνόματί μου (cf. ix. 38 f., xiii. 6, and
see 1 Regn. xxv. 5, Gal. iv. 14, Col. iv.
10, *Didache* 12 πᾶς δὲ ὁ ἐρχόμενος
ἐν ὀνόματι Κυρίου δεχθήτω), 'on the
ground of My Name,' i.e. the act
being based upon a recognition of his
connexion with Me, cf. WM., p. 490.
Other nearly equivalent phrases are
διὰ τὸ ὄνομα (Jo. xv. 21, Mc. xiii. 13,
Apoc. ii. 3), ὑπὲρ τοῦ ὀνόματος (Acts v.
40, ix. 16, xv. 26, 3 Jo. 7); cf. ἐν τῷ
ὀνόματι (Mc. ix. 38, 1 Pet. iv. 14), διὰ
τοῦ ὀνόματος (Acts iv. 30), εἰς τὸ ὄνομα
(Acts viii. 16). On the use of ὄνομα
in the papyri cf. Deissmann, *B. St.*,

pp. 146 f., 196 f. For the absolute use
of τὸ ὄνομα see Bp Westcott's note on
3 Jo. 7, and Lightfoot on Ign. *Eph.* 3.
Δέξηται...δέχηται: the particular act
of recognition is evidence of a state of
heart to which Christ Himself is a
welcome guest.

καὶ ὃς ἂν ἐμὲ δέχηται κτλ.] The action
passes into a region beyond that of
the visible order; to receive a lowly
brother in Christ's Name is to receive
Christ, and to receive Christ is to
receive the Eternal Father in Whose
Name He came. Cf. Mt. x. 40, Lc. x.
16, Jo. xii. 44, 45. Ὁ ἀποστείλας με
(ὁ πέμψας με Jo. *l.c.*, see Bp Westcott,
Add. Note on Jo. xx. 21), sc. ὁ
πατήρ, Jo. v. 36, vi. 57, x. 36, xvii. 18,
xx. 21 ; the Son is ὁ ἀπόστολος...τῆς
ὁμολογίας ἡμῶν (Heb. iii. 1). Other
references to the Mission of the Son
in the Synoptists will be found in Mt.
x. 40, xv. 24, Mc. i. 38 (note), xiii. 6,
Lc. iv. 18, 43, ix. 48, x. 16; the idea is
in the background of the whole Ministry, which rests on ἐξουσία, and supports itself by faith and prayer. On
δέχεσθαι see vi. 11, note. Οὐκ...ἀλλά,
not so much...as : Blass, *Gr.* p. 267,
n. 2.

38—40. THE USE OF THE NAME
BY A NON-DISCIPLE (Lc. ix. 49—50).

38. ἔφη αὐτῷ ὁ Ἰωάνης] This is the
only remark attributed by the Synoptists specifically to St John (cf. however
x. 35 Ἰάκωβος καὶ Ἰωάνης, xiii. 3 Πέτρος
καὶ Ἰάκωβος καὶ Ἰωάνης καὶ Ἀνδρέας),

τῷ ὀνόματί σου ἐκβάλλοντα δαιμόνια, καὶ ἐκωλύομεν
αὐτόν, ὅτι οὐκ ἠκολούθει ἡμῖν. ³⁹ ὁ δὲ Ἰησοῦς εἶπεν Μὴ 39
κωλύετε αὐτόν· οὐδεὶς γάρ ἐστιν ὃς ποιήσει δύναμιν
ἐπὶ τῷ ὀνόματί μου καὶ δυνήσεται ταχὺ κακολογῆσαί
με· ⁴⁰ ὃς γὰρ οὐκ ἔστιν καθ᾽ ἡμῶν ὑπὲρ ἡμῶν ἐστιν.⁑ 40 ⁑ syrʰⁱᵉʳ

38 και εκωλυομεν (εκωλυσαμεν ACNXΓΠ al minᵖˡ)] pr os ουκ ακολουθει ημω
A(D)NXΓΠΣ al minᵖˡ a b c ff i k l q r vg syrʰᶜˡ go arm (om אBCLΔΨ 1071 minᵖᵃᵘᶜ
f syrʳˢⁱⁿᵖᵉˢʰ me) | om οτι ουκ ηκ. (אBD åκ. rell) ημιν DX 1 13 28 69 604 alⁿᵒⁿⁿ
lattᵛᵗ⁽ᵉˣᶜ ᶠ⁾ ᵛᵍ arm   39 Ιησους] αποκριθεις D 2ᵖᵉ a b ff i k | ουδεις] ου Γ | ποιησει]
ποιει Δ arm ποιησας 1071 pr ου Ψ | επι] εν 13 69 346 alᵖᵃᵘᶜ | om ταχυ F* 1 28 209
a b c d ff i k rᵛⁱᵈ syrˢⁱⁿ arm   40 ημων bis אBCΔΨ 1 13 69 209 alᵐᵘ⁽ᵛⁱᵈ⁾ k syrˢⁱⁿ
arm] υμων᾽ bis ADNΓΠΣΦ minˢᵃᵗ ᵐᵘ a b c f ff i q vg syrʳᵖᵉˢʰ ʰᶜˡ ⁽ᵐᵍ⁾

and it creates an impression of candour
and conscientiousness not unworthy
of the future θεολόγος. His words are
in some measure a response (ἀποκριθείς, Lc.; cf. Mc. ix. 5) to the teaching
just received. The phrase ἐπὶ τῷ
ὀνόματί μου had put him in mind of a
recent occurrence, and he takes the
opportunity of laying the facts before
the Master. He and one or more of
the other disciples, probably during
their recent journey through northern
Galilee, had prohibited a non-disciple
from using the Master's Name for the
purpose of exorcising demoniacs.
Ought they rather to have welcomed
him as a brother? For the use of the
Lord's Name by non-Christian ex-
orcists cf. Acts xix. 13 (where see
Blass's note). Ἐκωλύομεν, the 'conative' imperf., Burton § 23; for κωλύειν
cf. x. 14, 1 Cor. xiv. 39. Οὐκ ἠκολούθει
ἡμῖν (Lc. μεθ᾽ ἡμῶν) is a frank confession
of jealousy for the honour of the Apostolate. In the light of the Lord's
words the action had began to wear a
different aspect to the mind of John.

39. μὴ κωλύετε αὐτόν κτλ.] The
sincerity of the speaker saves him
from censure; the Lord merely corrects the error. He does not say
δέχεσθε αὐτόν, for the man's motive
did not appear; but the attitude of
His disciples towards such an one
should have been at least neutral.

Οὐδεὶς γάρ ἐστιν κτλ. (Mc. only):
whatever his intention, the man is for
the time (οὐ...ταχύ) practically committed to a course of action which at
least cannot be unfriendly. For δύναμιν ποιεῖν see vi. 5, and with οὐ
δύνασθαι used in reference to a moral
impossibility cf. Mt. vi. 24, Heb. vi. 4 f.
To work a miracle in Christ's name
was not a test of moral character or
proof of spiritual affinity to Him (Mt.
vii. 22, Acts xix. 13), as childlike trust
and humility must always be; but it
was a safeguard against open and
immediate (οὐ ταχύ) hostility (for κακολογεῖν cf. vii. 10, Acts xix. 9), and
might be the beginning of better
things: Euth. συνεχώρει δὲ καὶ τούτοις
θαυματουργεῖν ἅμα μὲν εἰς βεβαίωσιν
τοῦ κηρύγματος, ἅμα δὲ καὶ εἰς βελτίωσιν
αὐτῶν δὴ τῶν θαυματουργούντων. Bede's
use of this incident is interesting:
"itaque in haereticis ac male catholicis
non sacramenta communia...sed divi-
siones pacis detestari et prohibere
debemus."

The Lord's answer finds a partial
parallel in Num. xi. 28 f.

40. ὃς γὰρ οὐκ ἔστιν καθ᾽ ἡμῶν κτλ.]
The indicative expresses the assumption that such a person exists (Blass,
Gr. p. 217). Lc. gives ὑμῶν bis. An
opposite rule appears to be laid down
in Mt. xii. 30=Lc. xi. 23, ὁ μὴ ὢν μετ᾽
ἐμοῦ κατ᾽ ἐμοῦ ἐστιν, καὶ ὁ μὴ συνάγων

41 ^{41} Ὃς γὰρ ἂν ποτίσῃ ὑμᾶς ποτήριον ὕδατος ἐν
ὀνόματι ὅτι Χριστοῦ ἐστε, ἀμὴν λέγω ὑμῖν ὅτι
42 οὐ μὴ ἀπολέσῃ τὸν μισθὸν αὐτοῦ. ^{42} καὶ ὃς ἂν

41 αν ποτιση] ποτισει Ψ | εν ονοματι ℵABC*LNXΓΠΣΦΨ min^{pl} syr^{sin}] εν τω ον.
DHMΔ min^{mu} εν τω ον. τουτω arm^{vid} + μου ℵ*C³DXΓΔΠ² al min^{pl} latt syr$^{hcl (mg) hier}$ me
go aeth (om μου ℵ$^{c.a}$ABC*KLNΠ* 1 1071 al^{pauc} syrr$^{sin pesh hcl (txt)}$ arm) | om οτι 2°
AC³NXΓΠ al^{pl} | απολεσει DE min^{nonn}

μετ' ἐμοῦ σκορπίζει. But the two rules
are in fact complementary (Gould); in
the latter words the Lord refers to
the relations of a man's inner life to
Himself, whilst in this context He
deals with outward conduct. Upon
conduct, in our partial ignorance, the
most hopeful construction should be
put; the man who is not a declared
enemy of the Christian brotherhood
may be provisionally regarded as a
friend. In the present case, indeed,
there was presumptive evidence of
something better than neutrality, since
the person in question had used the
Name of Christ.

41—50. THE TEACHING RESUMED:
ON THE CONSEQUENCES OF CONDUCT
TOWARDS BRETHREN IN CHRIST (Mt.
xviii. 6—9; cf. Mt. x. 42, Lc. xvii. 1,
2, xiv. 34).

41. ὃς γὰρ ἂν ποτίσῃ ὑμᾶς κτλ.]
The thread of the teaching, broken off
at v. 38 by John's question, is now
resumed. The spiritual significance
of help offered to a brother for
Christ's sake is independent of the
material value of the gift. A cup of
water may be judged worthy of an
eternal recompense. Victor: τοῦτο
λέγει διὰ τοὺς ἔνδειαν ἴσως προφασιζο-
μένους. For ποτίζειν τινά τι cf. Gen.
xxiv. 17 πότισόν με μικρὸν ὕδωρ,
1 Regn. xxx. 11, Job xxii. 7, Jer. xvi.
7 οὐ ποτιοῦσιν αὐτὸν ποτήριον. The
ποτήριον is the ordinary cup used both
for wine and water: cf. vii. 4, Lc. xi.
39, 1 Cor. xi. 25. Ὕδατος, Mt. (x. 42),
ψυχροῦ.

ἐν ὀνόματι ὅτι Χριστοῦ ἐστε] The Vg.
renders in nomine meo, quia Christi

estis; and so Wycliffe, Rheims, A.V.,
whilst Tindale has "for my name's
sake." But μου has no right to a place
in the text (see vv. ll.); and ἐν ὀνόματι
ὅτι κτλ. is nearly equivalent to διὰ τὸ
Χριστοῦ εἶναι, on the score of your
being Christ's—a use of ὀνόματι not unknown to class. Greek, cf. e.g. Thuc. iv.
60. Χριστοῦ εἶναι is a Pauline phrase,
Rom. viii. 9, 1 Cor. i. 12, iii. 23, 2 Cor.
x. 7; the anarthrous Χριστός is unique
in sayings attributed to our Lord by
the Synoptists; cf. Dalman, Worte,
i. p. 239 n. Mt.'s εἰς ὄνομα μαθητοῦ
is perhaps nearer to the original:
cf. εἰς ὄνομα προφήτου, δικαίου Mt. x.
41; "a later editor's hand is very
probably to be seen in" the words
which now stand here in Mc. (Hawkins,
Hor. Syn., p. 122). Οὐ μὴ ἀπολέσῃ
τὸν μισθὸν αὐτοῦ presents the recompense of eternity in a form appreciable
by the Jewish mind, cf. Mt. v. 12, vi.
1 f., xx. 1 ff., 1 Cor. iii. 8 ff., Apoc. xxii.
12; for the nature and conditions of
the μισθός see Mt. xxv. 34 ff. κληρονο-
μήσατε τὴν ἡτοιμασμένην ὑμῖν βασιλείαν
...ἐδίψησα καὶ ἐποτίσατέ με...ἐφ' ὅσον
ἐποιήσατε ἑνὶ τούτων τῶν ἀδελφῶν μου
τῶν ἐλαχίστων, ἐμοὶ ἐποιήσατε.

42. καὶ ὃς ἂν σκανδαλίσῃ κτλ.] The
converse is equally true. A wrong
done to a disciple however insignificant
will bring incalculable evil upon the
evil-doer. On σκανδαλίζειν see iv. 17,
note. It is possible to be an innocent
cause of stumbling; the Lord Himself
was such, cf. vi. 3, 1 Cor. i. 23, 1 Pet.
ii. 8. But He was careful to abstain
from placing unnecessary stumbling-
blocks in men's way (see Mt. xvii. 27,

σκανδαλίσῃ ἕνα τῶν μικρῶν τούτων τῶν πιστευόντων, καλόν ἐστιν αὐτῷ μᾶλλον εἰ περίκειται μύλος
ὀνικὸς περὶ τὸν τράχηλον αὐτοῦ, καὶ βέβληται εἰς

42 σκανδαλιζῇ D | των μικρων τουτων אABC*,²DLM²NΔΦ 1 604 1071 al^paᵘᶜ
b c i ff q vg syr^pesh hcl arm me go aeth] om τουτων EFGHKM*SUVXΓΠΣΨ min^pl
f των μ. υμων (ut vid) a k | πιστευοντων]+εις εμε ABC²LNXΓΠΣΦΨ min^pl c f q vg
syr^sin pesh hcl arm go al (om εις εμε אΔ b ff i k*) πιστιν εχοντων C*vid D a d | περιε-
κειτο D | μυλος ονικος אBCDLΔΨ min^nonn mola asinaria vel asinaricia latt^vt (exc q) vg
syr^sin pesh arm go aeth] λιθος μυλικος ΑΝΧΓΠΣΦ min^pl lapis molaris q syr^hel me^vid
μυλωνικος λιθος vel λ. μυλων 13 28 69 258 346 2^pe | περι] επι D min^perpauc a d f i vg |
εβληθη D

ἵνα δὲ μὴ σκανδαλίσωμεν αὐτούς), and
it is this scrupulous regard for the
infirmities of others that He enjoins
(cf. Rom. xiv. 21, 1 Cor. viii. 13, 2 Cor.
xi. 29), and the wilful or heedless
creation of σκάνδαλα that He condemns. Τῶν πιστευόντων at length
shews how τὰ τοιαῦτα παιδία (v. 37),
are to be understood : the little ones
(Zach. xiii. 7, usually in contrast with
οἱ μεγάλοι Apoc. xi. 18, xiii. 16, xix. 5,
18, xx. 12, or in the phrase ἀπὸ μικροῦ
ἕως μεγάλου 1 Regn. v. 9 etc., Heb.
viii. 11) who believe, i.e. the lowliest,
whether in their own eyes or in the
eyes of men, in the outward order of
the Church or even in the spiritual
order, cf. Mt. xi. 11, Lc. vii. 28, ὁ
μικρότερος ἐν τῇ βασιλείᾳ τοῦ οὐρανοῦ
(τοῦ θεοῦ) : the reference is here
especially to the last type of μικροί,
St Paul's ἀδύνατοι (Rom. xv. 1) or
ἀσθενεῖς, ἀσθενοῦντες τῇ πίστει (Rom.
xiv. 1, 1 Cor. viii. 10 ff., ix. 22).
καλόν ἐστιν αὐτῷ μᾶλλον] Mt. συμφέρει αὐτῷ ἵνα, Lc. (xvii. 2) λυσιτελεῖ
αὐτῷ εἰ. For καλὸν...μᾶλλον, 'it were
good...by comparison,' cf. Acts xx.
35, Gal. iv. 27 (Isa. liv. 1 LXX.); and
for καλὸν...εἰ, Mt. xxvi. 24; for ἐστίν
we should expect ἦν, as in Mt. l.c.,
but the present brings the alternative
before the reader more vividly : the
man is seen at the moment when the
weight is placed round his neck (περίκειται), and then lying at the bottom
of the sea (βέβληται) ; even under

these circumstances he is in a better
case than if he had caused the feeblest
brother to stumble; cf. Rom. xiv. 13 ff.,
1 Cor. viii. 9 ff. Instead of the simple εἰ
βέβληται (Lc. ἔρριπται) εἰς τὴν θάλασσαν,
Mt. has ἵνα καταποντισθῇ ἐν τῷ πελάγει
τῆς θαλάσσης. Cod. D corrects both
tenses ; see Blass, Gr. p. 215. Μύλος
ὀνικός Mt., Mc. ; Lc. λίθος μυλικός.
Μύλος in the LXX. is the handmill
(רֵחַיִם, see Driver on Deut. xxiv. 6,
and cf. Num. xi. 8) usually worked
by women, especially female slaves
(Exod. xi. 5, Jud. ix. 53, Mt. xxiv. 41);
the upper stone is the ἐπιμύλιον (LXX.,
Deut. l.c., Jud. l.c. (B), but the word
is not used in the N. T.). Distinct
from this handmill (χειρομύλη, χειρο-
μύλων, Xen. al.) was the larger sort
of mill, which was driven by an ass
(Ovid, fast. vi. 318, "pumiceas versat
asella molas"), the רֵחַיִם שֶׁל חֲמוֹר of
the Talmud (J. Lightfoot on Lc. xviii.).
Since the millstone ἐπιμύλιον is also
called ὄνος in classical Gk., it has been
thought that μύλος ὀνικός may have the
same sense here ; but the conjecture
is unnecessary. Cf. Origen: εἰσὶ γὰρ καὶ
μύλων διαφοραί, ὡς εἶναι τὸν μέν τινα
αὐτῶν, ἵν' οὕτως ὀνομάσω, ἀνθρωπικόν,
ἄλλον δὲ ὀνικόν. The stone of an 'ass-
mill' would be a μύλος μέγας (Apoc.
xviii. 21), and this is to the point :
the stone round the neck is heavy
enough to render escape impossible.
Schöttgen produces a parallel from

43 τὴν θάλασσαν. ⁴³καὶ ἐὰν σκανδαλίσῃ σε ἡ χείρ σου,
ἀπόκοψον αὐτήν· καλόν ἐστίν σε κυλλὸν εἰσελθεῖν
εἰς τὴν ζωήν, ἢ τὰς δύο χεῖρας ἔχοντα ἀπελθεῖν

43 σκανδαλιση אBLΔΨ minᵖᵃᵘᶜ a f ff k vg] σκανδαλιξη (-ξει) ACDFGN rell | αυτην]
+et proice abs te b (arm) | σε] σοι ADNXΓΠ al | ξωην]+αιωνιον arm | τας δυο] om
τας DΨ | απελθειν] βληθηναι D minᵖᵉʳᵖᵃᵘᶜ a f ff k

Kiddushin: "even though a man
had a millstone round his neck yet
ought he to attend to the study of the
Law." For an early instance of the
use of this saying of Christ see Clem.
Cor. 46 : κρεῖττον ἦν αὐτῷ περιτεθῆναι
μύλον καὶ καταποντισθῆναι εἰς τὴν θάλασσαν ἢ ἕνα τῶν ἐκλεκτῶν μου δια-
στρέψαι. The form, it will be observed,
does not agree with either Mt., Mc. or
Lc., but comes nearest to Mt.

43. καὶ ἐὰν σκανδαλίσῃ σε ἡ χείρ
σου κτλ.] "The offender of the little
ones is still more an offender against
himself" (Bruce). A man may place
moral stumbling-blocks in his own
path; the temptation may proceed
not from without, but from some part
of his own nature. As men submit
to the loss of a bodily organ or limb
in order to preserve the body as a
whole, so it is their interest to sacrifice powers and functions of their
spiritual nature which have been
found to be inevitable occasions of
sin. Better to live under a sense of
partial mutilation and incompleteness
than to perish in the enjoyment of
all one's powers. Origen: ὁμοίως
καὶ ἐπὶ τῆς ψυχῆς καλὸν καὶ μακά-
ριον ἐπὶ τοῖς βελτίστοις χρῆσθαί τῇ
δυνάμει αὐτῆς· εἰ δὲ μέλλομεν διά
τινα μίαν ἀπολέσθαι, αἱρετώτερον ἀπο-
βαλεῖν τὴν χρῆσιν αὐτῆς, ἵνα μετὰ τῶν
ἄλλων δυνάμεων σωθῶμεν. The word,
he adds, may be applied in various
ways : to the excision of an offending
member of the Christian brotherhood,
or to the surrender, for Christ's sake,
of a friend or near kinsman. For
ἀποκόπτειν τὴν χεῖρα see Deut. xxv.
12, Jud. i. 6. Καλόν ἐστιν...ἤ : see
WM., p. 302, and cf. Ps. cxvii. (cxviii.)

8 f. ἀγαθὸν...ἤ, Hos. ii. 7 (9), καλῶς
ἤ (כִּי טוֹב). Ἀπελθεῖν and εἰσελθεῖν
are in marked contrast ; for the
former cf. Mt. v. 30, xxv. 46. The
issues of life are on the one hand
an entrance into the higher life which
is its proper end, and, on the other,
a departure from it. On εἰσέρχεσθαι
εἰς τ. ζωήν see Dalman, *Worte,* i.
pp. 95, 127.

Κυλλός, used in class. Gk. of one
who has a crushed or crippled limb,
is employed here and apparently also
in Mt. xv. 30 (χωλούς, κυλλούς) with
special reference to the loss of a
hand. Τὴν ζωήν, the higher life; the
word is occasionally used in the N. T.
for physical existence (Acts xvii. 25,
I Cor. iii. 22, xv. 19 (ἡ ζ. αὕτη), 2 Pet.
i. 3), but in the great majority of
instances it means life in union with
GOD (cf. Mt. vii. 14, Jo. iii. 36, v. 24,
40, vi. 53 etc., esp. I Jo. v. 11 f.), often
more closely defined as ζωὴ αἰώνιος, ἡ
ὄντως ζωή (1 Tim. vi. 19), ἡ ζωὴ τοῦ
θεοῦ (Eph. iv. 18). In this context,
it is instructive to note, ἡ ζωή corresponds to ἡ βασιλεία τοῦ θεοῦ (*v.* 47).

Γέεννα, גֵּי בְנֵי־הִנֹּם, גֵּי בֶן־הִנֹּם, גֵּי הִנֹּם,
in the LXX. φάραγξ Ὀνόμ, Ἑννόμ, Ἐν-
νώμ (Jos. xv. 8, 2 Esdr. xxi. 30 (אᶜ·ᵃ)),
φ. υἱοῦ Ἑννόμ (Jer. vii. 31, 32) or
πολυάνδριον υἱοῦ Ἐ. (Jer. xix. 6), Γαὶ
Ὀννόμ (Jos. xviii. 16, A), Γαιβενθόμ (B)
or Γαμβὲ Ἑννόμ (A) (2 Chron. xxviii.
3), Γεβανὲ Ἐννόμ (2 Chron. xxxiii. 6),
Γαίεννα (Jos. xviii. 16, B). In the
O. T. the name denotes the ravine
which, starting from the N.W. of
Jerusalem, sweeps round the S.W.
angle of the city, and then, taking
a south-easterly course, meets the

εἰς τὴν γέενναν, εἰς τὸ πῦρ τὸ ἄσβεστον. ⁴⁵καὶ ἐὰν 45
ὁ πούς σου σκανδαλίζῃ σε, ἀπόκοψον αὐτόν· καλόν
ἐστίν σε εἰσελθεῖν εἰς τὴν ζωὴν χωλόν, ἢ τοὺς δύο

43 om εις την γ. syr^sin | εις το πυρ το ασβεστον] του πυρος F του π. του ασβεστου
syr^hel vid (om εις το π. το ασβ. א^c.aLΔΨ 604 al^perpauc syr^pesh) + (44) οπου ο σκωληξ
αυτων ου τελευτα και το πυρ ου σβεννυται ADNXΓΠΣΦ al min^pl latt^vt pl vg syr^pesh hel (go
aeth) (om v. 44 אBCLΔ 1 28 118 251 2^pe k syr^sin arm me)   45 σκανδαλιζη (-ξει)
(א)ABCDNΓΔΠΨ al min^pl] σκανδαλιση (-ει) (L) go* | αποκοψον αυτον] εκκοψον 1071 |
σε 2° אABCEF al^pl] σοι DNM*SUΓ al^pl | την ζωην]+αιωνιον D (sic) latt^vt pl vg arm |
χωλον] pr κυλλον η א

Kidron below the Pool of Siloam at
the well now called Bir Eyûb (Recovery, p. 6). This valley is the
traditional site (but see ib. p. 306 ff.)
of the fire-worship which began in
the reign of Ahaz (2 Chron. xxviii.
3, xxxiii. 6, Jer. vii. 31, xix. 2 ff.),
and after its desecration by Josiah
(2 Kings xxiii. 10) it became a common receptacle for the offal of the
city, and, in the later development
of Jewish thought, a symbol of the
supposed place of future punishments
(cf. Stanton, p. 325 ff.); the conception occurs already in Enoch xxvii. 1,
αὕτη ἡ φάραγξ κεκατηραμένη ἐστί, cf.
ib. xc. 24 ff., and the name is so used
in the Talmud, e.g. Aboth i. 6,
"[the sinner] desists from words of
Torah, and in the end he inherits Ge-
hinnom" (גֵּיהִנָּם, Dalman, Gr. p. 146,
Worte, i. p. 131 f.; Wünsche, neue
Beiträge, p. 596, gives other references). The N. T. form γέεννα (Mt.
v. 22, 29, 30, x. 28, xviii. 9, xxiii. 15,
33, Mc. ix. 43, 45, 47, Lc. xii. 5,
James iii. 6) is used exclusively in
the figurative sense, and only (as
the references shew) in Synoptic reports of sayings of Christ, and by
St James. It appears also in the
Sibyllines (i. 103, ἐς γέενναν μαλεροῦ
λάβρου πυρὸς ἀκαμάτοιο), and in the
transliteration gehenna it occurs in
the Latin version of 4 Esdr. (ii. 29,
vii. 36, "clibanus gehennae ostendetur
et contra eum iocunditatis paradisus":
cf. Tert. Apol. 47, "gehennam...quae

est ignis arcani subterraneus ad poe-
nam thesaurus...paradisum...locum
divinae amoenitatis recipiendis sanctorum spiritibus destinatum"), and
has established itself in the Latin Bible
(O. L. and Vg.). From Anglo-Saxon
times the word was rendered into
English by the ambiguous "hell," used
also for ἅδης; even R.V. keeps "hell"
here in the text.

τὸ πῦρ τὸ ἄσβεστον] The phrase
appears to be based on Isa. lxvi. 24
(see below v. 48); cf. also 4 Regn. xxii.
17, Isa. i. 31, Jer. vii. 20; the altar-
reference is perhaps to the altar-fire
Lev. vi. 9 (2), τὸ πῦρ τοῦ θυσιαστηρίου...
οὐ σβεσθήσεται. Ἄσβεστος, a revived
Homeric word, occurs as a variant in
Job xx. 26 (א^c.a mg A), and also in Mt.
iii. 12 = Lc. iii. 17. Here Mt. uses αἰώνιος as its equivalent. The fire which
devours sin belongs to the eternal
order and burns as long as sin remains to be consumed. For the
repeated article see note on iii. 29.

45. καὶ ἐὰν ὁ πούς σου σκανδαλίζῃ
σε] This mention of the foot naturally
follows that of the hand; if the two
members are to be distinguished in
the interpretation, the movements of
life will be represented by the foot
and its activities by the hand. On
both a check may be wisely placed, if
it is found that they minister to sin.

κ. ἐ. σε εἰσελθεῖν] On the readings
σε, σοι cf. Blass, Gr. p. 240 f. Βληθῆναι is substituted in vv. 45, 47 for
ἀπελθεῖν—the punishment is involun-

47 πόδας ἔχοντα βληθῆναι εἰς τὴν γέενναν. ⁴⁷καὶ ἐὰν ὁ
ὀφθαλμός σου σκανδαλίζῃ σε, ἔκβαλε αὐτόν· καλόν
σέ ἐστιν μονόφθαλμον εἰσελθεῖν εἰς τὴν βασιλείαν
τοῦ θεοῦ, ἢ δύο ὀφθαλμοὺς ἔχοντα βληθῆναι εἰς
48 γέενναν, ⁴⁸ὅπου ὁ σκώληξ αὐτῶν οὐ τελευτᾷ καὶ
49 τὸ πῦρ οὐ σβέννυται. ⁴⁹πᾶς γὰρ πυρὶ ἁλισθήσεται.

45 om εις την γεενναν 604 | γεενναν]+του πυρος F+του πυρος του ασβεστου c vg
syrʰᵉˡ+εις το πυρ το ασβεστον ΑΔΝΧΓΠΣΦ minᵖˡ a f ff i go aeth+(46) οπου ο σκωληξ
αυτων ου τελευτα και το πυρ ου σβεννυται ΑΔΝΧΓΠΣΦ minᵖˡ lattᵛᵗ ᵖˡ ⁽ⁿᵒⁿ ᵏ⁾ ᵛᵍ syrrᵖᵉˢʰ ʰᶜˡ
(go aeth) (om v. 46 אBCLΔ 1 28 92 118 218 251 253 2ᵖᵉ 19ᵉᵛ cˢᶜʳ k syrˢⁱⁿ arm me)
47 και ο οφθ. σου ει σκανδαλιζει σε D | σε 2°] σοι ACDMNΧΓΠ alᵖˡ | μονοφθ.] quacumque
parte corporis debilem k | βληθηναι] απελθειν D minᵖᵃᵘᶜ c i syrˢⁱⁿ | γεενναν]+του πυρος
ΑCΝΧΓΠΣΦ minᵖˡ f i l q r syrrᵖᵉˢʰ ʰᶜˡ go aeth+εις το πυρ το ασβεστον F   48 οπ.
το πυρ ου σβ. και ο σκ. κτλ. c k | τελευτησει 1 a b c ff i q | το πυρ]+αυτων Ψ 262 300
alᵖᵃᵘᶜ b me syrr | σβεσθησεται a b c ff i k q   49 om πας...αλισθησεται D 64 65*
a b c ff i | πας...αλισθ.] omnia autem substantia consumitur k | πας γαρ]+αρτος 11
230 alᵖᵉʳᵖᵃᵘᶜ παν γαρ armᵛⁱᵈ | πυρι] pr εν אC minᵖᵃᵘᶜ | αλισθησεται] δοκιμασθησεται 46
52 g (examinantur)+και πασα (πασα γαρ) θυσια αλι αλισθησεται ΑC(D)ΝΧΓΠΣΦ al
lattᵛᵗ ᵖˡ ᵛᵍ syrrᵖᵉˢʰ ʰᶜˡ me go aeth+και πασα πασα θυσια αναλωθησεται Ψ (cf. k) (om אBLΔ
1 61 73 118 604 alⁿᵒⁿⁿ k syrˢⁱⁿ arm)

tary, though it has been reached through successive acts of the will.

47. καὶ ἐὰν ὁ ὀφθαλμός κτλ.] The eye is here the symbol of the lust which works through it (ἡ ἐπιθυμία τῶν ὀφθαλμῶν, 1 Jo. ii. 16). Ἔκβαλε αὐτόν: Mt. ἔξελε αὐτ. καὶ βάλε ἀπὸ σοῦ, expanding Mc.'s compressed thought—'tear it out and cast it away.' Such a wrench may be necessary in the moral nature ; the love of visible beauty is a true and noble element in man, but if it becomes in any individual the occasion of sin, he must put it from him ; better to enter life with no eye but for the spiritual and eternal beauty than to indulge the lower taste to the loss of all. Μονόφθαλμος, one of the Herodotean words (Herod. iii. 16, iv. 29) revived in the κοινή but condemned by the Atticists ; cf. Lob. Phryn. 136, μονόφθαλμον οὐ ῥητέον ἑτερόφθαλμον δέ. Τὴν βασιλείαν τοῦ θεοῦ answers to τὴν ζωήν (v. 43 note).

48. ὅπου ὁ σκώληξ αὐτῶν κτλ.]

Cited from Isa. lxvi. 25, ὁ γὰρ σκώληξ αὐτῶν οὐ τελευτήσει (A, τελευτᾷ) καὶ τὸ πῦρ αὐτῶν οὐ σβεσθήσεται. The words have impressed themselves on more than one passage in Jewish writing outside the Canon; cf. Sir. vii. 17, ἐκδίκησις ἀσεβοῦς πῦρ καὶ σκώληξ: Judith xvi. 17, Κύριος...ἐκδικήσει αὐτοὺς...δοῦναι πῦρ καὶ σκώληκας εἰς σάρκας αὐτῶν. "Σκώληξ, animae" (Bengel). For the significance of such language as adopted by Christ cf. Thpht. : αἰσθητὴν τιμωρίαν εἶπεν, ἐκφοβῶν ἡμᾶς διὰ τούτου τοῦ αἰσθητοῦ ὑποδείγματος...σκώληξ δὲ καὶ πῦρ κολάζοντα τοὺς ἁμαρτωλοὺς ἡ συνείδησίς ἐστιν ἑκάστου καὶ ἡ μνήμη τῶν πραχθέντων, ἥτις ὥσπερ σκώληξ καταδαπανᾷ καὶ ὡς πῦρ φλέγει. Like the fire, the worm is undying: "the wounds inflicted on the man himself by his sins, the degradation and deterioration of his being, have no limitations [of time]." (Gould.) The presents οὐ τελευτᾷ, οὐ σβέννυται (cf. LXX.) state simply the law or normal condition of

⁵⁰καλὸν τὸ ἅλας· ἐὰν δὲ τὸ ἅλας ἄναλον γένηται, 50
ἐν τίνι αὐτὸ ἀρτύσετε; ἔχετε ἐν ἑαυτοῖς ἅλα, καὶ
εἰρηνεύετε ἐν ἀλλήλοις.

50 το αλας bis א^{c.a} (1°, א*) ABCDNXΓΠΣΦΨ min^{omn vid}] το αλα LΔ et 2°, א* |
γενησεται D | αρτυσεται ACDHLNΣ 126 al^{mu} αρτυθησεται Κ 1 14 al^{pauc} d f syr^{pesh} arm
me go aeth | εχετε] υμεις ουν εχ. 13 69 346 2^{pe} arm εχ. ουν υμεις 28 | αλα א*A*BDLΔ
1 28 al^{pauc}] αλας א^{c.a}A^aCNXΓΠΣΦ min^{pl} το αλας U 604 panem k

the σκώληξ and πῦρ. The question
of the eternity of punishment does
not come into sight.
The ‘Western’ and Syrian texts
add these words as a refrain to vv.
43, 45; see app. crit. supra.
49. πᾶς γὰρ πυρὶ ἁλισθήσεται]
‘Fire, I said, for with fire shall every
man be salted.’ The ‘Western’ gloss
πᾶσα γὰρ (or καὶ πᾶσα) θυσία ἁλὶ ἁλισθήσεται rightly seeks an explanation
in Lev. ii. 13 (πᾶν δῶρον θυσίας ὑμῶν
ἁλὶ ἁλισθήσεται). The sacrificial salt
was the symbol of a covenant-relation
with GOD (בְּרִית מֶלַח, Num. xviii. 19,
2 Chron. xiii. 5). In the case of
every disciple of Christ the salt of
the covenant is a Divine Fire (Mt. iii.
11, αὐτὸς ὑμᾶς βαπτίσει ἐν πνεύματι
ἁγίῳ καὶ πυρί) which purifies, preserves
and consummates sacrifice—the alternative to the Fire which consumes
(Mt. iii. 12, Heb. xii. 29). Cf. Euth. :
πᾶς πιστὸς πυρὶ τῆς πρὸς θεὸν πίστεως
ἢ τῆς πρὸς τὸν πλησίον ἀγάπης ἁλισθήσεται, ἤγουν τὴν σηπεδόνα τῆς κακίας
ἀποβαλεῖ. On the reading see WH.,
Intr. p. 101, Notes, p. 25 : the traditional text is defended by Burgon-
Miller, Causes of Corruption, p.
275.
50. καλὸν τὸ ἅλας κτλ.] ‘Good is
the salt’ implied in ἁλισθήσεται (v. 49).
῞Αλας (τό) is the late form of ἅλς (ὁ) ;
cf. Lev. ii. 13, Jud. ix. 45, 2 Esdr. vi.
9, vii. 22, Mt. v. 13, Lc. xiv. 34; the
dat. ἅλατι occurs in Col. iv. 6; the
nom. is also written ἅλα (cf. γάλα) in
Sir. xxxix. 26 (B), and as a variant
in each of the passages where ἅλας is
found in the N. T.; cf. Blass, Gr. p. 27,

WH., Notes, p. 158. ῎Αναλος insulsus
is used here only in the LXX. and N. T.,
but it is Aquila’s rendering for תָּפֵל
in Ezech. xiii. 10, 11, 15, xxii. 28. In
the parallel saying of Mt. v. 13=Lc.
xiv. 34, μωρανθῇ takes the place of
Mc.’s ἄναλον γένηται. Ἐν τίνι αὐτὸ
ἀρτύσετε; Mt. ἐν τίνι ἁλισθήσεται;
Ἀρτύειν ἅλατι occurs in Col. iv. 6,
where see Bp Lightfoot’s note; Symm.
gives ἀνάρτυτος for Aq.’s ἄναλος in
Ezech. ll. cc., and for ἄνευ ἁλός (LXX.)
in Job vi. 6.
In its immediate reference to the
Apostles the passage is well explained
by Mr Latham (p. 360): “if the preserving principle embodied in the
Apostles, and which was to emanate
from them, should itself prove corrupt [? inoperative], then where could
help be found ? If they, the chosen
ones, became selfish, if they wrangled
about who should be greatest, then
the fire which our Lord had come to
send upon earth was clearly not
burning in them, and whence could
it be kindled afresh?” For a wider
application cf. Victor: εἴτις οὖν χάριτος ἀξιωθεὶς καὶ κενὴν ταύτην ποιήσει,
οὗτος ἂν εἴη ἐν ᾧ οἱ ἅλες ἐμωράνθησαν.
ἔχετε ἐν ἑαυτοῖς ἅλα κτλ.] ‘Keep
the seasoning power, the preserving
sacrificial Fire, within your own hearts,
and as a first condition and indication
of its presence there, be at peace with
your brethren.’ Thus the discourse
reverts to the point from which it
started (v. 33). Disputes about precedence endangered the very existence of the new life. Εἰρηνεύειν is
elsewhere in the N. T. limited to

10. 1 ¹Καὶ ἐκεῖθεν ἀναστὰς ἔρχεται εἰς τὰ ὅρια τῆς
Ἰουδαίας καὶ πέραν τοῦ Ἰορδάνου, καὶ συνπορεύονται
πάλιν ὄχλοι πρὸς αὐτόν, καὶ ὡς εἰώθει πάλιν ἐδίδα-
¶ i σκεν αὐτούς.¶

X 1 κακειθεν ALNXΓΠ | ερχεται] ηλθεν N | και περαν אBC*LΨ me] om και C²DGΔ
1 13 28 69 124 209 604* 2ᵖᵉ alⁿᵒⁿⁿ latt syrrˢⁱⁿᵖᵉˢʰ arm go aethᵛⁱᵈ δια του περαν
ANXΓΠΦ al minᵖˡ του περαν Σ | συνπορευονται (συμπ. LNXΓΠΣΦΨ minᵖˡ) παλιν οχλοι]
συνερχεται π. ο οχλος D 2ᵖᵉ a b c ff i k q (r) (arm) | και ως ειωθει] ως ει. και D b ff i | om
παλιν 2° k syrˢⁱⁿ | εδιδασκεν] pr εθεραπευσεν και syrˢⁱⁿ

St Paul (Rom. xii. 18, 2 Cor. xiii. 11,
1 Thess. v. 13).

X. 1. DEPARTURE FROM GALILEE; JOURNEYS IN JUDAEA AND PERAEA (Mt. xix. 1—2).

1. καὶ ἐκεῖθεν ἀναστὰς ἔρχεται] This
phrase (which corresponds to the
Hebrew וַיֵּלֶךְ [מִשָּׁם] וַיָּקָם, Gen. xxii.
3, Num. xxii. 14, &c.) seems to be
used for the commencement of a
considerable journey, cf. vii. 24. On
the present occasion the Lord is
finally quitting Galilee (Mt. μετῆρεν
ἀπὸ τῆς Γαλειλαίας) and Capernaum
(ix. 33); His face is henceforth turned
towards Jerusalem (Lc. ix. 51, xvii.
11). The departure followed soon
after the teaching recorded in ix.
35—50, Mt. xviii. 1—35; cf. Mt. xix.
1, ὅτε ἐτέλεσεν ὁ Ἰησοῦς τοὺς λόγους
τούτους. The incident of the στατήρ
seems also to have occurred during
this interval (Mt. xvii. 24 ff.).

εἰς τὰ ὅρια τῆς Ἰουδαίας καί κτλ.]
These words cover the whole interval
between the end of the Galilean
Ministry and the final visit to Jerusalem. The time was spent partly
in Judaea, partly beyond the Jordan.
It seems to have included a journey
to Jerusalem in September for the
Feast of Tabernacles (Jo. vii. 14), and
another in December for the Feast of
the Dedication (Jo. x. 22), a retreat
to Bethany beyond the Jordan (Jo. x.
40), a visit to Bethany on the Mount
of Olives (Jo. xi. 1 ff.), a second
retreat to "Ephraim" (? Ophrah)

"near the wilderness" (Jo. xi. 54),
ending in the last journey through
Jericho. Τὰ ὅρια τ. Ἰ., not the frontier
only (as Origen in Mt. t. xiv. 15, οὐκ
ἐπὶ τὰ μέσα, ἀλλ' οἰονεὶ τὰ ἄκρα), but
the region as a whole; cf. vii. 24. Καὶ
πέραν: Mt. omits καί, and is followed
by the 'Western' text of Mc.; the
R. T. (διὰ τοῦ π.) is perhaps an attempt
to extract sense from the clause de-
nuded of καί.

συνπορεύονται πάλιν ὄχλοι] As in
Galilee before the departure to the
North (iii. 7 f., 20, iv. 1, v. 21, vi. 33,
54 f.), and even under Mt. Hermon
(ix. 14 f.). Ὄχλοι: Mc. uses the sing.
elsewhere, but the pl. occurs repeatedly
in Mt., Lc. With the return of the
ὄχλος, the Lord reverted to His old
methods of teaching; chiefly, no
doubt, as St Luke's account of this
period (Lc. ix. 31 ff.) suggests, employing the parable as the vehicle of
instruction. Ὡς εἰώθει: cf. Lc. iv. 16,
κατὰ τὸ εἰωθὸς αὐτῷ. The Gospels
reveal certain habits of thought and
action which invest the Lord with a
true human character. The Lord,
after an interval during which He
has devoted Himself to the training
of the Twelve, returns to His customary teaching of the multitude. The
reading of D and a few O. L. texts,
which refers ὡς εἰώθει to the ὄχλος,
looks like a correction and renders ὡς
εἰ. otiose, for it is implied in πάλιν.
Ἐδίδασκεν (cf. vi. 34)—the teaching
continued throughout the period,

²Καὶ προσελθόντες Φαρισαῖοι ἐπηρώτων αὐτόν 2
Εἰ ἔξεστιν ἀνδρὶ γυναῖκα ἀπολῦσαι; πειράζοντες
αὐτόν. ³ὁ δὲ ἀποκριθεὶς εἶπεν αὐτοῖς Τί ὑμῖν ἐνε- 3
τείλατο Μωυσῆς; ⁴οἱ δὲ εἶπαν Ἐπέτρεψεν Μωυσῆς 4

2 om προσελθόντες οι Φ. D a b k syrˢⁱⁿ | Φαρισαιοι ΑΒΛΓΔΠΦΨ minᵖˡ c ff] om D
pr οι ℵCNVXΣ minˢᵃᵗᵐᵘ | επηρωτων (επηρωτησαν ΑΝΧΓΠΣΦΨ minᵖˡ qᵛⁱᵈ)] pr πειρα-
ζοντες arm (cf. syrˢⁱⁿ Or) | om πειρ. αυτον arm

whenever opportunities offered themselves. Mt. refers only to the miracles
which incidentally accompanied the
teaching (καὶ ἐθεράπευσεν αὐτοὺς ἐκεῖ).
As before the journey to Hermon,
the teaching was doubtless chiefly
parabolic.

2—12. QUESTION OF DIVORCE (Mt.
xix. 3—9 : cf. Mt. v. 31—32 ; Lc. xvi.
18).

2. προσελθόντες Φαρισαῖοι ἐπηρώτων κτλ.] With the resumption of
the public teaching the Pharisees
return to the attack (cf. vii. 5, viii.
11 ; Victor: ὢ τῆς ἀνοίας· ᾤοντο ἐπιστο-
μίζειν αὐτὸν διὰ τῶν ζητημάτων, καίτοι γε
ἤδη λαβόντες τεκμήριον τῆς δυνάμεως).
But their present attitude marks an
advance ; for the first time they venture to test the Teacher's orthodoxy
by a leading question (πειράζοντες
αὐτόν : cf. Mc. viii. 11). Φαρισαῖοι
(anarthrous), individual members of
the party ; cf. ix. 14, γραμματεῖς. Οἱ
Φ. occurs elsewhere in Mc. quite
constantly, and has been substituted
here in the R.T. The reference to the
Pharisees is strangely omitted by D
and a few good O.L. authorities.

εἰ ἔξεστιν ἀνδρὶ γυν. ἀπολῦσαι] The
question appears to have been already
answered during the Galilean Ministry
(Mt. v. 31, 32), but possibly on an occasion when no Pharisees were present.
They may have heard a rumour as
to His view of the matter and wished
to verify it, but it is unlikely that
they hoped to draw Him in a moment·
of forgetfulness into a denial of His
earlier teaching (Euth.: ἐνόμισαν ὅτι
ἐπελάθετο...ἐὰν μὲν εἴπῃ ὅτι ἔξεστιν

ἀντιθήσουσιν ὅτι Καὶ πῶς προλαβὼν
ἐδίδαξας ὅτι οὐκ ἔξεστιν; cf. Jerome
in Mt.). Rather they expected a
negative reply, and were prepared to
turn it to their own purposes. It
might be used to excite the anger
of Antipas, who had put away his
first wife and married again (cf. vi.
17, note) ; more probably their intention was simply to place Him in apparent opposition to Moses, who had
permitted divorce. Mt.'s addition,
κατὰ πᾶσαν αἰτίαν, turns the edge of
the question, leaving an escape from
the alternative of an unconditional
'yea' or 'nay': cf. the exception
allowed in xix. 9 (μὴ ἐπὶ πορνείᾳ).

3. ὁ δὲ ἀποκριθεὶς εἶπεν κτλ.] The
Lord anticipates the appeal to Moses,
and asks for the Mosaic ruling upon
the point. Since they recognised the
authority of Moses, He will go to
Moses in the first instance (cf. vii.
10). Mt., who seems to have missed
this point, almost inverts the order
of the dialogue, and places τί Μωυσῆς
ἐνετείλατο in the mouth of the Pharisees, as an objection to the Lord's
appeal to Gen. i. 27. For M. ἐνετείλατο cf. Deut. vi. 6, Jos. iv. 12.

4. ἐπέτρεψεν Μωυσῆς κτλ.] They
refer to Deut. xxiv. 1 LXX., γράψει
αὐτῇ βιβλίον ἀποστασίου καὶ δώσει εἰς
τὰς χεῖρας αὐτῆς καὶ ἐξαποστελεῖ αὐτὴν
ἐκ τῆς οἰκίας αὐτοῦ. The words, as the
context shews, are simply permissive,
the general purpose of the passage
being to provide against a certain
contingency which might follow the
divorce. They recognise the validity
of the husband's act, but do not

5 βιβλίον ἀποστασίου γράψαι καὶ ἀπολῦσαι. ⁵ὁ
δὲ Ἰησοῦς εἶπεν αὐτοῖς Πρὸς τὴν σκληροκαρδίαν
6 ὑμῶν ἔγραψεν ὑμῖν τὴν ἐντολὴν ταύτην· ⁶ἀπὸ δὲ
ἀρχῆς κτίσεως ἄρσεν καὶ θῆλυ ἐποίησεν αὐτούς.

4 γραψαι] δουναι 61 b δουναι γραψαι D dare scriptum c d ff q rᵛⁱᵈ (syrˢⁱⁿ) |
απολυσαι]+αυτην N   5 ο δε I.] και αποκριθεις ο I. ΑΔΝΧΓΠΣΦ minᵒᵐⁿ ᵛⁱᵈ
lattᵛᵗ ᵖˡ ᵛᵍ syrˢⁱⁿ ᵖᵉˢʰ ʰᶜˡ arm go aeth | εγραψεν] επετρεψεν ΝΣΦ syrˢⁱⁿ + Μωυσης DΨ (90)
alᵖᵃᵘᶜ (b) c (f) k syrˢⁱⁿ Clem Al | ταυτην]+απολυσαι τας γυναικας υμων aeth   6 om
κτισεως D min² b ff q syrʳˢⁱⁿ ᵖᵉˢʰ | αυτους] om D 86* 219 b f ff k* go aeth+ο θεος
ΑΔΝΧΓΠΣΦΨ minᵒᵐ ᵛⁱᵈ a b f k q vg syrr arm go aeth

create the situation. Βιβλίον ἀποστασίου (=סֵפֶר כְּרִיתֻת, Aq. β. ἀποκοπῆς,
Symm. β. διακοπῆς), Vg. libellus re-
pudii, "a libel of forsakinge" (Wycliffe), "a testimoniall of devorse-
ment" (Tindale), occurs again in Isa.
l. 1, Jer. iii. 8; cf. ἔγραψεν συνγραφὴν
βιβλίου συνοικήσεως (Tob. vii. 13, א).
On the history of the word ἀποστ. see
Kennedy, Sources, p. 121; unlike the
Hebrew term it stamps the divorced
wife as disloyal, cf. the classical ἀποστασίου δίκη (Dem. 790. 2, 940. 15).
For γράψαι Mt. has δοῦναι; both acts
were essential to a valid divorce.
For a specimen of a Jewish 'bill of
divorce' see J. Lightfoot on Mt. v. 31.

5. ὁ δὲ Ἰησοῦς κτλ.] The Lord
does not deny that 'Moses' permitted
divorce; command it he did not.
The commandment (τὴν ἐντολὴν ταύτην—ταύτην is emphatic—this particular commandment) consisted of
"regulations tending to limit it and
preclude its abuse" (Driver). No
such regulations would have been
necessary but for the σκληροκαρδία
which had been innate in the Hebrew
people from the first (cf. Ezek. iii. 7,
πᾶς ὁ οἶκος Ἰσραὴλ...σκληροκάρδιοι).
The purpose of the legislation of
Deut. l.c. was to check this disposition,
not to give it head; and for the
Pharisees to shelter themselves under
the temporary recognition of a necessary evil was to confess that they had
not outgrown the moral stature of

their fathers (τὴν σκλ. ὑμῶν). Σκληροκαρδία (עָרְלַת לֵבָב), Aq. ἀκροβυστία
καρδίας, Vg. duritia cordis, occurs in
Deut. x. 16, Jer. iv. 4, Sir. xvi. 10;
in 'Mc.' xvi. 14 it goes along with
ἀπιστία. With this history the word
must be taken to mean a condition
of insensibility to the call of GOD, and
not only the want of consideration
for a fellow-creature which the present context suggests. But incapacity
for comprehending this Divine love
(Rom. ii. 4, 5) implies the absence of
an unselfish love for men, and both
result from the withering up of the
moral nature under the power of a
practical unbelief.

6. ἀπὸ δὲ ἀρχῆς κτίσεως κτλ.] From
the temporary permission of divorce
under the Deuteronomic law the Lord
appeals to the principle enunciated
in the original constitution of man.
Cf. Hort, Jud. Christianity, p. 33;
Victor: διὰ τῶν πραγμάτων ὑμῖν ἐξ
ἀρχῆς ὁ θεὸς ἐνομοθέτησε τὰ ἐναντία...
εἰ δὲ Μωσέα προβάλλῃ, ἐγὼ δὲ λέγω
σοι τὸν Μωσέως δεσπότην. With ἀπὸ
ἀρχῆς κτίσεως comp. xiii. 19 ἀπ' ἀρχῆς
κτ. ἣν ἔκτισεν ὁ θεός, Rom. i. 20 ἀπὸ
κτίσεως κόσμου, 2 Pet. iii. 4 (where
the exact phrase occurs again); and
see Dalman, Worte, i. p. 136. Κτίσις
is (1) the act of creation (Rom. l. c.),
(2) the totality of created things (cf.
e.g. Sap. xix. 6, Judith ix. 12, xvi. 14,
3 Macc. ii. 2, 7, vi. 2, Rom. viii.
19 ff., Col. i. 15, 23 (cf. Lightfoot)),

⁷ἕνεκεν τούτου καταλείψει ἄνθρωπος τὸν πατέρα 7
αὐτοῦ καὶ τὴν μητέρα, ⁸καὶ ἔσονται οἱ δύο εἰς σάρκα 8
μίαν. ὥστε οὐκέτι εἰσὶν δύο ἀλλὰ μία σάρξ. ⁹ὃ οὖν 9
ὁ θεὸς συνέζευξεν ἄνθρωπος μὴ χωριζέτω. ¹⁰καὶ εἰς 10

7 ἕνεκεν] pr και ειπεν DΝΣ 13 28 69 124 346 1071 2ᵖᵉ alᵖᵃᵘᶜ b c ff q arm | om αυτου DM*N | μητερα]+αυτου ℵ(D)M minᵖᵃᵘᶜ a b c f ff syrrˢⁱⁿᵖᵉˢʰ me go aeth (om ΑΒCLΝΧΓΔΠΣΦΨ minᵖˡ k q vg syrʰᶜˡ arm) | ad fin vers add και προσκολληθησεται προς την γυναικα (vel τη γυναικι) αυτου (AC)D(LΝ)ΧΓ(Δ)Π(Σ)Φ minᶠᵉʳᵉ ᵒᵐⁿ lattᵉˣᶜ ᶠᵒʳᵗ ᵏ syrrᵖᵉˢʰ ʰᶜˡ (arm) me aeth (om ℵBΨ 48ᵉᵛ syrˢⁱⁿ go) 8 σαρξ μια ℵACFKM²UΓΠΦ 604 alⁿᵒⁿⁿ 9 om ουν D ff k* 10 εις την οικιαν ℵBDLΔΨ minᵖᵃᵘᶜ b] εν τη οικια ΑCΝΧΓΠΣΦ minᵖˡ a f ffᵛⁱᵈ k q r vg me go

(3) a creature (Rom. viii. 39), 2 Cor. v. 17 (?), Heb. iv. 13. The senses run one into the other, so that it is sometimes difficult to decide between them, but (1) appears to predominate here. On the other hand in Apoc. iii. 14, where Christ speaks of Himself as ἡ ἀρχὴ τῆς κτίσεως τοῦ θεοῦ, (2) is to be preferred.

ἄρσεν καὶ θῆλυ ἐποίησεν αὐτούς] A verbal citation from Gen. i. 27, LXX. The subject of the verb is ὁ θεός (Gen. l.c.); Mt. supplies ὁ κτίσας.

7—8. ἕνεκεν τούτου κτλ.] Another nearly verbal citation from the LXX. (Gen. ii. 24), omitting καὶ προσκολλη-θήσεται τῇ γυναικὶ αὐτοῦ, which however is supplied by Mt. and finds a place in a great majority of the MSS. and versions of Mc. The passage is cited again in 1 Cor. vi. 16 (partly), and in Eph. v. 31 (cf. Ps. Clem. 2 Cor. 14), where there are some interesting variants.

8. καὶ ἔσονται οἱ δύο κτλ.] On εἶναι εἰς (לְ הָיָה) see WM., p. 229; BDB., p. 226. Ὥστε with ind. introduces an actual consequence which follows from the foregoing words, as in ii. 28, Rom. vii. 12, xiii. 2, 1 Cor. iii. 7, xi. 27. Μία σάρξ: cf. 1 Cor. vi. 16, ἐν σῶμα. But in the intention of the Creator the union is not carnal or corporeal only; Origen in Mt.: ὅπου γε ὁμόνοια καὶ συμφωνία καὶ ἁρμονία ἀνδρός ἐστι πρὸς γυναῖκα, τοῦ μὲν ὡς ἄρχοντος τῆς δὲ

πειθομένης τῷ Αὐτός σου κυριεύσει, ἀληθῶς ἐστιν εἰπεῖν τῶν τοιούτων τό Οὐκέτι εἰσὶ δύο.

9. ὁ οὖν ὁ θεὸς συνέζευξεν κτλ.] Tindale: "what GOD hath cuppled, let not man separat." In Genesis the words ἕνεκεν τούτου κτλ. are ascribed to Adam, not to the Creator (Mt. ὁ κτίσας...εἶπεν). But they point to a Divine purpose already revealed in the creation of mutually complementary sexes and in the blessing pronounced upon their union (Gen. i. 27 f.), and these constitute a Divine sanction that renders lawful wedlock indissoluble at the discretion of the individual (ἄνθρωπος, cf. Jo. iii. 4). For συνευγνύναι cf. Ezech. i. 11, 23, Jos. ant. i. 19. 10; and for χωρίζειν in this sense, 1 Cor. vii. 10 ff. This verse was introduced into the English Form of Matrimony in 1548, but it had previously stood in the Gospel of the Ordo sponsalium.

For a perverse use of this passage by certain Gnostics of the second century see the letter of Ptolemaeus to Flora in Epiph. haer. 33. 3 ff.

10. καὶ εἰς τὴν οἰκίαν κτλ.] The incident was at an end, so far as the Pharisees were concerned; but it led afterwards to a private conversation between the Lord and the Twelve (cf. vii. 17, ix. 28). Mt. overlooks the change of surroundings, and represents the Lord as still addressing the

τὴν οἰκίαν πάλιν οἱ μαθηταὶ περὶ τούτου ἐπηρώτων
11 αὐτόν. ¹¹καὶ λέγει αὐτοῖς Ὃς ἂν ἀπολύσῃ τὴν
γυναῖκα αὐτοῦ καὶ γαμήσῃ ἄλλην μοιχᾶται ἐπ' αὐτήν·

10 οἱ μαθηται]+αυτου ΑΔΝΧΓΠΣΦ min^pl b f ff^vid q vg syrr go aeth+κατ ιδιαν
c k | περι τουτου ΑΒCLMΝΧΓΔΣΨ 604 al^nonn a syrr^sin pesh me aeth] π. τουτων ℵ π.
του αυτου EFGHSUVIIΦ min^pl b fq vg syr^hcl arm^vid go π. του αυτ. λογου (vel π. τουτου)
D (c) f (ff) k om Κ min^8 | επηρωτησαν ΑΔΝΧΓΠΣΦ min^pl latt^vid   11—12 ord
verss mut syr^sin   11 om επ Clem Al om επ αυτην 1 28 2^pe al^paue syrr^sin pesh arm

Pharisees (λέγω δὲ ὑμῖν). Εἰς τὴν
οἰκίαν, when they had entered the
house (cf. ix. 33, and WM., p.
517; such a conjectural addition as εἰσελθόντα, εἰσελθόντος, or εἰσελθόντων αὐτῶν
is wholly unnecessary) where they were
lodging, probably in one of the villages
on the road to Jerusalem (Lc. ix. 51 f.,
x. 38, xiii. 22); opposed as in ix. 33 to
ἐν τῇ ὁδῷ understood in x. 1 f. Πάλιν
...ἐπηρώτων, they repeated the question which had been put by the
Pharisees (v. 2). The answer was
explicit and authoritative, as that of
a Master speaking to an inner circle
of disciples.

11. ὃς ἂν ἀπολύσῃ κτλ.] Of simple
divorce the Lord has spoken sufficiently; it is a dissolution of a Divinely
constituted union. He deals now with
the case of marriage after divorce,
and pronounces it to be adultery.
Μοιχᾶται ἐπ' αὐτήν, Vg. adulterium
committit super eam, "commits adultery in reference to her," sc. τὴν ἀπο-
λελυμένην (not, as Victor, ἐπὶ δευτέραν
ἣν ἐπεισάγει). Μοιχᾶσθαι is used by
the LXX. (Jer.⁶ Ezech.³) absolutely or
with the acc. of the object and with
either of the guilty parties for subject (Jer. xxxvi. (xxix.) 23; Ezech.
xvi. 32); in the N. T., outside the
present context (Mt., Mc.), it is used
only in Mt. v. 32^b, the ordinary practice being to write μοιχεύειν of the
man, and μοιχεύεσθαι (pass.) of the
woman (Mt. v. 28, 32), as in class. Gk.;
the LXX. uses μοιχεύεσθαι (mid.) of
the man in Lev. xx. 10 bis. Clement
of Alexandria, who reads μ. αὐτήν,

explains (strom. ii. 23): τουτέστιν,
ἀναγκάζει μοιχευθῆναι. On the construction (ὃς ἂν (or ἐὰν) ἀπολύσῃ...
μοιχᾶται) see Burton, § 312, and for
ἐπ' αὐτήν 'in reference to her,' and
so 'to her detriment,' cf. vi. 34, ix.
22, xiv. 48.

In both v. 32 and xix. 9, Mt.
qualifies ὃς ἂν ἀπολύσῃ τ. γ. αὐτοῦ by
adding παρεκτὸς λόγου πορνείας or μὴ
ἐπὶ πορνείᾳ. If we may assume (cf.
v. 12, note ad fin.) that these words
formed part of the Lord's judgement
on one at least of the occasions when
it was pronounced, He allows a solitary
exception to the indissolubility of
marriage, viz. in the case of unfaith-
fulness. Πορνεία, though it is to be
distinguished from μοιχεία when the
two are named in the same context
(vii. 21), can scarcely in this connexion
refer to an act of sin committed before
marriage; the word is used as in Hos.
ii. 5 (7) ἐξεπόρνευσεν ἡ μήτηρ αὐτῶν,
Am. vii. 17 ἡ γυνή σου ἐν τῇ πόλει
πορνεύσει. This then is the only
ἄσχημον πρᾶγμα (Deut. xxiv. 1) which
still justifies, under the law of Christ,
the use of divorce. Whether in such
a case the words added in Mt. permit
or tolerate re-marriage is a question
of much difficulty, which belongs to
the interpretation of the first Gospel.
The post-Christian history of the subject is treated by H. M. Luckock,
History of Marriage (1894), and
O. D. Watkins, Holy Matrimony
(1895); for contemporary and later
Jewish opinion upon the conditions
of a lawful divorce comp. Jos. ant. iv.

¹²καὶ ἐὰν αὐτὴ ἀπολύσασα τὸν ἄνδρα αὐτῆς γαμήσῃ 12
ἄλλον, μοιχᾶται.
¹³Καὶ προσέφερον αὐτῷ παιδία ἵνα αὐτῶν ἅψηται· 13

12 εαν αυτη…αλλον] εαν γυνη εξελθη απο του ανδρος και αλλον γαμηση D (13) 28
(69) 124 346 (2^{pe}) a b (c ff) arm | αυτη απολυσασα᾽ γυνη απολυση…και ΑΝΧΓΠΣΦ
min^{pl} f (k) vg syrr^{sin pesh} go | γαμηση αλλον אBC*DLΔΨ 1 13 28 69 124 346 al^{pauc}]
γαμηθη αλλω AC²ΝΧΓΠΣΦ min^{pl} | μοιχαται] (similiter) et qui dimissam (a viro)
ducit moechatur (a) b f (ff g)

8. 23, J. Lightfoot on Mt. v., Edersheim,
Life, ii., p. 332 ff., Schürer II. ii. 123,
Driver on Deut. *l. c.*, and *Marriage*
in Hastings, *D. B.*, and *Encycl. Bibl.*
12. καὶ ἐὰν αὐτὴ ἀπολύσασα κτλ.]
Mc. only. For ἀπολύειν used in reference to the action of the wife see
Diod. xii. 18 διωρθώθη νόμος ὁ διδοὺς
ἐξουσίαν τῇ γυναικὶ ἀπολύειν τὸν ἄνδρα.
Similarly in 1 Cor. vii. 12 f. ἀφιέναι is
used indiscriminately of both parties.
The divorce of the husband by the
wife was possible under both Greek
and Roman Law (see Plutarch, *Alc.*
8, Gaius i. 127, cited by Stanley on
1 Cor. vii. 13, and other reff. in Wetstein *ad loc.*); and St Paul (1 Cor. *l. c.*
γυνή…μὴ ἀφιέτω τὸν ἄνδρα) distinctly
recognises the legal right of Christian
women at Corinth to leave their
husbands on the mere point of incompatibility of religious belief, though
he prohibits them from using this
right. J. Lightfoot (on 1 Cor.) quotes
a Rabbinical opinion that the same
privilege was conceded to married
women by Jewish custom; on the
other hand Josephus (*ant.* xv. 7. 10),
writing of Salome, says quite posi-
tively: πέμπει…γραμμάτιον ἀπολυο-
μένη τὸν γάμον οὐ κατὰ τοὺς Ἰουδαίους
νόμους. See however Burkitt, *G. H.*
p. 99 ff. In any case it is unnecessary
to regard this view as "derived from
an Hellenic amplification of the tradition" (Meyer), a hypothesis which is
excluded by the general character of
the second Gospel. In His private
instruction to the Apostles, as Peter
remembered, the Lord completed His
teaching by a reference to the prac-

tice of the Pagan and Hellenised
circles which must have been already
familiar to the Twelve, and with
which they would shortly be called to
deal. See Burkitt in *J. Th. St.*, v. p. 628.
For the sequel see Mt. xix. 10—12.

13—16. BLESSING OF CHILDREN
(Mt. xix. 13—15, Lc. xviii. 15—17).

13. καὶ προσέφερον αὐτῷ παιδία]
This incident follows with singular
fitness after the Lord's assertions of
the sanctity of married life. Mt. regards the sequence as strictly chronological (τότε προσηνέχθησαν κτλ.), and
Mc. appears to locate the arrival of
the children at the house where the
Lord delivered to the Twelve His
judgement on marriages after divorce
(cf. x. 10, 17). Lc., whose narrative
here rejoins that of Mt. and Mc., has
no note of time or place, for Lc. xvii.
11 cannot be taken as a guide; but
the fact that from this point the three
Synoptists proceed in almost unbroken
order to the history of the Passion may
suggest that these events belong to the
last journey from Ephraim to Jericho
and Jerusalem. Προσφέρειν is repeatedly used of the ministry of
friends who brought their sick to the
Lord, Mt. iv. 24, viii. 16, ix. 2 (Mc.
ii. 4), 32, xii. 22, xiv. 35; young children needed the same service, and
now at length received it. It was a
sign of the growing reverence for the
great Rabbi when even infants (καὶ
τὰ βρέφη, Lc.) were brought to Him
for His blessing. Παιδίον, though
used of a child twelve years old (v.
39, 42), could be applied to an infant

14 οἱ δὲ μαθηταὶ ἐπετίμησαν αὐτοῖς. ¹⁴ ἰδὼν δὲ ὁ
Ἰησοῦς ἠγανάκτησεν καὶ εἶπεν αὐτοῖς Ἄφετε τὰ

13 επετιμησαν ℵBCLΔΨ] επετιμων ADNXΓΠΣΦ minᵒᵐⁿ ᵛⁱᵈ latt | αυτοις ℵBCLΔΨ
c k me] τοις προσφερουσιν (αυτα) ADNX(Γ)ΠΣΦ minᶠᵉʳᵉᵒᵐⁿ a b f ff q vg syrˢⁱⁿ ᵖᵉˢʰ ʰᶜˡ
arm go aeth   14 και]+επιτιμησας 1 13 28 69 124 346 2ᵖᵉ syrˢⁱⁿ ʰᶜˡ (ᵐᵍ) (arm)

eight days old (Gen. xvii. 12); whilst
βρέφος may be the unborn fetus (Lc. i.
41, 44), the babe in its cradle (Lc. ii.
12, 16) or at the breast (4 Macc. iv.
25), or the child who is learning his
first lessons at his mother's knee (2 Tim.
iii. 15). Those who were brought to
Jesus were doubtless of various ages,
from the infant in arms to the elder
children still under the mother's care.
The Lord Himself had passed through
all the stages of human immaturity
(Iren. ii. 22. 4), and this group of
children with their friends would
recall His own experience at Nazareth.
The youngest were not too young for
His benediction; Tertullian's "veniant
ergo dum adolescunt, veniant dum
discunt, dum quo veniant docentur"
(de bapt. 18) strikes a false note which
has been taken up and exaggerated
in later times. Contrast Victor: τὸ
τῆς φρονήσεως ἐνδεὲς οὐ κωλυτικὸν τῆς
προσόδου.

ἵνα αὐτῶν ἅψηται] Similarly Lc.
(ἅπτηται); Mt. ἵνα τὰς χεῖρας ἐπιθῇ
αὐτοῖς καὶ προσεύξηται—a commentary
on the briefer original. On the con-
junctive cf. WM., p. 358 ff. The custom of laying on of hands with prayer
upon children for the purpose of
benediction (εἰς χειροθεσίαν εὐλογίας,
Clem. Al. paed. i. 12) finds its archetype in Gen. xlviii. 14, 15 (see Hastings,
D. B. iii. p. 84 f.). Such benedictions,
it seems, were commonly obtained by
parents for their children from the
ἀρχισυνάγωγοι (Buxtorf de synag.
p. 138); and here was One greater
than any local synagogue-ruler. But
perhaps the purpose of the friends
was simply to secure a blessing by
contact with the wonder-working
Prophet (i. 41, viii. 22, cf. iii. 10, v. 28,

vi. 56). Cf. Orig. in Mt.: τάχα δὲ
καὶ...τὸ βούλημα τῶν προσφερόντων
τοιοῦτον ἦν, διαλαβόντων ὅτι οὐχ οἷόν τε
ἦν, ἁψαμένου Ἰησοῦ βρεφῶν ἢ παιδίων
καὶ δύναμιν διὰ τῆς ἁφῆς ἐναφιέντος
αὐτοῖς, σύμπτωμα ἢ δαιμόνιον ἤ τι ἄψ-
ασθαι οὗ φθάσας ὁ Ἰησοῦς ἥψατο.
Bengel [ἵνα]...ἄψηται : "modestum
petitum."

οἱ δὲ μαθηταὶ ἐπετίμησαν αὐτοῖς]
Vg.comminabantur; Wycliffe, "thret-
enyden to men offringe"; Tindale,
"rebuked"; cf. ix. 38 f., x. 48 f. The
Lord, who was in the house, was approached through the Twelve or one
or more of the senior members of
that body (cf. Jo. xii. 21 f.); and they
discouraged the attempt as idle or,
more probably, as derogatory to the
Master's dignity. Victor: τίνος δὲ
ἕνεκεν ἀπεσόβουν τὰ παιδία οἱ μαθηταί;
ἀξιώματος ἕνεκεν. Thpht.: νομίζοντες
ἀνάξιον τοῦτο εἶναι τοῦ χριστοῦ.

14. ἰδὼν δὲ ὁ Ἰησοῦς κτλ.] From
the house Jesus saw what was happening, and His displeasure was aroused
(ἠγανάκτησεν, Mc. only). Indignation
is attributed to Him on no other
occasion, but it is recognised by St
Paul as under certain circumstances
a Christian feeling (2 Cor. vii. 11 τὸ
κατὰ θεὸν λυπηθῆναι πόσην κατειργάσατο
ὑμῖν...ἀγανάκτησιν); cf. 4 Macc. iv. 21,
ἀγανακτήσασα ἡ θεία δίκη. That the
nature of His kingdom should still be
misunderstood and His work hindered
by the Twelve was just cause for
indignant surprise. Bengel: "ἠγα-
νάκτησε[ν]...propter impedimentum
amori suo a discipulis oblatum."

ἄφετε τὰ παιδία κτλ.] 'Let the
children come to Me, hinder them
not.' Both in Mt. (ἄφετε...καὶ μὴ
κωλύετε ἐλθεῖν) and Lc. (ἄφετε...ἔρ-

παιδία ἔρχεσθαι πρὸς μέ, μὴ κωλύετε αὐτά· τῶν γὰρ
τοιούτων ἐστὶν ἡ βασιλεία τοῦ θεοῦ. ¹⁵ἀμὴν λέγω 15
ὑμῖν Ὃς ἂν μὴ δέξηται τὴν βασιλείαν τοῦ θεοῦ ὡς
παιδίον, οὐ μὴ εἰσέλθῃ εἰς αὐτήν. ¹⁶καὶ ἐναγκαλισά- 16
μενος αὐτὰ κατευλόγει, τιθεὶς⁋ τὰς χεῖρας ἐπ' αὐτά.   ⁋ L

14 παιδια] παιδαρια D* | μη] pr και אACDLM² 1 13 al^{sat mu} latt syrr^{sin pesh hcl} arm go
aeth   15 ου μη...αυτην] ου μη εις αυτ. εισελευσεται D   16 εναγκαλισαμενος] προσκα-
λεσαμενος D convitans b convocans c d f ff q r syr^{sin} | κατευλογει אBC(L)NΔ(Ψ) 2^{pe}
al^{nonn}] ευλογει ADEHK*MSUVX(Γ)ΠΣΦ min^{pl} | τιθεις τας χειρας επ αυτα] ετιθει τ. χ.
επ αυτα και (ante κατευλ. vel ευλ.) D b c ff k q arm

χεσθαι...καὶ μὴ κ.) the words assume a
later form ; in Mc. we hear the Lord's
indignant call, as it startles the disciples in the act of dismissing the
party. Ἄφετε...μὴ κωλύετε : "an ex-
pressive *asyndeton*" (Bruce). With
μὴ κωλύετε cf. ix. 39 n. The children
are regarded as themselves coming
and being hindered ; cf. the Office for
Public Baptism : "we call upon Thee
for this infant that he, coming, &c."
Τῶν γὰρ τοιούτων κτλ. Cf. Dalman,
Worte, i. p. 104. Origen : τοιούτων ὁποῖά ἐστι τὰ παιδία. Victor : οὐ
γὰρ 'τούτων' εἶπεν ἀλλὰ 'τῶν τοιούτων,'
ἐπειδὴ πρόσεστι καὶ τὸ τῆς φρονήσεως
ἐνδεὲς τοῖς παισίν...ἵνα τῇ προαιρέσει
ταῦτα ἐργαζώμεθα ἃ τῇ φύσει τὰ παιδία
ἔχει. Cf. Ambrose *in Lc.* : "non aetas
praefertur aetati ; alioquin obesset
adolescere" ; Jerome *in Mt.* : "talium,
ut ostenderet non aetatem regnare
sed mores." That this teaching is
latent in the words the next verse
shews ; but it is their immediate purpose to assign a reason (γάρ) for the
Lord's command. To exclude children from the Kingdom of GOD is to
exclude those who of all human beings
are naturally least unfitted to enter
it, and whose attitude is the type of
the converted life (Mt. xviii. 3).

15. ἀμὴν λέγω ὑμῖν κτλ.] The Lord
confirms with His solemn ἀμήν (cf. iii.
28, note) the final lesson of His ministry in Galilee. Mt., who has preserved
the words on that occasion (Mt xviii.

3), omits them here ; but the repetition was clearly necessary under the
circumstances. Δέχεσθαι elsewhere
has for its object a person (ἐμέ, ὑμᾶς,
ix. 37), a message (τὸν λόγον, Lc. viii.
13, Acts xi. 1, Jas. i. 21), or a gift
(2 Cor. vi. 1, xi. 4) ; the kingdom
embraces all these ; to receive it is to
receive Christ, the Gospel, and the
grace of the Spirit. Δέξηται : Bengel,
"offertur enim." For the phrase εἰσελθεῖν εἰς τὴν βασ. τ. θεοῦ cf. ix. 47, x.
23, 25, Jo. iii. 5 ; with ὡς παιδίον cf.
Ps. cxxx. (cxxxi.) 2, ὡς ἀπογεγαλακ-
τισμένον, and for an early Christian
use of the words see Herm. *sim.* ix.
29, οἱ πιστεύσαντες...ὡς νήπια βρέφη
εἰσίν, οἷς οὐδεμία κακία ἀναβαίνει ἐπὶ
τὴν καρδίαν, οὐδὲ ἔγνωσαν τί ἐστι
πονηρία, ἀλλὰ πάντοτε ἐν νηπιότητι
διέμειναν. It is, however, not so much
the innocence of young children which
is in view, as their spirit of trustful
simplicity.

16. ἐναγκαλισάμενος κτλ.] He had
already called them to Him (Lc. προσεκαλέσατο), and as they came up in
succession, each was taken in His
arms and blessed (κατευλόγει). For
ἐναγκαλισάμενος see ix. 36, note ; the
repetition of the characteristic act
would perhaps recall to the minds of
the disciples the forgotten teaching
of the last days at Capernaum. Κατευλογεῖν, ἅπ. λεγ. in the N. T., occurs
in Tob. xi. 1, 17, and in Plutarch ;
as in καταγελᾶν (v. 40), and καταφιλεῖν

17 ^{17} Καὶ ἐκπορευομένου αὐτοῦ εἰς ὁδὸν προσδραμὼν
εἷς καὶ γονυπετήσας αὐτὸν ἐπηρώτα αὐτόν Διδάσκαλε

17 προσδραμων εις (πρ. τις 604)] ιδου τις πλουσιος προσδρ. ΑΚ(Μ)Π 13 28 69 124
736* 1071 2ᵖᵉ alⁿᵒⁿⁿ (syrʰᶜˡ(ᵐᵍ)) arm | γονυπετων D 28 69 124 346 | αυτον]+λεγων 13
69 124 346 2ᵖᵉ alᵖᵃᵘᶜ a b c k syrr arm me go Clem Al

(xiv. 45), the force of κατά seems to
be intensive—He blessed them fer-
vently, in no perfunctory way, but
with emphasis, as those who were
capable of a more unreserved benediction than their elders. Instead of
the mere touch for which the friends
had asked, He laid his hands on them
(τιθεὶς τὰς χεῖρας ἐπ᾽ αὐτά, Mt. ἐπιθεὶς
τὰς χ. αὐτοῖς) with the words of blessing. "Plus fecit quam rogatus erat"
(Bengel): cf. the Gelasian collect
(Wilson, p. 228): "abundantia pie-
tatis tuae et merita supplicum excedis
et vota."

In the N. African Church this incident seems to have been urged in
support of Infant Baptism as early as
the time of Tertullian (cf. v. 13, note).
Mt. xix. 13 ff. occurs as the Gospel of
the Baptismal Office in an *ordo* of the
12th century (Muratori, *De ant. eccl.
rit.*, i. p. 44), and was used as such in
the English Church until 1549, when
the more impressive and suggestive
narrative of Mc. was substituted by
Cranmer and his colleagues.

17—22. THE RICH MAN WHO
WANTED BUT ONE THING (Mt. xix.
16—22, Lc. xviii. 18—23).

17. ἐκπορευομένου αὐτοῦ εἰς ὁδόν]
Mt. (xix. 15) ἐπορεύθη ἐκεῖθεν. The
incident occurred when the Lord had
left the house, and was beginning His
journey again. For εἰς ὁδόν cf. vi. 8,
note, and contrast εἰς τὴν ὁδόν (xi. 8).

The text of Clement of Alexandria
throughout this context has been carefully examined by P. M. Barnard,
in *Texts and Studies*, v. 5, *q. v.*

προσδραμὼν εἰς κτλ.] He was an
ἄρχων (Lc.) and yet a νεανίσκος (Mt.).
Ἄρχων is a term of some latitude; it
is used by Mt. (ix. 18) for an ἀρχισυν-

ἀγωγος (Mc.) or ἄρχων τῆς συναγωγῆς
(Lc.), and by Lc. for a chief Pharisee
(xiv. 1, cf. Syr.ᶜᵘ· in xviii. 18); in Acts
iv. 5 τοὺς ἄρχοντας = τ. ἀρχιερεῖς; Jo.
(e.g. iii. 1, vii. 26 ff.) apparently understands by ἄρχων any member of the
great Sanhedrin. The word passed
into Rabbinic (ארכונא, ארכונטס, Dalman, *Gr.* p. 148 f.) as a general term
for a great man or prince (cf. Westcott
on Jo. iii. 1). If it is used by Lc. here
in this looser sense no difficulty arises
from the youth of this ἄρχων; his
large property (v. 22) sufficiently accounts for his local eminence, not to
urge that νεανίσκος is a relative term
which may be used of any age between
boyhood and middle life (Lob.,*Phryn.*,
p. 213; cf. Diog. Laert. 8. 10). Προσ-
δραμών (Mt. προσελθών), cf. ix. 15; for
εἷς (Mt., Mc.) 'one,'=τις (Lc.) cf. Mt.
viii. 19, ix. 18, Apoc. viii. 13, ix. 13,
xix. 17 (WM., p. 145, BDB., s.v. אֶחָד
(3)). Γονυπετήσας αὐτόν: cf. i. 40, note.
The ἀρχισυνάγωγος (v. 22) also pro-
strated himself; but the homage paid
by this ἄρχων is more remarkable
because he is not a suppliant for
material help. In his eagerness to
obtain spiritual advice he shews no
less zeal than if he had sought the
greatest of temporal benefits.

διδάσκαλε ἀγαθέ, τί ποιήσω] Similarly Lc. (δ. ἀ., τί ποιήσας...); Mt., who
throughout the story follows another
tradition, changes the point of both
question and answer (διδάσκαλε, τί
ἀγαθὸν ποιήσω...τί με ἐρωτᾷς περὶ τοῦ
ἀγαθοῦ;). Cf. Orig. *in Mt.* t. xv.: ὁ μὲν
οὖν Ματθαῖος ὡς περὶ ἀγαθοῦ ἔργου
ἐρωτηθέντος τοῦ σωτῆρος...ἀνέγραψεν·
ὁ δὲ Μᾶρκος καὶ Λουκᾶς φασι τὸν
σωτῆρα εἰρηκέναι Τί με λέγεις ἀγαθόν;
The change may be due to the shifting

ἀγαθέ, τί ποιήσω ἵνα ζωὴν αἰώνιον κληρονομήσω;
¹⁸ ὁ δὲ ᾿Ιησοῦς εἶπεν αὐτῷ Τί με λέγεις ἀγαθόν; οὐδεὶς 18

17 ποιησω ινα] ποιησας Ψ

of the place of the adjective in the
original—מַה הַטּוֹב רַבִּי has become
רַבִּי מַה הַטּוֹב (cf. Delitzsch *ad loc.*,
and Resch, *Paralleltexte zu Lc.*,
p. 494). Resch endeavours to shew
that both forms of the answer may
have sprung from מַה תֹּאמַר לִי הַטּוֹב;
see also J. T. Marshall, *Exp.* III. iv. p.
384, vi. 88, where the corresponding
Aramaic is given. ᾿Αγαθέ is probably
sincere, not a fulsome compliment,
still less intended for irony. But it
implies an imperfect standard of
moral goodness, since the speaker
regarded the Lord as a merely human
teacher; cf. Ambrose: "in portione
dixit bonum, non in universitate."

ἵνα ζωὴν αἰώνιον κληρ.] No more
appropriate question could have been
put to our Lord; Clem. Al. *quis
dives* 6 ἠρώτηται...ἐρώτημα καταλλη-
λότατον αὐτῷ, ἡ ζωὴ περὶ ζωῆς, ὁ σωτὴρ
περὶ σωτηρίας. It was put moreover
by an earnest enquirer; contrast Lc.
x. 25, where the same question is
asked by a νομικός as a test of orthodoxy (ἐκπειράζων αὐτόν). Κληρονομεῖν
(יָרַשׁ, sometimes נָחַל) τὴν γῆν (cf. Mt.
v. 5) is a phrase which runs through
the O.T.; but a more spiritual conception of the inheritance of the just finds
a place in the later books, e.g. Sir. iv.
13 (κλ. δόξαν), xxxvii. 26 (κλ. πίστιν),
Pss. Sal. xii. 8 (κλ. ἐπαγγελίας), xiv.
7 (κλ. ζωὴν ἐν εὐφροσύνῃ); cf. Philo,
quis rer. div. heres. The use of the
term ζωὴ αἰώνιος first appears in connexion with the hope of the Resurrection, cf. Dan xii. 2 (חַיֵּי עוֹלָם), Pss.
Sal. iii. 16, Enoch xxxvii. 4, xl. 9, lviii.
3, 2 Macc. vii. 9. In adopting these
words into its creed the Gospel transfigured their meaning; Christ had
ῥήματα ζωῆς αἰωνίου (Jo. vi. 68) which

were unknown to the Pharisees. But
the term itself, it is important to
remember, was of O. T. growth and
familiar to the Pharisaic Scribes.

18. τί με λέγεις ἀγαθόν;] The emphasis is on ἀγαθόν, not on the pronoun.
The Lord begins by compelling the
enquirer to consider his own words.
He had used ἀγαθέ lightly, in a manner
which revealed the poverty of his
moral conceptions. From that word
Christ accordingly starts. Clem. Al.
l. c. κληθεὶς δὲ ἀγαθός, ἀπ᾿ αὐτοῦ πρώτου
τοῦ ῥήματος τούτου τὸ ἐνδόσιμον λαβὼν
ἐντεῦθεν καὶ τῆς διδασκαλίας ἄρχεται,
ἐπιστρέφων τὸν μαθητὴν ἐπὶ τὸν θεὸν
τὸν ἀγαθὸν καὶ πρῶτον καὶ μόνον ζωῆς
αἰωνίου ταμίαν, ἣν ὁ υἱὸς δίδωσιν ἡμῖν
παρ᾿ ἐκείνου λαβών. The man is
summoned to contemplate the absolute ἀγαθωσύνη which is the attribute
of GOD, and to measure himself by that
supreme standard. Viewed in this
light the words are seen not to touch
the question of our Lord's human
sinlessness or of His oneness with the
Father; on the other hand they are
consistent with the humility which
led Him as Man to refrain from
asserting His equality with GOD (Phil.
ii. 6): cf. Athan. *c. Arian.* iii. 7, εἰ...
ὁ υἱὸς οὐχ ἑαυτὸν ἀλλὰ τὸν πατέρα
ἐδόξασε, λέγων μὲν τῷ προσερχομένῳ
Τί με λέγεις ἀγαθόν; οὐδεὶς ἀγαθὸς εἰ
μὴ εἷς ὁ θεός...ποία ἐναντιότης; Hilary
surely misreads the Lord's words
when he says: "nomine bonitatis
abstinuit...quod congrua in eum se-
veritate iudex esset usurus." Only
the supremely Good can be the perfect
Judge. To Christ both characters
belong, but this was not the moment
for revealing Himself in either. See
next note.

οὐδεὶς ἀγαθὸς εἰ μὴ εἷς ὁ θεός] Mt.
εἷς ἐστιν ὁ ἀγαθός. Justin (*dial.* 101),

19 ἀγαθὸς εἰ μὴ εἷς ὁ θεός. ¹⁹τὰς ἐντολὰς οἶδας Μὴ
φονεύσῃς, μὴ μοιχεύσῃς, μὴ κλέψῃς, μὴ ψευδομαρτυρήσῃς, μὴ ἀποστερήσῃς, τίμα τὸν πατέρα σου καὶ

18 εις ο θεος] μονος εις θ͞ς D (b) *solus deus* a ff εις ο θ͞ς ο πατηρ Or² arm^codd
19 μη φον. μη μοιχ. μη κλεψ. ℵ^a (om μη μοιχ. ℵ*) BCΔΨ min^perpauc syr^sin me] μη μοιχ.
μη φον. μη κλεψ. ΑΝΧΠΣΦ min^pl a b d ff q r^vid vg syr^hcl arm go aeth Clem Al μη
μοιχ. μη κλεψ. μη φον. syr^pesh μη μοιχ. μη πορνευσης μη κλεψ. D k μη μοιχ. μη κλεψ.
μη πορν. Γ μη φον. μη μοιχ. μη πορν. μη κλεψ. c | om μη φον. 1 118 209 300 f |
om μη αποστερ. B*ΚΔΠΨ 1 28 69* 118 209 al^nonn syr^sin arm Clem Al

Marcion, the Clementines (*hom.* xviii.
3), and Ephrem (*ev. conc. exp.*), add
in Mt. ὁ πατήρ (μου) ὁ ἐν τοῖς οὐρανοῖς,
and ὁ πατήρ is read by Origen (*in Jo.*
t. i. 35); see WH., *Notes*, p. 14.
Ephrem's commentary is interesting :
"et tu, Domine, nonne es bonus...et
adventus tuus nonne erat adventus
bonitatis ? Sed 'ego,' ait, 'non a me-
ipso veni.' Et opera tua nonne sunt
bona ? 'Pater meus,' ait, 'qui est in
me, ipse operatur haec opera.'" The
Son, as Origen points out (*in Jo.* t.
xiii. 25, 36), is the εἰκὼν τῆς ἀγαθότητος
τοῦ πατρός, and not, *qua* Son, τὸ
αὐτοάγαθον. Hence He disclaims the
title ἀγαθός, when it is offered to Him
without regard to His oneness with
the Father, and refers it to the Source
of Godhead (μὴ ἐνεγκόντι μηδὲ τὴν
ἀγαθός προσηγορίαν τὴν κυρίαν καὶ
ἀληθῆ καὶ τελείαν παραδέξασθαι, αὐτῷ
προσφερομένην, ἀλλὰ ἀναφέροντι αὐτὴν
εὐχαρίστως τῷ πατρί). Similarly Bengel : "non in se requiescebat, sed se
penitus ad Patrem referebat." On
the other hand Ambrose rightly pleads :
"si a Deo Filius non excipitur, utique
nec a bono Christus excipitur...cum
bonus Pater, utique et ille bonus
qui omnia habet quae Pater habet"—
"bonus ex bono," as Ephrem well says.
For Gnostic perversions of this text
see Iren. i. 20. 2, Hippol. *haer.* v. 7,
vii. 31, *Clem. hom. l.c.*, Epiph. *haer.*
33. 7. On the relation of the doctrine
of the Divine goodness to the harder
facts of life see Origen *in Mt. ad loc.*

For O.T. anticipations of the Lord's
saying cf. 1 Sam. ii. 2, Ps. cxviii. 1 ff.

19. τὰς ἐντολὰς οἶδας κτλ.] Having
fixed the standard of goodness the
Lord proceeds to rehearse the Divine
precepts which were regarded by the
Jew as the highest expression of the
θέλημα ἀγαθόν (Rom. xii. 2), and as
the source of all that is good in man
(cf. Weber, *Jüd. Theologie*, p. 20).
Mt. paraphrases εἰ δὲ θέλεις εἰς τὴν
ζωὴν εἰσελθεῖν, τήρει τὰς ἐντολάς, and
makes the enumeration which follows
an answer to a second question
(ποίας;). The Lord cites only the
commandments which regulate man's
duty to his neighbour, probably because they admit of a relatively simple
application to the conduct of life. He
cites these in the order vi., vii., viii.,
ix. (x.), v. (Mt., Mc.) or, according to
Lc., vii., vi., viii., ix., v. ; Mc.'s order
(on the vv. ll. cf. WH., *Notes*, p. 25)
is that of cod. A and of the M. T. in
Exod. xx. and Deut. v., whilst Lc.'s
agrees with that of cod. B in placing
vii. before vi. (cf. Rom. *l.c.*, Jas. ii. 11,
Philo, *de x orac.* 10, *de spec. legg.* iii.
2, and on the other hand, Jos. *ant.* iii.
5. 5 ; and see *Intr. to the O. T. in Gk.*,
p. 234). Μὴ ἀποστερήσῃς (Mc. only)
seems to be derived from Exod. xxi.
10, Deut. xxiv. 14 (A), cf. Sir. iv. 1,
Jos. *ant.* iv. 8. 38 ; but it may be
intended here to represent the tenth
commandment, while summing up the
sins committed against vi.—ix. ; on
the class. and later use of ἀποστερεῖν

τὴν μητέρα. ²⁰ὁ δὲ ἔφη αὐτῷ Διδάσκαλε, ταῦτα 20
πάντα ἐφυλαξάμην ἐκ νεότητός μου. ²¹ὁ δὲ Ἰησοῦς 21
ἐμβλέψας αὐτῷ ἠγάπησεν αὐτὸν καὶ εἶπεν αὐτῷ

19 μητερα]+σου ℵ*CFNΣ 28 124 238 al^nonn a b c f syrr^sin pesh me go aeth   20 ο δε
εφη ℵBΔΨ me] ο δε αποκριθεις ειπεν ADNXΓΣΦ min^fere omn latt syrr (arm) go (Clem
Al) και αποκρ. εφη C | ὸm διδασκαλε KΠ 1 209 al^pauc Clem Al | εφυλαξαμην
ℵBCNXΓΔΠΣΦΨ] εφυλαξα AD 28 Clem Al Or εποιησα 1 209 2^pe arm | μου]+τι ετι
υστερω KMNΠΣ 13 28 69 124 346 1071 2^pe al^nonn a c syr^hcl arm   21 αυτω 2°]+ει
θελεις τελειος ειναι KMNΠΣ(Φ) 13 28 69 124 346 736 2^pe al^nonn syr^hcl (arm) me aeth
Clem Al

see Field, *Notes*, p. 33 f., and for the N.T. use cf. 1 Cor. vi. 7 f., vii. 5. The fifth commandment is reserved to the last place, possibly in order to emphasise its importance in view of its practical abrogation by the oral law (vii. 10 ff.). Mt. adds the summary of the Second Table from Lev. xix. 18 (cf. Mc. xii. 31). The form μὴ φονεύσῃς κτλ. (Mc., Lc.) occurs also in Jas. ii. 11; Mt.'s οὐ φονεύσεις follows the LXX. (Exod., Deut.).

20. ταῦτα πάντα ἐφυλαξάμην] Mt., Lc. ἐφύλαξα. In the LXX. both voices are used in this connexion, with perhaps a preference for the mid. (cf. Gen. xxvi. 5, Exod. xx. 6, Deut. xxvi. 18, 3 Regn. ii. 3, viii. 61 (act.); Lev. xviii. 4, Deut. iv. 2, 1 Chron. xxviii. 7, 2 Esdr. xx. 29 (30), Ps. cxviii (cxix.) 4 ff. (mid.)). The N.T. elsewhere uses φυλάσσειν only in this sense (Lc. xi. 28, Jo. xii. 47, Acts vii. 53, xvi. 4, xxi. 24, Rom. ii. 26, Gal. vi. 13, &c.). Ἐκ νεότητός μου: Lc., ἐκ νεότητος, Mt., who calls the man a νεανίσκος, omits these words. The phrase ἐκ (or ἀπὸ) νεότητος with or without the pronoun following is frequent in the LXX., e.g. Gen. viii. 21 (ἐκ ν. αὐτοῦ=מִנְּעֻרָיו), 1 Regn. xii. 2, Ps. lxx. (lxxi.) 17; in the N. T. it is used again in Acts xxvi. 4.

The young man is relieved by the Lord's answer. If the eternal inheritance could be secured on so simple a condition as the keeping of the Decalogue, it was his already. He had

thought perhaps (as Mt.'s ποίας; seems to shew) of the precepts of the Halachah. Something more than the letter of the Torah must surely be necessary; what was it? (Mt. τί ἔτι ὑστερῶ;). The deeper meaning and larger requirements of the Law were yet hidden from him.

21. ὁ δὲ Ἰ. ἐμβλέψας αὐτῷ κτλ.] Mc. only; Mt. has merely ἔφη αὐτῷ, Lc., ἀκούσας...εἶπεν αὐτῷ. Ἐμβλέπειν (viii. 25, x. 27, xiv. 67, Lc. xxii. 61) is to fix the eyes for a moment upon an object,—a characteristically searching look turned upon an individual; cf. περιβλέπεσθαι (iii. 5, x. 23), which describes a similar look carried round a circle. Ἠγάπησεν αὐτόν. The look revealed that which attracted love, such as the Lord entertained for a genuine, however imperfect, disciple; cf. Jo. xiii. 1, 23, 34; xv. 9, 12. Tindale's endeavour to weaken the force of ἠγ. by translating "Jesus... favoured him" is unnecessary; still less can we adopt the rendering "caressed him" which Field (*Notes*, p. 34), though with some hesitation, suggests; the Lord loved in the man what He saw to be good and of GOD. Cf. Grotius: "Amat Christus non virtutes tantum sed et semina virtutum"; Godet: "ce regard d'amour était en même temps un regard plein de pénétration par lequel Jésus discerna les bonnes et les mauvaises qualités de ce cœur, et qui lui inspira la parole suivante." On the distinction between

῾Εν σε ὑστερεῖ· ὕπαγε, ὅσα ἔχεις πώλησον καὶ δὸς

21 σε ℵBCMΔII* 28 al^pauc] σοι ADNXΓΠ²ΣΦΨ min^pl Clem Al Or pr ετι ℵ min^nonn me | δος] διαδος k (*distribue*) Clem Al

ἀγαπᾶν and φιλεῖν (Jo. xi. 3, 36, xx. 2) see Trench, *syn.* 12, Westcott on Jo. v. 20, xi. 3. ἕν σε ὑστερεῖ] Lc. ἔτι ἕν σοι λείπει. Clem. Al. *quis dives* 10: ἕν σοι λείπει· τὸ ἕν τὸ ἐμόν, τὸ ἀγαθόν, τὸ ἤδη ὑπὲρ νόμον, ὅπερ νόμος οὐ δίδωσιν, ὅπερ νόμος οὐ χωρεῖ, ὁ τῶν ζώντων ἴδιόν ἐστιν (cf. Lc. x. 41). For ὑστερεῖν in this sense see Jo. ii. 3, and for the acc. of the person, cf. Ps. xxii. (xxiii.) ἵ οὐδέν με ὑστερήσει (אֶחְסָר לֹא), lxxxiii. (lxxxiv.) 12; the construction ὑστερῶ τι (Sir. li. 24, Mt. xix. 20, 2 Cor. xii. 11) or τινός (Lc. xxii. 35, Rom. iii. 23, &c.) is more usual in the N. T. Mt. represents the enquirer as asking τί ἔτι ὑστερῶ; and for ἕν σε ὑστερεῖ in the Lord's reply substitutes εἰ θέλεις τέλειος εἶναι. One thing was wanting to perfect the man's fitness for the inheritance of eternal life.

ὕπαγε, ὅσα ἔχεις πώλησον κτλ.] The sale and distribution of his property were the necessary preparations in his case for the complete discipleship which admits to the Divine kingdom. Euth. : ἐπεὶ τὰ ὑπάρχοντα...ἐμπόδια ἦσαν τοῦ ἀκολουθῆσαι, κελεύει ταῦτα πωλῆσαι. The words are not a general counsel of perfection, but a test of obedience and faith which the Lord saw to be necessary in this particular case. The demand of the Divine Lover of souls varies with the spiritual condition of the individual; for one equally great see Gen. xii. 1, Heb. xi. 8 ff. Whether this precept led to the sacrifices described in Acts ii. 44 f., iv. 34 ff. cannot now be known; the *Life of St Anthony* relates its effect on the great Egyptian hermit: chancing one day to hear Mt. xix. 21 read in the Gospel for the day, ὡς δι' αὐτὸν γενομένου τοῦ ἀναγνώσματος ἐξελθὼν εὐθὺς ἐκ τοῦ κυριακοῦ τὰς μὲν κτήσεις ἃς

εἶχον ἐκ προγόνων...ταύτας ἐχαρίσατο τοῖς ἀπὸ τῆς κώμης...τὰ δὲ ἄλλα ὅσα ἦν αὐτοῖς πωλήσας...δέδωκε τοῖς πτωχοῖς, τηρήσας ὀλίγα διὰ τὴν ἀδελφήν. The destitute poor (οἱ πτωχοί) were a numerous class in Palestine in the first century (cf. xii. 42, xiv. 5 ff., Lc. xvi. 20, Jo. xiii. 29, Jas. ii. 2 f.), and one for which no regular provision was made. The *Gospel acc. to the Hebrews* is eloquent on this point: "quomodo dicis, 'Legem fecisti et prophetas'...et ecce multi fratres tui, filii Abrahae, amicti sunt stercore, morientes prae fame, et domus tua plena est multis bonis et non egreditur omnino aliquid ex ea ad illos."

The self-sacrifice which the Lord imposed on this wealthy enquirer asserts in principle the duty of the rich to minister to the poor; the particular form which their ministry must take varies with the social conditions of the age. Of the form embodied in this precept it is probably safe to say ῾Ο δυνάμενος χωρεῖν χωρείτω. See Clem. Al. *quis dives* 13 ff. for some weighty remarks upon the question of a voluntary poverty. While discouraging the abandonment of wealth in a general way, he admits that there are cases in which it may be expedient: § 24 ἀλλ' ὁρᾷς σεαυτὸν ἡττώμενον ὑπ' αὐτῶν καὶ ἀνατρεπόμενον· ἄφες, ῥίψον, μίσησον, ἀπόταξαι, φύγε (adding a reference to Mt. v. 29). Cf. *paed.* ii. 3 § 36, ἕπου τῷ θεῷ γυμνὸς ἀλαζονείας, γυμνὸς ἐπικήρου πομπῆς, τὸ σόν, τὸ ἀγαθόν, τὸ ἀναφαίρετον μόνον, τὴν εἰς τὸν θεὸν πίστιν, τὴν εἰς τὸν παθόντα ὁμολογίαν, τὴν εἰς ἀνθρώπους εὐεργεσίαν κεκτημένος, κτῆμα τιμαλφέστατον.

καὶ ἕξεις θησαυρὸν ἐν οὐρανῷ] In contrast with θησαυροὶ ἐπὶ τῆς γῆς (Mt. vi. 19), cf. Lc. xii. 33 f.; compare

[τοῖς] πτωχοῖς, καὶ ἕξεις θησαυρὸν ἐν οὐρανῷ· καὶ
δεῦρο ἀκολούθει μοι. ²²ὁ δὲ στυγνάσας ἐπὶ τῷ 22
λόγῳ ἀπῆλθεν λυπούμενος, ἦν γὰρ ἔχων κτήματα
πολλά.

²³Καὶ περιβλεψάμενος ὁ Ἰησοῦς λέγει τοῖς μαθη- 23

21 πτωχοις ΑΒΝΧΓΔΣΨ 604 1071 al^mu arm go Clem Al] pr τοις אCDΦ 1 2^pe
al^mu | μοι]+αρας τον σταυρον (σου) A(G)ΝΧΓΠΣΦ al^pl et ante δευρο 1 13 28 69 al^pauc
a syrr^sin pesh aeth Ir item pro δευρο arm   22 στυγνασας] εστυγνασεν...και D b c ff q |
τω λογω] pr τουτω D 28 69 124 346 2^pe a b c f ff k q syrr^sin pesh | κτηματα] χρηματα D
116 b f ff k q syr^sin Clem Al | πολλα]+και αγρους b k Clem Al   23 λεγει] ελεγεν א*C

the remarkable parallel in Mt. xiii.
44, and the imagery of Apoc. iii. 17 f.

καὶ δεῦρο ἀκολούθει μοι] See ii.
14, note. The final test of character,
proposed to all candidates for eternal
life; cf. Jo. x. 27, xii. 26. This essential
condition is not necessarily involved
in even the greatest sacrifice of outward things; cf. Jerome: " multi
divitias relinquentes Dominum non
sequuntur."

22. ὁ δὲ στυγνάσας ἐπὶ τῷ λόγῳ]
Mc. only : Mt. ἀκούσας...τὸν λόγον τοῦτον, Lc. ἀκούσας...ταῦτα. As he heard
the sentence, his brow clouded over
(στυγνὸς καὶ κατήφης Clem. Al., quis
dives 4), the lighthearted optimism
of his mood broke down. Στυγνάζειν
is used of the saddening of either the
face of nature (Mt. xvi. 3, 'Western'
text) or the human face (Ezech. xxvii.
35, xxviii. 19 (A), xxxii. 10); the dark
and stormy night is στυγνή (Sap. xvii.
5); the στυγνός is the sombre, gloomy
man who broods over unwelcome
thoughts (Isa. lvii. 17, Dan. ii. 12
στυγνὸς γενόμενος καὶ περίλυπος, LXX.).
In the last passage the effect is partly
due to anger (Th. ἐν θυμῷ καὶ ὀργῇ),
but usually it is the result of dis-
appointment or grief, and that is
clearly what is intended here; cf. Vg.
contristatus in verbo; Wycliffe: "he
was ful sorie in the word." The
answer did not exasperate, but it
gave him pain which was visible on
his countenance: ἀπῆλθεν λυπούμενος

(Mt., Mc.), περίλυπος γενόμενος (Lc.).
His hopes were dashed; the one
thing he yet wanted was beyond his
reach; the price was too great to pay
even for eternal life. For the time
the love of the world prevailed. Yet
it is unnecessary with Origen and
Jerome to characterise his sorrow as
that of the world (2 Cor. vii. 10);
rather it may be the birth-
pangs of a spirit struggling for release. His riches were indeed as
thorns (Jerome) which threatened to
choke the seed of the word (iv. 7, 19),
but the end of the struggle is not
revealed. For the time, however, he
answered the Lord's δεῦρο by turning
his back on Him (ἀπῆλθεν).

ἦν γὰρ ἔχων κτήματα πολλά] Probably estates, lands; cf. Acts i. 18
(ἐκτήσατο χωρίον), iv. 34 (κτήτορες
χωρίων ἢ οἰκιῶν), v. 1, 3 (ἐπώλησεν
κτῆμα, ἀπὸ τῆς τιμῆς τοῦ χωρίου); in
Acts ii. 44 κτήματα are apparently
distinguished from the vaguer ὑπάρ-
ξεις. On ἦν...ἔχων—R.V. 'he was
one that had'—see Burton, § 432.
Cf. Bede: "inter pecunias habere et
pecunias amare multa distantia est.
multi enim habentes non amant, multi
non habentes amant."

23—27. THE RICH AND THE KING-
DOM OF GOD (Mt. xix. 23—26, Lc.
xviii. 24—27).

23. καὶ περιβλεψάμενος κτλ.] When
the man was gone the Lord's eye
swept round the circle of the Twelve

ταῖς αὐτοῦ Πῶς δυσκόλως οἱ τὰ χρήματα ἔχοντες
24 εἰς τὴν βασιλείαν τοῦ θεοῦ εἰσελεύσονται. ²⁴οἱ δὲ
μαθηταὶ ἐθαμβοῦντο ἐπὶ τοῖς λόγοις αὐτοῦ. ὁ δὲ
Ἰησοῦς πάλιν ἀποκριθεὶς λέγει αὐτοῖς Τέκνα, πῶς
δύσκολόν ἐστιν εἰς τὴν βασιλείαν τοῦ θεοῦ εἰσελθεῖν·
25 ²⁵εὐκοπώτερόν ἐστιν κάμηλον διὰ τρυμαλιᾶς ῥαφίδος

23 οι τα χρ. εχοντες] οι πεποιθοτες επι (? τοις) χρημασιν syrˢⁱⁿ | τα χρ.] om τα C
24 tot vers post 25 transpos D 235 a b ff om r | λεγει] ειπεν ΔΨ 1071 2ᵖᵉ alᵖᵃᵘᶜ | τεκνα
אBCDXΔ Clem Al τεκνια ΑΝΣΨ 1 1071 alᵖᵃᵘᵉ lattᵛⁱᵈᵉˣᶜᑫ om ΕΓΚΠ minᵛⁱˣ ᵐᵘ c k |
εστιν] + τους πεποιθοτας επι (τοις) χρημασιν ΑC(D)ΝΧΓΠΣΦ al minᵖˡ b f q vg
syrᵃ ⁱⁿ ᵖᵉˢʰ ʰᶜˡ arm meᵉᵈᵈ Clem Al (om אBΔ k meᶜᵒᵈᵈ) 25 ευκοπωτερον...εισελθειν]
τ[αχ]ειον καμηλος δια τρυμαλιδος ρ. διελευσεται η πλουσιος εις τ. βασ. τ. θ. D (a) |
καμιλον bˢᶜʳ* syrʰᶜˡ (‌ܩ‌ܠ‌ܝ‌ܢ‌) | τρυμαλιας (τρηματος א* Clem Al q. d. § 2
τρυπηματος 13 69 al Clem Al str. ii. 5. 22)] pr της ΒΕΓΗSVΧΦ minᵖˡ me Clem
Al | ραφιδος (βελονης 13 69 al Clem Al)] pr της ΒΕFHSVΧΓΦ minᵖˡ Clem Al

(iii. 5, note), as He drew for them the
lesson of the incident. So Mc. only;
Lc., ἰδὼν δὲ αὐτὸν εἶπεν. Πῶς δυσκόλως, Mc., Lc. ; ἀμὴν λέγω ὑμῖν ὅτι...
δυσκόλως, Mt. Δύσκολος and δυσκόλως occur in the N. T. only in this
context ; the LXX. use δύσκολος in
Jer. xxix. 9 (xlix. 8), δυσκολία in Job
xxxiv. 30 ; cf. εὔκολος in 2 Regn. xv.
3. The rarity of this class of words
in Biblical Gk. renders the occurrence
of δυσκόλως here in the three Synoptists the more significant. With πῶς
δ., 'with what difficulty,' comp. πῶς
παραχρῆμα, Mt. xxi. 20, πῶς συνέχομαι,
Lc. xii. 50. Οἱ τὰ χρήματα ἔχοντες,
'they who have money'; cf. v. 22 ἦν
ἔχων κτήματα. The wider word which
is preferred here includes all property whether in coin or convertible
into it (cf. Arist. eth. iv. 1 χρήματα δὲ
λέγομεν πάντα ὅσων ἡ ἀξία νομίσματι
μετρεῖται); for the former sense of χρήματα cf. Job xxvii. 17 (τὰ χρ. =כֶּסֶף),
2 Macc. iii. 7, 4 Macc. iv. 3, Acts iv.
37 (τὸ χρῆμα), viii. 18 ff., xxiv. 26 : for
the latter, 2 Chron. i. 11, 12 (נְכָסִים),
Sir. v. 1, 8, &c. Εἰς τ. βασιλείαν κτλ.;
cf. v. 15, note. For a partial parallel to
the saying see Sir. xxxiv. (xxxi.) 8, 9.

24. οἱ δὲ μαθηταὶ ἐθαμβοῦντο ἐπί
κτλ.] Mc. only. The Twelve were
thrown into consternation (for θαμβεῖσθαι see i. 27 n.) at (i. 22) the
Lord's sayings (λόγοις, contrast λόγῳ,
v. 22) on this occasion, but especially,
no doubt, at this last remark. What
manner of kingdom was this which
men must become as children to enter
(v. 15), and which men of substance
could scarcely enter at all? Their
surprise was probably expressed in
words, perhaps by Peter ; cf. Ev. sec.
Hebr. ap. Orig.: "conversus dixit
Simoni discipulo suo sedenti apud se
'Simon fili Ioanne, facilius est &c.'"

τέκνα, πῶς δύσκολόν ἐστιν κτλ.] For
τέκνα, which occurs here only (cf. Jo.
xiii. 33 τεκνία, xxi. 5 παιδία) in reference to the Twelve, see ii. 5 n. The
Lord, in sympathy with their growing
perplexity, adopts a tone of unusual
tenderness. Yet He repeats His hard
saying (πάλιν), and this time removes
the qualifying reference to the rich:
' it is hard to enter in any case, though
specially hard for such.' Euth.: ἐστι
δὲ τὸ πῶς βεβαιωτικόν, ἀντὶ τοῦ ἀληθῶς.
On the 'Western' addition, "inserted
to bring the verse into closer con-

διελθεῖν ἢ πλούσιον εἰς τὴν βασιλείαν τοῦ θεοῦ εἰσελθεῖν. ²⁶οἱ δὲ περισσῶς ἐξεπλήσσοντο, λέγοντες πρὸς 26

25 διελθειν BC(D)KΠ 1 69 124 1071 alsᵃᵗmu b c f ff q vg syrᵖᵉˢʰ hᶜˡ(ᵗᵉˣᵗ) arm me aeth]
εισελθειν אΑΝΧΓΔΣΦΨ minᵖˡ a k syrʳˢⁱⁿ hᶜˡ(mg) go (Clem Al) | om εισελθειν (D) a ff k
syrˢⁱⁿ Clem Al   26 om περισσως F | προς αυτον אBCΔΨ me] πρ. εαυτους ADM²N
ΧΓΠΣΦ minᶠᵉʳᵉᵒᵐⁿ latt syrr arm go aeth πρ. αλληλους M*

nexion with the context by limiting
its generality," see WH., *Notes*, p. 26;
and cf. Prov. xi. 28 for its probable
source.

25. εὐκοπώτερόν ἐστιν κτλ.] For
εὐκοπώτερόν ἐστιν see ii. 9, note. Διὰ
τρυμαλιᾶς ῥαφίδος : Mt. διὰ τρήματος
(al. τρυπήματος) ῥ., Lc. διὰ τρήματος
βελόνης. Τρυμαλιά, a late and rare
word, is a perforation, e.g. πέτρας Jud.
(vi. 2), xv. 8, 11 B (A has μάνδρα,
σπήλαιον, or ὀπή), Jer. xiii. 4, xvi. 16,
xxix. (xlix.) 16 ; τρῆμα, τρύπημα are
classical words of the same general
meaning. Of ῥαφίς and βελόνη Phrynichus says: β. καὶ βελονοπώλης ἀρχαία,
ἡ δὲ ῥαφὶς τί ἐστιν οὐκ ἄν τις γνοίη.
Nevertheless, as Rutherford shews
(*N. Phr.* p. 174 f.), ῥαφίς is the older
word, and reappears in late Gk.
In both cases Mc. has used the colloquial word ; in both Lc. prefers the
forms of literary Gk., while Mt. retains ῥαφίς, but excludes τρυμαλιά.
In the MSS. naturally the forms are
interchanged.

Similar sayings in reference to the
elephant are quoted from Rabbinical
writings by J. Lightfoot and Schöttgen
ad loc. The exact metaphor occurs in
the Koran (Plummer), and in proverbs
current among the Arabs (Bruce), but
in these it is possibly borrowed from
the Gospels. Celsus (Orig. *c. Cels.* vi.
16) held that the words ἄντικρυς ἀπὸ
Πλάτωνος εἰρῆσθαι, τοῦ Ἰησοῦ παρα-
φθείραντος τὸ Πλατωνικόν, referring to
Plat. *legg.* 743 A ἀγαθὸν δὲ ὄντα διαφερόντως καὶ πλούσιον εἶναι διαφερόντως ἀδύνατον. The general similarity and the
essential difference of the two sayings
are worthy of remark. The attempts
to soften the proverb which Christ

uses, either by taking κάμηλον (v. l.
κάμιλον, cf. WH., *Notes*, p. 151) for a
ship's cable (schol. οὐ τὸ ζῷον λέγει
ἀλλὰ τὸ παχὺ σχοινίον ᾧ δεσμοῦσι τὰς
ἀγκύρας, cf. Thpht., Euth., Arm.), or
explaining ῥαφίς as a narrow *wady*,
or a gate through which a camel
can scarcely pass, misses the point
of the simile, which is intended to
place the impossibility in the strong-
est light (*v.* 27). To contrast the
largest beast of burden known in
Palestine with the smallest of artificial apertures is quite in the manner of Christ's proverbial sayings :
cf. iv. 31 f., Mt. xxiii. 24. Origen in
his reply to Celsus *l.c.* rightly compares with the saying as a whole Mt.
vii. 14 (cf. Lc. xiii. 24) στενὴ ἡ πύλη καὶ
τεθλιμμένη ἡ ὁδὸς ἡ ἀπάγουσα εἰς τὴν
ζωήν. It is remarkable at how many
points the present context recalls
the language or the teaching of the
'Sermon on the Mount' (cf. e.g. *vv.*
17, 19, 21).

26. οἱ δὲ περισσῶς ἐξεπλήσσοντο
κτλ.] Their astonishment now passed
all bounds and broke out into a cry
of despair. Ἐξεπλήσσοντο, cf. i. 22, vi.
2, vii. 37. Καὶ τίς Mc., Lc., R.V. 'then
who ?' =τίς ἄρα Mt., cf. τίς οὖν Clem.
Al. *quis dives* 4; see WM., p. 345, and
Holtzmann *ad loc.*: "das καί nimmt
den Inhalt der vorhergehenden Rede
auf"; another ex. may be seen in Jo.
ix. 36. "Who can be saved if the rich
are excluded?" The Twelve have not
yet grasped the special difficulties of
the rich, who seem from their position
to have the first claim to admission
into the Kingdom. If they are excluded, they ask, who can dare to
hope ? Σωθῆναι = εἰσελθεῖν εἰς τὴν

27 αὐτόν Καὶ τίς δύναται σωθῆναι; ²⁷ἐμβλέψας αὐτοῖς
ὁ Ἰησοῦς λέγει Παρὰ ἀνθρώποις ἀδύνατον, ἀλλ' οὐ
παρὰ θεῷ· πάντα γὰρ δυνατὰ παρὰ θεῷ.

28   ²⁸ʸἬρξατο λέγειν ὁ Πέτρος αὐτῷ Ἰδοὺ ἡμεῖς
29 ἀφήκαμεν πάντα καὶ ἠκολουθήκαμέν σοι.   ²⁹ἔφη ὁ

27 αδυνατον] pr τουτο C³DNΣ 1071 alᵖᵃᵘᶜ b c syrʳˢⁱⁿ ᵖᵉˢʰ arm + εστιν D 1071 alᵖᵃᵘᶜ
a b c f ff k q vg arm | om αλλ ου π. θ. D r | παντα γαρ δυν. παρα θεω (τω θεω ΑΚΠΣΦ
minᵐᵘ)] παρα δε τω θεω δυνατον D 157 a ff (k) (Clem Al) om Δ 1 69 209 736* alⁿᵒⁿⁿ
1 armᶻᵒʰ | γαρ] δε r   28 ηρξατο] pr και D minᵛⁱˣ ᵐᵘ lattᵛᵗ ᵖˡ ᵛᵍ + δε ΚΝΠΣ
minˢᵃᵗ ᵐᵘ f + ουν 736 | ηκολουθηκαμεν BCD] ηκολουθησαμεν ℵΑΝΧΓΔΠΣΦΨ minᵒᵐⁿ ᵛⁱᵈ
Clem Al | σοι] +τι αρα εσται ημιν ℵ min² b   29 εφη ο I. ℵΒΔ me] και αποκριθεις
(vel αποκρ. δε) ο I. ειπεν Α(CDEFGHK)Μ(N)SUVXΓΠ²ΣΦ 604 alᵛⁱˣ ᵐᵘ a b c f ff (k) q r
vg syrʳˢⁱⁿ ᵖᵉˢʰ ⁽ʰᶜˡ⁾ arm go (aeth) (Clem Al) εφη αυτοις Ψ

βασιλείαν τοῦ θεοῦ (vv. 24, 25), or εἰς
ζωὴν αἰώνιον (v. 17); for this higher
sense of σῴζειν cf. viii. 35, xiii. 13,
[xvi. 16]. On δύναται Jerome well
remarks: "ubi difficile ponitur non
impossibilitas praetenditur."

27. ἐμβλέψας αὐτοῖς] Mt., Mc.;
the second ἐμβλέψας (cf. v. 21, note)
is wanting in Lc. In the words which
follow His searching look, He does
not retreat from His position, though
He reveals the true ground of hope.
The saying is based on Gen. xviii. 14
ἀδυνατήσει παρὰ τῷ θεῷ ῥῆμα; cf. Job
xlii. 2, Zech. viii. 6. Παρά (dat.),
penes, as in Mt. vi. 1, viii. 10, Rom. ii.
11, ix. 14; in Lc. i. 37 παρὰ τοῦ θεοῦ
introduces another thought, that the
power proceeds from God. 'The
power of God converts impossibilities
into facts.' The Western text of Mc.
(cf. WH., Notes, p. 26) limits the
saying to the particular case; Lc.
expresses its general truth in the epigrammatic form τὰ ἀδύνατα παρὰ ἀνθρώποις δυνατὰ παρὰ τῷ θεῷ ἐστίν. In
Lc., as Plummer notes, an incident
follows (xix. 1 ff.) which proves that
the salvation of the rich is "possible
with God." On the apparent limitation
of God's power by His goodness and
righteousness cf. the remark of Euth.:
φασὶ δέ τινες ὅτι ἐὰν πάντα δυνατὰ τῷ
θεῷ, δυνατὸν ἄρα τῷ θεῷ καὶ τὸ κακόν·

πρὸς οὓς λέγομεν ὅτι τὸ κακὸν οὐκ ἔστι
δυνάμεως ἀλλ' ἀδυναμίας.

28–31. THE REWARD OF THOSE
WHO LEAVE ALL FOR CHRIST'S SAKE
(Mt. xix. 27—30, Lc. xviii. 28—30).

28. ἤρξατο λέγειν ὁ Πέτρος] Mt.
τότε ἀποκριθεὶς ὁ Π. εἶπεν. The conversation which follows arose out of
the previous incident (ἀποκρ., cf. ix. 5),
yet it struck a new note. It was Peter
who characteristically broke in with
this fresh question (Mt., Mc., Lc.); cf.
Clem. Al. quis dives 2 ταχέως ἥρπασε
καὶ συνέβαλε τὸν λόγον. The call
δεῦρο ἀκολούθει μοι reminded him
that the sacrifice required from the
rich man and withheld had been
actually made by himself and his
brother. Victor, Euth.: ποῖα πάντα,
ὦ μακάριε Πέτρε; τὸν κάλαμον, τὸ
δίκτυον, τὸ πλοῖον, τὴν τέχνην, ταῦτά
μοι πάντα λέγεις; ναί, φησίν, ἃ εἶχον
καὶ ὅσα εἶχον. Ἀφήκαμεν πάντα (cf.
i. 18, 20, ii. 14): Lc., as if to soften
the tactless frankness of the speech,
ἀφέντες τὰ ἴδια. Mc.'s ἠκολουθήκαμεν
"we followed, and are following still"
is changed into the aor. in Mt., Lc.
It may be hoped that τί ἄρα ἔσται
ἡμῖν; (Mt. only) was left unspoken;
that it was in the speaker's mind, the
Lord's answer shews.

29. ἔφη ὁ Ἰησοῦς] Though Peter
only spoke, the Lord addresses the

Ἰησοῦς Ἀμὴν λέγω ὑμῖν, οὐδείς ἐστιν ὃς ἀφῆκεν
οἰκίαν ἢ ἀδελφοὺς ἢ ἀδελφὰς ἢ μητέρα ἢ πατέρα ἢ
τέκνα ἢ ἀγροὺς ἕνεκεν ἐμοῦ καὶ ἕνεκεν τοῦ εὐαγγελίου,
³⁰ἐὰν μὴ λάβῃ ἑκατονταπλασίονα νῦν ἐν τῷ καιρῷ 30

29 οικιαν] οικιας FMΨ min² syrrsin pesh aeth om D b | om η αδελφας go | η πατερα
η μητερα אΑΝΧΓΠΣΦΨ minᵖˡ b vgeddcoddpl syrr arm aeth | om η πατερα D a ff k |
η τεκνα] pr η γυναικα ΑϹΝΧΓΠΣΦΨ minᵖˡ f q syrr go aeth | om η αγρους Ψ | εμου] του
ε. ονοματος armᶜᵒᵈᵈ | ενεκεν 2°] om ΑΒ*Σ* minᵐᵘ c k ενεκα D   30 εαν] ος αν D
ος ου 28 2ᵖᵉ (k) | απολαβη א 1 (Clem Al) | εκατοντ.]+μετα διωγμων k | om νυν D 255
406 a k q syrsin

Twelve, whose thoughts Peter had
interpreted (εἶπεν αὐτοῖς, Mt., Lc.;
λέγω ὑμῖν, Mt., Mc., Lc.). The first
part of the answer is preserved by
Mt. only (v. 28, cf. Lc. xxii. 28 ff.), and
affects the Twelve only; the common
tradition related only what was of
importance to all believers.

οὐδεὶς ἐστιν ὃς ἀφῆκεν κτλ.] The
sacrifices contemplated embrace all
the material possessions included
under the three heads of home,
relatives, and property; the sacrifice
in life is not at present in view, since
none of the Twelve has been called
to that as yet. Lc. adds γυναῖκα
immediately after οἰκίαν, and omits
ἀγρούς. Of the Twelve, as we know,
Simon Peter had left house and wife
(i. 29 f.), the sons of Zebedee their
father, and Levi at least a lucrative
occupation; cf. Act. Thom. ad fin.
ἔπιδε ἐφ᾽ ἡμᾶς Κύριε, ὅτι τὴν ἰδίαν
κτῆσιν κατελείψαμεν διὰ σέ κτλ. Cf.
Philo de vit. cont. p. 50 (ed. Conybeare), καταλιπόντες ἀδελφούς, τέκνα,
γυναῖκας, γονεῖς...τὰς πατρίδας. Ἦ...
ἤ...ἤ: cf. v. 30 καί...καί...καί: " quae
relinquuntur disiunctive enumeran-
tur; quae retribuuntur, copulative "
(Bengel). Ἕνεκεν ἐμοῦ καὶ ἕνεκεν τοῦ
εὐαγγελίου: Mt., ἕνεκεν τοῦ ἐμοῦ ὀνόματος, Lc., εἵνεκεν τῆς βασιλείας τοῦ θεοῦ.
Mc.'s phrase has already occurred in
viii. 35, where Mt., Lc. have simply
ἕνεκεν ἐμοῦ (Dalman, Worte, i. p. 84):
perhaps it is an expansion of the

original ἕνεκεν ἐ. which was characteristic of Peter's Roman preaching;
references to 'the Gospel,' rare in Mt.
and altogether wanting in Lc., are
fairly frequent in Mc. (i. 1, 14, 15,
viii. 35, x. 29, xiii. 10, xiv. 9, [xvi.
15]). Victor: ἀδιάφορον δὲ τὸ λέγειν
'ἕνεκα τοῦ ἐμοῦ ὀνόματος,' ἢ 'ἕνεκα τοῦ
εὐαγγελίου,' ὡς ὁ Μᾶρκος, ἢ 'ἕνεκα τῆς
βασιλείας τοῦ θεοῦ,' ὡς ὁ Λουκᾶς· τὸ
γὰρ ὄνομα τοῦ χριστοῦ δύναμίς ἐστι τοῦ
εὐαγγελίου καὶ τῆς βασιλείας.

30. ἐὰν μὴ λάβῃ κτλ.] 'Without
receiving'; for the construction cf.
iv. 22, and see Blass, Gr. p. 215. The
rough but forcible phrase οὐδεὶς ἐστιν
ὅς...ἐὰν μὴ λάβῃ is avoided by Mt. (πᾶς
ὅστις...λήμψεται) and corrected by
Lc. (οὐδεὶς ἐστιν ὅς...ὃς οὐχὶ μὴ λάβῃ).
Ἑκατονταπλασίονα (2 Regn. xxiv. 3,
Lc. viii. 8, cf. 1 Chr. xxi. 3 ἑκατοντα-
πλασίως) is softened by Mt., Lc. into
πολλαπλασίονα (Dalman, Worte, i.
p. 53). On the reading of D in Mt.
(ἑπταπλασίονα) see Nestle, Philol.
sacr., p. 24. Νῦν ἐν τῷ καιρῷ τούτῳ:
ἐν τῷ κ. τ., Lc.; Mt. omits both this
and the corresponding ἐν τῷ αἰῶνι τῷ
ἐρχ. For καιρός see i. 15, note; ὁ
καιρὸς οὗτος for ὁ αἰὼν οὗτος is unique,
but ὁ νῦν κ. is a Pauline phrase (Rom.
iii. 26, viii. 18, xi. 5, 2 Cor. viii. 13, cf.
ὁ κ. ὁ ἐνεστηκώς, Heb. ix. 9, Westcott);
here, as contrasted with ὁ αἰὼν ὁ ἐρχ.,
ὁ κ. οὗτος seems to be the present
season, the era of the Advent, the
opportunity of sacrifice, beyond which

τούτῳ, οἰκίας καὶ ἀδελφοὺς καὶ ἀδελφὰς καὶ μητέρα[s]
καὶ τέκνα καὶ ἀγροὺς μετὰ διωγμῶν, καὶ ἐν τῷ αἰῶνι
§ L 31 ⁸τῷ ἐρχομένῳ ζωὴν αἰώνιον. ³¹πολλοὶ δὲ ἔσονται
πρῶτοι ἔσχατοι, καὶ οἱ ἔσχατοι πρῶτοι.

30 οικιας] pr ος δε αφηκεν D a b ff | om οικιας...διωγμων ℵ* c k | και μητερας
BEFGH(N)SUVΔΨ minᵖˡ ᵛⁱᵈ vg syrᵖᵉˢʰ armᶻᵒʰ me] και μητερα ℵᵃACD minᵖᵃᵘᶜ (a b)
f ff q syrˢⁱⁿ armᶜᵒᵈᵈ και μητερα και πατερα ℵᶜKMXII minˢᵃᵗᵐᵘ 604 736 l go aeth
pr (vel add) και πατερας ΝΣ 736* 1071 alⁿᵒⁿⁿ meᵉᵈᵈ | και τεκνα] pr και γυναικα 218 220
736* pˢᶜʳ | μετα διωγμων] εχειν μ. διωγμων εις που (sic: ? τινες -μου) Clem Al μ. διωγμου
D (cf. Nestle, T. C. p. 265) | om και 6° D aᶜᵒʳʳ ᵛⁱᵈ b ff | αιωνιον]+λημψεται D a b c ff
k+κληρονομησει 1071 syrˢⁱⁿ   31 δε] γαρ syrˢⁱⁿ arm | οι εσχατοι] om οι ℵADKLM
VΔΠΨ minᵐᵘ me go

spreads the yet limitless age of the realised Kingdom. Mc. alone specifies the present rewards, and he describes them in the terms of the sacrifice. Πατέρας is omitted, possibly for the reason mentioned in Mt. xxiii. 9, but καὶ μητέρας (if we accept that reading) suffices to shew that the relations enumerated in v. 30 are not to be understood literally; cf. Jo. xix. 26 f., Rom. xvi. 13. A moment's reflexion should have saved Julian from his senseless sneer (Theophylact: 'Ιουλιανὸς ἐκωμῴδει ταῦτα). Yet when Origen thinks only of the recompenses of "Paradise," he loses sight of a distinction which the Lord's promise certainly recognises (ἐν τῷ καιρῷ τούτῳ, ἐν τῷ αἰῶνι τῷ ἐρχομένῳ); and the promise was used with still less reason by the Millenarians (Jerome in Mt.). Without doubt the relations which the Lord offers "now in this time" in place of those which have been abandoned for his sake are the spiritual affinities which bind the members of the family of GOD (cf. iii. 34 f.). Victor appositely quotes 1 Tim. v. 2 (he might have added Rom. xvi. 13, Gal. iv. 19): ὥσπερ γὰρ ἀδελφοὺς δίδωσι τοὺς οὐκ ἀδελφοὺς καὶ γονεῖς τοὺς οὐ γονεῖς καὶ τέκνα τὰ οὐ τέκνα. In D and a few O. L. texts a new sentence begins after ἐν τῷ καιρῷ τούτῳ: ὃς δὲ ἀφῆκεν οἰκίαν καὶ ἀδελφὰς καὶ ἀδελφοὺς καὶ μητέρα καὶ

τέκνα καὶ ἀγροὺς μετὰ διωγμοῦ, ἐν τῷ αἰῶνι τῷ ἐρχομένῳ ζωὴν αἰώνιον λήμψεται. Μετὰ διωγμοῦ here, it will be seen, strengthens ἀφῆκεν, and does not, like μ. διωγμῶν in our other authorities, qualify λάβῃ.

As for οἰκίαι and ἀγροί, see 1 Cor. iii. 22 f. That even in this life the compensations of sacrifice are an hundredfold was matter of common experience in the age of the confessors. Μετὰ διωγμῶν: Mc. only; but cf. iv. 17, where Mt. confirms ἡ διωγμοῦ: even in the Sermon persecution is already foretold (Mt. v. 10 ff.). Not simply "in the midst of persecutions" (WM., p. 472; cf. Thpht. τουτέστι διωκόμενοι), but 'accompanied by' them, cf. Blass, Gr. p. 134; μετά adds an element which was to temper the compensations of the present, and warns against dreams of unbroken peace (Bengel: "ne discipuli sperarent felicitatem externam"). The qualifying clause is entirely in the manner of Christ, cf. Jo. xv. 20, xvi. 33. Ὁ αἰὼν ὁ ἐρχόμενος=ὁ αἰὼν ὁ μέλλων, Mt. xii. 32, ὁ αἰὼν ἐκεῖνος, Lc. xx. 35, the age which is to follow the παρουσία. Ζωὴν αἰώνιον: cf. the question of v. 18, to which the Lord looks back; Mt. makes the reference more distinct by adding κληρονομήσει.

31. πολλοὶ δὲ ἔσονται πρῶτοι κτλ.] A saying which occurs also in Mt. xx. 16, Lc. xiii. 30; Lc. omits it here.

³²ʾΗσαν δὲ ἐν τῇ ὁδῷ ἀναβαίνοντες εἰς Ἱεροσό- 32
λυμα, καὶ ἦν προάγων αὐτοὺς ὁ Ἰησοῦς, καὶ ἐθαμ-
βοῦντο· οἱ δὲ ἀκολουθοῦντες ἐφοβοῦντο. ⁸καὶ παρα-   § syrʰⁱᵉʳ
λαβὼν πάλιν τοὺς δώδεκα ἤρξατο αὐτοῖς λέγειν τὰ·

32 om και ην πρ. αυτ. ο I. k | προσαγων D | και εθαμ. οι δε ακ. εφοβουντο אBC*LΔΨ
2ᵖᵉ] και εθαμβ. και ακ. εφοβ. ΑΝΧΓΠ al minᵖˡ f q vg syrr go και εθαμβ. οι ακ. και
εφοβ. arm και εθαμβ. οι ακ. c (ff) k om 604* om οι δε ακ. εφοβ. D minᵖᵃᵘᶜ a b | om
παλιν syrʰⁱᵉʳ | τ. δωδεκα] + κατ ιδιαν armᵛⁱᵈ

As it stands it is a rebuke to the
spirit which is impelled to the sacrifice by the mere hope of the reward.
How much need there was of the
warning, the experience of Judas
Iscariot and of Simon Peter himself
was to shew. Bede : " vide enim
Iudam de Apostolo in apostatam ver-
sum...vide latronem in cruce factum
confessorem. et quotidie videmus
multos in laico habitu constitutos
magnis vitae virtutibus excellere, et
alios a prima aetate spiritali studio
servientes, ad extremum otio torpen-
tes flaccescere." The Lord's words
have a lesson for each successive age
of the Church.

32—34. THE PASSION FORETOLD
FOR THE THIRD AND LAST TIME (Mt.
xx. 17—19, Lc. xviii. 31—34).

32. ἦσαν δὲ ἐν τῇ ὁδῷ κτλ.] The
issue of the journey (v. 17) now
becomes apparent; the road leads to
Jerusalem, and to the Cross. Ἀναβαίνοντες (Mt. μέλλων ... ἀναβαίνειν);
the verb is used of any ascent (Gen.
xxxv. 3 εἰς Βαιθήλ, Num. xxi. 33 ὁδὸν
τὴν εἰς Βασάν, Jos. viii. 1 εἰς Γαί,
3 Regn. xxii. 12 εἰς Ῥεμμὰθ Γαλααδ),
but especially of journeys to Jerusalem
(4 Regn. xvi. 5, 2 Esdr. i. 3, 3 Macc.
iii. 16, Jo. ii. 13, v. 1, xi. 55, Acts xi.
2, xxv. 1, 9, Gal. ii. 1), which stands
near the highest point of the backbone of Palestine, and cannot be
approached from any quarter without
an ascent. Ἱεροσόλυμα: so Mc., Jo.ᵉᵛ·,
Josephus always; Ἱερουσαλήμ occurs
once in Mt. (xxiii. 27), thrice in the
Apocalypse (iii. 12, xxi. 2, 10), and

predominates in Lc. and Paul; for the
distinction which seems to regulate
St Paul's choice see Lightfoot on
Gal. iv. 25. Ἱερουσαλήμ is archaic,
and suggests the associations of
O. T. history; Ἱεροσόλυμα, the Greek
equivalent, was the geographical name
in common use. For the breathing
see WH., Intr., p. 313.

ἦν προάγων...ἐφοβοῦντο] Mc. only.
For προάγων see vi. 45, x. 32, xi. 9,
xiv. 28, xvi. 7 ; the acc. is frequent
after προάγειν and προέρχεσθαι (cf.
2 Macc. x. 1, Mt. ii. 9); but the
gen. with or without ἐνώπιον is also
used (Judith x. 22, Lc. i. 17). The
Lord walked in advance of the Twelve
with a solemnity and determination
which foreboded danger (cf. Lc. ix. 51
τὸ πρόσωπον ἐστήρισεν τοῦ πορεύεσθαι
εἰς Ἱερουσαλήμ), " more intrepidi
ducis " (Grotius); see Jo. x. 4. His
manner struck awe into the minds
of the Twelve, who were beginning
at length to anticipate an impending
disaster (ἐθαμβοῦντο, cf. i. 27, x. 24;
Eccl. xii. 5 θάμβοι ἐν τῇ ὁδῷ); whilst
the rest of the company (οἱ δὲ
ἀκολουθοῦντες, cf. vv. ll.), the crowd
who usually hung upon the Lord's
footsteps (cf. x. 1, 46), or His fellow-
travellers on their way to the Passover,
were conscious of a vague fear (ἐφοβοῦντο). There was risk of a real
panic, and the Lord therefore checks
His course, till the Twelve have come
up to Him.

καὶ παραλαβὼν πάλιν τοὺς δ.] He
admitted them again to His company;
for παραλαβεῖν in this sense cf. iv. 36,

§ i 33 μέλλοντα αὐτῷ συμβαίνειν, 33 §ὅτι Ἰδοὺ ἀναβαίνομεν
εἰς Ἱεροσόλυμα, καὶ ὁ υἱὸς τοῦ ἀνθρώπου παραδοθήσεται τοῖς ἀρχιερεῦσιν καὶ τοῖς γραμματεῦσιν· καὶ
κατακρινοῦσιν αὐτὸν θανάτῳ καὶ παραδώσουσιν αὐτὸν
34 τοῖς ἔθνεσιν, 34καὶ ἐμπαίξουσιν αὐτῷ καὶ ἐμπτύσουσιν

33 παραδίδοται Κ | και τοις γραμμ.] om א* om τοις CDEFGKMNSUVXΓΠ min^sat mu |
θανατου D*   34 και εμπαιξ. αυτω κ. εμπτυσ. αυτω] ad inridendum k

v. 40, ix. 2, xiv. 33. Mt. adds κατ᾽
ἰδίαν—the words that follow were not
intended for the crowd (οἱ ἀκολουθοῦντες), but for the Twelve only.
Thpht.: μυστήριον γὰρ ὂν τὸ πάθος
τοῖς οἰκειοτέροις ἔδει ἀποκαλυφθῆναι.
Ἤρξατο αὐτοῖς λέγειν: cf. vi. 2, note.
The subject was not a new one, but it
had been dropped for a while, and it
was in sharp contrast to the hopes of
reward which were uppermost in the
minds of the Twelve (x. 28 ff.). With
τὰ μέλλ. αὐτῷ συμβαίνειν cf. Lc. xxiv.
14, περὶ πάντων τῶν συμβεβηκότων
τούτων. The phrase is frequent in
the LXX. (cf. e.g. Gen. xlii. 4, 29, xliv.
29, Job i. 22, Esth. vi. 13, 1 Macc.
iv. 26).

33, 34. ἰδοὺ ἀναβαίνομεν κτλ.] The
Twelve shared the journey if not its
issue; contrast Jo. xx. 17 ἀναβαίνω
πρὸς τὸν πατέρα μου. Their destination
was self-evident (ἰδού), and there was
always risk involved in a journey to
Jerusalem (Jo. xi. 8 ff.); but the
Twelve had still to learn that this
particular journey was to end in the
Master's death (καὶ ὁ υἱὸς κτλ.). The
third and final prediction of the
Passion which follows is far more
explicit than the first or the second
(Mc. viii. 31 ff., ix. 31), and indeed
anticipates every important stage in
the history. Six successive steps are
clearly enumerated, and in their actual
order—(1) the betrayal (παραδοθήσεται
τοῖς ἀρχ. κ. τοῖς γραμμ.; the Elders,
who were mentioned in viii. 31, are
omitted here, as the least important
factor in the Sanhedrin), (2) the sentence of the Sanhedrin (κατακρινοῦσιν),

(3) the handing over of the Prisoner
to the Roman power (παραδώσουσιν
τοῖς ἔθνεσιν), (4) the mockery and its
details (ἐμπαίξουσιν...ἐμπτύσουσιν...
μαστιγώσουσιν), (5) the Crucifixion
(ἀποκτενοῦσιν, Mc., Lc.; cf. Mt. σταυ-
ρῶσαι), (6) the Resurrection (ἀναστήσεται, Mc., Lc.; Mt. ἐγερθήσεται).
The Resurrection finds a place in all
three predictions; of the other details
only (2), (5) are distinctly announced
in the earliest prediction, and (1), (5)
in the second. Lc. prefaces the whole
series by a reference to the Prophets
(τελεσθήσεται πάντα τὰ γεγραμμένα διὰ
τῶν προφητῶν, cf. Lc. xxiv. 44). For
the construction κατακρίνειν θανάτῳ cf.
Dan. iv. 34ᵃ (LXX.), WM., p. 263, Blass,
Gr. p. 111. Τὰ ἔθνη (or anarthr., ἔθνη)
= הַגּוֹיִם, Wycliffe, "hethene men";
cf. Ps. ii. 1, 8, Isa. lx. 2, Ezech. iv. 13,
Sir. x. 15 f., Bar. ii. 13, 1 Macc. ii. 18,
Rom. ii. 14 (SH.), 24, Gal. i. 16, ii. 12,
1 Tim. iii. 16. The Lord speaks as
a Jew to Jews; that He was to be
delivered to a heathen power, was no
small aggravation of His sentence
and of the national sin (cf. xii. 8,
Acts iii. 13).

34. ἐμπαίξουσιν αὐτῷ κτλ.] See xv.
19, 20, Jo. xix. 1, and cf. Isa. l. 6, Ev.
Petr. 3 ἐνέπτυον αὐτοῦ ταῖς ὄψεσι...καί
τινες αὐτὸν ἐμάστιζον. The formidable
punishment of scourging was kept by
Pilate in his own hands, the mockery
was left to the Procurator's soldiers,
but in both cases Gentiles were the
agents; over the mockery He was
to sustain at the hands of the High
Priest's servants (xiv. 65) and from
the chief priests themselves (xv. 31)

αὐτῷ καὶ μαστιγώσουσιν αὐτὸν καὶ ἀποκτενοῦσιν,
καὶ μετὰ τρεῖς ἡμέρας ἀναστήσεται.

³⁵ Καὶ προσπορεύονται αὐτῷ Ἰάκωβος καὶ Ἰωάνης 35
οἱ [δύο] υἱοὶ Ζεβεδαίου λέγοντες αὐτῷ Διδάσκαλε,
θέλομεν ἵνα ὃ ἐὰν αἰτήσωμέν σε ποιήσῃς ἡμῖν.

34 και μαστιγ. αυτον κ. εμπτυσ. αυτω ΑΝΧΓΠΣΦ min^pl syrr arm go om και εμπτυσ. αυτω 28 min^nonn om και μαστ. αυτον D min^pauc ff g k | αποκτενουσιν] crucifigent k + αυτον Α*CΝΧΓΠΨ al^pl | μετα τρεις ημερας אBCDLΔ (a) b (c) ff i k (q) syr^hcl (mg) me] τη τριτη ημερα ΑΝΧΓΠΣΦ min^omn vid f vg syrr^sin pesh hcl (txt) arm aeth Or   35 οι δυο υιοι BC me] om δυο אDEFGHLSVΓΔΠ²Ψ min^pl syr^hier om οι δυο AKMNUXΠ*Σ min^sat mu go | om αυτω ΑΝΧΓΠΨ al^pl | αιτησωμεν (-σομεν א^cA)] ερωτησωμεν D ɪ 2^pe | om σε ΧΓ al^pl

the Lord mercifully draws a veil. The order of the R. T. (vv. ll.) is probably based on the supposed order of the events (cf. Jo. *l.c.*). Μετὰ τρεῖς ἡμέρας = τῇ τρίτῃ ἡμέρᾳ Mt., τῇ ἡμ. τῇ τρ. Lc.; see viii. 31, note. Lc. adds that this third prediction, like the second (Mc. ix. 32), failed to reach the understandings of the Twelve, notwithstanding its explicitness (αὐτοὶ οὐδὲν τούτων συνῆκαν...ἦν τὸ ῥῆμα κεκρυμμένον...οὐκ ἐγίνωσκον τὰ λεγόμενα).

35—45. PETITION OF THE SONS OF ZEBEDEE. TEACHING BASED ON THE INCIDENT (Mt. xx. 20—28; cf. Lc. xxii. 25 f.).

35. καὶ προσπορεύονται αὐτῷ κτλ.] Mt. again (cf. xix. 27) fixes the sequence by beginning the sentence with τότε. The occasion was peculiarly inopportune, but there is nothing psychologically improbable in this; cf. ix. 30—34. The incident is wanting in Lc. Mt. agrees with Mc. in the dialogue, but represents the mother of James and John (i.e. Salome, Mt. xxvii. 56, Mc. xv. 40) as the actual petitioner; she was in the company (Mc. *l.c.*), and though the sons were certainly to some extent responsible (Mt. xx. 20, 22), it is more than probable that maternal ambition prompted their application to our Lord. The recent promise of Mt. xix. 28 would have suggested it; and her near relationship to the Lord (see

Bp Westcott's note on Jo. xix. 25) may have inspired her with some hope of success. Προσπορεύεσθαι is ἅπ. λεγ. in the N. T., but fairly frequent in the LXX. (cf. e.g. Exod. xxiv. 14, 1 Esdr. xx. 28 (29), Sir. xii. 14).

Ἰάκωβος καὶ Ἰωάνης] The usual order, probably that of seniority (i. 19, note); Lc. however inverts it occasionally (viii. 51, ix. 28, Acts i. 13), in view of the later pre-eminence of John. Mt. uses the phrase οἱ [δύο] υἱοὶ Z. without the personal names here and in xxvi. 37, xxvii. 56; cf. Jo. xxi. 2. Of Zebedee (cf. i. 19) no notice is taken after the parting from his sons; he may have died in the interval, or remained indifferent to the new movement.

λέγοντες αὐτῷ Διδάσκαλε κτλ.] According to Mt., Salome approaches with her sons, prostrates herself, and intimates that she has a request to make (προσκυνοῦσα καὶ αἰτοῦσά τι ἀπ' αὐτοῦ). Mc., who has for once lost the pictorial details, preserves the words, putting them, however, into the mouth of the sons. Both the homage offered and the terms of the petition (cf. vi. 23) suggest that the Lord is approached in the character of a King, who can gratify the desires of His subjects without limitation, as indeed in another sense He afterwards declared Himself able to do (Jo. xiv. 13, 14, xv. 16, xvi. 23, 24).

36 ³⁶ὁ δὲ εἶπεν αὐτοῖς Τί θέλετε [μὲ] ποιήσω ὑμῖν;
37 ³⁷οἱ δὲ εἶπαν αὐτῷ Δὸς ἡμῖν ἵνα εἷς σου ἐκ δεξιῶν καὶ
38 εἷς ἐξ ἀριστερῶν καθίσωμεν ἐν τῇ δόξῃ σου. ³⁸ὁ δὲ
Ἰησοῦς εἶπεν αὐτοῖς Οὐκ οἴδατε τί αἰτεῖσθε. δύνασθε

36 tot vers om k | om τι θελετε D | om θελετε abi | με ποιησω ℵ^{c.a}BΨ arm ποιησω
CD ποιησαι με ΑΝΧΓΠΣΦ min^pl go με ποιησαι ℵ^{c.b vid} L ποιησαι Δ min   37 αριστε-
ρων BLΔΨ] ευωνυμων ℵACDNΧΓΠΣΦ min^{omn vid} + (vel pr) σου (ℵ)AC(L)ΝΧΓΠΣΦ
min^pl a f vg syrr me go aeth | om καθισωμεν...σου k | δοξη] βασιλεια της δοξης 13 69
124 346   38 ειπεν] pr αποκριθεις D 1 13 28 69 124 346 2^pe abffikq syr^{sin hier}
arm

36. τί θέλετε [μὲ] ποιήσω ὑμῖν;] Mt.
τί θέλεις; Mc. blends the two forms
τί θέλετέ με ποιῆσαι and τί θ. ποιήσω.
On θέλ. ποιήσω (without ἵνα) cf. vi. 25,
note, WM., p. 256. The Lord will not
grant the prayer until the thing desired has been specified.
37. δὸς ἡμῖν ἵνα κτλ.] Mt. εἰπὲ ἵνα
καθίσωσιν οὗτοι οἱ δύο υἱοί μου κτλ.
Δὸς ἡμῖν ἵνα...καθίσωμεν : cf. WM.,
p. 423, Blass, Gr. p. 226. Ἐκ δεξιῶν...
ἐξ ἀριστερῶν (Mt. εὐωνύμων), next to
the King on either hand. The right
hand was the place of honour (2 Regn.
xvi. 6, 3 Regn. ii. 19, 1 Esdr. iv. 29, Ps.
cix. (cx.) 1, Sir. xii. 12, Acts vii. 55 f.,
Rom. viii. 34); and next to it, the
immediate left (Jos. ant. vi. 11. 9 παρα-
καθισθέντων αὐτῷ (τῷ βασιλεῖ) τοῦ μὲν
παιδὸς Ἰωνάθου ἐκ δεξιῶν, Ἀβενήρου δὲ
τοῦ ἀρχιστρατήγου ἐκ τῶν ἑτέρων). Ἐκ
in this phrase denotes the direction—
'starting from' the right hand (or the
left); WM., p. 459. The petition was
a bold attempt to raise afresh the
question τίς μείζων (ix. 34) which the
Lord had already dismissed. Ἐν τῇ
δόξῃ σου : cf. Mt. xix. 28 ἐπὶ θρόνου
δόξης αὐτοῦ. Ephrem thinks that the
idea was suggested by the vision of
the Transfiguration in which the Lord
appeared in glory between Moses and
Elijah.
38. οὐκ οἴδατε τί αἰτεῖσθε] So also
Mt., who agrees with Mc. (Bede) in
representing the answer as addressed
to the two and not to the mother.
Jerome : "mater postulat et Dominus

discipulis loquitur, intelligens preces
eius ex filiorum descendere voluntate." With αἰτεῖσθε following αἰτή-
σωμεν (v. 35) cf. vi. 22 ff. (αἴτησον...
αἰτήσῃς...αἰτήσωμαι...ῃτήσατο); the
middle perhaps calls attention to the
self-seeking which inspired the request
and was its deepest condemnation—
for ἡ ἀγάπη οὐ ζητεῖ τὰ ἑαυτῆς. But the
petition displayed ignorance (οὐκ οἴδατε : cf. Thpht., ὑμεῖς γὰρ νομίζετε
αἰσθητὴν εἶναι τὴν ἐμὴν βασιλείαν καὶ
αἰσθητὴν τὴν καθέδραν αἰτεῖσθε) as well
as lack of love ; of the latter the Lord
had already spoken at length; the
former he proceeds to expose.
δύνασθε πιεῖν κτλ.] The imagery of
the petition is sustained in this question. The cup belongs to the royal
banquet at which the King sits between His most honoured guests, cf.
Gen. xl. 11 f., 2 Regn. xii. 3, 2 Esdr.
xii. 1, Esth. 1. 7. But by an easy
transition the Lord passes in thought
to another set of associations which
connects the wine-cup with the allotted share of joy or suffering which
is the portion of men and of nations
in the course of their life (Ps. xxii.
(xxiii.) 5, lxxiv. (lxxv.) 9, cxv. 4 (cxvi.
13), Isa. li. 17 ff., Lam. ii. 13, iv. 21,
Ezech. xxiii. 31 ff.). What this cup
was in the present case both the
brethren afterwards learnt in Gethsemane (xiv. 36). Πίνειν ποτήριον=
πίν. πόμα (1 Cor. x. 4), or ἐκ ποτηρίου
(1 Cor. xi. 28); cf. 1 Cor. x. 21, xi. 26 f.
Ὁ ἐγὼ πίνω : the drinking of the cup

πιεῖν τὸ ποτήριον ὃ ἐγὼ πίνω, ἢ τὸ βάπτισμα ὃ ἐγὼ
βαπτίζομαι βαπτισθῆναι ; ³⁹ οἱ δὲ εἶπαν αὐτῷ Δυνά- 39
μεθα. ὁ δὲ Ἰησοῦς εἶπεν αὐτοῖς Τὸ ποτήριον ὃ ἐγὼ
πίνω πίεσθε, καὶ τὸ βάπτισμα ὃ ἐγὼ βαπτίζομαι

38 πειν D | η] και AC³XΓΠΣΦ minᵖˡ syrʳᵖᵉˢʰ ʰᵉˡ⁽ᵗˣᵗ⁾ go aeth | om ο εγω βαπτιζομαι
syrˢⁱⁿ   39 ειπαν] λεγουσιν Ψ | om αυτω D ι 28 alᵖᵃᵘᶜ a b c ff i k q syrʰⁱᵉʳ | δυνο-
μεθα B* | το μεν ποτ. AC³DNXΓΠΣΦΨ minᵒᵐⁿ ᵛⁱᵈ | om ο εγω βαπτ. k

was coextensive with the incarnate
life on earth, but the Passion is of
course chiefly in view (Mt. ὃ ἐγὼ μέλλω
πίνειν). Hilary: "de calice sacramenti
passionis interrogat."

ἢ τὸ βάπτισμα...βαπτισθῆναι] Mc.
only. The royal baths in which the
Herods delighted may possibly be in
view, though βάπτισμα and βαπτίζομαι are preferred to λουτρόν and
λούομαι, in order to bring the imagery
into line with the thought which is in
the Lord's mind. Of a 'baptism'
which awaited Him He had already
spoken to the Twelve (Lc. xii. 50),
and He now reminds the two of it.
The metaphorical use of βαπτίζεσθαι
is common in the later Gk., e.g. Isa.
xxi. 4 ἡ ἀνομία με βαπτίζει, Jos. B. J.
iv. 3. 3 ὃ δὴ (a false hope) ἐβάπτισεν
τὴν πόλιν, Plut. Galb. 21 ὀφλήμασι
βεβαπτισμένος: and the metaphor
itself is among the most usual in the
O. T.; the sufferer is regarded as
plunged and half-drowned in his grief
or loss, e.g. Ps. xviii. 16, xlii. 7, lxix.
1 ff., cxxiv. 4 f. A reference to the
cleansing virtue of the Cross com-
municated to the soul in Baptism
(Thpht. : βάπτισμα, ὡς καθαρισμὸν τῶν
ἁμαρτιῶν ποιησάμενον) is perhaps unnecessary; nor need we suppose an
anticipation of St Paul's thought εἰς
τὸν θάνατον αὐτοῦ ἐβαπτίσθημεν (Rom.
vi. 3). For the construction βάπτισμα
ὃ βαπτίζομαι cf. Jo. xvii. 26, Apoc.
xvi. 9 (WM., p. 281 f.).

39. δυνάμεθα] A lighthearted and
eager reply, which reveals the absence even in a disciple like John
of any clear understanding of the

Master's repeated warnings, and at the
same time the loyalty of the men who
were ready to share the Master's lot,
whatever it might be. This trustful
δυνάμεθα however falls short of the
meaning of the Lord's δύνασθε, which
had reference to spiritul power (ix.
23, x. 27); it is a mere profession of
moral courage at the best. Contrast
St Paul's πάντα ἰσχύω ἐν τῷ ἐνδυνα-
μοῦντί με (Phil. iv. 13).

πίεσθε, βαπτισθήσεσθε] This then
they shall do, since they have strength
for it; they shall share the Master's
cup and baptism. The promise was
fulfilled in the case of both brothers,
but in singularly different ways.
James, as Origen already points out
(in Mt. t. xvi. 6), fell under the sword
of Herod Agrippa I. (Acts xii. 2);
John was condemned by the Emperor to exile in Patmos (Apoc. i. 9).
Both suffered with Christ, one as a
martyr, the other as a confessor; one
by an early death, the other throughout a long life. The Lord's words
are thus seen to assign to these two
no more than He assigns to all disciples (Mc. viii. 34, Rom. viii. 17,
2 Tim. ii. 11 ff.). Yet it was natural
that in an age of persecution the
words should be felt to be peculiarly
applicable to martyrdom strictly so
called, and this application is early
and widespread; cf. Polyc. mart. 14
εὐλογῶ σε ὅτι κατηξίωσάς με...τοῦ λαβεῖν με μέρος ἐν ἀριθμῷ τῶν μαρτύρων
ἐν τῷ ποτηρίῳ τοῦ Χριστοῦ σου. Cyril.
Hier. cat. iii. 10 τὸ μαρτύριον γὰρ οἶδε
βάπτισμα καλεῖν ὁ σωτήρ, λέγων Δύνασθε κτλ. Victor: τουτέστιν 'μαρτυρίου

40 βαπτισθήσεσθε· ⁴⁰τὸ δὲ καθίσαι ἐκ δεξιῶν μου ἢ ἐξ
εὐωνύμων οὐκ ἔστιν ἐμὸν δοῦναι, ἀλλ᾽ οἷς ἡτοίμασται.
41 ⁴¹καὶ ἀκούσαντες οἱ δέκα ἤρξαντο ἀγανακτεῖν περὶ

40 η] και ΑϹΝΧΓΠΣΦ min^pl k syrr arm aeth | ευωνυμων]+μου Ψ min^vix mu
syrr^sin pesh aeth | δουναι] om syr^hier+υμιν c f (k) vg^edd codd pl aeth | αλλ οις] αλλοις
a b d ff k aeth αλλω syr^sin | ητοιμασται]+υπο του πατρος μου א^*c.b Φ 1 209 1071 al^perpauc
a syr^hel(mg)+υπο του π. 604   41 οι λοιποι δεκα D a b c ff q syr^hier me | ηρξαντο
αγανακτειν] ηγανακτησαν A 1 al^pauc q vg^sixt

καταξιωθήσεσθε καὶ ταῦτα πείσεσθε ἄπερ
ἐγώ.' The passage was regarded as
investing martyrdom with a baptismal
character, cf. the treatise *De rebapt.*
14 "homines non solum aqua verum
etiam sanguine suo proprio habere
baptizari, ita ut et solo hoc baptismate
baptizati fidem integram et digna-
tionem sinceram lavacri possint adi-
pisci." For examples of the abuse of
the Lord's words by Gnostic sects of
the second century, see Iren. i. 21. 2,
Hipp. *haer.* v. 8. The story of St
John's being compelled by Domitian
to drink a cup of poison (Tisch. *act.
App. apocr.*, p. 269) is possibly a
realistic attempt to shew that the
words received in his case a literal
fulfilment. The same may perhaps be
said of the statement said to be due
to Papias, that St John as well as
St James was slain by the Jews (see
Encycl. Bibl. ii., p. 2509 ff.).

40. τὸ δὲ καθίσαι κτλ.] The Lord
disclaims the right to dispose in an
arbitrary manner of the higher rewards of the Kingdom. Cf. Thpht.:
ὥσπερανεὶ βασιλεὺς δίκαιος προεκάθητο
ἀγῶνός τινος, εἶτα προέλθοιεν αὐτῷ
τινες φίλοι αὐτοῦ καὶ εἴποιεν Δὸς ἡμῖν
τοὺς στεφάνους, εἶπεν ἄν Οὐκ ἔστιν
ἐμὸν τὸ δοῦναι, ἀλλ᾽ εἴ τις ἀγωνίσεται
καὶ νικήσει, ἐκείνῳ ἡτοίμασται ὁ στέφ-
ανος. Euth.: οὐκ ἔστιν ὅπερ εἶπεν
ἀδυναμίας, ἀλλὰ δικαιοσύνης. Yet in
some sense He could not give what
was asked, seeing that it belonged to
Another to determine whose it should
be. Christ is indeed the appointed
Distributor of all eternal rewards

(2 Tim. iv. 8, Apoc. xxii. 12), but He
will distribute them in accordance
with the Father's dispositions. This,
which is implied in οἷς ἡτοίμασται, is
expressed by Mt., who adds ὑπὸ τοῦ
πατρός μου—a form of words frequent
in Mt. (vii. 21, x. 32 f., xi. 27 &c.) and
Lc. (ii. 49, x. 22, xxii. 29, xxiv. 49),
but not found in Mc. For ἑτοιμάζειν
(προετοιμ.) in reference to Divine
preparations see Dalman, *Worte*, i.
p. 104 ff., and cf. Ps. vii. 14, xxii. (xxiii.)
5, Mt. xxv. 34, 41, Lc. ii. 31, Rom. ix.
23, 1 Cor. ii. 9, Eph. ii. 10, 2 Tim. ii.
21, Heb. xi. 16; it is used, as the exx.
shew, either of persons or things, but
chiefly, as here, of the latter. Οἷς
ἡτοίμασται involves an ἐκλογή, but on
what the selection turns does not
appear. The ἀλλά which precedes
does not contrast those to whom the
Lord reserves the right of giving the
reward with others to whom it is not
His to give—which would have been
expressed rather by εἰ μή—but those
who shall receive with those who shall
not; i.e. the true complement of the
sentence is δοθήσεται, not ἐμόν ἐστιν
δοῦναι. In the sense which is here in
view the Son does not give to any.
On the reading ἄλλοις, implied in some
of the versions, see Nestle, *T. C.* p. 37.

41. καὶ ἀκούσαντες κτλ.] If the
rest of the Twelve were not present,
the report naturally reached them;
and it at once revived the spirit of
jealousy which had been checked by the
teaching of ix. 35 ff., and went far to
create a new group in the Apostolate
(οἱ δέκα, Mt., Mc.). Hitherto Peter,

Ἰακώβου καὶ Ἰωάνου. ⁴²καὶ προσκαλεσάμενος αὐτοὺς 42
ὁ Ἰησοῦς λέγει αὐτοῖς Οἴδατε ὅτι οἱ δοκοῦντες ἄρχειν
τῶν ἐθνῶν κατακυριεύουσιν αὐτῶν, καὶ οἱ μεγάλοι
αὐτῶν κατεξουσιάζουσιν αὐτῶν.   ⁴³οὐχ οὕτως δέ 43

41 Ιακ. κ. Ιωαν.] των δυο αδελφων Α 91   42 ο δε ιϲ προσκ. αυτους ΑΝΧΓ al
min^fereomn | οιδατε] pr ουκ 13 69 108 124 127 | κ. οι μεγαλοι αυτων] κ. οι βασιλεις
אC*^vid κ. οι μεγ. Σ om κ. οι μεγ. αυτ. κατεξ. αυτ. syr^sin   43 om δε D syr^sin arm

James and John had formed a recognised triumvirate; now Peter joins
and probably leads the other nine in
their indignation. The bitter feeling
was perhaps not expressed in the
presence of the two—both Mc. and
Mt. use ἀγανακτεῖν περί, not ἀγ. κατά
(Sap. v. 22)—but it threatened the
harmony and spiritual life of the
Apostolate, and called for immediate
correction. Euth. (in Mt.): οὕτω
πάντες ἦσαν ἀτελεῖς, μήπω τοῦ θείου
πνεύματος ἐπιφοιτήσαντος αὐτοῖς.

42. καὶ προσκαλεσάμενος κτλ.] On
προσκαλεῖσθαι see iii. 13, note. The
Lord called the ten to him, and without referring to the circumstances,
pointed out that neither ambition nor
jealousy had any place in the brotherhood of the Son of Man. The tone
of His words is singularly gentle; the
occasion (for there had been great
provocation) called for definite teaching rather than for censure.

οἴδατε ὅτι οἱ δοκοῦντες κτλ.] He
begins with matters within their cog-
nisance (cf. x. 19). They knew enough
of the Gentile world to be aware that
the sort of greatness which they desired was just that which the Gentiles
sought. Οἱ δοκοῦντες ἄρχειν, 'those
who are regarded as rulers,' Mt. οἱ
ἄρχοντες; for Mc.'s unusual phrase cf.
Gal. ii. 2, 6, 9, with Lightfoot's note
(cf. Hastings, D. C. G. ii. p. 538 b),
and see 3 Macc. v. 6 οἱ πάσης σκέπης
ἔρημοι δοκ. εἶναι, 22 τοῖς ταλαιπώροις
δοκοῦσιν, 4 Macc. xiii. 14 μὴ φοβηθῶμεν τὸν δοκοῦντα ἀποκτενεῖν, and esp.
Sus. 5 (LXX. and Th.) οἱ ἐδόκουν κυ-
βερνᾶν τὸν λαόν. The Master recognised the Empire and other institutions

of society as facts belonging to the
Divine order of things (xii. 17), but
He did not admit that the power of
such a ruler as Tiberius was a substantial dignity; it rested on a reputation which might be suddenly wrecked,
as indeed the later history of the
Empire clearly proved. Τῶν ἐθνῶν,
see v. 33, note (Thpht.: τὸ ἁρπάζειν
τὴν τιμὴν καὶ τῶν πρωτείων ἐρᾶν ἐθνικὸν
ἐστιν). As good Jews the disciples
would shrink from following Gentile
precedent (cf. Mt. vi. 32). Οἱ μεγάλοι
αὐτῶν, the great men of the heathen
world, the officials and other persons
in authority or influence (οἱ μεγιστᾶνες, vi. 21). These Gentile magnates
exercise arbitary rule over their subjects and inferiors, whether as lords
paramount (κατακυριεύουσιν, Mt., Mc.,
Vg. dominantur) or as subordinates
(κατεξουσιάζουσιν, Mt., Mc.). For
κατακυριεύειν see Gen. i. 28, ix. 1, Ps.
ix. 26, 31 (x. 5, 10), cix. (cx.) 2, Acts
xix. 16, and esp. 1 Pet. v. 3, where
there is possibly a reminiscence of the
Lord's saying; of κατεξουσιάζειν no
other example is quoted, but ἐξουσιά-
ζειν occurs in Lc. xxii. 25, 1 Cor. vi.
12, vii. 4 bis, and both verbs doubtless carry the sense of ἐξουσία
('derived authority,' cf. i. 22, note).
With κατακυριεύσουσιν, κατεξουσιάζουσιν, cf. κατάρχειν in Numbers xvi.
13.

43, 44. οὐχ οὕτως δέ ἐστιν ἐν ὑμῖν]
Another order prevails in (ἐν, denoting
the sphere, WM., p. 483) the new
Israel, whose standards of greatness
are wholly unlike those of the Gentile
world. Jesus had already inaugurated
these new conditions of social life—

¶ N   ἐστιν ἐν ὑμῖν· ἀλλ' ὃς ¶ ἂν θέλη μέγας γενέσθαι ἐν
44 ὑμῖν, ἔσται ὑμῶν διάκονος, ⁴⁴καὶ ὃς ἂν θέλη ἐν ὑμῖν
45 εἶναι πρῶτος, ἔσται πάντων δοῦλος· ⁴⁵καὶ γὰρ ὁ υἱὸς
τοῦ ἀνθρώπου οὐκ ἦλθεν διακονηθῆναι ἀλλὰ διακονῆσαι,
¶ syrʰⁱᵉʳ   καὶ δοῦναι τὴν ψυχὴν αὐτοῦ λύτρον ἀντὶ πολλῶν.¶

43 εστιν ℵBC*DLΔΨ lattᵛᵗ ᵖˡ ᵛᵍ] εσται AC³NXΓΠΣΦ minᵒᵐⁿ ᵛⁱᵈ q arm me go |
εσται] εστω ℵCXΔ 69 2ᵖᵉ alᵖᵃᵘᶜ | υμιν διακ. 604   44 εν υμιν ειναι πρωτος ℵBCLΔ(Ψ)
28 alᵖᵃᵘᶜ latt me] υμων γενεσθαι πρ. AC³(D)XΓΠ(Σ)Φ minᵖˡ go aeth | εσται] εστω
minᵖᵃᵘᶜ | παντων] υμων D 2ᵖᵉ alᵖᵉʳᵖᵃᵘᶜ a aeth

the true reading is ἐστίν, not ἔσται
(see app. crit.)—both by example
(v. 45), and precept (ix. 35). The
latter He now repeats with some
amplification. Service is henceforth
to precede greatness, preeminence
can only be secured by a true *servus
servorum Dei.* Comp. 1 Cor. ix. 19,
2 Cor. iv. 5, Clem. R. 1 *Cor.* 48, and for
the necessary safeguard of a Christian
ambition, see Gal. v. 13; the δουλεία
which ennobles is that of disinterest-
ed love, based on absolute submission
to God and Christ, and consistent
with a true ἐλευθερία. That the
Kingdom of God admits of degrees of
spiritual greatness is taught also in
Mt. v. 19 (ἐλάχιστος...μέγας κληθήσεται
ἐν τῇ βασ. τῶν οὐρανῶν). On διάκονος...
δοῦλος see ix. 35, note, and with πάντων
δοῦλος cf. 1 Cor. ix. 19, 2 Cor. iv. 5.

45. καὶ γὰρ ὁ υἱός] On καὶ γάρ,
Vg. *nam et,* see WM., p. 560. The
law of service is recommended by the
example of the Head of the race;
even the Son of God made its fulfilment the purpose of His life, when
He took upon Him the μορφὴ δούλου
and became the Son of Man. For
ἦλθεν in reference to the Lord's entrance into the world cf. i. 38, ii. 17;
it is used also of the Baptist (ix. 11 ff.,
Jo. i. 7) regarded as a Divine mes-
senger. The purpose of the Lord's
advent was to minister (Lc. xxii. 27,
Rom. xv. 8); His life as a whole was
a ministry (διακονῆσαι, not διακονεῖν);
if He received the services of others

(as of angels, i. 13, women, xv. 41),
it was not for this end He came.
Nothing could more clearly mark the
contrast between the Kingdom which
is not of this world (Jo. xviii. 36) and
earthly kingdoms as they existed in
the days of Christ. The pass. δια-
κονεῖσθαι occurs again in 2 Cor. iii.
3, viii. 19 f., but in connexion with
the service rendered; for its use with
reference to the person who receives
service cf. Blass, *Gr.* p. 184.

καὶ δοῦναι τὴν ψυχήν κτλ.] Vg. *et
daret vitam suam redemptionem pro
multis;* Wycliffe: "and ȝeue his lyf
aȝen biyinge for manye" (Tindale,
Cranmer, &c. "for the redemption of
many"; A.V., R.V., "a ransom for
many"). The ministry of the Son of
Man culminates in the sacrifice of
His life. He had required this supreme service from His disciples
(viii. 35), and He will be the first to
render it. Yet His sacrifice is to be
doubly unique. The disciple may lose
his life (ἀπολέσει τὴν ψυχὴν αὐτοῦ),
the Master only can give it in the
fullest sense (Jo. x. 18, Gal. i. 4,
1 Tim. ii. 6, Tit. ii. 14). Further,
whilst the disciple parts with his life
for the sake of Christ and the Gospel,
the Master gives it as a λύτρον ἀντὶ
πολλῶν—His Death is to be a supreme
act of service to humanity. For a
full discussion of λύτρον and its cog-
nate words see Westcott, *Hebrews,*
p. 295 f. Λύτρον, which occurs in the
LXX. fairly often (Exod.², Lev.⁵, Num.⁸,

⁴⁶*Καὶ ἔρχονται εἰς Ἰερειχω· καὶ ἐκπορευομένου* 46

46 ερχεται D min² syr^sin a b ff g i r Or^bis | Ιερειχω (1°) B² (om και ερχ. εις I. B*)
CFLΨ] Ιεριχω אADXΓΔΠΣΦ min^omn vid | εκπορευομενου...ικανου cum turba magna k

Prov.², Is.¹), and in various senses answering to כֹּפֶר, פִּדְיוֹן, גְּאֻלָּה, מְחִיר, is used in the N.T. only in this context (Mt., Mc.); *ἀντίλυτρον*, which is a variant for *λύτρωσις* in Ps. xlviii. (xlix.) 2, appears in 1 Tim. ii. 6, also in reference to the sacrifice of Christ. In certain cases the Law provided *λύτρα τῆς ψυχῆς* (or *λ. περὶ ψυχῆς*), a price for a life which had been dedicated or lost (Exod. xxi. 30, xxx. 12 ; cf. Num. xxxv. 31 f.). The Lord contemplates a *λύτρον* which is *ψυχὴ ἀντὶ ψυχῆς* (Lev. xxiv. 18), His own *ψυχή* (xiv. 34) given as a ransom for the *ψυχαί* of men. The idea was not unfamiliar to the later Jews, cf. 2 Macc. vii. 37, 38, 4 Macc. i. 11, and esp. xvii. 22 ...*ὥσπερ ἀντίψυχον γεγονότας τῆς τοῦ ἔθνους ἁμαρτίας· καὶ διὰ τοῦ αἵματος τῶν εὐσεβῶν ἐκείνων καὶ τοῦ ἱλαστηρίου θανάτου αὐτῶν ἡ θεία πρόνοια τὸν Ἰσραὴλ προκακωθέντα διέσωσεν*: something of this kind was probably in the mind of Caiaphas, Jo. xi. 50, and the disciples may have understood the Lord to say that He was about to offer himself as a victim for the redemption (Lc. ii. 38, xxiv. 21) of Israel. *Ἀντὶ πολλῶν*: St Paul writes *ὑπὲρ πάντων* (1 Tim. *l.c.*); St John, *περὶ ὅλου τοῦ κόσμου* (1 Jo. ii. 2). For the present the Lord is content with the less definite statement, which if it does not involve, certainly does not exclude the other. Jerome's comment "non dixit...'pro omnibus,' sed 'pro multis,' id est, pro his qui credere voluerint" is quite unwarranted ; cf. Rom. v. 12, 15, 18. *Ἀντί* belongs to the imagery of the *λύτρον*, cf. viii. 37 *ἀντάλλαγμα τῆς ψυχῆς*, and Mt. v. 38, xvii. 27 ; elsewhere *ὑπέρ* is used in this connexion (xiv. 24, Jo. xi. 50 f., xvii. 19, xviii. 14, Rom. v. 8, xiv. 15, 1 Cor. i. 13, xv. 3, 2 Cor. v.

15, Gal. i. 4, ii. 20, Eph. v. 2, 25, 1 Thess. v. 10, 1 Tim. *l.c.*, Tit. ii. 14, Heb. ii. 9, x. 12, 1 Pet. ii. 21, iii. 18, 1 Jo. iii. 16), or even *περί* (1 Jo. ii. 2, and as a variant in several of the passages cited for *ὑπέρ*). For an early expansion of *λύτρον ἀντὶ πολλῶν* see the beautiful passage in *Ep. ad Diogn.* ix. 2.

46—52. PASSAGE THROUGH JERICHO. BLIND BARTIMAEUS RESTORED TO SIGHT (Mt. xx. 29—34, Lc. xviii. 35—43).

46. *καὶ ἔρχονται εἰς Ἰερειχώ*] If the modern et-Taiyibeh is the site of Ephraim (Jo. xi. 54), the place of the Lord's last retirement (see note on x. 1), a road still "marked by Roman pavement" (G. A. Smith, *H. G.*, p. 269 n.) led straight from the spot to Jericho. The traveller from Ephraim who reached Jericho by this road would enter through a gate on the N. side of the city, and in order to proceed to Jerusalem, he would cross to the west gate : cf. *ἔρχονται εἰς* (Mc.), *ἐκπορευομ. ἀπό* (Mt., Mc.), *εἰσελθὼν διήρχετο* (Lc.). Jericho is mentioned in the Gospels only here and in the parable of Lc. x. 30 ff., but the Lord and His disciples had doubtless passed through it before, perhaps more than once, when journeying to Jerusalem ; the journey to Bethany from Peraea (Jo. x. 40, xi. 1, 7, 17) must at least have led Him past the town. Now however He enters with a crowd of followers (Lc. xviii. 36), as a great Rabbi on His way to the Passover; and His passage through the city bears the character of an ovation. *Ἔρχονται*, the 'historic' present (Hawkins, *H. S.*, p. 116).

The Jericho of our Lord's time (LXX. (B) and N. T. Ἰερειχώ, WH.,

αὐτοῦ ἀπὸ Ἰερειχὼ καὶ τῶν μαθητῶν αὐτοῦ καὶ
ὄχλου ἱκανοῦ ὁ υἱὸς Τιμαίου Βαρτιμαῖος, τυφλὸς

46 απο Ιερειχω אBCLΨ (απο Ιεριχω ΑΧΓΔΠΣΦ minᵒᵐⁿ ᵛⁱᵈ)] εκειθεν D a b f ff i q rᵛⁱᵈ
go Orᵇⁱˢ | και 3°] μετα DΨ a b f ff i l r arm go | o υιος] om o ΑΧΓΠΦ minᵖˡ go | om
o υιος Τιμ. Βαρτ. k | Βαριτειμιας D (a b d ff q) | τυφλος אBDLΔΨ 124 alᵖᵃᵘᶜ me go Or]
pr o ΑCΧΓΠΣΦ minᵖˡ

Notes, p. 155; Josephus, Ἰεριχοῦς or Ἰεριχώ, gen. -οῦς, represented by the modern *er Riha*) was about five miles W. of the Jordan and fifteen N.E. of Jerusalem, near the mouth of the *Wady Kelt*, and more than a mile south of the site of the ancient town. The fertility of the climate and soil, described in glowing terms by Jos. *B. J.* viii. 3, attracted Herod the Great and Archelaus, who adorned it with public buildings and a palace. Under the Procurators it seems to have been held by a Roman garrison (*B. J.* ii. 18. 6). Yet the town was not given over to a Hellenistic population like the cities of the Decapolis, or the neighbouring Phasaelis; Priests and Levites from Jerusalem found their way thither (Lc. x. 31 f.), and the Lord, who seems never to have entered Tiberias, did not hesitate to be a guest at a house in Jericho (Lc. xix. 5). His arrival there marks another distinct stage in the journey to the Cross; by publicly entering Jericho He places Himself in the power of the Procurator and the Great Sanhedrin.

καὶ ἐκπορευομένου αὐτοῦ κτλ.] Similarly Mt. Both Mt. and Mc. omit the striking story of Zacchaeus (Lc. xix. 2—10), which appears to have had no place in the common tradition. Further, they both differ from Lc. with regard to the time and place of the miracle (Lc. ἐν τῷ ἐγγίζειν αὐτὸν εἰς Ἰερειχώ, cf. xix. 1). Augustine's suggestion (*de cons. ev.* ii. 126) "duo similia similiterque miracula fecisse Iesum" is not recommended to the modern student by the alternative "mentiri evan-

gelium"; the trustworthiness of the Gospels is now seen to be maintained and not impeached by a frank recognition of their independence in details. In the present instance the statement of Mc., which is in every way fuller and more precise, is probably to be preferred to that of Lc. "Οχλον ἱκανοῦ: Mt. ἠκολούθησεν αὐτὸν (cf. Mc. x. 32) ὄχλος πολύς. Ἱκανός = πολύς, here only in Mc., is frequent in Lc. (Ev.⁶, Acts¹⁶), and occurs occasionally in the later books of the Canon (Hab. ii. 13 λαοὶ ἱκανοὶ...ἔθνη πολλά, Zach. vii. 3 ἤδη ἱκανὰ ἔτη), especially in 1—3 Macc.; the word was used in this sense by the comic poets, and in colloquial and the later literary Greek.

ὁ υἱὸς Τιμαίου Βαρτιμαῖος] Mc. only. Bengel is doubtless right in inferring: "notus apostolorum tempore Bartimaeus"; cf. Victor: ὀνομαστὶ δεδήλωκεν ὁ Μᾶρκος...ὡς ἐπιφανῆ τότε ὄντα. Cf. v. 22, xiv. 3, xv. 21. The Greek name Τίμαιος, familiar as that of the interlocutor in the *Timaeus* of Plato, probably covers an Aramaic name, which also underlies the patronymic Βαρτιμαῖος. According to Jerome (*interpr. hebr. nom.*, ed. Lagarde, p. 66), the true form of the latter word is Barsemia, *filius caecus* (ܒܪ ܣܡܝܐ); but our existing Greek mss. lend no support to this reading. Βαρτιμαῖος suggests בַּר טִמְאִי, where טִמְאִי may be either an adjective 'unclean' or a personal name. In either case the accent ought probably to follow the analogy of Βαρθολομαῖος (Bengel's "proparoxytonon ut ipsum Τίμαιος" rests upon the assumption that Βαρτ. is compounded of Βάρ, Τίμαιος).

προσαίτης, ἐκάθητο παρὰ τὴν ὁδόν.   ⁴⁷καὶ ἀκούσας 47
ὅτι ᾿Ιησοῦς ὁ Ναζαρηνός ἐστιν ἤρξατο κράζειν καὶ
λέγειν Υἱὲ Δαυεὶδ ᾿Ιησοῦ, ἐλέησόν με.   ⁴⁸καὶ ἐπετί- 48

46 προσαιτης ℵBLΔΨ k me] προσαιτων (post οδον) AC² (om C*) ΧΓΠΣΦ
minᶠᵉʳᵉᵒᵐⁿ επαιτων (item post οδ.) (D) 2ᵖᵉ: mendicans a b c d f ff q vg syrr go aeth
47 εστιν ο N. B | Ναζαρηνος BLΔΨ 1 118 209 a b c f k vg Or] Ναζωραιος ℵAC(E)Χ
(Γ)ΠΣΦ minᵖˡ q* go | ιϲ υιος Δ. 2ᵖᵉ | υιε] υιος DK 69 409 Or ο υιος AM*ΧΓΠ al
minᵖˡ | om Ιησου Ψ

It must be admitted that we should
have expected Mc. to write Βαρτιμαῖος,
ὅ ἐστιν υἱὸς Τιμαίου (cf. iii. 17, vii. 11,
34, xiv. 36); yet see v. 47 υἱὲ Δαυεὶδ
᾿Ιησοῦ. Both the Sinaitic Syriac and
the Peshitta read "Timaeus son of
Timaeus" (ܒܪ ܛܝܡܝ ܛܝܡܝ), as if Mc.
had written Τίμαιος ὁ υἱὸς Τιμαίου, but
this may be due to the difficulty of
rendering the Greek into Syriac exactly without iteration. On the whole
question see Nestle, Marg. p. 83 ff.,
and in Hastings, D. B. iv., p. 762; and
Schmiedel in Encycl. Bibl. i., s.v.
Bartimaeus.

τυφλὸς προσαίτης] Προσαίτης is a
late word (Plutarch, Lucian), found
also in Jo. ix. 8; Lc. uses ἐπαιτεῖν here
and in xvi. 3, and αἰτεῖν ἐλεημοσύνην
in Acts iii. 2. Παρὰ τὴν ὁδόν: cf. πρὸς
τὴν θύραν τοῦ ἱεροῦ Acts l. c.; on παρά
after a verb of rest see WM., p. 503,
Blass, Gr. p. 138. Probably Bartimaeus had his seat on the high road
just outside the wall, so as to attract
the attention of all who passed in
and out of the gate. Mt., who agrees
with Mc. against Lc. as to the
locality, differs from both in representing two men as subjects of the
miracle (ἰδοὺ δύο τυφλοὶ...ἀνέβλεψαν);
cf. Mt. viii. 28 δύο δαιμονιζόμενοι,
where Mc. has ἄνθρωπος and Lc.
ἀνήρ τις; in ix. 27 Mt. records
another miracle in which two blind
men are healed. See note on v. 2.
Thpht., following Aug., suggests:
ἐνδέχεται δὲ δύο μὲν εἶναι τοὺς ἰαθέντας,
τὸν δὲ ἐπιφανέστερον αὐτῶν τοῦτον εἶναι τὸν παρὰ τῷ Μάρκῳ μνημονευόμενον.

This is possible, but in such cases the
student may well be content to note
the apparent discrepancy in the two
traditions. If he must harmonise,
he will be wise to follow Tatian (Hill,
Diatess., p. 167), in constructing his
narrative on the basis of Mc. See
the curious fusion of this narrative
with that of Jo. ix. in Ev. Nicod. c. vi.

47. ἀκούσας ὅτι ᾿Ιησοῦς ὁ N. ἐστιν]
The tramp of many feet (Lc. ὄχλου
διαπορευομένου) told him that something unusual was happening; and in
answer to his enquiries (Lc. ἐπυνθάνετο
τί εἴη τοῦτο) he learnt that Jesus was
passing (Mt. παράγει, Lc. παρέρχεται).
῾Ο Ναζαρηνός, Lc. ὁ Ναζωραῖος: on
the distribution of the two forms in
the N. T. see i. 24, note, and on the
origin of the latter form cf. Dalman,
Gr. p. 141 note. ῞Ηρξατο κράζειν: Mt.
ἔκραξαν, Lc. ἐβόησεν (but ἔκραζεν later
on).

υἱὲ Δαυείδ κτλ.] Κύριε, υἱὲ Δ. Mt.,
᾿Ιησοῦ, υἱὲ Δ. Lc. Cf. Mt. ix. 27, xv.
22; in Mc., Lc. υἱὸς Δαυείδ as an
appellative occurs here only. Bengel:
"magna fides, quod caecus filium Da-
vidis adpellat quem ei Nazoraeum
praedicabat populus." The use of the
term reminds the reader that the
Lord is now on Judaean soil. Once
indeed the identification of Jesus
with the Son of David had been suggested in Galilee (Mt. xii. 23), but the
cry does not seem to have been taken
up. At Jerusalem all Jews thought
of David as their father, and of
Messiah as the Son of David in an
especial sense (xi. 10, xii. 35, Jo. vii.

μων αὐτῷ πολλοὶ ἵνα σιωπήσῃ· ὁ δὲ πολλῷ μᾶλλον
49 ἔκραζεν Υἱὲ Δαυείδ, ἐλέησόν με. ⁴⁹καὶ στὰς ὁ Ἰησοῦς
εἶπεν Φωνήσατε αὐτόν. καὶ φωνοῦσι τὸν τυφλὸν
§ Wᵍ 50 λέγοντες αὐτῷ Θάρσει, ἔγειρε· φωνεῖ σε. ⁵⁰§ὁ δὲ
§ ⁷ ἀποβαλὼν τὸ §ἱμάτιον αὐτοῦ ἀναπηδήσας ἦλθεν πρὸς

48 ο δε] αυτος δε Ψ 1071   49 φωνησατε αυτον ℵBCLΔ minᵖᵃᵘᶜ k syrʰᵉˡ⁽ᵐᵍ⁾ me]
αυτον φωνηθηναι ΑΔΧΓΠΣΦ minᵖˡ lattᵛᵗ ᵖˡ ᵛᵍ (syrrᵖᵉˢʰ ʰᶜˡ⁽ᵗˣᵗ⁾ arm) aeth | και φωνουσι τον
τυφλον λεγ. αυτω] οι δε λεγουσιν τω τυφλω D (2ᵖᵉ) a (b ff) i q | θαρσει] θαρρων (vel
θαρσ.) 1 13 28 69 209 346 | εγειραι U 736 alⁿᵒⁿⁿ εγειρου 1 13 28 69 209 346
50 αποβαλων] αποβαλλων Δ επιβαλων 2ᵖᵉ syrˢⁱⁿ ᵛⁱᵈ | αναπηδησας ℵBDLMᵐᵍΔΨ 1071
2ᵖᵉ alᵖᵉʳᵖᵃᵘᶜ latt syrʰᵉˡ⁽ᵐᵍ⁾ me go Or] αναστας ΑCMᵗˣᵗΧΠΣΦ⁷ minᵖˡ syrrˢⁱⁿ ᵖᵉˢʰ ʰᶜˡ⁽ᵗˣᵗ⁾
arm aeth om Γ | προς τ. I.] προς αυτον D minᵖᵃᵘᶜ lattᵛᵗ ᵖˡ ᵛᵍ

42; cf. Dalman, *Worte*, i. p. 262);
for the sources of the latter belief
see note on xii. 35.

The petition "O Son of David," &c.
in the English Litany of 1544, had
been used in some mediaeval devo-
tions (Blunt, *Ann. PB.*, p. 234), but
the corresponding versicle in the third
Sarum Litany for St Mark's Day had
Fili Dei vivi and not *Fili David*.
The *Kyrie eleison* of both East and
West is due to the Psalter of the
LXX. (Ps. vi. 2, ix. 13, &c.) and not
directly to the present context; see
Intr. to the O. T. in Gk., p. 473.

48. ἐπετίμων αὐτῷ πολλοί] The remonstrance came, Lc. says, from the
crowd in front (οἱ προάγοντες, cf. xi.
9), i.e. the man began his litany before Jesus Himself had reached the
spot. The cry spoilt the harmony of
the triumph. Why should this beggar
force his misery on the attention of
the great Prophet? Victor: οὐκ ἐπι-
τρέποντες τῷ τυφλῷ βοᾶν, ὥσπερ ἐπὶ
βασιλέως παριόντος. Cf. x. 13. The
indignant σιώπα (Mt., Mc., σίγα Lc.),
was general (πολλοί, Mc., ὁ ὄχλος,
Mt.). But it seemed only to add
vigour to the reiterated ἐλέησον
(πολλῷ μᾶλλον ἔκραζεν Mc., Lc., μεῖζον
ἔκραξαν, Mt.).

49. στὰς ὁ Ἰ. εἶπεν Φωνήσατε] Mt.
στὰς...ἐφώνησεν, Lc. σταθεὶς...ἐκέλευ-
σεν...ἀχθῆναι. On στάς, σταθείς, see

iii. 24 f. The procession was stopped,
and the call was passed on to the front
till it reached Bartimaeus. Reproofs
were at once changed into words of
encouragement, which Mc. alone has
preserved in a Greek sentence, the
music of which caught the fancy of
Longfellow. Θάρσει, Vg. *animaequior
esto*; cf. Gen. xxxv. 17, Exod. xiv. 13,
xx. 20, 3 Regn. xvii. 13 (=אַל תִּירָא),
&c., Mt. ix. 2, 22, xiv. 27 (Mc. vi. 50),
Jo. xvi. 33, Acts xxiii. 11. St Paul
(2 Cor.⁵) and Heb.¹ write θαρρεῖν,
and this form occurs also in Prov.
i. 21 (θαρροῦσα), xxxi. 11 א (θαρρεῖ),
Bar. iv. 21 B (θαρρεῖτε), 27 B (θαρρή-
σατε), 4 Macc. xiii. 11, xvii. 4 (θάρρει).
In view of the last four references it
is precarious to lay stress on the circumstance that in the N. T. θαρσ.
is limited to the imperative. Φωνεῖ
σε: so the Lord's φωνήσατε is rightly
interpreted by those who execute it.
He calls through the voices of His
messengers.

50. ὁ δὲ ἀποβαλών...ἀναπηδήσας...
πρὸς τὸν Ἰ.] Mc. only. The ἱμάτιον
is thrown aside in his haste; cf.
4 Regn. vii. 15 ἰδοὺ πᾶσα ἡ ὁδὸς
πλήρης ἱματίων...ὧν ἔρριψεν Συρία ἐν
τῷ θαμβεῖσθαι αὐτούς, Heb. xii. 1 ὄγκον
ἀποθέμενοι πάντα...τρέχωμεν: the point
is missed in the tame ἐπιβαλών of the
Syr.ˢⁱⁿ and one of the cursive MSS.
(vv. ll.). Ἀναπηδᾶν is ἅπ. λεγ. in the

τὸν Ἰησοῦν. ⁵¹καὶ ἀποκριθεὶς αὐτῷ ὁ Ἰησοῦς εἶπεν 51
Τί σοι θέλεις ποιήσω; ὁ δὲ τυφλὸς εἶπεν ¶ αὐτῷ   ¶ ⁊
Ῥαββουνεί, ἵνα ἀναβλέψω. ⁵²καὶ ὁ Ἰησοῦς εἶπεν 52
αὐτῷ Ὕπαγε, ἡ πίστις σου σέσωκέν σε. καὶ εὐθὺς
ἀνέβλεψεν, καὶ ἠκολούθει αὐτῷ ἐν τῇ ὁδῷ.

51 ειπεν] λεγει ΑΧΓΠᵐᵍ alᵖˡ | ποιησω] pr ινα 604 al·ᵖᵃᵘᶜ b c | ραββουνει Β (ραβ-
βουνι ℵΑCΕ²FΗΚLΜSUΧΓΠΣΦΨ minᵐᵘ ραββονι 604* alᵖᵃᵘᶜ f vg aeth) syrʰᶜˡ arm
(Or)] κυριε ραββει D a b ff i ραββι 38 k q syrᵖᵉˢʰ κυριε 409   52 ηκολουθησαν 121
346 409 alᵛⁱˣ ᵐᵘ rᵛⁱᵈ ηκολουθησε 604ᶜᵒʳʳ | αυτω 2°] τω Ιησου Μ⁽ᵗˣᵗ ᵉᵗ ᵐᵍ ²⁾ΧΓΠΣΦ minᵖˡ
syrʰᶜˡ⁽ᵗˣᵗ⁾ go Or | om εν τη οδω 736*

N. T., but occurs in 1 Regn. xx. 34
(קוֹם), xxv. 10, Tob.⁴ Esth.¹; cf. Acts
iii. 8, ἐξαλλόμενος ἔστη. With the
whole context cf. Luc. Catapl. 15 ἐγὼ
δὲ…ἄσμενος ἀπορρίψας τὴν σμίλην…
ἀναπηδήσας εὐθὺς ἀνυπόδητος…εἰπόμην.
Acc. to Lc. the blind man was led by
friendly hands (ἐκέλευσεν…ἀχθῆναι).

51. τί σοι θέλεις ποιήσω;] For the
construction see x. 36, note, and for
τί ποιήσω cf. xv. 12; on the position
of σοι see Blass, Gr. p. 288. Obvious
as was the meaning of the ἐλέησον,
the Lord will have the want specified.

ῥαββουνεί, ἵνα ἀναβλέψω] Mt. κύριε,
ἵνα ἀνοιγῶσιν οἱ ὀφθαλμοὶ ἡμῶν, Lc.
κύριε, ἵνα ἀναβλ. Mc. alone preserves
the Aramaic original of the κύριε: cf.
ix. 5, note. The form ῥαββουνεί appears again in Jo. xx. 16, where see
Westcott's note, with which compare
Dalman, Worte, i. p. 279; on the
broadening of the second vowel cf.
Dalman, Gr. p. 140 n. and Worte, i.
p. 267. The Syriac versions have
ܪܒܘܠܝ (sin.), ܪܒܝ (pesh.), ܪܒܘܠܝ
(hcl.); Syr.ˢⁱⁿ· has ܪܒܘܠܝ again in Jo.
l.c., Syr.ᶜᵘ· is unfortunately wanting
in both passages. The English versions before Rheims and A.V. render
"Master." Ἵνα ἀναβλέψω, sc. θέλω or
θ. ποιήσῃς: cf. vi. 25, note; for ἀναβλέπειν 'to recover sight' see Tob. xi. 8
(ℵ), xiv. 2, Isa. xlii. 18 (=hiph. of נבט),
and in the N. T., Mt. xi. 5, Jo. ix.
11 ff., Acts ix. 12 ff. To give ἀνάβλεψις
to the blind was a prerogative of the

Son of David (Is. lxi. 1, Lc. iv. 18,
vii. 22). Τὸ ἀναβλέψω Tatian and
Syr.ᶜᵘ· ⁽ᴹᵗ·, ᴸᶜ·⁾ add "that I may see
Thee"; cf. Hill, Diatess., p. 167 n.

52. ὕπαγε, ἡ πίστις σου σέσωκέν σε]
Lc. ἀνάβλεψον κτλ. Mt., who omits
the words, adds the customary sign:
σπλαγχνισθεὶς…ἥψατο τῶν ὀμμάτων.
The eulogistic ἡ π. σου κτλ. seems to
have been reserved for cases of more
than ordinary faith; see Mt. ix. 22,
Mc. v. 34, Lc. vii. 50. In such passages σῴζειν probably includes the
deeper sense; see v. 34, note. All the
Evangelists note that the cure was
immediate (Mc. εὐθύς, Mt. εὐθέως, Lc.
παραχρῆμα)—a contrast to the method
employed in more than one other case
of blindness (viii. 23 f., Jo. ix. 6 ff.).
Ephrem: "o felicem mendicum qui
manum extendens ut ab homine ob-
olum acciperet, dignus habitus est ut
donum a Deo acciperet."

καὶ ἠκολούθει κτλ.] Bartimaeus, no
longer blind or a beggar, joins the
crowd of followers "in the way,'" i.e.
on the road to Jerusalem (Bengel).
Lc. adds δοξάζων τὸν θεόν: possibly in
the words of some well-known Psalm
(cf. cxlv. (cxlvi.) 8), which may have
been taken up by the crowd (Lc. πᾶς
ὁ λαὸς ἔδωκεν αἶνον τῷ θεῷ). For an
admirable homiletic use of the story
see Orig. in Mt.: εἴθε καὶ ἡμεῖς…παρ'
αὐτὴν καθεζόμενοι τῶν γραφῶν τὴν ὁδόν,
ἀκούσαντες ὅτι Ἰησοῦς παράγει, διὰ τῆς
ἡμετέρας ἀξιώσεως στήσαιμεν αὐτόν, καὶ

11. 1   ¹ Καὶ ὅτε ἐγγίζουσιν εἰς Ἰεροσόλυμα εἰς Βηθφαγὴ
καὶ Βηθανίαν πρὸς τὸ ὄρος τὸ Ἐλαιών, ἀποστέλλει

XI 1 ἐγγιζουσιν] ἠγγιζεν (vel ηγγισεν) DE minᵖᵃᵘᶜ b c ff i k q | Ἰεροσολυμα]
Ἰερουσαλημ ΑΧΓΠΦ minᵖˡ me go + και ηλθεν 1071 (al) | εις Βηθφαγη (Βηθσφ. Β³FΓΣ
604 alⁿᵒⁿⁿ) και (+εις אC εις syrˢⁱⁿ) Βηθανιαν א(A)BC(L)ΧΓΔΠ(Σ)Φ minᶠᵉʳᵉ ᵒᵐⁿ f q
syrr⁽ˢⁱⁿ⁾ᵖᵉˢʰ ʰᵉˡ arm (me) go aeth] και εις Βηθανιαν D a b ff i (k) (r) vg Or εις Βηθφαγη
Ψ yˢᶜʳ (Βηθσφ.) the | το ελαιων B k (montem eleon) r] το καλουμενον ελ. Σ των ελαιων
aeth | αποστελλει] απεστειλεν FH 1 alᵖᵉʳᵖᵃᵘᶜ a b c f k** syrrˢⁱⁿ ᵖᵉˢʰ go aeth επεμψεν C

εἴποιμεν ὅτι θέλομεν ἵνα ἀνοιγῶσιν οἱ
ὀφθαλμοὶ ἡμῶν [cf. Ps. cxix. 18]· ὅπερ
ἐὰν εἴπωμεν ἀπὸ διαθέσεως ὀρεγομένης
τοῦ βλέπειν...σπλαγχνισθήσεται ὁ σωτὴρ ἡμῶν...καὶ ἁψαμένου αὐτοῦ φεύξε-
ται μὲν τὸ σκότος καὶ ἡ ἄγνοια, εὐθέως
δὲ οὐ μόνον ἀναβλέψομεν, ἀλλὰ καὶ ἀκο-
λουθήσομεν αὐτῷ.

XI. 1—11. SOLEMN ENTRY INTO
THE PRECINCT OF THE TEMPLE (Mt.
xxi. 1—11, Lc. xix. 29—45, Jo. xii. 1,
12—19).

1. ἐγγίζουσιν εἰς Ἰεροσόλυμα] The
road from Jericho (cf. Lc. x. 30) up
the Wady Kelt has brought the party
to the East slope of the Mount of
Olives, within three miles of Jerusalem ; for ἐγγίζειν εἰς cf. Tob. vi. 6,
10 (א), Lc. xviii. 35 ; the dat. is also
used, Acts ix. 3, x. 9. According to
Jo. the time was πρὸ ἐξ ἡμερῶν τοῦ
πάσχα, i.e. probably Nisan 8, the eve
of the Sabbath (cf. Lewin, fast. sacr.
p. 230 ; Westcott on Jo. xii. 1).

εἰς Βηθφαγὴ καὶ Βηθανίαν] Mt. εἰς
Βηθφαγή. More exactly, the spot
they approached was not Jerusalem,
but the villages nearest to the city
on the Jericho road ; for the repeated
εἰς, the second limiting the first, cf.
v. 11, εἰς Ἰ. εἰς τὸ ἱερόν. Bethphage
(v. l., Bethsphage) has not been identified, but the Talmud (Neubauer, p. 147
ff.) mentions a בית פאגי (or בית פגי,
Dalman, Gr. p. 152) which seems to
have been near Jerusalem ; cf. Eus.
onom., Βηθφ. κώμη πρὸς τῷ ὄρει τῶν
ἐλαιῶν. Βηθανία (or Βηθανιά indecl., Lc.
xix. 29, WSchm. p. 91,= בֵּית חֲנִיָּה,
Dalman, Gr. p. 143, the Talmudic בֵּית

הִינֵי, Neubauer, p. 149 f.) is the modern
el 'Azariyeh, the Lazarium of the
fourth century (Silvia, p. 57 : "Lazarium, id est, Bethania, est forsitan
secundo miliario a civitate"). The
village lies in a sheltered and fruitful
hollow, of which a picturesque description will be found in Stanley, S.
and P., p. 186 ff. As to the meaning
of the names, Jerome gives for Bethphage domus oris vallium, vel domus
bucae or (tr. in Mc.) d. maxillae
("Syrum est," he says, "non Hebrae-
um "), and for Bethany domus ad-
flictionis eius vel d. oboedientiae (בֵּית
עֲנִיָּה) ; a more usual etymology connects them respectively with the fig
(פַּגִּים, Cant. ii. 13, but see Buxtorf,
sub v.) and the date, which certainly
were grown in the neighbourhood.

πρὸς τὸ ὄρος τὸ Ἐλαιών] Cf. εἰς τὸ
ὄρος, iii. 13, vi. 46, ix. 2, xiv. 26 ; πρός·
with the acc. expresses motion towards, as in i. 5, iv. 3, 13, 32, &c. ; the
Mount was the object immediately in
view as they approached. The hill to
the East of Jerusalem is called in the
O.T. "the olive-trees" (2 Regn. xv. 30),
"the mountain of the olive-trees "
(Zach. xiv. 4), or simply "the mountain" (2 Esdr. xviii. 15). In the N.T.
τὸ ὄρος τῶν ἐλαιῶν predominates (Mt.³,
Mc.², Lc.²) ; but the hill is also known
as ὁ ἐλαιών, "the olive-grove" (Acts i.
12 ἀπὸ ὄρους τοῦ καλουμένου Ἐλαιῶνος,
where Blass corrects ἐλαιῶν in defiance
of the MSS.) ; cf. Jos. ant. vii. 9. 2 ἀνα-
βαίνοντος αὐτοῦ διὰ τοῦ Ἐλαιῶνος ὄρους.
As late as the fourth century the
name Ἐλαιών seems to have lingered

δύο τῶν μαθητῶν αὐτοῦ, ²καὶ λέγει αὐτοῖς Ὑπάγετε 2
εἰς τὴν κώμην τὴν κατέναντι ὑμῶν, καὶ εὐθὺς εἰσπορευόμενοι εἰς αὐτὴν εὑρήσετε πῶλον δεδεμένον,
ἐφ᾽ ὃν οὐδεὶς [οὔπω] ἀνθρώπων ἐκάθισεν· λύσατε

2 οὐδεὶς οὐπω ανθρ. BLΔΨ] οὐδ. ανθρ. οὐπω ℵC 13 69 al^pauc ουπω ουδ. ανθρ. ΚΠΣΦ
604 (736) ουδ. πωποτε ανθρ. A ουδεις ανθρ. DXΓ min^pl a c g k syrr^sin pesh arm aeth |
κεκαθικεν A(DEM)XΓΠ(Σ)Φ min^pl | λυσατε αυτ. κ. φερετε] λυσαντες αυτ. αγαγετε
ΑΔΧΓΠΣΦ min^pl λυσαντες αυτ. απαγαγετε 2^pe

on the spot, for Silvia (p. 70) gives it
as an alternative to the Latin *olivetum*,
and indeed appears to prefer *Eleon*.
These facts lend a high probability to
the reading of B(Σ)k r in the present
context, and tempt us to prefer Ἐλαιών
to ἐλαιῶν in Lc. xix. 29, xxi. 37; cf.
Deissmann, *Bible Studies*, p. 208 ff.,
where the objections raised by Blass
(*Gr.* p. 85) are sufficiently answered.
For the distance of the Mount of
Olives from the city see Acts i. 12, ὅ
ἐστιν ἐγγὺς Ἰερουσαλὴμ σαββάτου ἔχον
ὁδόν. Jo. xi. 18 ὡς ἀπὸ σταδίων δεκα-
πέντε. Jos. *ant.* xx. 8. 6, ἀπέχει στάδια
πέντε. Bethphage was one of the limits
of the Sabbatic zone round the city.

ἀποστέλλει κτλ.] According to Jo.
(xii. 1, 12) this occurred on the
morrow (τῇ ἐπαύριον) after the arrival
at Bethany, the events of Mc. xiv.
3—9 having intervened (Jo. xii. 2—
8); see note on Mc. xiv. 3. Ἀποστέλλει, 'gives them a commission to
execute' (iii. 14 note, vi. 7). Δύο τῶν
μαθητῶν, probably one of the six pairs
which made up the Apostolate, cf. vi.
7, Lc. x. 1; on the other hand cf. xiv.
12, note. The Baptist also seems to
have arranged his disciples in pairs,
cf. Lc. vii. 19, Jo. i. 35. The minute-
ness of Mc.'s account suggests that
Peter was one of the two selected on
this occasion.

2. ὑπάγετε εἰς κτλ.] Since according to John the Lord was now on His
way from Bethany to Jerusalem, the
village was probably Bethphage (cf.
Mt. xxi. 1), which seems to have been

on the opposite side of the ascent;
for κατέναντι (לִפְנֵי) see Exod. xxxii. 5,
Num. xvii. 4 (19), Mc. xii. 41, xiii. 3.
Εὐθὺς εἰσπορευόμενοι 'even as ye enter,'
cf. i. 10; Mt. is content with εὐθύς, Lc.
with εἰσπορ.; the combination in Mc.
is characteristically precise. Πῶλον
δεδεμένον: so Lc.; Mt. ὄνον δεδεμένην
καὶ πῶλον μετ᾽ αὐτῆς. Πῶλος may be
the young of any animal; the Greek
naturally used it for the most part of
the horse, the Greek-speaking Jew of
the ass; cf. Gen. xxxii. 15 (16), xlix.
11, Jud. x. 4, xii. 14, Zech. ix. 9.
Mt. who quotes Zech. *l. c.* (xxi. 4 ff.)
fills in the picture from the prophecy;
in Jo. (xii. 15) on the other hand the
prophecy is slightly modified to bring
it into correspondence with the event;
Mc. and Lc. simply state the facts.
The foal was unbroken, had never
been ridden (Mc., Lc.), as befitted an
animal consecrated to a sacred purpose
(Num. xix. 2, Deut. xxi. 3; cf. Hor.
epod. ix. 22, Verg. *georg.* iv. 540).
The Lord was born of one who ἄνδρα
οὐκ ἔγνω (Lc. i. 34), and was buried
οὗ οὐκ ἦν οὐδεὶς οὔπω κείμενος (Lc.
xxiii. 53). His choice of an animal not
ridden by any before Him is another
of those claims to uniqueness which
contrast forcibly with His usual con-
descension to the circumstances of an
ordinary human life. It is arbitrary
to refer the clause ἐφ᾽ ὅν κτλ. to the
narrator (Gould). Λύσατε...καὶ φέρετε:
the aorist and present imperatives are
both appropriate, cf. WM., p. 393 f.

3 αὐτὸν καὶ φέρετε. ³καὶ ἐάν τις ὑμῖν εἴπῃ Τί ποιεῖτε
τοῦτο; εἴπατε Ὁ κύριος αὐτοῦ χρείαν ἔχει, καὶ
4 εὐθὺς αὐτὸν ἀποστέλλει πάλιν ὧδε. ⁴καὶ ἀπῆλθον
καὶ εὗρον πῶλον δεδεμένον πρὸς θύραν ἔξω ἐπὶ τοῦ

3 τι ποιειτε τουτο] τι λυετε τον πωλον D 28 69 124 346 1071 2ᵖᵒ a b f ff i r arm Or
τι 1 109 syrˢⁱⁿ | ο κυριος] pr οτι ℵACDLXΓΠΣΦ minᵖˡ f q vg syrrᵖᵉˢʰ ʰᶜˡ arm go |
αποστελλει ℵABCDEFHKLMSVXΓΔΣ minˢᵃᵗ ᵐᵘ b c l go] αποστελει GUΠΦΨ 1 alᵐᵘ
a d f ff q rᵛⁱᵈ vg arm aegg aeth Or | παλιν ℵBC*DLΔ minᵖᵃᵘᶜ Orᵇⁱˢ] om AC²XΓΠΣΦΨ
minᵖˡ latt syrr arm aegg go aeth Or¹ | αποστ. παλιν αυτον B αυτον παλιν αποστ. C*
4—5 om k   4 πωλον] pr τον ℵCΔ 13 28 1071 alˢᵃᵗ ᵐᵘ arm the | θυραν] pr την
ℵACDXΓΠΣΦ minᶠᵉʳᵉ ᵒᵐⁿ Or¹ (om την BLΔ 2ᵖᵉ ᵛⁱᵈ aegg go Orᵇⁱˢ)

3. ἐάν τις ὑμῖν εἴπῃ κτλ. The
Lord provides against a possible
difficulty. The proceeding seemed
high-handed, and if it was witnessed
by any, the objection would certainly
be raised Τί ποιεῖτε τοῦτο ; = Lc. διὰ τί
λύετε; For answer they were instructed simply to state that the
Master (ὁ κύριος, cf. Jo. xiii. 13)
needed the foal (αὐτοῦ, Mt. αὐτῶν=
the mother and the foal). Χρείαν ἔχειν
= חָשַׁב Dan. iii. 16 (LXX. and Th.);
for the construction cf. ii. 17, xiv.
63, Jo. xiii. 29, Heb. v. 12, Apoc. xxi.
23, xxii. 5. Wycliffe: "seie ȝe that
he is nedeful to the Lord." The
words have reference chiefly to the
didactic purpose which the Lord had
in view; cf. Jerome ad l., and Victor:
οὐ γὰρ ἀπὸ τοῦ ὄρους τῶν ἐλαιῶν εἰς
Ἰερουσαλὴμ ἐξιόντι τῷ κυρίῳ χρεία τις
ἐπ᾽ ὄνου καθέζεσθαι, ὃς τὴν Ἰουδαίαν
καὶ Γαλιλαίαν ἅπασαν διῄει πεζός. Tertullian (de coron. 13) remarks quaintly
but suggestively: "dominus tuus ubi
...Hierusalem ingredi voluit nec asi-
num habuit privatum."

καὶ εὐθὺς αὐτὸν ἀποστ. πάλιν ὧδε]
The animal is not to be detained
longer than the occasion requires;
the Master will send him back to
Bethphage as soon as He has reached
Jerusalem. In Mt. the sentence has
taken quite another turn (εὐθὺς δὲ
ἀποστελεῖ αὐτούς sc. ὁ κύριος τῶν ὑπο-
ζυγίων), and the harmonisers have

imported this into Mc.'s text; see
vv. ll. Field, Notes, p. 34 f., offers
some defence of the R. T. on internal grounds which are not con-
vincing. Mt. adds here a reference
to Zech. ix. 9, in which he sees a
prophecy of the present incident (cf.
note on v. 2).

4. ἀπῆλθον καὶ εὗρον κτλ.] Lc. εὗρον
καθὼς εἶπεν αὐτοῖς. For other examples of this supernatural knowledge
of circumstances cf. xiv. 13, Mt. xvii.
27, Jo. i. 48. While they fall short
of a logical proof of omniscience (Gore,
Dissertations, p. 80 f.), they must be
allowed due weight in any estimate of
the powers of the Sacred Humanity
(Mason, Conditions, p. 157 ff.). In Mc.
the coincidences between the Lord's
anticipations and the event appear in
detail (vv. 4—8). The foal was tied
up πρὸς θύραν ἔξω, at (here nearly =
πρὸς θύρᾳ, cf. Blass, Gr. p. 139) a
house-door, but outside, not in the
house, but in the street. For θύρα
a house-door, see Gen. xix. 6, 9, Mc. i.
33, ii. 2, and for ἔξω 'out of doors,' iii.
31 f., Lc. xiii. 25, xxii. 62, Jo. xviii. 16.
Ἐπὶ τοῦ ἀμφόδου, Vg. in bivio, whence
Wycliffe "in the meeting of tweye
weyes,"Tindale, A.V."in a place where
two ways met"; R.V. "in the open
street." Ἄμφοδον occurs in Jer. xvii.
27, xxx. 16 (xlix. 27), as the equivalent
of אַרְמְנוֹת, where Aq. and Symm.
have βάρεις, but the Greek lexico-

ἀμφόδου, καὶ λύουσιν αὐτόν. ⁵καὶ τινες τῶν ἐκεῖ 5
ἑστηκότων ἔλεγον αὐτοῖς Τί ποιεῖτε λύοντες τὸν
πῶλον; ⁶οἱ δὲ εἶπαν αὐτοῖς καθὼς¶ εἶπεν ὁ Ἰησοῦς· 6 ¶F
καὶ ἀφῆκαν αὐτούς. ⁷καὶ φέρουσιν τὸν πῶλον πρὸς 7
τὸν Ἰησοῦν, καὶ ἐπιβάλλουσιν §αὐτῷ τὰ ἱμάτια αὐτῶν· §N
καὶ ἐκάθισεν ἐπ᾽ αὐτόν. ⁸καὶ πολλοὶ τὰ ἱμάτια 8

5 εστωτων ΜΓ 238 1071 al^nonn   6 ειπεν] ενετειλατο ΑΧΓΠΣΦ min^pl latt^vt4vg
syrr^peshhcl go ειρηκει D b c ff i q (dixerat)   7 φερουσιν ℵ^cΒΛΔΨ 1071] αγουσιν
ℵ*C 1 13 28 69 124 346 al^pauc ηγαγον ΑΔΧΓΠΣ min^pl | επεβαλον ΑΧΓΠΣΦ min^pl
a̦cfkq theb go aeth | αυτων] εαυτων Β αυτου D 256 om 1 28 299 b ff i k q arm |
εκαθισαν ℵ καθιζει (D) 1 28 91 209 241 299 2^pe | επ αυτον] επ αυτων 2^pe al^nonn επ αυτω
ΑΝΧΓΠ min^pl latt^vt pl vg

graphers explain the word by ἀγυιά, δίοδος, ῥύμη and the like: cf. Epiphanius cited by Wetstein: ἀμφόδων ἤτοι λαυρῶν ἐπιχωρίως καλουμένων ὑπὸ τῶν τὴν Ἀλεξανδρέων οἰκούντων πόλιν. Ἄμφοδον occurs again in the D text of Acts xix. 28 (δραμόντες εἰς τὸ ἄμφοδον ἔκραζον), where see Blass's note. Λύουσιν αὐτόν: cf. v. 2, and for other examples of this use of λύειν see Lc. xiii. 15, Apoc. ix. 14 f.

5—6. τινὲς τῶν ἐκεῖ ἑστηκότων] Idlers hanging about the lanes in the outskirts of the village, cf. Mt. xx. 3, 6; for the phrase see ix. 1, xv. 35. According to Lc. they were the owners (οἱ κύριοι), which is probable enough; they had tied up the animals while they enjoyed the gossip of the street. That they were satisfied with the answer Ὁ κύριος αὐτοῦ χρ. ἔχει κτλ. need cause no surprise; the Master was well known in the neighbourhood, and His disciples had been with Him before on a memorable occasion (Jo. xi. 7 ff.). The promise to return the animal at once could be trusted; for the present it was not required by the owners, and they might well be proud that it should be used by the Prophet. So they let the two go off (ἀφῆκαν αὐτούς) with the foal. It is quite unnecessary to say with Thpht.: οὐκ ἂν ἐγένετο εἰ μὴ θεία τις ἀνάγκη ἐπέκειτο τοῖς

κυρίοις. Τί ποιεῖτε λύοντες; (= τί ποιεῖτε τοῦτο; v. 3): cf. Acts xxi. 13, with Blass's note, and WM., p. 761.

7. φέρουσιν τὸν πῶλον κτλ.] Mt. τὴν ὄνον καὶ τὸν πῶλον: see v. 2. The foal, being yet unbroken, had no trappings (Gen. xxii. 3, Num. xxii. 21, 2 Regn. xvii. 23, 3 Regn. ii. 40, xiii. 13 ff.) and as a substitute for the ἐπίσαγμα (Lev. xv. 9), some spare clothing (τὰ ἱμάτια, cf. v. 28, 30) was hastily thrown (ἐπιβάλλουσιν, Lc. ἐπιρίψαντες: Mt. ἐπέθηκαν) over him (Mt. ἐπ᾽ αὐτῶν), and the Lord took His seat—for Lc.'s ἐπεβίβασαν τὸν Ἰησοῦν can scarcely be understood literally—the rope with which the foal had been tied serving for bridle. As Jerome remarks, Mt.'s ἐπάνω αὐτῶν cannot be taken strictly, and he seeks a solution in allegory ("cum historia vel impossibilitatem habeat vel turpitudinem, ad altiora transmittimus"). There can be little doubt that Mt.'s form of the story is coloured by the details of the prophecy which he quotes (see note on v. 2); Mc. on the other hand records the simple facts.

8. πολλοὶ τὰ ἱμάτια κτλ.] This was perhaps suggested by the use of ἱμάτια for the saddling of the foal. Other disciples, not to be outdone, stripped off their quadrangular wraps and carpeted the bridle path, and the enthusiasm spread to a crowd

αὐτῶν ἔστρωσαν εἰς τὴν ὁδόν, ἄλλοι δὲ στιβάδας,
9 κόψαντες ἐκ τῶν ἀγρῶν. ⁹καὶ οἱ προάγοντες καὶ
οἱ ἀκολουθοῦντες ἔκραζον Ὡσαννά· εὐλογημένος ὁ

8 εστρωσαν] εστρωννυον D 1 28 2ᵖᵉ alᵖᵃᵘᶜ | εις την οδον אBCDLXΓΔΦΨ minᵖˡ b ff i] εν
τη οδω ΑΚΜΝΠΣ minᵖˡ ā f k q vg | om αλλοι...αγρων syrˢⁱⁿ | στοιβαδας AC(N)SVXΓΣΦ
minᵖˡ | κοψαντες εκ των αγρων אB(C)LΔΨ the] εκοπτον εκ των δενδρων (αγρων syrʰᵉˡ⁽ᵐᵍ⁾)
και εστρωννυον εις την οδον (vel εν τη οδω) A(D)NXΓΠΣΦ minᵒᵐⁿ ᵛⁱᵈ latt syrrᵖᵉˢʰ ʰᶜˡ
arm go   9 εκραζον] + λεγοντες ADNXΓΠ al minᵖˡ a b f i q vg syrr arm aeth ελεγον
Ψ | ωσαννα] om D b ff rᵛⁱᵈ + τω υψιστω 13 69 1071 2ᵖᵉ al k arm + εν υψιστω 28 al + εν
υψιστοις 29 c i | om ο ερχ. X

of followers (πολλοί, Mt. ὁ πλεῖστος
ὄχλος). For the construction ἔστρωσαν
εἰς τὴν ὁδόν cf. Tob. vii. 16 (א) ἔστρωσεν
εἰς τὸ ταμεῖον. Lc. represents the
action as repeated along the line of
progress (πορευομένου δὲ αὐτοῦ ὑπε-
στρώννυον); cf. Mc.'s ἐστρώννυον infra.
All the commentators refer to Robinson,Researches in Palestine, i. p. 473,
ii. p. 162 for an illustrative incident;
an O.T. parallel will be found in 4
Regn. ix. 13.
    ἄλλοι δὲ στιβάδας κτλ.] Mt. ἄλλοι
δὲ ἔκοψαν κλάδους ἀπὸ τῶν δένδρων.
Στιβάδες (from στείβω—the form στοι-
βάς (R.T.) is incorrect, see Fritzsche,
though στοιβή occurs in the LXX.),
Vulg. frondes, Wycliffe "bowis or
braunchis," is a litter of leaves or
other green stuff from the meadows
or trees; cf. the Schol. on Theocr. vii.
67 cited by Wetstein: στ. δέ ἐστι
στρωμνὴ ἐπὶ τῆς γῆς ἐκ φύλλων. Mc.
uses the pl. for the materials of the
litter—boughs, long grass, &c., collected from the cultivated lands (ἀγρῶν,
cf. v. 14, vi. 36, 56, x. 29 f.) on either
side of the path. The word is fairly
distributed in class. and later Gk. (cf.
e.g. Plato, resp. 372 B; Philo, de vit.
cont., ed. Conybeare, p. 109), but ἅπ.
λεγ. in the LXX. and N. T.; Aq. uses it
in Ezech. xlvi. 23 for מְירוֹת, which he
perhaps understands as sheepfold enclosures constructed of interwoven
boughs (=ἐπαύλεις). Jo.'s ἔλαβον τὰ
βαΐα τῶν φοινίκων seems to refer to
another concourse which came from

Jerusalem: see next note. The
triumph of Judas Maccabaeus (1 Macc.
xiii. 51) may have been in the thoughts
of many.
    9. οἱ προάγοντες καὶ οἱ ἀκολου-
θοῦντες] So Mt. For the contrast cf.
x. 32 f. On this occasion the Lord
seems to have been in the middle of
two crowds (οἱ...καὶ οἱ...WM., p. 160);
see Stanley, S. and P., p. 191: "two
vast streams of people met on that
day. The one poured out from the
city...from Bethany [and Bethphage]
streamed forth the crowds who had
assembled there on the previous night.
...The two streams met midway. Half
the vast mass turning round preceded;
the other half followed." If this suggestion is accepted, οἱ προάγοντες are
the Galileans from Jerusalem (Jo. xii.
12, ὁ ὄχλος πολὺς ὁ ἐλθὼν εἰς τὴν
ἑορτήν, cf. Westcott's note), who bring
with them palm leaves (ib. 13, ἔλαβον
βαΐα τῶν φοινίκων), cut in the Kidron
or on the western slope of Olivet;
whilst οἱ ἀκολουθοῦντες are the villagers
who strew the path with garments and
foliage. Jerome allegorises: " qui
sunt qui praecedunt ? patriarchae et
prophetae. qui sequuntur ? apostoli
et gentilium populus. sed et in prae-
cedentibus et in sequentibus una vox
Christus est; ipsum laudant, ipsum
voce consona concrepant."
    ἔκραζον Ὡσαννά] The cry rose again
and again. It began πρὸς τῇ καταβάσει τοῦ ὄρους, as the 'city of David'
came into view: see Stanley, S.

ἐρχόμενος ἐν ὀνόματι Κυρίου· ¹⁰εὐλογημένη ἡ ἐρχο- 10
μένη βασιλεία τοῦ πατρὸς ἡμῶν Δαυείδ· ὡσαννὰ ἐν

9—10 εν ονοματι...βασιλεια] εις την βασιλειαν k   10 ευλογημενη] pr και
AD*KMΠ 736 1071 | om ερχομενη Δ 1 alᵖᵃᵘᶜ a | βασιλεια]+εν ονοματι κυριου
ΑΝΧΓΠΣΦ minᵖˡ q syrʰᶜˡ go aeth | ωσαννα εν τοις υψιστοις] ειρηνη εν τ. υψ. 604 syrˢⁱⁿ
ειρ. εν ουρανω και δοξα εν υψ. arm ωσ. ειρ. εν ουρ. κ. δ. εν υψ. 1 91 118 209 299 ειρ. εν
ουρ. κ. δ. εν υψ. ωσ. εν υψ. 251 syrʰᶜˡ⁽ᵗˣᵗ⁾

and P., p. 190. Ὡσαννά represents
הוֹשִׁיעָה־נָּא (Ps. cxviii. 25, LXX. σῶσον
δή), in the Aramaic form הוֹשַׁ֫ענא; see
Kautzsch, p. 173, Dalman, Gr. p. 198,
for the breathing cf. WH., Intr., p.
313; other views of the derivation of
the word are discussed by Cheyne in
Encycl. Bibl. s. v.; cf. Thayer in
Hastings D.B. ii. p. 418 f. Ps. cxviii.,
whether it celebrates the triumph of
Judas Maccabaeus (Cheyne, Origin of
the Psalter, p. 16), or the dedication
of the Second Temple (Delitzsch, Westcott), was intimately connected in the
minds of all loyal Jews with the hope
of national restoration, and its liturgical use at the Feast of the Tabernacles (cf. J. Lightfoot on Mt. xxi. 9;
the seventh day of the Feast is still
called "the Great Hosanna," Taylor,
Teaching, p. 79), and at the Passover
in the Hallel, rendered its words
doubly familiar. It appears that the
palm-branches which were carried in
procession round the altar (Ps. cxviii.
27, cf. Cheyne, Psalms, p. 315 ff.) were
waved at the words הוֹשִׁיעָה־נָּא (J.
Lightfoot, l. c., Edersheim, Temple,
p. 191 ff.); so that the palms of the
προάγοντες may have suggested the
use of this cry. The addition of τῷ
υἱῷ Δαυείδ (Mt.), if it was made at
the time, pointed to Jesus as the
Messiah through whom the salvation
of Israel was expected. But ὡσ. τῷ
υἱῷ Δ. was apparently an early liturgical form in Jewish-Christian churches
(Didache 10), and may have been introduced in this way into the evangelical tradition; it is worthy of note
that Mc. and Jo. agree to omit τ.

υἱῷ Δ. here. For an early Christian
interpretation of Hosanna see Clem.
Al. paed. i. 5 § 12 φῶς καὶ δόξα καὶ
αἶνος μεθ' ἱκετηρίας τῷ κυρίῳ· τουτὶ γὰρ
ἐμφαίνει ἑρμηνευόμενον Ἑλλάδι φωνῇ τὸ
ὡσαννά. Cf. Thayer in Hastings, l.c.
εὐλογημένος ὁ ἐρχόμενος κτλ.] From
Ps. cxviii. 26 (LXX.); Lc. alone inserts ὁ βασιλεύς. In the Psalm
the words are clearly a solemn welcome to the pilgrim, Israelite or
proselyte, who comes up to worship
at the Feast—the accents of the Heb.
shew that בְּשֵׁם יְהוָה is to be connected with בָּרוּךְ—the blessing in the
Name of the LORD (Num. vi. 27, Deut.
xxi. 5) is invoked upon every such
visitor (cf. Perowne ad l.). But the
words (as the next verse will shew) are
used with some perception that this
Visitor is ὁ ἐρχόμενος (הַבָּא) in a
deeper sense; cf. Mt. xi. 3, Jo. iii. 31,
xi. 27.

10. εὐλογημένη ἡ ἐρχ. βασιλεία κτλ.]
This clause, preserved by Mc. only, is
possibly the origin of the liturgical
addition to Hosanna (see on v. 9),
and also of Lc.'s βασιλεύς (Lc. xix.
38). It is a comment on the words
of the Ps., due perhaps to a few
among the crowd who realised more
fully than the rest the meaning of
this reception of the Galilean Prophet.
Ἡ βασιλεία may have been suggested
by the Lord's frequent phrase ἡ β.
τοῦ θεοῦ, or by the knowledge that
He had taught His disciples to pray
ἐλθάτω ἡ β. (Mt. vi. 10); τοῦ πατρὸς
ἡμῶν Δ. (not τοῦ υἱοῦ Δ.) betrays the
limitations which still beset their
highest hopes. To what extent the

§ ⫶ 11 τοῖς ὑψίστοις. ¹¹καὶ εἰσῆλθεν εἰς Ἱεροσόλυμα §εἰς

11 εἰς τὸ ἱερόν ℵBCLMΔΨ 13 28 60 69 115 225 346 1071 2ᵖᵉ aˢᶜʳ] pr καὶ
ΑΔΝΧΓΠΣΦ⫶ minᵖˡ q syrrˢⁱⁿ ʰᵉˡ go

Pharisaic conception of the Messianic kingdom admitted of spiritual ideas may be learnt from Pss. Sal. xvii., xviii. (cf. Ryle and James, *Intr.*, p. lvi. ff.).

ὡσαννὰ ἐν τοῖς ὑψίστοις] Τὰ ὕψιστα = מְרוֹמִים in the LXX. of Job xvi. 19, xxxi. 2, Ps. lxxi. 21, cxlviii. 1; in the N. T. ἐν (τοῖς) ὑψίστοις occurs only in this context and Lc. ii. 14, but St Paul has ἐν τοῖς ἐπουρανίοις (Eph. i. 3, vi. 12). As connected with ὡσαννά, unless the whole phrase is to be regarded simply as a shout of triumph like Ἰὴ παιάν, *Io triumphe* (Thayer *l.c.*), ἐν τοῖς ὑψ. must be taken to mean: 'let the prayer for our deliverance be ratified in high heaven.' Cf. 3 Regn. viii. 30 σὺ εἰσα-κούσῃ...ἐν οὐρανῷ, Mt. xvi. 19 ἔσται δεδεμένον...λελυμένον ἐν τοῖς οὐρανοῖς. GOD answers in heaven, and the result appears on earth. Lc. writes ἐν οὐρανῷ εἰρήνη καὶ δόξα ἐν ὑψίστοις, blending (as it seems) the Angelic Hymn with the welcome of the multitude; comp. the similar combination in the Clementine Liturgy (Brightman, p. 24). The use of the present passage in the 'Preface' of the Liturgy is ancient and wide-spread; cf. e.g. the Liturgy of St James (ib. p. 51), and the Gelasian *canon actionis* (Wilson, p. 234).

St Luke adds at this point (1) a remonstrance from certain Pharisees who were present, and our Lord's reply (xix. 39, 40); (2) the magnificent lamentation over Jerusalem (xix. 41—44).

11. εἰσῆλθεν εἰς Ἱεροσ. εἰς τὸ ἱερόν] On the double εἰς see note to *v.* 1. The Precinct of the Temple immediately overlooked the valley of the Kidron, and the Lord entered Jeru-salem when He passed within the great eastern gate of the ἱερόν. Τὸ ἱερόν in this sense occurs only in the Synoptists and in Acts; in the LXX. it is frequent, but only in the later books (chiefly 1 Esdras and 1—4 Macc.). On the distinction between ἱερόν and ναός see Westcott on Jo. ii. 14, and Trench, *syn.* § iii., who refers to Jos. *ant.* viii. 3. 9, περιέβαλε δὲ [ὁ Σολομὼν] τοῦ ναοῦ κύκλῳ γείσιον...τού-του δ᾿ ἔξωθεν ἱερὸν ᾠκοδόμησεν ἐν τετραγώνου σχήματι. Of the Herodian ἱερόν Josephus has left a description in *ant.* xv. 11. 3 f., *B. J.* vi. 5. 4; another account is to be found in the Mishna *Middoth* ii. 1. For a popular treatment of the subject see Edersheim, *The Temple, its ministry and services*; recent discoveries upon the spot are described in the *Recovery of Jerusalem* and other publications of the Palestine Exploration Fund. The Lord on entering the Precinct found Himself in the Court of the Gentiles, and probably did not go beyond it on the first day. But the report of His arrival and solemn entry spread through Jerusalem, and Mt. describes the excitement which the tidings caused (ἐσείσθη πᾶσα ἡ πόλις κτλ., xxi. 10 f.).

On the remarkable change of policy implied in this formal avowal of Messianic claims see Victor: πολλάκις ἐπέβη τῶν Ἱεροσολύμων πρότερον, ἀλλ᾿ οὐδέποτε μετὰ τοιαύτης περιφανείας... ἐπειδὴ δὲ...ὁ σταυρὸς ἐπὶ θύραις ἦν μειζόνως ἐκλάμπει λοιπόν. Bede: "nunc autem ubi passurus Hierosolymam venit, non refugit eos qui se regem faciunt...non reprimit voces, regnumque quod adhuc victurus in mundo suscipere noluit, iamiam exiturus per passionem crucis de mundo non negavit suscipere."

τὸ ἱερόν· καὶ περιβλεψάμενος πάντα ὀψίας ἤδη οὔσης
τῆς ὥρας ἐξῆλθεν εἰς §Βηθανίαν μετὰ τῶν δώδεκα.   § 33
   ¹²Καὶ τῇ ἐπαύριον⁷ ἐξελθόντων αὐτῶν ἀπὸ Βηθα- 12 ¶ ⁷
νίας ἐπείνασεν.   ¹³καὶ ἰδὼν συκῆν ἀπὸ μακρόθεν 13
ἔχουσαν φύλλα ἦλθεν εἰ ἄρα τι εὑρήσει ἐν αὐτῇ· καὶ

11 οψιας ΑΒDΝΧΓΠΣΦ⁷ minᵖˡ] οψε אCLΔ Or¹ | ηδη] επι 1071 | om της ωρας Β της
ημερας 13 28 69 124 346   13 συκην]+μιαν אΚΜΙΙ minⁿᵒⁿⁿ syrʳˢⁱⁿ ᵖᵉˢʰ arm | om απο
ΜᵐᵍΧΓΠΦ minᵖˡ | ει αρα τι ευρ.] ιδειν εαν τι εστιν D b c ff i k r ως ευρησων τι 2ᵖᵉ a f q
Orᵇⁱˢ

περιβλεψάμενος πάντα κτλ.] Jerome : "quasi cum lucerna quaereret
(Zeph. i. 12)...quaerens in templo, et
nihil quod eligeretur invenit." Euth. :
ὡς κύριος τοῦ τοιούτου οἴκου.   On περιβλέπεσθαι see iii. 5, 34, v. 32, ix. 8,
x. 23. Nothing escaped His comprehensive glance (περιβλ. πάντα), which
revealed much that would call for
serious work on the morrow (v. 15,
note). It was too late to begin that
evening. Ὀψίας ἤδη οὔσης τῆς ὥρας,
towards or after sunset, i. 32, iv. 35,
vi. 47, xiv. 17, xv. 42 ; with the reading of א (ὀψὲ ἤ. οὔσης) cf. v. 19, ὀψὲ
ἐγένετο.
   ἐξῆλθεν εἰς Βηθανίαν μ. τ. δ.] Cf.
xi. 19 (Mt. xxi. 17), xiii. 1, 3. The
nights of Sunday, Monday, and Tuesday before the Passion were spent at
Bethany, or rather in the open air
on the Mount of Olives in the neighbourhood of the village (Lc. xxi. 37 ;
comp. Lc. xxiv. 50 with Acts i. 12).
The bivouac among the hills offered
comparative security against the danger of a sudden arrest ; and the
conditions were favourable to medi-
tation and prayer ; cf. Euth. ἐξεπορεύετο εἰς τὰ προαστεῖα διὰ τὴν ἡσυχίαν.
The crowd of followers was at length
dispersed, and though the days were
passed in the busy Precinct, at night
the Lord found Himself alone with
the Twelve.
   12—14. THE FIGTREE IN LEAF
BUT WITHOUT FRUIT (Mt. xxi. 18—19).
   12. τῇ ἐπαύριον] On the morning
of the fourth day before the Passover

i.e. Monday, Nisan 11 (Jo. xii. 1, 12).
Ἐξελθ. αὐτ. ἀπὸ Βηθανίας must be
interpreted with the same latitude
which appears to belong to ἐξῆλθεν
εἰς Βηθανίαν (v. 11); Mt. more exactly,
ἐπαναγαγὼν εἰς τὴν πόλιν. Ἐπείνασεν :
cf. Mt. iv. 2. The Lord had not
broken His fast (cf. Jo. iv. 32 ff.), or
the morning meal had been scanty or
hurried ; a day of toil was before
Him, and it was important to recruit
His strength on which the spiritual
exercises of the night had perhaps
drawn largely. The wayside figtree
seemed to offer the necessary refreshment.
   13. ἰδὼν συκῆν ἀπὸ μακρόθεν κτλ.]
The fresh green foliage caught the eye
long before the tree was reached. It
was a solitary tree, standing by the
roadside (μίαν ἐπὶ τῆς ὁδοῦ, Mt.), a
derelict perhaps of some old garden
or vineyard (Lc. xiii. 6, Jo. i. 48), now
offering its fruit to every passer-by.
Ἀπὸ μ., cf. v. 6, note.
   ἦλθεν εἰ ἄρα τι εὑρήσει κτλ.] Εἰ ἄρα,
si forte, cf. Acts viii. 22 εἰ ἄρα ἀφεθήσεται, xvii. 27 εἰ ἄρα ψηλαφήσειαν
αὐτὸν καὶ εὕροιεν : the ἄρα reviews
the circumstances already recited and
infers from them the chance of success; for the constr. see Burton, § 276,
and on this use of ἄρα cf. WM., p. 556,
Blass, Gr. p. 250 f. The direct question might have run εἰ ἄρα τι εὑρήσω ;
The tree was prematurely in leaf ;
planted in some sheltered hollow, it
was already in leaf before the Passover, when other trees of its sort were

¶ Wᵃ 14 ἐλθὼν ἐπ᾿ αὐτὴν οὐδὲν εὗρεν εἰ μὴ φύλλα· ὁ γὰρ καιρὸς οὐκ ἦν σύκων¶. ¹⁴καὶ ἀποκριθεὶς εἶπεν αὐτῇ Μηκέτι εἰς τὸν αἰῶνα ἐκ σοῦ μηδεὶς καρπὸν φάγοι. καὶ ἤκουον οἱ μαθηταὶ αὐτοῦ.

13 om ελθων επ αυτην D b c ff i k r om επ αυτην a g | ουδεν ευρεν] μηδεν ευρων D (2ᵖᵉ) (a q) Or | φυλλα]+μονον C²ΝΣΦ 33 61 69 124 1071 2ᵖᵉ b c q aeth Or | ο γαρ καιρος ουκ ην συκων אΒC*ᵛⁱᵈΛΔΨ me] ου (vel ουπω) γαρ ην (ο) καιρος συκων ΑC²(D)ΝΧΓΠΣΦ minᵒᵐⁿ ᵛⁱᵈ latt go aeth Or   14 om και 1° D 2ᵖᵉ a q Or | om αποκριθεις f q r vg syrᵖᵉˢʰ | μηδεις] ουδεις minⁿᵒⁿⁿ | φαγη DU 1 13 69 346 604ᶜᵒʳʳ alᵖᵉʳᵖᵃᵘᶜ

only beginning to bud (xiii. 28); and it was reasonable to expect a corresponding precocity in regard to the figs. But when the Lord had come up to it (ἐπ᾿ αὐτήν, cf. v. 21, xv. 22, the result of motion towards, WM., p. 508), He found that the tree did not fulfil its promise. There were no figs under the leaves—not even the half-ripe figs which the peasants of Palestine ate with their bread in the fields (Edersheim ii. p. 375).

ὁ γὰρ καιρὸς οὐκ ἦν σύκων] 'For the season was not that of figs.' (Wycliffe, "for it was no tyme of figgis.") In Palestine the figtree yields more than one crop in the course of the summer (Smith, *D.B.*², p. 1066), but even the early figs are not in season before May. There was then no reason to expect fruit upon this tree beyond the promise of its leaves. Premature in foliage, it proved to be not earlier than the yet leafless trees in regard to its fruit. Bengel: "propior aspectùs arboris ostendit arborem non esse talem qualem folia singulariter promittebant." He is surely right in adding: "supersederi potuit tota quaestione de generibus ficuum arborum." Equally unnecessary is it to suppose that the Lord expected to find a few figs left over from the previous crop; see the curious theory built on this view by Ephrem (*ev. conc. exp.* p. 182).

14. ἀποκριθεὶς εἶπεν αὐτῇ κτλ.] The answer is to the invitation which the tree by its foliage had seemed to offer to the hungry traveller. For the address to an inanimate object, cf. iv. 39; such personifications of natural phenomena are in accordance with the genius of Hebrew poetry and prophecy, cf. Num. xx. 8, Ps. cxlviii. 3 ff., Dan. iii. 57 ff. Μηκέτι...μηδεὶς: for the (emphatic) double negative see WM., p. 625. The optative (WM., pp. 357, 627, Burton, § 175 f.) is replaced in Mt. by the subjunctive with οὐ μή, i.e. for the expression of a desire Mt. substitutes a negative which nearly amounts to a prohibition (Burton, § 167). Neither form can properly be called an imprecation or curse; contrast Gen. iii. 17, Heb. vi. 7 f., and see note on *v.* 21. Bengel: "quod Iesu Christo non servit, indignum est quod ulli mortalium serviat."

The sentence on the fruitless figtree repeated in a tangible form the lesson of a parable spoken during the Lord's recent journeyings (Lc. xiii. 6 ff.). But in repeating it extends the teaching of the parable. It is not mere fruitlessness which the Lord here condemns, but fruitlessness in the midst of a display which promises fruit. Cf. Origen *in Mt.* εὗρεν ἐν αὐτῇ...μόνον ζωῆς ἔμφασιν...καὶ ἔστιν εὑρεῖν τοιούτους τινάς...ἐμφήναντας ὅτι ζῶσι καὶ παντελῶς εἰσι ξηροί· οὓς διὰ τὸ μὴ καρποφορεῖν ἔστιν ἰδεῖν καὶ ἀφισταμένους παντελῶς τοῦ λόγου καὶ ξηρανθέντας. Bede: "arefecit Dominus arborem...ut homines...intellegerent sese divino condemnandos iudicio si absque operum fructu de plausu tan-

¹⁵ Καὶ ἔρχονται εἰς Ἱεροσόλυμα. καὶ εἰσελθὼν εἰς 15
τὸ ἱερὸν ἤρξατο ἐκβάλλειν τοὺς πωλοῦντας καὶ τοὺς
ἀγοράζοντας ἐν τῷ ἱερῷ, καὶ τὰς τραπέζας τῶν
κολλυβιστῶν καὶ τὰς καθέδρας τῶν πωλούντων τὰς

15 ερχονται] ηρχοντο C εισελθων D syr^sin + παλιν ΝΣ min^pauc (a) b f ff i | εισελθων
εις το ιερον] οτε ην εν τω ιερω D | εκβαλλειν] + εκειθεν D b | τους αγοραϛ.] om τους
DEGHSVXΓΔΦΨ min^pl Or | κολλυβιστων] + εξεχεεν ΝΣ (εξεχεσεν) 13 28 69 124 346
2^pe arm

tum sibi religiosi sermonis velut de
sonitu et tegumento blandirentur viri-
dantium foliorum." The immediate
reference is doubtless to the Jewish
people, so far in advance of the other
nations in knowledge and the forms of
worship, so nearly on a level with them
in regard to spiritual religion and the
love of God. Hilary: "in facie syna-
gogae positum exemplum est"; Victor:
τὴν μέλλουσαν κατὰ τὴν Ἱερουσαλὴμ
κρίσιν ἐπὶ τῆς συκῆς ἔδειξεν. Thpht.
compares Ezekiel xvii. 9.

καὶ ἤκουον οἱ μαθ. αὐτοῦ] Mc. only.
The sentence prepares the reader for
the sequel, v. 20 ff. All heard, one
remembered (v. 21).

15—19. SECOND DAY IN THE TEM-
PLE. BREAKING UP OF THE TEMPLE
MARKET (Mt. xxi. 12—17, Lc. xix.
45—48).

15. ἔρχονται...εἰσελθὼν κτλ.] Cf. v.
11. Ἤρξατο ἐκβάλλειν. He began the
day's work by ejecting the traffickers,
making no distinction between sellers
and buyers (τοὺς πωλ. καὶ τοὺς ἀγ.).
The market was within the Precinct
(ἐν τῷ ἱερῷ), and had already attracted the attention of Jesus at the
first Passover of His ministry (Jo. ii.
14, εὗρεν ἐν τῷ ἱ. τοὺς πωλοῦντας). It
was a recognised institution, under the
protection of the ἀρχιερεῖς and known
in Rabbinical writings as חֲנִיּוֹת בְּנֵי חָנָן,
the shops of the sons of Hanan, i.q.
Annas (see Lightfoot on Mt. xxi. and
Edersheim, Life, i. p. 369 ff.). The
sales were limited to Temple-requi-
sites, victims for the sacrifices (Jo.
l.c. βόας καὶ πρόβατα καὶ περιστεράς),

and the wine, oil, salt, &c., used in
the ritual. The purchasers were not
only pilgrims from a distance, but
probably all whose means enabled
them to buy on the spot and thus to
escape not only the trouble of bringing
the animals with them, but also the
official inspection which was compulsory in such cases (cf. Edersheim, l.c.).

καὶ τὰς τραπέζας τῶν κολλυβιστῶν
κτλ.] Cf. Jo. l.c. εὗρεν τοὺς κερματι-
στὰς καθημένους...τῶν κολλυβιστῶν ἐξέ-
χεεν τὰ κέρματα κτλ. Κέρματα is 'small
change,' κόλλυβος a small coin (Ar.
Pax 1200, οὐδεὶς ἐπρίατ' ἂν δρέπανον
κολλύβου), but the latter word acquired in practice the meaning 'rate
of exchange,' so that κολλυβιστής carries with it the thought of the (often
usurious) profit which the κερματισταί
secured. The κόλλυβος (קַלְבּוֹן) of the
Temple nummularii was a fixed sum
per half-shekel, the equivalent of a
third or fourth of a denarius (Edersheim, Life, i. p. 368, Temple, p. 48).
Since every Israelite was required to
pay his half-shekel yearly (Mt. xvii. 24,
cf. Exod. xxx. 13 ff.) to the support of
the Temple, and it could be paid only
in the Jewish coin (cf. Madden,
Jewish coinage, p. 43 f.), a large profit
would be reaped at the approach of
the Passover from the pilgrims who
assembled from Gentile countries (cf.
Jo. xii. 20, Acts ii. 5) and brought
with them Greek or Roman money.
To spill their piles of half-shekels
over the floor of the Court on the eve
of the Passover was to deal a blow to
their traffic at a time when it was at

16 περιστερὰς κατέστρεψεν· ¹⁶καὶ οὐκ ἤφιεν ἵνα τις
17 διενέγκῃ σκεῦος διὰ τοῦ ἱεροῦ. ¹⁷καὶ ἐδίδασκεν καὶ
ἔλεγεν [αὐτοῖς] Οὐ γέγραπται ὅτι ῾Ο οἶκός μου οἶκος

15 om κατεστρεψεν DK syrˢⁱⁿ   17 και ελεγεν] λεγων ADNXΓΠ alᵖˡ | om αυτοις
BΨ 28 b syrˢⁱⁿ | om ου D 1 28 2ᵖᵉ b c (ff) i k q me arm | om οτι CDΨ 69 alᵖᵃᵘᵉ c ff i k q
armᶜᵒᵈᵈ aeth

its height. The history of the Temple
tax will be found in Schürer ii. i. p.
249 ff. ; for a Rabbinical description
of the traffic see J. Lightfoot, l.c.
For τράπεζα in this connexion cp. Lc.
xix. 23 ; the moneychanger or broker
is a τραπεζείτης, Mt. xxv. 27. On the
whole subject see Hastings, D. B. iii.
p. 432 f. Origen (in Jo. t. x. 23)
applies the passage to abuses in the
Visible Church: πότε γὰρ ἐν τῇ ὀνομα-
ζομένῃ ἐκκλησίᾳ ἥτις ἐστὶν οἶκος θεοῦ
ζῶντος...οὐκ εἰσί τινες κερματισταὶ καθήμενοι δεόμενοι πληγῶν κτλ.

καὶ τὰς καθέδρας τῶν πωλ. τὰς περι-
στεράς] The doves (Wycliffe " culue-
ris ") required by the Law for the
purification of women (Lev. xii. 8, Lc.
ii. 22 f.), for the ceremonial cleansing
of lepers (Lev. xiv. 22), and on certain
other occasions (Lev. xv. 14, 29).
Every branch of the Temple trade suffered, and not only those forms which
were specially offensive or aggressive;
the Lord was opposed to it on principle, not on aesthetic grounds. The
Fathers regard the dove-sellers as representing allegorically ecclesiastics
who traffic in spiritual gifts, e.g.
Jerome ad l.: " vere cathedra pesti-
lentiae (Ps. i. 1) quae vendit columbas
vendit gratiam Spiritus sancti. multae
cathedrae sunt usque hodie quae ven-
dunt columbas."

16. καὶ οὐκ ἤφιεν κτλ.] Mc. only;
the incident, which in the midst of so
much that was more stirring passed
out of the recollection of the other
witnesses, was remembered and related by St Peter. Persons carrying
goods or implements were accustomed
to pass through the Precinct, from
the eastern to the western gate, or the

reverse, as a short cut between the
city and the Mt of Olives. The practice appears to have been interdicted
by the Jewish authorities: "what is
the reverence of the Temple ? that
none go into the mountain of the
Temple with his staff and his shoes,
with his purse, and dust upon his feet;
and that none make it his common
thoroughfare" (J. Lightfoot ad loc.);
cf. Jos. c. Ap. ii. 7 "denique nec vas
aliquod portare licet in templum"; cf.
Wünsche, neue Beiträge, p. 398 ; but
if the interdict existed, it had become
a dead letter, and the Lord did not
shrink from the invidious task of
putting it into execution. ῎Ηφιεν, see
WH., Notes, p. 167, WSchm. pp. 102,
123 ; for ἀφιέναι ἵνα, cf. Jo. xii. 7,
Burton, § 210. Σκεῦος : cf. iii. 27, note;
here probably any household goods,
tools, utensils, or the like. Jerome
remarks upon the whole incident :
"si hoc in Iudaeis, quanto magis in
nobis ? si hoc in lege, quanto magis
in evangelio ? "

17. καὶ ἐδίδασκεν καὶ ἔλεγεν κτλ.]
The Lord's action had brought a
crowd together, which afforded an
opportunity for continuous teaching
(imperf.). As His custom was, He
bases His lesson on Scripture (οὐ
γέγραπται...; Mt., cf. Jo. x. 34 οὐκ ἔστιν
γεγραμμένον ; Lc. γέγραπται, cf. Mc.
vii. 6, ix. 12 f., xii. 29, 36), an authority
against which no Jew could appeal.
῝Οτι, recitativum ; cf. WM., p. 683,
note. The quotation in Mc. and Mt.
is in the words of the LXX. (Isa. lvi. 7),
though Mt. stops short at κληθήσεται :
Lc. quotes loosely, writing ἔσται for
κληθήσεται (for the Hebraism cf. Mt.
v. 9, 19, Lc. i. 32, 35, Rom. ix. 7, 26),

προσευχῆς κληθήσεται πᾶσιν τοῖς ἔθνεσιν; ὑμεῖς δὲ
πεποιήκατε αὐτὸν σπήλαιον λῃστῶν. ¹⁸καὶ ἤκουσαν 18

17 πεποιηκατε BLΔ Or] εποιησατε ℵACDNXΓΠΣΦ minᶠᵉʳᵉᵒᵐⁿ   18 ηκουον ΔΨ

and like Mt. he omits πᾶσιν τοῖς
ἔθνεσιν, which he would scarcely have
done had Mc. been before him (cf.
Plummer). The last words have a
special appropriateness in the present
context; for the part of the ἱερόν
which the Lord had just reclaimed
from secular use was the Court of
the Gentiles, where only within the
Precinct Gentiles were at liberty to
pray.   So far as in them lay, the
authorities had defeated the fulfilment of the prophecy; for who could
pray in a place which was at once a
cattle-market and an exchange, where
the lowing of oxen mingled with the
clinking of silver and the chaffering
and haggling of the dealers and those
who came to purchase? Origen in Mt.:
ἐποίουν δὲ τὰ ἐναντία τῇ εὐχῇ ἐν αὐτῷ.
For the homiletic treatment of the
incident the whole passage in Origen
(t. xvi. 20 sqq.) is valuable; see also
in Jo. t. x. 23 (16).

ὑμεῖς δὲ πεποιήκατε κτλ.] There
was worse than this; the house of
prayer had not only become an οἶκος
ἐμπορίου (Jo. ii. 16), but a σπήλαιον
λῃστῶν (on λῃστής see Trench, syn.
xliv., and cf. xiv. 48, xv. 27); no
bandits' cave along the Jericho road
(Lc. x. 30), by which the Lord had
lately come, was the scene of such
wholesale robbery as the Mountain of
the House.   The words are from another prophet, Jer. vii. 11 μὴ σπήλαιον
λῃστῶν (מְעָרַת פָּרִצִים) ὁ οἶκός μου...ἐν-
ώπιον ὑμῶν; Ὑμεῖς, addressed to the
crowd, for in this matter all were to
blame, from the High Priest to the
pilgrims who encouraged the traffic by
purchasing, or the townsfolk who used
the Court as a thoroughfare. Πεποιήκατε is more exact than either Mt.'s
ποιεῖτε or Lc.'s ἐποιήσατε—the evil had
been stopped for the moment, but its

results were enduring. Neither the
salesmen nor money-changers were
better than λῃσταί—the pilgrims were
practically at their mercy, and they
did not content themselves with a
fair margin of profit; their extortion
was more than mere dishonesty, it
was downright robbery. The Talmudic
tract on the sale of doves relates how
Rabban Simeon ben Gamaliel, finding
that the dealers exacted a piece of
gold for each bird, insisted that they
should be content with a silver piece
(J. Lightfoot on Mt. l.c.). If this extortion was practised on poor women
who came to be purified, what may
not have been demanded of wealthy
Jews from Rome and the provinces?

18. καὶ ἤκ. οἱ ἀρχιερεῖς κτλ.] For
the first time in the Synoptic Gospels
the ἀρχιερεῖς are represented as combining with the γραμματεῖς against
Jesus. Jo. mentions two earlier occasions on which this coalition existed
(Jo. vii. 32 ff., xi. 47, 57); but there
can be no doubt that His attack upon
the Temple-market and exchange,
which contributed largely to the re-
venues of the Temple, and was under
their immediate protection, incensed
the priestly aristocracy in the highest
degree.   Henceforth they took the
lead in the conspiracy against the
Galilean Prophet, and the Scribes
were content to follow; the Elders
(Lc., οἱ πρῶτοι τοῦ λαοῦ) were naturally guided by the two professional
classes. Ἤκουσαν, the matter came
to their ears; the report seems to
have been brought by some of their
party who were on the spot, for Mt.
adds (xxi. 15 ff.) that they saw the
Lord working wonders and heard the
Hosannas of the Entry repeated by
children in the Temple-court. They
remonstrated with Him to no purpose,

οἱ ἀρχιερεῖς καὶ οἱ γραμματεῖς, καὶ ἐζήτουν πῶς
αὐτὸν ἀπολέσωσιν· ἐφοβοῦντο γὰρ αὐτόν, πᾶς γὰρ
19 ὁ ὄχλος ἐξεπλήσσετο ἐπὶ τῇ διδαχῇ αὐτοῦ. ¹⁹καὶ
ὅταν ὀψὲ ἐγένετο, ἐξεπορεύοντο ἔξω τῆς πόλεως.
20   ²⁰Καὶ παραπορευόμενοι πρωὶ εἶδον τὴν συκῆν

18 απολεσουσιν KM*SˢⁱˡΔ minᵐᵘ | om αυτον 2° AKΠ alⁿᵒⁿⁿ e ff | πας γαρ] οτι πας
ADLNXΓΠΣ minᵖˡ Or | εξεπλησσοντο ℵMΔ minᵖᵃᵘᵉ c vgᵉᵈᵈ   19 οταν ℵBCKLΔΠ*Ψ
28 33 2ᵖᵉ 1071 alᵖᵃᵘᶜ] οτε ADNXΓΠΣΦ minᵖˡ | εγινετο AE²GHV²X 69 alᵖᵃᵘᶜ | εξε-
πορευοντο ABKM*ΔΠΨ 124 2ᵖᵉ 1071 alⁿᵒⁿⁿ c d r syrrᵖᵉˢʰ ʰᶜˡ ⁽ᵐᵍ⁾ arm] εξεπορευετο
ℵCDEGHMᵐᵍNSUVXΓΣΦ minᵖˡ a b f ff k vg syrrˢⁱⁿ ʰᶜˡ ⁽ᵗˣᵗ⁾ me go aeth   20 πρωι
παραπ. ANXΓΠ om πρωι a c k

and withdrew to consider plans of
revenge.

ἐζήτουν πῶς...ἐφοβοῦντο γὰρ αὐτόν]
Cf. Acts xxi. 31. It was not easy to
find the way so long as He had the
ὄχλος with Him. The great majority
of the people who thronged the Court
were not drawn from Jerusalem, where
the priestly class were paramount,
but from Galilee and from Gentile
countries, and a crowd so constituted
might be dangerous in their present
humour ; death by stoning was not
impossible even within the Precinct
(Jo. x. 31), and might overtake the
priests themselves or the Levitical
guard (Lc. xx. 6, Acts v. 26, *Ev. Petr.*
10), if they attempted to arrest a
popular Prophet.

πᾶς γὰρ ὁ ὄχλος κτλ.] The effect of
the Lord's teaching on the populace
was the same at the end as at the
outset of His work, cf. i. 22. It was
still a καινὴ διδαχή, never losing its
freshness.

19. καὶ ὅταν ὀψὲ ἐγένετο κτλ.] Mt.
mentions only the return to the Mount
on Monday night (ἐξῆλθον...ηὐλίσθη) ;
Mc. states once for all the Lord's
practice on each of the first three
days of Holy Week ; cf. R.V. "every
evening He went forth out of the
city." Similarly Lc., xxi. 37. Field
(*Notes*, p. 35), while regarding ὅταν...
ἐγένετο as "a solecism—probably due
to St Mark himself," thinks that a

single action is intended. For ὅταν
with the ind. cf. iii. 11 ; the aor. is
used in this connexion again in Apoc.
viii. 1 (WM., p. 389 note). The day
had begun for Jesus and the Twelve
πρωί (Mt. xxi. 18) ; it ended ὀψέ.
Hunger (*v.* 12) and fatigue were forgotten in the work of GOD (cf. Jo. iv.
31 ff.). Only the approach of the hour
for closing the gates and the melting
away of the crowd in the Court (cf.
Edersheim, *Temple*, p. 116 ff.) induced
Him to retire for rest. Ἐξεπ. ἔξω
τῆς πόλεως, cf. *v.* 11 ; Mc. omits εἰς
Βηθανίαν here, but Mt. supplies it,
adding καὶ ηὐλίσθη ἐκεῖ.

20—25. CONVERSATION ON THE
WITHERING OF THE FIGTREE ; THE
OMNIPOTENCE OF FAITH, PRAYER,
AND LOVE (Mt. xxi. 19ᵇ—22).

20. παραπορευόμενοι πρωί κτλ.] In
the early light of the next (Tuesday)
morning the figtree (xi. 13 συκῆν) by
the wayside was as conspicuous for its
shrivelled leaves as it had been for
their freshness the day before. All
saw it (εἶδον), and marked how the tree
was blasted root and branch (ἐκ ριζῶν).
In Mt. the entire incident belongs to
the Tuesday morning, and the figtree
is withered under the eyes of the
Apostles (ἐξηράνθη παραχρῆμα), whose
astonishment is at once expressed ;
Augustine's "alio die viderunt alio
die mirati sunt" (*de cons. ev.* ii. 131)
is certainly not warranted by Mt.'s

ἐξηραμμένην ἐκ ῥιζῶν. ²¹καὶ ἀναμνησθεὶς ὁ Πέτρος 21
λέγει αὐτῷ 'Ραββεί, ἴδε ἡ συκῆ ἣν κατηράσω
ἐξήρανται. ²²§καὶ ἀποκριθεὶς ὁ Ἰησοῦς λέγει αὐτοῖς 22 § syr^hier
Ἔχετε πίστιν θεοῦ. ²³ἀμὴν λέγω ὑμῖν ὅτι ὃς ἂν 23
εἴπῃ τῷ ὄρει τούτῳ Ἄρθητι καὶ βλήθητι εἰς τὴν
θάλασσαν καὶ μὴ διακριθῇ ἐν τῇ καρδίᾳ αὐτοῦ ἀλλὰ

21 λεγει] ειπεν Ψ | ιδου D 435 1071 al^pauc | εξηρανθη DLNΔΣΨ 33 min^nonn
22 εχετε] pr ει ℵD 13 28 33^corr 61 69 124 1071 a b i r syr^sin arm | om θεου a c k r
23 αμην]+γαρ ACLXΓΔΠΣΦ min^pl q syrr^pesh hcl me go | om οτι 1° ℵD 33 2^pe
al^pauc k arm go aeth | os αν ειπη] εαν ειπητε 33 syr^sin

words. That the tradition has been
preserved in a more accurate form by
Mc. is scarcely open to doubt; cf.
Victor: ἀκριβέστερον ὁ παρὼν εὐαγγελιστὴς ἀπομνημονεύει τῆς ἱστορίας, ἐν
τῇ ἐφεξῆς ἡμέρᾳ λέγων τεθεωρῆσθαι ὑπὸ
τῶν μαθητῶν ἐξηραμμένην τὴν συκῆν.
The classical phrase ἐκ ῥιζῶν is ἅπ.
λεγ. in the N. T., but occurs in Job
xxviii. 9, xxxi. 12, Ezech. xvii. 9.
With ἐξηρ. ἐκ ῥιζῶν cf. Job xviii. 16
ὑποκάτωθεν αἱ ῥίζαι αὐτοῦ ξηρανθή-
σονται.

21. καὶ ἀναμνησθεὶς κτλ.] The connexion between the withered tree and
the Lord's words on the previous
morning flashed at once on Peter's
quick thought: cf. xiv. 72 ἀνεμνήσθη
ὁ Πέτρος τὸ ῥῆμα. 'Ραββεί: cf. ix. 5,
xiv. 45, Jo. i. 39. Κατηράσω: in the
light of the event the Lord's words
shaped themselves into a κατάρα to
the recollection of the disciple; see
note on v. 14. 'Εξήρανται, not ἐξηράνθη (Mt., see WM., p. 345)—the enduring effect of the 'curse' was before
the eyes of all; cf. πεποιήκατε, v. 17.
For ξηραίνεσθαι, of plants, see iv. 6,
Jo. xiv. 6, Jas. i. 11, 1 Pet. i. 24.

22. καὶ ἀποκριθεὶς κτλ.] The answer
is remarkable; the Lord does not
explain the lesson to be learnt from
the fate of the tree, but deals with a
matter of more immediate importance
to the Twelve, the lesson to be learnt
from the prompt fulfilment of His

prayer (μηκέτι...φάγοι, v. 14). The
answer is addressed not to Peter
only, but to all.

ἔχετε πίστιν θεοῦ] Sc. πίστιν (τὴν)
εἰς τὸν θεόν. The gen. is that of the
object, as in πίστις Ἰησοῦ (Χριστοῦ),
Rom. iii. 22, 26, Gal. ii. 26, &c. (cf.
WM., p. 232); πίστιν is anarthrous,
as being sufficiently defined by the
genitive—'a faith which rests on GOD.'
Compare Jo. xiv. 1 πιστεύετε εἰς τὸν
θεόν. Elementary as the command
may have seemed to be, it was necessary even for professed theists and
Jews (James ii. 14 ff.). Mt. omits θεοῦ
(ἐὰν ἔχητε πίστιν, cf. app. crit.).

23. ἀμὴν λέγω ὑμῖν] The solemn
preface which prepares for a specially
important saying (iii. 28, viii. 12, ix.
1, 41, x. 15, 29).

ὃς ἂν εἴπῃ κτλ.] The Twelve were
crossing the Mt of Olives; below
them, between the mountains of Judaea and the mountains of Moab, lay
the hollow of the Dead Sea. 'Faith,
cooperating with the Divine Will,
could fill yonder bason with the mass
of limestone beneath their feet.' The
metaphor was in use among the
Rabbis; e.g. J. Lightfoot quotes
from the Talmud: "he saw Resh
Lachish...as if he were plucking up
mountains"; a famous master in
Israel was known as עֹקֵר הָרִים, 'a
rooter up of mountains.' Of the Mt
of Olives Zechariah had foretold that

24 πιστεύῃ ὅτι ὃ λαλεῖ γίνεται, ἔσται αὐτῷ. ²⁴διὰ
τοῦτο λέγω ὑμῖν Πάντα ὅσα προσεύχεσθε καὶ αἰ-

23 πιστευσῃ ACDN(ΧΓ)ΠΣΦ minᵖˡ | ο] a ΑΧΓΠΦ | λαλει אB(L)N(Δ)ΣΨ 33 48ᶜᵛ
2ᵖᵉ a k] λεγει ΑΧΓΠΦ minᵖˡ f q vg | γινεται] εσται 2ᵖᵉ | εσται αυτω]+ο εαν ειπη
ΑΝΧΓΠΣΦΨ minᵖˡ a q syrrᵖᵉˢʰ ʰᶜˡ ʰⁱᵉʳ arm go το μελλον· ο αν ειπη γενησεται D b c ff i
γενησεται οσα αν ειπη 2ᵖᵉ   24 οσα]+αν (vel εαν) A(ΚΝ)ΧΓΠΣΦ minᵖˡ | προσευ-
χεσθε και] προσευχομενοι ΑΝΧΓΠΣΦ minᵒᵐⁿ ᵛⁱᵈ arm | αιτησθε ΓΠ 1 604 alⁿᵒⁿⁿ

when the feet of the LORD stood
upon it, the mountain should cleave
asunder and the two masses be removed to the north and south (xiv. 4).
Standing on Olivet, the Lord may
have had this prophecy in His
thoughts; but His saying had been
uttered before, under the heights of
Hermon (Mt. xvii. 20). For another
saying of the same type, see Lc.
xvii. 6. The teaching is substantially
that of ix. 23 (πάντα δυνατὰ τῷ πιστεύοντι); for a practical application
to common life see Thpht. ad loc.:
ὄρος...ἡ ὑπερήφανος γνώμη, ὑψηλή τις
οὖσα καὶ σκληρά· ὅστις οὖν ὁρᾷ τὸ τῆς
ὑπερηφανίας πάθος ἐνοχλοῦν αὐτῷ...ὁ
τοιοῦτος ὀφείλει ἐπιτιμᾶν τῷ ὄρει τούτῳ.
Victor's caution is important: δῆλον
δὲ ὡς οὐκ ἀχρεῖον τούτων ἕκαστον ἐπαγ-
γέλλεται Χριστός, οὐδὲ οἷον ἐπὶ θαυμα-
τουργίᾳ κενῇ...οὔτε γὰρ ὄρος οὔτε δὴ
κάρφος ἀχρείως μετακινηθείη ἂν κατὰ
δύναμιν θεοῦ, ἐπεὶ μηδὲ αὐτὸς ἀχρείως
τὴν συκῆν ἐξήρανεν. Ἄρθητι, βλήθητι:
the aorists point to momentary effects,
Burton, § 184 (98). Διακριθῇ, Vg. hae-
sitaverit, 'hesitate,' 'doubt'; cf. Acts
x. 20, xi. 2, Rom. iv. 20, xiv. 23, James
i. 6, ii. 4; in these passages διακρί-
νεσθαι = secum disceptare = dubitare
(Blass)—a sense "apparently confined to the N. T. and later Christian
writings" (Mayor on James i. 6, q.v.),
where διακρ. "appears as the proper
opposite" of πίστις, πιστεύω (SH.,
Romans, p. 115). Πιστεύῃ (see vv. ll.)
is more accurate than πιστεύσῃ: faith
is regarded as the normal attitude
of the heart, not a sudden emotion
or isolated act. Faith contemplates
the effect as potentially accompanying

its exercise (ὁ λαλεῖ γίνεται), though
the actual fulfilment may be delayed
(Mt. γενήσεται). It endows even a
passing utterance (λαλεῖ) with a power
to which there is no limit but the μέτρον πίστεως which GOD has bestowed
(Rom. xii. 3). On the construction
ἔσται αὐτῷ see Blass, Gr. p. 111 f.
St Paul, with this saying in view,
recognises the need of something
higher than the faith which could
move mountains (1 Cor. xiii. 2 κἂν
ἔχω πᾶσαν τὴν πίστιν ὥστε ὄρη μεθι-
στάνειν, ἀγάπην δὲ μὴ ἔχω, οὐθέν εἰμι.
The Lord, however, does not overlook
this higher principle, or proclaim a
πίστις χωρὶς ἔργων: see v. 25.

24. διὰ τοῦτο λέγω ὑμῖν κτλ.] A
practical instruction based (διὰ τοῦτο)
on ὃς ἄν...πιστεύῃ ὅτι ὃ λαλεῖ γίνεται,
ἔσται αὐτῷ. 'Since this is the cri-
terion of success in spiritual things,
let it be the constant attitude of
your minds when you pray.' Ὅσα
προσεύχεσθε καὶ αἰτεῖσθε, Mt. ὅσα ἂν
αἰτήσητε ἐν τῇ προσευχῇ. Προσεύχεσθαι is used absolutely, or followed by
ἵνα or ὅπως with a clause expressing
the desire (xiv. 38, Jas. v. 16), or by
τοῦ with the inf. (Jas. v. 17); the acc.
of the prayer is rare, but cf. Lc. xviii.
11 ταῦτα προσηύχετο, Rom. viii. 26 τί
προσευξώμεθα. As distinguished from
αἰτεῖν or αἰτεῖσθαι, προσεύχεσθαι implies a Divine Object of prayer; a
προσευχή is exclusively a religious
act, an αἴτημα may be addressed
either to GOD (Phil. iv. 6, 1 Jo.
v. 15) or to man (Lc. xxiii. 24); cf.
Dan. vi. 7 ὃς ἂν αἰτήσῃ αἴτημα παρὰ
παντὸς θεοῦ καὶ ἀνθρώπου. On the
mid. αἰτεῖσθαι see vi. 23, 24. Ἐλάβετε,

τεῖσθε, πιστεύετε ὅτι ἐλάβετε, καὶ ἔσται ὑμῖν. ²⁵καὶ 25
ὅταν στήκετε προσευχόμενοι, ἀφίετε εἴ τι ἔχετε
κατά τινος, ἵνα καὶ ὁ πατὴρ ὑμῶν ὁ ἐν τοῖς οὐρανοῖς
ἀφῇ ὑμῖν τὰ παραπτώματα ὑμῶν.¶   ¶ syrʰⁱᵉʳ

24 ελαβετε ℵBCLΔΨ me] λαμβανετε ΑΝΧΓΠΣΦ minᶠᵉʳᵉᵒᵐⁿ go ληмψεσθε D 1 2ᵖᵉ
latt aeth   25 στηκετε ACDHLM²VXΨ 1 124 alⁿᵒⁿⁿ] στηκητε BEGKM*SUVΔΠ(Σ)Φ
minᵖˡ Or στητε ℵ | αφετε C* | αφιη X αφησει D minᵖᵉʳᵖᵃᵘᶜ | υμων 2°]+(26) ει δε υμεις
ουκ αφιετε ουδε ο πατηρ υμων ο εν (τοις) ουρανοις αφησει (υμιν) τα παραπτωματα υμων
A(CD)EFᵛⁱᵈGH(KM)NUVXΓΠΣΦ minᵖˡ a b c f ff i m q r vg syrʳᵖᵉˢʰʰᵉˡ go (om ℵBLSΔΨ
minᵖᵃᵘᵉ k l syrˢⁱⁿ arm): postea add λεγω δε υμιν αιτειτε κτλ. (Mt vii. 7, 8) M minⁿᵒⁿⁿ

the petition was granted and potentially answered at the moment when
it was offered. Πιστεύετε ὅτι ἐλάβετε
καί = ἐὰν πιστεύητε ὅ. ἐλ., hypothetical
imperative for protasis, Burton, § 269.
Mt. omits this reference to the realising power of a successful faith, re-
ducing the promise to πιστεύοντες
λήμψεσθε. Λαμβάνειν is the correlative
of αἰτεῖσθαι, cf. Mt. vii. 8, Jas. iv. 3,
1 Jo. iii. 22, and see Wünsche, p. 102.

25. καὶ ὅταν στήκετε προσευχόμενοι
κτλ.] 'Whenever ye stand at prayer,
forgive.' Another condition of effective
prayer. The same lesson occurs in
another form and setting, Mt. vi. 14;
the R. T. adds here from Mt. the
converse εἰ δὲ ὑμεῖς οὐκ ἀφίετε κτλ.
and a few MSS. append Mt. vii. 7 f. As
the words stand in the true text of
Mc., they possess an individuality which
shews that they have not been imported from another context. Εἴ τι
ἔχετε κατά τινος: cf. Mt. v. 23 ἔχει τι
κατὰ σοῦ, Col. iii. 13 ἐάν τις πρός τινα
ἔχῃ μομφήν. Ἀφίετε balances πιστεύετε; the act of prayer must be
accompanied by love as well as by
faith. For στήκειν see WH., Notes,
p. 169; for ὅταν...στήκετε, cf. WM.,
p. 388, Burton, § 309, Blass, Gr. p.
218. Standing was the normal attitude in prayer (1 K. viii. 14, 22, Neh.
ix. 4, Ps. cxxxiv. 2, Jer. xviii. 20, Mt.
vi. 5; cf. Lightfoot on Mt. l.c.); in the
temple-court even the Publican stands,
though afar off (Lc. xviii. 11, 13); but
kneeling seems to have been preferred

on occasions of great solemnity or of
distress (1 K. viii. 54, Ezra ix. 5, Dan.
vi. 10, Mt. xxvi. 39, Acts vii. 50, xx.
36, xxi. 5, Eph. iii. 14): cf. the story
which is told of James 'the Just,' Eus.
H. E. ii. 23. In the ancient Church
kneeling was forbidden during the
Great Forty Days and on Sundays
(Tert. de coron. 3, can. conc. Nicaen.
20), and the Eastern Church adheres
to the practice of standing at prayer
(Stanley, E. C. p. 195 ff.). The Lord's
reference to the contemporary custom
imposes of course no ritual order
upon the future Church.

ἵνα καὶ ὁ πατὴρ ὑμῶν κτλ.] A reference to the Lord's Prayer, or the
early teaching connected with it, cf.
Mt. vi. 12, 14 f. This is the only place
where the phrase ὁ πατὴρ ὑμῶν [ὁ ἐν
τοῖς οὐρανοῖς] is found in Mc.; v. 26
(R. T.) is an interpolation from Mt.
Comp. however iii. 35, where the doctrine of a Divine family is implicitly
taught. Παράπτωμα occurs in the
Gospels only here and Mt. vi. 14 f.,
but it is fairly common in the later
books of the LXX. (cf. e.g. Ps. xviii.
(xix.) 12, Dan. vi. 4 (5) Th.) and in
St Paul. The word, which is coupled
with ἁμαρτία in Eph. ii. 1, means specifically a 'false step,' a fall from the
right course, whilst ἁμαρτία is a falling short of the true end or aim; see
Trench, syn. 16; παραπτ. is perhaps
preferred in this context because
offences against GOD are for the
moment placed in the same category

§F 27   ²⁷§Καὶ ἔρχονται πάλιν εἰς Ἱεροσόλυμα. καὶ ἐν
τῷ ἱερῷ περιπατοῦντος αὐτοῦ ἔρχονται πρὸς αὐτὸν
οἱ ἀρχιερεῖς καὶ οἱ γραμματεῖς καὶ οἱ πρεσβύτεροι,
28 ²⁸καὶ ἔλεγον αὐτῷ Ἐν ποίᾳ ἐξουσίᾳ ταῦτα ποιεῖς;
ἢ τίς σοι ἔδωκεν τὴν ἐξουσίαν ταύτην ἵνα ταῦτα

27 ερχεται DX b c ff i (k *exiit*) q aeth | om παλιν FΦ | και οι πρεσβ.] om 1 91
209+του λαου D   28 και ελεγον] κ. λεγουσιν ADNXΓΠ al^pl λεγοντες Ψ | om η
τις...ποιης D min^perpauc k | η τις] και τις ΑΝΧΓΠΣΦ min^pl latt^vt pl vg syrr^sin pesh hcl (txt)
arm go aeth | om ινα τ. ποιης 2^pe a b syr^sin arm

with those committed against men,
to which the lighter term properly
belongs.

27—33. THE AUTHORITY OF JESUS
CHALLENGED BY MEMBERS OF THE
SANHEDRIN (Mt. xxi. 23—27, Lc. xx.
1—8).

27. ἔρχονται πάλιν εἰς Ἱ.] A third
visit to the Temple (cf. *vv.* 11, 15)—
the day, apparently, Tuesday in Holy
Week.

ἐν τῷ ἱερῷ περιπατοῦντος] Probably
in the colonnades of the Court of the
Gentiles, either in the στοὰ βασιλική
on the S. side of the Court (see
Recovery, p. 9) or in the στοὰ Σολο-
μῶνος (Jo. x. 23) on the E. side. As
He passed along, or at intervals when
He was stopped by the crowd, He
taught (Mt. διδάσκοντι, Lc. διδάσκον-
τος αὐτοῦ τὸν λαόν...καὶ εὐαγγελιζομέ-
νου). While He was teaching, members
of each order in the Sanhedrin were
seen to approach (Mt. προσῆλθαν, Lc.
ἐπέστησαν). Mt. speaks of two orders
only (οἱ ἀρχ. καὶ οἱ πρεσβ.), but Lc.
agrees with Mc. in adding the Scribes;
it is conceivable that the latter, who
were our Lord's ordinary opponents,
kept in the background on this
occasion, since the question concerned
the custodians of the Temple rather
than the interpreters of the Law.
The repeated article (οἱ...καὶ οἱ...καὶ
οἱ) seems to indicate that those who
came were representatives of their
respective classes: cf. viii. 31, x. 33.
The united action of the three bodies

was probably resolved upon in conference the night before ; see *v.* 18,
note.

28. ἐν ποίᾳ ἐξουσίᾳ ταῦτα ποιεῖς;]
The question in itself was a reasonable
one, and the men who asked it felt that
they had a right to do so. The
Temple was in their charge, and by
forcibly ejecting the vendors whom
they allowed, Jesus had laid claim
to a superior jurisdiction. They now
ask Him publicly to produce His
credentials, to state (1) the nature
of His authority, (2) the name of the
person from whom He had received
it. Ποία, *qualis*, τίς, *quis*; cf. 1 Pet.
i. 11 τίνα ἢ ποῖον καιρόν, with Hort's
note, and see note on xii. 28. Ἐν π.
ἐξ., in right of what authority ? cf.
Acts iv. 7 ἐν ποίᾳ δυνάμει ἢ ποίῳ ὀνόματι. Ἵνα ταῦτα ποιῇς, Mc. only ; the
words further define the point at issue
(Burton, § 216) ; even if Jesus had
received some measure of authority,
was it such as to justify His interference in the control of the Temple ?
Ταῦτα, notably the expulsion of the
licensed salesmen (Euth. : ποῖα; τὸ
ἐκβάλλειν τοὺς πωλοῦντας καὶ ἀγοράζοντας ἐν τῷ ἱερῷ, τὸ ἀνατρέπειν τὰς
προρρηθείσας τραπέζας καὶ καθέδρας, τὸ
μὴ ἀφιέναι διενεγκεῖν σκεῦος διὰ τοῦ
ἱεροῦ, καὶ τοιαῦτα) ; but the vagueness
of the word covers a reference to the
whole career of Jesus, which from
their point of view had been continually in conflict with lawful authority,
in Galilee as well as in Jerusalem.

ποιῆς ; ²⁹ὁ δὲ ᾿Ιησοῦς εἶπεν αὐτοῖς ᾿Επερωτήσω ὑμᾶς 29
ἕνα λόγον, καὶ ἀποκρίθητέ μοι, καὶ ἐρῶ ὑμῖν ἐν ποία
ἐξουσίᾳ ταῦτα ποιῶ. ³⁰τὸ βάπτισμα τὸ ᾿Ιωάνου, ἐξ 30
οὐρανοῦ ἦν ἢ ἐξ ἀνθρώπων; ἀποκρίθητέ μοι. ³¹καὶ 31
διελογίζοντο πρὸς ἑαυτοὺς λέγοντες ᾿Εὰν εἴπωμεν

29 ειπεν] pr αποκριθεις ADNXΓΠΣΦ minᴾˡ a b f ff i q vg syrrˢⁱⁿ ʰᶜˡ arm go | υμας]+
καγω (vel και εγω) ℵD(EFH)GMN(SUVX)ΓΣΦΨ minᵐᵘ a b f ff i q r vg syrrᵖᵉˢʰ ʰᶜˡ καγω
υμας AKΠ 736 minᵖᵃᵘᶜ (syrˢⁱⁿ arm) go aeth (om καγω BCᵛⁱᵈLΔ minᵖᵉʳᵖᵃᵘᶜ k* me) | και
ερω υμιν] καγω υμιν ερω LΔ 33 c me και εγω λεγω υμειν D   30 το βαπτισμα] pr ει
Δ | το Ιωανου] om το NXΓΠΣΦΨ minᴾˡ | εξ ουρ.] pr ποθεν ην ℵCΦ 33 1071 alᵖᵉʳᵖᵃᵘᶜ
(k) syrᵖᵉˢʰ the aeth   31 διελογιζοντο ℵᶜ·ᵃ BCDGKLMΔΠΨ alⁿᵒⁿⁿ] προσελογιζοντο
ℵ*ᶜ·ᵇ ελογιζοντο AEFHNSUVXΓΣΦ minᴾˡ | προς εαυτους] εν εαυτοις 33 | εαν] pr τι
ειπωμεν DΦ 13 28 69 124 346 2ᵖᵉ a b c ff i (k) (r)

29. ἐπερωτήσω ὑμᾶς ἕνα λόγον]
Question is met by question (cf. x. 4,
18); Mt. ἐρωτήσω ὑ. κἀγώ, 'I also on
my part have a point to raise.' ῎Ενα
λόγον, 'just one preliminary matter
for consideration'; εἷς neither contrasts the Lord's single question with
the two put by the Sanhedrin, nor is it
a mere substitute for τις, but points to
the simplicity of the issue; the answer
to that one question will decide it.
Let them answer first (ἀποκρίθητέ μοι),
as became the teachers of Israel, and
He will then be prepared with His reply
(καὶ ἐρῶ ὑμῖν κτλ.). Baljon's κἂν ἀπο-
κριθῆτέ μοι is less after the style of Mc.

30. τὸ βάπτισμα τὸ ᾿Ιωάνου κτλ.]
The enquiry is pushed a stage further
back. Though Jesus had not received
His authority from John, John had
borne public and repeated testimony
to His Divine mission (Jo. i. 26 f.,
29 ff., 36). The question of the Sanhedrin therefore resolved itself into a
question as to the source of John's
teaching (Mt. πόθεν ἦν;). Τὸ βάπτισμα
τὸ ᾿Ιωάνου: i.e. the Baptist's work and
teaching as a whole, symbolised by
its visible expression, cf. Acts i. 22,
xviii. 25; for the form βάπτισμα see
i. 4, note. ᾿Εξ οὐρανοῦ, of heavenly
origin (Blass, Gr. p. 147 f.; cf. Wünsche,
p. 398 f., Dalman, Worte, i. p. 178),
i.e. from God, as the alternative ἐξ

ἀνθρώπων shews; cf. Acts v. 38, 39;
for the phrase, cf. Jo. iii. 27. The
Baptist knew himself to be personally
ἐκ τῆς γῆς, and recognised the limitations of his teaching (ἐκ τῆς γῆς λαλεῖ,
ib. v. 31); but his 'baptism,' his message and its seal, were Divine (Jo. i. 6).
᾿Αποκρίθητέ μοι: the Lord claims an
answer, as from authorised teachers
and men who were acquainted with
the facts.

Dr Bruce's use (comm. on Mt. xxi.
23 ff.) of the Lord's question as an
antidote to the "notion of church
sacraments and orders depending on
ordination" is entirely beside the
mark. The question refers to the
authority of a prophet, not to that of
a regular ministry; the latter derives
its powers from Christ (Jo. xx. 21)
through the hands of men (2 Tim. i.
6); the former, if not directly ἐξ οὐρανοῦ, can only be ἐξ ἀνθρώπων, and
is therefore futile.

31. διελογίζοντο πρὸς ἑαυτούς] Mt.
δ. ἐν ἑαυτοῖς, Lc. συνελογίσαντο πρὸς ἑ.
The Marcan phrase occurs in viii. 16,
where πρὸς ἑ. probably = πρὸς ἀλλήλους.
In the present instance conference
was scarcely possible, and Mt.'s ἐν
ἑαυτοῖς probably gives the true sense,
cf. Mc. ii. 6, 8. The same thought
flashed across the minds of all; they
realised that there was no way of

Ἐξ οὐρανοῦ, ἐρεῖ Διὰ τί οὖν οὐκ ἐπιστεύσατε αὐτῷ;
32 ³² ἀλλὰ εἴπωμεν Ἐξ ἀνθρώπων ; ἐφοβοῦντο τὸν
ὄχλον· ἅπαντες γὰρ εἶχον τὸν Ἰωάνην ὄντως ὅτι

31 ερει] λεγει υμιν (sic) D (arm^vid) | om ουν AC*LMSXΔΨ 1071 al^nonn a b c d ff k q
syr^sin 32 αλλα] εαν D min^nonn g q vg + εαν min^vix mu b f ff r (syrr) arm | εφοβουντο]
φοβουμεθα (D)ΝΣ 13 28 69 124 2^pe al^pauc a b f ff i q vg^codd arm | οχλον ℵBCΝΣΦ 33
106 syr^hcl(mg)] λαον ADLXΓΔΠΨ min^pl | ειχον] εχουσιν Σ ηδεισαν D 2^pe a b c f ff i k q
arm | οντως οτι προφητης ην ℵ^cBCLΨ 13 69 346] οντως ως προφητην Δ theb οτι οντως
(vel αληθως) προφ. ην A(D)ΧΓΠΦ min^pl latt^vt pl vg syrr^pesh hcl me go om οντως ℵ*ΝΣ 1
28 124 2^pe al^pauc c k syr^sin arm aeth

escape but one. Bede: "viderunt quod utrumlibet horum responderint in laqueum se casuros, timentes lapidationem, sed magis timentes veritatis confessionem."

ἐὰν εἴπωμεν Ἐξ οὐρανοῦ κτλ.] To acknowledge the Divine mission of John was to charge themselves with unbelief in having as a class rejected his baptism (Lc. vii. 30), and to give an advantage to their Questioner which He would not be slow to use (ἐρεῖ Διὰ τί κτλ.). They do not appear to have seen the real drift of the Lord's question, or the direct answer which the reply Ἐξ οὐρανοῦ would give to their own. For πιστεύειν with dat. cf. Gen. xv. 6 ἐπίστευσεν Ἀβρὰμ τῷ θεῷ, Jo. v. 46 εἰ γὰρ ἐπιστεύετε Μωυσεῖ, xiv. 11 πιστεύετέ μοι, 1 Jo. v. 10 ὁ μὴ πιστεύων τῷ θεῷ ψεύστην πεποίηκεν αὐτόν. As distinguished from πιστεύειν followed by ἐν, ἐπί, or εἰς, πιστεύειν τινί regards faith as placed in the word of another rather than in his person.

32. ἀλλὰ εἴπωμεν κτλ.] "Shall we then say 'Of men'?—they feared the crowd." The normal construction is given by Mt. (ἐὰν δὲ εἴπωμεν...φοβούμεθα τ. ὄ.); in Mc. the protasis takes the form of a question, and the apodosis disappears, the Evangelist supplying its place by narrative (WM., p. 725, Blass, Gr. p. 286). On the deliberative subjunctive cf. xii. 14, and WM., p. 356. Lc. specifies the fear which was uppermost in their minds: ὁ λαὸς ἅπας καταλιθάσει ἡμᾶς. From

Jo. viii. 57 it is clear that even within the Precinct the danger was a real one, if the susceptibilities of a Jewish crowd (ὄχλος, Mt., Mc.) were aroused. A denial of John's Divine mission might be treated by his adherents as blasphemy, since it would amount to an attribution to man of words which were held to be of the Holy Ghost.

ἅπαντες γὰρ εἶχον κτλ.] 'For as to John, all really held that he was a prophet' (cf. WM., p. 781). Mt. has softened this rough note into ὡς προφήτην ἔχουσιν τὸν 'Ι., whilst Lc. abandons ἔχω (πεπεισμένος γάρ ἐστιν (sc. ὁ λαὸς) Ἰωάνην προφήτην εἶναι). For ἔχειν 'to regard' cf. Lc. xiv. 18, Phil. ii. 29, Blass, Gr. pp. 231, 247; D's ἤδεισαν is a correction or a gloss, Ὄντως ὅτι is not = ὅτι ὄντως (cf. ix. 1, note), but the adverb is to be taken with εἶχον—the people were seriously impressed with a conviction of John's prophetic character. His martyrdom had perhaps deepened the reverence which was entertained for him by the thousands who had received his baptism. He had seemed to fulfil a long cherished hope (cf. i. 5, note), and to suggest that the confidence of the people had been misplaced would rouse a dangerous storm. Ὄντως occurs here only in Mc.; Lc. uses it twice, Jo. once, St Paul six times; in the LXX. it is rare, but well distributed (Num.[1], 3 Regn.[1], Sap.[1], Jer.[2]). Ἦν, 'had been': see Blass, Gr. p. 192.

προφήτης ἦν. ³³καὶ ἀποκριθέντες τῷ Ἰησοῦ λέ- 33
γουσιν Οὐκ οἴδαμεν. καὶ ὁ Ἰησοῦς λέγει αὐτοῖς
Οὐδὲ ἐγὼ λέγω ὑμῖν ἐν ποίᾳ ἐξουσίᾳ ταῦτα ποιῶ.
¹Καὶ ἤρξατο αὐτοῖς ἐν παραβολαῖς λαλεῖν Ἀμ- 1 **12.**
πελῶνα ἄνθρωπος ἐφύτευσεν, καὶ περιέθηκεν φραγμὸν

33 ο Ιησους]+(vel pr) αποκριθεις (AD)EFGH(KM)SUVX(Π)Φ minᵖˡ b ff (i q vg)
syrrˢⁱⁿʰᵉˡ arm go aeth | εις ποιαν εξουσιαν D   XII 1 λαλειν אBGLΔΨ 1 13 69 118
124 346 d f ff i q vg syrrˢⁱⁿ ᵖᵉˢʰ ʰᵉˡ(ᵐᵍ) aegg] λεγειν ACDNXΠΣΦ minᵖˡ k syrʰᵉˡ(ᵗˣᵗ) go +
και λεγειν arm (cf. b c) | περιεθηκεν]+αυτω C²NΨ 28 2ᵖᵉ al

33. ἀποκριθέντες τῷ Ἰησοῦ κτλ.]
They saved themselves from the
dilemma by a disgraceful profession
of ignorance. The Lord does not go
behind their answer, or expose its
disingenuousness; it was enough that
it released Him from His undertaking
to reply to their challenge (v. 29).
If they could not tell, the compact
had fallen through; and He refuses
accordingly to fulfil His part (οὐδὲ
ἐγὼ λέγω ὑμῖν). His position was un-
assailable, and they left Him without
a word. Οὐδέ takes up οὐκ in the
answer of the Sanhedrin: for a somewhat similar use cf. Mt. vi. 15, 'Jo.' viii.
11. Victor: οὐκ εἶπεν Οὐκ οἶδα, ἀλλ'
Οὐ λέγω· ἀντὶ τοῦ Οὐκ ἠβουλήθητε τὸ
ἀληθὲς εἰπεῖν· οὐδὲ τῆς παρ' ἐμοῦ τεύ-
ξεσθε ἀποκρίσεως. ἢ καὶ οὕτως· Οὐ
δύνασθε οὐδὲ ὑμεῖς περὶ ἐμοῦ ἀκούειν
ὅστις εἰμί, ἐπεὶ τὸν μάρτυρα οὐ δέχεσθε
ὃς ἦλθεν εἰς μαρτυρίαν.

XII. 1—12. THE HUSBANDMEN AND
THE HEIR. (Mt. xxi. 33—46, Lc. xx.
9—19.)

1. ἤρξατο...ἐν παραβολαῖς λαλεῖν]
A new commencement was made of
parabolic teaching, addressed to the
Sanhedrists (αὐτοῖς), and intended to
expose the true character of their
hostility. Ἐν παραβολαῖς, cf. Ps. lxxvii.
(lxxviii.) 2 (= בְּמָשָׁל), Mt. xiii. 3, 10, 13,
34 f., xxii. 1, Mc. iii. 23, iv. 2, 11, Lc.
viii. 10. Lc., who with Mc. relates but
one parable in this context, changes
the phrase (ἤρξατο...λέγειν τὴν παραβολὴν ταύτην): Mt. on the other hand,

who has already recorded the parable
of the 'Two Sons' (vv. 28—32), begins
Ἄλλην παραβολὴν ἀκούσατε. On the
connexion of this parable with the
foregoing narrative cf. Victor: ἡ παρα-
βολὴ δηλοῖ ὅτι μὴ μόνον περὶ τὸν Ἰωάννην ἠγνωμονήκασιν, ἀλλὰ καὶ περὶ
αὐτὸν τὸν κύριον, ἀρξάμενοι ἀπὸ τοῦ οἰ-
κέτου, προελθόντες δὲ ἐπὶ τὸν δεσπότην.

ἀμπελῶνα ἄνθρωπος ἐφύτευσεν] Mt.
ἄνθρ. ἦν οἰκοδεσπότης ὅστις κτλ. He
was not simply the owner of a vineyard, but a master who had slaves at
his command (v. 2 ff.; cf. Mt. xiii. 27,
Lc. xiv. 21). The land of Israel was
a land of the vine (Gen. xlix. 11, Deut.
viii. 8), and the planting of vineyards
was one of the cares of the prudent
householder (Deut. xxviii. 30, 39). The
vineyard had become a recognised
symbol of Israel itself, as the covenant people (Ps. lxxx. 8 f., Isa. v. 2 ff.,
Jer. ii. 21), and it was impossible for
the members of the Sanhedrin or for
the better-taught among the crowd to
mistake the drift of the parable (see
v. 12). The imagery and even the
language is largely derived from Isa.
l.c. (ἀμπελὼν ἐγενήθη...καὶ φραγμὸν
περιέθηκα...καὶ ᾠκοδόμησα πύργον...καὶ
προλήνιον ὤρυξα...καὶ ἔμεινα τοῦ ποιῆσαι σταφυλήν); cf. dial. Tim. et Aq.
(ed. Conybeare, p. 93) εἶπεν αὐτοῖς τὴν
παραβολὴν ἥνπερ τότε Ἡσαίας προεῖπεν.
Ἀμπελών, a word chiefly found in the
later Gk., is common in the LXX, where
it usually represents כֶּרֶם. For φυ-
τεύειν ἀμπ. (נָטַע כֶּ״) see Gen. ix. 20,

καὶ ὤρυξεν ὑπολήνιον καὶ ᾠκοδόμησεν πύργον, καὶ
2 ἐξέδετο αὐτὸν γεωργοῖς, καὶ ἀπεδήμησεν. ²καὶ

1 ωκοδομ.]+αυτω 1071 | εξεδοτο B³D(F²H)NXΓΔΠΣΦΨ min^fereomn

Deut. xx. 6, xxviii. 20, 39, Am. v. 11, Soph. i. 13, Isa. xxxvii. 30, lxv. 21, Ezech. xxviii. 26, 1 Macc. iii. 56, 1 Cor. ix. 7; the Vg. *vineam pastinavit* is more realistic: "dug and trenched the ground (to receive the vines)"; cf. *novellavit* (k).

περιέθηκεν φραγμόν] As a protection partly against human depredators, partly against wild animals (Ps. lxxix. (lxxx.) 13 f. ἵνα τί καθεῖλες τὸν φραγμὸν αὐτῆς καὶ τρυγῶσιν αὐτὴν πάντες οἱ παραπορευόμενοι;...ἐλυμήνατο αὐτὴν σῦς ἐκ δρυμοῦ καὶ ὄνος ἄγριος κατενεμήσατο αὐτήν). For φραγμός see Num. xxii. 24 (ἔστη ἐν ταῖς αὔλαξιν τῶν ἀμπέλων φραγμὸς ἐντεῦθεν καὶ φ. ἐντ.), Lc. xiv. 23, Eph. ii. 14. Lc. omits περιέθηκεν...πύργον.

ὤρυξεν ὑπολήνιον] Mt. ὤρυξεν ἐν αὐτῷ ληνόν. The ληνός, *torcular*, is properly the trough which receives the grapes, and where they are trodden (cf. Num. xviii. 30, Prov. iii. 10, Sir. xxx. 25 (xxxiii. 16), Isa. lxiii. 3, Thren. i. 15). It was usually excavated in the rock, see Moore on Jud. vi. 11 and cf. Joel i. 17. The vat was furnished with a προλήνιον (Isa. v. 2, cf. lxiii. 3) under which was the ὑπολήνιον, *lacus*, R.V. "pit for the winepress" (Joel iii. (iv.) 13, Hagg. ii. 17 (16), Zach. xiv. 10, Isa. xvi. 10 οὐ μὴ πατήσουσιν οἶνον εἰς τὰ ὑπολήνια = בְּקֶב), into which the juice ran. Mc. adheres to Isa. v. in referring to the בְּקֶב, but does not follow the lxx. rendering.

ᾠκοδόμησεν πύργον] Such towers were built in exposed places to protect cattle and vines (cf. 2 Chron. xxvi. 10, Mic. iv 8, Isa. *l.c.*), and for the convenience of the herdsmen and ἀμπελουργοί: similar structures may still be seen among the terraced hills about Hebron. On such traces of the former culture of the vine in Palestine see G. A. Smith, pp. 81, 208.

The patristic interpretation of these details is not quite consistent; e.g. Hilary sees "in turri eminentiam legis...ex qua Christi speculari posset adventus," whilst Jerome comments: "*turrim*, haud dubie quin templum": cf. Thpht.: φραγμὸς δὲ ὁ νόμος...πύργος δὲ ὁ ναός.

ἐξέδετο αὐτὸν γεωργοῖς] The owner, living at a distance, instead of employing his own slaves to work the vineyard, let it out to local cultivators, who were required to pay the rent in kind. In Palestine "such leases were given by the year or for life; sometimes the lease was even hereditary"(Edersheim, *L. and T.* ii. p. 423). This use of ἐκδίδοσθαι does not seem to occur in the lxx., but it is common in class. Gk.; for a close parallel see Plat. *legg.* 806 D γεωργίαι δὲ ἐκδεδομέναι δούλοις ἀπαρχὴν τῶν ἐκ τῆς γῆς ἀποτελοῦσιν ἱκανὴν ἀνθρώποις ζῶσι κοσμίως. On the form ἐξέδετο see WH., *Notes*, p. 167, W-Schm., p. 121. The tenants are γεωργοί here in Mt., Mc., Lc.; Lc. uses ἀμπελουργός in xiii. 7, but apparently in reference to the hired slave working under a master who is from time to time on the spot. Γεωργία as the wider word may include ἀμπελουργία, cf. Gen. ix. 20 ἤρξατο Νῶε ἄνθρωπος γεωργὸς γῆς, καὶ ἐφύτευσεν ἀμπελῶνα. On the other hand the words can be contrasted, as in Jer. lii. 16, where the ploughmen and the vine-dressers are regarded as two distinct classes.

καὶ ἀπεδήμησεν] The owner, having let his land, went into foreign parts (Vg. *peregre profectus est*); Lc. adds that his absence was a prolonged one (χρόνους ἱκανούς). Ἀποδημεῖν, ἀπόδημος in the N. T. are limited to the

ἀπέστειλεν πρὸς τοὺς γεωργοὺς τῷ καιρῷ δοῦλον,
ἵνα παρὰ τῶν γεωργῶν λάβῃ ἀπὸ τῶν καρπῶν

2 ινα...αμπελωνος] ινα απο του καρπου (του καρπου etiam AX al) του αμπ.
δωσουσιν αυτω D latt^{vt pl} (syr^{sin}) | παρα των γ. λαβη] λ. παρ αυτων 33 604 2^{pe} | λαβη Ψ
syr^{pesh}

Synoptists, occurring, besides this context, in Mt. xxv. 14 f., Mc. xiii. 34, Lc. xv. 13 : St Paul has ἐκδημεῖν in 2 Cor. v. 6 ff., where it is contrasted with ἐνδημεῖν, as Xenophon contrasts ἀποδημεῖν with ἐπιδημεῖν (Cyr. vii. 5.69). The GOD of Israel is represented in the light of an absentee proprietor. Origen (in Mt.) explains : ἀποδημία τοῦ δεσπότου ὅτι Κύριος ὁ συνὼν αὐτοῖς ἐν νεφέλῃ ἡμέρας καὶ στύλῳ νυκτὸς ἕως αὐτοὺς καταφυτεύσει εἰσαγαγὼν εἰς ὄρος ἅγιον αὐτοῦ...οὐκέτι αὐτοῖς ἐπεφαίνετο. The gradual withdrawal of visible interpositions, ending in the suspension of the gift of prophecy, had borne this aspect in the eyes of the nation (cf. e.g. Jer. xiv. 8), and the absence was real in the case of the dishonest teachers and unbelieving priesthood who were now the leaders of Israel. But, however prolonged, it was as yet but an ἀποδημία, not a dereliction, not an abandonment of the Divine claim upon Israel's allegiance. Even the temporary withdrawal had a gracious purpose; comp. the remark of Jerome: "abire videtur a vinea ut vinitoribus liberum operandi arbitrium derelinquat." Cf. Bengel: "invenitur tempus divinae taciturnitatis ubi homines agunt pro arbitrio"; and see Mc. iv. 26 ff.

2. καὶ ἀπέστειλεν κτλ.] The demand was not made till the vintage came ; Mt. ὅτε...ἤγγισεν ὁ καιρὸς τῶν καρπῶν (cf. xi. 13). Τῷ καιρῷ, dative of the point of time, cf. WM., p. 373 f. Origen : ὁ χρόνος ἦν τῶν προφητῶν ἀπαιτούντων τὸν καρπόν. On the mission of the Prophets see Isa. vi. 8, Jer. xxv. 4. The title δοῦλος Κυρίου is first given to Moses (Jos. xiv. 7, Ps.

civ. (cv.) 26) and Joshua (Jos. xxiv. 29); it is borne by David (2 Regn. iii. 18, vii. 4 ff.) ; and ultimately becomes the formal style and title of the prophet (Am. iii. 7, Zech. i. 6, Jer. vii. 25, xxv. 4, &c.). In Mt. groups of δοῦλοι are sent twice (vv. 34, 36); in Mc. each servant receives a separate mission, and there are many such (δοῦλον... πάλιν ἄλλον δοῦλον...καὶ ἄλλον...καὶ πολλοὺς ἄλλους), whilst Lc. stops, but perhaps without any special purpose, at the third (δοῦλον...ἕτερον...τρίτον). The groups in Mt. may be taken to represent successive periods of prophetic energy, whilst the reference to individuals in Mc. and Lc. accentuates the distinctness of the message entrusted to each true prophet. Or, as Thpht. suggests, each of the successive messengers may represent a prophetic era: δοῦλον ἕνα τάχα τοὺς περὶ τὸν Ἡλίαν προφήτας...δεύτερον δὲ... τοὺς περὶ Ὡσῆε καὶ Ἡσαίαν...τρίτον δὲ ...τοὺς ἐν τῇ αἰχμαλωσίᾳ. Comp. Origen on Mt. t. xvii. 16.

ἵνα...λάβῃ κτλ.] Whatever the form of the message, its general purpose was one and the same—that the owner might receive (Mt. λαβεῖν) his due. Ἀπὸ τῶν καρπῶν, the 'fruits' being the source from which (WM., p. 463) the landlord obtained his rent. He claimed merely the portion which by agreement belonged to him (τοὺς καρποὺς αὐτοῦ, Mt.) ; under the terms of the lease (v. 1, note) another portion would go to the cultivators (2 Tim. ii. 6). For the interpretation see v. 17 ἀπόδοτε...τὰ τοῦ θεοῦ τῷ θεῷ. In one sense GOD claims all, in another only a part ; cf. Bengel: "pars fructuum colonis concessa."

3 τοῦ ἀμπελῶνος· ³καὶ λαβόντες αὐτὸν ἔδειραν καὶ
4 ἀπέστειλαν κενόν. ⁴καὶ πάλιν ἀπέστειλεν πρὸς
αὐτοὺς ἄλλον δοῦλον, κἀκεῖνον ἐκεφαλίωσαν καὶ
¶ f 5 ἠτίμασαν.¶ ⁵καὶ ἄλλον ἀπέστειλεν· κἀκεῖνον ἀπέκτειναν, καὶ πολλοὺς ἄλλους, οὓς μὲν δέροντες οὓς

3 και λαβ.] οι δε λαβ. ACNX(Γ)ΠΣΦ min^pl | κενον]+προς αυτον D a b ff   4 om
παλιν X the | om εκεφαλιωσαν...κακεινον (v. 5) syr^sin | εκεφαλιωσαν και ℵBLΨ] εκε-
φαλαιωσαν και ACDNΣΦ rell min^omn vid arm κεφαλαιωσαντες 1 28 91 118 299 604 2^pe
decollaverunt k (? εκεφαλισαν) pr λιθοβολησαντες ACNXΓΠΣΦ 604 min^pl syrr^pesh hcl
go aeth | ητιμασαν (vel ητιμησαν) ℵB(D)LΨ 33 latt aegg] απεστειλαν ητιμωμενον (vel
ητιμασμενον) ACNXΓΠΣΦ min^pl syrr^pesh hcl arm go aeth   5 και 1°]+παλιν
ΑΝΧΓΠΣΦ min^pl f q vg syrr^pesh hcl arm go | om ους μεν...αποκτ. k r^vid | ους μεν...ους
δε ℵBLΔ 1 33 2^pe al^nonn] ους μεν...αλλους δε D ους μεν...τους δε Φ τους μεν...τους δε
ACNXΓΠΣ min^pl

3. καὶ...ἔδειραν καὶ ἀπέστειλαν κενόν] Δέρειν in the LXX. has its original meaning "to flay," but in the N.T. it is used only in the sense of "beating severely" or "scourging" (cf. xiii. 9, Lc. xii. 47 f., xxii. 63, Jo. xviii. 23, Acts v. 40, xvi. 37, xxii. 29), which it bears frequently in the comic poets (cf. Ar. *Vesp.* 485 ἣ δέδοκταί μοι δέρεσθαι καὶ δέρειν δι᾽ ἡμέρας, *Ran.* 619 μαστιγῶν, δέρων, στρεβλῶν). The first slave is let go after his beating, but without that which he had come for, 'empty-handed'; for this use of κενός cf. Job xxii. 9, Lc. i. 53. The repetition of λαβεῖν, ἀποστεῖλαι is remarkable; the servant, instead of taking anything, is taken; sent to receive, he is sent back empty. It is difficult to decide whether the play on these words is intentional, or due to the simplicity of the style of the common tradition; in favour of the second explanation it may be noted that this feature is most noticeable in Mc.

4. κἀκεῖνον ἐκεφαλίωσαν] Ἐκεφαλίωσαν is ἅπ. λεγ. in Greek literature (cf. Lob. *Phryn.*, p. 95), but formed quite regularly from κεφάλιον, a diminutive which occurs in late writers; according to the analogy of γναθοῦν, 'to hit on the cheek,' κεφαλιοῦν would be 'to wound on the

head.' This sense is supported by the Vg. *in capite vulneraverunt*; cf. Syrr.^pesh., hcl. *lapidaverunt et contuderunt*, Me. *vulneraverunt*. It agrees in a general way with Mt.'s ἐλιθοβόλησαν, and Lc.'s τραυματίσαντες, to which Mc.'s ἐκεφ. seems to correspond, and with the requirements of the context in Mc. The first servant was beaten, the third killed; the second, though not killed, fared worse than the first, for he was knocked about the head. Ἐκεφαλαίωσαν would seem to mean that he was summarily dispatched, and it is difficult to believe with Field (*Notes*, p. 35) that Mc. adopted it in the sense of ἐκεφάλωσαν, "a *vox nihili*." Baljon employs the extreme remedy of conjectural emendation, admitting into his text ἐκολάφισαν (cf. xiv. 65). This gives an excellent sense, but until it finds some documentary support it is safer to adhere to the reading of ℵBLΨ and interpret with Euth.: ἀντὶ τοῦ 'τὴν κεφαλὴν συνέτριψαν.' Καὶ ἠτίμασαν: in this and other ways they heaped contumely upon him; for this use of ἀτιμάζειν cf. 2 Regn. x. 5, Acts v. 40, 41.

5. κἀκεῖνον ἀπέκτειναν κτλ.] From insult the γεωργοί proceeded on the next occasion to murder; and so

δὲ ἀποκτεννύντες. ⁶ἔτι ἕνα εἶχεν, υἱὸν ἀγαπητόν· 6
ἀπέστειλεν αὐτὸν ἔσχατον πρὸς αὐτοὺς λέγων ὅτι
Ἐντραπήσονται τὸν υἱόν μου. ⁷ἐκεῖνοι δὲ οἱ γεωργοὶ 7
πρὸς ἑαυτοὺς εἶπαν ὅτι Οὗτός ἐστιν ὁ κληρονόμος·

5 αποκτεννυντες (Νᶜ)B(L) 150ᵉᵛ (minᵖᵃᵘᶜ)] αποκτεννοντες Ν*ACDΕ(FGHKN)UV(X) Γ(Π)Σ(Φ)Ψ 604 αποκτιναντες Δ αποκτεινοντες minᵛⁱˣᵐᵘ   6 ετι...εσχατον novissi-mum misit filium k | ετι] ετι ουν ACDNXΓΠΣΦ minᵖˡ q vg syrʰᶜˡ υστερον δε ετι 13 28 69 124 346 604 cˢᶜʳ (2ᴾᵉ) | υιον εχων ΝΧΓΠΣΦ minᵖˡ | αγαπητον]+(vel pr) αυτου ΑΝΧΓΠΣΦ (1 13 28 69 124 299) alᵖˡ syrʰᶜˡ go | αυτον] pr και ACNX*ΓΠΣΦΨ minᵖˡ syrʰᶜˡ go κακεινον D | εσχατον προς αυτους ΝBCLΔ 13 69 alⁿᵒⁿⁿ] προς αυτ. εσχ. ΑΝΧΓΠΣΦ alᵖˡ om εσχατον 1071 syrˢⁱⁿ om προς αυτους D 1071 a ff i k q | οτι] om LNΔΣ 33 alⁿᵒⁿⁿ c k ισως minᵖᵃᵘᶜ a b syrrˢⁱⁿ ᵖᵉˢʰ arm   7 εκεινοι δε οι γ.] οι δε γ. D a b ff i k vg arm the aeth+ιδοντες (vel θεασαμενοι) αυτον (+ερχομενον) ΝΣ (13 28 69 124 604 1071 alⁿᵒⁿⁿ syrʰᶜˡ⁽ᵐᵍ⁾ arm) | ο κληρ.] pr ο υιος αυτου (Δ) syrˢⁱⁿ

matters went on for a long time, each servant who was sent suffering death or maltreatment at their hands. Καὶ πολλοὺς ἄλλους, sc. ἐκάκωσαν, or the like; cf. WM., p. 728 f. Οὓς μέν... οὓς δέ: cf. iv. 4, and sèe WM., p. 130, Blass, *Gr.* p. 145 f. Δέροντες: see *v.* 3 note. Ἀποκτεννύντες is a very rare form but "probably right" here (WH., *Notes*, p. 169). For O. T. parallels see I Kings xviii. 13, xxii. 27, 2 Chron. xxiv. 20 ff., xxxvi. 15 f., Neh. ix. 26 (τοὺς προφήτας σου ἀπέκτειναν), Jer. xliv. (xxxvii.) 15 (ἐπάταξαν αὐτόν); and cf. Lc. vi. 23, xiii. 34, Acts vii. 52, 1 Thess. ii. 15, Heb. xi. 36 ff., Apoc. xvi. 6, xviii. 20 ff.

6. ἔτι ἕνα εἶχεν κτλ.] One remained whom the owner could send, and he was not a slave, but his own son. Υἱὸν ἀγαπητόν: Lc. τὸν υἱ. τὸν ἀγαπ., Mt. υἱὸν αὐτοῦ. On ἀγαπητός see i. 11, note, ix. 7; here it seems to be un-doubtedly an adjective qualifying υἱός, and not an appellation. The one and only Son (*dial. Tim. et Aq.*, τὸν υἱὸν αὐτοῦ τὸν μονογενῆ) is contrasted sharply with the many servants (πολλοὺς...ἕνα...ἀγαπητόν), cf. Heb. i. 1, 2, iii. 5, 6. He had been reserved to the end (ἔσχατον, cf. ἐπ᾽ ἐσχάτου Heb. i. 2). The mission of the Son

marked, from the N. T. standpoint, the fulness of time (Gal. iv. 4), syn-chronising with the completion of the ages (Heb. ix. 26).

λέγων ὅτι Ἐντραπήσονται κτλ.] Lc. qualifies ἐντρ. by prefixing ἴσως. But to the owner any other result was incon-ceivable, and the parable sets forth the improbability, from the human point of view, of such an issue as the Incar-nation actually had; cf. Thpht.: ἐντρ., τὸ εἰκὸς λέγων, Bengel: "exprimitur quid facere debuerint." Ἐντρέπεσθαί τινα, *revereri aliquem*, is a late con-struction; classical writers use the gen. of the person who is regarded with awe (Blass, *Gr.* p. 89). For other exx. of the acc. cf. Sap. ii. 10, Lc. xviii. 2, Heb. xii. 9.

7. ἐκεῖνοι δὲ οἱ γεωργοί κτλ.] Ἐ-κεῖνοι (which is wanting in Mt., Lc.) points back to the picture already drawn of the men: "those husband-men, being such as we know they were." Πρὸς ἑαυτοὺς εἶπαν, Mt. εἶπον ἐν ἑαυτοῖς, Lc. διελογίζοντο πρὸς ἀλλή-λους: with Mc.'s πρὸς ἑ. cf. xi. 31. Lc. has clearly given the general sense: when the heir was seen making his way to the vineyard at vintage time, a hurried consultation was held, and the resolution taken to destroy him.

οὗτός ἐστιν ὁ κληρονόμος] So Mt.,

δεῦτε ἀποκτείνωμεν αὐτόν, καὶ ἡμῶν ἔσται ἡ κλη-
8 ρονομία. ⁸καὶ λαβόντες ἀπέκτειναν αὐτόν, καὶ
9 ἐξέβαλον αὐτὸν ἔξω τοῦ ἀμπελῶνος. ⁹τί ποιήσει
ὁ κύριος τοῦ ἀμπελῶνος; ἐλεύσεται καὶ ἀπολέσει

8 εξεβαλον (-λαν B) αυτον] om αυτον LXΔ al minᵖˡ b k vg arm   9 τι...αμπε-
λωνος] tunc dominus indignatus veniet k | τι]+ουν ℵACDNXΓΔΠΣΦΨ minᵒᵐⁿ ᵛⁱᵈ
a b c ff i q vg syrrᵖᵉˢʰ ʰᶜˡ arm

Mc., Lc. There is perhaps a reference
to Gen. xv. 3, 4; the earlier messengers were but δοῦλοι and had no personal interest in the estate: the υἱός
ἀγαπητός is sole heir. Cf. Heb. i. 2
υἱῷ ὃν ἔθηκεν κληρονόμον πάντων, where
see Westcott's note. Elsewhere in
the N. T. the word is used only in reference to the adopted sons of the
Divine family; cf. Jas. ii. 5, Rom. iv.
13, viii. 17, Gal. iii. 29, iv. 1, 7, Tit. iii.
7, Heb. vi. 17, xi. 17; cf. the use of
κληρονομεῖν supra, x. 17, and of κλη-
ρονομία in Gal. iii. 18, Eph. i. 14 &c.
To the only Son belongs, however, an
unique heirship based on His unique
sonship: He is ὁ κληρονόμος by virtue
of the Eternal Generation. Δεῦτε
ἀποκτείνωμεν αὐτόν, Gen. xxxvii. 20,
LXX., the words of Joseph's brethren
at Dothan. The Beloved Son was
the Joseph of His own generation (cf.
Gen. xxxvii. 3, 4).

καὶ ἡμῶν ἔσται ἡ κληρονομία] The
inheritance to which the parable refers is the vineyard, i.e. Israel (Ps.
xxvii. (xxviii.) 9, xxxii. (xxxiii.) 12,
&c.). If even the heathen were to
be the inheritance of the Son (Ps.
ii. 8), much more was Israel. He had
claimed it for Himself (cf. Jo. i. 11),
and even the partial response He
received had awakened the jealousy
of its rulers, and led to His death,
which was due to a desperate effort
on their part to recover their failing
power over the people.

8. ἀπέκτειναν αὐτόν] The Jewish
rulers were in fact His murderers,
though they were compelled to leave
the execution in the hands of Gentiles

(Acts ii. 23, 36, iii. 15, 1 Thess. ii. 15).
Ἀπέκτειναν contemplates the Passion
as already accomplished history; it
was so in the purpose of the Sanhedrin and in the mind of Christ.

καὶ ἐξέβαλον αὐτὸν ἔξω τ. ἀμπ.]
In Mt. and Lc. the casting out precedes the death (Mt. λαβόντες αὐτὸν
ἐξέβαλον ... καὶ ἀπέκτειναν, Lc. ἐκβα-
λόντες...ἀπέκτειναν): in Mc. it seems
to follow; but such details can scarcely be pressed. According to the
imagery of the parable, casting forth
from the vineyard is excommunica-
tion, formal or practical. In Jerusalem a follower of Jesus had been
excommunicated some months before
this (Jo. ix. 22, 34), and even if
the Jerusalem synagogues had not
dared to extend the sentence to the
Master, He was treated as excom-
municate when He was condemned as
a blasphemer, and handed over for
punishment to the civil power. Origen: ὅσον ἐφ᾽ ἑαυτοῖς ἀλλότριον αὐτὸν
εἶναι ἔκριναν καὶ τοῦ ἀμπελῶνος καὶ τῶν
γεωργῶν, ἡνίκα κατεψηφίζοντο αὐτοῦ
τὴν πρὸς θάνατον ψῆφον. His crucifixion outside the gate of the Holy
city (Jo. xix. 17) symbolised this
virtual expulsion from the community
of Israel; cf. Heb. xiii. 12, 13.

9. τί ποιήσει ὁ κύριος τοῦ ἀμπελῶνος;] What is the next step which
the owner (for κύριος = בַּעַל, cf. Lc.
xix. 33) will take? He has no mes-
senger remaining; his only son is
dead: his servants are dead or their
efforts have failed. Will he abandon
his just claims and submit besides to
outrage of the grossest kind? The

τοὺς γεωργούς, καὶ δώσει τὸν ἀμπελῶνα ἄλλοις.
¹⁰οὐδὲ τὴν γραφὴν ταύτην ἀνέγνωτε Λίθον ὃν ἀπε- 10
δοκίμασαν οἱ οἰκοδομοῦντες, οὗτος ἐγενήθη εἰς κεφαλὴν

9 τους γεωργους]+τουτους (vel εκεινους) C²(GNΣ) (1) 33 al^nonn (syrr^sin pesh hcl arm aeth)   10 εγνωτε 604

answer is clear: he will come in person to chastise and eject the men who have done this. In Mt. this answer is put into the mouth of the audience, whether the Sanhedrists or the people; in Lc. the Lord answers His own question, and voices among the audience exclaim Μὴ γένοιτο, betraying their consciousness of the meaning of the parable; Mc. leaves the answer unassigned, but seems to treat it as part of the Lord's own teaching. The divergence is interesting. In Mc. we probably have the nucleus from which the two later accounts have grown; certainly it is difficult to suppose that Mt. xxi. 41 can have been uttered by the audience (Euth.: ἄκοντες προφητεύουσι καὶ αὐτοὶ τὸ μέλλον), though the words of Christ may well have awakened a response in their consciences and thus have become in a sense their own.

ἐλεύσεται καὶ ἀπολέσει κτλ.] Sc. ὁ κύριος τοῦ ἀμπελῶνος. The owner's coming will bring destruction upon the murderers, and the vineyard will be let (δώσει = ἐκδώσεται, Mt.) to other occupiers such as may be ready to pay him their yearly dues (Mt. only, οἵτινες ἀποδώσουσιν αὐτῷ τοὺς καρποὺς ἐν τοῖς καιροῖς αὐτῶν). The parable at this point becomes a scarcely veiled prophecy of the Divine visitation of wrath which befell Jerusalem, the call of the Gentiles, and the fruitfulness and permanence of the Catholic Church. Origen, followed by most of the ancient interpreters, explains ἄλλοις as referring to the Apostles (cf. 1 Cor. iii. 6 ff.); but a wider reference seems preferable— the 'other husbandmen' are the rulers

and guides of the Church throughout her generations. For ἔρχεσθαι in reference to Divine visitations cf. Ps. xcv. (xcvi.) 13, Amos v. 17, Enoch i. 9 (Jude 14); for another view of the substitution of the Gentile for the Jew, see Mt. viii. 11 f., xxi. 19, and esp. Rom. xi. 17 ff., where addressing Gentiles St Paul points out that their tenure of the privilege which the older Israel had for the time forfeited is conditional upon a continued response to the Divine call (vv. 21, 23); cf. Jerome in Mt.: "locata est autem nobis vinea, et locata ea conditione ut reddamus Domino fructum temporibus suis."

10. οὐδὲ τὴν γραφὴν ταύτην κτλ.] R. V. "Have ye not read even this scripture?" For οὐδέ 'not even' in a question cf. Lc. vi. 3, xxiii. 40. Mt. has here οὐδέποτε ἀνέγνωτε ἐν ταῖς γραφαῖς; Lc., who takes the question as an answer to a μὴ γένοιτο from the crowd, Τί οὖν ἐστιν τὸ γεγραμμένον τοῦτο; Γραφή is a portion of Scripture, as in xv. 28, Jo. vii. 38, 42, xix. 37 (ἑτέρα γραφή), 2 Tim. iii. 16 (πᾶσα γραφή), and almost always when the sing. is used; see Lightfoot on Gal. iii. 22. The passage was one in common use—hence οὐδέ: could it be that these students and teachers of the Scriptures were not acquainted even with the commonplaces of Holy Writ? (cf. v. 24).

λίθον ὃν ἀπεδοκίμασαν κτλ.] Ps. cxvii. (cxviii.) 22, 23, an exact quotation from the LXX., which gives here a word for word rendering of the M. T. The quotation was perhaps suggested by the Hosanna verses (xi. 9, cf. 18, note) which it almost immediately precedes. In the Psalmist's view the

11 γωνίας· ¹¹παρὰ Κυρίου ἐγένετο αὕτη, καὶ ἔστιν
12 θαυμαστὴ ἐν ὀφθαλμοῖς ἡμῶν; ¹²καὶ ἐζήτουν αὐτὸν

11 om παρα Κυριου εγεν. αυτη D

stone is Israel, and the builders are the world-powers engaged in raising the fabric of history—whether Assyria and Babylonia, or, if the Psalm be Maccabaean, Syria represented by Epiphanes (see Cheyne, *Origin of the Psalter*, p. 16 f.). Israel had been cast aside (cf. Jer. xxviii. (li.) 26) by men in high places, but had recovered its place among the nations —had again become the κεφαλὴ γωνίας (רֹאשׁ פִּנָּה), the bond of unity in the fabric, by reason of its unique office of witnessing to the One Living GOD. In our Lord's use of the words the conditions are changed ; He, as the true representative of Israel's witness to GOD, is the Stone which is designed to be 'head of the corner'; the builders who cast the Elect Stone aside are the present leaders of Israel (Jerome: "quos supra vinitores appellarat, nunc aedificatores"). This application of the words deeply impressed the Apostles, who reproduce it more than once after the Pentecost (Acts iv. 11, 1 Pet. ii. 4, 7) and connect with it the prophecy of Isa. xxviii. 16 (Rom. ix. 32, Eph. ii. 20, 1 Pet. ii. 6) ; Christ receives the title of λίθος ἀκρογωνιαῖος, *lapis angularis*, the bond of unity in the new Israel (Eph. *l.c.*). The metaphor was perhaps unduly pressed by the Greek and Latin expositors (cf. T. K. Abbott, *Ephesians*, p. 70), e.g. by Euth., who writes : καθάπερ γὰρ ἐκεῖνος [ὁ λίθος] ἐφ᾽ ἑαυτῷ συνδεῖ τοίχους δύο, τὸν αὐτὸν τρόπον καὶ ὁ χριστὸς ἐφ᾽ ἑαυτῷ συνδεσμεῖ τοὺς δύο λαούς, τόν τε ἐξ ἐθνῶν καὶ τὸν ἐξ Ἰουδαίων. But the 'Corner Stone' clearly emphasises the cohesion of believers in the Body of Christ, as the 'Foundation Stone' (1 Cor. iii. 11) implies their dependence on His work and strength.

Jerome points out that, while the builders of Israel rejected both these purposes of the Lord's coming, the wise master-builder of the Gentile Church ("iuxta Paulum architectum") overlooked neither. The old hymn of the Sarum Dedication office boldly fuses both together: "angulare fundamentum lapis Christus missus est, | qui compage parietum in utroque nectitur, | quem Syon sancta suscepit, in quo credens permanet."

11. παρὰ Κυρίου ἐγένετο αὕτη κτλ.] A continuation of the words of Ps. cxviii., omitted by Lc. Αὕτη (זֹאת), 'this thing,' a Hebraism (WM., pp. 39, 298, Blass, *Gr.*, p. 82), which is due to the text of the LXX. and not to the Synoptists themselves: for other exx. in the LXX. see Driver on 1 Sam. iv. 7. Attempts to explain αὕτη as referring to κεφαλήν or to γωνίας (פִּנָּה = זֹאת) are not only unnecessary, but yield an inferior sense ; see Field, *Notes*, p. 15. It is the elevation of the rejected stone into its predestined place at the head of the corner in which the Psalmist sees the hand of GOD (παρὰ Κυρίου, WM., p. 457), and which is a standing miracle in the eyes of the true Israel (θαυμαστὴ ἐν ὀφθ. ἡμῶν, WM., p. 482). The application of this to the Resurrection and Ascension is easy and attractive ; cf. Victor : ὅτι δὴ μετὰ θάνατον ζῶν φαίνεται Χριστός, βασιλεὺς ὢν οὐρανίων τε καὶ ἐπιγείων.

Mc. omits a striking saying which follows in Lc. (πᾶς ὁ πεσὼν ἐπ᾽ ἐκεῖνον τὸν λίθον κτλ.) and, after a slightly different form, in most texts of Mt.

12. ἐζήτουν αὐτὸν κρατῆσαι κτλ.] Sc. οἱ γραμματεῖς καὶ οἱ ἀρχιερεῖς, as Lc. reminds us. Κρατῆσαι, the inf. as object, see Burton § 387. For the second time (cf. xi. 18) the arrest

κρατῆσαι, καὶ ἐφοβήθησαν τὸν ὄχλον, ἔγνωσαν γὰρ
ὅτι πρὸς αὐτοὺς τὴν παραβολὴν εἶπεν. καὶ ἀφέντες
αὐτὸν ἀπῆλθαν.

¹³ Καὶ ἀποστέλλουσιν πρὸς αὐτόν τινας τῶν 13
Φαρισαίων καὶ τῶν Ἡρῳδιανῶν, ἵνα αὐτὸν ἀγρεύ-
σωσιν λόγῳ. ¹⁴καὶ ἐλθόντες λέγουσιν αὐτῷ Διδά- 14

12 τὴν παραβολὴν]+ταυτην 1071 al^nonn min^nonn b k vg syrr^sin pesh arm   13 om
προς αυτον D a c i k q | των Φαρισαιων] των γραμματεων syr^pesh pr εκ 69 346 g^ser syr^sin
arm | αγρευσωσιν] παγιδευσωσιν D 2^pe 604   14 και 1°] οι δε ΑΝΧΓΠΣΦ al min^pl
syrr^pesh hcl arm go | ελθοντες λεγ. αυτω] επηρωτων αυτον οι Φαρισαιοι D (c ff k) ελθ.
ηρξαντο ερωταν αυτον εν δολω λεγοντες G 1 13 28 69 (604) al^nonn (syr^sin) (arm)

would have been effected in the Precinct by the στρατηγὸς τοῦ ἱεροῦ (cf.
Acts iv. 1), if the people had not still
been with Jesus. On ἐφοβήθησαν τὸν
ὄχλον see xi. 32, note ; on καί in this
sentence cf. WM., p. 545. Mt. adds
that the crowd regarded Jesus as they
had regarded His forerunner (xi. 32),
in the light of a prophet. Mc. and
Lc. explain the cause of the growing
hostility of the Sanhedrists; they knew
that the Parable of the Husbandmen
was spoken in reference to them (πρὸς
αὐτούς : cf. Lc. xii. 41, Heb. i. 7, 8, xi.
18). For the moment they had no
alternative but to accept defeat and
return to their council-chamber to
mature their plots (ἀφέντες αὐτὸν
ἀπῆλθαν, Mc. only). Meanwhile the
Lord continued to teach in parables
(Mt. xxii. 1—14), addressing Himself
to His disciples and the crowd.

13—17. The Pharisees' Question
(Mt. xxii. 15—22, Lc. xx. 20—26).

13. ἀποστέλλουσιν πρὸς αὐτόν κτλ.]
The discomfiture which the Sanhedrin
had suffered when acting in concert
broke them up again into parties,
each of which took action for itself.
The Pharisees were the first to move
(Mt. τότε πορευθέντες οἱ Φ. συμβούλιον
ἔλαβον), and they decided to send
certain of their disciples (Mt. τοὺς
μαθητὰς αὐτῶν, Mc. τινὰς τῶν Φ.) who
knew how to combine the vigilance
of practised dissemblers with the ap-

parent innocence of young enquirers
(Lc. ἐγκαθέτους ὑποκρινομένους ἑαυτοὺς
δικαίους εἶναι). Their business was to
entrap the Master into some remark
by which He would be fatally com-
promised. Ἀγρεύειν (Mc.), παγιδεύειν
(Mt.), are both ἅπ. λεγόμενα in the N.T.,
but both are used by the LXX. and in
a metaphorical sense (ἀγρ., Prov. v. 22,
vi. 25 f., Job x. 16 ; παγ., 1 Regn.
xxviii. 9, Eccl. ix. 12) ; in ἀγρεύειν
λόγῳ, the dat. is instrumental or
modal ; speech—a question on their
side, an answer on His—was to be
the means employed in the capture of
their prey. Cf. Lc. xi. 54, where
θηρεύειν is similarly used ; in the
present context Lc. prefers the simpler
phrase ἐπιλαβέσθαι λόγου.

In this attempt the Pharisees associated with their own disciples
"certain...of the Herodians" (Mc.,
Mt.). The Greek and Latin expositors generally understand by
Ἡρῳδιανοί here soldiers from Herod's
army, referring to Lc. xxiii. 11 : but
both the form of the adj. (cf. Blass on
Acts xi. 26, and Gr. p. 63) and the
circumstances of its occurrence decide
for the meaning 'Herod's partisans'—
scarcely, as some authorities mentioned by Victor and Ps.-Tertull. adv.
omn. haer. 1, persons who regarded
Herod as the Messiah; see iii. 6, note.
These men were doubtless the Galilean Herodians who had already

σκαλε, οἴδαμεν ὅτι ἀληθὴς εἶ καὶ οὐ μέλει σοι περὶ
οὐδενός· οὐ γὰρ βλέπεις εἰς πρόσωπον ἀνθρώπων,
ἀλλ' ἐπ' ἀληθείας τὴν ὁδὸν τοῦ θεοῦ διδάσκεις.
ἔξεστιν δοῦναι κῆνσον Καίσαρι ἢ οὔ; δῶμεν ἢ μὴ

14 εξεστιν] pr ειπε (vel ειπον) ουν ημιν (+ει [vel τι] σοι δοκει) (C*²D)ΜΝΣ(Φ) 1071
al^pauc (a b ff i q) syr^pesh corr arm | κηνσον] επικεφαλαιον (D) 124 επικεφαλεον δ. κηνσον
1071 2^pe k (capitularium) arm^cod (cf. syrr^sin pesh) | η ου δωμεν η μη δωμεν] η ου
D a b c ff i l η ου δωμεν 225 vg syr^sin arm^cdd go dabimus aut non k

proved themselves useful to the
Pharisees, and might on the present
occasion render service again.

14. διδάσκαλε, οἴδαμεν κτλ.] The
preamble is skilfully arranged with
the view of disarming suspicion, and
at the same time preventing escape.
So independent and fearless a teacher
of truth could not from fear of consequences either refuse an answer to
honest and perplexed enquirers, or
conceal His real opinion. For οἴδαμεν
ὅτι κτλ. cf. Jo. iii. 2. Ἀληθής, true,
the opposite of ψευδής (1 Jo. ii. 8), as
ἀληθινός of ψευδώνυμος (cf. Trench,
syn. § viii.); the use of the word by
the Pharisees is an unconscious witness to the impression which Christ's
life and teaching had left even upon
enemies. Ἀληθής occurs here only
in the Synoptists, but both adj. and
noun are common in Jo.: truth is
one of the notes of the Lord's Divine
Mission as it is presented by St John
(e.g. i. 17, iii. 32, v. 31 ff., vii. 18,
viii. 13 ff., xiv. 6). Οὐ μέλει σοι περὶ
οὐδενός. There is veiled irony in the
words. He had shewn little consideration for men of learning and
hierarchical rank; doubtless He would
be equally indifferent to the views of
the Procurator and the Emperor
himself; when the truth was concerned, His independence would
assert itself with fearless impartiality.
For οὐ μέλει σοι cf. iv. 38, Lc. x. 40,
Jo. x. 13, 1 Pet. v. 7.

οὐ γὰρ βλέπεις κτλ.] Lc. οὐ λαμ-
βάνεις πρόσωπον. Cf. θαυμάζειν πρόσ-
ωπα (Jude 16), προσωπολημπτεῖν (Jas.

ii. 9) and the nouns προσωπολήμπτης
(Acts x. 34), προσωπολημψία (Jas. ii. 1,
Rom. ii. 11, Eph. vi. 9, Col. iii. 25):
the compounds are unknown to the
LXX., which employs λ. πρόσωπον (Lev.
xix. 15), θ. πρόσωπον (Job xiii. 10),
ἐπιγνῶναι (ὑποστέλλεσθαι, αἱρετίζειν,
αἰδεῖσθαι, ὁρᾶν εἰς) πρόσωπον, according
to the sense of the Heb. verb. Βλέπειν
(ὁρᾶν) εἰς πρ. (הִכִּיר פָּנִים) clearly is to
pay regard to the outward appear-
ance or the personal character or
position; for the more difficult λαμβάνειν πρ. (προσωπολημπτεῖν), which
answers to נָשָׂא פָנִים, see Lightfoot
on Gal. ii. 6, and Mayor on James l.c.

ἀλλ' ἐπ' ἀληθείας κτλ.] Teaching as
well as life was characterised by
truth. Ἐπ' ἀληθείας (cf. Job ix. 2, Isa.
xxxvii. 18, Dan. ii. 8 (LXX. and Th.),
Lc. iv. 25, xxii. 59, Acts x. 34), "according to truth" (Blass, Gr. p. 133)
—rather "with truth" (WM., p. 528).
Τὴν ὁδὸν τοῦ θεοῦ, not as in i. 3 'the
way along which He comes,' but 'the
way which He appoints for men,' cf.
Acts xviii. 25 f., also ἡ ὁδὸς τῆς ἀληθείας (2 Pet. ii. 2), or ἡ ὁδός simply,
as a term for the Christian faith and
its followers (Acts ix. 2, xix. 9, 23,
xxiv. 14, 22). This use of ὁδός is a
Hebraism (cf. B D B. s.v. דֶּרֶךְ), of
which there are frequent instances in
the LXX., e.g. in Gen. vi. 12, Ps. i. 1,
6, Jer. xxi. 8; comp. the opening of
the Didache (ὁδοὶ δύο εἰσί, μία τῆς
ζωῆς καὶ μία τοῦ θανάτου: Dr C. Taylor,
Teaching, p. 7 ff.), and the Lord's
words in Mt. vii. 13, 14.

ἔξεστιν δοῦναι κῆνσον κτλ.] They

δῶμεν; ¹⁵ ὁ δὲ εἰδὼς αὐτῶν τὴν ὑπόκρισιν εἶπεν 15
αὐτοῖς Τί με πειράζετε; φέρετέ μοι δηνάριον ἵνα

15 ειδως ℵᶜABCLNXΓΔΠΣΦΨ minᵖˡ a k vg syrrˢⁱⁿ ᵖᵉˢʰ ʰᶜˡ arm aegg] ιδων ℵ*(D) 13
28 69 346 2ᵖᵉ b c ff i q go | πειραζετε]+υποκριται FGNΣ 1 13 28 33 69 2ᵖᵉ alᵖᵃᵘᶜ q
syrʰᶜˡ ᶜᵒʳʳ arm | δηναριον]+ωδε ℵ* 1 b

can no longer refrain from putting
the question with which they had
been charged. Mt. begins εἰπὸν οὖν
ἡμῖν τί σοι δοκεῖ; but the abrupt
ἔξεστιν (Mc., Lc.) is perhaps more in
keeping with the impatience of these
young intriguers. Ἔξεστιν, 'does the
Torah permit it?' cf. ii. 24, 26, vi. 18,
x. 2. Κῆνσον, Mt., Mc.; Lc. φόρον:
the Latin word is transliterated as
in Aramaic (ℵסנק, Dalman, Gr. p. 147).
The census is the poll tax (ἐπικεφά-
λαιον in cod. D, Syrr.ˢⁱⁿ·, ᵖᵉˢʰ· ܟܣܐ

ܟܪܐ, ܟܪܝ) or tributum capi-
tis, as distinguished from the tributum
agri, and from the customs on articles
of commerce (τέλη, cf. Mt. xvii. 25).
The Judaean poll tax went into the
Emperor's fiscus, not into the aera-
rium, so that it was actually paid to
"Caesar." The payment was objection-
able both as a sign of subjection to a
foreign power (Mt. l.c.), and because of
the Emperor's effigy stamped on the
denarius in which the money was paid
(Madden, Jewish Coinage, p. 247).
The copper coins struck by the Procurators were free from the effigies,
usually bearing some device to which
no objection could be taken, cornu-
copiae, or leaves of the olive, vine, or
palm (Schürer I. ii., p. 77, Madden,
p. 135); but the silver denarius,
which was not a local coin, bore the
head of the Imperator, and its compulsory use could not but increase
the scruples of patriotic Jews. For
Καῖσαρ see Jo. xix. 12, 15, Acts xvii.
7, xxv. 8 ff., Phil. iv. 22. A summary
of Jewish opinion on the duty of
Israel towards its foreign rulers is
given by Weber, Jüd. Theologie, p.
78. Ἦ οὔ...ἦ μή, cf. WM., p. 595.

δῶμεν ἦ μὴ δῶμεν;] Deliberative

subj., as in iv. 30, vi. 24, 37. They
require a direct answer, 'yes' or 'no,'
as if the question called for no more.
A negative answer was of course desired; they hoped to hear him say
Οὐκ ἔξεστιν. Such a reply, in the
present temper of the crowd, might
have placed Him at once at the head
of a popular rebellion (Acts v. 37); at
the least it would have involved Him
in a charge of treason (Lc. xxiii. 2).
And, as they justly said, no fear of
consequences would have withheld
Him from making it, if it had been
true.

15. εἰδὼς αὐτῶν τὴν ὑπόκρισιν κτλ.]
Mt. γνοὺς τὴν πονηρίαν αὐτῶν, Lc. κατανοήσας αὐτῶν τὴν πανουργίαν. The
variations of both verb and noun are
instructive. Malice (πονηρία) lay at
the root of their conduct, unscrupulous
cunning (πανουργία) supplied them
with the means of seeking their end,
whilst they sought to screen themselves under the pretence (ὑπόκρισις)
of a desire for guidance and an admiration of fearless truthfulness. The
Lord detected their true character
intuitively (εἰδώς), He knew it by
experience (γνούς), and He perceived
it by tokens which did not escape
His observation (κατανοήσας). Thus
each Evangelist contributes to the
completeness of the picture. Ὑπόκρισις occurs here only in Mc.; for
ὑποκριτής see vii. 6, note; other instances of the Lord's power of detecting hypocrisy may be found in
ii. 8, iii. 1 ff., vii. 11 ff., x. 2 ff.

τί με πειράζετε;] For this use of
πειράζειν see i. 13, viii. 11 (note), x. 2.
Τί remonstrates, cf. ii. 7, v. 35, 39,
viii. 12, 17, x. 18, xi. 3, xiii. 6. What
was their object in provoking Him to

16 ἴδω. ¹⁶οἱ δὲ ἤνεγκαν. καὶ λέγει αὐτοῖς Τίνος ἡ εἰκὼν
αὕτη καὶ ἡ ἐπιγραφή; οἱ δὲ εἶπαν αὐτῷ Καίσαρος.
17 ¹⁷ὁ δὲ Ἰησοῦς εἶπεν Τὰ Καίσαρος ἀπόδοτε Καίσαρι

16 om οι δε (2°) AD a b i q vg | ειπαν (ειπον NXΓΙΙ al)] λεγουσιν A b d i q vg
17 ο δε I.] και αποκριθεις (vel αποκρ. δε) ο I. A(D)NXΓΠΣΦ min^pl (latt^(vt pl vg)) syrr^(sin hcl)
arm go | ειπεν]+αυτοις ℵACLNXΓΔΠΨ al min^(omn vid) (om BD) | Καισαρος] pr του D |
αποδοτε]+ουν M 13 69 604 2^pe al^nonn latt^(vt pl vg) syr^hcl | Καισαρι] pr τω D 1071 2^pe

deliver judgment upon a hotly contested point? The question lays bare
their veiled malignity. Mt. adds ὑποκριταί, which is implied in Mc⁰.s ὑπόκρισιν.

φέρετέ μοι δηνάριον ἵνα ἴδω] A denarius (דינרא cf. Dalman, *Gr.* p. 149)
was not likely to be ready at hand,
since only Jewish coins were current
in the Temple; they must fetch one
for Him to see (ἵνα ἴδω); Bengel's
suggestion, "Salvator tum primum
videtur tetigisse et spectasse dena-
rium," is improbable; the Lord wishes
to see the *denarius* that He may use
it to demonstrate His teaching. It
is easy to realise the pause which
followed, the fresh interest excited
by the production of the coin (οἱ δὲ
ἤνεγκαν), and the breathless silence
while all waited for the momentous
reply. Mt. and Lc. have missed this
characteristic feature in the story,
substituting ἐπιδείξατε (Lc. δείξατε).
For δηνάριον Mt. has τὸ νόμισμα
(2 Esdr. viii. 36, 1 Macc. xv. 6) τοῦ
κήνσου, the coin in which the tribute
was paid (see note on *v.* 14).

16. τίνος ἡ εἰκὼν αὕτη καὶ ἡ ἐπιγραφή;] Vg. *cuius est imago haec et
inscriptio (scriptio, superscriptio)?*
See the engraving of a *denarius* of
Tiberius in Madden, p. 247, or in
Hastings, *D. B.* iii. pp. 424—5; the
ἐπιγραφή is TI · CAESAR · DIVI · AVG ·
F · AVG ·, and on the reverse, PONTIF ·
MAXIM ·. In the Epp. εἰκών passes
into a theological term, the meaning
of which is exhaustively investigated
by Lightfoot on Col. i. 15.

οἱ δὲ εἶπαν κτλ.] There was no

escape from this answer, even if they
suspected the purpose it would serve.
They could not in this case plead οὐκ
οἴδαμεν (xi. 33), for both head and
legend proclaimed the fact.

17. τὰ Καίσαρος ἀπόδοτε κτλ.] "O
plenam miraculi responsionem et per-
fectam dicti caelestis absolutionem"
(Hilary). Ἀπόδοτε τὸ ἔχον τὴν εἰκόνα τῷ
εἰκονιζομένῳ...οὐδὲν ἐμποδίζει ὑμῖν πρὸς
θεοσέβειαν τὸ τελεῖν τῷ Καίσαρι (Thpht.).
The thought seems to be: 'The coin
is Caesar's; let him have his own.
The fact that it circulates in Judaea
shews that in the ordering of GOD's
providence Judaea is now under
Roman rule; recognise facts, so long
as they exist, as interpreting to you
the Divine Will, and submit.' Cf.
Rom. xiii. 7, 1 Pet. ii. 13 f., and see
the note on *The Church and the
Civil Power* in SH., *Romans*, p. 369.
Contrast with the Lord's answer the
teaching of another northern leader,
Judas the Gaulanite, Jos. *ant.* xviii. 1.
1 τὴν ἀποτίμησιν οὐδὲν ἄλλο ἢ ἄντικρυς
δουλείαν ἐπιφέρειν (cf. Origen *in Mt.*
t. xvii. 25). Granted that payment
was a badge of slavery, there are
circumstances, Christ teaches, under
which slavery must be borne. Ἀπο-
δοῦναι, which is substituted in the
answer for δοῦναι in the question,
implies that the tribute is a debt: cf.
Rom. *l.c.*, and see Mt. v. 26, xvii. 28 ff.

καὶ τὰ τοῦ θεοῦ τῷ θεῷ] The question rested on an implied incompatibility of the payment of tribute with
the requirements of the Law of GOD;
the Lord replies that there is no such
incompatibility: οὐ κωλύεταί τις ἀπο-

καὶ τὰ τοῦ θεοῦ τῷ θεῷ. καὶ ἐξεθαύμαζον ἐπ᾽ αὐτῷ.

¹⁸Καὶ ἔρχονται Σαδδουκαῖοι πρὸς αὐτόν, οἵτινες 18

17 εξεθαυμαζον אBΨ] εθαυμαζον D² (εθαυμαζοντο D*) LΔ 1071 2ᵖᵉ εθαυμασαν ACNXΓΠΣΦ minᵖˡ | επ αυτω] επ αυτον D(K) 28 8ᵖᵉ

διδοὺς Καίσαρι τὰ Καίσαρος ἀποδιδόναι τῷ θεῷ τὰ τοῦ θεοῦ (Origen). Debts to man and debts to GOD are both to be discharged, and the two spheres of duty are at once distinct and reconcileable; cf. Dalman, *Worte*, i. p. 113. Τὰ τοῦ θεοῦ in the narrower and immediate sense of the words may mean, as Jerome says, "decimas, primitias, et oblationes ac victimas"; in its wider application the term includes the best that man has to offer, his own nature, which bears the image of GOD (Lc. xv. 8—10): "quemadmodum Caesar a nobis exigit impressionem imaginis sui, sic et Deus ut...Deo reddatur anima" (Bede); "*Deo propria*...corpus, animam, voluntatem" (Hilary).

καὶ ἐξεθαύμαζον ἐπ᾽ αὐτῷ] 'They stood amazed (R. V. "wondered greatly") at Him.' Ἐκθαυμάζειν is ἅπ. λεγ. in the N. T., but occurs in Sir. xxvii. 23, xliii. 18, 4 Macc. xvii. 17; compare Mc.'s use of ἐκθαμβεῖσθαι, ἐκπερισσῶς, ἔκφοβος. The enquirers preserved a discreet silence (Lc. ἐσίγησαν), and presently took their leave (Mt. ἀφέντες αὐτὸν ἀπῆλθαν), "infidelitatem cum miraculo pariter reportantes" (Jerome). They wondered perhaps not so much at the profound truth of the words, which they could scarcely have realised, as at the absence in them of anything on which they could lay hold (Victor, θαυμάσαντες τὸ ἄληπτον τοῦ λόγου).

18—27. THE QUESTION OF THE SADDUCEES (Mt. xxii. 23—33 ; Lc. xx. 27—38).

18. καὶ ἔρχονται Σαδδουκαῖοι] I.e. τινὲς τῶν Σαδδουκαίων (Lc.). This party has not been mentioned by Mc. or Lc. hitherto (see however Mc. viii. 11,

note). It was nearly identified with the priestly aristocracy (Acts v. 17 ὁ ἀρχιερεὺς καὶ πάντες οἱ σὺν αὐτῷ, ἡ οὖσα αἵρεσις τῶν Σαδδουκαίων), and its headquarters were at Jerusalem, whilst the Pharisaic scribes were to be found in Galilee as well as in Judaea (Lc. v. 17); moreover, its adherents were relatively few (Jos. *ant.* xviii. 1. 4), and were not, like the Pharisees, in possession of the popular esteem (*ib.* xiii. 10. 6). The present opportunity of approaching Jesus upon the question which divided them from the Pharisees was probably the first which had offered itself; the discomfiture of the disciples of the Pharisees left the field free for their rivals.

οἵτινες λέγουσιν ἀνάστασιν μὴ εἶναι] Cf. Acts xxiii. 8 Σαδδουκαῖοι...λέγουσιν μὴ εἶναι ἀνάστασιν μήτε ἄγγελον μήτε πνεῦμα. Jos. *ant.* xviii. 1. 4 Σαδδουκαίοις δὲ τὰς ψυχὰς ὁ λόγος συναφανίζει τοῖς σώμασι. For further information as to the party and their tenets see Schürer, II. ii. p. 29 ff., Taylor, *Sayings*, Exc. iii., and cf. Jos. *B. J.* ii. 8. 14 ψυχῆς τε τὴν διαμονὴν καὶ τὰς καθ᾽ ᾅδου τιμωρίας καὶ τιμὰς ἀναιροῦσιν. For οἵτινες λ. cf. iv. 20, ix. 1, xv. 7, and see WM., p. 209, note, and Bp. Lightfoot on Gal. iv. 24, v. 19; the relative clause applies to the Sadducees in general, not only to the particular members of the party to whom reference has been made. Ἀνάστασις as a theological term appears first in 2 Macc. (vii. 14, xii. 43), Ps. lxv. (lxx.) tit. In the N.T., besides the present context and its synoptic parallels, it occurs Lc.ᵉᵛ. ², ᵃᶜᵗ. ¹¹, Jo.ᵉᵛ. ⁴, ᵃᵖᵒᶜ. ², Paul⁸, Heb.³, 1 Pet.², usually with a qualifying gen. (δικαίων, νεκρῶν, ζωῆς, κρίσεως, Ἰησοῦ Χριστοῦ)

λέγουσιν ἀνάστασιν μὴ εἶναι, καὶ ἐπηρώτων αὐτὸν
19 λέγοντες ¹⁹Διδάσκαλε, Μωυσῆς ἔγραψεν ἡμῖν ὅτι
¶ N ἐάν τινος ἀδελφὸς¶ ἀποθάνῃ καὶ καταλίπῃ γυναῖκα
καὶ μὴ ἀφῇ τέκνον, ἵνα λάβῃ ὁ ἀδελφὸς αὐτοῦ τὴν

18 αναστασιν μη ειναι] αναστασις ουκ εστιν 1 13 28 69 124 346 | επηρωτησαν
ΑΝΧΓΠΣΦ minᵖˡ   19 Μωσης ΑCEFGHLUVΧΓΦ minᵖˡ | om οτι D 69 108
ινα 1071 | καταλιπη BGKLUVΔΠΣΦΨ minᵖˡ] καταλειπη (vel -πει) Α(E)F(H)MSX(Γ)
minᵖᵉʳᵐᵘ καταλειψη (vel -ψει) ℵ (433 c) εχη D 28 (604) a b c ff i k q syrˢⁱⁿ | τεκνον
ℵᶜ·ᵃBLΔΨ 1 118 241 299 a c ff k arm me] τεκνα ℵ*ᶜ·ᵇΑCDΧΓΠΣΦ minᵖˡ b i q vg
syrrᵖᵉˢʰ ʰᵉˡ the go aeth | την γυναικα]+αυτου ΑΔΧΓΠΣ minᵖˡ a b c ff i q vg syrrᵖᵉˢʰ ʰᵉˡ
arm

or clause (ἡ ἐκ νεκρῶν), but once only
(Lc. ii. 34) in a non-technical sense.
Μὴ εἶναι; this negation of the resurrection was matter of opinion, not of fact
(οὐκ εἶναι); cf. WM., p. 604.

καὶ ἐπηρώτων αὐτόν] The question
was perhaps partly tentative; they
were curious to know the exact
position which this teacher, who was
known to be adverse to the Pharisees,
would take with regard to the main
point at issue between the Pharisees
and themselves. But their purpose
was hostile; the extreme case they
offer for His opinion is clearly intended as a reductio ad absurdum
of any view but their own.

19. διδάσκαλε] On their lips the
title is purely formal; there is here
no pretence of a desire to learn such
as may have dictated its use by the
disciples of the Pharisees (v. 14). The
actual question (ἐπηρώτων) does not
come before v. 23; but all that precedes is preamble to what they intended to ask.

Μωυσῆς ἔγραψεν ἡμῖν κτλ.] In
Deut. xxv. 5 ff. The exact words are
not cited by the Synoptists, nor do
they agree in the form adopted; Lc.
on the whole follows Mc., but Mt.
changes the awkward ἐάν τινος ἀδελφός
into ἐάν τις, and for λάβῃ uses the
technical ἐπιγαμβρεύσει (LXX.¹⁰, Aq. in
Deut. l.c.; ἅπ. λεγ. in N.T.). Josephus
(ant. iv. 8. 23) states the law of
levirate marriage thus: τὴν ἄτεκνον

τἀνδρὸς αὐτῇ τετελευτηκότος ὁ ἀδελφὸς
ἐκείνου γαμείτω καὶ τὸν παῖδα τὸν γενόμενον τῷ τοῦ τεθνεῶτος καλέσας ὀνόματι
τρεφέτω τοῦ κλήρου διάδοχον. On the
institution as it existed in Israel see
Driver, Deuteronomy, p. 280 ff., and
for an early instance of its use, cf.
Gen. xxxviii. 8 (a chapter assigned to
J, Driver, Intr., p. 15). For the attribution of Deut. to Moses see x. 3 f.
Ὅτι...ἵνα: a confusion of two constructions, ὅτι Ἐὰν...ἀποθάνῃ...λήμ-
ψεται and ἵνα ἐὰν ἀποθάνῃ...λάβῃ,
which Lc. avoids by omitting ὅτι.
Ἔγραψεν...ἵνα, i.e. γραφῇ ἐνετείλατο...
ἵνα, cf. xiii. 34.

ἐάν τινος ἀδελφὸς ἀποθάνῃ] The
Deuteronomic law is limited to a
special case: ἐὰν κατοικῶσιν ἀδελφοὶ
ἐπὶ τὸ αὐτό. "When the members of
the family were separated, the law
did not apply. It was a collateral
object of the institution to prevent a
family inheritance from being broken
up" (Driver).

καὶ μὴ ἀφῇ τέκνον] Heb. וּבֵן אֵין לֹו.
The Sadducees interpret בֵּן in the
widest sense (cf. LXX. σπέρμα δὲ μὴ ἦν
αὐτῷ), but the purpose of the law
seems to shew that its operation is
to be limited to cases where no male
issue was left. Comp. Wünsche on
Mt. xxii. 24. Καταλείπειν and ἀφιέναι
are employed indifferently in this passage in reference to the issue of the
marriage (19 ἀφῇ τέκνον, 20 ἀφῆκεν
σπέρμα, 21 καταλιπὼν σπ., 22 ἀφῆκαν

γυναῖκα καὶ ἐξαναστήσῃ σπέρμα τῷ ἀδελφῷ αὐτοῦ.
²⁰ἑπτὰ ἀδελφοὶ ἦσαν· καὶ ὁ πρῶτος ἔλαβεν γυναῖκα, 20
καὶ ἀποθνῄσκων οὐκ ἀφῆκεν σπέρμα· ²¹καὶ ὁ δεύτερος 21
ἔλαβεν αὐτήν, καὶ ἀπέθανεν μὴ καταλιπὼν σπέρμα,
καὶ ὁ τρίτος· ὡσαύτως ²²καὶ οἱ ἑπτὰ οὐκ ἀφῆκαν 22
σπέρμα· ἔσχατον πάντων καὶ ἡ γυνὴ ἀπέθανεν.
²³ἐν τῇ ἀναστάσει τίνος αὐτῶν ἔσται γυνή ; οἱ γὰρ 23

19 εξαναστησει ΑСΗΓ min^nonn   20 επτα αδελφοι ησαν] ησαν ουν παρ υμιν
επτα αδ. D a b i q (604) (1071) επτα ουν αδ. ησαν C²ΜΣ min^mu c vg arm aeth |
αποθνησκων ουκ αφ. σπερμα] απεθανεν και ουκ αφ. σπ. D 1 28 604 2^pe al^pauc ff i
syrr^sin pesh hcl (txt) arm *priusquam generaret filium decessit et non remisit semen* k
mortuus est non relicto semine b q vg και απεθανε και αποθνησκων ουκ αφ. σπ. 1071
21 ελαβεν αυτην]+*ad suscitandum semen fratris sui* c+*resuscitare semen fratri suo*
k | μη καταλιπων σπερμα אΒCLΔ 33] και ουδε αυτος αφηκεν σπερμα A(D)(X)ΓΔΠΣΦ
min^pl latt^(vt pl) vg syrr^pesh hcl arm go | και ο τριτος ωσαυτως om D ff i και ο τρ. ελαβεν
αυτην ωσαυτως 1 604 (cf. 2^pe) arm   22 και ελαβον αυτην (vel ωσαυτως και) οι επτα
και ουκ αφηκαν σπερμα (Α)(D)M^mgΧΓΠΣ min^pl (a) (i) (vg) syrr^pesh (hcl) (go) aeth | om
εσχατον παντων D c k | εσχατον] εσχατη AEFMSUVXΓΦ min^pl vg go | απεθανεν]+
ατεκνος c k (*sine filiis*)   23 εν τη αναστασει אΒC*EFHLSUVXΓΔΨ al^pl k q go]
εν τ. ουν αναστ. AC²(DG)ΚΜΠ(Σ) (1 28 604 1071 2^pe) syrr^sin pesh hcl (corr) arm aeth
+(post αναστασει) οταν αναστωσιν ΑΧΓΠΣΦ (13 69 346) al^pl a ff i q vg syrr^sin hcl arm
go (aeth) (om אΒCDLΔΨ) | αυτων]των επτα 1 91 209 299 om Δ c k | γυνη] pr η AD*
13 | οι γαρ επτα] παντες γαρ 1 91 299

σπ.), but καταλ. only is used of the
wife (19 καταλίπῃ γυναῖκα); see however Mt. xxii. 25 ἀφῆκεν τὴν γ. αὐτοῦ
τῷ ἀδελφῷ αὐτοῦ. On καταλείψῃ (א)
see Deissmann, *Bibl. Studies*, p. 190.

ἐξαναστήσῃ σπέρμα] So Lc.; Mt.
ἀναστήσει σπ. A reminiscence of Gen.
xxxviii. 8 ἀνάστησον σπέρμα τῷ ἀδελφῷ
σου. Ἐξανιστάναι σπέρμα occurs in
Gen. iv. 25, xix. 34, and the compound
verb is common in the LXX.; in the
N.T. it occurs again in Acts xv. 5 (cf.
ἐξανάστασις, Phil. iii. 11).

20—22. ἑπτὰ ἀδελφοὶ ἦσαν κτλ.]
Mt. writes as if they professed that
the case had actually occurred : ἦσαν
δὲ παρ᾽ ἡμῖν ἑ. ἀδ. The position of
ἑπτά draws attention to the number.
Victor is probably right : ἔπλασαν...
ἑπτά...ὥστε ἐκ περιουσίας κωμῳδῆσαι
τὴν ἀνάστασιν. Ἀποθνῄσκων, at his
death ; for the connexion of this pres.

part. with ἀφῆκεν see Burton, § 122 :
in the next verse ἀποθνῄσκων...ἀφῆκεν
becomes without change of sense
ἀπέθανεν...καταλιπών (Burton § 138).
Ὡσαύτως καί—so the words are best
arranged (cf. D, καὶ ὡσαύτως ἔλαβον
αὐτὴν οἱ ζ᾽ καὶ οὐκ ἀφῆκαν σπέρμα).
For ὡσ. καί see xiv. 31, 1 Cor. xi. 25,
1 Tim. v. 25. Οἱ ἑπτά : the ἑπτὰ
ἀδελφοί mentioned above (*v.* 20).
Ἔσχατον is used adverbially as in
Num. xxxi. 2, Deut. xxxi. 27, 29
(אַחֲרֹן), and with πάντων in 1 Cor.
xv. 8 ; Mt., Lc. substitute the more
usual ὕστερον. The wife survived all
the seven. She too (καί) was now
dead (ἀπέθανεν); so that the interest
of the case had passed over to the
future life, if such there were.

23. ἐν τῇ ἀναστάσει κτλ.] The drift
of their story at length appears ; it
is supposed to present a difficulty

24 ἐπτὰ ἔσχον αὐτὴν γυναῖκα. ²⁴ἔφη αὐτοῖς ὁ Ἰησοῦς
Οὐ διὰ τοῦτο πλανᾶσθε, μὴ εἰδότες τὰς γραφὰς μηδὲ
25 τὴν δύναμιν τοῦ θεοῦ ; ²⁵ὅταν γὰρ ἐκ νεκρῶν ἀνα-

24 εφη αυτοις ο I. אBCLΔ 33 syrᵖᵉˢʰ me] και αποκριθεις (vel αποκριθεις δε) ο I.
ειπεν αυτοις A(D)ΧΓΠΣΦ minᵖˡ b (c ff) q vg syrʳ⁽ˢⁱⁿ⁾ʰᶜˡ arm go aeth | om ου Δ a c i k
(syrˢⁱⁿ?) the | μη ειδοτες] μη γινωσκοντες D Or | του θεου] +οιδατε D

to believers in the Resurrection. Τῇ
ἀναστάσει: 'that resurrection for which,
on the shewing of the Pharisees, we are
to look'; for the art. cf. Lc. xiv. 14,
Jo. xi. 24, Acts xvii. 18, 1 Cor. xv. 40.
Mt. and Lc. insert οὖν: in Mc. the
moral of the story is produced with
characteristic bluntness (cf. v. 14 ἔξεστιν δοῦναι) without conjunction or
preface as in Mt. xxii. 17. Crude
as the question may seem, it must
have offered serious difficulties to
the Pharisees, who held materialistic
views as to the future state : cf.
Enoch x. 17 ἔσονται ζῶντες ἕως γεν-
νήσωσιν χιλιάδας, and Sohar cited by
Schöttgen on Mt. xxii. 28, "mulier illa
quae duobus nupsit in hoc mundo,
priori restituitur." For ἔχειν τινὰ
γυναῖκα cf. Mt. iii. 9, Acts xiii. 5,
Phil. iii. 17. On 'Western' readings
in this verse see WH., Notes, p. 26.
24. οὐ διὰ τοῦτο πλανᾶσθε κτλ.]
'Is not this the reason why ye go
wrong, that ye know not &c.?' The
difficulty which seemed to these men
insuperable was due to an error on
their own part, and the error was
the result of ignorance. For οὐ πλανᾶσθε; (cf. 1 Cor. xv. 33) Mt. has the
direct πλανᾶσθε, but the question is
characteristic of our Lord's manner ;
cf. οὐδὲ (οὐκ)...ἀνέγνωτε (vv. 10, 26).
On διὰ τοῦτο...μὴ εἰδ. see WM., p. 201;
μὴ follows δ. τ., because the ignorance
is viewed relatively to the error and
not simply as matter of fact (οὐκ εἰδ.,
cf. 1 Regn. ii. 12, Prov. vii. 23). The
ignorance was twofold : (1) ignorance
of Scripture, (2) ignorance of GOD
(cf. 1 Cor. xv. 34 ἀγνωσίαν θεοῦ τινὲς
ἔχουσιν); both inexcusable in members of the priesthood, as most of

these men probably were (see v. 18).
The Lord deals with the second of
these causes of error first, since it
is fundamental. For μή...μηδέ cf. vi.
11, xiii. 15 (WM., p. 612 f.), and for αἱ
γραφαί, 'the contents of the canon,'
see xiv. 49, Lc. xxiv. 27, 32, 44 f.
25. ὅταν γὰρ ἐκ νεκρῶν κτλ.] Mt.
ἐν γὰρ τῇ ἀναστάσει. Lc. recasts the
sentence : οἱ δὲ καταξιωθέντες τοῦ αἰῶνος ἐκείνου τυχεῖν καὶ τῆς ἀναστάσεως
τῆς ἐκ νεκρῶν. The Sadducees (and
the Pharisees also, so far as they
connected marriage and the propagation of the race with the future life)
shewed themselves incapable of con-
ceiving a power which could produce
an order entirely different from any
within their experience. They assumed either that GOD could not
raise the dead, or that He could raise
them only to a life which would be
a counterpart of the present, or even
more replete with material pleasures.
Thpht.: ὑμεῖς γὰρ δοκεῖτε ὅτι πάλιν
τοιαύτη κατάστασις σωματικωτέρα μέλλει εἶναι· οὐκ ἔστι δέ...ἀλλὰ θειοτέρα
τις...καὶ ἀγγελική. Compare St Paul's
answer to the question πῶς ἐγείρονται
οἱ νεκροί, ποίῳ δὲ σώματι ἔρχονται;
(1 Cor. xv. 35 ff.). Νεκροί is anarthrous in the phrase ἐκ νεκρῶν, with the
single exception of Eph. v. 14; on the
other hand we find ἀπὸ τῶν ν., Mt.
xiv. 2, xxvii. 64, xxviii. 7 (ἀπὸ ν., Lc.
xvi. 30, but in another connexion);
μετὰ τῶν ν., Lc. xxiv. 5; περὶ τῶν
ν. infra, v. 26; ὑπὲρ τῶν ν., 1 Cor.
xv. 29. Ὅταν...ἀναστῶσιν, 'when they
shall have risen,' i.e. in the life which
will follow the resurrection. Γαμίζε-
σθαι, γαμίσκεσθαι (Lc. has both forms,
cf. Blass, Gr. p. 52), of the woman,

στῶσιν, οὔτε γαμοῦσιν οὔτε γαμίζονται, ἀλλ᾽ εἰσὶν
ὡς ἄγγελοι [οἱ] ἐν τοῖς οὐρανοῖς. ²⁶περὶ δὲ τῶν νεκρῶν, 26
ὅτι ἐγείρονται, οὐκ ἀνέγνωτε ἐν τῇ βίβλῳ Μωυσέως

25 ουτε...ουτε] ου...ουδε D | γαμιζονται אBCGLUΔΨ 1 124 209 al^nonn] γαμισ-
κονται ΕΚΜSVΧΓΠΣΦ Or εκγαμισκονται AFH min^nonn εκγαμιζονται min^perpauc γαμι-
ζουσιν D 2^pe | αγγελοι] pr οι B Or+θεου 33 61 69 2^pe 1071 al^nonn vg^ed aeth | οι εν τ.
ουρ. ΑBEGHSVΧΓΦΨ min^mu] om οι אCDFKLMUΔΠΣ min^satmu   26 των νεκρων]
pr της αναστασεως 13 33 69 124 346 arm | βυβλω D | Μωσεως ACEFGHLSUVΧΓΦΨ
min^pl

'to be given in marriage'; both are
words of the later Gk.; for γαμίζειν
cf. I Cor. vii. 38 (WSchm., p. 126).
Γαμεῖν is used here, in its proper sense,
of the man; see note on x. 11 f., and
cf. Mt. xxiv. 38, Lc. xvii. 27.

ἀλλ᾽ εἰσὶν ὡς ἄγγελοι [οἱ] ἐν τοῖς οὐ.]
Similarly Mt.; Lc., who paraphrases
throughout: οὐδὲ γὰρ ἀποθανεῖν ἔτι
δύνανται, ἰσάγγελοι γάρ εἰσιν, καὶ υἱοί
εἰσιν θεοῦ (cf. Gen. vi. 2, Heb. and
LXX. cod. B) τῆς ἀναστάσεως υἱοὶ ὄντες.
See Dalman, Worte, i. p. 161. Their
equality with angels consists in their
deliverance from mortality and its
consequences: cf. Phil. de sacrif.
Ab. et Cain 2, Ἀβραὰμ ἐκλιπὼν
τὰ θνητὰ προστίθεται τῷ θεοῦ λαῷ
καρπούμενος ἀφθαρσίαν, ἴσος ἀγγέλοις
γεγονώς. Comp. Enoch xv. 4 ff. for
the Jewish view of the freedom of
Angels from the conditions which
render marriage necessary for mankind. The reference to angels meets
in passing another Sadducean tenet;
the Lord was with the Pharisees in
their maintenance of the doctrine of
Angels and spirits, as well as in their
belief in a future resurrection (cf. Acts
xxiii. 6 ff.). On Christ's doctrine of
the future life as disclosed in this passage see Latham, Service of Angels,
pp. 40 ff., 50 ff. Even if we omit οἱ
(vv. ll.), ἐν τοῖς οὐρανοῖς is to be connected with ἄγγελοι (cf. xiii. 32), not
with εἰσίν.

26. περὶ δὲ τῶν νεκρῶν κτλ.] 'It
is, then, possible for human life to
exist under new conditions which

will remove the supposed difficulty.
Now as to the general question.
God can create new conditions under
which a risen life may be possible.
But is there reason for supposing
that He will do so? The law itself,
rightly understood, implies that He
will.' For περί, quod attinet ad, at
the head of a sentence, introducing
the subject which is to be stated or
discussed, see WM., p. 467. Ἐγείρονται, "they rise," the 'gnomic
present'; see Burton § 12, and cf.
I Cor. xv. 16 εἰ γὰρ νεκροὶ οὐκ ἐγείρονται (see ib. 13 εἰ δὲ ἀνάστασις
νεκρῶν οὐκ ἔστιν). The appeal is now
to the γραφαί—οὐκ ἀνέγνωτε; For the
formula see ii. 25, Mt. xii. 5, xix. 4,
xxi. 16, 42, Lc. vi. 3.

ἐν τῇ βίβλῳ Μωυσέως κτλ.] The
Torah is elsewhere in the N.T. called
νόμος Μωυσέως (Lc. xxiv. 44, Jo. i. 45,
Acts xxviii. 23) or simply Μωυσῆς
(Lc. xvi. 29); but βίβλος or βιβλίον
M. is frequent in the LXX. (2 Chron.
xxxv. 12, I Esdr. v. 48, vii. 6, 9,
Tob. vi. 13, vii. 12 (א)); for a similar
use of βίβλος in the N.T. see Lc. iii.
4 ἐν βίβλῳ λόγων Ἠσαΐου, Acts vii. 42
ἐν β. τῶν προφητῶν. The Lord refers,
as the Sadducees referred, to the
Pentateuch, the authority of which
could not be disputed by any Jewish
party; on the attitude of the sect
towards the later books see Dr
Taylor's remarks, Sayings, p. 128 f.
and cf. Ryle, Canon, p. 175. In
adopting the ordinary title of the
Pentateuch the Lord does not of

ἐπὶ τοῦ βάτου πῶς εἶπεν αὐτῷ ὁ θεὸς λέγων Ἐγὼ
ὁ θεὸς Ἀβραὰμ καὶ θεὸς Ἰσαὰκ καὶ θεὸς Ἰακώβ;
27 ²⁷οὐκ ἔστιν θεὸς νεκρῶν ἀλλὰ ζώντων· πολὺ πλανᾶσθε.

26 του βατου ℵABCLXΓΠΦ minᵖˡ] της β. DMΣΨ minⁿᵒⁿⁿ Or | πως ℵBCLUΔΨ
minⁿᵒⁿⁿ] ως ADXΓΠΣ minᵖˡ Or | εγω]+ειμι MUΔ minⁿᵒⁿⁿ latt syrᵖᵉˢʰ arm aegg go
aeth Or½ | θεος 3°, 4° BD Orᵇⁱˢ] pr o ℵACLXΓΔΠΣΦΨ minᵒᵐⁿ ᵛⁱᵈ Orˡ   27 θεος] pr o
ℵACEFGHMᵗˣᵗSUVΓΨ minᵖˡ Orˡ+θεος 13 33 69 108 124 346 736 alˢᵃᵗ ᵐᵘ (om
BDKLMᵐᵍXˢⁱˡ ΔΠ alⁿᵒⁿⁿ) | ζωντων] pr θεος EGHMᵗˣᵗSVΓΦ minᵖᵉʳᵐᵘ q syrʰᶜˡ aeth |
πολυ πλανασθε] pr υμεις ουν ADXΓΠΣΦ minᵒᵐⁿ ᵛⁱᵈ lattᵛᵗ ᵖˡ ᵛᵍ syrrᵖᵉˢʰ ʰᶜˡ (arm) the aeth
υμεις δε G 1 229 299 604 2ᵖᵉ syrˢⁱⁿ (arm)

course dogmatically teach the Mosaic authorship of the Law or of any part of it in its existing form; see note on i. 44. Ἐπὶ τοῦ βάτου, "on the bousche" (Wycliffe), "in the busshe" (Tindale); rather "in the place concerning the bush" (R.V.), or "at 'the Bush,'" i.e. in the section of the Law which relates to the burning bush (Exod. iii. 1 ff., where an open *parashah* still begins); a similar indication of a "pre-Talmudic system of sections" (Ryle, p. 236) occurs in Rom. xi. 2 ἐν Ἠλείᾳ, where see SH. Βάτος is masc. in the LXX. (Exod. iii. 2 ff., Deut. xxxiii. 16), but fem. in Lc. xx. 37, Acts vii. 35 (cf. Moeris: ὁ β. ἀττικῶς· ἡ β. ἑλληνικῶς). The word belongs to the numerous class of Homeric nouns which re-appear in Aristophanes and the comedians (Kennedy, *Sources*, p. 77 f.).

πῶς εἶπεν αὐτῷ ὁ θεός] For this use of πῶς cf. v. 16, Acts ix. 27, xi. 13, xx. 18. Cf. Mt., τὸ ῥηθὲν ὑμῖν ὑπὸ τοῦ θεοῦ: Lc., less exactly, Μωυσῆς ἐμήνυσεν, attributing the Divine words to the supposed author of the book. The words were addressed to Moses (αὐτῷ Mc.), but the revelation they contained was for the latest generation of Israel (ὑμῖν Mt.).

ἐγὼ ὁ θεὸς Ἀ. καὶ θεὸς Ἰσ. καὶ θεὸς Ἰακ.] Exod. iii. 6, LXX., ἐγώ εἰμι ὁ θεὸς τοῦ πατρός σου, θεὸς Ἀ. κτλ. The article is not repeated, for the Person is One; the repetition of θεός on the other hand emphasises the distinct relation in which God stands

to each individual saint. In quoting this passage the Lord argues thus: ' In this place God reveals Himself as standing in a real relation to men who were long dead. But the living God cannot be in relation with any who have ceased to exist; therefore the patriarchs were still living in His sight at the time of the Exodus; dead to the visible world, they were alive unto God.' Origen: ἄτοπον λέγειν ὅτι ὁ θεὸς ὁ εἰπών Ὁ ὤν, τοῦτό μοί ἐστιν ὄνομα, τῶν οὐδαμῶς ὄντων θεός ἐστιν...ζῶσιν ἄρα αἰσθανόμενοι τοῦ θεοῦ καὶ τῆς χάριτος αὐτοῦ ὁ Ἀβραὰμ καὶ ὁ Ἰσαὰκ καὶ ὁ Ἰακώβ. This argument establishes the immortality of the soul, but not, at first sight or directly, the resurrection of the body. But the resurrection of the body follows, when it is understood that the body is a true part of human nature; comp. Westcott, *Gospel of the Resurrection*, pp. 140 ff., 155 ff. God would not leave men with whom He maintained relations in an imperfect condition; the living soul must in due time recover its partner; the death of the body could only be a suspension of vital activities which in some other form would be resumed. For partial parallels in Rabbinical writings see J. Lightfoot on Mt. xxii. 32.

27. οὐκ ἔστιν θεός κτλ.] 'He is not a God of dead men, but of living.' Lc. adds πάντες γὰρ αὐτῷ ζῶσιν. Death is a change of relation to the world and to men; it does not change our

²⁸ §Καὶ προσελθὼν εἷς τῶν γραμματέων ἀκούσας 28 § syrʰⁱᵉʳ
αὐτῶν συνζητούντων, εἰδὼς ὅτι καλῶς ἀπεκρίθη αὐτοῖς, ἐπηρώτησεν αὐτόν Ποία ἐστὶν ἐντολὴ πρώτη

28 των γραμματεων] γραμματευς F minᵖᵃᵘᶜ | ακουσας] ακουων 1 28 299 ακουοντων
2ᵖᵉ | om αυτ. συνζ. ειδως k (syrˢⁱⁿ) | ειδως ℵᶜΑΧΓΔ𝝭 minᵖˡ aegg] ιδων ℵ*CDLΣΦ 1 13
28 69 604 1071 alⁿᵒⁿⁿ a b c ff i q vg syrrᵖᵉˢʰ ʰᶜˡ arm | ποια] pr διδασκαλε D b c ff i k |
πρωτη πασων εντολη Μ* minᵐᵘ

relation to GOD. There are two striking parallels in 4 Maccabees, vii. 19 οἱ
πιστεύοντες ὅτι θεῷ οὐκ ἀποθνήσκουσιν·
ὥσπερ γὰρ οἱ πατριάρχαι ἡμῶν Ἀβραάμ,
Ἰσαάκ, Ἰακώβ, ἀλλὰ ζῶσιν τῷ θεῷ: xvi.
25 ἰδόντες ὅτι διὰ τὸν θεὸν ἀποθανόντες
ζῶσιν τῷ θεῷ, ὥσπερ Ἀβραὰμ καὶ
Ἰσαὰκ καὶ Ἰακὼβ καὶ πάντες οἱ πατριάρχαι. Lightfoot on Mt. quotes Rabbinical sayings to the same purpose.
With the anarthrous νεκρῶν, ζώντων cf.
1 Pet. iv. 3 κρῖναι ζῶντας καὶ νεκρούς.

πολὺ πλανᾶσθε] Mc. only. Not
only were they in error, but their
error was a great and far-reaching
one. The priestly aristocrats submitted to the reproof in silence (Mt.
ἐφίμωσεν τοὺς Σαδδουκαίους) ; the enthusiasm of the people rose yet higher
(Mt. ἐξεπλήσσοντο). Yet it was not a
logical victory which the Lord desired, but the recovery of the erring
(Mt. xviii. 12 f.). Πλανᾶν, πλανᾶσθαι,
are used in a moral sense by the LXX.
from Deut. iv. 19 onwards, esp. in the
sapiential books and the Prophets,
and by the N.T. writers exclusively.

28—34. THE SCRIBE'S QUESTION
(Mt. xxii. 34—40).

28. προσελθὼν εἷς τῶν γραμματέων]
Acc. to Mt. (xxii. 34) the discomfiture
of the Sadducees led to a fresh
gathering of their rivals, and the
question was proposed by the scribe
with a distinctly hostile purpose
(ἐπηρώτησεν εἷς...πειράζων: cf. Jerome
on Mt.: "non quasi discipulus sed
quasi tentator accedit"). In Lc., on
the other hand, some of the Scribes
openly approve of the Lord's answer
to the Sadducees (xx. 39), and Mc.

clearly regards the scribe who questioned the Lord as free from malicious
intent (v. 34). The Greek commentators endeavour to reconcile the two
traditions: cf. Victor: ἠρώτησε μὲν
γὰρ πειράζων παρὰ τὴν ἀρχήν, ἀπὸ δὲ
τῆς ἀποκρίσεως ὠφεληθεὶς ἐπηνέθη.
But the attempt cannot be regarded
as satisfactory. Doubtless the repulse of the Sadducees was received
by the Pharisees with very mixed
feelings; the majority, in whom hatred
of Jesus was stronger than zeal for a
dogma, were irritated by His fresh
victory; a few, among whom was this
scribe, were constrained to admire,
even if they were willing to criticise,
the Rabbi who, though not Himself a
Pharisee, surpassed the Pharisees as a
champion of the truth. Εἷς τῶν γρ.,
Mt. εἷς ἐξ αὐτῶν (sc. τῶν Φαρισαίων)
νομικός (see note on ii. 6); for another
instance of a solitary scribe approaching our Lord without hostile intentions
see Mt. viii. 19, and cf. Jo. iii. 1 f. The
Pharisees as a body were not present
during the interview with the Sadducees; this man had heard the
discussion (ἀκ. αὐτ. συνζητούντων,
Wycliffe, "sekynge togidere"), and
recognised (εἰδώς) the excellence of
the Lord's answer (καλῶς ἀπεκρίθη).
When they were gone he stepped
forward (προσελθών), and put another
question. Ἀκούσας αὐτῶν κτλ. supplies
the motive of προσελθών, and through
εἰδώς of ἐπηρώτησεν also (cf. Meyer).
For the construction ἀκούσας αὐτῶν
συνζ. cf. Acts x. 46, xi. 7 and WM.,
p. 434.

ποία ἐστὶν ἐντολὴ πρώτη πάντων;]

29 πάντων; ²⁹ἀπεκρίθη ὁ Ἰησοῦς ὅτι Πρώτη ἐστίν
Ἄκουε, Ἰσραήλ, Κύριος ὁ θεὸς ἡμῶν Κύριος εἷς
¶ c 30 ἐστιν¶. ³⁰καὶ ἀγαπήσεις Κύριον τὸν θεόν σου ἐξ
ὅλης [τῆς] καρδίας σου καὶ ἐξ ὅλης τῆς ψυχῆς σου καὶ
ἐξ ὅλης τῆς διανοίας σου καὶ ἐξ ὅλης τῆς ἰσχύος σου.

28 om παντων D 604 2ᴾᵉ a b c ff i k syrˢⁱⁿ arm   29 απεκριθη ο I.] ο δε I.
απεκριθη αυτω ΑϹΧΓΠΣΦ minᴾˡ vg syrʰᵉˡ go ο δε I. ειπεν αυτω 1 28 69 299 346 2ᴾᵒ
(a) k syrᵖᵉˢʰ arm αποκριθεις δε ο I. ειπεν αυτω D (604) b ff i q (syrˢⁱⁿ the aeth) | om
οτι D 1 28 91 209 299 2ᴾᵉ a b c ff i q syrˢⁱⁿᵖᵉˢʰ arm | om οτι πρωτη εστιν 229 k | πρωτη
εστιν אBLΔ me] παντων πρωτη D(Χ) 91 (209) (299) 2ᴾᵉ a b i syrˢⁱⁿ arm πρωτον παντων
28 (604) πρωτη παντων εντολη ΑϹΚΜ*²ΥΠΣΦ 33 alˢᵃᵗ ᵐᵘ syrʰᵉˡ go πρωτη παντων (vel
πασων) των εντολων ΕFGHS(V)Γ minᴾˡ syrᵖᵉˢʰ | ημων] υμων 2ᴾᵉ alⁿᵒⁿⁿ i σου Ψ minᵖᵃᵘᶜ
c me aeth | κυριος 2°] om F minᵖᵃᵘᶜ a b k syrˢⁱⁿ θεος vg Cyprᵇⁱˢ   30 om της 1°,
2°, 3° B (om της 1° etiam D*ΧΨ) | om και εξ ολης τ. ψυχης σου ΚΠ* minᵖᵃᵘᶜ k | om
και εξ ολης της διανοιας σου DH minᵖᵉʳᵖᵃᵘᶜ c ff k syrʰⁱᵉʳ Cyprᵗᵉʳ | σου ult]+αυτη πρωτη
(+παντων) εντολη ΑD(ΚΥ)ΧΓ(Π)Σ(Φ) minᵒᵐⁿ ᵛⁱᵈ latᵉˣᶜ ᵃ syrˢⁱⁿᵖᵉˢʰ ʰᶜˡ arm go

Mt. ποία ἐντ. μεγάλη ἐν τῷ νόμῳ; The
Vg. (interrogavit eum quod esset
primum omnium mandatum) and
the R.V. " what commandment is the
first of all?" overlook the distinction
between ποῖος and τίς which, though
faint, still exists in the N.T. (see note
on xi. 28). The Lord is not asked to
select one commandment out of the
Ten, but to specify a class of commandments, or a particular commandment as representative of a class, to
which the priority belongs; cf. Rom.
iii. 27 διὰ ποίου νόμου; τῶν ἔργων;
οὐχί, ἀλλὰ διὰ νόμου πίστεως. Πρώτη
πάντων, not πασῶν: as Alford points
out, πρῶτος πάντων is treated as a
single word—"first-of-all"; cf. WM.,
p. 222, Blass (Gr. p. 108), who explains
the construction by "a stereotyped
use of the neuter πάντων to intensify
the superlative." The construction is
perhaps without an exact parallel in
class. or contemporary Gk.; see Field,
Notes, p. 36, who disputes Fritzsche's
reference to Ar. Av. 471, and seeks an
example in Chrysostom.

29. πρώτη ἐστίν Ἄκουε κτλ.] The
Lord replies in the words of Deut. vi.
4 ff., part of the first clause of the
Shema, which was recited daily by

every Jew and written on the minia-
ture roll which the scribe carried in
his phylactery (Schürer, II. ii. pp. 84,
113). The words had thus already
been singled out by tradition as of
primary importance; the Shema was
regarded as including the Decalogue
(Taylor, Sayings, pp. 52, 132); and
the passage from Deut. vi. stood in
the forefront of this fundamental
confession of faith and duty, as if
claiming by its very position the
title of ἐντολὴ πρώτη πάντων: cf.
Wünsche, neue Beiträge, p. 399. On
the various renderings proposed for
יְהוָֹה אֱלֹהֵינוּ יְהוָֹה אֶחָד see Driver,
Deuteronomy p. 89, who decides in
favour of " J. our GOD is one J."

30. ἐξ ὅλης [τῆς] καρδίας κτλ.] The
present B text of the LXX. gives ἐξ
ὅλης τῆς διανοίας σου κ. ἐ. ὅ. τῆς ψυχῆς
σου κ. ἐ. ὅ. τῆς δυνάμεώς σου, but
διανοίας is a correction by the second
hand, probably for καρδίας, which is
the reading of codd. A and F. Καρδία
and διάνοια are often interchanged in
the LXX. and its MSS. (cf. Hatch, Essays,
p. 104), and almost the same may be
said of δύναμις and ἰσχύς. The three
Heb. words מְאֹד‎, נֶפֶשׁ‎, לֵבָב‎ together

³¹ δευτέρα αὕτη 'Αγαπήσεις τὸν πλησίον σου ὡς 31
σεαυτόν. μείζων τούτων ἄλλη ἐντολὴ οὐκ ἔστιν.

31 δευτερα] pr και Α(D)ΧΠ al^{pl} c (k) q syrr go arm aeth pr η ΔΨ | αυτη] ομοια
αυτη ΑΧΓΠΣΦ syrr^{sin pesh} arm ομ. ταυτη D 69 | σεαυτον] εαυτον ΗΧΠ*Σ min^{sat mu} |
μειζων…εστιν] hoc est magnum mandatum a

represent the sum of the powers which
belong to the composite life of man;
the first two are frequently combined,
especially in Deut., where the writer
desires to enforce "the devotion of
the whole being to GOD," the 'heart'
being in the psychology of the ancient
Hebrews the organ of intellect, and
the 'soul' of the desires and affections"
(Driver, Deuteronomy, pp. 73, 91);
the third word (used in this sense
only here and in 2 Kings xxiii. 25)
adds the thought of the forces which
reside in these parts of human nature,
and in the body through which they
act. See the scholastic treatment of
this subject by Thomas Aq., p. 2,
q. 27, art. 5; q. 44, art. 4 f.

Mt. follows the Heb. in substituting ἐν (בְּ) for ἐξ, ter; on the other
hand he agrees with Mc. in giving
the doublet καρδίας, διανοίας, and
altogether omits the important clause
וּבְכָל מְאֹדֶךָ. Lc. (in another context,
x. 27) combines Mt.'s presentation of
the passage with Mc.'s (ἐξ ὅλης καρδίας
σου καὶ ἐν ὅλῃ τῇ ψυχῇ σου, καὶ ἐν ὅλῃ
τῇ ἰσχύι σου, καὶ ἐν ὅλῃ τῇ διανοίᾳ σου).
Regarded from one point of view,
love dwells in the heart; from another,
it proceeds from it, overflowing into
the life of men.

On καρδία see ii. 6, note, iii. 5, vi.
52, vii. 19, 21; διάνοια, so far as it is
distinguishable from καρδία (cf. Lc. i.
51 διανοίᾳ καρδίας), is "the process of
rational thought" (Westcott on 1 Jo.
v. 20), or the faculty of thought itself,
the mind (cf. Plat. legg. 916 A ἢ κατὰ
τὸ σῶμα ἢ κατὰ τὴν διάνοιαν, and see
Cremer s.v.); see 1 Pet. i. 13, 2 Pet.
iii. 1.

'Αγαπήσεις, diliges, prescribes the
higher love which is due to GOD, and

under GOD to man regarded as His
creature (v. 31); cf. Trench, syn. xii.
It is ἀγάπη, not φιλία, which is the
sum of human duty. Neither the
LXX. nor the N.T. uses φιλεῖν of the
love due to GOD, in respect of His
essential Being; yet cf. Prov. viii. 17,
1 Cor. xvi. 22.

31. δευτέρα αὕτη κτλ.] Mt. adds
ὁμοία. In the question no reference
has been made to a second commandment, but the Lord adds it in order
to complete the summary of human
duty; cf. Victor: περὶ μιᾶς ἐρωτηθεὶς
οὐκ ἀπεσιώπησε τὴν ἀχώριστον αὐτῆς.
The citation is from Lev. xix. 18
LXX., verbatim; the passage is quoted
again in Jas. ii. 8 (where see Mayor's
note), Rom. xiii. 9, Gal. v. 14. As
Bp Lightfoot points out (Gal. l.c.), "in
the original text the word 'neighbour'
is apparently restricted to the Jewish
people," for τοῖς υἱοῖς τοῦ λαοῦ σου
occurs in the first member of the
parallelism; that Jesus used it in
the widest sense is clear from Lc. x.
29 ff. So understood the saying was
a recapitulation of the second part of
the Decalogue: see Rom. l.c. τὸ γάρ Οὐ
μοιχεύσεις κτλ. (cf. note on Mc. vii. 21)
καὶ εἴ τις ἑτέρα ἐντολή, ἐν τῷ λόγῳ
τούτῳ ἀνακεφαλαιοῦται: Gal. l.c. ὁ γὰρ
πᾶς νόμος ἐν ἑνὶ λόγῳ πεπλήρωται. On
the prominence given to it by Jewish
teachers see Wünsche on Mt. xxii. 39.
Acc. to Mt. the Lord added: ἐν ταύταις ταῖς δυσὶν ἐντολαῖς ὅλος (on ὅλος
see Hort, Jud. Chr., p. 21) ὁ νόμος
κρέμαται καὶ οἱ προφῆται. They were
the first two commandments because
they revealed the ultimate principles
of morality which it was the business
of the Law as a whole to enforce, and
on which the ripest teaching of the

32 ³²[καὶ] εἶπεν αὐτῷ ὁ γραμματεύς Καλῶς, διδάσκαλε,
§ ٦ ἐπ᾽ ἀληθείας §εἶπας ὅτι εἷς ἐστιν, καὶ οὐκ ἔστιν ἄλλος
33 πλὴν αὐτοῦ· ³³καὶ τὸ ἀγαπᾶν αὐτὸν ἐξ ὅλης [τῆς]
καρδίας καὶ ἐξ ὅλης τῆς συνέσεως καὶ ἐξ ὅλης τῆς
ἰσχύος, καὶ τὸ ἀγαπᾶν τὸν πλησίον ὡς ἑαυτὸν
περισσότερόν ἐστιν πάντων τῶν ὁλοκαυτωμάτων καὶ

32 και ειπεν] om και B syrrˢⁱⁿ ᵖᵉˢʰ aegg | ειπες א*DEFHLVXΔΠ² | εις εστιν]+(ο)
θεος (D)EF(G)H minˢᵃᵗ ᵐᵘ a b c ff i q vgᵉᵈ syrrˢⁱⁿ ʰᵉˡ⁽ᶜᵒʳʳ⁾ arm aegg | om αλλος D a
33 om και το αγαπαν...εαυτον k | της καρδιας] om της BUXΨ minᵖᵃᵘᶜ+σου אL
minᵖᵃᵘᶜ me | συνεσεως] δυναμεως D 2ᵖᵉ a b i q ισχνος 1 33 118 209 299 arm me+και
εξ ολης της ψυχης ADXΓΠΣΦ٦ minᵖˡ b c ff i q vg syrr⁽ˢⁱⁿ⁾ ᵖᵉˢʰ ʰᶜˡ the go aeth | και εξ
ολης της ισχνος] om D 33 b Hil εξ ολης τ. συνεσεως 1 118 209 299 arm me | εαυτον
BXΔ*ΠΣΦΨ٦ minᵖˡ a b c ff q vg] σεαυτον אADLSΓΔ² minᵖᵃᵘᶜ i k | περισσοτερον
אBLΔ 33] περισσοτερα Ψ om ABDXΓΠΨ minᵖˡ πλειον ADXΓΠΣΦ٦ minᶠᵉʳᵉ ᵒᵐⁿ |
om παντων arm

Prophets depended. As to the relative importance of the commandments
the Lord is content to say that these
fundamental laws of human life are
second to none—μείζων τούτων ἄλλη
ἐντολὴ οὐκ ἔστιν.

32. [καὶ] εἶπεν αὐτῷ ὁ γραμ. κτλ.]
This verse and the next two are
peculiar to Mc. Καλῶς, 'well said,' cf.
Jo. iv. 17, xiii. 13, and see note on
vii. 6; for ἐπ᾽ ἀληθείας cf. xii. 14. Ἐπ᾽
ἀλ. confirms καλῶς; the saying was
truly a fine one; Wycliffe, "in truthe
thou hast wel seide," R.V. "of a truth
...thou hast well said." Tindale, followed by Cranmer and A.V., connects
ἐπ᾽ ἀλ. with εἶπας ("well, master, thou
hast sayd the truthe"), but with less
probability. Ὅτι introduces the re-
hearsal of what the Lord had said,
"that" (R.V.), not "for" (A.V.); ὅτι
εἷς ἐστιν, "that He is one"; the Scribe
refrains from unnecessarily repeating
the Sacred Name. Οὐκ ἔστιν ἄλλος
πλὴν αὐτοῦ: an O.T. phrase, cf. Exod.
viii. 10 (6), Deut. iv. 35, Isa. xlv. 21.

33. καὶ τὸ ἀγαπᾶν...καὶ τὸ ἀγαπᾶν]
On ἀγαπᾶν see v. 30, note. The
repetition is due to a desire to
keep the two commandments separate. The scribe substitutes σύνεσις
for διάνοια and omits ψυχή. For
σύνεσις see Bp Lightfoot's note on
Col. i. 9, and the note on Mc. vii. 18
supra; according to Aristotle it
represents the critical side of the intellect (Eth. Nic. vi. 7 ἡ δὲ σ. κριτική)
which had special interest for men of
this class. From the scribe's ready
answer Bede gathers "inter scribas et
Pharisaeos quaestionem esse versatam
quod esset mandatum primum...qui-
busdam videlicet hostias et sacrificia
laudantibus, aliis vero maiore auctori-
tate fidem et dilectionis opera prae-
ferentibus." It is to the credit of this
scribe that he held the latter view.
Περισσότερόν ἐστιν κτλ.: the words
are based apparently on 1 Regn. xv.
22. Θυσίαι (זְבָחִים) are sacrifices in
general, ὁλοκαυτώματα (עֹלוֹת), eucharistic offerings, "nobilissima species
sacrificiorum" (Bengel): a more complete classification of the various
kinds of sacrifice is cited in Heb.
x. 5, from Ps. xxxix. (xl.) 7 (see
Westcott, Hebrews, p. 309). Περισσότερον, 'far more,' cf. vii. 36, xii.
40. For Rabbinical parallels to the
Scribe's saying see Wünsche ad l.

θυσιῶν. ³⁴καὶ ὁ Ἰησοῦς ἰδὼν αὐτὸν ὅτι νουνεχῶς 34
ἀπεκρίθη εἶπεν αὐτῷ Οὐ μακρὰν εἶ ἀπὸ τῆς βασιλείας
τοῦ θεοῦ. καὶ οὐδεὶς οὐκέτι ἐτόλμα αὐτὸν ἐπερωτῆσαι.
³⁵§Καὶ ἀποκριθεὶς ὁ Ἰησοῦς ἔλεγεν διδάσκων ἐν 35 § Tᵈ

33 θυσιων] pr των אLMΔ 13 28 33 69 2ᵖᵉ alᵐᵘ ᵛⁱᵈ   34 ιδων] ειδως Η*Ψ
minᵖᵃᵘᶜ | om αυτον 1° אDLΔ alⁿᵒⁿⁿ syrˢⁱⁿ arm | om ει א*ᶜ·ᵇ L | ουκετι] ουκ 61
1071 cˢᶜʳ

34. ἰδὼν αὐτὸν ὅτι κτλ.] Αὐτόν
forestalls the subject of the dependent
clause; cf. WM., p. 781. What the
Lord observed in reference to this
man was the intelligence displayed by
his answer. It was shewn not only
in accepting the Lord's judgement as
to the two primary commandments,
but in detecting and admitting the
principle on which the judgement
rested, viz. the superiority of moral
over ritual obligations. Νουνεχῶς, ἅπ.
λεγ. in Biblical Gk., occurs in Aristotle
and later writers, esp. Polybius, as
equivalent to νουνεχόντως (Lob. Phryn.
p. 599).

οὐ μακρὰν εἶ ἀπό κτλ.] For the
phrase οὐ μακρὰν εἶναι (ἀπέχειν, ὑπάρχειν) cf. Lc. vii. 6, Jo. xxi. 8, Acts xvii.
27. Under the old theocracy οἱ
μακράν are either exiled Jews (Isa.
lvii. 19), or the Gentiles (Eph. ii. 13);
distance from the new Kingdom is
measured neither by miles, nor by
ceremonial standards, but by spiritual
conditions. The man was to some
extent intellectually qualified for admission to the Kingdom; certainly he
had grasped one of its fundamental
principles. It would be interesting to
work out a comparison between this
scribe and the ἄρχων of x. 17 ff. In
both cases something was wanting to
convert admiration into discipleship.
If wealth was the bar in the one case,
pride of intellect may have been fatal
in the other. The mental acumen
which detects and approves spiritual
truth may, in the tragedy of human
life, keep its possessor from entering
the Kingdom of God. Bengel: "si

non procul es, intra; alias praestiterit
procul fuisse."

καὶ οὐδεὶς οὐκέτι ἐτόλμα κτλ.] After
this the policy of questioning Jesus
was abandoned; no one was bold
enough (ἐτόλμα, cf. Jo. xxi. 12, Jude 9)
to renew the attempt, and the Lord
continued His teaching for the short
remainder of His ministry in the
Temple without interruption. Mt.
places these words after the Lord's
question about David's Son, and adds
οὐδεὶς ἐδύνατο ἀποκριθῆναι αὐτῷ λόγον.
He had answered all their questions;
a single instance was enough to shew
that they could not answer His.

35—37ᵃ. THE LORD'S QUESTION
(Mt. xxii. 41—45, Lc. xx. 41—44).

35. καὶ ἀποκριθεὶς ὁ Ἰ. ἔλεγεν] On the
use of ἀποκρίνεσθαι where no question
precedes see ix. 5, 6, note. The
question which was now asked was in
fact a final answer to all opponents.
It was asked, according to Mt., in the
presence of the Pharisees and was in
fact addressed to them (συνηγμένων δὲ
τῶν Φ. ἐπηρώτησεν αὐτούς): the Lord
demands of them Τί ὑμῖν δοκεῖ περὶ
τοῦ χριστοῦ; and they answer "He is
David's Son." Mc.'s account of the
circumstances is different; the question is asked in the course of the
Lord's public teaching, which is resumed after He has silenced all His
adversaries (ἔλεγεν διδάσκων ἐν τῷ
ἱερῷ); and it is addressed, not to the
Scribes but to the people, who are
invited to consider one of the dicta
of the Scribes (πῶς λέγουσιν οἱ γρ.
κτλ.). Lc.'s εἶπεν δὲ πρὸς αὐτούς is
perhaps ambiguous, but in the ques-

τῷ ἱερῷ Πῶς λέγουσιν οἱ γραμματεῖς ὅτι ὁ χριστὸς
36 υἱὸς Δαυείδ ἐστιν; ³⁶ αὐτὸς Δαυείδ εἶπεν ἐν τῷ
πνεύματι τῷ ἁγίῳ Εἶπεν Κύριος τῷ κυρίῳ μου Κάθου
ἐκ δεξιῶν μου, ἕως ἂν θῶ τοὺς ἐχθρούς σου ὑποκάτω

36 αυτος] + γαρ ΑΧΓΠΣΦ⁷ minᵖˡ b i q vg syrrᵖᵉˢʰ ʰᶜˡ go aeth και αυτος Δ c d ff syrˢⁱⁿ
arm the και ουτος D | τω πνευματι τω αγιω אBDL(Tᵈ)UΔΨ 33 2ᵖᵉ aⁿᵒⁿⁿ] πνευματι
αγιω ΑΧΓΠΣΦ⁷ minᵖˡ | ειπεν 2°] λεγει ADEGHKM*SVΠΦ minᵐᵘ k q go | κυριος] pr o
אALTᵈΧΓΔΠ⁷ minᶠᵉʳᵉᵒᵐⁿ (om BD cˢᶜʳ) | καθου] καθισον B | υποκατω BDTᵈΨ 28 aegg]
υποποδιον אALΧΓΔΠΣΦ⁷ minᶠᵉʳᵉᵒᵐⁿ latt syrrˢⁱⁿ ᵖᵉˢʰ ʰᶜˡ arm go aeth

tion he follows the same tradition as
Mc. Πῶς λέγουσιν; 'how do they
make good their statement in view
of the fact about to be mentioned?'
Cf. I Cor. xv. 12, 15.

ὁ χριστὸς υἱὸς Δαυείδ ἐστιν] Cf. Jo.
vii. 42 οὐχ ἡ γραφὴ εἶπεν ὅτι ἐκ τοῦ
σπέρματος Δαυείδ...ἔρχεται ὁ χριστός;
The inference was drawn from such
passages as Ps. lxxxix. 3 ff., Is. xi. 1,
Jer. xxiii. 5 (cf. Edersheim, *Life*, ii.
pp. 724, 731). That the populace
recognised it as a truth was made
evident by their cries of ὡσαννὰ τῷ υἱῷ
Δαυείδ, but their convictions were
shared by the Scribes and indeed derived from them. Jesus does not on
the one hand dispute the inference,
or, on the other, press the identification; He contents Himself with
pointing out a difficulty, in the solution of which lay the key to the whole
problem of His person and mission.
On ὁ χριστός see viii. 29, and for υἱὸς
Δ., cf. x. 47, note.

36. αὐτὸς Δαυείδ εἶπεν κτλ.] The
difficulty is stated. It has to do with
the interpretation of a Psalm which
by common confession was Messianic
(Edersheim, ii. p. 720 f.). Ps. cx. is
assigned to David in the title (M.T.,
LXX.), and the attribution was probably undisputed in the first century, and
assumed by our Lord and His Apostles
(Acts ii. 34) on the authority of the
recognised guardians of the canon.
It is possible, however, that He mentions David simply as being the re-
puted author of the Psalter (cf. Lc.,

Δ. ἐν βίβλῳ ψαλμῶν: Heb. iv. 7 ἐν
Δαυείδ λέγων, where see Westcott's
note). It cannot fairly be claimed
that our Lord is committed by His
hypothetical use of a current tradition to the Davidic authorship of the
Psalter or of the particular Psalm:
see Sanday, *Inspiration*, pp. 414, 420;
Gore, *Incarnation*, p. 196 f.; Kirkpatrick, *Psalms*, pp. 662 f. His whole
argument rests on the hypothesis that
the prevalent view was correct. Ἐν
τῷ πνεύματι τῷ ἁγίῳ, Mt. ἐν πνεύματι:
cf. Acts ii. 30 προφήτης ὑπάρχων, Acts
iv. 25 (אABE, see WH., *Notes*, p. 92,
Blass *ad l.*). On ἐν πνεύματι see i. 23,
note, and on τὸ πν. τὸ ἅγιον, i. 10, note;
the Psalm was θεόπνευστος (2 Tim. iii.
16), the writer was ὑπὸ πνεύματος ἁγίου
φερόμενος (2 Pet. i. 21). The phrase is
not otiose; it gives authority to the
words on which the question turns.
Ps. cx. opens with a specific claim
to inspiration in a high degree (נְאֻם
יְהֹוָה).

εἶπεν Κύριος τῷ κυρίῳ μου κτλ.] The
words are cited from Ps. cix. (cx.) 1,
LXX., with two verbal changes, Κύριος
(יְהֹוָה) for ὁ κύριος—a reading which
serves to differentiate the word from τῷ
κυρίῳ (לַאדֹנִי)—and ὑποκάτω for ὑποπόδιον. Lc. restores ὑποπόδιον, and
the same reading appears in Acts ii.
35, Heb. i. 13. That Mt. supports
Mc.'s ὑποκάτω against both LXX. and
Heb. points to the probability that
the quotation came into the Synoptic
tradition from a collection of *testi-*

τῶν ποδῶν σου. ³⁷αὐτὸς¶ Δαυεὶδ λέγει αὐτὸν κύριον, 37 ¶ ٦
καὶ πόθεν αὐτοῦ ἐστιν υἱός;
Καὶ ὁ πολὺς ὄχλος ἤκουεν αὐτοῦ §ἡδέως.¶   ³⁸καὶ 38 §⸌ᵉ𝔗ᵈ

37 αυτος Δ.] pr ει Σ i ff syrˢⁱⁿ arm + ουν ΑΧΓΠΣΦ٦ minᵖˡ b vg syrrᵖᵉˢʰ ʰᶜˡ* arm
aeth om αυτος Σ b c syrˢⁱⁿ | Δαυειδ]+εν πνευματι Ψ | λεγει] καλει Μ²UΦΨ 33 2ᵖᵒ 48ᵉᵛ
c syrᵖᵉˢʰ | ποθεν] πως ℵ* Μ*ΣΨ 1 13 28 33 69 1071 2ᵖᵉ alᵖᵃᵘᶜ b the aeth | ο πολυς]
om o ℵD 604 2ᵖᵉ | ηκουσεν ΜΓ minᵖᵃᵘᶜ vgᵉˣᶜ ᶠᵘ

monia: see note on i. 2. On the form κάθου = κάθησο see WM., p. 98: it is used freely in the LXX. and in Jas. ii. 3, and occurs in the Gk. of the New Comedy (Kennedy, *Sources*, p. 162). For ἐκ δεξιῶν cf. x. 37, note. Ὑποκάτω τῶν ποδῶν σου looks back to the scene in Josh. x. 24: as cited by our Lord the words suggest (1) the ignominious defeat of His enemies which had just been witnessed; (2) the final collapse of all opposition to His work (1 Cor. xv. 24 ff.). No other O.T. context is so frequently cited or alluded to by Apostolic and sub-apostolic writers. In the N.T. besides this context and its parallels see the direct quotations in Acts ii. 34, Heb. i. 13, v. 6, vii. 17, 21, and the references in Mc. xiv. 62 and parallels, 'xvi. 19,' Acts vii. 56, Rom. viii. 34, 1 Cor. xv. 24 ff., Eph. i. 20, Col. iii. 1, Heb. i. 3, viii. 1, x. 12 f., 1 Pet. iii. 22, Apoc. iii. 21. Of early patristic writings cf. esp. Barn. 12. 10 αὐτὸς προφητεύει Δαυειδ... Εἶπεν Κύριος κτλ. ἴδε πῶς Δαυειδ λέγει αὐτὸν κύριον καὶ υἱὸν οὐ λέγει; Clem. R. 1 Cor. 36; Justin, *ap.* i. 45, *dial.* 76, 83. On the question what our Lord, if he quoted the words in Hebrew or Aramaic, would have substituted for the Tetragrammaton, see Dalman, *Worte*, i., p. 149 f.

37. αὐτὸς Δαυεὶδ λέγει κτλ.] See note on *v.* 36. Κύριον is here = אֲדֹנִי, sovereign lord; cf. Symm., τῷ δεσπότῃ μου. The title does not involve Divine sovereignty, yet it was a natural inference that a descendant who was David's lord was also David's GOD: cf. *Did.* 10 ὡσαννὰ τῷ θεῷ Δαυίδ, and

Dr C. Taylor's remarks (*Teaching*, p. 160). The Lord, however, is content to point out the superficial difficulty: καὶ πόθεν (Mt. κ. πῶς) αὐτοῦ ἐστιν υἱός; whence (= how, cf. Dem. *de cor.* (242) οὐκ ἔστι ταῦτα...πόθεν;) can the Davidic sonship be maintained in the face of this inspired assertion of a lordship to which David himself submits? For λέγειν = καλεῖν cf. x. 18, Acts x. 28.

Justin (*dial.* 32, 56, 83) says that the Jews of his day sought to escape from the Christian use of Psalm cx. by applying it to Hezekiah. For the predominant Jewish interpretation of the Psalm, see Perowne, ii. p. 256 ff.; and for recent opinion on its date and purpose comp. Cheyne, *Origin of the Psalter*, p. 20 ff.

37ᵇ—40. DENUNCIATION OF THE SCRIBES (Mt. xxiii. 1 ff., Lc. xx. 45—47).

37. καὶ ὁ πολὺς ὄχλος κτλ.] Ὁ π. ὄχλος, the great mass of the people, as distinguished from a relatively small minority led by the priestly and professional classes (Mt. οἱ ὄχλοι, Lc. πᾶς ὁ λαός); cf. Jo. xii. 9, 12 ὁ ὄχλος πολύς, where however ὄχλος πολύς is treated as a single word (cf. Westcott *ad l.*). For examples of this use of ὁ πολὺς ὄχλ. see Field, *Notes*, p. 37, who cites Plutarch, Pausanias, Dio Chrys., Lucian, and Diod. Sic. At the end of the "day of questions" the Lord's popularity with the non-professional majority of His audience was unabated. Two successive days of teaching had exhausted neither His resources nor their delight. The discomfiture of the Scribes added flavour to the teaching; Euth.: ὡς ἡδέως διαλεγομένου καὶ

¶ go ἐν τῇ διδαχῇ αὐτοῦ ἔλεγεν Βλέπετε ἀπὸ ¶ τῶν γραμματέων τῶν θελόντων ἐν στολαῖς περιπατεῖν καὶ
39 ἀσπασμοὺς ἐν ταῖς ἀγοραῖς ³⁹καὶ πρωτοκαθεδρίας ἐν

38 και εν τη διδαχη αυτου ελεγεν ℵ(A)BL(XΓ)Δ(Π)Ψ 33 (al^pl) c k (l q vg) aegg^me(the)
syrr^pesh hcl go aeth] ο δε διδασκων (+αμα) ελ. αυτοις (D) 2^pe (a) b d i (arm) | των
θελοντων] και των τελωνων D | στολαις] στοαις syr^sin hier | ασπασμους] pr ζητουντων Ψ pr
φιλουντων 11 238 346 736 al^nonn c syr^sin pesh | αγοραις]+ποιεισθαι DΦ 2^pe

εὐχερῶς αὐτοὺς ἀνατρέποντος. For ἡ-
δέως ἤκουεν compare vi. 20—a suggestive parallel.

38. ἐν τῇ διδαχῇ αὐτοῦ ἔλεγεν] The
Lord's teaching proceeded without
further interruption; the few sentences which follow are specimens of
its character and manner. Mt. and
Lc. help us to realise the scene; the
Twelve form, as in Galilee, an inner
circle round the Lord, and to them
His teaching is primarily addressed,
though it is not without interest or
profit for the wider audience by which
they are surrounded (Mt. ἐλάλησεν
τοῖς ὄχλοις κ. τοῖς μαθηταῖς αὐτοῦ, Lc.
ἀκούοντος δὲ παντὸς τοῦ λαοῦ εἶπεν τοῖς
μαθ. αὐτοῦ). Mt. has preserved a far
larger part of this teaching than Mc.,
who gives only a fragment; the two
traditions are moreover independent;
Mc. and Lc. have only three clauses
in common with Mt. (καὶ ἀσπασμοὺς...
δείπνοις, cf. Mt. xxiii. 6, 7).

βλέπετε ἀπὸ τ. γραμματέων] For
the construction cf. viii. 15. In Mt.
the discourse opens with a recognition of the official character of the
Scribes, and of the duty of the people
towards them as authorised teachers.
It is their conduct only which is de-
nounced (Mt. xxiii. 2, 3). Τῶν θελόντων...περιπατεῖν καὶ ἀσπασμοὺς is
an instance (WM., p. 722) of the
oratio variata, due to the use in the
same sentence of the two constructions, θέλω with inf. and θέλω τι. Lc.
avoids it by changing the verb (θελόντων περιπατεῖν...φιλούντων ἀσπ.). For
θέλειν τι see Mt. ix. 13 (Hos. vi. 6).

Στολή, stola, is 'equipment,' 'apparel,'
and hence esp. 'long, flowing raiment,' a vestis talaris. The word
is much used in the LXX., chiefly as
the equivalent of בֶּגֶד or לְבוּשׁ, for
priestly or royal robes (e.g. Exod. xxxi.
10 τὰς στολὰς τὰς λειτουργικάς, Esth.
viii. 15 τὴν βασιλικὴν στολήν, 1 Macc.
vi. 15 ἔδωκεν αὐτῷ τὸ διάδημα καὶ τὴν
στολήν), and in the N. T. for dress
worn on festive or solemn occasions
(e.g. Lc. xv. 22, Apoc. vii. 9). On the
singular change of meaning which has
led to the use of the word to describe
a mere ἐπιτραχήλιον see DCA. ii. 1935.
Syr.^sin. and two MSS. of Syr.^hier. presuppose στοαῖς, which was also the
reading before Syr.^cu. in Lc. xx. 46.
The variant is tempting at first sight,
but besides its lack of extant Greek
support, it fails to yield a quite satisfactory sense. The colonnades of the
Precinct were not the resort of a
privileged class of teachers only;
Christ Himself and the Apostles used
them freely (Jo. x. 23, Acts iii. 11,
v. 12). Mt. adds other tokens of the
love of display: πλατύνουσι γὰρ τὰ
φυλακτήρια...μεγαλύνουσι τὰ κράσπεδα.
Not the use of dignified costume is
condemned by Christ, but the use of
it for the sake of ostentation (θελόντων
...περιπατεῖν); see note on v. 39.

καὶ ἀσπασμοὺς ἐν ταῖς ἀγοραῖς] Sc.
θελόντων (cf. previous note). For
instances of such salutations cf. ix. 15,
xv. 18. Mt. adds epexegetically καὶ
καλεῖσθαι ὑπὸ τῶν ἀνθρώπων 'Ραββεί:
other titles which the Scribes affected
were Abba (Mt. πατέρα μὴ καλέσητε),

ταῖς συναγωγαῖς καὶ πρωτοκλισίας ἐν τοῖς δείπνοις·
⁴⁰οἱ κατέσθοντες τὰς οἰκίας τῶν χηρῶν καὶ προφάσει 40

39 πρωτοκλησιας AFHKLUXΓ min^permu   40 οι κατεσθοντες B (-θιοντες אALΨ
rell)] οι κατεσθιουσιν D 1 91 299 | χηρων]+και ορφανων D 13 28 69 124 346 2^pe
a b c ff i q syr^hier | om και D latt^exc e syr^sin pesh arm

and *Moreh* (*ib.* μηδὲ κληθῆτε καθη-
γηταί); cf. J. Lightfoot on Mt. *ad l.*,
Schürer, II. i. p. 316 f., Wünsche, p. 400,
and on the other hand Dalman, *Worte*,
i. p. 279. The Lord did not refuse
such titles, which were pre-eminently
due to Him (Jo. xiii. 13), but He did
not demand or desire them (Jo. v. 41).
'Αγοραί in Jewish towns have been
mentioned in vi. 56, vii. 4; cf. Mt. xi.
16, xx. 3.

39. καὶ πρωτοκαθεδρίας...κ. πρωτο-
κλισίας] Sc. θελόντων. The Scribes
not only received but claimed the
place of honour at all gatherings,
social as well as religious. The πρωτοκαθεδρία seems to be the bench in
the synagogues in front of the ark
and facing the congregation, which
was reserved for officials and persons
of distinction (Edersheim, *Life*, i. p.
436); the πρωτοκλισία is the place of
the most honoured guest on the couch
of the *triclinium*; cf. Lc. xiv. 8, and
Jos. *ant.* xv. 2. 4 παρὰ τὰς ἑστιάσεις
προκατακλίνων. Acc. to the Talmud
the chief guest lay in the middle, if
there were three on a couch; if there
were two, he lay on the right side of
the couch (Edersheim, ii. p. 207).
Both πρωτοκαθεδρία and πρωτοκλισία
appear to be ἅπ. λεγόμενα: Fritzsche
prints τὰ πρωτοκλίσια in 2 Macc. iv.
21, but though the passage is obscure,
πρωτοκλήσια is probably right in that
context. The Vg. here resorts to a
paraphrase; *in primis cathedris se-
dere...et primos discubitus:* similarly
all the English versions.

ἐν τοῖς δείπνοις] Guests were entertained either at breakfast (Mt. xxii. 4,
Lc. xi. 38, xiv. 12) or at supper, but
chiefly at the evening meal (vi. 21, Lc.
xiv. 16, Jo. xii. 2, &c.).
40. οἱ κατέσθοντες κτλ.] For

κατέσθ. cf. iv. 4, and for the form
in -θειν, i. 6 (note). Like birds or
locusts settling on the ripe crops, these
men who claimed the reverence of
Israel devoured the property of their
brethren, even of those most deserving
of consideration. Οἰκία is apparently
used here like οἶκος, in the sense of
τὰ ὑπάρχοντα: cf. Gen. xlv. 18, Heb.
(BDB., p. 110) and LXX., and see
the example cited by Wetstein from
Aelian, *V. H.* iv. 2, οἰκίαν αὐξῆσαι καὶ
πλοῦτον: the phrase ἐσθίειν or κατεσθ.
οἶκον is frequent in the Odyssey, and
the Latin poets have the corresponding
comedere (*devorare*) *patrimonium*,
bona, &c. As the women who were
attracted by our Lord's teaching
ministered to Him of their substance
(xiv. 3, Lc. viii. 2, 3), so doubtless the
Pharisaic Rabbis had their female
followers, whose generosity they
grossly abused. Widows were specially the object of their attack;
Thpht.: ὑπεισήρχοντο γὰρ εἰς τὰς
ἀπροστατεύτους γυναῖκας ὡς δῆθεν προ-
στάται αὐτῶν ἐσόμενοι: for instances see
Schöttgen on Mt. xxiii. 14, who shews
that such a course was familiarly
known as פרושין מכת, *plaga Pha-
risaeorum*. The practice was expressly forbidden in the Law; Exod.
xxii. 22 (21) πᾶσαν χήραν καὶ ὀρφανὸν
οὐ κακώσετε. Οἱ κατέσθοντες is an
asyndeton due to the note-like form
in which Mc. presents the fragments
of the longer discourses which he has
preserved (cf. e.g. vi. 7 ff. notes).
Lc., who gives the paragraph otherwise word for word, sets the construction right (οἱ κατεσθίουσιν...καὶ
προσεύχονται); cf. cod. D here.

καὶ προφάσει μακρὰ προσ.] Vg. *sub
obtentu prolixae orationis;* Wycliffe,
"undir colour of long preier," and

μακρὰ προσευχόμενοι· οὗτοι λήμψονται περισσό-
¶ e τερον κρίμα.¶

41   ⁴¹ Καὶ καθίσας κατέναντι τοῦ γαζοφυλακίου ἐθεώρει πῶς ὁ ὄχλος βάλλει χαλκὸν εἰς τὸ γαζο-

40 ουτοι]+και 2ᵖᵉ οιτινες 13 28 69   41 καθισας] καθεζομενος D εστως 1 13 28 69
346 2ᵖᵉ alᵖᵃᵘᶜ syrrˢⁱⁿ ʰᵉˡ⁽ᵐᵍ⁾ ʰⁱᵉʳ arm Or+o ⁱ̄ˢ ADXΓΠ al minᵒᵐⁿ ᵛⁱᵈ | κατεναντι] απεναντι
BUΨ 33 alⁿᵒⁿⁿ κατενωπιον 13 346 | γαζοφυλακειου BG (hiat H) MSV²XΠ² alᵐᵘ | θεωρει
ℵ* Or¹ | βαλλει] εβαλλε 13 69 124 | om βαλλει...πλουσιοι D | γαζοφυλακειον EFGM
V*Ψ alᵐᵘ

similarly Tindale, Geneva and Rheims:
A.V., R.V., "for a pretence make long
prayers." Προφάσει is the opposite
of ἀληθείᾳ (cf. Phil. i. 18). Men who
devoured the property of widows
could pray only in pretence. The word
carries with it, however, the further
sense of 'pretext' (Lightfoot on Phil.
l.c., 1 Thess. ii. 5); under colour of
a reputation for piety due to the
length of their prayers (προσχήματι
εὐλαβείας, Thpht.) they insinuated
themselves into the good opinion of
their victims. On the whole subject
see Mt. vi. 5 ff., and cf. J. Lightfoot on
Mt. xxiii. 15, who quotes the Rabbinical saying "Long prayers make a
long life." The Lord on certain occasions prayed long (Lc. vi. 12), but
not προφάσει, or with mere πολυλογία
(Mt. l.c.).

οὗτοι λήμψονται κτλ.] Religious
teachers who use prayer as a means of
securing opportunities for committing
a crime, shall receive a sentence in
excess of that which falls to the lot
of the dishonest man who makes no
pretension to piety; to the sentence
on the robber will be added in their
case the sentence on the hypocrite.
Κρίμα is the definitive issue of a
judicial process (κρίσις); for περισσότερον κρίμα cf. Jas. iii. 1 μεῖζον κρ.
λημψόμεθα, and Lc. xii. 47 f.

41—44. THE WIDOW'S TWO MITES
(Lc. xxi. 1—4).

41. καθίσας κατέναντι τ. γ.] The
teaching in the Court of the Gentiles
had ceased, and the Lord with the

Twelve passed within the low marble
wall which fenced off the inner precinct from the intrusion of non-Israel-
ites; and entering the Court of the
Women (Edersheim, Temple, p. 24 ff.,
Geikie, Life, p. 408) sat down opposite
to (κατέναντι, facing, cf. xi. 2, xiii. 3;
for ἀπέναντι see Mt. xxvii. 24, 61) the
Treasury: cf. Jos. ant. xix. 6. 1 τῶν
ἱερῶν ἐντὸς ἀνεκρέμασεν περιβόλων ὑπὲρ
τὸ γαζοφυλάκιον. A Temple Treasury
(τὸ γαζοφυλάκιον, or τὰ γαζοφυλάκια)
is mentioned in 2 Esdr. xx. 37, 38,
xxiii. 4 f., and 2 Macc. iii. 6 ff., iv. 42,
v. 18, 4 Macc. iv. 3. In the Herodian
temple there were thirteen chests
placed at intervals round the walls of
the Court of the Women, and known
from their trumpet-like form as
הַשׁוֹפָרוֹת, each marked with the purpose to which the offerings it received
were to be devoted (Edersheim, p. 26);
to these, or rather to the colonnade
under which they were placed, the
name of 'The Treasury' seems to
have been given; see Hastings, D.B.
iv. 809. Comp. Jo. viii. 20 ἐν τῷ
γαζοφυλακίῳ...ἐν τῷ ἱερῷ. Γάζα and
γαζοφυλάκιον belong to the later Gk.

ἐθεώρει πῶς ὁ ὄχλος βάλλει κτλ.] The
Lord's attention is attracted by the
rattling of the coin down the throats
of the Shopharoth. He looks up (Lc.
ἀναβλέψας, cf. Lc. xix. 5, 'Jo.' viii. 7
ἀνέκυψεν) from the floor of the Court
on which His eyes had been resting,
and fixes them on the spectacle
(ἐθεώρει, cf. v. 38, Lc. xxiii. 35, Jo. xii.
45): before Him is a study of human

φυλάκιον. καὶ πολλοὶ πλούσιοι ἔβαλλον πολλά·
⁴²καὶ ἐλθοῦσα μία χήρα πτωχὴ ἔβαλεν λεπτὰ δύο, 42

42 χηρα] pr γυνη ℵ | om πτωχη D 2ᵖᵉ a b c ff i k q arm | εβαλλεν K 13 69 124 alᵖᵃᵘᶜ

nature which is unique in its own way. 'Ο ὄχλος is as usual 'the masses,' and χαλκόν may therefore retain its proper meaning; though χαλκός like *aes* is used for money of all kinds (cf. vi. 8), yet the mention of the rich men's larger gifts, which immediately follows, points here to copper coins such as the *as* (ἀσσάριον, Mt. x. 29), and the *quadrans* (κοδράντης, Mt. v. 26): see note on v. 42. The movement of the tenses in this context is interesting: βάλλει...ἔβαλλον...ἔβαλεν (*vv.* 42, 43) ...ἔβαλον, ἔβαλεν (*v.* 44). See Burton, §§ 14, 21, 56.

καὶ πολλοὶ πλούσιοι κτλ.] From time to time, as He watched, rich men (and not a few of them) cast in large sums; the Passover was at hand and wealthy worshippers were numerous and liberal. Lc. speaks only of the rich and the widow; Mc. distinguishes three classes.

The wealth of the temple-treasury in the time of Pompey is illustrated by Josephus (*ant.* xiv. 4. 4; 7. 1).

42. καὶ ἐλθοῦσα μία χήρα πτωχή] Lc. εἶδεν δέ τινα χήραν πενιχράν. With Mc.'s μία cf. συκῆν μίαν, Mt. xxi. 19. The widow stands out on the canvas, solitary and alone, in strong contrast to the πολλοὶ πλούσιοι, and is detected by the Lord's eye in the midst of the surrounding ὄχλος. It may have been the intention of the two Synoptists to compare her simple piety with the folly of the rich widows who wasted their substance on the Scribes (Victor), or she may once have been one of the latter class, and reduced to destitution by Pharisaic rapacity; at least it is worthy of notice that Mt., who does not mention this feature in the character of the Scribes, omits also the incident of the mites, whilst Mc. and Lc. have both, and in the

same order of juxtaposition. The widow was πτωχή (Mc.), πενιχρά (Lc.); the latter word is a poetical form of πένης, which occasionally takes its place in late prose, e.g. Exod. xxii. 25 (עָנִי), Prov. xxviii. 15, xxix. 7 (רָשׁ). Hatch (*Essays*, p. 73 ff.) argues that πτωχός and πένης, which are contrasted in class. Gk. (e.g. Ar. *Plut.* 552 πτωχοῦ μὲν γὰρ βίος...ζῆν ἐστιν μηδὲν ἔχοντα· τοῦ δὲ πένητος ζῆν φειδόμενον), are used in Biblical Gk. for "one and the same class ... the peasantry or *fellahin*." But in the N.T. at least the πτωχός is distinctly the indigent and destitute man, the pauper rather than the peasant (x. 21, xiv. 5, 7, Lc. xvi. 20), and the extreme opposite of the πλούσιος (2 Cor. vi. 10, Jas. ii. 2 ff., Apoc. xiii. 16; cf. Trench, *syn.* xxxvi., T. K. Abbott, *Essays*, p. 78). That such was the condition of this widow is clear from the sequel.

ἔβαλεν λεπτὰ δύο κτλ.] Vg. *misit duo minuta quod est quadrans* (Wycliffe, "tweye minutis"; Tindale, "two mytes"). The λεπτόν (cf. Xen. *Cyrop.* i. 4. 11 τὸ λεπτότατον τοῦ χαλκοῦ νομίσματος) was half a *quadrans* (i.e. the eighth part of an *as* or the ₁₂₈th part of a *denarius*), as Mc. explains for the benefit of his Roman readers. It was a Greek coin, the seventh of a χαλκοῦς (Suidas), and no smaller copper coin was in circulation; cf. Lc. xii. 59 τὸ ἔσχατον λεπτόν, where D and the O.L. versions substitute the more familiar *quadrans*. Mc.'s ὅ ἐστιν κοδράντης is an explanation for Western readers; κοδράντης occurs also in Mt. v. 26, but Mt. was "familiar as a tax-gatherer with the Roman system of accounting by the lowest denomination in the Roman scale" (A. R. S. Kennedy, in Hastings, *D.B.* iii. p. 428).

43 ὅ ἐστιν κοδράντης. ⁴³καὶ προσκαλεσάμενος τοὺς
μαθητὰς αὐτοῦ εἶπεν αὐτοῖς Ἀμὴν λέγω ὑμῖν ὅτι
ἡ χήρα αὕτη ἡ πτωχὴ πλεῖον πάντων ἔβαλεν τῶν
44 βαλλόντων εἰς τὸ γαζοφυλάκιον· ⁴⁴πάντες γὰρ ἐκ
τοῦ περισσεύοντος αὐτοῖς ἔβαλον, αὕτη δὲ ἐκ τῆς
ὑστερήσεως αὐτῆς πάντα ὅσα εἶχεν ἔβαλεν, ὅλον τὸν
¶ syrʰⁱᵉʳ   βίον αὐτῆς.¶

43 εβαλεν ℵᶜABDLΔ 33 alⁿᵒⁿⁿ Or²] βεβληκεν EFGHKMᵐᵍSUVXΓΠΦ minᵖˡ |
γαζοφυλακιον (-κειον EFGMVΨ)]+τα δωρα 604   44 περισσευοντος αυτοις] περισσευ-
ματος αυτων U(Γ)Δ minᵐᵘ | om ολον...αυτης syrˢⁱⁿ

On the *quadrans* see Madden, *Jewish
Coinage*, p. 244 f.; Hastings, *l.c.*; and
Exp. T. x. pp. 185, 232, 286, 336.
The point of the present story lies
in the circumstance that the widow's
last *quadrans* was in two coins, and
that she parted with both. A Rabbinic rule seems to have prohibited
the offering of a single λεπτόν: "ne
ponat homo perutam (פְּרוּטָה, the
Jewish equivalent) in cistam eleemo-
synes" (Wetstein). On ὅ ἐστιν see
Blass, *Gr.* p. 77.

43. *καὶ προσκαλεσάμενος κτλ.*] The
Twelve, who were perhaps conversing
at a little distance, are beckoned to
come near (cf. iii. 13, note); here was
a lesson which they had overlooked
and which He would teach them.
How difficult a lesson it was for
them to learn, and how important
to their life, appears from the use
of the solemn formula ἀμὴν (Lc.
ἀληθῶς) λέγω ὑμῖν, on which see iii.
28, note. The lesson is taught, as
usual, by an example—in the con-
crete, not in the abstract. Ἡ χήρα
αὕτη η πτωχή: the position of the
adj. calls attention to her condition
(WM., p. 168); pauper as she was,
she had given more than the rich,
more than all. Lc. here exchanges
πενιχρά for πτωχή: see note on *v.* 42.
Euth. εἰ καὶ πτωχὴ τοῖς χρήμασιν ἦν,
ἀλλὰ πλουσία τῇ γνώμῃ καθίσταται
(cf. Jas. ii. 5).

44. *πάντες γὰρ ἐκ τοῦ περισσεύοντος
κτλ.*] Justification of the paradox
πλεῖον πάντων ἔβαλεν. Τὸ περισσεῦον,
the active equivalent of τὸ περίσσευμα
(comp. Mt. xiv. 20 with Mc. viii. 8)—
'that which aboundeth,' abundance,
rather than 'that which is left over.'
Superfluity is balanced by ὑστέρησις
(Aq. in Job xxx. 3, Phil. iv. 11), used
here instead of the commoner word
ὑστέρημα, which is the opposite of
περίσσευμα (2 Cor. viii. 14). The rich
cast in (on the aor. see Blass, *Gr.*
p. 193) πολλά, the widow πάντα.
Relatively to their respective means
the gift of the latter was incomparably
the greatest. The principle is stated
by St Paul, 2 Cor. viii. 12: εἰ γὰρ ἡ
προθυμία πρόκειται, καθ᾽ ὃ ἐὰν ἔχῃ
εὐπρόσδεκτος, οὐ καθ᾽ ὃ οὐκ ἔχει. Cf.
Arist. *eth. Nic.* iv. 2 κατὰ τὴν οὐσίαν
ἡ ἐλευθεριότης λέγεται· οὐ γὰρ ἐν τῷ
πλήθει τῶν διδομένων τὸ ἐλευθέριον, ἀλλ᾽
ἐν τῇ τοῦ διδόντος ἕξει· αὕτη δὲ κατὰ
τὴν οὐσίαν δίδωσιν· οὐδὲν δὲ κωλύει
ἐλευθεριώτερον εἶναι τὸν τὰ ἐλάττω
διδόντα, ἐὰν ἀπὸ ἐλαττόνων διδῷ. See
other exx. in Wetstein of the recognition of this principle by Greek and
Roman pagan writers. Ὅλον τὸν βίον
αὐτῆς, all that she had to live upon
until more should be earned. For
βίος, *victus*, see Lc. xv. 12, 30, 1 Jo.
iii. 17. The Lord not only noticed
the widow's action, which needed
nothing more than close observation,

¹Καὶ ἐκπορευομένου αὐτοῦ ἐκ τοῦ ἱεροῦ λέγει ι **13**
αὐτῷ εἷς τῶν μαθητῶν αὐτοῦ Διδάσκαλε, ἴδε ποταποὶ λίθοι καὶ ποταπαὶ οἰκοδομαί. ²§καὶ ὁ Ἰησοῦς 2 §e
εἶπεν αὐτῷ Βλέπεις ταύτας τὰς μεγάλας οἰκοδομάς;

XIII. 1 εκπορευομενων αυτων Ψ | εκ] απο Ψ | των μαθητων] pr εκ ADFXΔ 1 13 28
604 al^nonn latt | om διδασκαλε Ψ | ποδαποι, -παι D* | οικοδομαι]+του ιερου D b c ff k l q
2 o Ιησους] pr αποκριθεις A(D)(EFGH)K(MSUVXΓ)(ΔΠ)Σ(Φ) 1071 al^pl latt arm aeth |
αυτω] αυτοις D min^pauc a b e ff i k q om 1 118 | βλεπεις] βλεπετε DM^mg min^perpauc
a b c e ff i k q pr ου 2^pe b c ff i k* βλεπε syr^sin vid | ταυτας τας μεγ. οικοδ.] has omnes
magnas aedificationes vg (cf. ff i q) ista magna et aedificia vestra e omnia illa magna
k has omnes aedificationes arm hanc aedificationem syr^sin

but knew the precise circumstances
under which she gave the two
λεπτά.

XIII. 1—2. DESTRUCTION OF THE
TEMPLE FORETOLD (Mt. xxiv. 1—2,
Lc. xxi. 5—6).

1. ἐκπορευομένου αὐτοῦ ἐκ τ. ἱεροῦ]
As He left the Precinct. Mt. somewhat otherwise, ἐξελθὼν ἀπὸ τοῦ
ἱεροῦ ἐπορεύετο, i.e. He had left,
and was on His way (to Bethany).
According to Mt. His last remark
before leaving had been Ἀφίεται ὑμῖν
ὁ οἶκος ὑμῶν. The disciples inwardly
deprecated such a sentence upon so
majestic a pile; they began talking
(Lc. τινῶν λεγόντων) of its magnificence, and one of them, the spokesman of the rest (Mt. οἱ μαθηταί, Mc.
εἷς τῶν μαθτῶν), bade Him turn and
look at the glory of the buildings
(Mt. προσῆλθον ἐπιδεῖξαι, Mc. ἴδε);
" ut flecterent eum ad misericordiam
loci illius, ne faceret quod facere
fuerat comminatus " (Origen). The
conjecture may be hazarded that the
speaker was Peter, as on some other
notable occasions (viii. 29, 32, x. 28,
xi. 21, xiii. 3, xiv. 29). But his
name is not mentioned, since in this
instance nothing turned upon his
personality.

ἴδε ποταποὶ λίθοι κτλ.] On ἴδε as
distinguished from ἰδού see ii. 24, iii.
34, notes. Ποταπός is late Gk. for ποδα-
πός (Lob. Phryn., p. 56, Rutherford,

N. Phryn., p. 128 f.): the word does
not occur in the LXX., but it is found in
this form in Mt.¹, Mc.¹, Lc.², Jo.^epp.1,
2 Pet.¹, in a sense approaching to
ποῖος (Vg. qualis), but with a distinct
note of surprise which is wanting in
the latter word. As to the stones of
Herod's temple see Jos. ant. xv. 11. 3
(ᾠκοδομήθη ὁ ναὸς ἐκ λίθων μὲν λευκῶν
τε καὶ καρτερῶν, τὸ μέγεθος ἑκάστων
περὶ πέντε καὶ εἴκοσι πηχῶν ἐπὶ μῆκος,
ὀκτὼ δὲ ὕψος, εὖρος δὲ περὶ δώδεκα),
and for the buildings, B.J. v. 5. 1 ff.,
Edersheim, Temple, p. 20 ff. Οἰκοδομαί (Mt., Mc.) is perhaps preferred to
οἰκοδομή, as representing the mass of
separate edifices—enclosures, colonnades, halls, sanctuaries,—by which
the platform of the ἱερόν was occupied. The word οἰκοδομή is post-
classical (Lob. Phryn., p. 481 f.),
answering sometimes to οἰκοδόμησις
(e.g. Rom. xiv. 19, and so generally
in St Paul's metaphorical use of the
term), sometimes to οἰκοδόμημα (2 Cor.
v. 1, Eph. ii. 21, where see Abbott's
note). Lc. refers also to the costly
offerings which the buildings contained (ἀναθήμασιν κεκόσμηται).

2. βλέπεις ταύτας τὰς μ. οἰκοδ.;]
'Art thou looking at these great
edifices?' i.e. do they fill and satisfy
the eye, shutting out other objects of
vision? Cf. Lc. ταῦτα ἃ θεωρεῖτε. Mt.
misses the point by a change of phrase
(οὐ βλέπετε...;). The disciples are

οὐ μὴ ἀφεθῇ ὧδε λίθος ἐπὶ λίθον ὃς οὐ μὴ καταλυθῇ.

§n 3 [3] § Καὶ καθημένου αὐτοῦ εἰς τὸ ὄρος τῶν ἐλαιῶν κατέναντι τοῦ ἱεροῦ ἐπηρώτα αὐτὸν κατ᾽ ἰδίαν Πέτρος

2 ου μη] pr αμην λεγω υμιν οτι D(G)Σ (1) (13) 28 (69) 604 (2^{pe}) al^{nonn} a b (c) e ff i k l q arm | ωδε] om AEFHKM*SVXΓΠ min^{pl} ff i vg *in templo* e k Cypr | επι λιθω ADEFHKSVΣΦ min^{pl} | ου μη καταλυθη (ου καταλυθησεται ℵ*L min^{pauc})] + και δια τριων ημερων αλλος αναστησεται ανευ χειρων D lat$^{\text{vt exc q}}$ Cypr   3 εις] επι Σ | επηρωτα ℵBLΨ 13 28 33 69 al^{pauc} syr$^{\text{hcl (mg)}}$] επηρωτων ADXΓΔΠΣΦ min^{pl} latt syrr$^{\text{sin pesh hcl (txt)}}$ arm the aeth | ο Πετρος ℵD 2^{pe} (al^{pauc})

warned that the pride which as Jews they naturally felt in this grand spectacle was doomed to complete humiliation.

οὐ μὴ ἀφεθῇ κτλ.] Mt. introduces this saying with the solemn ἀμὴν λέγω ὑμῖν, but Mc.'s repeated οὐ μή (Burton, § 487) is scarcely less emphatic. For the fulfilment see Jos. *B. J.* vii. 1. 1 κελεύει Καῖσαρ ἤδη τὴν πόλιν ἅπασαν καὶ τὸν νεὼν κατασκάπτειν. It is the more remarkable because Titus made every effort to check the conflagration (Jos. *B. J.* vi. 4. 6 ff.); it was only when this was found to be impossible that he permitted the work of destruction to be completed (*ib.* 5. 2). Thpht. mentions that some in his day asserted that the old walls had not been completely demolished (καὶ μήν φασί τινες ὡς πολλὰ λείψανα τῆς Ἰερουσαλὴμ τῆς παλαιᾶς πόλεως), and the great bevelled stones still to be seen *in situ* at the S.E. corner of the Haram wall, and near Robinson's Arch, attest the fact; for particulars reference may be made to Hastings, *D.B.* ii. p. 596 ff. But while a part of the substructions remains, the buildings on the platform of the ἱερόν, to which the Lord referred, are wholly gone; not a stone there is left in its place. Ἐπὶ λίθον: so also Mt., Lc. The idea of motion which the acc. suggests (WM., p. 507 f.) is faintly present in οὐ μὴ ἀφεθῇ. See on the other hand Blass, *Gr.* p. 132. Ὃς οὐ μὴ καταλυθῇ, Mt. ὃς οὐ καταλυθήσεται. The story subsequently circulated by the ἀρχιερεῖς (xiv. 58, xv. 29, Acts vi. 14), that Jesus had undertaken Himself to destroy the Temple, may have arisen partly from the saying of Jo. ii. 19, but perhaps also from a misconception of the present saying, which may have been reported to them by Judas. On the remarkable addition in D and the O.L. authorities, see WH., *Notes*, p. 26; it is apparently suggested by xiv. 58 (cf. Jo. ii. 19).

3—13. The Question of the Four, and the first part of the prophetic Answer (Mt. xxiv. 3—14, Lc. xxi. 8—19).

3. καὶ καθημένου αὐτοῦ κτλ.] The very posture in which the Lord delivered His great prophecy was remembered and found a place in the earliest tradition (Mt., Mc.). He had crossed the Kedron, ascended the steep road over the Mt of Olives which led to Bethany, and was already resting and seated, when He was approached, not now by a solitary disciple (*v.* 1), but by four—the first two pairs among the Twelve, as Mc. alone appears to know (Mt. οἱ μαθηταί)—the other eight, who had possibly deputed the Four to act for them, remaining at a distance (κατ᾽ ἰδίαν). On the order of the Four see iii. 17, note, and cf. ix. 2; as on other occasions Peter is foremost—probably the spokesman (ἐπηρώτα αὐτὸν...Πέτρος). Καθημένου reminds us of the

καὶ Ἰάκωβος καὶ Ἰωάνης καὶ Ἀνδρέας¶ ⁴Εἰπὸν ἡμῖν 4 ¶θ
πότε ταῦτα ἔσται, καὶ τί τὸ σημεῖον ὅταν μέλλῃ
ταῦτα συντελεῖσθαι πάντα. ⁵ὁ δὲ Ἰησοῦς ἤρξατο 5

3 Ιωαν. και Ιακ. U 28 69 124 346 435   4 ειπε ΑΧΓΔΠΣΦ minᵖˡ | om παντα
Δ 13 2ᵖᵉ alᵖᵃᵘᶜ k   5 ο δε I.]+αποκριθεις A(DG)ΧΓΔΠΣΦ (13 28 69 124 604 2ᵖᵉ
alᵖᵃᵘᶜ latt arm) | ηρξατο λεγειν] ειπεν D 2ᵖᵉ alᵖᵃᵘᶜ a k n syrˢⁱⁿ arm

Sermon on the Mount (Mt. v. 1);
both the opening Instruction and the
concluding Prophecy were delivered
ex cathedra; a hill-side in each case
supplied the Teacher's chair. The
first discourse had set forth the principles of the new Kingdom; the last
deals with its ultimate issues. Only
Mc. adds that the prophecy was delivered in full view of the Precinct
(κατέναντι τοῦ ἱεροῦ, cf. xii. 41). On
καθ. εἰς see WM., p. 516).

4. εἰπὸν ἡμῖν κτλ.] The question
is twofold, (a) as to the time when
(πότε) the Temple is to perish, (b) as
to the signal (τὸ σημεῖον) for its approach. Mt. expands ὅταν μέλλῃ ταῦτα
συντ. πάντα (ὅ. μ. τ. γίνεσθαι, Lc.) into
τῆς σῆς παρουσίας καὶ συντελείας τοῦ
αἰῶνος, a phrase of much interest,
since it reveals the principle on which
the Apostolic Church after the fall of
Jerusalem interpreted the following
prophecy. Later opinion was much
divided, cf. Victor: οἱ μὲν γὰρ περὶ
τῆς συντελείας τοῦ αἰῶνος εἰρῆσθαι
ταῦτα ὑπολαμβάνουσιν, οἱ δὲ περὶ τῆς
ἐρημώσεως τῆς Ἰερουσαλήμ· καὶ τῆς
μὲν προτέρας δόξης Ἀπολινάριος καὶ
Θεόδωρος ὁ Μοψουεστίας, τῆς δὲ δευ-
τέρας Τίτος καὶ ὁ ἐν ἁγίοις Ἰωάννης ὁ
τῆς βασιλίδος ἐπίσκοπος. The term
συντέλεια (cf. Dalman, *Worte*, i. p.
126 f.) is apparently suggested by
συντελεῖσθαι (Mc.), but both συντέλεια
and παρουσία are words peculiar to
Mt. among the Synoptists (παρ., Mt.
xxiv. 3, 27, 37, 39; συντ., Mt. xiii. 39,
40, 49, xxiv. 3, xxviii. 20). Συντέλεια
and συντελεῖν, -λεῖσθαι, used in classical Greek chiefly in reference to contributions to the public service (so

even in the late Fayûm papyrus,
Grenfell-Hunt-Hogarth, p. 120), and
in later Greek also of finishing off
a piece of work, are of frequent occurrence in all parts of the LXX.,
where they generally answer to כלה
and its derivatives; for συντελεῖν,
συντελεῖσθαι in the N. T. cf. Lc. iv. 2,
13, Jo. ii. 3, Acts xxi. 27. Τὸ σημεῖον
is common to the three accounts; a
single sign seems to have been expected, probably one of portentous
character.

5. ὁ δὲ Ἰησοῦς ἤρξατο λέγειν] The
great Prophecy begins (Bengel: "ἤρξατο: antea non erat multum locutus his de rebus"). The Lord deals
first with the second part of the
question (τί τὸ σημεῖον). But the
answer (ἀποκριθεὶς εἶπεν, Mt.) is not
such as they expect; no one sign is
mentioned, and the tone of the prediction is wholly practical.

Many recent critics hold that portions of the discourse which follows
(*vv.* 7—8, 14—20, 24—27, possibly also
30—31) belong to a Jewish-Christian
apocalypse whose *disiecta membra*
were incorporated by the Synoptists
or their source. This opinion is based
on the belief that the excision of the
verses in question restores unity to
the context and removes ideas alien
from the teaching of Christ. But in
the entire absence of documentary
evidence it scarcely calls for serious
consideration here. The arguments
urged in support of it may be seen
in Charles, *Eschatology*, p. 325 ff.;
Moffatt, *Historical N. T.*, p. 637 ff.;
Schmiedel, art. *Gospels* in *Encycl.
Bibl.* ii. (col. 1857).

λέγειν αὐτοῖς Βλέπετε μή τις ὑμᾶς πλανήσῃ.
6 ⁶πολλοὶ ἐλεύσονται ἐπὶ τῷ ὀνόματί μου λέγοντες ὅτι
7 Ἐγώ εἰμι, καὶ πολλοὺς πλανήσουσιν. ⁷ὅταν δὲ
ἀκούσητε πολέμους καὶ ἀκοὰς πολέμων, μὴ θροεῖσθε·

5 μη τις] μηδεις Σ | πλανησει DHTΨ al^nonn   6 πολλοι]+γαρ ΑΔΧΓΔΠΣΦ
min^omn vid latt syrr arm aegg | επι τω ονοματι μου] +pseudiprofetae (sic) k | om οτι
D 33 604 al^paue b c ff k q | ειμι]+o χ̅ς̅ 13 28 69 124 346 604 1071 al^paue b c l arm aeth
7 ακουητε Β | μη] pr ορατε א* c.b(vid) 604 8^pe | μη θροεισθε] μη θορυβεισθε D min^paue
nolite turbari an nolite timere vel ne timuistis b c d ff g i k l g vg

βλέπετε μή τις ὑμᾶς πλανήσῃ] Mt.,
Mc.; βλ. μὴ πλανηθῆτε, Lc. Cf. βλέπειν ἀπό, viii. 15, xii. 38; βλ. μή
occurs again in 1 Cor. viii. 9, Gal.
v. 15, Col. ii. 8, Heb. iii. 12 (with
fut.), xii. 25. For πλανᾶν, πλανᾶσθαι,
in reference to religious error, see xii.
24, 27, Jo. vii. 12, 47, 1 Jo. ii. 26,
2 Tim. iii. 13, Apoc. ii. 20, xii. 9; cf.
the use of πλάνη, Eph. iv. 14, 2 Thess.
ii. 11, 1 Jo. iv. 6, and of πλάνος in
2 Jo. 7. This warning against impostors is not inconsistent with the
promise of the Spirit of truth (Jo.
xvi. 13), for the Divine Spirit is not
irresistible, and the spirit of error
(1 Jo. iv. 6) may be the stronger in
individual cases.

6. πολλοὶ ἐλεύσονται κτλ.] See v.
21 ff., notes. One such impostor is
described in Acts viii. 9 Σίμων...λέγων
εἶναί τινα ἑαυτὸν μέγαν, ᾧ προσεῖχον
πάντες ἀπὸ μικροῦ ἕως μεγάλου λέγοντες Οὗτός ἐστιν ἡ δύναμις τοῦ θεοῦ ἡ
καλουμένη μεγάλη. Josephus speaks
of another, ant. xx. 5. 1 : γόης τις
ἀνὴρ Θευδᾶς ὄνομα πείθει τὸν πλεῖστον
ὄχλον...προφήτης γὰρ ἔλεγεν εἶναι. Cf.
B.J. ii. 13. 4 πλάνοι γὰρ ἄνθρωποι καὶ
ἀπατεῶνες προσχήματι θειασμοῦ νεω-
τερισμοὺς καὶ μεταβολὰς πραγματευ-
όμενοι δαιμονᾷν τὸ πλῆθος ἐπειθον καὶ
προῆγον εἰς τὴν ἐρημίαν ὡς ἐκεῖ τοῦ
θεοῦ δείξοντος αὐτοῖς σημεῖα ἐλευ-
θερίας. Such impostors came ἐπὶ τῷ
ὀνόματι [τοῦ χριστοῦ], holding out a
false Messianic hope, claiming powers
which belonged to the true Christ,
even if they did not assume the title.

The vague boast ἐγώ εἰμι (Soph. ii.
15) becomes in Mt. ἐγώ εἰμι ὁ χριστός,
but of an actual usurpation of the
name we hear nothing before Bar-
cochba. For the phrase ἐπὶ τῷ ὀν. μου
see ix. 39 note; for ἐγώ εἰμι in a
Messianic sense, comp. note on vi. 50.

7. ὅταν δὲ ἀκούσητε κτλ.] A second
warning. The Apostles are not to
permit the political troubles which
would surely precede the end to dis-
tract them from their proper work.
Πολέμους καὶ ἀκοὰς πολέμων, wars in
actual progress, or commonly expected
and on all men's tongues; unless ἀκοὰς
πολέμων is simply a doublet, added to
explain the difficult ἀκούειν πολέμους.
For ἀκοή see i. 28 note; and for the
pl. in this sense cf. Dan. xi. 44 Th.
ἀκοαὶ...ταράξουσιν αὐτόν: ἀκούειν ἀκοήν
or ἀκοάς is a LXX. phrase, occurring
e.g. 1 Regn. ii. 24. Lc., who omits
κ. ἀκοὰς πολ., adds καὶ ἀκαταστασίας,
interpreting the words in the light
of events. The reference is primarily,
no doubt, to the disturbed state of
Palestine during the interval between
the Ascension and the fall of the
City; we may think e.g. of the expedition of Cuspius Fadus against
Theudas and of Felix against the
Egyptian Jew; the riots at Jerusalem
under Agrippa II.; the early movements of the last struggle which
began in A.D. 66. To the early Jewish
Church, which is immediately in view,
the suspense which these and other
outbreaks occasioned must have been
unsettling and disquieting. St Paul

δεῖ γενέσθαι, ἀλλ' οὔπω τὸ τέλος. ⁸ἐγερθήσεται 8
γὰρ ἔθνος ἐπ' ἔθνος καὶ βασιλεία ἐπὶ βασιλείαν,

7 δει ℵ*ΒΨ aegg]+γαρ ℵᶜΑDLΧΓΔΠΣΦ min ᵒᵐⁿ ᵛⁱᵈ latt syrr   8 εγερθησεται]
αναστησεται 604

uses the same word in deprecating
the restlessness which was occasioned
in a Gentile Church by the expectation of a speedy παρουσία (2 Thess. ii.
2 εἰς τὸ μὴ ταχέως σαλευθῆναι ὑμᾶς
...μηδὲ θροεῖσθαι), and the warning is
doubtless necessary at all seasons
of feverish unrest. Θροεῖν, in class.
Gk. 'to raise an outcry,' is used in
Biblical Gk. in the pass. only, of the
alarm occasioned by a sudden cry, or
of mental uneasiness in general; cf.
Cant. v. 4 ἡ κοιλία μου ἐθροήθη ἐπ'
αὐτόν, 2 Thess. ii. 2 εἰς τὸ μὴ ταχέως...
θροεῖσθαι...ὡς ὅτι ἐνέστηκεν ἡ ἡμέρα
τοῦ κυρίου: and see Kennedy, Sources,
p. 126. Θορυβεῖσθε is substituted here
by the 'Western' text, and Lc. has
πτοηθῆτε.

δεῖ γενέσθαι, ἀλλ' οὔπω τὸ τέλος]
Mt. δεῖ γὰρ γενέσθαι ἀλλ' οὔπω
ἐστὶν τὸ τ., Lc. δεῖ γὰρ ταῦτα γ.
πρῶτον ἀλλ' οὐκ εὐθέως τὸ τ. The
epigrammatic brevity of Mc. (Tisch.
on v. 6, "abiectis coniunctionibus
scribere adamat") is specially striking
in this context; cf. v. 6 πολλοὶ ἐλεύσονται (Mt., Lc. π. γὰρ ἐλ.); v. 8
ἔσονται σεισμοί...ἔσ. λιμοί· ἀρχή κτλ.
(Mt. καὶ ἔσ. λ. κ. σ., πάντα δὲ ταῦτα
ἀρχή, Lc. σεισμοί τε...καὶ...λιμοὶ ἔσονται). For δεῖ, 'such is the Divine
purpose,' cf. viii. 31, ix. 11, xiii. 10,
xiv. 31; the phrase δεῖ γενέσθαι is
from the O. T. (Dan. ii. 28). Τὸ τέλος
looks back to συντελεῖσθαι, and may
therefore be presumed to refer primarily to Jerusalem. But a more
distant end may also be in view; cf.
I Cor. xv. 24 ἐν τῇ παρουσίᾳ αὐτοῦ·
εἶτα τὸ τέλος, I Pet. iv. 7 πάντων δὲ
τὸ τέλος ἤγγικεν.

8. ἐγερθήσεται γὰρ ἔθνος κτλ.]
Nations will rush into warfare from
causes partly racial, partly political.

Cf. Isa. xix. 2 ἐπεγερθήσονται Αἰγύπτιοι
ἐπ' Αἰγυπτίους...πόλις ἐπὶ πόλιν καὶ
νομὸς ἐπὶ νομόν: supra, iii. 14 ἐὰν
βασιλεία ἐφ' ἑαυτὴν μερισθῇ. Other
disquieting events will mark the times
—σεισμοί, λιμοί, and λοιμοί (Lc.), unless λοιμοί is a primitive error due to
the confusion of λιμός and λοιμός in
the source (cf. 3 Regn. viii. 37, Ezech.
xxxvi. 29, vv.ll.); Field's remark (Notes,
p. 37) that λιμοί and λοιμοί have been
connected ever since Hesiod, op. 242,
loses its force if we assume an Aramaic original. On the addition καὶ
ταραχαί see WH., Notes, p. 26. The
commentators point out that such
troubles were frequent during the
period A.D. 30—70 (cf. e.g. Alford on
Mt. xxiv. 7); the famine of A.D. 44
(45—46, Ramsay) is familiar to us
from Acts xi. 28, and earthquakes are
reported to have taken place κατὰ
τόπους—in Crete and Asia Minor, and
at Rome and in Italy: in Lc. κατὰ
τόπους is connected with λοιμοί, but
see above. Such disasters are frequently foretold by the O.T. prophets
as marks of Divine visitation (e.g.
Isa. viii. 21, xiii. 13, xiv. 30, xxiv.
18—20, Jer. xxiii. 19, Ezek. v. 12;
cf. Apoc. vi. 8, xi. 13, xvi. 18, xviii.
8, Enoch i. 6, 4 Esdr. xvi. 36—40);
they belong to the imagery of an
apocalyptic passage, and while it is
interesting to notice particular fulfilments in the Apostolic age, the wider
reference is not to be left out
of sight. Each age brings public
troubles which excite disquietude,
and may at times suggest the near
approach of the end. Yet the end
is not reached by such vicissitudes;
they are but the beginning—the ἀρχή,
and not the τέλος, as men may be led
to suppose. "Talis et tanta creatura

ἔσονται σεισμοὶ κατὰ τόπους, ἔσονται λιμοί· ἀρχὴ
¶ b 9 ὠδίνων¹ ταῦτα. ⁹βλέπετε δὲ ὑμεῖς ἑαυτούς· παραδώσουσιν ὑμᾶς εἰς συνέδρια καὶ εἰς συναγωγὰς δαρή-

8 εσονται 1°] pr και ΑΧΓΔΠΣΦ minᵖˡ (latt) syrr arm the aeth | εσονται 2° א(*)ᶜ·ᵃ
BLΨ 28 me] και D 2ᵖᵉ lattᵛᵗ ᵖˡ ᵛᵍ pr και ΑΧΓΔΠΣΦ•minᵖˡ q syrrᵖᵉˢʰ ʰᶜˡ the aeth om εσ.
syrˢⁱⁿ arm | λιμοι]+και ταραχαι ΑΧΓΠΦ minᵒᵐⁿ ᵛⁱᵈ q syrr the Orⁱⁿᵗ+και λοιμοι και ταρ.
Σ arm | om αρχη ωδ. ταυτα Φ c | αρχαι AEFGHMS²VXΓΠ²Σ minᵖˡ | ταυτα]+παντα
1071 (cf. 13 28 69 124 299 346 2ᵖᵉ a g n)   9 om βλεπετε...εαυτους D 1 28 91 124
604 2ᵖᵉ a ff i n syrˢⁱⁿ arm | παραδωσουσιν υμας] π. γαρ υμ. אΑΧΓΔΠΣΦ minᵖˡ q vg
syrrᵖᵉˢʰ ʰᶜˡ the και π. υμ. 1 28 124 299 syrˢⁱⁿ arm ειτα υμ. αυτους παραδ. D 604 2ᵖᵉ
a ff i k n | εις συναγωγας] εν ταις συναγωγαις (+αυτων) minᵐᵘ (a ff k n q vg)

mundi...necesse est ante corruptionem ut langueat" (Origen).

ἀρχὴ ὠδίνων ταῦτα] 'Ωδίν is used of the sharp pangs of childbirth (Ps. xlvii. (xlviii.) 7 ἐκεῖ ὠδῖνες ὡς τικτούσης, 1 Thess. v. 3 ὥσπερ ἡ ὠδὶν τῇ ἐν γαστρὶ ἐχούσῃ), or of death (Ps. xvii. (xviii.) 5, 6 ὠδῖνες θανάτου, ᾅδου, Acts ii. 24). Either may be thought of here : these things are the first death-throes of the old order, or the first birth-pangs of the new ; but the hopefulness of Christian eschatology is in favour of the second thought being at least the more prominent ; cf. Jo. xvi. 21, Rom. viii. 22, and the doctrine of the παλιν-γενεσία (Mt. xix. 28), and the ἀπο-κατάστασις πάντων (Acts iii. 21, 2 Pet. iii. 12 ff.). Moreover there may possibly be a reference to the Rabbinic expectation of the חֶבְלֵי־הַמָּשִׁיחַ (J. Lightfoot ad l. ; and see esp. Schürer, II. ii. p. 154 f., Weber, p. 350 f.), or rather perhaps to the O. T. language which suggested it.

9. βλέπετε δὲ ὑμεῖς ἑαυτούς] 'Look ye to yourselves,' think not only of what is coming on the nation and on the world (Bengel : "cetera nolite curare, tantum vos ipsos spectate"). The late and rare βλέπειν ἑαυτόν occurs again in 2 Jo. 8, where it is followed by ἵνα μή—here it is used absolutely, with the added force which brevity gives ; Mt., who places the rest of this verse in the original charge to the Twelve (x. 17), paraphrases προσέ-

χετε δὲ ἀπὸ τῶν ἀνθρώπων. Lc. adds that the troubles will overtake the Christian community first (πρὸ τούτων πάντων); cf. 1 Pet. iv. 17 ὁ καιρὸς τοῦ ἄρξασθαι τὸ κρίμα ἀπὸ τοῦ οἴκου τοῦ θεοῦ.

παραδώσουσιν ὑμᾶς κτλ.] Their earliest sufferings would come from their own countrymen, and from the representatives of religion ; 'men will hand you over to the Sanhedrins, and flog you in the synagogues.' Who the παραδοταί will be appears below v. 12. Συνέδρια...συναγωγάς : the former term includes both the Great Sanhedrin of Jerusalem (cf. Acts iv. 15, v. 21 ff., vi. 12 ff., xxii. 30, xxiii. 1 ff.), and the local courts of discipline described by Josephus (ant. iv. 8. 14), i.e. the elders of the synagogues assembled for the purpose of exercising disciplinary powers ; see Hatch, Organization, p. 58. Lc.'s briefer παραδιδόντες εἰς τὰς συναγωγάς is correct, for the local court was attached to the synagogue, and its sentences were carried out in it (Acts ix. 2) ; the Lord foresees that His Apostles and disciples will be taken from the courts into the synagogues and there openly scourged—εἰς συνα-γωγὰς δαρήσεσθε, a pregnant con-struction, cf. Mt. (x. 17) ἐν ταῖς συνα-γωγαῖς αὐτῶν μαστιγώσουσιν ὑμᾶς. On δαρήσεσθε see xii. 3, 5 (to which passage the Lord possibly refers), and cf. Acts v. 40. St Paul, who

σεσθε, καὶ ἐπὶ ἡγεμόνων καὶ βασιλέων σταθήσεσθε
ἕνεκεν ἐμοῦ εἰς μαρτύριον αὐτοῖς. ¹⁰καὶ εἰς πάντα τὰ 10

9 και επι βασ. σταθ. και δαρ. επι ηγ. syrˢⁱⁿ | δαρησεσθε] pr και 604 | ηγεμονας κ.
βασιλεις 1071 | ηγεμονων]+δε ΑΚΓΠΨ 736 alⁿᵒⁿⁿ | σταθησεσθε] αχθησεσθε GU 1 13
33 alⁿᵒⁿⁿ the | ενεκα B

before his conversion had inflicted this punishment on Christians, underwent it himself five times (2 Cor. xi. 24, where see Schöttgen).

καὶ ἐπὶ ἡγεμόνων καὶ βασιλέων σταθήσεσθε] The secular power would follow the example set by the Synagogue. 'Ye shall be placed before high officials and kings.' In the N.T. the ἡγεμών is especially the Procurator of Judaea (Mt. xxvii. 2 παρέδωκαν Πειλάτῳ τῷ ἡγεμόνι, Acts xxiii. 24 πρὸς Φήλικα τὸν ἡγεμόνα). But the word, as contrasted with βασιλεύς, may be used of any subordinate governors; cf. 1 Pet. ii. 14 εἴτε βασιλεῖ ὡς ὑπερέχοντι, εἴτε ἡγεμόσιν ὡς δι' αὐτοῦ πεμπομένοις, where the Imperator and the provincial representatives of Rome, whether proconsuls, propraetors, legates, or procurators, are clearly intended; cf. Acts xvi. 20 ff., xviii. 12 ff. Ἐπὶ...βασιλέων σταθ. becomes in Mt. ἐπὶ...βασιλεῖς ἀχθήσεσθε, cf. Lc. ἀπαγομένους ἐπὶ βασιλεῖς, i.e. Mt. and Lc. represent the persecuted disciples as on their way to the court, whereas in Mc. they are already there, standing before the judge. For this use of ἵστασθαι comp. Mt. xxvii. 11, Acts xxiv. 20, xxv. 10. Ἔνεκεν ἐμοῦ, Lc. ἕνεκεν τοῦ ὀνόματός μου: cf. viii. 35, x. 29 ἕνεκεν ἐμοῦ καὶ [ἕνεκεν] τοῦ εὐαγγελίου, 1 Pet. iv. 16 ὡς Χριστιανός.

εἰς μαρτύριον αὐτοῖς] See notes on i. 44, vi. 11; the phrase occurs only in the Synoptics and in Jas. v. 3. Lc. gives here quite another turn to the clause—ἀποβήσεται ὑμῖν εἰς μαρτύριον, i.e. he seems to have had before him εἰς μαρτ. ὑμῖν. As it is presented by Mc. and Mt., the sense is that the appearance of Christians before the magistrates on a charge of loyalty to

the Name of Christ would be in itself a proclamation of the Name to those who from their social position might otherwise have failed to hear it. Mt. adds καὶ τοῖς ἔθνεσιν: the Gospel would in this way make its way into Gentile society, cf. 2 Tim. iv. 16 f.

10. καὶ εἰς πάντα τὰ ἔθνη κτλ.] The Lord foresees the extension of the Gospel to the whole Gentile world by the direct preaching of the word; there was a Divine necessity (δεῖ, cf. v. 7) that this should take place before the end came (πρῶτον, Mt. καὶ τότε ἥξει τὸ τέλος). Cf. xi. 17, xvi. 15, Mt. xxv. 32, xxviii. 19, Lc. xxiv. 47. The work which began in Galilee with the personal Ministry of the Lord (i. 14 ἦλθεν...κηρύσσων τὸ εὐαγγέλιον, cf. Heb. ii. 3 ἀρχὴν λαβοῦσα λαλεῖσθαι διὰ τοῦ κυρίου) was to be carried forward by the Apostolic ministry to the ever-expanding confines of the habitable world (Mt. ἐν ὅλῃ τῇ οἰκουμένῃ); and the execution of this purpose was perhaps the chief condition of the final issue being reached. The disclosure of this fact could not but be stimulating to the early preachers of the Gospel; they felt that it was in some sense within their power to hasten the end by extending the kingdom (2 Pet. iii. 12 σπεύδοντας τὴν παρουσίαν). Origen's remark here is interesting: "nondum est praedicatum evangelium regni in toto orbe; non enim fertur praedicatum esse evangelium apud omnes Aethiopas...sed nec apud Seras nec apud Orientem audierunt Christianitatis sermonem. quid autem dicamus de Britannis aut Germanis?...quorum plurimi nondum audierunt evangelii verbum, audituri sunt autem in ipsa

11 ἔθνη πρῶτον δεῖ κηρυχθῆναι τὸ εὐαγγέλιον. ¹¹καὶ
ὅταν ἄγωσιν ὑμᾶς παραδιδόντες, μὴ προμεριμνᾶτε τί
¶ 33 λαλήσητε, ἀλλ᾽ ὃ ἐὰν δοθῇ ὑμῖν¹ ἐν ἐκείνῃ τῇ ὥρᾳ,
τοῦτο λαλεῖτε· οὐ γάρ ἐστε ὑμεῖς οἱ λαλοῦντες

10 πρωτον]+δε minᵖᵃᵘᶜ a d ff(k) arm the+γαρ syrˢⁱⁿ | το ευαγγελιον]+εν πασιν
τοις εθνεσιν D ff καὶ οταν] οταν δε ΑΧΓΔΠΣΦ minᵖˡ q syrr arm | προμε-
ριμνατε] μεριμνατε ΜΓ 33 alⁿᵒⁿⁿ προμεριμνησηται 1071 προσμελετατε Ψ | τι λαλησητε
(-σετε U alⁿᵒⁿⁿ)] pr πως η 13 69 124 346 pr μηδε προμελετατε 604 (Or) pr μελετατε
(vel προμελ.) (28) 299 433 604 (2ᵖᵉ) arm (Or) + μηδε μελετατε ΑΧΓΔΠΦ minᵖˡ
syrrᵖᵉˢʰ ʰᵉˡ (om אΒDLΨ 1 33 69 alᵖᵃᵘᶜ c ff i k q vg syrˢⁱⁿ aegg aeth)

saeculi consummatione." For another
condition cf. 2 Thess. ii. 3 ἐὰν μὴ
ἔλθῃ ἡ ἀποστασία πρῶτον.

11. καὶ ὅταν ἄγωσιν ὑμᾶς κτλ.]
Verses 11—13 are placed by Mt. in
the original charge to the Twelve
(Mt. x. 19—22, cf. v. 9), but traces of
them occur also in Mt. xxiv. (9, 13);
Lc. also has reminiscences of this
teaching in an earlier chapter (Lc.
xii. 11 f.) as well as in the present
context. Such counsels may well have
been repeated.

The Lord returns to the personal
trials awaiting the disciples. First
of these was the fear with which
inexperienced provincials would anticipate an appearance before a Roman
judge, whether Proconsul or Imperator; on their way to the court (ὅταν
ἄγωσιν), besides the bitter sense of
being betrayed by friends and relations (παραδιδόντες, cf. v. 12), they
would be distracted by anxiety as
to their defence. The Lord provides
against this: 'the Holy Spirit will
be your παράκλητος, and speak by
your mouths.' Μὴ προμεριμνᾶτε: 'be
not anxious beforehand'; προμεριμνᾶν
is ἅπ. λεγ. in the N. T. and perhaps
in writers earlier than the close of
the canon; Mt. has μεριμνᾶν, Lc. the
classical προμελετᾶν, 'to prepare a
speech.' Τί λαλήσητε: Mt. πῶς ἢ
τί λ.—neither the matter nor the
words need be considered; for the
construction cf. vi. 36, ix. 6 (WM.,
p. 373). Ὃ ἐὰν δοθῇ...λαλεῖτε, Burton

§ 303. The whole passage resembles
the promise to Moses, Exod. iv. 11 ff.
τίς ἔδωκεν στόμα ἀνθρώπῳ; συμβιβάσω
σε ὃ μέλλεις λαλῆσαι κτλ.; in Lc. this
allusion to Exod. is yet more apparent
(ἐγὼ γὰρ δώσω ὑμῖν στόμα κτλ.). It
must be borne in mind that both the
command to speak ἐκ τοῦ αὐτοσχεδίου
and the promise of Divine assistance
in doing so are limited to an occasion
when effective premeditation would
be impossible.

οὐ γάρ ἐστε ὑμ. οἱ λαλοῦντες κτλ.]
Wycliffe: "for ȝe ben not spekinge
(or, spekeris) but the Hooly
Gost." The Holy Spirit would speak
for them and by their lips. For τὸ
πν. τὸ ἅγ. see iii. 29, note. Mt. has τὸ
πν. τοῦ πατρὸς ὑμῶν, in Lc. (see last
note) the Lord represents Himself
as the source of the inspiration—
a noteworthy variation, with which
compare Jo. xiv. 26, xv. 26. The
whole passage anticipates the promise
of the "other Paraclete" (Jo. xiv.
16). Mt. completes the sentence ἀλλὰ
τὸ πνεῦμα...τὸ λαλοῦν ἐν ὑμῖν: compare St Paul's doctrine of the Spirit's
agency in prayer (Rom. viii. 15, 26,
Gal. iv. 6). The present passage cannot properly be used to support a
theory of verbal inspiration either in
the speeches or the writings of the
apostolic age; the Holy Spirit does
not, like the evil spirits (cf. v. 6 ff.),
so identify Himself with the inspired
as to destroy or even to suspend their
responsibility or individuality.

ἀλλὰ τὸ πνεῦμα τὸ ἅγιον. ¹²καὶ παραδώσει ἀδελφὸς 12
ἀδελφὸν εἰς θάνατον καὶ πατὴρ τέκνον, καὶ ἐπαναστήσονται τέκνα ἐπὶ γονεῖς καὶ θανατώσουσιν αὐτούς.
¹³καὶ ἔσεσθε μισούμενοι ὑπὸ πάντων διὰ τὸ ὄνομά 13
μου· ὁ δὲ ὑπομείνας εἰς τέλος, οὗτος σωθήσεται.

12 και παραδ.] παραδ. δε ΑΧΓΔΠΣΦ min^{fereomn} ff i q vg syrr^{pesh hcl} aeth Or παραδ.
γαρ syr^{sin} | om και πατηρ τεκνον 1071 | επαναστησεται Β

12. καὶ παραδώσει κτλ.] The note
already struck in vv. 9, 11 is taken up
again. The thought of treachery on
the part of friends must have been
uppermost in the Lord's mind; He
was speaking in the presence of a
traitor who had been a friend. What
had befallen Himself must befall His
followers. The sentence is moulded
on Mic. vii. 6 υἱὸς ἀτιμάζει πατέρα,
θυγατὴρ ἐπαναστήσεται ἐπὶ τὴν μητέρα
αὐτῆς. Εἰς θάνατον, θανατώσουσιν—the
penalty of confessing Christ would be
more than stripes (v. 9); the Sanhedrins might be content with these, but
the civil rulers would inflict death.
Ἐπαναστήσονται, used properly of in-
surgents (e.g. Dan. xi. 2, 14), but in
the LXX. of revolt against any constituted authority. Θανατώσουσιν (so
all the Synoptists here), 'shall be the
cause of death' (Rheims, "shall worke
their death"), rather than ἀποκτενοῦσιν, 'shall put them to death.'
Lc. guards the sentence further by
substituting ἐξ ὑμῶν for αὐτούς: not
all would win the crown of martyrdom. One had been already marked
out for it in the Lord's foreknowledge
(x. 39, cf. Acts xii. 1); another was
about to be forewarned of his end
yet more distinctly (Jo. xxi. 18, cf.
2 Pet. i. 14).

13. καὶ ἔσεσθε μισούμενοι κτλ.]
This clause is given in identical words
by the three Synoptists; it must have
early passed into a commonplace
among Greek-speaking Christians.
No fact in the early history of the
Church is more certain or more sur-

prising than that which the Lord here
foretells. It is explained by Tacitus
as due to a suspicion of criminality
(ann. xv. 44, "per flagitia invisos...
Christianos"), but the mere name was
enough to provoke it (Justin, apol. i.
4 ἐφ' ἡμῶν τὸ ὄνομα ὡς ἔλεγχον λαμβά-
νετε : Tert. apol. 2 "id solum ex-
pectatur quod odio publico necessa-
rium est, confessio nominis"). It was
in fact the name of Christ Himself
(διὰ τὸ ὄνομά μου) which repelled the
unbelieving majority (cf. Jo. iii. 20,
vii. 7, xv. 23 ff.), and in this thought
there was infinite comfort for the
persecuted; cf. 1 Pet. iv. 14, Polyc.
Phil. 8 ἐὰν πάσχωμεν διὰ τὸ ὄνομα
αὐτοῦ, δοξάζωμεν αὐτόν, and Thpht.
ad l. τὸ γὰρ ἕνεκεν αὐτοῦ μισεῖσθαι
ἱκανόν ἐστιν πάσας ἐπικουφίσαι τὰς
συμφοράς. On the causes of the un-
popularity of the early Church see
Ramsay, Ch. in the Empire, p. 346 ff.,
and cf. Origen in Mt.: "cum haec
ergo contigerint mundo [the disorders
foretold in vv. 7, 8] consequens est
quasi derelinquentibus hominibus de-
orum culturam ut propter multitudi-
nem Christianorum dicant fieri bella
et fames et pestilentias." Ἔσεσθε
μισούμενοι is not an exact equivalent of
μισηθήσεσθε, but carries "the thought
of continuance" (Burton § 71, cf. WM.,
p. 438).

ὁ δὲ ὑπομείνας εἰς τέλος κτλ.] So Mt.
exactly, but in a somewhat different
connexion; Lc. paraphrases ἐν τῇ ὑπομονῇ ὑμῶν κτήσεσθε τὰς ψυχὰς ὑμῶν—
a valuable clue to the interpretation.
Εἰς τέλος does not look back to τὸ

14　　¹⁴ʹὍταν δὲ ἴδητε τὸ βδέλυγμα τῆς ἐρημώσεως

14 το βδελ. της ερημ.]+το ρηθεν υπο Δανιηλ του προφητου ΑΧΓΔΠΣΦ min⁽ᶠᵉʳᵉ ᵒᵐⁿ⁾
c (k) l syrrᵖᵉˢʰ ʰᶜˡ aeth

τέλος (vv. 4, 7), but as in Lc. xviii. 5,
Jo. xiii. 1 and in numerous passages
of the LXX., it is an adverbial phrase,
'finally,' 'at last,' 'to' or 'in the end';
cf. 1 Chron. xxviii. 9 (לְעַד), 2 Chron.
xxxi. 1 (לְכַלֵּה), Ps. xlviii. (xlix.) 9,
Job xx. 7 (לָנֶצַח). He who is finally
victorious, who perseveres in his confession till death puts an end to the
conflict, shall save his soul's life. The
teaching is similar to that of viii. 35,
but it strikes the note of ὑπομονή of
which from this time forth all Christian
teaching is full; cf. e.g. James i. 3 f.,
Rom. v. 3 f., viii. 25, 1 Thess. i. 3,
2 Thess. i. 4, iii. 5, Heb. xii. 1, Apoc.
i. 9, Tertullian de patientia, Cyprian
de bono patientiae; on the last two see
Archbp Benson's remarks, Cyprian,
p. 439 ff.; and on the characteristics of
Christian ὑπομονή comp. Trench, syn.
liii. For the higher sense of σώζειν cf.
viii. 35, x. 26; preservation from the
destruction which overtook the Jews
can hardly be in question here, or
again deliverance from the sword of
the persecutor; the thought is rather
of a salvation which is not fully
realised till death or the παρουσία.

14—23. TROUBLES CONNECTED
CHIEFLY WITH THE FALL OF JE-
RUSALEM (Mt. xxiv. 15—25, Lc. xxi.
20—24).

14. ὅταν δὲ ἴδητε κτλ.] The Lord
answers the question τί τὸ σημεῖον
in reference to the end of the City
and Temple, so far as an answer
was needed for practical guidance.
The sign is the βδέλυγμα τῆς ἐρημώσεως : Mt. adds, τὸ ῥηθὲν διὰ Δανιὴλ
τοῦ προφητοῦ, a later note which is
wanting in the true text of Mc.
The phrase occurs in the Greek
Daniel thrice : ix. 27 ἐπὶ τὸ ἱερὸν
βδέλυγμα τῶν ἐρημώσεων LXX., Th.

(עַל כְּנַף שִׁקּוּצִים מְשֹׁמֵם); xi. 31 βδ.
ἐρημώσεως, LXX., βδ. ἠφανισμένον Th.
(שִׁקּוּץ מְשֹׁמֵם); xii. 11 (τὸ) βδ. (τῆς)
ἐρημώσεως LXX., Th. (שִׁקּוּץ שֹׁמֵם);
cf. viii. 13 ἡ ἁμαρτία ἐρημώσεως LXX.,
Th. (הַפֶּשַׁע שֹׁמֵם). Difficulties connected with the Heb. text (see Bevan,
Daniel, ad ll., esp. p. 192 f.; Driver,
Daniel, pp. 151, 188, and in Hastings,
D.B. i. p. 11) do not directly con-
cern us here; if the Lord cited it,
He did so doubtless in the sense
which the Greek translations had long
impressed upon the passage. The
Greek phrase βδ. ἐρημώσεως occurs
also in 1 Maccabees, where it is applied to the altar of Zeus erected in
the Temple by Antiochus, B.C. 168
(1 Macc. i. 54, cf. v. 59, vi. 7). Βδέλυγμα is a frequent LXX. rendering of
שֶׁקֶץ or שִׁקּוּץ in the sense of an idol,
cf. Deut. xxix. 17 (16), or a false god
(Ezech. vii. 20), but as the passages
just cited from 1 Macc. shew, it is not
limited to an object of idolatrous worship; any symbol of heathenism which
outraged the religious feelings of the
Jewish people might be so described.
The defining genitive ἐρημώσεως limits
us to an outrage which was the pre-
lude of national ruin, a crisis corresponding in effect if not in circumstances with the invasion of Antiochus.
What this new βδ. ἐρημώσεως was
St Luke, taught by the event, plainly
tells us, for instead of ὅταν ἴδητε τὸ
βδ. κτλ. (Mt., Mc.) he writes ὅταν ἴδ.
κυκλουμένην ὑπὸ στρατοπέδων Ἰερουσαλήμ. The presence of the Roman
army round the Holy City was itself a
βδέλυγμα of the worst kind, and one
which foreboded coming ruin. The
words of Daniel seemed to find a
second fulfilment; Rome had taken
the place of Syria. Cf. Jos. ant. x.

ἑστηκότα ὅπου οὐ δεῖ—ὁ ἀναγινώσκων νοείτω—τότε

14 εστηκοτα אBL] εστηκος DΨ 28 εστος AEFG(KM)SUV(ΧΓ)ΔΠΣΦ 2ᵖᵉ minᵖˡ στηκον 1 13 28 69 91 299 346 | οπου] pr εν τοπω 1071 εν τοπω αγιω aethᵛⁱᵈ | νοειτω] +τι αναγεινωσκει D a (n)

11. 7 καὶ δὴ ταῦτα ἡμῶν συνέβη παθεῖν τῷ ἔθνει ὑπὸ 'Αντιόχου τοῦ 'Επιφα-νοῦς...τὸν αὐτὸν δὲ τρόπον ὁ Δανίηλος καὶ περὶ τῆς 'Ρωμαίων ἡγεμονίας ἀνέ-γραψε καὶ ὅτι ὑπ' αὐτῶν ἐρημωθήσεται. The patristic interpreters thought of Pilate's attempt to introduce the effigy of the emperor into the city (*B. J.* ii. 9. 2), or of similar insults offered to the Jewish faith by Hadrian (Jerome : "potest...accipi...aut de imagine Caesaris quam Pilatus posuit in templo aut de Hadriani equestri statua quae in ipso sancto sanctorum usque in praesentem diem stetit") or of acts committed at the time of the capture of the city (Victor : βδ. τινές φασι τοὺς στρατιώτας τοὺς εἰσελθόντας τῷ ἱερῷ, τινὲς δὲ τὸν ἀνδριάντα τοῦ τότε τὴν πόλιν ἑλόντος), or of the Roman standards, which bore the figure of the eagle (Ephrem).

ἑστηκότα ὅπου οὐ δεῖ] A *constructio ad sensum* (WM., p. 176) ; the βδέ-λυγμα is personified, or regarded as personal : 'when ye see...him standing where he ought not'; cf. 2 Thess. ii. 6 f. τὸ κατέχον...ὁ κατέχων. Mt. pre-fers ἑστός, and interprets ὅπου οὐ δεῖ as ἐν τόπῳ ἁγίῳ—a phrase which has confirmed the impression, based on 1 Macc. *l.c.*, that the sign must be sought within the sacred precinct. But his anarthrous τόπος ἅγιος is per-haps not equivalent to ὁ ἅ. τόπος (2 Macc. viii. 17, Acts vi. 13) or ὁ τόπος (Jo. xi. 48), ὁ τ. οὗτος (Acts xxi. 28). All Palestine, but especially Jerusalem (ἡ ἁγία γῆ, ἡ ἁγία πόλις, 2 Macc. i. 7, iii. 1) was to a Jew holy ground, where the Gentile had no right to be. On ὅπου οὐ δεῖ cf. Bengel : "sermo ad hominem ; Judaei putabant non oportere, et non oportebat quatenus locus erat sanctus."

ὁ ἀναγινώσκων νοείτω] This paren-thesis finds a place both in Mt. and Mc., and probably belonged to a com-mon source. The words may be either those of the Lord directing attention to the passages in Daniel, or those of the writer of a document on which both Mc. and Mt. drew, directing attention to the Lord's words in this place. But the former supposition is almost excluded by the fact that in Mc.—the earlier narrative—no men-tion is made of Daniel or any pro-phetic writing. If ὁ ἀναγινώσκων is the reader (Apoc. i. 3) of the docu-ment on which Mc. here depends, we are carried back to days before the first investment of Jerusalem (A.D. 66) when the sign yet needed interpreta-tion : "the time has not yet come...but it is near at hand" (Sanday, *Inspira-tion*, p. 292).

τότε οἱ ἐν τῇ 'Ιουδαίᾳ κτλ.] Not the Apostles themselves, but other Jew-ish Christians who remained in the country. Cf. Thpht. : καλῶς εἶπεν Οἱ ἐν τῇ 'Ιουδαίᾳ· οἱ γὰρ ἀπόστολοι οὐκ ἦσαν ἐν τῇ 'Ιουδαίᾳ, ἀλλά...πρὸ τοῦ πολέμου ἐδιώχθησαν ἀπὸ τῆς 'Ιερουσαλήμ, μᾶλλον δὲ ἐξῆλθον αὐτοί. So Mt., Mc., Lc. ; Lc. adds a special warning to those who should be in Jerusalem itself or its neighbourhood (καὶ οἱ ἐν μέσῳ αὐτῆς κτλ.). Acc. to Eus. *H. E.* iii. 5. 3 the Christians of Jerusalem were warned before the war broke out by a pro-phetic revelation (κατά τινα χρησμὸν τοῖς αὐτόθι δοκίμοις δι' ἀποκαλύψεως ἐκδοθέντα πρὸ τοῦ πολέμου) to leave the city and retire to Pella in Peraea; Epiphanius (*de pond. et mens.* 15) has nearly the same story, but attributes the revelation to an angel. Pella (Jos. *B. J.* iii. 3. 3, G. A. Smith, p. 593 ff., Merrill, *East of the Jordan*,

15 οἱ ἐν τῇ Ἰουδαίᾳ φευγέτωσαν εἰς τὰ ὄρη. ¹⁵ὁ ἐπὶ
τοῦ δώματος μὴ καταβάτω μηδὲ εἰσελθάτω τι ἆραι
16 ἐκ τῆς οἰκίας αὐτοῦ, ¹⁶καὶ ὁ εἰς τὸν ἀγρὸν μὴ ἐπι-
§ go στρεψάτω εἰς τὰ ὀπίσω ἆραι §τὸ ἱμάτιον αὐτοῦ.
17 ¹⁷οὐαὶ δὲ ταῖς ἐν γαστρὶ ἐχούσαις καὶ ταῖς θηλα-

14 εις] επι U 604 2ᵖᵉ aᴵᵖᵃᵘᶜ   15 ο επι BFH aegg] ο δε επι ℵAEGKLMSUVX
ΓΔΠΣΦΨ minᶠᵉʳᵉᵒᵐⁿ syrʰᵉˡ και ο επι D 604 2ᵖᵉ syrˢⁱⁿ arm a ff k n q vg | καταβατω]+εις
την οικιαν ΑΔΧΓΔΠΣΦ minᵖˡ a ff i n q vg syrrˢⁱⁿ ʰᶜˡ arm aeth (om ℵBL c k aegg syrᵖᵒˢʰ)
16 ο εις τον αγρον]+ων ΑΧΓΠΣΦ minᵖˡ | εις τα οπισω] om εις τα ℵD minᵖᵃᵘᶜ
17 om δε D | θηλαζομεναις D 28

p. 184 ff.) lay between Gerasa and
Hippos on the edge of the table-land,
scarcely among the mountains; but
the way to it from Judaea led across
both the Judaean and the Moabite
hills, so that εἰς τὰ ὄρη is a sufficient
index of the direction which the flight
was to take. Details as to the precise
locality would be more appropriately
given through one of the 'prophets'
of the Church of Jerusalem (cf. Acts
xi. 27 f., xxi. 10) when the time drew
near.

15, 16. ὁ ἐπὶ τοῦ δώματος κτλ.]
When the signal is given, not a
moment may be lost; the citizen
who is resting or praying on his roof
must not stop to collect his property,
or the countryman who is at work
to go after the clothing he has left
in another part of the field. Men
went up to the flat roofs of their
houses to sleep (1 Sam. ix. 25), to
worship (Jer. xix. 13, Zeph. i. 5, Acts
x. 9), to watch (Isa. xxii. 1), to proclaim tidings good or bad (Isa. xv. 3,
Mt. x. 27), to spend the Feast of
Tabernacles (Neh. viii. 16), and doubtless for many other purposes; so
usual a place of resort was the
roof that the law required it to be
fenced with a parapet (Deut. xxii. 8)
as a protection against accidental
falls. The roof was accessible from
without (ii. 4, note, cf. Lc. v. 19) by
a staircase, or ladder, so that the
man on the roof might escape with-

out entering his house. Ὁ εἰς τὸν
ἀγρόν, he who is at work on the
farm; εἰς calls attention to the
movement which attends labour—
the man has gone out to his plot of
ground (for ἀγρός see v. 14, vi. 36,
56, xi. 8, xv. 21, Lc. xv. 15), and
while there, is moving from place to
place; for this use of εἰς cf. ii. 1 (v.l.),
Acts viii. 40, Blass, Gr., p. 122 f.
Meanwhile his outer garment (τὸ ἱμάτιον) is left behind (εἰς τὰ ὀπίσω) at
home, or at the entrance of the field;
he is working γυμνός (Jo. xxi. 7) or
μονοχίτων, and he must be content
to make his escape as he is. Εἰς τὰ
ὀπίσω is a frequent phrase in the LXX.
(usually = אָחוֹר); for the N. T. cf. Lc.
ix. 62, Jo. vi. 66, xviii. 6, xx. 14. The
passage as a whole recalls Lot's escape
from Sodom (Gen. xix. 17 μὴ περιβλέ-
ψῃς εἰς τὰ ὀπίσω...εἰς τὸ ὄρος σώζου).
Lc. has these verses in another connexion, where the allusion to Sodom
is clear (Lc. xvii. 28 ff.).

17. οὐαὶ δὲ ταῖς κτλ.] Alas for
mothers with children at the breast,
and those who are soon to become
mothers, for whom a hasty flight is
impossible, who cannot leave their
burden. The horrors of the siege
would convert the joy of maternity
into a woe: cf. Lc. xxiii. 28 f. Οὐαί
has the true ring of apocalyptic prophecy; both the O. T. prophets and
the Apocalypse use it abundantly;
Mc. has it only here and in xiv. 21,

ζούσαις ἐν ἐκείναις ταῖς ἡμέραις. ¹⁸προσεύχεσθε δὲ 18
ἵνα μὴ γένηται χειμῶνος· ¹⁹§ἔσονται §γὰρ αἱ ἡμέραι 19 §b
ἐκεῖναι θλίψις οἵα οὐ γέγονεν τοιαύτη ἀπ᾽ ἀρχῆς §C
κτίσεως ἣν ἔκτισεν ὁ θεὸς ἕως τοῦ νῦν, καὶ οὐ μὴ

18 om δε Ψ και προσ. D a i n | γενηται אּ*ᶜ·ᵃ B (D) (L) (13) (28) alᵐᵘ c (d) ff l vg
arm] + η φυγη υμων אּᶜ·ᵇΑΧΓΔΠΣΦΨ minᵖˡ k syrrᵖᵉˢʰ ʰᶜˡ aegg go aeth | χειμωνος]+η
σαββατου (-των, -τω, εν σαββατω) L minⁿᵒⁿⁿ k (aut sabbato)+μηδε σαββατου Σ+μ.
σαββατω 1071+μ. εν σαββατω 736   19 εσονται γαρ αι ημ. εκειναι] εσται γαρ εν ταις
ημεραις εκειναις Γ (a b d k n q) syrrˢⁱⁿ ᵖᵉˢʰ | θλιψις οια ου γεγονεν τοιαυτη] θλιψεις οιαι ουκ
εγενοντο (vel ου γεγονασι) τοιαται D 299 (2ᵖᵉ) (yˢᶜʳ) latt arm θλιψεις οιαι ου γεγοναν
ουδεποτε τοιαυται Φ θλιψεις οιαι ου γεγονασι ποτε τ. 2ᵖᵉ θλιψις οια ου γεγονε ποτε
τοιαυτη 604 om τοιαυτη Ψ | om κτισεως 28 299 armᶜᵒᵈ | om ην εκτ. ο θεος D 27 2ᵖᵃ
a c ff k n arm | ην אּBCᵇLΨ 28] ης AC²ΧΓΔΠΦ minᶠᵉʳᵉ ᵒᵐⁿ | om εως του νυν Σ | και
ου μη] ουδε μη D ουδ ου μη FGΣ 1 13 69 157 253 346 2ᵖᵉ

but it is frequent in Mt., Lc. Θηλάζειν is used of the mother (Gen. xxi. 7,
Exod. ii. 9, 1 Regn. i. 23, 2 Macc. vii.
27), as well as of the child (3 Regn.
iii. 25, Ps. viii. 2, Joel ii. 16, Jer. li.
(xliv.) 7, Lc. xi. 27)—a fact which
appears to have been overlooked by
the 'Western' corrector who wrote
θηλαζομέναις for θηλαζούσαις (cf. vv.ll.).
Ἐν γαστρὶ ἔχειν is a Herodotean
phrase revived in late Greek; in the
lxx. it is the usual equivalent of
הָרָה.

18. προσεύχεσθε δὲ ἵνα μὴ γένηται]
Mt. supplies ἡ φυγή from φευγέτωσαν v. 16, but the reference may
well be wider—'pray that this sign
and all that must follow its appearance
come not to pass during the winter,
when the hardships of flight and
privation will be greater.' For the
gen. of time see WM., p. 258, and
cf. νυκτός, 1 Thess. v. 7. Mt. has the
interesting addition μηδὲ σαββάτῳ
'nor yet (at whatever season) on a
sabbath,' when many Jews, even
Christian Jews (cf. Acts xxi. 20 f.),
would be hindered by their scruples
from escaping beyond the immediate
vicinity of Jerusalem (Acts i. 12); in
the Maccabean wars such scruples had
borne deadly fruit (1 Macc. ii. 32 ff.),
and their influence was now perhaps

stronger than ever through the teaching of the Scribes. Mc.'s omission of
this point has been commonly explained by the fact that he wrote
for Gentile readers, to whom the
strength of Jewish feeling on the
subject would be unintelligible. But
it is quite possible that μηδὲ σαββάτῳ had no place in the common
tradition, though it had clung to the
memory or had been added by the
zeal of the Palestinian Church. For
προσεύχεσθαι ἵνα (ὅπως) cf. xiv. 35, 38 ;
Phil. i. 9, Jas. v. 16; for other constructions see Lc. xxii. 40, Jas. v. 17.

19. ἔσονται γὰρ αἱ ἡμέραι κτλ.]
'Those days shall be straitness the
like of which hath not come to pass'
&c. Mt. softens the harshness of
Mc.'s sentence, but at the same time
lessens its force (ἔσται γὰρ τότε θλίψις
μεγάλη οἵα οὐ γέγονεν). The Book of
Daniel is again in view: cf. Dan.
xii. 1 lxx. ἐκείνη ἡ ἡμέρα θλίψεως οἵα
οὐκ ἐγενήθη ἀφ᾽ οὗ ἐγενήθησαν ἕως
τῆς ἡμέρας ἐκείνης = Th. ἔσται καιρὸς
θλίψεως, θλίψις οἵα οὐ γέγονεν ἀφ᾽ ἧς
γεγένηται ἔθνος κτλ. Θλίψις is here
(see iv. 17, note, and cf. Lc.'s ἀνάγκη)
used almost in its literal sense for the
daily tightening of the meshes of the
siege; cf. Deut. xxviii. 53 (which is
also perhaps in the Lord's thoughts),

¶ n 20 γένηται.¶ ²⁰καὶ εἰ μὴ ἐκολόβωσεν Κύριος τὰς ἡμέρας,
οὐκ ἂν ἐσώθη πᾶσα σάρξ· ἀλλὰ διὰ τοὺς ἐκλεκτοὺς

19 γενωνται D 2ᵖᵉ lattᵉˣᶜᵏ   20 κυριος] ο θεος Ψ 13 28 69 299 1071 alⁿᵒⁿⁿ arm
the | τας ημερας]+εκεινας EFGMΔΨ 1 13 69 736 alⁿᵒⁿⁿ c g* syrrˢⁱⁿᵖᵉˢʰ arm aegg aeth
+δια τους εκλεκτους αυτου D a b ff i q arm

ἐν τῇ στενοχωρίᾳ σου καὶ ἐν τῇ θλίψει
σου ᾗ θλίψει σε ὁ ἐχθρός σου, reproduced in Jer. xix. 9, where the LXX.
has ἐν τῇ περιοχῇ καὶ πολιορκίᾳ ᾗ
πολιορκήσουσιν αὐτοὺς οἱ ἐχθροὶ αὐτῶν.
Οἷα...τοιαύτη for τοιαύτη οἷα is perhaps
unique; the passages quoted in
Grimm-Thayer (1 Cor. xv. 48, 2 Cor.
x. 11) are not exact parallels. Γέγονεν
represents the fact as standing in its
completeness on the page of history:
'no such event has ever occurred';
comp. Jos. B. J. prooem. 4 τὰ γοῦν
πάντων ἀπ᾽ αἰῶνος ἀτυχήματα πρὸς τὰ
Ἰουδαίων ἡττῆσθαι δοκῶ κατὰ σύγκρισιν.
Ἀπ᾽ ἀρχῆς κτίσεως κτλ.: cf. x. 6, note;
similar phrases occur in Exod. ix. 18,
Deut. iv. 32; with ἣν ἔκτισεν ὁ θεός,
cf. οὓς ἐξελέξατο (v. 20). Ἕως τοῦ νῦν,
cf. ἄχρι τοῦ νῦν, Rom. viii. 22, Phil. i.
5; ἀπὸ τοῦ νῦν, Lc. xxii. 18, 69, Acts
xviii. 6, 2 Cor. v. 16.

Lc. adds (xxi. 23ᵇ, 24) some remarkable words, based partly on
Zach. xii. 3, partly anticipating the
Pauline view of the relation between
the fall of Israel and the conversion
of the Gentile world (Rom. xi. 25 ff.).

20. εἰ μὴ ἐκολόβωσεν Κύριος κτλ.]
Mt. εἰ μὴ ἐκολοβώθησαν αἱ ἡμέραι ἐκεῖναι. Mc.'s form of the sentence has a
note of greater originality—the use of
the anarthrous Κύριος=יְהֹוָה which is
limited in the N.T. to O.T. quotations
and phrases, and a few passages where
a Hebrew or Aramaic original seems
to be directly in view (e.g. Lc. i. 5—
ii. 52, where it occurs eight times).
Κολοβοῦν is properly to 'amputate'
(cf. 2 Regn. iv. 12 κολοβοῦσιν τὰς χεῖρας
αὐτῶν καὶ τοὺς πόδας αὐτῶν, and cf.
the epithet κολοβοδάκτυλος applied to
St Mark, p. xxvi f.); hence to 'curtail,'
'cut short,' Vg. (Mt., Mc.) breviare.

With the thought of a Divine curtail-
ment of time comp. Barnabas 4. 3 εἰς
τοῦτο γὰρ ὁ δεσπότης συντέτμηκεν τοὺς
καιροὺς καὶ τὰς ἡμέρας, ἵνα ταχύνῃ ὁ
ἠγαπημένος αὐτοῦ καὶ ἐπὶ τὴν κληρονο-
μίαν αὐτοῦ ἥξῃ: but the purpose in
Barn. is different, and the reference
is to Dan. ix. 24 συνετμήθησαν, and
not to the Gospels. On the construction εἰ μὴ ἐκολόβωσεν...οὐκ ἂν
ἐσώθη see WM., p. 382.

οὐκ ἂν ἐσώθη πᾶσα σάρξ] לֹא יִוָּשַׁע
כָּל־בָּשָׂר (Delitzsch). Two Heb. idioms
are combined here—the use of כֹּל
בָּשָׂר for 'all men' (Gen. vi. 12), and
the use of כֹּל...לֹא for 'none' (Gen.
ix. 11); cf. Blass, Gr. pp. 162, 178,
WM., p. 214 f. For the construction
see WM., p. 382. Not a soul could
have escaped from Jerusalem, had
not the hand of GOD brought the
siege to a speedy end. It lasted five
months, from the Passover (Jos. B.J.
v. 3. 1) to September (ib. vi. 8. 4),
when Titus entered the city; but the
investment was not complete before
May. Notwithstanding the horrors
of the time the survivors were in-
credibly numerous, 97,000 acc. to
Josephus (B. J. vi. 9. 3). For the
causes which "combined to shorten
the siege" see Alford on Mt. xxiv. 22.

διὰ τοὺς ἐκλεκτούς κτλ.] In the
O.T. the ἐκλεκτοί (הַבְּחִירִים) are the
covenant people (Ps. civ. (cv.) 6, Isa.
xliii. 20), but more especially Israel
idealised and responding to GOD's
choice (Isa. xlii. 1, lxv. 9 ff.). In Enoch
the term is used for the righteous in
Israel (En. i. 1 εὐλόγησεν ἐκλεκτοὺς
δικαίους) for whom the Messianic
Kingdom is reserved. The Gospels
retain this general sense, transferring

οὓς ἐξελέξατο ἐκολόβωσεν τὰς ἡμέρας. ²¹§καὶ τότε 21 § Wᵇ
ἐάν τις ὑμῖν εἴπῃ ῞Ιδε ὧδε ὁ χριστός, ἴδε ἐκεῖ, μὴ
πιστεύετε· ²²ἐγερθήσονται γὰρ ψευδόχριστοι καὶ 22

21 ιδε (1°) אBL] ιδου ACDXΓΔΠΣΦ minᵒᵐⁿ ᵛⁱᵈ | ιδε (2°) אBDL 28 2ᵖᵉ] ιδου
AWᵇXΓΔΠΣΦ minᵖˡ om C 63 me pr και B the pr η A(C)DXΓΔΠΣΦ minˢᵃᵗᵐᵘ a b c ff i q
syrʰᶜˡ arm (me) go aeth | πιστευσητε GKMSUWᵇXΓΠΣΦ   22 γαρ ABDLΦ] δε
אC | om ψευδοχριστοι και D 124 i k

the word to those of the κλητοί who
answer to the call and prove themselves worthy of it (Mt. xxii. 14, cf.
Lightfoot on Col. iii. 12). Here the
elect, for whose sake the siege was
shortened, are probably the faithful
members of the Church of Jerusalem,
the ἅλας τῆς γῆς, whose intercession
or whose presence secured this privilege, though it did not avail to save
the city (Gen. xviii. 32); Thpht. would
include those of the Jews who should
afterwards be brought to the faith,
τοὺς ἐξ ᾿Εβραίων...ὕστερον μέλλοντας
πιστεύειν. Οὓς ἐξελέξατο is omitted
by Mt.; cf. v. 19 τῆς κτίσεως ἣν
ἔκτισεν ὁ θεός, where Mt. has merely
τοῦ κόσμου.

21. καὶ τότε ἐάν τις ὑμῖν εἴπῃ κτλ.]
The warning of v. 6 is resumed, with
special reference to the circumstances
of the last days of Jerusalem. Such a
crisis would be sure to call up a host
of pretenders to Messiahship, whether
the title were used or not (see note to
v. 6). ῎Ιδε ὧδε...ἴδε ἐκεῖ: Mt. expands
this: ἐὰν οὖν εἴπωσιν ὑμῖν ᾿Ιδοὺ ἐν
τῇ ἐρήμῳ ἐστίν, μὴ ἐξέλθητε· ᾿Ιδοὺ ἐν
τοῖς ταμείοις, μὴ πιστεύσητε. Too little
is known of the life of the Church at
Pella to enable us to say whether it
was disturbed by such reports. But the
tidings of the siege which reached
the refugees from time to time would
have predisposed them to accept any
stories which chimed in with their
growing belief that the παρουσία was
at hand. Μὴ πιστεύετε: incredulity is
sometimes a Christian duty. On the
pres. imperative see Burton § 1656.

22. ψευδόχριστοι καὶ ψευδοπρο-
φῆται] The ψευδοπροφήτης is known
to the lxx. (Zach. xiii. 2, Jer.⁹=נָבִיא),
for there were such under the old
covenant (2 Pet. ii. 1, cf. Deut. xiii.
1 ff.); and the Lord had at the outset
of the Ministry warned His disciples
against this class of men (Mt. vii. 15),
for the return of a true prophecy
would bring back the spurious imita-
tions. One such appears in Acts xiii.
6; many such were abroad before the
end of the Apostolic age (1 Jo. iv. 1,
see Westcott's note; cf. Apoc. xix. 20,
xx. 10); they were familiar to the
writer of the Didache (11 πᾶς δὲ
προφήτης διδάσκων τὴν ἀλήθειαν, εἰ
ἃ διδάσκει οὐ ποιεῖ, ψευδοπροφήτης
ἐστίν). The ψευδόχριστος is necessarily a far less common character,
and the word is probably a creation of the Evangelists or their
Greek source. St John's ἀντίχριστος
(1 Jo. ii. 22, iv. 3, 2 Jo. 7) presents a
different conception; the Antichrist
opposes Christ, the Pseudochrist is
merely a "pretender to the Messianic
office" (Westcott on 1 Jo. ii. 22, cf.
Trench, syn. xxx.). The pretended
Messiahs were scarcely a source of
serious danger to the Church, after the
end of the Jewish polity, and it is to
these only that the Lord's words directly refer. Even the earlier Church
writers however do not always observe
this distinction; cf. Hegesippus ap.
Eus. H. E. iv. 22 ἀπὸ τούτων (he has
named various early heretical sects)
ψευδόχριστοι...οἵτινες ἐμέρισαν τὴν
ἕνωσιν τῆς ἐκκλησίας φθοριμαίοις λόγοις
κατὰ τοῦ θεοῦ καὶ κατὰ τοῦ χριστοῦ
αὐτοῦ. Similarly Justin (dial. 82)

ψευδοπροφῆται καὶ δώσουσιν σημεῖα καὶ τέρατα
πρὸς τὸ ἀποπλανᾶν εἰ δυνατὸν τοὺς ἐκλεκτούς.
23 ²³ὑμεῖς δὲ βλέπετε· προείρηκα ὑμῖν πάντα.
§ e 24   ²⁴§'Ἀλλὰ ἐν ἐκείναις ταῖς ἡμέραις μετὰ τὴν θλί-

22 δωσουσιν] ποιησουσιν D 13 28 69 91 124 299 346 2ᵖᵉ a d | τους εκλεκτους] pr και
ACLWᵇXΓΔΠΣΦ minᵒᵐⁿ ᵛⁱᵈ latt syrr arm aegg go aeth om τους Ψ   23 προειρηκα]
pr ιδου ℵACDWᵇXΓΔΠΣΦ minᶠᵉʳᵉᵒᵐⁿ lattᵉˣᶜᵃ syrr arm go Cypr

quotes the present context with the
remark ὅπερ καὶ ἔστι· πολλοὶ γὰρ
ἄθεα καὶ βλάσφημα καὶ ἄδικα ἐν ὀνόματι
αὐτοῦ παραχαράσσοντες ἐδίδαξαν. But
these are the ἀντίχριστοι of 1, 2 Jo.
rather than the ψευδόχριστοι of the
Gospels.

δώσουσιν σημεῖα καὶ τέρατα] The
words look back to Exod. vii. 11, 22,
and are based on Deut. xiii. 1 (2) ἐὰν...
προφήτης...δῷ σοι σημεῖον ἤ τέρας (וְנָתַן
אֵלֶיךָ אוֹת אוֹ מוֹפֵת) κτλ. The combination σημεῖα καὶ τέρατα is common in
the O.T. (e.g. Deut. xxviii. 46, xxix. 3
(4), xxxiv. 11, 2 Esdr. xix. 10, Ps.
cxxxiv. (cxxxv.) 9, Isa. viii. 18; what
Dr Driver (*Deut.* p. 75) says of the
corresponding Heb. words is true of
the Greek—σημεῖον is "a *sign*, i.e.
something, ordinary or extraordinary,
as the case may be, regarded as significant of a truth beyond itself," whilst
τέρας is "a *portent*, an occurrence
regarded merely as something extraordinary"; cf. Trench, *syn.* xli. The
Gospels prefer σημεῖον and δύναμις in
reference to the miracles of Jesus;
the Jews sought for startling τέρατα
(Jo. iv. 48), but the Lord's work did
not usually assume this form; the
latter word, however, is used freely in
the Acts (ii. 22, 43, iv. 30, v. 12, vi. 8,
xiv. 3, xv. 12), and occasionally by
St Paul (Rom. xv. 19, 2 Cor. xii. 12),
to describe the effect which the Christian miracles produced, rather than
their actual character or their purpose.
To exhibit portents belongs especially
to the false prophet or false Christ,
whose ambition it is to startle and

excite admiration. But his τέρατα
are as false as his pretensions (2
Thess. ii. 9 τ. ψεύδους).

πρὸς τὸ ἀποπλανᾶν κτλ.] 'With the
view of misleading'; cf. WM., p. 505.
Ἀποπλανᾶν, 'to lead astray by divert-
ing from the right path,' used absolutely (2 Chron. xxi. 11, Prov. vii. 21,
Sir.³, 2 Macc. ii. 2), or followed by
ἀπό and a gen. (1 Tim. vi. 10 ἀπεπλα-
νήθησαν ἀπὸ τῆς πίστεως). Τοὺς ἐκλεκτούς, cf. *v.* 20, note; Mt. emphasises
the boldness of the aim by prefixing
καί. Εἰ δυνατόν, sc. ἐστίν, *si potest fieri*,
R. V. "if possible"; the phrase leaves
the possibility undetermined, cf. xiv.
35, Rom. xii. 18.

23. ὑμεῖς δὲ βλέπετε] 'But ye,
for your part, be on your guard'; cf.
vv. 5, 9; βλ. is used absolutely again
in *v.* 33. Προείρηκα ὑμῖν πάντα: 'all
that is necessary to direct your conduct'; if the prediction was not full
or exact enough to gratify curiosity, it
was sufficient to create responsibility
and supply practical guidance. Προει-
πεῖν is used of prophetic announce-
ments; cf. Acts i. 16 προεῖπε τὸ πνεῦμα
τὸ ἅγιον, Rom. ix. 29 προείρηκεν
Ἡσαίας.

24—27. THE END OF THE DISPEN-
SATION FORETOLD (Mt. xxiv. 29—31,
Lc. xxi. 25—28).

24. ἀλλὰ ἐν ἐκείναις ταῖς ἡμέραις
μετὰ κτλ.] 'But (ἀλλά) there is more
to follow; in those days, &c.' The
prophecy now carries us beyond the
fall of the city (μετὰ τὴν θλίψιν ἐκείνην,
cf. *v.* 19). Ἐν ἐκείναις ταῖς ἡμέραις is
indefinite (i. 9, note), merely connecting

ψιν⁋ ἐκείνην ὁ ἥλιος σκοτισθήσεται, καὶ ἡ σελήνη οὐ   ⁋ b
δώσει τὸ φέγγος αὐτῆς, ²⁵καὶ οἱ ἀστέρες ἔσονται ἐκ 25
τοῦ οὐρανοῦ πίπτοντες, καὶ αἱ δυνάμεις αἱ ἐν τοῖς

24 εκεινην] των ημερων εκεινων Σ 11 69 346 1071 al^nonn arm^cod   25 εσονται εκ
τ. ουρ. πιπτοντες] οι εκ του ουρ. εσ. πιπτ. D c ff (q) του ουρ. εσ. πιπτ. (vel εκπιπτ.)
L(W^bΧΓΔΠ²ΣΦ) min^pl (εκπιπτ. etiam A vg) πεσουνται εκ των ουρανων 604 | αι εν τοις
ουρ.] των ουρανων DK 115 a c ff g i syrr^sin pesh arm^codd me aeth

the sequel with what has gone before, so that the destruction of the Jewish polity is regarded as the starting point of the era which will be ended by the παρουσία. Mt., interpreting the Lord's words by the conviction which possessed the first generation, prefixes εὐθέως, with which compare the ταχύ of Apoc. xxii. 20; the original form of the sentence, as we see it in Mc., leaves the interval uncertain. The Lord merely foretells that His personal coming will follow the capture of Jerusalem, and not precede and prevent it, as many might be tempted to expect (*v.* 21 f.). Lc. has lost the note of time altogether.

ὁ ἥλιος σκοτισθήσεται κτλ.] The symbolical description which follows is gathered from O.T. predictions of the ruin of nations hostile to Israel; cf. Isa. xiii. 10 (of Babylon) οἱ γὰρ ἀστέρες τοῦ οὐρανοῦ...τὸ φῶς οὐ δώσουσιν, καὶ σκοτισθήσεται τοῦ ἡλίου ἀνατέλλοντος, καὶ ἡ σελήνη οὐ δώσει τὸ φῶς αὐτῆς: *ib.* xxxiv. 4 (of Edom) τακήσονται πᾶσαι αἱ δυνάμεις τῶν οὐρανῶν...καὶ πάντα τὰ ἄστρα πεσεῖται: Ezech. xxxii. 7 (of Egypt) ἥλιον ἐν νεφέλῃ καλύψω, καὶ σελήνη οὐ μὴ φάνῃ τὸ φῶς αὐτῆς. Joel (ii. 30=iii. 3) connects similiar portents with the dispensation of the Spirit (cf. Acts ii. 17 ff.). In all these cases physical phenomena are used to describe the upheaval of dynasties, or great moral and spiritual changes; and it is unnecessary to exact any other meaning from the words when they are adopted by Christ. The centuries which followed the fall of Jerusalem were destined to witness

dynastic and social revolutions greater and wider than any which swept over Babylon and Egypt, and to these portents of Christian history the Lord's words may reasonably be referred. On the other hand they do not exclude, perhaps they even suggest, a collapse of the present order of Nature immediately before the παρουσία (2 Pet. iii. 12). One of the phenomena described accompanied the Crucifixion (Lc. xxiii. 45); the Return may well be signalised by greater disturbances of the visible order. Φέγγος is used specially, though not invariably, of the 'lights that govern the night'; see Trench, *syn.* clxxxvii., and cf. Joel ii. 10, iii. (iv.) 15; this word is stronger than φῶς, the brightness or lustre of light; cf. Hab. iii. 4 φέγγος αὐτοῦ ὡς φῶς ἔσται.

25. οἱ ἀστέρες ἔσονται...πίπτοντες] The conception is that of individual stars (not τὰ ἄστρα as in Lc. xxi. 25) falling at various times: cf. Apoc. vi. 13, viii. 10, ix. 1. For the periphrasis ἔσονται...π. cf. *v.* 13 ἔσεσθε μισούμενοι. Mt. has πεσοῦνται, but it is unsafe to infer (WM., p. 437) that Mc.'s expression is a simple substitute for the future; as usual, Mc. is more precise in his descriptive language than Mt. Σαλευθήσονται on the other hand is equally accurate, for the disturbance is in this case regarded as final (Heb. xii. 26). The "powers in heaven" (Mt. 'of heaven') are the צְבָא הַשָּׁמַיִם of Isa. xxxiv. 4; the heavenly bodies in general. Σαλεύεσθαι (used here by the three Synoptists) is frequently employed by the LXX. for earthquake

26 οὐρανοῖς σαλευθήσονται. ²⁶καὶ τότε ὄψονται τὸν
υἱὸν τοῦ ἀνθρώπου ἐρχόμενον ἐν νεφέλαις μετὰ δυνά-
27 μεως πολλῆς καὶ δόξης· ²⁷καὶ τότε ἀποστελεῖ τοὺς

26 εν νεφελαις] επι των νεφελων D syrˢⁱⁿ ᵛⁱᵈ μετα τ. νεφελων (ut vid) a d ff i q om X
e g | δυν. και δοξης πολλης ΑΜΔΙΙ minˢᵃᵗ ᵐᵘ syrʰᵉˡ arm aeth   27 om τοτε Σ |
αποστελλει HᵛⁱᵈLΔΣ minᵖᵃᵘᶜ | τους αγγελους]+αυτου ℵACWᵇΧΓΔΠΣΦΨ minᵒᵐⁿ ᵛⁱᵈ vg
syrr arm aegg go aeth Orⁱⁿᵗ (om αυτου BDL a e ff i k q)

(Ps. xvii. (xviii.) 8, xlv. (xlvi.) 7, lxxvi.
(lxxvii.) 19, lxxxi. (lxxxii.) 5 &c.), with
special reference to the scene of the
Law-giving; here the movement is
extended to heaven and the heavenly
hosts, as in Hagg. ii. 6 (Heb. *l.c.*).
Lc. adds a striking description of the
distress which these extraordinary
phenomena will produce on earth (καὶ
ἐπὶ γῆς συνοχὴ ἐθνῶν κτλ.).
26. καὶ τότε ὄψονται κτλ.] This
time of unrest and fear will culminate
in the Vision of the Son of Man foreshadowed by Daniel (vii. 13 LXX.
ἐθεώρουν ἐν ὁράματι τῆς νυκτός, καὶ
ἰδοὺ ἐπὶ (μετά, Th.) τῶν νεφελῶν τοῦ
οὐρανοῦ ὡς υἱὸς ἀνθρώπου ἤρχετο (ἐρχόμενος, Th.)). In Daniel the Man
(בַּר־אֱנָשׁ) who comes in the clouds
represents the kingdom of saints which
is to supersede the heathen empires
indicated by the Four Beasts (cf.
Stanton, *J. and Chr. Messiah*, p. 109;
Bevan, *Daniel*, p. 118; Driver, *Daniel*,
p. 102 ff.). The Lord had from the
beginning of His Ministry assumed
the title of the Son of Man (ii. 10,
where see note), and now at length
He identifies Himself with the object
of Daniel's vision; in Him the kingdom of regenerate humanity will find
its Head, and His manifestation in
that capacity is to be the crowning
revelation of the future (cf. xiv. 62,
Apoc. i. 7, xiv. 14). Ὄψονται, 'men
shall see,' cf. *v.* 9; the Apocalypse
(i. 7) paraphrases ὄψεται αὐτὸν πᾶς
ὀφθαλμός. On ἐν νεφέλαις see Dalman,
Worte, i. p. 198.
Mt. prefixes καὶ τότε φανήσεται τὸ
σημεῖον τοῦ υἱοῦ τοῦ ἀνθρώπου ἐν οὐρα-

νῷ. Cf. *Didache* 16: τότε φανήσεται
τὰ σημεῖα τῆς ἀληθείας· πρῶτον, σημεῖον
ἐκπετάσεως ἐν οὐρανῷ. Cyril. Hier. *cat.*
xv. 22: σημεῖον δὲ ἀληθῶς ἰδικὸν τοῦ
χριστοῦ ἐστιν ὁ σταυρός· φωτοειδὲς
σταυροῦ σημεῖον προάγει τὸν βασιλέα:
PW., *Sarum Breviary, Sanct.*, p. 278
"hoc signum crucis erit in caelo cum
Dominus ad iudicandum venerit."
But the meaning may be simply "the
sign which is the Son of Man" (Bruce);
the Vision of the Christ will itself be
the signal for the συντέλεια (*v.* 4).
Μετὰ δυνάμεως πολλῆς καὶ δόξης, cf.
viii. 38, Mt. xxv. 31; the conception
is based on Dan. vii. 14 (ἐδόθη αὐτῷ...
τιμὴ βασιλικὴ κτλ.).

27. καὶ τότε ἀποστελεῖ κτλ.]
Another link in the chain of events
(cf. καὶ τότε, *v.* 26). "The Son of
Man shall send the Angels"—"His
Angels," Mt. (cf. Mt. xiii. 41, Heb. i.
6, and see Mc. i. 13, viii. 38); Mt. adds
μετὰ σάλπιγγος μεγάλης, with a reference to the scene of the Law-giving
(Exod. xix. 16; cf. 1 Cor. xv. 52,
1 Thess. iv. 16)—"and shall assemble
(Mt. ἐπισυνάξουσιν, sc. οἱ ἄγγελοι, cf.
xiii. 41 συλλέξουσιν) His elect." Such
a gathering of men into a true and
lasting brotherhood had proved to be
impossible under the conditions of
Judaism (Mt. xxiii. 37 ποσάκις ἠθέλησα
ἐπισυναγαγεῖν τὰ τέκνα σου), but would
be realised in the Israel of GOD,
at the παρουσία; cf. 2 Thess. ii. 1
ἡμῶν ἐπισυναγωγῆς ἐπ' αὐτόν. Ἐπι-
συναγωγή is suggestively used for the
ordinary gatherings of the Church,
which are anticipations of the great
assembling at the Lord's Return

ἀγγέλους καὶ ἐπισυνάξει τοὺς ἐκλεκτοὺς αὐτοῦ ἐκ
τῶν τεσσάρων ἀνέμων ἀπ' ἄκρου γῆς ἕως ἄκρου
οὐρανοῦ.¶   ¶ e
²⁸'Απὸ δὲ τῆς συκῆς μάθετε τὴν παραβολήν. ὅταν 28

27 τους εκλεκτους αυτου] om αυτου DLΨ 1 28 91 299 2ᵖᵉ a c ff i k Orⁱⁿᵗ | ακρου 1°]
ακρων D minᵖᵃᵘᶜ (a) aeth | της γης U 1 13 28 69 736 2ᵖˡ alⁿᵒⁿⁿ | ακρου 2°] ακρων 1
alᵖᵃᵘᶜ aeth | του ουρανου UΨ 13 28 69 736* 2ᵖᵉ alⁿᵒⁿⁿ

(Heb. x. 25). Both noun and verb are
employed by the LXX. in passages
where the reassembling of the scattered tribes of Israel into the Messianic kingdom is in view: see Deut.
xxx. 4 (συνάξει), Tob. xiii. 13, xiv. 7
(א), Ps. cv. (cvi.) 47, cxlvi. (cxlvii.) 2,
Zach. ii. 6 (συνάξω), 2 Macc. ii. 7.
Τοὺς ἐκλεκτοὺς αὐτοῦ. The Father
elects (v. 20), but in the Son (Eph.
i. 4); and the elect belong to the Son
by the Father's gift (Jo. x. 27, xvii.
6, 10).

ἐκ τῶν τεσσάρων ἀνέμων κτλ.] From
Zach. ii. 6 (10) ἐκ τῶν τεσσάρων ἀνέμων
τοῦ οὐρανοῦ συνάξω ὑμᾶς, and Deut.
xxx. 4 ἐὰν ᾖ ἡ διασπορά σου ἀπ' ἄκρου τοῦ
οὐρανοῦ ἕως ἄκρου τοῦ οὐρανοῦ, ἐκεῖθεν
συνάξει σε Κύριος: cf. also Deut. iv.
32; Deissmann (B. St. p. 248) quotes
ἐκ τεσσάρων ἀνέμων from a Fayûm
papyrus. 'The four winds' (cf. Apoc.
vii. 1) stand for the four points of the
compass. The Lord's thought is still
dwelling on the new Israel, in which
are to be fulfilled the O.T. anticipations of the reassembling of the tribes.
Mc.'s phrase ἀπ' ἄκρου γῆς ἕως ἄκρου
οὐρανοῦ is unusual and difficult; the
LXX. has ἀπ' ἄκρου τῆς γῆς ἕως ἄ. τ.
γ. (Deut. xiii. 7 (8), Jer. xii. 12), as
well as ἀπ' ἄ. τ. οὐρ. ἕως ἄ. τ. οὐρ. (Deut.
xxx. 4, Ps. xviii. (xix.) 7), and even
speaks of τέσσαρα ἄκρα τοῦ οὐρανοῦ
(Jer. xxv. 16 (xlix. 36)), but the contrast
of the ἄκρον γῆς and the ἄκρον οὐρανοῦ
appears only here; the sense seems
to be, "from any one to any other
opposite meeting-point of earth and
sky" (Bengel: "ab extremo caeli et

terrae in oriente usque ad extremum
caeli et terrae in occidente"), i.e. round
the whole horizon of the world. But
the phrase is perhaps colloquial rather
than exact, and intended only to
convey the impression that no spot on
the surface of the earth where any of
the elect may be will be overlooked.

28—29. THE LESSON OF THE BUD-
DING FIG-TREE (Mt. xxiv. 32—33, Lc.
xxi. 29—31).

28. ἀπὸ δὲ τῆς συκῆς κτλ.] 'From
the fig-tree learn the parable (it offers),' i.e., the analogy which will serve
to illustrate this particular point. The
first article is generic (WM., p. 132),
the second possessive (WM., p. 135).
On παραβολή see iii. 23. The illustration is not worked out in the customary
form ὁμοία ἐστὶν ἡ βασιλεία τοῦ θεοῦ
συκῇ κτλ., or the like, but is merely
suggested in passing; nevertheless
the essence of the 'parable' is here.
With μάθετε (the Master's call to the
μαθηταί) cf. Mt. ix. 13, xi. 29. Under
Christ's guidance teaching may be
extracted from (ἀπό) the most familiar
of natural objects. The fig-tree was
among the commonest products of the
neighbourhood of Jerusalem; yet twice
within two days it furnished Him with
materials of instruction (cf. xi. 13 ff.).
Lc. lessens the interest of the passage
by adding καὶ πάντα τὰ δένδρα.

ὅταν ἤδη ὁ κλάδος κτλ.] The tree is
not yet in full leaf like the precocious
specimen of xi. 13 (ἔχουσαν φύλλα); at
the Passover the leaves would be just
escaping from their sheaths. 'Απαλός
is used of young vegetation in Lev. ii.

ἤδη ὁ κλάδος αὐτῆς ἀπαλὸς γένηται καὶ ἐκφύῃ
τὰ φύλλα, γινώσκετε ὅτι ἐγγὺς τὸ θέρος ἐστίν·
29 ²⁹οὕτως καὶ ὑμεῖς, ὅταν ἴδητε ταῦτα γινόμενα,
¶ go γινώσκετε ὅτι ἐγγύς ἐστιν¶ ἐπὶ θύραις.

28 εκφύη FSUΓΨᵛⁱᵈ minᵐᵘ a (procreaverit) k (germinaverit) syrʰᶜˡ me aeth] εκφυῇ EGKMVWᵇΠ minᵖᵉʳᵐᵘ d i q vg (nata fuerint) ff (nascuntur) syrˢⁱⁿ ᵖᵉˢʰ arm the | φυλλα]+εν αυτη D 28 91 124 604 2ᵖᵉ alᵖᵃᵘᶜ q arm | γινωσκετε ℵB*CEFGHKMSUV WᵇΧΓΠΣΦ minᵖˡ a ff i k q vg (cognoscitis) syrr arm the go] γινωσκεται AB³DLΔ minᵐᵘ aeth | θερος] τελος K   29 ταυτα] pr παντα D 36ᵉᵛ (c ff) i (q) arm (aeth) | θυραις]+το τελος k (finis)+η βασιλεια του θεου l (regnum dei)

14, Aq. ἀπαλὰ λάχανα, cf. Ezech. xvii.
4 τὰ ἄκρα τῆς ἀπαλότητος [sc. τῆς κέδρου]; here it denotes the result of the softening of the external coverings of the stem, as it grows succulent under the moisture and sunshine of spring. This stage has been already (ἤδη) reached; and it is succeeded by another, ὅταν ἐκφύῃ τὰ φύλλα: the branch puts forth its leaves. The Latin versions and the Sinaitic and Peshitta Syriac support ἐκφυῇ (see vv. ll.), which might certainly stand (WSchm., p. 110); but φύειν trans. occurs in Cant. v. 13, Sir. xiv. 19, and ἐκφύειν trans. in Ps. ciii. (civ.) 14 Symm., and there is no sufficient reason for changing the subject here. Field's argument that if the transitive were used "we should have expected the aor. ἐκφύσῃ" overlooks the fact that the parable represents vegetation as still in its first stage. The bursting of the fig-tree into leaf is the earliest sign of the approach of summer; cf. Cant. ii. 11 ff. For θέρος, the season of summer, cf. Gen. viii. 22, Ps. lxxiii. (lxxiv.) 17, Jer. viii. 20; the noun is elsewhere anarthrous, and the article, which occurs here in all the accounts, is perhaps emphatic—"the summer," as contrasted with the leafless winter. Meyer's identification of θέρος in this place with θερισμός is out of keeping with the context; though the παρουσία is elsewhere regarded as the harvest time of the world (Mt. xiii. 30, 39,

Apoc. xiv. 15), another train of ideas prevails here: cf. Origen: "unusquisque eorum qui salvantur...in se absconditam habet vitalem virtutem; Christo autem inspirante,...quae sunt abscondita in iis progrediuntur in folia aestate instante." Thpht.: [ἡ] τοῦ χριστοῦ παρουσία...θέρος τῷ ὄντι τοῖς δικαίοις ἀπὸ χειμῶνος. Γινώσκετε, indic., not imper., Vg. cognoscitis; 'experience tells you.' On the reading γινώσκεται—a common itacism—see Field, Notes, p. 37 f.

29. οὕτως καὶ ὑμεῖς κτλ.] The lesson of the parable enforced. Οὕτως καί, 'so in like manner' (WM., p. 548); ὑμεῖς, 'ye disciples,' as distinguished from the rest of men. As all men (and you among them) recognise the signs of approaching summer, so ye, with your special opportunities, ought to recognise (γινώσκετε, imper.; Vg. scitote) the premonitions of the παρουσία. Ἐγγύς ἐστιν ἐπὶ θύραις: Lc. ἐγγύς ἐ. ἡ βασιλεία τοῦ θεοῦ. If we are to supply a subject in Mt. and Mc., ἡ συντέλεια or τὸ τέλος will naturally suggest itself; but the impersonal ἐγγύς ἐ. is in better accord with the mysterious vagueness of an apocalypse; on the phrase see Dalman, Worte, i. p. 87. Ἐπὶ θύραις: with foot already firmly set upon the doorstep; cf. Prov. ix. 14 ἐκάθισεν ἐπὶ θύραις τοῦ ἑαυτῆς οἴκου ἐπὶ δίφρου, Sap. xix. 17 ἐπὶ ταῖς τοῦ δικαίου θ. (cf. Gen. xix. 11 τοὺς ὄντας ἐπὶ τῆς

³⁰Ἀμὴν λέγω ὑμῖν ὅτι οὐ μὴ παρέλθῃ ἡ γενεὰ 30
αὕτη μέχρις οὗ ταῦτα πάντα γένηται. ³¹ὁ οὐρανὸς 31
καὶ ἡ γῆ παρελεύσονται, οἱ δὲ λόγοι μου οὐ [μὴ]

---

30 μεχρις ου] μ. οτου Β μεχρι ℵ εως ου D min^{pau}✦εως αν 1 13 28 69 124 al^{pauc} εως
2^{pe} | om ταυτα 1071   31 παρελευσονται 1° ℵΒDUXΓΠ 1 al^{pl} c ff g i l q vg] παρε-
λευσεται AC^{vid}EFGHLMSVW^bXΔΣΦ min^{sat mu} a k | om μη BD* (hab ℵACL rell)

θύρας τοῦ οἴκου [Λώτ]); James v. 9
ὁ κριτὴς πρὸ τῶν θυρῶν ἔστηκεν is perhaps a reminiscence of this saying;
cf. also Phil. iv. 5, Apoc. i. 3, xxii. 10,
and the Aramaic watchword μαρὰν
ἀθά in 1 Cor. xvi. 22, *Didache* 10.

30—32. THE EVENT CERTAIN; THE
EXACT TIME KNOWN TO NONE BUT
THE FATHER (Mt. xxiv. 34—36, Lc.
xxi. 32—33).

30. ἀμὴν λέγω ὑμῖν ὅτι κτλ.] Having
answered the question τί τὸ σημεῖον
the Lord addresses Himself to the
other point raised in *v.* 4, πότε ταῦτα
ἔσται. An introductory ἀμὴν λέγω
ὑμῖν demands serious attention (cf. xii.
43). The difficult saying which follows is given in nearly identical words
by the three Synoptists. Ἡ γενεὰ
αὕτη is frequent in the Gospels (cf. e.g.
viii. 12 (note), 38, Mt. xi. 16, xii. 41 ff.,
xxiii. 36, Lc. xvii. 25), referring apparently in every instance to the
generation to which the Lord Himself belonged. In the LXX. γενεά
(=דּוֹר) occasionally means 'a class of
men,' with an ethical significance
(Victor: οὐκ ἀπὸ χρόνων...μόνον, ἀλλὰ
καὶ ἀπὸ τρόπου; cf. Ps. xi. (xii.) 8
(where see Dr Kirkpatrick's note),
xiii. (xiv.) 5, xxiii. (xxiv.) 6; and there
are passages in the N. T. where this
use of the word comes into sight (e.g.
Mt. xvii. 17, Mc. ix. 19, Acts ii. 40,
Phil. ii. 15). In the present context it
is certainly more natural to take γενεά
in its normal signification; the passage
is similar to Mt. xxiii. 36, where there
can be no doubt as to the meaning.
Men who were then alive would see

the fulfilment of the sentence pronounced upon Jerusalem (*v.* 2). If
ταῦτα πάντα be held to include, as the
words are probably meant to include,
the συντέλεια and παρουσία, γενεά must
be widened accordingly: cf. e.g. Theod.
Mops. *ap.* Victor.: γενεὰν λέγει πονη-
ρὰν τῷ τρόπῳ καὶ οὐ τοῖς προσώποις:
Jerome: "aut genus hominum signi-
ficat, aut specialiter Iudaeorum";
Thpht.: ἡ γενεὰ αὕτη, τουτέστι τῶν
πιστῶν. It is possible that a word
was purposely employed which was
capable of being understood in a
narrower or a wider sense, according
to the interpretation assigned to the
passage by the hearer or reader. On
οὐ μὴ παρελθῇ see Burton, § 172: in
v. 31 the future is used without change
of meaning.

31. ὁ οὐρανὸς καὶ ἡ γῆ κτλ.] The
disturbances of Nature and Society
foretold in *vv.* 24 ff. would leave the
great revelation of the Father's Love
and Will unshaken (cf. Isa. li. 6, Heb.
xii. 25 ff.). The Lord claims for the
Gospel a permanence even more absolute than that which at the outset
of His Ministry He had claimed for
the Law (Mt. v. 18, Lc. xvi. 17, cf.
Hort, *Jud. Chr.* p. 16). Οἱ λόγοι μου,
not this particular apocalypse only (οἱ
λόγοι οὗτοι, Mt. vii. 24, Lc. ix. 28), but
Christ's teaching as a whole (οἱ ἐμοὶ
λόγοι, viii. 38 = ὁ ἐμὸς λόγος, Jo. viii.
31 ff.). Ὁ οὐρ. καὶ ἡ γῆ παρελεύσονται:
cf. 2 Pet. iii. 10 οἱ οὐρανοὶ ῥοιζηδὸν
παρελεύσονται: Apoc. xxi. 1 ὁ γὰρ
πρῶτος οὐρανὸς καὶ ἡ πρώτη γῆ ἀπῆλθαν,
καὶ ἡ θάλασσα οὐκ ἔστιν ἔτι.

§ f 32 παρελεύσονται. ³²§περὶ δὲ τῆς ἡμέρας ἐκείνης ἢ τῆς ὥρας οὐδεὶς οἶδεν, οὐδὲ οἱ ἄγγελοι ἐν οὐρανῷ οὐδὲ ὁ υἱός, εἰ μὴ ὁ πατήρ.

§ e 33 ³³§Βλέπετε, ἀγρυπνεῖτε· οὐκ οἴδατε γὰρ πότε

31 παρελευσονται 2° אBL minᵖᵃᵘᶜ] παρελθωσιν ACDWᵇΧΓΔΠΣΦ minᵖˡ 32 η ABCEGHKLMS²UVWᵇΧΓΔΠΨ 1071 alᵐᵘ] και אDFS* 1 13 28 69 124 alˢᵃᵗ ᵐᵘ a g i k q syrˢⁱⁿ ᵖᵉˢʰ arm aegg aeth | της ωρας] om της AEFGHSVWᵇΧΦ minˢᵃᵗᵐⁿ ωρας εκεινης Σ syrˢⁱⁿ ᵖᵉˢʰ | οι αγγελοι] αγγελος B | εν ουρανω] pr οι ACEFGHK²MSVΧΓΔΠΦ(Ψ) minᵖˡ syrʰᶜˡ the των ουρανων UΣ 28 1071 alⁿᵒⁿⁿ a g syrᵖᵉˢʰ aeth | om ουδε ο υιος X (cf. Ambr de fide v. 16) | ο πατηρ] μονος ο π. Δ c (solus pater) ο π. μονος Φ 13 61 124 238 1071 2ᵖᵉ alᵖᵃᵘᶜ a k armᶜᵒᵈᵈ the aeth 33 βλεπετε] om syrˢⁱⁿ + ουν D (c) ff i q + δε και 13 28 69 299 346 2ᵖᵉ (k) aeth | αγρυπνειτε]+και προσευχεσθε אACLWᵇΧΓΔΠ(Σ)ΦΨ minᶠᵉʳᵉ ᵒᵐⁿ f ff i q vg syrr arm aegg aeth (om BD 122 a c k)

32. περὶ δὲ τῆς ἡμέρας ἐκείνης κτλ.] Ἡ ἡμέρα ἐκείνη is here apparently (cf. xiv. 25, Lc. xxi. 34, 2 Thess. i. 10, 2 Tim. i. 18) the day of the final Return in which "those days" (vv. 17, 19, 24) will find their issue; elsewhere described as ἡ ἐσχάτη ἡμ. (Jo., passim), ἡ ἡμ. τοῦ κυρίου ['I. X.] (Paul), or simply ἡ ἡμέρα (Mt. xxv. 13, 1 Thess. v. 4). The end is assured, it belongs to Revelation; but the time has not been revealed, and shall not be. Οὐδεὶς...οὐδὲ...οὐδέ, 'no one...not even (ne quidem)...nor yet': for the sequence cf. Mt. vi. 26, Apoc. v. 3, and for οὐδέ ne quidem, vi. 31. Οὐδὲ οἱ ἄγγελοι, who are to be employed in the work of 'that day,' cf. v. 27. Comp. the Rabbinical parallels cited by Wünsche, p. 404; and for other references to the limitations of angelic knowledge see Eph. iii. 10, 1 Pet. i. 12. Οὐδὲ ὁ υἱός. Not ὁ υἱὸς τοῦ ἀνθρώπου, but ὁ υἱός absolutely, as contrasted with ὁ πατήρ: cf. Mt. xi. 27, Lc. x. 22, Jo. v. 19 ff., vi. 40, xvii. 1, 1 Jo. ii. 22 &c. By the Father's gift all things that the Father hath are the Son's (Jo. v. 20, xvi. 15), and as the Eternal Word it would seem that He cannot be ignorant of this or any other mystery of the Divine Will (Mt. xi. 27, Jo. i. 18). But the time of the predestined end is one of those things

which the Father has "set within His own authority" (Acts i. 7), and the Son had no knowledge of it in His human consciousness, and no power to reveal it (Jo. viii. 26, 40, xiv. 24, xv. 15). See upon the whole context Mason, Conditions, p. 120 ff.

The patristic treatment of the passage is fully examined by Bp Gore, Dissertations, p. 111 ff. Irenaeus (ii. 28. 6) is content to call attention to the practical reproof which the Lord's words administer to idle curiosity. In Origen (in Mt. ad l.) the exegetical difficulty comes into view, and he offers alternative explanations; the ignorance of which the Lord speaks belongs either to His human nature, or to the Church, as whose Head He speaks. Later expositors, influenced by a just indignation at the Arian argument εἰ ἦν ἀιδίως ὑπάρχων ὁ υἱὸς πρὸς τὸν θεόν, οὐκ ἂν ἠγνόησε περὶ τῆς ἡμέρας, regarded the ignorance as 'economic' only; whilst others understood εἰ μὴ ὁ πατήρ as nearly equivalent to χωρὶς τοῦ πατρός: cf. Basil, ep. 236. 2 τουτέστιν, ἡ αἰτία τοῦ εἰδέναι τὸν υἱὸν παρὰ τοῦ πατρός· οὐδ᾽ ἂν ὁ υἱὸς ἔγνω, εἰ μὴ ὁ πατήρ.

That the day is known to GOD was taught in Zech. xiv. 7; cf. Pss. Sol. xvii. 23 εἰς τὸν καιρὸν ὃν οἶδας σύ, ὁ θεός (Dalman, Worte, i. p. 235).

ὁ καιρός ἐστιν. ³⁴§ὡς ἄνθρωπος ἀπόδημος ἀφεὶς 34 § Wᵗ
τὴν οἰκίαν αὐτοῦ καὶ δοὺς τοῖς δούλοις αὐτοῦ τὴν
ἐξουσίαν, ἑκάστῳ τὸ ἔργον αὐτοῦ, καὶ τῷ θυρωρῷ

33 ποτε ο καιρος εστιν] ποτε ο καιρος D a τον καιρον (ut vid) c syrˢⁱⁿ   34 ως]
ωσπερ Σ 1 13 28 69 124 alⁿᵒⁿⁿ | αποδημων DX 1 28 209 245 299 2ᵖᵉ cˢᶜʳ | αυτου 1°, 2°]
εαυτου B | εκαστω אBC*DLΨ 238 248 2ᵖᵉ 8ᵖᵉ a c ff me aeth] pr και AC²WᵇΧΓΔΠΣΦ
minᵖˡ i syrrᵖᵉˢʰ ʰᶜˡ arm

33—37. THE FINAL WARNING,
BASED ON THE UNCERTAINTY OF THE
TIME (Mt. xxiv. 42 ff., Lc. xxi. 36).
    33. βλέπετε, ἀγρυπνεῖτε κτλ.] Wy-
cliffe : "se ʒe wake ʒe and preie
ʒe." For βλέπετε cf. vv. 5, 9, 23; it
is the keynote of the discourse.
Ἀγρυπνεῖτε, 'do not permit yourselves to sleep'; cf. 1 Esdr. viii. 58
ἀγρυπνεῖτε καὶ φυλάσσετε, Ps. cxxvi.
(cxxvii.) 1 ἠγρύπνησεν ὁ φυλάσσων,
Cant. v. 2 ἐγὼ καθεύδω καὶ ἡ καρδία μου
ἀγρυπνεῖ. In the Epistles the verb
is used in reference to prayer (Eph.
vi. 18) and spiritual work (Heb. xiii.
17) : cf. Lc. ἀγρυπνεῖτε δὲ ἐν παντὶ
καιρῷ δεόμενοι. Bede mentions other
forms of spiritual ἀγρυπνία : "vigilat
autem qui ad adspectum veri luminis
mentis oculos apertos tenet, vigilat
qui servat operando quod credit,
vigilat qui se torporis et neglegentiae
tenebras repellit." Οὐκ οἴδατε γὰρ
πότε κτλ. If the Master Himself
does not know, the disciples must
not only acquiesce in their ignorance,
but regard it as a wholesome stimulus
to exertion (γάρ). On ὁ καιρός see i.
15 ; each appointed time of Divine
visitation is a καιρός, occurring at the
moment predestined for it in the
ordering of events.
    34. ὡς ἄνθρωπος ἀπόδημος κτλ.]
Another παραβολή (v. 28), and as
appears from Mt. xxiv. 43 ff., xxv.,
one of a series delivered at this time.
With ἄνθρ. ἀπόδημος 'a man on his
travels' (Wycliffe, "a man the which
gon far in pilgrimage"), comp. xii. 1
ἄνθρ. ἀπεδήμησεν, and Mt. xxv. 14
ἄνθρ. ἀποδημῶν (cf. xiii. 45 ἄνθρ. ἔμ-

πορος). The traveller is here and in
Mt. l.c. the Son of Man, and the
journey is His return to the Father
(Jo. xiv. 3). Ὡς, "it is as if," cf.
ὥσπερ, Mt. xxv. 14 (Blass, Gr., p. 270,
cf. WM., p. 578 n.). The construction
of the sentence which follows is broken
by the intrusion of καί before ἐνετείλατο; the reader desiderates either
ἀφεὶς...καὶ δοὺς...ἐνετείλατο or ἀφεὶς
...ἔδωκεν...καὶ ἐνετ., or ἀφεὶς...καὶ δοὺς
...καὶ ἐντειλάμενος (Vg. qui peregre
profectus...reliquit...et dedit...et
praecipiat, v.l. praecepit; see Wordsworth-White ad l.); Fritzsche's and
Meyer's expedient of taking the last
καί as = etiam (WM., p. 578) is adopted
by R.V., but seems to be unnecessary
in view of other indications of grammatical laxity in Mc.'s style.
    τοῖς δούλοις...τὴν ἐξουσίαν, ἑκάστῳ
τὸ ἔργον] The authority is committed
to the servants collectively (Bengel :
"hanc dedit servis coniunctim"), the
task is assigned individually. On
ἐξουσία see i. 22, vi. 7, notes ; for
δοῦλος in this reference cf. xii. 2,
Jo. xiii. 16, xv. 15, 20 ; the Apostolic
writers glory in the title Ἰησοῦ Χριστοῦ δοῦλος (James i. 1, Jude 1, Apoc. i.
1, Rom. i. 1, Phil. i. 1 ; cf. δοῦλος θεοῦ
Tit. i. 1, 1 Pet. ii. 16). Here apparently
the δοῦλοι are the disciples in general,
the θυρωρός is the Apostolate and the
ministry (cf. Jo. x. 3 τούτῳ ὁ θυρωρὸς
ἀνοίγει), to whom especially belongs the
responsibility of guarding the house
and of being ready to open the door to
the Master at His return (Lc. xii. 36,
cf. Ezek. xxxiii. 2 ff.). Bede : "ordini
pastorum ac rectorum ecclesiae curam

35 ἐνετείλατο ἵνα γρηγορῇ. ³⁵γρηγορεῖτε οὖν, οὐκ
οἴδατε γὰρ πότε ὁ κύριος τῆς οἰκίας ἔρχεται, ἢ ὀψὲ
36 ἢ μεσονύκτιον ἢ ἀλεκτοροφωνίας ἢ πρωί· ³⁶μὴ ἐλθὼν
¶ e 37 ἐξαίφνης εὕρη ὑμᾶς καθεύδοντας.¶ ³⁷ὃ δὲ ὑμῖν λέγω
πᾶσιν λέγω Γρηγορεῖτε.

34 γρηγορη] αγρυπνη Γ   35 om η 1° ADWᵇΧΓΠΣΦ minᵒᵐⁿ ᵛⁱᵈ latᵛᵗ ᵖˡ ᵛᵍ
syrrˢⁱⁿ ᵖᵉˢʰ ʰᵉˡ(ᵗˣᵗ) arm | μεσονυκτιου ADWᵇΧΓΠΦ μεσονυκτιω Σ 604˙ alᵖᵉʳᵖᵃᵘᶜ | αλεκτο-
ροφωνιου D αλεκτοροφωνια Δ   36 ελθων] εξελθων DΓ minᵖᵃᵘᶜ | εξαιφνης ABEFG
MSUWᵇΧΠΣΦ] εξεφνης ℵCDKLUΓΔ al | ευρησει 238 300 1071 cˢᶜʳ   37·0] a
AWᵇΓΠ²ΣΦ minᵖˡ q syrʰᵉˡ | ο δε υμ. λ. πασιν λ.] εγω δε λ. υμιν D (2ᵖᵉ) a (cf. ff i) quod
autem uni dixi omnibus vobis dico (om γρηγ.) k

solerti observantia iubet impendere,"
adding, however, "vigilare praeci-
pimur universi ianuas cordium." Ἵνα
γρηγορῇ: γρηγορεῖν, a late formation
from ἐγρήγορα, condemned by the
Atticists (Lob. *Phryn.* p. 118, cf.
Rutherford, p. 200 f., WSchm., p.
104 *n.*), is found in the later books
of the LXX. (2 Esdr.¹ Jer.³ Bar.¹
Thren.¹ Dan. (Th.¹) 1 Macc.¹), and
in the N. T. (Syn.¹⁴ Acts¹ Paul⁴
1 Pet.¹ Apoc.³). The passage in
1 Macc. (xii. 27) is an interesting
illustration of its use here: ἐπέταξεν
Ἰωναθὰν τοῖς παρ' αὐτοῦ γρηγορεῖν...δι'
ὅλης τῆς νυκτός. For early Christian
use cf. Ign. *Polyc.* 1 γρηγορεῖ, ἀκοί-
μητον πνεῦμα κεκτημένος.

35. γρηγορεῖτε οὖν κτλ.] Ὁ κύριος
τῆς οἰκίας ἔρχεται answers here to
ὁ καιρός ἐστιν in *v.* 33 and explains
its ultimate meaning (cf. Mt. xxiv. 3
τῆς σῆς παρουσίας). With the phrase
ὁ κ. τῆς οἰκίας = ὁ οἰκοδεσπότης cf. Mt.
x. 25, xx. 1 ff., Lc. xiii. 25, and esp.
Heb. iii. 5 Χριστὸς δὲ ὡς υἱὸς ἐπὶ τὸν
οἶκον αὐτοῦ. Mt. (xxiv. 42) substitutes ὁ κύριος ὑμῶν, cf. Heb. iii. 6 οὗ
οἶκός ἐσμεν ἡμεῖς.

ἢ ὀψὲ ἢ μεσονύκτιον κτλ.] In any
one of the four watches of the night;
cf. Lc. xii. 38 κἂν ἐν τῇ δευτέρᾳ κἂν
ἐν τῇ τρίτῃ φυλακῇ ἔλθη. A three-
fold division of the night is mentioned
in the O. T., cf. Jud. vii. 19 τῆς
φυλακῆς μέσης (τῆς μεσούσης, A): the

first two Gospels speak of a fourth
watch (Mt. xiv. 25, Mc. vi. 48, where
see note; cf. Jos. *ant.* v. 6. 5 κατὰ
τετάρτην μάλιστα φυλακὴν προσῆγε
τὴν ἑαυτοῦ στρατιάν: *Berachoth*, cited
by Wetstein, "quatuor vigiliae fue-
runt noctis")—a Roman arrangement
(Blass on Acts xii. 4), but not unknown in classical Greece (Eur. *Rhes.*
5, cited by Kypke: τετράμοιρον νυκτὸς
φρουράν). The watches were distinguished as *vigilia prima*, *secunda*,
&c.; ὀψέ, μεσονύκτιον, κτλ. are
popular equivalents, not to be too
strictly interpreted. For ὀψέ see xi.
11, 19; for μεσονύκτιον, Jud. xvi. 3,
Ps. cxviii. (cxix.) 62, Isa. lix. 10
(where it is the opposite of μεσημβρία), Lc. xi. 5, Acts xvi. 25, xx. 7;
ἀλεκτοροφωνία, ἅπ. λεγ. in biblical
Gk. (but cf. 3 Macc. v. 23, 24), is
used in Aesop, *fab.* 44: πρωί corresponds to the φυλακὴ ἑωθινή of Exod.
xiv. 24, 1 Regn. xi. 11 (A, πρωινή), or
φ. πρωία of Ps. cxxix. (cxx.) 6. On
the acc. μεσονύκτιον see WM., p. 288.

36. μὴ ἐλθὼν ἐξαίφνης κτλ.] See
Mt. xxv. 5, Rom. xiii. 11, 1 Thess. v.
6; the need of the caution was
soon to be forcibly illustrated (xiv.
37 ff.). For the orthography of
ἐξαίφνης see WH., *Notes*, p. 151, and
cf. ix. 8, note; for the ethical import
cf. Lc. xii. 40 ᾖ ὥρᾳ οὐ δοκεῖτε: the
suddenness is not due to caprice on
the part of the Master, but to

¹῏Ην δὲ τὸ πάσχα καὶ τὰ ἄζυμα μετὰ δύο ἡμέρας. 1　**14**
καὶ ἐζήτουν οἱ ἀρχιερεῖς καὶ οἱ γραμματεῖς πῶς αὐτὸν

XIV 1 το πασχα και τα αζ.] τα αζ. και το πασχα Ψ om και τα αζ. D pascha azu-
morum k (cf. syrr^{sin pesh}) | πως] οπως MX το πως Σ

neglect of duty on that of the servant.

37. ὁ δὲ ὑμῖν λέγω πᾶσιν λέγω] Comp. Peter's question in Lc. xii. 41, which here receives a direct answer. Watching was not to be limited to the θυρωρός, all must keep vigil till He returned ; priest and people, the man of the world as well as the recluse ; cf. Thpht.: πᾶσι δὲ ταῦτα παραγγέλλει ὁ κύριος, καὶ τοῖς κοσμικωτέροις καὶ τοῖς ἀναχωρηταῖς. The early Church expressed her sense of the importance of this charge by the institution of the παννυχίδες or *vigiliae*; see Batiffol, *hist. du bréviaire Romain*, p. 2 ff.

XIV. 1—2. THE DAY BEFORE THE PASCHAL MEAL. DESIGNS OF THE PRIESTS AND SCRIBES (Mt. xxvi. 1—5, Lc. xxii. 1—2).

1. ἦν δὲ τὸ πάσχα κτλ.] Πάσχα (Aram. אסחפ, אספפ, cf. Dalman, *Gr.* pp. 107, 126) is the prevalent transliteration of פסח in the LXX. (Pent.²⁰ Jos.¹ 4 Regn.³ 1 Esdr.¹⁴ 2 Esdr.³ Ezech.¹), the alternative form φάσεκ or φάσεχ occurring only in 2 Chron. (xxx.⁶ xxxv.¹²), Jer. xxxviii. (xxxi.) 8 ; in the N. T. πάσχα is used uniformly (Mt.⁴ Mc.⁵ Lc.⁷ Jo.⁹ Acts¹ Paul¹ Heb.¹). Philo also has πάσχα (e.g. *de decal.* ἦν Ἑβραῖοι πατρίῳ γλώττῃ πάσχα προσαγορεύουσιν); in Josephus the MSS. vary between πάσχα and φάσκα (see Niese's text and app. crit. *ant.* v. 1. 4, xiv. 2. 1, xvii. 9. 3, *B. J.* ii. 1. 3). Τὸ πάσχα is either (*a*) the lamb (Exod. xii. 11, 21, &c.), or (*b*) the feast at which it was eaten, or (*c*) the Paschal festival as a whole (Jos. *ant.* xvii. 9. 3 φάσκα δ' ἡ ἑορτὴ καλεῖται, Lc. ἡ ἑορτὴ τῶν ἀζύμων ἡ λεγομένη πάσχα); for (*a*) see *v.* 12 ; in the present passage (*b*) seems

to be intended, since τὸ π. is distinguished from τὰ ἄζυμα, the opening meal from the period of abstinence from leaven. Τὰ ἄζ., "the azymes" (המצּות), are properly the ἄρτοι ἄζυμοι or λάγανα ἄζυμα (Lev. ii. 4) which were eaten throughout the Paschal week, but here = 'the Feast of Azymes,' ἡ ἑορτὴ τῶν ἀζύμων (Exod. xxxiv. 18) or αἱ ἡμέραι τῶν ἀζ. (Acts xii. 3, xx. 6). The word lends itself easily to this sense, the neut. pl. being commonly employed for the names of festivals, cf. τὰ ἐγκαίνια, Jo. x. 22 and the class. τὰ Διονύσια, τὰ Παναθήναια (Blass, *Gr.* p. 84 f.).

ἦν...μετὰ δύο ἡμέρας] Lc. less precisely, ἤγγιζεν : Mt. represents the Lord as calling attention to the approach of the Feast (εἶπεν...Οἴδατε ὅτι μετὰ δύο ἡμέρας τὸ πάσχα γίνεται). Mc.'s ἦν = ἤμελλεν εἶναι is noticeable ; the Evangelist looks back on the event as past. Μετὰ δύο ἡμέρας = τῇ ἐχομένῃ ἡμέρᾳ, if we are to follow the analogy of μετὰ τρεῖς ἡμ. (viii. 31, note); cf. Hos. vi. 2 where μετὰ δύο ἡμέρας is distinguished from ἐν τῇ ἡμέρᾳ τῇ τρίτῃ and, as Field points out (on Mt. xvi. 21), is equivalent to ἐν τῇ ἡμέρᾳ τῇ δευτέρᾳ.... The day will thus, on the Synoptic reckoning, be Wednesday, Nisan 13; cf. Exod. xii. 6. Thpht.: τῇ τετράδι τὸ συμβούλιον (v. *infra*) συνέστη, καὶ διὰ τοῦτο νηστεύομεν καὶ ἡμεῖς τὰς τετράδας (see *Did.* 8, *Ap. Const.* v. 15).

καὶ ἐζήτουν οἱ ἀρχιερεῖς κτλ.] Cf. xi. 18, xii. 12. The plot was now under discussion at a meeting consisting of representatives of each order in the Sanhedrin: Mc., Lc. οἱ ἀρχ. καὶ οἱ γρ., Mt. συνήχθησαν οἱ ἀρχ. καὶ οἱ πρεσβύτεροι τοῦ λαοῦ (cf. Mc. xi. 27). Mt. adds that the meeting was held in the

2 ἐν δόλῳ κρατήσαντες ἀποκτείνωσιν· ²ἔλεγον γάρ Μὴ
  ἐν τῇ ἑορτῇ, μή ποτε ἔσται θόρυβος τοῦ λαοῦ.

3   ³Καὶ ὄντος αὐτοῦ ἐν Βηθανίᾳ ἐν τῇ οἰκίᾳ Σίμωνος

2 γαρ אBC*DLΨ a c fff i k l q syrrˢⁱⁿ ʰᵉˡ(ᵐᵍ) me] δε ACᶜWᵇΧΓΔΠΣΦ minᵒᵐⁿ ᵛⁱᵈ vgᵉᵈ
syrr⁽ᵖᵉˢʰ⁾ʰᵉˡ ⁽ᵗˣᵗ⁾ arm the aeth | μη...μη ποτε] μη ποτε εν τη εορτη D a (c) ff i (k) q
3 αυτου] του Ιησου D c fff i q the | τη οικια] om τη א*Φ 11 106 229 238 604 2ᵖᵉ alᵖᵃᵘᶜ

house of Caiaphas, who for some time
had advocated the policy of sacrificing
Jesus to the Roman power (Jo. xi. 49 f.).
There was no division of opinion now
as to the principle, or as to the
character of the means to be employed
for the arrest (ἐν δόλῳ, Mc., δόλῳ, Mt.;
cf. Mc. vii. 22); only the opportunity
(πῶς) was still wanting. On the subj.
after πῶς see WM., p. 373 f.; in direct
discourse the question would run
Πῶς αὐτὸν...ἀποκτείνωμεν; and the
mood is retained notwithstanding the
tense of ἐζήτουν (WM., p. 374).

2. ἔλεγον γάρ Μή κτλ.] An echo
from the council chamber which
reached the Apostles and found its
place in the traditions of the Church.
Voices were heard deprecating an
arrest after the Paschal week had
well begun (ἐν τῇ ἑορτῇ); it must be
made during the next few hours, or
postponed till after the Feast. Μή,
used elliptically, cf. Blass, Gr. p. 293 f.,
and Lightfoot on Gal. v. 13; if we are
to supply a verb, the previous words
suggest κρατήσωμεν αὐτόν. Μή ποτε
ἔσται, more vivid than Mt.'s ἵνα μὴ
γένηται; the use of εἶναι and the ind.
fut. represents the danger as real and
imminent, and adds force to the
deprecation: cf. Lightfoot on Col. ii.
8, Westcott on Heb. iii. 12, and Field,
Notes, p. 38. The Sanhedrists lived
in fear of their own people (Lc. ἐφοβοῦντο γὰρ τὸν λαόν: cf. xi. 18, note,
xii. 12). Θόρυβος τοῦ λαοῦ, not merely
"clamour," "uproar" (v. 28), but as
Vg. tumultus, a riot, or its precursor,
an outbreak of disorder (Acts xx. 1,
xxiv. 18).

3—9. THE EPISODE OF THE ANOINT-

ING AT BETHANY (Mt. xxvi. 6—13,
Jo. xii. 2—8).

3. καὶ ὄντος αὐτοῦ ἐν Βηθανίᾳ]
There is nothing either in Mc. or Mt.
to raise a doubt as to the historical
sequence; indeed Mt.'s γενομένου following upon ὅτε ἐτέλεσεν κτλ. (v. 1)
may seem to suggest that the supper
occurred immediately after the Lord's
arrival at Bethany on the evening
of the "Day of questions." St John,
however, places it before the Triumphal
Entry (Jo. xii. 1 ff., 12; see Mc. xi. 1,
note); and his order has been generally accepted from the time of Tatian
(cf. Hill, p. 196 f.). Augustine (de
cons. ev. ii. 78) rightly points out that
the two Synoptists do not definitely
contradict the Fourth Gospel: at the
same time it may be questioned
whether either of them consciously
connected the event with the first
day at Bethany ("recapitulando ergo
ad illum diem redeunt in Bethaniam
qui erat ante sex dies paschae").
For some reason which does not lie
upon the surface (cf. vv. 4, 10, notes)
this episode had been dislodged from
its historical order in the tradition
to which Mc. and Mt. were indebted
for their account. On the whole
question and the history of opinion
upon it see Hastings, D.B. iii. p. 279 ff.
Ὄντος αὐτοῦ...ἀνακειμένου αὐτοῦ: the
double gen. absolute accords with Mc.'s
often disjointed style.

ἐν τῇ οἰκίᾳ Σίμωνος κτλ.] Tatian
rightly limits himself here to Mt. Mc.
Jo., placing Lc. vii. 36 ff. in another
and much earlier connexion (Hill,
p. 100 ff.), and this view was held at
a later time by Apollinaris and Theo-

τοῦ λεπροῦ κατακειμένου αὐτοῦ ἦλθεν γυνὴ ἔχουσα ἀλάβαστρον μύρου νάρδου πιστικῆς πολυτελοῦς·

3 ηλθεν] προσηλθεν αυτω 13 69 124 346 | om ναρδου πιστ. πολυτ. D | πιστικης] *spicati* c ff q r^{vid} vg *optimi* a | πολυτελους] πολυτιμου AGM^{mg} 1 13 28 69 1071 2^{pe} al^{nonn}

dore of Mopsuestia (Victor). Origen, however, speaks of the two narratives as commonly confused in his time (*in Mt. ad l.* "multi quidem existimant de una eademque muliere quatuor evangelistas exposuisse"). There are points of resemblance—the name of the host, and the use of an ἀλάβαστρος, to which Jo. adds the anointing of the Feet, and the wiping them with the hair—but, as Origen points out, there is an essential difference in the persons whose act is described ("non enim credibile est ut Maria quam diligebat Iesus...peccatrix in civitate dicatur"). That the circumstances were intentionally modified by Lc. (Holtzmann, see Plummer *ad l.*) is scarcely less incredible in view of Lc.'s own statement of his historical principles (i. 3).

According to Jo. the supper at Bethany was given in the house of Martha (ἡ Μάρθα διηκόνει, cf. Lc. x. 38 ff. and Mc. i. 31). It is not necessary to regard the reference to Simon in Mt. and Mc. as due to the influence of Lc.'s story. Simon the leper (on the commonness of the name see i. 16, note) may have been Martha's husband, now dead or parted from her by his disease, or the father of the family (Thpht.: φασί τινες καὶ πατέρα εἶναι τοῦ Λαζάρου, ὃν ἀπὸ τῆς λέπρας καθαρίσας εἱστιᾶτο παρ' αὐτῷ). The epithet ὁ λεπρός may have clung to the leper after his recovery; Jerome, who compares Μαθθαῖος ὁ τελώνης (Mt. x. 3), remarks: "sic et *leprosus* Simon iste vocatur antiquo nomine, ut ostendatur a Domino fuisse curatus." The suggestion of Ephrem (*ev. conc. exp.* p. 205) is improbable: "quomodo lepra in corpore Simonis permanere poterat, qui purificatorem leprae in domo sua recumbentem vidit? forsitan...pro sua hospitalitate mercedem accepit purificationem." That Simon was the actual host and present at the feast cannot be inferred from ἐν οἰκίᾳ Σίμωνος.

ἦλθεν γυνή κτλ. Jo. ἡ οὖν Μαριάμ (cf. Jo. xi. 2): her anonymity in the Synoptists is perhaps due to the Galilean origin of the synoptic tradition. In the cycle of events hitherto described by Mc. Mary of Bethany had no place; Lc.'s reference to her (x. 38 ff.) comes from another source. Ἔχουσα ἀλάβαστρον μύρου: so Mt.; Jo., λαβοῦσα λίτραν μύρου. On the gen. see WM., p. 235. Ἀλάβαστρος (so Mc., cf. τὴν ἀλ., *infra*; also ὁ ἀλ. (B) and τὸ ἀλάβαστρον (A) 4 Regn. xxi. 4) is an alabaster flask such as was commonly used for preserving precious unguents; cf. Herod. iii. 20 δῶρα φέροντας...μύρου ἀλάβαστρον; Plin. *H. N.* xiii. 2 "unguenta optume servantur in alabastris." This 'alabaster' held a λίτρα (i.e. a Roman *libra*) of fragrant oil of the most costly kind (Mt. βαρυτίμου, Jo. πολυτίμου)—for πολυτελής cf. Prov. i. 13 (κτῆσις), xxxi. 10 (λίθος), Sap. ii. 7 (οἶνος), 1 Tim. ii. 9 (ἱματισμός). On the genitives μύρου νάρδου see WM., pp. 235, 238; the first expresses the local relation of the μύρον to the ἀλάβαστρος, the second defines the former as of the particular kind known as νάρδος πιστική. Νάρδος (Heb. נֵרְדְּ, from a Sanscrit root), a product of the *Nardostachys nardus jatamansi*, a native of the Himalayas (Tristram, *N. H. of the Bible*, p. 485), was used by luxurious Israelites (Cant. i. 12, iv. 13 f., cf. Driver *Intr.*, p. 422, note 2; Enoch xxxii. 1), and at a later time by the Greeks (Athen. xv. 691 B ναρδίνου δὲ μύρου μέμνηται

συντρίψασα τὴν ἀλάβαστρον κατέχεεν αὐτοῦ τῆς
§ go 4 κεφαλῆς. ⁴§ἦσαν δέ τινες ἀγανακτοῦντες πρὸς ἑαυτούς

3 συντριψασα אBLΨ me] pr και ACDWᵇΧΓΔΠΣΦ minᵒᵐⁿ ᵛⁱᵈ latt syrr arm
θραυσασα D 2ᵖᵉ | την αλαβ. אᶜBCLΔ] τον αλαβ. א*ADEFHKSUVWᵇΧΓΠ 1071 alᵖˡ
το αλαβ. GMΦ 1 13 69 | της κεφαλης] pr κατα AWᵇΧΓΠΣΦ minᵖˡ pr επι D 20ᵉᵛ (et ut
vid a ff q vg) τη κεφαλη Ψ 4 ησαν δε τινες...εαυτους] οι δε μαθηται αυτου διε-
πονουντο D 2ᵖᵉ a ff i (arm) om προς εαυτους c k

Μένανδρος) and Romans (Plin. H. N.
xiii. 5, Hor. Od. ii. 11, iv. 12, Ov. de
arte am. iii. 443, Tib. ii. 2. 7, iii. 6. 9).
The epithet πιστική (Mc., Jo.) is not
without difficulty. Πιστικός occurs in
the sense of 'trustworthy,' 'genuine,'
in late writers, e.g. Artemid. Onir.
2. 32 γυναῖκα πιστικὴν καὶ οἰκοῦρον, and
πιστικῶς is found nearly in the sense
of πιστῶς. The epithet has therefore
been taken to mean that the nard
was genuine, not a cheap imitation;
cf. Thpht.: τὴν ἄδολον νάρδον καὶ
μετὰ πίστεως κατασκευασθεῖσαν, Plin.
H. N. xii. 12 "adulteratur et pseu-
donardi herba...sincerum quidem
levitate deprehenditur et colore
rufo odorisque suavitate." Jerome
(tr. in Mc.) plays lightly on this
meaning of the word: "ideo vos vo-
cati estis 'pistici,' fideles : ecclesia...
dona sua offert...fidem credentium."
Something however may be said for
the alternative offered by Thpht., εἴ-
δος νάρδου οὕτω λεγόμενον. The word
is transliterated in the Sinaitic
Syriac (ܘܢܪܕܝܢ ܦܝܣܛܝܩܝ), and in
some O.L. texts (e.g. nardi piscicae (sic),
k; n. pistici, d), whilst the Vg. nardi
spicati suggests that πιστικός may be
an attempt to represent spicatus; cf.
Galen cited in Wetstein : ἐπὶ δὲ τῶν
πλουσίων γυναικῶν καὶ τὸ καλούμενον
ὑπ᾽ αὐτῶν...σπίκατον προσφέρουσι.
For πιστικός potabilis, i.e. liquid, there
is no good authority. Πολυτελοῦς : cf.
v. 5, note. Clem. Al. paed. ii. 8 § 61
ὅπερ ἡγεῖτο τὸ κάλλιστον εἶναι παρ᾽ αὐτῇ,
τὸ μύρον, τούτῳ τετίμηκε τὸν δεσπότην.
συντρίψασα τὴν ἀλ.] A detail peculiar to Mc. Vg. fracto alabastro ; she
crushed or knocked off the head of

the thin alabaster flask ; it had served
its purpose and would not be used
again. Renan (Vie, p. 385) gives
another reason : "selon un vieil usage
qui consistait à briser la vaisselle dont
on s'était servi pour traiter un étran-
ger de distinction," adding "j'ai vu
cet usage se pratiquer encore à Sour."
For this use of συντρίβειν cf. Ps. ii. 9
(ὡς σκεῦος κεραμέως συντρίψεις, cf.
Apoc. ii. 27), Sir. xxi. 14 (ὡς ἄγγιον
συντετριμμένον).

κατέχεεν αὐτοῦ τῆς κεφαλῆς] Mt.
ἐπὶ τῆς κεφ. αὐτοῦ ἀνακειμένου. Mc.
has already represented the Lord as
lying on the triclinium (κατακειμένου
αὐτοῦ); the woman is standing behind and over Him. The gen. κεφαλῆς
answers to the downward direction of
the fluid, expressed in κατέχεεν, cf.
WM., pp. 477, 537 n.; Blass, Gr. p. 106;
and see Gen. xxxix. 21, Ps. lxxxviii.
(lxxxix.) 46. Such an act was not an
unusual attention to a guest; cf. Ps.
xxii. (xxiii.) 5, Cant. i. 12, and the
passages from Roman poets cited
above ; and add Plat. resp. iii. 398 A
μύρον κατὰ τῆς κεφαλῆς καταχέαντες.
Acc. to Jo. the Feet were anointed—
a reminiscence, possibly, of the earlier
anointing described by Lc. The woman may, however, as Aug. supposes,
have performed both acts, though we
cannot unreservedly admit his canon,
"ubi singuli evangelistae singula com-
memorant, utrumque factum intelle-
gere [oportet]." To anoint the feet of
a recumbent guest would have been
possible (see note on v. 18), but less
easy and usual, and on this occasion
perhaps less appropriate.

4. ἦσαν δέ τινες κτλ.] Mt. ἰδόντες

Εἰς τί ἡ ἀπώλεια αὕτη τοῦ μύρου γέγονεν; ⁵ἠδύνατο 5
γὰρ τοῦτο τὸ μύρον πραθῆναι ἐπάνω δηναρίων τριακοσίων καὶ δοθῆναι τοῖς πτωχοῖς· καὶ ἐνεβριμῶντο

4 εις τι Ψ] pr και λεγοντες AC²WᵇΧΓΔΠΣΦ minᶠᵉʳᵉᵒᵐⁿ lattᵛᵗᵖˡᵛᵍ pr και ελεγον D 2ᵖᵉ
syrrˢⁱⁿᵖᵉˢʰ arm aeth | αυτη] τουτου k syrᵖᵉˢʰ arm | om του μυρου minᵖᵃᵘᶜ a c l | om
γεγονεν D 64 a ff i   5 om γαρ D k arm aeth | τουτο το μυρον] om τουτο ℵ om
το μυρον EFGHMSVXΓ minᵖᵃᵘᶜ c k syrrˢⁱⁿᵖᵉˢʰ me | ενεβριμουντο ℵC* cˢᶜʳ

δὲ οἱ μαθηταὶ ἠγανάκτησαν, Jo. λέγει δὲ
Ἰούδας ὁ Ἰσκαριώτης. The indefinite-
ness of Mc.'s statement may be an
indication of the early date of his
source; personal considerations still
had weight in dictating reserve under
such circumstances. Cf. xiv. 47 εἰς δέ
τις τῶν παρεστηκότων, where again Jo.
supplies the name. The feeling expressed aloud by Judas may have been
shared by others in the Apostolic body;
as men unaccustomed to luxury they
might naturally resent the apparent
waste. Ἦσαν ἀγ. πρὸς ἑαυτούς, not as
Vg., erant indigne ferentes intra
semet ipsos, but rather as R.V. "had
indignation among themselves," i.e.
exchanged remarks or looks which
betrayed their sympathy with Judas.
For ἦσαν ἀγαν. see WM., p. 438, and
for πρὸς ἑαυτούς ad invicem, cf. xvi. 3,
and the nearly equivalent πρὸς ἀλλήλους in iv. 41, viii. 16.

εἰς τί ἡ ἀπώλεια αὕτη κτλ.] 'What
end can it have served?'—the plausible
cui bono of a shortsighted utilitarian-
ism. For εἰς τί cf. xv. 34, Mt. xiv. 31,
and esp. Sir. xxxix. 17 (26) οὐκ ἔστιν
εἰπεῖν Τί τοῦτο; εἰς τί τοῦτο; (לָמָּה זֶּה?).
Ἀπώλεια in the active sense of wasting
(Vg. perditio) is perhaps unique in
Biblical Gk.; the commentators refer
to Polyb. vi. 59. 5, where ἀπ. is contrasted with τήρησις. For ἀπόλλυσθαι
'to be wasted' cf. ii. 22. Γέγονεν: the
perfect calls attention to the act as
complete and still abiding in its
sensible effects; cf. v. 33, ix. 21.

5. ἠδύνατο γὰρ τοῦτο τὸ μύρον κτλ.]

The unguent might well be said to
have been wasted, in view of (γάρ) the
good which the owner might have
done with it. Δηναρίων τριακοσίων is
not governed by ἐπάνω (WM., p. 313),
but is the gen. of price (WM., p. 258,
cf. Jo. xii. 5); as to the amount see
Pliny H.N. xiii. 4, who speaks of certain
unguents which "excedunt quadra-
genos denarios librae." Mt.'s πολλοῦ
seems to indicate a fading interest in
such details. On τοῖς πτωχοῖς see x. 21,
note, and cf. Gal. ii. 10. The Passover
was perhaps a time when alms of this
kind were specially demanded; cf. Jo.
xiii. 29. How many of the poor of
Jerusalem might have been relieved
and gladdened by the money wasted
on an extravagance! The force of the
remark becomes apparent when it is
remembered that the labourer's daily
wage was a denarius (Mt. xx. 2) and
that two denarii sufficed for the inn-
keeper's payment in Lc. x. 35, whilst
two hundred (Mc. vi. 37) would have
gone some way to feed a multitude.

On ἠδύνατο without ἄν see WM., p.
352, and on the augment, WSchm.,
p. 99. Ἐνεβριμῶντο αὐτῇ, Mc. only.
The remarks were directed against
the woman, for no one ventured to
complain of the Lord's acceptance
of the offering. For ἐμβριμᾶσθαι see
note on i. 43; the word takes its note
whether of strictness or harshness
from the occasion. Here the Vg.
rendering is doubtless right: freme-
bant in eam. Cf. Thpht.: ἐνεβριμῶντο αὐτῇ· τουτέστιν, ἠγανάκτουν,
ὕβριζον, ἐπεπλήκτουν αὐτῇ.

6 αὐτῇ.　⁶ὁ δὲ Ἰησοῦς εἶπεν Ἄφετε αὐτήν· τί αὐτῇ
κόπους παρέχετε; καλὸν ἔργον ἠργάσατο ἐν ἐμοί·
7 ⁷πάντοτε γὰρ τοὺς πτωχοὺς ἔχετε μεθ᾽ ἑαυτῶν, καὶ
ὅταν θέλητε δύνασθε αὐτοῖς [πάντοτε] εὖ ποιῆσαι· ἐμὲ

5 αυτη] pr εν D*　　6 ειπεν]+αυτοις D 238 2ᵖᵉ a c ff i k q syrˢⁱⁿ arm aegg |
αφες k | καλον]+γαρ ℵG 13 28 69 2ᵖᵉ alᵖᵃᵘᶜ c syrˢⁱⁿ arm | ηργασατο ℵ*B*D 69 150ᵉᵛ]
ειργ. ℵᶜAB³CLWᵇΧΓΔΠΣΦΨ minᵖˡ | εν εμοι] εις εμε 𝖲 minᵖᵃᵘᶜ　　7 μεθ εαυτων]
μεθ υμων D 91 299 | αυτους ΑΧΠΣΦ minᵖˡ | om παντοτε 2° ℵ*ACDUXΓΔΣΦ minᵖˡ
latt syrr arm (hab ℵᶜ·ᵃ BL aegg) | ποιειν D*ΔΨ minᵖᵃᵘᶜ

6. ὁ δὲ Ἰησοῦς εἶπεν Ἄφετε αὐτήν
κτλ.] Ἄφετε αὐτήν is "let her alone"
(R.V.) rather than "suffer ye her"
(Vg., Wycliffe), as the next words shew.
Κόπους (κόπον) παρέχειν occurs again
in Lc. xi. 7, xviii. 5, Gal. vi. 17, and is
found in Aristotle; but as Wetstein
points out, class. writers prefer παρε-
χειν πράγματα [or πόνον, ὄχλον]. The
interference was unreasonable (τί;),
and the woman should rather have
been commended; her act was a καλὸν
ἔργον, one which possessed true moral
beauty; cf. Jo. x. 32 (Westcott), 1 Tim.
v. 10ᵃ, 25, vi. 18, Tit. iii. 8, 14, Heb. x.
24; the more usual phrase is ἔργον
ἀγαθόν (Acts ix. 36, Rom. xiii. 3, Eph.
ii. 10, 1 Tim. v. 10ᵇ, 2 Tim. iii. 17).
Mc.'s ἐν ἐμοί becomes εἰς ἐμέ in Mt.
—both perhaps answering to בִּי. The
goodness of the act lay in the grateful
love which it displayed (cf. Lc. vii.
47 ἠγάπησεν πολύ); no sacrifice was
too costly to offer to One who had
restored her brother to life. The
Lord's tacit acceptance of supreme
devotion as His due is not less remarkable than Mary's readiness to render
it; cf. viii. 35, Mt. xxv. 40 (ἐμοὶ
ἐποιήσατε), Jo. xxi. 15 ff. (ἀγαπᾷς...
ἀγαπᾷς...φιλεῖς με;). The beauty of
a good act varies according to the
relation in which it stands to Christ.

7. πάντοτε γὰρ τοὺς πτωχοὺς κτλ.]
Cf. Deut. xv. 11 οὐ γὰρ μὴ ἐκλίπῃ ἐνδεὴς
ἀπὸ τῆς γῆς. The first and third clauses
of this saying of Christ are preserved
in almost identical words by Mt., Mc.,

Jo., but Mc. alone has καὶ ὅταν θέλητε...
εὖ ποιῆσαι. There was no intention
on the Lord's part to contrast services
rendered to Himself in person with
services rendered to the poor for His
sake—the two are in His sight equivalents (Mt. xxv. 40, 45); His purpose is
to point out that the former would very
soon be impossible, whilst opportunities for the latter would abound to
the end of time. Ὅταν θέλητε: the
will was not wanting to the Apostolic
Church (Rom. xv. 26, Gal. ii. 10, 2 Cor.
viii. 1 ff.); the faith of Christ yielded
a new ground of sympathy with the
needy (δι᾽ ὑμᾶς ἐπτώχευσεν) which in
all ages has made the Church a refuge
of the destitute. As to the power
to execute this goodwill see 2 Cor.
viii. 3, and for the juxtaposition of will
and power cf. i. 40. Ἐμὲ οὐ πάντοτε
ἔχετε is true in the sense in which it
was said (cf. Jo. xvii. 11 οὐκέτι εἰμὶ
ἐν τῷ κόσμῳ), although in another
sense the Lord could teach Ἐγὼ μεθ᾽
ὑμῶν εἰμι πάσας τὰς ἡμέρας. Jerome:
"videtur in hoc loco de praesentia
dicere corporali." Εὖ ποιεῖν (not
εὐποιεῖν) occurs here only in the N.T.,
though fairly frequent in the LXX.,
where it usually stands for הֵיטִיב; the
acc. commonly follows (e.g. Gen. xxxii.
9 (10) εὖ σε ποιήσω), but the dat. is
also found, cf. Sir. xii. 1 f. ἐὰν εὖ ποιῇς,
γνῶθι τίνι ποιεῖς...εὖ ποίησον εὐσεβεῖ,
καὶ εὑρήσεις ἀνταπόδομα, where the
whole context is instructive as to the
Jewish conception of εὐποιία.

δὲ οὐ πάντοτε ἔχετε. ⁸ὃ ἔσχεν ἐποίησεν· προέλαβεν 8
μυρίσαι τὸ σῶμά μου εἰς τὸν ἐνταφιασμόν. ⁹ἀμὴν 9
δὲ λέγω ὑμῖν 'Όπου ἐὰν κηρυχθῇ τὸ εὐαγγέλιον εἰς

8 εσχεν] ειχεν Φ min^nonn γαρ syr^sin | εποιησεν אBLΨ 1 13 28 69 209 346 2^pe a me
syr^hel] pr (vel+) αυτη ACDW^bΧΓ(Δ)ΠΣΦ min^pl c f f i q vg om k^vid   9 om δε
ACFHMUXΣ min^pl f ff i k q vg syrr^sin hel arm aegg go aeth | οπου] pr οτι 124 604
a c d f i k | το ευαγγ.]+τουτο ACW^bΧΓΔΠΣΦΨ min^pl (c f) q vg syrr^pesh hel arm aegg go

8. ὃ ἔσχεν ἐποίησεν] Mc. only.
Ἔσχεν sc. ποιῆσαι. For this use of
ἔχειν cf. Mt. xviii. 25 (Lc. vii. 42), Lc.
xii. 4, xiv. 14, 'Jo.' viii. 6, Acts iv. 14,
Heb. vi. 13; the infinitive is not
always expressed, as Kypke shews,
quoting e.g. Dion. Hal. ant. vii. p. 467
οὐκ εἶχον δὲ ὅτι ἂν ἄλλο ποιῶσιν. For
the general sense see 2 Cor. viii. 12
καθὸ ἐὰν ἔχῃ εὐπρόσδεκτος, οὐ καθὸ οὐκ
ἔχει. Mary could not prevent the Lord's
Death; what she did He accounts as
a supreme effort to do honour to His
dead body. Προέλαβεν μυρίσαι, prae-
venit ungere: Mt. πρὸς τὸ ἐνταφιάσαι
με ἐποίησεν. Προλαμβάνειν 'anticipate'
is used in class. writers with a case,
or absolutely; for the inf. see Kypke
ad l. and Blass, Gr. p. 227, who compare Jos. ant. xviii. 7 προλαβὼν ἀνελεῖν
and Ps. Clem. 2 Cor. viii. 2 ἐὰν δὲ προ-
φθάσῃ...βαλεῖν. Μυρίζειν is ἅπ. λεγ. in
Biblical Gk., but occurs in Herodotus
and the comic poets. Fragrant unguents were used for anointing the
dead body after it had been washed
(Lucian de luct. 11 λούσαντες αὐτοὺς...
καὶ μύρῳ τῷ καλλίστῳ χρίσαντες τὸ
σῶμα)—a process to be distinguished
from embalming, which, as we see
from Jo. xix. 39, consisted of laying
myrrh and aloes in the folds of the
grave clothes. Acc. to Ev. Petr. 6
the Lord's Body was washed, and Mc.
(xvi. 1) relates how on Saturday night
the women ἠγόρασαν ἀρώματα ἵνα
ἀλείψωσιν αὐτόν. But the Resurrection prevented the fulfilment of their
design, and thus as it seems the only
anointing which the Lord received
was this anticipatory one at Bethany

a week before He lay in the tomb.
Εἰς τὸν ἐνταφιασμόν 'with a view to
its preparation for burial.' Ἐνταφιά-
ζειν (חָנַט), ἐνταφιαστής (רֹפֵא) occur in
Gen. l. 2 (LXX.) in connexion with the
embalming of Jacob, and ἐνταφιαστής
is found in the papyri in this sense
(Deissmann, B. St., p. 120 f.). But
words derived from ἐντάφιος may be
used to include everything belonging
to the preparation of a dead body for
the grave; cf. Test. xii. patr. Iud. 26
μηδείς με ἐνταφιάσῃ πολυτελεῖ ἐσθῆτι.
St John follows another tradition
in his report of this saying: ἄφες αὐτήν,
ἵνα εἰς τὴν ἡμέραν τοῦ ἐνταφιασμοῦ μου
τηρήσῃ αὐτό (אBD), or acc. to an
easier but less strongly supported
reading, ἄφες αὐτήν· εἰς τ. ἡμ. τ. ἐντ.
μου τετήρηκεν αὐτό. Mt. confirms Mc.'s
account, but in other terms (βαλοῦσα
γὰρ αὕτη τὸ μύρον τοῦτο ἐπὶ τοῦ σώμα-
τός μου πρὸς τὸ ἐνταφιάσαι με ἐποίησεν). The obscurity of the words
may have led to these variations. For
their general meaning comp. Euth.:
καθάπερ προφητεύουσα τὸν πλησιάζοντά
μου θάνατον.

9. ἀμὴν δὲ λέγω ὑμῖν κτλ.] Omitted
by Jo., but reported by Mt., Mc., in
almost identical words. For τὸ εὐαγγέλιον see i. 1, 14 f., viii. 35. The
world-wide proclamation of the Gospel
is explicitly foretold in xiii. 10; on
this earlier occasion it is assumed, as
if it were a matter of course. Εἰς
ὅλον τὸν κόσμον (Mt. ἐν ὅλῳ τῷ κόσμῳ)
is new, as an equivalent for εἰς πάντα
τὰ ἔθνη, but see Mt. v. 14, xiii. 38,
and for the phrase, Mc. viii. 36. The
thought of the κόσμος as the field of

ὅλον τὸν κόσμον, καὶ ὃ ἐποίησεν αὕτη λαληθήσεται
εἰς μνημόσυνον αὐτῆς.

10   ¹⁰ Καὶ Ἰούδας Ἰσκαριὼθ ὁ εἷς τῶν δώδεκα ἀπῆλθεν

10 Ιουδας] pr ιδου 13 63 64 69 124 alᶠᵒʳᵗᵉ pr o FGHKSUVX alᵖˡ | Ισκαριωθ
ℵ*BC*ᵛⁱᵈLΨ (o Ισκ.) (a f i Scarioth)] (o) Ισκαριωτης ℵᶜAC²LWᵇΧΓΔΠΣΦ minᵒᵐⁿᵛⁱᵈ
Or Eus Σκαριωτης D (c)(f) k l q Scariota syrr arm | om o εις τ. δωδ. A | o εις
ℵBC*ᵛⁱᵈLMΨ] om o C²WᵇΧΓΔΠΣΦ minᵒᵐⁿᵛⁱᵈ Or Eus εις εκ D 2ᵖᵉ lattᵛⁱᵈ

the activities of Christ and the Church, though much more abundant and more fully developed in the Fourth Gospel, is present in the oldest Synoptic sources. For κηρύσσειν εἰς cf. i. 39, 1 Thess. ii. 9, and see Blass, *Gr.* p. 124.

καὶ ὃ ἐποίησεν αὕτη κτλ.] This second prediction (Thpht. : δύο προφητείας, ὅτι τε τὸ εὐαγγέλιον κηρυχθήσεται...καὶ ὅτι τὸ ἔργον τῆς γυναικὸς συγκηρυχθήσεται) secured its own fulfilment ; an incident marked by so striking a comment was naturally enshrined in the earliest tradition, and became the property of the Catholic Church in the Gospels of Mt. and Mc. That the saying has not been reported by Lc. and Jo. is an interesting indication of the independence of those Evangelists. Καὶ ὃ ἐπ., together with the preaching of the Gospel this story shall also be told, and become a commonplace of Christian tradition. Εἰς μνημόσυνον αὐτῆς, cf. Acts x. 4 εἰς μνημόσυνον ἐνώπιον τοῦ θεοῦ. The word μνημ., which is of frequent occurrence in the LXX. as the equivalent of זִכָּרוֹן, זֵכֶר, or אַזְכָּרָה, is also found in early and late class. Gk., especially in the pl. (cf. τὰ εὐαγγέλια, i. 1, note). The Lord erects a memorial for all time to her who had done her best to honour Him (1 Regn. ii. 30 τοὺς δοξάζοντάς με δοξάσω). He who received not glory from men (Jo. v. 41) knew how to appreciate to the full the homage of a sincere love. Victor: ἐγὼ γὰρ (φησί) τοσοῦτον ἀπέχω τοῦ καταδικάσαι αὐτὴν ὡς κακῶς πεποιηκυῖαν...ὅτι οὐδὲ ἀφήσω λαθεῖν τὸ γεγενημένον, ἀλλ᾽ ὁ

κόσμος εἴσεται τὸ ἐν οἰκίᾳ εἰργασμένον καὶ ἐν κρυπτῷ· καὶ γὰρ μεγάλης διανοίας ἦν τὸ γεγενημένον καὶ πολλῆς τεκμήριον πίστεως.

10—11. INTERVIEW OF JUDAS WITH THE PRIESTS (Mt. xxvi. 14—16, Lc. xxii. 3—6).

10. καὶ Ἰούδας Ἰσκαριὼθ κτλ.] Judas Iscariot is mentioned by Mc. only in this chapter (*vv.* 10, 43), and in the Apostolic list (iii. 19) ; for Ἰσκαριώθ —the only form of that name used by Mc.—see the note on the latter passage. As to the sequence, Mc. as usual connects by a simple καί, while Mt. uses τότε, and thus appears to place the application of Judas to the Priests immediately after the supper at Bethany. Some reason there must have been for this early grouping ; if Jo. is right as to the date of the supper (see note on *v.* 3), the sequence in Mt. Mc. is probably ethical ; its purpose may be either (*a*) to place in sharp contrast the piety of Mary and the baseness of Judas (Thpht. : ἵνα δείξῃ τὴν ἀναίδειαν τοῦ Ἰούδα), or (*b*) to indicate that the latter incident arose in some way out of the former ; whether it was that the Lord's persistent reference to His death drove Judas to despair, or that he resented the expenditure of money which might have found its way into his own hands (Jo. xii. 4), or that the Lord's look or manner convinced him that his habit of pilfering and his treacherous intentions were known. Or (*c*) the arrangement of the narrative may be chiefly due to a desire to bring together the Lord's words about His approaching

πρὸς τοὺς ἀρχιερεῖς, ἵνα αὐτὸν παραδοῖ αὐτοῖς. ¹¹οἱ 11
δὲ ἀκούσαντες ἐχάρησαν, καὶ ἐπηγγείλαντο αὐτῷ

10 παραδοι Β (-δω אΑLΨ rell exc C de quo non liq)] προδοι D (*proderet* i k vg) |
om αυτοις D 28 91 299 2^{pe} a cffik syr^{sin} Or Eus   11 om ακουσαντες D a cffik
Eus | επηγγειλαν Ψ

burial, and the story of the treachery
which precipitated the end. The last
solution is perhaps the best, as being
the simplest; but it does not necessarily exclude the first two; the first
at least may have been also present
to the thoughts of those who originally drew up the common tradition.
ʼΟ εἷς τῶν δώδεκα : Mt. εἷς τ. δ., Lc.
ὄντα ἐκ τοῦ ἀριθμοῦ τῶν δ. This reference to the position held by Judas in
the Apostolate is not without meaning:
cf. Thpht. : οὐ γὰρ ἁπλῶς κεῖται τὸ ʼεἷς
τῶν δώδεκα,ʼ ἀλλʼ ἵνα δείξῃ ὅτι εἷς τῶν
προκρίτων, ἐκλεκτὸς καὶ αὐτὸς ὤν. The
art. is difficult to explain, especially
as there is no trace of it in *vv.* 20, 43.
ʼΟ εἷς naturally implies a contrast to
ὁ ἕτερος (cf. e.g. Lc. vii. 41, xvii.
34 f.) ; here, if it is to stand, the
contrast is apparently with οἱ λοιποί,
'that one, the only one, of the Twelve
who proved a traitor or was capable
of the act,' or 'the notorious member
of the body,' as opposed to εἷς τις, an
unknown individual ; unless ὁ εἷς =
εἷς ὤν, cf. ὁ εἷς τῶν ἁγίων ἀγγέλων
in Enoch xx. ff. Another explanation,
however, has been suggested which
deserves consideration. Since Judas
is frequently described in the Gospels
as εἷς τῶν δώδεκα (Mt. xxvi. 47, Mc.
xiv. 10, 20, 43, Lc. xxii. 47 (cf. 3), Jo.
vi. 71), the article may be intended to
mark the words as a familiar designation of the traitor—'that One
of the Twelve' who is notorious.
ʼΑπῆλθεν πρὸς τοὺς ἀρχιερεῖς. He
realised that in Jerusalem it was
with this class rather than with the
Scribes that the issue lay. Probably
they were still sitting in the palace
of Caiaphas (*v.* 1) ; with them were
the heads of the Levitical Temple

police (Lc. συνελάλησεν τοῖς ἀρχ. καὶ
στρατηγοῖς, sc. τοῦ ἱεροῦ, cf. Acts iv. 1,
v. 24). His business with them was
to arrange the terms of the Betrayal
(ἀπῆλθεν...ἵνα παραδοῖ); cf. Bede: "ostendit eum non a principibus invita-
tum, non ulla necessitate constrictum,
sed sponte propria sceleratae mentis
inesse consilium." On the form παραδοῖ see iv. 29, note. Even at this
climax παραδοῦναι is preferred by the
Evangelists to προδοῦναι: cf. i. 14,
iii. 19, ix. 31, notes.

11. οἱ δὲ ἀκούσαντες ἐχάρησαν κτλ.]
The proposal came from Judas, not
from the Priests, but it was received
by them with more delight than they
would care to shew—ἐχάρησαν, not
ἠγαλλιάσαντο: cf. Mt. v. 12, Apoc.
xix. 7 ; both words may be used of
interior joy (Lc. i. 47, Jo. xvi. 22),
but the former is the more suggestive
of the inward feeling, the latter of its
audible or visible expression. ʼΕπηγ-
γείλαντο αὐτῷ: the promise was a
response to a direct question from
Judas (Mt. εἶπεν Τί θέλετέ μοι δοῦναι;).
Mt. alone mentions the amount promised, which was therefore not a
matter of common tradition; probably
he was struck by its agreement with
the sum named in Zach. xi. 12 ff.
The ἀργύριον (τριάκοντα ἀργύρια Mt.,
τρ. ἀργυροῦς sc. σίκλους, Zach.) was
doubtless paid in shekels or the
equivalent tetradrachms which were
current (Mt. xvii. 24, cf. Madden,
p. 240, Hastings, *D.B.*, iii. 428). For
the loss of the 300 denarii Judas
consoled himself by a compact which
yielded 30 staters (perhaps two-fifths
of what Mary had spent on the
spikenard ; see Jos. *ant.* iii. 8. 2,
Madden, p. 246). Jerome : "infelix

ἀργύριον δοῦναι. καὶ ἐζήτει πῶς αὐτὸν εὐκαίρως
παραδοῖ.

12 ¹²Καὶ τῇ πρώτῃ ἡμέρᾳ τῶν ἀζύμων, ὅτε τὸ πάσχα
ἔθυον, λέγουσιν αὐτῷ οἱ μαθηταὶ αὐτοῦ Ποῦ θέλεις

11 αργυρια ΑΚΥΓΠΣ min^{sat mu} syr^{hcl} Eus | παραδοι BD (-δω ℵΑΛΨ rell ut vid)]
+αυτοις Δ min^{pauc} the   12 εθυον] ησθιον syr^{sin vid} | om αυτου D a ff^{vid} vg arm

Judas damnum quod ex effusione
unguenti se fecisse credebat vult Magistri pretio compensare." Small as
this sum was, Judas seems to have
been satisfied, the more so perhaps
because it was paid on the spot (Mt.
ἔστησαν αὐτῷ). He went back to the
Master and the Eleven with the price
of blood in his girdle.

καὶ ἐζήτει πῶς κτλ.] The Priests
had transferred their anxieties to the
traitor (cf. xii. 12, xiv. 1); it was for
him now to contrive and plot. They
had sought an opportunity of arresting
an enemy; it was the business of Judas
to seek an opportunity of betraying a
friend. Πῶς αὐτὸν εὐκαίρως παραδοῖ
Mc.; Mt. ἐζήτει εὐκαιρίαν (so also Lc.) ἵνα
αὐτὸν παραδῷ. For εὐκαίρως cf. 2 Tim.
iv. 2 ἐπίστηθι εὐκαίρως ἀκαίρως, and see
Mc. vi. 21, note. The problem which
presented itself to Judas was the same
which had perplexed the Priests—
how to elude the crowd of Galileans
and other visitors at the Feast who
were still with Jesus (Lc. τοῦ παραδοῦναι αὐτὸν ἄτερ ὄχλου). But his
position in the inner circle of disciples clearly gave him an advantage
in dealing with it, which the Priests
did not possess.

12—16. PREPARATIONS FOR THE
PASCHAL MEAL (Mt. xxvi. 17—19,
Lc. xxii. 7—13).

12. τῇ πρώτῃ ἡμ. τῶν ἀζύμων] See
v. 1, note. Lc. calls it ἡ ἡμέρα τῶν
ἀζύμων, and in both Mc. and Lc. it is
further defined as the day on which
the Paschal lamb was killed (Mc. ὅτε
τὸ πάσχα ἔθυον = Lc. ᾗ ἔδει θύεσθαι τὸ
π.). Euth.: πρώτην δὲ τῶν ἀζ. τὴν πρὸ
τοῦ πάσχα φασὶν ἡμέραν, τὴν τρισκαι-

δεκάτην μὲν τοῦ μηνός, πέμπτην δὲ τῆς
ἑβδομάδος. The lamb was killed and
eaten on Nisan 14 (Exod. xii. 6, Lev.
xxiii. 5, Num. ix. 3, 5, 11, xxviii. 16,
2 Chron. xxx. 2, 15, 1 Esdr. i. 1, vii. 10,
2 Esdr. vi. 19 f., Ezech. xlv. 21), and
though the ἑορτὴ τῶν ἀζύμων began
on Nisan 15 (Lev. xxiii. 6, Num.
xxviii. 17), yet unleavened bread was
eaten from the evening of Nisan 14
(Exod. xii. 18), and by custom from
noon on that day (J. Lightfoot ad l.,
Edersheim, Temple, p. 189). Later
Jewish usage identified the first day
of unleavened bread (לחג ראשׁון יום
המצות) with Nisan 15, but it is precarious on this ground to charge the
Synoptists with inconsistency (J. Th.
St. iii., p. 359). The phrase θύειν
τὸ π. is from the LXX. (Exod. xii. 21
(שׁחט), Deut. xvi. 2 (זבח) &c.); cf.
1 Cor. v. 7 τὸ π. ἡμῶν ἐτύθη Χριστός.
Θύειν does not necessarily convey the
idea of sacrifice (cf. Lc. xv. 23, Jo.
x. 10), yet the slaying of the πάσχα
was a sacrificial act performed in the
Court of the Priests, normally by the
head of the household (Exod. xii. 6),
but on occasions by Levites (2 Chron.
xxx. 15 ff., xxxv. 3 ff., Ezr. vi. 19); see
the ceremonial described in Edersheim, Temple, p. 190 ff. Ἔθυον 'it
was customary to kill'; imperf. of
repeated action (Burton, § 24).

λέγουσιν αὐτῷ οἱ μαθ. αὐτοῦ] They
approached Jesus (Mt. προσῆλθον),
perhaps under the impression that
He had overlooked the necessity for
immediate preparation; Lc. seems to
represent the Lord as taking the
initiative. Ποῦ θέλεις...ἑτοιμάσωμεν;

ἀπελθόντες ἑτοιμάσωμεν ἵνα φάγῃς τὸ πάσχα; ¹³καὶ 13
ἀποστέλλει δύο τῶν μαθητῶν αὐτοῦ καὶ λέγει §αὐτοῖς   § l'
'Υπάγετε εἰς τὴν πόλιν, καὶ ἀπαντήσει ὑμῖν ἄνθρωπος
κεράμιον ὕδατος βαστάζων· ἀκολουθήσατε αὐτῷ.
¹⁴καὶ ὅπου ἐὰν εἰσέλθῃ εἴπατε τῷ οἰκοδεσπότῃ ὅτι 14

12 ετοιμασωμεν]+σοι DΔ 2ᵖᵉ alᵖᵃᵘᶜ c f g i k l q vg syrᵖᵉˢʰ Orⁱⁿᵗ   13 των μαθ.]
pr εκ D latt Orⁱⁿᵗ | και λεγει αυτοις] λεγων D 604 1071 2ᵖᵉ a ff i q the Orⁱⁿᵗ | και 3°]
+εισελθοντων υμων εις την πολιν Σ 13 28 69 91 124 299 346 2ᵖᵉ arm Orⁱⁿᵗ   14 om
οτι Σ 604

cf. WM., p. 356, Burton, § 171, and see x. 36, 51, xv. 9; for ἑτοιμάζειν ἵνα φάγῃς τὸ π. Mt. has ἑτ. σοι φαγεῖν τὸ π.: so the three Synoptists below, ἑτ. τὸ πάσχα; the harsher ἑτ. ἵνα appears again in Apoc. viii. 6.

13. ἀποστέλλει δύο] Mt. does not specify the number; Lc. on the other hand gives their names—ἀπέστειλεν Πέτρον καὶ 'Ιωάνην, a grouping which is frequent in the early chapters of the Acts, iii. 1 ff., iv. 13 ff., viii. 14. Edersheim (Life, p. 487, Temple, p. 190) supposes that the two were entrusted with the purchase and sacrifice of the lamb; but the directions which the Lord gives relate only to the room and its arrangement. If the meal was (as the Synoptists imply) the Paschal supper, it seems possible that the lamb was provided by the οἰκοδεσπότης (v. 14), i.e. that the Lord and the Twelve shared the one which he had provided; if the household was a small one, such an arrangement would have been in accordance with the spirit of Exod. xii. 4 (cf. Edersheim, Life, ii. p. 483).

ὑπάγετε εἰς τὴν πόλιν] The Lord was therefore still outside, probably at or near Bethany. The two are sent into Jerusalem πρὸς τὸν δεῖνα (Mt. ; Thpht. : πρὸς ἄνθρωπον ἀγνώριστον, cf. Euth. : παρεσιώπησε μὲν τοῦ ἀνδρὸς τὴν κλῆσιν, ὅπως μὴ μαθὼν τὴν οἰκίαν 'Ιούδας ἐκδράμῃ πρὸς τοὺς ἐπιβούλους καὶ εἰσαγάγῃ τούτους αὐτῷ πρὸ τοῦ παραδοῦναι τὸ μυστικὸν δεῖπνον

τοῖς μαθηταῖς). Mc. and Lc. add the remarkable direction ἀπαντήσει (Lc. συν.) ὑμῖν ἄνθρωπος κτλ. The man was probably a servant (Deut. xxix. 11 (10), Jos. ix. 27, 29, 33 (21, 23, 27)): he had been sent to fetch a supply of water, probably from Siloam or Bir Eyûb (Recovery, p. 10 ff., D. B.² p. 1590 ff.) and for use at the Feast (cf. Jo. ii. 6, xiii. 4 ff.), and entering the city on his return by a gate at the S.E. corner (cf. Neh. ii. 14 שַׁעַר הָעַיִן), he crossed the path of the two, who were coming in from Bethany. Κεράμιον ὕδατος, an earthen pitcher filled with water; see WM., p. 235, and cf. κ. οἴνου Jer. xlii. (xxxv.) 5; for βαστάζειν see Jo. xix. 17 β. τὸν σταυρόν, Gal. vi. 2, 5 β. βάρη, φορτίον. The man would act as an unconscious guide through the network of narrow and unfamiliar streets to the appointed place; the two were to follow in silence, and enter the house into which they saw him pass (Lc. ἀκ. αὐτῷ εἰς τὴν οἰκίαν).

Tertullian sees in the pitcher of water a prophecy of the great baptismal rite which signalised the approach of Easter in the ancient Church (de bapt. 19 : " diem solemniorem pascha praestat...nec incongruenter ad figuram interpretabitur quod... Dominus...paschae celebrandae locum de signo aquae ostendit ").

14. εἴπατε τῷ οἰκοδεσπότῃ κτλ.] The message is not for the servant whose part is fulfilled when he had led them

Ὁ διδάσκαλος λέγει Ποῦ ἐστιν τὸ κατάλυμά μου
ὅπου τὸ πάσχα μετὰ τῶν μαθητῶν μου φάγω ;
15 ¹⁵καὶ αὐτὸς ὑμῖν δείξει ἀνάγαιον μέγα ἐστρωμένον
16 ἕτοιμον, καὶ ἐκεῖ ἑτοιμάσατε ἡμῖν. ¹⁶καὶ ἐξῆλθον

14 ο διδ.]+ημων syrʳˢⁱⁿ(ᵛⁱᵈ)ᵖᵉˢʰ k | που] pr ο καιρος μου εγγυς εστιν syrˢⁱⁿ | om μου 1°
APWᵇXΓΠΦ minᵖˡ c ff i k syrˢⁱⁿᵖᵉˢʰʰᶜˡ(ᵗˣᵗ) arm go aeth Orⁱⁿᵗ (hab אBCDLΔΨ 1 13
28 69 1071 alⁿᵒⁿⁿ a f l q vg the syrʰᶜˡᵐᵍ Orⁱⁿᵗ) | φαγομαι Dᵍʳ 13 (28) 69 124 209 346
15 ανωγαιον B³MSUX(ΓΣΨ) minⁿᵒⁿⁿ οικον armᶜᵒᵈ | μεγα εστρωμ.] οικον εστρωμ. μεγαν
Dᵍʳ | om ετοιμον AM*Δ minⁿᵒⁿⁿ a vg arm | και εκει BCL 346 1071 (κακει אD 2ᵖᵉ)]
om και APWᵇXΓΔΠΣΦ minᵖˡ a c ff i k q syrr arm the   16 εξηλθον]+ετοιμασαι
124 2ᵖᵉ arm+ετ. αυτω 1071

to the house, but for the head of the
house. Its terms are remarkable : ὁ
διδάσκαλος λέγει (cf. λέγει Ἰησοῦς in
the Oxyrhynchus fragment, Lc. λέγει
σοι ὁ δ.), and seem to imply that
Jesus was known, and His character
as a Rabbi acknowledged by the οἰκοδεσπότης. The conjecture which makes
him the father of Mark (cf. Acts xii.
12 ; Edersheim, Life, ii. p. 485) is
interesting, but unsupported by any
evidence beyond the faint clue offered
by Acts xii. 12. On ὁ διδ. see iv. 38,
note.

ποῦ ἐστιν τὸ κατάλυμά μου κτλ.]
Κατάλυμα, Vg. refectio, better, as some
O. L. authorities, refectorium or di-
versorium : the word belongs to the
κοινή (Moeris : καταγώγιον καὶ κατά-
γεσθαι Ἀττικῶς, κατάλυμα καὶ καταλύειν
Ἑλληνικῶς), but the verb at least is
used by good authors in a kindred
sense (e.g. Plat. Gorg. 447 B παρ'
ἐμοὶ γὰρ Γοργίας καταλύει). For κατάλυμα, 'guest-room,' in Biblical Gk. cf.
1 Regn. i. 18 (where see Driver's note),
ix. 22 (לִשְׁכָּה), Sir. xiv. 25 ; in Exod.
iv. 24 (מָלוֹן), Lc. ii. 7, it is used in the
wider sense (=πανδοχεῖον Lc. x. 34).
Here the meaning is defined by v. 15.
Μου (Mc. only) claims perhaps right
of use rather than ownership, 'the
room for Me,' which for the time is to
be Mine. Even so, the language is
remarkable, though not unique (cf.
xi. 3); and Mt. softens it into πρὸς

σὲ ποιῶ τὸ πάσχα. The Lord's manner
is changed in this last week ; He is
now the revealed King of Israel (see
xi. 7 ff., notes). For ὅπου...φάγω see
Burton, § 318 f., Blass, Gr. p. 217.

15. καὶ αὐτὸς ὑμῖν δείξει κτλ.] The
man will take you to the room ; αὐτός
(Lc. κἀκεῖνος) is perhaps not emphatic
(cf. viii. 29, note), but it implies
the readiness of the οἰκοδεσπότης to
render personal service. Ἀνάγαιον
μέγα ἐστρωμένον, Mc. Lc.; Mt. is relatively vague throughout this section.
On the form ἀνάγαιον see Lob. Phryn.
p. 297, WSchm., pp. 47, 51, and cf.
what Rutherford says as to κατάγαιον
(N. Phryn., p. 357) ; ἀνάγαιον is ἅπ.
λεγ. in Biblical Gk., the usual word
being ὑπερῷον (=עֲלִיָּה, see Moore on
Jud. iii. 20), cf. Acts i. 13, ix. 37,
39, xx. 8. Each of these passages
implies a room spacious enough for
a considerable gathering, but the
size varied of course with the character of the house. This upper room
was ἐστρωμένον, i.e. carpeted (xi. 8),
or more strictly perhaps provided with
carpeted divans, see Smith's B. D.²,
p. 1406 f.; cf. Ezech. xxiii. 41 ἐκάθου
ἐπὶ κλίνης ἐστρωμένης, Xen. Cyrop. viii.
2. 6 κλίνην στρώννυσι, τράπεζαν κοσμεῖ,
Aristoph. Ach. 1089 τὰ δ' ἄλλα πάντ'
ἐστὶν παρεσκευασμένα, | κλῖναι, τράπεζαι,
προσκεφάλαια, στρώματα (cited by
Field, Notes, p. 39, q. v.). Ἡμῖν, 'for
Me and you'; the Lord does not
often use the pl. in this inclusive way,

οἱ μαθηταὶ¹ καὶ ἦλθον εἰς τὴν πόλιν, καὶ εὗρον καθὼς   ¶ go
εἶπεν αὐτοῖς· καὶ ἡτοίμασαν τὸ πάσχα.
¹⁷Καὶ ὀψίας γενομένης ἔρχεται μετὰ τῶν δώδεκα. 17
¹⁸καὶ ἀνακειμένων αὐτῶν καὶ ἐσθιόντων ὁ Ἰησοῦς 18
                                    ●

16 οι μαθ.]+αυτου ACDPWᵇΧΓΠΣΦ minᵖˡ latt syrr arm aeth | ευρον] εποιησαν D
a c ff i q armᶜᵒᵈ   18 ο Ιησους ειπεν] λεγει ο I. D 2ᵖᵉ

but cf. ix. 39. The keeping of the
Paschal festival was absolutely common
to Master and disciples.

16. ἐξῆλθον...ἦλθον...εὗρον] The
minute explicitness of one who had
part in the transaction shews itself
here : contrast Lc. ἀπελθόντες...εὗρον,
Mt. ἐποίησαν. Καθὼς εἶπεν αὐτοῖς : all
the particulars were as the Master
foretold—the servant with the pitcher,
the οἰκοδεσπότης ready to oblige, the
large divan-spread upper room; cf.
xi. 1 ff. For the second time in that
week the Lord had shewn a superhuman knowledge of circumstances
as yet unrealised; see Mason, Conditions, p. 159.

ἡτοίμασαν τὸ πάσχα] Supposing
the lamb to have been already slain
and returned to the house, there still
remained much to be done: the roast-
ing of the lamb, the provision of the
unleavened cakes, the bitter herbs,
the Charoseth (see below), and the
four cups of wine, the preparation of
the room and the lamps; and in the
preparation of the food there were
many ritual niceties to be observed (cf.
e.g. Edersheim, Temple, pp. 199, 204).
Tὸ πάσχα is here apparently the paschal meal (cf. v. 1, note), but it implies
the provision of the paschal lamb.

17—21. THE PASCHAL SUPPER :
THE TRAITOR INDICATED (Mt. xxvi.
20—25; Lc. xxii. 14, 21—23; Jo. xiii.
2, 21—30).

17. ὀψίας γενομένης] So Mt.; Lc.
more vaguely ὅτε ἐγένετο ἡ ὥρα. On
ὀψίας see i. 32, vi. 47, xiii. 35, notes.
The lambs were not slain in the Precinct till after the offering of the
Evening Sacrifice (Temple, p. 190 f.;

cf. Exod. xii. 6 πρὸς ἑσπέραν, בֵּין
הָעַרְבָּיִם), and though the latter was
on this occasion offered an hour earlier
than usual, the subsequent ceremonial must have lasted till late in the
afternoon. The meal was in its original associations nocturnal (Exod. xii.
8 φάγονται τὰ κρέα τῇ νυκτὶ ταύτῃ), and
motives of prudence would probably
have prevented the Master from
making His way through the city
before sunset. Ἔρχεται μετὰ τῶν δώδεκα : unless οἱ δώδεκα is here used
loosely for οἱ μαθηταί, the two had
returned to report that all was
ready, and to guide the party to the
place.

18. ἀνακειμένων αὐτῶν καὶ ἐσθιόν-
των] The meal has now begun (Jo.
δείπνου γινομένου). We see the Twelve
and the Lord reclining on the divans
which were ready for their use (v. 15).
For ἀνακεῖσθαι see ii. 15, note, vi. 26;
Lc. uses here the correlative ἀναπίπτειν. It seems to have been part of the
original ritual of the Passover to eat
standing (cf. Exod. xii. 11), but the
recumbent posture had become customary, and was interpreted as a sign
of the freedom from slavery which
had been inaugurated by the Exodus
(Temple, p. 201). The guests lay on
their left side with their feet resting
on the ground, and the couches seem
to have been grouped in sets of two
or three; when these were placed
together, the central position was that
of greatest dignity; see J. Lightfoot on
Mt. xxvi., and cf. Jo. xiii. 23 ff., from
which it appears that the Lord reclined between St Peter and St John.
On this occasion the arrangement was

εἶπεν Ἀμὴν λέγω ὑμῖν ὅτι εἷς ἐξ ὑμῶν παραδώσει με,
¶ G 19 ὁ ἐσθίων μετ᾽ ἐμοῦ.⁣ ¹⁹ἤρξαντο λυπεῖσθαι καὶ λέγειν
20 αὐτῷ εἷς κατὰ εἷς Μήτι ἐγώ; ²⁰ὁ δὲ εἶπεν αὐτοῖς Εἷς

18 ο εσθιων] των εσθιοντων B aegg   19 ηρξαντο אBLΨ me] pr οι δε ADPWᵇX
ΓΔΠΣΦ minᵖˡ latt syrr arm pr και C 238 | λυπ_εισθαι] + και αδημονειν 1071 | εις κατα
εις אBLΔΨ (εις καθ εις ADPWᵇXΓΠΣΦ minᵒᵐⁿ ᵛⁱᵈ)] εις εκαστος C om k | μητι εγω]
+ ειμι ραββει A+ειμι Σ 13 28 69 alᵖᵃᵘᶜ+και αλλος μητι εγω ADWᵇXΓΠ(Σ)Φ minᵖˡ
a (c) f ff i (k) q syrʰᶜˡ⁽ᵐᵍ⁾ (arm) Or (om אBCLPΔ vg aegg syrʳᵃⁱⁿ ᵖᵉˢʰ ʰᵉˡ⁽ᵗˣᵗ⁾ arm aeth)
20 ο δε]+αποκριθεις APWᵇXΓΔΠΣΦ minᵒᵐⁿ ᵛⁱᵈ k syrʰᶜˡ arm aeth | ειπεν] λεγει DΨ
2ᵖᵉ dicit k ait a ff i q vg | εις των δωδεκα אBCLΨ minᵖᵃᵘᶜ] εις εκ τ. δ. ADPWᵇX
ΓΔΠΣΦ minᵖˡ om M k

possibly 3+3+3+2+2, or it may
have been that there was but one set
of three, that in which the Lord was.
Ἐσθιόντων : the meal had proceeded
some way and the *pedilavium* had
already taken place (see Jo. xii. 2 ff.);
in Lc. the institution of the Eucharist
also precedes the revelation of the
traitor, but the order of the older
Gospels is here almost certainly to
be preferred, as Tatian already saw
(Hill, p. 221).

ἀμὴν λέγω ὑμῖν ὅτι εἷς κτλ.] Hitherto they had known only that He should
be delivered into the hands of His
enemies (ix. 31, x. 33), and probably
no suspicion had been entertained of
Judas ; even Jo. vi. 70 is indefinite,
and the event alone shewed its significance. It is difficult to remember
this in view of the repeated reference
to the treachery of Judas wherever
his name is mentioned in the Gospel
history (cf. iii. 19, note). Εἷς ἐξ ὑμῶν
revealed a new feature in the history
of the Passion which was more intolerable than any, involving the
Twelve in a horrible charge from
which they could only escape when
the traitor was made known. Jerome:
"mittit crimen in numero ut conscius
agat paenitentiam." Ὁ ἐσθίων μετ᾽
ἐμοῦ is peculiar to Mc. : the words
probably refer to Ps. xl. (xli.) 10, which
the Lord quoted (Jo. xiii. 18); cf. Lc.
ἡ χεὶρ τοῦ παραδιδόντος με μετ᾽ ἐμοῦ ἐπὶ
τῆς τραπέζης.

19. ἤρξαντο λυπεῖσθαι] The omis-

sion of the copula adds to the dramatic
power of the narrative. Gloom fell at
once on the company (cf. x. 22, Mt.
xvii. 23). Mt. adds σφόδρα, but the
simple λυπεῖσθαι tells us enough ; cf.
St Paul's account of a λύπη κατὰ θεόν,
2 Cor. vii. 11. The ἀπολογία came at
once in the question which went round,
Μήτι ἐγώ; is it—yet surely it cannot
be—I ? (cf. iv. 21, note). On εἷς κατὰ
εἷς (Mt. εἷς ἕκαστος) see WM., p. 512,
Blass, *Gr.*pp. 145,179 ; cf. Apoc. xxi. 21
ἀνὰ εἷς ἕκαστος. Καθ᾽ εἷς appears in the
LXX. (Lev. xxv. 10 (A), 1 Esdr. i. 31,
Isa. xxvii. 12 (κατὰ ἕνα), 3 Macc. v. 34,
4 Macc. xv. 12, 14) ; in such phrases
the prep. appears to be used adverbially. See the discussion in Deissmann,
B. St. p. 138 ff.

20. ὁ δὲ εἶπεν αὐτοῖς κτλ.] The
Fourth Gospel fills in the picture.
The question addressed to the Lord
(αὐτῷ v. 19, Mt. κύριε) was followed
by a perplexed and perhaps suspicious
look at one another (Jo. xiii. 22).
When the Lord's answer came, it was
given to John, and perhaps not audible beyond the neighbourhood of the
divan on which He reclined between
Peter and John. The form of the
reply in Jo. is so distinct from that
in Mt. Mc., that Tatian gives them
separately, placing the Synoptic tradition first ; but it seems clear that
an answer to the whole party would
have rendered Peter's enquiry (Jo.,
v. 23 f.) superfluous. John's account
is probably the more precise, since it

τῶν δώδεκα, ὁ ἐμβαπτόμενος μετ' ἐμοῦ εἰς τὸ [ἐν]
τρύβλιον. ²¹ ὅτι ὁ μὲν υἱὸς τοῦ ἀνθρώπου ὑπάγει 21
καθὼς γέγραπται περὶ αὐτοῦ, οὐαὶ δὲ τῷ ἀνθρώπῳ

20 εμβαπτομενος] ενβαπτιζομενος D εμβαψας Σ | μετ εμου]+την χειρα A a c f ff q
vg^codd aliq ed aegg | om εν ℵAC²D*2LPΨ rell (hab BC*vid) 21 om οτι ACDPWᵇX
ΓΔΠΣΦ min^omn vid a arm (hab ℵBLΨ aegg) | υπαγει] παραδιδοται D a c i 21 γε-
γραπται] εστιν γεγραμμενον D

was he who received the answer
directly from the Lord.

ὁ ἐμβαπτόμενος κτλ.] The reference
is probably to the sauce חֲרֹסֶת, "a
compound of dates, raisins, &c., and
vinegar" (*Temple*, pp. 204, 208), into
which at a certain moment the master
of the house dipped pieces of the unleavened cake with bitter herbs between them, which were then distributed to the company (J. Lightfoot
on Mt.). The sign consisted in the
singling out of Judas to receive the
'sop' from the Master's hands (Jo.
ἐγὼ βάψω τὸ ψωμίον καὶ δώσω αὐτῷ).
Commentators who deny that the
meal described in Jo. xiii. is the
paschal supper regard the ψωμίον as
the "'tid-bit' which an Oriental host
is accustomed to offer to any favourite
guest" (Dr M. Dods on Jo. xiii. 25 ;
cf. Bp Westcott *ad l.*). In Mt. Mc.,
where the paschal meal is clearly in
view, it is natural to connect the sign
with the *Charoseth*. Ὁ ἐμβαπτόμενος,
present "used to describe vividly a
future event," Burton §§ 15, 130 ; the
middle marks the act as that of Judas
himself (Mt. ἐμβάψας...τὴν χεῖρα).
Τρύβλιον is perhaps a bowl (cf. Ar.
Ach. 278 εἰρήνης ῥοφήσει τρ., *Plut.*
1108 ἐς ταὐτὸν ὑμᾶς συγκυκήσας τρ.)
rather than a dish (Vg. *catinus*;
Wycliffe, Tindale, "plater," "platter";
A.V., R.V., "dish" ; Euth. : ἐστὶν εἶδος
πίνακος) ; on the accent see Chandler
§ 350. Μετ' ἐμοῦ εἰς τὸ ἕν τρ. The
act is difficult to realise under the
circumstances of the paschal feast,
and in connexion with the *Charoseth*;
but the words, esp. in Mc., who alone
has ἕν, point to the baseness of the

treachery which sacrificed an intimate
friend. To dip into the same dish
was a token of intimacy, cf. Ruth ii.
14 βάψεις τὸν ψωμόν σου [ἐν] τῷ ὄξει.

21. ὅτι ὁ μὲν υἱὸς τοῦ ἀνθρώπου κτλ.]
This weighty saying is given in identical words by Mt. Mc., and in a shorter
form by Lc. Ὑπάγει, 'goeth His way,'
used frequently in Jo. of the Lord's
Death (viii. 14, 21 f., xiii. 3, 33 ff., xiv.
4 ff.) as beginning His return to the
Father (vii. 33, xiv. 6, xvi. 10, 17) ; cf.
Thpht. : ὡσανεὶ γὰρ ἀποδημία ἦν ὁ
θάνατος τοῦ χριστοῦ, οὐχὶ θάνατος.
Lc.'s πορεύεται (= הָלַךְ in reference to
the last journey of death, e.g. 2 Regn.
xii. 23, cf. BDB., p. 234) partly misses
this point. Καθὼς γέγραπται περὶ
αὐτοῦ: Lc. κατὰ τὸ ὡρισμένον, acc. to
the Divine purpose expressed in the
symbolism and predictions of the
O.T. ; cf. Mc. ix. 13. The saying has
no flavour of Pharisaic fatalism ; it is
not a blind ἀνάγκη, but a Personal
Will, long revealed and accepted,
which the Son of Man consciously
obeys (Phil. ii. 8). Περὶ αὐτοῦ: cf. ix.
12 γεγρ. ἐπὶ τὸν υἱὸν τοῦ ἀνθρώπου,
and see the note there.

οὐαὶ δὲ τῷ ἀνθρώπῳ ἐκείνῳ κτλ.] The
Divine purpose does not palliate the
traitor's sin or relieve him of responsibility in any degree. Οὐαί is not
vindictive, or of the nature of a curse ;
it reveals a misery which Love itself
could not prevent (cf. xiii. 17) ; cf.
Ephrem, *ev. conc. exp.* :' "quibus verbis iniquum hunc proditorem in cari-
tate deplorabat." Δι' οὗ...παραδί-
δοται: the traitor was the last link
in the chain which connected purpose
and result, so that διά in this context

ἐκείνῳ δι' οὗ ὁ υἱὸς τοῦ ἀνθρώπου παραδίδοται· καλὸν
αὐτῷ εἰ οὐκ ἐγεννήθη ὁ ἄνθρωπος ἐκεῖνος.

§ n 22   ²²Καὶ ἐσθιόντων αὐτῶν λαβὼν ἄρτον εὐλογήσας
ἔκλασεν καὶ ἔδωκεν αὐτοῖς καὶ εἶπεν Λάβετε, τοῦτό

21 om ο υιος του ανθρ. (2°) D 604 a | καλον]+ην אACDPWᵇΧΓΔΠΣΦΨ minᵒᵐⁿ ᵛˡᵈ
(om BL)   22 λαβων]+ο Ιησους א*ᶜACLPWᵇΧΓΔΠΣΨ minᶠᵉʳᵉ ᵒᵐⁿ f q vg syrrᵖᵉˢʰ ʰᶜˡ
arm me aeth (om ο I. אᵃBD 2ᵖᵉ affik syrˢⁱⁿ the) | αρτον] pr τον ΜΣ minⁿᵒⁿⁿ |
ευλογησας (ευλογησεν και D)] ευχαριστησας U pr και Π 1071 alⁿᵒⁿⁿ | εδωκεν] εδιδου 1
13 69 124 209 346 | αυτοις]+και εφαγον εξ αυτου παντες kᵛˡᵈ | λαβετε] om k+φαγετε
EFHM²SVWᵇΧΓΣ minᵖˡ ff

(Mt. Mc. Lc.) is more exact than
ὑπό or ἀπό would have been; besides
the good Will of God which decreed
the Passion and of which he had no
knowledge, there was behind his act
the instigation of Satan (Lc. xxii. 3,
Jo. xiii. 2) working on his passions.
Origen in Mt.: "non dixit...a quo traditur, sed per quem traditur, osten-
dens...Iudam ministrum esse tradi-
tionis." Yet his intervention was
deliberate, and his responsibility
therefore complete. The Divine necessity for the Passion was no excuse
for the free agent who brought it
about: "non et malum oportuerit esse.
nam et Dominum tradi oportebat, sed
vae traditori" (Tert. praescr. 30).

καλὸν αὐτῷ εἰ οὐκ κτλ.] Mt. supplies ἦν with καλόν: in the apodosis of
a conditional clause where the supposition is contrary to fact, ἄν is sometimes omitted; cf. WM., p. 383, Burton, § 249, and on εἰ οὐκ for εἰ μή in
the protasis, cf. Burton § 469 r., Blass,
Gr. p. 254; for καλὸν...εἰ cf. ix. 42 ff.,
notes. The blessing of birth is turned
into a curse by a sin which leaves no
hope of a true repentance. Jerome:
"simpliciter dictum est multo melius
esse non subsistere quam male subsistere." The form of the saying is
Rabbinical, cf. Chagigah ed. Streane,
p. 55 "it were better for him that he
had not come into the world." A
somewhat similar saying, but less
severe, is attributed to the Lord in

ix. 42; the two are brought together
by Clem. R., 1 Cor. 46.

22—25. INSTITUTION OF THE EU-
CHARIST (Mt. xxvi. 26—29, Lc. xxii.
17—20; cf. 1 Cor. xi. 23—25).

22. ἐσθιόντων αὐτῶν] Cf. v. 18.
Another stage in the Paschal meal
has been reached. The eating of the
lamb seems to have been by custom
reserved to the end (Edersheim,
Temple, p. 208—9); the food up to this
point consisted only of the unleavened
cakes and bitter herbs, and possibly
the Chagigah (see Edersheim, op.
cit., p. 186, Streane, Chag., p. 35 f.,
notes).

λαβὼν ἄρτον κτλ.] Jerome: "ad
verum paschae transgreditur sacramentum." The Lord took one of the
cakes (for ἄρτος a bread-cake, cf. viii.
14) which were placed before Him as
president, and gave thanks (εὐλογήσας
Mt. Mc. = εὐχαριστήσας, Lc. Paul, cf.
vi. 41, note, and see J. Th. St. iii.
p. 163), probably in the customary
form; fraction (cf. Acts ii. 46, xx. 7,
11, 1 Cor. x. 16, xi. 24, Ign. Eph. 20)
accompanied or immediately followed
(vi. 41) the benediction (cf. Burton
§ 141—3), and then distribution. Cf.
1 Regn. ix. 13 εὐλογεῖ τὴν θυσίαν καὶ
μετὰ ταῦτα ἐσθίουσιν οἱ ξένοι. The
procedure as a whole corresponded to
the preliminaries of the two miracles
of the loaves, but on this occasion the
broken bread was given to the disciples primarily for their own use; they

ἐστιν τὸ σῶμά μου. ²³καὶ λαβὼν ποτήριον εὐχαρι- 23
στήσας ἔδωκεν αὐτοῖς, καὶ ἔπιον ἐξ αὐτοῦ πάντες.
²⁴καὶ εἶπεν αὐτοῖς Τοῦτό ἐστιν τὸ αἷμά μου 24

22 το σωμα μου] + quod pro multis confringitur in remissionem peccatorum a
23 ποτηριον] pr το ΑΡΓΠΦ minᵖˡ | om παντες syrˢⁱⁿ   24 om αυτοις B

must first 'take and eat' before they
gave to the multitude (contrast vi.
l.c., viii. 6). Λάβετε Mt. Mc.; Mt. adds
φάγετε, Lc. and Paul omit both directions. Comp. Cant. v. 1 φάγετε, πλη-
σίοι, καὶ πίετε...ἀδελφοί.

τοῦτό ἐστιν τὸ σῶμά μου] So Mt.
Mc. Lc.; Paul' (cf. Lc.), τοῦτό μού
ἐστιν τὸ σῶμα τὸ ὑπὲρ ὑμῶν. The
words would have recalled those
spoken at the supper at Bethany
six days before (xiv. 8), and perhaps
also the teaching at Capernaum just
before the previous Passover (Jo. vi.
48 ff.). The bread which is now given
(τοῦτο) is identified with (ἐστίν) the
Body of His Flesh (Col. i. 22); to eat
it is to partake in the great Sacrifice
(τὸ ὑπὲρ ὑμῶν, cf. x. 45). St Paul adds
(and the words have found their way
into all but the 'Western' texts of
Lc., see WH., Notes, p. 63): τοῦτο
ποιεῖτε εἰς τὴν ἐμὴν ἀνάμνησιν. But,
for whatever reason, this clause had
no place in the primitive tradition.

23. καὶ λαβὼν ποτήριον] R. V.
rightly, "He took a cup." So Mt.
Mc.; Paul (cf. Lc.) identifies the cup
with that which followed the meal
(τὸ ποτήριον μετὰ τὸ δειπνῆσαι). The
Talmud prescribes four cups at the
Paschal feast (J. Lightfoot on Mt.
xxvi. 27); the third was known as
the כּוֹס הַבְּרָכָה or "cup of blessing"
(cf. 1 Cor. x. 16), and it has been
usual to regard this as the Cup of
the Eucharist. If with WH. (Notes,
p. 64) we hold that Lc. xxii. 19ᵇ, 20
was "absent from the original text
of Lc.," it seems to follow that acc.
to Lc.'s tradition the blessing of the
Cup preceded that of the Bread
(cf. Didache 9 πρῶτον περὶ τοῦ ποτηρίου, and see J. Th. St. iii. p. 362),

and on this hypothesis the Eucharistic
Cup must probably be placed at an
earlier stage. But Lc.'s order in this
narrative is somewhat discredited by
the fact that he places the institution
of the Eucharist before the detection
of the traitor (see note on v. 18); and
St Paul's μετὰ τὸ δειπνῆσαι, written in
A.D. 57, or acc. to Harnack in A.D. 53,
must be held to be decisive. On εὐχαριστήσας see last note. The gift of
the Cup had been foreshadowed in
the discourse at Capernaum (Jo. vi.
55 τὸ αἷμά μου ἀληθής ἐστι πόσις).

καὶ ἔπιον ἐξ αὐτοῦ πάντες] Mt.,
whose account adheres generally to
Mc.'s, shapes these words into the command πίετε ἐξ αὐτοῦ πάντες, corresponding to λάβετε, φάγετε. Πάντες:
no such inclusive direction is given in
the case of the Bread, which represents a gift equally necessary to the
life of the soul (Jo. vi. 53). The R. C.
commentator Knabenbauer suggests
that πάντες was added "quoniam
quidem alias non unum poculum
omnibus destinabatur," but the ritual
of the Paschal meal (cf. Edersheim,
Temple, p. 204) renders this explanation improbable. Perhaps the solution
is to be sought in the words which
accompanied the gift of the Cup (see
v. 24, note).

24. καὶ εἶπεν αὐτοῖς] There is no
reason to regard Mc.'s εἶπεν as differ-
ing in substance from Mt.'s λέγων.
Mc. does not say that the words
followed the delivery or the drinking
of the cup, although the insertion of
καὶ ἔπιον κτλ. compels him to detach
the words from the gift.

τοῦτό ἐστιν τὸ αἷμά μου τῆς διαθήκης]
So Mt., Mc.; Paul (cf. Lc.): τοῦτο τὸ
ποτήριον ἡ καινὴ διαθήκη ἐστὶν ἐν τῷ

¶ P 25 τῆς διαθήκης τὸ ἐκχυννόμενον ὑπὲρ πολλῶν.¶ ²⁵ ἀμὴν

24 της διαθηκης] της καινης διαθ. ΑΡΨᵇΧΓΔΠΣΦ minᶠᵉʳᵉᵒᵐⁿ a f q vg syrr arm aeth pr το AD*FHKMPSUΓΔΠΣΦ | εκχυνομενον EFHKMSVWᵇΧΓΠ²ΦΨ minᵖˡ + εις αφεσιν αμαρτιων 9 13 18 69 1071 13ᵉᵛ cˢᶜʳ a me | υπερ] περι ΑΡΨᵇΧΓΠΣΦ minᵖˡ

ἐμῷ αἵματι. The original words are clearly based on Exod. xxiv. 8 ἰδοὺ τὸ αἷμα τῆς διαθήκης ἣν διέθετο Κύριος πρὸς ὑμᾶς περὶ τούτων τῶν λόγων, i.e. the blood which ratified the 'Book of the Covenant' (see Westcott on Heb. ix. 20). A new covenant (Jer. xxxviii. (xxxi.) 31 ff.) was on the point of being ratified by the Blood of a better Sacrifice with a greater Israel, whose representatives all drank of it, as the whole congregation (Heb. ix. 19) had been sprinkled with the blood shed under the mountain of the Lawgiving. On the Biblical sense of διαθήκη see Westcott, Hebrews, p. 298 ff.; the present context excepted, it is used in the N.T. with a distinct reference to the Christian dispensation only in 2 Cor. iii. 6, 14 (δ. καινή), and Hebrews vii. 22, viii. 6 (δ. κρείττων), ix. 15 (δ. καινή), xii. 24 (δ. νέα), xiii. 20 (δ. αἰώνιος). The two genitives (μου, τῆς διαθήκης), both dependent on αἷμα, indicate different relations (WM., p. 239); the Blood is Christ's, and in another sense it is that of the Covenant which it seals and executes. For the comparison of wine to blood cf. Gen. xlix. 11, Isa. lxiii. 1 ff.; the Blood of the Covenant was the fruit of "the holy Vine of David" (Did. 9, ed. Taylor, p. 69).

τὸ ἐκχυννόμενον ὑπὲρ πολλῶν] "Which is being shed on behalf of many"; the shedding is imminent and regarded as already present (Burton, § 131). The O. L. and many MSS. of the Vulgate render effundetur, and the future still stands in the canon of the Roman mass. On the form χύννειν see Blass, Gr. p. 41, WSchm., p. 132; for ὑπὲρ πολλῶν, cf. x. 45, note: Mt. adds here εἰς ἄφεσιν ἁμαρτιῶν, a result which is elsewhere connected with repentance and bap-

tism (Mc. i. 4, Lc. xxiv. 47, Acts ii. 38, v. 31), but ultimately rests on the Covenant ratified by the Sacrifice of Christ (Eph. i. 7, Col. i. 14, Heb. ix. 22).

The Gospels (if we except the doubtfully genuine words in Lc.) shew no trace of the direction τοῦτο ποιεῖτε εἰς τὴν ἐμὴν ἀνάμνησιν (1 Cor. xi. 24, 25). While the theory of a Pauline origin of the Eucharist (Hastings, D. B. ii. p. 638) is excluded by the position assigned to the institution in the early Jewish-Christian sources on which Mc. and Mt. drew, it is possible that the command which secures the permanence of the Eucharist may belong to the special revelation bestowed on St Paul (consult, but with caution, M°Giffert, Apostolic Age, p. 68, note).

For an Apostolic interpretation of the words τοῦτό ἐστιν τὸ σῶμα, τὸ αἷμά μου, see 1 Cor. x. 15, 16, xi. 27, 29; the belief of the second century is perhaps most characteristically expressed in Did. 9 ff.; Ignatius, Smyrn. 6, Philad. 4, Trall. 8, Rom. 7; Justin, apol. i. 66, dial. 70, 117; Iren. iv. 18. 4 f., 33. 2, v. 2. 2 f. A true note is struck by Euth.: χρὴ μὴ πρὸς τὴν φύσιν τῶν προκειμένων ὁρᾶν, ἀλλὰ πρὸς τὴν δύναμιν αὐτῶν: and by Hooker, E.P., v. 67. 13 "this Bread hath in it more than the substance which our eyes behold, this Cup...availeth to the endless life and welfare both of soul and body...to me which take them they are the Body and Blood of Christ; His promise in witness hereof sufficeth, His word He knoweth which way to accomplish." For a catena of patristic teaching on the subject see Pusey, Doctrine of the Real Presence, p. 315 ff.; the ante-Nicene teaching is collected in J. Th. St. iii. p. 161 ff.

§λέγω ὑμῖν ὅτι [οὐκέτι] οὐ μὴ πίω ἐκ τοῦ γενήματος § N
τῆς ἀμπέλου ἕως τῆς §ἡμέρας ἐκείνης ὅταν αὐτὸ πίνω § G
καινὸν ἐν τῇ βασιλείᾳ τοῦ θεοῦ. ²⁶Καὶ ὑμνήσαντες ἐξῆλθον εἰς τὸ ὄρος τῶν ἐλαιῶν.¶ 26 ¶ the

25 om ουκετι אCDL bˢᶜʳ* a c f k me aeth (hab ABNWᵇΧΓΠΨ minᶠᵉʳᵉᵒᵐⁿ ff g i l q
vg syrr arm the) | ου μη πιω] ου μη προσθω πειν D (2ᵖᵉ) a f arm | γεννηματος
DKNΓΦ minᵐᵘ

25. ἀμὴν λέγω ὑμῖν ὅτι οὐκέτι κτλ.]
A mysterious saying not to be lightly
dismissed as a "poetic utterance"
(Bruce). The Lord solemnly foretells
that this shall be His last Passover,
His last meal. But his prophecy
looks beyond His Death to a day of
reassembling round another board
(ἕως τῆς ἡμέρας ἐκείνης ὅταν κτλ.). The
saying recalls the parables of Lc. xiv.
16 ff., Mt. xxii. 1 ff.; in Lc. (xxii.
29 f.) it is expanded into the form
διατίθεμαι ὑμῖν...βασιλείαν ἵνα ἔσθητε
καὶ πίνητε ἐπὶ τῆς τραπέζης μου ἐν τῇ
βασιλείᾳ μου. The Messianic Kingdom is a banquet at which Christ
and His elect will drink in a new
and glorious way of the fruit of the
mystical Vine (Jo. xv. 1 ff.); for
illustrations from Jewish sources see
Wünsche, p. 334. Καινότης (see ii. 21,
note) is the characteristic mark of all
that belongs to the kingdom of God
(cf. Trench, syn. x.); the καινὴ διαθήκη
inaugurates a καινὴ κτίσις, in which
at length all things are to become
new (Apoc. xxi. 5). The saying has a
partial fulfilment in the Eucharists of
the universal Church; its ultimate accomplishment belongs to the risen life,
for which the Bridegroom has "kept
the good wine" (cf. Apoc. xix. 9).
Origen: "implebitur in regno Dei hoc
pascha et manducabit [panem] Jesus
cum discipulis suis et bibet...veram
escam et verum potum manducabi-
mus et bibemus in regno Dei, aedifi-
cantes per ea et confortantes veris-
simam illam vitam." The reading of
D οὐ μὴ προσθῶ πεῖν is noteworthy.
Γένημα, as distinguished from γέννημα

(Mt. iii. 7), is 'a fruit of the earth';
see WH., Notes, p. 148, WSchm., p.
55 f., Deissmann, B. St., p. 184; this
use of the word is non-Attic, but not
limited to Biblical Gk. (cf. Rutherford,
p. 348, Deissmann (B. St., p. 109, who
cites τὰ γενήματα τῶν ὑπαρχόντων μοι
παραδείσων from a papyrus of B.C. 230).
Τὸ γένημα τῆς ἀμπέλου is an O.T. phrase
for wine (cf. Num. vi. 4, Hab. iii. 17,
Isa. xxxii. 12), and as such it is suitable
to a rite which was based on the law
of the O.T.; moreover it occurred in
the ordinary form for the benediction
of the cup, "blessed be He that
created the fruit of the vine" (J. Lightfoot on Mt. xxvi.).

26—31. DEPARTURE TO THE MOUNT
OF OLIVES. THE DESERTION AND DE-
NIAL FORETOLD. (Mt. xxvi. 30—35,
Lc. xxii. 31—39; cf. Jo. xiii. 36—38,
xiv. 31, xviii. 1.)

26. καὶ ὑμνήσαντες] The singing of
Psalms followed the meal; Wycliffe:
"the ympne seid," Tindale: "when
they had sayd grace"; cf. Victor:
ηὐχαρίστησαν μετὰ τὸ λαβεῖν καὶ ὑμνή-
σαν, ἵνα καὶ ἡμεῖς αὐτὸ τοῦτο ποιῶμεν.
For this use of ὑμνεῖν, ὕμνος cf. Ps.
lxxi. (lxxii.) 20 ἐξέλιπον οἱ ὕμνοι Δαυείδ, 2 Chron. vii. 6 ἐν ὕμνοις Δ., 2 Macc.
i. 30 οἱ δὲ ἱερεῖς ἐπέψαλλον τοὺς ὕμνους,
Jos. ant. vii. 12. 3 ὁ Δαυΐδης...ὕμνους
συνετάξατο. The Psalms which were
sung at the end of the Paschal supper,
after the filling of the fourth cup,
were probably those which formed
the second part of the 'Hallel,' viz.:
Pss. cxv.—cxviii.; see Edersheim,
Temple, p. 210, J. Lightfoot ad l.,
Schöttgen i., p. 231, Schürer, II.i.p. 291,

27 ²⁷καὶ λέγει αὐτοῖς ὁ Ἰησοῦς ὅτι Πάντες σκανδαλισθήσεσθε, ὅτι γέγραπται Πατάξω τὸν ποιμένα, καὶ

27 και 1°] τοτε Dcff om syrˢⁱⁿ | παντες]+υμεις D 13 69 124 alᵖᵃᵘᶜ affikq vg syrrˢⁱⁿ ᵖᵉˢʰ
the | σκανδαλισθησεσθε אBC*DHLSVWᵇΧΓΔΠ²Ψ minˢᵃᵗ ᵐᵘ ff q]+εν εμοι GΨᶜᵒʳʳ
minᵖᵉʳᵖᵃᵘᶜ afikl syrˢⁱⁿ+εν τη νυκτι ταυτη minᵖᵃᵘᶜ vgᶜᵒᵈᵈ+εν εμοι εν τη ν. τ.
AC²EFKMNUΠ*³ minᵖˡ vgᵉᵈ aegg syrrᵖᵉˢʰ ʰᶜˡ arm aeth | οτι γεγρ.] γεγρ. γαρ ΝΣ

note. Others suppose that Ps. cxxxvi.
is intended. Bede thinks of the
intercessory prayer of Jo. xvii. For
an interesting but grotesque attempt
to place an original hymn in the lips
of Christ and the Eleven, see *Acta
Joh.* (*Apocr. anecd.*, ed. James, ii.
p. 10). That the Gospels contained
a reference to this Paschal hymn is
mentioned by Justin (*dial.* 106 μετ᾽
αὐτῶν διάγων ὕμνησε τὸν θεόν, ὡς καὶ
ἐν τοῖς ἀπομνημονεύμασι τῶν ἀποστόλων
δηλοῦται γεγενημένον), who finds in it
a fulfilment of Ps. xxi. (xxii.) 23.

ἐξῆλθον εἰς τὸ ὄρος τῶν ἐλαιῶν] This
movement seems to correspond to that
of Jo. xiv. 31 ἐγείρεσθε, ἄγωμεν ἐντεῦθεν
(so Tatian, Hill, p. 226); the discourses
of Jo. xv., xvi., and the prayer of Jo.
xvii. were uttered either on the way
to the Kidron or possibly in the
Precinct (cf. Westcott on Jo. xv. 1, 2).
On τὸ ὄρος τ. ἐλ. see xi. 1, note; on
ἐξῆλθον, see xi. 11. Lc. adds κατὰ τὸ
ἔθος. The nightly departure for the
Mount had become habitual, and the
Eleven felt no surprise when they
were summoned to leave the κατάλυμα: no provision had been made
for spending the night in Jerusalem.

27. καὶ λέγει αὐτοῖς ὁ Ἰ. κτλ.] Mt.
τότε λέγει (see note on x. 13); Lc. and
Jo. appear to place the conversation
in the supper-room, but the three
traditions (Mt.-Mc. Lc. Jo.) are distinct and independent. The Fayûm
fragment (acc. to Zahn's reconstruc-
tion, *Kanon*, ii. p. 785) leaves the
point open: [ὑμνησάντων δὲ αὐτῶν μετὰ
τὸ φ]αγεῖν ὡς ἐξ ἔθους πά[λιν εἶπε
Ταύτη]κτλ. Πάντες σκανδαλισθήσεσθε,
Mt. π. ὑμεῖς σκ. ἐν ἐμοὶ ἐν τῇ νυκτὶ
ταύτῃ. The frequent warnings against

σκάνδαλα (iv. 17, ix. 42 ff., cf. Mt. xxiv.
10, Lc. vii. 23, Jo. xvi. 1) gave to
this prophecy a terrible significance.
Moreover, hitherto this fate had over-
taken only the enemies of Jesus (vi. 3,
Mt. xv. 12), or disloyal followers (Jo.
vi. 61); but now the Apostles themselves are warned that they will fall
without exception, and that very
night.

ὅτι γέγραπται κτλ.] The Lord confirms His prophecy by a quotation from
the O.T.: cf. ix. 12 f., xiv. 21. The
words which are cited differ materially from the B text of Zach. xiii. 7
πατάξατε τοὺς ποιμένας, καὶ ἐκσπάσατε
τὰ πρόβατα (cf. Tert. *de fug.* 11 "evel-
lite oves"); the A text comes nearer
with πάταξον τὸν ποιμένα, καὶ διασκορπισθήσονται τὰ πρ. τῆς ποίμνης (cf.
Mt.), and it has on its side the
support of Justin (*dial.* 53 πάταξον τὸν
ποιμένα καὶ διασκ. τὰ πρόβατα αὐτοῦ),
while the loose reference in Barn.
5. 13 (ὅταν πατάξωσιν τὸν ποιμένα ἑαυτῶν
τότε ἀπολεῖται τὰ πρόβατα τῆς ποίμνης)
seems to blend B's πατάξατε with A's
conclusion. But all known forms of
the Greek text agree with the M.T.
in beginning the clause with an imperative, whilst Mt. and Mc. concur
in πατάξω. The latter reading is
possibly due to a collection of *testimonia* from which the common tradition drew (cf. i. 2, note); it is noteworthy that it is found not only in
Mt. Mc., but in the Fayûm fragment,
which gives [κατὰ] τὸ γραφέν Πατάξω
τὸν [ποιμένα καὶ τὰ] πρόβατα διασκορ-
πισθήσ[ονται]. On the import of the
prophecy see Kirkpatrick, *Doctrine
of the Prophets*, p. 465. The general
law was to find its most terrible ful-

τὰ πρόβατα διασκορπισθήσονται. ²⁸ἀλλὰ μετὰ τὸ 28
ἐγερθῆναί με προάξω ὑμᾶς εἰς τὴν Γαλειλαίαν. ²⁹§ὁ δὲ 29 § ¬¹²
Πέτρος ἔφη αὐτῷ Εἰ καὶ πάντες σκανδαλισθήσονται,
ἀλλ᾽ οὐκ ἐγώ.¶ ³⁰καὶ λέγει αὐτῷ ὁ Ἰησοῦς Ἀμὴν 30 ¶ W¹
λέγω σοι ὅτι [σὺ] σήμερον ταύτῃ τῇ νυκτὶ πρὶν [ἢ δὶς]

27 τα προβ.]+της ποιμνης EFKMΠ* 736*ᵛⁱᵈ 1071 alⁿᵒⁿⁿ a c | διασκορπισθησεται
EHMSUVWᵇXΓΠΦ minᵖˡ   28 αλλα μετα] και μ. C μ. δε minⁿᵒⁿⁿ   29 εφη]
λεγει DΨ αποκριθεις λ. 1 13 69 124 209 346 604 2ᵖᵉ (c k) arm | ει και אBCGLΨ
1 13 69 1071 alᵖᵃᵘᶜ arm] και ει AEFHKMNSUVWᵇXΓΔΠΣΦ alᵖˡ και εαν D καν 604
2ᵖᵉ | εγω]+ου σκανδαλισθησομαι Dᶠᶠq aeth   30 om συ אCDΔ minᵐᵘ aᶠᶠilq |
om σημερον DS 604 2ᵖᵉ aᶠᶠiq arm | ταυτη τη νυκτι] εν τη ν. ταυτη ANWᵇXΓΔΠΣΦ
minᵖˡ om S | om η אD 69 238 604 2ᵖᵉ alᵖᵃᵘᶜ | om δις אC*D 238 150ᵉᵛ aᶜᶠᶠik arm
aeth (hab ABC²LNWᵇXΓΔΠΣΦΨ minᵖˡ fq vg aegg syrr)

filment in the dispersion of the flock
(Lc. xii. 32) of the Good Shepherd.

28. ἀλλὰ μετὰ τὸ ἐγερθῆναι κτλ.]
Ἀλλά contrasts the hope of the
Resurrection with the deepening
gloom of the Passion; the Lord
rarely mentions the one without the
other (cf. viii. 31, ix. 31, x. 34).
Euth.: προειπὼν τὰ λυπηρά, προλέγει
καὶ τὰ παραμυθούμενα. On μετά with
the inf. see Burton § 406—7. With
the promise προάξω ὑμᾶς εἰς τὴν Γ.
cf. xvi. 7, Mt. xxviii. 10, 16, Ev. Petr.
12; it was natural that the Eleven
should return to Galilee after the
Passover, and the Lord reassures
them by promising to be there before them. Of this return to the
North Lc. says nothing, whilst Mc.
(so far as we can judge from his
unfinished work) and Mt. are equally
silent as to appearances in Jerusalem
subsequent to the day of the Resurrection. But their silence is not
unnatural in view of the Galilean
character of their record, which is
abandoned only in the case of the
narrative of the Passion and Resurrection. On προάγειν τινά see x. 32,
note.

29. ὁ δὲ Πέτρος ἔφη αὐτῷ κτλ.]
Peter is stung to the quick by the
suggestion of disloyalty, and repu-
diates it for himself. His speech is

well characterised by Euth.: ὁ δὲ
τρία ὁμοῦ πταίει· πρῶτον ὅτι ἀντεῖπε—
he ought rather to have prayed
'Lord help me'—δεύτερον, ὅτι τῶν ἄλλων ἑαυτὸν προέθηκε...τρίτον, ὅτι ἑαυτῷ
μόνῳ καὶ οὐ τῇ βοηθείᾳ τοῦ θεοῦ τεθάρ-
ρηκε. Εἰ καί, "even admitting that it
is true"; the Fayûm fragment has
καὶ εἰ, which emphasises the improbability (Burton § 280). At all events
there will be one exception to the
rule—ἀλλ᾽ οὐκ ἐγώ. For ἀλλά beginning the apodosis see WM., p. 552;
on the ellipse cf. Blass, Gr. p. 291.
The expansion of this characteristic
saying in Mt. is instructive. In Lc.,
whose report however may relate to
another occasion, Peter says Κύριε,
μετὰ σοῦ ἕτοιμός εἰμι καὶ εἰς φυλακὴν
καὶ εἰς θάνατον πορεύεσθαι, cf. Jo. τὴν
ψυχήν μου ὑπὲρ σοῦ θήσω. Tatian
brings the three sayings into one
(Hill, p. 223 f.).

30. καὶ λέγει αὐτῷ ὁ Ἰησοῦς κτλ.]
Peter's boast is turned into the prophecy of a greater downfall: "pro-
missio eius audax...facta est ei causa
ut non solum scandalizaretur, verum
etiam ter denegaret" (Origen). "Thou
(emphatic σύ, answering to Peter's
ἐγώ) to-day, in this night, before the
morning watch, shalt deny me not
once but thrice." According to the
Jewish reckoning the day of the

31 ἀλέκτορα φωνῆσαι τρίς με ἀπαρνήσῃ. ³¹ ὁ δὲ ἐκπερισσῶς ἐλάλει Ἐὰν δέῃ με συναποθανεῖν σοι, οὐ μή
σε ἀπαρνήσομαι. ὡσαύτως δὲ καὶ πάντες ἔλεγον.

32 ³²Καὶ ἔρχονται εἰς χωρίον οὗ τὸ ὄνομα Γεθσημανεί,

31 ο δε]+Πετρος ACGMNSU al^nonn syr^hcl arm aeth+μαλλον 1 13 69 (? arm) |
εκπερισσως ℵBCDΨ min^perpauc] εκ περισσου AW^bΧΓΠΣΦ min^pl περισσως L 13 69
124 346 2^pe εκ περισιας (sic) Δ | ελαλει ℵBDLΨ loquebatur f ff i k q r vg] ελεγεν
ACNW^bΧΓΔΠΣΦ min^omn vid dicebat a syrr me+μαλλον ANW^bΧΓΔΠΣΦ min^fere omn
(c ff) k (om μ. ℵBCDL 2^pe a f i q vg syr^hcl aegg) | συναποθανειν σοι] συν σοι αποθανειν
L 1 115 1071 2^pe al^perpauc | απαρνησομαι ABCDHLNW^bΔΠ*Ψ al] απαρνησωμαι
ℵEFGKMSUVXΓΠ² min^sat mu | om ωσαυτως...ελεγον Ψ | ωσαυτως] ομοιως ℵ* | om δε
B 1 209 al^pauc a c ff k | om και D min^perpauc   32 ερχεται 2^pe | ου] ω C 282
latt^vt plvg | Γεθσημανει ℵAB³CKLMNSUVΓΔΠ min^pl (Γετσημ. B* Γησαμ. D arm^codd vtt
Γεσσημ. EFGHXΣ min^mu)] Γεθσημανη Φ min^nonn syr^hcl Γεσσιμανη Ψ

Passion has already begun (σήμερον);
it commenced with the night of the
Paschal Supper. Δίς (cf. v. 72) is
peculiar to Mc. among the canonical
Gospels, but it is supported by the
Fayûm papyrus. The word is suggestive, cf. Bengel: "valde notabilis
circumstantia primo cantu Petrum se
non collecturum esse." The papyrus
substitutes ἀλεκτρυών for the old
poetical form ἀλέκτωρ (cf. Rutherford,
N. Phryn., p. 307 f.; ἀλέκτωρ occur in
another papyrus of c. A.D. 100 (Fayûm
Towns, p. 275), and κοκκύζειν (Theocr.
vii. 48) for φωνεῖν: [ἔφη Πρὶν] ὁ ἀλεκ-
τρυὼν δὶς κοκ[κύξει.σήμερον, σὺ τρίς με
ἀ]παρν[ήσῃ] (Zahn, l.c.). Comp. 3 Macc.
v. 23 ἄρτι δὲ ἀλεκτρυών ἐκέκραγεν
ὄρθριος, and see the references to the
second cockcrowing in Ar. Eccl. 390,
Juv. ix. 106: for the time indicated,
see the note on ἀλεκτοροφωνία (supra,
xiii. 35). On ἀπαρνήσῃ cf. viii. 34
note; on πρὶν ἤ with the inf. see
Burton § 380 f.

31. ὁ δὲ ἐκπερισσῶς ἐλάλει] Peter's
profession of confidence is intensified
by his mortification : he continued to
talk (ἐλάλει, cf. vv. ll.) with excessive
vehemence (cf. ὑπερπερισσῶς, vii. 37);
Euth.: ὅσον διαβεβαιοῦται ὁ Χριστός,
τοσοῦτον ὁ Πέτρος ἀντισχυρίζεται. Unconsciously, no doubt, yet in point of
fact, as Origen says, he gave the

lie to the Master: "dominum nostrum
profitebatur facere mendacem per ea
quae sibi confidens dicebat." The
protest was probably uttered more
than once (ἐλάλει), as passionate remarks are apt to be. Ἐὰν δέῃ κτλ.,
"though it be necessary"; Mt.'s κἂν
suggests the improbability of this
contingency (Burton § 281). The idea
of sharing the Lord's Death had
originated, as it seems, with the less
demonstrative Thomas (Jo. xi. 16); it
was afterwards to pass in St Paul's
writings into the language of theology
(Rom. vi. 2 ff., Col. ii. 12, iii. 1 ff.;
the word συναποθ. occurs in the λόγος
cited in 2 Tim. ii. 11). Both συνθανεῖν
and συναποθανεῖν are classical forms;
for the latter cf. Plat. Phaed. 88 τοῦ
ἀποθανόντος οὐ συναποθνῄσκει ἡ ψυχή,
Sir. xix. 10 ἀκήκοας λόγον; συναπο-
θανέτω σοι. Οὐ μή σε ἀπαρν. : on this
future see Blass, Gr., p. 204 f.
Ὡσαύτως δὲ καὶ πάντες ἔλεγον. All
had been included in the first prophecy of impending failure, and
Peter's passionate protest stirred the
rest to similar (Mt. ὁμοίως) professions
of loyalty. In Lc. and Jo. Peter
only is warned and the other ten
do not appear.

32—42. THE AGONY IN GETHSE-
MANE (Mt. xxvi. 36—46, Lc. xxii.
40—46: cf. Jo. xviii. 1 ff.).

καὶ λέγει τοῖς μαθηταῖς αὐτοῦ Καθίσατε ὧδε ἕως
προσεύξωμαι. ³³καὶ παραλαμβάνει τὸν Πέτρον καὶ 33

32 τοις μαθ. αυτου] om αυτου A δ arm αυτοις D a | καθισαι Δ | ωδε] om B* αυτου
1 209 | προσευξωμαι (-ξομαι DHXΓΨ 1071 al^{nonn})] pr απελθων MNUΣ min^{nonn} aeth
33 τον Πετρον] om τον א* al^{pauc}

32. ἔρχονται εἰς χωρίον...Γεθσημα-
νεί] The name is not given by Lc.
(γενόμενος δὲ ἐπὶ τοῦ τόπου) or Jo.,
but the latter mentions that the
place was a garden which lay on
the further side of the Kidron
(πέραν τοῦ χειμάρρου τοῦ Κέδρων...
κῆπος). Γεθσημανεί (R.T. -νή), Syr.^{sin.}
ܓܣܡܢ, Syr.^{pesh.} ܓܣܡܢ,
"nichts Anderes sein kann als
שְׁמֵנִי גַּת = גַּת שְׁמָנִי" (Dalman, Gr.,
p. 152; see his note on the length-
ening of the second vowel); cf. Γεθε-
ρεμμῶν (Jos. xxi. 24), Γεθχόβερ (4
Regn. xiv. 25). On the other hand
the forms Γησαμανεί, Γεσσημανεί, suggest גַּיְא שְׁמָנִים (Encycl. Bibl. s.v.). As
the name in its more usual spelling
denotes, the estate (χωρίον, praedium,
villa, cf. 2 Chron. xxvii. 27 ἐν τοῖς
χωρίοις τοῦ οἴνου, Acts iv. 34 κτήτορες
χωρίων ἢ οἰκιῶν) may at one time have
had an oil press upon it, but it was now
apparently one of the private gardens
which were to be found in the outskirts of Jerusalem (cf. Jo. xix. 41),
and (doubtless by the favour of its
owner) it had been a favourite resort
of Jesus (Jo. πολλάκις συνήχθη Ἰ.
ἐκεῖ μετὰ τῶν μαθητῶν αὐτοῦ). There
is no reason to doubt that the enclo-
sure still known as the Latin Gethsemane occupies the site of that
which was already identified with
the Garden of the Agony in the
fourth century; cf. Eus. onom. s. v.
ἐν ᾧ καὶ νῦν τὰς εὐχὰς οἱ πιστοὶ
ποιεῖσθαι σπουδάζουσιν: Jerome, lib.
interpr. "est autem ad radices montis
Oliveti nunc ecclesia desuper aedifi-
cata": Silvia, peregr. p. 62, describes
in detail the Holy-Week procession
to Gethsemane, the reading of the

Gospel on the spot, the wailing and
weeping of the excited crowd of
pilgrims. The church has disappeared, but the traditional spot is
marked by olive trees of venerable
age, whether planted by Christian
hands, or sprung from the roots of
those which Titus cut down (Jos.
B. J. vi. 1. 1).

καὶ λέγει...Καθίσατε ὧδε κτλ.] All
appear to have entered the garden
(Jo. εἰσῆλθεν αὐτὸς καὶ οἱ μαθηταὶ
αὐτοῦ), but eight of the Eleven were
bidden to rest near the entrance,
that the Master might retire for
prayer. In this there was probably
nothing unusual; cf. i. 35, vi. 46.
On ἕως (Mt. ἕ. οὗ) προσεύξωμαι see
Burton, § 321 ff., who translates,
"while I pray"; so A. V., R. V.,
though both render the parallel
ἕως φάγω καὶ πίω in Lc. xvii. 8
"till I have eaten and drunken."
The Vg. has donec orem, on which
see Madvig, §§ 339. 2 b, 360. 1. In
Mt. we see the Lord pointing to the
spot which He will make His oratory
(ἀπελθὼν ἐκεῖ). It is such a detail
as might have been expected in Mc.,
who however omits it.

33. καὶ παραλαμβάνει κτλ.] This
again was not an entirely new step:
the eight would remember the Transfiguration, when, as now, the purpose of the retirement was to pray
(Lc. ix. 28); Thpht.: παραλ. δὲ τοὺς
τρεῖς μόνους...ἵνα οἱ ἰδόντες τὰ ἔνδοξα
ἴδωσι καὶ τὰ σκυθρωπά. On παραλαμβάνει see iv. 36, v. 40, ix. 2, x. 32,
notes; on the order of the names
(Πέτρος, Ἰάκωβος, Ἰωάνης) cf. iii. 17,
v. 37, ix. 2, notes, and, on the repetition of the article, the notes on

τὸν Ἰάκωβον καὶ τὸν Ἰωάνην μετ᾽ αὐτοῦ, καὶ ἤρξατο

§ the 34 ἐκθαμβεῖσθαι καὶ ἀδημονεῖν· ³⁴ §καὶ λέγει αὐτοῖς Περί-

33 τον Ιακωβον] om τον אCDEFGHMNSUVWᵇΧΓΔ al | τον Ιωανην] om τον אCDEFGHLMNSUVWᵇΧΓΔ al | μετ αυτου] μεθ εαυτου ALNWᵇΧΓΔΠΣΦΨ minᵖˡ om syrˢⁱⁿ | ηρξαντο LS | εκθαμβεισθαι] λυπεισθαι 1 118 syrʳˢⁱⁿᵖᵉˢʰ arm | αδημονειν] ακηδεμονειν D* (ακηδημ. Dᶜᵒʳʳ) ακηδιαν cˢᶜʳ taediari cdffiq taedere f taedium pati k acediari et deficere a 34 και 1°] τοτε D 13 69 124 346 604 2ᵖᵒ a arm | λεγειν Ψ

v. 37, ix. 2. Mc. sets each individuality before the mind separately, while Mt. (τὸν Πέτρον καὶ τοὺς δύο υἱοὺς Ζεβεδαίου) brings Peter prominently into the foreground.

καὶ ἤρξατο ἐκθαμβεῖσθαι καὶ ἀδημονεῖν] Wycliffe : " began for to drede and to henge." The shadow of death begins to fall upon Him as He passes with the Three into the depths of the olive-grove. Mt. writes ἤρξ. λυπεῖσθαι: Mc.'s ἐκθαμβεῖσθαι— the word is peculiarly Marcan, see note on ix. 15—strikes another note, that of amazed awe. It is unnecessary either to abandon in this place the proper sense of θάμβος, or to find with Meyer a truer psychology in Mt.'s λυπεῖσθαι. The Lord was overwhelmed with sorrow (see next verse), but His first feeling was one of terrified surprise. Long as He had foreseen the Passion, when it came clearly into view its terrors exceeded His anticipations. His human soul received a new experience—ἔμαθεν ἀφ᾽ ὧν ἔπαθεν, and the last lesson of obedience began with a sensation of inconceivable awe. With this there came another, that of overpowering mental distress —ἤρξατο...ἀδημονεῖν (Mt., Mc.). The verb occurs only once again in the N. T. (Phil. ii. 26 ἐπιποθῶν καὶ ἀδημονῶν, where see Lightfoot's full note), and does not appear in the LXX., but it is used by Aquila (Job xviii. 20, LXX. στενάζειν) and Symmachus (Ps. lx. = lxi. 3, LXX. ἀκηδιᾶν, cxv. 2 = cxvi. 11, LXX. ἐν τῇ ἐκστάσει, Eccl. vii. 17 (16), LXX. ἐκπλαγῆναι, Ezech. iii. 15, LXX. ἀναστρεφόμενος, Th. θαυμάζων). Plato couples ἀδημονεῖν with ἀπορεῖν more

than once ; see esp. Phaedr. 251 D : ἀδημονεῖ τε τῇ ἀτοπίᾳ τοῦ πάθους καὶ ἀποροῦσα λυττᾷ. These references shew that ἀδημονεῖν forms a natural sequel to ἐκθαμβεῖσθαι, representing the distress which follows a great shock, "the confused, restless, half-distracted state" (Lightfoot) which may be worse than the sharp pain of a fully realised sorrow. Bede : "timet Christus, cum Petrus non timeat." The reading of D seems to have arisen from a confusion of ἀδημονεῖν with ἀκηδιᾶν, unless ἀκηδεμονεῖν is a true form meaning 'to be listless, the reverse of a κηδεμών.'

34. καὶ λέγει αὐτοῖς Περίλυπος κτλ.] The Lord reveals to His three witnesses a part of His distress. His words recall Ps. xli. (xlii.) 6, 12, xliii. (xliii.) 5 ἵνα τί περίλυπος εἶ, ἡ ψυχή— in an earlier utterance of the Holy Week He had referred to the rest of the refrain (ἵνα τί συνταράσσεις με, cf. Jo. xii. 27 ; see Kirkpatrick on Ps. xliii.). But His sorrow exceeds the Psalmist's ; it is ἕως θανάτου, a sorrow which well-nigh kills. Comp. Jon. iv. 9 σφόδρα λελύπημαι ἕως θανάτου (עַד מָוֶת). As for the cause of this overwhelming grief, Jerome's remark, "contristatur...anima...non propter mortem, sed usque mortem," is doubtless true, but the narrative does not encourage the view which prevails in many patristic commentaries, that the Lord's sorrow and prayers were only for the sins and woes of men (cf. e.g. Ambr. in Lc. "cum in se nihil haberet quod doleret nostris tamen angebatur aerumnis"). His human

λυπός ἐστιν ἡ ψυχή μου ἕως θανάτου· μείνατε ὧδε
καὶ γρηγορεῖτε. ³⁵καὶ προελθὼν μικρὸν ἔπιπτεν ἐπὶ 35
τῆς γῆς, καὶ προσηύχετο ἵνα εἰ δυνατόν ἐστιν παρέλθῃ

34 om μεινατε ω. κ. γρηγ. syrˢⁱⁿ | γρηγορειτε]+μετ εμου G 1 28 alᵖᵃᵘᶜ q r the
35 προελθων אBFKMNΠ*³Φ minᵐᵘ lattᵛᵗᵖˡᵛᵍ syrˢⁱⁿ] προσελθων ACDEGH*LSUV
WᵇΧΓΔΠ²ΣΨ minᵖˡ ff syrrᵖᵉˢʰ ʰᶜˡ | επιπτεν אBLΨ] επεσεν ACDNWᵇΧΓΔΠΣΦ minᵒᵐⁿ ᵛⁱᵈ
lattᵛⁱᵈ+επι προσωπον DGΣ 1 13 69 124 346 604 2ᵖᵉ alᵖᵃᵘᶜ k syrˢⁱⁿ arm | επι την γην
13 69 124 346 604 2ᵖᵉ alᵖᵉʳᵖᵃᵘᶜ

soul shrank from the Cross, and the
fact adds to our sense of the greatness of His sacrifice.

Though the Gospels yield abundant
evidence of the presence of human
emotions in our Lord (e.g. iii. 5, vi. 6,
x. 14, Jo. xi. 33), this direct mention
of His 'soul' has no parallel in them
if we except Jo. xii. 27 ; for in such
passages as x. 45, Jo. x. 11 ψυχή
is the individual life (see Cremer s.v.)
rather than the seat of the emotions.
The present passage was from the first
eagerly used for polemical purposes
both by Christians (Iren. i. 8. 2, iii.
22. 2) and unbelievers (Orig. c. Cels.
ii. 24).

μείνατε ὧδε καὶ γρηγορεῖτε] The
Three are placed where they can see
and hear (cf. v. 35), for they are to be
witnesses of the Agony. For the
same reason they are to keep themselves awake (cf. Lc. ix. 32) ; but
γρηγορεῖτε (Mt. γρ. μετ' ἐμοῦ) has
besides an ethical meaning, as in xiii.
35 ff. ; a great crisis was near, which
demanded a wakeful spirit (v. 38).
Origen : "maneamus ubi praecepit
Jesus (1 Cor. vii. 20)...ut cum eo
pariter vigilemus qui non dormit
neque dormitat custodiens Israel."
On the tenses see Blass, Gr. p. 196.

35. καὶ προελθὼν μικρόν κτλ.] The
Lord went forward (for προελθ., cf.
vi. 33, Acts xii. 10) into the olive-
grove, as if to isolate Himself from
the Three, who could not share His
present sorrow ; comp. the noteworthy
parallel in Gen. xxii. 5. Μικρόν (Lc.,

ὡσεὶ λίθου βολήν) is more frequently
used of time than of space (cf. Cant.
iii. 4 ὡς μικρὸν ὅτε παρῆλθον, Hos. i. 4
ἔτι μικρόν, Jo. vii. 33, xii. 35 ἔτι
χρόνον μ., ἔτι μ. χρ.), but Meyer cites
from Xenophon μικρὸν πορεύεσθαι,
προπέμπειν. There He fell upon His
face (Mt. ἐπὶ πρόσωπον αὐτοῦ, cf. Gen.
xvii. 3, 17, Lc. v. 12, xvii. 16) on the
earth (Mc. only ; cf. Jud. xiii. 20
ἔπεσαν...ἐπὶ τὴν γῆν, and for the gen.
see WM., p. 470) ; the imperf. ἔπιπτεν
(Mt. ἔπεσεν) describes the prostration
as taking place under the eyes of the
narrator (cf. WM., p. 226). Lc. speaks
only of kneeling (θεὶς τὰ γόνατα), a
not infrequent attitude in prayer (cf.
Acts viii. 60, ix. 40, xx. 36, xxi. 5 ; see
note on xi. 25).

προσηύχετο ἵνα κτλ.] The Lord's
habit of prayer has already been
noticed in i. 35, vi. 46 (see notes) : on
the prayers of the Agony comp. Heb.
v. 7 with Westcott's notes. Ἵνα...ἡ
ὥρα is a note peculiar to Mc., sum-
marising and interpreting the prayers
which follow. For προσεύχεσθαι ἵνα,
cf. xiii. 18, note ; ἡ ὥρα, the appointed
time (v. 41, Jo. xvii. 1), cf. ἡ ὥρα
αὐτοῦ Jo. vii. 30, viii. 20, ἡ ὥ. ἵνα
δοξασθῇ Jo. xii. 23, ἡ ὥ. αὕτη ib.
27 bis, ἡ ὥ. ἵνα μεταβῇ Jo. xiii. 1 ;
comp. the phrase ὥρα (τῆς) συντελείας
in Dan. xi. 40, 45 (LXX.), and Jo. xvi.
4 ἡ ὥρα αὐτῶν sc. ὧν λελάληκα, 21 ἡ
ὥρα αὐτῆς sc. τικτούσης. Παρέλθῃ, 'may
pass by without bringing its allotted
suffering.' Εἰ δυνατόν ἐστιν, cf. xiii. 22,
note, and see more on next verse.

36 ἀπ᾽ αὐτοῦ ἡ ὥρα. ³⁶καὶ ἔλεγεν Ἀββὰ ὁ πατήρ,
¶ i πάντα δυνατά σοι·¶ παρένεγκε τὸ ποτήριον τοῦτο
37 ἀπ᾽ ἐμοῦ· ἀλλ᾽ οὐ τί ἐγὼ θέλω ἀλλὰ τί σύ. ³⁷καὶ

35—36 om απ αυτου...παρενεγκε k   36 αββα ο πατηρ] πατερ μου syr^sin vid |
δυναται Ψ | παρενεγκαι אACKW^bΠ* min^mu | αλλ] pr πλην Ν πλην Or | ου τι]
ουχ ο D 70 ου το Σ ουχ ως 13 346 2^pe c d ff | θελω] λεγω a (dico) | αλλα τι] αλλ ο
D 70 αλλ ως 13 69 346 2^pe c d ff αλλ οτι GΣ 1 al^pauc αλλ ει τι CUΦΨ min^nonn | συ]+
θελεις D a c f ff q arm aegg aeth

36. καὶ ἔλεγεν Ἀββὰ ὁ πατήρ] The
words of the prayer are given with
minor variations by the three Synoptists. Mt. begins πάτερ μου, Lc. πάτερ,
Mc., as in v. 41, vii. 34, preserves
the Aramaic word uttered by Jesus
(אַבָּא, Dalman, Gr. p. 157; Worte,
i. p. 257). Ὁ πατήρ is either (1) an
interpretative note due to the Evangelist or his source, and nearly equivalent to ὅ ἐστιν πατήρ, or (2) a part
of the original prayer, cf. SH. on
Rom. viii. 15 ("it seems better to
suppose that our Lord Himself, using
familiarly both languages ... found
Himself impelled spontaneously to
repeat the word"), and Schöttgen ad
loc., who quotes instances of a similar
duplication, e.g. מרי בירי (where the
second word represents the Galilean
pronunciation of κύριε), and ναί, ἀμήν,
Apoc. i. 7, cf. xxii. 20. Or, accepting
Schöttgen's explanation, we may regard Ἀββὰ ὁ πατήρ as (3) a formula
familiar to the bilingual Palestinian
Church, which naturally found its way
in place of the simple Ἀββά or ὁ
πατήρ into the earliest cycle of oral
teaching, and thence into this Gospel.
Dr Chase (Lord's Prayer in the
Early Church, p. 24) suggests that
the words were the current equivalent of the initial Πάτερ of the
Lord's Prayer in its shorter form
(Lc. xi. 2), and that they are used
with a reference to that Prayer both
by Mc. and in Rom. l.c., Gal. iv. 6.

πάντα δυνατά σοι] Mt. εἰ δυνατόν
ἐστιν (cf. v. 35), Lc. εἰ βούλει. Comp.
x. 27. The Lord realises in His own

case the truth He had impressed on
the Twelve. Seeing that nothing is
per se impossible to the Father, He
can pray, even on the eve of the
Passion, that it may be averted. In
perfect faith He believes that even
now it is possible to defeat Judas and
the Sanhedrin (Mt. xxvi. 53), to resist
Pilate and the power of Rome (Jo.
xix. 11), even to defy death (Jo. x. 17,
18); and He asks (but with a reserva-
tion which will immediately appear)
for deliverance in whatever way.
Παρένεγκε, 'carry past,' i.e. cause it to
pass by; so Lc., Mt., παρελθάτω: cf.
Jud. vi. 5, A τὰς σκηνὰς αὐτῶν παρέ-
φερον, where B has αἱ σκηναὶ αὐτῶν
παρεγίνοντο, and see the illustrations
from Plutarch in Field, Notes, p. 39.
Τὸ ποτήριον τοῦτο: cf. x. 38, note; in
Jo. the reference to the Cup of the
Passion comes further on, in the
incident of Simon and Malchus (Jo.
xviii. 11). The Cup corresponds to
'the hour' in v. 35.

ἀλλ᾽ οὐ τί ἐγὼ θέλω κτλ.] For ἀλλά
Mt. has πλήν here, see Blass, Gr.
p. 268. On this use of τί where a
classical writer would have written
ὅ τι see WM., p. 210, and Blass, Gr.
p. 175, who cites a saying of Euergetes
in Ath. x. 438 E τίνι ἡ τύχη δίδωσι,
λαβέτω (cf. his comm. on Acts xiii. 25).
The interrogative sense of τίς in such
cases does not perhaps wholly disap-
pear; we may paraphrase : 'however,
the question is not (οὐ, not μή) what
is My will,' &c. Mt. (πλὴν οὐχ ὡς...
ἀλλ᾽ ὡς...) and Lc. (πλὴν μὴ τὸ θέλημά
μου ἀλλὰ τὸ σὸν γινέσθω) avoid the

ἔρχεται καὶ εὑρίσκει αὐτοὺς καθεύδοντας, καὶ λέγει
τῷ Πέτρῳ Σίμων, καθεύδεις ; οὐκ ἴσχυσας μίαν ὥραν
γρηγορῆσαι ; ³⁸ γρηγορεῖτε, καὶ προσεύχεσθε ἵνα μὴ 38

37 ερχεται] + προς τους μαθητας 1071 | ισχυσατε D 1 69 124 209 346 al^nonn ff k |
γρηγορησαι] + μετ εμου F min^pauc + ουν 1071   38 ινα...πειρασμον] ut transeat a
vobis (vos) temptatio c ff i (k) | om ινα D

colloquial τί, regarding it perhaps as
unsuitable in a solemn prayer. The
words, as a whole, seem to look back
to the Lord's Prayer as given by Mt.
⟨γενηθήτω τὸ θέλημά σου⟩, and in Lc.
and Mt.'s second version of them (v. 42)
the resemblance is closer. The Divine
Will, which is the expression of the
Divine righteousness and love, limits
the exercise of the Divine power, and
therefore supplies a necessary check
to the expectations which might otherwise arise from belief in the omnipotence of GOD; cf. 1 Jo. v. 14. The
practical teaching of this passage
is well stated by Origen : " quare
proprium est omnis hominis fidelis
primum quidem nolle pati aliquid
doloris, maxime quod ducit usque ad
mortem ; si autem sic voluerit Deus,
acquiescere etiam contra voluntatem
suam." The words occupy an important place in the history of the
doctrine of the Person of Christ. The
Church found in Christ's οὐ τί ἐγὼ
θέλω ἀλλὰ τί σύ conclusive evidence of
the existence in our Lord of a true
human will, distinct from the Divine
Will, although even in this supreme
crisis absolutely submissive to it; for
a catena of the patristic passages see
Petav. de Incarn. ix. 6. 4 sqq., and
comp. esp. John of Damascus, de fide
orth. iii. 18 εἶχε μὲν οὖν φυσικῶς καὶ ὡς
θεὸς καὶ ὡς ἄνθρωπος τὸ θέλειν· εἵπετο
δὲ καὶ συνετάσσετο τῷ αὐτοῦ θελήματι
τὸ ἀνθρώπινον...ταῦτα θέλον ἃ τὸ θεῖον
αὐτοῦ ἤθελε θέλημα...αὐτεξουσίως δὲ
ἤθελε τῷ θείῳ καὶ ἀνθρωπίνῳ θελήματι
...ὥστε ἤθελε μὲν αὐτεξουσίως κινουμένη
ἡ τοῦ κυρίου ψυχή, ἀλλ᾽ ἐκεῖνα αὐτεξουσίως ἤθελεν ἃ ἡ θεία αὐτοῦ θέλησις
ἤθελε θέλειν αὐτήν. On the difficult

questions connected with the personality of the Lord's human nature the
student may consult Dorner (E. T.
II. i., p. 201 ff.), and Westcott on Jo. i.
14. Ἐγὼ θέλω identifies the Person
of Christ with the action of His human
will, but does not necessarily affirm
that the personality resides in His
humanity.

37. καὶ ἔρχεται καὶ εὑρίσκει κτλ.]
The Lord rises again (Lc. ἀναστὰς ἀπὸ
τῆς προσευχῆς), and returning to the
Three finds that His warning (v. 34)
has been in vain ; all are asleep (cf.
xiii. 36). Lc. explains their sleep as
resulting ἀπὸ τῆς λύπης, i.e. from the
exhaustion produced by their deepening realisation of the Passion (cf.
v. 19, Jo. xvi. 20). Peter is addressed
as the first of the Three ; but the
rebuke is partly personal, as Mc. at
least is aware (Σίμων, καθεύδεις ; οὐκ
ἴσχυσας... ; cf. Mt., οὐκ ἰσχύσατε... ;).
Mc. has not used the personal name
Σίμων since Peter's call to the Apostolate (iii. 16), and its appearance here
is certainly suggestive ; cf. Jo. xxi.
15 ff. Σίμων Ἰωάνου, where the reference to natural, perhaps hereditary,
character is still more plainly emphasised. For the time he is 'Peter'
no more ; the new character which
he owes to association with Jesus is
in abeyance. He who was ready to
die with the Master (v. 31) has been
proved not to possess the strength
of will (οὐκ ἴσχυσας) requisite for
resisting sleep during the third part
of a single watch (μίαν ὥραν); cf.
Euth. : σὺν ἐμοὶ ἀποθανεῖν ἐπηγγείλασθε,
καὶ οὐκ ἰσχύσατε μίαν ὥραν γρηγορῆσαι
μετ᾽ ἐμοῦ.

38. γρηγορεῖτε, καὶ προσεύχεσθε

ἔλθητε εἰς πειρασμόν· τὸ μὲν πνεῦμα πρόθυμον, ἡ δὲ

38 ελθητε א*B 346 q] εισελθητε אᶜACDLNWᵇXΓΔΠΣΦΨ minᶠᵉʳᵉᵒᵐⁿ a f vg

κτλ.] "Watch ye, and pray that" &c. (R.V. mg.). The Lord now addresses the Three and not Simon only. He reveals the deeper purpose of His injunction; wakefulness of spirit was chiefly important as necessary to prayer; cf. 1 Pet. iv. 7 νήψατε εἰς προσευχάς, v. 8 ν., γρηγορήσατε. Already, as they took their places in Gethsemane, He had said γρηγορεῖτε (v. 34), and προσεύχεσθε μὴ εἰσελθεῖν εἰς πειρασμόν (Lc. xxii. 40); He repeats this now, for there was still time. Ἵνα μὴ ἔλθητε κτλ.: another reference to the Lord's Prayer. Dr Chase (Lord's Prayer, p. 61 f.) points out that the Syriac versions use the same verb in different conjugations for εἰσφέρειν in Mt. vi. 13, Lc. xi. 4, and ἔρχεσθαι here. Similarly, no doubt, one root would have been used in the Hebrew or Aramaic originals of both passages (cf. Delitzsch, אַל־תְּבִיאֵנוּ = μὴ εἰσενέγκῃς, אַל־תָּבֹא פֶּן=μὴ ἔλθητε). Πειρασμός is used in the O.T. "of the trying or proving of GOD by man, but more commonly of the trying or proving of man by GOD" (Hatch, Essays, p. 71); and since GOD tries men by affliction, the word acquires the latter meaning (e.g. Sir. ii. 1 ἑτοίμασον τὴν ψυχήν σου εἰς πειρασμόν). The N.T. writers also employ it with this connotation (cf. Lc. xxii. 28, Acts xx. 19, Gal. iv. 14, 1 Pet. i. 6, and see Mayor's note on Jas. i. 2), but not exclusively, for the Gospel reveals another form of temptation which does not come from GOD (James i. 13), and is not limited to the infliction of suffering. Πειράζεσθαι ὑπὸ τοῦ σατανᾶ (i. 13, note) is 'to be solicited to commit sin' (cf. Jas. i. 13 f.), and the context shews that this sense predominates here and in the Lord's Prayer. With ἐλθεῖν εἰς π. comp. περιπεσεῖν (Jas. i. 2), ἐμπίπτειν (1 Tim.

vi. 9); the present phrase implies that the temptation may be escaped by an act of the will (cf. 1 Cor. x. 13, Jas. v. 7). Jerome, Bede: "non ait...ne tentemini sed ne intretis in tentationem, hoc est, ne tentatio vos superet et intra suos casses teneat."

τὸ μὲν πνεῦμα πρόθυμον κτλ.] So Mt. A saying of peculiar interest, especially as finding a place in the older Synoptists, since it anticipates the teaching of St Paul and St John. It is quoted already by Polycarp (Phil. 7), whether from the Gospels or from current tradition. On the contrast πνεῦμα, σάρξ, see Westcott on Jo. iii. 6, and SH. on Rom. viii. 9. It begins in the O.T. (see e.g. Num. xvi. 22, xxvii. 16, Isa. xxxi. 3), where 'the flesh' is man "as belonging to the sphere of material life," under the limitations of a corporeal nature, frail, mortal, and in fact impure (Gen. vi. 12); and 'the spirit' is the vital force (Gen. vi. 17) which in man is directly dependent on the Spirit of GOD (Gen. ii. 7) and the organ of communication with GOD and the spiritual world; cf. Schultz, O. T. Theology, E. T., II. p. 242 ff. In the Eleven the human spirit was already under the influence of the Spirit of GOD through their intercourse with Christ (Jo. xiv. 17, see Westcott's note). It was therefore πρόθυμον (cf. 2 Chron. xxix. 31 πρόθυμος τῇ καρδίᾳ, 2 Cor. viii. 11, ἡ προθυμία τοῦ θέλειν), willing and eager (cf. Lc. xxii. 33 ἕτοιμός εἰμι), through the energy of the רוּחַ נְדִיבָה (Ps. li. 14). But its προθυμία was not a match for the vis inertiae of its colleague, the frail flesh (cf. Rom. vi. 19 διὰ τὴν ἀσθένειαν τῆς σαρκὸς ὑμῶν, viii. 3 τὸ ἀδύνατον τοῦ νόμου ἐν ᾧ ἠσθένει διὰ τῆς σαρκός). In the Epp. the 'flesh' is regarded as not merely weak and impotent, but actively op-

σὰρξ ἀσθενής. ³⁹καὶ πάλιν ἀπελθὼν προσηύξατο 39
τὸν αὐτὸν λόγον εἰπών. ⁴⁰καὶ πάλιν ἐλθὼν εὗρεν 40
αὐτοὺς καθεύδοντας, ἦσαν γὰρ αὐτῶν οἱ ὀφθαλμοὶ
καταβαρυνόμενοι, καὶ οὐκ ᾔδεισαν τί ἀποκριθῶσιν
αὐτῷ. ⁴¹καὶ ἔρχεται τὸ τρίτον καὶ λέγει αὐτοῖς 41

39 om τον αυτον λογον ειπων D a c ff k   40 παλιν ελθων ευρεν αυτους אBLΨ
(q me)] om παλιν D a c ff k υποστρεψας ευρ. αυτ. παλιν AC(N)Wᵇ(X)ΓΔΠΣΦ al
minᵒᵐⁿ ᵛⁱᵈ f l vg syrr arm aeth | καταβαρυνομενοι אᶜABKLNUΔΠ*ΣΨ 1 11 13 69
alˢᵃᵗ ᵐᵘ] καταβαρουμενοι D 238 253 καταβεβαρημενοι א* βεβαρημενοι CEFGHSVWᵇXΓΠΦ
minᵖˡ βαρυνομενοι M 56   41 λεγει] pr ubi adoravit k

posed to the 'spirit,' Gal. v. 17 ff.,
the seat of the lower ἐπιθυμίαι which
wage war upon the true life of men
(1 Pet. ii. 11); the contrast between
the two has become sharper and
deeper through the mission of the
Holy Spirit, Who gives new force and
a new direction to the spiritual side
of human nature (Rom. viii. 9 ff.).

39. καὶ πάλιν ἀπελθὼν προσηύξατο
κτλ.] The injunction to pray is again
confirmed by example. The Lord's
second prayer was substantially a repetition of the first (τὸν αὐτὸν λόγον
εἰπών), yet not identical with it, 'the
same petition' rather than "the same
words"; the answer to the first prayer
seems to have been vouchsafed in a
growing consciousness of the Father's
Will, and the second prayer assumes
the form Εἰ οὐ δύναται τοῦτο παρελθεῖν
ἐὰν μὴ αὐτὸ πίω, γενηθήτω τὸ θέλημά
σου (Mt.). The last clause is taken
verbally from Mt. vi. 10; cf. Acts xxi.
14. On τὸ θέλημα (τοῦ θεοῦ) see iii.
35, note : Lightfoot, Revision, p. 106.
Προσηύξατο...εἰπών: part. of identical
action, Burton, § 139.

40. καὶ πάλιν ἐλθών κτλ.] Returning to the Three He again finds them
asleep, their eyes weighed down with
slumber (καταβαρυνόμενοι, Mt. βεβαρη-
μένοι, sc. ὕπνῳ (Lc. ix. 32) ; cf. Joel ii.
8 καταβαρουμένοι ἐν τοῖς ὅπλοις αὐτῶν
πορεύσονται, Gen. xlviii. 10 οἱ δὲ ὀφθαλμοὶ Ἰσραὴλ ἐβαρυώπησαν). During the
Transfiguration (Lc. l. c.) the Three

had experienced the same overpowering drowsiness and the same
inability to give expression to their
thoughts ; with οὐκ ᾔδεισαν τί ἀποκρ.
αὐτῷ comp. ix. 6 οὐκ ᾔδει τί ἀποκριθῇ
(note). They were as men in a dream
who could not say what they would.
On the earlier occasion these were
the effects of fear (Mc. l. c. ἔκφοβοι
γὰρ ἐγένοντο); in Gethsemane the
cause was grief (see note on v. 37).

41. καὶ ἔρχεται τὸ τρίτον κτλ.] A
third interval of prayer had intervened (Mt. προσηύξατο ἐκ τρίτου τὸν
αὐτὸν λόγον εἰπών). Tatian connects
with this third prayer the narrative
of the Bloody Sweat, guided perhaps
by its position in the third Gospel.
But the inference from position is
precarious, for (1) St Luke recognises
only one prayer in Gethsemane, and
(2) the narrative in question, though
a precious and probably genuine relic
of primitive tradition, seems to have
had no place in the original Lc. (cf.
WH., Notes, p. 66 f.).

καὶ λέγει...Καθεύδετε κτλ.] The time
for watchfulness and prayer has gone
by, and the injunction is not repeated:
in place of it comes a permission to
sleep. The permission is surely ironical : 'sleep then, since it is your will
to do so; rest, if you can'; cf. Thpht.:
εἰρωνευόμενος δὲ τοῦτο λέγει πρὸς
αὐτούς...ἐπιγελῶν τῷ ὕπνῳ αὐτῶν.
Euth. : ἐντρέπων αὐτοὺς...καὶ καθαπτό-
μενος...'ἐπεὶ μέχρι τοῦ νῦν οὐκ ἐγρηγο-

Καθεύδετε τὸ λοιπὸν καὶ ἀναπαύεσθε. ἀπέχει· ἦλθεν

§ go ἡ ὥρα, §ἰδοὺ παραδίδοται ὁ υἱὸς τοῦ ἀνθρώπου εἰς

42 τὰς χεῖρας τῶν ἁμαρτωλῶν. ⁴²ἐγείρεσθε, ἄγωμεν·

ἰδοὺ ὁ παραδιδούς με ἤγγικεν.

41 το λοιπον] om το ACDEFLSV²ΧΨ min^{sat mu} om το λοιπον syr^{sin}   41—42 και ἀναπαυεσθε...ηγγικεν] ecce adpropinquavit qui me tradit. et post pusillum excitavit illos et dixit iam ora est ecce traditur filius hominis in manu peccatorum surgite eamus k   41 om απεχει Ψ | απεχει...ωρα] απεχει το τελος και η ωρα D 1071 (c) q απ. το τελος (και) ηλθεν η ωρα Φ a f(ff) syrr^{pesh hcl} arm | ωρα]+ηγγικεν το τελος syr^{sin vid} | τας χειρας] om τας AFKNUW^bΠΣ 1 11 69 604 2^{pe} al^{nonn} | των αμ.] om των 13 69 435 604   42 παραδιδων D | με] μου 1071 | ηγγικεν ABDLNΣΦ rell] ηγγισεν ℵC

ρήσατε, τὸ λοιπὸν καθ. καὶ ἀναπ., εἰ δύνασθε.' The Lord did not hesitate to use irony (cf. vii. 9) when there was occasion for it; exhortation and reproof had in this instance failed, and no other means of rousing the Three to a sense of duty remained. As Augustine (de cons. ev. iii. 11) admits, "recte fieret, si esset necesse"; but who can say that the necessity did not exist? Τὸ λοιπόν, 'in future,' 'henceforth,' cf. 1 Cor. vii. 29, Heb. x. 13=εἰς τὸ λ., εἰς τὰ λοιπά, 2 Macc. xi. 19, xii. 31. 'Ye shall not be interrupted by any further call to prayer.' ἀπέχει· ἦλθεν ἡ ὥρα κτλ.] His irony has produced the desired effect, the Apostles are roused, and the Lord at once reverts to His customary tone of serious direction. 'Απέχει (Mc. only) marks the transition. 'Απέχειν is frequently used in the papyri in forms of receipt (see Deissmann, B. St. p. 229; Fayûm Towns, general index s.v.; Herwerden, lex. supplet. et dial. s.v.); cf. Mt. vi. 2 ff., Lc. vi. 24, Phil. iv. 18. The impersonal ἀπέχει is peculiar to Mc., and only one other ex. has been discovered (Ps.-Anacr. xv. 33 ἀπέχει· βλέπω γὰρ αὐτήν), cf. Num. xvi. 3 ἐχέτω ὑμῖν=רַב לָכֶם). But the sense is doubtless correctly given by the Vg. sufficit, 'enough!' see Field, Notes, p. 39. The question remains whether ἀπέχει refers to the

sleep of the Apostles, or to the ironical reproof. The latter seems the better interpretation; the Lord breaks off the momentary play of irony—it is as if He would say, 'this is no time for a lengthened exposure of the faults of friends; the enemy is at the gate.' The 'Western' text seeks to interpret ἀπέχει by adding τὸ τέλος from Lc. xxii. 37; see WH., Notes, p. 26 f., and cf. Euth. ἀπέχει τὰ κατ᾽ ἐμέ· ἤγουν πέρας ἔχει. Ἡ ὥρα, cf. v. 35, note; on ἦλθεν, 'is come,' see Burton § 52 (p. 26 f.). Παραδίδοται ὁ υἱὸς τοῦ ἀνθρώπου: the present is used even in ix. 31 (note) as the equivalent of παραδοθήσεται (x. 33), so vivid was the Lord's anticipation of the event; here it points to the event as now imminent, as in xiv. 21. Εἰς τὰς χ. τῶν ἁμαρτωλῶν, cf. εἰς χ. ἀνθρώπων (ix. 31), τοῖς ἔθνεσιν (x. 33); on ἁμαρτωλοί see ii. 15, viii. 38; the word may be used technically, or in its deeper sense. In this context it would mean to the disciples 'the Gentiles,' i.e. the Roman officials; but in the Lord's own thought the Scribes and Priests were doubtless included. He had sought the company of sinners who were willing to receive Him, for He came to call them (ii. 16, 17); but to be delivered to the will of sinners who refused His call was one of the bitterest ingredients of His Cup.

42. ἐγείρεσθε, ἄγωμεν κτλ.] 'Rise

43 Καὶ εὐθὺς ἔτι αὐτοῦ λαλοῦντος παραγίνεται [ὁ] 43
Ἰούδας εἷς τῶν δώδεκα καὶ μετ' αὐτοῦ ὄχλος μετὰ
μαχαιρῶν καὶ ξύλων παρὰ τῶν ἀρχιερέων καὶ τῶν

43 om ευθυς DΣ 1 13 69 346 604 2^{pe} latt^{vt pl vg} syrr^{sin pesh} arm | o Ιουδας AB] Ιουδας ℵCDLNW^bΧΓΔΠΨ min^{fere omn} + o Ισκαριωτης A(D)KMUW^bΠΦ min^{sat mu} latt syrr^{pesh hcl} arm aeth Or (om ℵBCEGHLNSVΧΓΔΣΨ min^{pl} syr^{sin} aegg go) | εις]+ων EFGHM VΧΓ 1 al^{pl vid}+εκ Δ min^{pauc} | οχλος]+πολυς ACDNW^bΧΓΔΠΣΦ min^{pl} k vg syrr^{sin pesh} Or | παρα] απο B pr απεσταλμενοι 1 al^{nonn} c ff the | των γραμμ.] om των ACKMNΔ min^{nonn} pr απο D

ye, let us go.' They were still lying
on the ground; He was standing
by. At this moment the traitor and
his party are seen to be approaching
(on ἤγγικεν see i. 14, note). Ὁ παραδιδούς points back to the revelation of
the supper-chamber (xiv. 18 ff.), which
Peter and John at least had understood. The call to 'go' ends the scene
in Gethsemane, but cannot be intended
to suggest flight, for the Lord had
always reserved Himself for this
'hour,' and had now finally embraced
the Divine Will concerning it; cf.
Euth.: οὐ μόνον οὐκ ἔφυγεν, ἀλλὰ καὶ
εἰς ἀπάντησιν αὐτῶν ἐξιέναι παρασκευά-
ζεται. On the arrival of Judas the
Lord went forth to meet him (Jo.
xviii. 4), and called the Three to
accompany Him.

43—50. ARRIVAL OF THE TRAITOR.
ARREST OF JESUS (Mt. xxvi. 47—56,
Lc. xxii. 47—53, Jo. xviii. 2—12).

43. καὶ εὐθὺς ἔτι αὐτοῦ λαλοῦντος
κτλ.] The words ἰδού...ἤγγικεν had
hardly left the Lord's lips (cf. v. 35,
note), when Judas arrived (παραγίνεται,
venit, cf. Mt. iii. 1, Jo. iii. 23; in the
LXX. the verb is with rare exceptions
an equivalent of בוא). Lc. adopts the
original phrase ἔτι αὐτ. λαλ. (Mt. Mc.),
but seems to connect it with another
saying (cf. Lc. xxii. 46 with Mt. xxvi.
41, Mc. xiv. 38). Jo. explains how it
came to pass that Judas sought the
Master in Gethsemane (ᾔδει...τὸν τόπον, ὅτι πολλάκις συνήχθη Ἰησοῦς ἐκεῖ
μετὰ τῶν μαθητῶν αὐτοῦ). Possibly it
was matter of notoriety among the

Twelve that the garden would be
visited after the Paschal meal. Εἷς
τῶν δώδεκα, cf. vv. 10, 20; Jo. vi. 71;
the phrase appears to belong in this
place to the original tradition, for it
is common to the three Synoptists;
"the literary reflection of the chronic
horror of the Apostolic Church that
such a thing should be possible"
(Bruce). There is force in the remark of Euth.: οὐκ ἐπαισχύνονται
τοῦτο γράφοντες οἱ εὐαγγελισταί, πανταχοῦ γὰρ τῆς ἀληθείας φροντίζουσιν.
Cf. Origen, c. Cels. ii. 15.

καὶ μετ' αὐτοῦ ὄχλος κτλ.] Judas came
first, as guide to the party (προήρχετο
αὐτούς, Lc., Acts i. 16), but was closely
followed (μετ' αὐτοῦ) by an armed
crowd. Their arms (ὅπλα, Jo.) consisted only of μάχαιραι (used here
probably in the stricter sense), short
swords or knives, such as even private
persons carried (infra, v. 47, Lc. xxii.
36, 38; cf. Gen. xxii. 6, 10, Jud. iii.
16 ff., where see Moore's note), and
ξύλα, stout sticks (cf. Jos. B. J. ii. 9. 4),
or perhaps clubs, such as the fullers
of Jerusalem used in their work (cf.
Hegesippus ap. Eus. H. E. ii. 23)—
such weapons in fact as could be
hastily collected by an irregular body
of men called out to deal e.g. with a
brigand (v. 48, ὡς ἐπὶ λῃστήν). But
the men who followed Judas did not
belong to the ὄχλος who thronged
Jesus in the temple courts; they came
from (WM., p. 457) the Sanhedrists
(παρὰ τῶν ἀρχ. κ. τ. γραμμ. κ. τ. πρεσβ.
=Mt. ἀπὸ τῶν ἀρχ. καὶ πρεσβ.=Jo.

44 γραμματέων καὶ τῶν πρεσβυτέρων. ⁴⁴δεδώκει δὲ ὁ παραδιδοὺς αὐτὸν σύσσημον αὐτοῖς λέγων ʽΟν ἂν φιλήσω αὐτός ἐστιν· κρατήσατε αὐτὸν καὶ ἀπάγετε

43 των πρεσβ.] om των א*AU 1 69 346 604 al^pauc   44 δεδωκει] εδωκεν D | συσσημον (συνσ. אΔ συσ. FL)] σημειον D 2^pe al^pauc | om αυτοις D 2^pe a cff k q arm | αυτος] ουτος Ψ | και απ. ασφαλως] ασφ. και απ. syrr^sin peshvid | απαγετε אBDL 604 al^pauc] απαγαγετε ACEGHKMNSUVW^bΧΓΔΠΣΦΨ min^pl αγαγετε F min^pauc

ἐκ τῶν ἀρχ. καὶ ἐκ τῶν Φαρισαίων ὑπηρέτας : each of the orders is regarded as separately responsible). These ὑπηρέται were probably members of the temple police (Jo. vii. 32, Acts v. 26 ; see Schürer, II. i. p. 264 f., Edersheim, Temple, p. 119) ; if the νυκτοφύλακες could not be withdrawn from the Precinct, the ἡμεροφύλακες were doubtless available in emergencies. With them were regular troops from the Antonia, whose assistance had doubtless been secured through the influence of the High Priest (Jo. λαβὼν τὴν σπεῖραν, 'the maniple,' or perhaps 'the cohort,' under its tribune (χιλίαρχος), see Westcott on Jo. xviii. 3, 12) ; but of these the Synoptists seem to know nothing. The ὄχλος included personal servants of the High Priest (v. 47) and individuals who were attracted by curiosity or some other interest (v. 51) ; Lc. adds that members of the Sanhedrin were also present (xxii. 52). Mc. mentions the three orders in the Sanhedrin separately (τῶν ἀρχ. καὶ τῶν γρ. καὶ τῶν πρ., cf. Jo.), for their action was due to a concurrence of class interests rather than to a formal vote of the whole body ; cf. viii. 31, x. 33, xi. 18, 27, xiv. 1, xv. 1. Renan goes beyond the evidence when he writes (Vie, p. 305) "le mandat d'arrestation émanait ... du Sanhédrin."

44. δεδώκει δὲ ὁ παραδιδούς κτλ.] Such details might have been arranged after the departure of Judas from the supper. Σύσσημον is a word condemned by Phrynichus, who classes

it with κίβδηλα ἀμαθῆ (Rutherford, p. 493); but in the later prose style it is used freely (e.g. Diod. Sic. xx. 52 τὸ συγκείμενον πρὸς μάχην σύσσημον), and it occurs in the LXX. (Jud. xx. 38, 40, B, Isa. v. 26, xlix. 22, lxii. 10, cf. Ign. Smyrn. 1); more precisely than σημεῖον, which Mt. has here, it denotes a signal or token agreed upon between two parties, a tessera. It was Judas again (cf. v. 10, note) who took the initiative ; the token was of his proposing. On the omission of the augment in the plup. δεδώκει see WM., p. 85, Blass, Gr. p. 37.

The σύσσημον was a kiss, the customary mode of saluting a Rabbi ; see Wünsche, p. 339. Φιλεῖν osculari is frequent in the LXX. (e.g. Gen. xxvii. 26, xlviii. 10, Prov. vii. 13, Cant. i. 2, viii. 1), as in class. Gk., but the N. T. uses it only in this context ; φίλημα, however, occurs in the Epistles (Paul⁴, 1 Pet.¹), where the kiss consecrated by the Gospel becomes the σύσσημον of brotherly love (φ. ἅγιον, ἀγάπης). Αὐτός ἐστιν, 'he is the man'; cf. Blass, Gr. p. 264.

κρατήσατε αὐτὸν κτλ.] The undertaking of Judas was fulfilled by the kiss, which betrayed the Lord to His enemies ; the rest belonged to the agents of the Sanhedrists. Yet he volunteers advice : 'seize and carry Him off securely.' The words reveal the interest which Judas, when committed to the scheme, had learnt to take in its success. It might even now be frustrated by the escape of Jesus before there was time to arrest Him, or by a rescue on the way to the city or

ἀσφαλῶς. ⁴⁵καὶ ἐλθὼν εὐθὺς προσελθὼν αὐτῷ 45
λέγει 'Ραββεί, καὶ κατεφίλησεν αὐτόν.¶ ⁴⁶οἱ δὲ 46 ¶ ר¹²
ἐπέβαλαν τὰς χεῖρας αὐτῷ καὶ ἐκράτησαν αὐτόν.

45 om ελθων D 1 al^nonn a c ff k q syrr^sin(vid) pesh arm | om ευθυς D 251 604 2^pe a cff kq |
προσελθων] pr και ℵ* min^perpauc | ραββει]+ραββει (-βι) AEFGHKNSUVWᵇΧΓΠΣ
syrr^peshhcl(txt) arm go pr χαιρε C²Φ 1 13 69 124 346 2^pe al^nonn a c vg^ed syr^hcl(mg) the
46 επεβαλαν ℵB] επεβαλον ACDLNΣΦΨ rell | τας χειρας αυτω ℵᶜBDL 1 11 13 69 118
346 604 1071 2^pe a k q syrr arm τας χ. αυτων ℵ*CΔΣ επ αυτον τας χ. M*S min^pauc
τας χ. επ αυτον Ψ επ. αυτον τ. χ. αυτων (A)EF²GH(K)M²UVWᵇΧΓ(Π)Φ min^pl | εκρα-
τησαν] εδησαν k^vid

in the streets; hence the double direction. For κρατεῖν 'to arrest,' cf. vi.
17; for ἀπάγειν 'to carry off in custody,' see xiv. 53, xv. 16, Mt. xxvii. 31,
Acts xii. 19. 'Ασφαλῶς caute, Tindale
"warely" (Acts xvi. 23), cf. ἀσφαλί-
ζεσθαι, Acts xvi. 24, Jos. B. J. iii. 8.
8 φρουρεῖν μετὰ πάσης ἀσφαλείας.
There must be no risk of miscarriage,
and Jesus had often shewn a supernatural power of eluding His enemies;
"tamquam si dicat, 'nisi diligenter
eum tenentes abduxeritis, cum voluerit effugiet vos.'" (Origen.)

45. καὶ ἐλθὼν εὐθὺς προσελθὼν κτλ.]
No sooner had Judas reached the
spot than he approached Jesus; not
a moment was lost. Mt.'s εὐθέως
προσελθών is comparatively tame.
He uttered the name of attachment
by which he had so long been used to
accost Jesus (ix. 5, note), and sealed
it by a fervent kiss (κατεφίλησεν, Mt.
Mc.). Καταφιλεῖν is frequent in the
LXX. where, like φιλεῖν osculari, it
usually represents פָּשַׁק, and perhaps
implies no particular vehemence or
fervour. But the proper force of the
compound verb (cf. Xen. mem. ii. 6.
33 τοὺς δ' ἀγαθοὺς καταφιλήσοντος) is
apparent in N. T. usage, cf. Lc. vii. 38,
45, xv. 20, Acts xx. 37; comp. v. 40
note. The kiss was not repeated;
contrast Lc. vii. 38, 45 κατεφίλει, οὐ
διέλιπεν καταφιλοῦσα, Acts l.c. κατεφί-
λουν. Lc., as if he shrank from
realising the scene, contents himself
by saying ἤγγισεν τῷ 'Ιησοῦ φιλῆσαι

αὐτόν. There is much difficulty in
harmonising the accounts of our
Lord's answer. Acc. to Mt. He
replied 'Εταῖρε, ἐφ' ὃ πάρει ('do
the work for which thou art here,'
cf. Jo. xiii. 27); acc. to Lc., 'Ιούδα,
φιλήματι τὸν υἱὸν τοῦ ἀνθρώπου παρα-
δίδως; acc. to Jo., who omits the
incident of the kiss, the Lord
comes forward and asks the party
τίνα ζητεῖτε; Both Tatian and Augustine (de cons. ev. iii. 15) place these
evidently distinct sayings in the
order Lc., Mt., Jo., but a satisfactory
adjustment is hardly possible without
fuller knowledge. Such a moment of
surprise and terror would naturally
leave different impressions on the
minds of the witnesses. If Mc. represents Peter's testimony, his silence
at this point is suggestive. That
Apostle, we may imagine, was torn
by a conflict of feelings which left his
memory a blank in reference to the
Master's words; the treachery of
Judas, the arrest of Jesus, filled his
thoughts.

46. οἱ δὲ ἐπέβαλαν κτλ.] The arrest
was effected without resistance on
the Master's part. For ἐπιβάλλειν
τὰς χεῖρας (τὴν χεῖρα) in a hostile
sense see Jo. vii. 30, 44, Acts iv. 3,
v. 18, xii. 1, xxi. 27; in the LXX. the
phrase is used for יָד שָׁלַח (Gen. xxii.
12, 2 Regn. xviii. 12) with ἐπί (אֶל)
followed by the acc., which is also
the usual construction in the N. T.;

47 ⁴⁷εἰς δὲ [τὶς] τῶν παρεστηκότων σπασάμενος τὴν μάχαιραν ἔπαισεν τὸν δοῦλον τοῦ ἀρχιερέως καὶ 48 ἀφεῖλεν αὐτοῦ τὸ ὠτάριον. ⁴⁸καὶ ἀποκριθεὶς ὁ Ἰησοῦς εἶπεν αὐτοῖς Ὡς ἐπὶ λῃστὴν ἐξήλθατε μετὰ μαχαιρῶν

47 εις δε τις BCEFGHKNSUVXΓΔΠΣΦ minᵖˡ a vg syrʰᶜˡ go] εις δε אALMΨ 604 alᵖᵃᵘᶜ c f ff k q aegg aeth και τις D | om των παρεστ. D a | τ. αρχιερεως]+Καιαφα Ψ | ωταριον אBDΦΨ 1 syrʰᶜˡᵐᵍ] ωτιον ACLNWᵇXΓΔΠΣ minᶠᵉʳᵉᵒᵐⁿ + το δεξιον go 48 και αποκρ. ο I.] ο δε I. D a ff q ο δε I. αποκρ. 604 (2ᵖᵉ) k | om ως D | εξηλθετε FKMSU VWᵇΓΠ alᵖˡ

see however Esth. vi. 2 ἐπιβαλεῖν χεῖρας Ἀρταξέρξῃ, and the frequent ἐπιβαλεῖν τινι (e.g. Esth. i. 1). On the form ἐπέβαλαν cf. WH., *Notes*, p. 165.

47. εἰς δέ τις τῶν παρεστ. κτλ.] Mc.'s vague phrase (cf. xiv. 69 f., xv. 35, Jo. xviii. 22) becomes in Mt. εἷς τῶν μετὰ Ἰησοῦ, and in Lc. εἷς τις τῶν ἐξ αὐτῶν, Jo. only supplying the name (Σίμων Πέτρος). On εἷς τις see Blass, *Gr.* pp. 144, 178. During the early days of the Church of Jerusalem when the evangelical tradition was being formed, prudential reasons (cf. Jo. xviii. 26) may have suggested reticence as to the name of the offender and even the fact of his connexion with the Christian body. In the Gospels we see the reserve gradually breaking down, and finally abandoned when the danger had ceased. Σπασάμενος τὴν μάχαιραν (cf. Acts xvi. 27), 'having drawn his knife' (see *v.* 43, note ; the art. connects the weapon with the subject of the verb, cf. Mt. τὴν μ. αὐτοῦ) 'out of its sheath' (θήκη, Jo. xviii. 11). The verb is used both in act. and mid., and with reference to μάχαιρα or ῥομφαία, cf. Jud. ix. 54 (B, A), Ps. xxxvi. (xxxvii.) 14, cli. 7 ; Mt. has here ἀπέσπασεν. The Apostles, who had a couple of knives at hand (Lc. xxii. 38), when they saw violence offered to the Master eagerly asked, Κύριε, εἰ πατάξομεν ἐν μαχαίρᾳ (Lc.) ; Peter, true to his impetuous nature, did not wait for the answer ; to draw his knife and strike at the

nearest of the party was the work of a moment.

ἔπαισεν τὸν δοῦλον κτλ.] The blow fell on the High Priest's slave (δοῦλον, Mt. Mc. Lc. Jo.; to own no slaves was a peculiarity of the Essenes, Jos. *ant.* xviii. 1. 5). The sufferer was a Malchus (Jo.), Μάλχος, or Μάλιχος i.e. מַלִּיךְ (Dalman, p. 104)—a common name, for Josephus mentions five persons who bore it (see Niese's index). He was doubtless foremost in the business of the arrest, and thus provoked his punishment. Lc. and Jo. mention that the ear which was 'taken off' (ἀφεῖλεν Mt. Mc. Lc., ἀπέκοψεν Jo.) was the right one. Ὠτάριον Mc. Jo. (ὠτίον Mt. Lc.) is a dim. of the New Comedy, which had perhaps become colloquial ; cf. γυναικάριον (2 Tim. iii. 6), κυνάριον (Mc. vii. 27), παιδάριον (Jo. vi. 9); Blass, *Gr.* p. 63 f. For the Lord's remonstrance with Peter, which Mc. omits, see Mt. xxvi. 52—54, Lc. xxii. 51, Jo. xviii. 11 ; the substance is well given by Ephrem : "cuius verbum gladius est gladium non indiget." Lc. alone adds ἁψάμενος τοῦ ὠτίου ἰάσατο αὐτόν.

48. ὡς ἐπὶ λῃστὴν κτλ.] The Lord remonstrates not against the arrest, but against the manner in which it was effected. Why this armed multitude ? He was not a λῃστής (cf. Jo. xviii. 14), but a religious teacher. Why this nocturnal sally (ἐξήλθατε) ? If His teaching or conduct merited punishment, He had given them

καὶ ξύλων §συλλαβεῖν με ; ⁴⁹καθ᾽ ἡμέραν ἤμην πρὸς 49 §P
ὑμᾶς ἐν τῷ ἱερῷ διδάσκων, καὶ οὐκ ἐκρατήσατέ με·
ἀλλ᾽ ἵνα πληρωθῶσιν αἱ γραφαί. ⁵⁰καὶ ἀφέντες 50
αὐτὸν ἔφυγον πάντες.

---

49 ουκ εκρατησατε] ουκ εκρατει (sic) B ου κρατησατε (sic) L | αι γραφαι] + των
προφητων ΝΦ 13 69 124 346 2ᵖᵉ alᵖᵃᵘᶜ syrʰᶜˡ arm the   50 και] τοτε οι μαθηται
Ν(Σ) 13 69 124 346 alᵖᵃᵘᶜ c vg syrr⁽ˢⁱⁿ⁾ᵖᵉˢʰ ʰᶜˡ arm the aeth | εφυγον παντες אBCLΔΨ
61 258 435 me go] παντες εφ. ADPWᵇΧΓΠ alᵖˡ latt syrʰᶜˡ al | εφυγον] pr οι μαθηται
1071 | om παντες א 13 124 346 alⁿᵒⁿⁿ syrᵖᵉˢʰ

---

abundant opportunities of arresting Him publicly in the Precinct. For other exx. in Biblical Greek of the class. συλλαβεῖν, 'to arrest,' cf. Jer. xliii. (xxxvi.) 26, xliv. (xxxvii.) 13, Jo. xviii. 12, Acts i. 16, xii. 3.

It is possible that the σπεῖρα (see note on v. 43) had been obtained from the Procurator on the plea that Jesus was a dangerous insurgent (cf. Lc. xxiii. 2), and robbery and other outrages would readily be associated with the career of such a leader (Lc. xxiii. 19, Jo. xviii. 40; cf. Polyc. mart. 7 ἐξῆλθον διωγμῖται καὶ ἱππεῖς μετὰ τῶν συνηθῶν αὐτοῖς ὅπλων ὡς ἐπὶ λῃστὴν τρέχοντες).

49. καθ᾽ ἡμέραν κτλ.] Cf. Acts ii. 46 f., iii. 2; the Lord had visited the Precinct on three consecutive days in that week alone. Ἤμην πρὸς ὑμᾶς, eram apud vos; Lc. ὄντος μου μεθ᾽ ὑμῶν: on πρός with acc., apud, see WM., p. 504, and cf. ix. 19, note. This familiar intercourse, this daily presence in the Precinct, was now a thing of the past (ἤμην: on the form see WM., p. 95 f.). Καὶ οὐκ ἐκρατήσατέ με, Vg. et non me tenuistis; the καί is not really adversative, see note on vii. 24. The Lord does not upbraid them with the cowardice which had been at the root of their inaction during the earlier days of the Holy Week; their own consciences would supply the reproof; cf. xii. 12. Ἀλλ᾽ ἵνα κτλ. The treachery of Judas, the secrecy

of the arrest, belonged to the order of events foreshadowed by the Spirit of prophecy. Mt. supplies the ellipse: τοῦτο δὲ ὅλον γέγονεν ἵνα κτλ.; in Mc. the context suggests ἀλλ᾽ ἐξῆλθατε, or ἀλλ᾽ οὐκ ἐκρατήσατέ με. For similar exx. of the elliptic ἀλλ᾽ ἵνα see Jo. i. 8, ix. 3, xiii. 18; it is akin to the use of ἵνα in v. 23, but there the word mentally supplied gives the dependent clause the force of an imperative, which is not to be thought of here. Αἱ γραφαί, cf. xii. 24, Lc. xxiv. 27 ff., Jo. v. 39, Acts xvii. 2 ff., 2 Pet. iii. 16. Mt. adds τῶν προφητῶν, but perhaps without intending to limit the reference to the prophetic books of the Canon.

50. καὶ ἀφέντες αὐτὸν ἔφυγον πάντες] Sc. οἱ μαθηταί (Mt.), both the three in Gethsemane and the eight without. The sheep were scattered (v. 27), the Shepherd was left alone (Jo. xvi. 32); cf. Bede: "impletur sermo Domini quem dixerat quod omnes discipuli scandalizarentur in illo in ipsa nocte." Ἔφυγον πάντες: the position of πάντες calls attention to the fulfilment of Christ's warning (v. 27): not even Peter formed an exception to the general desertion. All fled. Yet two at least recovered themselves so far as to follow afterwards, if at a safe distance (v. 54, Jo. xviii. 15).

51—52. THE YOUNG MAN WHO FOLLOWED. (Mc. only.)

51   ⁵¹ Καὶ νεανίσκος τις συνηκολούθει αὐτῷ περιβεβλημένος σινδόνα ἐπὶ γυμνοῦ, καὶ κρατοῦσιν αὐτόν·
¶f 52 ⁵²ὁ δὲ καταλιπὼν τὴν σινδόνα γυμνὸς ἔφυγεν.¶
53   ⁵³Καὶ ἀπήγαγον τὸν Ἰησοῦν πρὸς τὸν ἀρχιερέα,
καὶ συνέρχονται [αὐτῷ] πάντες οἱ ἀρχιερεῖς καὶ οἱ

51 νεανισκος τις אBC(D)LΨ] εις τις ν. AEFGHKMNSUVWᵇΧΓΔΠΣΦ minᶠᵉʳᵉᵒᵐⁿ
(cf. Nestle *T. C.* p. 265) | συνηκολουθει אBCLΨ] ηκολουθει DΦ 1 alᵐᵘ ηκολουθησεν
ΑΝΡΧΓΔΠΣ minᵖˡ συνηκολουθησεν Δ | αυτω] αυτους D 42 ff | επι γυμνου] γυμνος 13
69 346 2ᵖᵉ om 1 118 209 c k syrˢⁱⁿ the | κρατουσιν αυτον אBC*DLΔΨ a c f k l me]
+οι νεανισκοι AC²NPWᵇΧΓΠΣΦ minᵖˡ q syrʰᵉˡ arm go aeth οι δε ν. κρατουσιν αυτον 1
13 (69) 124 (209) 346 604 2ᵖᵉ the   52 εφυγεν]+απ αυτων ΑDΝΡΧΓΔΠΣΦ minᵒᵐⁿ ᵛⁱᵈ
a f q r vg syrrˢⁱⁿ ʰᵉˡ arm go   53 τον αρχιερεα]+(vel pr) Καιαφαν ΑΚΜΠ 11 13 69
124 604 736* ᵛⁱᵈ 1071 2ᵖᵉ alⁿᵒⁿⁿ syrr⁽ᵖᵉˢʰ⁾ʰᵉˡ arm (Or) | αυτω ΑΒΝΡΧΓΠΣΦΨ minᵖˡ
(ad eum syrˢⁱⁿ⁽ʔ⁾ᵖᵉˢʰ arm)] προς αυτον C αυτου 1 209 om אDLΔ 13 64 69 124 346 2ᵖᵉ
latt aeth | om παντες C ff | οι πρ. και οι γρ. אBCLΝPWᵇΧΓΔΨ minᵖˡ syrʰᵉˡ me go]
οι γρ. και οι πρ. A(D)KΠ 604 2ᵖᵉ alᵖᵉʳᵖᵃᵘᶜ latt syrᵖᵉˢʰ arm aeth Or

51. καὶ νεανίσκος τις συνηκολούθει
κτλ.] One there was, not an Apostle,
who followed boldly and at once, going
along with the Lord (συνηκολούθει
αὐτῷ, cf. 2 Macc. ii. 4, 6, Mc. v. 37,
Lc. xxiii. 49) until he was seized by
the ὑπηρέται. His attire would excite
attention, a σινδὼν ἐπὶ γυμνοῦ i.e. a
linen garment or wrap, see J. Lightfoot *ad l.* and Moore on Jud. xiv. 12,
13 ; cf. Prov. xxix. 42 (xxxi. 24),
where the γυνὴ ἀνδρεία makes σινδόνες
(סָדִין) for sale ; 1 Macc. x 64 (A)
περιβεβλημένον αὐτὸν σινδόνα. In the
present case the σινδών was either a
light summer 'square' hastily caught
up, or, possibly, a night-dress ; cf.
Galen cited by Wetstein, μὴ γυμνὸς
κοιμίζεσθαι ἀλλὰ περιβεβλημένος σινδόνα, and Field, *Notes*, p. 40. In
either case Bengel's inference is just :
"locuples igitur erat." Ἐπὶ γυμνοῦ is
in this case 'on the naked body' ; for
a more restricted sense of γυμνός see
Tob. i. 16, Isa. xx. 2 ff., 2 Macc. xi. 12.

52. καταλιπὼν τὴν σινδόνα] The
incident recalls Joseph's flight from
the wife of Potiphar (Gen. xxxix. 12 ff.).
The σινδών, if of the nature of an
ἱμάτιον, a rectangular wrap and not a

close-fitting garment, could easily be
detached.

The νεανίσκος has been identified
with St John (Ambr., Chrys., Bede),
James the brother of the Lord (Epiph.
haer. lxxviii.), a resident in the house
where the Lord had eaten the Passover (Thpht.), or the Evangelist himself
(many recent commentators). The
last two views are not incompatible,
if John Mark was the son of the
οἰκοδεσπότης (*v.* 14, note). It has also
been suggested that Gethsemane was
the property of his mother Mary
(*Exp.* IV. iii. p. 225). That the incident
was drawn by Mark from his own
recollection or from his stores of local
knowledge may be regarded as certain ; it formed no part of the common
tradition or (as we may assume) of St
Peter's preaching.

53—65. TRIAL BEFORE THE HIGH
PRIEST (Mt. xxvi. 57—68, Lc. xxii.
54ᵃ, 63—71; cf. Jo. xviii. 12—14,
19—24).

53. καὶ ἀπήγαγον τὸν Ἰησοῦν κτλ.]
They followed the traitor's advice (*v.*
44), and for greater security bound
their Prisoner first (Jo. ἔδησαν αὐτὸν
καὶ ἤγαγον). He was taken from

πρεσβύτεροι καὶ οἱ γραμματεῖς. ⁵⁴καὶ ὁ Πέτρος ἀπὸ 54
μακρόθεν ἠκολούθησεν αὐτῷ ἕως ἔσω εἰς τὴν αὐλὴν
τοῦ ἀρχιερέως· καὶ ἦν συνκαθήμενος μετὰ⁋ τῶν   ⁋ F

54 om απο L^vidΔΨ | ηκολουθει GΨ 1 13 69 604 | om εσω D 1 209 al^pauc syr^sin | εις
την αυλην] της αυλης 1 209 al^pauc | ·καθημενος D latt^vt pl vg vid

Gethsemane direct to the house of the
High Priest (πρὸς τὸν ἀρχ., Lc. εἰς τὴν
οἰκίαν (Mc. *infra*, Jo. εἰς τὴν αὐλὴν)
τοῦ ἀρχιερέως), who that year was
Caiaphas (Mt. Jo.); acc. to Jo., they
led Him first to Annas, who as an
ex-High Priest and father-in-law of
Caiaphas (Jo.) was possibly still an
inmate of the official residence (see
Westcott on Jo. xviii. 15). Annas
(חָנָן, ʺΑννας, Jos. ʺΑνανος) had been
High Priest A.D. 7—14; Joseph Caiaphas (קַיָּפָא, Dalman, p. 127, Ἰώσηπος
ὁ καὶ Καιάφας, Jos. *ant.* xviii. 2. 2)
held the office A.D. 18—36. At the
house of the latter, notwithstanding
the early hour, the whole hierarchy
(Mc. πάντες οἱ ἀρχιερεῖς, cf. Acts iv. 6)
were assembled, and with them were
members of the other orders which
composed the Sanhedrin. Mc. pic-
tures the assembly as flocking together
(συνέρχονται) to the palace (cf. Field,
Notes, p. 40), Mt. represents them as
already in session when Jesus arrived
(συνήχθησαν) ; all were probably on or
near the spot, awaiting the result of
Judas's mission. With συνέρχ. αὐτῷ
cf. Jo. xi. 33, and see WM., p. 269,
and Field, *l.c.*

54. καὶ ὁ Πέτρος ἀπὸ μακρόθεν κτλ.]
Peter's flight (*v.* 50) was checked
perhaps by the recollection of his
boast, and he followed the party, but
at a safe distance (ἀπὸ μακρ., v. 6, note,
viii. 3, xi. 13, xv. 40). On arriving at
the High Priest's house Peter passed
into the αὐλή (Vg. *atrium*), i.e. the
open court round which the chambers
were built, and which was entered
through a προαύλιον (*infra v.* 68)
opening into the street; αὐλή is con-

stantly used in the LXX. for the חָצֵר
or court of the Tabernacle (Exod.
xxvii. 9) or Temple (3 Regn. vi. 36),
but also in reference to a large private
house (2 Regn. xvii. 18, 4 Regn. xx. 4,
Dan. ii. 49 (תְּרַע), 3 Macc. v. 10, 46).
He gained admission through the
influence of St John, who was an
acquaintance of the High Priest (Jo.
xviii. 15 ff.), and had entered with
Jesus (συνεισῆλθεν τῷ Ἰησοῦ, Jo.).
His purpose was to see how the trial
would end (ἰδεῖν τὸ τέλος, Mt.); meanwhile he took up his place with the
members of the Levitical guard (μετὰ
τῶν ὑπηρετῶν, see note on *v.* 43) who
had been engaged in the arrest, and
were warming themselves over a
charcoal fire (ἀνθρακιὰν πεποιηκότες
Jo.) in the court (ἐν μέσῳ τῆς αὐλῆς
Lc.). Peter sat (Mt. Mc. Lc.) or stood
(Jo.) among them, glad of the heat
after his long exposure to the night
air, but forgetful that the blaze lit up
his features (πρὸς τὸ φῶς, so Mc. Lc.),
and exposed him to the scrutiny of
enemies; cf. Bengel: "saepe sub cura
corporis neglegitur anima." The alti-
tude of Jerusalem causes the nights
to be cold; the mean annual tempe-
rature is variously given as 66° or
62°, and the two or three hours which
precede sunrise are everywhere the
coldest. For other Biblical references
to the use of fires in Jerusalem for
the purpose of giving warmth see Isa.
xliv. 16 θερμανθεὶς εἶπεν Ἡδύ μοι ὅτι
ἐθερμάνθην καὶ εἶδον πῦρ, Jer. xliii.
(xxxvi.) 22 ἐκάθητο ἐν οἴκῳ χειμερινῷ
καὶ ἐσχάρα πυρὸς κατὰ πρόσωπον αὐτοῦ.
For the form ἦν συνκαθ. see WM.,
p. 438.

55 ὑπηρετῶν καὶ θερμαινόμενος πρὸς τὸ φῶς. ⁵⁵οἱ δὲ ἀρχιερεῖς καὶ ὅλον τὸ συνέδριον ἐζήτουν κατὰ τοῦ Ἰησοῦ μαρτυρίαν εἰς τὸ θανατῶσαι αὐτόν, καὶ οὐχ 56 ηὕρισκον. ⁵⁶πολλοὶ γὰρ ἐψευδομαρτύρουν κατ' αὐτοῦ, 57 καὶ ἴσαι αἱ μαρτυρίαι οὐκ ἦσαν. ⁵⁷καί τινες ἀναστάντες ¶r 58 ἐψευδομαρτύρουν κατ' αὐτοῦ λέγοντες ὅτι¶ ⁵⁸ᶜΗμεῖς

54 και θερμ. μετα τ. υ. Σ | om προς το φως 1 alᵖᵃᵘᶜ syrˢⁱⁿ   55 μαρτυριαν] ψευδομαρτυριαν AS* minᵖᵃᵘᶜ k the | εις το θανατωσαι] ινα θανατωσουσιν D (2ᵖᵉ) et ut vid syrr arm ινα αυτον θανατωσουσιν 1071 | ευρισκον אACNWᵇXΓΠ minᵖˡ 56 εψευδομαρτυρουν]+και ελεγον D | αυτου] του Ιησου Ψ   57 και τινες] και αλλοι D a ff k q Orⁱⁿᵗ αλλοι δε 13 69 124 346 604 c alii arm | εψευδ. κατ αυτου λεγοντες] εψευδ. και ελεγον κατ αυτου D (k)   58 οτι ημεις ηκουσ. αυτου λεγοντος] οτι ειπεν א hic dixit c k

55. οἱ δὲ ἀρχιερεῖς κτλ.] While Peter sits in the αὐλή, the Lord is standing in one of the chambers above (v. 66) before His judges. It was a full (ὅλον) if informal meeting of the Sanhedrin (Edersheim, Life, ii. p. 553). For the word συνέδριον 'see xiii. 9: here and in xv. 1 it is used in an exclusive sense of the national council (cf. Acts iv. 15, v. 21 ff., vi. 12 ff., xxii. 30, xxiii. 1 ff.), the סַנְהֶדְרִין of the Talmud, on the history and character of which see Schürer, II. i. 163 ff. As a first step Caiaphas appears to have examined Jesus as to His disciples and teaching (Jo. xviii. 19ff.). The day had begun to dawn (Lc. xxii. 66), when the actual trial took place. Witnesses had meanwhile been brought together, but when they came to give their evidence, the result was disappointing, indeed practically nothing (ἐζήτουν... μαρτυρίαν...καὶ οὐχ ηὕρισκον); it failed to establish a capital offence, which was the purpose in view (εἰς τὸ θανατῶσαι αὐτόν, Mt. ὅπως αὐτ. θανατώσωσιν=לַהֲמִיתוֹ), or indeed any offence at all; "sic omnia irreprehensibiliter et dixit et fecit ut nullam verisimilitudinem reprehensionis invenirent in eo" (Origen). On θανατοῦν see xiii. 12, note. Οὐχ ηὕρισκον: such was the

situation at the moment to which the narrative refers.

56. πολλοὶ γὰρ ἐψευδομαρτύρουν κτλ.] Of witnesses there was no lack, but their evidence was palpably false; they contradicted one another. Ἴσαι αἱ μαρτυρίαι οὐκ ἦσαν, Vg. convenientia testimonia non erant, they did not correspond; see J. Lightfoot ad l. No two witnesses could be found to bear the joint testimony which was legally requisite to justify a capital sentence (Deut. xix. 15). The proposal to render ἴσος 'adequate' (Erasmus, Grotius) is unnecessary, and without support. On καί in this sequence see on v. 49.

57—58. καί τινες ἀναστάντες κτλ.] Mt. ὕστερον δὲ προσελθόντες δύο. The conditions seemed to be satisfied at last; the scene recalls 3 Regn. xx. 13 καὶ ἦλθον δύο ἄνδρες οἱ υἱοὶ παρανόμων καὶ ... κατεμαρτύρησαν αὐτοῦ. The Lord had been heard to say that He would overthrow the Temple. Similarly Stephen was charged with having affirmed that He would do so (Acts vi. 14 ἀκηκόαμεν γὰρ αὐτοῦ λέγοντος ὅτι Ἰησοῦς ὁ Ναζωραῖος οὗτος καταλύσει τὸν τόπον τοῦτον). The question arises how this idea impressed itself on the Jews. Did the words

ἠκούσαμεν αὐτοῦ λέγοντος ὅτι Ἐγὼ καταλύσω τὸν
ναὸν τοῦτον τὸν χειροποίητον, καὶ διὰ τριῶν ἡμερῶν
ἄλλον ἀχειροποίητον §οἰκοδομήσω· 59καὶ οὐδὲ οὕτως 59 §1
ἴση ἦν ἡ μαρτυρία αὐτῶν. 60καὶ ἀναστὰς ὁ ἀρχιερεὺς 60
εἰς μέσον ἐπηρώτησεν τὸν Ἰησοῦν λέγων Οὐκ ἀποκρίνῃ

58 καταλυω ΑΠ* 2 vg^codd | om τουτον D k syr^sin | οικοδομησω] αναστησω D a cff k
60 εις το μεσον DMΦΨ min^mu pr εστη Ψ

spoken at the first Passover of the
Ministry (Jo. ii. 19) rankle in the
minds of the hearers till they were
used as evidence against Him three
years afterwards? Or were they
repeated in a fuller form during the
teaching of the Holy Week? or did
the witnesses base their testimony on
a distorted report by Judas of words
spoken to the Twelve on the Mount
of Olives (xiii. 2, note)? Mt. gives
the testimony in the simpler form
Οὗτος ἔφη Δύναμαι καταλῦσαι τὸν ναὸν
τοῦ θεοῦ καὶ διὰ τριῶν ἡμερῶν οἰκοδο-
μῆσαι. It has been suggested (Bruce)
that this "comes nearest to what the
witnesses actually said," and that Mc.
"puts into their mouths, to a certain
extent, the sense" afterwards attached
to the saying of Christ. But this
is not after Mc.'s manner; when he
repeats a saying in a longer form,
there is reason to regard the longer
form as original. Some such saying
as this is possibly behind the words
of Stephen (Acts vii. 48 οὐχ ὁ ὕψιστος
ἐν χειροποιήτοις κατοικεῖ) and St Paul
(Acts xvii. 24; cf. 2 Cor. v. 1, Heb.
ix. 11, 24). On the history and meaning of χειροποίητος, ἀχειροποίητος, see
Lightfoot's note on Col. ii. 11.

If the Lord said the words as
they stand in Mc., He said what
the event has proved to be true; His
death destroyed the old order, and
His resurrection created the new. In
this case the ψευδομαρτυρία consisted
in wresting the *logion* from its context and giving it a meaning which
His character and manner of life

proved to be impossible; cf. Jerome
in Mt.: "falsus testis est, qui non in
eodem sensu dicta intellegit quo dicuntur." On διὰ τρ. ἡμερῶν see ii. 1
and viii. 31, note; and with οἰκοδο-
μήσω cf. Mt. xvi. 18; the Western
ἀναστήσω recalls the ἐγερῶ of Jo. ii. 19.

59. καὶ οὐδὲ οὕτως κτλ.] Mt. omits
this verse; in Mc. it looks back to
v. 56, and expresses the disappoint-
ment felt by the Sanhedrists when
even this last resource failed them.
For οὐδὲ οὕτως cf. Isa. lviii. 5, 1 Cor.
xiv. 21: 'not even under these circumstances' (οὐδέ as in v. 3, vi. 31,
xii. 10, xiii. 32, xvi. 13). Mc. does
not explain the nature of the ἀνι-
σότης; possibly the witnesses broke
down under examination or contradicted one another as to matters of
detail.

60. καὶ ἀναστὰς ὁ ἀρχιερεύς κτλ.]
Caiaphas rose, for greater solemnity,
in the assembly (cf. iii. 3 εἰς τὸ μέσον),
and endeavoured to extort a statement from Jesus, urging that His
silence suggested that He had no
answer to make and that the witness
was true. The rendering of the Vg.
and several of the O.L. authorities
(*ff*, *q*; cf. *a*, *c*, *k*), which brings the
two questions into one ("non respondes
quicquam ad ea quae tibi obiciuntur
ab his?"), is, as Blass points out
(*Gr.* p. 176 n.), impossible, since it
would require ἀποκρ. πρὸς ἅ (cf. Mt.
xxvii. 14). Οὐκ...οὐδέν, a combination
which intensifies the negation; cf.
iii. 27 and see Blass, *Gr.* p. 256. Τί =
τί ἐστιν ὅ (Blass, p. 177 n.), what is

§ 33 61 οὐδέν; §τί οὗτοί σου καταμαρτυροῦσιν; ⁶¹ὸ δὲ ἐσιώπα
¶ P καὶ οὐκ ἀπεκρίνατο οὐδέν. πάλιν ὁ ἀρχιερεὺς ἐπηρώτα¶
αὐτὸν καὶ λέγει αὐτῷ Cὺ εἶ ὁ χριστός, ὁ υἱὸς τοῦ

60 τι] οτι LΨ (k)   61 ο δε] ο δε Ιησους ℵA minⁿᵒⁿⁿ syrᵖᵉˢʰ aeth εκεινος δε
D | ουκ απεκρινατο ουδεν ℵBCLΨ 33 1071] ουδεν απεκρινατο (vel απεκριθη) A(D)IN
PWᵇXΓΔΠΣΦ minᵖˡ Or om k | επηρωτα αυτον] επηρωτησεν αυτ. FIΦ 604 2ᵖᵉ alᵐᵘ
Or+εκ δευτερου Φ 13 69 124 346 604 2ᵖᵉ syrˢⁱⁿ arm Or | και λεγει αυτω] λεγων Φ
346 2ᵖᵉ (arm) Or+ο αρχιερευς D q | om ο χριστος Γ k | του ευλογητου] του θεου ℵ*
(του ευλ. ℵᶜ) του θ. του ευλ. ΑΚΠ 346 alⁿᵒⁿⁿ vg armᶻᵒʰ του ευλογημενου Ψ

the value of this testimony? what
construction is to be put upon it?
Καταμαρτυρεῖν: frequent in the Ora-
tors and used by the LXX. (3 Regn.
xx. (xxi.) 10, Job xv. 6, Prov. xxv. 18,
Dan. vi. 24 (25)); in the N. T. only in
the Synoptic accounts of the Passion
(Mt. xxvi. 62 = Mc. xiv. 60; Mt. xxvii.
13).

61. ὁ δὲ ἐσιώπα κτλ.] The Lord
refused the opportunity of either
denying the charge, or justifying the
words if they were His. This was
not the time for serious instruction,
nor were these the men to whom it
could be profitably addressed; nor
could He admit the authority of an
assembly which was following up an
unjust arrest by the employment of
perjured witnesses. It was a καιρὸς
τοῦ σιγᾶν, and He kept silence (ἐσιώπα,
imperf.) accordingly. Cf. Origen
in Mt.: "discimus ex hoc loco con-
temnere calumniantium et falsorum
testium voces ut nec responsione
nostra dignos eos habeamus, nec de-
fendere nosmetipsos ubi non sunt
convenientia quae dicuntur adversus
nos." The Lord's silence before His
judges afterwards recalled to the
minds of the disciples Isa. liii. 7;
cf. Acts viii. 32 ff., 1 Pet. ii. 23. The
classical ἀπεκρινάμην occurs in the
LXX. and N.T. but rarely (LXX.[5], Mt.[1],
Mc.[1], Lc.ᵉᵛ·[5], act·[1], Jo.[2]), ἀπεκρίθην elsewhere taking its place; ἀπεκρινάμην
itself was a substitute for the earlier
ἠμειψάμην, ἀπημειψάμην (Rutherford,
p. 186 f.).

πάλιν ὁ ἀρχιερεύς κτλ.] A second

and successful attempt to obtain an
answer; to the direct question "Art
Thou the Christ?" solemnly put to
Him on oath (Mt. ἐξορκίζω σε κατὰ
τοῦ θεοῦ τοῦ ζῶντος ἵνα ἡμῖν εἴπῃς εἰ
σὺ εἶ ὁ χρ.) by the ecclesiastical head
of the nation, Jesus at once replies.
Thpht.: ἵνα μὴ ἔχωσιν ὕστερον λέγειν
ὅτι 'ἐὰν σαφῶς εἰπόντος αὐτοῦ ἠκούσαμεν, ἐπιστεύσαμεν ἄν.' Σὺ εἶ, 'art
Thou?' as in xv. 2; cf. Rom. xiv. 4,
Jas. iv. 12; ὁ χριστός, see notes on viii.
29, xii. 35. Τοῦ εὐλογητοῦ, Mt. τοῦ θεοῦ:
the title is based on the doxology
הוּא (Aram. קַדִּישׁ בְּרִיךְ (קֻדְשָׁא בְּרִיךְ
(cf. Schöttgen on Rom. ix. 5, Dal-
man, i. p. 163 f., Burkitt in J. Th. St.,
v. p. 453). The High Priest admits
the Divine Sonship of Messiah; the
Christ was the Son of GOD, since He
inherited the promises made to David
(2 Sam. vii. 14, Ps. ii. 7, lxxxix. 26 f.).
The alternative to this inference is
that Caiaphas is quoting words which
were attributed to Jesus (cf. Mt.
xxvii. 43) and demanding that He
should either admit or deny them;
but the form of the sentence favours
the view that Caiaphas himself identified the Messiah with the Son. In
the Psalms of Solomon the χριστὸς
κύριος is merely Son of David (cf.
James and Ryle, p. liv. ff.); but
Enoch cv. 2 and 4 Esdr. vii. 28 f., xiv.
9 recognise His Divine Sonship, and
the idea seems to have been familiar
during the Lord's lifetime; see Jo. i.
49, xi. 27, Mt. xvi. 16 (cf. Mc. viii. 29).
The Messianic Sonship was perhaps
not regarded as specifically different

εὐλογητοῦ; ⁶²§ὁ δὲ Ἰησοῦς εἶπεν Ἐγώ¶ εἰμι· καὶ 62 §f ¶Φ
ὄψεσθε τὸν υἱὸν τοῦ ἀνθρώπου ἐκ δεξιῶν καθήμενον
τῆς δυνάμεως καὶ ἐρχόμενον μετὰ τῶν νεφελῶν τοῦ
οὐρανοῦ. ⁶³ὁ δὲ ἀρχιερεὺς διαρήξας τοὺς χιτῶνας 63

62 ο δε I.]+αποκριθεις DG 1 13 69 124 346 1071 2ᵖᵉ aff k q syrˢⁱⁿ arm the |
εγω ειμι] pr συ ειπας οτι 13 69 124 346 604 1071 2ᵖᵉ arm Or | om και ερχομενον D |
μετα] επι G 1 11 28 33 alⁿᵒⁿⁿ a syrrˢⁱⁿᵖᵉˢʰ the   63 διαρηξας (B*N)]+ευθεως 124 604
2ᵖᵉ a arm Or | τον χιτωνα S syrᵖᵉˢʰ armᶜᵒᵈ

from the Sonship of Israel; see the
Rabbinical references in Edersheim,
Life, ii. pp. 716, 719, Weber, *Jüd.
Theol.*, p. 153, and on the whole sub-
ject consult Schürer, II. ii. p. 158 ff.;
Hastings, *D.B.* iv. p. 570 ff.

62. ὁ δὲ Ἰησοῦς εἶπεν Ἐγώ εἰμι] Cf.
Lc.: ὑμεῖς λέγετε ὅτι ἐγώ εἰμι. The
phrase σὺ εἶπας (Mt. xxvi. 25, 64), or
σὺ λέγεις (Mt. xxvii. 11=Mc. xv. 2=
Lc. xxiii. 3=Jo. xviii. 37), has since
Erasmus usually been regarded as an
idiomatic affirmative, on the strength
of certain classical and Rabbinical
parallels; but it has been shewn by
Dr Thayer (in the *Journal of Bibl.
Literature*, xiii. p. 40 ff.) that the
balance of ancient opinion is against
this view, and that the words mean
simply what they say, while the context, the tone, and the circumstances
must in each case determine the exact
inference which is to be drawn from
them. Mc. has seen in this Σὺ εἶπας
a direct affirmation, and interprets it
accordingly; but it is possible that the
Lord purposely preferred the vaguer
form; cf. Origen *in Mt.* (cited by
Thayer): "quia non erat dignus princeps ille sacerdotum Christi doctrina,
propterea non eum docet, nec dicit
quia *Ego sum*, sed verbum oris eius
accipiens in redargutionem ipsius con-
vertit dicens *Tu dixisti*, ut eo modo
videretur argui non doceri."

καὶ ὄψεσθε τὸν υἱόν κτλ.] The words
point to Dan. vii. 13 Th. ἰδοὺ μετὰ
(LXX. ἐπί, cf. Mt.) τῶν νεφελῶν τοῦ
οὐρανοῦ ὡς υἱὸς ἀνθρώπου ἐρχόμενος
(cf. xiii. 26, note), and Ps. cix. (cx.) 1,

κάθου ἐκ δεξιῶν μου. Both passages
seem to have been regarded by
the Jews as Messianic (cf. xii. 36,
note, and for Dan. *l.c.* see Edersheim,
Life, ii. p. 733 f.), and to claim that
they would be fulfilled in Himself
was equivalent to an assertion of His
Messiahship. But the words of Jesus
are also a solemn warning that His
position and that of His judges would
one day be reversed, and a final but
ineffectual summons to repentance
and faith; cf. Victor: ἐπιφέρει δὲ τὸ
τῆς κρίσεως, ἀπειλῶν ὅτι ὄψονται αὐτὸν
ἐν τῇ οὐρανίῳ δόξῃ φαινόμενον…ἀλλ'
ὅμως ἀκούσαντες οὐκ ἐφυλάξαντο…τὸν
λόγον…οὕτως οὐκ εἰς ὠφέλειαν τοῖς
ἀνηκόοις αἱ τῶν μυστηρίων ἀποκαλύψεις,
ἀλλ' εἰς κατάκρισιν. Mt. prefixes
ἀπ' ἄρτι to ὄψεσθε, and Lc. ἀπὸ τοῦ
νῦν: the vision of the Son of Man
sitting on the Right Hand of the
Power of GOD (τῆς δυνάμεως τοῦ θεοῦ
Lc.; ἡ δύναμις = הַגְּבוּרָה, which was
technically used for GOD, cf. Thpht.,
δύναμιν γὰρ ἐνθάδε τὸν πατέρα φησίν,
and see Dalman, *Worte*, i. p. 164 f.)
began from the year of the Crucifixion (cf. Acts ii. 33 f., vii. 55, Rom.
viii. 34, Heb. i. 3 f., 1 Pet. iii. 22,
Apoc. ii. 21, xii. 5, 'Mc.' xvi. 19), and
is to be followed in due course by
the vision which all must see of His
Return (Apoc. i. 7). The Jewish leaders by their rejection of His Messiahship secured His exaltation (Phil. ii.
9) and their own ultimate confusion.

63. ὁ δὲ ἀρχιερεὺς διαρήξας κτλ.]
This old sign of mourning or horror
is mentioned first in Gen. xxxvii. 29;

64 αὐτοῦ λέγει Τί ἔτι χρείαν ἔχομεν μαρτύρων; 64ἠκού-
σατε τῆς βλασφημίας· τί ὑμῖν φαίνεται; οἱ δὲ
65 πάντες κατέκριναν αὐτὸν ἔνοχον εἶναι θανάτου. 65καὶ

64 ηκουσατε] pr ιδε νυν ℵ (min^perpauc syrr^sin pesh arm) + παντες GNΣ 1 124 2^pe al^nonn
syr^sin arm | της βλασφημιας] την βλασφημιαν ADG 1 13 2^pe al^pauc + αυτου DGINΣ
min^nonn q syr^sin go aeth + του στοματος αυτου 13 61 69 (124) 346 (2^pe) syrr^pesh hcl (mg)
arm | φαινεται] δοκει DNΣ 28 2^pe

the phrase is usually διαρηγνύναι τὰ
ἱμάτια (cf. Mt., and so more than forty
times in the LXX.), but τοὺς χιτῶνας
occurs in Judith xiv. 19, Ep. Jer. 31,
2 Macc. iv. 38, and is strictly accurate
in the present case: cf. Maimonides
ap. Buxtorf: "laceratio non fit in
interula seu indusio linteo nec in
pallio exteriori; in reliquis vestibus...
omnibus fit." What was originally a
natural act of passionate grief is reduced in the Talmud to minute and
stringent rules: "laceratio fit stando
(*v.* 60), a collo anterius non posterius,
non ad latus neque ad fimbrias...lon-
gitudo rupturae palmus est." The
law forbade the High Priest to rend
his garment in private troubles (Lev.
x. 6, xxi. 10), but when acting as a
judge, he was required by custom to
express in this way his horror of any
blasphemy uttered in his presence (cf.
J. Lightfoot on Mt.). On the form διαρήξας see WH., *Notes*, p. 163, WSchm.,
p. 56; on χιτῶνες pl., see vi. 9, note.

τί ἔτι χρείαν ἔχομεν μαρτύρων;] The
relief of the embarrassed judge is
manifest. If trustworthy evidence
was not forthcoming, the necessity for
it had now been superseded; the
Prisoner had incriminated Himself. On
χρείαν ἔχειν τινός see ii. 17, xi. 3, notes.

64. ἠκούσατε τῆς βλασφημίας] WH.
places a mark of interrogation after
βλασφ., but perhaps unnecessarily; cf.
Mt. ἴδε νῦν ἠκ. τὴν βλασφημίαν. The
gen. rei after ἀκούειν is on the whole
less usual than the acc., but cf. Lc.
xv. 25, Acts vii. 34; in Acts xxii. 1
both person and thing are in the gen.
(ἀκούσατέ μου τῆς...ἀπολογίας): the
gen. is perhaps more realistic than

the acc (cf. Buttmann, *Gr.* p. 144 f.).
On βλασφημία see iii. 28, vii. 22, notes.
The blasphemy in this case is the claim
to Messianic honours and powers,
which is assumed to be groundless.

τί ὑμῖν φαίνεται;] 'What is your
view?' (Mt. τί ὑ. δοκεῖ;), cf. Ar. *Eccl.*
875 ὀρθῶς ἔμοιγε φαίνεται (*me iudice*).
The formula as prescribed in *Sanhedrin* iii. 7 (see Edersheim, *Life* ii. p.
561 note) is סברי מרנן, to which the
answer is either לחיים (for life) or
למיתה (for death) as the case may be.
On this occasion the conclusion was
foregone; no one proposed to test the
claim of Jesus before condemning it
as blasphemous; all condemned Him
to be worthy of death. Κατέκρ. αὐτὸν
ἔνοχον εἶναι θανάτου is under the circumstances more exact than κατέκριναν θανάτῳ (x. 33); the court could
not pass a capital sentence (see on xv.
1). On ἔνοχος θανάτου cf. iii. 29, note.
Death was the legal penalty of blasphemy (Lev. xxiv. 16, 1 Kings xxi.
10 ff.), and stoning the manner of
execution in such cases (1 K. *l.c.*, Jo.
x. 30 ff., Acts vii. 55 ff.). Πάντες, i.e.
all who were present (πάντας γὰρ ἐπ-
εσπάσατο διὰ τὸ ῥῆξαι τὸν χιτωνίσκον,
Victor); those who, like Joseph (Lc.
xxiii. 51) and Nicodemus (Jo. vii.
50 ff.), were opposed to the whole
plot against Jesus would not have
been summoned to this meeting.

65. καὶ ἤρξαντό τινες ἐμπτύειν αὐτῷ
κτλ.] Mt. abridges: τότε ἐνέπτυσαν
εἰς τὸ πρόσωπον αὐτοῦ, omitting the
covering of the Lord's Face; Lc., who
retains the latter particular, substitutes
ἐνέπαιζον for ἐνέπτυον. The prophecy

ἤρξαντό τινες ἐμπτύειν αὐτῷ καὶ περικαλύπτειν
αὐτοῦ τὸ πρόσωπον καὶ κολαφίζειν αὐτὸν καὶ λέγειν
αὐτῷ Προφήτευσον· καὶ οἱ ὑπηρέται ῥαπίσμασιν
αὐτὸν ἔλαβον.

65 εμπτυειν (ενπτ. DΔ)]+τω προσωπω αυτου D (604) af syrᵖᵉˢʰ arm aegg go | om
και περικαλ. αυτου το πρ. D af syrˢⁱⁿ και περικ. αυτου το πρ. 1071 | κολαφιζειν και
λεγειν] εκολαφιζον και ελεγον D a c velantes faciem eius clarificabant (sic) eum k |
προφητευσον]+νυν G 1 118+ημιν Ψ k+νυν ημιν 1071 syrˢⁱⁿ+ημιν χ͞ε τις εστιν ο παισας
σε IUXΔΣ (13) 33 (69) 108 124 604 736ᶜᵒʳʳ 1071 2ᵖᵉ alⁿᵒⁿⁿ syrʰᶜˡ arm aegg aeth |
om οι υπηρεται D c(k) | ελαβον אABCIKLNSVΓΔΠΨ minⁿᵒⁿⁿ] ελαμβανον DG 1
13 69 2ᵖᵉ alⁿᵒⁿⁿ syrʰᶜˡ me εβαλλον HWᵇΣ minᵖᵉʳᵐᵘ εβαλον EMUWᵇX 33 604 minˢᵃᵗᵐᵘ

of x. 34 includes both indignities
(ἐμπαίξουσιν καὶ ἐμπτύσουσιν) among
those which Jesus would receive at
the hands of the Gentiles, and it was
fulfilled by the Procurator's soldiers
(xv. 19, 20); but certain of the Sanhedrists anticipated this pagan outrage.
In Ev. Petr. 4 the Jews are unjustly
charged with the subsequent mockery:
[ὁ Πειλᾶτος] παρέδωκεν αὐτὸν τῷ λαῷ...
καί τις αὐτῶν ἔνεγκεν στέφανον ἀκάνθινον...καὶ ἕτεροι ἑστῶτες ἐνέπτυον αὐτοῦ
ταῖς ὄψεσι. See the remarkable parallel cited by Wetstein from Seneca de
consol. 13: "ducebatur Athenis ad
supplicium Aristides, cui quisquis oc-
currerat deiciebat oculos et ingemis-
cebat...tanquam in ipsam iustitiam
animadvertentes; inventus est tamen
qui in faciem eius inspueret." 'Εμ-
πτύειν conspuere is a late equivalent
in the LXX. (Num. xii. 14, Deut. xxv.
9) and N.T. of the Attic καταπτύειν;
cf. Rutherford, N. Phryn., p. 66. Περικαλύπτειν (Exod. xxviii. 20, 3 Regn.
vii. 17): with reference, perhaps, to
the Roman practice of covering the
heads of the condemned (Cic. pro
Rabir. (ed. Heitland) iv. 13 "i lictor,
...caput obnubito, arbori infelici sus-
pendito"; ib. v. 16 "obductio capitis
et nomen ipsum crucis absit"), as well
as for the purpose of concealing from
Him the persons of His tormentors.
καὶ κολαφίζειν αὐτόν κτλ.] So Mt.;
Lc. δέροντες (cf. Mc. xii. 3, xiii. 9).

Κολαφίζειν is specific: the blows were
inflicted with the fist (κόλαφος, Att.
κόνδυλος; cf. Ter. Adelph. ii. 2. 36
"colaphis tuber est totum caput").
Προφήτευσον as it stands alone in
Mc. is scarcely intelligible; Mt. gives
a clue to its meaning (προφ. ἡμῖν,
χριστέ, τίς ἐστιν ὁ παίσας σε); 'use
Thy supernatural powers, Messiah, to
detect the offender.' Our Lord was
not the first prophet in Israel who
had been smitten on the face; cf.
1 Kings xxii. 24, Mic. v. 1. On the
Jewish conception of Messiah as a
Prophet see Stanton, J. and Chr.
Messiah, p. 126 ff., and cf. vi. 4, note.
καὶ οἱ ὑπηρέται κτλ.] Mt. also distinguishes this class of offenders (οἱ
δὲ ἐράπισαν), but without identifying
them. They were the members of the
Temple guard who had effected the
arrest (v. 43, note), and were still in
charge of their Prisoner (cf. Lc. οἱ ἄνδρες οἱ συνέχοντες αὐτόν). Embolden-
ed by the conduct of their superiors,
they added their own form of insult.
For ῥαπίζειν, ῥάπισμα see Lobeck,
Phryn., p. 175, and Rutherford's important discussion (N. Phryn., p.
257 ff.); the words are used in reference
to blows delivered by a stick (ῥαπίς),
or by the palm of the open hand; in
the latter case the Attic form was ἐπὶ
κόρρης πατάξαι, but later writers, beginning with Plutarch, use ἐπὶ κ. ῥαπίζειν. In two at least of the three LXX.

66 ⁶⁶Καὶ ὄντος τοῦ Πέτρου κάτω ἐν τῇ αὐλῇ ἔρχεται
67 μία τῶν παιδισκῶν τοῦ ἀρχιερέως, ⁶⁷καὶ ἰδοῦσα τὸν
Πέτρον θερμαινόμενον ἐμβλέψασα αὐτῷ λέγει Καὶ

66 om κατω DIΨ 1 69 2ᵖᵉ alᵖᵃᵘᶜ a c ff q syrˢⁱⁿ⁽ᵛⁱᵈ⁾ aegg | αυλη]+του αρχιερεως
syrˢⁱⁿ | ερχεται] om syrˢⁱⁿ+προς αυτον D | μια παιδισκη ℵC syrˢⁱⁿ ᵖᵉˢʰ arm   67 om
και 2° D

instances of ῥαπίζειν, it refers to a blow
on the face by the hand of another
person (1 Esdr. iv. 30, Hos. xi. 4), and
ῥάπισμα is used in the same sense
in Isa. l. 6 τὰς δὲ σιαγόνας μου [ἔδωκα]
εἰς ῥαπίσματα. The Vg. adopts this
meaning here (alapis eum caedebant);
the English versions vary (Wycliffe,
"beeten him with strokis or boffatis";
Tindale, Cranmer, "boffeted him on
the face"; Geneva, "smote him with
their rods of office"; R.V. offers the
alternative "blows of their hands"
(text), "strokes of rods" (marg.)). Cf.
Field, Notes, p. 105 (on Jo. xviii. 22).
The difficult phrase ἔλαβον ῥαπίσμασιν
has been changed in many secondary
uncials and cursives into ἔβαλλον or
ἔβαλον (see app. crit.); the confusion
of βαλεῖν and λαβεῖν is one of the
commonest in MSS. Field (Notes, p.
40) supports the latter reading by
arguments which deserve consideration, but the harder ἔλαβον (or ἐλάμ-
βανον, cf. Nestle, T. C. p. 266), supported as it is by the great majority
of the older and better authorities,
claims preference; and it finds a
parallel in a papyrus of the first
century which has the phrase κονδύ-
λοις λαβεῖν τινα (Blass, Gr. p. 118).
Moreover, 'they caught Him with
blows' is more realistic than 'they
struck Him,' and therefore more true
to Mc.'s usual manner. Cf. Origen in
Mt.: "et nunc qui iniuriant unum aliquem de ecclesia et faciunt ei haec, in
faciem exspuunt Christi, et Christum
colaphis caedentes castigant et pugnis."

66—72. Peter denies the Master
thrice (Mt. xxvi. 69—75, Lc. xxii. 56
—62, Jo. xviii. 17, 25—27).

66, 67. ὄντος τοῦ Π. κάτω ἐν τῇ
αὐλῇ κτλ.] The story of Peter's ad-
venture in the court of the High
Priest's official residence (cf. v. 54,
note), which had been interrupted by
the account of the trial, is now resumed. He is κάτω (Mc.), ἔξω (Mt.),
outside the council chamber, and
below it, in the open area beneath the
room where the Sanhedrin had met,
and he sat there (v. 54) by the charcoal fire. While he is there a servant
maid (μία παιδίσκη, Mt., π. τις, Lc.),
one of the High Priest's domestics
(Mc.), comes to the fire (ἔρχεται); she
notices Peter sitting in the firelight
(ἰδοῦσα τὸν Π. θερμαινόμενον, Lc. καθήμενον πρὸς τὸ φῶς: cf. v. 54), and
after gazing at him intently for a
moment (ἐμβλέψασα αὐτῷ), she crosses
to the place where he is sitting (προσῆλθεν αὐτῷ, Mt.) and charges him
with belonging to the party of Jesus.
Παιδίσκη is a slave-girl employed in
domestic service (Gen. xii. 16, xvi. 1 ff.,
Lc. xii. 45, Acts xii. 13, xvi. 16), the
female equivalent of παῖς in the sense
of δοῦλος (Ps. cxv. 7 (cxvi. 16), Eccl. ii.
7, Sap. ix. 5, Esth. vii. 4 = שִׁפְחָה); the
wider meaning (=κόρη, νεᾶνις) disappears in Biblical Gk., see Lightfoot
on Gal. iv. 22. For ἐμβλέπειν cf. viii.
25, x. 21, 27, notes. The first glance
revealed the presence of a stranger;
closer attention enabled her to recognise Peter. St John tells us why—she
was the portress who at his desire had
let Peter in (ἡ παιδίσκη ἡ θυρωρός, cf.
Acts xii. 13). For Ναζαρηνός, the less
common form which Mc. uniformly
adopts, see i. 24, note. The order τοῦ
Ναζαρηνοῦ...τοῦ Ἰησοῦ suits an excited,

σὺ μετὰ τοῦ Ναζαρηνοῦ ἦσθα τοῦ ᾽Ιησοῦ.¶ ⁶⁸ ὁ δὲ 68 ¶ Wᵇ
ἠρνήσατο λέγων Οὔτε οἶδα οὔτε ἐπίσταμαι σὺ
τί λέγεις· καὶ ἐξῆλθεν ἔξω εἰς τὸ προαύλιον.

67 μετα του Ναζ. ησθα του Ι. BCLΨ] μετα του Ι. ησθα του Ν. א syrrˢⁱⁿ ᵖᵉˢʰ μετα
του Ι. του Ν. ησθα DΔ minᵖᵃᵘᶜ latt syrʰᶜˡ arm go aeth Eus μετα του Ν. Ι. ησθα
ΑΝΧΓΠΣ minᵖˡ | Ναζωραιου Δ 238 ff Eus (cf. Ναζορηνου D *Nazoreno* k l* q)
68 ουτε οιδα ουτε επισταμαι אBDL 1071 2ᵖᵉ Eus] ουκ οιδα ουτε (vel ουδε) επ.
GH(KMNU)V(ΧΓ)Δ(ΠΣ) minᵖᵉʳᵐᵘ ουκ οιδα k syrᵖᵉˢʰ | συ τι אBCLNUΔΣΨ 1 33
108 209 1071 2ᵖᵉ] τι συ ΑΙΧΓΠ minᵖˡ τι D minᵖᵃᵘᶜ latt | εξω εις το προαυλιον] εξω εις
την προαυλην D εις το εξω προαυλιον 2ᵖᶜ εις την εξω αυλην (vel προαυλην) 1 (13
69) 209 (604) kᵛⁱᵈ (*in exteriorem atrii locum*) syrˢⁱⁿ arm+και αλεκτωρ εφωνησεν
ACDINΧΓΔΠΣ minᶠᵉʳᵉᵒᵐⁿ a f ff k q vg syrrᵖᵉˢʰ ʰᶜˡ arm go aeth (om κ. αλ. εφ. אBLΨ
17ᵉᵛ c syrˢⁱⁿ me)

hurried, utterance ; 'that Nazarene…
Jesus.' ᾽Ησθα μετὰ τοῦ ᾽Ιησοῦ gives
an exact description of Peter's relation
to the Lord (iii. 14, cf. Acts iv. 13);
on ἦσθα see WM., p. 96. All the
Evangelists give the words of the παιδίσκη, but with much variation (Mt.
καὶ σὺ ἦσθα μετὰ ᾽Ι. τοῦ Γαλειλαίου, Lc.
καὶ οὗτος σὺν αὐτῷ ἦν, Jo. μὴ καὶ σὺ
ἐκ τῶν μαθητῶν εἶ τοῦ ἀνθρώπου τούτου;).
68. ὁ δὲ ἠρνήσατο κτλ.] Cf. v. 30 f.
Had Peter been called to go with the
Master to judgement and death, probably he would gladly have done so.
The trial came in an unexpected form,
and discovered a weak point—his
lack of moral courage (cf. Gal. ii. 11 ff.).
Οὔτε οἶδα οὔτε ἐπίσταμαι σὺ τί λέγεις.
Again the Gospels vary, Mt. being
nearest to Mc., and Jo. most remote
(Mt. οὐκ οἶδα τί λέγεις, Lc. οὐκ οἶδα
αὐτόν, γύναι, Jo. οὐκ εἰμί, sc. ἐκ τῶν
μαθητῶν αὐτοῦ), and again the words
as given by Mc. seem specially appropriate ; the eager repetition οὔτε οἶδα
οὔτε ἐπ. betrays the effort to hide
embarrassment, and the order of the
words σὺ τί λ. suggests unusual emotion (unless we punctuate with WH.
marg., οὔτε ἐπίσταμαι· σὺ τί λέγεις;).
Οἶδα and ἐπίσταμαι differ as *novi* and
scio, though the Vg. reverses the distinction here : 'I neither know nor
understand what you are saying,' i.e.

I am neither conscious of the fact,
nor is the statement intelligible to
me. Or οἶδα may refer to the Master
as in Lc. οὐκ οἶδα αὐτόν. ᾽Επίσταμαι
occurs here only in the Gospels,
and rarely in the Epistles (Paul¹,
Heb.¹, Jas.¹, Jude¹), but is frequent in
the Acts, where it appears in connexion and partial contrast with
γινώσκω (Acts xix. 15); οἶδα and
ἐπίσταμαι appear together again in
Jude 10. Blass (*Gr.* p. 265) rejects
οὔτε…οὔτε as inadmissible in the case
of 'two perfectly synonymous' verbs,
but the objection disappears when
their meanings are seen to be distinct.
καὶ ἐξῆλθεν ἔξω εἰς τὸ προαύλιον]
Mt. ἐξελθόντα δὲ εἰς τὸν πυλῶνα. The
πυλών is properly the gateway of a
mansion (Gen. xliii. 19, Lc. xvi. 20,
Acts xii. 13 f.), a temple (3 Regn. vi. 8),
or a city (3 Regn. xvii. 10, Apoc. xxi.
12 ff., xxii. 14) ; the προαύλιον (ἅπ. λεγ.)
is doubtless the vestibule by which
access was gained to the αὐλή, and
which was contiguous to the πυλών.
Peter left the fire, and retreated into
the comparative darkness of the vestibule, but only to fall again into the
hands of his persecutor. Jo., who
apparently connects the first denial
with the moment of Peter's admission
to the αὐλή, places the second at the
fire (v. 25).

69 ⁶⁹καὶ ἡ παιδίσκη ἰδοῦσα αὐτὸν ἤρξατο πάλιν λέγειν
70 τοῖς παρεστῶσιν ὅτι Οὗτος ἐξ αὐτῶν ἐστιν· ⁷⁰ὁ δὲ
¶ f πάλιν ἠρνεῖτο. καὶ μετὰ μικρὸν¶ πάλιν οἱ παρεστῶτες
¶ ι ἔλεγον τῷ Πέτρῳ Ἀληθῶς ἐξ αὐτῶν¶ εἶ, καὶ γὰρ

69 και η παιδ. ιδ. αυτον ηρξ. παλιν אCLΔΨ 108 127] και η παιδ. ιδ. αυτον παλιν
ηρξ. ΑΙΝΧΓΠΣ minᵖˡ παλιν δε (ε)ιδ. αυτον η παιδ. D 604 2ᵖᵉ c f(k)q vg syrˢⁱⁿ
arm Eus om παλιν BM 50 f aegg aeth | ηρξατο...λεγειν] ειπεν B aegg aeth | παρ-
εστηκοσιν ΑΔΝΧΓΠ²Σ minᵖˡ | ουτος] και αυτος D και ουτος 13 59 69 106 124 251 346
604 2ᵖᵉ ac ff syrrˢⁱⁿ ᵖᵉˢʰ arm aeth   70 ηρνησατο (D)FGMNΧΔΣ 1 13 69 124
604 2ᵖᵉ alⁿᵒⁿⁿ Eus | παρεστωτες (-στηκοτες D)] περιεστωτες G 1

69. καὶ ἡ παδίσκη ἰδοῦσα αὐτόν
κτλ.] The portress (cf. v. 66, note),
who has returned to her post, recognises and points Peter out to the idlers
in the vestibule. Mt. ἄλλη, another
maid, not the portress; cf. Thpht.:
Ματθαῖος μὲν ἄλλην ταύτην λέγει, Μᾶρκος
δὲ τὴν αὐτήν, οὐδὲν δὲ ἡμῖν τοῦτο πρὸς
τὴν ἀλήθειαν τοῦ εὐαγγελίου· μὴ γὰρ
ἐν μεγάλῳ τινὶ καὶ συνεκτικῷ τῆς σωτηρίας ἡμῖν διαφωνοῦσι; Augustine,
in order to harmonise Mc. with Jo.,
suggests that the maid was at the
fire, and that Peter, overhearing her
remark, turned to defend himself :
" rediens et rursus ad ignem stans
resistebat negando verbis eorum."
Aug. adds : "liquido...colligitur col-
latis de hac re omnibus evangelistarum testimoniis non ante ianuam
secundo Petrum negasse sed intra
in atrio ad ignem; Matthaeum autem
et Marcum...regressum eius brevi-
tatis causa tacuisse." He does not
feel the difficulty of reconciling Mt.'s
ἄλλη with Mc.'s ἡ παιδίσκη, which
in his Latin codex is simply ancilla;
and Lc.'s ἕτερος is taken to be one
of the bystanders who joins in the
attack on Peter. The last supposition,
which is supported by Jo.'s εἶπον, is
not improbable ; the loquacity of the
maid would naturally communicate
itself to some of the company. Mc.'s
account places Peter's conduct in the
least favourable light; if the remark
came only from the maid to whom
he had already replied, and was ad-

dressed to those about her and not
to the Apostle, his second denial was
without excuse.

70. ὁ δὲ πάλιν ἠρνεῖτο] Mt. adds
μετὰ ὅρκου (cf. xxvi. 63), and gives the
words of the denial : οὐκ οἶδα τὸν
ἄνθρωπον (Lc. Jo. οὐκ εἰμί). Thpht. :
ἐπιλαθόμενος τοῦ λόγου οὗ εἶπεν ὁ
κύριος ὅτι τὸν ἀρνησάμενόν με...ἀρνή-
σομαι κἀγώ.
καὶ μετὰ μικρὸν πάλιν κτλ.] So Mt.;
Lc. διαστάσης ὡσεὶ ὥρας μιᾶς, and for
οἱ παρεστῶτες, ἄλλος τις. During the
interval Peter's Galilean accent had
attracted attention and confirmed the
suspicions of the bystanders. At
length they accosted Peter (προσελθόντες, Mt.), or, according to Lc., one
of them affirmed (διισχυρίζετο) in his
presence that he was assuredly what
he had denied himself to be. Καὶ
γὰρ (Vg. nam et, cf. Ellicott on 2
Thess. iii. 10) Γαλειλαῖος εἶ, Mc. (Lc.),
'for, besides other considerations,
thou art from Galilee'; Mt. καὶ γὰρ ἡ
λαλιά σου δῆλόν σε ποιεῖ: for the form
which these words assume in some
MSS. of Mc. see the app. crit. On
the dialectic peculiarities of Galilean
Aramaic comp. Neubauer, géogr. du
Talmud, p. 184 f., Dialects of Palestine
in Stud. Bibl. i. p. 49 ff.; Dalman, Gr.
p. 4 f., 31 ff., 42 ff., Worte, i. p. 64,
and the older literature mentioned by
Schürer ii. i. p. 10, note; and for an
earlier reference to local differences
of pronunciation in Palestine see Jud.
xii. 8. Jo., whose acquaintance with

Γαλειλαῖος εἶ· ⁷¹ ὁ δὲ ἤρξατο ἀναθεματίζειν καὶ ὀμνύναι 71
ὅτι Οὐκ οἶδα τὸν ἄνθρωπον τοῦτον ὂν λέγετε. ⁷²καὶ 72
εὐθὺς ἐκ δευτέρου ἀλέκτωρ ἐφώνησεν· καὶ ἀνεμνήσθη
ὁ Πέτρος τὸ ῥῆμα, ὡς εἶπεν αὐτῷ ὁ Ἰησοῦς ὅτι Πρὶν

70 Γαλειλαιος ει]+και η λαλια σου ομοιαζει ΑΧΓΔΠ minᵖˡ q syrrᵖᵉˢʰʰᶜˡ arm go+
και η λ. σου δηλοι ΝΣ (33)   71 ομνυναι ΒΕΗLSUVXΓ minˢᵃᵗᵐᵘ] ομνυειν
ℵΑCGKΜΝΔΠΣΨ minᵖᵉʳᵐᵘ Eus+και λεγειν D (a) q arm | om τουτον ον λεγετε ℵ
om τουτον DΚΝΣ arm om ον λ. k   72 om ευθυς ΑCΝΧΓΔΠΣΨ minᵖˡ syrrˢⁱⁿʰᶜˡ
aegg go | om εκ δευτερου ℵL c | το ρημα ως] το ρ. ο DΝΧΓΠΣ minˢᵃᵗᵐᵘ του ρηματος
ου Μ 69 alᵛⁱˣᵐᵘ | το ρημα...Ιησ.] του ρηματος του Ιησου ειποντος I 209 syrrᵖᵉˢʰʰᶜˡ⁽ᵗˣᵗ⁾
armᶜᵒᵈᵈ aeth | om οτι...απαρνηση D 142* a

the High Priest gave him special
opportunities of knowing the fact,
states that at this crisis a slave of
Caiaphas who was a relative of
Malchus, clinched the charge with
the question Οὐκ ἐγώ σε εἶδον ἐν τῷ
κήπῳ μετ᾽ αὐτοῦ ;
71. ὁ δὲ ἤρξατο ἀναθεματίζειν κτλ.]
Peter, growing desperate as he sees the
meshes closing round him, invokes an
anathema on himself if his denials are
false. Ἀνάθεμα, ἀναθεματίζειν are LXX.
equivalents for חֵרֶם, הֶחֱרִים, cf. e.g.
Num. xviii. 14, xxi. 3 f., Deut. xiii. 15
(16) ff. ; an ἀνάθεμα (a late collateral
form of ἀνάθημα as εὕρεμα of εὕρημα,
cf. H. H. A. Kennedy, Sources, p. 117,
and SH. on Rom. ix. 3) is an object
devoted to destruction ; see the discussion in Driver's Deuteronomy, p.
98 f. and the interesting illustration
which he cites from the Moabite stone,
and cf. Lightfoot on Gal. i. 8, 9. The
practice of laying oneself under a
conditional anathema is exemplified
in Acts xxiii. 12 (ἀνεθεμάτισαν ἑαυτούς). In Mt., Mc., the verb is used
absolutely ; cf. Vg. coepit anathe-
matizare, English versions from
Wycliffe onwards, "he began to curse";
but the usage of the words shews that
the imprecation was directed against
himself. Mt. employs the stronger
καταθεματίζειν (cf. κατάθεμα, Apoc. xxii.
3). On the alternative forms ὀμνύναι,
ὀμνύειν (Mt.), see WH., Notes, p. 168 f.,

WSchm. p. 123, Blass, Gr. p. 47 f.
Οὐκ οἶδα τὸν ἄνθρωπον τοῦτον ὂν λέγετε :
the indirect denial of the Lord has
grown into the direct : ' I am not one
of His ' into 'I know Him not'; the
former, indeed, involved the latter :
"negavit ipsum cum se negavit eius
esse discipulum" (Bede). Ὃν λέγετε,
nearly =περὶ οὗ λ. ; cf. Jo. vi. 71 ἔλεγεν
δὲ τὸν Ἰούδαν, 1 Cor. x. 29 συνείδησιν
δὲ λέγω.

72. καὶ εὐθὺς ἐκ δευτέρου ἀλέκτωρ
ἐφώνησεν] 'That moment, as he
spake (Lc. παραχρῆμα, ἔτι λαλοῦντος
αὐτοῦ), for the second time a cock
crew.' Ἐκ δευτέρου (Jos. v. 2, Mt.
xxvi. 42, Jo. ix. 24, Acts x. 15, Heb.
ix. 28, a non-classical phrase = (τὸ)
δεύτερον, cf. Blass on Acts, l.c.) is
here peculiar to Mc., corresponding
to δίς in v. 30 and below in this verse
(72ᵇ). On the textual history of the
passage see WH., Intr.² pp. 243, 330,
Notes, p. 27 ; on ἀλέκτωρ, φωνεῖν, cf.
v. 30, note.

καὶ ἀνεμνήσθη ὁ Πέτρος κτλ.] Mt.
ἐμνήσθη τοῦ ῥήματος, Lc. ὑπεμνήσθη
τοῦ ῥ. The second cockcrowing recalled to Peter's mind the forgotten
saying. Mc., according to the best
text (see v. 68, app. crit.), has not
referred to an earlier cockcrowing ;
Peter may not have noticed the first,
but from the lapse of time he would
recognise that this was the second—
the ἀλεκτοροφωνία of the third watch

ἀλέκτορα [δὶς] φωνῆσαι τρίς με ἀπαρνήσῃ. καὶ ἐπιβαλὼν ἔκλαιεν.

15. 1 ¹Καὶ εὐθὺς πρωὶ συμβούλιον ποιήσαντες οἱ ἀρχι-

72 δις φωνησαι B 2ᵖᵉ k aegg] φ. δις AC²LNXΓΔΨ alᵖˡ om δις אC* ᵛⁱᵈΔ 251
c ff l q aeth | και επιβαλων (επιλαβων Δ 247) εκλαιεν (εκλαυσεν אC)] και ηρξατο κλαιειν
D latt syrrˢⁱⁿ ᵖᵉˢʰ ʰᶜˡ arm the go και εκλαιεν (? εκλαυσεν) aethᵛⁱᵈ   XV- 1 πρωι] pr
επι το (vel τω) A(E)N(S)XΓΔΠΣ minᶠᵉʳᵉᵒᵐⁿ | ποιησαντες AB(D)NXΓΔΠΣΨ minᵖˡ
(a ff k q) vg syrr arm go (aeth) Or] ετοιμασαντες אCL

(xiii. 35). For ῥῆμα of a particular
saying of Jesus cf. ix. 32, Lc. ii. 50,
Jo. v. 47. It is instructive to note
that in quoting the saying Mc. does
not quite verbally reproduce his own
report of it (v. 30). On ἀναμιμνή-
σκεσθαί τι see WM., p. 256, Blass, Gr.
p. 102.

καὶ ἐπιβαλὼν ἔκλαιεν] Mt., Lc. καὶ
ἐξελθὼν ἔξω ἔκλαυσεν πικρῶς. From
the second century onwards Mc.'s
ἐπιβαλών has been felt to be a difficulty. (a) The 'Western' text substitutes καὶ ἤρξατο κλαίειν (Vg. et
coepit flere), cf. Thpht., Euth., ἐπιβ.
ἀντὶ τοῦ 'ἀρξάμενος' (for the part.
cf. Acts xi. 4 ἀρξάμενος ἐξετίθετο).
(b) Thpht.'s alternative ἢ ἐπικαλυψά-
μενος τὴν κεφαλήν is supported with
great learning by Dr Field (Notes,
p. 41 ff.), but he fails to produce any
instance in which ἐπιβάλλειν is used
in this sense without ἱμάτιον (cf. e.g.
Lev. xix. 19 ἱμάτιον...κίβδηλον οὐκ
ἐπιβαλεῖς σεαυτῷ) or some explanatory
word. (c) There is more to be said for
the interpretation adopted by the A.V.
and R.V. (text): "when he thought
thereon." Wetstein cites from Galen
the phrase ἐπιβάλλειν τινὶ τὴν διάνοιαν,
and the analogy of προσέχειν, ἐπέχειν,
ἐνέχειν (vi. 19) affords some justification for understanding ἐπιβαλών in this
sense. (d) The word is used by late
writers intransitively in such phrases
as ἐπιβαλών φησι, ἐπιβ. ἐρωτᾷ, with the
meaning sermonem excipiens, and
Mc. may have employed it here in
some such sense; Peter's weeping
was his answer to the Lord's words

recalled to his memory by the second
cockcrowing. On the whole it must
be confessed that the word remains
one of the unsolved enigmas of Mc.'s
vocabulary; but of current interpretations the choice seems to lie
between (c) and (d). Ἔκλαιεν, the
weeping continued some while; Mt.'s
and Lc.'s ἔκλαυσεν, even with the
added πικρῶς, is less suggestive.

XV. 1—15. THE TRIAL BEFORE
THE PROCURATOR (Mt. xxvii. 1—26,
Lc. xxiii. 1—3, 18—25, Jo. xviii.
28—40, xix. 4—16).

1. εὐθὺς πρωί] At daybreak, as
soon as it was morning; Mt. πρωίας
γενομένης (cf. ἅμα πρωί, Mt. xx. 1).
For εὐθύς in this sense cf. i. 10, 21,
23. The precise meaning of πρωί
must be determined by the context;
in this case, since the second cockcrowing was past and the Crucifixion
followed at the third hour (v. 25), it
is natural to understand the hour of
daybreak—from 5 to 6 a.m.

συμβούλιον ποιήσαντες κτλ.] Vg.
consilium facientes, R.V. "held a
consultation." Mommsen (cited by
Deissmann, B. St. p. 238) shews that
the late and rare word συμβούλιον
was used as a technical term to represent the Latin consilium; cf. Plut.
Rom. 14 κωνσίλιον γὰρ ἔτι νῦν τὸ συμβούλιον καλοῦσι. Deissmann quotes
from an Egyptian inscription of the
time of Antoninus Pius καθημένων ἐν
συμβουλίῳ ἐν τῷ πραιτωρίῳ. In Biblical Greek the word occurs only in
4 Macc. xvii. 17 ὅλον τὸ συμβούλιον
(אV, συνέδριον A), Mt. xii. 14, xxii. 15,

ἐρεῖς μετὰ τῶν πρεσβυτέρων καὶ γραμματέων καὶ
ὅλον τὸ συνέδριον δήσαντες τὸν Ἰησοῦν ἀπήνεγκαν

1 γραμματεων] pr των א(C)D 1 2ᵖᵉ aegg Or | απηνεγκαν] απηγαγον CDGNΣ 1 124
604 2ᵖᵉ alᵖᵃᵘᶜ Or + εις την αυλην D *in atrium* a c ff q + *in praetorium* k

xxvii. 1, 7, xxviii. 12, Mc. iii. 6, xv. 1,
Acts xxv. 12; in the first and last of
these passages (see Blass on Acts *l.c.*)
it answers to *concilium*, but in the
rest the abstract sense is to be preferred. Mc.'s ποιεῖν συμβ. is equivalent
to Mt.'s λαβεῖν συμβ. This seems not
to have been realised by the (? Alexandrian) correctors, who have changed
ποιήσαντες into ἑτοιμάσαντες (cf. *app.
crit.*).

The consultation was held between
the hierarchy on the one hand, and
the rest of the Sanhedrin on the
other (μετὰ τῶν πρ. καὶ γρ.; contrast
xiv. 53); the priesthood led by Caiaphas now openly take the lead, as
they have done in fact since the affair
of the Temple market. The purpose
of their deliberations would be to
resolve on a way of giving effect to
the judgement of the Sanhedrin (xiv.
64); cf. Mt. κατὰ τοῦ Ἰησοῦ ὥστε
θανατῶσαι αὐτόν. Καὶ ὅλον τὸ συνέδριον. Mt. πάντες: the three orders
were agreed, the result was practically the act of the whole Sanhedrin,
though there were individuals who
held aloof from the proceedings (Lc.
xxiii. 51, Jo. xix. 39, cf. vii. 50 f.). On
the irregular and informal character
of the whole trial see Edersheim,
Life, ii. p. 553 ff.

δήσαντες…παρέδωκαν Πειλάτῳ] The
Sanhedrists' resolve was immediately
followed by action. There was no
time to be lost; the Feast had begun
(cf. xiv. 2), and the multitudes would
presently assemble; they must place
the Lord in the hands of the Procurator before a rescue could be
attempted. Δήσαντες Mt., Mc. He
had been bound on His arrest (Jo.
xviii. 12), but the manacles or cords

had probably been removed while He
was in the High Priest's house; now
that the streets had to be traversed
again, they were replaced. Origen:
"Christus…volens tradidit se ad
vincula, seponens in se divinitatis
virtutem." Παρέδωκαν. The nemesis
which overtook these betrayers was
swift and precise: παρέδωκαν οἱ Ἰουδαῖοι τοῖς Ῥωμαίοις τὸν κύριον· παρεδό-
θησαν δὲ αὐτοὶ ὑπὸ Κυρίου τῶν Ῥωμαίων
χερσί (Thpht.). Πειλάτῳ: Mt. adds
τῷ ἡγεμόνι (cf. Tac. *ann.* xv. 44), Jo.
substitutes εἰς τὸ πραιτώριον (cf. *v.* 16
infra).

Since the fall of Archelaus in A.D. 6
Judaea had been under a *procurator*
(ἐπίτροπος) who governed it subject
to the supervision of the *legatus* of
Syria; cf. Jos. *ant.* xvii. 13. 5, xviii.
1. 1, *B. J.* ii. 8. 1, and compare
Marquardt, *Staatsverwaltung*, i. p.
250 ff., Schürer I. ii. p. 44 ff. Pontius
Pilatus—Mc. uses only the *cognomen*—
(Lc. iii. 1, Acts iv. 27, 1 Tim. vi. 13;
cf. Tac. *ann.* xv. 44 "Christus Tiberio
imperitante per procuratorem Pon-
tium Pilatum supplicio adfectus erat"),
the fifth Procurator, entered upon his
office in A.D. 25—6, and held it for
ten years. A fortunate accident en-
ables us to compare with the portrait
which the Gospels draw of this man
the estimates formed by Josephus and
Philo; cf. Jos. *ant.* xviii. *passim*,
B. J. ii. 9. 2 ff.; Phil. *de leg.* 38. The
latter cites a letter of Agrippa I. in
which Pilate is described as τὴν φύσιν
ἀκαμπὴς καὶ μετὰ τοῦ αὐθάδους ἀμεί-
λικτος, and a terrible picture is drawn
of the blots upon his official life, τὰς
δωροδοκίας, τὰς ὕβρεις, τὰς ἁρπαγάς, τὰς
αἰκίας, τὰς ἐπηρείας, τοὺς ἀκρίτους καὶ
ἐπαλλήλους φόνους, τὴν ἀνήνυτον καὶ

¶ L 2 καὶ παρέδωκαν Πειλάτῳ.⁴ ²καὶ ἐπηρώτησεν αὐτὸν ὁ
Πειλᾶτος Cὺ εἶ ὁ βασιλεὺς τῶν Ἰουδαίων; ὁ δὲ ἀπο-
3 κριθεὶς αὐτῷ λέγει Cὺ λέγεις. ³καὶ κατηγόρουν αὐτοῦ
4 οἱ ἀρχιερεῖς πολλά. ⁴ὁ δὲ Πειλᾶτος πάλιν ἐπηρώτα
αὐτὸν λέγων Οὐκ ἀποκρίνῃ οὐδέν; ἴδε πόσα σου

1 Πιλατ. CLNΓΔΠΣΨ min^{omn vid} (Πειλ. ℵABD)   2 o Πειλ.]+λεγων 13 69 124
346 556 c k arm the | αυτω λεγει] ειπεν αυτω ANX^{vid}ΓΔΠΣ min^{pl}   3 κατηγορουσιν
D | πολλα]+αυτος δε ουδεν απεκρινατο NUΔΨ 13 33 69 124 1071 a]^{sat mu} a c syrr^{sin hcl}
arm aeth Or   4 επηρωτα BU 13 33 69 124 2^{pe} a]^{nonn} a k syr^{hcl(mg)} arm]
επηρωτησεν ℵACDNXΓΔΠΣ min^{pl} ff q vg syrr^{pesh hcl(txt)} | om λεγων ℵ* 1 209 2^{pe}
a arm the | om ουδεν B*

ἀργαλεωτάτην ὠμότητα. This last feature of his administration is well illustrated by Lc. xiii. 1. But the picture
is perhaps overdrawn; see Renan,
Vie, p. 413 ff. The Pilate of the
Gospels is not altogether wanting in
the sense of justice which characterised the better class of Roman
officials; and if he is compared with
the Jewish leaders, the result is distinctly in his favour.
The Procurator resided at Caesarea
by the sea (Acts xxiii. 23 ff., Jos. B.J.
ii. 9. 2), but he spent the Paschal
week in Jerusalem, where his presence
might be needed in case of an outbreak of fanaticism; cf. Jos. B. J. ii.
14. 8, 15. 5. As to the quarters he
occupied at Jerusalem see xv. 16, note.
2. καὶ ἐπηρώτησεν αὐτὸν ὁ Π. κτλ.]
The preliminaries are related by Jo.
The Sanhedrists are too punctilious
to enter the pagan Procurator's house
during the Paschal season, and the
interview takes place outside. He
asks the nature of the charge, and
gathers from their answer that the
Prisoner is accused of a capital offence. Then he calls Jesus into the
praetorium; the Lord stands before
him (Mt.), and the Procurator enquires, Σὺ εἶ κτλ. (Mt. Mc. Lc. Jo.).
Many causes may have cooperated to
suggest this question—the tradition
of the coming of the Magi (Mt. ii.
1 ff.), the report of the Lord's preach-

ing concerning the Kingdom of GOD,
the cries raised at the Triumphal
Entry; or it may refer simply to
His claim of Messiahship, for ὁ
βασιλεὺς τῶν Ἰουδαίων is merely ὁ
χριστός interpreted from the standpoint of a Roman official. According
to Lc. the Priests had already accused
Jesus of sedition (ἤρξαντο κατηγορεῖν
αὐτοῦ λέγοντες Τοῦτον εὕραμεν δια-
στρέφοντα τὸ ἔθνος ἡμῶν...λέγοντα ἑαυτὸν χριστὸν βασιλέα εἶναι), but the
words are possibly intended to express
at the outset the substance of the
charge upon which He was tried
before the Procurator. On οἱ Ἰουδαῖοι see vii. 3, note; the term is
appropriate on the lips of an alien; to
the Priests and Scribes the Christ is
ὁ βασιλεὺς Ἰσραήλ (infra, v. 32).
"The form of the sentence (σὺ εἶ...)
suggests a feeling of surprise in the
questioner" (Westcott); see however
xiv. 61, Lc. vii. 19 f., where the
pronoun appears merely to emphasise
the identity: 'art thou the person...?'
ὁ δὲ ἀποκριθεὶς αὐτῷ κτλ.] The
answer is given more fully by Jo. (σὺ
λέγεις ὅτι βασιλεύς εἰμι), who narrates
the whole conversation between Jesus
and Pilate. Σὺ λέγεις neither affirms
nor denies (cf. xiv. 62, note; Thpht.:
ἀμφίβολον ἀπόκρισιν δίδωσι), but
leaves the matter to Pilate's judgement (see, however, Blass, Gr. p. 260).
But according to Jo., the Lord pro-

κατηγοροῦσιν. ⁵ὁ δὲ Ἰησοῦς οὐκέτι οὐδὲν ᵀ ἀπεκρίθη, 5 ¶ q
ὥστε θαυμάζειν τὸν Πειλᾶτον. ⁶§κατὰ δὲ ἑορτὴν 6 §F

4 κατηγορουσιν אBCDΨ 1 604 48ᵉᵛ lattᵛⁱᵈ me aeth] καταμαρτυρουσιν AEGHKM
NSUVXΓΔΠΣ minᵖˡ syrr arm the go   5 απεκρινατο G 1 13 69 alᵖᵃᵘᶜ | τον Π.]+λιαν
armᵛⁱᵈ   6 την εορτ. D

ceeded to reveal the sense in which He claimed kingship (ἡ βασιλεία ἡ ἐμὴ οὐκ ἔστιν ἐκ τοῦ κόσμου τούτου...πᾶς ὁ ὢν ἐκ τῆς ἀληθείας ἀκούει μου τῆς φωνῆς). The contrast between His reply to Pilate and that to Caiaphas (xiv. 62) is of great interest; in dealing with Pilate He appeals to conscience only, and makes no reference to the Messianic hopes raised by the O.T.

3—5. καὶ κατηγόρουν αὐτοῦ κτλ.] Pilate and Jesus are now again standing outside the Praetorium (cf. Jo. xviii. 38); the Priests and other members of the Sanhedrin (Mt. καὶ πρεσβυτέρων) are still there, and the crowd has begun to assemble (Lc. καὶ τοὺς ὄχλους). Pilate, satisfied of the innocence of Jesus, announces, Οὐδὲν εὑρίσκω αἴτιον ἐν τῷ ἀνθρώπῳ τούτῳ (Lc., cf. Jo.). He is answered by a storm of fresh accusations (πολλά), which are audaciously contrary to fact (cf. Lc. xxiii. 2, 5). The Lord preserves a strict silence, as He had done when false witnesses gave contradictory evidence before Caiaphas (xiv. 60, 61, notes). To Pilate this self-restraint was incomprehensible; he invited answers from the Prisoner, and, when He remained silent, expressed great astonishment (θαυμάζειν...λίαν, Mt.); cf. Victor: ἐθαύμασεν ὁ Πειλᾶτος πῶς ὁ λογιώτατος διδάσκαλος...οὐκ ἀπολογεῖται. Οὐδέν...πόσα: the charges were many—πόσα answers to πολλά, v. 3,—and to not one of them did the Lord vouchsafe a reply. His reserve was the more remarkable, because He had answered Pilate before; but now His lips were sealed (οὐκέτι οὐδὲν ἀπεκρίθη, Vg. amplius nihil respondit). Cf. Origen: "nec enim erat dignum respondere ut

dubitanti utrum debeat adversus accusationes eorum falsas respondere"; see also his remarks in c. Cels. praef. (ad init.). Ambrose: "bene tacet qui defensione non indiget."

6. κατὰ δὲ ἑορτήν κτλ.] 'At (the) feast' = at the Passover, Vg. per diem festum, Wycliffe, "by a solemne day"; cf. Ps. xciv. (xcv.) 8 κατὰ τὴν ἡμέραν τοῦ πειρασμοῦ, and Westcott's note on Heb. iii. 8: κατὰ τὴν ἑορτήν occurs in Jos. ant. xx. 9. 3. The alternative rendering (Fritzsche) 'feast by feast' (cf. καθ' ἡμέραν, κατ' ἐνιαυτόν) is perhaps less probable, notwithstanding the absence of the article; the Passover was so clearly in view that ἑορτή required no definition. Of the custom (Mt. εἰώθει ὁ ἡγεμών, Jo. ἔστιν δὲ συνήθεια ὑμῖν) there seems to be no other evidence than that which the Gospels furnish. Mc.'s ἀπέλυεν (cf. ἐποίει, v. 8) does not compel us to look further back than Pilate's own term of office for the origin of the custom; a precedent of the kind would ripen into a claim almost at once. The commentators find a partial parallel in Livy's account of the lectisternium (v. 13 "vinctis quoque demta in eos dies vincula")—a passage which shews at least that the practice was not foreign to Roman feeling. ᵃΟν παρητοῦντο, 'for whose life (or liberty) they begged.' Παραιτεῖσθαι is usually to deprecate censure or punishment, cf. 4 Macc. xi. 2 οὐ μέλλω, τύραννε, πρὸς τὸν...βασανισμὸν παραιτεῖσθαι, Acts xxv. 11 οὐ παραιτοῦμαι τὸ ἀποθανεῖν, or with an acc. of the person addressed, Esth. vii. 7 παρητεῖτο τὴν βασίλισσαν. Here it is followed by an acc. of the object desired (WM.,

7 ἀπέλυεν αὐτοῖς ἕνα δέσμιον ὃν παρῃτοῦντο.   ⁷ἦν δὲ

ὁ λεγόμενος Βαραββᾶς μετὰ τῶν στασιαστῶν δεδε-

6 απελυεν] απελυσεν 1071 ειωθει ο ηγεμων απολυειν 13 69 124 346 (solebat dimit-
tere a (c) ff vg consueverat remittere k: cf. syrᵖᵉˢʰ) | om δεσμιον 604 | ον παρητουντο
ℵ*AB*(Δ) et ut vid k syrᵖᵉˢʰ aegg] οντερ ητουντο ℵᶜB³CNXΓΠΣΨ minᵖˡ ον αν ητ.
DG 2ᵖᵉ 13 69 alᵖᵃᵘᶜ ον ητ. 1 quemcunque petissent a cff k vg   7 Βαβαρραβας
(sic) Δ | στασιαστων ℵBCDKNΨ 1 13 69 minⁿᵒⁿⁿ] συνστασιαστων (συστ.) A(E)GH
(MSU)V(XΓ)Δ(Π)Σ minᵐᵘ

p. 284), like the uncompounded verb;
cf. Lc. xxiii. 25 ὃν ᾐτοῦντο, Acts iii. 14
ᾐτήσασθε ἄνδρα φονέα χαρισθῆναι ὑμῖν.
Mt.'s ἤθελον colours the fact by suggesting that the request implied a
choice. The alternative reading ὅνπερ
ᾐτοῦντο (see app. crit.) is defended by
Field, Notes, p. 43, cf. Burgon-Miller,
Causes, p. 32. Ὅσπερ occurs nowhere
else in the N.T. (Blass, Gr. p. 36, who
on grammatical grounds prefers (p.
207) the reading of D).

7. ἦν δὲ ὁ λεγόμενος Βαραββᾶς κτλ.]
The form of the sentence is remarkable, when it is compared with the
notices of Barabbas in the other
Gospels: "there was the man known
as B." &c., not ἦν δὲ δέσμιός τις λεγ.
B. as one might have here expected.
When the Marcan tradition was being
formed the name of Barabbas was
still perhaps remembered at Jerusalem
as that of a once formidable person
(Mt. δ. ἐπίσημον). The name was
probably secondary, a surname, or, as
the form suggests, a patronymic (for
ὁ λεγόμενος in this connexion see Mt.
i. 16, ix. 9; on the other hand cf. Lc.
xxii. 47, Jo. ix. 11, where the personal
name follows); the man was commonly
called בַּר־אַבָּא (Dalman, p. 142), "a
very usual name in the Talmudists"
(J. Lightfoot on Mt. xxvii. 16) and
borne by two Rabbis, R. Samuel Bar
Abba, and R. Nathan Bar Abba.
According to Jerome in Mt., "in
evangelio quod scribitur iuxta Hebraeos filius magistri eorum inter-
pretatur"; cf. the schol. in cod. S (cited
by Tischendorf on Mt. xxvii. 17) ὁ
Βαραββᾶς, ὅπερ ἑρμηνεύεται διδασκάλου

υἱός. The conclusion has been drawn
that another tradition gave the name
as Bar-Rabba (Renan, Vie, p. 419, cf.
Hilgenfeld, ev. sec. Hebr. etc., p. 28,
WH., Notes, p. 20, Resch, p. 339,
Nestle, T. C. p. 259). According to
some, apparently most, of the copies
of Mt. known to Origen (in Mt. l.c.),
the personal name of Bar-Abba was
the same as our Lord's, and the
reading Ἰησοῦν τὸν Βαραββᾶν survives
in four cursive mss. of Mt., and in
the Sinaitic Syriac and the Armenian
versions of Mt.; but it probably
originated in an early error (see
WH. l.c. and the supplementary note
in WH.² p. 144). Nothing is actually
known of this Bar-Abba beyond the
facts mentioned in the Gospels. He
was a λῃστής (Jo.) who had been
engaged with others in a notable disturbance of the peace within the city
(Lc. γενομένην ἐν τῇ πόλει) in which
blood had been shed, and who was
now in custody with his comrades on
the double charge of faction and
murder (διὰ στάσιν καὶ φόνον, Lc.).
Στάσις is either 'standing,' 'posture'
(LXX., Heb. ix. 8), or 'faction,' 'disturbance' (Acts xv. 2, xix. 40, xxiii. 7,
10, xxiv. 5); the latter meaning exclusively appears in στασιάζειν (Judith
vii. 15, 2 Macc. iv. 30, xiv. 6) and its
derivative στασιαστής. Στασιαστής
(ἅπ. λεγ. in Biblical Gk.) occurs also
in Josephus, but is non-classical; cf.
Moeris: στασιώτης Ἀττικῶς, στασιαστής Ἑλληνικῶς. Οἵτινες (cf. Lc.
ὅστις) characterises the men: they
were such desperate characters that
they had gone to the length of

μένος οἵτινες ἐν τῇ στάσει φόνον πεποιήκεισαν. ⁸καὶ 8
§ἀναβὰς ὁ ὄχλος ἤρξατο αἰτεῖσθαι καθὼς ἐποίει αὐ- § r
τοῖς. ⁹ὁ δὲ Πειλᾶτος ἀπεκρίθη αὐτοῖς λέγων Θέλετε 9
ἀπολύσω ὑμῖν τὸν βασιλέα τῶν Ἰουδαίων ; ¹⁰ἐγίνω- 10
σκεν γὰρ ὅτι διὰ φθόνον παραδεδώκεισαν αὐτὸν [οἱ

7 πεποιηκασιν Ψ   8 αναβας אBD a ff vg aegg go] αναβοησας אᶜˑᵇACΝΧΓΠΣΨ
minᵒᵐⁿ ᵛⁱᵈ syrʳᵛⁱᵈ arm om k | ο οχλος] pr ολος D a k go | αιτεισθαι]+αυτον D k | εποιει
αυτοις] pr αει ACDΝΧΓΠΣ minᵒᵐⁿ ᵛⁱᵈ a ff r syrʰᶜˡ go+καθ εορτην c k εθος ην αυτοις ινα
τον Βαραββαν απολυση αυτοις 604 (arm): cf. k   9 αποκριθεις λεγει αυτοις D 2ᵖᵒ
a ff | om υμιν D ff   10 εγινωσκεν] επεγινωσκεν AKΠ minᵖᵃᵘᶜ εγνωκει א* ηδει D
1 13 69 346 604 2ᵖᵒ | παραδεδωκεισαν (παρεδωκεισ. AEGΝVΧΔΣ minᵐᵘ)] παρεδωκαν
DHS 1 13 69 alᵖᵃᵘᶜ | om οι αρχιερεις B 1 13ᵉᵛ 47ᵉᵛ (k) syrˢⁱⁿ me

murder. Πεποιήκεισαν : cf. δεδώκει xiv.
44, παραδεδώκεισαν, v. 10; see WSchm.
p. 99. For φόνον ποιεῖν, facere homi-
cidium, cf. Deut. xxii. 8.

8. καὶ ἀναβὰς ὁ ὄχλος κτλ.] The
crowd, which had begun to assemble
before the visit to Antipas (v. 3, note),
now forced its way up to the head-
quarters of the Procurator (cf. Acts
xxi. 35 ὅτε δὲ ἐγένετο ἐπὶ τοὺς ἀνα-
βαθμούς...ἠκολούθει τὸ πλῆθος τοῦ
λαοῦ), and demanded the release of
a prisoner according to Pilate's usual
practice at the Passover (ἐποίει=εἰώθει
ποιεῖν, cf. ἀπέλυεν, v. 6, note). Another
tradition represents the Procurator as
taking the initiative by reminding the
crowd of the custom (Jo. xviii. 39 ἔστιν
δὲ συνήθεια ὑμῖν ἵνα ἕνα ἀπολύσω κτλ.);
Mc. alone suggests that he was influenced by their attitude and cries.
Ἀναβοήσας (see app. crit.) is a scriptio
proclivis which falls in readily with
the context (cf. vv. 13, 14), but misses
a feature in the story which is of some
importance; the advance of the crowd
was no less menacing than their
shouts. Ἀναβοᾶν, ἀναβῆναι are liable
to be confused in MSS., see Fritzsche
ad l., who refers to 2 Regn. xxiii. 9,
4 Regn. iii. 21, Hos. viii. 9.

9. ὁ δὲ Πειλᾶτος ἀπεκρίθη κτλ.]
Pilate's proposal was an answer to
the demands of the populace, who
seem to have been animated by the

desire of claiming a right, rather than
by any special goodwill towards Jesus.
Possibly the majority consisted of
citizens, and not of the Galileans who
had welcomed their Prophet in the
Temple courts. Θέλετε ἀπολύσω : for
the construction see vi. 25, x. 36, notes.
The full form of the question is given
by Mt. (τίνα θ. ἀ. ὑμῖν, τὸν Βαραββᾶν
ἢ Ἰησοῦν), but τὸν βασιλέα τῶν Ἰουδαίων (Mc., Jo.) is doubtless original;
the cynicism of the Roman finds pleasure in connecting that title with this
harmless dreamer, as he considers
Jesus to be.

10. ἐγίνωσκεν γὰρ ὅτι διὰ φθόνον
κτλ.] A note belonging to the earliest
tradition (Mc., Mt.), added to explain
Pilate's motive. From the first he
was aware of the feeling which lay at
the root of the Sanhedrists' animosity
to Jesus, and this knowledge was partly intuitive, partly due to impressions
left on Pilate by their conduct (ἐγίνωσκεν, Mt. ᾔδει). The pretence of loyalty
to the Emperor was too flimsy to
deceive a man of the world, and he
detected under this disguise the
vulgar vice of envy. The Prophet of
Galilee had earned a reputation, and
gained a hold upon the conscience of
the nation which the priestly rulers at
Jerusalem failed to secure, and His
success explained their resentment.
But the people were free from the

11 ἀρχιερεῖς]. ¹¹οἱ δὲ ἀρχιερεῖς ἀνέσεισαν τὸν ὄχλον
12 ἵνα μᾶλλον τὸν Βαραββᾶν ἀπολύσῃ αὐτοῖς. ¹²ὁ δὲ
Πειλᾶτος πάλιν ἀποκριθεὶς ἔλεγεν αὐτοῖς Τί οὖν
§ P 13 ποιήσω ὃν λέγετε τὸν βασιλέα τῶν §᾽Ιουδαίων; ¹³οἱ
14 δὲ πάλιν ἔκραξαν Σταύρωσον αὐτόν. ¹⁴ὁ δὲ Πει-

11 οι δε αρχ.] οιτινες και 604 arm | ανεσεισαν] επεισαν D ανεπεισαν Γ min^nonn (similiter a c ff k r syr^sin hcl arm the)   12 ελεγεν αυτοις] ειπεν αυτ. ADNXΔΠΣΨ min^fere omn αυτ. λεγει Γ απεκριθη αυτ. 604 2^pe | ποιησω] pr θελετε ADNXΓΠΣ min^pl latt syrr arm go aeth | om ον λεγετε AD 1 13 69 118 604 2^pe al^perpauc latt arm the om ον B | τον βασιλεα] om τον ΝΧΓΠΣ min^pl go βασιλει D* (τω β. D^corr)   13 εκραξαν] εκραζον G 1 13 69 al^pauc arm εκραυγασαν 604 (2^pe) c^scr + λεγοντες ADKMΠ 604 al^nonn a c ff aeth + ανασειομενοι υπο των αρχιερεων και ελεγον G 13 69 124 346 556 c^scr syr^hcl(mg) (arm)

prejudices of the hierarchy, and might be trusted to demand the release of Jesus, especially when the alternative was such as Pilate proposed. Διὰ φθόνον : cf. Sap. ii. 24, 3 Macc. vi. 7, Phil. i. 15. On the pluperfect after ἐγίνωσκεν see Blass, *Gr.* p. 200.

11. οἱ δὲ ἀρχιερεῖς ἀνέσεισαν τὸν ὄχλον κτλ.] An interval followed during which the hierarchy brought their influence to bear upon a crowd already perhaps divided upon the personal question submitted to them. What arguments were used to lead them to prefer Barabbas (μᾶλλον τὸν B.) is matter for conjecture; if Barabbas was a Jerusalemite, and the crowd consisted largely of his follow-townsmen, an appeal may have been made to local prejudice; but there may have been also a lurking sympathy with the στασιασταί, which the Sanhedrists knew how to evoke. They would pose as advocates of Barabbas rather than as enemies of Jesus; to obtain the release of the one was to condemn the other (Mt. τὸν δὲ ᾽Ιησοῦν ἀπολέσωσιν). With them were the elders (Mt.), who represented the people, and whose influence perhaps secured the triumph of the less popular Sadducean aristocracy. ᾽Ανασείειν in the metaphorical sense (= ἀναπείθειν, Hesych.), a word of the later Gk. which occurs again Lc. xxiii. 5 and is occasionally

used by Aq. and Symm., though not by the LXX.

12. ὁ δὲ Πειλᾶτος πάλιν ἀποκριθείς κτλ.] After a space Pilate put the question again and received the answer " Barabbas" (Mt.). His next move was to test the popular feeling with regard to Jesus : τί οὖν ποιήσω; (deliberative subjunctive, cf. Burton, § 168), 'what in that case would you have me do with Him,' &c. For the construction ποιεῖν τινά τι see Blass, *Gr.* p. 90; the more usual phrase is ποιεῖν τινί (ἔν τινι, μετά τινος) τι. ⁸Ον λέγετε τὸν βασιλέα τῶν ᾽Ιουδαίων : see note on v. 9. Mt. has in both instances τὸν λεγόμενον Χριστόν.

13. οἱ δὲ πάλιν ἔκραξαν Σταύρωσον αὐτόν] There was now no hesitation : again the Procurator was answered by a shout in which all joined (Mt.). Perhaps the crowd were nettled by Pilate's imputation (ὃν λέγετε κτλ.), perhaps they resented his desire to dictate their answer, and with the fickle cruelty of an irresponsible multitude they clamoured for the death of one whose release they had a few minutes before been disposed to demand (v. 8). Lc. represents the cry as repeated again and again (ἐπεφώνουν λέγοντες Σταύρου σταύρου; cf. Jo. xix. 6, 15). Σταυροῦν in class. Gk. is 'to fence with a palisade,' ἀνασταυροῦν being reserved from Herodotus downwards for the

λᾶτος ἔλεγεν αὐτοῖς Τί γὰρ ἐποίησεν κακόν; οἱ
δὲ περισσῶς ἔκραξαν Σταύρωσον αὐτόν. ¹⁵ὁ δὲ 15
Πειλᾶτος¶ βουλόμενος τῷ ὄχλῳ τὸ ἱκανὸν ποιῆσαι ¶ a
ἀπέλυσεν αὐτοῖς τὸν Βαραββᾶν, καὶ παρέδωκεν τὸν
Ἰησοῦν φραγελλώσας ἵνα σταυρωθῇ.

14 om αυτοις Ψ | περισσως] περισσοτερως ΕΝPSUVXΓΠ^mgΣ min^pl | εκραξαν]
εκραξον ADGKMPΠ* 1 69 346 al^nonn latt syr^pesh arm me εκραυγαξον 1071 2^pe
15 om βουλομενος…ποιησαι D ff k | ποιειν B 1071 | φλαγελλωσας D*

punishment of impaling; but σταυροῦν is used in Esth. vii. 9, viii. 13 for
תָּלָה (cf. Deut. xxi. 23, Gal. iii. 13),
and in the later sense by Polybius.

14. ὁ δὲ Πειλᾶτος ἔλεγεν αὐτοῖς κτλ.]
Pilate, still reluctant, condescends to
expostulate. Τί γὰρ ἐποίησεν κακόν;
Vg. quid enim mali fecit? where γὰρ
(WM., p. 559) looks back to σταύρωσον, and invites an explanation :
'what evil has he done?—for that
there has been wrongdoing as implied
in your demand for punishment.' But
a mob has no reasons to give beyond
its own will, and the only answer is a
louder and wilder clamour (περισσῶς,
cf. x. 26, xiv. 31 ; Lc. ἐπέκειντο φωναῖς,
μεγάλαις).

15. ὁ δὲ Πειλᾶτος βουλόμενος κτλ.]
Pilate's choice is made at last; his
scruples, though quickened by his
wife's message (Mt. xxvii. 19), are
overruled by the immediate necessity
of pacifying the mob. Βούλεσθαι, a
rare word in the Gospels (Mt.², Mc.¹,
Lc.², Jo.¹), implies more strongly than
θέλειν the deliberate exercise of voli-
tion ; see Lightfoot on Philem. 13.
Τὸ ἱκανὸν ποιῆσαι, satisfacere; a
Latinism which occurs in Polybius,
Appian, and Diogenes Laertius, and
once in the lxx. (Jer. xxxi. (xlviii.)
30 οὐχὶ τὸ ἱκανὸν αὐτῷ οὐχ οὕτως
ἐποίησεν; unless the passage should
be punctuated οὐχὶ τὸ ἐκ. αὐτῷ; οὐχ
κτλ.) ; cf. Acts xvii. 9 λαβόντες τὸ
ἱκανόν, with Blass's note. Either at
this juncture or just before the final
surrender (see next note) Pilate went

through the ceremony of washing his
hands (Mt. xxvii. 24, Ev. Petr. 1, where
see note).
ἀπέλυσεν…παρέδωκεν κτλ.] In St
John's circumstantial account (xix.
1—16) we can see the order of the
events which followed. Pilate seems
to have pronounced no formal sentence
(see Westcott on Jo. xix. 16 ; Lc.'s
ἐπέκρινεν should probably be taken as
expressing the substantial result of
his decision), and even made a last
effort to save Jesus by an appeal ad
misericordiam. The scourging was
perhaps intended to be a compro-
mise ; comp. Lc. παιδεύσας…αὐτὸν
ἀπολύσω. But the Procurator's ecce
homo had no further effect than to
elicit from the Priests the real
charge : υἱὸν θεοῦ ἑαυτὸν ἐποίησεν.
A second private interview between
Pilate and Jesus followed, and then
another attempt on Pilate's part to
escape from his false position. It was
frustrated by the menace Ἐὰν τοῦτον
ἀπολύσῃς οὐκ εἶ φίλος τοῦ Καίσαρος,
upon which Pilate finally gave way.

φραγελλώσας] 'When he had
scourged Him': aor. of antecedent
action, Burton § 134; cf. Vg. tradidit
Iesum flagellis caesum. Φραγελλοῦν,
flagellare, a Latinism which has found
its way also into Mt.; Jo. uses μαστιγοῦν,
Ev. Petr. μαστίζειν. Φραγέλλη, φρα-
γέλλιον (Jo. ii. 15), φλαγελλιον are cited
in the lexicons from late Greek writers; of φραγελλοῦν no example seems
to have been found excepting in this
context and in Christian writings (e.g.

§ syr^hier 16   ¹⁶§ Οἱ δὲ στρατιῶται ἀπήγαγον αὐτὸν ἔσω τῆς

16 εσω...πραιτωριον] *in praetorium* k | εσω της αυλης אABC*NXΓΔΠΣΨ min^pl syrr
the go aeth] εσω εις την αυλην DP 1 13 69 346 556 604 al^pauc arm εις την αυλην (του
Καιαφα) C³(M) al^satmu εξω της αυλης Δ 1071

Ev. Nic. 9, 16, *Test. xii. patr., Ben.* 2).
The punishment of scourging usually
preceded crucifixion; cf. Jos. *B. J.* ii.
14. 9 μάστιξιν προαικισάμενος ἀνεσταύ-
ρωσεν: *ib. infra,* μαστιγῶσαί τε πρὸ
τοῦ βήματος καὶ σταυρῷ προσηλῶσαι:
ib. v. 11. 1; Lucian, *reviv.* ad init.: ἐμοὶ
μὲν ἀνεσκολοπίσθαι δοκεῖ αὐτὸν νὴ Δία
μαστιγωθέντα γε πρότερον, and for an
earlier instance of this Roman bar-
barity see Livy, xxxiii. 36, "alios
verberatos crucibus adfixit." It was
inflicted with the *horribile flagellum,*
reserved for slaves and condemned
provincials (Cic. *pro Rabir.* 4 "Porcia
lex virgas ab omnium civium corpore
amovit; hic misericors flagella retu-
lit"), a lash usually composed of leather
thongs (contrast Jo. ii. 15) loaded at
intervals with bone or metal (see the
Class. Dictionaries *s.v. flagrum,* and
cf. Lipsius *de cruce* c. 3). The sufferer
was sometimes lashed to a column;
see Lipsius, c. 4, and Westcott on
Jo. xix. 1.

παρέδωκεν...ἵνα σταυρωθῇ] The last
stage in the παράδοσις, cf. xiv. 10, 44,
xv. 1, 10. The Lord is now delivered
to the soldiers, whose business it is
to execute the sentence (cf. οἱ στρατιῶται...παραλαβόντες, Mt.), or from
another point of view to the Priests
and people (Jo. xix. 16, 17, *Ev. Petr.*
3), to whose will the soldiers readily
gave effect. Cf. Thpht.: τὸ στρατιω-
τικὸν φῦλον ἀεὶ ἀταξίαις χαῖρον καὶ
ὕβρεσι τὰ οἰκεῖα ἐπεδείκνυτο.

16—20ᵃ. THE LORD IS MOCKED
BY THE PROCURATOR'S SOLDIERS (Mt.
xxvii. 27—31ᵃ, Jo. xix. 2—3).

16. οἱ δὲ στρατιῶται κτλ.] Mt. οἱ
στρ. τοῦ ἡγεμόνος, a distinct body
from the στρατεύματα Ἡρῴδου (Lc.
xxiii. 11). They were members of
the σπεῖρα which was quartered in
the Antonia (Acts xxi. 31; cf. *supra*

xiv. 43, note), and belonged to the
auxilia (Marquardt, v. p. 388), who
were of provincial birth—not Jews,
since the Jews were exempt from the
conscription, but other Palestinians
and foreigners, serving under Roman
orders and at the disposal of the Procurator (Schürer 1. ii. p. 49 ff.). The
soldiers in question were probably the
centurion (*infra v.* 39 ff.) and the
handful of men sent with him to carry
out the sentence. After the scourging,
which had been inflicted outside, they
brought the Lord 'within the court
which is (known as) Praetorium' (ἔσω
τῆς αὐλῆς ὅ ἐστιν πρ.—on the gender
of the relative see WM., p. 206—Mt.
εἰς τὸ πρ.). A difficulty has been
found in Mc.'s identification of the
αὐλή with the *praetorium,* and Blass
(*Exp. T.* x. 186) proposes τῆς αὐλῆς
τοῦ πραιτωρίου, relying on Jerome's
atrium praetorii; whilst others regard
.ὅ ἐστιν πρ. as a gloss from Mt. But
the explanatory clause is quite in Mc.'s
manner (iii. 17, vii. 11, 34, xii. 42, xv.
42), and the most public part of the
praetorium may well have been known
by the Latin name of the whole. The
word *praetorium* (as Lightfoot has
shewn, *Philippians,* p. 97) may mean
(1) headquarters in a camp, or (2) the
residence of a governor, or other
mansion. In the Gospels and Acts it
bears the second sense, cf. Acts xxiii.
35 ἐν τῷ πραιτωρίῳ τοῦ Ἡρῴδου, i.e.
the palace built by Herod the Great
at Caesarea, which was used by the
Procurators as their official residence.
It has been inferred (Schürer 1. ii.
p. 48) that Herod's palace at Jerusalem, a fortified building on the
Western hill, served as the *praetorium*
when the Procurator visited the Holy
City; certainly it was sometimes so
used (cf. e.g. Jos. *B. J.* ii. 14. 8 Φλῶρος

αὐλῆς, ὅ ἐστιν πραιτώριον, καὶ συνκαλοῦσιν ὅλην τὴν σπεῖραν. ¹⁷καὶ ἐνδιδύσκουσιν αὐτὸν πορφύραν, καὶ 17 περιτιθέασιν αὐτῷ πλέξαντες ἀκάνθινον στέφανον·

16 ο εστιν] ubi erat arm^codd pl | συνκαλουσιν] καλουσιν D   17 ενδιδυσκουσιν ℵBCDFΔΨ 1 13 69 al^pauc] ενδυουσιν ΑΝΡΧΓΠΣ min^pl | πορφυραν] χλαμυδα κοκκινην min^perpauc the χλ. κοκκ. και πορφ. 13 69 124 346 604 1071 2^pe al^pauc syr^hier arm | περιτιθεασιν] επιτιθεασιν D imponunt vel imposuerunt c ff vg superponunt k | αυτω] capiti eius arm | om πλεξαντες D (cf. c d ff)

δὲ τότε μὲν ἐν τοῖς βασιλείοις αὐλίζεται, ib. 15. 5 Φλῶρος...ἐξῆγε τῆς βασιλικῆς αὐλῆς τοὺς σὺν αὐτῷ), and apparently by Pilate himself (Philo, leg. ad Cai. 38 ἐν τοῖς κατὰ τὴν ἱερόπολιν Ἡρῴδου βασιλείοις). But Westcott (on Jo. xviii. 28, xix. 13) regards the Antonia as the scene of the trial, and there is much to be said in favour of his view; the proximity of this great fortress to the Temple and its means of communication with the Precinct (Acts xxi. 35, cf. supra, v. 8, note) accord with the picture presented by the Gospels, while on the other hand it is difficult to reconcile their account with the other hypothesis; a procession of the Sanhedrists across the city would have been at once indecorous and dangerous. Moreover, the citadel was the natural headquarters of the σπεῖρα, and on the occasion of the Passover would have served the purpose of the Procurator's visit better than Herod's palace. For an account of the Antonia see Jos. ant. xv. 11. 4, B. J. i. 5. 4, v. 5. 8; and for a summary of the traditional evidence which connects it with the Praetorium, see Sir C. Wilson's art. Jerusalem in Smith's B.D.², p. 1655.

συνκαλοῦσιν ὅλην τὴν σπεῖραν] The cohort had been concerned in the arrest (Jo. xviii. 3, 12), and were therefore interested in the trial and its issue. Σπεῖρα (1) a coil, (2) a band of men, is used in inscriptions for θίασος (Deissmann, B. St., p. 186), and by Polybius and later writers for the Roman cohort (Polyb. xi. 21 τρεῖς σπείρας, τοῦτο δὲ καλεῖται τὸ σύνταγμα

τῶν πεζῶν παρὰ 'Ρωμαίοις κόορτις), or perhaps (see Westcott on Jo. l.c.) for the maniple; in the N.T., however, the σπεῖρα seems to be the cohors, for it is commanded by a χιλίαρχος i.e. a tribunus cohortis (Jo. xviii. 12, Acts xxi. 31); cf. Vg. convocat totam cohortem. The strength of the cohort varied with that of the legion, but it would in any case reach several hundreds; ὅλην τ. σπ. must of course be taken loosely for all who were at hand or not on duty at the time. On the whole subject see Marquardt v. p. 453 ff.

17. ἐνδιδύσκουσιν αὐτὸν πορφύραν κτλ.] They had first stripped off His own clothing (Mt., cf. v. 10), except perhaps the χιτών (cf. Jo. xix. 23). Πορφύραν, Jo. ἱμάτιον πορφυροῦν, Mt., more precisely, χλαμύδα κοκκίνην (cf. Hor. sat. ii. 6. 102, 106); i.e. the garment was a scarlet (Apoc. xvii. 4, xviii. 16) paludamentum or sagum (see Trench, syn. 4)—the cloak of one of the soldiers, possibly a cast-off and faded rag, but with colour enough left in it to suggest the royal purple (cf. Dan. v. 7 ff., 29, 1 Macc. x. 20, xi. 58, xiv. 43 f.). The Romans of an earlier time οὐ περιεβάλλοντο πορφύραν (1 Macc. viii. 14), but the Augustan age was not indifferent to such Eastern luxuries; the Lord, moreover, is regarded by His mockers as a pretender to an Oriental throne. Ἐνδιδύσκειν is a late form of ἐνδύειν which occurs in the LXX. (e.g. 2 Regn. i. 24 τὸν ἐνδιδύσκοντα ὑμᾶς κόκκινα); in the N.T. it appears again in Lc. xvi. 19 ἐνεδιδύσκετο πορφύραν.

περιτιθέασιν αὐτῷ πλέξαντες κτλ.]

18 ¹⁸καὶ ἤρξαντο ἀσπάζεσθαι αὐτόν Χαῖρε, βασιλεῦ τῶν
19 Ἰουδαίων· ¹⁹καὶ ἔτυπτον αὐτοῦ τὴν κεφαλὴν καλάμῳ
§ P καὶ ἐνέπτυον §αὐτῷ, καὶ τιθέντες τὰ γόνατα προσ-

18 ασπαζεσθαι αυτον] +και λεγειν (vel+λεγοντες) אC²(M)NUΣ 11 33 346 736
al^{sat mu} arm | βασιλευ אBDMPSVXΨ al^{mu}] ο βασιλευς AC²EFGHKNUΓΔΠΣ min^{mu}
19 αυτου την κεφ. καλαμω] αυτον καλ. εις την κεφ. D 2^{pe} c ff k | om και ενεπτυον αυτω
U | αυτω] faciei eius arm | om και τιθεντες...προσεκυνουν αυτω D min^{perpauc} k

Cf. 1 Macc. x. 20 ἀπέστειλαν αὐτῷ
(i.e., to Jonathan)...στέφανον χρυσοῦν:
2 Macc. xiv. 4 ἦλθεν πρὸς τὸν βασιλέα
Δημήτριον...προσάγων αὐτῷ στέφανον
χρυσοῦν. The proper badge of Oriental royalty was the διάδημα : see Isa.
lxii. 3, Esth. vi. 8 (א^{c.a}), 1 Macc. i. 9,
xi. 13, and cf. Apoc. xix. 12 ; the στέ-
φανος was the victor's wreath, which
was presented to royal personages
as a tribute to military prowess, or
as a festive decoration (see Trench,
syn. xxiii.). If this distinction is to be
maintained here the soldiers seem
to have had in view the laurel
wreath of the Imperator ; see Westcott on Jo. xix. 2, who refers to
Suetonius (Tib. 17 "triumphum ipse
distulit...nihilominus urbem praetex-
tatus et laurea coronatus intravit").
The wreath which they plaited (for
πλέκειν στέφανον cf. Isa. xxviii. 5) was
of thorns (ἀκάνθινον, Vg. spineam, cf.
Isa. xxxiv. 13, =ἐξ ἀκανθῶν Mt. Jo.),
i.e. composed of twigs broken off from
some thorny plant which grew on
waste ground hard by (iv. 7), not improbably the Zizyphus spina-Christi
or nubk tree, of which "the thorns
are long, sharp and recurved, and
often create a festering wound"
(Tristram, N.H. p. 430, adding "I
have noticed dwarf bushes of the Z.
growing outside the walls of Jerusalem"). Twigs of nubk may have
been used in callous thoughtlessness
rather than out of sheer brutality—
"there were thorns on the twigs, but
that did not matter" (Bruce). On the
other hand G. E. Post in Hastings
D. B. iv. prefers the Calycotome

villosa, which is easily plaited into
the shape of a crown.
18. ἤρξαντο ἀσπάζεσθαι αὐτόν κτλ.]
According to Ev. Petr. the Lord was
seated on an extemporised βῆμα, as a
King sitting in judgment (ἐκάθισαν
αὐτὸν ἐπὶ καθέδραν κρίσεως λέγοντες
Δικαίως κρῖνε βασιλεῦ τοῦ Ἰσραήλ, cf.
Justin, apol. I. 35 ἐκάθισαν ἐπὶ βήματος
καὶ εἶπον Κρῖνον ἡμῖν); that He was
placed on a seat to receive the mockery of homage is at least not improbable. A reed was placed in His
right hand to represent a sceptre
(Mt.). Cf. the remarkable parallel
cited by Wetstein from Philo, in
Flacc. § 6 βύβλον μὲν εὐρύναντες ἀντὶ
διαδήματος ἐπιτιθέασιν αὐτοῦ τῇ κεφαλῇ
...ἀντὶ δὲ σκήπτρου βραχύ τι παπύρου
τμῆμα τῆς ἐγχωρίου καθ᾽ ὁδὸν ἐρριμμέ-
νον ἰδόντες ἀναδιδόασιν· ἐπεὶ δὲ...διε-
κόσμητο εἰς βασιλέα...προσῇεσαν οἱ μὲν
ὡς ἀσπασόμενοι οἱ δὲ ὡς δικασόμενοι.
Another interesting illustration will
be found in Field, Notes, p. 21 f.
Χαῖρε, β. τ. Ἰ., have rex Iudaeorum,
in imitation of the well-known have
Caesar. St John by using the imperf. (ἤρχοντο πρὸς αὐτὸν καὶ ἔλεγον,
cf. Westcott ad l.) recalls the scene
yet more vividly.
19. ἔτυπτον ... προσεκύνουν αὐτῷ]
Mc. represents the mimic homage as
mingled with brutal insult ; in Mt.
the brutality follows the mimicry.
Pseudo-Peter adds some further details : ἕτεροι ἑστῶτες ἐνέπτυον αὐτοῦ
ταῖς ὄψεσι, καὶ ἄλλοι τὰς σιαγόνας
αὐτοῦ ἐράπισαν (cf. Jo. ἐδίδοσαν αὐτῷ
ῥαπίσματα, and Isa. l. 6)· ἕτεροι καλάμῳ
ἔνυσσον αὐτόν, καί τινες αὐτὸν ἐμάστιζον

ἐκύνουν αὐτῷ. ²⁰καὶ ὅτε ἐνέπαιξαν αὐτῷ, ἐξέδυσαν 20
αὐτὸν τὴν πορφύραν καὶ ἐνέδυσαν αὐτὸν τὰ ἱμάτια
αὐτοῦ.

§Καὶ ἐξάγουσιν αὐτὸν ἵνα σταυρώσωσιν αὐτόν·   § L
²¹καὶ ἀγγαρεύουσιν παράγοντά τινα Σίμωνα Κυρη- 21

20 om ενεπαιξαν αυτω D | την πορφ.] την χλαμυδα al^perpauc τ. χλαμ. και τ. πορφ. 12
13 69 124 346 604 (1071) syr^hier arm (the) | τα ιματια αυτου BCΔΨ] τα ιματια D τα
ιμ. τα ιδια ΑΝΡΧΓΠΣ min^pl τα ιδια ιμ. αυτου א c^ser | εξαγουσιν] αγουσιν A | αυτον]
+εξω Ψ | ινα σταυρωσουσιν ACDLNPΔΣ 33 69 al^pauc ωστε σταυρωσαι 1 ινα σταυρωθη
28 131   21 εγγαρευουσιν א*B* ανγ. D | παραγοντα τινα Σιμ. Κυρ.] τον Σιμ.
παραγοντα τον Κυρ. D Σιμ. τον Κυρ. παραγοντα 2^pe arm om παραγοντα N

λέγοντες Ταύτῃ τῇ τιμῇ τιμήσωμεν τὸν
υἱὸν τοῦ θεοῦ. Τιθέντες...προσεκ. αὐτῷ:
Mt., γονυπετήσαντες ἔμπροσθεν αὐτοῦ
ἐνέπαιξαν αὐτῷ. For τιθέναι τὰ γόνατα,
Vg. ponere genua = κάμπτειν τὰ γ.,
γονυπετεῖν, see Lc. xxii. 41, Acts vii.
60.

20. καὶ ὅτε ἐνέπαιξαν αὐτῷ κτλ.]
Their humour spent itself, or the
time allowed for their savage sport
came to an end, or there was no insult left to add (Victor : ἔσχατος ὅρος
ὕβρεως τὸ γενόμενον ἦν) ; accordingly,
the sagum was taken off and the
Lord's own outer clothing restored.
Of the crown and the wreath there is
no mention, but they were doubtless
cast aside when they had served their
purpose. The prophecy of x. 34 had
now been fulfilled. For ἐκδιδύσκειν
τινά τι see Blass, Gr. p. 92.

20^b—22. The Way to the Cross
(Mt. xxvii. 31^b—33, Lc. xxiii. 26—33ᵃ,
Jo. xix. 16, 17).

20. καὶ ἐξάγουσιν αὐτόν κτλ.] 'They
lead Him forth'; cf. Jo., ἐξῆλθεν:
Mt., Lc., ἀπήγαγον αὐτόν, but Mt.
continues ἐξερχόμενοι δέ. Ἐξάγειν
(הוֹצִיא) is usually followed by a reference to the place which is left (cf. e.g.
Gen. xi. 31 ἐκ τῆς χώρας τῶν Χαλδαίων,
xx. 13 ἐκ τοῦ οἴκου, Num. xix. 3 ἔξω
τῆς παρεμβολῆς, 3 Regn. xx. (xxi.) 13
ἔξω τῆς πόλεως, Acts xii. 17 ἐκ τῆς
φυλακῆς). Here we may supply either
ἔξω τοῦ πραιτωρίου or ἔξω τῆς πόλεως ;

the latter is supported by Heb. xiii.
12 ἔξω τῆς πύλης ἔπαθεν. No distinct
tradition indicates the route : the
name of Via Dolorosa, given to the
lane which crosses the city and leads
to the Church of the Holy Sepulchre,
appears to be later than the 12th
century (Robinson, Later Researches,
p. 170).

The condemned carried their own
crosses to the place of execution ; cf.
Plutarch, de ser. Dei vind.: τῶν
κολαζομένων ἕκαστος τῶν κακούργων
ἐκφέρει τὸν αὑτοῦ σταυρόν. The Lord
accordingly started with this burden
upon Him (Jo. βαστάζων αὑτῷ τὸν σταυρὸν ἐξῆλθεν) ; cf. viii. 34, note. As
the ancient commentators point out,
there is no inconsistency here between
the Fourth Gospel and the Synoptists
(Jerome : "intellegendum est quod
egrediens de praetorio Iesus ipse
portaverit, postea obvium habuerit
Simonem cui portandam crucem im-
posuerint").

21. καὶ ἀγγαρεύουσιν παράγοντά τινα
κτλ.] Mt. ἐξερχόμενοι δὲ εὗρον ἄνθρω-
πόν τινα. The words suggest that the
man came into sight as they issued
from the gate. He was on his way
from the country (ἀπ' ἀγροῦ, Mc., Lc.,
cf. εἰς ἀγρόν 'Mc.' xvi. 12 ; the Vg. de
villa would better represent ἀπὸ τοῦ
ἀγροῦ, cf. v. 14, vi. 36, xiii. 16), and
was passing by (παράγοντα, cf. i. 16,
ii. 14) when the soldiers seized (Lc.,

ναῖον ἐρχόμενον ἀπ᾽ ἀγροῦ, τὸν πατέρα ᾿Αλεξάνδρου
22 καὶ ῾Ρούφου, ἵνα ἄρῃ τὸν σταυρὸν αὐτοῦ. ²²καὶ

21 απ ακρου A | om και Ρουφου ff

ἐπιλαβόμενοι) and pressed him into their service. ᾿Αγγαρεύειν, *angariare* (cf. the Aramaic אַנְגַּרְיָא, Dalman, *Gr.* p. 147), a word of Persian origin; see Herod. viii. 98 τοῦτο τὸ δράμημα τῶν ἵππων (the service of the royal couriers) καλέουσι Πέρσαι ἀγγαρήιον. Since the Persian ἄγγαροι were impressed, the verb ἀγγαρεύειν was used in reference to compulsory service of any kind. Hatch (*Essays,* p. 37) was able to quote an instance of ἀγγαρεύειν from an Egyptian inscription of A.D. 49; Deissmann (*B. St.* p. 87) has since discovered it in a papyrus of B.C. 252, so that the word had long been established in Egyptian Gk., though it has no place in the LXX.; even the remarkable form ἐγγαρεύειν (see *app. crit.*) finds a parallel in a papyrus of A.D. 340 which has ἐνγαρίας (Deissmann, *B. St.* p. 182). Besides this context, in which it is common to Mt., Mc., the verb is used in Mt. v. 41, where compulsory service is clearly intended.

The man's name was Simon (cf. i. 16, note), and he was of Cyrene (Mt., Mc., Lc.). Cyrene received a Jewish settlement in the time of Ptolemy I. (Jos. *c. Ap.* ii. 4; cf. 1 Macc. xv. 23), and the Jews formed an influential section of the inhabitants (Jos. *ant.* xiv. 7. 2). At Jerusalem the name of Cyrene was associated with one of the synagogues (Acts vi. 9), and Jewish inhabitants of Cyrenaica were among the worshippers at the Feast of Pentecost in the year of the Crucifixion (Acts ii. 10), whilst a Lucius of Cyrene appears among the prophets and teachers of the Church of Antioch about A.D. 48 (*ib.* xiii. 1). Whether this Simon had become a resident at Jerusalem, or was a visitor at the Passover (cf. Lc. xxiv. 18), it is impossible to decide. Mc. alone further describes

him as "the father of Alexander and Rufus." An Alexander is mentioned in Acts xix. 33, 1 Tim. i. 20, 2 Tim. iv. 14, but in each case he is an antagonist of St Paul. Rufus has with some probability been identified with the person who is saluted in Rom. xvi. 13; see SH. *ad l.*, who point out that the epithet ἐκλεκτὸν ἐν Κυρίῳ bestowed on the Roman Rufus implies eminence in the Roman Church; to his mother also, who if the identification is correct was probably the wife or widow of Simon, St Paul bears high testimony (τὴν μητέρα αὐτοῦ καὶ ἐμοῦ). If Mc. wrote for Roman Christians, and the sons of Simon were well known at Rome, his reference to Alexander and Rufus is natural enough. In any case it implies that the sons became disciples of repute whose identity would be recognised by the original readers of the Gospel. See further Zahn, *Einl.* ii. p. 251. Origen points out the practical teaching of the incident: "non autem solum Salvatorem conveniebat accipere crucem suam, sed et nos conveniebat portare eam, salutarem nobis angariam adimplentes." An early form of Docetism taught that Simon was crucified instead of Jesus (Iren. i. 24. 4).

ἵνα ἄρῃ τὸν σταυρὸν αὐτοῦ] So Mt.; the use of αἴρειν is perhaps intended to recall viii. 34 (Mt. xvi. 24); Lc. represents Simon as passive in the matter (ἐπέθηκαν αὐτῷ τὸν σταυρὸν φέρειν ὄπισθεν τοῦ ᾿Ιησοῦ).

22. φέρουσιν αὐτὸν ἐπὶ τὸν Γολγοθάν κτλ.] Mt. εἰς τόπον λεγόμενον Γολγοθά, Lc. ἐπὶ τὸν τόπον τὸν καλούμενον Κρανίον, Jo. εἰς τὸν λεγ. Κρανίου τόπον ὃ λέγεται ᾿Εβραϊστὶ Γολγοθά. The transliteration represents the Aram. גֻּלְגָּלְתָּא, = Heb. גֻּלְגֹּלֶת, translated by

φέρουσιν αὐτὸν ἐπὶ τὸν Γολγοθὰν τόπον, ὅ ἐστιν
μεθερμηνευόμενον Κρανίου τόπος.

²³Καὶ ἐδίδουν αὐτῷ¶ ἐσμυρνισμένον οἶνον, ὃς δὲ 23 ¶ Ν

22 φερουσιν] αγουσιν D 13 69 846 2ᵖᵉ latt^{exck} (perducunt, adducunt, duxerunt) |
Γολγοθαν אBFGK(L)MNSUVΓΔ min^{satmu}] Γολγοθα AC*DEHPXII min^{satmu} | om
τοπον א* c | μεθερμηνευομενος ABNΣ   23 εδιδουν αυτω] διδουσιν αυτω (Ψ) 2ᵖᵉ+πιειν
AC²D (πειν) PXΓΠΣ min^{omn} c ff k vg syrr^{peshhclhier} the go aeth | ος δε אBΓ*ᵛⁱᵈ Σ 33]
ο δε ACLPXΓ¹²ΔΠΨ min^{fereomn} και D 1 ff k n vg+γευσαμενος G 1

κρανίον in Jud. ix. 53, 4 Regn. ix.
35 ; for the form Γολγοθάν (Mc. only),
cf. Βηθσαιδάν vi. 45, viii. 22 (WH.,
Notes, p. 160, WSchm., p. 63 f.). Κρανίου τόπος (Vg. *calvariae locus*, whence
the 'Calvary' of the English versions
in Lc.) answers precisely to Γολγ.
τόπος, and enabled the Greek reader
to picture to himself the low skull-
shaped mound (see Meyer-Weiss on
Mt. xxvii. 32) where crucifixions were
wont to take place. A curious legend
connected the *calvariae locus* with the
burial place of Adam's skull, and with
the saying in Eph. v. 14; see Jerome
on Mt. xxvii., who wisely remarks :
" favorabilis interpretatio...nec tamen
vera." The place seems to have been
known in the fourth century (Eus.
onom. ὃς καὶ δείκνυται ἐν Αἰλίᾳ πρὸς
τοῖς Βορείοις τοῦ Σιὼν ὄρους. Cyril.
Hier. *cat.* xiii. ὁ Γολγοθᾶς...μέχρι σήμερον φαινόμενος. Silv. *peregr.* p. 54
"in ecclesia maiore quae appellatur
Martyrio quae est in Golgotha").
From Jo. we learn that, though outside the walls (*v.* 20, note), it was
near the city (Jo. xix. 20), apparently
among the gardens or paradises of the
wealthier inhabitants (*ib.* 41). It seems
to have been ascertained that the
present Church of the Holy Sepulchre
is beyond the second of the ancient
walls (*Encycl. Bibl.* ii. 1753, 2430).
But a knoll near *Jeremiah's Grotto*
and the road to Damascus is by some
recent investigators regarded as the
true site, and the question as a whole
is still *sub iudice* ; for a brief discussion of the various theories see Smith

B.D.² p. 1655. On ὅ ἐστιν μεθ. see
v. 41, note. Mc.'s φέρουσιν has been
thought to imply that the Lord
needed support; cf. i. 32, ii. 3, and
contrast Heb. i. 3. But the word may
mean simply to lead, as a prisoner
to execution or a victim to the sacrifice : cf. Jo. xxi. 18, Acts xiv. 13.

23—32.   THE CRUCIFIXION AND
FIRST THREE HOURS ON THE CROSS
(Mt. xxvii. 34—44, Lc. xxiii. 33ᵇ—43,
Jo. xix. 18—26).

23.   καὶ ἐδίδουν αὐτῷ κτλ.] The
'conative imperfect' (Burton, § 23)
prepares the reader for the refusal by
which the offer was met; Mt., less
precisely, ἔδωκαν. A draught of οἶνος
ἐσμυρνισμένος (Vg. *murratum vinum*), wine drugged with myrrh, was
usually offered to condemned male-
factors (J. Lightfoot on Mt. xxvii. 34,
Wünsche, p. 354; cf. *Sanhedr.* 43. 1),
through the charity, it is said, of the
women of Jerusalem (cf. Lc. xxiii.
27 ff.), the intention being to deaden
the sense of pain : cf. Prov. xxiv. 74
=xxxi. 6 δίδοτε μέθην τοῖς ἐν λύπαις,
καὶ οἶνον πίνειν τοῖς ἐν ὀδύναις. Mt.
describes the potion as οἶνον μετὰ
χολῆς μεμιγμένον, perhaps with a mental reference to Ps. lxviii. (lxix.) 22,
Lam. iii. 15 ; as Cyril (*cat.* xiii. 29)
points out, gall and myrrh possess a
common property (χολώδης δὲ καὶ
κατάπικρος ἡ σμύρνα), and Mt. with
the prophecy in view may have described the myrrh as χολή. Ps. Peter
(c. 5) confuses this draught of drugged
wine which was refused with the
posca (*infra, v.* 36) which was accepted,

24 οὐκ ἔλαβεν.　²⁴καὶ σταυροῦσιν αὐτὸν καὶ διαμερίζονται τὰ ἱμάτια αὐτοῦ, βάλλοντες κλῆρον ἐπ᾽ αὐτὰ

24 σταυρουσιν BLΨ c d ff h arm aegg aeth] σταυρωσαντες (om και 2°) ℵACDPX
ΓΔΠΣ min^{omn vid} n vg syrr^{peshhcl(txt)} go | διεμεριζοντο (vel -σαντο) vel -σαν Σ 69 124
604 1071 al^{nonn} (k) syrr arm | βαλοντες KLMV min^{nonn}

and mistakes the purpose of both
offers. On the other hand Burgon-
Miller, *Traditional Text*, p. 253, with
equal improbability regard the οἶνον
(or ὄξος, as they read) μ. χ. as distinct
from the οἶνον ἐσμ. The answer of
Macarius Magnes (ii. 17) to a pagan
objector indicates the true line of
defence for the Christian apologist in
such cases : ἄλλος ἄλλως εἰπόντες [οἱ
εὐαγγελισταὶ] τὴν ἱστορίαν οὐκ ἔφθειραν.
Σμυρνίζειν, 'to drug with myrrh,'
appears to be ἅπ. λεγ. ; the verb
occurs elsewhere as an intrans., 'to
resemble myrrh.' On the use of aro-
matic wines see Pliny, *H. N.* xiv. 15,
19. The Lord tasted the mixture
(Mt.), but declined to drink it ; He
had need of the full use of His human
faculties, and the pain which was
before Him belonged to the cup
which the Father's Will had appointed (xiv. 36 ff.), of which He
would abate nothing. For ὃς δέ without a preceding ὃς μέν, cf. Jo. v. 11,
and see *app. crit.*

24. καὶ σταυροῦσιν αὐτόν] Mc.
keeps the realistic present through
nearly the whole of this context
(20 ἐξάγουσιν, 21 ἀγγαρεύουσιν, 22
φέρουσιν, 24 διαμερίζονται, 24, 27 σταυροῦσιν). The process of crucifixion is
sufficiently described in the Bible
Dictionaries *s. vv. cross, crucifixion*,
which may also be consulted for the
bibliography of the subject. The
Lord's Hands were nailed to the
patibulum (Jo. xx. 20, 25, *Ev. Petr.*
6) ; whether the Feet were also nailed
does not appear, though Christian
writers from Justin (*dial.* 97) downwards have affirmed it, influenced
perhaps by Ps. xxi. (xxii.) 17. The

work was done by the soldiers on
duty (Jo. xix. 23), but the guilt lay at
the door of the Jewish people (Acts
ii. 23 διὰ χειρὸς ἀνόμων προσπήξαντες
ἀνείλατε, *ib.* 36 ὃν ὑμεῖς ἐσταυρώσατε,
cf. 1 Thess. ii. 15, Apoc. i. 7).

καὶ διαμερίζονται τὰ ἱμάτια αὐτοῦ
κτλ.] The Lord's clothing, which had
been removed before crucifixion (cf.
Col. ii. 15), is now divided by the
quaternion of soldiers on duty (Jo.
xix. 23 ἐποίησαν τέσσαρα μέρη, ἑκάστῳ
στρατιώτῃ μέρος); for the woven seam-
less χιτών (ἄραφος...ὑφαντός) they cast
lots. St John, who was an eyewitness,
recollects the exact procedure, and,
whether consciously or not, corrects
the impression which the Synoptists
convey, that the whole was distributed
by lot ; the Fourth Gospel also alone
supplies the reference to Ps. xxi.
(xxii.) 19, which must have been in
the minds of all ; the words received
a striking fulfilment at the death of
the Son of David, whatever may
have been their primary meaning (cf.
Cheyne, *Bk. of Psalms*, p. 64). Ps.
Peter draws a remarkable picture of
the scene : τεθεικότες τὰ ἐνδύματα ἔμπροσθεν αὐτοῦ διεμερίσαντο, καὶ λαχμὸν
ἔβαλον ἐπ᾽ αὐτοῖς. The lot was perhaps
cast with dice which they had brought
to pass the time ; the game known as
πλειστοβολίνδα may be intended, cf.
D. Heinsii *exerc. ad Nonn. paraphr.*
p. 507. Ἐπ᾽ αὐτά, cf. ἐπὶ τὸν ἱματισ-
μόν, Ps. xxi. *l.c.* ; the clothing was
the object to which the lottery was
directed (WM., p. 508; cf. v. 21, vi.
34, x. 11). Τίς τί ἄρῃ, Vg. *quis quid*
tolleret, a blending of two interrogative sentences (τίς ἄρῃ; τί ἄρῃ;)
familiar in class. Gk., but rare in the

τίς τί ἄρη. ²⁵ἦν δὲ ὥρα τρίτη καὶ ἐσταύρωσαν 25
αὐτόν. ²⁶καὶ ἦν ἡ ἐπιγραφὴ τῆς αἰτίας αὐτοῦ 26
ἐπιγεγραμμένη 'Ο βασιλεὺς τῶν 'Ιουδαίων. ²⁷καὶ 27

24 om τις τι αρη D min^Perpauc k n syr^sin   25 ωρα τριτη (ωρα γ̄ D τρ. ωρα
AC*KΠ* min^pauc)] ωρα εκτη k^scr2 syr^hcl(mg) aeth | και] οτε 13 69 124 346 556 1071
syr^pesh | εσταυρωσαν] εφυλασσον D ff k n r   26 γεγραμμενη Ψ | ο βασιλευς] pr
ουτος εστιν D (33) syr^sin pesh go pr *hic est Iesus* c+ουτος 33 1071

N.T.; cf. Lc. xix. 15 in cod. A (ἵνα
γνῷ τίς τί διεπραγματεύσατο) and see
Blass, *Gr.* p. 173, Field, *Notes*, p. 43 f.
25. ἦν δὲ ὥρα τρίτη καί κτλ.] 'Now
it was the third hour when they
crucified him'—a note of time in
which ἐσταύρωσαν looks back to σταυροῦσιν (v. 24), and καί coordinates
(Blass, *Gr.* p. 262; cf. *app. crit.*) the
arrival of the hour with the act. This
mention of the third hour is peculiar
to Mc., and appears to be inconsistent
with Jo. xix. 14. Attempts were early
made to remove the difficulty either
by changing τρίτη into ἕκτη (cf. *Acta
Pil. ap.* Tisch. *Ev. apocr.* 283 f.: ἀνε-
βίβασαν αὐτὸν καὶ ἐκάρφωσαν ἐν τῷ
σταυρῷ ὥρᾳ ἕκτη: Ps. Hier. *brev. in
Ps.* lxxvii., who suggests that τρίτη
has arisen out of a confusion between
F̄ and Γ̄), or by less satisfactory
methods (cf. e.g. Aug. *cons. ev.* iii. 42
"intelligitur ergo fuisse hora tertia
cum clamaverunt Judaei ut Dominus
crucifigeretur, et veracissime demonstratur tunc eos crucifixisse quando
clamaverunt"). The problem cannot
be said to have been solved yet; Bp.
Westcott's contention that St John
followed the modern Western reckoning, so that his ὥρα ἕκτη=6 a.m., has
been considerably shaken by recent
research (see Prof. Ramsay in *Exp.*
IV. vii. p. 216, v. iii. p. 457, and cf.
A. Wright, *N. T. problems*, p. 147 ff.).
It may be noticed that while Jo. is
perhaps intentionally vague (ὡς ἕκτη),
Mc. is precise. In Jerusalem there
could be no uncertainty about the
principal divisions of the day (cf. Acts
ii. 15, iii. 1), even if the intermediate
hours were not strictly noted.

26. καὶ ἦν ἡ ἐπιγραφή κτλ.] Another
detail which Mc. stops to note. The
cross bore an inscription (ἐπιγραφή,
xii. 16), setting forth the charge on
which the Crucified had been condemned (for αἰτία, Vg. *causa*, cf.
Ar. *Ach.* 285 f. XO. σὲ μὲν οὖν κατα-
λεύσομεν... ΔΙ. ἀντὶ ποίας αἰτίας; and
Acts xiii. 28, xxv. 18). The technical
name for this record was *titulus* (τίτλος, Jo.): the board (σανίς) on which
it was written was carried before the
criminal or affixed to him (Suet.
Calig. 32 "praecedente titulo qui
causam paenae indicaret"). Other
examples of *tituli* remain; e.g. Suetonius (*Domit.* 10) mentions a sufferer
who bore the inscription IMPIE ·
LOCVTVS, and the Viennese letter in
Eus. *H. E.* v. 1 speaks of a martyr
who was preceded in the amphitheatre
by a board on which was apparently
inscribed HIC · EST · ATTALVS · CHRES-
TIANVS (πίνακος αὐτὸν προάγοντος ἐν ᾧ
ἐγέγραπτο 'Ρωμαιστί Οὗτός ἐστιν "Αττα-
λος ὁ Χριστιανός). The title on the
Lord's cross was written by Pilate in
Aramaic and Greek, as well as in
the official Latin (Jo.), so as to be
intelligible to all Jews—Hellenists
from the provinces as well as any
Palestinians who were not bilingual.
The text of the inscription as given
by the Evangelists varies remarkably
(ὁ βασιλεὺς τῶν 'Ιουδαίων (Mc.), ὁ β. τ.
'Ι. οὗτος (Lc.), οὗτός ἐστιν 'Ιησοῦς ὁ β.
τ. 'Ι. (Mt.), 'Ιησοῦς ὁ Ναζωραῖος ὁ β.
τ. 'Ι. (Jo.). The words ὁ βασιλεὺς
τῶν 'Ιουδαίων, on which all agree, form
the αἰτία; it was usual to prefix the
name, and we may accept the evidence
of St John, who saw the *titulus*,

§ ꓶ   σὺν αὐτῷ σταυροῦσιν δύο λῃστάς, §ἕνα ἐκ δεξιῶν καὶ
29 ἕνα ἐξ εὐωνύμων αὐτοῦ. ²⁹καὶ οἱ παραπορευόμενοι
ἐβλασφήμουν αὐτὸν κινοῦντες τὰς κεφαλὰς αὐτῶν καὶ

27 συν αυτω σταυρουσιν δυο λῃστας] συνσταυρουσιν δ. λ. Δ συν αυτω εσταυρωσαν δ.
λ. B c d ff k n syrᵖᵉˢʰ go συν αυτω σταυρουνται β̄ λῃσται D* (λῃστας Dᶜᵒʳʳ) | αυτου] om
C³D 1 2ᵖᵉ 7ᵖᵉ alᵖᵃᵘᶜ c ff k n + (28) και επληρωθη η γραφη η λεγουσα και μετα των ανομων
ελογισθη EFG(H)KLMPSU(V)ΓΔΠΣꓶ¹² 13 69 604 alᵖˡ ff n r vg syrrᵖᵉˢʰ ʰᵉˡ ʰⁱᵉʳ arm (me)
go aeth (om אABC*·³DXΨ minˢᵃᵗᵐᵘ k syrˢⁱⁿ the)   29 παραπορευομενοι] παραγοντες
E Eus

that the local designation was added.
The Latin text therefore may probably have been—with or without a
preliminary *hic est*—IESVS · NAZA-
RENVS · REX · IVDAEORVM. In the last
two words the grim irony of Pilate is
apparent ; Ps. Peter misses their
point by representing the inscription
as the work of the Jews, and reading
Οὗτός ἐστιν ὁ βασιλεὺς τοῦ Ἰσραήλ
(see *v.* 2, note).

27. καὶ σὺν αὐτῷ σταυροῦσιν κτλ.]
The two had been His companions on
the way to Golgotha (Lc.), and were
now hanging one on either side of
Him (Jo. ἐσταύρωσαν...ἄλλους δύο,
ἐντεῦθεν καὶ ἐντεῦθεν, μέσον δὲ τὸν
Ἰησοῦν) ; to St John the spectacle
may well have recalled words spoken
by Jesus not many weeks before (Mc. x.
37 ff.). Viewed in the light of Luke's
narrative (xxiii. 39 ff.) it reminds
the reader also of Mt. xxv. 39 ; the
Cross which divides the penitent from
the obdurate anticipates the θρόνος
δόξης. Λῃστάς, so Mt. ; Lc., κακούρ-
γους. They were outlaws and doubtless desperate men (cf. xi. 17, xiv. 48,
Lc. x. 30, Jo. x. 1, 2 Cor. xi. 26) ;
possibly they had been members of
the band led by Barabbas (Trench,
Studies, p. 293). Yet the λῃστής
might be of very different moral
calibre from the κλέπτης—one who
had been driven into crime by the
circumstances of his life or of the
times. It may be assumed that this
was so in the case of the penitent.
Nearness to Christ (ὁ ἐγγύς μου ἐγγὺς

τοῦ πυρός) revealed his latent capacity
for a nobler life as well as the malignity of his comrade. The secondary
uncials (see *app. crit.*) add a reference
to Isa. liii. 12, borrowed perhaps from
Lc. xxii. 37, which Burgon-Miller
(*Causes of Corruption,* p. 75 ff.)
vigorously defend ; but see WH.,
Notes, p. 27. As Alford points out,
it is not after Mc.'s manner to ad-
duce prophetic testimony. A curious
gloss in the O. L. ms. *c* supplies the
names of the λῃσταί : "unum a dextris
nomine Zoathan et alium a sinistris
nomine Chammatha." In the Acts of
Pilate (ed. Tisch.² pp. 245, 308) they
are *Dysmas* and *Gestas*, in the Arabic
Gospel of the Infancy (p. 184), *Titus*
and *Dumachus* (Θεομάχος), while *l*
gives *Ioathas* and *Maggatras*; see
Thilo, *cod. apocr. N. T.* i. pp. 143,
580, Wordsworth and White *ad l.*
and on Lc. xxiii. 32, and cf. Nestle,
T. C. p. 266.

29. καὶ οἱ παραπορευόμενοι κτλ.]
Either country folk on their way to
the city (cf. *v.* 21), or citizens whose
business called them into the country
(Lc. xxiv. 13). Neither class would
have much knowledge of Jesus beyond
hearsay, and common report credited
him with dangerous fanaticism. Οἱ
παραπορευόμενοι, הָעֹבְרִים, cf. Isa. li. 23,
Thren. ii. 15 πάντες οἱ παραπ. ὁδόν...
ἐκίνησαν τὴν κεφαλὴν αὐτῶν : the
Evangelists seem to have specially in
view Ps. xxi. (xxii.) 8 πάντες οἱ θεω-
ροῦντές με ἐξεμυκτήρισάν με (cf. Lc.),
ἐλάλησαν ἐν χείλεσιν, ἐκίνησαν κεφαλήν.

λέγοντες Οὐὰ ὁ καταλύων τὸν ναὸν καὶ οἰκοδομῶν ἐν τρισὶν ἡμέραις, ³⁰σῶσον σεαυτὸν καταβὰς ἀπὸ τοῦ 30 σταυροῦ. ³¹ὁμοίως καὶ οἱ ἀρχιερεῖς ἐμπαίζοντες 31 πρὸς ἀλλήλους μετὰ τῶν γραμματέων ἔλεγον ''Ἄλλους ἔσωσεν, ἑαυτὸν οὐ δύναται σῶσαι· ³²ὁ χριστὸς ὁ 32 βασιλεὺς Ἰσραὴλ καταβάτω νῦν ἀπὸ τοῦ σταυροῦ,

29 ουα (ουαι minᵖᵃᵘᶜ Eus)] om ℵᶜ·ᵃL*ΔΨ d k | om εν ADPV minᵖᵉʳᵐᵘ 30 καταβας ℵBDLΔΨ k l n vg me] και καταβα (-βηθι) AC(P)ΧΓΠΣ minᵖˡ 31 ομοιως] om D 238 c ff k n + δε C³M² alᵐᵘ the | προς αλληλους (εις αλλ. D 2ᵖᵉ Eus)] om 13 28 69 alᵖᵃᵘᶜ c k 32 ο χριστος] pr ει 1071 | Ισραηλ] pr του ACPΧΓΣ minᵖˡ aegg Eus + εστιν 1071 | καταβα L

Ἐβλασφήμουν...κινοῦντες τὰς κεφ.: they spared neither words nor gestures of derision; cf. (besides the passages cited above) 4 Regn. xix. 21, Job xvi. 5, Sir. xiii. 7.

οὐὰ ὁ καταλύων κτλ.] Οὐά, va, vah, expresses admiration, real or ironical, not, as οὐαί, commiseration; e.g. οὐὰ Αὔγουστε (Dio Cass.), ἐπαίνεσόν με, εἰπέ μοι Οὐὰ καὶ Θαυμαστῶς (Arrian), 'vah homo impudens' (Plaut.). On ὁ καταλύων κτλ. see xiv. 58, note: with the construction cf. Lc. vi. 25 οὐαὶ ὑμῖν οἱ ἐμπεπλησμένοι, Apoc. xviii. 10, 16 οὐαὶ οὐαὶ ἡ πόλις ἡ μεγάλη...ἡ περιβεβλημένη. Σῶσον σεαυτόν: in Mt. the ground of this raillery appears (εἰ υἱὸς εἶ τοῦ θεοῦ); the Sanhedrists had spread the report of the Lord's answer to the question of Caiaphas (xiv. 61 f.). The jest was the harder to endure since it appealed to a consciousness of power held back only by the self-restraint of a sacrificed will. Hilary: "non erat difficile de cruce descendere, sed sacramentum erat paternae voluntatis explendum."

31. ὁμοίως καὶ οἱ ἀρχιερεῖς κτλ.] The Sanhedrists condescended to share the savage sport of the populace; members of the priestly aristocracy were seen in company with scribes and elders (Mt.) deriding the Sufferer, not indeed directly addressing Him, or mingling with the crowd, but remarking to one another (πρὸς ἀλλήλους) on His in-

ability to save Himself. Ἔσωσεν... σῶσαι: the verb is used in two shades of meaning: 'He saved others from disease, He cannot save Himself from dying'; or with Justin we may understand ἔσωσεν in reference to Lazarus (ap. i. 38 ὁ νεκροὺς ἀνεγείρας ῥυσάσθω ἑαυτόν). Even in the act of mocking, they bear witness to the truth of His miraculous powers. The Lord had not claimed the character of a σωτήρ, as His frequent saying ἡ πίστις σου σέσωκέν σε shews; but the fact that His touch or word gave new life to men was nevertheless notorious. It could not be denied, though it might be discredited or used against Him.

32. ὁ χριστὸς ὁ βασιλεύς κτλ.] Mt. βασ. Ἰσραήλ ἐστιν· καταβάτω κτλ., Lc. εἰ οὗτός ἐστιν ὁ χριστὸς τοῦ θεοῦ ὁ ἐκλεκτός. Unable to induce Pilate to remove or alter the τίτλος, they give their own complexion to it, substituting Ἰσραήλ for τῶν Ἰουδαίων, and explaining ὁ βασ. by ὁ χριστός, or ὁ ἐκλεκτός. If He will even now (νῦν) substantiate His claim of Messiahship by a miracle wrought in His own behalf, they profess themselves ready to believe (Mt. καὶ πιστεύσομεν ἐπ' αὐτόν; with Mc.'s ἵνα ἴδ. καὶ πιστ. cf. Jo. iv. 48, vi. 30); to which Jerome well replies: "resurrexit et non credidistis; ergo si etiam de cruce descenderet, similiter non crederetis."

¶ syr^{hier} ἵνα ἴδωμεν καὶ πιστεύσωμεν.¶ καὶ οἱ συνεσταυ-
¶ r
¶ the ρωμένοι σὺν¶ αὐτῷ¶ ὠνείδιζον αὐτόν.

§ i 33   ³³Καὶ γενομένης ὥρας ἕκτης §σκότος ἐγένετο ἐφ'

32 πιστευσωμεν] + αυτω C³DFGHM*PV²ΓΠ²Σ min^{satmu} c ff k l n syr^{pesh} arm
the aeth Eus | συν αυτω] om συν ΑCΡΧΓΔΠΣ min^{omn vid} (hab אBL) μετ αυτου Ψ om D
33 και γεν.] γεν. δε ΑCEFHKUVXΓΠ min^{pl} | εφ ολης της γης D min^{perpauc} Eus
om syr^{sin}

In Mt. they proceed with strange obtuseness to quote Ps. xxii. 8 (cf. Edersheim, *Life*, ii. p. 718). καὶ οἱ συνεσταυρωμένοι κτλ.] So Mt.; Lc. εἶς δὲ τῶν κρεμασθέντων κακούργων ἐβλασφήμει αὐτόν. The traditions are distinct but not inconsistent; the pl. in Mt. Mc. is used with sufficient accuracy if one of the two spoke, at least for the time, on behalf of both (cf. Mt. viii. 28 ff., xx. 30 ff., with the corresponding accounts in Mc., Lc.). Lc.'s fuller statement explains ὠνείδιζον: in the mouth of the λῃστής the raillery which he had borrowed from the crowd became a reproach ; the Lord professed to have power to save His fellow-sufferers as well as Himself (σεαυτὸν καὶ ἡμᾶς), and would not use it.

It is interesting to note that συνσταυροῦσθαι, used of the λῃσταί by Mt. Mc. Jo., is applied by St Paul (Rom. vi. 6, Gal. ii. 20) to the sharing of the Cross by the members of Christ in Baptism.

33—37. THE LAST THREE HOURS ON THE CROSS (Mt. xxvii. 45—50, Lc. xxiii. 44—45ᵃ, 46, Jo. xix. 28—30). 33. γενομένης ὥρας ἕκτης κτλ.] Lc. ἦν ἤδη ὡσεὶ ὥρα ἕκτη, but the use of ὡσεί with numerals is characteristic of the Third Gospel and the Acts (cf. Lc. iii. 23, ix. 14, 28, xxii. 59, Acts i. 15, ii. 41, x. 3, xix. 7). Mt., like Mc., speaks definitely (ἀπὸ ἕκτης ὥρας); cf. Ἐυ. Petr. 5 ἦν δὲ μεσημβρία. Ps. Peter is doubtless right in interpreting ὅλην τὴν γῆν as Judaea (σκότος κατέσχε πᾶσαν τὴν Ἰουδαίαν; cf. Origen,

"tantummodo super omnem terram Judaeam"). Though the phrase is usually employed in a wider sense (cf. e.g. Gen. i. 26, xi. 9, Ps. xxxii. (xxxiii.) 8, Lc. xxi. 35, Apoc. xiii. 3), the compilers of the original tradition had probably in view the limited darkness of Exod. x. 22 (ἐγένετο σκότος...ἐπὶ πᾶσαν γῆν Αἰγύπτου τρεῖς ἡμέρας), and in adopting the words thought only of the land of Israel. Lc. explains that the darkness which fell on the land at the Crucifixion was due to a failure of the sun's light (ἐκλείποντος τοῦ ἡλίου); in *Acta Pilati* (ed. Tisch., p. 234), the Jews, in defiance of astronomy, attribute it to an ordinary eclipse (ἔκλειψις τοῦ ἡλίου γέγονεν κατὰ τὸ εἰωθός)—an event which, as Origen points out, could not have occurred at the time of the Paschal full moon. On the obscuration of the sun's light mentioned by Phlegon see Orig. *in Mt.*, *c. Cels.* ii. 33. Irenaeus (iv. 33. 12) refers to Amos viii. 9 (δύσεται ὁ ἥλιος μεσημβρίας); acc. to Ps. Peter, men went about with lamps, supposing that the sun had set and it was already night. The original account (Mt. Mc.) seems to be satisfied by the hypothesis of an extraordinary gloom due to natural causes and coinciding with the last three hours of the Passion. The purpose of the darkness was variously explained by the Gk. and Latin fathers ; cf. Cyril. Hier.: ἐξέλιπεν ὁ ἥλιος διὰ τὸν τῆς δικαιοσύνης ἥλιον: Jerome: "videtur mihi clarissimum lumen mundi...retraxisse radios ne... pendentem videret Dominum"; Leo:

ὅλην τὴν γῆν ἕως ὥρας §ἐνάτης. ³⁴καὶ τῇ ἐνάτῃ ὥρᾳ 34 § N
ἐβόησεν ὁ Ἰησοῦς φωνῇ μεγάλη Ἐλωί ἐλωί λαμὰ
σαβαχθανεί; ὅ ἐστιν μεθερμηνευόμενον Ὁ θεός μου
ὁ θεός μου, εἰς τί ἐγκατέλιπές με; ³⁵καί τινες τῶν 35

34 τη εν. ωρα אBDFLΨ 1 69 1071 al^pauc] τη ωρα τη εν. ACPXΓΔII al min^pl |
εβοησεν] ανεβοησεν MN min^pauc εφωνησεν D | om ο Ιησους D k syr^sin | φωνη μεγ.]
+λεγων ACNPXΓΔIIΣ min^pl vg syrr^pesh hcl arm go (om λ. אBDLΨ 604 2^pe al^pauc
ff k n syr^sin me) | ελωι bis] ηλει bis D 2^pe 131 c d i k n (heli) arm Eus (cf. syr^pesh) |
λαμα BDΣ 1 ff (i) n] λεμα אCLΔΨ⁻ λιμα (λειμα) A(EFGH)KMP(S)U(V)XΓII min^mu
λαμμα min^pauc ϛ | σαβαχθανει (-νι) א° (σαβακτ. א*) (A)C(EF)GHKLMN(P)UV(Γ)ΔIIΣ
min^pl ζαβαχθανει B (⁻vid i) ζαφθανει D zaphtani d zaphani k | ο θεος μου bis
אCDHLMSUVΣ min^permu c ff k n vg syrr arm me go aeth] ο θεος μου semel B ο θεος
ο θεος μου AEFGKPΓΔII⁻ min^sat mu Eus | εγκατελιπες (ενκ. APΔΣ -λειπες EGLII*⁻
-λειπας K^min pauc) με] με εγκατελ. (A)CN(P)XΓ(Δ)II min^pl ωνειδισας με D c (exprobrasti me)
i (me in opprobrium dedisti) k (me maledixisti : cf. J. Th. St. i. p. 278 ff.) Mac Magn
(i 12)   35 om και...ακουσαντες Δ om ακουσαντες C

"in vos, Iudaei, caelum et terra
sententiam tulit"; Victor : γέγονεν
ὅπερ ἤτουν τὸν Ἰησοῦν ἐξ οὐρανοῦ
σημεῖον.

34. τῇ ἐνάτῃ ὥρᾳ ἐβόησεν ὁ Ἰ. κτλ.]
The only word uttered on the Cross
which finds a place in the earliest
tradition as given by Mt. Mc.: for
the other six recorded words see
Lc. xxiii. 34 (WH., Notes, p. 67 f.),
43, 46; Jo. xix. 26, 28, 30. The
present word shares with the final
one (v. 37, Lc. xxiii. 46) the distinction of having been spoken in a loud
voice—a cry or shout (ἐβόησεν) rather
than, like our Lord's ordinary sayings
(cf. Mt. xii. 19), a calm and deliberate utterance. The cry is given by
both Gospels in the transliterated form
ἐλωί ἐλωί λαμὰ (Mt. λεμὰ) σαβαχθανεί
=שְׁבַקְתָּנִי לְמָא אֱלָהִי אֱלָהִי (where
the Hebrew vocalization of the first
word has taken the place of the pure
Aramaic אֱלָהִי, Dalman, Gr. p. 123,
n., Worte i. p. 42 f., Kautzsch, p.
11, n.), answering to the Heb. of Ps.
xxii. 1 (אֵלִי אֵלִי לְמָה עֲזַבְתָּנִי) : for the
root שְׁבַק, Syr. ܫܒܩ, see Dan. iv.
12, 20, 25, where it is rendered by
ἀφιέναι (LXX.), ἐᾶν (Th.). On the form

which cod. D substitutes for σαβαχθανεί and the rendering ὠνείδισάς
με, see the next note. Both Mt.
and Mc. append a version which is
practically that of the LXX. (ὁ θεός
μου ὁ θεός μου...ἵνα τί ἐγκατέλιπές με;),
but omit the words πρόσχες μοι which
have nothing corresponding to them
in the M. T. and apparently were
not represented in the Heb. text
of our Lord's time (Jerome ad l.:
"intende mihi in hebraeis codicibus
non habetur et adpositum vox Domini
declarat quae illud etiam in evangelio
praetermisit"; in Hexaplaric mss.
the words are obelised, cf. Field,
Hexapla, ad l.). The remarkable
rendering in Ev. Petr. (ἡ δύναμίς
μου ἡ δύναμις κατελειψάς με) seems
to presuppose the 'Western' reading
ἠλεί ἠλεί, and to treat אֵל as=חַיִל
(BDB., p. 43); cf. Aq. ἰσχυρέ μου ἰσχ.
μου with the remarks of Eusebius,
d. e., p. 494.

35. καί τινες τῶν ἑστηκότων κτλ.]
The remark was probably meant
for banter, cf. v. 31 f. On the connexion in Jewish thought of Elijah
with the Messiah see vi. 15, viii.
28, ix. 11 f., notes; Elijah was moreover regarded as a deliverer in time

¶ P ἑστηκότων ἀκούσαντες ἔλεγον ῎Ιδε ᾿Ηλείαν φωνεῖ.¶
36 ³⁶δραμὼν δέ τις γεμίσας σπόγγον ὄξους περιθεὶς

35 εστηκοτων B] εκει εστηκοτων A παρεστωτων אDV 33 2ᵖᵉ alⁿᵒⁿⁿ παρεστηκοτων
CLNPΠΣΨ minᵖˡ | ιδε (ειδε) אBFLUΔΨ 13 33 69 (1071) alᵖᵃᵘᶜ] ιδου AEGHMNPSVΓΣ⁷
minᵖˡ οτι ιδου KII minᵖᵃᵘᶜ οτι C 2ᵖᵉ minᵖᵃᵘᶜ syrˢⁱⁿ armᶻᵒʰ om D 604 c k syrᵖᵉˢʰ armᶜᵒᵈ
Eus | φωνει]+ ουτος D c ff   36 δραμων δε...λεγων] και δραμοντες εγεμισαν σπ. οξ.
και περιθεντες καλ. εποτιζον αυτ. λεγοντες 13 69 124 346 | τις אBLΔΨ] εις ACDNPΓΣ
minᵒᵐⁿ ᵛⁱᵈ latt go+και אACDNPΓΔΠΣ⁷ minᵒᵐⁿ ᵛⁱᵈ (om BLΨ c) | γεμισας] πλησας D
604 2ᵖᵉ | περιθεις] επιθεις D+τε ACPXΓΔΠΣ minᵖˡ pr και 1 (69) alᵖᵃᵘᶜ (om אBDLΨ
33 67 1071 2ᵖᵉ me go)

of trouble, cf. Wünsche, p. 356. It would seem that the word which was taken for an invocation of Elijah (אֱלִיָּהוּ, אֵלִיָּה) must have been אֵלִי, not אֱלֹהִי or אֱלָהִי, and this consideration has led Resch (*Paralleltexte*, p. 357 f.; but cf. Dalman, *Worte*, i. p. 43) to the conclusion that the Lord cited the words of the Psalm in Heb., and that the remarkable form ζαφθανεί in cod. D represents the Heb. עֲזַבְתַּנִי ; cf. Chase, *Syro-Latin Text*, p. 106 f., who suggests ܚܣܕܬܢܝ for which he thinks D's ὠνείδισάς με may be an equivalent. The problem is discussed further by König and Nestle in *Exp. T*. xi. pp. 237 f., 287 f., 334 ff., but with no assured result. It is remarkable that in Macarius Magnes the objector knew both ὠνείδισας and ἐγκατέλιπες and regarded them as distinct utterances: ὁ δέ...ἵνα τί με ἐγκατέλιπες; ὁ δέ...εἰς τί ὠνείδισάς με; In Mt. the T. R. reads ἠλί while retaining σαβαχθανί ; cf. Epiph. *haer*. lxix. 68 cited by Resch: λέγων 'ἠλί ἠλί' ᾿Εβραικῇ τῇ λέξει...καὶ οὐκέτι ᾿Εβραικῇ ἀλλὰ Συριακῇ διαλέκτῳ 'λημὰ σαβαχθανί.' On ἐστηκότων see ix. 1 note.

36. δραμὼν δέ κτλ.] The three accounts of this incident vary considerably; St John's, as we might expect, is the fullest and probably it is also the most exact. Near the Cross there lay a vessel full of sour wine (σκεῦος ἔκειτο ὄξους μεστόν, Jo.), the ὄξος ἐξ οἴνου of Num. vi. 1, which was the or-

dinary drink of labourers in the field (Ruth ii. 14), and of the lower class of soldiers (Plutarch, *Cato maior*, p. 336 ὕδωρ δ' ἔπινεν ἐπὶ τῆς στρατείας, πλὴν εἴποτε διψήσας περιφλεγὼς ὄξος ᾔτησεν), and known by them as *posca* (Plaut. *mil*. iii. 2. 25, *trucul*. ii. 7. 48); on this occasion it had probably been brought by the quaternion on guard, and acc. to Lc. (xxiii. 36) a drink of it had already been offered by them to Christ in derision. The Lord, who had refused the drugged wine at the beginning of His sufferings, now exclaimed 'I thirst'; upon which one of the by-standers (τις, Mc., εἷς ἐξ αὐτῶν, Mt.) ran to the wine jar, and gave Him drink. The sponge is mentioned here only in Biblical Gk., but it is mentioned by Gk. writers from Homer (*Od*. i. 111) downwards, and must have been familiar in countries bordering on the Mediterranean. The reed on which the sponge was raised (Mt., Mc.) is described by Jo. as 'hyssop,' a plant prescribed by the Law for use in certain ritual acts (Lev. xiv. 4 ff., Num. xix. 6 ff.; cf. Ps. l. (li.) 9, Heb. ix. 19 ff.). ῞Υσσωπος represents the Heb. אֵזוֹב, a wallplant, acc. to 1 Kings iv. 33, and therefore not of great size; but a stalk three or four feet in length would probably have sufficed to reach the lips of the Crucified. On the identification of the plant see the Bible Dictionaries *s.v.*, and Tristram, *N. H.*, p. 457 f., who inclines to the caper (*Capparis spi-*

καλάμῳ ἐπότιζεν αὐτόν, λέγων "Αφετε ἴδωμεν εἰ
ἔρχεται §'Ηλείας καθελεῖν αὐτόν. ³⁷ὁ δὲ 'Ιησοῦς ἀφεὶς 37 § q
φωνὴν μεγάλην ἐξέπνευσεν.¶   ¶ P

36 om εποτιζεν αυτον λεγων D | αφετε] αφες ℵDV 1 13 69 604 2ᵖᵉ alⁿᵒⁿⁿ cikⁿⁿⁱᵈ
armᶻᵒʰ go

nosa). The stem stripped of its thorns
passed for a reed, but St John, who
stood by the Cross and paid close
attention to everything (Jo. xix. 25,
35), remembered that it belonged to
the hyssop. For περιθεῖναί τινί τι, 'to
put upon,' cf. Prov. vii. 3, 1 Cor. xii. 23,
and *supra*, *v.* 17; the phrase is common here to Mt., Mc., Jo.; Vg. *cir-
cumponens calamo*. Δραμών...γεμίσας
...περιθείς, without an intervening
conjunction (see *app. crit.*), is rough
even for Mc.; yet see x. 30, xiv. 23,
67, xv. 21. 'Επότιζεν is perhaps an
allusion to Ps. lxviii. (lxix.) 22 εἰς τὴν
δίψαν μου ἐπότισάν με ὄξος : cf. Jo.
xix. 28 ἵνα τελειωθῇ ἡ γραφή.
λέγων "Αφετε κτλ.] Mt. distinctly
assigns this saying to the rest of
the party, who desire the man to
desist and wait for Elijah to intervene (οἱ δὲ λοιποὶ εἶπαν "Αφες κτλ.).
The independence of the two Evangelists at this point is significant. Archbishop Benson (*Apocalypse*, p. 146)
would detach λέγων in this context
from the subject of the verb, and
render it "one saying." But there
is no example of so loose a construction elsewhere in the Gospels, and it
is impossible to admit it here. Aug.'s
"unde intelligimus et illum et ceteros
hoc dixisse" does not touch the heart
of the difference; Mc.'s ἄφετε is a
rebuke addressed by one of the company to the rest, whilst Mt.'s ἄφες,
if it is to be pressed, inverts the situation; if Mt.'s account is to be preferred, the mockery was kept up to
the end. See however WM. p. 356 n.
for another explanation of ἄφες. Εἰ
ἔρχεται, Burton, § 251. Καθελεῖν αὐτόν
sc. ἀπὸ τοῦ σταυροῦ, cf. *v.* 46, Lc. xxiii.

53, Acts xiii. 29; Mt., σώσων αὐτόν:
on καθελεῖν as a technical word see
v. 46, note.
37. ὁ δὲ 'Ιησοῦς ἀφείς κτλ.] Mt.
πάλιν κράξας φωνῇ μεγάλῃ, with a
reference to the cry at the ninth hour
(*v.* 34). 'Αφιέναι φωνήν, *emittere vocem*;
cf. Dem. *de cor.* p. 339 ὁ κῆρυξ...
φωνὴν ἀφίησι : for φωνὴν μεγ. cf. *ib.*
c. *Eubul.* p. 537 ἐβλασφήμει κατ' ἐμοῦ
καὶ πολλὰ καὶ μεγάλῃ τῇ φωνῇ. Two
final utterances are recorded (Jo. ὅτε
οὖν ἔλαβεν τὸ ὄξος ὁ 'Ι. εἶπεν Τετέ-
λεσται : Lc., φωνήσας φωνῇ μ. ὁ 'Ι.
εἶπεν Πάτερ, εἰς χεῖράς σου παρατί-
θεμαι τὸ πνεῦμά μου); the second seems
to be especially intended by Mt., Mc.;
it was uttered in a loud voice, and
its contents connect it with the
moment of departure. Like the other
loud cry it is taken from the Psalms
(Ps. xxx. (xxxi.) 6). 'Εξέπνευσεν, so
Lc.; the aor. calls attention to the
moment of departure, contrast ἐπότιζεν, *v.* 36. The word does not occur
elsewhere in Biblical Gk.; in classical
writers it is the opposite of ἐμπνεῖν,
and used absolutely, 'to expire,' or
followed by βίον or ψυχήν. Mt. (ἀφῆκεν
τὸ πνεῦμα), Jo. (παρέδωκεν τὸ πν.) call
attention to the fact that the Death
of the Lord was a voluntary surrender,
not a submission to physical necessity;
see Westcott on Jo. xix. 30, and cf.
Orig. *in Jo.* t. xix. 16 ὡς βασιλέως
καταλείποντος τὸ σῶμα καὶ ἐνεργήσαντος
μετὰ δυνάμεως καὶ ἐξουσίας ὅπερ ἔκρινεν
εὔλογον εἶναι ποιεῖν. On Ps. Peter's
ἀνελήμφθη see note *ad l.*
38—41. EVENTS WHICH IMMEDI-
ATELY FOLLOWED THE DEATH OF JESUS
(Mt. xxvii. 51—56, Lc. xxiii. 45ᵇ, 47—
49, Jo. xix. 31—37).

38   ³⁸ Καὶ τὸ καταπέτασμα τοῦ ναοῦ ἐσχίσθη εἰς δύο

¶ F 39 ἀπ' ἄνωθεν ἕως κάτω.   ³⁹ἰδὼν δὲ ὁ κεντυρίων¶ ὁ παρε-

¶ ד   στηκὼς ἐξ ἐναντίας αὐτοῦ ὅτι¶ οὕτως ἐξέπνευσεν εἶπεν

38 το καταπ.] pr ιδου N | εις δυο]+μερη D cffikn (q)   39 ο παρεστ.] om ο ד |
εξ εναντιας αυτου] εκει D 2ᵖᵉ inq arm om minᵖᵉʳᵖᵃᵘᶜ | ουτως] + κραξας ΑϹΧΓΔΠΣ
minᵖᵉʳᵐᵘ ff nq vg syrrᵖᵉˢʰʰᶜˡ go aeth κραξας 2ᵖᵉ (syrˢⁱⁿ) arm ουτως αυτον κραξαντα και
D | εξεπνευσεν] εκραξεν kᵛⁱᵈ | om ειπεν D

38. καὶ τὸ καταπέτασμα κτλ.] There were two curtains in the ναός, the outer one, through which access was gained to the Holy Place, and the inner, which covered the entrance to the Holy of Holies (Edersheim, *Temple*, p. 35 f.). See Heb. ix. 3, where the writer, who however has the Tabernacle and not the Temple in his thoughts, speaks of the latter as τὸ δεύτερον καταπέτασμα, and cf. Philo *gig.* 12 τὸ ἐσώτατον καταπέτασμα. In the LXX. the latter is called simply τὸ καταπέτασμα Exod. xxvi. 31 ff. (Heb. פָּרֹכֶת), the other (Heb. מָסָךְ) being properly but not uniformly distinguished as τὸ κάλυμμα (see Westcott on Heb. vi. 19). The rending of the inner curtain of the Temple is reported by Mt., Mc., Lc.; Mt. seems to connect it with an earthquake which followed the Lord's Death, Lc. places it before the end; cf. Ps. Peter: αὐτῆς [τῆς] ὥρας διεράγη τὸ καταπέτασμα. The Gospel according to the Hebrews, as represented by Jerome (*in Mt.*, cf. *ad Hedib.* 120), had another version of the incident: "superliminare (cf. ἀπ' ἄνωθεν) templi infinitae magnitudinis fractum esse atque divisum." The mystical import of the rent veil is pointed out in Heb. x. 19 ff.; cf. Victor: ἵνα λοιπὸν εἴργοντος οὐδενὸς εἰς τὴν ἐσωτέραν τρέχωμεν σκηνὴν οἱ κατ' ἴχνος ἰόντες Χριστοῦ. With ἀπ' ἄνωθεν, ἕως κάτω, cf. ἀπὸ μακρόθεν, v. 6, note.

39. ἰδὼν δὲ ὁ κεντυρίων κτλ.] For *centurio* Mt. and Lc. use ἑκατόνταρχος (-χης), which was familiar through the LXX., where it answers to שַׂר הַמֵּאוֹת; Mc. prefers a Latinism already employ-

ed by Polybius (vi. 24 τοὺς δὲ ἡγεμόνας κεντυρίωνας [ἐκάλεσαν]); the word is also freely used by Ps. Peter (*ev.* 8 ff.), who like Mc. does not employ ἑκατόνταρχος. On the centurions see Marquardt, p. 357 ff. The traditional name of this centurion was Longinus (*Acta Pilati*, ed. Tisch., p. 288); the same name is also given to the soldier who pierced the side of Christ and the prefect charged with the execution of St Paul (*D.C.B.*, *s.v.*). In the fourth century Longinus the centurion was already believed to have subsequently become a saint and a martyr (Chrys. *hom. in Mt. ad l.*); but the testimony which the Gospels attribute to him is merely that of a man who was able to rise above the prejudices of the crowd and the thoughtless brutality of the soldiers, and to recognise in Jesus an innocent man (Lc.), or possibly a supernatural person (Mt., Mc.). Υἱὸς θεοῦ is certainly more than δίκαιος, but the centurion, who borrowed the words from the Jewish Priests (Mt. xxvii. 41 ff.), could scarcely have understood them even in the Messianic sense; his idea is perhaps analogous to that ascribed to Nebuchadnezzar in Dan. iii. 25, where בַּר־אֱלָהִין is an extraordinary, superhuman, being. This impression was produced on the centurion when he saw the Lord expire as He did (ἰδὼν ὅτι οὕτως ἐξέπνευσεν, cf. Origen: "miratus est in his quae dicta fuerant ab eo ad Deum cum clamore et magnitudine sensuum"), or (Mt.) when he saw the earthquake and other occurrences (τὰ γινόμενα), or (Lc.) reflected on the whole trans-

Ἀληθῶς οὗτος ὁ ἄνθρωπος υἱὸς θεοῦ ἦν.   ⁴⁰ἦσαν δὲ 40
καὶ γυναῖκες⁋ ἀπὸ μακρόθεν θεωροῦσαι, ἐν αἷς καὶ   ⁋ i
Μαρία ἡ Μαγδαληνὴ καὶ Μαρία ἡ Ἰακώβου τοῦ

39 υιος θεου ην ο ανθρ. ουτος 1071   40 ησαν δε]+εκει C | εν αις]+ην ACDN
ΓΔΠΣΨ min^pl arm om syrr^sin pesh | om εν αις και syrr^sin pesh | om και 2° C³DGUΓ 1 33
1071 al^sat mu c ff k n q vg^ed, codd pl syrr arm me go | Μαρια 1°] Μαριαμ BC 1 al^panc

action (τὸ γενόμενον). The conduct
and sayings of Jesus, so unique in
his experience of crucifixions, culmi-
nating in the supernatural strength
of the last cry, the phenomena which
attended the Passion—the darkness,
the earthquake, perhaps also the
report of the event in the Temple,
impressed the Roman officer with the
sense of a presence of more than
human greatness. The Roman in
him felt the righteousness of the
Sufferer, the Oriental (v. 16, note)
recognised His Divinity. Mt. includes
the other soldiers (οἱ μετ᾽ αὐτοῦ...
ἐφοβήθησαν σφόδρα λέγοντες κτλ.). Ἐξ
ἐναντίας, Vg. ex adverso, a phrase
used in class. Gk. and frequent in
LXX.; cf. ὁ ἐξ ἐν., Tit. ii. 8. Being on
duty, he had stood facing the crosses,
and nothing had escaped him.

40. ἦσαν δὲ καὶ γυναῖκες κτλ.] There
were others besides the centurion who
viewed the crucifixion seriously, and
were present throughout. 'There
were also women'—many women (Mt.)
—'looking on at a long distance,'
where they could be safe from the
ribaldry of the crowd, and yet watch
the Figure on the Cross—not the
"daughters of Jerusalem" who had
bewailed Jesus on the way to Golgotha,
but followers from Galilee. Mt., Mc.,
mention three by name (ἐν αἷς καὶ...
καὶ...καί, both...and...and).
Μαρία ἡ Μαγδαληνή] Mary (on the
forms Μαρία, Μαριάμ, see WSchm.,
p. 91 n.) the Magdalene had been the
subject of a remarkable miracle (Lc.
viii. 2 ἀφ᾽ ἧς δαιμόνια ἑπτὰ ἐξεληλύθει,
cf. 'Mc.' xvi. 9), and had in consequence devoted her property and

time to the work of personal attendance on Jesus (Lc. l.c.). The epithet
Μαγδαληνή, which everywhere distinguishes her from other women of the
same name, is doubtless local (cf.
Syr.^sin. ⲁ, like Ἀδραμυν-
τηνός, Ναζαρηνός; she may have belonged to the Magdala now represented by el-Mejdel, at the south
end of Gennesaret (vi. 53); cf. Neubauer, géogr. du Talm., p. 216 f. A
confused story in the Talmud represents this Mary as a woman's hair-
dresser (מגדלא נשיא); see Chagigah,
ed. Streane, p. 18, and cf. Laible, J. Chr.
in the Talmud, tr. by Streane, p. 16 f,
and Wünsche p. 359; a graver error in
western Christian tradition has identified her with the γυνὴ ἁμαρτωλός of
Lc. vii. 37 ff. For other references to
her in the N.T. and tradition see note
on xvi. 9.
καὶ Μαρία ἡ Ἰακώβου τοῦ μικροῦ
καὶ Ἰωσῆτος μήτηρ] Mt. M. ἡ τοῦ Ἰακ.
καὶ Ἰωσήφ μ., Jo. M. ἡ τοῦ Κλωπᾶ.
She is called ἡ Ἰωσῆτος (infr. v. 47),
ἡ [τοῦ] Ἰακώβου (xvi. 1, Lc. xxiv. 10), ἡ
ἄλλη M. (in contrast to the Magdalene)
Mt. xxvii. 61, xxviii. 1. If by ἡ
Κλωπᾶ is meant 'the wife of Cl.,' and
Κλωπᾶς=Ἀλφαῖος (חַלְפִּי), this Mary
was the mother of the second James
in the Apostolic lists (cf. iii. 18,
note); but it is against the identification that the extant Syriac versions
render Ἀλφ. by ⲁⲗⲫ, ⲁⲗⲫ,
but Κλωπ. by ⲕⲗⲱⲡ, ⲕⲗⲱⲡ
(Lightfoot, Galatians, p. 267; Syr.^sin.
and Syr.^cu. are unhappily wanting in
Jo. xix. 25). A Clopas is mentioned
by Hegesippus (cf. Eus. H.E. iii. 11,

§ ٦ 41 §μικροῦ καὶ 'Ιωσῆτος μήτηρ καὶ Σαλώμη, ⁴¹αἳ ὅτε ἦν
ἐν τῇ Γαλειλαίᾳ ἠκολούθουν αὐτῷ καὶ διηκόνουν αὐτῷ,
καὶ ἄλλαι πολλαὶ αἱ συναναβᾶσαι αὐτῷ εἰς 'Ιεροσόλυμα.

¶ N 42   ⁴²Καὶ ἤδη ὀψίας γενομένης,¶ ἐπεὶ ἦν Παρα-

40 Ιωσητος אᶜBDL(Δ) (ι) 13 69 346 2ᵖᵒ k n me] Ιωση א*ACEGHKMNSUVΓΠΣΨ
minᵖˡ syrrᵖᵉˢʰ ʰᶜˡ arm go Ιωσηφ (ut vid) d ff i q vg syrˢⁱⁿ Aug   41 αι 1° אBΨ 32 131 1071
c d ff k q me syrʰᵉˡ arm aeth] και ACLΔ minⁿᵒⁿⁿ vg go Aug αι και DNXΓΠΣ minᵖˡ
syrʰᵉˡ | ηκολουθησαν DΣ minᵖᵃᵘᶜ | om αυτω 1° Ψ | om και διηκονουν αυτω CDΔ minⁿᵒⁿⁿ
n | om αυτω 2° N | αλλαι] ετεραι A (αιτ.) | αι συναναβ.] om αι LΨ | Ιλημ̄ 2ᵖᵒ
42 και ηδη…προσαββατον] et erat in sabbato syrˢⁱⁿ

22, 32, iv. 22), who was brother of
Joseph the husband of Mary the
Virgin, and father of the Symeon
who succeeded James the Just in
the presidency of the Church of
Jerusalem (cf. Mayor, St James,
p. xvi f.). Τοῦ μικροῦ, sc. τῇ ἡλικίᾳ
(cf. Lc. xix. 3); Deissmann, however
(B. St. p. 144 f.), offers some evidence
of the word being used in reference to
age (μικρός = minor). Whether from
stature or age this James was thus
distinguished in the Church of Jerusalem. 'Ιωσῆτος : see vi. 3, note.
καὶ Σαλώμη] Mt. καὶ ἡ μήτηρ τῶν
υἱῶν Ζεβεδαίου, but according to the
Gospel acc. to the Egyptians Salome
was childless (καλῶς οὖν ἐποίησα μὴ
τεκοῦσα); Jo. (apparently, see Westcott ad l.) καὶ ἡ ἀδελφὴ τῆς μητρὸς
αὐτοῦ. See notes on i. 19, x. 35 ff.
The name, which is given only by
Mc. (here and xvi. 1), is left without identification, for it was well
known in the Church, and among
women connected with the Gospel
narrative it was unique. It is the
Heb. fem. name שְׁלֹם with a Gk.
ending, like Μαριάμνη (Dalman, Gr.
p. 122, cf. Blass, Gr. p. 30). The name
belonged to several members of the
Herod family; see vi. 22, note, and
cf. the indices to Josephus (ed. Niese).

41. αἳ ὅτε ἦν ἐν τῇ Γαλειλαίᾳ
κτλ.] Cf. Lc. viii. 2, where besides

Mary of Magdala are mentioned 'Ιωάνα
γυνὴ Χουζᾶ ἐπιτρόπου Ἡρῴδου (xxiv.
10) καὶ Σουσάννα καὶ ἔτεραι πολλαί.
Thése were doubtless among the
ἄλλαι πολλαὶ αἱ συναναβᾶσαι. Their
names had less significance than those
which Mc. mentions; they probably
returned to their homes in Galilee
after the Passover, and thus faded
out of the memory of the Christian
community at Jerusalem. Διηκόνουν
αὐτῷ : Lc. adds ἐκ τῶν ὑπαρχόντων αὐταῖς. Their ministry continued
to the end (Mt. ἠκολούθησαν…διακο-
νοῦσαι αὐτῷ); Jerome : "ceteris re-
linquentibus Dominum mulieres in
officio perseverant…et ideo meruerunt
primae videre resurgentem." For
ἀναβαίνειν εἰς 'Ιεροσόλυμα see x. 32,
note; for συναναβαίνειν cf. Gen. l. 7,
Exod. xii. 38, 1 Esdr. viii. 5, Acts
xiii. 31.
42—47. THE BURIAL OF THE
LORD (Mt. xxvii. 57—61, Lc. xxiii.
50—55, Jo. xix. 38—42).
42. ἤδη ὀψίας γενομένης] It was
already 3 p.m. when the Lord expired,
and some interval must be allowed for
the subsequent interview of Joseph
with Pilate (v. 43 ff.), so that sunset
was not far off when all was ready
for the burial. 'Οψία is a relative
term (cf. i. 32, iv. 35, vi. 47, xiv. 17,
notes), and an hour before sunset
would be relatively late in view of the
approaching Sabbath.

σκευή, ὅ ἐστιν προσάββατον, ⁴³§ἐλθὼν Ἰωσὴφ ὁ ἀπὸ 43 § syrʰⁱᵉʳ
Ἀρειμαθαίας εἰσχήμων βουλευτής, ὃς καὶ αὐτὸς ἦν

42 προσαββατον אB*CKMΔΠ*Ψ 1 33 69 alᵐᵘ] προς σαββατον (προσσ.) AB³EGH
LSUVΓΠ² minˢᵃᵗᵐᵘ arm πριν σαββατον DΣ 604 ante sabbatum ff n q vg   43 ελθων]
ηλθεν DEGHSV minᵐᵘ | Ιωσηφ] Ioses k | ο απο Αρ.] om ο D minᵖᵃᵘᶜ | Αρειμαθαιας
אB*] Αριμ. rell -μαθιας אᶜ·ᵃᵛⁱᵈ D 69 yˢᶜʳ lattᵛᵗ ᵛᵍ ᵉᵈᵈ ᵖˡ

ἐπεὶ ἦν Παρασκευή κτλ.] Reason
for immediate action on the part of
Joseph : the day was the eve of a
Sabbath. Παρασκευή, 'preparation,'
had become a technical name for
Friday, which is still so called in the
Greek East; cf. Jos. ant. xvi. 6. 2 ἐν
σάββασιν ἢ τῇ πρὸ αὐτῆς παρασκευῇ,
Did. 8 τετράδα καὶ παρασκευήν. Mt.
(xxvii. 62) uses it without explanation;
Mc. for the benefit of his Western
readers adds ὅ ἐστιν προσάββατον—a
word already employed in Judith viii.
6 and in the titles of Psalms xci. (xcii.)
א, xcii. (xciii.) אB. Jo. (xix. 14) calls
the day of the Crucifixion παρασκ. τοῦ
πάσχα, but further on (xix. 31) he describes it as immediately preceding
the Sabbath; on the problem raised
by his account see Westcott, Introduction to the Gospels, p. 329 ff. The
Jews had already taken steps to provide for the removal of the bodies
before the Sabbath (Jo. v. 31 ff., cf.
Ev. Petr. 2, 5, notes); had they not
been anticipated, the Lord's Body
would have been committed to the
common grave provided for criminals
who had been hanged (cf. Lightfoot
on Mt. xxvii. 58: cf. Ev. Petr. 2),
and acc. to Deut. xxi. 23, this would
have happened before nightfall.

43. ἐλθὼν Ἰωσὴφ ὁ ἀπὸ Ἀρ. κτλ.]
Eusebius onom. s.v., followed by Jerome
de situ, identifies Arimathaea with
Ἀρμαθέμ (-θάιμ), Σειφά, πόλις Ἐλκανὰ
καὶ Σαμουήλ (1 Regn. i. 1, הָרָמָתַיִם צוֹפִים :
on the name see Driver ad l.), a
Ramathaim or Ramah in Mt Ephraim
which is possibly identical with er-Ram
a few miles N. of Jerusalem. Eus., however, places it near Diospolis (Lydda),
cf. 1 Macc. xi. 34 Λυδδὰ καὶ Ῥαθαμεΐν

(v. l. Ῥαμαθέμ). On the breathing
(Ἀρ.) see WH., Intr., p. 313. Ἀπὸ Ἀρ.,
even if not preceded by the art., is probably to be connected with Ἰωσήφ, not
with ἐλθών, cf. Lc. Jo., and comp. Jos.
ant. xvi. 10. 1 Εὐρυκλῆς ἀπὸ Λακεδαί-
μονος; for other instances of ἀπὸ in this
sense cf. Jo. i. 45, Acts vi. 9 (Blass, Gr.
p. 122). Joseph was a βουλευτής (Mc.
Lc.; the word passed into Rabbinic,
see Dalman, Gr. p. 148), a senator i.e. a
member of the Sanhedrin, as appears
from Lc.'s statement (v. 51) that he
had not consented to the resolution
which condemned Jesus. Mc.'s εὐσχή-
μων seems to answer to Mt.'s πλούσιος,
cf. Acts xiii. 50, xvii. 12 : this sense of
the word was severely condemned by
Phryn. (τοῦτο μὲν οἱ ἀμαθεῖς ἐπὶ τοῦ πλουσίου καὶ ἐν ἀξιώματι ὄντος τάττουσιν),
and Rutherford adds that it "seems
confined to Christian writers," but he
overlooks the exx. cited by Wetstein
from Plutarch and Josephus; the
latter (vit. 9) writing of the state of
Tiberias says: στάσεις τρεῖς ἦσαν κατὰ
τὴν πόλιν, μία μὲν ἀνδρῶν εὐσχημόνων...
ἡ δευτέρα δὲ στάσις ἐξ ἀσημοτάτων.
Similarly honesti homines are contrasted by Pliny with the plebs.

ὃς καὶ αὐτὸς ἦν προσδεχόμενος κτλ.]
So Lc.; Mt. ἐμαθητεύθη (v. l. ἐμαθή-
τευσεν) τῷ Ἰησοῦ, Jo. ὢν μαθητὴς τοῦ
Ἰησοῦ, κεκρυμμένος δέ. The three
statements seem to describe successive stages in the man's religious
history. Originally he had been in the
position of Simeon (Lc. ii. 25); there
were not a few such in Jerusalem at
the beginning of the century (Lc. ii.
38). The preaching of Jesus, perhaps
at the first passover, made him a
secret disciple; after the Resurrection

προσδεχόμενος τὴν βασιλείαν τοῦ θεοῦ, τολμήσας
εἰσῆλθεν πρὸς τὸν Πειλᾶτον καὶ ἠτήσατο τὸ σῶμα
¶ Η 44 τοῦ 'Ιησοῦ.¶ ⁴⁴ὁ δὲ Πειλᾶτος ἐθαύμασεν εἰ¶ ἤδη
¶ ˥ τέθνηκεν, καὶ προσκαλεσάμενος τὸν κεντυρίωνα
45 ἐπηρώτησεν αὐτὸν εἰ ἤδη ἀπέθανεν· ⁴⁵καὶ γνοὺς ἀπὸ
§ ˥ τοῦ §κεντυρίωνος ἐδωρήσατο τὸ πτῶμα τῷ 'Ιωσήφ.

43 om τολμησας syrʰⁱᵉʳ | εισηλθεν] ηλθεν D 26ᵉᵛ | σωμα] πτωμα D k   44 εθαυ-
μαζεν אD cﬀkqvg ᴬᵘᵍ | ει] pr και ειπεν Δ (arm) | ηδη BD armᵛⁱᵈ] παλαι
אACEGKLMSUVXᵛⁱᵈΓΠΣΨ minᶠᵉʳᵉᵒᵐⁿ om syrˢⁱⁿ | τεθνηκει D   45 om και
γνους...Ιωσηφ ﬀ | om απο του κεντ. k syrᵖᵉˢʰ | απο] παρα D 124 2ᵖᵉ alᵖᵃᵘᶜ | πτωμα
אBDL 2ᵖᵉ] σωμα ACEGKMSUVXΓΔΠΣΨ˥¹² minᶠᵉʳᵉᵒᵐⁿ k | Ιωσηφ] Ιωση B

he became a member of the Church
(ἐμαθητεύθη, cf. Mt. xxviii. 19).

τολμήσας εἰσῆλθεν πρὸς τὸν Πειλᾶτον
κτλ.] Acc. to Ps. Peter, Joseph is a
friend of Pilate, and his petition is
tendered immediately after the sentence has been pronounced; Pilate
refers him to Herod, but the Body is
ultimately given to Joseph by the
Jews (Ev. Petr. 2, 6). Τολμήσας creates
quite a different impression of Joseph's
act. He summons up his courage to
face the Procurator (on the phrase
see Field, Notes, p. 44). The circumstances of the Passion, which wrecked
the brave resolutions of the Apostles,
made this secret disciple bold. The
aor. part. has almost the force of an
adv., cf. Vg. audacter introiit; see
Field, l. c.

44, 45. ὁ δὲ Πειλᾶτος ἐθαύμασεν
κτλ.] Peculiar to Mc. Pilate wondered whether Jesus was already
dead, and was not satisfied until he
had ascertained the fact from the
responsible officer. Θαυμάζειν εἰ (cf.
1 Jo. iii. 13) leaves the fact slightly
doubtful; contrast θ. ὅτι in Jo. iv. 27,
Gal. i. 6. The perfect τέθνηκεν represents the Death as an existing
state, whilst ἀπέθανεν in the indirect
question which follows refers to it as
momentary effect; 'is He dead?'
Pilate asks himself, but to the centurion he says 'did you see Him

die?' (cf. WM., pp. 339, 679). Death
seldom supervened so soon in the
case of the crucified; they lived for
two or three days, and in some cases
died at last of starvation rather than of
their wounds (Eus. H. E. viii. 8). Cf.
Origen: "miraculum enim erat quoniam post tres horas receptus est qui
forte biduum victurus erat in cruce."
Our Lord died first of the three, cf.
Jo. xix. 33.

45. καὶ γνοὺς ἀπὸ τοῦ κεντυρίωνος
κτλ.] The centurion had returned to
head-quarters, and was able to report
the fact (cf. v. 39). Upon this Pilate
granted the Body (donavit corpus), as
Mc. says in language which savours of
an official character (cf. Mt. ἐκέλευσεν
ἀποδοθῆναι, Jo. ἐπέτρεψεν [ἵνα ἄρῃ]);
δωρεῖσθαι is used especially of royal
or Divine bounty, see Gen. xxx. 20,
1 Esdr. i. 7, viii. 55, Esth. viii. 1,
2 Pet. i. 3 f. (the only other example
in the N.T.). Πτῶμα has the same
ring; the Body which 'saw no corruption' is not elsewhere called 'a
corpse' (cf. vi. 29, Apoc. xi. 8 f.), but
to Pilate it would appear merely in
that light; τὸ σῶμα (τοῦ 'Ιησοῦ, αὐτοῦ)
is substituted in Mt. Lc. Jo. Πτῶμα is
used of the carcases of animals, e.g.
Jud. xiv. 8 τὸ πτ. τοῦ λέοντος: when
employed for the dead body of a
human being it carries a tone of contempt (cf. e.g. Sap. iv. 19 πτῶμα ἄτιμον,

⁴⁶καὶ ἀγοράσας σινδόνα καθελὼν αὐτὸν ἐνείλησεν τῇ 46
σινδόνι καὶ ἔθηκεν αὐτὸν ἐν μνήματι ὃ ἦν λελατο-

46 και 1°] ο δε Ιωσηφ DΣ 38 106 435 2ᵖᵉ latt syrrᵖᵉˢʰʰᶜˡ arm Aug | καθελων]
λαβων D (? syrˢⁱⁿ) pr και ACEGKMSUVΓΔΠΣ minᵒᵐⁿ ᵛⁱᵈ vg syrr arm go aeth | τη
σινδονι] εις την σινδονα D | εθηκεν ℵBC²DLΣΨ minⁿᵒⁿⁿ] κατεθηκεν AC*EGKMSUVXΓΠ
minᵖˡ | αυτον] αυτο AMⁱ 435 | 'μνηματι ℵB] μνημειω ACDLXΓΔΠΣΨⁱ¹² minᵒᵐⁿ ᵛⁱᵈ

Ezech. vi. 5, A). The majority of the uncial MSS. avoid the word here, and borrow σῶμα from Mt. Lc. Jo.; and the Latin versions similarly prefer *corpus* to *cadaver*.

46. καὶ ἀγοράσας σινδόνα κτλ.] On his way back to Golgotha Joseph provides himself with linen; on σινδών see xiv. 51; the word is used here of linen in the piece, not of a garment; it was still, as Mt. says, καθαρά, fresh and unused (cf. xi. 2, note). His next task was to remove the Body from the Cross. Καθελών, cf. *v.* 36, Acts xiii. 29; the word is common in this sense, cf. e.g. Jos. x. 27 καθεῖλεν αὐτοὺς ἀπὸ τῶν ξύλων, Phil. *in Flacc.* § 10 ὅδ' οὐ τετελευτηκότας ἐπὶ σταυρῶν καθαιρεῖν...προσέταττεν. Joseph. *B. J.* iv. 5. 2 τοὺς ἀνασταυρουμένους πρὸ δύντος ἡλίου καθελεῖν τε καὶ θάπτειν. Other examples will be found in Field, *Notes,* p. 44. The Romans used *detrahere* in a similar sense; cf. Petron. *sat.* iii. "miles...cruces servabat ne quis ad sepulturam corpora detraheret." In this work Joseph was probably not alone; though the little crowd of assistants with which the poetry of Rubens' great picture surrounded him is imaginary, St John's account (*v.* 39 f.) leads us to suppose that his brother Sanhedrist Nicodemus was already on the spot. Nicodemus had brought a large supply of the spices used for embalming the dead (ἕλιγμα σμύρνης καὶ ἀλόης ὡς λίτρας ἑκατόν, a hundred pounds of aromatics made up in a compact roll). The Body was then taken by the two men (ἔλαβον, Jo.), bathed perhaps (Ps. Peter, cf. Acts ix. 37), and wrapped

(ἐνετύλιξεν, Mt. Lc.) or swathed (ἐνείλησεν, Mc., εἴλησε, Ps. Pet.; cf. 1 Regn. xxi. 9) in the linen between the folds of which the spices were finely crumbled (μετὰ τῶν ἀρωμάτων, Jo.), and finally bound with strips of cloth (ἔδησαν ὀθονίοις, Jo.), after the Jewish manner of burying (Jo.). The picture may be completed by comparing what is said of Lazarus in Jo. xi. 44, and the account of the grave clothes in Jo. xx. 7 : the Hands and Feet were bound with ὀθόνια (= κειρίαι, xi. 44), and the Face was covered with a face-cloth (σουδάριον). All was now ready for the interment.

καὶ ἔθηκεν αὐτὸν ἐν μνήματι κτλ.] Mc. knows only that the tomb was artificially constructed, cut out of a rock, the resting-place of some rich citizen; cf. Isa. xxii. 16 ἐλατόμησας σεαυτῷ ὧδε μνημεῖον, καὶ ἐποίησας σεαυτῷ ἐν ὑψηλῷ μνημεῖον, καὶ ἔγραψας σεαυτῷ ἐν πέτρᾳ σκηνήν; Such rock-hewn chambers abound on the S., W., and N.W. of the city; see Robinson, *Researches,* i. p. 517 ff., and Mr Fergusson's art. *Tombs* in Smith's *B. D.* This tomb was a new one which had never been used (Mt. Lc. Jo.), and had been prepared by Joseph for his own burial (Mt.); it was in a garden adjacent to the place of crucifixion (Jo.). The garden was presumably the property of Joseph, a 'paradise'; according to *Ev. Petr.* 6 the spot bore the name Κῆπος Ἰωσήφ. On the custom of burying in gardens see 4 Regn. xxi. 18, 26, 2 Esdr. xiii. 16. For ἔθηκεν the more technical word κατέθηκεν has been substituted in most of the MSS.

394 / Commentary on Mark

μημένον ἐκ πέτρας, καὶ προσεκύλισεν λίθον ἐπὶ τὴν
47 θύραν τοῦ μνημείου. ⁴⁷ἡ δὲ Μαρία ἡ Μαγδαληνὴ καὶ
Μαρία ἡ Ἰωσῆτος ἐθεώρουν ποῦ τέθειται.

16. 1 ¹ Καὶ διαγενομένου τοῦ σαββάτου¶ Μαρία ἡ
¶ 7

46 πετρας] της π. D 1 2ᵖᵉ alᵖᵉʳᵖᵃᵘᶜ εν τη πετρα 13 69 346 | προσεκυλισεν] προσ-
κυλισας D 1 | επι] εις Δ 1071 | μνημειου] + και απηλθεν (D)G 1 59 157 209
47 Ιωσητος ℵᶜBLΔΨ 1 k me] Ιωση CEGKMSUVΓΠ minᵖˡ syrr go Ιωσηφ ΑΣ 258 vg
aeth Ιακωβου D ff n q syrˢⁱⁿ Ιακ. και Ιωσητος 13 69 124 346 2ᵖᵉ ᵛⁱᵈ syrʰⁱᵉʳ arm | εθεωρουν]
εθεασαντο D 2ᵖᵉ | που] τον τοπον οπου D c ff q arm | τεθειται ℵᶜABCD(L)ΔΠΣΨ(7¹²)
33 69 131 229 alᵖᵃᵘᶜ k] τιθεται EGKMSUVΓ (604) minᵖˡ   XVI 1 om διαγενομενου
...Σαλωμη D n (q) | om Μαρια 1°...Σαλωμη k | Μαρια 1°] pr η B*L min¹

καὶ προσεκύλισεν λίθον κτλ.] Λίθον
μέγαν, Mt., cf. xvi. 4 ἦν γὰρ μέγας
σφόδρα: in Lc. cod. D adds ὃν μόγις
εἴκοσι ἐκύλιον, while Ps. Peter represents the matter as requiring the
services of all who were present (ὁμοῦ
πάντες οἱ ὄντες ἐκεῖ ἔθηκαν); the stone
was afterwards, at the desire of the
Jews, sealed and guarded (Mt.), cf.
Ev. Petr. 6. The opening was usually
closed with a stone, if any of the
loculi were occupied; cf. Jo. xi. 38
ἔρχεται εἰς τὸ μνημεῖον· ἦν δὲ σπήλαιον
καὶ λίθος ἐπέκειτο ἐπ' αὐτῷ. The stone
was rolled to the opening (προσκυλίειν
here only and in the corresponding
context in Mt.; cf. Jos. x. 18 κυλίσατε
λίθους ἐπὶ τὸ στόμα τοῦ σπηλαίου.
Mr Latham (Risen Master, p. 33,
and illustr. 1; cf. E. Pierotti, Jerusalem Explored (E. Tr., 1864), ii.,
plate lvi. fig. 3) imagines "a massive
circular disc of stone, much like a
grindstone of four feet diameter,"
rolled along "a furrow grooved out
of the rocky soil"; but κυλίειν λίθον
does not in itself suggest more than
the rolling of a mass of stone along
the ground: cf. 1 Regn. xiv. 33,
Prov. xxvi. 27, Zech. ix. 16. Μνῆμα
and μνημεῖον seem to be employed
indiscriminately (cf. v. 2 ff.), unless
μνῆμα is here a loculus; the Vg. uses
monumentum for both words. According to Jo. (v. 42) the Body was
placed in Joseph's tomb on account of
its proximity to the Cross—till the

Sabbath was over, perhaps, and not
with a view to a permanent interment;
cf. Jo. xx. 13, 15.
47. ἡ δὲ Μαρία ἡ Μαγδ. κτλ.] The
Magdalene and the other Mary (v. 40)
had remained on the spot, and were
watching the action of Joseph and
Nicodemus; cf. Origen: "caritas
duarum Mariarum colligavit eas ad
monumentum novum, propter corpus
Iesu quod fuerat ibi." Ambrose:
"sexus nutat, devotio calet." They
sat opposite to the place of sepulture
(Mt., ἀπέναντι τοῦ τάφου), and saw the
Body carried in, so that they knew
where it lay. Τέθειται, Lc. ἐτέθη:
for the perf. cf. τέθνηκεν (v. 44). Their
thought was, 'He is there (contrast xvi.
6 οὐκ ἔστιν ὧδε), and there we shall find
Him when the sabbath is past.' Victor remarks: ἀναγκαία καὶ κατὰ θεὸν ἡ
παραμονὴ τῶν γυναικῶν εἰς τὸ γνῶναι
ποῦ τίθεται, ἵνα ἀπαντήσωσι καὶ τῆς
ἀναστάσεως τὴν ἐπαγγελίαν κομίσωσι
τοῖς μαθηταῖς. Μαρία ἡ Ἰωσῆτος sc.
μήτηρ (v. 40); cf. the 'Western' text substitutes Ἰακώβου (see app. crit.).

XVI. 1—8. VISIT OF THE WOMEN
TO THE TOMB ON THE THIRD DAY
(Mt. xxviii. 1—8, Lc. xxiv. 1—10; cf.
Jo. xx. 1 ff.).

1. διαγενομένου τοῦ σαββάτου κτλ.]
When the Sabbath was over (i.e. after
sunset on the day which followed the
Crucifixion), the three women named
in xv. 40 went forth to purchase
aromatics for the anointing of the

Μαγδαληνὴ καὶ Μαρία ἡ τοῦ Ἰακώβου καὶ Σαλώμη
ἠγόρασαν ἀρώματα ἵνα ἐλθοῦσαι ἀλείψωσιν αὐτόν.
²καὶ λίαν πρωὶ τῇ §μιᾷ τῶν σαββάτων ἔρχονται ἐπὶ 2 §ꓶ
τὸ μνημεῖον ἀνατείλαντος τοῦ ἡλίου. ³καὶ ἔλεγον 3

1 του Ιακ.] om του ℵ*CGMSUVXΓΨ minⁿᵒⁿⁿ | ηγορασαν] ηνεγκαν (ut vid) c k pr
πορευθεισαι D (c ff) k n (q) syrʰⁱᵉʳ arm | αρωματα] pr unguentum et syrˢⁱⁿ | om ελθουσαι
D c ff k n q | αυτον] τον Ιησουν K²MX 13 69 124 346 1071 alˢᵃᵗᵐᵘ vgᵉᵈ   2 om λιαν
D c k n syrʳˢⁱⁿ ᵖᵉˢʰ arm | om πρωι c q | τη μια ℵ(B)LΔΨ (1) 33 1071 2ᵖᵉ alᵖᵃᵘᶜ me Eus]
της μιας AC(D)EGKMSUVXΓΠΣ minᵖˡ | των σαββατων ℵBKLΔ 33 69 2ᵖᵉ alᵖᵃᵘᶜ]
σαββατων ACEGMSUVXᵛⁱᵈΓΔ*ΠΣ minᵖˡ του σαββατου D 1071 alᵖᵃᵘᶜ c k q | μνημειον
ℵᶜABC³DLXΓΔΠΣΨ minᵒᵐⁿ ᵛⁱᵈ] μνημα ℵ*C* 2ᵖᵉ | ανατειλαντος] ανατελλοντος D c n q
Tyc Aug pr ετι KΠ* 1 2ᵖᵉ alᵖᵃᵘᶜ Aug

Body (Mc. Lc.). According to D the purchase apparently took place on Friday (before the Sabbath began). They had probably seen Joseph and Nicodemus use spices freely in the process of wrapping it for burial (Jo. xix. 40, cf. xv. 46 f., notes), but they desired to add more externally, and to apply fragrant oils (Lc. καὶ μύρα, cf. Mc. ἵνα...ἀλείψωσιν αὐτόν); the incident at Bethany (xiv. 3 ff.) was perhaps fresh in their memory, and suggested this final ministry. For διαγίνεσθαι 'to intervene' in reference to intervals of time cf. Acts xxv. 13, xxvii. 9; the verb is used in this sense from Demosthenes downwards. For ἀρώματα, cf. 2 Chr. xvi. 14 ἔθαψαν αὐτὸν (sc. Ἀσά)...καὶ ἔπλησαν ἀρωμάτων καὶ γένη μύρων μυρεψῶν, and the list of spices in Sir. xxiv. 15; and see xiv. 3, 8, notes.

2. λίαν πρωὶ τῇ μιᾷ τῶν σαββ. κτλ.] Mt. ὀψὲ δὲ σ. τῇ ἐπιφωσκούσῃ εἰς μίαν σ., Lc. τῇ δὲ μιᾷ τῶν σ. ὄρθρου βαθέως, Jo. τῇ δὲ μιᾷ τῶν σαββάτων... πρωὶ σκοτίας ἔτι οὔσης (cf. Ps. Pet. 9, 11 τῇ δὲ νυκτὶ ᾗ ἐπέφωσκεν ἡ κυριακή...ὄρθρου δὲ τῆς κυριακῆς). All the canonical accounts, notwithstanding a remarkable independence of expression, point one way. The last hours of Saturday night were already giving place to the first signs of dawn when the three women started

for Joseph's garden; the morning watch had begun, but it was yet dark. Mc. adds ἀνατείλαντος τοῦ ἡλίου, words which are scarcely less inconsistent with his own λίαν πρωί than with Jo.'s σκοτίας ἔτι οὔσης. The harmonists have from the first been exercised by the apparent contradiction, as the reading of D and some other 'Western' authorities seems to shew : see note on i. 32, and cf. Aug. cons. ev. iii. 65 "oriente iam sole, id est, cum caelum ab orientis parte iam albesceret." But the correction (for such it seems to be) gives little relief; the same moment of time can hardly be described as λίαν πρωί and as 'sunrise.' It is better to regard Mc.'s note as a compressed statement of two facts; the two women started just before daybreak and arrived just after sunrise (ἔρχονται = ἐξελθοῦσαι...ἦλθον). Τῇ μιᾷ τῶν σαββάτων (Acts xx. 7, 1 Cor. xvi. 2), on the first day after the Sabbath (Bede: "prima sabbatorum prima dies est a die sabbatorum"), εἰς being used by a common Hebraism for πρῶτος (WM., p. 311, Blass, Gr. p. 140); cf. πρώτῃ σαββάτου, v. 9, where however σάββατον is probably used for 'the week,' as in Lc. xviii. 12.

3. ἔλεγον πρὸς ἑαυτάς κτλ.] Mc. only. On the way they remembered the stone which they had seen Joseph

πρὸς ἑαυτάς Τίς ἀποκυλίσει ἡμῖν τὸν λίθον ἐκ τῆς
4 θύρας τοῦ μνημείου; ⁴καὶ ἀναβλέψασαι θεωροῦσιν
ὅτι ἀνακεκύλισται ὁ λίθος, ἦν γὰρ μέγας σφόδρα.
5 ⁵καὶ εἰσελθοῦσαι εἰς τὸ μνημεῖον εἶδον νεανίσκον
καθήμενον ἐν τοῖς δεξιοῖς περιβεβλημένον στολὴν

3 προς εαυτους D | εκ] απο CDΨ min^paue latt (ab) Eus   4 και αναβλεψασαι...
σφοδρα] ην γαρ μεγας σφοδρα και ερχονται και ευρισκουσιν αποκεκυλισμενον τον λιθον
D 2^pe c ff n syr^(sin) hier (Eus) *subito autem ad horam tertiam tenebrae diei* (leg. *diei
tenebrae*) *factae sunt per totum orbem terrae et descenderunt de caelis angeli et sur-
gent* (leg. *surgentes*, nisi forte *surgente* cf. F. C. Burkitt, *Itala*, p. 94) *in claritate
vivi dei simul ascenderunt cum eo et continuo lux facta est tunc illae accesserunt ad
monimentum et vident revolutum lapidem fuit enim magnus nimis* k | ανακεκυλισται
אBL] αποκεκ. AC(D)XΓΔΠΣ min^omn vid   5 εισελθουσαι] ελθουσαι B 127 | om εν
τοις δεξιοις syr^hier

roll to the entrance of the tomb and leave there, and they began to talk (ἔλεγον) about it. It would require more than the strength of three women to remove it. Ps. Peter (c. xi.) expands τίς ἀποκυλίσει κτλ. into a set speech which is at once feeble and confused. For πρὸς ἑαυτάς=πρὸς ἀλλήλας, cf. xi. 31, xiv. 4, notes. Ἀποκυλίειν, the opposite of προσκυλίειν (xv. 46); the form κυλίειν begins in Aristophanes to take the place of the older κυλίνδειν or κυλινδεῖν, which is unknown to Bibl. Gk. The compound ἀποκυλ. occurs in Gen. xxix. 3 ff. in reference to the removal of a stone from the mouth of a well. Ἐκ τῆς θύρας: Lc. less exactly, ἀπὸ τοῦ μνημείου (cf. WM., p. 454).

4. καὶ ἀναβλέψασαι κτλ.] By this time they are near the knoll out of the side of which the tomb had been cut; the sun has risen, and involuntarily looking up at the mention of the stone they see that it has been displaced. The change from ἀποκυλίειν to the rarer and more difficult ἀνακυλίειν is evidence of Mc.'s care for accuracy in detail; the stone was not rolled right away, but rolled back so as to leave the opening free; cf. *Ev. Petr.* 9 ὁ δὲ λίθος...ἀφ' ἑαυτοῦ κυλισθεὶς ἐπεχώρησε παρὰ μέρος, καὶ ὁ τάφος

ἠνοίγη. The perf., as in xv. 44, 47, adds to the vividness of the narrative: we hear the women exclaim Ἀνακεκύλισται—their τίς ἀποκυλίσει; has been answered, and their wish, idle as it had seemed, is realised. Ἦν γὰρ μέγας σφόδρα either accounts for their being able to see what had occurred before they reached the spot, or it explains why the sight arrested their attention. Mt. attributes the removal of the stone to the descent of an Angel, accompanied by an earthquake; the Angel sits upon the stone which he has rolled away, and is there apparently when the women arrive. It is impossible to feel any·confidence in Thpht.'s attempt to reconcile the two accounts: ἐνδέχεται γὰρ ὃν εἶδον ἔξω καθήμενον...τοῦτον ἰδεῖν πάλιν ἔσω, προλαβόντα τὰς γυναῖκας καὶ εἰσελθόντα. A remarkable gloss follows *v.* 3 in *k* (see *app. crit.*); cf. the story in *Ev. Petr.* 9.

5. καὶ εἰσελθοῦσαι κτλ.] Lc. εἰσελθοῦσαι δὲ οὐχ εὗρον τὸ σῶμα. Mt. does not mention the fact of their entering; see last note. In Jo. Mary Magdalene arrives at the tomb alone, and all the circumstances are different. The attempt to harmonise these independent narratives is beset with difficulty; see however Tatian's scheme (Hill, p. 252 ff.), and the provisional

λευκήν,¶ καὶ ἐξεθαμβήθησαν. ⁶ὁ δὲ λέγει αὐταῖς Μὴ 6 ¶ ㄱ
ἐκθαμβεῖσθε· Ἰησοῦν ζητεῖτε τὸν Ναζαρηνὸν τὸν
ἐσταυρωμένον· ἠγέρθη, οὐκ ἔστιν §ὧδε· §ἴδε ὁ τόπος   §ꟼ §ㄱ

5 εξεθαμβηθησαν] εθανβησαν D n syrᴾᵉˢʰ arm   6 ο δε λ. αυταις] και λ. αυταις ο
αγγελος (D) ff (cf. c n) | εκθαμβεισθε] φοβεισθαι D n syrᴾᵉˢʰ arm | τον Ναζαρηνον] τ.
Ναζωραιον LΔ k om ℵ* (hab ℵª) D | ιδε ο τοπος] ειδετε εκει (+ τον D²) τοπον αυτου
D ιδε εκει ο τ. αυτου 2ᴾᵉ : similiter cff k n q

arrangement proposed by Bp Westcott (*St John*, p. 288 f.). On the special appearance to Mary Magdalene, which characterises the Johannine tradition, see below, *v.* 9 f., notes. According to Mc. the women on entering were startled and awestricken (ἐκθαμβεῖσθαι, cf. ix. 15, xiv. 33, notes) to see a young man sitting ἐν τοῖς δεξιοῖς (cf. τὰ δεξιὰ μέρη τοῦ πλοίου, Jo. xxi. 6), on the right hand side of the tomb, clad in a long robe (στολήν, cf. xii. 38, note) of dazzling whiteness (λευκήν, cf. ix. 3, note). Mt., who identifies the νεανίσκος as an Angel, has a fuller description : ἦν δὲ ἡ εἰδέα αὐτοῦ ὡς ἀστραπὴ καὶ τὸ ἔνδυμα αὐτοῦ λευκὸν ὡς χιών. In Lc. the women see two men standing over them in flashing raiment (ἐπέστησαν αὐταῖς ἐν ἐσθῆτι ἀστραπτούσῃ). The very diversity of the accounts strengthens the probability that the story rests upon a basis of truth; the impressions of the witnesses differed, but they were agreed upon the main facts. The conception of the Angel as a young man clad in bright attire finds an interesting parallel in 2 Macc. iii. 26, 33 δύο ἐφάνησαν αὐτῷ νεανίαι... διαπρεπεῖς τὴν περιβολήν...οἱ αὐτοὶ νεανίαι πάλιν ἐφάνησαν τῷ Ἡλιοδώρῳ ἐν ταῖς αὐταῖς ἐσθήσεσι ἐστολισμένοι. Similarly Josephus (*ant.* v. 8. 2) describes the Angel who appeared to Manoah's wife as φάντασμα ...νεανίᾳ καλῷ παραπλήσιον μεγάλῳ. Cf. also *Ev. Petr.* 9, 11. On καθήμενον see WM., p. 434 ; περιβάλλεσθαι στολήν, Blass, *Gr.* pp. 92, 113, and cf. xiv. 51, Apoc. vii. 13, x. 1 ; on στολὴ

λευκή see ix. 3, and Apoc. vi. 11, vii. 9, 13.

6. ὁ δὲ λέγει αὐταῖς κτλ.] The Angel is not an apparition merely (vi. 50) ; he speaks to the women and answers (ἀποκριθείς Mt.) their unspoken fears. Lc. follows another tradition of the Angel's words, but Mt. is in substantial agreement with Mc. ; Mc.'s account, however, derives peculiar life and freshness from the absence of conjunctions in the first five clauses. Μὴ ἐκθαμβεῖσθε : Mt. adds ὑμεῖς, for he has just mentioned the terror which struck the guards at the sight of the Angel ; but the contrast would have no meaning for the women, and can scarcely have found a place in the original words. Τὸν Ναζαρηνόν (Mc. only) strikes a familiar note in the memories of these Galilean women (cf. i. 24, x. 47, xiv. 67, notes) ; τὸν ἐσταυρωμένον (Mt. Mc.) rather than τὸν σταυρωθέντα, for the event is recent, and the Person is still living ; cf. 1 Cor. i. 23, Gal. iii. 1, and contrast Jo. xix. 20, 2 Cor. xiii. 4, Apoc. xi. 8, where the aor. suffices to express the historical circumstance. Ἠγέρθη, the Resurrection is an accomplished fact, the moment is already past ; contrast ἐγήγερται in 1 Cor. xv. 4, 20, where the purpose is to emphasise the abiding truth of the Lord's risen life. Ἴδε ὁ τόπος κτλ. 'here is the *loculus* where the Body lay ; you can see for yourselves that it is not there' (Jerome : "ut si meis verbis non creditis vacuo credatis sepulchro"). In Mt. the Angel reminds the women that the Lord had foretold the issue of the

¶ a*

7 ὅπου ἔθηκαν αὐτόν. ⁷ἀλλὰ ὑπάγετε εἴπατε τοῖς μαθηταῖς αὐτοῦ καὶ τῷ Πέτρῳ ὅτι Προάγει ὑμᾶς εἰς¶ τὴν
8 Γαλειλαίαν· ἐκεῖ αὐτὸν ὄψεσθε, καθὼς εἶπεν ὑμῖν. ⁸καὶ
ἐξελθοῦσαι ἔφυγον ἀπὸ τοῦ μνημείου, εἶχεν γὰρ

7 ειπατε] pr και C*D 33 2ᵖᵉ k | προαγει] ιδου προαγω D k syrʰⁱᵉʳ ιδου προαγει
2ᵖᵉ syrʳˢⁱⁿᵖᵉˢʰ arm ηγερθη απο των νεκρων και ιδου προαγει 1 59 118 209 604 | αυτον] με
D k | ειπεν] ειρηκεν Δ ειρηκα D (ειπον 40 72) a³ ff k q   8 εξελθουσαι...μνημειου]
ακουσαντες εξηλθον απο του μνημειου και εφυγον Ρ | εξελθουσαι] ακουσαντες 2ᵖᵉ (sic)
syrʳˢⁱⁿᵖᵉˢʰʰᵉˡ(ᵐᵍ) arm + ταχυ E minⁿᵒⁿⁿ ς | om απο του μνημειου...εκστασις syrˢⁱⁿ | γαρ]
δε ACLΓΔΠ minᵒᵐⁿᵛⁱᵈ go

Crucifixion (καθὼς εἶπεν); in Lc. this
passing reference is expanded into a
citation of the prophecy (μνήσθητε ὡς
ἐλάλησεν ὑμῖν κτλ.), the Evangelist
adding, καὶ ἐμνήσθησαν τῶν ῥημάτων
αὐτοῦ. But the prophecy was addressed, so far as we know, to the
Twelve only, and the reference to it, or
at least the citation, probably formed
no part of the earliest tradition.

7. ἀλλὰ ὑπάγετε κτλ.] Ἀλλά (WM.,
p. 551) recalls their thoughts from the
wonder and awe of the announcement
which they had just received to the
duty which lay immediately before
them; it "breaks off the discourse
and turns to a new matter" (Alford).
They must go with speed (ταχύ, Mt.)
and deliver a message to the disciples.
Mc. adds καὶ τῷ Πέτρῳ, 'and in particular to Peter'; cf. Acts i. 14 σὺν
γυναιξὶν καὶ Μαριάμ, and the less complete parallel in i. 5 ἡ Ἰουδαία χώρα
καὶ οἱ Ἱεροσολυμεῖται (cf. WM., p. 546).
Peter is named, both as the first of
the Eleven, and probably also to assure
him that his denials are forgiven
(Thpht.: ὡς κορυφαῖος...ἢ...ἵνα μὴ σκαν-
δαλισθῇ...ὡς αὐτὸς μὴ λόγου ἀξιωθεὶς
οἷα ἀρνησάμενος—cf. Bede: "vocatur
ex nomine ne desperaret ex nega-
tione"); cf. 1 Cor. xv. 5 ὤφθη Κηφᾷ,
εἶτα τοῖς δώδεκα. The message would
open of course with the tidings of the
Resurrection (εἴπατε ὅτι Ἠγέρθη, Mt.),
but its purpose was to turn the steps
of the Apostles to Galilee whither

the Master would precede them.
Προάγει ὑμᾶς εἰς τὴν Γαλειλαίαν (Mt.
Mc.); cf. xiv. 28, note; the reminder
is necessary, for the words of Christ
would be forgotten for the while in
the excitement of the great events
which had occurred. It is more difficult to understand why the matter
should have been so urgent if a
week at least was to intervene before
the Risen Christ left Jerusalem (Jo.
xx. 26). Perhaps it was important to
dispel at the outset any expectations
of an immediate setting up of the
Kingdom of GOD in a visible form at
Jerusalem (cf. Acts i. 6). Καθὼς εἶπεν
ὑμῖν: Mt., with a complete change of
reference, ἰδοὺ εἶπον ὑμῖν.

8. καὶ ἐξελθοῦσαι ἔφυγον κτλ.] The
picture is true to psychological probability. At first the Angel's words
only increased their terror; they
turned and fled from the tomb,
trembling and unable for the moment
to collect their thoughts or control
themselves. On ἔκστασις see v. 42 note,
and cf. Lc. v. 26, Acts iii. 10, x. 10;
εἶχεν=ἔλαβεν (Lc. l.c., cf. Field, Notes,
p. 44 f. and Deissmann, B. St. p. 293),
κατείχεν, cf. Jos. ant. v. 1, 18 κατά-
πληξις εἶχε τοὺς ἀκούοντας: for other
exx. see Field ad l. As they came to
themselves and began to realise the
truth, joy mingled with their fear and
predominated (Mt. μετὰ φόβου καὶ
χαρᾶς μεγάλης), and their flight was
changed into an eager haste to de-

αὐτὰς τρόμος καὶ ἔκστασις· καὶ οὐδενὶ οὐδὲν εἶπαν,

ἐφοβοῦντο γάρ ¶ ⁕ ⁕ ⁕ ⁕ ⁕ ⁕   ¶ ℵB syr^sin

[⁹ Ἀναστὰς δὲ πρωὶ πρώτη σαββάτου ἐφάνη 9

8 τρομος] φοβος DΠ*^vid arm^vid | om και εκστασις arm   9 δε C²] κ̓αι C*^vid om δε 13 69 124 604* al^nonn arm^zoh+o Ιησους F^w 13 28 69 124 604 1071 al^nonmu c ff vg^sixt arm^codzoh | om πρωι Ϸ | πρωτη] τη μια Eus syr^hier | σαββατων ΚΙΙ 1 al^satmu Eus⅔ | εφανη πρωτον] εφανερωσεν πρωτοις D εφανη πρωτη 2^pe om πρωτον syr^hier arm me Eus^l

liver their message (ἔδραμον ἀπαγγεῖλαι κτλ.). But Mc.'s narrative comes to an abrupt end before this second stage of feeling has been reached; fear still prevails, and the shock has been too severe to permit them to say a word about what had occurred. Οὐδενὶ οὐδὲν εἶπαν is too general a statement to justify the limitation κατὰ τὴν ὁδόν (cf. Lc. x. 4); until their terrors had subsided they had no thought for the Angel's message and no tongue to tell it. According to Lc. xxiv. 9 it was delivered by them afterwards ; cf. vv. 10, 11, notes, and Jo. xx. 18. With the abrupt ending comp. ix. 6, ἔκφοβοι γὰρ ἐγένοντο: the parallel however is not exact, and it is perhaps improbable that the Evangelist deliberately concluded a paragraph with ἐφοβοῦντο γάρ (cf. WH., Notes, p. 46). As Mr Burkitt suggests (Two Lectures, p. 28), some object may have followed the verb. For an instance of a broken sentence at the end of an imperfect document see 1 Esdr. ix. 55, compared with 2 Esdr. xviii. 13.

9—11. THE APPEARANCE TO MARY MAGDALENE (Jo. xx. 11—18).

9. ἀναστὰς δὲ πρωὶ κτλ.] The sequence is suddenly broken, and Mary Magdalene, who is one of the three women mentioned in xvi. 1, becomes, as in Jo. xx., the subject of a distinct narrative which in form at least is not consistent with the Marcan tradition. She is introduced to the reader, as if she had not been named before (παρ' ἧς κτλ.); alone of the three she sees the Lord, and announces the Resur-

rection to the Eleven, and no explanation is given of this unexpected turn in the events. Lastly, the paragraph has evidently been detached from some document in which the Lord has been the subject of the preceding sentence; in its present position ὁ Ἰησοῦς is imperatively required (cf. WH., Notes, p. 51). On the general question of the authorship of the fragment xvi. 9—20 and its relation to the Gospel, see the Introduction. Πρωί is doubtless to be taken with ἀναστάς, not with ἐφάνη, and thus it determines the time when the Resurrection took place—on the third day, as the Lord had foretold, though before daybreak, perhaps in the earliest hour of the morning watch.

πρώτη σαββάτου] Cf. τῇ μιᾷ τῶν σαββάτων (v. 1, note); the use of πρῶτος in this phrase is apparently unique, though we have πρώτη ἡμέρα τῶν ἀζύμων in xiv. 12, Mt. xxvi. 17. The Gospels moreover seem to prefer σάββατα in this connexion, but cf. 1 Cor. xvi. 2 κατὰ μίαν σαββάτου. Ἐφάνη occurs here only in reference to an appearance of the risen Christ; see, however, Num. xxiii. 4 ἐφάνη ὁ θεὸς τῷ Βαλαάμ, Lc. ix. 8 Ἠλείας ἐφάνη. A more usual term is ὤφθη, Lc. xxiv. 34, 1 Cor. xv. 5 ff.; cf. ὀπτανόμενος Acts i. 3, and ὄψεσθε v. 7, supra. That the Lord appeared first to the Magdalene may have been inferred from the narrative of Jo. xx. 11 ff. St Paul's Κηφᾷ εἶτα τοῖς δώδεκα (1 Cor. xv. 5) determines only the relative order of the appearance to Peter and the other Apostles.

πρῶτον Μαρία τῇ Μαγδαληνῇ παρ' ἧς ἐκβεβλήκει ἑπτὰ
¶ ¶ 10 δαιμόνια. ¹⁰ἐκείνη πορευθεῖσα ἀπήγγειλεν τοῖς μετ'¶

9 παρ C*DLΨ⊓¹² 33] αφ AC³EGKMSUVXΓΔΠΣ℘ minᶠᵉʳᵉᵒᵐⁿ   10 εκεινη] + δε
C*ᵛⁱᵈ minᵖᵃᵘᶜ cfflq sinᵖᵉˢʰ arm | πορευθεισα] απελθουσα KΠ minᵖᵃᵘᶜ videns 1 | τοις
μετ αυτου] pr αυτοις D τοις μ. αυτης syrʰⁱᵉʳ

παρ' ἧς ἐκβεβλήκει ἑ. δ.] The fact
was known also to Lc. (viii. 2 ἀφ' ἧς δ.
ἑ. ἐξεληλύθει). 'Εκβάλλειν παρά occurs
here only: for παρά with the gen.
indicating the quarter from which a
movement proceeds see viii. 11, xii. 2,
xiv. 43, and on its distinction from ἀπό
cf. WM., p. 456f. 'Επτὰ δαιμόνια ("septenarii spiritus," Tertullian, cited
above p. 95) recalls Mt. xii. 45, ἑπτὰ
ἕτερα πνεύματα πονηρότερα, and the
striking contrast in Apoc iii. 1 τὰ ἑ.
πνεύματα τοῦ θεοῦ. Cf. Thpht.: ἑπτὰ
δαιμ., τὰ ἐναντία τῶν ἑπτὰ τῆς ἀρετῆς
πνευμάτων. To Celsus it appeared to
be a fatal objection to the Christian
faith that the earliest witness of the
Resurrection should have been, on
the shewing of the Gospels themselves,
a γυνὴ πάροιστρος. The objection repeats itself, though the tone is widely
different, in the last words of Renan's
chapter on Jésus au tombeau: "pou-
voir divin de l'amour! moments sacrés
où la passion d'une hallucinée donne
au monde un Dieu ressuscité!" But
the hallucination of the Magdalene
belongs to the μωρὸν τοῦ θεοῦ, which
is at once wiser and stronger than
men. Renan, however, has ludicrously
overestimated the place which Mary
Magdalene holds among the witnesses
of the Resurrection; cf. Les Apôtres,
p. 13, "la gloire de la résurrection
appartient donc à Marie de Magdala;
après Jésus, c'est Marie qui a le plus
fait pour la fondation du christianisme."
So far was this from being recognised
by the Apostolic age that St Paul
does not even mention her in his
summary of the evidence (1 Cor. xv.
5 ff.).

10. ἐκείνη πορευθεῖσα ἀπήγγειλεν
κτλ.] Cf. Jo., ἔρχεται...ἀγγέλλουσα
τοῖς μαθηταῖς. Both accounts are
singularly devoid of the animation
which such a moment would suggest;
contrast ἔδραμον, Mt. xxviii. 8, and
praecurrens, which some O.L. texts
substitute here. 'Εκείνη, illa, cf. v.
13: the pronoun is neither emphatic
nor antithetic, merely indicating the
subject, as in Jo. v. 46, vii. 45—a non-
Marcan use; cf. Blass, Gr. p. 168.
Mc. seems also to have avoided the
colourless πορεύεσθαι, which occurs
abundantly in the other Gospels, and
thrice in this context; in ix. 30, if
genuine, it has the specific sense of
taking a journey. Τοῖς μετ' αὐτοῦ
γενομένοις: 'to those who had been
with Him,' cf. ii. 19, iii. 14, Jo. xiii.
33, xvii. 12, Acts iv. 13. In their
strictest sense the words describe
only the Apostolic body, yet see Acts
i. 21; all the other μαθηταί who were
in Jerusalem at the time were probably in the company (comp. v. 12,
note, Acts i. 13 ff.). Though Jerusalem was keeping the Feast, the disciples were occupied in mourning and
bewailing their loss; cf. Jo. xvi. 20
κλαύσετε καὶ θρηνήσετε ὑμεῖς. The
combination πενθεῖν καὶ κλαίειν is
frequent, cf. 2 Regn. xix. 1, 2 Esdr.
xi. 4, xviii. 9, Lc. vi. 25, Jas. iv. 9,
Apoc. xviii. 11, 15, 19; the present
passage is apparently imitated by
Ps. Pet. (ev. 7 ἐνηστεύομεν (Mc. ii.
20) καὶ ἐκαθεζόμεθα πενθοῦντες καὶ
κλαίοντες νυκτὸς καὶ ἡμέρας ἕως τοῦ
σαββάτου, cf. ib. 12 ἡμεῖς δὲ οἱ δώδεκα
μαθηταὶ τοῦ κυρίου ἐκλαίομεν καὶ ἐλυ-
πούμεθα).

αὐτοῦ γενομένοις, πενθοῦσι καὶ κλαίουσιν· ¹¹ κἀκεῖνοι 11
ἀκούσαντες ὅτι ζῇ καὶ ἐθεάθη ὑπ' αὐτῆς ἠπίστησαν.
¹² Μετὰ δὲ ταῦτα ¶ δυσὶν ἐξ αὐτῶν περιπατοῦσιν 12 ¶ g⁰

10 γινομενοις 69 | πενθουσιν AL   11 κακεινοι AC³D*ΧΓΔΙΣ minᵖˡ n vg]
εκεινοι δε C* c ff q me εκεινοι LUΨⱣ 127 1071 cˢᶜʳ syrʰᵉˡ arm | ηπιστησαν] και ουκ
επιστευσαν αυτη (-τω D*) D   12 om περιπατουσιν 1 syrʰⁱᵉʳ arm

11. κἀκεῖνοι ἀκούσαντες ὅτι ζῇ κτλ.]
According to Jo., Mary's report was
conveyed in the words Ἑώρακα τὸν
κύριον. This writer's account goes
further ; Mary can testify that the
Master is alive (ζῇ) ; what she had
seen was not a mere vision. This
was the constant belief of the eye-
witnesses : Lc. xxiv. 5, 23, Acts i. 3,
xxv. 19, Rom. vi. 10, Apoc. i. 18,
ii. 8. Ἐθεάθη : this word, which is
not used in the genuine work of Mc.
but occurs frequently in Jo., seems to
point to the beauty and wonderful-
ness of what she saw ; cf. Jo. i. 14, 32,
Acts i. 11, xxii. 9, 1 Jo. i. 1, iv. 12, 14.
For the aor. pass. see Mt. vi. 1, xxiii. 5.
Our writer uses θεᾶσθαι again in v. 14,
but in the middle.

ἠπίστησαν] Of this result Jo. says
nothing ; Lc. connects it with the
message of the women (xxiv. 11 ἐφάνησαν...λῆρος τὰ ῥήματα ταῦτα καὶ ἠπί-
στουν αὐταῖς)—the occasion is possibly
the same, for no Evangelist mentions
both visits ; cf. v. 8, note. Ἀπιστεῖν,
which is common in class. Gk., occurs
but seldom in the N. T. (Lc.ᵉᵛ· ², ᵃᶜᵗ·¹,
Paul², 1 Pet.¹, and twice in this fragment, vv. 11, 16) ; the stronger ἀπει-
θεῖν is more frequent in Biblical Gk.
(LXX.⁴⁸, N.T.¹⁴) ; the relative meanings
of the two may be studied in Heb. iii.
12, 18 f., iv. 11, where ἀπιστία is seen
to pass readily into ἀπείθεια. The
disciples had reached only the first
stage ; see v. 14, note.

12—13. Appearance to two Disciples on their way into the
country (Lc. xxiv. 13—32).

12. μετὰ δὲ ταῦτα δυσίν κτλ.] The

writer knows only that this manifestation was subsequent to that which
was vouchsafed to the Magdalene (cf.
πρῶτον, v. 9) ; from Lc. we learn that
it took place on the same day (ἐν αὐτῇ
τῇ ἡμέρᾳ, xxiv. 13). Μετὰ ταῦτα (τοῦτο)
is not a Marcan phrase, but occurs
frequently in Lc. and Jo. (Lc.ᵉᵛ· ⁵, ᵃᶜᵗ·⁴,
Jo.¹²). The two belonged to the
company of the Eleven, for ἐξ αὐτῶν
apparently looks back to ἐκεῖνοι in
the preceding verse ; in Lc., where
the same phrase occurs, the reference
is less distinct, but the Apostolic
party are probably intended (cf. v. 10).
They were walking when they met
Him, on their way to the country (εἰς
ἀγρόν, cf. ἀπ' ἀγροῦ, xv. 21), i.e., as Lc.
explains, εἰς κώμην ἀπέχουσαν σταδίους
ἑξήκοντα ἀπὸ Ἰερουσαλήμ, ᾗ ὄνομα
Ἐμμαούς. A walk of about seven
English miles brought them to this
place, which cannot therefore have
been Emmaus Nicopolis, now Am-
wâs, 22 miles from Jerusalem on the
Jaffa road (1 Macc. iii. 40, 57, iv. 3,
Jos. ant. xiii. 1. 3, etc. ; cf. Eus.
onom. αὕτη ἐστὶν ἡ νῦν Νικόπολις, and
see Neubauer, géogr. du T., p. 100 f.).
Josephus (B. J. vii. 6. 6) mentions a
χωρίον of the same name, distant
from Jerusalem σταδίους τριάκοντα
(v.l. ἑξήκοντα) which may be identical
with Lc.'s κώμη. Caspari suggests
Mozah (Josh. xviii. 26), which in
some MSS. of the LXX. appears as
Ἀμωσά or Ἀμμουσά (הַמֹּצָה). The
site is necessarily undetermined, but
el-Kubeibeh, Kulonieh, and el-Kham-
asa have been proposed, places which
lie respectively N.W., W., and S.W. of

ἐφανερώθη ἐν ἑτέρᾳ μορφῇ, πορευομένοις εἰς ἀγρόν·
13 ¹³κἀκεῖνοι ἀπελθόντες ἀπήγγειλαν τοῖς λοιποῖς· οὐδὲ
¶ n   ἐκείνοις ἐπίστευσαν.¶

§o 14   ¹⁴§ᵈ Ὕστερον [δὲ] ἀνακειμένοις αὐτοῖς τοῖς ἕνδεκα

13 εκεινοι L ff arm   14 υστερον δε ΑΔΣ 2ᵖᵉ aᵖᵃᵘᶜ syrrᵖᵉˢʰ ʰᶜˡ* me aeth] om δε
CEGKLMSUVXΓΔΠΨϷ minᵖˡ ff vg syrʰᶜˡ* arm | om αυτοις L 13 syrrᵖᵉˢʰ ʰᶜˡ arm

the city. Of these *Kulonieh*, or rather
the adjacent *Beit Mizza* (Mozah),
seems to have the best claim.
Lc. gives the name of one of the
two disciples as Κλεόπας, i.e. Κλεόπατρος (cf. Ἀντίπας = Ἀντίπατρος, Apoc.
ii. 13, and see Lightfoot, *Galatians*,
p. 267).

Ἐν ἑτέρᾳ μορφῇ suggests a transfor-
mation analogous to that described
in ix. 2, but the account in Lc. forbids
this; there was clearly nothing in
the Lord's appearance to distinguish
Him from any other wayfaring man.
The words must be explained as contrasting the Magdalene's impression
(*v.* 9) with that received by the two;
to her He had seemed to be a κηπου-
ρός (Jo. xx. 15), to them He appeared
in the light of a συνοδοιπόρος. Lc.
explains that their inability to recognise Him was due to their own in-
fatuation (xxiv. 16); when that was
removed, they knew Him at once
(*ib. v.* 31). Ἐν ἑτέρῳ σχήματι might
have been expected in this connexion,
but σχῆμα, as Lightfoot suggests, may
have been "avoided instinctively, as
it might imply an illusion or an im-
posture" (*Philippians*, p. 129). For
the Gnostic notion that the Lord's
humanity possessed the power of
assuming different forms see *Acta
Johannis*, 1 ff. (ed. James, p. 3). A
similar property is ascribed to St
Thomas (*Acta Thomae*, 34, ed. Tisch.,
p. 219, ἄνθρωπος γὰρ εἰ δύο μορφὰς
ἔχων, καὶ ὅπου ἂν θέλῃς ἐκεῖ εὑρίσκῃ).

13. κἀκεῖνοι…ἀπήγγειλαν τοῖς λοιποῖς κτλ.] Vg. *et illi euntes nuntiave-
runt ceteris* (cf. ἐκείνη, *v.* 10, note; on
the crasis κἀκ. see Gregory, *prolegg.* i.

p. 96). The circumstances are given
by Lc. (xxiv. 33 f.). Οὐδὲ ἐκείνοις
ἐπίστευσαν. The writer of the fragment is evidently not indebted to Lc.
for his knowledge of the facts, for
according to Lc. the two were met by
their brethren at Jerusalem with the
cry ἠγέρθη ὁ κύριος καὶ ὤφθη Σίμωνι.
Those who shared this conviction
would certainly not have been unwilling to find a confirmation of their
hopes in the tidings from Emmaus.
At the same time there may have
been and probably was (cf. Mt. xxviii.
16, Jo. xx. 24 ff.) another current of
feeling which was adverse to the
testimony of Simon, and those who
were under its influence would have
rejected the story of the two. Aug.
is possibly right in his view of this
apparent discrepancy: "quid intellegendum est nisi aliquos ibi fuisse qui
hoc nollent credere?" Οὐδέ takes up
and accentuates the negative implied
in ἠπίστησαν (*v.* 11). The two men did
not fare better than the solitary woman
who had been the first to announce
the Resurrection.

14—18. APPEARANCES TO THE
ELEVEN (Lc. xxiv. 36—43, Jo. xx.
19—23, Mt. xxviii. 16—20: cf. 1 Cor.
xv. 5 ff.).

14. ὕστερον δέ κτλ.] At length,
after manifestations vouchsafed to an
individual and to two disciples not of
Apostolic rank, the Lord revealed
Himself to the Apostolic college. The
paragraph which follows seems to
be a summary of the various narratives within the writer's knowledge
which spoke of appearances to that
body. It is without note of time or

ἐφανερώθη, καὶ ὠνείδισεν τὴν ἀπιστίαν αὐτῶν¹ καὶ   ¶ Σ

§σκληροκαρδίαν ὅτι τοῖς θεασαμένοις αὐτὸν ἐγηγερ-   § H

14 ἐγηγερμενον] om X + (et) nuntiantibus (illis) o q

place, and *v*. 19 suggests that it is intended to cover the whole period between the evening of the Resurrection-day and the Ascension. Ὕστερον δέ, another non-Marcan phrase, completes the series started by πρῶτον (*v*. 9) and continued by μετὰ δὲ ταῦτα (*v*. 12); cf. Mt. xxi. 34 ff. ἀπέστειλεν...πάλιν ἀπέστειλεν...ὕστερον δὲ (Mc. ἔσχατον) ἀπέστειλεν : xxii. 25 ff. ὁ πρῶτος...ὁ δεύτερος...ὕστερον δὲ (Mc. ἔσχατον) πάντων. Ἀνακειμένοις αὐτοῖς τοῖς ἕνδεκα ἐφ.: the first visit of the risen Christ to the Eleven themselves was paid when they were at table. This circumstance agrees with the time of day (Lc. xxiv. 29, 33, Jo. xx. 19), and moreover seems to be implied in Lc. xxiv. 41, where they answer the Lord's question ἔχετέ τι βρώσιμον by producing some cooked fish (ἰχθύος ὀπτοῦ μέρος). Αὐτοῖς τοῖς ἕνδεκα, *ipsis* (not *illis*, Vg.) *undecim*: αὐτοῖς contrasts the Eleven as a body with the isolated witnesses who had brought reports of the earlier manifestations. The use of οἱ ἕνδ. (cf. Lc.) does not decide the question whether the writer was aware of the absence of Thomas : 'the Eleven' are the Apostolic body regarded as an unit, cf. the use of οἱ δώδεκα in Jo. xx. 24, 1 Cor. xv. 5, *Ev. Petr.* 12. Ἐφανερώθη : a favourite word with St John, especially in reference to the self-manifestations of Christ (Jo. i. 31, ii. 11, vii. 4, xxi. 1 *bis*, 14, 1 Jo. i. 2 *bis*, ii. 28, iii. 5, 8).

καὶ ὠνείδισεν τὴν ἀπιστίαν αὐτῶν κτλ.] The writer is still upon the note which he struck in *vv*. 11, 13. He shews himself independent both of Jo., whose account seems to leave no place for this rebuke, and Lc., who represents the Eleven as disbelieving their own senses (*vv*. 37, 41); in our

fragment a middle course is taken which agrees with the previous context (τοῖς θεασαμένοις αὐτόν...οὐκ ἐπίστευσαν). Ὠνείδισεν is not used elsewhere of a censure pronounced by the Lord on the Apostles. He 'reproached' Bethsaida, Chorazin and Capernaum for their impenitence (Mt. xi. 20), but His unfavourable judgements on His disciples are expressed in rebukes (viii. 33), not in reproaches. It may have been that something sharper than rebuke (cf. xiv. 41, note) was necessary to rouse them from the faithless despondency into which they had been plunged by the Crucifixion ; but the use of the word is more probably one sign among many of a handling less delicate and psychologically exact than that to which we are accustomed in the canonical gospels. Τὴν ἀπιστίαν αὐτῶν καὶ σκλ. Nowhere else is σκληροκαρδία laid to the charge of the Apostles (cf. x. 5), or even ἀπιστία : they are ὀλιγόπιστοι (Mt. vi. 30, viii. 26, xiv. 31, xvi. 8); their faith is immature, wanting in promptness, and sometimes on the point of collapse (Mc. iv. 40, xi. 22, Lc. xxii. 32); there is a real danger lest they should drift into final unbelief (Jo. xx. 27 μὴ γίνου ἄπιστος), but ἄπιστοι in the strict sense they are not. Similarly the Lord complains of the callousness (viii. 17), rather than of the hardness of their hearts ; the latter state goes along with impenitence (Rom. ii. 5), and implies the absence or failure of love. The words are harsher than any which the Lord is elsewhere reported to have used towards His disciples, although it is possible, as has been suggested, that a peculiarly drastic treatment was necessary at this moment. Ὅτι, for that ; cf. WM., p. 551. Ἐγηγερμένον, not ἐγερθέντα :

15 μένον [ἐκ νεκρῶν] οὐκ ἐπίστευσαν. ¹⁵καὶ εἶπεν αὐτοῖς
Πορευθέντες εἰς τὸν κόσμον ἅπαντα κηρύξατε τὸ

14 om εκ νεκρων C³DEFGHKLMSUVΓΠΨϸ minᵖˡ latt syrrᵖᵉˢʰ ʰⁱᵉʳ me aeth (hab
AC*ΧΔ minⁿᵒⁿⁿ syrʰᵉˡ arm) 15 αυτοις] προς αυτους D | om απαντα D syrʰⁱᵉʳ
me | το ευαγγελιον]+μου syrrᵖᵉˢʰ ʰⁱᵉʳ (cf. Act. Pil. A cod. E ap. Tisch. p. 259)

they had seen Him in His risen state;
cf. 2 Tim. ii. 8 μνημόνευε...ἐγηγερμένον,
'have Him in remembrance as (not
raised merely but) risen.' See note on
v. 6.

Jerome (c. Pelag. ii. 15) found here
in some copies of the Gospel, chiefly
Greek, the remarkable addition: "Et
illi satisfaciebant dicentes, Saeculum
istud iniquitatis et incredulitatis sub
Satana est qui (codd. quae) non sinit
per immundos spiritus ueram dei
apprehendi uirtutem. idcirco iam
nunc reuela iustitiam tuam." The
Greek text of this passage with its
context has now come to light in the
Freer ms. of the Gospels (W), which
after οὐκ ἐπίστευσαν proceeds: κἀκεῖνοι
ἀπελογοῦντο (cod. -ντε) λέγοντες ὅτι Ὁ
αἰὼν οὗτος τῆς ἀνομίας καὶ τῆς ἀπιστίας
ὑπὸ τὸν σατανᾶν ἐστιν τὸν μὴ ἐῶντα
ᵗπὸ πνευμάτων ἀκαθάρτων (cod. ὁ μὴ
ἐῶν τὰ ὑπὸ τῶν πν. ἀκάθαρτα) τὴν ἀλήθειαν τοῦ θεοῦ καταλαβέσθαι καὶ δύναμιν.
διὰ τοῦτο ἀποκάλυψόν σου τὴν δικαιο-
σύνην ἤδη. ἐκεῖνοι ἔλεγον [?ταῦτα] τῷ
χριστῷ. καὶ ὁ χριστὸς ἐκείνοις προσέ-
λεγον ὅτι Πεπλήρωται ὁ ὅρος τῶν ἐτῶν
τῆς ἐξουσίας τοῦ σατανᾶ. ἀλλὰ ἐγγίζει
ἄλλα δεινὰ καὶ [?ἐκείνοις] ὑπὲρ ὧν ἁμαρ-
τησάντων ἐγὼ παρεδόθην εἰς θάνατον ἵνα
ὑποστρέψωσιν εἰς τὴν ἀλήθειαν καὶ
μηκέτι ἁμαρτήσωσιν, ἵνα τὴν ἐν οὐρανῷ
πνευματικὴν καὶ ἄφθαρτον τῆς δικαιοσύνης δόξαν κληρονομήσωσιν. ἀλλὰ
πορευθέντες εἰς τὸν κόσμον ἅπαντα κτλ.
On the text and interpretation of
this fragment and its relation to the
Marcan Appendix see Two new Gospel fragments in Lietzmann's Kleine
Texte (E. tr., Cambridge, 1908),
pp. 9—12.

15. καὶ εἶπεν αὐτοῖς Πορευθέντες κτλ.]
The words are in strange contrast to
the stern reproof of the previous
verse; the extreme compression which
the writer of the fragment practises
has led him to connect two occasions
which were separated by more than
a week. At the first interview the
Eleven were entrusted with a new
mission (πέμπω ὑμᾶς, Jo.), but the
particulars were reserved for the
meeting in Galilee (Mt.). On the
whole the present passage follows the
lines of the Galilean charge; πορευθέντες κτλ. corresponds to Mt.'s πορ.
οὖν μαθητεύσατε πάντα τὰ ἔθνη, and in
each account there is a reference to
baptism as connected with the world-
wide teaching. Yet there is no indication of dependence on Mt.; our
writer pursues his own course (vv.
17 f.), and probably fuses later instructions with those which belong to
the interview among the Galilean hills.

In Act. Pil. A (c. xiv.) these verses
(15—18) are quoted with the preface
εἴδομεν τὸν Ἰησοῦν καὶ τοὺς μαθητὰς
αὐτοῦ καθιζόμενον εἰς τὸ ὅρος τὸ καλούμενον Μαμίλχ (al. Μαμβήχ); see the
note on this in Thilo, p. 617 ff.

That the Eleven were to be the
heralds of the Gospel to the world, as
the Master had been its herald in
Galilee (i. 14), was a revelation reserved for the days after the Resurrection; but the catholic mission of
the Gospel had been foretold before
the Passion, in nearly the same words
that are used here (Mt. xxvi. 13,
Mc. xiv. 9, notes). Πάσῃ τῇ κτίσει has,
however, a Pauline ring: in Mc. κτίσις
is used only in the phrase ἀπ' ἀρχῆς
κτίσεως (x. 6, xiii. 19, notes); in
St Paul we find it in its present connexion (Col. i. 23 τοῦ εὐαγγελίου οὗ
ἠκούσατε τοῦ κηρυχθέντος ἐν πάσῃ

εὐαγγέλιον⁋ πάσῃ τῇ κτίσει. ¹⁶ὁ πιστεύσας καὶ 16 ⁋ D*
βαπτισθεὶς σωθήσεται, ὁ δὲ ἀπιστήσας κατακριθή-
σεται. ¹⁷σημεῖα δὲ §τοῖς πιστεύσασιν ἀκολουθήσει 17 § syrᵉᵘ
ταῦτα· ἐν τῷ ὀνόματί μου δαιμόνια ἐκβαλοῦσιν,

16 ο πιστευσας] ο πιστευων 1071 pr οτι D 1071 2ᵖᵉ 6ᵖᵉ   βαπτισθεις pr ο LΔ
17 ακολουθησει C*LΨ] παρακολουθησει AC²DⲢ 33 | εν] επι L | εκβαλλουσιν D

κτίσει, where see Lightfoot's note).
Πᾶσα ἡ κτίσις is 'the whole creation'
(R.V.), as in Rom. viii. 22: cf. Judith
ix. 12 βασιλεῦ πάσης κτίσεώς σου, xvi.
14 σοὶ δουλευσάτω πᾶσα ἡ κτίσις σου,
3 Macc. ii. 2, 7, vi. 2. Here probably
the phrase = πάσῃ τῇ οἰκουμένῃ (Euth.)
sc. to all men, cf. πάντα τὰ ἔθνη, Mt.;
not however without an outlook upon
the inanimate world, to which the
Gospel offers the hope of an ἀποκατάστασις πάντων (Rom. l.c., 2 Pet. iii. 13).
16. ὁ πιστεύσας καὶ βαπτισθείς κτλ.]
Vg. qui crediderit et baptizatus fuerit: the aor. participles describe
acts which are past in relation to the
time of the principal verb, for both
the acceptance of the Gospel and the
ministration of baptism precede salvation (cf. Burton § 134 f.). Βαπτισθείς,
pass., corresponds to βαπτίζοντες in
Mt.; converts were to receive baptism
at the hands of the Eleven or of other
disciples; the middle is used (Acts
xxii. 16) where the voluntary submission of the recipient is chiefly in view.
For σώζεσθαι in the deeper sense of
gaining restoration to spiritual health
see viii. 35 (2°), x. 26, xiii. 13, notes.
The connexion between πίστις and
σωτηρία is illustrated in the Gospels
by the miracles of healing, and in the
Epistles takes its place as an axiom of
Christian soteriology; baptism is less
commonly but as distinctly associated
with 'salvation' in the Apostolic
writings (1 Pet. iii. 21 ὑμᾶς...νῦν σώζει
βάπτισμα, Tit. iii. 5 ἔσωσεν ἡμᾶς διὰ
λουτροῦ παλινγενεσίας: cf. Lc.'s use of
οἱ σωζόμενοι in Acts ii. 47). Σωθήσεται is of course not an unconditional
promise of final restoration; cf. Euth.:

σωθήσεται εἴγε τὰ τῆς πίστεως καὶ τὰ
τοῦ βαπτίσματος ἐπιδείξεται.
ὁ δὲ ἀπιστήσας κατακριθήσεται] There
is no need to repeat the reference to
baptism: ἀπιστήσας carries with it the
neglect of the sacrament of faith, but
in itself it is sufficient to secure condemnation. Throughout the fragment
this writer lays the greatest emphasis
on the primary obligation of belief
and the sinfulness of unbelief. The
present words are strongly Johannine
in tone (cf. Jo. iii. 18), though κατακρίνειν does not belong to the vocabulary of the Fourth Gospel. Neither the
nature nor the ground of the sentence
on unbelief appears here; the latter
comes into sight in Jo. iii. 19 f.
17. σημεῖα δὲ τοῖς πιστ. ἀκολουθήσει
ταῦτα] Cf. Jo. xiv. 12 ὁ πιστεύων
εἰς ἐμὲ τὰ ἔργα ἃ ἐγὼ ποιῶ κἀκεῖνος ποιήσει. The promise is not limited to the
Apostles; τοῖς πιστεύσασιν includes
their converts, and indeed seems specially to point to them (Vg. eos qui credi-
derint, cf. v. 16). That it was fulfilled
is evident from casual references in the
Epp. of St Paul, e.g. 1 Cor. xii. 28,
Gal. iii. 5, though the former passage
shews that the σημεῖα did not, even
in the Apostles' age, attend every
believer (τοῖς π., not τῷ πιστεύσαντι).
Their purpose was to be 'signs' of the
Divine mission of the Church, not to
accredit the faith of the individual.
On σημεῖον see xiii. 22, note; standing
by itself as it does here, the word is
characteristic of St John (Jo.¹⁶). In
σημεῖα...ταῦτα the pronoun is quasi-
predicative: 'these are the signs which
shall follow.'
ἐν τῷ ὀνόματί μου κτλ.] The first

¶ p

¶ II*

18 γλώσσαις λαλήσουσιν [καιναῖς], ¹⁸[καὶ ἐν ταῖς χερσὶν]
ὄφεις ἀροῦσιν, κἂν θανάσιμόν τι πίωσιν¶ οὐ μὴ
αὐτοὺς βλάψῃ· ἐπὶ ἀρρώστους χεῖρας ἐπιθήσουσιν
καὶ καλῶς¶ ἕξουσιν.

17 om γλωσσαις λαλ. καιναις ℞ | om καιναις C*LΔΨ arm me (hab AC²DX rell syrʰⁱᵉʳ) 18 om και εν ταις χερσιν AD syrᵖᵉˢʰ ʰⁱᵉʳ (hab C*²LMᵐᵍXΔ 1 22 33 604 2ᵖᵉ 6ᵖᵉ 6ᵉᵛ syrᵉᵛ ʰᶜˡ* arm) | ποιωσιν D* | ου μη AC³L] ουδεν C* arm | βλαψει minᵐᵘ

'sign' had already 'followed' the Apostles in their Galilean mission (vi. 13), and the Seventy also (Lc. x. 17 ff.); indeed, the Name had been occasionally used in this way by believers who were not even formally disciples (ix. 38). The post-Apostolic Church believed itself to retain this power : cf. e.g. Justin, *dial.* 30 σήμερον καὶ ἐξορκιζόμενα κατὰ τοῦ ὀνόματος Ἰησοῦ Χριστοῦ...ὑποτάσσεται : *ib.* 76 καὶ νῦν ἡμεῖς οἱ πιστεύοντες...τὰ δαιμόνια πάντα καὶ πνεύματα πονηρὰ ἐξορκίζοντες ὑποτασσόμενα ἡμῖν ἔχομεν.

γλώσσαις λαλήσουσιν] Cf. Acts ii. 3 f. ὤφθησαν αὐτοῖς διαμεριζόμεναι γλῶσσαι...καὶ ἤρξαντο λαλεῖν ἑτέραις γλώσσαις, x. 46 ἤκουον γὰρ αὐτῶν λαλούντων γλώσσαις, *ib.* xix. 6, 1 Cor. xii. 28 ἔθετο ὁ θεὸς ἐν τῇ ἐκκλησίᾳ...γένη γλωσσῶν, and the full treatment of the subject *ib.* c. xiv. Late in the second century Irenaeus (cf. Eus. *H. E.* v. 7) bears witness : πολλῶν ἀκούομεν ἀδελφῶν ἐν τῇ ἐκκλησίᾳ παντοδαπῶς λαλούντων διὰ τοῦ πνεύματος γλώσσαις. For various opinions as to the γλωσσολαλία of the primitive Church see Stanley, *Corinthians*, p. 243 ff., Plumptre's art. *Gift of Tongues* in Smith's *B. D.* (iii. 1555 ff.) and A. Robertson's art. in Hastings (iv. p. 793 ff.), McGiffert, *Hist. of Christianity*, pp. 50 ff., 521 ff., A. Wright, *Some N.T. problems*, p. 277 ff. Καιναῖς may have been suggested by the analogy of καινὴ διαθήκη, καινὸς ἄνθρωπος, or the O. T. καινὸν ᾆσμα.

18. ἐν ταῖς χερσὶν ὄφεις κτλ.] Cf. Lc. x. 19 ἰδοὺ δέδωκα ὑμῖν τὴν ἐξουσίαν τοῦ πατεῖν ἐπάνω ὄφεων...καὶ οὐδὲν

ὑμᾶς οὐ μὴ ἀδικήσει. The incident in Acts xxviii. 3 f., though not a direct illustration, belongs to this class of σημεῖα. More exact fulfilments are described by non-canonical writers, e.g. Papias according to Eus. *H.E.* iii. 39 tells of Barsabbas ὡς δηλητήριον φάρμακον ἐμπιόντος καὶ μηδὲν ἀηδές... ὑπομείναντος. The legend of St John and the cup of poison in *Act. Joh.* (Tisch. p. 270) may owe its origin to the saying which our fragment embodies : such stories abounded at a later time, cf. Thpht. : πολλοὶ γὰρ καὶ φάρμακα πιόντες διὰ τῆς τοῦ σταυροῦ σφραγῖδος ἀβλαβεῖς διετηρήθησαν. For the use made of this passage by pagan objectors in the fourth century see Macar. Magn. iii. 16 ὁ πιστεύων καὶ μὴ ποιῶν ταῦτα ἢ γνησίως οὐ πεπίστευκεν, ἢ πιστεύων γνησίως οὐ δυνατὸν ἀλλ' ἀσθενές ἔχει τὸ πιστευόμενον. St Paul's doctrine of Love (1 Cor. xiii. 8 ff.) suggests an answer to the dilemma. The classical θανάσιμος occurs here only in Biblical Gk., which elsewhere uses the poetical θανατηφόρος (LXX.⁵, Jas. iii. 8).

ἐπὶ ἀρρώστους χεῖρας ἐπιθήσουσιν κτλ.] The Twelve had been commissioned to heal the sick, but while the Lord was with them they seem to have used unction, leaving to Him the imposition of hands (vi. 13, note). After the Ascension both signs were employed (see Acts ix. 12, xxviii. 8, Jas. v. 14), and the latter still lingers in the *unctio extrema* of the West and the εὐχέλαιον of the Eastern Church; an office for the anointing of the sick was provided in the first

¹⁹§ʿΟ μὲν [οὖν] κύριος ['Ιησοῦς] μετὰ τὸ λαλῆσαι 19 § F
αὐτοῖς ἀνελήφθη εἰς τὸν οὐρανὸν καὶ ἐκάθισεν ἐκ

19 μεν ουν] om ουν C*L go arm (hab AC²D) δε syrr | om κυριος H minᵖᵃᵘᶜ | om
Ιησους AC³DEGMSUVXΓΗΨ minᵖˡ (hab C*KLΔ 1 22 33 124 1071 2ᵖᵉ alᵖᵃᵘᶜ c ff o vg
syrr arm me aeth Irⁱⁿᵗ)   ανελη's μφθη] ανεφερετο 36 40 ανελ. και ανεφ. 68 | τον
ουρανον] τους ουρανους 13 69 124 346 | εκ δεξιων] εν δεξια CΔ minᵖᵃᵘᶜ εν δεξιων D

English Prayerbook, but disappeared
in 1552. It is interesting to note the
concurrence of the same two signs in
the ceremonial which followed Baptism (cf. Mason, *Confirmation*, p. 12 f.).
The classical καλῶς ἔχειν occurs here
only in the N. T.: cf. 1 Esdr. ii. 18;
for ἄρρωστος see vi. 5, 13.

19—20. THE ASCENSION, AND ITS
SEQUEL (Lc. xxiv. 50 ff., Acts i. 9; cf.
1 Pet. iii. 22, Rom. viii. 34, Heb.
viii. 1).

19. ὁ μὲν οὖν κύριος 'Ιησοῦς κτλ.]
On μὲν οὖν followed by δέ see WM.,
p. 556, n.; while οὖν looks back to the
preceding narrative with its usual
consequential force, μὲν...δέ (*v.* 20)
contrasts the new life into which the
Lord passed by the Ascension with
the work of those whom He left on
earth. Mc. very seldom uses either
οὖν (x. 9, xi. 31, xiii. 25, xv. 12), or
μὲν...δέ (xii. 5, xiv. 21, 28); ὁ κύριος
'Ιησοῦς is without example in the
Gospels, with the possible exception
of Lc. xxiv. 3, though common in the
Acts and occurring occasionally in
St Paul (1 Cor. xi. 23, xvi. 23). Μετὰ
τὸ λαλῆσαι αὐτοῖς : the phrase seems
to connect the preceding verses (15—
18) with the Ascension, as though
they were an outline of the farewell
discourse; cf. Lc. xxiv. 51 ἐν τῷ εὐλογεῖν αὐτὸν αὐτοὺς διέστη ἀπ᾿ αὐτῶν,
Acts i. 9 ταῦτα εἰπών...ἐπήρθη. But,
regard being had to the general
character of the fragment, μετὰ τὸ λ.
may be interpreted, 'after the series
of interviews with the Eleven of which
a specimen has been given'; cf. Euth.:
μετὰ τὸ λαλῆσαι οὐ μόνον τοὺς λόγους
τούτους, ἀλλὰ πάντας ὅσους ἐλάλησεν
αὐτοῖς ἀπὸ τῆς ἡμέρας τῆς ἀναστάσεως

μέχρι συμπληρώσεως τῶν τεσσαράκοντα
ἡμερῶν. This verse is cited by Irenaeus
(iii. 10. 6) with the preamble "in fine
autem evangelii ait Marcus"; see
Introduction.
ἀνελήμφθη εἰς τὸν οὐρανόν κτλ.] Cf.
Acts i. 2, 11, 22, 1 Tim. iii. 16. The
use of ἀναλημφθῆναι for the Ascension
was perhaps suggested by 4 Regn.
ii. 11 ἀνελήμφθη 'Ηλειού...ὡς εἰς τὸν
οὐρανόν, comp. Sir. xlviii. 9, 1 Macc. ii.
58. Other N.T. terms are ἀναβῆναι
(Jo. vi. 62, xx. 17 *bis*, perhaps from Ps.
xxiii. (xxiv.) 3), ἐπαρθῆναι (Acts i. 9),
πορευθῆναι εἰς οὐρανόν (1 Pet. iii. 22),
διεληλυθέναι τοὺς οὐρανούς (Heb. iv.
14), ἁρπασθῆναι πρὸς τὸν θεόν (Apoc.
xii. 5). The Creeds generally employ
ἀναβαίνειν (*ascendere*) or ἀνέρχεσθαι,
possibly because ἀνελήμφθη (*adsump-
tus est*) would have admitted a
Docetic interpretation (*Apostles'
Creed*, p. 71 f.); but the festival of
the Ascension was known in the East
as the Assumption (ἡ ἀνάληψις, ἡ ἑορτὴ
τῆς ἀναλήψεως).
When the author of the fragment
adds καὶ ἐκάθισεν κτλ. he passes beyond the field of history into that of
Christian theology. The belief that
the risen and ascended Christ stands
or sits at the Right Hand of GOD is
one of the earliest and most cherished
of Christian ideas (Acts vii. 55 f.,
Rom. viii. 34, Eph. i. 20, Col. iii. 1,
Heb. i. 3, viii. 1, x. 12, xii. 2, 1 Pet.
iii. 22, Apoc. iii. 21), based on the
Lord's own use of Ps. cx. 1 (xii. 36,
xiv. 62), and it is not unlikely that
the writer has adopted here a primitive formula, or echoes a creed-like
hymn; cf. 1 Tim. iii. 16 ἀνελήμφθη ἐν
δόξῃ. 'Εκ δεξιῶν : so xii. 36, xiv. 62;

20 δεξιῶν τοῦ θεοῦ. ²⁰ἐκεῖνοι δὲ ἐξελθόντες ἐκήρυξαν πανταχοῦ, τοῦ κυρίου συνεργοῦντος καὶ τὸν λόγον βεβαιοῦντος διὰ τῶν ἐπακολουθούντων σημείων.]

19 θεου]+πατρος 1* cˢᵉʳ me arm^cod   20 om δια L | σημειων]+αμην C*EFʷGKL MSUVXΓΔΨ c o me aeth (om AC² 1 33 a1^mu a³ q vg syrr arm)
Subscr κατα Μαρκον Β ευαγγελιον κατα Μ. ℵACEHKLUΓΔΨ k syr^eu τελος του κατα Μ. (αγιον) ευαγγελιον min^mu om MSX

the Epistles use ἐν δεξιᾷ in this connexion. The Creeds show the same variation (Hahn³, p. 384).

20. ἐκεῖνοι δὲ ἐξελθόντες κτλ.] Another rapid summary. The writer passes over without mention the return to Jerusalem, and the founding of the Palestinian Churches, and hurries on to the fulfilment of the Catholic mission confided to the Eleven after the Resurrection (v. 15); the contrast to Lc. xxiv. 52 f. is instructive. Ἐκεῖνοι are here clearly the Eleven (v. 14), but the Eleven reinforced by accessions to the Apostolate and by the self-propagating life of the Ecclesia. Ἐξελθόντες, from Jerusalem in the first instance (Acts i. 8); but the word may include all the fresh departures by which the Gospel was carried from one region to another (cf. Acts xv. 40, xvi. 3, 10, 40, xx. 1, 2 Cor. ii. 13, Phil. iv. 15), till the Kingdom of God seemed to have been proclaimed everywhere. Ἐκήρυξαν πανταχοῦ clearly does not belong to the earliest form of Gospel-tradition, but it might have been written as early as the period of St Paul's Roman imprisonment (Col. i. 23). Cf. Clem. R. 1 Cor. 42 οἱ ἀπόστολοι...ἐξῆλθον εὐαγγελιζόμενοι, Herm. sim. ix. 25 ἀπόστολοι καὶ διδάσκαλοι οἱ κηρύξαντες εἰς ὅλον τὸν κόσμον: Justin, apol. i. 45 ἀπὸ Ἱερουσαλὴμ οἱ ἀπόστολοι αὐτοῦ ἐξελθόντες πανταχοῦ ἐκήρυξαν.

τοῦ κυρίου συνεργοῦντος κτλ.] Συνεργεῖν, συνεργός are used by St Paul of

human cooperation (e.g. Rom. xvi. 3, 9, 21, 1 Cor. iii. 9, xvi. 16), but not of the cooperation of the ascended Lord,— a thought which is expressed in other ways. Βεβαιοῦν is another Pauline word (Rom. xv. 8, 1 Cor. i. 6, 8), and the phrase βεβαίωσις τοῦ εὐαγγελίου (Phil. i. 7) comes very near to our author's βεβαιοῦν τὸν λόγον: on the technical meaning of βεβαίωσις cf. Deissmann, B. St., p. 104 ff. The whole context has also a striking affinity to Heb. ii. 3, 4 ἀρχὴν λαβοῦσα λαλεῖσθαι διὰ τοῦ κυρίου ὑπὸ τῶν ἀκουσάντων εἰς ἡμᾶς ἐβεβαιώθη, συνεπιμαρτυροῦντος τοῦ θεοῦ σημείοις. An instance of the combination of βεβαιοῦν and συνεργεῖν is cited by Wetstein from Plutarch: τοῦ βεβαιοῦντος καὶ συνεργοῦντος πρὸς νόησιν καὶ πίστιν. On the participles see Burton, § 449. Ἐπακολουθεῖν occurs again in 1 Tim. v. 10, 24, 1 Pet. ii. 21.

In the Apostolic age, probably within the experience of the writer, the cooperation of the ascended Christ was manifested 'by the accompanying signs' which had been promised to it. Other ages need and receive in other ways indications no less fruitful or sure of His continual Presence with the workers of His Church (Mt. xxviii. 20). Cf. Bede: "numquid quia ista signa non facimus minime credimus?...sancta quippe ecclesia quotidie spiritaliter facit quod tunc per apostolos corporaliter faciebat......miracula tanto maiora sunt quanto magis spiritalia."

NORTHERN PALESTINE
to illustrate
Mark 1 thru 10

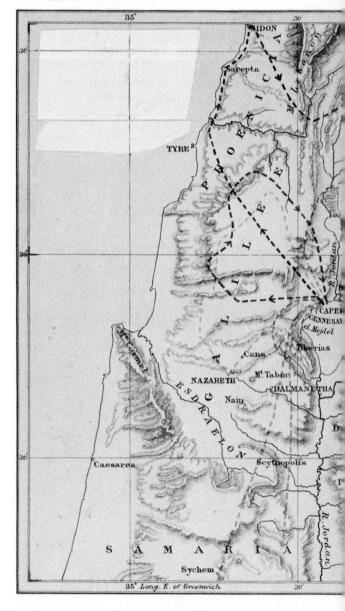

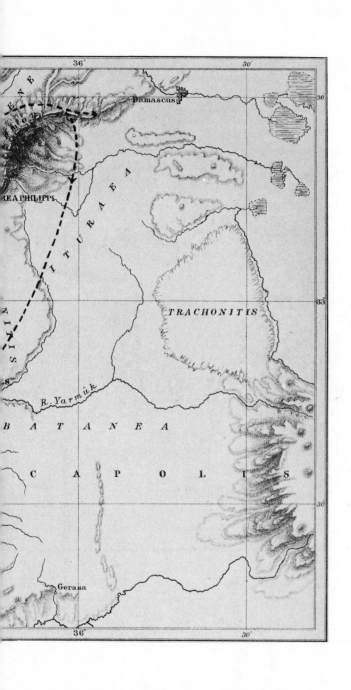

SEA OF GALILEE
and its environs
to illustrate
Mark 1 thru 10

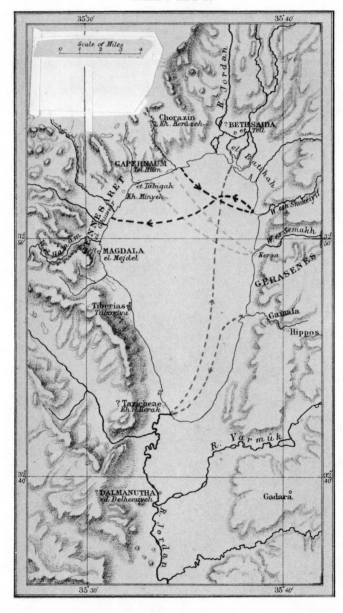

Index of the Greek Words Used in Mark
as printed in this Edition

An asterisk denotes that the word is not used elsewhere in the N.T.

418 / Index of Greek Words

κτίζειν xiii. 19
κτίσις x. 6, xiii. 19, xvi. 15
κύκλῳ iii. 34, vi. 6, 36
*κυλίεσθαι ix. 20
κυλλός ix. 43
κῦμα iv. 37
κυνάριον vii. 27, 28
κύπτειν i. 7
Κυρηναῖος xv. 21
κύριος i. 3 (LXX.), ii. 28, v. 19, vii. 28,
  xi. 3, 9 (LXX.), xii. 9, 11 (LXX.), 29
  (LXX.), 30 (LXX.), 36 (LXX.), 37 (LXX.),
  xiii. 20, 35, xvi. 19, 20
κωλύειν ix. 38, 39, x. 14
κώμη vi. 6, 36, 56, viii. 23, 26, 27, xi. 2
*κωμόπολις i. 38
κωφός vii. 32, 37, ix. 25

λαῖλαψ iv. 37
λαλεῖν i. 34, ii. 2, 7, iv. 33, 34, v. 35,
  36, vi. 50, vii. 35, 37, viii. 32, xi. 23,
  xii. 1, xiii. 11 ter, xiv. 9, 31, 43, xvi.
  17, 19
λαμά xv. 34
λαμβάνειν iv. 16, vi. 41, vii. 27, viii. 6,
  14, ix. 36, x. 30, xi. 24, xii. 2, 3,
  8, 19, 20, 21, 40, xiv. 22 bis, 23, 65,
  xv. 23
λανθάνειν vii. 24
λαός vii. 6, xiv. 2
λατομεῖν xv. 46
λάχανον iv. 32
λέγειν passim
λεγιών v. 9, 15
λέπρα i. 42
λεπρός i. 40, xiv. 3
λεπτόν xii. 42
Λευείς ii. 14
λευκαίνειν ix. 3
λευκός ix. 3, xvi. 5
λῃστής xi. 17, xiv. 48, xv. 27
λίαν i. 35, vi. 51, ix. 3, xvi. 2
λίθος v. 5, xii. 10 (LXX.), xiii. 1, 2, xv.
  46, xvi. 3, 4
λιμός xiii. 8
λόγος i. 45, ii. 2, iv. 14, 15 bis, 16, 17,
  18, 19, 20, 33, v. 36, vii. 13, 29,
  viii. 32, 38, ix. 10, x. 22, 24, xi. 29,
  xii. 13, xiii. 31, xiv. 39, xvi. 20
λοιπός iv. 19, xiv. 41, xvi. 13
λύειν i. 7, vii. 35, xi. 2, 4, 5
λυπεῖσθαι x. 22, xiv. 19
λύτρον x. 45
λυχνία iv. 21
λύχνος iv. 21

Μαγδαληνή, ἡ xv. 40, 47, xvi. 1, 9
μαθητής ii. 15, 16, 18 quater, 23, iii. 7, 9,
  iv. 34, v. 31, vi. 1, 29, 35, 41, 45,
  vii. 2, 5, 17, viii. 1, 4, 6, 10, 27 bis,
  33, 34, ix. 14, 18, 28, 31, x. 10, 13,

23, 24, 46, xi. 1, 14, xii. 43, xiii. 1,
  xiv. 12, 13, 14, 16, 32, xvi. 7
Μαθθαῖος iii. 18
μακράν xii. 34
μακρόθεν, ἀπό, v. 6, viii. 3, xi. 13, xiv.
  54, xv. 40
μακρός xii. 40
μᾶλλον v. 26, vii. 36, ix. 42, x. 48, xv. 11
μανθάνειν xiii. 28
Μαρία, Μαριάμ, (1) ἡ μήτηρ τοῦ Ἰησοῦ
  vi. 3; (2) ἡ Μαγδαληνή xv. 40, 47,
  xvi. 1, 9; (3) ἡ Ἰακώβου, ἡ Ἰωσῆτος
  xv. 40, 47, xvi. 1
μαρτυρία xiv. 55, 56, 59
μαρτύριον i. 44, vi. 11, xiii. 9
μάρτυς xiv. 63
μαστιγοῦν x. 34
μάστιξ iii. 10, v. 29, 34
μάτην vii. 7 (LXX.)
μάχαιρα xiv. 43, 47, 48
μέγας i. 26, iv. 32, 37, 39, 41, v. 7, 11,
  42, x. 42, 43, xiii. 2, xiv. 15, xv. 34,
  37, xvi. 4
μεγιστάν vi. 21
μεθερμηνεύεσθαι v. 41, xv. 22, 34
μείζων iv. 32, ix. 34, xii. 31
μέλει iv. 38, xii. 14
μέλι i. 6
μέλλειν x. 32, xiii. 4
μέν iv. 4, ix. 12, xii. 5, xiv. 21, 38,
  xvi. 19
μένειν vi. 10, xiv. 34
μερίζειν iii. 24, 25, 26, vi. 41
μέριμνα iv. 19
μέρος viii. 10
μεσονύκτιον xiii. 35
μέσος iii. 3, vi. 47, vii. 31, ix. 36, xiv.
  60
μετά (1) w. gen., i. 13, 20, 29, 36, ii.
  16 bis, 19 bis, 25, iii. 5, 6, 7, 14,
  iv. 16, 36, v. 18, 24, 37, 40, vi. 25,
  50, viii. 10, 14, 38, ix. 8, x. 30,
  xi. 11, xiii. 26, xiv. 7, 14, 17, 18, 20,
  33, 43, 48, 54, 62, 67, xv. 1, 7, 31,
  xvi. 10; (2) w. acc., i. 14, viii. 31,
  ix. 2, 31, x. 34, xiii. 24, xiv. 1, 28,
  70, xvi. 12, 19
μεταμορφοῦσθαι ix. 2
μετανοεῖν i. 15, vi. 12
μετάνοια i. 4
μετρεῖν iv. 24
μέτρον iv. 24
μέχρις xiii. 30
μή ii. 4, 7, 19, 21, 22, 26, iii. 20, iv. 5,
  6, v. 7, 36, 37, vi. 4, 5, 8 quater,
  9, 11, 34, 50, viii. 1, 14, ix. 1, 8,
  9, 39, 41, x. 9, 14, 15 bis, 18, 19
  (quinquies: LXX.), xi. 13, 23, xii. 14,
  18, 19, 21, 24, xiii. 2, 5, 7, 11, 15,
  16, 19, 20, 21, 30, 32, 36, xiv. 2, 25,
  31, xvi. 6, 18

420 / Index of Greek Words

424 / Index of Greek Words

Index to the Introduction and Notes